THE PAPERS OF MARTIN LUTHER KING, JR.

Initiated by

The King Center

in association with

Stanford University

Martin Luther King, Jr., and Coretta Scott King say grace with their children Yolanda King and Martin Luther King III, 1961. Photo by William Diehl.

THE PAPERS OF MARTIN LUTHER KING, JR.

VOLUME VI

Advocate of the Social Gospel
September 1948–March 1963

Senior Editor

Clayborne Carson

Volume Editors

Susan Carson
Susan Englander
Troy Jackson
Gerald L. Smith

UNIVERSITY OF CALIFORNIA PRESS

Berkeley   Los Angeles   London

University of California Press, one of the most distinguished university presses in the United States, enriches lives around the world by advancing scholarship in the humanities, social sciences, and natural sciences. Its activities are supported by the UC Press Foundation and by philanthropic contributions from individuals and institutions. For more information, visit www.ucpress.edu.

University of California Press
Berkeley and Los Angeles, California

University of California Press, Ltd.
London, England

Library of Congress Cataloging-in-Publication Data
King, Martin Luther, Jr., 1929–1968.
    The papers of Martin Luther King, Jr.
        V. 6. Advocate of the social gospel, September 1948–March 1963.
            Contents: V. 1. Called to serve, January 1929–June 1951—
    V. 2. Rediscovering precious values, July 1951–November 1955—
    V. 3. Birth of a new age, December 1955–December 1956—
    V. 4. Symbol of the movement, January 1957–December 1958—
    V. 5. Threshold of a new decade, January 1959–December 1960.
        p.   cm.
    Includes bibliographical references and index.
    ISBN-10 0-520-24874-0   ISBN-13 978-0-520-24874-8 (cloth: alk. paper).
        1. Afro-Americans—Civil rights.   2. Civil rights movements—United States—History—20th century.   3. King, Martin Luther, Jr., 1929–1968—Archives.   4. United States—Race relations.
    I. Carson, Clayborne, 1944–   .   II. Carson, Susan.
    III. Englander, Susan.   IV. Jackson, Troy.   V. Smith, Gerald L.
    VI. Title.

E185.97.K5A2   2007
323′.092—dc22   91–42336

Manufactured in the United States of America

15   14   13   12   11   10   09   08   07   06
10   9   8   7   6   5   4   3   2   1

The paper used in this publication meets the minimum requirements of ANSI/NISO Z39.48-1992 (R 1997) (Permanence of Paper).

To Coretta Scott King
(1927–2006)
whose vision inspired these volumes

On the one hand I must attempt to change the soul of individuals so that their societies may be changed. On the other I must attempt to change the societies so that the individual soul will have a chance. Therefore, I must be concerned about unemployment, slums and economic insecurity. I am a profound advocator of the social gospel.

MARTIN LUTHER KING, JR.
Fall 1948

The editors of the Martin Luther King, Jr., Papers Project wish to acknowledge the generosity of the following major contributors, without whose support this volume would not have been possible:

Martin Luther King, Jr., Research and Education Institute
Founding Endowment Donors
Ronnie Lott / All Stars Helping Kids
The Mumford Family—Agape Foundation

Sustaining Contributors
Ronnie Lott / All Stars Helping Kids
Myra Reinhard Family Foundation / All Stars Helping Kids

Major Contributors
Betty A. Williams Curtis and G. Russell Curtis, Sr.
The Flora and William Hewlett Foundation
Lilly Endowment Inc.
National Endowment for the Humanities
National Historical Publications and Records Commission
The Peninsula Community Foundation
Stanford University
Woodside Summit Group, Inc.

Patrons
Wayne Duckworth
Mary McKinney Edmonds
Bonnie Fisher and Boris Dramov
Indy MAC Bancorp, Inc. (in honor of Lydia Kennard Reeves)
Leonard Merrill Kurz and the Kurz Family Foundation
Carolyn and Cordell Olive
Jim C. Robinson
Mario and Rachelle Shane
Jean and Lewis Wolff (the Wolff Family Private Foundation)

The Papers of Martin Luther King, Jr.

CLAYBORNE CARSON,
Senior Editor

1. *Called to Serve, January 1929–June 1951*
Volume editors: Ralph E. Luker and Penny A. Russell

2. *Rediscovering Precious Values, July 1951–November 1955*
Volume editors: Ralph E. Luker, Penny A. Russell, and Peter Holloran

3. *Birth of a New Age, December 1955–December 1956*
Volume editors: Stewart Burns, Susan Carson, Peter Holloran,
and Dana L. H. Powell

4. *Symbol of the Movement, January 1957–December 1958*
Volume editors: Susan Carson, Adrienne Clay, Virginia Shadron,
and Kieran Taylor

5. *Threshold of a New Decade, January 1959–December 1960*
Volume editors: Tenisha Armstrong, Susan Carson, Adrienne Clay,
and Kieran Taylor

6. *Advocate of the Social Gospel, September 1948–March 1963*
Volume editors: Susan Carson, Susan Englander, Troy Jackson,
and Gerald L. Smith

The publisher gratefully acknowledges the many individuals and foundations that have contributed to the publication of the Papers of Martin Luther King, Jr., and the General Endowment Fund of the University of California Press Foundation for its contribution toward the publication of this volume.

Our special thanks to Maya Angelou, Sukey Garcetti, Maxine Griggs, Mary Jane Hewitt, Franklin Murphy, Joan Palevsky, and Marilyn Solomon for their leadership during the campaign.

Challenge Grant
Times Mirror Foundation

Leadership Grants
The Ahmanson Foundation
AT&T Foundation

Partners
ARCO Foundation
William H. Cosby and Camille O. Cosby
The George Gund Foundation
The Walter and Elise Haas Fund
LEF Foundation
Sally Lilienthal
J. Michael Mahoney
The Andrew W. Mellon Foundation
National Historical Publication and Records Commission
Peter Norton Family Foundation
Joan Palevsky
The Ralph M. Parsons Foundation

CONTENTS

ILLUSTRATIONS

Photographs

Facsimiles

Charts

Map

ACKNOWLEDGMENTS

The Martin Luther King, Jr., Papers Project continues to rely on the generous contributions of many individuals who are drawn together by a common desire to disseminate the ideas of King and the social justice movements he inspired. The participants in the Project's editorial and research activities constitute a uniquely dedicated and talented community. As the Project's director, I have appreciated the opportunity to work closely with my colleagues, both staff members and student researchers, and with supporters who contributed funding, historical information, documents and permission to use them, and generous encouragement. In the previous five volumes of this edition, I have described the contributions of many individuals whose association with the Project has been long-term. Thus, I will focus attention here on those individuals whose contributions have been of particular significance during the final stages of preparation of *Volume VI: Advocate of the Social Gospel.*

Institutional Support

The King Papers Project relies on the support of the Martin Luther King, Jr., Estate and the continuing cooperation of the King Center in Atlanta. Before her passing in 2006, Coretta Scott King, the King Center's founding president, was particularly steadfast in her support of the Project, which she initiated. She generously made available the documents that form the core of this volume and that previously had been stored among family materials in her basement. For myself and those of my colleagues who had the pleasure of working with Mrs. King (often in her home), our sense of loss is measured in our grief and in our awareness of her singular, tireless effort to preserve her husband's intellectual legacy. Mrs. King's former assistant Lynn Cothren was consistently helpful, as were members of her office staff, including Patricia Latimore, especially in providing access to documentary materials that are not part of the King collection at the King Center.

Other King Center officials and staff members have also been helpful. I have continued to collaborate with Dexter Scott King in his roles as head of the King Estate and president of the King Center. I also conferred with Martin Luther King III while he served as president of the Center. King Center administrators supported the Project's work in various ways. In addition to Dexter King, we have appreciated the support of Rosalind McGinnis and her predecessor, Tricia Harris. We are also grateful for the support of the King Library and Archive staff, particularly Director of Archives Cynthia Lewis and her assistant, Elaine Hall. Other King Center staff members who have been helpful to us include Alice Eason, Michael England, Barbara Harrison, Steve Klein, and Robert Vickers. I have also enjoyed working with Jennifer Quirk from Intellectual Properties Management.

Since 1997, when the responsibility for the administration of the Project's federal grants was transferred from the King Center to Stanford University, we have benefited more than ever from Stanford's research resources and administrative

Acknowledgments

support. The Project has counted on the enthusiastic backing of President John Hennessy and Provost John Etchemendy as well as that of LaDoris Hazzard Cordell, Vice Provost for Campus Relations and Special Counselor to the President. Regarding the Project's ongoing needs, I have had the pleasure of consulting with Vice Provost for Undergraduate Education John Bravman and Director of Undergraduate Research Programs Susan Brubaker-Cole. Dean of Humanities and Sciences Sharon Long and former Dean Russell Berman have been consistently gracious and supportive. We also appreciate the concern of Ian Gotlib, Senior Associate Dean, and Deans Judith Goldstein and Robert Gregg. We are also thankful for the encouragement of History Department chair Aron Rodrigue and former chair Carolyn Lougee Chappell. The personnel of the Humanities and Sciences Dean's Office helped us find our way through the bureaucratic maze. On personnel matters, we have received vital assistance from Human Resource manager Amber Triplett. James Henry, Director of Finance, was also helpful. In the Office of Sponsored Research we appreciate the assistance of Lillie Ryans-Culclager, Deputy Director; Blanca Rebuelta, Associate Grant and Contract Officer; Linda Erwin, Assistant Director; Marie Mui, Senior Research Accountant; Dora Yu, Research Accountant; Diven Sharma, Research Accountant; and Cecile Imbert, Accounting Associate. Former Associate Dean of Development David Voss has assisted the Project in its never-ending pursuit of additional funding. We are also deeply grateful for the continuing interest and assistance of the staff at Stanford's Cecil H. Green Library, especially Mary-Louise Munill in the interlibrary borrowing office.

Contributing editor Gerald L. Smith would particularly like to thank University of Kentucky Dean Howard Grotch and Richard Greissman, Cliff Swauger, and Christian Ecker from the College of Arts and Sciences; Fitzgerald Bramwell and the staff of the Office of Research and Graduate Studies; and Evangeline Johnson, staff support in the African American Studies Program.

The King Papers Project has had a supportive relationship with the publisher of our edition, the University of California Press. We have enjoyed working with the all of the staff members involved in the painstaking work of producing our volumes. Those involved with this volume include Director Lynne Withey, History editor Niels Hooper, former History editor Monica McCormick, Randy Heyman, and Rachel Lockman. Kathleen MacDougall's enthusiasm and organizational skills in coordinating this effort at UC Press are especially noteworthy.

The involvement of the Project's Advisory Board has declined in recent years but we continue to appreciate the advice we receive from this extraordinary group of distinguished scholars and former associates of Dr. King, who are listed in this volume's opening pages. In addition to Mrs. King and Mrs. Farris, I wish to acknowledge in particular the critical comments regarding Volume VI that we received from David J. Garrow. His thoughtful criticism on the manuscript drafts was a valuable addition to the volume. In addition to benefiting from the advice of these members of the Advisory Board, the Project has also relied on its Stanford University Advisory Committee, which has expanded its role in recent years. They included the committee's chair, Harold Boyd, and the following members: Barton J. Bernstein, Vicki Brooks, Capri Silverstri Cafaro, Roy Clay, Greg Crossfield, Karl Cureton, Betty A. Williams Curtis and G. Russell Curtis, Sr., George Fredrickson, Morris Graves, Julie Anne Henderson, Henry Organ, John Rickford, Alene Smith, and David Tyack.

The King Papers Project could not have survived without funding from numerous generous donors. Major contributors to this volume include Betty A. Wllliams Curtis and G. Russell Curtis, Sr., the Flora and William Hewlett Foundation, the Lilly Endowment Inc., Ronnie Lott / All Stars Helping Kids, the National Endowment for the Humanities (NEH), the National Historical Publications and Records Commission (NHPRC), the Peninsula Community Foundation, Myra Reinhardt Family Foundation/All Stars Helping Kids, Stanford University, and the Woodside Summit Group, Inc. Individuals at these institutions have often demonstrated a concern for the Project far outside the bounds of professional responsibilities. I acknowledge in particular Chairman Bruce Cole and former Chairman William R. Ferris, Grants Administrator Alice Hudgins, and Senior Program Officer Michael Hall and former Program Officer Daniel P. Jones of the NEH. NHPRC Executive Director Max J. Evans and his predecessor, Ann C. Newhall, Deputy Executive Director Kathleen Williams and her predecessor, Roger Bruns, Program Officer Daniel Stokes, Management and Program Analyst Nancy T. Copp, and Archivist Allen Weinstein and his predecessor, John W. Carlin, have been generous in their assistance to the Project. In addition, I have appreciated the support of Lilly Endowment Inc., Program Director Jacqui Burton, and Program Officer Jean Smith and former Program Director Jeanne Knoerle. I offer a special thanks to Lilly Endowment Inc., which provided the primary funding for Volume VI and gave us vital support.

Patrons of this volume include Wayne Duckworth, Mary McKinney Edmonds, Bonnie Fisher and Boris Dramov, Indy MAC Bancorp, Inc. (in honor of Lydia Kennard Reeves), Leonard Merrill Kurz and the Kurz Family Foundation, Carolyn and Cordell Olive, Jim C. Robinson, Mario and Rachelle Shane, and Jean and Lewis Wolff (the Wolff Family Private Foundation).

Donors include Rosalina and Charles Abboud, Patricia and Royal Alsup, Bettina Aptheker, Herbert Aptheker, Carolyn and John Barnes, Jacqueline Bowles, Sara and Harold Boyd, Richard P. and Jane F. Brummel, Harvey L. Cole, Rabbi Sidney Akselrad (Congregation Beth Am), George Counts, Nadine Cruz and Laurence Ulrich, Candace Falk, George M. Fredrickson, Lettie and Dr. Robert Green, Kris S. Hanamoto, John and Marthelia Hargrove, Evelyn Brooks Higginbotham, Rosalind C. Hooper, Evelyn Kelsey, Jenna Klein, Earl Lawson, Steven F. Lawson, Edward and Stephanie Leland, Jay and Elise Miller, Keith Miller, R. V. Oakford, Laura F. and Keisho Okayama, Henry P. Organ, Steven Phillips, Pittsburg Branch NAACP, Judith Prather, Arnold Rampersad, Joan S. Reid, Eric Roberts and Lauren Rusk, Beverly Ryder, Susana G. and John Smith, Robert Tasto and Sallie Reid, Gautam Venkatesan, Merti Walker, Kimberly and Tyrone Willingham, Rosalind Wolf, and Peter Zeughauser (the Zeughauser Group).

Sustainers include Althea Anderson, Bobbie Armstrong, Kimberly Baker, Ellen Broms, Lea E. Byrd, Sharon H. Carson, John A. Dittmer, Andrea and Brian Dowdy, Matt Doyle, Tina Ebey, First Hebrew Congregation of Oakland (Temple Sinai), Patricia Handley, Hanan Hardy, Robert and Muriel Herhold, Peter H. Holloran, Wah Tung Lau, Delia McGrath, M. Brigid O'Farrell, Bevin Parker-Evans, Damani Rivers, Bill and June Sale, the Salzman Family, Stephanie Shoffner, Vonda Stanford, Demetrius Stanley, Commieolla D. Thierry, David Tyack and Elizabeth Hansot, Tamara Walton, and Rega and Allen Wood.

This volume, as with all the volumes of King's papers, has been the result of a long-term collaboration involving student and post-graduate researchers, in which academic credentials counted for less than demonstrated ability and dedication. From its inception, the mission of the King Papers Project has not only been to produce a definitive edition of King's papers but to provide an opportunity for able and dedicated students to acquire research skills and to increase their understanding of the modern African-American freedom struggle. As the Project has evolved, a few veteran staff members have provided an essential degree of stability amidst the continual turnover of student researchers. The editors listed on the title page have each made vital contributions.

Amidst the many changes in the King Project's personnel, Susan Carson has continued to be a vital and steadfast source of guidance for me and for those who have joined the staff. In addition to training new staff members, Susan has been involved in every aspect of the Project's work, from preparation of grant proposals to document acquisition to manuscript preparation. Her contribution was especially important in the laborious process of locating and carefully cataloging the documents we acquired from the basement of the King home. As the significance of these documents became clear, she suggested that the King Project undertake this thematic volume.

This volume would not have been initiated without the efforts of several editors and research assistants. University of Kentucky associate professor of history Gerald L. Smith joined the Project as a contributing editor in 1998 to begin the work on this volume. His insights as a historian and as a active minister have guided the work of the volume from its inception. University of Kentucky Ph.D. candidate and University Christian Church of Cincinnati minister Troy Jackson also became a contributing editor soon afterward. They were both instrumental in maintaining the focus on King's religious faith and ministerial practice in crafting this volume. Associate editors Kerry Taylor and Adrienne Clay worked effectively with the contributing editors during the first stages of document selection and annotation. After Taylor's departure (in 2001 to pursue doctoral studies at the University of North Carolina), Susan Englander joined the staff as assistant editor and ably coordinated the work of the contributing editors and onsite Stanford editorial staff. Sue's scholarly preparation, her remarkable ability to facilitate collaboration with offsite editors, and her growing experience in the annotation of religious documents all served to ensure this volume's timely completion. Her dedication inspired her colleagues. Sue's work was initially assisted by the capable and energetic research assistant Rebecca Engels, who left the Project in 2002. Research assistant Stewart Walker joined the staff several months later and provided Volume VI with his organizational skills, intellectual curiosity, and his recovering pitching arm. Now in graduate studies at New York University, Stewart skillfully digitized most of the images that appear in this volume.

Although not assigned to this volume, other staff members made substantial contributions to it. Associate editor Tenisha Armstrong has been a solid resource of information and common sense. Elizabeth Brummel brought enthusiasm to the demanding amount of details needed to maintain control of our database and valuable insights to our editorial meetings and the annotation process. Madolyn Orr proofread parts of this manuscript with a keen eye. Research assistants Brandon Smith and Louis Jackson demonstrated great attention to detail and gladly performed any task given them. No longer with the Project but contributing to this volume were Lauren Araiza, Elizabeth Baez, Andrea Dowdy, Alice Endamne, Damani Rivers, and Erin Wood.

Although not directly involved in the research or writing of this volume, other staff members provided essential administrative support, especially Project Administrator Jane Abbott and Assistant Administrator Regina Covington. Jesika Gandhi supervises our computer networking needs and Paula Wirth coordinated the online dissemination of the Project's documents and research material.

Student Researchers

The King Papers Project is immensely grateful for the many hours of thoughtful, though sometimes tedious, research conducted by undergraduate and graduate students over the years. These students, representing many disciplines, brought their methods and perspectives to bear upon the important task of locating King's words in time and place. They plotted his daily movements against the sweep of events in a region too often shadowed by racial violence. With diligence they discovered unknown documents and patiently deciphered recordings of King's voice, sometimes barely audible, to produce some of this volume's most distinctive documents. Their individual and collective contributions are many, as are their number.

The Project has always depended on the skills, dedication, and exceptional talents of Stanford students. These students, working as interns, volunteers, or for academic credit, have contributed much to our work through their deep interest in and enthusiasm for the material. Undergraduate researchers who worked on Volume VI or whose work was not acknowledged in previous volumes include David Agu, India Alston, Kristy Anwuri, Kaara Baptiste, Pat Bomhack, Taurean Brown, Tracie Bryant, Nkechi Chukwueke, Jennifer Clark, Antonio Colvin, Tambi Cork, Matthew Cowan, LaTasha Crow, Brannon Cullum, Brian DeChesare, Robert DeSpain, Tabari Dossett, Georgia Duan, Karis Eklund, Kristin Ferrales, Crystal Garland, Adia Gooden, Claire Henderson, Margot Isman, Alicia James, Quaneisha Jenkins, Theresa Johnson, Prisilla Juarez, Monique King, Eric Kramon, David Lai, Vanessa Lawrence, Christy Machida, Kahdeidra Martin, Lauren McCoy, Marina McCoy, Alice McNeill, Danielle Moore, Laura Nugent, Chika Okafor, Sheila Ongwae, Aysha Pamukcu, Jill Parker, Krystal Quinlan, Ashley Rayner, Meghana Reddy, Christina Richers, Bill Ridgway, Abigail Rosas, Mercedes Roy, Anna Sale, Kate Skolnick, Ari Steinberg, Adriana Stewart-Hernandez, Manon Terrell, Brandi Thompson, Christopher Vaughan, Albert Wang, Clara Webb, Christopher Williams, Tessa Yeager, Reid Yokoyama, and Jenny Zhao. In addition Chien Le, Andrew Mo, and Mike Lewis provided the Project with dependable computer expertise, helping maintain our website and electronic databases, and addressing our endless questions. During this period the following volunteers greatly enhanced the Project's work and productivity: Erin Hill, Helen Kaufman, Marilyn Mayo, Lindsey Thomson-Levin, and William Tucker.

King Summer Research Fellows

The Project has also gained immensely from the contributions of graduate and undergraduate students from other colleges and universities who worked at the Stanford office as part of the Martin Luther King, Jr., Summer Research Fellowship. The Summer Fellows for 2003 and 2005 were Sarah Allen, Gina Bateson, Rob Boyle, and Christopher Williams (Stanford University), Donelle Boose (University of North Carolina at Chapel Hill), Jeneka Joyce (University of Notre Dame), Treva Lindsey (Oberlin College), Jane Metcalf (Yale University), Benjamin Peters (University of Washington), and Joel Rogers (Lawrence University).

Acquisition and Research Assistance

Volume VI, like the volumes that preceded it, would not have been possible without the King-related documents that have been provided to us by numerous individuals and institutions. The King collections at Boston University and the King Center have been at the core of our selection. We are especially grateful for the generous assistance of Boston University Special Collections Director Howard Gotlieb and Assistant Director Charlie Niles, as well as Cynthia Lewis of the King Center.

In addition to documents obtained from the King Center and Boston University, we identified many manuscript collections with King-related material important for this volume. Institutions, archives, libraries, and individuals that assisted us in locating documents for this volume include Betty Layton (American Baptist Historical Society); American Friends Service Committee Archives, Amistad Research Center (Tulane University); Fran O'Donnell (Andover-Harvard Theological Library, Harvard Divinity School); Carolyn Hunt Anderson; Cathy Lynn Mundale (Atlanta University Center); John Brooke; Jim Bull (Central United Methodist Church Archives); Chicago Historical Society; Dorsey Blake (Church for the Fellowship of All Peoples); Colgate-Rochester Divinity School; Columbia Broadcasting System; DePauw University; Fred O. Doty, Decatur Office of Vital Records; Elaine Kisner (Metroplitan Christian Council: Detroit-Windsor); Dexter Avenue King Memorial Baptist Church; Ebenezer Baptist Church; Wayne H. Kempton (Episcopal Diocese of New York); Christine King Farris; Julian O. Grayson; Howard University; Lawrence Edward Carter, Sr. (Morehouse College); Coretta Scott King; Library of Congress; Montgomery County Courthouse; Montgomery City Public Library; Joellen El Bashir (Moorland-Springarn Research Center); Noah Phelps (Muskegon County Museum Archives); Alton B. Pollard III (Chandler School of Theology, Emory University); John T. Porter; African American Resource Center of Portsmouth, N.H; Presbyterian Department of History; Bridget Arthur Clancy (Presbyterian Historical Society); Reigner Recording Library (Union Theological Seminary); Riverside Church; Schomburg Center for Research in Black Culture; Taffy Hall (Southern Baptist Historical Library and Archives); Southern Baptist Theological Seminary; Time Inc.; Kevin Sykes; Unitarian Church of Germantown; University of Massachusetts; Walter P. Reuther Library of Labor and Urban Affairs; Mervyn A. Warren, Philadelphia, Pa.; Wesleyan University; Corey Thomas (Wheaton College); White Rock Baptist Church; Wisconsin Historical Society; and Martha Smalley (Yale Divinity School Library).

A special thanks goes to the Rare Book and Manuscript Department at the New York office of Sotheby's for providing us with access to many valuable King sources. We especially extend our appreciation to Vice Chairman of Print and Manuscript Americana David Redden, Vice President of Books and Manuscripts Elizabeth Muller and Lauren Gioia, Chloe Schon, and Carly Krum.

King's colleagues and acquaintances, and their families, have been among the most important sources of King-related documents. Of those whom we were able to contact, many assisted us immeasurably in our research. Some graciously allowed us to make photocopies of the documents in their possession, which until now have not been available, and many kindly consented to interviews in connection with this volume. These individuals include Elaine Gardner Andrews, Ruth Copplin, Jethro English, Ernestine Farr, Hunton Green, Michael Haynes (Twelfth Baptist Church), Gwendolyn Hurley, James A. Kilgore (Friendship Baptist Church), Ella Ivey, Ernestine Robinson, Elizabeth Shepperd, and Evelyn Gardner Winston.

Individuals who gave permission for publication of their documents or those of relatives include Monica Karales, executrix for photographer James Karales; Sandra Weiner and John Broderick for the estate of photographer Dan Weiner; and the estate of John Steinbeck.

Several institutions and individuals assisted the Project on our audiovisual acquisitions and research for this volume: the Associated Press/Wide World Photos, Black Star, Boston University, Jim Bull (Central United Methodist Church Archives), Corbis-Bettman Archives, Christine King Farris, Getty Images, International Center for Photography, the Library of Congress, Magnum Photos, the Martin Luther King, Jr., Estate, and the *New York Daily News*.

Many scholars without official ties to the Project also provided assistance to the editors. These include Lewis V. Baldwin, Chris Beard, James H. Cone, Arnold Eisen, Walter Fluker, David J. Garrow, Robert Gregg, Vincent Harding, Peter Holloran, Richard Lischer, Scotty McClennan, Keith Miller, Barbara D. Savage, Robert Smith, and Mervyn Warren.

A few individuals have enhanced the work of the Project simply by visiting us and talking about their involvement with or scholarship on the civil rights movement or other movements for social change. Among the Project's recent invited guests have been Bettina Aptheker, Orlando Bagwell, Claus Bedenbrock, Aldo Billingslea, Ed Blankenheim, Harold and Sara Boyd, Michael Collopy, Cheo Hodari Coker, Jimmy Collier, Claudette Colvin, Mary McKinney Edmunds, Janice Edwards, Lindsey Ford, Arun Gandhi, Kateri Harnetiaux, Tricia Harris, Bruce Hartford, Bob Herhold, Matt Herron, Ericka Huggins, Jesse Jackson, Peniel Jackson, Tom Jackson, Carolyn Johnson, Martin Luther King III, Leonard Kurz, Earl Lawson, Ronnie and Karen Lott, Awele Makeba, Steve McCutchen, Rosalind McGinnis, John, Chris, and Jacky Mumford, Kim Oden, Charles Ogletree, Dylan Pennigroth, Nicholas Stanton Sharman, George P. Schultz, Fred Shuttlesworth, Kiron Skinner, Juliane Strubel, and Kitrra Sutherland.

Gerald L. Smith would like to extend his appreciation to Teresa, Elizabeth, and Sarah Smith, Romano and Mary Crawford, Mamie Mayfield, Octavene Turner,

Pastor Richard Gaines and the members of the Consolidated Baptist Church in Lexington, Kentucky, and the Farristown Baptist Church in Berea, Kentucky, for their support. Troy Jackson would like to thank Amanda, Jacob, Emma, and Ellie Jackson, and the University Christian Church for providing a community of encouragement for his academic pursuits.

Certainly there are other individuals and organizations that participated in and contributed to the success of the King Papers Project. Failure to mention them simply reflects the limits of my memory rather than of my gratitude.

CLAYBORNE CARSON
FEBRUARY 2006

Christians are always to begin with a bias in favor of a movement which protests against unfair treatment of the poor, but surely Christianity itself is such a protest. The Communist Manifesto might express a concern for the poor and the oppressed, but it expresses no greater concern than the manifesto of Jesus, which opens with the words, "The spirit of the Lord is upon me, because He hath anointed me to preach the gospel to the poor; He has sent me to heal the broken-hearted, to preach deliverance to the captive, recovering the sight of the blind; to set at liberty them that are bruised, to proclaim the acceptable year of the Lord."[1]

Martin Luther King, Jr.
"Can a Christian Be a Communist?"
30 September 1962

When Martin Luther King, Jr., preached "Can a Christian Be a Communist?" to the Ebenezer Baptist Church congregation in Atlanta during the fall of 1962, he returned to familiar homiletic themes that had been evident since the start of his ministry. King developed both the ideas and language for this sermon early in his preaching career. During the summers of 1952 and 1953, while a graduate student at Boston University, he prepared earlier versions of this sermon, titled "Communism's Challenge to Christianity," to preach at Ebenezer and insisted, as he would in his 1962 message, that Christians should respond to the threat of communism by strengthening their commitment to social justice.[2] Using similar phrasing and drawing on the Bible verse Luke 4:18–19 in his 1953 version as he did in 1962, King demonstrated his enduring commitment to the social duty of the Christian.[3] Throughout his career he returned to this passage in Luke as a declaration of the driving force behind his ministry.[4]

---

1. Luke 4:18–19.

2. "'Communism's Challenge to Christianity,' King Jr's Topic, Ebenezer," *Atlanta Daily World,* 10 August 1952, and King, "Communism's Challenge to Christianity," 9 August 1953, pp. 146–150 in this volume.

3. In Luke 4:18–19, Jesus quotes and adapts Isaiah 61:1–2: "The Spirit of the Lord God is upon me; because the Lord hath anointed me to preach good tidings unto the meek; he hath sent me to bind up the brokenhearted, to proclaim liberty to the captives, and the opening of the prison to them that are bound; To proclaim the acceptable year of the Lord, and the day of vengeance of our God; to comfort all that mourn."

4. In his 2 May 1954 acceptance speech at Montgomery's Dexter Avenue Baptist Church, King declared, "I have felt with Jesus that the spirit of [*the*] Lord is upon me, because he hath anointed me to

King consistently embraced this message from his first years as his father's associate minister at Ebenezer Baptist Church, through his years of theological training, and during his tenure in the pulpits of Dexter Avenue Baptist Church in Montgomery, Alabama, and Ebenezer. He similarly professed his identity as a social gospel minister in a paper written during his first term at Crozer Theological Seminary. "I must be concerned about unemployment, [slums], and economic insecurity," he averred. "I am a profound advocator of the social gospel."[5] Throughout his life, he professed a commitment to be involved with the daily concerns of congregation members as well as with their souls. King regarded salvation as a social as well as an individual process.[6]

Although King's academic writings were extensively examined in Volumes I (1992) and II (1994) of *The Papers of Martin Luther King, Jr.*, little was known about King's early homiletic expressions until the King Papers Project obtained a substantial body of such materials. In 1997 Mrs. Coretta Scott King granted the King Papers Project permission to examine papers kept in boxes in the basement of the home that became the King residence in 1965 and to identify items that were appropriate for the Project's mission. The most significant discovery resulting from this exploration was a private file of sermon materials King kept in his study. A battered cardboard box held over two hundred folders containing handwritten outlines, drafts, and prayers as well as academic papers, published articles, and correspondence.[7] This volume interrupts the chronology of the *Papers* to present a

---

preach the gospel to the poor, to heal the brokenhearted, to preach deliverance to the captives, and to set at liberty them that are bruised" (King, Acceptance Address at Dexter Avenue Baptist Church, 2 May 1954, p. 167 in this volume). King's father had also relied on the same biblical passage when he defined "the true mission of the Church" at a gathering of Atlanta's Missionary Baptist Association in 1940. King, Sr. introduced this biblical passage by commenting, "The church is to touch every phase of the community life. Quite often we say the church has no place in politics, forgetting the words of the Lord." After reciting the passage, he continued, "God hasten the time when every minister will become a registered voter and a part of every movement for the betterment of our people. . . . We can not expect our people to register and become citizens until we as leaders set the standard" (Martin Luther King, Sr., "Moderator's Annual Address" [Cartersville, Ga.: *Minutes of the Thirty-Sixth Annual Session of the Atlanta Missionary Baptist Association,* 1940], p. 18). For more on King, Sr.'s view of the ministry and his early activism, see Introduction, in *The Papers of Martin Luther King, Jr.,* vol. 1: *Called to Serve, January 1929–June 1951,* ed. Clayborne Carson, Ralph E. Luker, Penny A. Russell (Berkeley and Los Angeles: University of California Press, 1992), pp. 33–34.

5. King, "Preaching Ministry," 14 September–24 November 1948, p. 72 in this volume.

6. At the turn of the twentieth century, a significant number of American Protestants responded to the slums and poverty engendered by the massive wave of immigration, industrialization and urbanization by calling for social reform based in religious faith and action. These adherents to social-gospel Christianity maintained that Christian belief and doctrine was a genuine engine for the moral regeneration of American life and saw a social purpose in Christianity. They were intent upon "Christianizing the social order," as Baptist minister Walter Rauschenbusch put it, and seeking justice for the poor and disadvantaged (Rauschenbusch, *Christianizing the Social Order* [New York: Macmillan, 1912]). Proponents also envisioned a time of ever-increasing social progress. King's father and other African American ministers of this era took up the call for the social gospel on behalf of their own communities, publicly appealing for racial justice and for an end to Jim Crow laws and the practice of lynching (Introduction, in *Papers* 1:33–34).

7. This collection constitutes nearly half of all of King's homiletic materials currently catalogued by the King Papers Project and 129 of the 147 sermons and outlines dated prior to 1956. Although this volume focuses on those documents that illuminate his sermon preparation, King's sermon file contains

selection of documents from King's sermon file along with other previously unpublished materials that bear on his religious development before and during his rise to international acclaim.[8] In retracing his student years, the volume explores the role of Crozer and Boston University in shaping his skills in the ministry. Finally, it offers greater understanding of the origin, drafting, and editing of King's most familiar collection of sermons, *Strength to Love*.

This volume illuminates aspects of King's preaching ministry that have received little scholarly attention. The selected documents offer insight into the process through which brief handwritten outlines and sketches, many of which were prepared for Crozer preaching classes, were refined and expanded into complete and distinctive sermons that King delivered to appreciative audiences at Dexter, Ebenezer, and elsewhere. King continually revised his favorite sermons to increase their rhetorical effectiveness as well as to incorporate new themes and contemporary references. The documents illustrate his characteristic ability to weave together biblical texts and ideas drawn from varied sources—the sermons of other ministers, the insights of philosophers, passages from literature and Christian hymns, contemporary news, and set pieces—into a coherent, persuasive presentation. King actively drew on the ideas of such renowned preachers as Harry Emerson Fosdick, Frederick M. Meek, George Buttrick, and Robert J. McCracken, recasting their messages to reflect the needs and concerns of the African American community as well as his own sentiments.[9] Often he kept related homiletic material in the same folder in his sermon file. His folder titled "A Knock at Midnight" contained a mimeographed copy of D. T. Niles's August 1954 sermon "Evangelism," which was published later that year in the *Christian Century* as "Summons at Midnight." King drew heavily on Niles's prose for his own sermon "A Knock at Midnight."[10] He stored five

more than homiletic materials. Many folders in the file contain a variety of materials. For example, one labeled "Creating the Abundant Life" / "A Moment of Difficult Decision" includes two thematically related sermons with these titles, a copy of Douglas Malloch's poem "Be the Best of Whatever You Are," notes on the attorney Clarence Darrow's life, and the sermon outline "The Sea of Life," which deals with topics similar to those discussed in the folder's other documents. Another folder titled "The Fellow Who Stayed at Home" holds J. Wallace Hamilton's sermon "That Fellow Who Stayed at Home" and King's sermon on that theme. For a detailed rendering of King's sermon file, see Sermon File Inventory, pp. 609–627 in this volume.

8. King referred to this file in a 26 October 1960 letter to Coretta Scott King written from Georgia State Prison at Reidsville. He asked his wife to bring him a number of "sermons from my file" (in *The Papers of Martin Luther King, Jr.,* vol. 5: *Threshold of a New Decade, January 1959–December 1960,* ed. Clayborne Carson, Tenisha Armstrong, Susan Carson, Adrienne Clay, Kieran Taylor [Berkeley and Los Angeles: University of California Press, 2005], p. 532).

9. Robert J. McCracken succeeded Harry Emerson Fosdick as pastor of New York's Riverside Church in 1946 and served until 1967. Frederick M. Meek presided over Boston's Old South Church from 1946 until 1973. George Buttrick pastored Madison Avenue Presbyterian Church for twenty-eight years, beginning in 1927, and was best known for his 1928 book, *The Parables of Jesus.* For examples of King's sermons that were influenced by these ministers, see "Communism's Challenge to Christianity," 9 August 1953; "A Religion of Doing," 4 July 1954; "Opportunity, Fidelity, and Reward," January 1955; and "Our God Is Able," 1 January 1956, pp. 146–150, 170–174, and 243–246 in this volume, respectively. See also Chart 3, p. 38 in this volume.

10. For more on this sermon and its sources, see King, "A Knock at Midnight," 14 September 1958, pp. 347–350 in this volume.

sermons by Meek in a file labeled "Sermons by Other Ministers" and based his sermon "Our God Is Able" on two additional homilies by Meek that can be found in the folder that King titled "Our God Is Able."[11] King also drew upon the books in his personal study for his sermons, annotating some of these volumes with notes for his homilies.[12]

This volume also includes transcriptions of tape recordings of King's most famous sermons, such as "The Three Dimensions of a Complete Life" and "Paul's Letter to American Christians." The transcriptions, however, must be read in the context of King's oral presentation style. King's voice, initially low and measured, resounds in these audiotapes as he moves into the body of his sermon, elaborating his theme. His cadence becomes louder and more emphatic as the sermon progresses toward a conclusion. Some listeners responded to King's message with shouts of encouragement, urging him to "Preach!" and endorsing his line of thought with a "Yes!" or an "Oh, Lord!" King often responded to his audience. These transcriptions of recorded sermons and audience responses convey King at the height of his oratorical power, bring the outlines and sermon notes to life, and provide a basis of comparison between his sermon drafts and delivered sermons.

Collectively these documents shed considerable light on the theology and preaching preparation of one of America's most noted orators. The publication of this material reveals that, though King's ministerial skills benefited from his upbringing in a religious household, he worked diligently to develop his craft and forge a religious message the world could understand and appreciate. Using the sermon file, King's recorded sermons, and his 1963 volume of published sermons, *Strength to Love,* as benchmarks, one can trace King's progress from a novice to his status as a preacher with a global audience. As an associate minister at Ebenezer and as pastor at Dexter, King took up the call of the social gospel and applied it to the concrete realities of his own congregations. King's religious ideas, when linked to the precept of nonviolent resistance, would provide a powerful impetus for the burgeoning civil rights struggles of the 1950s.

These sermon materials reveal that King's concern for poverty, human rights, and social justice is clearly present in his earliest handwritten sermons. Even his early seminary student writings conveyed a message of faith, hope, and love for the dispossessed. During his first years of preaching in the late forties and early fifties, King was drawn to such issues as atomic-age anxiety, family disintegration, capitalism, the Cold War, and racism. His early sermons at Dexter were sprinkled not only with discussions of race relations but also with references to the hallmarks of the African American experience during the 1950s: the *Brown v. Board of Education* decision, the Emmett Till lynching, Autherine Lucy's attempt to integrate the University of Alabama, and the desegregation of public schools in Little Rock, Arkansas. King's social gospel message remained grounded in a faith in humanity and a belief in the power, protection, and promise of God but he rejected the

---

11. For more on this sermon and its sources, see King, "Our God Is Able," 1 January 1956, pp. 243–246 in this volume.

12. For a catalog of books kept in King's study that were relevant to his sermon preparation, see King's Personal Library: Selected Works, pp. 629–655 in this volume.

boundless optimism and unquestioning confidence in human progress that the term originally implied. He saw himself as an heir not only to social gospel proponents such as Harry Emerson Fosdick but also to an African American preaching tradition that demanded racial equality and acknowledged that the struggle for racial justice was a necessary part of the nation's social salvation. By the time he assembled the manuscript for *Strength to Love,* King could draw upon his theological training and years of experience as a pastor and civil rights leader to fulfill his mission of bringing "the Christian message to bear on the social evils that cloud our day."[13]

When he arrived at Crozer in 1948, King had already started his apprenticeship as a preacher. Overcoming adolescent religious skepticism and lingering doubts about his calling during the summer of 1947, King responded to his irrepressible "desire to serve God and humanity" and "to accept the challenge to enter the ministry."[14] In October 1947, King delivered his trial sermon at Ebenezer; the following February he was licensed to preach and ordained as a minister, serving as the church's associate pastor during his holiday breaks and vacations from Crozer and Boston University.[15] In the summers, King took over his father's duties and pulpit while King, Sr., "got away for some much needed rest."[16]

The younger King remembered differing "a great deal" with his father over theological matters during his undergraduate years at Morehouse College, particularly as he broke free of "the shackles of fundamentalism." He would, however, come to acknowledge his father's "noble example" as an important factor in his decision to enter the ministry.[17] A primary aspect of King, Sr.'s example was his dedication to the social gospel, a term he used freely. "My ministry has never been otherworldly—solely oriented toward life after death," he explained in a 1973 autobiography. "It has been equally concerned with the here and the now, with improving man's lot in <u>this</u> life. I have therefore stressed the social gospel."[18] King's father acknowledged the social gospel as a sometimes unpopular way of preaching, and chided the minister who "preached what his congregation <u>wanted</u> to hear—not what they <u>needed</u> to hear."[19]

King, Jr.'s mentors at Morehouse, especially president Benjamin E. Mays and reli-

13. King, *Strength to Love* (New York: Harper & Row, 1963), p. ix.

14. King, My Call to the Ministry, 7 August 1959, p. 368 in this volume.

15. Lillian D. Watkins, Certification of Minister's License for Martin Luther King, Jr., 4 February 1948, in *Papers* 1:150. In an unpublished autobiography, King, Sr., said of his son's trial sermon, "M.L. gave an excellent account of himself in his initial sermon. He preached like a veteran—like a man with years of experience behind him" (King, Sr., "A Black Rebel: The Autobiography of M. L. King, Sr. As Told to Edward A. Jones" [unpublished manuscript, 1973], p. 107). For more on King's early years as a preacher, see Introduction, in *Papers* 1:37–46).

16. King, Sr., "A Black Rebel," p. 108.

17. King, "Autobiography of Religious Development," 12 September–22 November 1950, in *Papers* 1:363.

18. King, Sr., "A Black Rebel," p. 23.

19. King, Sr., "A Black Rebel," p. 64.

gion professor George D. Kelsey, also became appealing role models as erudite advocates of liberal theology.[20] The influence of Mays and Kelsey at Morehouse doubtless encouraged King's belief that formal theological training was important. His early development as a minister was also shaped by his lifelong exposure to the preaching craft at Ebenezer and other nearby churches. King acknowledged, however, that in addition to needing personal experience, a good preacher must exhibit a strong intellect. King would insist during his first year at Crozer that "the minister must be both sincere and intelligent. [*Too*] often do our ministers possess the former but not the latter. This, I think, is a serious problem facing the ministry."[21]

Having rejected fundamentalism while at Morehouse, King arrived at Crozer ready "to fall in line with the liberal tradition there" while still affirming "the noble moral and ethical ideals that I grew up under."[22] In an early Crozer paper, he resolutely expressed his belief that liberal theology "is the best, or at least the most logical system of theology in existence" and lauded critical biblical scholarship—"the real theologian must be as open-minded, as unbiased, and as disinterested as the scientist." He was skeptical about biblical literalism, conceding "that the whale did not swallow Jonah, . . . or that Jesus never met John the Baptist." But King maintained that skepticism was not enough: "After the Bible has been stripped [*of*] all of its mythological and non-historical content, the liberal theological must be able to answer the question—what then?" [23]

King's own experiences, his reading of theologian Reinhold Niebuhr, and his desire to address the meaning of Jesus' teachings in the context of twentieth-century life shaped his view of liberal theology. He questioned the liberal belief in inherent human goodness and its neglect of sin as a factor in human nature and noted his skepticism in several papers that he wrote during his years at Crozer and at Boston.[24] His questioning of liberal theology resulted in his nuanced under-

---

20. Although King's later writings often minimized the influence of his time at Morehouse, Mays played a significant role in shaping King's early canon of sermonic themes. While King was a student, chapel was compulsory, and Mays spoke at the Tuesday chapel almost every week. Mays later acknowledged that the themes of his weekly Tuesday morning chapel sermons often corresponded with those of his weekly columns published in the nationally syndicated and widely read *Pittsburgh Courier,* an African American weekly newspaper. A comparison of Mays's columns with King's early sermons provides firm evidence that Mays had a major impact on the language and themes that became staples of King's preaching and thought. Each week, Mays addressed social issues such as voting rights, the myth of black inferiority, the necessity of sacrifice for social change, the social responsibilities of the church, the nature of evil in American society, and a profound optimism for justice. For an example of Mays's influence, see "The Mastery of Fear" / "Mastering Our Fears," 21 July 1957, pp. 317–321 in this volume.

21. King, "Preaching Ministry," 14 September–24 November 1948, pp. 69–72 in this volume. In his sermon file, King kept a copy of a speech by Kelsey titled "The Present Crisis in Negro Ministerial Education" (19 January 1948). In it, Kelsey expressed grave concerns regarding the level of scholarly preparation of most African American ministers.

22. King, "Autobiography of Religious Development," 12 September–22 November 1950, in *Papers* 1:363.

23. King, "The Weaknesses of Liberal Theology" I, 1948, pp. 78, 80 in this volume. For more on King's early adherence to liberal theology, see *Papers* 1:46–51.

24. For an early example of his thinking on sin, see King, " Mastering Our Evil Selves" / "Mastering Ourselves," 5 June 1949, pp. 96–97 in this volume.

standing of the social gospel that was influenced by Niebuhr's neo-orthodox thinking. King wrote, "The modern Christian must see man as a guilty sinner who must ask forgiveness and be converted."[25] He viewed Niebuhr's notion of original sin as "symbolic or mythological categories to explain the universality of sin" and "the necessary corrective of a kind of liberalism that too easily capitulated to modern culture."[26] However, King's formative experiences with the South's "vicious race problem" not only convinced him of the reality of sin; they made him question "the essential goodness of man." King recalled that he "had grown up abhorring not only segregation but also the oppressive and barbarous acts that grew out of it. . . . I had seen police brutality with my own eyes, and watched Negroes receive the most tragic injustice in the courts. All of these things had done something to my growing personality."[27]

Despite these experiences, King retained an "ever present desire to be optimistic about human nature." The act of repentance, King averred, was "an essential part of the Christian life" and made possible a "fellowship with God." Encouraged by the "noble possibilities in human nature," he found himself searching for the middle ground between social gospel optimism and neo-orthodox skepticism. King recalled going through a "transitional stage" while at Crozer, describing himself as "a victim of eclecticism" and attempting "to synthesize the best in liberal theology with the best in neo-orthodox theology and come to some understanding of man."[28]

In his 1949 sermon "Mastering Our Evil Selves" / "Mastering Ourselves" King rejected the neo-orthodox notion of a human "make-up that was predominantly evil."[29] Similarly, in "Splinters and Planks," he noted, "Sin is a well of water that each of us has drawn from" but he also denied that an individual's nature was irrevocably evil; one had a choice to either succumb to the temptation of sin or strive for goodness.[30] He maintained that the struggle between good and evil could be resolved and that through a conscious attempt to do this, "we actually master ourselves." Eventually, he declared, "we will somehow rise above evil thoughts. We will no longer possess two personalities but only one."[31]

Although King preached at his father's church before entering Crozer, he wel-

---

25. King, "How Modern Christians Should Think of Man," 29 November 1949–15 February 1950, in *Papers* 1:278. For more on King's thinking on Reinhold Niebuhr, see Introduction, in *Papers* 1:55.

26. King, "The Theology of Reinhold Niebuhr," April 1953–June 1954, in *The Papers of Martin Luther King, Jr.*, vol. 2: *Rediscovering Precious Value, July 1951–November 1955*, ed. Clayborne Carson, Ralph E. Luker, Penny A. Russell, Peter Holloran (Berkeley and Los Angeles: University of California Press, 1994), pp. 274, 278; see also King, "Reinhold Niebuhr's Ethical Dualism," 9 May 1952, in *Papers* 2:141–151.

27. King, "How Modern Christians Should Think of Men," 29 November–15 February 1950, in *Papers* 1:274. King, "My Pilgrimage to Nonviolence," 1 September 1958, in *The Papers of Martin Luther King*, vol. 4: *Symbol of the Movement, January 1957–December 1958*, ed. Clayborne Carson, Susan Carson, Adrienne Clay, Virginia Shadron, Kieran Taylor (Berkeley and Los Angeles: University of California Press, 2000), p. 473.

28. King, "How Modern Christians Should Think of Man," 29 November 1949–15 February 1950, in *Papers* 1:278, 274.

29. King, "Mastering Our Evil Selves" / "Mastering Ourselves," 5 June 1949, p. 95 in this volume.

30. King, "Splinters and Planks," 24 July 1949, pp. 97–99 in this volume.

31. King, "Mastering Our Evil Selves" / "Mastering Ourselves," 5 June 1949, pp. 96, 97 in this volume.

comed the opportunity to augment his already considerable oratorical skills with the theological sophistication he could acquire in his classes. As King wrote in his early papers on preaching, he knew that he "must somehow take profound theological and philosophical views and place them in a concrete framework" to become an effective preacher.[32] In essays for his preaching courses at Crozer, he derided ministers who left the people "lost in the fog of theological abstractions," arguing that instead, "I must forever make the complex, the simple."[33]

The ability to be an effective minister did not come readily to King, however, as indicated in the assessment of one of his ministerial evaluators who found in his pastoral approach "a smugness that refuses to adapt itself to the demands of ministering effectively to the average Negro congregation."[34] King, nevertheless, impressed most of his Crozer mentors, who gave him generally high grades and strong recommendations. George Washington Davis saw him becoming "an excellent minister or teacher," while Morton Scott Enslin predicted King would "probably become a big strong man among his people." Enslin recognized King's skill for retaining and refashioning information that could prove useful in the pulpit, writing, "All is grist that comes to his mill."[35]

King's time at Crozer proved to be the wellspring of concepts and practices that would become central to his preaching life. Unlike the essays he wrote to address theological debates, his homiletic writings—most of which were outlines or fragmentary drafts—reveal his struggle to deal with the practical concerns he would face as a clergyman while developing a solid intellectual foundation for his preaching. Many of these fragmentary drafts did not become complete sermons but they allowed him to experiment with homiletic themes and explore the meanings of biblical texts. The raw material for his future sermons, the sermon sketches and outlines that he may have prepared for preaching classes at Crozer, rely mainly on theological subjects and questions such as human immortality and death; repentance and forgiveness; and salvation, prayer and faith in human life. These writings reveal King's desire to communicate his biblical understanding and theological concerns in plain language. [36]

Central to King's approach to preaching was the concept of a knowable God. King retreated from any notion that God was, as theologian Karl Barth put forward,

---

32. King, "Preaching Ministry," 14 September–24 November 1948, p. 72 in this volume.

33. King, "Karl Barth," 14 September 1948–15 February 1950, and "Preaching Ministry," 14 September–24 November 1948, pp. 103 and 72 in this volume, respectively. King wrote both of these essays for Robert Keighton, from whom he took ten classes on preaching. He kept Keighton's 1956 work *The Man Who Would Preach* (New York: Abingdon Press, 1956) in his personal library and annotated the book, writing in a page margin, "Preaching is not merely saying something, but having something to say."

34. William E. Gardner, Crozer Theological Seminary Field Work Department: Rating Sheet for Martin Luther King, Jr., in *Papers* 1:381. Gardner, a friend of the King family, was pastor of the First Baptist Church in East Elmhurst, Queens, in New York City.

35. Davis, Crozer Theological Seminary Placement Committee: Confidential Evaluation of Martin Luther King, Jr., in *Papers* 1:334; Enslin, Crozer Theological Seminary Placement Committee: Confidential Evaluation of Martin Luther King, Jr., in *Papers* 1:354. For more on Davis's and Enslin's influence on King at Crozer, see *Papers* 1:48–49.

36. For examples of these drafts, see the section on Undated Homiletic Material, pp. 559–600 in this volume.

"'wholly other.' God is not a process projected somewhere [*in*] the lofty blue. God is not a divine hermit hiding himself in a cosmic cave."[37] While admitting that "we never find all of God," King scorned Barth's and the crisis theologians' "disdain for the very use of the word experience in a religious context" and contended that "the very idea of God is an outgrowth of experience."[38] To King, God was a readily perceivable entity, comprehendible and immanent. He preached that the knowable God maintained a personal interest in each human soul and was most discernable through biblical stories of Jesus' life. In a 1952 Christmas sermon King addressed "the Christlikeness of God" and asserted that Jesus "brought God nearer to earth."[39] He also affirmed that "God has set us a plan for the building of the soul, the life of Christ as it is revealed in the New Testament."[40] Ultimately, King stated, one could not escape God: "Fleeing into darkness or forgetting God is no escape from him."[41]

According to King, Jesus' example in the Bible provided Christians with a personal life path. He challenged his parishioners to examine themselves before condemning the sins of others and urged personal contrition for one's transgressions. In one of his earliest known complete sermons, King explained, "When we would criticise others for their shortcomings and insist that they be turned out of church, we hear Jesus saying, 'he who is without sin cast the first stone.'"[42] In a sermon sketch, he observed, "God always reserves for man the possibility of repentance" and characterized atonement as "a change of conduct as well as of heart." He then counseled forgiveness of others' sins: "Forgiveness does not take away the fact of sin. But it restores the offender to communion with us, which he had forfeited through his offense."[43] Forgiveness is necessary as it "is a process of life <u>and</u> the Christian weapon of social redemption. . . . the Christian weapon against social evil."[44]

In line with that notion of redemption, King concluded that Christian forgiveness "is the solution of the race problem." He urged his listeners to "go out with the spirit of forgiveness, heal the hurts, right the wrongs and change society."[45] King believed that this kind of "moral progress" was not only humanly possible but socially necessary for human survival.[46] For whites, he prescribed empathy, advising, "If the white man was closer to the Negro he would know more about the Negro and understand him better."[47] In an early outline inspired by the writings of Thomas Aquinas, King remarked that differences among people were a creation of God

37. King, "Mastering Our Evil Selves" / "Mastering Ourselves," 5 June 1949, p. 97 in this volume.

38. King, "The Place of Reason and Experience in Finding God," 13 September–23 November 1949, in *Papers* 1:231, 233, 234. For more on King's view of the importance of religious experience, see Introduction, in *Papers* 1:52.

39. King, After Christmas, What? 28 December 1952, p. 129 in this volume.

40. King, Sermon Conclusions, 30 November 1948–16 February 1949, p. 85 in this volume; see also "O That I Knew Where I Might Find Him!" 1948–1954, pp. 591–598 in this volume.

41. King, "God the Inescapable," 1948–1954, p. 574 in this volume.

42. King, "Facing Life's Inescapables," 3 March 1949, p. 90 in this volume.

43. King, Sermon Sketches II, 30 November 1948–16 February 1949, pp. 82, 83 in this volume.

44. King, "The Meaning of Forgiveness," 1948–1954, pp. 580–581 in this volume.

45. King, "The Meaning of Forgiveness," 1948–1954, p. 581 in this volume.

46. King, "Civilization's Great Need," 1949, p. 86 in this volume.

47. King, "I Sat Where They Sat," 1948–1954, p. 581 in this volume.

"because God brought things into being in order that his goodness might be represented by his creatures. And because his goodness could not be represented by one creature alone, He produced many and diverse creatures." He maintained that God intended that people "Black, red, yellow, white" were meant to co-exist, and concluded, "Our biological differences are but [*varying*] expressions of the richness and complexity of the divine nature."[48]

Seeking to reconcile modern social science with theology, King often used psychology and sociology to buttress the assertions in his sermons. In an early conclusion to "Life Is What You Make It," King noted, "Modern psychology affirms that vital religious faith is unequaled in its resources to make life worth living."[49] He referred to psychologist Carl Rogers's "permissive environment" when articulating the need for all Christians to put themselves in others' shoes, avowing that "unless you sit where others sit you cannot really know them or understand them."[50] King also endorsed the gift of reason and intelligence, maintaining that while conscientiousness was honorable, if it was not accompanied "by intelligence it can become the most ruinous force in human nature."[51] While he characterized scientific innovations as "tangible and amazing victories" and viewed the status of contemporary education as "astounding," King also distrusted advances that were used without regard to their impact on human life. He emphasized that science "alone will not save us at this moment. With the most amazing means of production in history we have unemployment. With the most amazing world contacts on record we make world wars." He concluded that "unless we can reestablish the moral and spiritual ends of living in personal character and social justice, our civilization will ruin itself with the misuse of its own instruments."[52] Without the reinforcement of Christian values, King believed, the sciences could as easily be forces of destruction as advancement.

In the post–World War II era, when many questioned God's existence and the purpose of faith in the wake of fascism and the atomic age, King maintained his confidence in God's ability to guide human life and history and in Christianity's force as a vehicle for social change. He detailed this vision of Christianity as a moral force in an early essay, "The Philosophy of Life Undergirding Christianity and the Christian Ministry." In his estimation, "Christianity is a value philosophy," one which judged the worth of human life and quality of earthly existence to be its greatest concern. Rather than disdain daily existence, King expressed his belief that the

---

48. King, "The Distinctions in God's Creation," 1948–1954, p. 579 in this volume. King drew on the writings of Thomas Aquinas's *Summa Theologica* (Anton C. Pegis, ed., *Introductions to St. Thomas Aquinas* [New York: Modern Library, 1948], pp. 259, 261). King referred to this volume in "The Distinctions in God's Creation."

49. King, Sermon Conclusions, 30 November 1948–16 February 1949, p. 86 in this volume. For other examples of this practice, see King, "A Way Out," 22 May 1949; "Mastering Our Evil Selves" / "Mastering Ourselves," 5 June 1949; and "First Things First," 2 August 1953, pp. 90–94, 94–97 and 143–146 in this volume, respectively.

50. King, "I Sat Where They Sat," 1948–1954, p. 581 in this volume.

51. King, Sincerity Is Not Enough, 3 June 1951, p. 119 in this volume.

52. King, "Civilization's Great Need," 1949, pp. 86, 87 in this volume; see also King, "Science and Religion," September 1948–May 1951, pp. 108–109 in this volume.

world "is a place in which God is fitting men and women for the Kingdom of God." Similarly, he felt that "Christianity at its highest and best has always insisted that persons are intrinsically valuable. And so it is the job of the Christian to love every man because God [*loves*] love."[53]

In the fall of 1951, King began his graduate studies in systematic theology at Boston University. Like his other academic writings as a doctoral student, King's dissertation was flawed by extensive use of unattributed sources, but it nonetheless expressed his maturing theological beliefs.[54] In his dissertation King rejected the theological abstractions of Paul Tillich and Henry Nelson Wieman in favor of a knowable and personal God more worthy of worship: "In God there is feeling and will, responsive to the deepest yearnings of the human heart; this God both evokes and answers prayers."[55] King's own optimism was not rooted in human acts but in his belief that "God and the universe are on the side of right."[56]

This skepticism regarding human acts extended to the economic milieu. King expressed disdain for capitalism in a letter written to Coretta Scott in the course of their courtship. Lonely during their separation in the summer of 1952, King first expressed his longing for Scott before thanking her for a copy of Edward Bellamy's socialist utopian novel, *Looking Backward 2000–1887*.[57] After reflecting on the book's merits and weaknesses, King agreed with Bellamy that capitalism "has outlived its usefulness. It has brought about a system that takes necessities from the masses to give luxuries to the classes." He concluded the letter with his assessment

---

53. King, "The Philosophy of Life Undergirding Christianity and the Christian Ministry," September 1948–May 1951, pp. 110, 111 in this volume; see also King, "God's Love," 5 September 1954, pp. 179–181 in this volume.

54. For King's dissertation in its entirety, see "A Comparison of the Conceptions of God in the Thinking of Paul Tillich and Henry Nelson Wieman," 15 April 1955, in *Papers* 2:339–544. For information on King's use of unattributed sources in student papers and a more detailed evaluation of King's dissertation, see Introduction, in *Papers* 2:6, 25–26.

55. King, "A Comparison of the Conceptions of God in the Thinking of Paul Tillich and Henry Nelson Wieman," 15 April 1955, in *Papers* 2:512. After being introduced to personalist theology at Crozer, King pursued his interest in this philosophical school with Edgar S. Brightman and L. Harold DeWolf during his graduate studies at Boston University. King's professors reinforced his belief in a God that could be perceived through personal events such as conversion and known as a concrete entity, one capable of intervening directly in human life and history. In his dissertation, King argued that denying that God had a distinct and knowable personality was "a rejection of rationality, goodness and love of God in the full sense of the words." To think this was to render God into "an unconscious process devoid of any true purpose." King, on the other hand, believed in a " 'living' God," one that was both immanent in the universe and possessed a personality: "The religious man has always recognized two fundamental religious values. One is fellowship with God, the other is trust in his goodness. Both of these imply the personality of God. . . . There may be interactions between impersonal beings, but not fellowship" (King, "A Comparison of the Conceptions of God in the Thinking of Paul Tillich and Henry Nelson Wieman," 15 April 1955, in *Papers* 2:506, 534, 512).

56. King, Index of Sermon Topics, 20 February–4 May 1951, p. 116 in this volume.

57. Edward Bellamy, *Looking Backward 2000–1887* (New York: Modern Library, 1951). Scott inscribed the book, writing, "I should be interested to know your reactions to Bellamy's predictions about our society. [¶] In some ways it is rather encouraging to see how our social order has changed since Bellamy's time. There is still hope for the future . . . Lest we become too impatient" (Scott, Inscription to Martin Luther King, Jr., 7 April 1952).

that "our economic system is going through a radical change, and certainly this change is needed. I would certainly welcome the day to come when there will be a nationalization of industry." He vowed to "hope, work, and pray that in the future we will live to see a warless world, a better distribution of wealth, and a brotherhood that transcends race or color. This is the gospel that I will preach to the world."[58]

While home from Boston in the summer of 1953 King explored the idea of worship as a counter to the intrusions of modern secular life in a sermon series at Ebenezer that may have been broadcast on Atlanta radio station WERD. He began by explaining that humanity's need to worship was instinctual and as natural "as the rising of the sun is to the cosmic order." King preached about the danger of turning one's natural "worship drive into false channels" and revering "false gods." The misdirected force of spiritual zeal had consequences that were national and international in scope. King warned his listeners of the dangers in viewing science and human effort as the source of salvation without recognizing that "the god of science which we so devoutly worshipped has brought about the possibility of universal annihilation."[59] He dedicated the second sermon in his series on false gods to an examination of the god of nationalism and castigated the purveyors of an unbridled chauvinism that led to wars and potential nuclear destruction. He also suggested that such impulses were also the source of white supremacy and "imperialistic greed." King called upon his listeners to join other "believers of the christian principle" and consider themselves as part of a larger world community: "If we are to avoid the drudgery of war; if we are to avoid being plunged across the abyss of atomic destruction, we must transcend the narrow confines of nationalism. Nationalism must give way to internationalism."[60] King's last sermon on false gods explored what was to his mind the most prevalent form of this sin: the worship of money and material goods. King charged, "This is the danger forever threatening our capitalistic economy which places so much emphasis on the profit motive," and he condemned the elevation of the dollar "to the status of a god. It becomes a power that corrupts and an instrument of exploitation."[61] In each case, King asked his listeners to return to the worship of the one God, focus their attention on national and world affairs, and regard social issues as part of their spiritual existence.

Racism appeared as a false god in King's thematic series. In "False God of Nationalism," King wondered, "Will we continue to serve the false god of racial prejudice or will we serve the God who made of one blood all men to dwell upon the face of the earth."[62] In his early attempts to grapple with prejudice, he recalled, "I had also learned that the inseparable twin of racial injustice is economic injustice. I saw how the systems of segregation ended up in the exploitation of the Negro as well as the poor whites."[63] King broadened his accusation of race prejudice, in his

---

58. King to Scott, 18 July 1952, pp. 123–126 in this volume.

59. King, "The False God of Science," 5 July 1953, pp. 130–132 in this volume.

60. King, "The False God of Nationalism," 12 July 1953, pp. 132–133 in this volume.

61. King, "The False God of Money," 19 July 1953, pp. 134, 135 in this volume; see also "Will Capitalism Survive?" 14 September 1948–15 February 1950, pp. 104–105 in this volume.

62. King, "The False God of Nationalism," 12 July 1953, p. 133 in this volume.

63. King, "My Pilgrimage to Nonviolence," 13 April 1960, in *Papers* 5:421–422.

1953 version of "Communism's Challenge to Christianity," to include the Christian church. "Segregation and discrimination could not exist in America today without the sanction of the Church," he maintained. "I am [*ashamed*] and appalled at the fact that Eleven O'clock on Sunday morning is the most segregated hour in Christian America. How tardy we have been. The Church has [*too*] often been an institution serving to crystalize the patterns of the status quo."[64]

Even early in his career, King used Jesus' teachings to espouse the use of love as a means of resolving conflict on personal, national and international levels. He counseled his listeners that Jesus' "new and revolutionary" call to "love even your enemies" was "the solution of the world's problem." King characterized Jesus' words as those of a "practical realist" that were "an absolute necessity for the survival of our civilization." Acknowledging that this tactic seemed unfeasible, King directed his congregants to evaluate themselves and their adversaries in life. Warning that "there might be causes on your end," conversely, King offered, "Always be willing to see the good points in your enemy." Finally, King proposed, love your enemies "because love has within [*it*] a redemptive power."[65] King's rejection of the goal of utterly defeating and humiliating one's opponent based in Christ's precepts had a telling effect on his pursuit of justice in future years.

King's early sermons and writings exhibited his desire to present the ideas inspired by his theological training and his own meditations on his faith in ways relevant and meaningful to his congregants. He readily drew on the notion of a knowable God to communicate the power and vision of his own Christological beliefs, and to preach the gospel of justice in a way that revealed his concern for his congregants' social and economic realities as well as their spiritual welfare. These abilities would later hold him in good stead as he met the challenge of his first pastorate at Dexter Avenue Baptist Church.

            ∾⊙≈⊙≈⊙≈

Following his marriage to Coretta Scott in 1953 and subsequent completion of the required course work for his doctorate at Boston University, King began to explore various career paths. While he entertained offers from academic institutions, he was also interested in serving as pastor of a community church. Among those King considered was Dexter Avenue Baptist Church in Montgomery, Alabama, a historic congregation near the Alabama State Capitol building with a membership that could boast of many of the city's black professionals including several faculty members from Alabama State College. The highly educated young pastor believed that he and the congregation could work well together.[66]

---

64. King, "Communism's Challenge to Christianity," 9 August 1953, p. 149 in this volume; see also King, "Is the Church the Hope of the World," 14 September–15 February 1950, pp. 105–106 in this volume. To King, race prejudice was a form of human sin. He observed that "the average white southerner . . . goes to church every Sunday. He worships the same God we worship . . . Yet at the same time He will spend thousands of dollars in an attempt to keep the Negro segregated and discriminated" (King, "Mastering Our Evil Selves" / "Mastering Ourselves," 5 June 1949, p. 96 in this volume).

65. King, "Loving Your Enemies," 31 August 1952, pp. 127–128 in this volume.

66. For a description of King's job opportunities, his interest in Dexter, and the history of the church, see Introduction, in *Papers* 2:28–30.

Invited to preach in January 1954 as a candidate to fill the congregation's pastoral vacancy, King elected to deliver one of his time-tested sermons, "The Dimensions of a Complete Life."[67] Based loosely on a sermon by Phillips Brooks, the scope of King's message expanded beyond personal and domestic affairs to consider issues of global concern, noting the negative effects of self-interested nations. While he recalled feeling some pressure to alter "Dimensions" in order to impress the congregation, in the end he reminded himself, "Keep Martin Luther King in the background and God in the foreground and everything will be all right."[68] In the sermon, King urged his listeners to maximize their personal abilities, move beyond their own lives by fostering genuine concern for others, and pursue a fulfilling relationship with God.[69]

After receiving the call to be the church's new pastor, King returned to Dexter early in April to preach "Going Forward by Going Backward."[70] The sermon included a harsh critique of society's pursuit of knowledge and materialism without also cultivating the timeless moral principles and a devotion to God that would truly make of the world a "brotherhood." Still, King sounded a chord of hope because of his conviction that the "universe hinges on moral foundations." He affirmed:

> There is something in this universe that justifies Carlyle in saying, "No lie can live forever." There is something in this universe which justifies William Cullen Bryant in saying, "Truth crushed to earth will rise again." There is something which justifies James Russell Lowell in saying, "Truth forever on the scaffold, wrong forever on the throne, yet that scaffold sways the future." [71]

The Dexter congregation would often hear this set piece advocating faith in the ultimate triumph of justice and righteousness.

Soon after his April visit, King wrote Dexter Avenue Baptist Church and agreed

---

67. Coretta Scott King claims "Three Dimensions" was the first sermon she heard King preach (Coretta Scott King, *My Life with Martin Luther King, Jr.* [New York: Holt, 1969], p. 59). King had also delivered a sermon with this title in September 1953 while serving as associate pastor at Ebenezer ("King Jr. to End Summer Series of Sermons; Ebenezer," *Atlanta Daily World*, 5 September 1953).

68. In his recollections of his first sermon at Dexter, King adds, "The congregation was receptive, and I left with the feeling that God had used me well, and that here was a fine church with challenging possibilities" (King, *Stride Toward Freedom: The Montgomery Story* [New York: Harper & Brothers, 1958], p. 17).

69. King, "The Dimensions of a Complete Life," Sermon at Dexter Avenue Baptist Church, 24 January 1954, pp. 150–156 in this volume.

70. King, "Going Forward by Going Backward," Sermon at Dexter Avenue Baptist Church, 4 April 1954, pp. 159–163 in this volume; see also Robert D. Nesbitt and Thomas H. Randall to King, 7 March 1954, in *Papers* 2:256.

71. King, "Going Forward by Going Backward," 4 April 1954, p. 162 in this volume; Thomas Carlyle, *The French Revolution* (1837), Bryant, "The Battlefield" (1839), and Lowell, "The Present Crisis" (1844). These three passages became commonplace in King's oratory. In a February 1960 letter from Dexter parishioners Cynthia and Julius Alexander, the couple remembered King's recitation of Lowell's 1844 poem as they recalled that "many months ago you said we must be prepared to face some real dark days ere freedom comes, . . . Yet if I may quote you 'Beyond the dim unknown God keeps watch over His own'" (Cynthia and Julius Alexander to King, 14 February–21 February 1960, in *Papers* 5:375). For King's use of this stanza of Lowell's poem, see "Discerning the Signs of History," 26 June 1955, p. 219 in this volume.

to become its pastor.[72] He returned to Montgomery on 2 May 1954 to give the sermon "Accepting Responsibility for Your Actions." In this third sermon at Dexter he challenged congregation members not to allow the circumstances of heredity or environment to determine their lives, but instead to focus on individual accountability as an effective response to crises and setbacks in life. King suggested Marian Anderson and Roland Hayes as African American role models who had achieved in spite of, and as a result of their reactions to, hindrances and injustice. However, King tempered his emphasis on individual responsibility and put his new congregation on notice regarding the type of leadership he would provide by stating, "I happen to be a firm believer in what is called the 'social gospel.' " While King's written text did not flesh out his definition of the term, he emphasized the necessity of pursuing "social reform."[73] King's fundamental commitment to advocating social justice remained constant.[74]

After that morning's service, King formally accepted the church's call with an afternoon address before his new congregation. He told them, "I come to the pastorate of Dexter at a most crucial hour of our world's history." He also humbly noted that he was neither a "great preacher" nor a "profound scholar" and came with "nothing so special to offer." Despite his self-effacement, King exhorted the congregation to "give our generation an answer. Dexter, like all other churches, must somehow lead men and women of a decadent generation to the high mountain of peace and salvation."[75]

Within two weeks of King's acceptance, the U.S. Supreme Court issued its first decision in the case of *Brown v. Board of Education,* ruling school segregation unconstitutional.[76] During the hopeful summer after the court's unanimous decision, King commuted between Boston and Montgomery a few times a month as he completed work on his dissertation. During this time, King continually urged his new congregation to take courageous stands for justice while bemoaning the cowardice and hypocrisy of whites regarding issues of race. In his May 1954 sermon "Mental and Spiritual Slavery," King reflected on Pilate's acquiescence to the crowd's demand that Jesus be crucified while condemning the reluctance of many Christians to be true to their consciences when it came to issues of race.[77] Although King was aware that his congregation included many who felt daily pressure to conform to white southern mores in order to maintain their jobs and insure their safety and that of their families, he did not hesitate to question the morality of this sub-

---

72. King, To Dexter Avenue Baptist Church, 14 April 1954, in *Papers* 2:260.

73. For an earlier version of this 2 May 1954 sermon, see King, "Accepting Responsibility for Your Actions," 26 July 1953, pp. 139–142 in this volume.

74. King did occasionally get involved in efforts to challenge injustice prior to his arrival at Dexter. For instance, in 1950 he and three friends charged a New Jersey bar owner with violating the state's civil rights laws. The case was eventually dropped ("Statement on Behalf of Ernest Nichols, S*tate of New Jersey vs. Ernest Nichols,* by W. Thomas McGann," 20 July 1950, in *Papers* 1:327–329).

75. King, Acceptance Address at Dexter Avenue Baptist Church, 2 May 1954, p. 166 in this volume.

76. *Brown et al. v. Board of Education of Topeka et al.,* 347 U.S. 483 (1954).

77. King, "Mental and Spiritual Slavery," Sermon at Dexter Avenue Baptist Church, May 1954, pp. 167–170 in this volume.

Biblical source text

Romans 12:2—"And be not conformed to this world:
but be ye transformed by the renewing of your mind."

Romans 12:2

The source of our strength and our love is God. We are not called to be reformers, but to be transformed nonconformists—to be men who live differently. Paul's word here is the Greek word from which we get our English derivative "metamorphosis." Paul is saying that God will radically and thoroughly change us. Jesus' word for it was to be "born again," and Paul's testimony was that when he opened his life to God in Christ "all things became new."
—*James E. Will, Sermon: "Men Who Live Differently," July 1951*

Mark 15:5— "And so Pilate, willing to content the people, released
Barabbas unto them, and delivered Jesus to be crucified."

Now at a point we must all be conformist. (We are tied to an extent to the folkways and mores) There is no virtue in being a nonconformist just to be a non conformist. Some people are non conformist just to get attention and to be different. This type of nonconformity I am not speaking of. I am speaking of a non conformity which is based on high and noble purposes. . . . {Quote Paul} We Christians are not called upon to be the conformist, but the non-conformist.
—*King, Sermon: "Mental and Spiritual Slavery," May 1954*

Romans 12:2

So Paul gives us a [*formula*] for constructive nonconformity which is found in the second half of the text. In order to discern the true will of God and become constructive nonconformist we must accept a new mental outlook. We must be transformed. Jesus' phrase for this experience was the new birth. And so only when we have been born again can we be true nonconformist. We are called upon to be transformed nonconformist. This is our eternal challenge as christians.
—*King, Sermon: "Transformed Nonconformist," November 1954*

Romans 12:2

So Paul gives us the [*formula*] for constructive nonconformity in the second half of the text. "Be ye transformed by the renewing of your mind." In other words nonconformity can only be creative ~~when~~ when it is controlled and directed by a transformed life. In order to be a constructive nonconformist we must accept a new mental outlook. We must so open our lives to God in Christ that he makes us new creatures. Jesus' phrase for this experience was the new birth. So only when we have been born again can we be true nonconformists. We are called upon not merely to be nonconformist, but to be transformed nonconformists.
—*King, Sermon: "Transformed Nonconformist," July 1962–March 1963*

mission to convention.[78] King may have felt more comfortable presenting this ethical problem because he knew that his predecessor at Dexter, Vernon Johns, had consistently challenged the congregation to display greater courage in confronting racism.[79]

King lacked some of Johns's abrasiveness but he did not intend to allow the members of his new congregation to comfortably conform to the immorality of apartheid. He warned that "most people today are in Pilate's shoes i.e. conformist. Most people would take stands on their ideas but they are afraid of being non-conformist." King made an example of "the [*minister*] choosing between truth and . . . being popular with the [*brethren*]," and concluded, "The great progressive moves of history have been ruined by the [*perpetuity*] of 'Pilateness.'" For a congregation filled with African American teachers and professors whose jobs were in the hands of white government officials, nonconformity could come at a great cost. King let his parishioners know early on that he expected them to make sacrifices on behalf of the "great progressive moves of history."[80]

"Mental and Spiritual Slavery" also demonstrates King's usage of other ministers' sermons for themes, phrases, and organization. James Will's homily "Men Who Live Differently," published in 1951, provided King with the sermon's key argument—that nonconformity for a moral purpose may be the truly Christian path. Although King did not follow Will's organization, he did re-title this sermon "Transformed Nonconformist," a subheading found in Will's sermon. It became one of his most enduring homilies.[81]

As he became more comfortable with his new congregation, and buoyed by the recent Supreme Court *Brown* decision, King continued to advocate for the necessity of the social gospel during his first summer as Dexter's pastor. He boldly reminded his audience of the twin scourges of conformity and hypocrisy that obstruct the way to justice, noting that the same whites "who lynch Negroes worship Christ," and that the "strongest advocators of segregation in America also worship Christ."[82] On 11 July 1954 he again called on Dexter members to accept the Christian imperative to work for social change: "We can talk all we want to about saving souls from hell and

---

78. Several Alabama State College faculty members attended Dexter, including Jo Ann Robinson, James E. Pierce, Mary Fair Burks, Norman Walton, and president H. Councill Trenholm. Robinson said that Dexter "had always been made up of many of the elite—the professionals and intellectuals—of Montgomery's black communities. Most of the church members were well educated, with good jobs and high positions because of their college and university training" (Robinson, *The Montgomery Bus Boycott and the Women Who Started It*, David J. Garrow, ed. [Knoxville: The University of Tennessee Press, 1987], p. 67). While some of Dexter's members may have been careful not to upset those in power, Robinson lobbied for social change throughout her tenure. In 1954, she penned a letter to Montgomery Mayor W. A. Gayle suggesting a bus boycott would be possible if conditions on the local buses did not improve (Jo Ann Robinson to W. A. Gayle, 21 May 1954).

79. Johns's boldness and stubbornness eventually convinced the board to accept his resignation in late 1952. For a description of King's impression of Johns, see Introduction, in *Papers* 2:29–30 and note 2, King to Thurman, 31 October 1955, in *Papers* 2:584.

80. King, "Mental and Spiritual Slavery," May 1954, pp. 169, 170 in this volume.

81. For more on the influences on this sermon, see Chart 1.

82. King, "A Religion of Doing," Sermon at Dexter Avenue Baptist Church, 4 July 1954, p. 173 in this volume.

preaching the pure and simple gospel, but unless we preach the social gospel our evangelistic gospel will be meaningless."[83]

Despite his growing ease with his new position, King remained sensitive to Dexter's exclusive reputation. While he accepted the congregation's staid responses to his preaching, King later admitted that he had been "anxious to change the impression in the community that Dexter was a sort of silk-stocking church."[84] King was convinced that true worship would transcend class distinctions, as he believed all were at a level place before God. In a sermon titled "Worship," King expressed a vision to inspire his congregation:

> Worship at its best is a social experience where people of all [*levels*] of life come together and communicate with a common father. Here the employer and the employee, the rich and the poor, the white collar worker and the common laborer all come [*together*] in a vast unity. Here we come to see that although we have different callings in life we are all the children of a common father, who is the father of both the rich and the poor.[85]

Some Dexter members have recounted strong impressions of King's preaching. Thelma Rice recognized the high quality of both the content and presentation of his sermons: "I was impressed with the command that he had over what he wanted to say and the way he said it, with [*conviction*]."[86] Another parishioner, Mrs. O. B. Underwood, also called young King "an outstanding preacher." She was impressed with King's delivery: "His voice was soothing; he could gain your attention almost immediately; you didn't wander when he was speaking; you listened when he was speaking, whether it was a mass meeting or a church service or a social gathering, feeling extremely elated." Underwood remembered resistance to his messages as well: "Many people didn't like his way of delivering Sunday morning messages. But most of the younger people and certainly most of his friends were very much in accord with his thoughts." She admired his directness: "The way he was able to deliver a message, it always hit, and it probably hit too hard. We used to laugh about many of the messages because you could sit in the back of the church and point out certain people that you knew said, 'looks like this message was aimed at that particular person.' "[87]

---

83. King, "What Is Man?" Sermon at Dexter Avenue Baptist Church, 11 July 1954, p. 176 in this volume.

84. King, *Stride Toward Freedom*, p. 25.

85. King, "Worship," Sermon at Dexter Avenue Baptist Church, 7 August 1955, p. 225 in this volume. In his annual report, King informed the congregation that new members would no longer be "voted in the church from the floor" but seen by the head of the Deacon Board, the church clerk, and the New Members Committee. They would then be "listed in the Church Bulletin on the Sunday after they join, and they will be officially welcomed into the church on the First Sunday night with the right hand of fellowship" (King, "Annual Report, Dexter Avenue Baptist Church," 1 October 1954–31 October 1955, in *Papers* 2:582, 583).

86. Thelma Rice, interview by Norman Lumpkin, 22 August 1973, in *Statewide Oral History Project*, Vol. 3, interview #052, Special Collections, Alabama State University Library, Montgomery. Alabama.

87. Mrs. O. B. Underwood, interview by Norman Lumpkin, 17 August 1973, in *Statewide Oral History Project*, Vol. 4, interview #054.

While King continued to preach moral nonconformity to his parishioners, many of his sermons and speeches over the next year contained a note of optimism regarding desegregation and greater racial justice.[88] Just a few days after Martin and Coretta King permanently made their home in Dexter's parsonage, King attended the National Baptist Convention in St. Louis, where he delivered an address before its Woman's Convention Auxiliary. His words indicate an increasing confidence in the inevitability of racial progress, desegregation, and social change: "Ultimately history brings into being the new order to blot out the tragic reign of the old order." King stressed that "the tide has turned" and "segregation is passing away."[89]

Not content to merely confront the moral comfort of his parishioners, King began to focus on mobilizing his new congregation to take advantage of the singular opportunity to challenge segregation presented by the *Brown* decision. In his sermon "Creating the Abundant Life," King advised his parishioners, "First if we are to create the abundant life we must give ourselves to some great purpose and some great cause that transcends ourselves."[90] Soon after relocating to Montgomery, King presented a plan for the future: "Since the gospel of Jesus is a social gospel as well as a personal gospel seeking to save the whole man, a Social and Political Action Committee shall be established for the purpose of keeping the congregation intelligently informed concerning the social, political, and economic situation," he announced. "This committee shall keep before the congregation the importance of the N.A.A.C.P."[91]

King's skill as a preacher rapidly became known throughout the community, and his reputation garnered him speaking opportunities outside his home church.[92] At the 23 January 1955 meeting of the Birmingham National Association for the Advancement of Colored People (NAACP), King spoke on "A Realistic Approach to Progress in Race Relations," and charged his audience to take action: "You must do more than pray and read the Bible" to eliminate segregation and discrimination.[93] He delivered the baccalaureate sermon at Alabama State College's graduation on 15 May 1955. His talk to the graduating students and their families described three mountains that had to be surmounted: "rugged individualism and national isolationism, the mountain of [*mediocrity*] in our various fields of endeavor, [*and*] the

---

88. This volume contains almost 20 extant sermons preached in the year before the beginning of the bus boycott at the end of 1955, more than any other period in King's early preaching career. It illuminates a period of King's preaching ministry that was previously arcane.

89. King, "The Vision of a World Made New," 9 September 1954, pp. 183, 184 in this volume.

90. King, "Creating an Abundant Life," Sermon at Dexter Avenue Baptist Church, 26 September 1954, p. 189 in this volume.

91. King, "Recommendations to the Dexter Avenue Baptist Church for the Fiscal Year 1954–1955," 5 September 1954, in *Papers* 2:290.

92. King's father remarked on his son's growing reputation: "Alexander called me yesterday just to tell me about how you swept them at Friendship Sunday. Every way I turned people are [*congratulating*] me for you. You see young man you are becoming very popular. As I told you you must be much in prayer. Persons like yourself are the ones the devil turns all of his forces aloose to destroy" (King, Sr. to King, Jr., 2 December 1954, in *Papers* 2:320).

93. "Apathy Among Church Leaders Hit in Talk by Rev. M. L. King," 25 January 1955, in *Papers* 2:330, 331.

mountain of hate and bitterness."[94] He was then invited to address the Montgomery NAACP chapter in June. In his speech, titled "The Peril of Superficial Optimism in the Area of Race Relations," King acknowledged the amazing progress in the area of race relations that had been made in recent years but warned against the potential onset of complacency:

> The danger facing the American Negro is that because of these astounding advances he will become complacent and feel that the overall problem is solved. And with the further assertion that that which is not solved will move inevitably toward solution. We might fall victims to the cult of inevitable progress. We must be realistic realizing that the problem might creep back into the window at any time. So long as one spark of prejudice lies latent in the heart of any white American, there is a possibility for it to develop into a flame of [*intolerance*] at the unpredictable moments. [95]

Yet even while rejecting shallow, naive optimism, King believed that there was reason for hope. A few weeks later, in an early version of "Death of Evil Upon the Seashore," he proclaimed, "Segregation is drowning today in the rushing waters of historical necessity."[96] Although King did not dismiss the persistence of racism, he encouraged his congregation to overcome the temptation "to look upon all white persons as evil." He observed that when an African American "looks beyond his circumstances and sees the whole of the situation, he discovers that some of the most implacable and vehement advocates of racial equality are consecrated white persons."[97] As evidence of this goodwill, King cited the founding white members of the NAACP.

Events during the coming months would temper King's optimism regarding white people, especially those in the South. The murder of young Emmett Till on 28 August 1955 was a brutal reminder of the vital and horrific reality of racism. The September acquittal of his murderers by an all-white Mississippi jury revealed the pervasive sanctioning of racist brutality. After bemoaning the hypocrisy of imperialist nations who have claimed to worship Christ while crushing "Africa and Asia with the iron feet of oppression," King commented in his sermon "Pride Versus Humility," "That jury in Mississippi, which a few days ago in the Emmett Till case, freed two white men from what might be considered one of the most brutal and inhuman crimes of the twentieth century, worships Christ."[98]

---

94. King, "Other Mountains," Baccalaureate Sermon at Alabama State College, 15 May 1955, p. 214 in this volume; for a similar talk see "Keep Moving from This Mountain," Address at Spelman College on 10 April 1960, in *Papers* 5:409–419.

95. King, "The Peril of Superficial Optimism in the Area of Race Relations," 19 June 1955, p. 215 in this volume.

96. King, "The Death of Evil Upon the Seashore," Sermon at Dexter Avenue Baptist Church, 24 July 1955.

97. King, "Looking Beyond Your Circumstances," Sermon at Dexter Avenue Baptist Church, 18 September 1955, p. 227 in this volume.

98. King, "Pride Versus Humility: The Parable of the Pharisee and the Publican," Sermon at Dexter Avenue Baptist Church, 25 September 1955, p. 232 in this volume.

As 1955 drew to a close, and in the wake of the Till verdict, King made charges in his sermons directed at the heart of the oppressive conditions faced by the black community. In an October 1955 sermon on the parable of the rich man and Lazarus, he pointed out that structural injustices become so ingrained that they are not seen as wrong or unjust. King warned that the "inequalities of circumstance" can only be overcome with great effort and sacrifice.[99] His concern for structural change was also prominent in a sermon titled "The One-Sided Approach of the Good Samaritan" that he delivered less than two weeks before the arrest of Rosa Parks. King questioned the long-term effectiveness of the Good Samaritan's actions: "He was concerned [*merely*] with temporary [*relief*], not with thorough reconstruction. He sought to [*soothe*] the effects of evil, without going back to uproot the causes." He concluded by calling his congregation to couple the compassion of the Good Samaritan with a willingness "to tear down unjust conditions and build anew instead of just patching things up."[100]

King's sermons as a pastor in the segregated South combined messages of hope with a stiff dose of social realism. While he was increasingly cognizant of the intransigence of white supremacy, he continued to encourage his congregation to embrace a gospel of social action and social change. Although he was shaken by the hypocrisy of white Christians evidenced by the Emmett Till case, King reminded himself and his congregation that there was still cause for optimism and hope.

On the first day of December 1955, police arrested Rosa Parks for violating local segregation laws. Early the next morning community activist E. D. Nixon called King and requested his support for a plan for a one-day boycott of the city's buses. Jo Ann Robinson, president of the Women's Political Council, had been threatening a boycott for nearly two years, as frustrations over the treatment of African Americans on Montgomery city buses multiplied. With Parks's arrest, Robinson saw an opportunity to make her dream a reality. Working past midnight on Friday, 2 December, she made thousands of copies of an announcement calling for a boycott of city buses for the following Monday.[101]

When Nixon called King that morning to announce the boycott, King agreed to join the planning, and the first meeting was set for Dexter that evening. Though the meeting was contentious, dozens of pastors in Montgomery agreed to communicate the boycott plans to their congregations that Sunday.[102] King's scheduled sermon title on that morning was "Why Does God Hide Himself?" King's sermon notes reveal a theme in his preaching over the coming year: the pervasiveness of evil and

---

99. King, "The Impassable Gulf (The Parable of Dives and Lazarus)," Sermon at Dexter Avenue Baptist Church , 2 October 1955, p. 237 in this volume.

100. King, "The One-Sided Approach of the Good Samaritan," 20 November 1955, p. 240 in this volume.

101. For a more detailed description of the beginnings of the boycott, see Introduction, in *The Papers of Martin Luther King, Jr.*, vol. 3: *Birth of a New Age, December 1955–December 1956*, ed. Clayborne Carson, Stewart Burns, Susan Carson, Peter Holloran, Dana L. H. Powell (Berkeley and Los Angeles: University of California Press, 1997), pp. 1–9.

102. Introduction, in *Papers* 3:3–4.

injustice. Bemoaning the ubiquity of evil throughout the globe, King proclaimed, "We have seen imperialistic nations trampling over other nations with the iron feet of oppression." Unfortunately, while atrocities continued, "the awful silence of heaven remained unbroken."[103] With the commencement of the bus boycott, King continued to wrestle with the "silence" of God in the midst of daily struggle.

During his Sunday message, King encouraged his congregation to not ride the city buses but he had no idea he would soon be thrust into the spotlight as spokesperson of the movement. On Monday afternoon, 5 December, leaders of Montgomery's black community elected King president of the newly formed Montgomery Improvement Association (MIA). That evening, at a mass meeting following the successful one-day boycott, King delivered a call to love and action in his rousing Holt Street address. In the speech, King incorporated a phrase he had used the day before in his sermon at Dexter, announcing to thunderous applause, "And you know, my friends, there comes a time when people get tired of being trampled over by the iron feet of oppression."[104] Within months, King became one of the most sought-after preachers in the nation. He refined a canon of sermons and speeches that he delivered over and over again to congregations, universities, and community organizations throughout the United States. While the number of his sermons at Dexter decreased as his fame increased, he continued to preach regularly for his home congregation.

By the dawn of 1956, any hope of a quick end to the boycott seemed to fade. Four weeks into the protest, and with no end in sight, King delivered a sermon titled "Our God Is Able" at Dexter. As would be true often during the coming year, King acknowledged the difficulty of the struggle, and yet clung to an ultimate hope in the power of God: "Much of my [ministry] has been given to fighting against social evil. There are times that I get despondent, and wonder if it is worth it. But then something says to me deep down within God is able." King implored his congregation to remain stalwart: "So this morning I say to you we must continue to struggle against evil, but [don't worry], God is able. [Don't] worry about segregation. It will die because God is [against] it."[105] As King's personal involvement in the struggle deepened and intensified, he forged a resilient and hope-filled faith in God in the face of the brutal realities of racism.

In "Our God Is Able," King broached the issue of theodicy, wondering why evil exists if God is truly good. King returned this to very question in his 15 January sermon, which asked, "Why do we believe in a good God in the midst of glaring evil?"[106] As vicious phone calls increased and threatening mail piled up, evil was no longer an idea; its presence was a glaring reality that had to be addressed.

As King's leadership and involvement grew, his strategic thinking about how to make the social gospel a reality began to take shape. His 22 January 1956 sermon, titled "Redirecting Our Missionary Zeal," called for a vigilant movement to

103. King, "Why Does God Hide Himself?" 4 December 1955, p. 242 in this volume.

104. King, MIA Mass Meeting at Holt Street Baptist Church, 5 December 1955, in *Papers* 3:72.

105. King, "Our God Is Able," 1 January 1956, p. 246 in this volume.

106. King, "How Believe in a Good God in the Midst of Glaring Evil," 15 January 1956, p. 248 in this volume.

redeem the souls of Southern whites: "Along with our work on the foreign field we must begin to do missionary work right here. Each of us must do this. And we must begin with the white man." Of course King was well aware that many white Southerners considered themselves devout Christians. Lest his congregation dismiss the call to be missionaries to Christian whites, he reminded them that the men who brutally murdered Emmett Till were churchgoers. While "the white man considers himself the supreme missionary," in reality, King pointed out, their "hands are full of blood." Rather than descending into hatred, he called on his congregation to be missionaries to whites by loving them and sitting down and preaching to them.[107] Less than two months into the boycott, King's dream for the South was not only the end of segregation but also a call for a redeemed community.

During a restless and frightening time late that month, King experienced a realization of the depth of evil as well as a renewal of this faith. Harried by late-night phone threats and an arrest after picking up passengers at a car pool station for bus boycotters, King confessed that "there were moments when I wanted to give up." Later, in a 27 January 1957 sermon, he particularly recalled "a sleepless morning in January 1956" after a particularly nasty phone call. He sat anxiously nursing a cup of coffee in his kitchen and praying for guidance when "almost out of nowhere I heard a voice that morning saying to me: 'Preach the Gospel, stand up for the truth, stand up for righteousness.'" King continued, "Since that morning I can stand up without fear. So I'm not afraid of anybody this morning."[108] He would need that fortitude in the near future.

On 30 January 1956, while King was wrapping up a mass meeting, a bomb went off on the porch of his house. Although his wife, Coretta, and their new baby were home at the time, nobody was hurt. Upon hearing the news, King rushed home and calmed the angry crowd that had gathered by citing a biblical injunction against violence.[109] The following Sunday, King delivered a sermon titled "It's Hard to Be a Christian." Frustrated by the Protestant church's conformity to culture, King lamented that "we have substituted a cushion for a cross" and "we have a high blood [*pressure*] of creeds and an anemia of deeds."[110] Citing the excesses of both "the shouting church" and "the dignified church," he claimed that many congregations were "regimenting men not regenerating them." In defining the true nature of Christianity, King noted it "is hard because it demands a dangerous and costly altruism." This "costly altruism" was missing in the lives of moderate whites who had chosen to remain silent during the struggle: "There are many white people who are for justice and fair play but they are afraid to speak."[111] With the bomb-

---

107. King, "Redirecting Our Missionary Zeal," 22 January 1956, p. 250 in this volume.

108. "King Says Vision Told Him to Lead Integration Forces" 28 January 1957, in *Papers* 4:114. King also wrote of this evening in his account of the Montgomery bus boycott (King, *Stride Toward Freedom*, pp. 134–135).

109. Joe Azbell, "Blast Rocks Residence of Bus Boycott Leader," 31 January 1956, in *Papers* 3:114–115.

110. King, "It's Hard to Be a Christian," 5 February 1956, p. 251 in this volume.

111. In his sermon "It's Hard to Be a Christian," King noted, "Give example of preachers" (5 February 1956, p. 252 in this volume).

ing of his home in the collective conscious of the congregation, King implored them to remember that "taking up the cross" demanded "putting our whole being in the struggle against evil, whatever the cost."[112]

Even as the bus boycott continued, other events revealed that the civil rights struggle was expanding its focus. In February 1956, the courts ordered the University of Alabama to admit its first African American student, Autherine Lucy. Some students and white community members responded to the news with threats and, when she was finally admitted, with violence. As he preached on 26 February 1956, King cited both the Till murder and the growing crisis at the University of Alabama: "We have looked to [*Mississippi*] and seen supposedly Christian and civilized men brutally [*murdering*] the precious life of a little child. We have looked to Alabama and seen a ruthless mob take the precious law of the land and crush it." Again in this sermon, despite overwhelming evidence to the contrary, King continued to maintain faith in both man and God: "If men are willing to submit their wills to God's will and to cooperate with him in his divine purpose, we will be able to turn the world upside down, outside in, and right side up."[113]

With the black citizens of Montgomery staunchly refusing to return to the buses, city officials decided to further test their endurance, arresting nearly one hundred participants in the protest, including King, for violating Alabama's anti-boycott law. The morning before King's 19 March trial for this arrest, he responded to the continued pressure from the city by preaching "When Peace Becomes Obnoxious." He noted, following riots by segregationists, University of Alabama officials had asked Autherine Lucy to leave the university for, as King sardonically put it, "her own safety and the safety of the university."[114] He cited an editorial in the *Tuscaloosa News* following Lucy's expulsion, which proclaimed "Yes, there's peace on the University campus this morning. But what a price has been paid for it!"[115] King built on this sentiment, charging: "It was peace that had been purchased at the price of capitulating to the forces of darkness. This is the type of peace that all men of goodwill hate. It is the type of peace that stinks in the nostrils of the almighty God." King derided the forces pursuing "obnoxious peace" in Montgomery: "I had a long talk the other day with a man about this bus situation. He discussed the peace being destroyed in the community, the destroying of good race relations." King conceded "that if the Negro [*accepts*] his place, accepts exploitation, and injustice, there will be peace," but insisted he was not interested in peace for the sake of peace. "If peace means accepting second class [*citizenship*],

---

112. King, "It's Hard to Be a Christian," 5 February 1956, p. 252 in this volume. During this dark time, King received a boost in a letter from fellow minister and Crozer classmate Marcus Garvey Wood. Wood advised King to be like the prophet Isaiah and "walk the streets barefooted until the waters of hate roll back to the ocean of eternity" (Cf. Isaiah 20:1–3). He continued, "I know you are preaching like mad now. You have thrown Crozer aside and you have found the real God and you can tell the world now that he is a God who moves in a mysterious way. That he will be your battle ax in the time of war and preserve you from your enemy." Wood concluded, "Kind regards to Mrs. King. Together you all are writing history" (Wood to King, 16 February 1956, in *Papers* 3:130).

113. King, "Faith in Man" I and II, 26 February 1956, pp. 253–255 in this volume.

114. King, "When Peace Becomes Obnoxious," 18 March 1956, p. 258 in this volume.

115. "What a Price for Peace," *Tuscaloosa News*, 7 February 1956.

I [*don't*] want it. If peace means keeping my mouth shut in the midst of injustice and evil, I [*don't*] want it."[116]

In the fall of 1956, as weariness set in among many boycott participants, King encouraged his congregation by preaching "Living Under the Tensions of Modern Life." He invoked their ancestors' struggle: "I'm glad the slaves were the greatest psychologists that America'd ever known, for they learned something that we must always learn. And they said it in their broken language, 'I'm so glad that trouble don't last always.'" Imparting hope and faith in God and in the ultimate triumph of good over evil, he assured his harried parishioners:

> All that they are saying are merely the last-minute breathing spots of a system that will inevitably die. For justice rules this world, love and goodwill, and it will triumph. They begin to wonder all over the nation, how is it that we can keep walking in Montgomery? How is it that we can keep burning out our rubber? How is it that we can keep living under the tension? And we can cry out to the nation, "We can do it because we know that as we walk God walks with us."[117]

Within a few months, the U.S. Supreme Court ruled that segregation on Montgomery's buses was unconstitutional. Over the course of the previous twelve months, the trajectory of King's life and ministry had been radically redirected. Within the crucible of a community in struggle, King forged a foundation of personal faith and refined his religious conviction. By the fall of 1956, King was no stranger to the "tensions of modern life," and as he stared evil in the face daily, he became a preacher of passionate conviction that could stir a nation.

As the demands on his time during and after the boycott continued to increase, King tried to preach as often as possible to his home congregation while also expanding his ministry beyond Montgomery. Delivering frequent sermons to diverse audiences, he rarely had time to prepare written texts. Responding to a request from *Pulpit Digest* for a sermon on race relations, King noted that he mainly preached from "a rather detailed outline."[118] King's busy schedule resulted in part

---

116. King, "When Peace Becomes Obnoxious," 18 March 1956, pp. 258, 259 in this volume.

117. King, "Living Under the Tensions of Modern Life," Sermon Delivered at Dexter Avenue Baptist Church, September 1956, p. 269 in this volume.

118. King to Samuel McCrea Cavert, 27 November 1959, p. 381 in this volume. Coretta King later emphasized the contrast between his preparation for preaching before the boycott as opposed to after the boycott had begun: "Perhaps the most important part of Martin's busy schedule was the fifteen hours a week he spent, in those early days, preparing his sermons. He would start Tuesday and work off and on until Saturday night, first writing his sermon out completely, then memorizing it. On Sunday morning, he would stand up in the pulpit and preach without a manuscript. The congregation always marveled that he could speak, apparently extemporaneously, for thirty-five or forty minutes. [¶] Later on, when the tremendous pressure of his leadership of the bus boycott gave him no time to write his sermons out, they really were extemporaneous. He would get ideas and discuss them with me. He would say, 'I've been thinking of such and such a thing for next Sunday.' . . . Then he would prepare an outline of his three or four main topics and would preach from that. It was very good training for him; in his later years he almost always preached from an outline" (Scott King, *My Life with Martin Luther King, Jr.,* p. 103). Art Carter also reported that King "preaches without manuscript" in his *Baltimore Afro-American* article written during the Montgomery bus boycott ("Rev. King Is 'King' in Montg'ry," 12 May 1956).

from his role as president of the Southern Christian Leadership Conference (SCLC), a group founded in early 1957. The nascent organization needed a steady stream of donations to fund their administrative staff, voter registration efforts, and other initiatives designed to challenge segregation. Due to his national renown as spokesperson during the boycott, King was SCLC's most effective ambassador and fundraiser, and he traveled throughout the nation and the world during the remainder of his life.

Increasingly, King saw significant connections between the movement for freedom in the United States and the worldwide struggle against western imperialism. In 1957, King received an invitation from Gold Coast, Africa, to the country's independence ceremonies. Global race relations and the decline of colonialism were on his mind while traveling to the newly renamed Ghana. In notes probably written at that time, King questioned the position of the segregated United States in this international move toward independence: "With her [*injustice*], her segregation and discrimination America is not fit to be the leading power of the world."[119] Upon his return to Montgomery, King preached a 7 April sermon reflecting on the struggle for freedom in nations around the world.[120]

Soon after his return from Africa, King used a Palm Sunday sermon on Jesus' struggle and resolve in the garden of Gethsemane to remind his congregation that despite the backlash following bus desegregation they could rely on God: "You can stand up amid despair. You can stand up amid persecution. You can stand up amid disappointment. You can stand up even amid death. But you don't worry because you know God is with you." King added, "Not my will, but Thy will be done. And when you can cry that, you stand up amid life with an exuberant joy. And you know that God walks with you."[121] For King and his congregation, the firm belief in God's presence gave them the courage to continue the struggle to live out the social gospel even in times of great duress.

The next week, on Easter Sunday, King shared some of his heartfelt questions regarding the persistence and power of evil in the world:

> I begin to despair every now and then. And wonder why it is that the forces of evil seem to reign supreme and the forces of goodness seem to be trampled over. Every now and then I feel like asking God, "Why is it that over so many centuries the forces of injustice have triumphed over the Negro and he has been forced to live under oppression and slavery and exploitation? Why is it God? Why is it simply because some of your children ask to be treated as first-class human beings they are trampled over, have their homes bombed, their children are pushed from their classrooms and sometimes little children are thrown into the deep waters of Mississippi?"[122]

---

119. King, God's Judgment on Western Civilization, March 1957.

120. King, "The Birth of a New Nation," Sermon Delivered at Dexter Avenue Baptist Church, in *Papers* 4:155–167.

121. King, Garden of Gethsemane, Sermon at Dexter Avenue Baptist Church, 14 April 1957, p. 282 in this volume.

122. King, Questions That Easter Answers, Sermon at Dexter Avenue Baptist Church, 21 April 1957, p. 289 in this volume.

Despite the challenges of life in the segregated South, King's faith remained stead-fast. He declared that Easter "answers the profound question that we confront in Montgomery. And if we can just stand with it, if we can just live with Good Friday, things will be all right. For I know that Easter is coming and I can see it coming now. As I look over the world, as I look at America, I can see Easter coming in race rela-tions. I can see it coming on every hand. I see it coming in Montgomery."[123]

King used this Easter service to address global issues as well. Concerned about the arms proliferation that accompanied the Cold War, King proclaimed: "I wish this morning that you would go tell Russia, go tell America, go tell the nations of the world that atomic bombs cannot solve the problems of the universe. Go back and tell them that hydrogen bombs cannot solve the problems of the world, but it is only through love and devotion to the justice of the universe that we can solve these problems."[124] Even though faced with the continuing exigency of the local struggle, King did not abandon his emergent global awareness. The interconnectedness of peace and justice throughout the world remained an overriding theme of King's preaching.

King's personal resources were being stretched thin by his increasingly demand-ing commitments to SCLC. His prophetic scope and faith in the transformative power of nonviolence was expanding beyond Montgomery city limits and American borders, yet he remained aware of the needs and worries of his individual parish-ioners. He addressed their lives and struggles through the teachings of Jesus and helped put their bitter experiences in the context of a global push and imperative for justice. During the summer of 1957, King delivered a series of sermons at Dexter, titled "Problems of Personality Integration." The messages in this series served to challenge damaging self-perceptions held by many African Americans as a result of the legacy of racism. King began the series with "Overcoming an Inferior-ity Complex," in which he asserted that black Americans "feel inferior because we have lived so long amid the tragic midnight of injustice and oppression." In the face of these challenging realities, King called his congregation to look to God's love as a firm basis for true dignity and self-respect.[125] In the second sermon of the series, King drew on homilies of Fosdick, McCracken, and Mays to preach "The Mastery of Fear." He proposed that "the Negro fears the White man and the White man the [*Negro*]," and highlighted the destructive nature of fear domestically and through-out the globe: "The basic cause of war is fear. Of course there are other causes— economic, political, racial—but they all spring from and are shot through with fear." As antidotes to the power of fear, King suggested leading a moral life, guided by "goodwill and love," and "possessing adequate interior Resources," and faith in God which gives one "the awareness [*that*] he is a child of God."[126]

---

123. King, Questions That Easter Answers, 21 April 1957, p. 289 in this volume.

124. King, Questions That Easter Answers, 21 April 1957, p. 292 in this volume.

125. King, "Conquering Self-Centeredness," Sermon Delivered at Dexter Avenue Baptist Church, 11 August 1957, in *Papers* 4:248; King, "Overcoming an Inferiority Complex," Sermon Delivered at Dexter Avenue Baptist Church, 14 July 1957, p. 315 in this volume.

126. King, The Mastery of Fear, 21 July 1957, pp. 319, 320, 321 in this volume. For more on King's development of this sermon, see Chart 2. For a third sermon in this series, see "Conquering Self-Centeredness," 11 August 1957, in *Papers* 4:248–259.

Chart 2. COMPARISON OF TEXT DEVELOPMENT FOR THE SERMON
"MASTERY OF FEAR" / "MASTERING OUR FEARS," 1957–1963

Biblical source text

1 John 4:18— "There is no fear in love; but perfect love casteth out fear; because fear hath torment. He that feareth, is not made perfect in love."

Fear of the dark, fear of water, fear of closed places, fear of open places, fear of altitude, fear of death, fear of hell, fear of cats, fear of Friday the thirteenth, fear of walking under a ladder—anybody who knows that hinterland and slum district of the mind knows how tragic it is. . . . and at last many face what the psychiatrists call phobophobia, the fear of fear, being afraid of being afraid.
—*Harry Emerson Fosdick, Sermon: "The Conquest of Fear," 1933*

Emerson even said that "He has not learned the lesson of life who does not every day surmount a fear."

One of the chief services of ministers and psychiatrists is to be listening-posts, where crammed bosoms, long burdened with surreptitious fears, can unload themselves.

It was a psychiatrist, Dr. Sadler, who, having said in one place, "Ridicule is the master cure for fear and anxiety," struck a deeper note when he said in another, "The only known cure for fear is *faith.*"
—*Harry Emerson Fosdick, Essay: "Dealing with Fear and Anxiety," 1943*

Fear is the greatest enemy of mankind. It is the foundation of many wars. Fear is the basis of the tension that seems to exist between the United States and Russia. It is at the root of the hatred and ill will that exist between members of different races.
—*Benjamin Elijah Mays, Article: "Two Fears," 20 July 1946*

King's public ministry in the United States gave him the opportunity to address a wider audience and to demonstrate clearly his own ecumenism. In December 1957 King spoke at the General Assembly of the National Council of Churches in St. Louis. In his speech, titled "The Christian Way of Life in Human Relations," King relied upon his experiences in Montgomery to universalize his message to his largely white audience:

> Those of us who struggle against racial injustice must come to see that the basic tension is not between the races. As I like to say to the people of Montgomery, Alabama, "The tension in this city is not between white people and Negro people. The tension is at bottom between justice and injustice, between the forces of light and the forces of darkness."[127]

---

127. King, The Christian Way of Life in Human Relations, Address Delivered at the General Assembly of the National Council of Churches, 4 December 1957, p. 324 in this volume. The previous

Chart 2. (continued)

The first is that we make a practice of looking fairly and squarely at our fears.
—*Robert J. McCracken, Sermon: "What to Do with Our Fears?" 1951*

Of primary importance in dealing with fear is making a practice of looking fairly and [*squarely*] at the object of our dread. Emerson "He has not [*learned*] the lesson of life who does not [*everyday*] surmount a fear."

One of the chief services of ministers and psychiatrists is to be listening-posts, where crammed bosoms, long [*burdened*] with surreptitious fears, can unload themselves.

Fear of dark, of water, of closed places, of high place, of cats, of Friday, of walking [*under*] a ladder, fear of [*responsibility*]; of old age and death

Dr Sadler said "Ridicule is the master cure of fear and [*anxiety*]. . . ."

The cure of fear is Faith

Russia fears America and America Russia

The Negro fears the White man and the White man the [*Negro?*]
—*King, Sermon: "The Mastery of Fear"/"Mastering Our Fears," 21 July 1957*

> *II Timothy 1:7*—"For God hath not given us the spirit of fear; but of power, and
> of love, and of a sound mind."

Fear is one of the major causes of war. We usually think that war comes from hate, but a close scrutiny of responses will reveal a different sequence of events—first fear, then hate, then war, then deeper hatred. If a nightmarish nuclear war engulfs our world—God forbid—it will not be because Russia and America first hated each other, but because they first feared each other.
—*King, Sermon: "The Mastery of Fear or Antidotes for Fear," March 1963*

A few weeks later, speaking at Beth Emet the Free Synagogue in Evanston, Illinois, King denounced the tendency of liberals to not take a stand: "What we find too often in the North is a sort of quasi-liberalism which is based on the philosophy of looking sympathetically at all sides, and it becomes so involved in seeing all sides that it doesn't get committed to either side." Instead, King called for a "positive, genuine liberalism" that would result in committed action to insure all people have "justice and freedom."[128]

---

day, speaking at a public event sponsored by the National Council of Church's Division of Christian Life and Work, King challenged white Christians to "take a definite stand in the name of Jesus Christ" (The Oneness of Man in American Intergroup Relations, Address delivered at the National Council of Church's Division of Christian Life and Work visitors program, 3 December 1957).

128. King, A Great Time to Be Alive, Address delivered at Beth Emet the Free Synagogue, 13 January 1958. In a letter written concerning King's visit to Evanston, Aviva Polish, wife of the synagogue's rabbi David Polish, noted, "Despite the fact, that as I recall, this was Dr. King's first visit to Evanston, very few

In June 1958, King criticized advocates of another liberal pitfall, gradualism, while addressing a group representing the newly formed United Presbyterian Church. In this sermon, again before a largely white Northern audience, King challenged, "If moderation means slowing up in the move for justice and capitulating to the whims and caprices of the guardians of a deadening status quo, then moderation is a tragic vice which all men of goodwill must condemn."[129] King's complete commitment to transformative social change demanded the action and involvement of all people of goodwill.

King continued to believe the church had the responsibility to be a powerful beacon for peace and justice. King frequently bemoaned the self-help qualities of many churches and ministers, while the world longed for something more substantive.[130] In a sermon titled "A Knock at Midnight," he chided the church's failure: "Hundreds and [*thousands*] of men and women in quest for the bread of social justice [*are*] going to the church only to be disappointed."[131] Once again, King viewed the number of conservative, comfort-oriented church members as one of the greatest impediments to true social change.

King's audience grew wider still with the publication of *Stride Toward Freedom*, King's account of the Montgomery bus boycott and his own spiritual journey during that challenging time. In conjunction with its release, King traveled to New York to sign copies of the book at a Harlem bookstore. While there, Izola Curry, a mentally disturbed black woman, stabbed King. The near-fatal wound caused King to be hospitalized for several days. During his weeks of recuperation, King had the opportunity to send inscribed copies of *Stride* to several friends and acquaintances, including Harry Emerson Fosdick, to whom King wrote, "If I were called upon to select the greatest preacher of this century, I would choose your name."[132]

Because of King's injury, he was forced to delay a planned visit to India. Finally, in early 1959 King had the opportunity to travel to India where he met with many of Gandhi's followers, including prime minister Jawaharlal Nehru. King had often cited the influence of Gandhi's life and commitment to nonviolence on his public ministry and on the burgeoning civil rights movement, giving this visit particular significance.[133] On the return trip from India, King spent several days in the Middle East traveling to Bethlehem, Jericho, and Jerusalem and seeing many of the major sites associated with the life and ministry of Jesus. Upon his return to Montgomery,

---

members of the Afro-American community attended" (Aviva F. Polish to King Papers Project Staff, 10 October 1996).

129. King, Paul's Letter to American Christians, Sermon Delivered to the Commission on Ecumenical Missions and Relations, United Presbyterian Church, U.S.A., 3 June 1958, p. 343 in this volume.

130. In particular, King complained of the religious approach given in minister Norman Vincent Peale's 1956 *The Power of Positive Thinking* (Englewood Cliffs, N.J.: Prentice Hall), which King labeled "escape religion," one which promised readers that they could avoid "trouble in life, any trials and tribulations." For an example of this, see The Rewards of Worship, Sermon Delivered at Dexter Avenue Baptist Church, 28 April 1957, p. 299 in this volume.

131. King, "A Knock at Midnight," 14 September 1958, p. 350 in this volume.

132. King, Inscription to Harry Emerson Fosdick, November 1958. For other references to King's stabbing, see Messages Following the Stabbing, pp. 603–608 in this volume.

133. For more on King's trip to India, see Introduction, in *Papers* 5:4–11.

King preached at Dexter the sermon A Walk Through the Holy Land. Espousing the value of broadening one's life experience, he mused, "I think if more of our white brothers in the South had traveled a little more, many of our problems would be solved today." More than anything else, however, the sermon reveals how powerful and moving King found the places associated with the crucifixion of Jesus. Noting that Simon of Cyrene helped Jesus carry the cross to Golgotha, King stated, "I think one day God will remember that it was a black man . . . who picked up that cross for him, and who took that cross on up to Calvary." He also recalled his emotions as he stood at the traditional site of the crucifixion: "There was a captivating quality there, there was something that overwhelmed me, and before I knew it I was on my knees praying at that point. And before I knew it I was weeping. This was a great world-shaking, transfiguring experience." King punctuated his sermon by emphasizing the significance of the Easter story: "The important thing is that that Resurrection did occur. [*The*] important thing is that that grave was empty."[134] For a pastor who consistently proclaimed a message of hope in the face of overwhelming challenges, the story of Jesus' victory over death remained central.[135]

After a busy spring and summer filled with speaking engagements and his re-election as vice president of the National Sunday School and Baptist Training Union, King delivered "A Tough Mind and a Tender Heart" at Dexter. Preached during the late summer of 1959, this sermon reveals King's pointed approach toward the resistance of white Southerners and the flaws in their rationalization of segregation: "The soft minded always fears change. The most pain of all pain for them is the pain of a new idea. They get a security in the status-quo." If the people of Dexter were to continue to pursue the social gospel, they must realize the nature of their foes and the consequences of their soft-mindedness: "Racial [*prejudice*] grows out of fears, which are [*groundless*] . . . There is little hope for us in our personal or collective lives until we become tough minded [*enough*] to rise [*above*] the shackles of half-truth and legends. The shape of the world today does not permit us the luxury of [*soft-mindedness*]."[136]

King also challenged the temptation of conformity and silence during threatening times. He sternly asserted: "We as Negroes must [*combine*] tough mindedness and tender heartedness if we are to attain the goal of freedom and equality. There are those soft minded individuals among us who feel that the only way to deal with oppression is to adjust [*to*] it. They acquiesce to the fate of segregation. They have been oppressed so long that they have become conditioned to oppression. . . . But this isn't thy way. It is only for soft minded cowards."[137]

---

134. King, A Walk Through the Holy Land, Easter Sunday Sermon Delivered at Dexter Avenue Baptist Church, 29 March 1959, in *Papers* 5:165, 169, 172.

135. King often preached that Easter was a season of eternal hope founded on human tragedy (King, "Living Under the Tensions of Modern Life," September 1956; Questions That Easter Answers, 21 April 1957; "The Christian Way of Life in Human Relations," 4 December 1957; Loving Your Enemies, Sermon Delivered at the Detroit Council of Churches' Noon Lenten Service, 7 March 1961, pp. 262–270, 283–293, 322–328, and 421–429 in this volume, respectively).

136. King, "A Tough Mind and a Tender Heart," 30 August 1959, pp. 374, 375 in this volume.

137. King, "A Tough Mind and a Tender Heart," 30 August 1959, p. 376 in this volume.

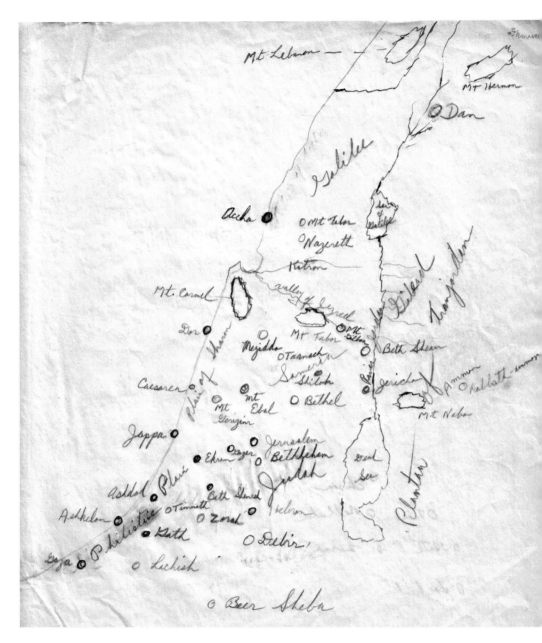

King drew this map of the Holy Land for Crozer Theological Seminary professor James B. Prichard's class Introduction to the Old Testament, a course he took during his first term at Crozer during the fall of 1948.

By 1959, his overcrowded schedule was adversely affecting both King and SCLC. At an SCLC administrative meeting in April 1959 that focused on the organization's financial woes and lack of solid planning, Lawrence Reddick, SCLC historian and King's companion on the India trip, noted that he and acting director Ella Baker had pressed King to cut back on speaking events that pulled him away from fundraising for SCLC. King's petulant response, recalled Reddick, was that an artist should not "be denied his means of expression. That he liked to preach and felt that he should do it." Reddick had already spoken with King on this subject during their India trip, advising him that he must abandon the ministry "and all other means of assured income," and give himself "fulltime to Crusading." However, Reddick averred, "I know that he will never do this."[138]

King turned to a solution that promised one form of relief from his relentless schedule conflicts. On 16 November, Ebenezer Baptist Church held a business meeting called by its Trustee Board and Board of Deacons to consider a recommendation that King be called to serve as its co-pastor with Martin Luther King, Sr. The full congregation voted unanimously in favor of this appointment.[139] Almost two weeks later, King announced his resignation from Dexter and his return to Atlanta and to Ebenezer. In his resignation statement, he described his pastorate of Dexter as "a great and creative spiritual venture." He admitted, however, that having been "catapulted into the leadership of the Montgomery movement" and as "a multiplicity of new responsibilities poured in upon me in almost staggering torrents" in the wake of the boycott, he had been rendered unable to attend to his pastoral duties. Having been "pulled into the mainstream by the rolling tide of historical necessity" he could not balance his pastoral and secular roles, futilely "attempting to be four or five men in one."[140] In the end, King felt his pastorate suffered the most neglect and stated that "I have not been able to do all that I had hoped to do at Dexter." He remembered "a program that I put on paper," and regretted that due to the demands of the bus boycott and the movement, "much of that program is still on paper."[141]

---

138. Lawrence Dunbar Reddick, Notes on Southern Christian Leadership Conference Administrative Committee Meetings on 2 April and 3 April 1959, April 1959 in *Papers* 5:178, 179.

139. Ebenezer Church Clerk P. O. Watson, the Board of Deacon's Acting Chair Robert J. Collier, Board of Trustees Chair J. H. Reese, and Pastor M. L. King, Sr. notified King of the call by mail the following day (Ebenezer Baptist Church to King, 17 November 1959, in *Papers* 5:323–324).

140. Draft, Resignation from Dexter Avenue Baptist Church, 29 November 1959, in *Papers* 5:328, 329.

141. King, Address Delivered during "A Salute to Dr. and Mrs. Martin Luther King" at Dexter Avenue Baptist Church, 31 January 1960, in *Papers* 5:352. King spoke too modestly of the outcome of his first set of annual recommendations for Dexter. During his first year at the church, many of his proposals came to fruition. The congregation initiated birthday clubs that competed to raise funds for Dexter; implemented many of King's structural improvements including new carpeting, a new public address system, and a new communion table; commenced a summer vacation Bible School; activated a Social and Political Action Committee that registered voters and generated support for the NAACP; and hired a full-time secretary. However, King had set his sights quite high. He concluded his vision of a new Dexter, saying, "With . . . the determination to keep God in the forefront, Dexter will rise to such heights as will stagger the imagination of generations yet unborn, and which even God himself will smile upon" (King, "Recommendations to the Dexter Avenue Baptist Church for the Fiscal Year 1954–1955," 5 September 1954, in *Papers* 2:293–294).

King's return to Atlanta and his new role as co-pastor of Ebenezer with his father marked a shift in his responsibilities as a minister. In one sense, because this pastorate reduced his church responsibilities by dividing them with his father, it completed the transition to his assumption of SCLC's leadership. It also allowed him to retain his position and identity as a pastor, something that King felt was at the center of his sense of self and that provided him with a wellspring for his political activities.[142]

At the end of January 1960, King bid farewell to Dexter Avenue Baptist Church and returned to Atlanta where he could focus more of his energies and attention on the growing work of SCLC. In some ways, King left Montgomery very much the same as when he arrived six years earlier. His theology and commitments had changed very little. He continued to be suspicious of the excesses of capitalism, to call for greater international cooperation and an end to colonialism, and to hope for an end to segregation and racism and the establishment of a beloved community in America. In other ways, however, King was a transformed person. He considered evil a continual presence, something he and his fellow workers faced day in and day out. Its passing was not inevitable, but would require tireless struggle and sacrifice. He knew full well the resolve of those in power to maintain the status quo, and was prepared to suffer and even die to resist this evil. Now King's ministry was about leading a community to trust in the power, justice, and righteousness of God even while evil seemed to triumph. When King left Montgomery, he knew "It's Hard to Be a Christian." He also knew that "Our God Is Able," and that as his people walk on, "God walks with us." He was now far more than an advocate for social gospel Christianity. With a profound faith in God, King left Dexter as a committed activist and part of the broader community who live the social gospel each day.[143]

⚬⚬⚭⚬⚭⚬⚭⚬⚮

On 7 February, King formally began his tenure at Ebenezer. Emphasizing that he had come to Atlanta "to serve the people of Ebenezer" as well as to "give time and assistance to the Negro's southwide struggle," King told his new congregation, "I do not consider myself an agitator. I do not consider myself a dangerous rabble rouser. I consider myself a minister of Jesus Christ."[144] He vowed to preach a "social gospel" as part of his duties at Ebenezer. Newspaper accounts recorded a crowd that "lined

---

142. According to preaching schedules for July 1962 until August 1963, King and his father planned to alternate times at the pulpit for most of the year, and to spell each other off in July and August, giving each pastor a month of vacation (King, Preaching schedule, 1 July 1962–28 July 1963; King, Preaching schedule for Ebenezer Baptist Church, 1 July 1962–25 August 1963).

143. For more on King's last sermon at Dexter, see "Dexter Honors Dr. And Mrs. King!!" 3 February 1960, in *Papers* 5:364–365. This sermon may have been "God in History: Four Proverbs," a sermon King composed after his stabbing (1959–1968, pp. 599–600 in this volume). For more on Dexter's farewell event for the Kings, see King, Address Delivered during "A Salute to Dr. And Mrs. Martin Luther King" at Dexter Avenue Baptist Church, 31 January 1960, in *Papers* 5:351–357.

144. Paul Delaney, "'Follow Way of Love,' Dr. King Asks People," *Atlanta Daily World,* 9 February 1960. King's denial that he planned to be a "rabble rouser" was probably in reaction to Georgia governor Ernest Vandiver's accusation that King's purpose in returning to Georgia was to cross "our state lines with the avowed intention of breaking laws" ("Ga. Governor Warns Dr. King He'll Be Watched," *New York Amsterdam News,* 19 December 1959). For more on King's return and his first Sunday at Ebenezer, see Introduction, in *Papers* 5:22–23.

the walls and stood in the rear of the main floor and balcony" to hear King preach "The Three Dimensions of a Complete Life," the same sermon he had delivered to secure his position at Dexter. Still more participants sat in the basement and listened to the two-and-a-half-hour long service over loudspeakers.[145]

Despite the burden of an Alabama indictment in mid-February charging him with filing fraudulent state tax returns, King resumed his role as a minister of national stature.[146] He traveled continuously through the late winter and spring of 1960 to preach from coast to coast, relying on tried-and-true sermons such as "Going Forward by Going Backward," its predecessor, "Rediscovering Lost Values," "Paul's Letter to American Christians," and "Three Dimensions of a Complete Life" to supply him with familiar themes and stories for these out-of-town engagements.[147]

In the midst of his legal preparations for the tax fraud case and preaching on the road, King reflected on his own "personal sufferings" in a 27 April 1960 *Christian Century* article, observing, "There are some who still find the cross a stumbling block, and others consider it foolishness, but I am more convinced than ever before that it is the power of God unto social and individual salvation." In the end, King may have been reflecting on his 1958 stabbing when he maintained that his travails, like the Apostle Paul's, caused him to "proudly say, 'I bear in my body the marks of the Lord Jesus,'" and to reinforce his faith in "the reality of a personal God."[148]

King's thoughts also returned to one of the demands that he had found hard to fulfill in Montgomery, a book of sermons promised early in 1957 to the publisher Harper & Brothers. Melvin Arnold, head of Harper's Religious Books Department, had welcomed King's "proposed collection of sermons; we hope that they will have a heavy emphasis on permanent religious values, rather than on topical events."[149]

---

145. "Dr. King Asks Love Returned for Hate," *Atlanta Constitution*, 8 February 1960 and Delaney, "'Follow Way of Love,'" 9 February 1960.

146. The Montgomery County Grand Jury indicted King on two counts of felony perjury for allegedly making false statements on his 1956 and 1958 tax returns (King, Interview on Arrest following Indictment by Grand Jury of Montgomery County, 17 February 1960, in *Papers* 5:370–372).

147. For example, King delivered versions of "Paul's Letter to American Christians" at Howard University on 24 April 1960 (Maude L. Ballou to Daniel G. Hill, 20 April 1960). He preached "Going Forward By Going Backward" at the Chicago Sunday Evening Club on 21 February 1960 (*The A.M.E. Church Review* 77 [April–June 1960]: 62–67). King gave "The Three Dimensions of a Complete Life" (28 February 1960, pp. 395–405 in this volume), on 13 March 1960 at Princeton University Chapel (Richard Stockton Conger to King, 15 March 1960), and on 30 April 1960 at Andrew Rankin Chapel at Howard University (Edward Peeks, "Rev. King Views Sitdowns in Life's Three Dimensions," *Baltimore Afro-American*, 7 May 1960).

148. King, "Suffering and Faith," 27 April 1960, in *Papers* 5:443, 444.

149. Arnold to King, 5 February 1957. For more on Melvin Arnold, see Arnold to King, 5 May 1958, in *Papers* 4:404. King had been encouraged to consider "a volume of your sermons" by William Robert Miller, who had heard him preach "Death of Evil Upon the Seashore" at St. John the Divine on 17 May 1956. He advised King, "Some of the best and most widely read works of men like Paul Tillich and Harry Emerson Fosdick came before the public in that way, and I am sure that a number of leading publishers—Harper, Scribners, Macmillan, or the religious book houses—might consider you a good bet financially" (Miller to King, 18 May 1956, in *Papers* 3:262).

Despite his best intentions and Arnold's repeated urging for a manuscript, King still had not produced the promised sermon book by the fall of 1959.[150]

Harper's director of religious publishing, Eugene Exman, continued to press King for a manuscript in early 1960, but King's indictment on tax fraud and his active support of the burgeoning sit-in movement delayed any attempts to put much effort into writing.[151] Ever hopeful, Exman contacted King in the spring of 1961, wishing to hear that he was "making good progress" on the sermon volume, and offering him "an advance on royalty [*to*] help you and your wife to get away for a little while from the tumult."[152]

While the circumstances were far from ideal, King was able to start working on the sermons during a fortnight in the Albany, Georgia, jail in July 1962. Having been arrested for holding a prayer vigil outside the Albany city hall, King and Ralph Abernathy shared a jail cell for fifteen days. Although by King's account the jail was "dirty, filthy and ill-equipped" and "the worse I have ever seen," he was able to spend a fair amount of uninterrupted time "reading and writing on my book on Negro sermons."[153] King claimed in his preface to *Strength to Love* that he prepared the drafts for "Loving Your Enemies," "Love in Action," and "Shattered Dreams" while in jail. The first set was mailed out in the early fall and included several sermons that had become King standards: "Paul's Letter to American Christians," "What Is Man?" and "Loving Your Enemies."[154] The voices of other preachers were still evident in the drafts King submitted to the press. In his draft of "Our God Is Able," a sermon he had delivered in 1956 and again in the early sixties, King continued to draw on the words and themes of Frederick Meek.[155]

---

150. Responding to a 2 September 1959 letter from Arnold, King apologized, "My schedule has been so heavy for the last few months that I have not had a chance to follow through" (King to Arnold, 29 September 1959). Arnold's 5 October 1959 reply suggested that King should "turn down some speaking engagements on the grounds that you have an obligation to reach an ever larger audience with a book of printed sermons!"

151. Before King visited Scarsdale, New York, in the spring to preach during a Lenten service at that city's Community Baptist Church, Exman made plans to meet there with King to discuss "your book of sermons" (Exman to King, 28 January 1960). Eugene Exman worked for Harper & Brothers, and then Harper & Row Publishers, as manager of the religious books department (1928–1944), as the department's director (1944–1955), and as its vice-president (1955–1965). Arnold wrote King to congratulate him on his victory in the tax fraud case, calling it "the latest installment in the cliff-hanger drama, the Perils of Martin." He continued, "We continue to hope that you will be able to get a breathing spell that will permit you to turn out your book of sermons. Your audience is waiting for it" (Arnold to King, 2 June 1960).

152. Exman to King, 5 May 1961. King refused several other writing offers that fall, but a 1 April 1962 deadline also fell by the wayside (McDonald to H. Claude Shostal, 13 November 1961; McDonald to John Hicks, 27 December 1961; McDonald to King, 20 February 1962). Referring to the ongoing desegregation campaign in Albany, Georgia that spring, King wrote to Exman, "So many things have come up in the Civil Rights struggle recently that I have had to give virtually all of my time to the movement. Frankly, I cannot see a let-up for the next few months" (King to Exman, 9 March 1962).

153. King, "Rev. M. L. King's Diary In Jail," *Jet Magazine*, 23 August 1962.

154. King, *Strength to Love*, p. ix. He first approached his work on the sermons for publication by laboriously writing out each sermon in longhand. The handwritten drafts were typed, probably by his secretary Dora McDonald. After King corrected these typescripts, McDonald mailed these initial drafts to Arnold.

155. For more on this influence, see Chart 3.

In his 5 October 1962 letter commenting on these sermons, Arnold not only had words of encouragement but enclosed a commentator's report. As he had noted in an early letter to King that "books of sermons have rather special requirements," Arnold apparently decided that, with sermonic material, King might respond more easily to criticism from a fellow minister. He brought in Charles Wallis, a minister and English professor at Keuka College and editor of *Pulpit Preaching*, to review King's manuscripts.[156]

Wallis saw *Strength to Love* as a "word profile" of King that would provide for those who saw him as merely an distant icon or "disturber of the peace" with the words of the minister who addressed his congregation with messages of "warmth, immediate application, and poetic verve." In particular, Wallis observed that King's writing "makes clear a pattern of Christian behavior" that the "scraps and pieces" of the publicly available knowledge of his life and beliefs had only suggested. [157]

However, in his critiques of the individual sermons, Wallis also cautioned King on some characteristics of his language that Wallis believed did not translate well into print, such as his repetition of thoughts and sentences and his expression of controversial ideas. He also urged King to compose a sermon that spoke specifically to white Christians. Overall, however, Wallis judged the manuscripts to be "excellent" and "will be good for Dr. King and all he represents."[158] Spurred on by this support, King followed through on his initial momentum and was able to spend parts of November and December working furiously on the book in order to meet a late December deadline. By late November, King and Arnold agreed on a title for the volume: *The Strength to Love*.[159]

By early March, Harper & Row representative Frank Elliott sent King the page proofs for the volume with an accompanying letter advising King that editorial changes were still in progress. Elliot remarked, "I do hope you understand that we want nothing to go into print without your approval, and that our few changes in manuscript were made partly to avoid repetition from one chapter to another, partly to prevent critics from misquoting you out of context, and partly for purposes

---

156. Arnold to King, 5 February 1957. Arnold participated in the preparation of the manuscript of King's *Stride Toward Freedom*, his account of the Montgomery bus boycott. During the revision of *Stride*'s manuscript, Arnold explained his revisions of King's comments on communism. In advising King, Arnold cited his experiences as an editor of controversial books at Beacon Press. Arnold wrote, "I learned what the enemies of freedom and of liberalism can do. Therefore, I made—and am now making—every effort to see that not even a single sentence can be lifted out of context and quoted against the book and the author" (Arnold to King, 5 May 1958, in *Papers* 4:404).

157. Charles L. Wallis, Editorial notes on *Strength to Love*, 3 October 1962.

158. Wallis, Editorial notes on *Strength to Love*, 3 October 1962. King followed most of Wallis's proposals, but did not write a sermon addressed strictly to white Christians.

159. Arnold proposed two alternate titles, "The Strength to Love" and "The Cost of Love," in a 26 November 1962 telegram to King. Three days later, Arnold requested King's contractual terms for the sermon book *The Strength to Love* (Arnold to King, 29 November 1962). Dora McDonald began sending out drafts of the sermons to Arnold in October 1962 (McDonald to Arnold, 15 October 1962 and 23 October 1962). King turned in the final drafts for sixteen sermons on 26 December 1962 and wrote that he aimed to complete his work "in a few days" (King to Arnold, 26 December 1962).

Biblical source text

Jude 1:24—"Now unto Him that is able to keep you from falling."

Jude 1:24

Meanwhile "Our God is able" is a conviction stressed and exulted in, over and over and over in the New Testament.

Believe me, it is not a weak God, it is not an incompetent God with Whom we have to deal.

Today, or soon, look up at the Sun. It is 93,000,000 miles *out there*. In six months from now you and I and our old Earth will be on the other side, the far side of the Sun—93,000,000 miles beyond it. And in a year from now we will have swung completely around the Sun and back to where we are now.
—*Frederick M. Meek, Sermon: "Our God Is Able," 4 January 1953*

All the great religions have so pictured life in terms of conflict. Hinduism called it a conflict between reality and illusion; Zoroastrianism a conflict between light and darkness; Platonism a conflict between spirit and matter; traditional Judaism and Christianity a conflict between God and Satan.
—*Harry Emerson Fosdick, Sermon: "How Believe in a Good God in a World Like This?" 1951*

Romans 8:31—"If God be for us, who can be against us?"

I Corinthians 15:28—". . . that God may be all in all."

Victor Hugo is describing the Battle of Waterloo. And Hugo concludes his description with these words: "Was it possible that Napoleon should win this battle? I answer 'No.' Because of Wellington? 'No.' Because of Blucher? 'No.'—because of God. Waterloo is not a battle; it is a change in the front of the universe."
—*Frederick M. Meek, Sermon: "Perhaps Your God Is Not Big Enough," 11 October 1953*

Jude 1:24

There is no better way to begin this year than with the conviction that there is a God of Power Who is able to do [*exceedingly abundant things*] in our lives and in the life of the universe. . . . The conviction that "Our God is able" is stressed and exulted in, over and over again in [*both*] the New and Old Testaments. This conviction stands at the [*center*] of our

Chart 3 (continued)

Christian faith. Theologically, it is expressed in the doctrine of the omnipotence of God. The God that we worship is not a weak God, He is not an incompetent God and consequently he is able to beat back gigantic mountains of opposition and to bring low prodigious hill tops of evil.

There is the sun. It often looks near. But it is 93,000,000 miles from the earth. In six month we will be on the other side of that sun, 93,000,000 miles beyond it. And in a year from now we will have swung completely around it and back to where we are now. We we notice the vastness of the cosmic [*order*] . . . we must cry out, "Our God is able."

Give Victor Hugo's description of Waterloo. He asks "Was it possible that Napolean should win this battle? I answer no. Because of Wellington? No. But because of God. Waterloo is not a battle; it is a change in the front of the universe." Waterloo is the symbol of the eternal doom of every Napolean

There is a tension or a struggle at the core of the universe. All the great religion have discovered this conflict: Hinduism (illusion & reality); Zoroastrianism (light and darkness; Platonism (spirit and matter) traditional Judaism & Christianity (God & Satan).
—*King, Sermon: "Our God Is Able," 1 January 1956*

Jude 1:24

At the center of the Christian faith is the conviction that there is a God of Power in the universe who is able to do exceedingly abundant things in nature and history. This conviction is stressed over and over again in the Old and New testaments. Theologically, it is expressed in the doctrine of the omnipotence of God. The God that we worship is not a weak and incompetent God.

Look at that sun again. It may look rather near. But it is 93,000,000 miles from the earth. In six months from now we will be on the other side of the [*sun*]—93,000,000 miles beyond it—and in a year from now we will have swung completely around it and back to where we are right now.

Go back to another century. Victor Hugo is describing the Battle of Waterloo in <u>Les Miserables</u>. He concludes his graphic account with these pointed words: "Was it possible that Napoleon should win this battle? I answer 'No.' Because of Wellington? 'No.' Because of Bluchen? 'No.'—because of God. Waterloo is not a battle; it is a change in the front of the universe." In a real sense, Waterloo is a symbol of the doom of every Napoleon.
—*King, Sermon: "Our God Is Able," July 1962–March 1963*

of clarity and construction."[160] The book made its formal appearance in early June.[161]

King had worried that the force of his spoken words would not make the transition to the printed page. "I have been rather reluctant to have a volume of sermons printed," he admitted in the preface for *Strength to Love*. "My misgivings have grown out of the fact that a sermon is not an essay to be read but a discourse to be heard. It should be a convincing appeal to a listening congregation." Even as the book went to press, he conceded, "I have not altogether overcome my misgivings."[162]

Reviewers offered mixed comments on *Strength to Love*. The critic for the *Christian Science Monitor* characterized the published sermons as "eloquent" and continued, "It is good to find a clergyman whose concept of Deity is so solidly based on Bible teaching, a God of spiritual power and love." While activist Staughton Lynd praised the book as "a spiritual handbook for Christians seeking to overcome hate" that "reaches out beyond the Negro's struggle to the other great social ills of war and economic exploitation," yet he found King's prose "often encumbered by clichés."[163] Despite the fact that the book had been released with much fanfare in both the mainstream and religious press and was selected as a featured book of the Religious Book Club, its sale figures two months after its publication were less than had been hoped.[164]

As the first major volume of sermons by an African American preacher widely available to a white audience, *Strength to Love* had much to contribute. The book consisted of a range of King's sermons, some developed early in his career and some that were crafted in his last years at Dexter and his first years back at Ebenezer's pulpit, and all familiar to audiences and congregations across the nation. They brought to the forefront King's essential identity as a preacher at a time when most people mainly knew him as a civil rights leader.

Readers who had heard King preach may have been disappointed by what they encountered within the pages of *Strength to Love*. While Harper officials Wallis, Arnold, and Exman agreed with King's broad view of race relations and may have privately cheered his methods and his language calling for the attainment of social justice, in their editing of King's sermons, they reworked his sentences with the purpose of toning down what they saw as the militant character of his speech. They removed phrases that they feared might offend readers such as King's disapproval of colonialism, capitalism, and hallmarks of Western civilization such as the

---

160. Frank Elliott to King, 1 March 1963.

161. Exman to King, 28 May 1963.

162. King, *Strength to Love*, p. ix.

163. Geoffrey Godsell, "From the Bookshelf," *Christian Science Monitor*, 19 July 1963; Lynd, "The New Negro Radicalism," *Commentary*, September 1963, p. 252.

164. On 17 September 1963, Arnold wrote a letter to King's agent, Joan Daves telling her that the publishers had overshot their projected percentage of sales spent on advertising for *Strength to Love* by eight percent. "If an 18% outlay on a sale of 12,686 books is a disappointment to you and to Martin, then Gene and I are disappointed, in turn. With this outlay, we are publishing the book without profit" (Arnold to Daves, 17 September 1963). For the book's selection by the Religious Book Club, see Exman to King, 28 May 1963. He noted that the Club feared that they might "suffer through the loss of subscribers in the south."

Enlightenment and the Industrial Revolution. King's assessment of segregation as one of "the ugly practices of our nation," his call that capitalism must be transformed by "a deep seated change," and his depiction of colonialism as "evil because it is based on a contempt for life" were stricken from the text.[165] King's contention that Jesus' response to his crucifixion was not hate but "a radical love" was revised to depict it as "an aggressive love."[166]

Wallis and the other editors seemed particularly sensitive to King's vivid anti-military and anti-war statements. In his draft sermon of "Transformed Nonconformist," King warned Americans, "When we would seek to build our nations on military power and put our abiding trust in a policy of massive retaliation, Jesus reminds us that 'he who lives by the sword will perish by the sword,'" and further challenged the military establishment by writing that "there are millions of people in our country who are tired of the arms race." He went on to characterize the early Christian church as anti-war: "Its views on war were clearly known because of the refusal of every Christian to take up arms." These statements were removed from the sermon's published version.[167]

The editors also stripped some of the familiar set pieces King used to illustrate points in his sermons. Wallis found that King's use of an illustration about human beings' chemical value in his sermon "What Is Man?" was "almost too widely known to bear added repetition." While it was readily available in a Harry Emerson Fosdick sermon, the illustration had also become a familiar element in King's homilies.[168] King's memorable characterization of political tyranny as "the iron feet of oppression" was repeatedly stricken from the version published in *Strength to Love*.[169] His references to world figures such as Ghanaian independence leader and eventual president Kwame Nkrumah and Indian prime minister Jawaharlal Nehru, whose position of non-alignment was assailed during the Cold War, were also edited out of the book as was King's reference to Mahatma Gandhi as "the Saint of India."[170]

The Harper & Row editors reduced the emphatic nature of King's statements and softened his direct calls to act or change. In the draft sermon "Transformed Nonconformist," he challenged those who upheld the status quo and submitted to

---

165. King, Draft of Chapter III, "On Being a Good Neighbor"; Draft of Chapter II, "Transformed Nonconformist"; Draft of Chapter XIII, "Our God Is Able," July 1962–March 1963, pp. 480, 471, and 530 in this volume, respectively. In reaction to King's biting statement on colonialism in his draft for "Our God Is Able," Charles Wallis asked in his comments on the sermon, "Was colonialism altogether a blight? Did not the enlightened colonialism of England bring in its wake the trained leadership which made possible the assuming of government by former colonials?" (Wallis, Editorial notes on *Strength to Love*, 3 October 1962).

166. King, Draft of Chapter IV, "Love in Action," July 1962–March 1963, p. 489 in this volume.

167. King, "Transformed Nonconformist," July 1962–March 1963, p. 473 in this volume.

168. King, Draft of Chapter XI, "What Is Man?" July 1962–March 1963; Wallis, Editorial notes on *Strength to Love*, 3 October 1962.

169. King, "What Is Man?" July 1962–March 1963; and Draft of Chapter VIII, "The Death of Evil Upon the Seashore," July 1962–March 1963, p. 505 in this volume.

170. King, Draft of Chapter I, "A Tough Mind and a Tender Heart," July 1962–March 1963, p. 461 in this volume; and Draft of Chapter VIII, "Death of Evil Upon the Seashore," July 1962–March 1963, p. 508. Wallis claimed that such references would "date the ms" (Wallis, Editorial notes on *Strength to Love*, 3 October 1962).

peer pressure, saying, "So many forces in our world are saying if you want to live a respectable life, just conform! Don't take a stand for unpopular causes; and don't allow the glaring search light of public opinion to catch you standing in an isolated minority of two or three. Choose the line of least resistance. Conform!"[171] Wallis and company revised those sentences to read: "Many voices and forces urge us to choose the path of least resistance, and bid us never to fight for an unpopular cause and never to be found in a pathetic minority of two or three."[172] The exclamatory force of King's disdain and the direct nature of his appeal were lost.

King's tendency to hammer home his point through repetition or a reiteration of his message also fell before the editor's pencil. In his sermon "How Should a Christian View Communism?" King began, "There are at least three reasons why the preacher should feel obligated to speak to his people about Communism."[173] He repeated a variant of this sentence at the head of the paragraphs that discussed these reasons. In the published version, these echoing pronouncements were eliminated. King would also use reiteration to stress a point that he had made. In his draft of "A Tough Mind and a Tender Heart," King counseled his listeners, "We must combine the toughness of the serpent with the softness of the dove." The editors struck most of his following words that reiterated the sermon's topic: "In other words, Jesus is saying that individual life at its best requires the possession of a tough mind and a tender heart."[174]

In the end, editors blunted the spirit of King's sermons in an attempt to introduce King to a broader audience and protect him from political attack. Just as Melvin Arnold sought changes to *Stride Toward Freedom* that played down any affinity to communism and moderated sentiments considered too extreme, Charles Wallis recommended that King temper his criticism of American institutions and conventions. He advised King to remove the rhythmic cadences and set pieces that marked his delivered sermons; for the most part, King accepted Wallis's recommendations. King's desire to place his sermons before the public and to broaden his audience may have justified his acquiescence in the publication of sermons that lacked a significant measure of their original poignancy.

Yet despite its omissions and changes and its inability to communicate King's voice from the pulpit in full throat, *Strength to Love* remains a concrete testament to his lifelong commitment to preaching the social gospel. His fusion of Christian teachings and social consciousness remains in print and continues to promote King's visions of love as a potent social and political force for change, of the value of redemptive suffering, of the efficacy of religious faith in surmounting evil, and of the vital need for true human integration, or as he defined it, "genuine intergroup and interpersonal living."[175]

---

171. King, "Transformed Noncomformist," July 1962–March 1963, p. 467 in this volume.

172. King, *Strength to Love*, p. 8.

173. King, Draft of Chapter XII, "How Should a Christian View Communism?" July 1962–March 1963 (TADd).

174. King, "A Tough Mind and a Tender Heart," July 1962–March 1963, p. 460 in this volume, and *Strength to Love*, p. 2.

175. King, *Strength to Love*, p. 23.

King certainly recognized the worth of producing a volume of his best-known sermons but also knew its shortcomings. As an African American minister imbued with the heritage of preaching's oral tradition and the potency of the spoken word, King rightly had doubts regarding the viability of his sermons' life force in print. He regarded worship as a social, collective experience and advised his congregation that services and sermons heard over the radio could be no substitute for the communion between pastors and congregations as well as the contact among members of the body religious.[176] For King, his ear was as important a preaching organ as his tongue, and a good sermon required listeners. Surely the spontaneous and sometimes fervent response of parishioners to his words, evident in many of King's recorded homilies, demonstrated how he depended on others' reactions to his illustrations, set pieces, metaphors, and use of contemporary events to shape what was to come. As a seasoned preacher who sermonized mainly from outlines, many quickly drafted on a handy piece of paper, King's sense of his audience and condence in his own ability to cobble together oratory based on a spare sketch and his own memory carried him through many Sundays and calls to worship.

Strength to Love represented a necessary step for King, one that would spread his message through a different medium, the commercial press, and allow him to seek a larger audience for that mode of communication he prized above all others, the sermon. His words circulated in a way typical of mid-century renowned white ministers such as Harry Emerson Fosdick and George Buttrick. Thus, despite its limitations, *Strength to Love* is a fitting tribute to King's early preaching life. The published sermons, developed during the first half of his public career, represent King's choice of those sermons that demonstrated his homiletic range and his identity as a minister. While King was already renowned as a political activist and movement spokesperson, the publication of *Strength to Love* served as another confirmation of his significant stature as a preacher, one whose preachings merited a volume of sermons. It perpetuates his legacy as a spiritual as well as political leader.

The body of foundational sermons King produced and preserved in his sermon file and the audio recordings of his preachings allow us to move beyond *Strength to Love*'s limitations. The artifacts of King's earliest years as a preacher lend dimension and texture to this crucial time in his development, help to regain the potency of his prophetic voice, and offer the best available examples of his power as a preacher. In tracing the development of his weekly messages from jottings and brief notes to full-fledged homilies, it is clear that King remained steadfast to his faith in human and social redemption and optimism in a just world. His consistent calls for social justice and to love one's enemy invigorated his words from the pulpit whether they emanated from Ebenezer, Dexter, or the many other houses of worship across the nation and the world in which he delivered his message. These pulpits provided a forum for his belief that only the pursuit of Christian values, of "the moral and spiritual ends for living," would bring about spiritual salvation and social change.

The controversial nature of issues at the heart of these sermons, such as world

---

176. King, The Rewards of Worship, Sermon Delivered at Dexter Avenue Baptist Church, 28 April 1957, pp. 293–301 in this volume.

peace and anti-militarism, nuclear disarmament, the failings of organized religion, and the pursuit of economic as well as social equality, foreshadowed the difficulties that King and the movement would face in light of his contentious rhetoric. His firm belief in "a warless world, a better distribution of wealth, and a brotherhood that transcends race or color" would bring forth extreme reactions, deepen his differences with the liberal mainstream, and result in his profound alienation from certain elements of the movement. King's nascent desire to be "a profound advocator of the social gospel" would uplift him and drive the spiritual character of the modern civil rights movement. It would also be a source of great sacrifice.

This Chronology and Sermon List includes King's sermon titles through 1959. Later sermon titles will be listed in the chronologies of appropriate volumes. Titles of delivered sermons are set in regular type while sermon titles and descriptions found only in press announcements or press releases prior to the sermon's delivery are italicized.

1947

Fall   King preaches a trial sermon at Ebenezer Baptist Church, Atlanta, Georgia.

1948

25 Feb   King is ordained and appointed associate pastor at Ebenezer.

25 Apr   *"Life is What You Make It"* and *"The Meaning of Christian Living,"* Liberty Baptist Church, Atlanta, Georgia.

Summer   King serves as associate pastor of Ebenezer.

1 Aug   *"External Versus Internal Religion,"* Ebenezer.

8 Aug   *"The Tests of Goodness,"* Ebenezer.

22 Aug   *"God's Kingdom First,"* Ebenezer.

Fall   King begins his first term at Crozer Theological Seminary.

1949

20 Feb   *Youth Day sermon,* Ebenezer.

3 Mar   *"Facing Life's Inescapables,"* Chester, Pennsylvania.

Summer   King serves as associate pastor at Ebenezer.

22 May   *"A Way Out,"* Ebenezer.

5 June   *"Mastering Our Evil Selves"* / *"Mastering Ourselves,"* Ebenezer.

19 June   *Men's Day sermon,* Mt. Vernon Baptist Church, Atlanta, Georgia.

3 July   *"The Voice of Hope,"* Ebenezer.

17 July   *"The Supremacy of Love,"* Ebenezer.

24 July   *"Splinters and Planks,"* Ebenezer.

31 July   *"Two Challenging Questions,"* Ebenezer.

7 Aug   *"Worship"* and *"On Being Converted,"* Ebenezer.

14 Aug   *Youth Day sermon,* Zion Hill Baptist Church, Atlanta, Georgia.

21 Aug   *"Who is Truly Great,"* Ebenezer.

4 Sept   *"The Great Paradox"* and *"The Significance of the Cross,"* Ebenezer.

11 Sept   *"Modern Baals,"* Ebenezer.

1 Jan	*"Impending Mountains,"* Ebenezer.
19 Feb	*"Walking with the Lord,"* Ebenezer.
Summer	King serves as associate pastor at Ebenezer.
28 May	*"Three Levels of Fellowship,"* Ebenezer.
4 June	*"I had Fainted Unless . . . !"* Ebenezer.
18 June	*"The Lord God Omnipotent Reigneth,"* Ebenezer.
25 June	*"Unanswered Prayer,"* Ebenezer.
2 July	*"Propagandizing Christianity"* and *"Forgiveness,"* Ebenezer.
16 July	*"Two Eternal Truths,"* Ebenezer.
23 July	*"Thou Fool"* and *"Having the Moral Courage to Speak Out,"* Ebenezer.
30 July	*Youth Day sermon,* Liberty Baptist Church, Atlanta, Georgia.
6 Aug	*"Christ or Shaos"* and *"What the Cross Means to Me,"* Ebenezer.
20 Aug	*"The Conquest of Fear,"* Ebenezer.
27 Aug	*"Worship,"* Ebenezer.
24 Dec	*"The Light Amid Darkness,"* Ebenezer.
31 Dec	*"A Religion of Doing,"* Ebenezer.

1951

18 Feb	*"Nothing in Particular,"* Ebenezer.
6–8 May	King graduates from Crozer Theological Seminary.
Summer	King serves as associate pastor at Ebenezer.
13 May	*"The World Crisis and a Mother's Responsibility,"* Ebenezer.
27 May	*"Beyond Condemnation,"* Ebenezer.
Summer	King serves as associate pastor at Ebenezer.
3 June	*"Sincerity Is Not Enough"* and *"The Courtesy of God,"* Ebenezer.
17 June	*"Where Is God Found?"* Ebenezer.
24 June	*"Procrastination,"* Ebenezer.
1 July	*"Witnessing for Christ,"* Ebenezer.
8 July	*"The Meaning of Faith,"* Ebenezer.
22 July	*"Doing the Best with What You Have,"* Ebenezer.
5 Aug	*"The Necessity of the Second Birth"* and *"Beyond Good Deeds,"* Ebenezer.
19 Aug	*"God's Kingdom First,"* Ebenezer.
2 Sept	*"What is Man?"* and *"What Think Ye of Christ?"* Ebenezer.
Fall	King begins his first term as a doctoral student at Boston University School of Theology.

1952

16 Mar	King is scheduled to preach at Ebenezer's celebration of its sixty-fifth anniversary and of King, Sr.'s twentieth anniversary as its pastor.
18 May	*"Relevance of the Holy Spirit,"* Ebenezer.

25 May	*"The Prevalence of Practical Atheism,"* Ebenezer.
Summer	King serves as associate pastor at Ebenezer.
27 July	*"The Divine Shepherd,"* Ebenezer.
3 Aug	*"The Power and Wisdom of the Cross,"* Ebenezer.
10 Aug	*"Communism's Challenge to Christianity,"* Ebenezer.
17 Aug	*"Faith in Man,"* Ebenezer.
31 Aug	*"Loving Your Enemies,"* Ebenezer; *Youth Day sermon,* Pilgrim Baptist Church, Atlanta, Georgia.
7 Sept	*"Mental and Spiritual Slavery"* and *"The Permanence of Christ,"* Ebenezer.
26 Oct	"Going Forward by Going Backward," People's Baptist Church, Portsmouth, New Hampshire.
28 Dec	*After Christmas, What?* Ebenezer.

1953

5 Apr	*Easter sermon,* Metropolitan Baptist Church, Boston, Massachusetts.
12 Apr	*"What Does It Mean to Believe in God?"* First United Baptist Church, Lowell, Massachusetts.
Summer	King serves as associate pastor at Ebenezer.
21 June	*"By These Things Men Live"* and *"Does It Pay to Be Faithful?"* Ebenezer.
28 June	*"Accepting Responsibility for Your Actions,"* Ebenezer.
5 July	Atlanta's WERD begins broadcasting from Ebenezer for several months. "The False God of Science," Atlanta, Georgia; *"When God Seems to Deceive Us,"* Ebenezer.
12 July	"The False God of Nationalism," Atlanta, Georgia; *"Transformed Non-Conformists,"* Ebenezer.
19 July	"The False God of Money," Atlanta, Georgia.
26 July	*"God's Revelation to the World,"* Ebenezer; "Accepting Responsibility for Your Actions," radio station WERD, Atlanta, Georgia.
2 Aug	*"Dressing Christ in False Robes,"* Ebenezer; *"First Things First"* *("God's Kingdom First"),* radio station WERD, Atlanta, Georgia.
9 Aug	*"The Tragedy of Almost"* and *"Communism's Challenge to Christianity,"* Ebenezer; *"A Half Baked Civilization,"* radio station WERD, Atlanta, Georgia.
16 Aug	*"Lord, Is It I?"* and *"Going Forward by Going Backward,"* Ebenezer; *"The Challenge of the Book of Jonah,"* radio station WERD, Atlanta, Georgia.
23 Aug	*"Self-Examination,"* Ebenezer; *"The Prevalence of Practical Atheism,"* radio station WERD, Atlanta, Georgia.
30 Aug	*"Opportunity, Fidelity, and Reward,"* Ebenezer, Atlanta, Georgia; *"The Peril of Conformity,"* radio station WERD, Atlanta, Georgia.
6 Sept	*"The Dimensions of a Complete Life,"* Ebenezer; *"What Is Man?"* radio station WERD, Atlanta, Georgia.

17 Jan	King is scheduled to preach an initial sermon at First Baptist Church in Chattanooga, Tennessee.
24 Jan	King preaches his initial sermon at Dexter Avenue Baptist Church. "The Three Dimensions of a Complete Life," Dexter, Montgomery, Alabama.
28 Feb	Rediscovering Lost Values, Second Baptist Church, Detroit, Michigan.
4 Apr	"Going Forward by Going Backward," Dexter.
14 Apr	King accepts the call to Dexter's pastorate.
May	"Mental and Spiritual Slavery," Dexter.
2 May	"Accepting Responsibility for Your Actions," Dexter. In the evening King gives his acceptance address at Dexter.
16 May	"What Is Man?" Thirty-third annual memorial service, Pullman Porters' Benefit Association of America, Union Baptist Church, Cambridge, Massachusetts.
30 May	"Loving Your Enemies," Dexter.
4 July	"A Religion of Doing," Dexter.
11 July	"What Is Man?" Men's Day sermon, Dexter.
1 Sept	King begins his pastorate at Dexter.
5 Sept	"God's Love," Dexter.
9 Sept	"The Vision of a World Made New," Woman's Convention Auxiliary of the National Baptist Convention, St. Louis, Missouri.
12 Sept	"Propagandizing Christianity," Dexter.
26 Sept	"Creating the Abundant Life," Dexter.
17 Oct	"New Wine in New Bottles," Dexter.
Nov	"Transformed Nonconformist," Dexter.
28 Nov	Men's Day sermon, Friendship Baptist Church, Atlanta, Georgia.

1955

Jan	On Worshiping False Gods
Jan	False God of Pleasure
20 Mar	Sixty-eighth anniversary sermon, Ebenezer.
8 May	*Crisis Facing Present-Day Family Life in America,* Dexter.
15 May	"Other Mountains," Baccalaureate sermon, Alabama State College, Montgomery, Alabama.
31 May	The faculty of Boston University votes to confer the doctorate on King.
19 June	"Who Is Truly Great," Dexter.
26 June	"Discerning the Signs of History," Dexter.
17 July	*Am I My Brother's Keeper?* Dexter.
24 July	"The Death of Evil Upon the Seashore," Dexter.
28 Aug	*Men's Day sermon,* Jackson Street Baptist Church, Birmingham, Alabama.
2 Oct	"The Impassable Gulf (The Parable of Dires and Lazarus)," Dexter.

16 Oct	"The Three Dimensions of a Complete Life," Southern University, Baton Rouge, Louisiana.
23 Oct	"The Death of Evil Upon the Seashore," Religious Emphasis Week, Fort Valley State College, Fort Valley, Georgia.
30 Oct	"The Seeking God," Dexter.
20 Nov	"The One-sided Approach of the Good Samaritan," Dexter.
4 Dec	"Why Does God Hide Himself," Dexter.
5 Dec	The Montgomery bus boycott begins.
25 Dec	"The Light That Shineth Amid Darkness," Dexter.

1956

1 Jan	"Our God Is Able," Dexter.
8 Jan	"The Death of Evil on the Seashore," Ebenezer.
15 Jan	"How Believe in a Good God in the Face of Glaring Evil?" Dexter.
22 Jan	"Redirecting Our Missionary Zeal," Dexter.
29 Jan	YMCA Sunday sermon, Dexter.
5 Feb	"It's Hard to Be a Christian," Dexter.
19 Feb	"What Is Man?" Religious Emphasis Week, Fisk Memorial Chapel, Nashville, Tennessee.
20 Feb	"Three Dimensions of a Complete Life," Religious Emphasis Week, Meharry Medical College, Nashville, Tennessee.
21 Feb	"Going Forward by Going Backward," Religious Emphasis Week, Tennessee State University, Nashville, Tennessee.
26 Feb	"Faith in Man," Dexter.
18 Mar	"When Peace Becomes Obnoxious," Dexter.
22 Apr	Youth Day sermon, Good Street Baptist Church, Dallas, Texas.
29 Apr	"Fleeing from God," Dexter; *Men's Day sermon,* Hunters' Chapel AME Zion Church, Tuscaloosa, Alabama.
13 May	"The Role of the Negro Mother in Preparing Youth for Integration," Dexter.
17 May	"The Death of Evil Upon the Seashore," National Day of Prayer and Thanksgiving, Cathedral of St. John the Divine, New York, New York.
20 May	*Youth Peoples Choir Day sermon,* Ebenezer Baptist Church, Pittsburgh, Pennsylvania.
23 May	*Youth Emphasis Week sermon,* Ebenezer Baptist Church, Pittsburgh, Pennsylvania.
22 July	Men's Day sermon, New Hope Baptist Church, Niagara Falls, New York.
12 Aug	"Rediscovering Lost Values," Mount Olivet Baptist Church, New York, New York.
7 Sept	"Paul's Letter to American Christians," National Baptist Convention, Denver, Colorado.
Oct	"The Prodigal Son," Dexter.

Oct	"The Fellow Who Stayed at Home," Dexter.
4 Nov	"Paul's Letter to American Christians," Dexter.
6 Nov	"The Most Durable Power," Dexter.
18 Nov	Men's Day address, Mount Zion First Baptist Church, Baton Rouge, Louisiana.
6 Dec	"Remember Who You Are!!" Andrew Rankin Memorial Chapel, Howard University, Washington, D.C.
20 Dec	The Montgomery Improvement Association votes to end the bus boycott.

1957

6 Jan	"Great Expectations," Dexter.
11 Jan	"The Ways of God in the Midst of Glaring Evil," Dexter.
20 Jan	Paul's Letter to American Christians, Ebenezer.
21 Jan	"Paul's Letter to American Christians," Twenty-fifth Anniversary of the Minnesota State Pastors Conference, Gloria Dei Lutheran Church, St. Paul, Minnesota.
27 Jan	At Dexter's Sunday service, King reveals to the congregation his vision of a year earlier in which a divine voice told him to lead the Montgomery movement without fear.
10 Feb	From pulpits across the nation, pastors read King's "For All—A Non-Segregated Society," a message he wrote for Race Relations Sunday sponsored by the National Council of Churches.
27 Feb	"Remember Who You Are," Annual Week of Prayer, Virginia Union University, Richmond, Virginia.
28 Feb	"Going Forward by Going Backward," Annual Week of Prayer, Virginia Union University, Richmond, Virginia.
1 Mar	"The Three Dimensions of a Complete Life," Annual Week of Prayer, Virginia Union University, Richmond, Virginia.
7 Apr	"The Birth of a New Nation," Dexter.
14 Apr	Garden of Gethsemane, Dexter.
21 Apr	Questions That Easter Answers, Dexter.
28 Apr	The Rewards of Worship, Dexter.
3 June	"Paul's Letter to American Christians," American Baptist Convention, Philadelphia, Pennsylvania.
14 July	"Overcoming an Inferiority Complex," Dexter.
21 July	"The Mastery of Fear," Dexter; "Going Forward by Going Backward," Woman's Day sermon, First Baptist Church, Montgomery, Alabama.
4 Aug	"Factors That Determine Character," Dexter.
11 Aug	"Conquering Self-Centeredness," Dexter.
12 Aug	"Propagandizing Christianity," National Missions Conference, Green Lake, Wisconsin.

18 Aug	"Paul's Letter to American Christians," Central Methodist Church, Detroit, Michigan.
22 Sept	*Men's Day sermon*, Liberty Baptist Church, Atlanta, Georgia.
27 Oct	"The Things That Are God's," Dexter.
10 Nov	"Love Your Enemies," Convocation of the School of Religion, Andrew Rankin Memorial Chapel, Howard University, Washington, D.C.
17 Nov	"Loving Your Enemies," Dexter.
1 Dec	"Structure and Destiny," Dexter.
3 Dec	The Oneness of Man in American Intergroup Relations, Division of Christian Life and Work Visitors Program of the National Council of Churches, St. Louis, Missouri.
4 Dec	The Christian Way of Life in Human Relations, General Assembly of the National Council of Churches, St. Louis, Missouri.

1958

12 Jan	"Structure and Destiny," Ebenezer; "What Is Man?" Chicago Sunday Evening Club, Chicago, Illinois.
16 Feb	"Not By Bread Alone," Dexter.
12 Mar	"The Christian Doctrine of Man," Detroit Council of Churches' Noon Lenten Services, Central Methodist Church, Detroit, Michigan.
23 Mar	"I Thirst," Dexter.
6 Apr	"The Lord God Omnipotent Reigneth," Dexter.
9 Apr	"What Is Man?" and "The Peril of Conformity," Shaw University, Raleigh, North Carolina.
13 Apr	"Is It Un-Christian to Judge Others?" Dexter.
23 Apr	"The Three Dimensions of a Complete Life," Bucknell University Chapel, Lewisburg, Pennsylvania.
4 May	"The Unpardonable Sin," Dexter.
11 May	"The Problem of Unanswered Prayer," Dexter.
25 May	"Did Jesus Believe in Chance?" Dexter.
1 June	"Did Jesus Disapprove of Wealth?" Dexter.
3 June	Paul's Letter to American Christians, Founding Convention of the United Presbyterian Church, U.S.A., Pittsburgh, Pennsylvania.
15 June	"Will Christ Visibly Return to Earth?" Dexter.
22 June	"Nature of Heaven," Dexter.
29 June	"The Nature of Hell," Dexter.
6 July	"The Mystery of Life," Dexter.
31 July	"A Knock at Midnight," Alabama State Sunday School and Baptist Training Union Congress, Selma University, Selma, Alabama.
3 Aug	"Catching the Wrong Train," Dexter.
10 Aug	"In Life's Storms," Dexter.
17 Aug	"The Greatest Power in the World," Dexter.

24 Aug	*"Going Forward by Going Backwards,"* Central Methodist Church, Detroit, Michigan.
31 Aug	"A Knock at Midnight," Central Baptist Church, Pittsburgh, Pennsylvania.
7 Sept	"Getting Along With Other People," Dexter.
14 Sept	"A Knock at Midnight," Woman's Convention, National Baptist Convention, Chicago, Illinois.
7 Dec	Eighty-first anniversary sermon, Dexter.
14 Dec	"Worship at Its Best," Dexter.
21 Dec	"Christ Our Starting Point," Dexter.

1959

4 Jan	"Inner Calm Amid Outer Tension," Dexter.
18 Jan	"The Blinding Power of Sin," Dexter.
8 Feb	"Looking Beyond Our Circumstances," Dexter (sermon delivered by tape recording in King's absence).
22 Mar	Palm Sunday sermon on Mohandas K. Gandhi, Dexter.
29 Mar	A Walk Through the Holy Land, Easter Sunday sermon, Dexter.
Apr	King's *The Measure of a Man* is published by Christian Education Press.
5 Apr	"Unfulfilled Hopes," Dexter.
12 Apr	"Making Use of What You Have," Dexter.
19 Apr	"The Dimensions of a Complete Life," Chicago Sunday Evening Club, Chicago, Illinois.
20 Apr	"Paul's Letter to American Christians," McCormick Theological Seminary, Chicago, Illinois.
26 Apr	"The Art of Getting Along with Others," Dexter.
3 May	"Sleeping Through a Revolution," Dexter.
10 May	"A New Challenge for Modern Mothers," Dexter.
31 May	"The Service of the Church to Mental Health," Dexter; "The Dimensions of a Complete Life," Baccalaureate service, Dillard University, New Orleans, Louisiana.
14 June	"Unconditioned Faith," Dexter.
21 June	"On Knowing How to Live with Prosperity," Dexter.
28 June	"On Knowing How to Live with Poverty," Dexter.
9 Aug	"Man's Helplessness Without God," Dexter.
16 Aug	*"The Conflict in Human Nature,"* Dexter.
23 Aug	"Loving Your Enemies," Central Methodist Church, Detroit, Michigan.
30 Aug	"A Tough Mind and a Tender Heart," Dexter.
20 Sept	*Youth Day sermon,* Second Baptist Church, Los Angeles, California.
27 Sept	"Understanding Life's Injustices," Dexter.
25 Oct	"Remember Who You Are," Rockefeller Memorial Chapel, University of Chicago, Chicago, Illinois.

2 Nov	In Chester, Pennsylvania, Crozer honors King with its first Alumni Achievement Award.
8 Nov	*Men's Day sermon,* Zion Baptist Church, Philadelphia, Pennsylvania.
22 Nov	*Seventy-first anniversary sermon,* Union Grove Baptist Church, Columbus, Ohio.
29 Nov	King resigns from Dexter during Sunday morning services.
20 Dec	"The Significance of the Manger," Dexter.
27 Dec	"After Christmas, What?" Dexter.

The central goal of the Martin Luther King, Jr., Papers Project is to produce an authoritative, multivolume edition of King's works. The edition contains accurate, annotated transcriptions of King's most important sermons, speeches, correspondence, published writings, unpublished manuscripts, and other papers, and is in general arranged chronologically. This volume, however, is thematic in nature and traces King's development as a preacher through his sermons, homiletic materials, and other supporting documents. As with the other volumes in the edition, it is internally arranged chronologically.

We assign highest priority to King's writings, public statements, and publications, although such materials may not be included when they repeat significant portions of the text of other documents from the period. When one of King's sermons or addresses is available in different versions, we prefer recordings rather than printed or published transcripts, complete versions rather than excerpts, and versions that have greater rather than lesser public impact. We also include correspondence containing significant information about King's thought or activities and incoming letters illuminating his relationships with or impact on others.

This volume, however, draws primarily on the contents of King's sermon file, which held the materials he used to prepare and to preach sermons. The file, which King maintained in his office, contained over five hundred documents. In addition, we have selected homiletic material not published in previous volumes, as well as correspondence, audiotapes, and other materials that provide insight into King's life as a minister. We included those documents that most clearly demonstrated King's development as a preacher, as opposed to his theological evolution, which was covered in volumes I and II of *The Papers of Martin Luther King, Jr.* The date range of this thematic volume begins with King's ordination in February 1948 and progresses through the submission of the complete manuscript for his sermon collection, *Strength to Love,* in March 1963.

This volume also contains sections designed to provide information useful to lay and scholarly readers alike. The Chronology and Sermon List presents the titles of King's delivered sermons and announced sermon topics as well as the major events and activities related to his career prior to his return to Ebenezer Baptist Church in 1960. Titles of delivered sermons are set in regular type while sermon titles and descriptions found only in press announcements or press releases prior to the sermon's delivery are italicized in the Sermon List. The Introduction is a narrative essay based on the documentary records assembled by the King Papers Project. It is intended to place King's papers in a historical and religious context rather than to substitute for a thorough biographical or historical treatment of King's life. The documents in this volume conclude with an addendum containing documents of significant historical value that were acquired following the publication of volume IV of *The Papers of Martin Luther King, Jr.* We have also included a complete inventory of the contents of King's sermon file, with documents published in this volume boldfaced, and a bibliography of selected works contained in King's personal library that he may have had available in preparing his sermons. Items found in this bibliography may have been added or removed since King's death. Finally, to assist scholars and others seeking further information regarding King-related primary documents, this volume includes a Calendar of Documents that provides full citations for items cited in annotations. It also contains other significant King-related documents including all documents in the sermon file not selected for publication.

Editorial Annotations

Documents are introduced by a title, date, and place of origin. Existing titles are used when available and are designated by quotation marks. For untitled items, we have created descriptive titles reflecting their content (e.g., Wedding Prayer). When necessary we have corrected titles with errors or irregularities in punctuation, capitalization, and spelling and we have standardized names, but these titles are not designated by quotation marks. Sermon or speech titles indicate the occasion of the address. A number of sermons and sermon outlines were found in folders with the location of the sermon written on them; this location is indicated in the descriptive title. In correspondence, the title contains the author (e.g., From John Steinbeck) or recipient (e.g., To Coretta Scott), leaving King's participation implied. When the date was not specified on the document but has been determined through research, it is rendered in italics and enclosed in square brackets. When a specific date could not be determined through research, we have provided a range date. King's sermons and a selection of school papers constitute the bulk of documents published in this volume. Many of these school papers and some sermon outlines lack identifying information and an examination of King's class notes and syllabi, available handwriting samples, and other documentary material determined their provenance. In this way, many documents from King's three years at Crozer could be assigned to a time span corresponding to one of the courses King completed during that period. Documents that could not be identified with a specific course were assigned a range date concurrent with the period that King studied with a particular professor, the years King spent as a seminary student, or the seven years King spent in graduate studies. We have also gathered related documents with the same or very similar dates under one headnote. If the place of origin appears on the document, it is included; if not and it could be determined through research, it is provided for King-authored documents only. (A more detailed explanation of procedures for assigning titles, dates, and other cataloging information appears at the end of the volume in the Calendar of Documents.)

Annotations are intended to enhance readers' understanding of documents. Headnotes preceding documents provide information necessary to the reader's understanding, and call attention to the overall significance of the document; in the case of longer documents a brief summary may be offered. Editorial footnotes explain specific references to individuals, organizations, events, literary quotations, biblical allusions, and other references in the document, as well as relevant correspondence or related documents. Biographical sketches describe the background and relationship to King of individuals who corresponded with him or are mentioned prominently in documents. We have not included such sketches for individuals featured in previous volumes. Editorial footnotes, on occasion, refer to alter-

My Call to the Ministry ———— Title

7 August 1959 —— Date
[*Montgomery, Ala.*] —— Place of origin

Joan Thatcher, publicity director of the American Baptist Convention, asked King to compose this statement. In her request, Thatcher noted, "Apparently many of our young people still feel that unless they see a burning bush or a blinding light on the road to Damascus, they haven't been called." [1] —— Headnote

My call to the ministry was neither dramatic nor spectacular. It came neither by some miraculous vision nor by some blinding light experience on the road of life. Moreover, it did not come as a sudden realization. Rather, it was a response to an inner urge that gradually came upon me. This urge expressed itself in a desire to serve God and humanity, and the feeling that my talent and my commitment could best be expressed through the ministry. At first I planned to be a physician; then I turned my attention in the direction of law. But as I passed through the preparation stages of these two professions, I still felt within —— Document that undying urge to serve God and humanity through the ministry. During my senior year in college I finally decided to accept the challenge to enter the ministry. I came to see that God had placed a responsibility upon my shoulders and the more I tried to escape it the more frustrated I would become. A few months after preaching my first sermon I entered theological seminary. [2] This, in brief, is an account of my call and pilgrimage to the ministry.

Martin Luther King, Jr.

THD. MLKP-MBU: Box 21.

Physical description codes

Document's archival code

Brief reference; full citation in Calendar of Documents

1. Thatcher to King, 30 July 1959. Maude Ballou enclosed this statement in a 7 August 1959 reply to Thatcher. Thatcher's letter indicated that King's message was to be included in a leaflet for the January 1960 observance of Life Service Sunday.

2. King preached his trial sermon at Ebenezer in the fall of 1947 and was —— Editorial footnote ordained in February 1948. He graduated from Morehouse College in May of that year and entered Crozer Theological Seminary the following September.

native accounts of events and to variations among versions (e.g., sentences altered or added by King when he modified a sermon or address for a different occasion). Marginal notes on the document, particularly those written by King, are also noted. Annotations may contain implicit or abbreviated references to documents (e.g., "King replied in a 20 October 1959 letter"); full bibliographic information for such documents can be found in the Calendar of Documents. Biblical citations in footnotes refer to the King James version of the Bible unless King drew on another version in the text. In citations that might refer to the synoptic gospels of Matthew, Mark and Luke, we have chosen the one text that best represents King's intent.

The source note following each document provides information on the characteristics of the original document and its provenance. Codes are used to describe the document's format, type, version, and form of signature. The code ADS, for example, identifies the document as written in the author's hand with a signature. The location of the original document is described next, using standard abbreviations from *USMARC Code List for Organizations*. (See List of Abbreviations for all codes used.) The source notes for documents located in King's sermon file also include the folders' titles. Folder labels handwritten by King appear in quotation marks. Many of the documents published and referred to in this volume, including all sermon file documents, with the archival codes CSKC, CSKCH, and MLKJP-GAMK:Vault are part of a large collection of King material acquired in June 2006 by Morehouse College in Atlanta, Georgia.

Transcription Practices

Transcriptions are intended to reproduce all documents accurately, adhering to the exact wording and punctuation of the original. In general, errors in spelling, punctuation, and grammar, which may offer important insights into the author's state of mind and conditions under which a document was composed, have been neither corrected nor indicated by *sic*. Capitalization, boldface, subscripts, abbreviations, hyphenation, strikeouts, ellipses, and symbols are likewise replicated.

This rule has certain exceptions, however. Single-letter emendations by the author have been silently incorporated, and typographical errors, such as malformed and superimposed characters, have been corrected. In published documents, spelling and grammatical errors have been retained unless an earlier draft revealed the author's intention. Moreover, some formatting practices such as outlining, underlining, paragraph indentation, and spacing between words or lines of text have been regularized to maintain consistency within the edition (e.g., continuous rather than discontinuous underscoring). Em-dashes, which appeared in several styles in the original manuscripts, have been regularized. The overall appearance of the source document (e.g., line breaks, pagination, vertical and horizontal spacing, end-of-line hyphenation) has not been replicated, and some features that could not be readily reproduced such as letterheads and typographic variations are described in annotations (in a few cases, visually interesting documents such as sermon outlines or book inscriptions have been reproduced as facsimiles). The internal address, salutation, and complimentary closing of a letter have been reproduced left-aligned, regardless of the original format. Insertions in the text by the author (usually handwritten) are indicated by curly braces ({ }) and placed as precisely as possible within the text. Hand-drawn lines separating text in a document or page breaks are indicated by an extra space in the text.

Editorial explanations are rendered in italics and enclosed by square brackets. Conjectural renderings of text are set in italic type followed by a question mark and placed within brackets: [*There's?*]. Instances of illegible text are indicated: e.g., [*strike-out illegible*] or [*word illegible*]. If the strikeout was by someone other than the author, it has not been replicated, but is described in a footnote. If part of a document is lost, the condition is described: [*remainder missing*]. In some instances, long documents may be excerpted to highlight passages that were most significant with respect to King. Editorial deletions to eliminate repetitive or extraneous segments are indicated by ellipses or by explanatory comment: [. . .] or [*King pauses mid-sentence*].

The King Papers Project's transcriptions of audio recordings are intended to replicate, to the extent possible, King's public statements as they were delivered, excluding only those utterings that do not convey significant meaning (e.g., unintentional stutters and pause words, such as "uh"). Certain sharply stressed phrases are rendered in italics to indicate the speaker's emphasis. When available, King's written text is used to clarify ambiguous phrases and as a guide to delineating sentences, paragraphs, and punctuation. In cases where the written text is not available, we have supplied punctuation for clarity. Transcriptions also attempt to convey some of the quality of the speech event, particularly the interplay between speaker and audience. When practical, audience responses to King's orations are enclosed in parentheses and placed appropriately within King's text. Editorial descriptions of audience participation are enclosed in square brackets. The first instance of a verbal audience response to a sermon is indicated as follows: [*Congregation:*] (*Preach*). Subsequent audience interjections are enclosed, as is appropriate, in brackets or parentheses: e.g., [*applause*] or [*singing*] or [*laughter*]; and (*Yes*) or (*Lord help him*). Multiple audience responses are indicated in order of occurrence, separated with commas: e.g., (*Tell it, Don't stop*). In addition, transcriptions occasionally suggest the loudness or duration of audience responses: e.g., [*sustained applause*]. In cases where a recording or its transcription is incomplete or unintelligible, that status is indicated within the text proper: e.g., [*gap in tape*] or [*words inaudible*].

ABBREVIATIONS

Collections and Repositories

64VF-CtW	1964 General Vertical File, Wesleyan University Special Collections, Wesleyan University, Middletown, Conn.
ABPC	Alton B. Pollard, III, Collection (in private hands)
AFSCR-PPAFS	American Friends Service Committee Records, American Friends Service Committee Archives, Philadelphia, Pa.
AJC-ICHi	Archibald James Carey Collection, Chicago Historical Society, Chicago, Ill.
BRP-DLC	Bayard Rustin Papers, Library of Congress, Washington, D.C.
BStPC	Black Star Publishing Collection, New York, N.Y.
CBSNA-NNCBS	Columbia Broadcasting System News Archives, Columbia Broadcasting System, Inc., New York, N.Y.
CCCSU	Clayborne Carson Collection (in private hands)
CHAC	Carolyn Hunt Anderson Collection (in private hands)
CKFC	Christine King Farris Collection (in private hands)
CRO-NRCR	Crozer Theological Seminary Records, Colgate-Rochester Divinity School, Rochester, N.Y.
CSKC	Coretta Scott King Collection*
CSKCH	Coretta Scott King Home Study Collection*
CtY-D	Yale Divinity School Library, Yale University, New Haven, Conn.
DABCC	Dexter Avenue King Memorial Baptist Church Collection (in private hands)
EBCR	Ebenezer Baptist Church, Miscellaneous Records (in private hands)
FODC	Fred O. Doty Collection (in private hands)
InGrD	DePauw University, Greencastle, Ind.
JBC	John Brooke Collection (in private hands)
JOG	Julian O. Grayson Papers (in private hands)
JTPP	John T. Porter Papers (in private hands)
JWD-ARC-LNT	John Wesley Dobbs Papers, Amistad Research Collections, Tulane University, New Orleans, La.

---

*Some materials from these collections of King-related documents, with archival codes CSKC, CSKCH, and MLKJP-GAMK: Vault, were acquired in June 2006 by Morehouse College in Atlanta, Georgia.

KyLoS	Southern Baptist Theological Seminary, Louisville, Ky.
LDRP-NN-Sc	Lawrence Dunbar Reddick Papers, Manuscript, Archives and Rare Books Division, Schomburg Center for Research in Black Culture, The New York Public Library, Astor, Lenox and Tilden Foundations, New York, N.Y.
LMC-DLC	Look Magazine Collection, Library of Congress, Washington, D.C.
MAWC	Mervyn A. Warren Collection (in private hands)
MCDA-AMC	Montgomery County District Attorney's Files, Montgomery County Courthouse, Montgomery, Ala.
MDCC-MiDW-AL	Metropolitan Detroit Council of Churches Collection, Wayne State University, Walter P. Reuther Library of Labor and Urban Affairs, Archives of Labor History and Urban Affairs, Detroit, Mich.
MiDCUMA	Central United Methodist Church Archives, Detroit, Mich.
MLKEC	Martin Luther King, Jr., Estate Collection (in private hands)
MLKJP-GAMK	Martin Luther King, Jr., Papers, 1950–1968, Martin Luther King, Jr., Center for Nonviolent Social Change, Inc., Atlanta, Ga.*
MLKP-MBU	Martin Luther King, Jr., Papers, 1954–1968, Howard Gotlieb Archival Research Center, Boston University, Boston, Mass.
MNAACP-NN-Sc	Montgomery Branch, National Association for the Advancement of Colored People Minutes, 1954–1955, Manuscripts, Archives and Rare Books Division, Schomburg Center for Research in Black Culture, The New York Public Library, Astor, Lenox and Tilden Foundations, New York, N.Y.
NCCP-PPPrHi	National Council of the Churches of Christ in the United States of America Papers, Presbyterian Department of History, Philadelphia, Pa.
NNAPWW	AP/Wide World Photos, New York, N.Y.
NNICP	International Center for Photography, New York, N.Y.
NNMAGPC	Magnum Photos, Inc., Collection, New York, N.Y.
NNRC	Riverside Church Archives, New York, N.Y.
NNTI	Time, Inc., New York, N.Y.
PBC-NhPoAA	People's Baptist Church Collection, African American Resource Center, Portsmouth, N.H.
PCUSAP-PPPrHi	Presbyterian Church (U.S.A.) Papers, Presbyterian Department of History, Philadelphia, Pa.
PPUCGC	Unitarian Church of Germantown Collection, Philadelphia, Pa.
PrRE	Evangelical Seminary, Rio Piedras, Puerto Rico
RRL-ViRUT	Reigner Recording Library, Union Theological Seminary, Richmond, Va.

SCLCR-GAMK	Southern Christian Leadership Conference Records, Martin Luther King, Jr., Center for Nonviolent Social Change, Inc., Atlanta, Ga.
SLP	Samuel P. Long, Jr., Papers (in private hands)
UPIR-NNBETT	UPI and Reuters Photo Collection, Corbis-Bettman Archives, New York, N.Y.
WEBD-MU	W. E. B. (William Edward Burghardt) Du Bois Papers, University of Massachusetts, Amherst, Mass.
WRBC	White Rock Baptist Church, Philadelphia, Pa. (in private hands)

Abbreviations Used in Source Notes

The following symbols are used to describe the original documents:

Format

A	Autograph (author's hand)
H	Handwritten (other than author's hand)
P	Printed
T	Typed

Type

At	Audio record
Aw	Art work
D	Document
F	Film
Fm	Form
L	Letter or memo
LP	Phonograph record
Ph	Photo
Ta	Audio transcript
Tv	Video transcript
Vt	Video tape
W	Wire or telegram

Version

c	Copy
d	Draft
f	Fragment

Signature

I	Initialed
S	Signed
Sr	Signed with representation of author

The Papers

I: CROZER YEARS

"Preaching Ministry"

[*14 September–24 November 1948*]
[*Chester, Pa.*]

During his first term at Crozer Theological Seminary, King submitted this hand-
written outline for Robert E. Keighton's course Preaching Ministry of the Church.[1]
The outline reveals King's early commitment to addressing societal needs and ills:
"I must be concerned about unemployment, [slums], and economic insecurity. I
am a profound advocator of the social gospel." Keighton marked the paper B+.

I. The Developement of significant trends

1. The first significant trend developing in the Christian era of preaching was the rise of the Apostolic fathers.[2] Here we get an emphasis placed on the resurrection and immanent return of Christ. This period is divided into two groups
    (1) the Diciple
    (2) Paul

2. The second significant trend ~~d~~ which developed in the Christian era was the Age of the Apologist.[3] This was the period in which there was an attempt to [~~vindicate~~?] give vindication for the Christian faith.

3. The third significant trend which developed in the Christian era was that of the Reformation. Immediately after the middle ages two event came about which affected the trend of preaching to a great extent.
    (1) the passing of the fudal system.[4]
    (2) The rise of the Renaissance.
    These event brought about a great change in the method of preaching.[5] During this period preaching [*strikeout illegible*] fell into three phases.
    (1) Scholastic
    (2) doctrinal
    (3) allegorical.

---

1. King took ten courses from Keighton at Crozer Theological Seminary. For a list of these courses, see Introduction, in *Papers* 1:48.

2. The Apostolic Fathers were first and second century CE Christian writers, including Clement of Rome, Ignatius, and Polycarp, whose personal relationships with the Apostles are said to have influenced their writings. According to a syllabus that was included in the instructions for Crozer's comprehensive examination, the course Preaching Ministry addressed the history of preaching, including "the distinguishable periods of Christian preaching" (Crozer Theological Seminary, "Syllabus in preaching and worship," September 1950).

3. The Apologetic period began in the second century CE and included writers such as Justin Martyr, Tatian, and Tertullian.

4. Keighton circled the misspelling "fudal."

5. Keighton added an "s" to the word "event."

King poses with his father in front of the family car in 1948. Courtesy of
Christine King Farris

It was during this period that we find such men as Luther, Calvin, and Knox.[6] Each of these men were more or less doctrinal preachers.[7] It is significant to know that this period marked the beginning of the modern era of preaching.

4. Immediately after the reformation many different schools of thought developed. Each school of thought had its method of preaching. It is out of this that we get German, French, British and American preaching.[8] The trend at this time appeared to be evangelical.

---

6. Martin Luther (1483–1546), John Calvin (1509–1564), and John Knox (1513?–1572) were leading figures in the Protestant Reformation.

7. Keighton inserted the word "was" over the word "were" and added the word "a" between "less" and "doctrinal." He also crossed out the "s" in "preachers."

8. Keighton put a question mark at the end of this sentence.

It is significant to know that preaching did not start with Christianity.
It had its roots [*far?*] in the soil of Hebrew culture.
(1) From Moses to Samuel[9]
(2) to the eighth century prophets[10]
(3) Rise of the Synagogue
Preaching was found in each of these groups.

(2) The preaching of the first four centuries was mainly apologetic. After Christ had failed to return, there had to be some justification for the validity of the Christian gospel.[11] ~~For this reason that the apologist arose~~. They were out at every turn to defend the Christian religion. Such man as Origen and Justin were forever attempting to prove the divinity of Christ.[12] It was doing the period that the Trinitarian doctrine arose.[13] It is also significant to know that the preaching of this period was mainly scriptural. The condition of the age required apologetic preaching.

Twentieth century preaching, on the contrary, deals with great social problem. Moreover, much of our twentieth century preaching is an attempt to adjust individuals to the complexities of modern society. The problem of the virgin birth and the trinity is not the most important features in twentieth century preaching, as was the case in the first four centuries of preaching.[14]

Also we find that twentieth century preaching is not as scriptural as was the preaching of the first four centuries.[15] The twentieth century preacher uses the Bible as a basis, in many instances, then he bring in all the empirical knowledge he can find to supplement that found in the Bible. On the other hand twentieth century preaching might grow out of a novel or a newspaper article. This was not the case in the first four centuries. The differences between these two types are inevitable, for preaching grows out of the times in which the preacher lives.

3. I fell that preaching is one of the most vital needs of our society, if it is used correctly.[16] There is a great paradox in preaching, on the one hand it may be very helpful and on the other it may be very pernicious. It is my opinion that sincerity is not enough for the preaching ministry. The minister must be both sincere and intelligent. To often do our ministers possess the

---

9. Samuel was a prophet prior to and during the early part of the united monarchy in Israel, including the reigns of Saul and David.

10. Eighth century BCE prophets included Amos, Hosea, Micah, and Isaiah.

11. Keighton put a question mark between the words "there" and "had."

12. Origen (185?–?254 CE) was an early church leader and prolific author. Justin Martyr (ca. 100–ca. 165 CE) was one of the earliest theologians and apologists for the Christian church and was put to death.

13. Keighton circled the word "doing." The Trinitarian doctrine, which holds that the Father, Son, and Holy Spirit are one entity, was established through decisions at the Nicene Council (325 CE) and the Council of Constantinople (381 CE).

14. Keighton added an "s" to the word "problem" and inserted the word "are" between the words "trinity" and "not."

15. Keighton wrote the word "so" between the words "not" and "scriptural."

16. Keighton inserted another "e" over the first "l" in the word "fell."

former but not the latter.[17] This, I think, is a serious problem facing the ministry.[18]

I also think that the minister should possess profundity of conviction. We have to many minister in the pulpit who are great spellbounders and to few who possess spiritual power.[19] It is my profound conviction that I, as an aspirant for the ministry, ~~will~~ should possess these powers.

I think that preaching should grow out of the experiences of the people. Therefore, I as a minister must know the problems of the people that I am pastoring.[20] To often do educated minister leave the people lost in the fog of theological abstractions, rather than presenting that theology in the light of the people's experiences.[21] It is my conviction that the minister must somehow take profound theological and philosophical views and place them in a concrete framework. I must forever make the complex, the simple.

Above all I see the preaching ministry as a duel process.[22] On the one hand I must attempt to change the soul of individuals so that their societies may be changed. On the other I must attempt to change the societies so that the individual soul will have a change. Therefore, I must be concerned about unemployment, slumms, and economic insecurity.[23] I am a profound advocator of the social gospel.

[*signed*] M. L. King[24]

AHDS. CSKC: Sermon file, folder 36, "Sermon Notes."

---

17. Keighton added another "o" to the word "To."

18. For a fuller treatment of this theme, see King, Sincerity Is Not Enough, 3 June 1951, pp. 119–120 in this volume.

19. Keighton crossed out the "ou" in the word "spellbounders," changing it to "spellbinders." He also added another "o" to the word "to" in both occurrences.

20. Keighton added commas to set off the phrase "as a minister."

21. Keighton added another "o" to the word "To."

22. Keighton circled the word "duel."

23. Keighton crossed out the second "m" in the word "slumms."

24. Following common practice for his Crozer assignments, King folded these sheets lengthwise and signed his name on the verso of the last page.

Preaching Ministry

I - The Developement of significant trends

1. The first significant trend developing in the Christian era^(preceding) was the rise of ~~the~~ Apostolic fathers. Here we get an emphasis placed on the resurrection and immanent return of Christ. This period is divided into two groups (1) the Disciples (2) Paul

2. The second significant trend ~~to~~ which developed in the Christian era was the Age of the Apologist. This was the period in which there was an attempt to ~~provide~~ give vindication for the Christian faith.

3. The third significant trend which developed in the Christian era was that of the Reformation. Immediately after the middle ~~ages~~ two event came about which affected the trend of preaching to a great extent. (1) the passing of the feudal system. (2) the rise of the Renaissance. These events brought about a great change in the method of preaching. During this period preaching ~~rose~~ fell

into three phases. (1) Scholastic (2) doctrinal (3) allegorical. It was during this period that we find such men as Luther, Calvin, and Knox. Each of these men were more or less a doctrinal preacher. It is significant to know that this period marked the beginning of the modern era of preaching.

4. Immediately after the reformation many different schools of thought developed. Each school of thought had its method of preaching. It is out of this that we get German, French, British and American preaching? The trend at this time appered to be evangelical.

It is significant to know that preaching did not start with Christianity. It had its roots for in the soil of Hebrew culture. (1) From Moses to Samuel (2) to the eighth century prophets (3) Rise of the Synagogue Preaching was found in each of these groups.

(2) The preaching of the first four centuries was mainly apologetic. After Christ had failed to return, there had to be some justification for the validity of the Christian gospel. For this reason that the apologist arose. They were out at every turn to defend the Christian religion. Such men as Origen and Justin were forever attempting to prove the divinity of Christ. It was during the period that the Trinitarian

doctrine arose. It is also significant to know that the preaching of this period were mainly scriptural. The condition of the age required apologetic preaching.

Twentieth century preaching, on the contrary, deals with great social problems. Moreover, much of our twentieth century preaching is an attempt to adjust individuals to the complexities of modern society. The problems of the virgin birth and the trinity are not the most important features in twentieth century preaching, as was the case in the first four centuries of preaching.

Also we find that twentieth century preaching is not as scriptural as was the preaching of the first four centuries. The twentieth century preacher uses the Bible as a basis, in many instances, then he brings in all the empirical knowledge he can find to supplement that found in the Bible. On the other hand twentieth century preaching might grow out of a novel or a newspaper article. This was not the case in the first four centuries. The differences between these two types are inevitable, for preaching grows out of the times in which the preacher lives.

3. I feel that preaching is one of the most vital needs of our society, if it is used correctly. There is a great paradox in preaching, on the one hand it may be very helpful and on the other it may be very pernicious. It is my opinion that sincerity is not enough for the preaching ministry. The minister must be both sincere and intelligent. Too often do our ministers possess the former but not the latter. This, I think, is a serious problem facing the ministry.

I also think that the minister should possess profundity of conviction. We have too many ministers in the pulpit who are great spellbinders and too few who possess spiritual power. It is my profound conviction that I, as an aspirant for the ministry, should possess these powers.

I think that preaching should grow out of the experiences of the people. Therefore, I, as a minister, must know the problems of the people that I am pastoring. Too often do ministers leave the people lost in the fog of theological abstractions, rather than presenting that theology in the light of the people's experiences. It is my conviction that the minister must somehow take profound theological and philosophical views and place them in a concrete framework. I must forever make the complex, the simple.

Above all I see the preaching ministry as a (duel) process. On the one hand I must attempt to change the soul of individuals so that their societies may be changed. On the other I must attempt to change the societies so that the individual soul will have a change. Therefore, I must be concerned about unemployment, slums, and economic insecurity. I am a profound advocator of the social gospel.

BF

"The Weaknesses of Liberal Theology"

These two essays, probably prepared for George W. Davis's course Great Theologians, reveal that King began questioning some of his previous theological ideals during his first year at Crozer.[1] In these assignments, he laments that liberal theologians often neglect the question, "What relevance does Jesus have in 1948 A.D.?"

"The Weaknesses of Liberal Theology" I

1948
[*Chester, Pa.*]

For the last few years we have heard a great deal of talk about liberal theology. Ever since the turn of the century this system of theology has been gaining great recognition. This theology grew out of an attempt to wed theology to the dominant thought pattern of the day, which is science. It insists that the real theologian must be as open-minded, as unbaised, and as disinterested as the scientist. Therefore, he can never speak in terms of the absolute. Moreover, liberal theology insists that truth is not a one-act drama that appeared once and for all on the Biblical stage, but it is a drama of many acts continually appearing as the curtain of history continues to open. The liberal believes that the light of God is forever shining through history as the blosom shines through the bud.[2] Therefore, there can be no set theology. Liberal theology can never be static. It must forever adjust itself to the changing conditions of history.[3]

Personally I think this is the best, or at least the most logical system of theology in existence.[4] But at the same time I must admit that there are certain weaknesses found in liberal theology which are well worth our attention. In this paper I will only discuss one of the weaknesses found in liberal theology; others will be discussed next week.

One of the great weaknesses of liberal theology is that it to often loses itself in "higher criticism."[5] In other words, the liberal theologian, in many instances,

---

1. King's reference to 1948 suggests he wrote this paper for Great Theologians, his only theology course that calendar year. For more on Davis's role in the development of King's theology, see Introduction, in *Papers* 1:49–50.

2. King repeated the previous three sentences in a 1949 assignment for Davis's course Christian Theology for Today (see King, "The Sources of Fundamentalism and Liberalism Considered Historically and Psychologically," 13 September–23 November 1949, in *Papers* 1:239).

3. In his course notes, King recorded that theology was partly determined by "the [*pressures?*] conditions of the environment in which the theologian lives. These pressures causes them to seek the nature of God." His notes continue: "<u>Is our day propitious for great theologians</u>. If ever the stage was set for great theological thinking, it is today. There are two major forces which must be present in society 1. New form and way of thinking 2. Crisis if a great theology is to come" (King, Class notes I, Great Theologians, 30 November 1948–16 February 1949).

4. Davis added a comma after the word "logical."

5. "Higher criticism," a type of biblical analysis that examined the historic accuracy of biblical texts, emerged in the eighteenth and nineteenth centuries. Davis added another "o" to the word "to."

IN THE MINISTER'S WORKSHOP

senses and attention which the modern world makes. Coleridge's ancient mariner felt the competition of distracting noise:

The Wedding-Guest here beat his breast,
For he heard the loud bassoon.

The bassoon has been particularly loud in recent years. Often it has been a literal, physical bassoon, swing music, calling youth like the flute of the Pied Piper. Always it has been a figurative bassoon, whose notes beat on the ears and minds of an audience which a speaker is trying to hold with a story of great matters.

The preacher must be baptized into a new conviction of the importance of preaching in a world increasingly distracted. He needs Paul's overpowering sense, expressed in the passage just quoted, of being the trustee of a word of salvation in a world increasingly damned. The relationship of that word to our world was strikingly drawn in blazing letters over a hundred years ago by a German Jew who saw with a penetrating eye, Heinrich Heine. He wrote in 1834: "Should that subduing talisman, the cross, ever break, then the old stone gods will rise from the long-forgotten ruins and rub the dust of a thousand years from their eyes, and Thor, leaping to life with his giant hammer, will crush the Gothic cathedrals." Was ever a prophecy more literally and tragically fulfilled? The cross did break for multitudes in Europe, and Thor crushed the Gothic cathedrals. That sentence of Heine's might well be carved on a plaque to be set in the rebuilt cathedrals of Coventry and Cologne. For it affirms the basic moral and spiritual reality of the world. It affirms that the proclaimer of "the talisman of the cross" is not marooned off on a side road but is in the very center of all the world's conflict and traffic. But if there is no undebatable compulsion to proclaim God's imperishable word, there will just be a rear-end action in a defeatist mood.

Every great movement in history has been prepared for and partly, at least, carried through by preaching—the beginning of the Christian church, the Crusades, the abolition of slavery, the Reformation, the Evangelical Revival, the labor movement, Marxian Communism, German Nazism. Not, surely, always Christian preaching, but preaching as a powerful instrument. For we have been living in a world

38

THE IMPORTANCE OF PREACHING

many with sermons. They blare through the radio, they shriek from headlines, they are dropped by the ton as leaflets over cities. They often go under the head of "psychological warfare"; but they are preaching, arguments, persuasions, appeals for conversion. They are major instruments. "Ideas are weapons." One fear that grips the hearts of multitudes today in America is that while possessing an amazing effectiveness of technical achievement in war—in the heaven's above, the earth beneath, and the waters under the earth—the United States may fail in the realm of the warfare of ideas, fail to sound any saving word in a doomed world.

Preaching, if it is to have adequate depth and height and breadth, must be theological preaching. Indeed, there is no other kind that is much more than a respectable embellishment of a comfortable life.

This has been expressed with rugged force in the challenge to the church: "If you have anything peculiarly Christian to say at this hour, for God's sake say it! But if you can do nothing but mouth over the clichés of the street corner, or the usual banalities of the Chamber of Commerce, for God's sake, keep still!" Those are rough words, but so were many of the words of Paul, and of Jesus. If preaching is not basically theological, not the proclamation of a God who has acted, but merely an anthology of moral maxims, it soon comes to resemble the description of Matthew Arnold as "a mournful evangelist who had somehow contrived to mislay his gospel." It is seductively easy to mislay a gospel. The old distinction, made again and again, is always valid and of first importance, that preaching should be a matter of the circumference and not an arc. An arc is a portion of the circumference of a circle; a sector is a V-shaped wedge in a circle, which includes a portion of the circumference but goes by radii to the center. "Arc preaching" deals with a segment of the circumference of life; "sector preaching" includes circumference but goes to the center. A true, as well as clever, description of preaching that stays on the circumference is found in the oft-quoted remark of Arnold Lunn: "There is no market for sermons on the text: God so loved the world that he inspired a certain Jew to inform his contemporaries that there was a great deal to be said for loving one's neighbors." Paul did "sector" preaching; he dealt with the varied circumferences of life in the

39

In his copy of Halford Edward Luccock's 1944 book *In The Minister's Workshop*, King writes, "Every great movement in history has been prepared for and partly carried out through preaching," and "If preaching is to have any depth, height and breadth, it must be theological preaching" (pp. 38–39).

becomes so involved in "higher criticism that he unconsciously stops there.[6] This is certainly a weakness that the liberal theologian should attempt to avoid. After the Bible has been stripped of all of its mythological and non-historical content, the liberal theologian must be able to answer the question—what then?[7] It is certainly justifiable to be as scientific as possible in proving that the Pentateuch was written by more then one author, that the whale did not swallow Jonah, that Jesus was not born a virgin, or that Jesus never met John the Baptist.[8] But after all of this, what relevance do these scriptures have?[9] What moral implications do we find growing out of the Bible? What relevance does Jesus have in 1948 A.D.?[10] These are question which the liberal theologian must of necessity answer if he expects to influence the average mind.[11] To often do we find many of the liberals dodging these vital questions.[12] This is the first great weakness of liberal theology.

{lost in a vocabulary}

[*signed*] M. L. King[13]

TAHDS. CSKC: Sermon file, folder 118, "Sermon Material."

"The Weaknesses of Liberal Theology" II

[*1948*]
[*Chester, Pa.*]

Last week we concluded that one of the great weaknesses of liberal theology is that it becomes so involved in higher criticism, in many instances, that it fails to answer certain vital questions. Today we will discuss another weakness of liberal theology which is equally pernicious. This weakness lies in its failure to contact the masses. Liberal theology seems to be lost in a vocabulary. Moreover, it seems to be too divorced from life.

This tendency to move out of the market-place of everyday life has led liberal theology to become so theoretical that it forgets the practical.[14] This is certainly a danger to any system of theology, for it presupposes that all life is theory, when in reality theory is not effective until it can be reproduced in the realm of the practical. This is certainly a point of warning, for it is the danger that faced the scholastics when they lost their heads to logic. Liberal theology

---

6. Davis added a quotation mark after the word "criticism."

7. Davis crossed out the second "of" in this sentence.

8. The Pentateuch refers to the first five books of the Hebrew Bible. Davis added the word "of" between the words "born" and "a."

9. Davis crossed out the word "of."

10. Davis indicated that "A.D." should have come before "1948."

11. Davis added an "s" to the word "question."

12. Davis added another "o" to the word "To."

13. King folded this assignment lengthwise and signed his name on the verso of the last page.

14. Davis drew a star between the words "market" and "place" to indicate one word, not two.

will only be recognized when it begin to grappel with the problems of the un-
sophisticated man.[15]

[*signed*] M. L. King[16]

AHDS. CSKC: Sermon file, folder 165.

---

15. Davis circled the word "only," drew an arrow to move it between the words "recognized" and
"when," and circled the misspelling "grappel."

16. King folded this document lengthwise and signed his name on the verso of the last page.

Sermon Sketches

[*30 November 1948–16 February 1949?*]
[*Chester, Pa.?*]

King probably wrote these exercises for the course Preparation of the Sermon.[1]
Throughout his life, he would revisit many of these themes and utilize many
of these titles, including "Facing Life's Inescapables" and "What Is Man?"[2]

Sermon Sketches I

I   Title—The Assurance of Immortality
         Job 19:25[3]
Theme—We are able to attain immortality through the men and women that we
influence, and through the children who are touched by the flame of our spirits.
Purpose—To show that the desire for immortality will not be in vain.
             In this sermon I purpose to show that the actual meaning of this text
has often been misunderstood. Actually this was a developing concept of
immortality. The word redeemer comes from the Hebrew word go'el mean-

---

1. The organization of these sketches reflects King's class notes for Preparation of the Sermon, which
defined the components of a sermon as the title, theme, purpose, introduction, body, and conclusion.
King recorded in his notes that a sermon's title "is not the theme or subject," but that it "is primarily for
advertising purposes." His notes also indicated that the theme was "the thing you are saying to the people," while the purpose was what "you expect to accomplish in your particular sermon. I must attempt to
get people to see, do, or be something." King characterized the sermon's conclusion as a recapitulation
"bringing the audience to a place where there is emotional impact" (King, Class notes, Preparation of
the Sermon, 30 November 1948–16 February 1949).

2. King, "Facing Life's Inescapables," 3 March 1949, and "What Is Man?" Sermon at Dexter Avenue
Baptist Church, 11 July 1954, pp. 88–90 and 174–179 in this volume, respectively.

3. "For I know that my redeemer liveth, and that he shall stand at the latter day upon the earth."   81

ing next-kin.[4] In other words the author believed he would live on through his "next-kin." This whole concept grew out of the view of levirate marriage.[5]

II Title—Beyond Asceticism
    Colossians 2:21[6]
Theme—True religion goes beyond asceticism and ritualistic practices; it is a new life.
Purpose—To show how to attain this new life.

III Title—Almost Persuaded
    Acts 26:28[7]
Theme—Procrastination is the thief of time
Purpose—To show the listeners that great experiences are often missed when we procrastinate.
    In this sermon I will assume that Agrippa's words were serious. Of course, it is difficult to tell whether the words of Agrippa are ironical or spoken seriously.

IV Title—Looking Toward The Hills
    Ps. 121:1[8]
Theme—God is always found in the highest and best things of life
Purpose—To show that God is the highest good.

V Title—The Misused Covenant
    In this sermon I purpose to show that this covenant is a threat rather than a benediction. From this point I will go on to say that man should rise above the watchful state: In other words, ~~he should~~ he should be able to conform in that area where the law does not reach.

[*signed*] M. L. King, Jr.[9]

AHDS. CSKC: Sermon file, folder 36, "Sermon Notes."

Sermon Sketches II

I Title—"Repentance"
Theme—Repentance means a [*change?*] of conduct as well as of heart.
Purpose—to show that God always reserves for man the possibility of repentance

---

4. Keighton wrote a question mark in the margin next to this sentence.

5. Levirate marriage calls for the closest male relative to marry the widow and to name their first son after the deceased man in the event that a husband dies without a son. For illustrations of levirate marriage, see Deuteronomy 25:5–10, and Ruth 3–4. Keighton wrote another a question mark in the margin next to this sentence.

6. "Touch not; taste not; handle not."

7. "Then Agrippa said unto Paul, Almost thou persuadest me to be a Christian." Herod Agrippa II (27 CE–ca. 100 CE) was the Roman-appointed authority in the first century CE over the region that included Jerusalem.

8. "I will lift up mine eyes unto the hills, from whence cometh my help."

9. King folded this assignment lengthwise and signed his name on the verso of the last page.

II   Title—"Forgiveness"[10]

theme—Forgiveness does not take away the fact of sin. But it restores the offender to communion with us, which he had forfeited through his offence. Purpose—To show that the forgiving spirit is one of the greatest experiences in life.

III "Facing life's Inescapables"[11]

Theme—There are certain great inevitables in life which cannot be escaped Purpose—To show the listeners how to face these inevitables.

[*signed*] M. L. King[12]

AHDS. CSKC: Sermon file, folder 36, "Sermon Notes."

Sermon Introductions

Why Religion?

INTRODUCTION

Recently, a very serious minded friend of mine asked me the question, why religion?[13] I found myself unable to give a concrete answer to this question, for I had never given it a thought. I could have probably answered his question by saying, if you have religion you will go to heaven, but in reality I know nothing about heaven. Or I could have said, if you dont have religion you will go to hell, but personally I dont believe in hell in the conventional sense.[14] Or maybe I could have quoted sone scriptural passage, but suppose he doubted even the authority of the Bible. He wanted sone concrete evidence on the necessity for religion. And so after giving the question sone serious thought, I will attempt to answer it in this sermon. Why Religion?

Life Is What You Make It

INTRODUCTION

Many people wander into the world, and they pick up everything they can get their hands upon looking for life.[15] They never get it. What they get is existence.

---

10. King developed a more complete outline of this sermon using Luke 15:20 as a text (King, "The Meaning of Forgiveness," 1948–1954, pp. 580–581 in this volume).

11. For an expanded version of this sermon, see King, "Facing Life's Inescapables," 3 March 1949, pp. 88–90 in this volume.

12. King folded this assignment lengthwise and signed his name on the verso of the last page. Keighton gave these three sketches an A.

13. King developed an essay with a similar theme (King, "The Purpose of Religion," September 1948–May 1951, pp. 109–110 in this volume). Keighton crossed out the comma after "Recently" and added a dash between "serious" and "minded."

14. King explored his belief in the afterlife in "What Happened to Hell?" (January 1961, p. 411 in this volume).

15. King's announced sermon topic for 25 April 1948 at Atlanta's Liberty Baptist Church was "Life Is What You Make It" ("Rev. M. L. King Jr. at Liberty Sunday," *Atlanta Daily World,* 24 April 1948). He

Existence is what you find; life is what you create. Therefore, if life ever seems worth while to you, it is not because you found it that way, but because you made it so.[16]

Civilization's Great Need

INTRODUCTION

The greatest need of civilization is not political security; the greatest need of civilization is not a multiplicity of wealth; the greatest need of civilization is not the superb genuis of science, as important as it is; the greatest need of civilization is moral progress[17]

The Effects of Conversion

There is no greater revolution in the world than conversion to God.

It might be profitable to those who have not yet undertaken this internal revolution of their spirits, to acquaint themselves with the three beautiful results of conversion.[18]

What Is Man?

One of the most pertinent and pressing problems of our time was raised by an ancient poet of Israel when he asked, "What is man?"[19] What men have believed about themselves, what they have thought was their nature and destiny, have been among the most potent facts in history.[20]

[*signed*] M. L. King Jr.[21]

AHDS. CSKC: Sermon file, folder 36, "Sermon Notes."

---

expanded upon this theme in the sermon "Creating the Abundant Life," Sermon at Dexter Avenue Baptist Church (26 September 1954, pp. 187–192 in this volume).

16. Keighton joined the words "worth" and "while."

17. For a complete version of this sermon, see King, "Civilization's Great Need," 1949, pp. 86–88 in this volume.

18. In a March 1948 radio address titled "The Effects of Conversion," Fulton J. Sheen stated: "Friends: There is no greater revolution in the world than conversion to God. It might be profitable to those who have not yet undertaken this internal revolution of their spirits, to acquaint themselves with the four beautiful results of conversion." King kept a copy of this address in his sermon file. Fulton J. Sheen, head of the American branch of the Catholic Church's Society for the Propagation of the Faith from 1951 until 1966, began radio broadcasts in 1930 while a professor at Catholic University in Washington, D.C.

19. Cf. Psalm 8:4. King may have preached this sermon on the radio as early as 6 September 1953 (see King, "Radio Sermons," 26 July–6 September 1953, p. 136 in this volume). He delivered it the following summer at Dexter Avenue Baptist Church and also gave it in 1958 as part of the Detroit Council of Church's Noon Lenten Services (King, "What Is Man?" 11 July 1954, and "The Christian Doctrine of Man," 12 March 1958, pp. 174–179 and 328–338 in this volume, respectively). "What Is Man?" was included in King's published volume of sermons (King, *Strength to Love* [New York: Harper & Row, 1963], pp. 87–92).

20. Keighton noted at the bottom of the assignment, "These are varied & all very good; especially the first."

21. King folded this assignment lengthwise and signed his name on the verso of the last page.

Sermon Conclusions

Facing Life's Inescapables

This is the conclusion of the whole matter. We can't escape ourselves; we can't escape sacrifice; we can't escape Jesus. We had better accept these as the great inevitables of life.

The House We are Building

When the Brooklyn Bridge was in course of construction, Roebling, the architect, was sick in bed. He was unable personally to watch its construction and could only direct the builders from his sick room. Finally the vast structure was finished. But before it was opened the master builder was taken out in a little boat, propped up with pillows, to a position in the East River beneath the great span. There he lay for a long time in silence with the plans of the bridge before him, looking now at the blueprints and now at the bridge, until it was all gone over. Then he sank back among the pillows with a satisfied smile. "It is like the plan."[22]

God has set us a plan for the building of the soul: the life of Christ as it is revealed in the New Testament.[23] No one can fail if he follows that plan. It is your lasting opportunity.

The Misuse of Prayer

Let us hear the conclusion of the whole matter.[24] We should never pray for God to abrogate the natural laws, neither should we make prayer a substitute for work and intelligence. Rather, we should prayer for an understanding mind so that we may know and understand God's expression of Himself in the ways of nature, and for an obedient heart so that as we learn to know and understand God's way and God's will we may dare to act and live in harmony with this understanding. This is true prayer.

Success In Life

There is an old saying, "If wishes were horses beggars would ride."[25] Friends, the great highroad of success lies along the old high-way of steadfast well-doing; and they who are the most industrious and the most persistent, and work in the truest spirit, will invariably be the most successful. Success treads on the heels of every right effort.

---

22. John A. Roebling, the original architect of the Brooklyn Bridge, died in 1869, fourteen years before the bridge opened. His son, Washington A. Roebling, carried on the project and became ill near the end of construction.

23. Keighton crossed out the comma after the word "soul" and inserted a colon.

24. King developed a more complete version of this theme (King, "The Misuse of Prayer," 1948–1954, pp. 590–591 in this volume).

25. King refers to the nursery rhyme "If Wishes Were Horses."

Modern psychology affirms that vital religious faith is unequaled in its resources to make life worth living. The church holds before us this fact—confirmed in the lives of Paul, Augustine, John Wesley, Tolstoy, Schweitzer in Africa—that you can be more than a conqueror, and that can be what you choose to make it.[26] {enellage}

[*signed*] M. L. King Jr.

AHDS. CSKC: Sermon file, folder 36, "Sermon Notes."

---

26. Cf. Romans 8:37. King refers to Augustine (354–430 CE), bishop of Hippo and Father of the Church; John Wesley (1703–1791), the founder of the Methodist Church; Leo Tolstoy (1828–1910), the Russian author of *War and Peace* (1865–1869); and Albert Schweitzer (1875–1965), a medical humanitarian and Nobel Peace Prize winner. Keighton underlined the word "that" and inserted "antecedent?"

"Civilization's Great Need"

1949
[*Atlanta, Ga.*]

This 1949 message, an early example of one of King's most consistent themes of his lifelong ministry, was probably preached while he was serving during the summer as Ebenezer's associate pastor.[1] *"On the whole our material and intellectual advances have outrun our moral progress," he asserts. In a closing prayer, handwritten at the end of this typed message, King implores God, "Help us to work with renewed vigor for a warless world, a better distribution of wealth, and a brotherhood that transcends race or color."*

The greatest need of civilization today is not political security; the greatest need of civilization today is not a well rounded United Nations Organization; the greatest need of civilization today is not a multiplicity of material goods; the greatest need of civilization today is not the superb genuis of science as important as it is; the greatest need of civilization today is moral progress. On the whole our material and intellectual advances have outrun our moral progress. Who can argue with any degree of logic that we have not progressed scientifically. Science can point to so many remarkable achievements, such tangible and amazing victories. It has freed

---

1. King was ordained and appointed associate pastor at Ebenezer Baptist Church in February 1948. He functioned in this capacity during summer vacations and school holidays.

man from many of his physical limitations. It has equipped man to see further, reach higher, travel faster, and communicate more speedily. One of my colleagues from China related to me that He flew from Shaghai to San Franscisco in only three days. As late as 1709 it took five days for a letter to go from New York to Washington. Yes science has dwrafed time and placed distance in chains. IT has stamped out many of man's dread plagues and diseases, alleviated his pain, prolonged his life and given him greater security and physical well-being.

Let us turn to the realm of education. Certainly man's progress educationally has been astounding. Illiteracy stands at a very ebb today, and is likely to vanish within a few generations. Our colleges and universities have more students today than ever before in their history. We know more about mathematics, chemistry, social science, and philosophy than we have ever known. Yes the scientific and educational means by which we live can hardly be surpassed, but the moral and spiritual ends for which we live stand almost in a state of oblivion. Thoreau was not indulging in wishful thinking when he wrote the phrase: "Improved means to an unimproved end."[2] This phrase could well characterize our modern life.

Truly it seems that our moral standards are lagging behind, in fact they are breaking down. Homes are disintergrating. The purity of family life is disappearing. Gambling, drunkenness, prostitution, and all sorts of pathological vices flourish as never before. Human brotherhood seems to be something foreign to the peoples of the world. Races stand against races, nations against nations, religions against religions.

Truly I sometimes cry "where are the moral and spiritual ends for living."

Unless we can reestablish the moral and spiritual ends of living in personal character and social justice, our civilization will ruin itself with the misuse of its own instruments. As Dr. Trueblood states in his book, "The Predicament Of Modern Man," Modern man has built up a complex civilization, but he may loose it, because in his proud hour of achievement he has failed to apply moral direction to his modern advances."[3] Our [~~knowledge?~~] {Scientific means} alone will not save us at this moment. With the most amazing means of production in history we have unemployment. With the most amazing world contacts on record we make world wars. With all of our knowledge and training, we hardly know enough to avoid sowing the seeds of another war. I tell you it is not enough to have the power of concentration, but worthy objectives upon which to concentrate. IT is not enough to have the accumulated knowledge of the race, but also the accumulated experiences of social liv-

---

2. Henry David Thoreau, *Walden; or, Life in the Woods* (1854), p. 57: "Our inventions are wont to be pretty toys, which distract our attention from serious things. They are but improved means to an unimproved end, an end which it was already but too easy to arrive at; as railroads lead to Boston or New York."

3. D. Elton Trueblood, *The Predicament of Modern Man* (New York: Harper & Brothers, 1944), p. 16: "This is the predicament of Western man. He has built up a complex civilization, but he may lose it because, in his proud hour of achievement, he has so largely lost or never developed the inner resources that are needed to keep a possible boon from becoming a calamity." At Crozer, King was required to read a portion of this text for Kenneth Smith's course Christianity and Society (Smith, Syllabus, Christianity and Society, 20 February–4 May 1951). Trueblood, a professor of philosophy at Earlham College from 1946 until 1966, hosted a visit by King on 23 April 1959 as one of the speakers in the college's Convocation series (King to Trueblood, 18 May 1959).

ing. It is not enough to know truth. We must love truth and sacrifice for it. We need not only knowledge which is power but wisdom which is control.

I warn you this morning my friends, we of 1949 A.D. will not escape the question of our Lord. What does it profit a man if he gains the whole world of means—airplanes, automobiles, skyscrapers, and subways—and lose the end the soul?[4] The words that the apostle Paul wrote in a letter to the church of Phillippi are still pertinent today. Finally, brethren, whatsoever things are true, whatsoever things are honest, whatsoever things are just, whatsoever things are pure, whatsoever things are of good report; if there be any virtue, and if there be any praise, think on these things."[5] If civilization is to survive she must rediscover the moral and spiritual ends for living.

{Eternal God Out of whose mind this great cosmic un we bes thee. Help us to seek that which is high, noble and Good Help us in the moment of difficult discision. Help us to work with renewed vigor for a warless world, a better distribution of wealth, and a brotherhood that transcends race or color.}

TAD. CSKC: Sermon file, folder 119, "Civilization's Greatest Need" / "Faith in Man."

---

4. Cf. Mark 8:36.
5. Cf. Philippians 4:8.

"Facing Life's Inescapables"

[*3 March 1949?*]
[*Chester, Pa.?*]

Preaching a few days after Joe Louis announced his retirement from boxing, King cites Louis, Marian Anderson, Paul Robeson, and Roland Hayes as examples of those who confronted and overcame the inevitable challenges of life.[1]

One of the tragic tendancies that has characterized man ever since the dawn of recorded history has been his attempt to escape his moral responsibilities. Man is forever trying to escape the realities of life. He is forever trying to make the false seem true; the evil seem good; the ugly seem beautiful; and the unjust seem just.

---

1. The sermon's date is based on King's reference to Joe Louis's announcement of retirement from boxing, a well-publicized event that occurred on 1 March 1949. Louis would return to boxing for financial reasons in 1950 and 1951. King may have delivered this sermon at J. Pius Barbour's Calvary Baptist Church in Chester, Pennsylvania. Barbour, a graduate of Crozer, was the editor of the *National Baptist Voice*. He hosted King in his home and frequently invited him to preach at his church while King attended Crozer (Barbour, "Meditations on Rev. M. L. King, Jr., of Montgomery, Ala.," *National Baptist Voice* [March 1956]; King to Alberta Williams King, October 1948, in *Papers* 1:161–162).

Moreover, man has to often concluded that he is a helpless victim of environment. This mistaken idea encourages him to blame everything but himself for his mistakes and weaknesses. As long as each individual refuses to accept his moral responsibility, there can never be any hope for a better life either for him or for the world.

One of the most amazing things about Jesus was his superb acceptance of life's great inescapbles. He never ran away from anything. He faced life each day and thereby developed the capacity within himself to meet the inevitables as they came. When you know exactly what you must face, you are more likely to develope within yourself the capacity to meet those things which no one can ever escape.

First, you cannot escape yourself. You are the one person from whom you can never get a divorce. You can get a divorce from Tom, Dick, or Mary, but never from yourself. You will always have yourself before you. We talk a great deal about adjusting man to his environment. But it is my opinion that man will never become adjusted to his environment until he becomes adjusted to himself. A prisoner serving a long prison sentence once said, "Even if a man does escape the police there is something inside him. . . . its no use trying to beat. Death is mild compared to the thing a criminal finds himself up against. I give it up. I can't explain it." He could not get away from himself, his own conscience his own sense of guilt. You may try to escape self by daydreaming. You may try to escape ~~it~~ self by flight into an imaginary utopian world. You may try to escape self by running into a mad world of pleasure. You may try to escape self by sucide. But the only ~~to~~ way to escape self is to accept self.

Second, we cannot escape sacrifice. No one ever accomplishes anything in this life without sacrificing themselves for one thing or another. We say that Beetovan was a great composer and we marvel when we hear his fifth symphony or his moonlight sonata, but we must ~~remb~~ remember that he sacrificed unbelievable hours a day for practice.[2] We say that Leonardo da Vinci was a great painter and we become captivated when we observe his beautiful picture, "The Last Supper", but we must remember that when a young lad he spent many hours at home painting pictures.[3] We say that Joe Louis is a great boxer and only two nights ago we marvelled as we heard him end a colorful career as probably the greatest boxer in history, but Joe Louis realized early that he could not stay up all night drinking and carraising if he was to be the chapion of the world.[4] We say that Marion Anderson, Paul Roberson and Roland Hayes are great singers, and as they sing the very fibers of souls are shaken, but we must remember that they spent many hours practicing while other boys and girls were spending all of their time playing and having a good time.[5] We say that Jesus has been the most influential character in Western civilization, and as

---

2. Ludwig van Beethoven (1770–1827) was a German composer.

3. Leonardo da Vinci (1452–1519) was a Renaissance artist and inventor.

4. Joe Louis (1914–1981) held the world heavyweight boxing championship title longer than any other man in history, successfully defending it twenty-five times between 1937 and 1949.

5. Marian Anderson (1897–1993) became the first African American to join New York's Metropolitan Opera and sang at the inaugurals of Presidents Eisenhower and Kennedy. Singer, actor, and political activist Paul Robeson (1898–1976) starred in a number of films and Broadway plays. Roland Hayes (1887–1977) garnered critical praise for his interpretations of spirituals and classical German folk songs.

we read his sermon on the mount there is something about it that penetrates our very souls, but we must remember that at a very early age he sacrificed his time to God, and finally he sacrificed even his life.[6] There are people who expect the best in life without effort. But I tell you this morning whatever your potentialities may be, they will amount to little or nothing unless you subject yourself to hard work and discipline.

Finally we cannot escape Jesus. For 19 centuries we have tried to escape him. But only to find that every time we attempt to escape him he stands right before us. When management would attempt to exploit labor, we hear Jesus saying, "If ye do it unto the least of these my brethern ye do it unto me."[7] When we would stand on the street coner and lust after women, we hear Jesus saying, "ye have heard it said in old times thou shall not comit adultry, but I say unto you whosoever shall look on a woman to lust after her hath already comitted adultry in his heart."[8] When we would criticise others for their shortcomings and insist that they be turned out of church, We hear Jesus saying, "he who is without sin cast the first stone."[9] When we would hate members of another race, or of another nationality, or of another religion, we hear Jesus saying, "there went a certain man down the Jerico road who fell among thieves and the man who helped him was the man of another race.[10] Everywhere we turn we see that disturbing man Jesus. So I say that the only way to escape Jesus is to accept him.

This is the conclusione of the whole matter: We cant escape ourselves, we cant escape sacrifice and we cant escape Jesus. We had better accept these as the great inevitables of life

AD. CSKC: Sermon file, folder 75, "Facing Life's Inescapables."

------

6. The Sermon on the Mount is the common designation for Jesus' teachings found in Matthew 5–7.
7. Matthew 25:40.
8. Matthew 5:27–28.
9. John 8:7.
10. Luke 10:25–37.

"A Way Out"

[*22 May 1949*]
[*Atlanta, Ga.*]

This handwritten document, the earliest known text of any sermon King delivered as associate pastor at Ebenezer,[1] illustrates his use of personal experiences and

------

1. King's announced sermon topic for 22 May 1949 at Ebenezer was "A Way Out" ("'A Way Out' Rev. M. L. King Jr.'s Subject," *Atlanta Daily World,* 21 May 1949).

relationships in his preaching. In the sermons he delivered at his home church during   22 May 1949
the summer of 1949, King displayed a willingness to address the issue of
race relations.

{That is the way out and the only successful way.}

A few days ago I had a very long conversation with one of my very close classmates. In the course of the conversation he related to me some of the tragic experiences that came to him a year before entering the seminary. He said, "you know King, just ~~before~~ a year ago I lost my wife and my mother within three weeks time. My wife died the first week in May and my mother died the last week in May. These were very tragic experience for me mainly because I wasn't prepared for them. At the funeral of both my wife and mother the minister said, 'this is the will of God, therefore it cannot be wrong.' But the great conflict that faced me at this [*moment*] was that it was not my will that my wife and mother should die. Here my will was in direct conflict with God's will. It was at this point that I almost cracked up. I had almost lost all hope in life. But finally after paryer and hard work I was able to balence myself. I came to see with the poet that into each life some rain must fall.[2] It is my firm belief that if I had not had a deep faith in God and a strong belief in the efficacy of prayer I would have never pulled through this crisis."

~~Jesus found himself in a similar crisis. We have set ourselves over the years to believe that Jesus wanted to die.~~

These types of experiences are not only peculiar to my friend, but they present themselves in all levels of human nature. Men are forever confronted with crisis situations Sometime ago Jesus found himself in a similar situation. He found himself confronted with the question of life or death. Of course many of us have set our minds to believe that Jesus was never confronted with this question. Moreover we have come to believe that He wanted to die in the beginning. But a close analysis of the scripture reveals the contrary. In fact it states clearly that Jesus had a deep-seated desire to escape death. In Luke's gospel we find these words, "Father, if thou be willing, remove this cup from me." Here we see that Jesus' will is the direct anthersis of God's will. At this moment Jesus didn't want to die, but his father in Heaven saw the necessity of his death. The question immediately arises, how was it that Jesus in the same verse could say, "nevertheless not my will, but thine, be done."[3] In other words, what resource did Jesus have to make his will become God's will? What was his way out in this moment of crisis? This is the question that I will attempt to answer before this sermon is ended.[4]

Before answering this question let us place this familiar picture in a modern frame and show the weakness of many of the resources that men turn to in crisis situation. I need not dwell on the fact that most people are at some time confronted with crisis: both the rich and the poor; the young and the old; the ups and ins; the

---

2. Henry Wadsworth Longfellow, "The Rainy Day" (1841): "Thy fate is the common fate of all, / Into each life some rain must fall."

3. Luke 22:42.

4. King also reflected on these questions in a 1957 Palm Sunday sermon (King, Garden of Gethsemane, Sermon Delivered at Dexter Avenue Baptist Church, 14 April 1957, p. 275–283 in this volume).

downs and outs. Of course the forms of these crisis may be as diverse as the number of human beings. It may result from the death of a love one; it may result from an unsuccessful love affair; it may result from the lose of some economic security, it may result from the failure to make the antiscipated grade in school; or it may result from a childs failure to [*come?*] up to his parents expectation. Although the form of these situations is different, the result is the same—crisis, crisis, crisis.

When men find themselves in these crisis situations they are forever trying to find a way out. They are forever attempting to rise above the mighty tempestuous seas of confusion to the smooth seas of comfort. What are some of the methods that men have used to come out of these crisis.

First, men have used the method of escapism. This was the method that the disciples used when they were confronted with the crisis of the death of their leader. They saw the solution of their problem in their feet. So they ran back to Galilee. But was this a solution to the problem? Had not the personality of this dynamic leader so intoxicated the minds of these men that a escape to Galilee was only a temporary escape from a problem which could not be so easily solved.

Modern man has attempted to use this method of escapism through such media as drunkeness, sensual indulgence, and even suicide. It seems that the contemporary soul is turning almost haphazardly to these avenues of escape. But do these methods actually solve the gigantic problems that we face in moments of crisis, or do they only push the problems back a step futher. It seems to me that the latter is the more logical. for we never solve problem by attempting to run from them. Our running only gives a tempory allevation not a permanent solution. For an instance, if I owe John Doe $50 and find myself unable to pay him, will getting drunk solve the problem for me. It may help me to forget my debt for a few hours, but when I get sober I still owe John $50.

The psychaitrists tell us that there is also a psychological danger in the use of drugs and alcohol in the moment of crisis. They tell us that the more we use these methods to escape the grim realities of life, the thiner and thiner our personalities become until ultimately they split. This may account for the increasing split personalities that we have today. So let us not turn to the various methods of escapism when we come to the crisis of life.

Men have turned to a second source in moments of crisis, namely to the companionship of friends. It seems that man's social instinct is most conspicuous in moments of crisis. So that words of friends in moments of crisis may be very consoling. N.P. The late Dr. George Truit of Texas, tells the story, in one of his books, of a great fire that broke out in a hotel of one of the southern cities.[5] The firemen were on the job with their net and ladder until it was believed that all in the building had been rescued. Suddenly a cry of dismay came from the top floor of the hotel, and immediatly the crowd began looking up. There they saw the white face of a little girl. Speedily the

---

5. George W. Truett was the pastor of First Baptist Church in Dallas, Texas, from 1897 until his death in 1944 and served as president of the Southern Baptist Convention from 1927 until 1929. King refers to an illustration from Truett's sermon "What To Do With Life's Burdens" (Truett, *A Quest for Souls: Comprising All the Sermons Preached and Prayers Offered in a Series of Gospel Meetings, Held in Fort Worth, Texas* [New York: George H. Doran, 1917], p. 22).

chief set forth the longest ladder and sent the youngest and bravest fireman. The crowd stood tense as this young fireman ascending the ladder. Finally he reached the little girl and began slowly to descend the ladder. Just at the time that he had gotten half way down the ladder billows of smoke began to flow from the window below him and flames began to leap from each side. Here the young fireman lost his courage. He began to hesitate falter and sway. Immediately the fire chief at the bottom of the ladder shouted, "Cheer him up boys, cheer him up," and cheer after cheer rang out.

Very soon the sound of the cheers from below reached the young fireman on the ladder. The crowds watched as the young firemen regained his strength and courage and once again began to descend the ladder until he finally brought the little girl to safty.

I guess many men have been able [*strikeout illegible*] to go through many crisis because of the cheers and kind words of friends ringing in their ears. But is this alway the case? Can we always rely on friends in moments of crisis? Suppose Jesus had relied on this source. Would he have been able to master this crisis. Did not his friend Peter deny him?[6] Did not his frind Judus betray him?[7] Did not the other disciples run to Galilee?[8] Yes, when Jesus faced the bitter cup, when he stood in Pilates judgment hall, when he bore his cross up the slopes of Calvery, there were no cheers. So we cannot alway depend on our friend in moment of crisis. You see, your susposedly best friend may be your worst enemy. And this type of enemy is more dangerous than an obvious enemy, for he knows your inner secrets, your weaknesses and your shortcomings. He knows the definite point of attact.

Again friend may only stick with you in moment of triumph and victory. These types of friend are quite prevelant in our world. They are present in our victory but absent in our defeat. So friendship might not be the best source toward which to turn in moment of crisis, for friendship might only be an external front with no internal basis.

Where then shall we turn, what road shall we travel, in the endless, basic, and all important attempt to remain stable in moments of crisis.

This brings us directly to original question. How did Jesus finally cone to the point that his will, which had in the beginning been contrary to God's will, become one with God will. The scripture tells us that he prayed. In other word Jesus turned to God in his moment of crisis It is this method that I recomend to you this morning. I guess many of you are saying that solution is to naive, too often do preachers tell us to pray and turn to God.

Why is it that on one occasion we hear Jeremiah saying, "cursed be the day wherein I was born" and on another occasion we hear him saying; "the word of God was in mine heart as a burning fire shut up in my bones.[9] It was because he turned to God in moments of crisis. Why is it that on one occasion we hear Deutero Isaiah saying, "Verily thou art a God that hidest thyself, O God of Israel, the Saviour," but on another occasion we hear him saying, "the grass withereth, the flower fadeth: but

6. For an example of Peter's denials of Jesus, see Matthew 26:69–75.

7. For an example of Judas' betrayal of Jesus, see Luke 22.

8. Matthew 26:56.

9. Jeremiah 20:14, 20:9.

the word of our God shall stand forever."[10] It is because he turned to God in moments of crisis. Why is it that on one occasion we hear Habakkuk crying, "O Lord how long shall I cry, and thou wilt not hear," but on another occasion we hear him crying, "The Lord God is my strength, and he will make my feet like hinds feet, and he will make me to walk upon mine high places."[11] Why is it that on an occasion we hear Job saying, "O that I knew where I could find him that I might come to his dweeling. And I would set my case in order before him," but on another occasion we hear him saying, "I know that my redeemer liveth, and that he shall stand at the ladder day upon earth.[12]

AD. CSKC: Sermon file, folder 13, "A Way Out."

---

10. Isaiah 45:15, 40:8.
11. Habakkuk 1:2, 3:19.
12. Job 23:3–4, 19:25.

"Mastering Our Evil Selves"
"Mastering Ourselves"

[*5 June 1949*]
[*Atlanta, Ga.*]

As he often did throughout his career, King uses psychology and race relations to illustrate his sermon.[1] Exploring the internal struggle between good and evil, he cites the actions of the typical white southerner: "He goes to church every Sunday. He worships the same God we worship. He will send thousands of dollars to Africa and China for the missionary effort. Yet at the same time He will spend thousands of dollars in an attempt to keep the Negro segregated and discriminated."

{Why is it that from the same lips that truth falls lies also fall? Why is it that ~~from~~ the same mother's heart that is overflowing with love is also overflowing with hate}

A few day ago the <u>New York times</u> carried the story of a man who under the influence of achohol had lost control of his automobile ~~killing an~~ and had run on the sidewalk of one of the main streets of New York, killing instantly two little boys coming from school. He was being held in the city jail without ~~trial~~ fine until his trial. The article futher stated that this man was an outstanding citizen of his community and also a Christian gentleman, in fact he was a decon in his local church. This arti-

---

1. King's announced sermon topic for 5 June 1949 at Ebenezer was "Mastering Our Evil Selves" ("Ebenezer to Hear Father, Son Sunday," *Atlanta Daily World*, 4 June 1949). In folder 110 of King's sermon files (which is titled "Mastering Our Evil Selves"), this document carries two titles: "Mastering Our Evil Selves" and "Mastering Ourselves."

cle immediately brought a pullingly element in my mind. Why ~~was it that~~ would a man, who had had such a [*strikeout illegible*] good reputation in his community, ~~would~~ let the element of evil overtake him. Why is it that good people are sometimes worse than the worst people and bad people sometimes better than the best people? Modern psychology attempts to get at this problem by saying that man is a duel personality. It sees man as a bundle of contradictions, contraries, and conflicts. To some psychologists the conflict is between the conscious and the unconscious mind; other pschologists sees it as a tension between ego and environment; to others it is the results of a duel between instinct and ideals.

There is a modern school of theology ~~that~~ which argues that the conflict resulted from the fall of man. They argue that in the beginning man was mad in the image of God, but soon he rebelled against God which brought about the fall.[2] And in the great fall the image of God was somewhat efaced, leaving man with a make-up that was predominantly evil. They argue that this conflict is a result of this evil nature that is in man forever fighting against the element of good that is left in him. Actually I dont know what causes the conflict. But I do know that there is a conflict. There is something paradoxical and contradictory about human nature. {~~In Memoriam Dea. J. W. Johnson~~}[3]

Let me hasten to say that this isn't an original discovery with modern psychology and modern theology for it must be remembered that the human race has always been aware of conflict. Plato, ~~has seen the personality~~ speaking figratively, discribed the personality as a charioteer driving two head-strong steeds, each wanting to go in different directions.[4] Listen to Ovid the Latin poet, "I see and approve the better things of life but the evil things I follow."[5] Goethe once said there was enough material in him to make both a rogue and a gentleman.[6] Our text for the morning brings out this conflict quite clearly, ~~Listen to the Apostle Paul as he decla~~ "The good that I would I do not: but the evil which I would not that I do."[7] This is Apostle writing in his epistle to the Romans. Whether Paul was speaking here of a conflict that had [*come?*] in his personal experience we do not know. But we do know that this is a paradigm of life. When we would want to do good there seems to be something telling us to do evil. When we would want to do evil there seems to be something telling us to do good.

This element of conflict ~~is~~ presents itself in all areas of life. We find it on the international scene. I think most of the peoples of the world want peace. That is the unrelenting the cry the world over. Yet at the same time we do everything contrary to peace.

On the national scene this conflict is evident in the area of racial prejudice. The

---

2. King refers to neo-orthodoxy or crisis theology. Genesis 1:26–27 and Genesis 3.

3. J. W. Johnson was a deacon at Ebenezer.

4. Plato *Phaedrus* 246a-247c.

5. Ovid *Metamorphoses* 7.20.

6. Fulton J. Sheen, *Peace of Soul* (New York: Whittlesey House, 1949), p. 36: "Goethe regretted that God had made only one man of him when there was enough material in him for both a rogue and a gentleman." Johann Wolfgang von Goethe (1749–1832) was a German poet, novelist, and playwright.

7. Romans 7:19.

average white southerner is not bad. He goes to church every Sunday. He worships the same God we worship. He will send thousands of dollars to Africa and China for the missionary effort. Yet at the same time He will spend thousands of dollars in an attempt to keep the Negro segregated and discriminated Yes, we must admit that there is something contradictory and paradoxical about human nature. {Cassady's Quarterly}

But the question immediately arises, can this situation be mastered? Are we capable of doing something to [*minimize?*] this conflict or is it something that will forever remain in the life of individuals? In other words, can we master ourselves? ~~To this question I would say, certainly we can partially master~~ ourselves

For the next few moment I would like to point out certain ways that we can rid ourselves of this duel personality and come to the point that we actually master ourselves.

First we must go through a process of self analyzation. In this process we must ascertain what our weaknesses are. No one can ever make improvements unless he knows the points at which he is weakest. Before the wise psysician gives a patient medicine he finds out where the sickness lies. This process of self analyzation is of primary importance, for it the open door which leads to the room of improvement.

Second, after the individual has found his weakness through this process of self analyzation he must admit that it is a weakness. To often do we rationalize for our sins by convicing ourselves that they are both healthy and normal. (It is at this very point that the eminent Catholic scholar Monsinor Sheen critizise many modern psychitrists, in his recent book, *Peace Of Soul*).[8] One of the tragedies of human nature is that man has the power to adjust his mind to believe anything that he wants to He has the power to convince himself that the wrong is right, (William James) that the false is true, that the low is high, and that the bad is good.[9] So, if we do not admit that our weaknesses are weaknesses the whole whole process of self analyzation has no meaning.

Now that we have found our weaknesses we come to the point of getting rid of them. What proceedures should we use? What steps should we take?

Before answering this question completely we must place it in a negative framework. We never get rid of our weaknesses by repressing them. This is the ringing cry of the psychitrists. Repressed desires only lead to greater frustration and in the final analysis the problem isn't solved.

First, we must use the method of substitution. That is, we must find one good thing that we like to do as well as we like the evil thing, and everytime we are persuaded to do the evil thing the good will overwelm it. This mean that we must not concentrate on the eradication of evil, but on the developing of Virtue. To cast an evil habit out without replacing it by a good one is a purposeless procedure.

Secondly, we must find some profitable way to use our leisure time. We must learn to appreciate good books and learn to love great music. I'm not speaking of the type of popular books that we to often read nor the type of trashy music that we

---

8. See Sheen, *Peace of Soul*, p. 73.

9. King refers to William James (1842–1910), whose essay "The Will To Believe" (1897) explores the role of the will in human thought, existence, and religion.

to often learn to love. But I am hear speaking of the type of books that have stood throughout the ages and the music that grew out of hearts and souls of men. When we have reached this stage our lives will become well-rounded. And then we will no longer desire the evil things of life for our mind will be lost in those thing which are high and noble.

Finally, we may master our evil selves by developing a continuous prayer and devotional life. Through this process the soul of man will become united with the life of God. Yes this is possible. [*Man?*] can know God. This has been the ringing cry of the mystic throughout the ages. God is not "wholly other." God is not a process projected somewhere the lofty blue. God is not a divine hermit hiding himself in a cosmic cave. But God is forever present with us. The God of religion is the God of of life. He somehow trancends the world, yet at the same time he is immanent in the world. And so by identifing ourselves with this knowable God our wills will somehow become his will. We will no longer think of our selfish desires. We will somehow rise above evil thoughts. We will no longer possess two personalities but only one. We will be true, because God is truth; we will be just, because God is justice; we will love, because God is love; we will be good, because God is goodness; we will be wise, because God is wisdom.

My friends, there is an evil way opened to you and there is a good way open to you in the final analysis you must desid which way your soul will go. God grant that you will choose your good self thereby mastering your evil self. Rember the words of John Oxenham.

Poem[10]

AD. CSKC: Sermon file, folder 110, "Mastering Our Evil Selves."

---

10. King probably refers to Oxenham's poem "The Ways" (1916), as he does in the sermon "Creating the Abundant Life," Sermon at Dexter Avenue Baptist Church (26 September 1954, p. 191 in this volume).

"Splinters and Planks"

[*24 July 1949*]
[*Atlanta, Ga.*]

In this handwritten sermon King suggests acknowledging one's own shortcomings before judging others. He applies this principle to the areas of international affairs and race relations, noting, "While we see the splinters in Russia's eye we fail to see the great plank of racial segregation and [discrimination] which is blocking the progress of America." Additionally, King notes, "Negroes see the splinters in the white man's eye and fail to see the planks in their own eye." According to a newspaper announcement, King was scheduled to deliver a version of this sermon at Ebenezer.[1]

---

1. King's announced sermon topic for 24 July 1949 at Ebenezer was "Splinters and Planks" ("'Splinters and Planks' to be King's Topic," *Atlanta Daily World*, 23 July 1949).

Why do you note the Splinter in your brother's eye and fail to see the plank in your own eye? (Matt. 7.3) (MOFFATT).[2]

These words of our text found in a recent translation of the New Testament, do nothing to change the meaning of the words found in the Authorized Version; Rather they place this familiar question in a modern framework.[3] This text is presented in words that modern man is well familar with. We know splinters. We frequently run them through our fingers. Sometimes they are so small that we can hardly see them. Moreover, we know planks. We know that in many instances a plank is large enough to stop a street car.

This figure of speech used by Jesus might seem for the moment quite exaggerated. But if we stop for the moment and analysize human actions with a disintirested eye, we will find that this contrast is not big enough, for it is a common human trait to see the weaknesses of others and never see ones own weakness

The splinter and plank scandal has presented itself throughout human history. In colonial Virginia a man could be sent to jail for failing to attend church twice on [*Sundays?*], while at the same time the slave trade went on with the saction of the church and religions.

Many parents of today spend much time denouncing the actions modern youth and at the same time they fail to supply an example of true Christian living. Sociologists have remainded us that juvenile delinquency has its origin in adult dilinquency. But how easy it is for the adutl to see the splinter in young peoples eye and fail to see the plank in their own eyes.

Remember how this familar situation expressed itself in Biblical times. One day the scribes and Pharisees brought unto Jesus a woman [*strikeout illegible*] who had comitted adultery. In an attempt to follow the Mosaic law they had decided to stone her. Adultry always stood out in ~~ancient times~~ Hebrew society as a great sin. Before stoning the woman they decided to question Jesus on the issue. Of course they were all but sure that Jesus would saction the stoning of this woman. But his reply to this question was quite different; it was a reply filled with psychological meaning. In substance he says, "He who is without sin cast the first stone."[4] Here Jesus is expressing the well known truth that when it comes to prue and undefied morality we all fall short of the mark. It seems that sin is a well of water that each of us has drawn from

---

2. Matthew 7:3 in James Moffatt, trans., *The New Testament* (New York: George H. Doran Co., 1926). James Moffatt (1870–1944), a Scottish biblical scholar and translator, published a modern version of the New Testament in 1913 and the Hebrew Bible in 1924. (Subsequent cites of biblical verses from Moffatt's translation are noted as MOFFATT, in parentheses.) King later referred to Christ's admonition in describing Gandhi's capacity for self-criticism and his critique of the Indian people in the midst of his campaign for independence from Great Britain (King, Palm Sunday Sermon on Mohandas K. Gandhi, Delivered at Dexter Avenue Baptist Church, 22 March 1959, in *The Papers of Martin Luther King, Jr.,* vol. 5: *Threshold of a New Decade, January 1959–December 1960,* ed. Clayborne Carson, Tenisha Armstrong, Susan Carson, Adrienne Clay, and Kieran Taylor [Berkeley and Los Angeles: University of California Press, 2005], p. 152).

3. The King James Version renders this text: "And why beholdest thou the mote that is in thy brother's eye, but considerest not the beam that is in thine own eye?"

4. John 8:7.

or to change the figure, sin is an ever present shower that sprinkles every one of us. And so none can boast of total purity.

The irony of Jesus still comes to our own day with blistering truth. Let us look on the international scene. {Take the conflict between Russia and America} Our criticism of Russia have been quite severe. We have argued that Russian Communism is the most injurious force in the world today. Any reader of the American newspaper is left with the impression that America is all right and Russia is all wrong. We are forever talking of the imperalistic tendencies of Russia. We talk glibly about her denial of individual freedoms. We dwell on the fact that Communism denies the existence of God. And so our criticisms of the weaknesses of Russia go on ad infinitum. But when we turn the coin to the other side the picture is quite different. We never find ourselves seeing the weaknesses of America. I am not at all saying that there are not some weaknesses in the Russian form of govenment. I must admit that it does not appeal to me directly. But have we not failed to see the gigantic planks in our eyes. While we see the splinters in Russia's eye we fail to see the great plank of racial segregation and dicrimination which is blocking the progress of America

2. National scene

   Race relation

   Negroes see the splinters in the white man's eye and fail to see the planks in their own eye

   1   segreting and discriminating each other.

   2.

3. Church life

   We as church members see the splinter in the worlds eye and fail to see the blank in our own eye.

4. Personal lives

5. [*Cxn?*]—Jesus as an example.

Only by removing the ~~splinter~~ planks from our eyes can we see clearly how to remove the splinters in our brothers eye.

We must attract people into goodness. Remember the words of Jesus, "If I be lifted up from the earth I will draw all men unto me"[5]

It is this same Jesus who has become the most influential character in Western Civilization etc.

ADS. CSKC: Sermon file, folder 114, "Splinters and Planks."

---

5. John 12:32; see also Johnson Oatman's hymn "Lift Him Up."

Four Papers on Preaching Issues

[*14 September 1948–15 February 1950*]
[*Chester, Pa.*]

King submitted the following assignments for preaching courses at Crozer taught by Keighton. They demonstrate the breadth of topics and issues that influenced King's emerging understanding of homiletics. "Karl Barth," a review of a sermon by this theologian, includes a harsh critique of the theological complexity of Barth's homily: "The preaching of theology must be presented in the light of the experiences of the people. This Barth fails to do."[1] Keighton gave the paper an A. In "The Limitation of Experience," King criticizes ministers who fail to read regularly and learn from others, claiming they "starve the people for the gospel." He questions the viability of capitalism in "Will Capitalism Survive?" claiming it "has seen its best days." In the final assignment, "Is the Church the Hope of the World?" King challenges the church, calling it "one of the chief exponents of racial bigotry."

"Karl Barth"

Karl Barth, round whose name centres the great discussions now agitating the theological world, was born at Basle, in Switzerland, in 1886.[2] He was born in the atmosphere of theology, for his father was a Professor of the Reformed Church and author of two useful books.[3] Barth first went to school at Berne, and proceeded thence to the other Universities at Berlin, Tubingen and Marburg.[4] The Neo-Kantian school at Marburg has left its mark upon the philosophical outlook of

---

1. King also criticized Barth in an essay he wrote for Davis's course at Crozer, Christian Theology for Today (King, "The Place of Reason and Experience in Finding God," 13 September–23 November 1949, in *Papers* 1:230–236). During his first semester of graduate studies at Boston University, King also focused on Barth's theology in L. Harold DeWolf's Seminar in Systematic Theology. In an essay for DeWolf, King challenged Barth's theology, commenting, "Most of my criticisms stem from the fact that I have been greatly influenced by liberal theology, maintaining a healthy respect for reason and a strong belief in the immanence as well as the transcendence of God" (King, "Karl Barth's Conception of God," 2 January 1952, in *The Papers of Martin Luther King, Jr.*, vol. 2: *Rediscovering Precious Values, July 1951–November 1955*, ed. Clayborne Carson, Ralph E. Luker, Penny A. Russell, and Peter Holloran [Berkeley and Los Angeles: University of California Press, 1994], p. 104).

2. Karl Barth (1886–1968) was a Swiss Reformed Church theologian. He studied at a series of universities between 1904 and 1909, including the University of Bern and the University of Marburg. After his ordination as a pastor in 1908 and the publication of *Epistle to the Romans* (1919), which established his reputation as a theologian, he became a professor of Reformed Theology at Göttigen (1921), Münster (1925), and finally at Bonn (1930), despite never receiving a doctorate. He was eventually exiled from Germany in 1935 because he refused to take an oath of loyalty to Adolf Hitler. His later writings include *Fide Quaerens Intellectum* (1931) and the multi-volume *Church Dogmatics* (1932–1968). Barth held that theology should be based solely on the Bible and the figure of Jesus Christ instead of human experience and reason. Keighton inserted an "a" before "round."

3. Fritz Barth (1856–1912) was the author of several books, including *The Gospel of St. John and the Synoptic Gospels* (New York: Eaton & Mains, 1907), *Die Hauptprobleme des Lebens Jesu* (Gütersloh, Germany: Bertelsmann, 1918), and *Einleitung in das Neue Testament* (Gütersloh, Germany: Bertelsmann, 1921).

4. Keighton corrected Tubingen to Tübingen.

King and Karl Barth outside the Princeton University chapel with James McCord in the background, 29 May 1962. Courtesy of Associated Press/Wide World Photos.

Barth.[5] Barth gives interesting information concerning the writers who later influenced his thought. His "ancestral line runs back through [*Søren*] Kierkegaard to [*Martin*] Luther and [*John*] Calvin and so to Paul and Jeremiah." To understand Mr. Barth's views one must know something of how he came to his present point of view. He has told us that most of his views came from the principles of the Reformed

---

5. Neo-Kantianism was a late nineteenth-century outgrowth of the philosophy of Immanuel Kant (1724–1804). One of its main expressions was the Marburg school, founded by Hermann Cohen (1842–1918), which developed a philosophical system emphasizing Kant's critical, *a priori* idealism as foundational in logic, ethics, and aesthetics.

Churches.[6] Such a dogmatic assumption as the utter depravity of man as a consequence of the Fall, is an example of the influence that the Reformed Churches had on Barth. All of this helps us to understand the views expressed by Barth in many of his books and also in the sermon that will be discussed at this point.

Karl Barth opens his sermon, "Repentance," with the moving Biblical pharse, Jesus calls us: "Come unto me!"[7] He states that Jesus desires to speak truth to us. He wants to talk God to us. He, who lets himself be told, repents. "Repentance," according to Barth, "is turning about to that which is nearest and which we always overlook."[8]

Mr. Barth makes it very clear that other voices also call us. He uses the church as an example. Today she calls men to thanksgiving, repentance, and prayers. But when the church says something, it is always an open question.[9] Repentance must go beyond the church, for in many instances the church is the greatest hindrance to repentance. The church, in many instances, has betrayed God to the needs and humours of men. If we want to hear the call of Jesus we must hear it despite the church.[10]

The question arises, who is Jesus? We know him best by those whom he calls to himself.[11] Jesus says, "Come unto me, all ye!" He is free enough to invite all to himself. It is essentially at this point, says Barth, that Jesus differs from other great men, other aims and movements. Even the church is not for all men.

Again the question arises, who is Jesus? He is the one who calls the laboring and the heavy laden to Himself. Because we labor and are heavy laden we belong to the "all" to whom the invitation is given.[12]

In conclusion the quistion arises, what does Jesus want of us? He wants nothing of us but that we come. Here Barth makes it very clear that Jesus does not want "ours" but "us". Of course to come to Jesus means to labor and to be heavy laden, therefore it is hard to come.[13] But we must see, says Barth, that coming to Jesus begins with the knowledge that something difficult is asked of us.

---

6. Reformed Churches are the Reformed, Congregational, United, and Presbyterian denominations, which have their theological roots in the works of John Calvin.

7. Cf. Matthew 11:28. Keighton indicated the "a" and "r" in the word "pharse" should be reversed.

8. "Jesus calls us: 'Come unto me!' He seeks to tell us what is true. He desires to speak truth to us. He wants to talk God to us. He, who lets himself be told, repents. Repentance is turning about to that which is nearest and which we always overlook; to the center of life which we always miss; to the simplest which is still too high and hard for us" (Karl Barth, *Come Holy Spirit: Sermons* [New York: Round Table Press, 1933], p. 67).

9. Barth, *Come Holy Spirit,* p. 69: "Other voices also call us: 'Come unto me!' The voice of the church, for example. Today she calls us to the Confederation's service of thanksgiving, repentance, and prayer . . . When the church says something, it is always an open question."

10. Barth, *Come Holy Spirit,* p. 71: "The call of Jesus resounds despite the church. But the church is a great, perhaps the greatest, hindrance to repentance. If we wish to hear the call of Jesus, then we must hear it despite the church."

11. Barth, *Come Holy Spirit,* p. 71: "*Who is Jesus?* We know him best by those whom he calls to himself."

12. Cf. Matthew 11:28.

13. Barth, *Come Holy Spirit,* p. 78: "What does Jesus want of us? He wants nothing of us but that we come. He does not want *ours* but *us.* If we come as we are, all is well. For this is the new and all-important thing, the mystery that confronts us in Christ. Our coming consists in this, that we permit Jesus to tell us that we labor and are heavy laden. On this account it is so hard for us to come."

It is very clear that many of Barth's theological concepts creep into this sermon, such as God, "the Wholly other." Of course, one complaint that I must make is that Barth sets up an obstruse mode of expression which only the learned can understand. He leaven the average mind lost in the fog of theological abstractions.[14] I am not saying that one must not preach theology, but I am contending that the preaching of theology must be presented in the light of the experiences of the people. This Barth fails to do.

Another complaint is that Barth doesn't fully explain his views; great terms like God, Faith, Repentance, are thrown out without adequate definition, as though their meaning were self-evident. For these reasons I found this sermon very boring.

[*signed*] M. L. King Jr.[15]

THDS. CSKC: Sermon file, folder 36, "Sermon Notes."

"The Limitation of Experience"

In historical theology three different things have been put forward as the source of Authority in Religion: the church, The Bible and experience. Luther and his friends destroyed the Church as the central Religious Authority for the Protestants and put the Bible in its place. Most Protestants are confused on this issue as they lean on both the Bible and Experience. The Protestants talk about the Bible and then proceed to rely on experience. But experience has its limitations.

What is experience? In philosophy according the [*Immanuel*] Kant, Experience is a compound out of sensation and the activity of the understanding. According to psychology, it is a change in a set pattern of behavior. According to the "man in the streets" it is simply living a ~~log~~ long time. And this is the danger.

Just because a man has lived a long time is no sign that he is a man of experience. There are plenty people thirty who have had more experience than a person fifty.[16] A farmer who has spent fifty years on the same plantation has certainly not had as much experience as a son who has been roaming all over Europe and the USA and is now thirty.

It is therefore a sign of mature judgment when you rely absolutely on your own experiences. The teachers in our schools have been pounding this in the heads of [*strikeout illegible*] students to long.[17] We must come to see that lives are enriched by the experiences of others.

A minister who therefore tries to preach out of his own experiences all the time soon becomes shallow. He should let the great souls of the world enrich his life. The run around all the week and never look in a book and then get up on Sunday and

---

14. Keighton crossed out the "n" in leaven and replaced it with an "s."

15. King folded this assignment lengthwise and signed his name on the verso of the last page.

16. Keighton placed a question mark before the word "thirty," placed brackets around the words "plenty people thirty," and circled the words "person fifty." He also placed a question mark above the word "fifty."

17. Keighton added "to" to the word "in," and added an "o" to the word "to."

preach what rises from inside you is to fool yourself and starve the people for the Gospel.[18]

[*signed*] M. L. King Jr.[19]

AHDS. CSKC: Sermon file, folder 36, "Sermon Notes."

"Will Capitalism Survive?"

Karl Marx, the German philosopher, once stated that capitalism carries the seed of its own destruction.[20] There is an obvious fallacy in this statement. The fallacy lies in its limitation. He speaks of capitalism as if it is the only social institution that carries the seed of its own destruction.[21] The actual fact is that every social institution carries the seed of its own destruction, its survival depends on the way the seed is nourished.[22] Therefore, just as every social institution carries the seed of its own destruction it also carries the seed of its own perpetuation.

Now after admitting that there is a definite fallacy in Marx' statement, do we find any truth therein?[23] It is my opinion that we do. I am convinced that capitalism has seen its best days in America, and not only in America, but in the entire world. It is a well known fact that no social institution can survive after it has outlived its usefullness.[24] This capitalism has failed to do.[25] It has failed to meet the needs of the masses.

Strikes and labor troubles are but surface indications of the deep dissatisfaction and distress in this country.[26] There is a definite revolt by, what Marx calls, "the proletariat", against "the bourgeoisie." Every we turn we hear the demand for socialize

---

18. Keighton circled the word "The" and placed a question mark in front of it. He also wrote a large question mark in the paper's margin next to the entire sentence. In the same sermon file folder as this essay, King kept a copy of a speech by George Kelsey, his professor at Morehouse College. Kelsey noted, in a speech given in Atlanta at the Joint Committee on Negro Ministerial Education of the Northern, Southern, and National Baptist Conventions, the presence of "scores of ignorant preachers who compensate for their ignorance by claiming that the entire message of the preacher comes from God, and not from books" (Kelsey, "The Present Crisis in Negro Ministerial Education," 19 January 1948).

19. King folded this assignment lengthwise and signed his name on the verso of the last page.

20. King paraphrases Karl Marx: "But capitalist production begets, with the inexorability of a law of Nature, its own negation" (Marx, *Capital: A Critique of Political Economy* [Chicago: Charles H. Kerr, 1906], 1:837). King also prepared a handwritten version of this paper (King, Notes on American Capitalism, 14 September 1948–15 February 1950, in *Papers* 1:435–436). Similar analyses of capitalism became a regular theme in King's writings and sermons for years to come (King to Coretta Scott, 18 July 1952; "Communism's Challenge to Christianity," 9 August 1953; "Can a Christian Be a Communist?" Sermon Delivered at Ebenezer Baptist Church, 30 September 1962, pp. 123–126, 146–150, and 445–454 in this volume, respectively).

21. Keighton crossed out the word "is" and wrote "were" above it.

22. Keighton made the comma after the word "destruction" into a semicolon.

23. Keighton inserted a comma after the word "now."

24. Keighton inserted a dash between the words "well" and "known."

25. Keighton crossed out the words "failed to do" and wrote "done" above it.

26. In the handwritten version of this paper this sentence reads: "We need only to look at the underlying developments of our society" (King, Notes on American Capitalism, 14 September 1948–15 February 1950, in *Papers* 1:435–436).

medicine.[27] In fact, what is more socialistic than the income tax, the T.V.A., or the N.R.B.[28] What will eventually happen is this: labor will become so powerful (this was certainly evidenced in the recent election) that she will be able to place a president in the White House.[29] This will in all probability bring about a nationalization of industry. This will be the end of capitalism.

What will the new movement be called in America? I must admit that I dont know. It might well be called socialism, communism, or socialistic democracy.[30] But what does it matter anyway, "a rose called by a different name smells just as sweet."[31] The point is that we will have a definite change. Capitalism finds herself like a losing football team in the last quarter trying all types of tactics to survive. We are losing because we failed to check our weaknesses in the beginning of the game.

[*signed*] M. L. King Jr.[32]

THDS. CSKC: Sermon file, folder 36, "Sermon Notes."

"Is the Church the Hope of the World?"

It is a common saying in religious circles that the church is the hope of the world. This question inevitably leads the objective mind to a bit of doubt. He immediately asks, "how can the church be the hope of the world when it is the most reactionary institution in society."[33] In other words, the church is suppose to be the most radical opposer of the status quo in society, yet, in many instances, it is the greatest preserver of the status quo.[34] So it was very easy for slavery to receive a religious saction.[35] The church is one of the chief exponents of racial bigotry. Monopoly capitalism has always received the saction of the church.[36]

Since this is the case, we must admit that the church is far from Christ. What has happened is this: the church, while flowing through the stream of history has picked up the evils of little tributaries, and these tributaries have been so powerful

---

27. Keighton inserted "where" after the word "every" and added "d" to the end of the word "socialize."

28. The 16th Amendment to the U.S. Constitution, ratified by the states in 1913, authorized a federal income tax. The Tennessee Valley Authority (TVA) was established by Congress in 1933 for the purposes of electrical generation, navigation, and flood control. King may refer to either the National Recovery Act enacted in 1933 or the National Labor Relations Board (NLRB) established in 1935, each of which sought to insure fair collective bargaining between businesses and unions. Keighton inserted a question mark following "N.R.B."

29. Organized labor played a key role in the election of Harry S. Truman in 1948.

30. Keighton crossed out "might" and wrote "may" over it.

31. King paraphrases William Shakespeare, *Romeo and Juliet*, act 2, sc. 2: "What's in a name? That which we call a rose / By any other name would smell as sweet." Keighton drew a line to this quotation and wrote at the end of the document, "Want to check this quotation? Romeo & Juliet II-ii-43-4."

32. King folded this assignment lengthwise and signed his name on the verso of the last page.

33. Keighton drew an arrow to indicate that "asks" should come before "immediately," and added a question mark at the end of the sentence.

34. Keighton added a "d" to the end of the word "suppose."

35. Keighton inserted an "n" in the word "saction."

36. Keighton bracketed the phrase "monopoly capitalism" and wrote a question mark in the margin.

that they have been able to overwhelm the main stream. In other words, the church has picked up a lot of historical vices. This is the tragedy of the church, for it has confused the vices of the church with the virtues of Christ. The church has been nothing but the slave of society; Whenever the mores call for evil practicies, society runs to the church to get its sanction.

Therefore, I conclude that the church, in its present state, is not the hope of the world. I believe that nothing has so persistently and effectively blocked the way of salvation as the church. On the other hand, the church can be the hope of the world, but only when it returns to Christ. If we take Christ to the world, we will turn it upside down, but the tragedy is that we to often take Christianity.[37] It is our job as ministers to bring the church back to the center of the human race. But we can only bring the church back to the center of the human race when we bring Christ back to the center of the church.[38]

[*signed*] M. L. King Jr.[39]

AHDS. CSKC: Sermon file, folder 36, "Sermon Notes."

---

37. Keighton added an "o" to the end of the word "to."

38. Keighton circled the word "only" and drew an arrow to indicate that it should have come in between the words "race" and "when." At the end of this essay, Keighton wrote: "You are careless in writing,—a characteristic that seems new! <u>Personal Comment</u> Beware of making words carry the burden of thoughts. Do not substitute the one for the other. Would you be willing to debate your meanings of the words 'Church', 'Christianity' & 'Christ'? It is far too easy to make these things the whipping boys! Don't begin your ministry by taking this path."

39. King folded this assignment lengthwise and signed his name on the verso of the last page.

Preaching Problems That I Have Encountered

[29 November 1949–15 February 1950]
[Chester, Pa.]

King probably prepared this brief handwritten document while enrolled in Keighton's course Preaching Problems.

1. Difficulty in preaching on special days that appear in the Christian year.[1]
2. Difficulty in applying the Old Testament to modern life.

---

1. For examples of sermons that King drafted for holidays, see King, After Christmas, What? 28 December 1952; "Crisis in the Modern Family," Sermon at Dexter Avenue Baptist Church, 8 May 1955; and Questions That Easter Answers, Sermon Delivered at Dexter Avenue Baptist Church, 21 April 1957, pp. 128–129, 209–213, and 283–293 in this volume, respectively.

3. I often get criticisms from laymen and unlettered ministers for using a modern Sept 1948–
translation of the Bible as a source of preaching May 1951
resurrection
    Christmas is an Incarnation. It is the meeting of two worlds
    Outline of a Christmas sermon.

AD. MLKP-MBU: Box 113.

Three Levels of Fellowship

[28 May 1950]
[Atlanta, Ga.]

Following his second year at Crozer, King returned to Ebenezer for the summer,
where he preached a sermon that may have been based on the following handwritten
outline.[1]

Subject Three Levals of Fellowship
Text 1 Cor 1:2, 9[2]

1. Gasterism—lower leval—the thing that holds this leval together is sensuality[3]
2. Communism—middle leval—the thing that holds this leval together is
   economics
3. Spirit — Higher leval — the thing that hold this leval together is love.

AD. CSKC: Sermon file, folder 100, "Sermons by Other Ministers."

---

1. King's announced sermon topic at Ebenezer for 28 May 1950 was "Three Levels of Fellowship" ("Rev. M. L. King, Jr. to Fill Ebenezer Pulpit Tomorrow," *Atlanta Daily World,* 27 May 1950).

2. 1 Corinthians 1:2: "Unto the church of God which is at Corinth, to them that are sanctified in Christ Jesus, called to be saints, with all that in every place call upon the name of Jesus Christ our Lord, both theirs and ours"; 1 Corinthians 1:9: "God is faithful, by whom ye were called unto the fellowship of his Son Jesus Christ our Lord."

3. *Gaster* is the Greek word for "stomach."

Three Essays on Religion

In the following three essays, King wrestles with the role of religion in modern society.
In the first assignment, he calls science and religion "different though converging
truths" that both "spring from the same seeds of vital human needs." King emphasizes
an awareness of God's presence in the second document, noting that religion's purpose
"is not to perpetuate a dogma or a theology; but to produce living witnesses and

107

testimonies to the power of God in human experience." In the final handwritten
essay King acknowledges the life-affirming nature of Christianity, observing that
its adherents have consistently "looked forward for a time to come when the law
of love becomes the law of life."

"Science and Religion"

[*September 1948–May 1951*]
[*Chester, Pa.*]

There is widespread belief in the minds of many that there is a conflict between science and religion. But there is no fundamental issue between the two. While the conflict has been waged long and furiously, it has been on issues utterly unrelated either to religion or to science. The conflict has been largely one of trespassing, and as soon as religion and science discover their legitimate spheres the conflict ceases.

Religion, of course, has been very slow and loath to surrender its claim to sovereignty in all departments of human life; and science overjoyed with recent victories, has been quick to lay claim to a similar sovereignty. Hence the conflict.

But there was never a conflict between religion and science as such. There cannot be. Their respective worlds are different. Their methods are dissimilar and their immediate objectives are not the same. The method of science is observation, that of religion contemplation. Science investigates. Religion interprets. One seeks causes, the other ends. Science thinks in terms of history, religion in terms of teleology. One is a survey, the other an outlook.

The conflict was always between superstition disguised as religion and materialism disguised as science, between pseudo-science and pseudo-religion.

Religion and science are two hemispheres of human thought. They are different though converging truths. Both science and religion spring from the same seeds of vital human needs.

Science is the response to the human need of knowledge and power. Religion is the response to the human need for hope and certitude. One is an outreaching for mastery, the other for perfection. Both are man-made, and like man himself, are hedged about with limitations. Neither science nor religion, by itself, is sufficient for man. Science is not civilization. Science is organized knowledge; but civilization which is the art of noble and progressive communal living requires much more than knowledge. It needs beauty which is art, and faith and moral aspiration which are religion. It needs artistic and spiritual values along with the intellectual.

Man cannot live by facts alone. What we know is little enough. What we are likely to know will always be little in comparison with what there is to know. But man has a wish-life which must build inverted pyramids upon the apexes of known facts. This is not logical. It is, however, psychological.

Science and religion are not rivals. It is only when one attempts to be the oracle at the others shrine that confusion arises. Whan the scientist from his laboratory, on the basis of alleged scientific knowledge presumes to issue pronouncements on God, on the origin and destiny of life, and on man's place in the scheme of things he is [*passing?*] out worthless checks. When the religionist delivers ultimatums to the scientist on the basis of certain cosomologies embedded in the sacred text then he is a sorry spectacle indeed.

When religion, however, on the strength of its own postulates, speaks to men of God and the moral order of the universe, when it utters its prophetic burden of justice and love and holiness and peace, then its voice is the voice of the eternal spiritual truth, irrefutable and invincible.,

TD. CSKC: Sermon file, folder 50, Sermons Not Preached.

"The Purpose of Religion"

[*September 1948–May 1951*]
[*Chester, Pa.*]

What is the purpose of religion?[1] Is it to perpetuate an idea about God? Is it totally dependent upon revelation? What part does psychological experience play? Is religion synonymous with theology?

Harry Emerson Fosdick says that the most hopeful thing about any system of theology is that it will not last.[2] This statement will shock some. But is the purpose of religion the perpetuation of theological ideas? Religion is not validated by ideas, but by experience.

This automatically raises the question of salvation. Is the basis for salvation in creeds and dogmas or in experience. Catholics would have us believe the former. For them, the church, its creeds, its popes and bishops have recited the essence of religion and that is all there is to it. On the other hand we say that each soul must make its own reconciliation to God; that no creed can take the place of that personal experience. This was expressed by Paul Tillich when he said, "There is natural religion which belongs to man by nature. But there is also a revealed religion which man receives from a supernatural reality."[3] Relevant religion therefore, comes through revelation from God, on the one hand; and through repentance and acceptance of salvation on the other hand.[4] Dogma as an agent in salvation has no essential place.

This is the secret of our religion. This is what makes the saints move on in spite of problems and perplexities of life that they must face. This religion of experience

---

1. King may have also considered the purpose of religion in a Morehouse paper that is no longer extant, as he began a third Morehouse paper, "Last week we attempted to discuss the purpose of religion" (King, "The Purpose of Education," September 1946–February 1947, in *Papers* 1:122).

2. "Harry Emerson Fosdick" in *American Spiritual Autobiographies: Fifteen Self-Portraits,* ed. Louis Finkelstein (New York: Harper & Brothers, 1948), p. 114: "The theology of any generation cannot be understood, apart from the conditioning social matrix in which it is formulated. All systems of theology are as transient as the cultures they are patterned from."

3. King further developed this theme in his dissertation: "[Tillich] finds a basis for God's transcendence in the conception of God as abyss. There is a basic inconsistency in Tillich's thought at this point. On the one hand he speaks as a religious naturalist making God wholly immanent in nature. On the other hand he speaks as an extreme supernaturalist making God almost comparable to the Barthian 'wholly other'" (King, "A Comparison of the Conceptions of God in the Thinking of Paul Tillich and Henry Nelson Wieman," 15 April 1955, in *Papers* 2:535).

4. Commas were added after the words "religion" and "salvation."

by which man is aware of God seeking him and saving him helps him to see the hands of God moving through history.

Religion has to be interpreted for each age; stated in terms that that age can understand. But the essential purpose of religion remains the same. It is not to perpetuate a dogma or theology; but to produce living witnesses and testimonies to the power of God in human experience.

[*signed*] M. L. King Jr.[5]

ADS. CSKC: Sermon file, folder 36, "Sermon Notes."

"The Philosophy of Life Undergirding Christianity and the Christian Ministry"

[*September 1948–May 1951?*]
[*Chester, Pa.?*]

Basically Christianity is a value philosophy. It insists that there are eternal values of intrinsic, self-evidencing validity and worth, embracing the true and the beautiful and consummated in the Good. This value content is embodied in the life of Christ. So that Christian philosophy is first and foremost Christocentric. It begins and ends with the assumption that Christ is the revelation of God.[6]

We might ask what are some of the specific values that Christianity seeks to conserve? First Christianity speaks of the value of the world. In its conception of the world, it is not negative; it stands over against the asceticisms, world denials, and world flights, for example, of the religions of India, and is world-affirming, life affirming, life creating. Gautama bids us flee from the world, but Jesus would have us use it, because God has made it for our sustenance, our discipline, and our happiness.[7] So that the Christian view of the world can be summed up by saying that it is a place in which God is fitting men and women for the Kingdom of God.

Christianity also insists on the value of persons. All human personality is supremely worthful. This is something of what Schweitzer has called "reverence for life."[8] Human being must always be used as ends; never as means. I realize that there have been times that Christianity has short at this point. There have been periods in Christians history that persons have been dealt with as if they were means rather than ends. But Christianity at its highest and best has always insisted that persons are intrinsically valu-

---

5. King folded this assignment lengthwise and signed his name on the verso of the last page.

6. King also penned a brief outline with this title (King, "The Philosophy of Life Undergirding Christianity and the Christian Ministry," Outline, September 1948–May 1951). In the outline, King included the reference "see Enc. Of Religion p. 162." This entry in *An Encyclopedia of Religion*, ed. Vergilius Ferm (New York: Philosophical Library, 1946) contains a definition of Christianity as "Christo-centric" and as consisting "of eternal values of intrinsic, self-evidencing validity and worth, embracing the true and the beautiful and consummated in the Good." King kept this book in his personal library.

7. Siddhartha Gautama (ca. 563–ca. 483 BCE) was the historical Buddha.

8. For an example of Schweitzer's use of the phrase "reverence for life," see Albert Schweitzer, "The Ethics of Reverence for Life," *Christendom* 1 (1936): 225–239.

able. And so it is the job of the Christian to love every man because God love love. We must not love men merely because of their social or economic position or because of thier cultural contribution, but we are to love them because ~~God~~ they are of value to God.

Christianity is also concerned about the value of life itself. Christianity is concerned about the good life for every ~~child,~~ man, ~~and~~ woman and child. This concern for the good life and the value of life is no where better expressed than in the words of Jesus in the gospel of John: "I came that you might have life and that you might have it more abundantly."[9] This emphasis has run throughout the Christian tradition. Christianity has always had a concern for the elimination of disease and pestilence. This is seen in the great interest that it has taken in the hospital movement.

Christianity is concerned about increasing value. The whole concept of the kingdom of God on earth expressing a concern for increasing value. We need not go into a dicussion of the nature and meaning of the Kingdom of God, only to say that Christians throughout the ages have held tenaciouly to this concept. They have looked forward for a time to come when the law of love becomes the law of life.

In the light of all that we have said about Christianity as a value philosophy, where does the ministry come into the picture?[10]

AD. CSKC: Sermon file, folder 49, "Sermon Notes."

---

9. John 10:10.

10. In his outline for this paper, King elaborated: "The Ministry provides leadership in helping men to recognize and accept the eternal values in the Xty religion. a. The necessity of a call b. The necessity for disinterested love c. The [*necessity*] for moral uprightness" (King, "Philosophy of Life," Outline, September 1948–May 1951).

"Science Surpasses the Social Order"

[20 February–4 May 1951?]
[Chester, Pa.?]

In this essay, probably written for Kenneth L. Smith's Christianity and Society course
at Crozer, King explores the tensions between religion and science in the atomic era.[1]
He argues for greater world cooperation and a shared ethical code.

---

1. In Smith's course, students were required to deliver oral reports and give two-page summaries to each member of the class. King kept a copy of a paper titled "The Ethical Implications of the Atomic Bomb," probably written by a fellow student on an assigned topic in the section of the course called Christianity and the International Order ("The ethical implications of the atomic bomb," Paper for Christianity and Society, and Smith, Syllabus, Christianity and Society, both dated 20 February–4 May 1951).

August 6, 1945, the date that the first atomic bomb was dropped on Japan, marked the end of an age already passe, and the beginning of a new world era, the atomic age.

During the five years in which scientists harnessed the power of the atom as a weapon of war, man's scientific progress leaped forward at least 500 years. The tragic situation now faced by mankind is that man's social order has not leaped the 500 years parellel with science.[2] This is a supreme example of what the sociologists call "cultural lag."[3] Man's social progress has failed to keep abreast with his scientific progress. Unless man by his will can bridge the gap, he is doomed to destruction.

Many, therefore, stand looking at the world's calamity as at a gigantic spectacle, feeling that the problem is well-nigh insoluble. I do not see how we can take that position, however, if we perceive what the gist of the world's problem really is: a lack of world brotherhood. I am convinced that if our civilization is to survive, we must rise from the narrow horizon of clashing nationalism to the wide horizon of world cooperation. No longer can we be content with a national ethical code, but instead we must have an international ethical code. This is truly what Mr. Wendall Wilkie called "one world," and we can readily make an addition to that prase by saying, one world or none.[4] World brotherhood is no longer a beautiful ideal, but an absolute necessity for civilization's survival. We must come to see that all humanity is so interwoven in a single process that whatever affects the man in Russia also affects the man in America. As Prime Minister Attlee said, "we cannot make a heaven in our country and leave a hell outside."[5] We had better realize that before it is to late.[6] We must erase the centuries of waiting and quickly achieve that world brotherhood. This is our great opportunity. This is our only hope.[7]

THD. CSKC: Sermon file, folder 36, "Sermon Notes."

---

2. King's misspelling of the word "parallel" was corrected.

3. For this course, Smith assigned *The Christian Response to the Atomic Crisis,* which discussed "the 'lag' of ethics behind technics" (Edward Leroy Long, *The Christian Response to the Atomic Crisis* [Philadelphia: Westminster Press, 1950], p. 39).

4. Wendell L. Wilkie, the Republican nominee for president in 1940, decisively lost the election to Franklin Delano Roosevelt and later authored the book *One World* (New York: Simon & Schuster, 1943). *The Christian Response to the Atomic Crisis* contained a chapter discussing Wilkie's *One World* and Dexter Master and Katharine Way's *One World or None* (New York: McGraw-Hill, 1946). The words "Wendall" and "Wilkie" were circled and crossed out and an "h" was inserted into the word "prase."

5. In his address to the joint session of the U.S. Congress on 13 November 1945, British prime minister Clement Attlee (1883–1967) described the Labour Party's views on foreign policy, saying, "We believe that we cannot make a heaven in our own country and leave a hell outside and we believe this not only from the moral basis of our movement which is founded on the brotherhood of man, without distinction of race or creed, but also from an entirely practical standpoint" (Address of the Prime Minister of Great Britain, 71st Cong., 1st sess., *Congressional Record* 91 [13 November 1945]: 10623).

6. An additional "o" was added to the word "to."

7. King's last name was written on the verso of the document.

Index of Sermon Topics

[20 February–4 May 1951 ?]
[Chester, Pa. ?]

While at Crozer, King used various methods for collecting and organizing homiletic material. Writing on a series of forms titled "Topic, Text and Subject Index," he sketches sermon ideas, noting biblical texts and other sources. King probably wrote these notes in 1951, as he refers to courses he took at Crozer during the spring of that year.

Matt. 7 12[1]   "The Rule Of Life" (To be prepared)
                "Our Uncivilized Civilization"

Hosea 4 10[2]   "What is Enough"
                1. Economic security is not
                2. Family is not enough
                3. Justice not enough
                4. We can only be filled.
                "When Religion Becomes too tolerant"

Brahminism has often been too tolerant. It has tolerated magic and all manner of superstitions. Far from attempting to reform the cruel social injustices of the caste system, it has found a moral justification for them. The religion has founded no church; it has developed no social activities; it has cared little to serve humanity. Salvation is to be won by inner meditation by oneself. One is taught to conceive himself in an intellectual manner to be identical with one's neighbor and love him as oneself, but little motivation is afforded to incite one to go actively to a neighbor's material assistance in any manner.[3]

---

1. "Therefore all things whatsoever ye would that men should do to you, do ye even so to them: for this is the law and the prophets."

2. "For they shall eat, and not have enough: they shall commit whoredom, and shall not increase: because they have left off to take heed to the Lord."

3. William Kelley Wright, *A Student's Philosophy of Religion* (New York: Macmillan, 1922), pp. 78–79: "On the contrary, the defects in Brahminism have been serious enough. It has been only too tolerant. It has for this reason failed to be a reforming religion. It has tolerated magic and all manner of degrading superstitions. Far from attempting to reform the cruel social injustices of the caste system, it has found a moral justification for them. This religion has founded no church; it has developed no social activities; it has cared little to serve humanity. Salvation is to be won by inner meditation by oneself. One is taught to conceive himself in an intellectual manner to be identical with one's neighbor and love him as oneself, but little motivation is afforded to incite one to go actively to a neighbor's material assistance in any manner." This book was on the syllabus for King's spring 1951 class Philosophy of Religion with George W. Davis (Bibliography and term assignments, Philosophy of Religion and Advanced Philosophy of Religion, 28 November 1950–4 May 1951).

Book	Chapter	Verse	Location Under Red ABC Tabs	TOPIC TEXT OR SUBJECT

File speeches, articles, studies, illustrations, etc., under Red ABC Tabs according to *first letter* of subject symbol used in 4th column. See Instruction, Pages VIII, IX and X.
Reserve the entire sheet where you expect to index many sermons, articles or studies under the same Book of the Bible or under some one subject heading.

Book	Chapter	Verse		TOPIC TEXT OR SUBJECT
Matt.	7	12		"The Rule Of Life" (To be prepared)
				"Our Uncivilized Civilization"
1 Peter	4	10		"What is Enough"
				1. Economic security is not 2. Family is not enough. 3. Justice is not enough 4. We can only be filled
				"When Religion Becomes Too Tolerant"
				Brahminism has often been too tolerant. It has tolerated magic and all manner of superstitions. Far from attempting to reform the cruel social injustices of the caste system, it has found a moral justification for them. The religion has founded no church; it has developed no social activities; it has cared little to serve humanity. Salvation is to be won by inner meditation by oneself. One is taught to conceive himself in an intellectual manner to be identical with one's neighbor and love him as oneself; but little motivation is afforded to incite one to go actively to a neighbor's material assistance in any manner.
				"The Need for an Agressive Liberalism" As a basis see, W. K. Wright, A Students Philosophy of Religion, p. 83, 84. this is a good article to write
Matt.	7	21		"The Quintessence of Religion" (See notes of Philosophy of Rel. I)
Rev.	3	20		The Courtesy of God C. God never forces his will upon an individual
Heb.	5	4		On Being Called of God to preach.

Form 5

| | "The Need for an Agressive Liberalism" | 20 Feb– |
| | As a basis see, W. K. Wright, <u>A Students Philosophy of Religion</u>, p.83, 84.[4] This is a good article to write | 4 May 1951 |

Matt. 7 21[5]   "The Quintessence of Religion"
(See notes of Philosophy of Rel. I)[6]

Rev. 3 20[7]   The Courtesy of God
(God never forces his will upon an individual

Heb 5 4[8]   On Being Called of God to preach.

Heb. 13 8[9]   "The Permenence of Christ"
The quest of the ages has been to find something un-changeable
Man's truth is always limited by the <u>Zeitgeist</u>, But the truth which Christ revealed is eternal.[10]

"The war of Spirit"
Every man must declare war on himself
He must struggle to conque his low evil and selfish nature and subject it to the higher nature
Every man is capable of becoming more that he is. "I look upon man as a fragment of the future." Nietsche[11]

23rd Psm[12]   "The Cosmic Shephard"

---

4. Wright, *A Student's Philosophy of Religion*, p. 84: "If religious liberals hope to preserve their more scientific conceptions of God and their emphasis upon the moral values of toleration, social service and progress, they cannot permit the masses in church and synagogue to go on unenlightened. The future of religion will never be assured in this country so long as more intelligent worshippers are indifferent to the obligation upon all true Christians and Jews to make their places of worship frequented by all classes and strata of society."

5. "Not every one that saith unto me, Lord, Lord, shall enter into the kingdom of heaven; but he that doeth the will of my Father which is in heaven."

6. In King's class notes for Philosophy of Religion, he wrote: "What is the fifth essence (quintessence) of religion. i.e. its highest essence. The question arises which is most important: belief in God or loyalty to the highest ideals. It seems that with Jesus the ~~good~~ of humanity was more important than theoretical belief in God. So that the quintessence of religion is devotion to the highest ideals." King also noted, "If loyalty to God does not make for the devotion to highest ideals in our lives then he might as well be dismissed" (28 November 1950–15 February 1951).

7. "Behold, I stand at the door, and knock: if any man hear my voice, and open the door, I will come in to him, and will sup with him, and he with me."

8. "And no man taketh this honour unto himself, but he that is called of God, as was Aaron."

9. "Jesus Christ the same yesterday, and to day, and for ever."

10. "Zeitgeist" is a German word referring to the prevalent spirit or ideas of a particular era.

11. King refers to philosopher Friedrich Nietzsche's observation: "I walk amongst men as the fragments of the future: that future which I contemplate" (*Thus Spake Zarathustra*, trans., Thomas Common [New York: Macmillan, 1916], p. 168).

12. "The Lord is my shepherd. I shall not want. He maketh me to lie down in green pastures: he leadeth me beside the still waters. He restoreth my soul: he leadeth me in the paths of righteousness for his name's sake. Yea, though I walk through the valley of the shadow of death, I will fear no evil: for thou art with me; thy rod and thy staff they comfort me. Thou preparest a table before me in the presence of mine enemies: thou anointest my head with oil; my cup runneth over. Surely goodness and mercy shall follow me all the days of my life; and I will dwell in the house of the Lord for ever."

This Psalm stress the fact that men has companion in his struggle for good. God and the universe are on the side of right.

When this Psalm came the world was made a better place in which to live

Acts 11:24[13]	"A Plea For Goodness"
	Curiousity: Vice or Virtue
	{See the Story of The Burning Bush in Exodus}[14]
{Matt 23:25	"Beyond Good Deeds"
Matt 15:19}[15]	It is not only the deed but the motive See Spurrier, Chapter 2[16]
Isaiah 40:15,17[17]	The Sin Of Nationalism[18]
	(see Spurrier, chaptr 3 pp. 56F)[19]
Gen 18 23 F[20]	"Irrelevant Goodness"
Gen 18 23F	(attempt to show that there were probably 10 good men in Sodom, but that there goodness was irrelevant.)

"God's Judgment upon America"

(The sin of America is that it combinds the pride of virtue (which was Israels defect), (with the pride of power, which was Babylons defect.[21]

---

13. "For he was a good man, and full of the Holy Ghost and of faith: and much people was added unto the Lord."

14. Exodus 3:1–4:17.

15. Matthew 23:25: "Woe unto you, scribes and Pharisees, hypocrites! for ye make clean the outside of the cup and of the platter, but within they are full of extortion and excess." Matthew 15:19: "For out of the heart proceed evil thoughts, murders, adulteries, fornications, thefts, false witness, blasphemies."

16. King refers to a chapter in *Power for Action: An Introduction to Christian Ethics* titled "Conflict with the Pharisees," in which William A. Spurrier argues: "Jesus attacked the ideal that a man's goodness or righteousness is determined by what he does. While it is true that a really good man should and will do good deeds and that 'by your fruits ye shall be known,' it is not necessarily true that he who does a so-called good deed is actually a good man" (Spurrier, *Power for Action: An Introduction to Christian Ethics* [New York: Charles Scribner's Sons, 1948], pp. 8–9). Kenneth Smith assigned this book for his course Christianity and Society (Syllabus, Christianity and Society, 20 February–4 May 1951).

17. Isaiah 40:15–17: "Behold, the nations are as a drop of a bucket, and are counted as the small dust of the balance: behold, he taketh up the isles as a very little thing. And Lebanon is not sufficient to burn, nor the beasts thereof sufficient for a burnt offering. All nations before him are as nothing; and they are counted to him less than nothing, and vanity."

18. For a developed sermon with this theme, see King, "The False God of Nationalism," 12 July 1953, pp. 132–133 in this volume.

19. Spurrier noted in a chapter of *Power for Action* titled "War and Peace": "Nations are subject to laws of right and wrong as well as its individuals. No nation or group of nations can say that they are God— the determiners of destiny, the final answers to all the problems of life. Nations come and go, rise and fall, but life with its purposes, meanings, creative abilities, right and wrong remains. 'Behold, the nations are as a drop of a bucket. All the nations before Him (God) are as nothing and they are counted to Him less than nothing and vanity' (Isaiah 40:15, 17). Nationalism is therefore a colossal expression of collective sin, the pride of man at its height" (*Power for Action*, p. 58).

20. Genesis 18:23–33 tells of Abraham bargaining with God to save the city of Sodom, a site of sin and depravity. God agreed to refrain from destroying Sodom if even only ten righteous people could be found.

21. Babylon was a Mesopotamian empire that conquered Israel in the sixth century BCE.

Gen. 3^{22}	"The Fall of Man"	20 Feb–
	(Show an individual fall. The conception of original sin receives validity in the light of the universality of sin.	4 May 1951
Gen. 3	"Beyond a Good Environment"	
	(Take the story of the fall of man. Here man was in a perfect environment. Yet he sinned. Man may have the best of environment, but unless he has something of God in he can change the perfect environment into literal hell.	
	"The Unlimited Christ"	
	(See Folder on <u>Christian Social Phi II</u>)^{23}	
Romans 3	"Man is unity in a great separation"	
2~~23~~ 24^{24}	All me are united in their separation from God. We are all sinners (our unity) needing to be reconciled with God (our separation)	
	"A Peace the passeth All Understanding"^{25}	
	Text "Peace I leave with you, my peace I give unto you.^{26}	
	"Religion does not aim to save us from the troubles and reverses of life, these came alike to all, but ~~that~~ it aims to support us under them and to teach us the divine purpose in them. Not outward prosperity, but this inward calm is the great legacy of the Christian. Men wonder how God's true child can keep his heart in such a rest amid the most distracting circumstanses—the answer is—"Peace I leave with thee." See Knudson's RTOT 289.^{27}	
Ephesians 4:6^{28}	God transcendent and Immanent	
Ephesians 6:11F^{29}	The Christian Warrior	
Lord's Prayer	Our Father	

---

22. Genesis 3 recounts Eve's temptation by the serpent, her temptation of Adam to eat from the tree of knowledge, and their banishment by God from the Garden of Eden.

23. During the spring of 1951, King was enrolled in Kenneth L. Smith's Christian Social Philosophy II, a course that surveyed nineteenth-century philosophy and the rise of the social gospel. Although King's notes do not mention "the Unlimited Christ" specifically, they do address the role of Christianity in society (King, Class notes, Christian Social Philosophy II, 20 February–4 May 1951).

24. "Even the righteousness of God, which is by faith of Jesus Christ, unto all and upon all them that believe: for there is no difference: For all have sinned, and come short of the glory of God; Being justified freely by his grace through the redemption that is in Christ Jesus."

25. Cf. Philippians 4:7.

26. John 14:27.

27. Albert C. Knudson, *The Religious Teaching of the Old Testament* (New York: Abingdon Press, 1918), p. 289: "It is good to know that our sufferings may be a trial of our faith, a test of our righteousness, that they may in the providence of God be vicarious and redemptive, that they have a disciplinary value, and that they will ultimately give way to a happier future; but it is better still to have a vision of God so rapturous that the sufferings of the present lose their sting, and life is permitted to go on in unruffled peace."

28. "One God and Father of all, who is above all, and through all, and in you all."

29. Ephesians 6:11–16 includes the command to "put on the whole armour of God" to engage in a spiritual battle against the devil.

see Abingdon Commentary 164.[30]

Sermon On Freedom Of Will

Text: Choose ye This Day When ye shall serve[31]

Acts 19:2[32]

The Relevance of the Holy Spirit

Most people have either forgotten that there is such a concept or they have a misconception of it. It remains true, however, that this is one of the most important doctrines in the Christian religion.

(1) It stresses the fact that God did not limit his revelation to one period (e.g. biblical time). God is revealing himself now.

(2) It stresses the immanense of God. This is needed in the face of much modern theology which speak of the total "otherness" of God. Quote Tennerson (Closer than hands)[33]

(3) It stresses the fact that God is continually working through history.

Matt 5:

Blessed are the pure in heart[34]

"Seeing God."

Seeing God is a matter of the heart and not the head. The practice of religion must be substituted for argument about it. As the poem says,

It were not hard, we think, to serve Him,
    If we could only see!
If he would stand with that gaze intense
    Burning into our bodily sense,
If we might look on that face most tender,
The brow where the stars are turned to splendour;
Might catch the light of His smile so sweet,
And view the marks of His hands and feet,
    How loyal we should be!
It were not hard, we think, to serve Him,
    If we could only see!
It were not hard, He says, to see Him,
    If we would only serve:
"He that doeth the will of heaven,
To him shall knowledge and sight be given."
While for His presence we sit repining,

---

30. King refers to *The Abingdon Bible Commentary*, which states: "Here it was that Jesus transcended the O.T. He conceived of God as Father and as Father of all men in a way that rendered obsolete all earlier nationalistic, particularistic, legalistic, and royalistic conceptions of him" (Frederick Carl Eiselen, Edwin Lewis, and David G. Downey, eds., *The Abingdon Bible Commentary* [New York: Abingdon Press, 1929], p. 164).

31. Cf. Joshua 24:15.

32. "He said unto them, Have ye received the Holy Ghost since ye believed? And they said unto him, We have not so much as heard whether there be any Holy Ghost."

33. King may be referring to a stanza from Alfred Lord Tennyson's poem "The Higher Pantheism" (1869): "Speak to Him thou for He hears, and Spirit with Spirit can meet— / Closer is He than breathing, and nearer than hands and feet."

34. Matthew 5:8.

Never we see His countenance shining:
They who toil where His reapers be
The glow of his smile may alway see,
And their faith can never swerve.
It were not hard, He says, to see Him,
If we would only serve.

See McCracken's <u>Questions People Ask</u>[35]
Sermon: How does one acquire Religious Experiences
"Why Does God Hide Himself?"[36]
When we deal with the finite we can be plain and even
somewhat certain. But as soon as we touch the fringe of the
infinite there is:

A deep beyond the deep
And a heigh beyond the height,
And our hearing is not hearing
And our seeing is not sight![37]

AFm. CSKC: Sermon file, folder 118, "Sermon Material."

---

35. The preceding poem is quoted from Robert J. McCracken's sermon "How Does One Acquire Religious Experience?" which was the first sermon in his collection *Questions People Ask* (New York: Harper & Brothers, 1951), pp. 11–19. Robert J. McCracken (1904–1973) succeeded Harry Emerson Fosdick as pastor of New York's Riverside Church. He served from 1946 to 1967 and used his pulpit to speak out against racial injustice and militarism.

36. King preached a sermon with this title on 4 December 1955 at Dexter Avenue Baptist Church (see King, "Why Does God Hide Himself?," pp. 241–242 in this volume).

37. McCracken, "Why Does God Hide Himself?": "We can be plain, precise, specific while we are dealing with what is finite, but as soon as we begin to touch the fringe of the infinite there is A deep beyond the deep, / And a height beyond the height, / And our hearing is not hearing, / And our seeing is not sight." McCracken and King quote Alfred Lord Tennyson's poem "The Voice and the Peak" (1874). In his sermon file, King kept a copy of McCracken's pamphlet "Why Does God Hide Himself?" 27 April 1947.

Sincerity Is Not Enough

[*3 June 1951*]
[*Atlanta, Ga.*]

Following his graduation from Crozer in May 1951, King returned to Atlanta for the summer and preached occasionally at Ebenezer where he delivered a sermon sharing the title of the following handwritten outline and brief manuscript.[1] He argues for the importance of intelligence in religion and cautions: "If sincerity is not [buttressed?] by intelligence it can become the most [ruinous] force in human nature."

---

1. King's announced sermon topic for 3 June 1951 was "Sincerity Is Not Enough" ("Rev. M. L. King, Sr. On Leave From Ebenezer Baptist," *Atlanta Daily World*, 2 June 1951).

Sincerity Is Not Enough, Sermon outline

Subject—Sincerety Is Not Enough
Text Roman 10:2[2]
I   Introduction
II   Text
     a   Historical background
III The revelation of this fact in various areas
     1.   History
     2.   Our contempory ~~political~~ life
          1.   The people who think that ou economic system can survive without a
               deep seated change
          2.   The people who cry up war.
          3.

AD. CSKC: Sermon file, folder 118, "Sermon Material."

Sincerity Is Not Enough

From the earliest moments of the Christian era the church has admonished
men to be sincere, conscientious, kind-hearted, and well intentioned. Christianity
inherited this emphasis from its Jewish ancestors, for Judaism always insisted that
morality and religion were one, not two. Certainly this is a noble inheritance. But to
say to a man that he must be sincere and conscientious, important though they be,
does not cover the ground. Sincerity is not enough. If sincerity is not [*buttressed?*] by
intelligence it can become the most runious force in human nature.

Indeet, the Apostle Paul was quite cognizant of this fact. He had the experience
of having his life's work opposed on every hand by a group of men who were profoundly sincere yet despreately stupid. These men, refered to as Judaizers, insisted
that before a Gentile could come into the Christian church he must first be cir-
cumsized and accepts the tenents of the Jewish law. Paul, on the ~~contrary~~ other
hand, did not insist on the necessity of a Gentile becoming a Jew before he could
become a Christian. Because of his liberal open-minded leanings these Judaizers
attempted to undermine Paul's efforts on every [*strikeout illegible*] hand. They followed him from shore to shore with the desire to defeat him. O how sincere they
were in there attempt to defeat this great Christian missionary. They felt that they
were doing the will of God. And so in his letter to the Roman Church in a verse
which seems certain to be referring to these men, Paul says: "For I bear them record
that they have a zeal of God, but not according knowledge."[3] How true this is of so
many Christians. How easily this passage of scripture can be applied to 1951 A. D.

Surely this text needs to be repeated over and over again, especially in religious
circles. All of the moral voices in the world seem to tell us to have a zeal of God, to
be sincere, and to be conscientious, but how few voices tell us to be intelligent.
Sincerity void of intelligence will never solve the spiritual problems of mankind. I
must hasten to say that by intelligence I do not mean mere formal education.

AD. CSKC: Sermon file, folder 55, "Propagandizing Christianity."

---

2. "For I bear them, record that they have a zeal of God, but not according to knowledge."
3. Romans 10:2.

II: BOSTON YEARS

[18 July 1952]
[*Atlanta, Ga.*]

In Atlanta to serve as associate pastor of Ebenezer after completing his first year at Boston University, King corresponded with Coretta Scott, whom he began dating during the spring of 1952. This letter from King refers to a possible trip by Scott to Atlanta to meet his parents, a trip she made during August. He also comments extensively on Edward Bellamy's Looking Backward 2000–1887, *a book Scott had given King.[1] King calls Bellamy a "social prophet" and a "social scientist" and offers reflections regarding the relative merits and shortcomings of capitalism, communism, and socialism, writing, "I am much more socialistic in my economic theory than capitalistic."*

Friday Morning

Dearest,

Fortunately, I am in a better mood today. your letter was sweet and refreshing to my heart, which had well-nigh grown cold toward you.[2] Of course I have become convinced in the last few days that my love for you is based on such a solid foundation that the stormy winds of anger cannot blow it assunder. Love is such a dynamic force isn't it? It is the most inexplicable and yet the most beautiful force in life. O how joyous it is [*to?*] be in it.

Darling I miss you so much. In fact, much to much for my own good. I never realized that you were such an intimate part of my life. My life without you is like a year without a spring time which comes to give illumination and heat to the atmosphere which has been saturated by the dark cold breeze of winter. Can you imagine the frustration that a King without a throne would face? Such would be my frustration if I in my little kinghood could not reign at the throne of Coretta. O excuse my darling. I didn't mean to go off on such a poetical and romantic flight. But how else can we express the deep emotions of life other than in poetry. Isn't love to ineffable to be grasped by the cold calculating heads of intellect?

By the way (to turn to something more intellectual) I have just completed Bellamy's <u>Looking Backward</u>. It was both stimulating and facinating. There can be no doubt about it Bellamy had the insight of a social prophet as well as the fact finding mind of the social scientist. I welcomed the book because much of its content is in line with my basic ideas. I imagine you already know that I am much more

1. Edward Bellamy, *Looking Backward 2000–1887* (New York: Modern Library, 1951). Bellamy's novel, originally published in 1888, envisions Boston in the year 2000 as part of a world that had experienced a moral and material transformation. In this new society, capitalism has been replaced by a more socialist form of production and distribution, society has become classless, and individuals acknowledge their common bond and responsibility for all members of society.

2. In a previous letter, King had reacted angrily when Scott implied she was against staying with the King family during a visit to Atlanta (King to Scott, 14 July 1952).

During their courtship, Coretta Scott gave King a copy of Edward Bellamy's *Looking Backward 2000–1887* and wrote this inscription (7 April 1952).

socialistic in my economic theory than capitalistic. And yet I am not so opposed to capitalism that I have failed to see its relative merits. It started out with a noble and high motive, viz, to block the trade monopolies of nobles, but like most human system it fail victim to the very thing it was revolting agaist. So today capitalism has outlived its usefulness. It has brought about a system that takes necessities from the masses to give luxuries to the classes. So I think Bellamy is right in seeing the gradual decline of capitalism.

I think you noticed that Bellamy emphasized that the [*change?*] would be evolutionary rather than revolutionary. This, it seems to me, is the most sane and ethical way for social change to take place. This, it will be remembered, is one of the points at which socialism differs from communism, the former [*strikeout illegible*] emphasizing evolution and the latter revolution. Communist would insist that the means justify the end. So if killing a thousand people will bring about a good end the act is ethically justifiable. It is at the point that I am radically opposed to communism Destructive means cannot bring about constructive ends. The mean does not necessarily justify the end, for, I would insist that the end is pre existent in the mean.

Also I am quite bitterly opposed to the metaphysical structure of communism as well as Marxism. It is based on what is known as <u>Dialectical Materialism</u>.[3] I, being an idealist, rather [*than?*] [*remainder missing*] materialist, would therefore reject Marx at this point.

There is [*one?*] point however, that I have learned from reading Marx and books like Bellamys, and that is that religion [*can?*] so easily become a tool of the middle class to keep the proletariant oppressed. To often has the church talked about a future good "over yonder" totally forgetting the present evil over here. As a theologian and one deeply convinced that the way of Christ is the only ultimate way to man's salvation, I will try to avoid making religion what Marx calls the "opiate of the people."[4]

On the negative side of the picture Bellamy falls victim to the same error that most writers of Utopian societies fall victim to, viz., idealism not tempered with realism. In other words, such systems are impractical. Bellamy with his over optimism fails to see that man is a sinner, and that he is give better economic and social conditions he will still be a sinner until he submits his life to the Grace of God. Ultimately our problem is [*a?*] theological one. Man has revolted against God, and through his humanistic endeavors he has sought to solve his problem by himself only to find that he ~~ha~~ has ended up in disillusionment.

Again Bellamy fails to see [*strikeout illegible*] that social systems dont die over night I dont think he gave capitalism long enough time to die. It is probably true that capitalism is on its death bed, but social systems have a way of developing a long and powerful death bed breathing capacity. Remember it took feudalism more than 500 years to pass out from its death bed. Capitalism will be in America quite a few more years my dear.

Yet with his basic thesis I would concur. Our economic system is going through a

---

3. King later preached a sermon in which he elaborated on these thoughts (King, "Communism's Challenge to Christianity," 9 August 1953, pp. 146–150 in this volume).

4. Karl Marx, "Contribution to the Critique of Hegel's *Philosophy of Right:* Introduction" (1844).

radical change, and certainly this change is needed. I would certainly welcome the day to come when there will be a nationalization of industry. Let us continue to hope, work, and pray that in the future we will live to see a warless world, a better distribution of wealth, and a brotherhood that transcends race or color. This is the gospel that I will preach to the world. At this point I must thank you a million times for introducing me to such a stimulating book. you are sweet and thoughtful indeed.

As to your visit to Atlanta, I would rather not go into a detail discussion over it because I see that it can break up a beautiful relationship. I see that you are much more influenced by other people than you are by me, as maybe you would rather spend your vacation with them since they have all the answers. Nevertheless [*I?*] still extend to you the invitation and hope that you will come. It hurt me very much to know that you believe that I would invite you to Atlanta and then mistreat you, especialy as nice as Ive been to you in the past. Oh well I guess all of us have a little of the unappreciative attitude in us.

If you are coming let me know so that I can make the arrangements. If you dont desire to come also let me know soon and I assure you that [*I?*] wont mention it to you any more. Of course if you dont come I will know that you have no confidence in me and I will proceed to think out our courtship in those lines. I hope [*strikeout illegible*] we wont have to break up about this trip.

Give my regards to [*Scottie?*] and the other member of the gang.[5] Be sweet and remember that daddy still loves you.

Eternaly yours

[*signed*] "Martin"

P.S. Hope you can read my bad writing

ALS. CSKC.

---

5. King may refer to Scott's sister Edythe Scott.

"Loving Your Enemies"

[*31 August 1952*]
[*Atlanta, Ga.*]

In this handwritten outline, the earliest known version of this oft-given sermon, King invokes Jesus' call for people to love their enemies as a solution to the problems facing modern society.[1] He contends that Jesus's teaching was not "the pious injunction of a

---

1. "'Loving Your Enemies' Rev. King, Jr.'s Subject," *Atlanta Daily World*, 30 August 1952. For a later example of this sermon that follows this early outline, see King, "Loving Your Enemies," Sermon Delivered

utopian dreamer." King continues, "This command is an absolute necessity for the
survival of our civilization. Love is the key to the solution of the world's problem, yes
even love for enemies. "

I   Int. In the 5th Chapter of Matthew's gosple verses 42 and 3 we find these pressing words flowing from the lips of our Lord and Master: "ye have heard that it
hath been said, Thou shalt love thy neighbour and hate thine enemy. But I say
unto you, Love your enemies, bless them that curse you, do good to them that
hate you, and pray for them which despitefully use you, and persecute you."[2]
   A. Historical setting
       (1) Hebrew idea of tooth for tooth[3]
       (2) Tribal God idea
       (3) Love was binding only in the tribe.
            In the midst of this Jesus comes out with a new and revolutionary idea.
       He says in substance love not only your neighbors and friends, but love
       even your enemies
   B. Man's reaction to this command
       (1) Over the years men have looked upon this command as an impractical
            ideal. Many people are convinced that it just isn't possible Many would
            say that this is just additional proof that Jesus was an impractical ideal-
            ist of yesterday who never quite came down to earth.
                 Yet far from being the impractical idealist, Jesus has become the
            practical realist and the words of our text glitter in our eyes with a
            new pertinance. Instead of being the pious injunction of a utopian
            dreamer, this command is an absolute necessity for the survival of our
            civilization. Love is the key to the solution of the world's problem, yes
            even love for enemies.

II   The ~~inevitability of enemies~~ [*strikeout illegible*] ~~all of us have enemies~~ hardness of
     the command. I think Jesus realized that it was hard

III How does one go about Loving his enemy
     (1) First analyze self: We may be somewhat [*responsible?*]
          (a) It is true that some people hate others for no reason
          (b) However there might be causes on your end. You might have done
               something in the past
          c.   Notice the international situation Communism is our enemy because
               of many of our blunders.

---

at Dexter Avenue Baptist Church, 17 November 1957, in *The Papers of Martin Luther King*, vol. 4: *Symbol of the Movement, January 1957–December 1958*, ed. Clayborne Carson, Susan Carson, Adrienne Clay, Virginia Shadron, Kieran Taylor (Berkeley and Los Angeles: University of California Press, 2000), pp. 315–324; see also King, Loving Your Enemies, Sermon Delivered at Detroit Council of Churches' Noon Lenten Services, 7 March 1961, pp. 421–429 in this volume, and King, *Strength to Love*, pp. 34–41.

2. Matthew 5:43–44.
3. This idea can be found throughout the Pentateuch; for an example, see Exodus 21:24.

      Quote Jesus: "How can you see the ~~beam~~ mote. etc.[4]

(2) Always be willing to see the good points in your enemy.

(3) Whe the possibility of defeating your enemy presents itself, you must not do it

  This would not follow with all out war between nations. This deals with enimity between individuals

IV Why Should one Love his enemy

(1) Because the process of hate for hate brings disaster to all involved

(2) Because hate distort the whole personality

3

(3) Because love has within in a redemptive power

AD. CSKC: Sermon file, folder 1, "Loving Your Enemies."

---

  4. Cf. Matthew 7:3–5.

After Christmas, What?

[*28 December 1952*]
[*Atlanta, Ga.*]

During his holiday break from graduate school, King delivered a version of the
following handwritten sermon outline at Ebenezer.[1] He asks, "Will Christmas
mean just another item in our social calendar or will it mean a new life and new
attitudes resulting from our encounter with Christ."

Luke 2:28[2]

Introduction: For the past few days we have made our symbolic journeys and pilgrimages to Bethlehem. We have symbolically knelt before the infant Jesus at his manger. There we have beheld him in all of his grandeur and glory. And In the midst of this sublime experience we have sung melodious [*tunes?*] that have ~~shaken the very fiber of our soul~~ reached high heaven. Now as ~~must make~~ [*our way?*] ~~back to our various homes~~ we leave Bethlehem and make our way back to our various

---

  1. "'After Christmas, What?' to Be Rev. M. L. King, Jr.'s Topic," *Atlanta Daily World*, 27 December 1952. King also preached a sermon with this title as one of his final homilies at Dexter Avenue Baptist Church in December 1959 (Dexter Avenue Baptist Church, Program, Sunday services, 27 December 1959).

  2. "Then he took him up in his arms, and blessed God, and said, Lord, now lettest thou thy servant depart in peace, according to thy word: For mine eyes have seen thy salvation, Which thou hast prepared before the face of all people: A light to lighten the Gentiles, and the glory of thy people Israel" (Luke 2:28–32). Luke 2:25–35 concerns Simeon, a man who had been waiting for a messiah for Israel.

homes the question poses itself, What did we gain? What is the value of our meeting with Christ? What is Christmas going to do for us in terms of chanced attitudes and better social conditions? Will Christmas mean just another item in our social calendar or will it mean a new life and new attitudes resulting from our encounter with Christ. After we have sung "[*Joy?*] to the World" and "O Little Town of Bethlehem, [*remainder missing*] What then?[3] After we have exclaimed "Peace On earth [*remainder missing*] good will toward men," What then?[4] Will we go back [*remainder missing*] home with our same old ways and our same [*remainder missing*] thought? Or will or lives and thoughts be [*remainder missing*] transformed that men will be able to [*recognize?*] [*remainder missing*] that we have been with Christ?[5] ~~The test~~ that [*remainder missing*] be the real test. The test of th value of Christmas [*remainder missing*] you will not be in terms of how many carol [*you?*] [*remainder missing*] have sung or how many eloquent [~~*phrases?*~~] words [*you?*] [*remainder missing*] repeated. <u>Text</u>

I You must go away with the conviction that [*remainder missing*] is near. The men who behell Christ in the manger [*remainder missing*] those who later encounted him were convinced that [*remainder missing*] brought God nearer to earth.
  (1) He represented a bit of [*remainder missing*] forth into time
  (2.) The Christlikeness of God
  (3) Jesus as the [*supreme?*] [*remainder missing*] of God
  (4) Christianity has always insisted that God is [*remainder missing*] and concerned.
  (5) Aristotle God[6]
  (6) There are times [*remainder missing*] we doubt the [*concern?*] about God
  (7) Christmas and [*remainder missing*] coming of Christ should dispel all our [*remainder missing*] No matter where I go God's love is there [*remainder missing*]

II We should go away with the conviction that Christ is the revelation of what man ought to be. Jesus reveald not only what God is but what man ought to be.
  1. The gap between what we actually are and what we ought to be
  2. Christ stand in judgment upon that which is law
  3. When I stand in the face of Christ I am ashamed of myself. His noble character cause me to cry not "I thank God that I am not like other men. but "God be merciful unto me a sinner.[7]
  We should go away with the conviction that Christ way is our eternal hope.

AD. CSKC: Sermon file, folder 57, Luke 2:28.

---

3. A portion of the right margin of the paper on which this sermon was written was torn and is missing.

4. Cf. Luke 2:14.

5. Cf. Acts 4:13.

6. In a paper written at Crozer, King noted: "He is not the Aristotelian God who merely contemplates upon himself; not only is God a self-knowing father, but he is an ~~ever~~ {other} loving Father" (King, "What a Christian Should Believe About Himself," 29 November 1949–15 February 1950, in *Papers* 1:281).

7. Cf. Luke 18:9–14.

False Gods We Worship

In July 1953, while King assisted his father at Ebenezer for the fifth consecutive summer, Atlanta's WERD, the first black-owned radio station in the United States, began broadcasting "messages" from Ebenezer and featured King as the speaker.[1] The brevity of these typed manuscripts and the dates written thereon suggest that he wrote them for the WERD broadcasts.[2] King filed these sermons together in a folder that he titled "False Gods We Worship."[3] In "The False God of Science," King challenges humanity's overdependence on the promises of science by revealing its shortcomings: "The god of science which we so devoutly worshipped has brought about the possibility of universal annihilation." In "The False God of Nationalism," he argues that God and nationalism are "incompatible" and asks, "Will we continue to serve the false god of racial prejudice or will we serve the God who made of one blood all men to dwell upon the face of the earth." In his concluding sermon of the series, King reflects on "the tragic consequences which develop when men worship the almighty dollar." Using language that would reappear often in his oratory, he asserts that his listeners must choose between "the transitory god of money which is here today and gone tomorrow" and "the eternal God of the universe who is the same yesterday, today and forever."

"The False God of Science"

5 July 1953
[*Atlanta, Ga.*]

Dr. William Ernest Hecking has said that all life is divided into work and worship; that which we do for ourselves and that which we let the higher than ourselves do.[4] Certainly worship is as natural to man as the rising of the sun is to the cosmic order.

---

1. "Ebenezer Begins WERD Broadcast Sunday Morning," *Atlanta Daily World,* 4 July 1953.

2. King dated these three manuscripts 5, 12, and 19 July 1953, respectively, while the *Atlanta Daily World* announced different topics for the services at Ebenezer on those same Sundays ("'When God Seems to Deceive Us,' Rev. M. L. King, Jr.'s Subject," *Atlanta Daily World,* 4 July 1953; "'Transformed Non-Conformists' to Be King Jr.'s Topic," *Atlanta Daily World,* 11 July 1953; "Mrs. Burney, 'Women's Day' Speaker at Ebenezer Sunday," *Atlanta Daily World,* 18 July 1953).

3. On the inside of the folder containing these sermons, King noted that he also preached the "False Gods" series at Dexter Avenue Baptist Church in January 1955. At that time, he included the sermon False God of Pleasure in the series (King, January 1955, p. 206 in this volume). He filed a sermon titled On Worshiping False Gods, which incorporated ideas espoused in these shorter addresses in the folder as well (King, January 1955, pp. 203–206 in this volume).

4. Harry Emerson Fosdick used similar language in his sermon "Why Worship?" (in Fosdick, *Successful Christian Living: Sermons on Christianity Today* (New York: Harper & Brothers, 1937), pp. 173–174: "Professor Hocking is right in saying that all man's life can be reduced to two aspects, work and worship—what we do ourselves, and what we let the higher than ourselves do to us." Fosdick may be referring to the tenor of William Ernest Hocking's *The Meaning of God in Human Experience,* which deals with the subject of work (New Haven, Conn.: Yale University Press, 1912). Fosdick was a Baptist preacher who served as pastor at the nondenominational Riverside Church in New York from 1925 until 1946 and was one of liberal Protestantism's most influential figures. King kept a copy of *Successful Christian Living* in his personal library and annotated it.

Men always have worshipped and men always will worship. There is the ever present danger, however, that man will direct his worship drive into false channels. It is not so {much} disbelief as false belief that is the danger confronting religion. It is not so much downright atheism as strong, determined polytheism which impedes the progress of religion. The scripture furnishes numerous examples of this ever present tendency of man to substitute false gods for the One true God. {Judges 2:12}[5]

When we move from the pages of the Bible to the scene of the modern world, we find this same tendency present in even greater proportions. On every hand modern man has turned from the One true God of the universe to the worship of false gods round about him. These false gods that modern men worship are numerous in number. I want to deal with three of them. Because of limited time, I will deal with only one of these false gods this morning. The other two will be discussed on the following two Sundays.

Let us notice this morning how modern man has made a god of science. It was quite easy for modern man to put his ultimate faith in science because science had brought about such remarkable advances, such tangible and amazing victories. He realized that man through his scientific genius had dwarfed distances and placed time in chains. He noticed the new comforts that had been brought about by science, from the vast improvements in communication to the elimination of many dread plagues and diseases. And so after noticing these astounding successes modern man ushered in a new god and a new religion. Individual scientist became the high priests, chemical and biological instruments became sacramental agencies through which the invisible grace of the scientific god became visibly manifested, and scientific laboratories became the sanctuaries. And so modern man dutifully worshipped at the shrine of the god of science.

But today we are confronted with the tragic fact that the god of science which we so devoutly worshipped has brought about the possibility of universal annihilation, and so man today stands on the brink of atomic destruction aghast, panic-stricken and petrified. He realizes now that his greatest need is not science which is power, but wisdom which is control.

Doubtless some one has been saying, but is it not right to devote ourselves to scientific adventure? Is not science important for the progress of civilization? To this I would answer yes. No person of sound intelligence could minimize science. It is not science in itself that I am condemning, {but it is the tendency of projecting it to the status of God that I am condemning.} We must come to see that science only furnishes us with the means by which we live, but never with the spiritual ends for which we live. And so we must turn back and give our ultimate devotion to the God who integrates the whole of life, to the God in whom we live and move and have our

---

5. "And they forsook the Lord God of their fathers, which brought them out of the land of Egypt, and followed other gods, of the gods of the people that were round about them, and bowed themselves unto them, and provoked the Lord to anger."

being, to the God who has been our help in ages past, our hope for years to come, our shelter from the stormy blast, and our eternal home.[6]

Preached July 5, 1953

TAD. CSKC: Sermon file, folder 18, "False Gods We Worship."

"The False God of Nationalism"

12 July 1953
[*Atlanta, Ga.*]

Last Sunday I spoke on the false god of science. This morning I would like to speak of another false god which seems to be receiving even greater devotion than the god of science—namely the god of nationalism.. If time permitted, I would trace the history of this new religion, unravel the strands that, woven together, have produced it. In its present form it is a modern phenomenon developing from the eighteenth century on, but that it is now dominant in the world is clear.[7] Our age is one in which men have turned away from the eternal God of the universe, and decided to worship at the shrine of the god of nationalism.

We are all familiar with the creed of this new religion. It affirms that each nation is an absolute sovereign unit acknowledging no control save its own independent will.[8] The watchword of this new religion is: "My country right or wrong." This new religion has its familiar prophets and preachers. In Germany it was preached by Hitler. In Italy it was preached by Mussilini. And in America it is being preached by the McCarthy's and the Jenners, the advocators of white supremacy, and the America first movements.[9] Strangely enough all of these nationalistic preachers have an amazing amount of homilectical skill, so much so that the number of their converts has risen to astronomical proportions.

The preachers of this new religion are so convinced of its supremacy that they are determined to persecute anyone who does not accept its tenets. And so today many sincere lovers of democracy and believers of the christian principle are being scorned and persecuted because they will not worship the god of nationalism. We live in an age when it is almost heresy to affirm the brotherhood of man. And so the new god marches on.

---

6. Acts 17:28. King quotes from Isaac Watts's hymn "O God, Our Help in Ages Past" (1719).

7. Fosdick, "Christianity's Supreme Rival," in *The Hope of the World* (New York: Harper & Brothers, 1933), p. 159: "Were there time, one might trace the history of this dogma, unravel the strands that, woven together, have produced it. In its present form it is a modern phenomenon developing from the eighteenth century on, but that it is now dominant in the world is clear." King annotated a copy of *The Hope of the World* and kept it in his personal library.

8. Fosdick, *The Hope of the World*, p. 158: "First, that each nation is a sovereign unit acknowledging no control save its own independent will."

9. Republican U.S. senator Joseph R. McCarthy (1908–1957), a noted exponent of Cold War anti-communism, accused the Truman administration and the military of harboring communists. His Republican Senate colleague William Ezra Jenner (1908–1985) supported McCarthy's early efforts. The America First Committee, founded in 1940, was an influential isolationist group that disbanded four days after the 7 December 1941 bombing of Pearl Harbor.

Yet, we all know of the great tragedies that have resulted from the worship of this false god of nationalism. More than anything else nationalism makes for war. And so long as this dogma obtains, men and nations will be plunged into the meshes of war. War, that dread force that leaves men physically handicapped and psychologically upset. War, that leaves our nations with orphans and widows. War, that piles our national debts higher than mountains of gold. War, that causes our moral standards to disintegrate. Such is the tragic consequence of nationalism.

If we are to avoid the drudgery of war; if we are to avoid being plunged across the abyss of atomic destruction, we must transcend the narrow confines of nationalism. Nationalism must give way to internationalism. This does not mean that we must not love our native lands. No other nation can mean to us what our nation means. Here are the roots of our heritage.[10] So it is not the total concept of nationalism that I am condeming; it is nationalism perverted into chauvinism and isolationism that I am condemning. One cannot worship this false god of nationalism and the God of christianity at the same time. The two are incompatible and all the dialectics of the logicians cannot make them exist together. We must choose whom we will serve.[11] Will we continue to serve the false god that places absolute national sovereignty first or will we serve the God in whom there is no east nor west?[12] Will we continue to serve the false god of imperialistic greed or will we serve the God who makes love the key which unlocks the door of peace and security. Will we continue to serve the false god of racial prejudice or will we serve the God who made of one blood all men to dwell upon the face of the earth.[13]

Today we need prophetic voices willing to cry out against the false god of nationalism. I realize that such a venture might bring about the possibility of being called many undesirable names. But speak we must if we are to acknowledge the sovereignty. {of God.} Against the claims of the false god nationalism we must affirm the supremacy of the eternal God of the universe, the Father of all mankind. This is the God we must worship if we are to sail through the tempestuous seas of confusion to the harbor of peace.

Preached July 12, 1953

TAD. CSKC: Sermon file, folder 18, "False Gods We Worship."

"The False God of Money"

[Atlanta, Ga.]

For the last two Sundays we have given a series of messages on the false gods we worship. This afternoon we conclude this series with a discussion of the false god of

---

10. Fosdick, *The Hope of the World,* p. 157: "No other nation can mean to us what our nation means. Here are the roots of our heritage."

11. Joshua 24:15.

12. King evokes John Oxenham's hymn "In Christ There Is No East or West" (1908).

13. Acts 17:26.

money. I consciously reserved this discussion for the last because the worship of the false god of money has had a much longer history and at many points is far more prevalent than the worship of other false gods. Every age has had those individuals who falsely elevated the economic means by which they lived to the status of ends for which they lived.

We have been attempting to stress throughout this series that a man's God is not his theory about God, picked up on the surface of his mind because he happens to live in the twentieth century, but a man's real God is that to which he gives his ultimate devotion, that unifying loyalty which draws his life together and gives it centrality and singleness of aim.

As soon as the matter is so stated, it becomes clear that millions today have made a god of money. Daily within our lives, altars smoke with sacrifices to this idol god. We attribute to the almighty dollar an omnipotence equal to that of the eternal God of the universe. We are always on the verge of rewriting the Scriptures to read, "Seek ye first money and its power and all these other things will be added unto you," or "Money is my light and my salvation, what shall I fear."[14]

The temptation to worship this money god is one that faces us all. To resist it we need to take high ground. This god of money is forever standing before us saying, "Worship me, I'll be your god. I'll teach you how to get rich quick; I'll teach you the shrewd methods of exploitation; I'll show you how to get a cadillac car or a Buick convertible with little effort. Just worship me." Oh how many have responded to the call of this god of money. Millions today are dutifully worshipping at the shrine of the god of money.

We do not have to look very far to see the tragic consequences which develop when men worship the almighty dollar. First it causes men to be more concerned about making a living than making a life. This is the danger forever threatening our capitalistic economy which places so much emphasis on the profit motive under more or less competitive conditions. There is the danger in such a system that men will become so involved in the money getting process that they will unconsciously forget to pursue those great eternal values which make life worth living. When men arrive at the point of making money a God they become more concerned with what they can get out of society than with what they can give to society in terms of service. How many individuals do we find entering important professions more concerned about the money they can make than the service they can render? How many young people do we find entering colleges and universities more concerned with gaining methods and techniques for making money than gaining methods and techniques for living a worth while life? When men bow down and worship at the shrine of money they are being deprived of their most precious endowment—the possibility of living life in its fullness and its endless beauty.

Another tragic attitude which the worship of money leads to is that of selfishness. The individual who really worships money will seek to get it at any cost. It might come through exploitation, cheating, or even robbery; the how is unimportant. The aim is to get rich. The person who accepts this philosophy has no concern for the

14. King parodies Matthew 6:33 and Psalm 27:1.

welfare of others. Other people become mere depersonalized means by which he exploits his economic ends.

A third tragedy that results from the deification of money is that it causes men to surrender their ideals. Who can doubt that the mad desire of gaining money and the fear of losing it are our chief breeders of moral cowardice and corruption. When men worship money they will compromise with honour and principle, keep silent when they should speakout, and engage in sharp practices that are morally degrading and socially pernicious; for money, mothers will constrain their daughters into loveless marriages; for money, public officials will sanction crime; for money, men will live their lives in the deep valleys of racketeering and gambling; for money, there are those who will sell their bodies and corrupt their souls. What will men not do for money when it becomes an object of worship? "The love of money," as Paul said to Timothy, "is the root of all evil."[15]

Doubtless some one has been saying, but are you minimizing the importance of money? Are you saying that we must not pursue economic goals? To which I would answer, of course not. No one can really minimize the importance of money. Even if he minimizes money in theory, he cannot do it in fact, for it is necessary for survival itself. Without it men are deprived not only of luxuries, but also of necessities. So it would be sheer nonsense to attempt to minimize the importance of money. It is not the possession of money that I am condemning; rather it is the inordinate worship of it that I am condemning. Money in its proper place is a worthwhile and necessary instrument for a well rounded life; but when it is projected to the status of a god it becomes a power that corrupts and an instrument of exploitation. Man is more than a dog to be satisfied with a few economic bones. Man is a child of God born to have communion with that which transcends the material. Man cannot live by bread alone.[16]

So long as we worship this false god of money, we will not be true worshippers of the One eternal God. Would today there were another Elijah to summons the peoples of the earth to meet him on the crest of some Mount Carmel, confronting them there with the choice between their baals and the true God. For still that ancient word might well ring across this modern world: "How long go ye limping between two sides? If the Lord be God, follow Him; but if Baal, then follow him."[17] So today man does stand between the god of money and the eternal God of the universe. Choose which ye will serve.[18] Will you serve the transitory god of money which is here today and gone tomorrow or will you serve the eternal God of the universe who is the same yesterday, today and forever.[19] Will you serve the god who is with us only in moments of prosperity or will you serve the God who walks with us through the valley of the shadow of death and causes us to fear no evil.[20] Will you

---

15. 1 Timothy 6:10.
16. This phrase is found in both the Hebrew Bible and New Testament; for example, see Deuteronomy 8:3 and Matthew 4:4.
17. 1 Kings 18:21.
18. Joshua 24:15.
19. Hebrews 13:8.
20. Psalm 23:4.

serve the god whose power is limited to stacking up stocks and bonds or will you serve the God whose creative power stacked up the gigantic mountains as if to kiss the skies and set forth the stars to bedect the heavens like swinging lanterns of eternity. Choose ye this day whom ye shall serve, the god of money or the eternal God of the universe.

Preached July 19, 1953.

TD. CSKC: Sermon file, folder 18, "False Gods We Worship."

"Radio Sermons"

[*26 July–6 September 1953*]
[*Atlanta, Ga.*]

King may have prepared this handwritten list of sermon titles as he planned for upcoming radio broadcasts on Atlanta station WERD.[1]

✓Accepting Responsibility for Your Action[2]—	July 26
God's Kingdom First[3]—	August 2
The Prevalence of Practical Atheism—	Aug 23
What Is Man[4]—	Sept 6
A Half Baked Civilization—	Aug 9
The Challenge of the Book of Jonah[5]—	Aug 16
The Peril of Conformity[6]—	August 30
{of many or the eternal God of the universe}[7]	

AD.CSKC: Sermon file, folder 11, "Our God Is Able."

---

1. King took Keighton's course The Minister's Use of Radio during his final year at Crozer.

2. King, "Accepting Responsibility for Your Actions," 26 July 1953, pp. 139–142 in this volume.

3. King retitled this sermon "First Things First" (2 August 1953, pp. 143–146 in this volume).

4. For versions of this sermon, see King, "What Is Man?" 11 July 1954 and "The Christian Doctrine of Man," Sermon Delivered at the Detroit Council of Churches' Noon Lenten Services, 12 March 1958, pp. 174–179 and 328–338 in this volume, respectively.

5. For an outline of this sermon, see King, "The Challenge of the Book of Jonah," 1951–1955, in *Papers* 2:325–326.

6. King was influenced by Eugene Austin's homily "The Peril of Conformity" and later developed a sermon titled "Transformed Nonconformist" (see note 18 to King, Draft of Chapter II, "Transformed Nonconformist," *Strength to Love*, July 1962–March 1963, p. 470 in this volume).

7. King wrote this phrase on the verso of the document.

"Prayers"

[*5 July–6 September 1953*]
Atlanta, Ga.

*King begins this collection of prayers with a radio announcement regarding services
and ministries at Ebenezer, indicating he prepared them for radio broadcast.[1] Most of
these handwritten prayers would serve the function of confession or repentance in a
worship service.*

We are very happy to greet you again from the Eb baptist Church. We are hoping
that through this broadcast you are gaining something that is spiritually uplifting.
you are alway invited to worship with us here at Ebenezer. Our doors are opened to
peoples of all races, all nationalities and all religious backgrounds. Our morning
worship begins at 11:00 A.M. and our evening worship begins at 7:30 P.M. Next
Sunday I will fill the pulpit both morning and evening. at the evening worship hour
we will observe the Lord's Supper Always feel free to worship at Ebenezer
1. Bible School.
2. We have opened a council clinic at Ebenezer Church for the benefit of the members of Eb in particular and the people of the community in general. The conselors
are Mrs Phoely Burney Professor William Nix and the Pastor.[2] The hour are from
5:00 to 8:00 on Mon Wed and Thurs at the A. D. Wh center.[3] Feel free to consul this
competant staff concening your problem and difficulties.

O thou Eternal God, out of whose absolute power and infinite intelligence the
whole universe has come into being. We humbly confess that we have not loved thee
with our hearts, souls and minds and we have not loved our neighbors as Christ
loved us.[4] We have all too often lived by our own selfish impulses rather than by the
life of sacrificial love as revealed by Christ. We often give in order to receive, we love
our friends and hate our enemies, we go the first mile but dare not travel the second,
we forgive but dare not forget.[5] And so as we look within ourselves we are confronted with the appalling fact that the history of our lives is the history of an eternal revolt against thee. But thou, O God, have mercy upon us. Forgive us for what

---

1. King's radio broadcasts from Ebenezer began on 5 July and ended on 6 September 1953
("Ebenezer Begins WERD Broadcast Sunday Morning" and "King Jr. to End Summer Series of Sermons;
Ebenezer," *Atlanta Daily World*, 4 July and 5 September 1953).

2. William M. Nix was a professor and dean of men at Morehouse College at this time. Phoebe Burney was dean of women at Atlanta's Clark College from 1943 until 1958 and served as a reference on
King's behalf when he applied to Crozer (Phoebe Burney to Charles E. Batten, 9 March 1948, in *Papers*
1:154).

3. King refers to the A. D. Williams Center, named for King's maternal grandfather and former
Ebenezer pastor. During Ebenezer's August 1953 publicity campaign, an announcement for this clinic
appeared weekly in the *Atlanta Daily World*.

4. Cf. Matthew 22:37.

5. Cf. Matthew 5:41–43.

we could have been but failed to be. Give us the intelligence to know thy will. Give us the courage to do thy will. Give us the devotion to love thy will. In the name and spirit of Jesus we pray. Amen.

O God our eternal Father, we praise thee for gifts of mind with which thou hast endowed us. We are able to rise out of the half-realities of the sense world to a world of ideal beauty and eternal truth. Teach us, we pray Thee, how to use this great gift of reason and imagination so that it shall not be a curse but a blessing. Grant us visions that shall lift us [*strikeout illegible*] from worldliness and sin into the light of thine own holy presence. Through Jesus Christ we pray. Amen.

Most Gracious and all wise God; Before whose face the generations rise and fall; Thou in whom we live, and move, and have our being.[6] We thank thee [*for?*] all of thy good and gracious gifts, for life and for health; for food and for raiment; for the beauties of nature and the love of human nature. We come before thee painfully aware of our inadaqucis and shortcomigs. We realize that we stand surrounded with the mountains of love and we deliberately dwell in the valley of hate. We stand amid the forces of truth and deliberately lie; We are forever offered the high road and yet we choose ~~the lo~~ to travel the low road. For these sins O God forgive. Break the spell of that which blinds our minds. Purify our hearts that we may see thee. O God in these turbulent day when fear and doubt are mounting high give us broad visions, penetrating eys, and power of endurance. Help us to work with rewed vigor for a warless world, for a better distribution of wealth, and for a brotherhood that transcends race or color. In the name and spirit of Jesus we pray. Amen.

O God, the Creator and Presever of all mankind; In whom to dwell is to find peace and security; toward whom to turn is to find life and life eternal, we humbly beseech Thee for all sorts and conditions of men; that thou wouldst be pleased to make thy ways known unto them, Thy saving health unto all nations. We also pray for Thy holy Church universal; that it may be so guided and governed by thy Spirit, that all who profess and call themselves Christians may be led into the way of truth, and hold the faith in unity of spirit, in the [*land?*] of peace, and in righteousness of life. Finally we commend to thy Fatherly goodness all those who are in any way afflicted or distressed in mind or body. Give them patience under the suffering and power of endurance This we ask in the name of Jesus. Amen.

First

Our Holy Father, we confess the weakness and sinfulness of our lives. We have often turned away from thee to seek our own desires. And often when we have done no evil, we have undertaken nothing of good, and so have been guilty of uselessness and neglect. From this sin of idleness and indifference set us free. Lead us into fruit-

---

6. Cf. Acts 17:28.

ful effort, and deliver us from profitless lives. We ask ~~this~~ in the name of Jesus. 26 July 1953
Amen.

Second

Our loving Father, from Thy hand have come all the days of the past. To Thee we look for whatever good the future holds. We are not satisfied with the world as we have found it. It is too little the kingdom of God as yet. Grant us the privilege of a part in its regeneration. ~~We wish the joy of fellowship with those sons of God who are bringing in the new day.~~ We are looking for a new earth in which dwells righteousness. It is our prayer that we may be children of light, the kind of people for whose coming and ministry the world is waiting.—Amen.

AD. CSKC: Sermon file, folder 97.

"Accepting Responsibility for Your Actions"

26 July 1953
[Atlanta, Ga.]

King most likely delivered this sermon as a radio address for Atlanta's WERD while serving as associate pastor at Ebenezer during the summer of 1953.[1] The following May, when King delivered his acceptance address at Dexter Avenue Baptist Church, he also preached a version of this sermon, explicitly emphasizing his commitment to the social gospel.[2]

One of the most common tendencies of human nature is that of placing responsibility on some external agency for sins we have commited or mistakes we have made. We are forever attempting to find some scapegoat on which we cast responsibility for our actions. Herein lies the tragic misuse of much of our modern psychology, particularly what is known as depth psychology or psychoanalysis. This school of thought affirms that many of our conscious actions are due to unconscious motives. Now there is a kernal of truth in this theory and we owe a great debt to Sigmund Freud for opening to us the uncharted regions of the sub conscious. But the tragedy lies in the fact that many modern men have used this theory as an attractive defense mechanism. How easy it was to say that unconscious emotions and repressed sex drives were responsible for our actions rather than plain everyday sin.

---

1. At the end of this document, King wrote "Preached July 26, 1953," the date he assigned to this title in his list of his radio sermons for the summer of 1953 (King, "Radio Sermons" 26 July–6 September 1953, p. 136 in this volume). King's announced sermon on 28 June 1953 was "Accepting Responsibility for Your Actions" ("Rev. King Jr. Slated at Ebenezer Sunday," *Atlanta Daily World*, 27 June 1953).

2. King wrote "Preached at Dexter, May 2, 1954" at the end of this document and also noted, "ARYA Preached at Dexter May 2, 1954" on the inside of the file folder containing this document (King, Acceptance Address at Dexter Avenue Baptist Church, 2 May 1954, pp. 166–167 in this volume). 139

The word sin was gradually eliminated from the modern vocabulary and there emerged in its place a series of bombastic psychological phrases such as phabias, complexes, and inhibitions. And so modern man was convinced that psychology had given him explanations which relieved him of any responsibility for his actions.

This tendency to thrust responsibility for our actions on some eternal agency is by no means a new one. The Genesis writers found it present in the very beginning of history. Remember the story of Adam and Eve in the Garden of Eden? God had placed Adam and Eve in the garden to dress it. They were given liberty to make use of everything in the garden with the exception of one thing: "They were not to eat of the tree of good and evil." Very soon a serpent appeared on the scene and said: "Hath God said, ye shall not eat of every tree of the garden?" And Eve answered: "We may eat of the fruit of the trees of the garden, but of the tree of good and evil God has commanded that we not eat or touch lest we die." And the nserpent answered "Ye shall not surely die, for God doth know that in the day ye eat thereof then your eyes shall be opened, and ye shall be as gods, knowing good and evil." After listening to these cogent words by the subtle serpent, Eve yielded to the temptation and very soon Adam and Eve were found eating from the tree that God had forbidden them to touch. When God came back on the scene to ascertain why this sin had been committed, he found each shifting responsibility on some external agency. Adam's answer was that the woman caused him to eat of the tree. Eve claimed that the serpent caused her to eat of the tree.[3] Neither Adam nor Eve stopped to realize that although they were tempted by external agencies, they were, in the final analysis, responsible for yielding to the temptation. Ultimately individual responsibility lies not in the external situation but in the internal response.

We are all familiar with the most common agencies on which we project responsibility for our actions. First we turn to environment. How easy it is for one to affirm that one's whole personality make-up and indeed one's very destiny itself is determined by one's environment. Here is a man about forty now whose life has been given in riotous living. Now as he looks back over these wasted years his comment is: "I would have been if I had been {in} a rich family with prestige and fame or if I had been in a more progressive community. It is my environment that has corrupted me." Yet such persons as this fail to realize that many individuals rise from the very lowest of environments to be some of the most noble characters of human history. There is a Marian Anderson, born in a poverty stricken area of Phila. Pa. She could have very easily given up in despair and cried out that she was born in the wrong environment. But she was not one to make excuses. This same Marian Anderson rose from a poverty stricken environment to be one of the world's greatest contraltoes, so that a Toscanni can say that a voice like this comes only once in a century and a Seballius of Finland can say, "My roof is too low for such a voice."[4] There is a Roland Hayes, born on the red hills of Gordon County Georgia under

---

3. Cf. Genesis 2:15–17, 3:1–13.

4. Arturo Toscanini (1867–1957), an internationally recognized conductor, and Finnish composer Jean Sibelius (1865–1957) made these comments on Anderson's singing during her concert tours of Europe in the 1930s (Anderson, *My Lord, What a Morning* [New York: Viking Press, 1956], pp. 149, 158). King owned Anderson's autobiography and kept it in his personal library.

the most crippling restrictions. At a very early age he found himself working in an iron foundry of Chatanooga Tenn. But from these red hills of Georgia, he rose to the palace of Queen Mother of Spain. From this iron foundry in Chatanooga, Tenn., he rose to the palace of King George the 5th.[5] There was an Abraham Lincoln, born in poverty and insecurity, later working as a Kentucky rail splitter. Yet this same Abraham Lincoln rose from a Kentucky rail splitter to be one of the greatest characters in the great drama of history. These are but few of the many examples that could be used to refute the claim that one is completely determined by his environment. Those who hold such a position fail to see that many fine and noble persons stem from bad environments and many very bad and corrupt persons stem from comfortable and desirable environments.

Another external agency on which we readily cast responsibility for our actions is heredity. There are those who would affirm that one is completely determined by heredity. How easy it is to say, "I would have been better if I had had better hereditary circumstances."

Here again those who project total responsibility for their actions on hereditary circumstances fail to see that numerous individuals rise above such circumstances. There is a John Bunyan, deprived of his physical sight, and yet he wrote a <u>Pilgrim's Progress</u> that generations will cherish so long as the cords of memory shall lengthen.[6] There is a Franklin D. Roosevelt, inflicted with infantile paralysis and yet he rises up to leave such an imprint in the sands of our nations history, that future history books will be incomplete without his name. There is a Hellen Keller, burdened with blindness and deafness, and she rises up to live such a sublime and noble life that millions have come to admire her as one of the choicest fruits on yhe tree of history.[7] These are but few of those who have proved that man is not finally caught in the cluches of heredity. He has within himself the power to transcend the disadvantages of bad hereditary conditions. As a world famous psychologist has said: "After going through the experimental and clinical literature, the thoughtful reader will conclude that the effects of personality upon glands are more impressive and easier to illustrate than are the effects of the glands upon personality."[8]

I must hasten to say that the above assertions do not mean to imply that heredity and environment are not important. I happen to be a firm believer in what is called the "social gospel." Indeed, no one can intelligently care for personal life without caring about genetics and social reform. Moreover, the above assertions do not mean to imply that our actions are not somewhat conditioned by external influences. When one considers the cosmic setting of our lives, our absolute dependence on the maintenance of the earth's heat and moisture, the determining effect on each individual of the race's biological evolution, the momentous consequences of

---

5. King refers to tenor Roland Hayes's successful singing tour of Europe.

6. John Bunyan (1628–1688) was an English preacher and Christian writer who, in 1678, published *Pilgrim's Progress,* an allegory of the Christian path to salvation.

7. Helen Keller (1880–1968).

8. Fosdick included this quotation in his sermon "Shouldering Responsibility for Ourselves," in *On Being a Real Person* (New York: Harper & Brothers, 1943), p. 7. King drew a line next to it in his copy of *On Being a Real Person* and wrote, "quote." Fosdick attributed the quotation to Starke R. Hathaway's *Physiological Psychology* (New York: D. Appleton-Century Co., 1942), p. 203.

heredity, and the conditioning effect of environment, one cannot lightly talk about being the master of one's fate and the captain of one's soul.[9] Far from saying that environment and heredity have no importance in human personality, what I am really saying is that there is another factor which is the ultimate determining factor (<u>viz</u>) personal response. And herein lies our responsibility. We are not responsible for the environment we are born in, neither are we responsible for our hereditary circumstances. But there is a third factor for which we are responsible namely, the personal response which we make to these circumstances.

And so the challenge which confronts all of us is to respond to our circumstances with strength and courage rather than with weakness and despair. Who in all history can serve as a better example for us at this point than our Lord and Master, Jesus Christ? There was nothing so comfortable and advantageous about His environmental and hereditary circumstances. He was born in a stable and raised on a carpenter's bench. His mother and father were not menbers of the upper crust of Jewish society. They did not enjoy the power of the aristocratic Pharisee or the prestige of the cosmopolitan Saducee. Jesus was born in plain unpretentious circumstances. But Jesus had within himself a power of personal response which was destined to transform his circumstances. This same Jesus who was born in an ox stable, rose up to be the strongest and tallest oak in the great forest of history. This same Jesus, rose from a carpenter's bench to give impetus to a movement which has grown from a group of 12 men to more than 700,000,000 today. This same Jesus split history into A.D. and B.C. This same Jesus so convinced men that His message is eternal and universal that they have triumphantly sung

> Jesus shall reign where ere the sun
> Does his successive journeys run;
> His kingdom spread from shore to shore,
> Till moons shall wax and wane no more.[10]

Not environment; not heredity; but personal response is the final determining factor in our lives. And herein lies our area of responsibility.[11]

Preached July 26, 1953

{Preached at Dexter, May 2, 1954}

TAD. CSKC: Sermon file, folder 66, "Accepting Responsibility for Your Actions" / "Faith In Man."

---

9. King paraphrases William E. Henley's 1875 poem "Invictus": "It matters not how strait the gate / How charged with punishments the scroll / I am the master of my fate: / I am the captain of my soul."

10. King quotes from Isaac Watts's hymn "Jesus Shall Reign Where'er the Sun" (1719).

11. Fosdick, *On Being a Real Person*, p. 4: "Three factors enter into the building of personality: heredity, environment, and personal response." Next to these words, King wrote "quote (environment)" in his copy of Fosdick's book. He also underlined the words "personality: heredity, environment and personal response."

2 August 1953
[*Atlanta, Ga.*]

In this typed manuscript prepared as a radio sermon and later used at Dexter, King elaborates upon Harry Emerson Fosdick's sermon "Righteousness First."[1] King comments on domestic and international affairs, including American race relations and the recent conflict in Korea: "So long as America places 'white supremacy' first we will never have peace. Indeed the deep rumbling of discontent in our world today on the part of the masses is [actually] a revolt against the imperialism, economic exploitation, and colonialism that has been perpetuated by western civilization for all these many years." He maintains that "only through placing love, mercy, and justice first can we have peace."

This mystery called life is so constructed that there are certain material goods that man has to have. The Sociologists and Psychologist tell us that there are certain basic drives inherent in the very nature of man which must inevitably be satisfied. Jesus himself realized this.[2] Throughout the Gospels of Jesus is pictured as wanting men to have physical well-being, economic security, food, clothing and health. There are some who are so dipped and dyed in extreme spirituality that they would have us believe that Jesus placed no emphasis on these earthly needs. They are the people who are so absorbed in a futute good "over yonder" that they are content with the present evils over here. The Communist are right in calling this type of religion the opiate of the people.[3] Far from saying that the basic necessities of life are not important, what Jesus really says is this: "your heavenly Father knoweth that ye have need of all these things. But seek ye first the kingdom of God, and his righteousness, and all thses things shall be added unto you."[4]

Here we human beings are wanting the good things of life. We are saying. I want what I want when I want it; and Jesus is saying you ought to have they. But they will never come until you fulfill a prior condition: righteous first. Unless first things are placed first then and only then will these things be added unto you.[5]

So this afternoon I will speak to you about two things we want that we will never get unless we follow the path that was set forth by Jesus: righteousness first.

---

1. King, "Radio Sermons," 26 July–6 September 1953, p. 136 in this volume; Fosdick, *A Great Time to Be Alive* (New York: Harper & Brothers, 1944), pp. 21–30. King kept a copy of this book in his personal library and annotated it.

2. In another version of this sermon that King titled "God's Kingdom First," he mentioned specific human drives: food and drink, intellectual development, security, sexuality, and love ("God's Kingdom First," 2 August 1953).

3. Karl Marx, "Contribution to the Critique of Hegel's *Philosophy of Right:* Introduction" (1844).

4. Matthew 6:32–33.

5. Fosdick, *A Great Time to Be Alive*, p. 22: "Here we human beings are, wanting the good things of life and trying to get them by anxiously pouncing on them like leopards, saying, I want what I want when I want it; and Jesus says, You ought to want such things but you will never enduringly get them until you fulfill a prior condition: righteousness first; then, and only then, shall these things be added unto you."

So let us turn first to the domestic scene. We all want a happy marriage life and happy family life. Throughout our nation there is the unrelating cry for less divorces. People have come to see that divorces rarely ever bring about the happiness and emotional freedom expected of them. People have come to see that divorces make for maladjustment within men and women. They have come to see that divorces cause broken homes, and often lead perfectly normal children into juvenile delinquency. But why is it that the family seems to be disintegrating like a stack of cards. At least one reason is that newly-weds have failed to see that righteousness must be placed first. in our age of distarted values we place such things as economic security and physical attraction first, failing to see that money and physical attraction alone cannot make a marriage permanently successful.

If some one would ask most of us what we expect out of marriage, we would probably answer, security and peace, happy children and beautiful home life that grows with the years. The msater would say to us, "your heavenly Father knoweth that ye have need of all these things" But if you do not place righteousness first what a wreckage can come to all of these. My friends, the foundation of any great home life is built upon righteousness.. Romance can start a home but romance alone cannot sustain a home.[6] Righteousness must be placed first. One of the wisest statements ever made is that solemn assertion in the Bible, "except the Lord build the house they labor in vain that build it."[7] It simply states the ~~irrevbcalle~~ irrevocable fact that you cannot build a successful marriage upon any other basis than the principles of love, beauty, natural respect and faith. Unless the house of marriage is built upon the rock of righteousness the storms and winds of disagreement will blow it apart.

Now let us turn for the moment to our great desire in the National and International scene. For one thing we want <u>peace</u>. Today the cry that is ringing in the ears of the peoples of the world is peace, peace, peace. I thinkf that the peoples of the world have come to realize that there are no gains from rwar. They realize that was sends men home physically handicapped and psychologically upset. They realize that war piles up a national debt higher than a mountain of gold and fills our nations with orphans and widows. So everybody is crying for peace. Yet we have no peace. Even the temporary let us in Korea is for from an assurance of peace. A Truce is not a peace.[8] And there is the danger that the flames of war might arise at any time to redden the skies of our dark and dreary world. Why is it that we have no peace in the world today? It is because we have failed to follow the principles of that gentle Prince of Peace who died on a Roman cross atop a Judean hill centuries ago.. In other words we have failed to place righteousness first. So long as we place our selfish economic gains first we will never have peace. So long as the nations of the

---

6. Fosdick, *A Great Time to Be Alive*, p. 23: "The things they want, they ought to want—security and peace, happy children, and lovely memories accumulating with the years. The Master would say to them again, 'Your heavenly Father knoweth that ye have need of all these things.' But what wreckage can come to homes that forget the rest of what he said! The ultimate foundations of a great home are ethical. Romance can start a home but romance alone cannot sustain one—only fidelity can maintain a fine family."

7. Psalm 127:1.

8. The Korean conflict effectively ended with the signing of an armistice agreement by the United Nations and North Korea on 27 July 1953, six days prior to the delivery of this sermon.

world are contesting to see which can be the most impeaialistic we will nver have peace. So long as America places "white supremacy" first we will never have peace. Indeed the deep rumbling of discontent in our world today on the part of the masses is acturlly a revolt against the imperialism, economic exploitation, and colonialism that has been perpetuated by western civilization for all these many years. All of these injustices must be eliminated. if we are to have peace. When will a stupid world rise up to see that a "get tough" ploicy cannot bring peace; universal military training cannot bring peace; the threat of the atomic bomb cannot bring peace; but only through placing love, mercy, and justice first can we have peace.

Our civilization may possess all knowledge of power. We may know all about atomic energy and radar. We may be able to use our minds to probe into the storehouse of nature. We may know all about the science of genetics and psyco-physical changes within human nature. All of these are fine, but if we do not place righteousness first these very things which are capable of being used constructively will be used destructively.[9]

My friends if you would look through the long corridors of human history you will see that major tragedies that have come to nations and individuals have come chiefly because they failed to place rightousness first. The historic Arnold Toybee tells us that some twenty two civilizations have risen upon the face of the earth all but about seven have ended in destruction.[10] Close observation will reveal that most of these civilizations fell because they did not place righteousness first. The The Roman Empire decided to place her military power first. For years she boasted of her superior roads, her great economic system, and her powerful political machinery. But in the fifth centure A.D., Alaric, with his hordes of Visigoths, swept across Italy and finally captured Rome.[11] And so the mistress of the world which had boasted so much of its militay power had fallen before the barbarians. She failed to place righteousness first. Moussalini decided to place his Fascistic government first, but today Italy is defeated and Musolini dead, killed by the very people whom he once ruled. Hitler placed Germandy and the idea of the master race first. He boasted that Germany would one day rule the world. As the German armies marched through many of the smaller nations of Europe the bands played and the crowds cheered in honor of Hitler. But today this same Germany and this same Hitler have been defeated and the German nations is jut now through a state of reconstruction. They failed to place righteousness first. The British empire placed

9. In "God's Kingdom First," King reversed the order of the sermon, first considering the international scene and then highlighting the family. In his transition between the two sections, King wrote: "We cannot stop with the obligation of the nation as a whole, but we must think of the individuals that make up the nation. If the nation and the world ever place righteousness first it will be because enough individuals have done it. We can never have peace so long as the minds of men are at war. The greatest peace table is not at Lake Success, neither will it be found massive assemblies in Paris or Moscow. The greatest peace table in the world is the breakfast table. Until we place righteousness first in our individual lives, our families, and our communities we will never have peace" (King, 2 August 1953).

10. British historian Arnold Toynbee (1889–1975) analyzed the development and disintegration of world civilizations throughout history, most fully explored in his twelve-volume work, *A Study of History* (London: Oxford University Press, 1934–1961).

11. Alaric (ca. 370–410 CE), king of the Visigoths, led his troops to capture Rome in 410 CE.

empirialism first. For years she stood as an island no larger thatn the State of Georgia, ruling almost a third of the world. She boasted that "the sun never sets on her empire". But today the British empire with all of her massive power is diminishing to such a state that we can almost say, "the sun never rises on her empire". America is placing economic power first. We are boasting that we are the richest nation in the world and that we possess the power of the atom bomb. But if we do not place something deeper than this first we to will be plunged across the abyss of destruction.

The voice of Christ is sounding yet. Ah, Christ, you have been saying it a long time. God help us as individuals and as a world to hear it now before it is to late: "Seek ye first the kingdom of God and his righteousness and all these other things shall be added unto you."

Preached 8–2–53
{Preached at Dexter, Third Sunday Sept. 19, 1954}

TAD. CSKC: Sermon file, folder 112, "First Things First."

"Communism's Challenge to Christianity"

9 August 1953
[*Atlanta, Ga.*]

King wrestles with the relationship between communism and Christianity, arguing that they are ultimately incompatible.[1] *Influenced by Riverside Church pastor Robert J. McCracken, he encourages the Ebenezer congregation to learn from communism, noting "It should challenge us first to be more concerned about social justice."*

I hope that all of you will listen to me very attentively this afternoon as I humbly attempt to speak to you about one of the most important issues of our day. There are at least two reasons why I as a Christian Minister feel obligated to talk to you about Communism.

The first has to do with the wide spread influence of Communism. It is believed in by more than 200,000,000 people covering one fifth of the earth's surface. Multitudes have embraced it as the most coherent philosophy and the greatest single emotional drive they know.

A second reason why the Christina minister should speak about it is that

---

1. King filed this typed version and a handwritten outline of this sermon in the same file folder (King, "Communism's Challenge to Christianity," Sermon outline, 9 August 1953). He also preached a sermon with this title at Ebenezer on 10 August 1952 ("'Communism's Challenge to Christianity,' King Jr's Topic, Ebenezer," *Atlanta Daily World,* 9 August 1952). King later developed this theme in "Can a Christian Be a Communist?" Sermon Delivered at Ebenezer Baptist Church (30 September 1962, pp. 445–454 in this volume, and "How Should a Christian View Communism?" in *Strength to Love,* pp. 93–100).

Communism is the only serious rival to Christianity.[2] Other historic world religions such as Judaism, Mohammedanism, Buddhism, Hinduism, may be listed as possible alternatives to Christianity, but for Christianity's greatest rival we must look elsewhere. Certainly no one in touch with the realities of the contemporary situation can deny that in the crisis confronting civilization Christianity's most formidable competitor and only serious rival is communism.

Let us begin by stating that communism and Christianity are at the bottom incompatible. One cannot be a true Christian and a true Communist simultaneously. How then is Communism irreconcilable with Christianity.

In the first place it leaves out God and Christ. It is avowedly secularistic and materialistic.[3] It regards religion phychologically as mere wishfull thinking, intellectually as the product of fear and ignorance, and historically as serving the ends of exploiters. Because of public opinion authorities have had to modify some of their anti-religious doctrines, but the official policy of the communistic party is still atheistic.[4]

In the second place the methods of communism are diametrically opposed to Christianity. Since for the Communist there is no Divine government, no absolute moral order, there are no fixed, immutalbe principles. Force, violence, murder, and lying are all justifiable means to the millennial end. Said Lenin, "we must be ready to employ tricking, deceit, and lawbreaking, withholding and concealing truth."[5] That the followers of Lenin have been willing to act upon his instructions is a matter of history.

In the third place, the end of communism is the state. I shall qualify this by saying that the state in Communist theory is a tempory reality which is to be eliminated when the classless society emergies. But it is true that the state is the end while it lasts. Man becomes only a means to that end. And if any man's so called rights or liberties stand in the way of that end, they are simply swept aside. His liberties of press or pulpit expression, his freedom to vote, his freedom to listen to what news he likes or to choose his books and even his friendships are all restricted. Man has to be a servant, dutiful and submissive, of the State, and the state is omnipotent and supreme.

Now there can be no doubt that all of this is the negation not only of the

---

2. McCracken, "What Should Be the Christian Attitude to Communism," in *Questions People Ask,* p. 164: "No one in touch with the realities of the contemporary situation will deny that in the crisis confronting civilization Christianity's most formidable competitor and only serious rival is Communism."

3. Morehouse professor and Ebenezer member Melvin Watson attended the 1952 service where King first preached this sermon and commented in a 14 August letter to King: "In discussing Communist theory in the early part of the sermon it was not clear to me whether you understood Communist materialism. The Communist theorists were definitely not materialists after the fashion of the Greek atomists. Marx's position was that the culture, thoughts, in fact, the whole life of man is conditioned (seems to use the word, determine, at times by the means of production by his relationship to the instruments necessary to the making of a living. This variety of materialism is very difficult to refute and is a very disturbing phenomenon. Whether a man stands in relation to the means of production as an owner or a mere user does make a difference in the way he thinks, acts, etc. It is exceedingly difficult to deny this and make it stick!" (*Papers* 2:156–157).

4. McCracken, *Questions People Ask,* p. 168: "Because it is avowedly secularistic and materialistic."

5. McCracken, *Questions People Ask,* pp. 168–169: "'We must be ready,' wrote Lenin, 'to employ trickery, deceit, lawbreaking, withholding and concealing truth.'"

Christian belief in God and the moral order that he has established, but also of the Christian estimate of man. I am cognizant of the fact that the record of the Christian Church has been smeared in the past by infamous persecutions and the irremovable strain of the inquisition, but even so Christianity at its best has never let go the ideal that man is an end because he is a child of God, and that the end of all life is the glory of God. The Christian ethic would affirm that destructive means can never justify constructive ends, because in the final analysis the end is pre-existant in the mean.

So let us not fool ourselves these two systems of thought are too contradictory to be reconciled. They represent diametrically opposed ways of looking at the world. and transforming the world. We must try to understand Communism, but never can we accept it and be true Christians.

Yet we must realize that there is something in Communism which challenges us all. It was the late Archbishop of Cantebury, William Temple that referred to Communism as a Christian hersy. By this he meant that Communism had laid hold on certain truths which are essential part of the Christian view of things, but that it had bound up with them concepts and practices which no Christian can ever accept or profess.[6] In other words, although Communism can never be accepted by a Christian, it emphasizes many essential truths that must forever challenge us as Christians. Indeed, it may be that Communism is a necessary corrective for a Christianity that has been all to passive and a democracy that has been all to inert.

It should challenge us first to be more concerned about social justice. However much is wrong with Communism we must admit that it arose as a protest against the hardships of the underpriviledged. The Communist Manifesta which was published in 1847 by Marx and Engels emphasizes throughout how the middle class has exploited the lower class. Communism emphasizes a classless society. Along with this goes a strong attempt to eliminate racial prejudice. Communism seeks to transcend the superficialities of race and color, and you are able to join the Communist party whatever the color of your skin or the quality of the blood in your veins.[7] {Marx was a Jew & later Christian}

With this passionate concern for social justice Christians are bound to be in

---

6. McCracken, *Questions People Ask*, pp. 165–166: "William Temple, the late Archbishop of Canterbury, was a distinguished philosopher and a man of affairs. He was a great Christian as well as a great churchman. From all over Christendom men looked to him for light and leading. He once described Communism as a 'Christian heresy.' What did he mean by that? He meant that Communism had laid hold on certain truths which are an essential part of the Christian scheme of things and which every Christian should acknowledge and profess, but that it had bound up with them concepts and practices which no Christian can ever acknowledge or profess."

7. Watson remarked, "Stalin would certainly not make the question of <u>race</u> a sub-point as you did on Sunday. With him it is a major point." He continued, "I think there can be no doubt about it that the appeal of communism to the Eastern nations today can be traceable to a large degree to the Soviet attitude <u>toward race</u>. This is a strategic policy with Russia" (Watson to King, 14 August 1952, in *Papers* 2:157).

8. McCracken, *Questions People Ask*, p. 166: "With a passionate concern for social justice Christians are bound to be in the completest accord. It is implicit in the Christian doctrines of the Fatherhood of God, the Brotherhood of man, the infinite worth of the human soul and explicit in passage after passage of the Bible."

accord. Such concern is implicit in the Christian doctrine of the Fatherhood of God and the brotherhood of man.[8] The Christian ought always to begin with a bias in favor of a movement which protests against unfair treatment of the poor, for surely Christianity is itself such a protest. The <u>Communist Manifesta</u> might express a concern for the poor and oppressed, but it expresses no greater concern than the Manifesta of Jesus with this as its opening sentence: "The spirit of the Lord is upon me, because He hath anointed me to preach the gospel to the poor; Je hath sent me to heal the brokenhearted, to preach deliverance to the captives, and recovering of sight to the blind, to set at liberty them that are bruised, to proclaim the acceptable year of the Lord."[9] And so a passionate concern for social justice must be a concern of the Christian religion.

We must admit that we as Christians have often lagged behind at this point. Slavery could not have existed in America for more than two hundred and fifty years if the Church had not sanctioned it. Segregation and discrimination could not exist in America today without the sanction of the Church. I am ashame and appalled at the fact that Eleven O'clock on Sunday morning is the most segregated hour in Christian America.[10] How tardy we have been. The Church has to often been an institution serving to crystalize the patterns of the status quo. Who can blame Karl Marx for calling such a religion an opiati.[11] When religion becomes involved in a future good "over yonder" that it forgets the present evils "over here" it is a dry as dust religion and needs to be condemned. {We must be concerned about the gulf between [*superfluous?*] wealth and abject poverty. Marx revealed the danger of the profit motive as the sole [*basis?*]} [*remainder missing*]

Communism also challenges us to invite all Christian forces for action. Too often have we been preoccupied with debates about orders and sacraments and ritual and denominationalism while civilization is engaged in a race with catastrophe. If we are to win the world to Christ we must rise above our differences realizing that we have unity of purpose and that God is not a denominational God.

Lastly we are challenged to dedicate and devote our lives to the cause of Christ as the Communist do to Communism. We cannot accept their creed, but we must admire their zeal, and their readiness to sacrifice themselves to the very uttermost and even to lay down their lives for a cause that they believe is going to make the world a better place. I have seen communist in universities passionately attempting

---

9. Luke 4:18–19. McCracken also quoted this passage in "What Should Be the Christian Attitude to Communism" (*Questions People Ask,* pp. 166–167).

10. In a speech before the Women's Society of New York's Riverside Church, Helen Kenyon labeled eleven o'clock on Sunday morning as "the most segregated time" in the United States and maintained that interracial churches existed as "oases in a great desert" ("Worship Hour Found Time of Segregation," *New York Times,* 4 November 1952). At that time, Kenyon chaired the policy committee of the National Council of Churches' Department of United Church Women. See also Robert J. McCracken, "Discrimination—The Shame of Sunday Morning," *The Pulpit* (February 1955): 4.

11. Karl Marx, "Contribution to the Critique of Hegel's *Philosophy of Right:* Introduction" (1844). On Marx and religion, Watson commented, "When you set Marx's attitude toward religion in the context of the history of the Christian church in Russia, the conclusion you reach is likely to be very sobering and will probably not make especially good sermonizing material" (Watson to King, 14 August 1952, in *Papers* 2:157).

to win their associates to communism. How many Christian students in our universities today have ever tried to win other students to Christ? How many of you on your jobs have ever attempted to win others to Christ? Would today that the Christian fire were burning with the same intensity in the hearts of Christians as the Communist fire is burning in the hearts of Communists. We must match the evangelistic passion of the Communists. We must unreservedly commit ourselves to the cause of Christ.

It seems that I can hear a voice crying through the vista of time: "ye shall be witnesses unto me both in Jerusalem, and in Judea and in Samaria, and unto the uttermost part of the earth."[12] I can hear the same voice saying, "go out into the highways and hedges and compel men to come."[13] I can hear the same voice saying, "Go ye into all the world, and preach the gospel to every creature."[14] Who this afternoon will answer saying: "Here am I O Lord, and I unreservedly commit myself to thy cause."

Preached Aug. 9, 1953

TAD. CSKC: Sermon file, folder 10, "Communism's Challenge to Christianity."

---

12. Acts 1:8.
13. Luke 14:23.
14. Mark 16:15.

"The Dimensions of a Complete Life," Sermon at Dexter Avenue Baptist Church

[24 January 1954]
[Montgomery, Ala.]

King delivered a version of this sermon at Dexter in Montgomery, Alabama, as the congregation considered him as a candidate to be their new pastor.[1] In a letter sent prior to King's appearance, Dexter deacon and choir director Joseph T. Brooks advised

1. King's sermon title for the Dexter service was "The Three Dimensions of a Complete Life" (Mary K. Frazier, "News of Colored People," *Montgomery Examiner,* 28 January 1954). He filed this document with another handwritten draft of this sermon that contained a discussion of only two of the three dimensions referred to in the sermon ("The Three Dimensions of a Complete Life," 24 January 1954). King wrote on the folder "Preached at Dexter January 1954." This was the first sermon that Coretta Scott heard King deliver, indicating it was developed by the early part of 1952 (Coretta Scott King, *My Life with Martin Luther King, Jr.* [New York: Holt, Rinehart & Winston, 1969], p. 59). He preached a version of the sermon on 6 September 1953 at Ebenezer Baptist Church and in 1960 during a fund-raising tour of California for the Southern Christian Leadership Conference (SCLC) ("King Jr. to End Series of Summer Sermons; Ebenezer," *Atlanta Daily World,* 5 September 1953; King, "The Three Dimensions of a Complete Life," Sermon Delivered at Friendship Baptist Church, 28 February 1960, pp. 395–405 in this volume). For other versions of this sermon, see King, *The Measure of a Man*

"The Dimensions of A Complete Life"

Text "the Length and the Breadth and the Height of it are equal." Rev. xxi 16.

One day out on a lonely obscure island called Patmos a man by the name of John caught vision of "the holy Jerusalem" descending out of heaven from God. To him it was the picture of humanity as it should be in its completeness. It was the picture of the new Jerusalem, new in structure new in outlook, new in character. One of the greatest glories of the new heavenly city which he saw was its completeness. It was not partial and one-sided; but in all three dimension it was complete. And so we read in our text. "the length and the breadth and the height of it are equal." The new city of God, the city of ideal humanity is not up on one side and down on the other; it is not an unbalanced entity; it is complete

First page of handwritten draft from which King may have preached his initial sermon, "The Dimensions of a Complete Life," at Dexter Avenue Baptist Church (January 1954).

*that he "plan a sermon which will not require too much dependence on a manu-
script."[2] According to a local newspaper account King was heard by "a large and
appreciative audience."[3]*

*In this handwritten draft, King draws on the theme, structure, and some of the
language of Phillips Brooks's "The Symmetry of Life."[4] King urges his listeners to
fulfill their God-given purposes in life, to develop concern for the welfare of others,
and to seek God. Regarding the need to be concerned about others, he concludes,
"No man should become so involved in his personal ambitions that he forgets that
other people exist in the world. Indeed if my life's work is not developed for the good
of humanity, it is [meaningless] and Godless."*

Text "The Length and the Breadth and the Height of it are equal." Rev. xxi 16.[5]

One day out on a lonely obscure island called Patmos a man by the name of John
caught vision of "the holy Jerusalem" descending out of heaven from God.[6] To him
it was the picture of humanity as it should be in its completeness. It was the picture
of the new Jerusalem, new in structure, new in outlook, new in character. One of the
greatest glories of the new heavenly city which he saw was its completeness. It was
not partial and one-sided, but in all three dimension it was complete.[7] And so we
read in our text: "The length and the breadth and the height of it are equal." The
new city of God, the city of ideal humanity is not up on one side and down on the
other; it is not ♭ an unblanced entity; it is complete on all sides.

John is saying something in this text which has eternal significance.[8] Behind his

---

(Philadelphia: Christian Education Press, 1959), pp. 19–34; *Strength to Love*, pp. 67–77; and "Three
Dimensions of a Complete Life," Sermon Delivered at the Unitarian Church of Germantown, 11
December 1960, in *Papers* 5:571–579.

2. Brooks also wrote King: "We are glad that you can come to us for the fourth Sunday" (J. T. Brooks
to King, 16 January 1954, in *Papers* 2:234).

3. Frazier, "News of Colored People," *Montgomery Examiner,* 28 January 1954.

4. Phillips Brooks, "The Symmetry of Life," in *Selected Sermons,* ed. William Scarlett (New York: E. P.
Dutton, 1949), pp. 195–206. In a later interview King acknowledged that Brooks's sermon was the inspi-
ration for this sermon (Mervyn Warren, "A Rhetorical Study of the Preaching of Doctor Martin Luther
King, Jr., Pastor and Pulpit Orator" [Ph.D. diss., Michigan State University, 1966], p. 105).

5. Revelation 21:16: "And the city lieth foursquare, and the length is as large as the breadth: and he
measured the city with the reed, twelve thousand furlongs. The length and the breadth and the height
of it are equal."

6. Cf. Revelation 1:9, 21:2.

7. Brooks, *Selected Sermons,* p. 195: "St. John in his great vision sees the mystic city, 'the holy Jerusalem,'
descending out of heaven from God. It is the picture of glorified humanity, of humanity as it shall be
when it is brought to its completeness by being thoroughly filled with God. And one of the glories of the
city which he saw was its symmetry. Our cities, our developments and presentations of human life, are
partial and one-sided. This city out of heaven was symmetrical. In all its three dimensions it was complete.
Neither was sacrificed to the other."

8. In the sermon's other draft, King added, "For most of us the book of revelation is a very difficult
book, puzzling to decode. We see it as a great enigma wrapped in mystery. Now it is true that if we look
upon the book of Revelation as the record of actual historical occurences, it is a very difficult book,
shrouded with impenetrable mysteries. But if we will look beneath the peculiar jargon of the author and
the prevailing apocalyte's symbolism we will be able to find there many eternal truths which forever challenge us" ("The Three Dimensions of a Complete Life," 24 January 1954).

poetic imagination and apocalyptic symbolism there is an eternal truth which we must forever recognize, and that is that life at its best and life as it should be is the life that is complete on all sides. So much of the noblest life which we have seen, both collective and individual, dissatisfies us with its partialness; so many of the greatest men we see are great only upon certain sides and have their other sides so flat and small; so many of our greatest civilization are great only on certain sides and have their other sides so low and degrading.

And yet life as it should be is the life that is rich and strong all round, complete on every side.[9] There are then three dimensions of the complete life to which we can fitly give the three names of our text, Length, Breath and Height. The Length of life, as we shall use it, is, of course, not its duration. It is rather the push of a life forward to its own personal ends and ambitions. It is the inward concern for achieving our own pernal end and ambitions. The Breadth of life is the outward concern for the welfare [of?] others. The Height of life is the upward reach toward God. These are the three dimensions of life, and without the due development of all no life becomes complete.[10] Give [illustration?] of a triangle.[11]

Think first about the Length of life, [word illegible] that dimention of life in which every man seeks to [strikeout illegible] developm his inward powers.[12] Every man has the responsibility to discover his mission in Life. God has created every normal [person with?] a capacity to achieve some end. Some are probably [endowed?] with more talent than other, but not none of us of left talentless.

---

9. Brooks, *Selected Sermons*, p. 195: "So much of the noblest life which the world has seen dissatisfies us with its partialness; so many of the greatest men we see are great only upon certain sides, and have their other sides all shrunken, flat, and small, that it may be well for us to dwell upon the picture, which these words suggest, of a humanity rich and full and strong all round, complete on every side, the perfect cube of human life which comes down out of heaven from God."

10. Brooks, *Selected Sermons*, p. 196: "There are, then, three directions or dimensions of human life to which we may fitly give these three names, Length and Breadth and Height. The Length of a life, in this meaning of it, is, of course, not its duration. It is rather the reaching on and out of a man, in the line of activity and thought and self-development, which is indicated and prophesied by the character which is natural within him, by the special ambitions which spring up out of his special powers. It is the push of a life forward to its own personal ends and ambitions. The Breadth of a life, on the other hand, is its outreach laterally, if we may say so. It is the constantly diffusive tendency which is always drawing a man outward into sympathy with other men. And the Height of a life is its reach upward towards God; its sense of childhood; its consciousness of the Divine Life over it with which it tries to live in love, communion, and obedience. These are the three dimensions of a life,—its length and breadth and height,—without the due development of all of which no life becomes complete."

11. In the sermon's other draft, King wrote out the illustration: "At one angle stands the individual person, at the other angle stands other persons, and at the tip top stands God. Unless these three are concatenated, working harmoniously together in a single life, that life is incomplete" ("The Three Dimensions of a Complete Life," 24 January 1954).

12. In the sermon's other draft, King added: "This is really the selfish dimension of life. There is such a thing as rational and moral self-interest. As the late Joshua Liebman said in an interesting chapter in his book entitled Peace of Mind, we must first love ourselves properly before we can adequately love others. Many people have been plunged across the abyss of emotional fatalism because they didn't love themselves" (King, "The Three Dimensions of a Complete Life," 24 January 1954). Joshua Loth Liebman (1907–1948) was a Reformed Jewish rabbi who served temples in Chicago and Boston. King most likely refers to the book's third chapter, "Love Thyself Properly" in *Peace of Mind* (New York: Simon and Schuster, 1946), pp. 38–58.

(1) Use what you have. Dont worry about others. Discover what you have and what you can do

(2) After you have discoved what you are made for, seek to do it with all the power there is in your system.[13] Do it as if God ordained you to do it. Let nothing cause you to lose sigh of you ultimate aim. Use the ill of Jesus. (For this cause came I into the world)[14]

(3) Never consider you life's work insignificant.[15] Quote Malloch[16]

(4) Set yourself earnestly to see what you were made to do, and then set yourself earnestly to do it

This clear onward push the the end is the length of a man's life.

~~Now there are some men who never get beyond this first dimension of living. I'm sure youve seen such people. These people are only concerned about themselves~~

Now although this is an important dimension of life, it is not the only dimension. If a life is to be complete we must not stop with this dimension. There are some people who never get beyond this first dimension of life.[17] I'm sure you have seen such people. These people are only concerned about themselves. They seek to achieve their ambitions at any cost. So if life is to be complete it must move beyond length to what we have called breadth. I have ventured to call this quality of breadth in a man life its outreach for the welfare of others. No man has lerned to live until he can rise out of his mere concern for self to the broader concern for others. Indeed the prayer that every man should learn to pray is: "Lord teach me to unselfishly serve humanity." No man should become so involved in his personal ambitions that he forgets that other people exist in the world. Indeed if my life's work is not developed for the good of hunanity, it is [*meaningless?*] and Godless. Length without Breadth is dead and narrow. I say to you whatever you do in life do it for the good

---

13. In the sermon's other draft, King wrote, "He should seek to do it so well that the living, the dead, and the unborn could do it no better" ("The Three Dimensions of a Complete Life," 24 January 1954).

14. Cf. John 18:37.

15. In the sermon's other draft, King wrote: "If it is for the uplifting of humanity, it has cosmic significance, however small it is. If you are called to a little job, seek to do it in a big way. If your life's work is confined to the ordinary, seek to do it in an extraordinary way. If you discover that you are called to be a street sweeper, sweep streets like Micheal Angelo painted pictures, like Beetovan composed music, and like Shakespeare wrote poetry. Sweep streets so well that all the host of heaven and earth will have to pause and say, 'here lived a great street sweeper who swept his job well'" (King, "The Three Dimensions of a Complete Life," 24 January 1954). King once attributed this illustration to Benjamin Mays (King, "Facing the Challenge of a New Age," Address Delivered at NAACP Emancipation Day Rally, 1 January 1957, in *The Papers of Martin Luther King, Jr.,* vol. 4: *Symbol of the Movement, January 1957–December 1958,* eds. Clayborne Carson, Susan Carson, Adrienne Clay, Virginia Shadron, Kieran Taylor [Berkeley and Los Angeles: University of California Press, 2000], p. 79).

16. In the sermon's other draft, King wrote out Douglas Malloch's 1926 poem "Be the Best of Whatever You Are" ("The Three Dimensions of a Complete Life," 24 January 1954). For the entire poem, see King, "The Three Dimensions of a Complete Life," 28 February 1960, pp. 398–399 in this volume.

17. In the sermon's other draft, King wrote: "They brilliantly develop their inner powers, but they live as if nobody else lives in the world but themselves. Other persons become mere steps by which they climb to their personal ambitions. There is nothing more tragic than to see a person bogged down in the length of life devoid of breadth" ("The Three Dimensions of a Complete Life," 24 January 1954).

of humanty. Dont do it merely for the prestige that it brings or the money that it brings, but do it for the serving of humanty[18]

(Bring in the relevance of this truth on the international scene[19] How nations have tried to live to themselves) Along with this comes the realization that we are not independent. The thinking man realizes that real life is interdependent. (Show the ill. of how before breakfast is over we are dependent on the whole world?)[20] All life is involved in a single process so that whatever effects one directly affects all indirectly. Quote John Donne "No man is an island . . . "[21]

Now one more dimension of the complete life still remains, viz the Height. The Height of life is its reach upward toward something distinctly greater than humanity.[22] Man must rise above earth to that great eternal reality who is the source and end of life. And so when we add Height to length and breath we have the complete life.

There are many men who who are wholly creative of the earth. There are those who never look up, who never seem to have anything to do with anything above this flat and level plain of human life.[23] The tragedy of much of modern life is that in quest of our [*personal?*] and social goals we have unconsciously forgotten God. We have pursued the length and breadth of life and neglected the Height. And so we find ourselves living a disorganized, incomplete and disconected life. (Quote H. G. Wells)[24]

In our age of science and materialism so many things have come which seem to make God [*irrelevant?*] Illustrate.

In our age we have set forth so many substitutes for God. (Inventions, money)

But my friends televisions and automobiles, subways and automobiles, dollars and cents can never be substitutes for God. For long before these came into exis-

---

18. At this point, King began using a second pen. In the sermon's other draft, King paraphrased the parable of the Good Samaritan in this section ("The Three Dimensions of a Complete Life," 24 January 1954; see also King, "The Three Dimensions of a Complete Life," 28 February 1960, p. 399 in this volume).

19. In a later version of this sermon King discussed the international implications of the breadth of life with regard to world poverty and health care ("The Three Dimensions of a Complete Life," 28 February 1960, pp. 400–401 in this volume).

20. For an example of this illustration taken from minister Leslie Weatherhead, see King, The Man Who Was a Fool, Sermon Delivered at the Detroit Council of Churches' Noon Lenten Services, 6 March 1961, pp. 415–416 in this volume.

21. King refers to John Donne's poem "Meditation XVII," *Devotions Upon Emergent Occasions* (1624). King wrote Donne's poem on the folder containing this sermon.

22. Brooks, *Selected Sermons*, p. 202: "The Height of life is its reach upward toward something distinctly greater than humanity."

23. Brooks, *Selected Sermons*, p. 202: "Evidently all that I have yet described, all the length and breadth of life, might exist, and yet man be a creature wholly of the earth. . . . He might even enter into living sympathy with his brother-men; and yet never look up, never seem to have anything to do with anything above this flat and level plain of human life."

24. King may refer to the following H. G. Wells quote: "Religion is the first thing and the last thing, and until a man has found God and been found by God, he begins at no beginning, he works toward no end" (Wells, *Mr. Britling Sees It Through* [New York: Macmillan, 1916], p. 442). For an example of King's use of this quote, see "Creating an Abundant Life," Sermon at Dexter Avenue Baptist Church, 26 September 1954, p. 191 in this volume.

tence we needed God and long after they shall have passed away we will still need God. Look up beyond your self interest. Look up beyond your concern for humanity. Look up to the very height of life itself and then you find God who makes life comple. We are commanded to love ourselves and we are commanded to love our neighbors as we love ourselves, but still there is a greatr commandments which say "Love the Lord thy God . . ."[25]

God is the end of life. We were made for God and we will be restless until we find rest in him.[26]

AD. CSKC: Sermon file, folder 21, "The Three Dimensions of a Complete Life."

---

25. Cf. Matthew 22:36–39.

26. King probably refers to Augustine *Confessions* 1.1: "Thou awakest us to delight in Thy praise; for Thou madest us for Thyself, and our heart is restless, until it repose in Thee."

III: DEXTER AVENUE BAPTIST CHURCH

"Going Forward by Going Backward,"
Sermon at Dexter Avenue Baptist Church

4 April 1954
Montgomery, Ala.

Dexter's congregation voted unanimously to call King as their new pastor in early March 1954.[1] Several weeks after the vote, King returned to meet with the church's pulpit committee regarding the details of their offer. At that time, he preached the following sermon, which has the same text, themes, and structure as Rediscovering Lost Values, a sermon he had delivered at Detroit's Second Baptist Church five weeks earlier.[2] In this typed manuscript, King reasons with his audience, "If we are to go forward we must go back and find God." Furthermore, he asserts, "Our problem lies in the fact that through our scientific genius we have made of the world a neighborhood, but through our moral genius we have failed to make of it a brotherhood."

There is something wrong with our world; something fundamentally and basically wrong. When we stop to analyze the cause of our world's ill, many things come to mind. We wonder if it is due to the fact that we don't know enough. But certainly it can't be that, for in terms of accumulated knowledge we know more today than men have known in any period of human history. We wonder if it is due to a failure to keep our scientific progress abreast with our progress in other areas. But certainly it can't be this, for our progress scientifically has been amazing. Man through his scientific genius has been able to draft distance and place time in chains. Moreover, through his scientific genius, man has stamped out many of his dread plagues and diseases, alleviated his pain, prolonged his life and given himself greater security and physical well-being. And so our problem cannot be in the scientific realm.

It seems to me that if we are to find the cause of our world's ill we must turn to the hearts and souls of men. Our problem lies in the fact that our material and intellectual advances have outrun our moral progress. Everywhere when we compare ourselves with previous generations with reference to our means for living, we are supreme. Yes, the scientific and educational means by which we live can hardly be surpassed, but the moral and spiritual ends for which we live stand almost in a state of oblivion. How much of our modern life is summarized in that shrewd phrase of

---

1. Dexter church clerk Robert D. Nesbitt and deacon chairman Thomas H. Randall sent King a telegram informing him of the church's vote. They expressed an interest in meeting with him on 20 March but King had other commitments and suggested rescheduling the meeting for the first Sunday in April (Nesbitt and Randall to King, 7 March 1954, and King to Pulpit Committee, Dexter Avenue Baptist Church, 10 March 1954, in *Papers* 2:256 and 258–259, respectively).

2. King, Rediscovering Lost Values, 28 February 1954, in *Papers* 2:248–256. King preached a version of "Going Forward by Going Backward" as early as 26 October 1952 in Portsmouth, New Hampshire (People's Baptist Church, Program, "Fifty-ninth anniversary service") and, according to a date written on this document, also delivered this sermon on 16 August 1953, during his time as Ebenezer's associate pastor. King also gave a version of this sermon before the Chicago Sunday Evening Club on 21 February 1960, which was later published (King, "Going Forward by Going Backward," *The A.M.E. Church Review* [April–June 1960]: 62–67).

Thoreau, "Improved means to an unimproved end."[3] Our problem lies in the fact that through our scientific genius we have made of the world a neighborhood, but through our moral genius we have failed to make of it a brotherhood. And the great danger confronting us today is not the atomic bomb created by physical science, not the atomic bomb that we can put in an airplane and drop on hundreds and thousands of people, but the atomic bomb which we have to fear today is that atomic bomb which lies in the hearts and souls of men, capable of exploding into the vilest of hate and into the most damaging selfishness.

My friends, if our civilization is to go forward today, we must go back and pick up those precious moral values that we have left behind. And unless we go backward to rediscover these moral and spiritual values, we will certainly not move forward to the city of peace and happiness. Our situation in the world today reminds one of a situation that took place in the life of Jesus. As you remember Jesus's parents went to Jerusalem every year at the feast of the passover. When Jesus was twelve years old, they went up to Jerusalem after the custom of the feast. After they had fulfilled their days they set out to return to Nazareth. Jesus being a very serious minded and inquisitive child remained behind in Jerusalem, asking and hearing questions, and his parents knew not of it. The story goes that the parents of Jesus travelled a whole day's journey before they missed him. And then Luke says: "When they found him not, they turned back to Jerusalem seeking him."[4] In other words the parents of Jesus realized that they had left a mighty precious value behind, and before they could go forward to Nazareth, they had to go backward to Jerusalem to rediscover this something of value they had lost.

There are many precious values that our civilization needs to rediscover. Unless we go back and pick them up we can not go forward to the city of peace. First, we need to go back and pick up the principle that all reality hinges on moral foundations. We must rediscover the value that there are moral laws of the universe just as abiding as the physical laws.[5] We have lost these values today. At least two things convince me that modern man has strayed away from the principle that there is a moral order of the universe. The first is that most people today have adopted a sort of relativistic ethic. By this I mean that most people feel that right and wrong are relative to their taste and their customs and their particular communities. So that there is really nothing absolutely right and absolutely wrong. It just depends on what the majority of the people are doing. This philosophy has invaded the whole of modern life. Now I admit that there are certain customs and folkways which aren't right or wrong. They are simply amoral, they have no moral value. But on the other hand there are certain things that are absolutely right and absolutely wrong. The eternal

---

3. Henry David Thoreau, *Walden; or Life in the Woods*, p. 57.

4. Luke 2:45.

5. In the 1960 version of this sermon, King elaborated: "Now I have no doubt of the fact that we believe in the physical laws, in their efficacy and their validity, and so we don't just go out disobeying them. We don't go out in Chicago and climb up to the highest building, to the last floor of that building, and decide to jump off, or to jump out of an airplane just to be jumping, for we unconsciously realize that there is a final law of gravitation in this universe, and if we fail to obey that law we will suffer the consequences. And even if we do not know it in its mathematical Newtonian formulation, we unconsciously know it, and so we follow it" (King, "Going Forward by Going Backward," April–June 1960, pp. 63–64).

King speaks with a parishioner on the steps of Dexter Avenue
Baptist Church, 1956. Photo by Dan Weiner; courtesy of Sandra
Weiner and the Collection of the International Center of
Photography.

God of the universe has ordained it to be so. It's wrong to be dishonest and unjust;
it's wrong to use your brother as a means to an end; it's wrong to waste the precious
life that God has given you in rioteous living, it is eternally and absolutely wrong; it's
wrong to hate, it always has been wrong and it always will be wrong. It was wrong in
two thousand B.C. and it's wrong in 1953 A.D. It's wrong in India, it's wrong in
Russia, it's wrong in China, it's wrong in America. It always has been wrong and it
always will be wrong.

A second thing that convinces me that modern man has strayed away from the
principle that there is a moral order of the universe is that most people today have
adopted a sort of pragmatic test of right and wrong; that is to say, whatever works is
right. And so the only sin for the average modern man is to disobey the Eleventh   161

commandment: "Thou shalt not get caught." It doesn't matter what you do, but just don't get caught. This attitude has lead to a philosophy of the survival of the slickest. It says, it's all right to lie, but just do it with a bit of finess; it's alright to rob, but be a dignified robber. This philosophy has invaded the whole of modern life. But my friends we must come to see that some things are right and some things are wrong, whether we are caught or not. This universe hinges on moral foundations. There is something in this universe that justifies Carlyle in saying, "No lie can live forever."[6] There is something in this universe which justifies William Cullen Bryant in saying, "Truth crushed to earth will rise again."[7] There is something which justifies James Russell Lowell in saying, "Truth forever on the scaffold, wrong forever on the throne, yet that scaffold sways the future."[8] There is something in this universe that justifies the Biblical writer in saying, "You shall reap what you sow."[9] God's universe has moral foundations and if we are to go forward we must go back and pick up this precious value.[10]

Another principle that we have left behind and that we need to go back and rediscover is the principle that all reality has spiritual control. This simply means that we must rediscover the principle that there is a God behind the process of life, and that He has supreme control of His creation. In our age of materialism we have gotten away from this principle.[11] You remember the text said that the parents of

---

6. Thomas Carlyle, *The French Revolution* (1837).

7. Bryant, "The Battlefield" (1839).

8. James Russell Lowell, "The Present Crisis" (1844). This passage, as well as the two earlier ones from Bryant and Carlyle, became a commonplace set piece in King's oratory. His phrasing closely resembles that in a sermon by Harry Emerson Fosdick titled "Why We Believe in God," in *On Being Fit To Live With: Sermons on Post-war Christianity* (New York: Harper & Brothers, 1946), p. 94: "There is something in this universe besides matter and motion. There is something here that justifies Carlyle in saying, 'No Lie can live for ever'; and Shakespeare in saying, 'There's a divinity that shapes our ends, / Rough-hew them how we will'; and Lowell in saying, 'Truth forever on the scaffold, Wrong forever on the throne, — / Yet that scaffold sways the future.'" In the published version of King's sermon "The Death of Evil Upon the Seashore," he corrected and lengthened his quotation from Thomas Carlyle (King, *Strength to Love*, p. 77).

9. Cf. Galatians 6:7.

10. In the 1960 version of this sermon, King added: "There is something deep down in our tradition that reminds us that the basic thing about a man is not his specificity but his fundamentum. The basic thing about a man is his dignity and his worth to the Almighty God. . . . Thereby we see a universality at the center of the Gospel. Then we find the Apostle Paul reiterating it on Mars' Hill: 'Out of one blood God made all men to dwell upon the face of the earth.'" King continued, "This is the great American dream, a beautiful and a sublime dream. But the tragedy is that we have so often scarred the dream. We have trampled over the dream. And it is one of the ironies of history, that in a nation founded upon the principle that all men are created equal, men are still arguing over whether the color of a man's skin determines the content of his character" (King, "Going Forward by Going Backward," April–June 1960, p. 65).

11. In the 1960 version, King added: "Now many people have overlooked this basic principle, and left it behind. Some have done it for very honest reasons. Some men have neglected it because they have looked out in the world and noticed the colossal and glaring reality of evil, that something that the poet Yeats calls 'the giant agony of the world,' and they have wondered how a good, all-powerful God could allow this evil to exist. Others have neglected it because they have found it difficult to square their intellectual world views with the sometimes irrational and unscientific dogmas of religion. And so there are some people who neglect this principle for honest reasons. [¶] But I suspect that most people neglect it

Jesus travelled a whole day before they missed him. They had unconsciously lost Jesus. So have we in the modern world unconsciously left God behind? We didn't kneel before God and say: "Good-bye God, we are going to leave you now, we are going to spend our time trying to get rich and in having a good time." The materialism in America was an unconscious process. It began with the Industrial Revolution in England, then mass production, then the invention of gadgets such as automobiles, radios, movies and television. Man became more concerned about these gadgets than about God. Man became so involved in attempting to get a big bank account and riding in a big car that he unconsciously forgot God. Man became so involved in looking at the man made lights of the city that he unconsciously forgot to think about that great cosmic light that gets up in the eastern horizon and paints its technicolor across the blue, a light man could never make. He became so involved in the intricacies of television and movies that he unconsciously forgot to think about the beautiful stars that appear as shining silver pins sticking in the magnificent blue pin cushion. He became so fascinated with his scientific progress that he unconsciously came to believe that man could usher in a new world unaided by any divine power. And so when we came to ourselves, we had travelled a day's journey and discovered that we had left God behind. My friends, if we are to go forward we must go back and find God. We must put God back into the center of our thinking. Television and automobiles, sub-ways and airplanes, dollars and cents, can never be substitutes for God, for long before any of these came into being, we needed God and after they will have passed away, we will still need God.

> Our God, our help in ages past,
> Our hope for years to come,
> Our shelter from the stormy blast,
> And our eternal home![12]

Preached at Dexter Avenue Baptist Church, First Sunday, April 1954
Preached August 16, 1953

TDc. CSKC: Sermon file, folder 97.

---

because they have just become involved in other things. These people are not theoretical doubters. They are not theoretical atheists. They are practical atheists" (King, "Going Forward by Going Backward," April–June 1960, p. 66).

12. King cites Isaac Watts's hymn "O God, Our Help in Ages Past" (1719). In the 1960 version of this sermon, King used a different ending: "And since 1941, one tragedy then has followed another, as if history were designed to refute the vain delusions of modern man. Maybe H. G. Wells was right: 'The man who is not religious begins at nowhere and ends at nothing,' for religion is like a mighty wind that breaks down doors and knocks down walls, and makes that possible, and even easy, which seems difficult and impossible. [¶] And so I say to you, discover God, and with this faith you will be able to adjourn the councils of despair, and bring new light to the dark chambers of pessimism." He concluded, "This is the challenge. Reach out and grab it, not tomorrow, not next week, not next year, but this moment. Go back and find Him. [¶] A tiny little minute, just sixty seconds in it. / I didn't choose it. I can't refuse it. It's up to me to use it. / A tiny little minute, just sixty seconds in it, / But eternity, eternity, eternity is in it. [¶] Let us use the moment, and God will be with us" (King, "Going Forward by Going Backward," April–June 1960, pp. 66–67).

You the people of Dexter Avenue Baptist Church have called me to serve as pastor of your historic Church; and I have gladly accepted the call. It is more than perfunctory gratitude that I express my appreciation to you, for bestowing upon me this great honor. I accept the pastorate dreadfully aware of the tremendous responsibilities accompanying it. Contrary to some shallow thinking, the responsibilities of the pastorate both stagger and astound the imagination. They take the whole man.

It is a significant fact that I come to the pastorate of Dexter at a most crucial hour of our world's history; at a time when the flames of war might arise at any time to redden the skies of our dark and dreary world; at a time when men know all to well that without the proper guidance the whole of civilization can be plunged across the abyss of destruction; at a time when men are experiencing in all relations disruption & and conflict, self-destruction and meaningless despair and anxiety. Today men who were but yesterday predicting the church of Christ are now asking the church the way to its paradise of peace and happiness. We must somehow give our generation an answer. Dexter, like all other churches, must somehow lead men and women of a decadent generation to the high mountain of peace and salvation. We must give men and women who are all but on the brink of despair a new bent on life. I pray God that I will be able to lead Dexter in this

King's notes for his acceptance address at Dexter (2 May 1954).

urgent mission.

I come to you with nothing so special to offer. I have no pretense to being a great preacher or even a profound scholar. I certainly have no pretense to infallibility — that is reserved for the height of the divine rather than the depth of the human. At every moment I am conscious of my finiteness, knowing so clearly that I have never been bathed in the sunshine of omniscience or baptized in the waters of omnipotence. I come to you with only the claim of being a servant of Christ, and a feeling of dependence on his grace for my leadership. I come with a feeling that I have been called to preach and to lead God's people. I have felt like Jeremiah the word of God was in my heart like burning fire shut up in my bones. I have felt with Amos, that when God speaks who can but prophesy. I have felt with Jesus that the spirit of Lord is upon me, because he hath anointed me to preach the gospel to the poor, to heal the brokenhearted, to preach deliverance to the captives, and to set at liberty them that are bruised.

Acceptance Address
at Dexter Avenue Baptist Church

[2 May 1954]
Montgomery, Ala.

Following King's second visit to Dexter, he wrote a letter conditionally accepting the
congregation's call to be its next pastor.[1] After a church meeting on 18 April, clerk
Robert D. Nesbitt wrote to King agreeing to his conditions and asking that he conduct
the church's 2 May morning communion service.[2] In these notes for his remarks
following the service, King expresses appreciation for the call to Dexter and notes
that he arrives "at a most crucial hour of our world's history." He humbly asserts,
"I have no pretense to being a great preacher or even a profound scholar," but adds,
"I come with a feeling that I have been called to preach and to lead God's people."

You the people of Dexter Avenue Baptist Church have called me to serve as ~~your~~
pastor of your historic Church; and I have gladly accepted the call. It is with more
than perfuctory gratitude that I again express my appreciation to you for bestowing
upon [*me?*] this great honor. I accept the pastorate dreadfully aware of the tremendous responsibilities accompaning it. [*strikeout illegible*] ~~to~~ Contrary to some shallow
thinking, the responsibilities of the pastorate both stagger and astound the imagination. They tax the whole man.

~~I come to you with no pretense to infallibility~~

It is a significant fact that I come ~~to you [the pastorate] at a most crucial h~~ to the
pastorate of Dexter at a most crucial hour of our world's history; At a time when the
flame of war might arise at any time to reden the skies of our dark and dreary world;
at a time when men know all to well that without the proper guidance the whole of
civilization can be plunged across the abyss of destruction; at a time when men are
experiencing in all realms of life disruption and conflict, self-destruction and meaningless, despair and anxiety. Today men who were but yesterday ridiculing the
Church of Christ are now asking the Church the way to the paradise of peace and
hapiness. We must somehow give our generation an answer. Dexter, like all other
churches, must somehow lead men and women of a decadent generation to the
high mountain of peace and ~~happiness~~ salvation. We must give men and women,
who are all but on the brink of despair, a new bent on life. I pray God that I will be
able to lead Dexter in this urgent mission.

I come to you with nothing so special to offer. I have no pretense to being a great
preacher or even a profound scholar. I certainly have no pretence to infallibility—
that is reserved for the height of the divine rather than the depth of the human. At
every moment I am conscious of my finiteness, knowing so clearly that I have never

---

1. King to Dexter Avenue Baptist Church, 14 April 1954, in *Papers* 2:260.
2. Nesbitt to King, 19 April 1954, in *Papers* 2:262–263. King noted on his 26 July 1953 manuscript of
"Accepting Responsibility for Your Actions" that he had also preached this sermon on 2 May 1954 at
Dexter (p. 139 in this volume).

been bathed in the sunshine of omnicience or baptized in the waters of omnipotence. I come to you with only the claim of being a servant of Christ, and a feeling
of dependence on his grace for my leadership. I come with a feeling that I have
been called to preach and to lead God's people. I have felt like Jeremiah that the
word of God is in heart like burning fire shut up in my bones.[3] I have felt with Amos
that when God speaks who can but prophesy.[4] I have felt with Jesus that the spirit of
Lord is upon me, because he hath anointed me to preach the gospel to the poor, to
heal the brokenhearted, to preach deliverance to the captives, and to set at liberty
them that are bruised.[5]

AD. CSKC: Sermon file, folder 118, "Sermon Material."

---

3. Cf. Jeremiah 20:9.
4. Cf. Amos 3:8.
5. Cf. Luke 4:18.

"Mental and Spiritual Slavery,"
Sermon at Dexter Avenue Baptist Church

May 1954
Montgomery, Ala.

*King made several trips from Boston to Montgomery before moving permanently in
September 1954. For one such trip, he preached from this handwritten outline.[1] King
calls on his new congregation to consider Pontius Pilate, who acquiesced to the crowds
and sentenced Jesus to death. He criticizes conformity: "Many white people are against
many of the practices of their group, but they are afraid to take a stand."[2] The following outline was compiled from fragments found in two different sermon folders.[3]*

"They are slaves who fear to speak,
for the fallen and the weak;
They are slaves who will not choose,
Hatred, scoffing and abuse,
Rather than in silence shrink,

---

1. King's announced 7 September 1952 sermon at Ebenezer Baptist Church was also titled "Mental
and Spiritual Slavery" ("Rev. King, Jr. Will Deliver Last Summer Sermon Sun," *Atlanta Daily World,* 6 September 1952).

2. King reworked this theme for a sermon titled "Transformed Nonconformist" (November 1954, pp.
195–198 in this volume, and "Transformed Nonconformist," *Strength to Love,* pp. 8–15).

3. This document's pages were found in two separate folders in King's sermon file. The first two pages
were stored in the folder titled "Mental Slavery." The last four pages were filed in an untitled folder (Sermon File Inventory, pp. 609 and 621 in this volume).

From the truth they needs must think;
They are slaves who dare not be,
In the right with two or three"[4]

I Int. These words from the pen of James Russel Lowell are quite expressive of all that I intend to say this morning. Usually we think of slavery in the physical sense, as an institution inflicted on one group of people by another group. But there is another type of slavery which is probably more prevelent and certainly more injurious than physical bondage, namely mental slavery. This is a slavery that the individual inflicts upon himself. History abounds with individuals who have enjoyed physical freedom and who have at the same time inflicted mental and spiritual freedom upon themselves. Deep down in their souls and minds they were slaves. (Notice the mental slavery of the Negro.)

II This morning I would like to use Pilate as an example of one whose mind was caught in the clutches of slavery

1. His mind and soul were enslaved to the crowd. In other words Pilate found security in conforming to ideas of the mob. Listen to the account. "And so Pilate, willing to content the people, released Barabbas unto them, and delivered Jesus to be crucified."[5] Pilate did not have the moral ~~courage~~ stamina to stand alone on his convictions

1. Most people today are in Pilate's shoes i.e. conformist. Most people would take stands on their ideas but they are afraid of being non-conformist. {This particular slavery has lead us to a philosophy of a numerical test of truth.}

(a) Many white people ~~feel~~ are against many of the practices of their group, but they are afraid to take a stand.

(b) Many people divelope undesirable habits in an attempt to conform

(c) Notice how the Church has often conformed

Now at a point we must all be conformist. (We are tied to an extent to the folkways and mores) There is no virtue in being a non-conformist just to be a non conformist.[6] Some people are non conformist just to get attention and to be different. This type of non-conformity I am not speaking of. I am speaking of a non conformity which is based on high and noble purposes. This type is both legitimate and necessary. Whenever the mores and patterns of our society conflict with our highest ideals and tend to degrade human personality then it is our moral obligation to revolt against them. {1. Agaist War 2. Agaist the inequalities of Capitalism 3. Many white people 4 Young people}

(D) Quote Emerson[7]

---

4. James Russell Lowell, "Stanzas on Freedom" (1892).

5. Cf. Mark 15:15. Pontius Pilate, who ordered Jesus' execution, was the fifth Roman governor of Judea and ruled for a decade (26–37 CE).

6. The remainder of this document was filed in a separate folder.

7. King may be referring to Ralph Waldo Emerson, *Self Reliance* (1841): "Whoso would be a man must be a nonconformist."

(E) The truely great men of history have been those who could stand up before the crowd and not bow. The great creative insights have come from men who were in a minority. It was the minority that fought for popular education, for religious liberty, for freedom of scientific research

F Professor Bixler of ~~Harvard~~ Coby College has made some interesting comments on our new psychological talk about the well adjusted life[8]

(G) {Quote Paul}[9] We Christians are not called upon to be the conformist, but the non-conformist. (Use ill of Thermostats and themon)[10] Being a Christian is serious business. It is more than reciting a few creeds. It is more than singing a few beatiful hymns. It is more than partaking of the sacraments.

2. ~~Pilates~~ Let us look at Pilate again. We find that his mind and soul were slaves to his own selfish interest. Pilate made it clear that he didn't believe Jesus to be guilty of the charges heaped upon him and he continually said "I find no fualt in him."[11] So Pilate's problem was not that of deciding whether Jesus was guilty or innocent. He knew he was innocent. The problem was whether he should free an innonent man and lose he secure position with the people, or sentence an innocent man to death and so establish himself more securely in the affections of his subjects. He did not want to condemn Jesus to death. But to free him would jeopodise his own position. And so he crucified upon the cross of his self interest

(1) ~~Not~~ Now it is easy for us to look back and condemn Pilate for such an action, but we must also see that many of us are just as much victims of this sort of thing as Pilate.

(a) Take the politician choosing between truth and votes

(b) Take the business man choosing between truth and some sharp business practice which mean more money

---

8. Harry Emerson Fosdick, "Facing the Challenge of Change," in *The Hope of the World* (New York: Harper and Brothers, 1933), p. 112: "Dr. Seelye Bixler, of Harvard University, has lately made some shrewd comments on our new psychological talk about the well-adjusted life." Julius Seelye Bixler was a professor of theology at Harvard University from 1933 until 1942 and served as president of Colby College from 1942 until 1960.

9. King probably refers to Paul's words in Romans 12:2: "And be not conformed to this world: but be ye transformed by the renewing of your mind, that ye may prove what is that good, and acceptable, and perfect, will of God." He also used this text as the basis for the November 1954 version of "Transformed Nonconformist" and the version that was submitted for publication in *Strength to Love* (see King, "Transformed Nonconformist," November 1954, and King, Draft of Chapter II, "Transformed Nonconformist," July 1962–March 1963, pp. 195–198 and 466–476 in this volume, respectively). See also Chart 1 (p. 16), which compares King's explication of this biblical text in this document with passages in his several versions of "Transformed Nonconformist."

10. "And so the christian is called upon not to be like a thermometer conforming to the temperature of his society, but he must be like a thermostat serving to transform the temperature of his society" (King, "Transformed Nonconformist," November 1954, p. 196 in this volume).

11. Cf. John 18:38 and 19:4, 6.

(c) Take the mininstr choosing between truth and keeing in with the member and being popular with the breathen

The great progressive moves of history have been ruined by the purpetuity of "Pilateness"[12]

Conclusion—Who has been the most influential character in history Jesus or Pilate Who is it that has been the most influential character of human history—Jesus or Pilate? Who is it that was able to change a Simon of sand into a Peter of Rock.[13] Who is it that was able to change a persecuting Peter into a Apostle Paul—Jesus or Pilate?[14] Who is it that has been able to split history into A.D. and B.C.—Jesus or Pilate? Who is it that so captivated the soul of man that they shook the hinges from the gates of the Roman empire—Jesus or Pilate? Who is that gave impetus to a movement that has grown from a group of eleven men to more than 600,000,000 followers today—Jesus or Pilate. Who is it whose influence has outlasted the Caesar and whose majestic power has towered above empires—Jesus or Pilate? Who is it that has given a message so universal and international that choirs the world ove can sing In Christ there is no East nor West—Jesus or Pilate?[15] Who is it that has so convinced men that his message is eternal and lasting that they have cry out with Handel of oll Halululia, Halulia[16]

Preached at Dexter May, 1954[17]

ADf. CSKC: Sermon file, folder 113, "Mental Slavery"; and Sermon file, folder 124.

---

12. King added this sentence in a second pen.
13. Cf. John 1:42.
14. Cf. Acts 9:1–28.
15. King cites John Oxenham's hymn "In Christ There Is No East or West" (1908).
16. King cites the "Hallelujah Chorus" in George Frideric Handel's oratorio *Messiah* (1741).
17. King added this sentence in a second pen.

"A Religion of Doing,"
Sermon at Dexter Avenue Baptist Church

4 July 1954
Montgomery, Ala.

During another weekend trip from Boston to Montgomery, King preached the following sermon at Dexter. Drawing ideas from Harry Emerson Fosdick's "Christianity Not a Form but a Force," King asserts: "Christ is more concerned about our attitude towards racial prejudice and war than he is about our long processionals. He is more concerned with how we treat our neighbors than how loud we sing his praises."[1]

---

1. Fosdick, *A Great Time to Be Alive,* pp. 89–97.

In the seventh chapter of Matthew's Gospel we find these pressing words flowing from the lips of our Lord and Master: "Not every one that saith unto me, Lord, Lord, shall enter into the kingdom of heaven; but he that doeth the will of my father which is in Heaven."[2] In these words Jesus is placing emphasis on a concrete practical religion rather than an abstract theoretical religion. In other words he is placing emphasis on an active religion of doing rather than a passive religion of talk. Religion to be real and genuine must not only be something that men talk about, but it must be something that men live about. Jesus recognized that there is always the danger of having a high blood pressure of creeds and an anemia of deeds. He was quite certain that the tree of religion becomes dry and even dead when it fails to produce the fruit of action.

Let us turn for the moment to some of the truths implicit in our text which must forever challenge us as christians. The first truth implied in our text is that the test of belief is action. This is just another way of saying that a man will do what he believes and in the final analysis he is what he does. There can be no true divorce between belief and action. There might be some divorce between intellectual assent and action. Intellectual assent is merely agreeing that a thing is true; real belief is acting like it is true. Belief always takes a flight into action. The ultimate test for what a man believes is not what he says, but what he does. Many people, for example, say that they believe in God, but their actions reveal the very denial of God's existence. Indeed the great danger confronting religion is not so much theoretical atheism as practical atheism; not so much denying God's existence with our lips as denying God's existence with our lives. How many of us so-called Christians affirm the existence of God with our mouths and deny his existence with our lives. It causes many to wonder if we believe in God after all. And there is warrant for such a wonder. If a man believes that there is a God that guides the destiny of the universe, and that this God has planted in the fiber of the universe an inexorable moral law that is as abiding as the physical laws, he will act like it. And if he doesn't act like it all of his impressive eloquence concerning his belief in God becomes as sounding brass and a tinkling cymbal.[3] Belief is ultimately validated in action. The ultimate test of a man's sincerity in crying Lord, Lord, is found in his active doing of God's will.

A second truth implied in our text is that real religion is not a mere form but a dynamic force. Now there can be no doubt that this is one area in which we have failed miserably. Dr. Moffatt's translation of that familiar passage in the second letter to Timothy is a true description of much of our conventional christianity. It reads: "Though they keep up a form of religion, they will have nothing to do with it as a force."[4]

Certainly that describes many people. There are about 700,000,000 christians in the world today, and were Christ's faith and way of life a vital force in anything like that number, the condition of this world would be far better than it is. How much truth there is in the lines of a modern poet who speaks about our worshipping congregation:

---

2. Matthew 7:21.
3. Cf. 1 Corinthians 13:1.
4. 2 Timothy 3:5 (MOFFATT).

They do it every Sunday,
They'll be all right on Monday;
It's just a little habit they've acquired.[5]

How much of our contemporary christianity can be described as a mere Sunday habit. To put it fugutively, christianity is not a garment that we wear in everyday life, but it is a Sunday suit which we put on on Sunday morning and hang up neatly in the closet on Sunday night never to be touched again until the next Sunday. We have a form of religion but have nothing to do with it as a force. As E. Stanley Jones put it, "innoculated with a mild form of christianity, we have become immune to the genuine article."[6] Yet if religion is to be real and genuine in our lives it must be experienced as a dynamic force. Religion must be effective in the political world, the economic world, and indeed the whole social situation. Religion should flow through the stream of the whole {of} life. The easygoing dicotymy between the sacred and the secular, the god of religion and the god of life, the god of Sunday and the god of Monday has wrought havoc in the portals of religion. We must come to see that the god of religion is the god of life and that the god of Sunday is the god of Monday.

One of the things that prevents the church from being the dynamic force that it could be is the deep division within. We argue endlessly over creeds and ritual and denominationalism while the forces of evil are marching on. My friends the forces of evil in the world today are too strong to be met by isolated denominations. We must come to see that we have a unity of purpose that transcends all of our differences and that the God whom we serve is not a denominational God. When we come to see this we will meet the forces of evil, not with a mere form, but with strong organized forces of good. Let it not be said that we have a form of religion but have nothing to do with it as a force. {Quote Shakespeare Othello}

A final truth implied in our text is that we must never substitute esthetics for ethics. As Dr. Harry Emerson Fosdick has said, "There are two sets of faculties in (all of) us, the esthetic and the ethical—the sense of beauty and the sence of duty— and Christ appeals to both."[7] And there is the ever present danger that we will become so involved in singing our beautiful hymns about Christ and noticing our beautiful architecture and ritual, that our religion will end up in emotional adorations only, saying, "Lord, Lord!"

---

5. Fosdick, *A Great Time To Be Alive*, p. 89: "In the United States today there are between fifty and sixty million members of Christian churches, and were Christ's faith and way of life a vital force in anything like that number, the condition of this country would be far better than it is. Gratefully appreciating the genuine faith and character in our churches, yet when one surveys the scene as a whole, one understands the lines of a modern poet about our worshiping congregations: 'They do it every Sunday, / They'll be all right on Monday; / It's just a little habit they've acquired.'"

6. E. Stanley Jones, *The Christ of the Indian Road* (New York: Abingdon, 1925), p. 119: "We are inoculating the world with a mild form of Christianity, so that it is now practically immune against the real thing." Cf. Fosdick, *A Great Time To Be Alive*, p. 90. E. Stanley Jones (1884–1973) was a Christian missionary and evangelist.

7. Fosdick considers these themes in his sermon "Christianity More Than Duty—Not Weight but Wings" in *The Hope of the World*, pp. 167–175.

What we are seeing in our world today is countless millions of people worshipping Christ emotionally but not morally. The white men who lynch Negroes worship Christ. The strongest advocators of segregation in America also worship Christ. Many of the greatest economic exploiters worship Christ. Much of the low, evil and degrading conditions existing in our society is perpetuated by people who worship Christ. The most disastrous events in the history of Christ's movement have not come from his opposers, but from his worshippers who said, "Lord, Lord!"

My friends may I say that a Christianity that worships Christ emotionally and does not follow him ethically is a conventional sham. Let us be well assured amid our beautiful churches, and our lovely architecture, that Christ is more concerned about our attitude towards racial prejudice and war than he is about our long processionals. He is more concerned with how we treat our neighbors than how loud we sing his praises. Christ is more concerned about our living a high ethical life than our most detailed knowledge of the creeds of christendom. Not every one, not any one, who merely says, "Lord, Lord!" but he that doeth the Father's will!

A very interesting story comes to us from the pen of Dr. Hugh Price Hughes. I will tell it as used by Dr. Howard Thurman.[8] The story takes place in the city of everywhere. It is the tale of a man who might have been I, for I dreamed one time of journeying to that city. I arrived early one morning. It was cold, there were flakes of snow on the ground and {as} I stepped from the train to the platform I noticed that the baggageman and the red cap were warmly attired in heavy coats and gloves, but oddly enough, they wore no shoes. As I looked further I found that no one in the station wore any shoes. Boarding the streetcar, I saw that my fellow travellers were likewise barefoot, and upon arriving at the hotel I found the bellhop and the clerk both devoid of shoes.

Unable to restrain myself longer, I asked the ingratiating manager what the practice meant.

"What practice?" said he.

"Why," said I, pointing to his bare feet, "why don't you wear any shoes in this town?"

"Ah," said he, "that is just it. Why don't we?"

"But what is the matter? Don't you believe in shoes?"

"Believe in shoes, my friend! I should say we do. That is the first article of our creed, shoes. They are indispensable to the wellbeing of humanity."

"Well, then, why don't you wear them?" said I, bewildered.

"Ah," said he, that is just it. Why don't we?"

After I checked in the hotel I met a gentleman who wanted to show me around the city. The first thing we noticed upon emerging from the hotel was a huge brick structure of impressive proportions. To this he pointed with pride.

"You see that?" said he. "That is one of our outstanding shoe manufacturing establishments!"

"A what?" I asked in amazement. "You mean you make shoes there?"

---

8. In the folder containing this sermon, King kept a typescript of the story by Hughes (1847–1902), a Methodist minister who founded the periodical *Methodist Times* in 1885. Thurman retold the story in his book *The Growing Edge* (New York: Harper & Brothers, 1956), pp. 143–146.

"Well, not exactly," said he, "we talk about making shoes there, and believe me, we have got one of the most brilliant young fellows you have ever heard. He talks most thrillingly and convincingly every week on this subject of shoes. He has a most persuasive and appealing way. Just yesterday he moved the people profoundly with his exposition of the necessity of shoe wearing. Many broke down and wept. It was really wonderful!"

"But why don't they wear them?" said I, insistantly.

"Ah," said he, "that is just it. Why don't we?"

And coming out of "The City of Everywhere" into the "Here," over and over that query rang in my ears: "Why don't we? Why don't we? Why don't we?"

My friends we say that we believe in wearing the way of Christ. We build beautiful churches in which we preach and sing with moving eloquence about the necessity of wearing his way. But why don't we?

"Why call ye me, Lord, Lord, and do not the things I command you?"[9]

"Why don't we? Why don't we? Why don't we?

{Preached at Dexter on July 4th, 1954}

TAD. CSKC: Sermon file, folder 91, "Religion of Doing."

---

9. Cf. Luke 6:46.

"What Is Man?" Sermon
at Dexter Avenue Baptist Church

[*11 July 1954*]
Montgomery, Ala.

In this handwritten and dated version of a sermon King had been developing since his seminary years, he stresses that all people are created in God's image and bear a responsibility to live accordingly.[1] King draws upon Harry Emerson Fosdick in calling

---

1. King indicates on the folder containing this sermon that he preached this sermon at Dexter on 9 July 1954, a Friday. He may have erred on the precise date he delivered the sermon, which according to the *Montgomery Examiner*'s 15 July report of the Men's Day service, occurred on 11 July 1954. For early uses of this sermon title, see King, Sermon Introductions, 30 November 1948–16 February 1949, and "Radio Sermons," 26 July 1953–6 September 1953, pp. 84 and 136 in this volume, respectively. King's personal library contained a copy of Crozer professor Edwin Ewart Aubrey's *Living the Christian Faith* (New York: Macmillan, 1939), which King annotated. He underlined the following portion of the preface: "'What is man?' becomes an acute problem once again, and its answer lies outside the descriptions of the average psychological textbook, greatly as these contribute to our understanding of the ways in which men express themselves" (Aubrey, *Living the Christian Faith*, p. viii). King later published a version of this sermon in his 1959 book *The Measure of a Man* (Philadelphia: Christian Education Press, 1959), pp. 1–18 and in his 1963 sermon collection (King, "What Is Man?" in *Strength to Love*, pp. 87–92).

for "a church that shall be a fountainhead of a better social order. We can talk all we want to about saving souls from hell and preaching the pure and simple gospel, but unless we preach the social gospel our evangelistic gospel will be meaningless."

"What is man that thou art mindful of him?"[2] This question flowing from the lips of the Psalmist is one of the most important questions facing any generation. The whole political, social and economic structure of any society is largely determined by its answer to this pressing question. Indeed, the conflict which we witness in the world today between totalitarianism and democracy is at bottom a conflict over the question, what is man?—whether man is a cog in the wheel of the state or whether he is a free creative being capable of facing responsibility.

In our generation the asking of this question has grown to extensive propotions. But though there is widespread agreement in asking the question, there is fantastic disagreement in answering it. A few modern thinkers would probably agree with the writer of yesterday who spoke of man as the supreme clown of creation. Others would probably share the materialistic thinking of the recent writer who described man as "a chemical laboratory driven about by sex impulse."[3] Others would probably join in with the optimism of Shakespeare's Hamlet:

> What a piece of work is man! how noble in reason: how infinite in faculty: In form and moving how express and admirable: In action how like an angel: in apprehension how like a God: the beauty of the world! the paragon of animals![4]

Still others would agree with [*Thomas*] Carlyle in saying,

> There are depths in man that go to the lowest hell, and heights that reach the highest heaven, for are not both heaven and hell made out of him, everlasting miracle and mystery that he is.[5]

And so we can see that the attempt to answer the question—what is man—has brought about many answers. For the moment let us turn to this significant question and see what we can do in terms of answering it. Our answer will obviously be conditioned by the Christian doctrine of the nature of man.[6]

Let us begin by stating that man is an animal with a material body. This is some-

---

2. Cf. Psalm 8:4.

3. King may be referring to Arthur Schopenhauer, *The World as Will and Idea*, trans. R. B. Haldane and J. Kemp (London: Routledge & Kegan Paul, 1948), 3:314: "Indeed, one may say man is concrete sexual desire; for his origin is an act of copulation and his wish of wishes is an act of copulation, and this tendency alone perpetuates and holds together his whole phenomenal existence."

4. Shakespeare, *Hamlet*, act 2, sc. 2.

5. Carlyle, *The French Revolution* (1837).

6. King submitted an outline entitled "The Nature of Man" as part of an assignment based on William Newton Clarke's *An Outline of Christian Theology* (1898) for George W. Davis's course at Crozer called Christian Theology for Today. The outline parallels his points in this sermon (see King, "Six Talks in Outline," 13 September–23 November 1949, in *Papers* 1:242–243).

what obvious, but nevertheless it should be stressed. Man is properly a part of animated nature and cannot disown his kinship with the earth and the creatures that live upon it. No one can doubt the fact that the organization of man's body resembles the bodies of animals in general. And like all other animals man is dependent on his environment for food, raiment and shelter.

This means that man's body is significant. This is what distinguishes Christian from Greek thought. And so because man is an animal with a material body, we must forever be conserned about his material well being. To often have we talked about the primacy of the spiritual with little concern for the material. It might be true that man cannot live by bread alone, but the mere fact that the alone is added to the passage implies that man cannot live without bread.[7] My friends man is body as well as soul, and any religion that pretends to care for the souls of people but is not interested in the slums that damn them, the city government that corrupts them, and the economic order that cripples them, is a dry, passive do nothing religion in need of new blood. As I look at the economic and social injustices existing in our world, I plead for a church that shall be a fountainhead of a better social order.[8] We can talk all we want to about saving souls from hell and preaching the pure and simple gospel, but unless we preach the social gospel our evangelistic gospel will be meaningless. Man is an animal with a material body, and he who overlooks this is overlooking an essential part of man's nature

Yet we cannot stop here. Man is more than an animal. Man is more than flesh and blood. Some year ago a chemist attempted to determine the worth of man in terms of material value. The results of the study revealed that in terms of the markets of that day man was worth only 99 cents in ~~terms of~~ material value. This simply means that the stuff of man's bodily make-up is worth only 99 cents.[9] (I guess now that the standards of living are a little higher man is worth a little more). But is it possible to explain the whole of man in terms of 99 cents. Can we explain the literary genius of a Shakespere in terms of 99 cents? Can we explain the artistic [*genius?*] of a Micalangelo in terms of 99 cents? Can we explain the musical genius of a

---

7. This phrase is found in both the Hebrew Bible and New Testament; for example, see Deuteronomy 8:3 and Matthew 4:4.

8. Fosdick, "Christianity's Stake in the Social Situation," in *The Hope of the World*, p. 25: "I plead instead for a church that shall be a fountainhead of a better social order. Any church that pretends to care for the souls of people but is not interested in the slums that damn them, the city government that corrupts them, the economic order that cripples them, and international relations that, leading to peace or war, determine the spiritual destiny of innumerable souls—that kind of church, I think, would hear again the Master's withering words: 'Scribes and Pharisees, hypocrites!'"

9. Fosdick, "There Is No Death," in *Successful Christian Living* (New York: Harper & Brothers, 1937), pp. 265–266: "Certain chemists, we are told, with a flair for statistics, figured out the chemical constitution of an average man and put the result into easily understandable terms, thus: An average man contains enough fat to make seven bars of soap, enough iron to make a medium-sized nail, enough sugar to fill a shaker, enough lime to whitewash a chicken-coop, enough phosphorus to make twenty-two hundred match tips, enough magnesium for a dose of magnesia, enough potassium to explode a toy cannon, together with a little sulphur. And the chemists figured that at market rates then current these chemical elements could be obtained for about ninety-eight cents. That's what we are made of. That's what all our seers and prophets, the great musicians, the great poets, the great leaders of the race, have been made of, about ninety-eight cents worth of chemical materials." King annotated a copy of this book and kept it in his personal library.

King writes a brief outline for "What Is Man?" the opening page of his copy of Reinhold Niebuhr's 1932 book *Moral Man and Immoral Society*.

Beetoven in terms of 99 cent? Can we explain the spiritual genius of Jesus of Nazareth in terms of nighty nine cents? Can we explain the ongoing processes of our own ordinary lives in terms of 99¢. My friends there is something in man that cannot be calculated in materialistic terms. Man is a being of spirit. This is ultimately that which distingushes man from his animal ancestry. He is in time, yet above time; He is in nature, yet above nature. He is made to have communion with that which is eternal and everlasting. We cannot imagine an animal writing a

177

Shakesperian play. We have never seen a group of animals sitting down discussing intricate problems concerning the political and economic structure of a society. We have never come across a group of animals [*strikeout illegible*] speculating on the nature and destiny of the universe. But man, that being that God created just a little lower than the angels, is able to think a poem and write it; he's able to think a symphony and compose it.[10] He's able to imagine a great civilization and create it. Through his amazing capacity for memory and thought and imagination, man is able to leap oceans, break through walls, and rise above the limitations of time and space. Through his powers of memory man can have communion with the past; through his powers of imagination man can embrace the uncertainties of the future.

Along with this strong intellectual capacity in man, there is a will. Man has within himself the power of choosing his supreme end. Animals follow their natures. But man has the power of acting upon his own nature almost as if from without; of guiding it within certain limits; and of modifying it by the choice of [*strikeout illegible*] of meaninful ends. Man entertains ideals, and ideals become his inspiration. Man can be true or false to his nature. He can be a hero or a fool. Both possibilities, the noble and the base alike, indicate man's greatness.

All that has just been said concerning the spiritual element in man gives backing to the Christian contention that man is made in the image of God.[11] Man is more than flesh and blood. Man is a spiritual being born to have communion with the eternal God of the universe. God creates every individual for a purpose—to have fellowship with him. This is the ultimate meaning of the image of God. It is not that man as he is in himself bears God's likeness, but rather that man is designated for and called to a particular relation with God. This concept of the image of God assures us that we, unlike our animal ancestry and the many inanimat objects of the universe, are priveledged to have fellowship with the divine.

Now we must admit that through our sinfulness some of the image of God has left us. God's image has been terribly scarred by our sin. In our modern world we have tried to get away from this term sin. We have attempted to substituted for it high sounding psychological phrases and other explanation that will relieve us of responsibility. But my friends whether we want to accept it or not man is a sinner in need of God's divine grace. Whenever a man looks deep down into the depths of his nature he becomes painfully aware of the fact that the history of his life is the history of a constant revolt against God. "All we like sheep have gone astray."[12] Every nation, every class and every man is apart of the gonewrongness of human nature. Of all the silly, sentimental teachings which have ever characterized any generation the denial of human sin is one of the worst.

Yet man is not made to dwell in the valleys of sin and evil; man is made for for that which is high and noble. When I see how we fight vicious wars and destroy human life on bloody battlefields, I find myself saying: "Man is not made for that."

---

10. The phrase "a little lower than the angels" is found in both the Hebrew Bible and New Testament; for example, see Psalm 8:5 and Hebrews 2:7.

11. Cf. Genesis 1:27.

12. Cf. Isaiah 53:6.

When I see how we live our lives in selfishness and hate, again I say: "man is not made for that" When I see how we often throw away the precious lives that God has given us in rioteous living, again I find myself saying: "Man is not made for that. My friends man is made for the stars, created for eternity, born for the everlasting. Man is a child of the almighty God, born for his everlasting fellowship. "What is man that thou art mindful of him? and the son of man, that thou visitest him? For thou hast crowned him with glory and honour. Thou madest him to have dominion over the works of thou hands; thou hast put all things under his feet. All sheep and oxen, yea and the beasts of the field. The fowl of the air, and the fish of sea, and whatsoever passeth through the paths of the sea."[13] This is man's kingly perogative. Who this afternoon will rise out of the dark and dreary valleys of sin and evil, realizing that man's proper home is in the high mountain of truth, beaty and goodness; yea even where God the eternal dwells forever.

Preached at Dexter, July 9, 1954

AD. CSKC: Sermon file, folder 22, "What Is Man?"

---

13. Cf. Psalm 8:4–8.

"God's Love," Sermon
at Dexter Avenue Baptist Church

[5 September 1954]
Montgomery, Ala.

After a summer commuting from Boston, King moved to Montgomery and began to serve as the full-time pastor of Dexter Avenue Baptist Church on 1 September 1954. For his first sermon following the move, he preached from John 3:16 and 1 John 4:8, emphasizing God's universality: "God's love is [too] broad to be limited to a particular race."

Text: John 3:16 [1]

I   Introduction:
(1) F.W. Myers question: Is the universe friendly?[2] This has been the question

---

1. "For God so loved the world, that he gave his only begotten Son, that whosoever believeth in him should not perish, but have eternal life."

2. F. W. H. Myers was a British scholar and member of the Society for Psychical Research in England in the 1880s. Harry Emerson Fosdick used this quote in *The Meaning of Faith* (New York: Association Press, 1917), p. 51: "F. W. Myers, when asked what question he would put to the Sphinx, if he were given only one chance, replied that he would ask, 'Is the universe friendly?'"

that the questing minds of philosophers and theologians have asked over the years. Some have answered no to the question. Others have answered yes.

   a.   The answer of Shakespeare's MacBeth[3]

   b.   The answer of Paul Lawrence Dunbar[4]

   c.   The positive answer that Christianity gives. God, we are told is love.

(2) One of the familiar passages affirming this love of God is John 3:16. "For God so loved the world that he gave his only begotten Son, that whosoever believest in him should not perish, but have everlasting life." And another states "God is Love." 1 John 4:8.[5] Both of these passages reveal several characteristics of God's love.

II   The characteristics of God's love

(1) <u>God's love is unceasing and eternal,</u> Love is an essential part of God's nature. Notice the text says "God is Love." This can never be said about man. We can never say that man is love. We can only say that man loves. Love is not an essential part of [*strikeout illegible*] man's nature. But God is love. God's love is not a single act, but is the abiding state of God's heart. God does not begin to love. God's love have no beginning and will have no ending. God always has loved and always will love. Civilizations might rise and fall, but God love will be here. Empires might crumble and perish, but God's love will be here. Even there might be a day when the stars cease to bedeck the heavens, but the love of God will be here. Man's love might waver and even dry up, but God's love will be here. God's love is eternal.

(2) ~~God~~ Notice secondly that God so loved the <u>world</u>. In other words, God's love has breath. It is all inclusive. It a big love; its a broad love. This is one of the things that distinguishes the N.T. from the O.T. (ill. The O.T. God is a tribal and national God.). Jesus came on the scene saying "our Father" meaning that he is everybodies Father. God's love is to broad to be limited to a particular race. It is to big to be wrapped in a particularistic garment. It is to great to be encompassed by any single nation. God is a universal God. This fact has been a ray of hope and has given a sense of belonging to hundreds of disinherited peope. ([*strikeout illegible*] Use the illustration of the old slave preacher.[6] Show how we as a minority group can gain consolation from it) All of the hate in the world cannot destroy the universal effect of God's love. Along with its breath, it is personal and indivial. God's [*loves?*] infinitessimal <u>me</u>.

---

3. King may refer to Shakespeare, *Macbeth,* act 5, sc. 5, as he does in "Creating the Abundant Life," Sermon at Dexter Avenue Baptist Church, 26 September 1954, p. 188 in this volume.

4. King may refer to the poem "Life" by Paul Laurence Dunbar (1895) as he does in "Creating the Abundant Life," 26 September 1954, p. 188 in this volume.

5. "He that loveth not knoweth not God; for God is love."

6. In an audio recording of "God's Love," a sermon delivered on 23 December 1962 at Ebenezer, King used this illustration: "This is what the old slave preacher used to say. He didn't have his grammar right but he knew God, and he would stand before the people caught in the dark night of slavery with nothing to look forward to the next morning but the long row of cotton ahead, the sizzling heat, and the rawhide whip of the overseer. He would stand up before them after they had worked from [*words inaudible*]. He said now, 'You ain't no slave. You ain't no nigger. But you're God's child.'" This anecdote may have been drawn from Howard Thurman's *Jesus and the Disinherited* (New York: Abingdon-Cokesbury Press, 1949), p. 50.

(3) God so love the world that he <u>gave</u>. God's love is ~~self~~ self-giving and sponta-neous. No body commanded God to give his love. It is just God's nature to give. God's gift to man was given not because God was asked to give it, but because he wanted to give it. Man didn't even ask for it. (Give ill of wife).[7] So it is with God's love. Can't you see what the hymn writer meant when he said:

Were the whole realm of nature mine
That were a present far to small
Love so amazing so divine
Demands my life, my all and all[8]

(4) God's love is redemptive. God's love gives life and new light. It saves us from death.

III Conclusion: All that I have said about the characteristics of God's love is brought to clearer light when we turn our eyes toward Calvery, for it is here that we find the supreme example of God's love. ~~And~~ The scene on Calvery is more than a meaningless drama that took place on an earthly stage, but it is a telescope through which we look out into the long vista of eternity and see the love of God breaking forth into time. It is God's way of saying to wayward man, "Come home I still love you." (Tell story of the musician who went to France.)

Paul was right. "Nothing can separate us from the love of God."[9]

Preached at Dexter Sept. 3, 1954[10]

AD. CSKC: Sermon file, folder 69, "God's Love."

---

7. King used the following illustration in his sermon "God's Love," Sermon notes, 5 September 1954, in *Papers* 2:327: "So God's gift to man was given not because God was asked to give it but because he wanted to give it. e.g. a gift that a man gives his wife which she doesn't ask for is more appreciated than one which is given which she ask for."

8. King cites Isaac Watts's hymn "When I Survey the Wondrous Cross" (1707).

9. Cf. Romans 8:35–39.

10. King may have misdated the sermon since 3 September was a Friday.

"The Vision of a World Made New"

[*9 September 1954*]
[*St. Louis, Mo.*]

At the invitation of Nannie Helen Burroughs, president of the Woman's Convention Auxiliary, National Baptist Convention, King spoke at the organization's annual meeting on the theme of the convention, "The Vision of the World Made New."[1] He rejects colonialism and imperialism and condemns segregation, noting, "The tragedy is that the Church sanctioned it." Still he remains hopeful: "Today we stand between

---

1. Burroughs to King, 3 August 1954, in *Papers* 2:282–283.

two worlds, a world that is gradually passing away and a world that is being born. We stand between the dying old and the emerging new." Burroughs later wrote King to thank him for sharing with the delegates: "What your message did to their thinking and to their faith is 'bread cast upon the water' that will be seen day by day in their good works in their communities." [2]

Frequently there appears on the stage of history individuals who have the insight to look beyond the inadequacies of the old order and see the necessity for the new. These are the persons with a sort of divine discontent. They realize that the world as it is is far from the world that it ought to be. They never confuse the "isness" of an old order with the "oughtness" of a new order.[3] And so in every age and every generation there are those persons who have envisioned some new order. Plato envisioned it in his Republic as a time when justice would reign throughout society and philosophers would become kings and kings philosophers. Karl Marx envisioned it as the emergence of a classless society in which the proletariant would ultimately conquer the reign of the bourgeoisie. Out of such a vision grew the slogan "From each according to his ability, to each [*according to his need?*]"[4] Edward Bellamy envisioned it Looking Backward as a time when the inequalities of monopoly capitalism would be blotted out and all men would live on a relatively equal plane with all of the conveniences of life.[5] The Christian religion envisioned it as the kingdom of God, a time when God would reign supreme in all life, and love, brotherhood and right relationship would be the order of society. In every age men have quested and longed for a new order.

Many centuries ago ~~there~~ [*strikeout illegible*] a man by the name of John was in prison on a lonely, obscure island called Patmos. In such a situation he was deprived of almost every freedom, but the freedom to think. He thought about many things. He thought about a possible new world and a new social order. He meditated on the need for a change in the old pattern of things. So one day he cried out: "I saw a new heaven and a new earth . . . I saw the holy city, new Jerusalem, coming down from God out of heaven."[6]

John could talk meaningfully about the new Jerusalem because he had experienced the old Jerusalem with its perfunctory ceremonialism, its tragic gulfs between

2. Burroughs to King, 21 September 1954, in *Papers* 2:295–296; see also Notes on Speech by Martin Luther King, Jr., at Woman's Auxiliary, National Baptist Convention on 9 September 1954, September 1954, in *Papers* 2:294.

3. Reinhold Niebuhr, *Beyond Tragedy: Essays on the Christian Interpretation of History* (New York: Charles Scribners' Sons, 1937), pp. 137–138: "The problem of maturity is not only to achieve unity amidst complexity of impulses but to overcome the particular conflict between the IS and the OUGHT of life, between the ideal possibilities to which freedom encourages man and the drive of egoism, which reason sharpens rather than assuages."

4. Marx, *Critique of the Gotha Programme* (New York: International Publishers, 1938), p. 10.

5. King refers to Bellamy's *Looking Backward 2000–1887*, a copy of which Coretta Scott gave to him during the spring of 1952. For his thoughts on the book, see King to Coretta Scott, 18 July 1952, pp. 123–126 in this volume.

6. Cf. Revelation 21:1–2.

abject poverty and inordinate wealth, its political domination and economic exploitation. John could see this old Jerusalem passing away and the new Jerusalem coming into being.[7]

John is saying something quite significant here. He realized that the old earth did not represent the earth as it should be. He knew that the conditions of the old Jerusalem did not represent the permanent structure of the universe. The old Jerusalem represented injustice, crushing domination, and the triumph of the forces of darkness. The new Jerusalem reprensented, justice, brotherhood and the triumph of the forces of light. So when John said he saw the new Jerusalem, he was saying in substance that he saw justice conquering injustice, he saw the forces of darkness consumed by the forces of light. Ultimately history brings into being the new order to blot out the tragic reign of the old order.

II   Now if we will look far enough we will see the truth of John's vision being revealed in the contemporary world. Today we stand between two worlds, a world that is gradually passing away and a world that is being born. We stand between the dying old and the emerging new.

    A. On a world scale we have seen the old order in the form of colonialism and imperialism. These lead to domination and exploitation.

       (1) Number of persons in the world as compared with number of colored.

       (2) Fifty years ago the vast majority of these persons were under some colonial power.

India under British
Africa under British, French and Dutch
China   "   "   "   "   "
Indonesia under the Dutch

       (3) One of the tragedies of the Church was that it became allied to the old order. Note South Africa and India.

       (4) But in spite of this we have gradually seen the old order pass away. Most of these colonial people are now free.[8]

       (5) So, like John, we can say we see a new heaven and a new earth. The old order of ungodly exploitation and crushing domination is passing away.

    B. On a national scale we have seen the old order in the form of segregation and discrimination.

       (1) Segregation has been an instrument all along to remind the Negro of his inferior status. Its presupposition is that the group that is segregated is inferior to the group th is segregating

---

7. Cf. Revelation 21:4.

8. King made similar points in notes for a speech he may have delivered in Ghana in March 1957. He chronicled how Western nations have exploited India, China, and Africa while also celebrating freedom. King charged: "With her [*injustice?*], her segregation and discrimination America is not fit to be the leading power of the world. And if she doesn't [*straighten*] up God will break the backbone of her power." He filed these notes in the same homiletic folder as this sermon (King, God's Judgment on Western Civilization, March 1957).

(2) Through segregation the Negro has been dominated politically . . .

(3) The tragedy is that the Church sanctioned it.

(4) But the tide has turned now. Segregation is passing away

III Notice one other point of the text. It mentions that this new city decends out of heaven from God rather than ascends out of earth from man.

AD. CSKC: Sermon file, folder 80, "God's Judgment on Western Civilization" / "The Vision of a World Made New."

"Propagandizing Christianity,"
Sermon at Dexter Avenue Baptist Church

[*12 September 1954*]
Montgomery, Ala.

King preached this homily, one of his most overtly evangelistic messages, during his first month as Dexter's pastor. Encouraging his listeners to become "propaganda agents" for the cause of Jesus, he poses this challenge: "If Hitler could do all of this with an evil idea it seems that we could rock the world with the truth of the saving power of the gospel."

Text: Acts 1:8[1]

Introduction: For the average person, the word propaganda has evil and viscious overtones. Propaganda is considered something used by the demagogue to spread evil ideologies. Because of the high state of development that propaganda has reached in totalitarian nations, it is readily dismissed as something to be condemned and avoided. But propaganda does not have to be ~~good or~~ evil. There is a noble sense in which propaganda can be used. Remember that the term originated in the Catholic Church. Propaganda is simply an attempt to disseminate principles or ideas by organized effort. ~~And so when Jesus says to his disciples "go ye into all the world and preach my gospel," he is saing int in effect, propagandize my word, spread it, disseminate it, push it into every nock and crock of the universe.~~[2]

---

1. "But ye shall receive power, after that the Holy Ghost is come upon you: and ye shall be witnesses unto me both in Jerusalem, and in all Judaea, and in Samaria, and unto the uttermost part of the earth."

2. Cf. Mark 16:15. In another sermon with a similar theme, King wrote an alternate introduction that refers to Harry Emerson Fosdick's sermon "The Fine Art of Making Goodness Attractive" (Fosdick, *The Hope of the World*, pp. 195–203). King's introduction reads: "In these days of modern transition confusion, when the forces of evil seem to stand before us like the beaming sun and the forces of good seem to be lost behind the dim fog of obscurity, one is almost forced to question the validity of ~~religion~~ Xtny. Has ~~religion~~ Xnt lost its power of directing and guiding the spiritual life of society? Has ~~religion~~ Xty been relegated to a mere creedal system with no transforming power? These are serious question. They are questions which are probbably lurking in the minds of all well thinking Christians and even non-Christians. Amid this situation I am lead to ask another question which to me is all important: Have we as Xns properly and adaquately propagandized Christianity? I can imagine that many of you are now quite astonished after hearing me use the word propaganda in relation to religion. The word propaganda for most of you has usually carried an unpleasant connotation. We often think of propaganda as a means of

~~On one occas~~ In the 1 chapter of the book of Acts Jesus is reported to have said to his disciples, "ye shall be witnesses unto me in Jerusalem, and in all Judae, and in Samaria, and unto the uttermost part of the earth." I would like to use this text as a basis of our discussion this morning, for ~~it~~ in these words Jesus is calling upon his disciples to ~~propagandize his word~~ be true propagandizers. He is saying in effect, propagandize my word, spread it, dissiminate it, push it into every nock and crok of the universe, carry it to every tribe and every race, every nation and every village; Propagandize my word to the uttermost part of the earth. This command comes to every generation of Christians. Jesus is still saying to Christians everywhere, ye shall be my witnesses, ye shall be my propaganda agents, ye shall be the spreader of my truth in all the world.

Now let us look at this text more closely and see what Jesus means by our being his witnesses. How are we to propagandize Christianity. The word witness ~~goes through~~ has three meanings in the New Testament, and these three meanings of the words witness set forth our responsibility in propagandizing Christianity.

I   The first meaning of the word is found in the Gopels and Acts. Here witness means simply to go out and talk about the resurrection. In other words it means verbal affirmation. Now this is important. We are forever confronted with the pressing demand to go out and [*strikeout illegible*] talk about Christianity. Never underestimate the power of words. (Advetizing has discovered it; Hitler discoved it). If Hitler could do all of this with an evil idea it seems that we could rock the world with the truth of the saving power of the gospel. If the advertizers can convince ~~the~~ men that they cant do without their products, we ought to be able to convince men of the productive power of God in Christ. (I can remember as a little boy how my grandmother cooked biskets and how I would run around the community and share them. They were too good to hold.) Do you really believe in this thing called Christianity. Do you believen that herein lies the solution to the world's problems. Do you believe that Christiainty has the power to give new meaning to life. Well tell the world about it. Tell your collegues about it, your workers, your franternity brothers, your playmates.

And Don't be afraid to defend the Church where necessary. Certainly the Church is not perfect, It has often stood in the way of social and scientific progress and as I will show in a few minutes I am often ashamed of the Church, but in spite of its errors I would hate to see what the world would be like without it.

(a) If someone tells you that all preachers are racketeers and insincere, go back and tell

(b) If they tell you that the church sanction ingnorance, go back and tell them.

(c) you dont have to be a philosopher [*or?*] theologian to talk about it. Be able to say as the man of old, "I was blind but now I see[3]

---

propagating evil and vicious ideologies. Yet we can by no means limit the word propaganda to such narrow confind. Propaganda may be good or bad depending on the merit of the cause urged. If you will turn to your Funk and Wagnalls' Dictionary you will find the word defined thus: '1. Any institution or scheme for propagating a doctrine or system'" (King, "Propagandizing Religion," 1948–1954).

3. Cf. John 9:25; see also John Newton's hymn "Amazing Grace" (1779).

SUCCESSFUL CHRISTIAN LIVING

turns its evil instincts! We thought that patriotism might save us, but see the murderous consequence which now we face! No! Something greater than science, deeper than education, more inclusive than patriotism, must save us. I am not ashamed of the gospel of Christ.

Indeed, in these difficult days one seems to discover its deep meaning all over again. In the gospel stands the most sober, realistic statement of the tragic need of man that the race has ever faced. Why should we walk at the great word "salvation" in view of our desperate want of it? Does not scientific medicine set itself to save us from disease? Do not schools exist because we need salvation from ignorance? Do we not institute philanthropies and pioneer more equitable economic orders because we need to be saved from poverty? Salvation is the chief preoccupation of all intelligent and earnest minds. But behind disease, ignorance, poverty, and running through the causes which produce and perpetuate them, is this deeper thing, the tragic selfishness of the unredeemed human soul. That is the sober, realistic fact. So the gospel of Christ has always taught. We may well be ashamed of much that is associated with the history of organized Christianity and with much that goes on in the churches today, but the gospel of Christ—that presents the soberest statement of realistic human need the world has ever faced.

For another thing, I am not ashamed of the gospel of Christ in its insistence on the prodigious lifting power of vicarious sacrifice. Vicarious sacrifice is the most impressive fact in the moral world. What one of us has not been saved from something because another, who did not need to do it, voluntarily took on himself our calamity or sin and by self-sacrifice redeemed us? And wherever that spirit of the cross appears and the ancient words come alive again, "He saved others; himself he cannot save," there is the

[80]

ON BEING CHRISTIANS UNASHAMED

most subduing, humbling, impressive fact we see. How can a man be ashamed of that?

This last week we buried Mrs. Anne Macy, Helen Keller's lifelong friend and teacher. Nearly fifty years ago, a little girl barely seven years of age—imprisoned behind doors so firmly locked it seemed they could not be unclosed and walls so high it seemed they could not be overpassed—was given to the care of this sacrificial teacher. For Mrs. Macy too had met blindness and, having partially surmounted it, vicariously gave herself to the blind. How subtly she passed through those fast closed doors! How marvelously she overpassed those high, strong walls and became to that imprisoned child the great emancipator! Years went by and Helen Keller passed her entrance examinations to college. Years went by and Helen Keller graduated from college *cum laude*. More years passed and Helen Keller was a world figure, known by every one. Still in the background was this magician, this self-effacing teacher, putting her life into another's and liberating it. It is one of the most amazing stories in the human record. And so powerful is such sacrifice that, because of this example of what can be done, new hopes have come, new methods, new open doors for blind and deaf folk everywhere, and the story has no end. Once more vicarious sacrifice works its miracle. How can one be ashamed of that?

To be sure, our world is disgraceful with the opposite of it; man's callous selfishness. Has some one here supposed that Paul, a man of piety and faith, must have been, therefore, a sentimentalist and looked at life through rosy spectacles? You should read the whole of this first chapter of the letter to the Romans, where our text appears. It is one of the most vehement eruptions of disgust with human life ever written. Listen to Paul in his denunciatory summary of humankind, "filled with all unrighteousness, wickedness, covetousness, maliciousness; full of envy, murder,

[81]

King writes, "I am ashamed of Christianity, but not of Christ" in the margins of his copy of Harry Emerson Fosdick's 1937 book *Successful Christian Living* (pp. 80–81).

II The second meaning of witness comes from Paul. For him witness means living a triumphant life. Its not enough to talk about it but we must live about it. (Quote Edgar Guest)[4] The most indisputable fact in all the universe is a pernal example. As we look around we see divorces rampant, the liquor traffic on the march, gambling almost legalized, sex turned into an immoral plaything. And involved in all of these is Christians—

(a) The Church has been too soporific

(b) The ministers are not to be excused.

{Preached at Dexter Sept. 10 1954}[5]

ADf. CSKC: Sermon file, folder 55, "Propagandizing Christianity."

4. King probably refers to Edgar A. Guest's poem "It Couldn't Be Done": "Somebody said that it couldn't be done / But he with a chuckle replied / That 'maybe it couldn't,' but he would be one / Who wouldn't say so till he tried. / So he buckled right in with the trace of a grin / on his face. If he worried he hid it. / He started to sing as he tackled the thing / That couldn't be done, and he did it!" (Guest, *Breakfast Table Chat* [Detroit: n.p., 1914], p. 148).

5. King wrote this date, a Friday, next to the sermon's title. He probably preached this sermon on Sunday, 12 September. He was also scheduled to deliver a version of this sermon on 2 July 1950 ("Ebenezer Baptist Reveals Slate," *Atlanta Daily World,* 1 July 1950).

"Creating the Abundant Life," Sermon at Dexter Avenue Baptist Church

26 September 1954
Montgomery, Ala.

In this handwritten text, King explains that each person can have a meaningful life: "Discover your calling. Then give your heart soul and mind to it. And thereby life will present you with meaning that you never thought was there. You are on the road to creating the abundant life."[1]

Subject: "Creating the Abundant Life"

Text: I come that you might have life John 10:10

1. King filed several outlines and illustrations in the same file folder, all of which contain themes found in "Creating the Abundant Life." These themes included the importance of dreaming, the value of persistence and hard work, and the worth of every human life (see King, Creating the Abundant Life, Sermon outline, 1948–1954; King, Be the Best of Whatever You Are by Douglas Malloch, 1948–1954; King, Notes on Clarence Darrow, 1948–1954; King, "A Moment of Difficult Decision," 1948–1954.

I

It is a very common thing to see people wandering into the world looking for life. They never get it. What they get is existence. Existence is something that you find; life is something that you create. Existence is the mere raw material from which all life is created. Therefore if life ever seems worth while to you it will not be because you found it that way, but because, by the help of God, you made it so. Life is not something that you find. Life is something that you create.

It was always Jesus' conviction that life is worth living and that men through the proper adjustment and attitudes could create a meaningful life. On one occasion Jesus said "I am come that they might have life, and that they might have it more abundantly." In other words Jesus is saying that a part of his mission on earth is to help men create the abundant life. He came not to negate life but to affirm it.

Yet in spite of Jesus' words we are confronted with the tragic fact that so many people today are disillusioned about life, feeling that life has no meaning. Suicides are quite prevalent and frustration and bewilderment are on the march. So many people today have decided to cry with Shakespeare's MacBeth

> Life is a tale told by an
> idiot, full of sound and
> fury signifying nothing[2]

Others have decided to cry with Paul Lawrence Dunbar,

> A crust of bread and a corner to sleep in;
> A minute to smile and an hour to weep in;
> A pint of joy to a peck of trouble,
> and never a laugh that the mourns
> came double; and that is life[3]

Still others have decided to cry with the philosopher [*Arthur*] Schopenhaur that "life is a tragic comedy played over and over again with slight changes in costume and scenery."[4]

Why is it that so many people have taken this attitude? Why is it that so many people have concluded that life has no meaning and that their [*strikeout illegible*] names are written in the diary of fate? I think that one reason among others is that many of us fail to see that life is largely what we make it, by the help of God. Many of us are unhappy and disillusioned about life because we are trying to find life ready made. We are looking for it to be handed to us on a silver platter. But it doesn't happen like that. Life is not something that you find. Life is something that you create.

---

2. Shakespeare, *Macbeth*, act 5, sc. 5.

3. Dunbar, "Life" (1895).

4. King distills a number of ideas from Schopenhauer's chapter "On History" in *The World as Will and Idea*, 3: 224–227.

Now we may well ask how do we create this abundant life that Jesus came bring? What should we do and what attitudes should we ~~developed~~ develope to make life worth living.

(The miserable life is the unextended life)

(1) First if we are to create the abundant life we must give ourselves to some great purpose and some great cause that transcends ourselves. This is what Jesus meant when he said he who loseth his life shall find it.[5] In other words he who loseth his life in some great purpose or cause transcending himself shall find his life.

This giving of oneself to some purpose transcending oneself might take place through ones life's work, provided that this life's work is decent and honest. Every man should learn to love his job. And there is a joy and an eternal satisfaction that comes out of a job well done. Whatever your life's work may be do it well. Do it as if God Almighty called you at this particular moment in history to do it. Do it so well that nobody could do it any better.

Whatever your life's work may be I admonish you to consider it significant. If God has endowed you with some great and extraordinary talent, use it well. If God has endowed you with just ordinary talent use that well, for ultimately God's standard of measurement is not in terms of how much we have but what we do with what we have. If your life's work is street sweeping, sweep them well. Be determined to sweep streets like Micaelangelo painted pictures, like Beetoven composed music, like Shakespeare wrote literature.[6] Sweep streets so well that all the heavenly host will have to pause and say, "here is a job well done and a life well lived."[7] The words of Douglas Malloch are relevant still:

> If you can't be a pine on the top of the hill,
> Be a shrub in the valley. But be
> the best shrub on the side of the
> rill; be a bush if you cant be a tree.
> If you can't be a highway, just be
> a trail. If you can't be the Sun,
> be a star. It isn't by size that
> you win or you fail. Be the best
> of whatever you are.[8]

Discover your calling. Then give your heart soul and mind to it. And thereby life will present you with meaning that you never thought was there. You are on the road to creating the abundant life.

(2) A second thing that is necessary to make life worth living is to live everyday

---

5. Cf. Matthew 10:39.

6. Michelangelo Buonarroti (1475–1564) and Ludwig van Beethoven (1770–1827).

7. At a 1 January 1957 rally in Atlanta, King attributed this illustration to Benjamin Mays (see King, "Facing the Challenge of a New Age," in *Papers* 4:79).

8. Malloch, "Be the Best of Whatever You Are" (1926).

to our highest and best selves. We dont have to go very far in life to see that it is possible to live to our lowest and worst selves. We all observe within ourselves something of what psychitrist and psychologist call Schizophrenia or split personality. We see a conflict between what we actually are and what we ought to be. The "isness" of our present natures is out of propotion with the eternal "oughtness" forever confronting us.[9] This is what the apostle Paul meant when he talked of the conflict between flesh and spirit. This is what he meant when he "the good that I would, I do not, and the evil that I would not, that I do."[10] This is what Ovid, the Latin poet meant when he said, "I see and approve the better things of life, but the evil things I do."[11] This is what Plato meant when he compared the personality to a Charioteer with two head strong [*strikeout illegible*] horses each wanting to go in different directions.[12] This is what Saint Augustine meant when he said, "Lord make me pure, but not yet."[13] The conflict between what we know we ought to be and what we actually are is one that confronts us all.

The wider the gap is between our higher selves and our lower selves, the more disintegrated we are; the less meaning we find in life. The more we live up to our higher natures, the more integrated we are and the more meaning we find in life. No man can be permanently happy who lives on the low planes of existence. Any man who lives out of harmony with his higher nature, is living out of harmony with his true essence, and such disharmony bring unhappiness and cynicism. Such with the plight of that Prodical Son who had gone into a far country and wasted all, living on the low and evil planes of existence. But then one day out in a swine pasture he came to himself. He came to see that the life that God had given him was to precious to throw away in low and evil living, and he knew that so long as he remaind their he would be frustrated and disillusioned, finding no meaning in life.[14] My friends we must come to see that we are not made to live on the low planes of existence. When I see how the nations of the world fight wars and destroy hundreds and thousands of lives on battlefields I find myself saying, man isn't made for that. When I see how we often live our lives in selfishness and hate envy and jealousy I find myself saying, man is not made for that. When I notice how so many of us throw away the precious lives that God has given us in rioteous living, I find myself saying, man is not made for that. Man is a child of God, [*strikeout illegible*] made for the stars, created for eternity, born for the everlasting, and so long [*strikeout illegible*] as man lives out of harmony with this high called he will find life a frustrated and meaningless drama played over and over again with slight changes in costume and scenery.[15] Go out and choose my friends to live up to your highest and best self, and

---

9. Cf. Niebuhr, *Beyond Tragedy*, pp. 137–138.
10. Cf. Romans 7:19.
11. Ovid *Metamorphoses* 7.20.
12. Plato *Phaedrus* 246a–247c.
13. Cf. Augustine *Confessions* 8.7.
14. Cf. Luke 15:11–32.
15. King paraphrases segments of Schopenhauer's chapter "On History" in *The World as Will and Idea*, 3: 224–227.

thereby create the abundant life. John Oxenham's words at this point have become immortal:

> To every man there openeth a way
> and ways and a way. The high
> soul climbs the high way, and
> the low soul grasps the low.
> And in between on the midst
> flats the rest drift to and
> fro. But to every man there openeth
> a high way and a low a ~~way~~ Each
> man decideth which way his
> soul shall go.[16]

(3) The third thing that we must do to create the abundant life is to choose to have an abiding religious faith. In other words we must have a lasting faith in God. H. G. Wells was right, "the man who is not religious begins at nowhere and ends at nothing, for religion is like a might wind that breaks down doors and knocks down walls and makes that possible and even easy which seems difficult and impossible."[17] It is religion which gives meaning to life. Religion keeps alive the conviction that life is meaningful and that there is purpose in the universe. Religion gives the individual a sense of belonging. It instills the awareness that in all of his struggles man has cosmic companionship.

On the surface it might appear that religion is a sort of unnecessary past time, which we can really do without. But then one day the tidal waves of confusion roll before us; the storms and winds of tribulation beat against our doors, and unless we have a deep and patient faith we will be blown assunder. You see religion doesn't gaurantee us that we wont have any problems and difficulties. What religion does is to give us the power to confront the problems of life with a smile. Religion does not aim to save us from the troubles and reverses of life, these come alike to all; but it aims to support us under them and to teach us the divine purpose in them. Religion does not say that everything which happens to us is good in itself, but it does say that if you love good properly all things work together for good.[18] It assures us that although we walk through the valley of the shadow of death, God is there.[19] It assures us that life has meaning because God controls the process of life.

In our scientific age there is a great temptation to usher God out of the universe. We are prone to believe that only that exist which we can see and touch and feel, i.e. things which we can apply our five senses to. But my friends this is certainly false. Science can never make God and unseen realities irrelavant, for in a real sense the everything that we see owes its existence to something that we do not see. You may see my body, but you can never see my personality. You may see the beautiful archi-

---

16. King paraphrases Oxenham's poem "The Ways," which was published in a collection of poems entitled *All's Well!* (New York: George H. Doran, 1916), p. 91.

17. Wells, *Mr. Britling Sees It Through,* p. 442.

18. Cf. Romans 8:28.

19. Cf. Psalm 23:4.

tecture of this building, but you can never see the mind of the architech who drew the bluprint or the faith and hope and love of the individuals who made it so. You may see the stars at night, but you can never see the law of gravitation that holds them there. Everything that we see is a shadow cast by that which we do not see. The visible is a shadow cast by the invisible.

So this morning let us go out with the conviction that God is still most certain Fact of the universe. Let us realize that all of the avances of modern science and all of the conforts that it has brought about can never be substitutes for God, as significant as they are. Televisions and radioes, airoplanes and subways, dollar and cents can never be substitutes for God, for long before any of these came into existence we needed God, and long after they have passed away we will still need God. Have faith in God, the God of the universe, the God who is the same yesterday, today and forever, the God who threw up the gigantic mountains kissing the skys, the God who threw up the stars to bedeck the heavens like swinging latterns of eternity, the God in who we live and move and have our being, the God who has been our help in ages past and our hope for years to come, our shelter in the time of storm and our eternal home.[20] This is the God that commands our faith, and only by have faith in him do we create the abundant life.

III

The priveledge and responsibility of creating life is one that confronts us all. Who this morning will start out on this great creative work, by giving oneself to some great purpose that transcends oneself, by living up to ones highest and best self, and by having an abiding faith in God.

The story goes

Preached at Dexter, Sept. 26, 1954

AD. CSKC: Sermon file, folder 71, "Creating the Abundant Life" / "A Moment of Difficult Decision."

---

20. Cf. Hebrews 13:8; cf. Acts 17:28. King cites Isaac Watts's hymn, "Our God, Our Help In Ages Past" (1719).

"New Wine in New Bottles,"
Sermon at Dexter Avenue Baptist Church

17 October 1954
Montgomery, Ala.

King warns that throughout history, "new and creative ideas" were not accepted when the "historical atmosphere at that time was not sufficiently new and strong to contain them." He cites Henry Wallace's "vision of Racial equality" as a recent example of an idea ahead of its time and, in contrast, highlights the timeliness of Martin Luther, Abraham Lincoln, and Jesus Christ.

"Neither do men put new wine into old bottles: else the bottles break, and the wine runneth out and the bottles perish: but they put new wine into new bottles, and both are preserved."—Matt. 9:17.

Introduction: Jesus came in the world conscious that he was bringing something essentially new. The long caravan of humanity had been moving in one direction for centuries, now it was to stop and change its course. Wherein it had been moving toward the city of legalism, it was now to move toward the city of Grace. Wherein it had been moving toward an earthly Kingdom of God political in scope, it was now to move toward a spiritual kingdom which is both "now" and "not yet."[1] It was the recognition of this newness which funished the figure which Christ is using in our text [*strikeout illegible*] as he thinks his own new ideas, He is compelled to think also how it will adapt itself to the old ways and thoughts and habits which it finds. To put this new life into the old patterns of thinking was like putting fresh flowing wine in a dry and rotten bottle. It is inevitable that the bottle will break and the wine will run out. The old will not hold the new.

It is not necessary to go into the full application of Christ [*strikeout illegible*] figure. By now we can see the central idea which it imparts: <u>that what is new and strong</u> and creative needs something new and strong to <u>hold</u> it.

I   Note how the truth of this text can be applied to historical events. There have been times in history when ~~good~~ new and creative ideas appeared on the scene, but they ended up unaccepted because the very historical atmosphere at that time was not sufficiently new and strong to contain them. This is the meaning of the statement that a man is ahead of his times. It often happens that an individual comes forth with a new dynamic ideas, only to find that it ~~perishes~~ is temporarily defeated because it can only find abode in an old worn out bottle.{As he thinks his own new ideas, he was compelled to think also how they would adapt themselves to the old way thoughs and habits which they found. To put this new life into the old pattern was like putting fresh flowing wine. . It is inevitable that the bottle will break and the wine will run out.} (use ill of Wilson and League of Nations.[2] (Wilkie's vision of one World.[3] (Wallace vision of Racial equality)[4]

On the other hand there are times when history is ready to accept a new event. This was the case in the event of the coming of Jesus. That is why it can

---

1. "The Kingdom Present" and "The Kingdom Not Yet" are chapter subheadings in L. Harold DeWolf's *A Theology of the Living Church* (New York: Harper, 1953), pp. 302–303. DeWolf was King's advisor at Boston University.

2. President Woodrow Wilson (1856–1924) presented the idea of the League of Nations as part of his fourteen-point plan for a post–World War I world in a speech given before Congress on 8 January 1918. Although adopted and implemented by many nations, the United States Senate refused to ratify this provision.

3. Wilkie, *One World*.

4. King refers to Henry A. Wallace (1888–1965), vice president under Franklin Delano Roosevelt (1941–1945) and the unsuccessful 1948 Progressive Party candidate for the presidency. During the 1948 campaign, Wallace spoke out against segregation and for voting rights for African Americans. A student poll conducted at Morehouse College during the campaign supported Wallace's candidacy (see note 146 to Introduction, in *Papers* 1:45).

be said that he came at the fullness of time.[5] The atmosphere of time and history had been so impregnated with a newness and fullness that the new event of God's revelation that appeared in his person was destined to succeed. The new event which appeared in the coming of Jesus was so world shaking because it was contained in a new bottle of historical receptivity. Time and history were ready for his coming. (ill Luther's reformation (Lincoln's ending of slavery)

II   This text has not only meaning for history
Note how the truth of this text applies to our personal lives.
We often attempt to get rid of bad habits. Here is a made who has a new and fresh desire to stop drinking, to be more honest etc, but in a few days he is doing the same thing. The real problem lies in the fact that this new fresh resolution is not coupled with a change in one general or overall structure of life. He has a new and fresh desire to change one segment of his life, but this new desire is placed in the same old worn out general structure.

1.   Deal with our concern for internationalism
2.   Give example of people ~~going~~ coming to Church In revivals. They bring a new emotional determination to an old mental framework. We must teach people that when they get new wine to get a bottle strong and new enought to contain it.

III   Within this text is the ultimate meaning of Jesus answer to Nicodemus. The partake of the new moving that comes as a results of salvation, you've got to born anew. You must be born all over.[6]

Why is it that we find it difficult to follow resolutions?

1. We concentrate on changing this one bad habit, forgetting that this one bad habit infiltrates the whole personality, and to change this habit means changing the whole habit structure, the whole general make up. The fresh new desire for changing is poured back into the same old general framework.

2. We often accept a thing intellectually, but not emotionally. The new intellectual change must be poured into an [*strikeout illegible*] old rotten emotional make up. (White students)

3. We often accept a thing emotionally, but not intellectually. (Revivals)

Preached at Dexter Third Sunday Oct. 17, 1954

AD. CSKC: Sermon file, folder 73, "New Wine in New Bottles."

---

5. Cf. Galatians 4:4 and Ephesians 1:10.
6. Cf. John 3:1–8.

[November 1954]
[Montgomery, Ala.]

Shortly after being installed as Dexter's twentieth pastor, King preached a sermon he would deliver frequently later his ministry.[1] He draws on James E. Will's thematically similar "Men Who Live Differently," a copy of which he filed in the same folder as this sermon.[2] In his remarks, King observes, "I have seen many white people who sincerely oppose segregation and [discrimination], but they never took a [real] stand against it because of fear of standing alone."

"And be not conformed to this world: but be ye transformed by the renewing of your mind." Romans 12:2

"We are a colony of heaven." Philippians 3:20[3]

{We must not be "astronomically intimidated"}

Both of these passages suggest that every true Christian is a citizen of two worlds: the world of time and the world of eternity.[4] The christian finds himself in the paradoxical situation of having to be in the world yet not of the world.[5] Indeed this is what is meant by one of the passages just read in which christians are referred to as a colony of heaven. This figure of speech should have special relevance for us in America, since the early days of our nation's history were days of colonialism. Thirteen of the states of our union were originally British colonies. Although our forefathers had relative freedom in forming their institutions and systems of law their ultimate allegiance was to the King of England. And so although the christian finds himself in the colony of time his ultimate allegiance is to the empire of eternity. In other words the christian owes his ultimate allegiance to God and if any earthly institution conflicts with God's will it is the christian duty to revolt against it.

---

1. Dexter Avenue Baptist Church, Program, "The installation of Rev. Martin L. King, Jr. as pastor," 31 October 1954. On the inside of the file folder containing this sermon, King wrote "TN Preached at Dexter, Nov. 1954." For a more developed version of this sermon, see King, Draft of Chapter II, "Transformed Nonconformist," July 1962–March 1963, pp. 466–476 in this volume.

2. Will, *The Pulpit* 22 (July 1951): 5–7. Will's sermon included the subheading "Transformed Nonconformists." James E. Will was assistant pastor of the Evangelical United Brethren Church in Aurora, Illinois, and was also attending Evangelical Theological Seminary in Naperville, Illinois at the time of the sermon's publication. He preached this sermon at the Chicago Sunday Evening Club on 27 May 1951 as its "Seminarian Sermon of 1951."

3. Cf. Philippians 3:20 (MOFFATT).

4. This theme was prominent in Reinhold Niebuhr's writings. A few months before preaching this sermon King referred to this theme in a paper presented to the dialectical society in Boston on "The Theology of Reinhold Niebuhr": "Eternity is always relevant to, and yet ever tensionally set against earth at every moment of time. Eternity may never be identified with earth, but earth may never declare independence from eternity" (King, April 1953–June 1954, in *Papers* 2: 270). For more of King's writings on Niebuhr, see also King, "Reinhold Niebuhr," 2 April 1952, and "Reinhold Niebuhr's Ethical Dualism," 9 May 1952, in *Papers* 2:139–152.

5. Cf. John 17:14–16.

Now there can be no doubt that the command of our text—do not conform—is difficult advice for any modern person. The pressure of the herd is ever strong upon us.[6] Even our intellectual disciplines attempt to convince us on the necessity of conforming. Some of our philosophical sociologists have gone so far as to tell us that morality is merely group consensus. In sociological lingo, this means that there is little difference between mores and morals. In plain language, it means that you tell the difference between right and wrong by a sort of Gallop poll method of finding what the majority thinks. The answer of certain psychologists to all maladjusted people is, simply, to learn to conform to this world. If we only dress and act and think like other people, then we shall be happy and mentally healthy.[7]

Yet the command of our texts still stand before us with glaring urgency: "Be not conformed to this world; but be ye transformed by the renewing of your mind." As Christians we are a colony of heaven thrown out, as pioneers, in the midst of an unchristian world to represent the ideals and way of living of a nobler realm until the earth should be the Lord's and the fullness thereof. I'm sure that many of you have had the experience of dealing with thermometers and thermostats. The thermometer merely records the temperature. If it is seventy or eighty degrees it registers that and that is all. On the other hand the thermostat changes the temperature. If it is too cool in the house you simply push the thermostat up a little and it makes it warmer. And so the christian is called upon not to be like a thermometer conforming to the temperature of his society, but he must be like a thermostat serving to transform the temperature of his society.[8]

In spite of this imperitive demand to live differently we are producing a generation of the mass mind. We have moved from the extreme of rugged individualism to the even greater extreme of rugged collectivism. Instead of making history we are made by history. The philosopher Nietzche once said that every man is a hammer or an anvil, that is to say every man either molds society or is molded by society.[9] Who can doubt that most men today are anvils continually being molded by the patterns of the majority.

Along with this has grown a deep worship of bigness. Especially in this country many people are impressed by nothing that is not big-big cities, big churches, big corporations. We all are tempted to worship size. We live in an age of "Jumboism" whose men find security in that which is large in number and extensive in size.[10]

---

6. Will, *The Pulpit*, p. 5: "The pressure of the herd is ever strong upon us."

7. Will, *The Pulpit*, p. 5: "Some of our philosophical sociologists have gone even further and have told us that morality is only group consensus. In sociological lingo, this means that there is little difference between folkways and morals. In plain language, it means that you tell the difference between right and wrong by a sort of Gallop poll method of finding what the majority thinks. The answer of certain psychologists to all maladjusted people is, similarly, to learn to conform to this world. If we only will dress and act and think like other people, then we shall be happy and mentally healthy."

8. A probable source of this illustration is a sermon by Henry H. Crane (Crane, "Thermometers Versus Thermostats," in *These Prophetic Voices* [New York: Abingdon-Cokesbury Press, 1942], pp. 26–40).

9. Frederick Nietzsche, *Thus Spake Zarathustra* (Thomas Common, trans.), p. 123: "Ye know only the sparks of the spirit: but ye do not see the anvil which it is, and the cruelty of its hammer!" See also Henry Wadsworth Longfellow, *Hyperion* (1892): "In this world a man must either be anvil or hammer."

10. Fosdick, "The Hope of the World in Its Minorities," in *The Hope of the World*, p. 4: "Again, this truth of Jesus is deflected from many modern minds because of our worship of bigness. One of my friends calls it 'Jumboism.'"

Men are afraid to stand alone for their convictions. There are those who have high and noble ideals, but they never reveal them because they are afraid of being nonconformist. I have seen many white people who sincerely oppose segregation and discimination, but they never took a rea stand against it because of fear of standing alone. I have seen many young people and older people alike develop undesirable habits not because they wanted to do it in the beginning, not even because they enjoyed it, but because they were ashame of saying "no" when the rest of the group was saying "yes". Even the Christian church has often been afraid to stand up for what is right because the majority didn't sanction it. The church has too often been an institution serving to crystalize and conserve the patterns of the crowd. The mere fact that slavery, segregation, war, and economic exploitation have been sanctioned by the church is a fit testimony to the fact that the church has too often conformed to the authority of the world rather than conforming to the authority of God. Even we preachers have manifested our fear of being non-conformist. So many of us turn into showman and even clowns, distorting the real meaning of the gospel, in an attempt to conform to the crowd. How many minister's of Jesus Christ have sacrificed their precious ideals and cherished convictions on the altar of the crowd. O how many people today are caught in the shackles of the crowd. Many of us think we find a sort of security in conforming to the ideas of the mob. But my friends it is the nonconformists that have made history, Not those who always look to see which way the majority is going before they make a decision. not those who are afraid to say no when everybody else is saying yes; but history has been made by those who caould stand up before the crowd and not bow. The great creative insights have come from men who were in a minority. It was the minority that fought for religious liberty; it was the minority that brought about the freedom of scientific research. In any cause that concerns the progress of mankind, put your faith in the nonconformist.

Now let us make it clear that non-conformity in itself might not be good. There is a type of bad nonconformity. There is no virtue in being a nonconformist just to be a nonconformist. Some people are nonconformist just to get attention and to be different. So Paul gives us a farmula for constructive nonconformity which is found in the second half of the text. In order to discern the true will of God and become constructive nonconformist we must accept a new mental outlook. We must be transformed. Jesus' phrase for this experience was the new birth.[11] And so only when we have been born again can we be true nonconformist. We are called upon to be transformed nonconformist. This is our eternal challenge as christians.

The courage of three Hebrew boys—Shadrach, Meshach, and Abednego is still a challenge to us today. The King Nebuchadnezzar had ordered that all were to bow down and worship the golden image. But there stood in the midst three Hebrew boys who were determined not to bow down and serve the golden image and they said to the King, if it be so, our God whom we serve is able to deliver us, but if not we will not bow.[12] Who today can stand up and refuse to bow in a crowd where everybody else is bowing.

---

11. Cf. John 3:3–7.
12. Daniel 3.

The spiritual strength and moral courage of Jesus amid the temptation in the wilderness is our eternal challenge.[13] Jesus was born at a time when the majority of people thought of the Kingdom as a political Kingdom and thought of the Messiah as the one who would restore this political kingdom with all of his power and pomp and riches. And all of the temptations that Satan offered Christ were temptations to fall in line with this type of material political kingdom. In other words he was urging Christ to conform to wishes of the mob. But in the midst of such a plea we can hear Christ saying in no uncertain terms: "Get thee behind me Satan."[14] As if to say, "I will not bow, for I have orders from an authority not of this world to build a new kind of kingdom, a kingdom that will one day rock the world, a kingdom that will shake the hinges from the gates of the Roman Empire. It will not be a kingdom political in structure and materialistic in outlook; it will be a kingdom of the spirit. I realize that at this time this type of kingdom does not conform to the majority opinion. But I will not bow."

Who will take the attitude of Jesus and be a sincere nonconformist. Today we stand on the brink of moral and physical destruction and the great need of the hour is sincere nonconformist. Men who will stand amid a world of materialism and treat all men as brothers; men who will stand up in a world that attempts to solve its problems by war and declare that he who lives by the sword will die by the sword.

Who this afternoon will go away with the determination not to be a slave to the crowd and not to bow to the desires of the mob.[15] Remember Christian friends we are now in the colony of time, but our ultimate allegiance is to the empire of eternity. "Be not conformed to this world, but be ye transformed by the renewing of your mind."

{NonConformity is costly. I must admit this}

{Close with John Oxman}[16]

TAD. CSKC: Sermon file, folder 14, "Transformed Non-Conformist."

---

13. Jesus is tempted in the wilderness in Luke 4:1–13.

14. Cf. Matthew 16:23.

15. In an outline of this sermon, King continues: "The need of the hour is sincere non-conformist. (1) Against materialism (2) nationalism (3) militarism" ("Transformed Nonconformist," Sermon outline, November 1954).

16. King probably refers to John Oxenham's poem "The Ways" (1916), as he does in "Creating the Abundant Life," Sermon at Dexter Avenue Baptist Church, 26 September 1954, p. 191 in this volume.

"Beyond Condemnation,"
Sermon at Dexter Avenue Baptist Church

[*November 1954*]
[*Montgomery, Ala.*]

Jesus' encounter with the Pharisees and a female adulterer serves as the basis of this handwritten sermon.[1] "Let us be slow to condemn others," King comments, reasoning that most people "need to be given new confidence in their power to do the good. They need not our condemnation, but our help."

And early in the morning he came again into the temple, and all the people came unto him; and he sat down, and ~~thought~~ taught them. And the scribes and Pharisees brought unto him a woman taken in adultery; and when they had set her in the midst, they say unto him, Master, this woman was taken in adultery, in the very act. Now Moses in the law commanded us, that such should be stoned: but what sayest thou? This they said, tempting him, that they might have to accuse him. But Jesus stooped down, and with his finger wrote on the ground, as though he heard them not. So when they continued asking him, he lifted up himself, and said unto them, He that is without sin among you let him cast the first stone at her. And again he stooped down and wrote on the ground. And they which heard it, being convicted by their own conscience, went out one by one, beginning at the eldest, even unto the last: and Jesus was left alone, and the woman standing in the midst. When Jesus had lifted up himself, and saw none but the woman, he said unto her, Woman, where are those thine accusers? hath no man condemned thee? She said, no man, Lord. And Jesus said unto her, Neither do I condemn thee, go, and sin no more. John 8:2–11.

Introduction: One of the basic responsibilities that ~~Jesus h religion~~ Christianity has to society and to individuals is that of condemnation. The Church must forever stand in judgement upon every political, social and economic system, condemning evil wherever they exist. The Church can never condone evil either in its social or [*strikeout illegible*] ind. dimensions. Jesus realized this, and throughout the gospel he is pictured condemning evil in no uncertain terms.

(1) He goes in the temple . . .[2]

(2) He see the Pharisess and says "ye serpents, ye generation of vipers, how can ye escape the damnation of hell.[3]

---

1. King wrote "BC Preached at Dexter Nov., 1954" on the inside of the folder containing this document. King was scheduled to give this sermon as early as 27 May 1951 ("Rev. M. L. King, Jr. to Fill Ebenezer Pulpit Sunday A.M.," *Atlanta Daily World*, 26 May 1951). A few months after joining his father as co-pastor of Ebenezer in 1960, King again delivered this sermon (see Ebenezer Baptist Church, Program, Sunday services, 24 July 1960).

2. King may be referring to Jesus' eviction of the moneychangers from the Temple; see, for example, Matthew 21:12–13.

3. Cf. Matthew 23:33.

On one occasion however we find Jesus failing to condemn a person who has committed an obvious sin, and we wonder why. Our discussion for the morning grows out out of this situation. Why did Jesus go beyond condemnation on this occasion.

1. In his assessment of sins, her sin was no worse than the sins of those who sought to stone her. Dont mistake the argument. Jesus is not making light of adultry.

   a. He looked at the Pharasees. They boasted how the followed the law from the dotting of an I to the crossing of a T. They could say suppiciliously: I thank thees Lord that I am not like other men.[4] And as he looked deeper he saw their tragic pride, their poinant hypocracy. And Jesus is saying all of this is as bad or worse than adultry. Here was these pompous, self-righous, arrogant Pharasees standing up ready to stone this women.
      They were victims of the gravest sin that one can committ, and that is the sin of feeling that one has risen above the capacity for sin.

   b. How many of us are ready to stone our contemporaries. We to often have something of the Pharisee in us.[5] We so easily see the faults of others. We are so ready to condemn. Yet we never stop to see that some of the sins we are committing are just as bad. Pride, bad temper, refusing to make up a quarrel, spreading lies, indulging in malicious gossip, mental crulty and social injustice are all terrible sins that we to often think lighty of.

   c. How we turn up our noses at those who commits sins like stealing or drunkenness or murder or crimes of the criminal courts. We think that we should never be tempted to committ them. Surely it comes as a shock to hear Christ saying, "But you do things which are far worse."
      You might not rob [*strikeout illegible*] a bank, but you steal others good names
      You might not be a drunkard, but you are drunk with hate, jealousy
      If our sins were punished ~~by~~ in society by Christ assessment, all of us would be in Jail.
      Jesus is not making light of adultry, but he is stirring the consciences of men and compelling them to see the gravity of all sin.

2. A second reason why Jesus did not condemn the woman was because she had already condemned herself. The object of condemnation is to produce a sense of guilt, then of penitence, and thus to inaugurate a new beginning

   a. Jesus was continually condenning the Pharasees because they felt no sense of guilt. They thought themselves the moral examples which all should emulate.

   b. The woman had a burning and terrible sense of guilt. Further condemnation would have been unecessary and cruel.

   c. How we Christians have often been cruel at this point. Give examples of people who have made mistakes.

   D. Let us be slow to condemn others. Most of the people we meet in daily life

---

4. Cf. Luke 18:9–14.

5. For more on King's analysis, see "Pride Versus Humility: The Parable of the Pharisee and the Publican," Sermon at Dexter Avenue Baptist Church, 25 September 1955, pp. 230–234 in this volume.

are not hardened hypocrites demanding fierce words. Most of the people we meet are not like the Pharisees thinking to highly of themselves, but they think too little of themselves. They need to be given new confidence in their power to do the good. They need not our condemnation, but our help. As Jung say in the last chapter of his great work, <u>Modern man In Search of a Soul</u>:

> Condemnation does not liberate, it oppresses. I am the oppressor of the person I condemn, not his friend and fellow sufferer. . . . Modern man has heard enough about guilt and sin. He is sorely beset by his own bad conscience and wants rather to learn how he is to reconcile himself with his own nature, how he is to love the enemy in his own heart and call the wolf his brother. (pp 271, 274)[6]

In the private interview a psychologist must always learn to identify himself with the patient, walking along the same road with him, never condemning or being shocked, trying to understand how the patient got into the distress which troubles him.[7]

3. Notice Jesus final words to this [*strikeout illegible*] woman. "Neither do I condemn thee, Go and sin no more" He bids her to look at the future, and not to the pass. We are to concentrate on the hights we are determined to attack, not look back into the depth in which he once wallowed.

AD. CSKC: Sermon file, folder 43, "Beyond Condemnation."

---

6. C. G. Jung, *Modern Man in Search of a Soul* (New York: Harcourt, Brace, 1933).
7. King also referred to this therapeutic method in "I Sat Where They Sat," 1948–1954, p. 581 in this volume.

"Christ, The Center of Our Faith"

[*1953–1955?*]

In this handwritten sermon outline, King reflects on the human tendency, for better or worse, to support causes based on personalities rather than ideologies. As he explores the impact of others on his life, King refers to Morehouse professor George D. Kelsey, who influenced his decision to attend seminary and his approach to pastoral ministry.

I Before men can devote their lives to a cause or a movement, they must find some person who, for them, becomes the personification or incarnation of that cause or movement. People always seek, not so much for some thing as for some one to believe in. They seek for some person that for them becomes the center of the cause. We often tell people to love the cause. But people cannot love a cause in abstract.

(1) People do not love Nazism first and foremost. They love Hitler and then Nazism through Hitler.

(2) Mussolini and Fasism

(3) Democracy and Lincoln & Jefferson Roosevet and Wilson, Truman and Eisenhower.[1]

We humans inevitably believes at last not in isms but in incarnations.

II ~~This~~ It is ultimately personality that shapes the course of history. We live in a generation in which impersonal forces are considered the the determining factors of human life.

(1) The biological materialist—heredity & [*genes?*]

(2) There are those who would say that geography and climate account for the whole human story.

(3) The Marxist are economic determinists.

But when we look further we discover that it is persons that most deeply influence our lives.

(a) Experience in college with George Kelsey[2]

(b) Throughout life that which influence us most is persons.

What does all of this have to do with our central theme.

III Christianity has no meaning devoid of Christ. The noble principles of Christianity remain abstract until they are personified in a person called Christ.

(a) Christ becomes the center or the pivotal point around which everything ~~revolves~~ in the Christian faith revolves.

(b) This is what the book of revelation means when it says He King of Kings and Lord of Lord.[3] He is the center not only of our faith, but of history and all nations must bow before him.

This is the ringing affirmation of Christmas—that a personality has come in the world to split history into A.D. and B.C.

(C) The thing that Christ brought into the world was not a new set of doctrines, not new teachings, but a great personality.

AD. CSKC: Sermon file, folder 70, "Christ the Center of Our Faith" / "How to Believe in a Good God in the Midst of Glaring Evil."

---

1. King's inclusion of Eisenhower at the end of a list of presidents suggests that he prepared this sermon after January 1953. It is also likely that he composed it before the Montgomery bus boycott began in December 1955, since afterwards he spoke of his own leadership in more humble terms: "I want you to know that if M. L. King had never been born this movement would have taken place" (Willie Mae Lee, Notes on Montgomery Improvement Association [MIA] Mass Meeting at First Baptist Church, 30 January 1956, in *Papers* 3:114).

2. Regarding Kelsey's influence, King later noted: "Two men, Dr. Benjamin Mays, president of Morehouse, and Dr. George Kelsey, professor of philosophy and religion, made me stop and think. Both were ministers, both deeply religious, and yet both were learned men, aware of all the trends of modern thinking. I could see in their lives the ideal of what I wanted a minister to be" (William Peters, "Our Weapon Is Love," *Redbook* [August 1956]: 72).

3. Cf. Revelation 17:14, 19:16.

On Worshiping False Gods

On Worshiping False Gods and The False God of Pleasure appear to be a reformulation of King's 1953 sermon series on false gods.[1] In the first document, a handwritten outline, King summarizes the dangers of turning to the false gods of science, money, and pleasure. He asserts that pursuing these ends may result in some material satisfaction, saying, "Ultimately man can not live by bread alone." In False God of Pleasure, which was not included in the original series, King stresses, "The more he fed his hunger, the closer he came to famine."

On Worshiping False Gods

[*January 1955*]

I   Introduction—
  a   The Necessity of worshp
  b.   There is always the danger that man will direct his worship instinct in spurious channeals
  C.   Text: The scripture funishis nunerous examples of the ever present tendecy of [*man?*] to substitute false gods for the One true God. And so in the Book of Judges we read: "And they [*forsook?*]"[2]
  D.   Meaning of Baal[3]
  E.   Many men today have turned to Baal or false gods.
II   The false gods that [*man?*] has set up
  1.   Science—
    a.   The success of science
    b.   Man's deifying of science
    c.   Results of the deification
  2.   ~~Eco~~Money or Economic forces
    a.   Critique of both communisn and captil
    b.   The money God stands before all of us saying "Worship me [*etc?*] I get cars for you, and big bank account
    C.   Result of deification

---

1. King kept these documents in the same file folder as the sermons in the 1953 series (King, "The False God of Science," 5 July 1953; "The False God of Nationalism," 12 July 1953; and "The False God of Money" 19 July 1953, pp. 130–132, 132–133, and 133–136 in this volume, respectively). On the outside of the folder, King wrote "Preached at Dexter Jan, 1955" twice. King also wrote "<u>FGP</u> Preached at Dexter Jan. 1955" on the outside of the folder containing this document.

2. Cf. Judges 2:12–13: "And they forsook the Lord God of their fathers, which brought them out of the land of Egypt, and followed other gods, of the gods of the people that were round about them, and bowed themselves unto them, and provoked the Lord to anger. And they forsook the Lord, and served Baal and Ashtaroth."

3. Baal was a fertility deity in ancient Canaan, often depicted in the Hebrew Bible as the false god that most enticed the people of Israel.

1. Men concerned about money can make rather than service that can be render

    (compare average student in college)

    (desire to be doctor, layer, minister merely for the money)

    2. Exploitation—Get rich no matter how Take from masses

3. God of Pleasure

    a   The Epicurean creed—eat, drink, and be merry. [*etc?*] Louis Jordan[4]

    b.   Here spiritual values have given away to temporary bodily satifaction Life has no meaning beyond a bottle of wisky, a pair of dice, and a beautiful night club

4   Both reason and experience reveal to us that these false gods can never reach the claims of the true God, if for no other reason than that they are to transitoy and short lived to satisfy the ultimate longings hunger of the human soul. They might satisfy some temporary desires, but ultimately man can not live by bread alone.[5] And so long as he places his [*ultimate?*] faith in these temporal finite gods he will walk through the valleyes of life distorted ambitions and frustrated hopes.

Those who worship the god of science fail to see that this god only funishes us with the material means by which we live never with the spiritual ends for which we live. Those who worship the god of ~~science~~ money fail to see that this god can only satisfy our material necessities. But man is more than a dog to be satisfied by a few economic bones. Those great intangible values which are so basic to the human soul cannot be bought with money.

Those who worship the god of pleasure fail to see that the Epicurean creed may be wrong. Maybe ~~it not be that~~ tomorow we dont really die. May it not be that this life is but an embryonic prelude to a new awaking. Maybe death is not a period which ends this sentence of life, but a coma that puntuates it to more loftier significance

As for me I [*strikeout illegible*] have decided not to ~~put~~ give my ultimate faith and devotion to these trasitory, ephemeral, and changing false gods. I have decided to give my ultimate faith to something unchangable and eternal. Not to those gods that are here today and gone tomorrow, but to the God that is the same yesterday, today and forever.[6] Not to the gods that give us a few dollars in moments of prosperity, but the God that walks with us through the valley of the shadow of death and causes us to fear no evil.[7] Not to the gods that give us a few moments of bodily satifaction, but to the God that gives us peace amid confusion and hope amid despair. Not to the gods that can invent for us a few beautiful automobiles, but to the God that ~~can~~ rolled out the mighty seas and the massive oceans. Not to the gods that

---

4. Epicurus (341–270 BCE), a Hellenistic philosopher, taught that the essence of life was the attainment of pleasure and the avoidance of pain. Louis Jordan (1908–1975) was a jazz and blues musician.

5. Cf. Deuteronomy 8:3 and Matthew 4:4.

6. Cf. Hebrews 13:8.

7. Cf. Psalm 23:4.

set up a few sky scraping buildings, but to the God that threw up the gigantic mountain bathing their peaks in the lofty blue. Not to the gods whose inventive power is limited to televisions and electric light bulbs, but to the God that threw up the radiant stars to bedeck the heavens like swinging laterns of eternity.

AD. CSKC: Sermon file, folder 18, "False Gods We Worship."

The False God of Pleasure

[January 1955]
[Montgomery, Ala.]

It is an old dream, as old as the Garden of Eden with its luscious forbidden fruit so pleasing to the eye. It was the fascinating dream of the hedonist. Epicurus built for it a cautious prudent philosophy. It has been presented in the lacelike poetry of Omar Khayyam. He says "Take the cash and let the credit go, nor heed the rumble of a distant drum."[8] He goes on to say: "A book of Verses undeneath the Bough, a Jug of Wine, a Loaf of Bread—and thou"[9]

But this doesn't work. For one thing we are mortal. Thrills play out, sensations are short lived, pleasures pall. Happiness is the harmony of all desires—mental, emotional social, spiritual

The more he sought life through pleasure, the more it eluded him. The more he fed his hunger, the closer he came to famine. The more he did what he liked, the less he liked what he did. The path was disappointing. It didn't arrive. It didn't lead to liberty.

AD. CSKC: Sermon file, folder 18, "False Gods We Worship."

---

8. Omar Khayyám (1048?–1122) was a Persian mathematician and poet whose book of four-line poems, *Rubáiyát,* became well known in the Western world through Edward Fitzgerald's English translation. King quotes a portion of *Rubáiyát* 13 (Khayyám, *Rubáiyát* [London: Macmillan, 1929], p. 31).

9. King quotes from Khayyám's *Rubáiyát* 12 (p. 31).

"Opportunity, Fidelity, and Reward"

text (The parable of the Talents (Matt 25. 14-30

Introduction - (1) The significance of the parable. (2) The story in brief.

I. ~~Unto one he gave five~~ Let us notice first that this ~~and~~ is a clear and sober denial of the equality of human endowment. (Unto one he gave five talents, to another two, to another one; to each according to his several abilities a) The findings of The I. Q. test are not new. They were stated long ago in this story. As ~~soon~~ as we reach maturity we come to realize ~~that~~ that certain gifts are ours without measure and that certain others have been denied us.

(a) Elaborate on the phrase equality of all men (all men are created equal.)

(b) Life is a landscaping job. We are handed a site, large or small, rugged or flat, picturesque or commonplace, whose general outlines and contours are largely

Handwritten sermon outline titled "Opportunity, Fidelity, and Reward," based on the parable of the talents (January 1955).

"Opportunity, Fidelity, and Reward,"
Sermon at Dexter Avenue Baptist Church

[*January 1955*]
Montgomery, Ala.

Drawing on George Buttrick's published lecture, "Opportunity, Fidelity, and Reward," King acknowledges in this handwritten outline that the wicked often prosper while the righteous suffer.[1] He highlights the "inner peace" and "unsurpassable joy" of those with the ability to be faithful.[2]

Text (The parable of the Talent [Matt 25:14–30])

Introduction—

   (1) The significance of the parable.

   (2) The story in brief.

I ~~Unto one he gave five~~ Let us notice first that the [*parable?*] is a clear and sober denial of the equality of human endowment. (Unto one he gave five talents, to another two, to another one; to each according to his several abilities.) The findings of the I.Q. tests are not new. They were stated long ago in this story. As soon as we reach maturity we come to realize ~~with~~ that certain gifts are ours within measure and that certain others have been denied us.[3]

   (a) Elaborate on the phrase equality of all men (All men are created equal.)

   (b) Life is a Landscaping job. We are handed a site, large or small, rugged or flat, picturesque or commonplace, whose general outlines and contours are largely determined for us. Both limitation and opportunity are involved in every site[4]

---

1. Buttrick, *The Parables of Jesus* (New York: Harper & Brothers, 1928), pp. 241–250. George Arthur Buttrick (1892–1980) was born in Northumberland, England. In 1915 he received degrees in philosophy from Lancaster Independent Theological College and Victoria University, and became minister at the First Union Congregational Church in Quincy, Illinois. Buttrick accepted the post as minister of New York City's Madison Avenue Presbyterian Church in 1927, and during his twenty-eight years there, taught homiletics at Union Theological Seminary. He served as president of the Federal Council of Churches, the predecessor of the liberal National Council of Churches, from 1940 to 1942. Buttrick wrote numerous other books including *Jesus Came Preaching* (1931), based on lectures he delivered at Yale University.

2. At the end of the document, King wrote "Preached at Dexter Jan., 1954." He did not preach regularly at Dexter until May 1954, which suggests he wrote the wrong year on the document and probably meant 1955. King was also scheduled to give a sermon with this title on 30 August 1953 ("'Opportunity, Fidelity, and Reward,' King Jr.'s Subject at Ebenezer," *Atlanta Daily World,* 29 August 1953).

3. Buttrick, *The Parables of Jesus,* p. 244: "The findings of the intelligence testers are not new: they were succinctly expressed long ago in this story. . . . On reaching years of maturity we begin to realize (with some heartburning, perhaps) that certain gifts and graces are ours within measure and that certain others have been denied us."

4. Fosdick, *On Being a Real Person,* p. 69: "Life is a landscaping job. We are handed a site, ample or small, rugged or flat, picturesque or commonplace, whose general outlines and contours are largely determined for us. Both opportunity and limitation are involved in every site . . . " On the page containing this quote, King wrote "Life Is a Landscaping Job" in his personal copy of *On Being a Real Person.*

(c) to avoid any charge of favoritism, the story represents every man as having some talent. No one is left talentless.[5]

II Let us notice second that an individual is judged not by the number of talents he possesses, but by his faithful in handling what he has. It is significant to notice that the commendation of the two talent man is in identical language as that of the five talent man. Thus we are introduced to a new systen of measurement. Other standarts stressed quantity. Jesus stressed quality. (Tell the story of the widows mite)[6] In terms of quantity she gave less than anybody. In terns of quality she gave more. So in computing success Jesus had his own revolutionary standards. The question is not "how much talent have you earned" but "how much faithfulness have you ~~applied~~ manifested."[7]

(a) No greater thing can be said in a person funeral than: "he has been faithful and loyal."

(b) This is a note that needs to be sounded in the ears of so many Christians in [*our?*] churches. A plea to young people to be faithful. One thing that appalls me most is the unfaithfulness of most Christian. The average deacon doesn't takes it seriously.
~~The man who is faithful in his ingorance is~~

(C) You dont need a broad cultural background (PhD) or a large bankaccount to be faithful.

(D) ~~I cant be~~ If you are an usher in the Church dont take it slight, but look upon it with honor and be faithful in doing it.

(E) The story of the faithful minister in N. J.

(F) Quote Douglas Mallach.[8]

III Let us notice finally that there is a reward for faithfulness. "Well done, good and faithful servant: thou hast been faithful over a few things, I will set thee over

---

5. Buttrick, *The Parables of Jesus*, p. 245: "Again, it must be noted, lest Heaven be charged with a gross favoritism, that the story represents every man as having some talent. No one is left empty-handed."

6. Cf. Luke 21:1–4.

7. Buttrick, *The Parables of Jesus*, p. 246: "It is significant therefore that the commendation of the two-talent man is in identical language with that spoken to his more gifted brother. Not a word is changed, not an accent of the voice is different. Thus we are introduced to a new system of measurements. There is a widow-woman in the portrait gallery of the Gospels who cast a farthing into the Temple treasury and of whom Jesus said that she gave 'more than they all together.' By what reckoning did Jesus arrive at such an estimate? Judging her gift by monetary value she gave less than anybody. Judging it by love-value she gave more than the total gifts of all the other worshippers. So in computing success Jesus has His own revolutionary standards. The question is not, 'How many talents have you earned?' but rather, 'How many, compared with the number entrusted to you?'" In another undated handwritten draft of this sermon, King offered the following variation on this theme: "II The parable proclaims the significance of one talent. The ruler was angry because one talent was not used. Every talent is needed in the divine economy. This man lacked the imagination to see that every talent is precious A. The real reason for his failure was his fear. I was afraid. He dared no venture. He lacked faith in God and life. He failed to see how much he is needed. He would not speak out" (Opportunity, Fidelity, and Reward, Sermon outline, January 1955).

8. King probably refers to Malloch's 1926 poem "Be the Best of Whatever You Are" as he does in his sermon "Overcoming an Inferiority Complex," Sermon Delivered at Dexter Avenue Baptist Church, 14 July 1957, p. 308 in this volume.

many things; enter thou into the joy of thy lord."[9] Here we find the answer to that question which has always gripped the religionist: Is there a reward for righteousness? Indeed the whole question of why the wicket prosper and the righteous suffer is another form of the same question. Religion answers this question with an insistence that there is a reward for faithfulness.

(a) Now it must be stressed that this reward is not necessirily material. Some of the most unfaithful and even wicket people enjoy material prosperity. Many of these even go to their graves prosperous.

(b) Deal with the Deuteronomic Idea. The Deuteronimist did catch hold to an eternal truth.[10]

(c) The true reward for faithfulness comes first in terms of an inner peace. There is a sort of unsurpassable joy that comes when a man lives consistently with his own ideals.

Preached at Dexter Jan., 1954[11]

AD. CSKC: Sermon file, folder 68, "Opportunity, Fidelity, and Reward."

---

9. Cf. Matthew 25:21, 23.

10. King refers to the argument formulated during the Babylonian exile that explained God's judgment of Israel as punishment for the nation's disobedience of Mosaic law. He answered a test question on this subject for George Kelsey's class on the Bible at Morehouse (King, Examination answers, Bible, 3 December 1946).

11. King wrote this in a second pen.

"The Crisis in the Modern Family,"
Sermon at Dexter Avenue Baptist Church

[8 May 1955]
[Montgomery, Ala.]

In this typed Mother's Day sermon, King blames war, urbanization, industrialization, and individualism for the disintegration of the family.[1] "In the average modern family," King affirms, "there is a civil war in progress in which the parents are revolting against each other and the children are revolting against the parents. In the modern family individualism has gone mad." He concludes by challenging his listeners to develop some practical ways to increase intimacy within the family, such as developing a family altar and attending church together.

---

1. King wrote "Preached at Dexter on Mother's Day 1955" on the outside of the folder containing this document. His announced sermon topic for 8 May 1955 at Dexter was "Crisis Facing Present-Day Family Life in America" ("Special Mother's Service," *Montgomery Advertiser,* 6 May 1955).

Every well-thinking American is deeply concernced about the decadent state into which the American family is falling. For sometime now, both religious and secular thinkers have sought to find the cause and cure of this disintigration that is gradually mortifying the American family. They are mindful of the fact that this decay in the family is the first step toward the decay of the nation, for the family constitutes the basic unit of the nation.

It would be impossible for me to go into the broad ramification of this immense problem this morning. Such a venture would require a book, and I should have to speak of marriage problem, of many sex problems, of the training of children, and of the basic structure of the family generally. But perhaps even in the limited time before me I can touch some of the more pressing aspects of this great problem. I would like to have you think first of the nature of the crisis confronting the family and some of the causes of its development.

Much of the disintegration of family life can be attributed to the war. It is true that the disintegration of home life began before the war, but the war years immeasurably complicated the situation. Many boys and girls were taken out of the atmosphere of a fine home and placed in an atmosphere filled with wild adventures. This situation placed them in contact with immorality of the basest sort. Gambling, sex promicurity and all sorts of pathological vices were constantly presented as alternatives to lonliness. Many boys and girls, caught in the shackles of the system, embraced these habits, not wholly aware of the fact that they would inevitably lead to their moral and spiritual doom. One of the greatest objections that I have to war is that it leads to a breakdown of the moral and ethical standards of society.

Again, the general frustration that comes as a result of war caused many persons to make unwise links with the opposite sex. War engagements and war marriages took place between people who never had a chance to know each other under normal conditions and for a sufficient length of time. Even worse, many young persons indulged in sexual intimacies who did not have the slightest intention of making a home together. Further, many a beautiful and wholesome marriage ~~together were~~ {was} separated for many years. This separation often lead the man to become emotionally and sexually attracted to other women, while the women become attracted to other men, so that the relatively smooth sailing that had characterized the marriage prior to separation was now interrupted by the tidal wave of unfaithfulness, resulting in deceit, suspicion, and misunderstanding.

But even more, the long separation often brought about a change in the personalities of those who were separated. I have heard so many times in counciling with people: "He just isn't the same since he has returned from the army." This is often true. No two individual, ~~often~~ {after} being separated for several years, can take up where they left off. Personality is not a static thing. It is dynamic, constantly growing and developing. So even when there has been complete fidelity and love, it was necessary to make new adjustments and attempt to know each other over again.

As strong as the war was in leading to the breakdown of American family, it was not the only factor. A second source of the problem was the fact that the growing industrialization of our society and the complex structure of the economic system made it necessary for many wives and mothers to go out and aid in securing the economic means of the family. This has led many women to a position of economic independence. The role that the woman once played in the family was now greatly modified. She could demand more rights and privileges than she had heretofore enjoyed because of her general economic status. Unconsciously, she was aware of the fact that if things didn't go well she could go out and make it on her own. The era in which the woman was completely dependent on the husband gradually passed away under the demands of a growing economic and industrial system.

Another factor which lead to the crisis in the modern family was the fact that the growing trend toward urbanization and industrialization led people away from the home for recreation and social outlet. There was a time when the home afforded the highest form of recreation. Families assembled together and had great joy in ~~chattering~~ {talking} and laughing among themselves. But with the emergence of the movies, automobiles, and night clubs, individuals were slowly pulled out of the homes for social outlet.

Probably a more basic source of the present crisis in the family is found in the modern emphasis on individualism. Ever since the coming of the Renaissance the watchword of modern man has been individualism. In economics, this emphasis expressed itself in Laissez-Faire capitalism; in politics it expressed itself in democracy; in religion it expressed itself in Protestantism; and in education it expressed itself in progressive education. Now this emphasis on endividualism was a healty revolt against a crippling authoritarianism. But the tragedy was that modern man allowed individualism to run wild. He indulged in the tragic luxury of rugged individualism. This rugged individualism seeped into the family. And so today every individual in the family asserts his or her rights with little regard for the thoughts of the family as a whole. All persons in the family are individualists in their pleasures and individualists in their suffering. Their rights are individual rights, their problems individual problems, their responsibility individual responsibility. Home is now merely a useful place to eat and sleep. It is not the center of communal life where the interests of one are the interests of all, where the joys of one are gladly shared by all, and where the troubles of one are regarded as burdens of all. In the average modern family there is a civil war in progress in which the parents are revolting against each other and the children are revolting against the parents. In the modern family individualism has gone mad. {There is an individualism that destroys the individual.}

All of these factors have converged to make for the breakdown in the American family. Homes have disintegrated like stacks of of cards. The National Office of Vital Statistics reports that in 1950 there were 1,669,000 marriages in America. In that same year there were 385,000 divorces. Now you can see that in that year there was approximately one divorce for every four marriages. In 1946 the marriage records reached an all time high. In that year there were 2,291,000 marriages. But compare that to the fact that in that same year there were 610,000 divorces. In that year there was approximately one divorce to every three marriages.

Now think of the tragic consequences of this. It means that hundreds and thousands of young people are forced to be brought up in broken homes. We all know the possible psychological difficulties that might arise as a result of being brought up in a broken home. It is God's plan that every child shall have a good father and a good mother. If either goes, the child's sense of security is underminded and h{is} emotional stability threatened. A family should be an intimate group of people living together in an atmosphere of good will, where the joys and successes of one are the joys and successes of all, and where the problems and failures of one are the concern of all. This sense of unity is threatened in the modern world.

The tragic disintegration of the modern family also means the possible loss of our national security. Family life is still the basic unit of the life of the nation, and on healthy family life depends the moral and spiritual life of the nation. You will remember that the historian Gibbon, in his analysis of the decline and fall of the Roman Empire, held that one of the main things that brought Rome to the junk heep of destruction was not the opposition of the enemy without the gate, but the disintegration of family life within the homes.[2] Home life in Rome frequently decended into orgies of sexuality and licence in which the true value perished. If we aren't careful the same thing will happen in America and our nation will sink to the level of a third or fourth rate power in world affairs. The relentless lesson of history cannot be escaped, and that is when the family structure begins to break down the structure of the nation itself begins to crack and crumble.

I think I can best use the time that remains by attempting to set forth some of the things that we can do to restore the family to the noble position that God intends for it. I may say at the outset that I do not think we will get at the problem by making a dogmatic decree that there should be no divorces. Such an easy solution fails to get at the root of the problem, and fails to see that there are times when divorces are not only necessary, but even healthy.

The first thing that can be done to restore the family to a harmonious unit is for each individual to respect the dignity and worth of every other individual in the family. The parents must respect each other, and the children must respect and be respected by the parents. Men must accept the fact that the day has passed when the man can stand over the wife with an iron rod asserting his authority as "boss." This does not mean that women no longer respect maculinity, i.e., strong, dynamic manliness; woman will always respect that. But it does mean that the day has passed when women will be trampled over and treated as some slave subject to the dictates of a despotic husband. One of the great contributions that Christianity has made to the world is that of lifting the status of womanhood from that of an insignificant child-bearer to a position of dignity and honor and respect. Women must be respected as human beings and not be treated as mere means. Strictly speaking, there is no boss in the home; it is no lord-servant relationship. The family should be a cooperative enterprise [*strikeout illegible*] {where} all members are working together for a common goal.

The child must also be respected as a member of the family. The day has gone forever in which parents ~~could~~ {can} afford to live in a haughty, superior world of their own, in which "children are seen and not heard." This does not mean that children must not be disciplined; nor does it mean that chil ren should not be taught to respect their parents. It does mean, however, that ~~children~~ {a child} must be respected and treated as {a} person~~s~~ with utmost significance. He has his little thoughts and his little rights that must be respected. When each member of a fam-

---

2. King refers to English historian Edward Gibbon (1737–1794) and his work *The History of the Decline and Fall of the Roman Empire* (1776–1788).

ily begins to respect the dignity of every other, that family is moving toward the start of love, and harmony and mutual respect which God intends for it.

A second thing that needs to be done to restore the family to its central position is for each individual to instill within himself a new awareness of the sacredness of marriage and the family. Marriage for so many has been relegated to a state of sexual experiment ~~when~~ {where} people live together until the fascination has worn off. Hollywood has become the Holy City for many Americans, and thousands have bowed before [*strikeout illegible*] {its} shrine, feeling that the more divorces they receive, the more they would receive the grace of glamour. Love has been eliminated as a necessity for marriage, and in its place has appeared such things as economic security, status, physical attraction, etc. All of these things have led to an almost complete disregard for the sacredness of marriage. But if the impending doom into which the family is gradually being plunged is to be avoided, we must again stress the sacredness of the marriage. In a sense marriage is man's greatest perogative, for in and through it God allows man to aid him in his creative activity. For this reason marriage will always stand as one of the most sacred institutions of mankind. That is why the marriage vows insist that it be enter into wisely, discreetly, reverently and in the fear of God.

{A third thing that needs to be done is to seek some ~~conditions~~ way to re establish the intimacies of the family.

(1)   Family altar
(2)   Make the children know you are concerned
(3)   Get connected with some church together}[3]

TAD. CSKC: Sermon file, folder 76, "The Crisis in the Modern Family."

---

3. King wrote this section in pen.

"Other Mountains,"
Baccalaureate Sermon at Alabama State College

15 May 1955
Montgomery, Ala.

Delivered at Alabama State College for baccalaureate sermon on May 15, 1955[1]

1. Rugged Individualism and national isolationalism
2. the mountain of meadiocrity in our various fields of endeavor
3. The mountain of hate and bitterness[2]

AD. CSKC: Sermon file, folder 78, "Keep Moving From This Mountain."

---

1. In a 2 May 1955 letter, Alabama State College president H. Councill Trenholm invited King to serve as the baccalaureate minister for the college's May commencement (in *Papers* 2:550–551) and also asked Martin and Coretta King to be dinner guests at his home prior to the ceremony. The day after the event, King's father boasted in a letter to J. Raymond Henderson, "They tell me he swept. He is already in great demand" (in *Papers* 2:556–557).
2. In his 1960 Founder's Day address at Atlanta's Spelman College, King spoke of four symbolic mountains that must be surmounted "if civilization is to survive." He described "the mountain of hatred and violence" that could be overcome with the use of "nonviolent resistance" and "the love ethic of Jesus Christ" (King, "Keep Moving from This Mountain," Address at Spelman College on 10 April 1960, in *Papers* 5:411–417).

"The Peril of Superficial Optimism
in the Area of Race Relations"

[*19 June 1955?*]

In this outline for a speech before an afternoon meeting of the Montgomery National Association for the Advancement of Colored Peoples (NAACP) King warns against complacency in the fight against prejudice in the United States and around the world for "so long as one spark of prejudice lies latent in the heart of any white American, there is a possibility for it to develop into a flame of intolerance."[1]

---

1. Montgomery NAACP secretary Rosa Parks's notes about the meeting mirrored the points made in this outline. According to Parks's notes, Dexter church clerk Robert D. Nesbitt introduced King, commenting, "He is a great asset to Montg' by activity in everything for the betterment of the community. He has launched an intensive campaign in the church for NAACP membership and voters" (Rosa Parks, Minutes, Mass meeting at First C.M.E. Church, 19 June 1955).

I   We ~~the~~ have come a long long way in race relation in the last few years. (Use 19 June 1955
analogy of Football game)[2]

   A. In Education

   B. In better economic status

   C. In social integration. Segregation is dying. He is dying hard, but there is no doubt that his corspe awaits him

   D. All who have contributed to these advances should be praised.

      (1) NAACP

      (2) inconspicuous groups

      (3) sincere and ethically minded whites

II   But the danger facing the American Negro is that because of these astounding advances he will become complacent and feel that the overall problem is solved. And with the further assertion that that which is not solved will move inevitably toward solution. We might fall ~~fa~~ victims to the cult of inevitable progress.

III We must be realistic realizing that the problem might creep back into the window at any time.[3]

    So long as one spark of prejudice lies latent in the heart of any white American, there is a possibility for it to develop into a [*strikeout illegible*] flame of intolerence at the unpredictable moments.

IV We must not become so complacent that we forget the struggles of other minorities. We must unite with oppressed minorities throughout the world. (Africa & Asia).

    We must be concernced because we are a part of humanity. Whatever affects one effects all. Science has so drafted time and place distance in chains that the has become a literal neighborhood.

AD. CSKC: Sermon file, folder 149, "Speeches."

---

2. On another occasion, King elaborated: "To use an analogy at this point, since the turn of the century we have brought the football of civil rights to about the fifty-yard line. And now we are advancing in the enemy's territory. The problem for the next few years will be to get the ball over the goal line. Let's not fool ourselves, this job will be difficult. The opposition will use all the power and force possible to prevent our advance. He will strengthen his line on every hand. But if we place good leaders in the back field to call the signals and good fellows on the line to made the way clear, we will be able to make moves that will stagger the imagination of the opposition. Some mistakes will be made, yes, the ball might be fumbled, but for God's sake, recover it! Teamwork and unity are necessities for the winning of any game" (King, "The Negro Past and Its Challenge for the Future," Address at Twelfth Baptist Church, 1951–1954).

3. King elaborated on a "realistic position" on race relations in "The 'New Negro' of the South: Behind the Montgomery Story, Address on 17 May 1956" (June 1956, in *Papers* 3:280–286).

"Discerning the Signs of History"

[*26 June 1955*]
[*Montgomery, Ala.*]

The following three versions of this sermon include a brief outline written on a notecard, a handwritten draft, and a typed manuscript.[1] *King cites numerous examples from world history demonstrating that "evil carries the seed of its own destruction."*

"Discerning the Signs of History," Sermon notes

I am convinced that what human life, man-centered, has torn down, human life, God-centered can build up.

1. He who oppresses another will ultimately suffer as a results of such oppression

3. Whenever the secular super-structure is cut alose from religious foundations disintegration sets in.

2. A breakdown in the moral structure of a society leads to the ultimate breakdown of the physical structure

AD. CSKC: Sermon file, folder 79, "Discerning the Signs of History."

"Discerning the Signs of History," Sermon outline

{And}

Luke 12:54, 55[2]

"ye can discern the face of the sky and of the earth; how is it that ye know not how to interpret this time?"[3] What is Jesus' indictment? He ~~was~~ is saying that these people had an amazing awarness of the the trends of astronomy and an appalling ignorance of the trends of history. They could read the face of the sky, but they could not read the face of the past. They had mastered the art of noticing the succession in the natural world. They were so ingenious that they could apply the law of cause and effect to the natural order. If a cloud appeared in the west they knew that a shower would soon emerge. If the south wind blew they knew that the tropical heat would soon appear The sequence was certain. They knew that one was the harbinger of the other [*Three pages are missing*]

---

1. According to a 26 June 1955 Dexter program, King preached a sermon with this title. Reinhold Niebuhr's book *Discerning the Signs of the Times: Sermons for Today and Tomorrow* may have inspired King's title for this sermon (New York: Charles Scribner's Sons, 1946). King wrote "discerning the signs of the time" above the passage Matthew 16:3 in his copy of the Bible.

2. "And he said also to the people, When ye see a cloud rise out of the west, straightway ye say, There cometh a shower; and so it is. And when ye see the south wind blow, ye say, There will be heat: and it cometh to pass."

3. Cf. Luke 12:56.

He started underestimating the power of his opponent. He invaded Russia in
1812. The Battle of Leipzig in 1813. His ultimate doom was the Battle of Waterloo in 1815.[4] Waterloo is but the eternal symbol of the doom of every Napoleon. He lived by the sword and die by it.[5]

    (b) Hitler set out to rule the world. Cite how he invaded Ethiopia and Halla Silassis had to flee his throne. But today Hitler is dead and Halla Sillasis still holds his throne[6]

    (c) Mussilini tried the sword, and ended up being killed by the very people that he once ruled.[7]

    This is the ever present story of history.

(3) A third lesson that history teaches is that whenever the secular superstructure is cut alose from religious foundations disintegration sets in. In other words whenever a civilization looses a moral and religious consciousness, it is headed for doom.

    (a) Toynbee teaches that 26 civilizations have risen and all but 10 have fallen.[8] They did not fall because of armies without but because of inner decay. Whenever emphemal institutions and techniques are raised to absoluteness decay sets in

    (b) Gibbon reports of what immorality meant in the fall of the Roman empire.[9]

    (c) I am worried about America because of its materialism. We affirm God with our lips while denying him with our lives. The white man is gradually repenting. He becoming more churchy. He has come to see the futility of materialism. <u>But I am still worried about the Negro</u>. He emptying his churches while the white man is filling them.

    (D) Cite what religion meant to the Negro in the past.

    (E) place God back into the center of your lives.

    I do not mean to leaves a message of doom this morning. This is hope if we will but read the signs of history and profit by its mistakes. I am convinced that what human life, man-centered, has torn down, human life God centered can build up.

    Conclude with story of wise man in Virginia

ADf. CSKC: Sermon file, folder 79, "Discerning the Signs of History."

---

4. Napoleon Bonaparte invaded Russia and captured Moscow on 14 September 1812. The Russians, however, set the city ablaze, leaving the French army with no place to stay during the winter. This led to the French army's retreat on 19 October 1812. At the battle of Leipzig, Russian, Austrian, Prussian, British, Portuguese, Spanish, and Swedish forces defeated Napoleon's troops on 19 October 1813 and forced the French army to flee Germany. Napoleon's final defeat at the battle of Waterloo on 18 June 1815 ended the Napoleonic Wars.

5. Cf. Matthew 26:52.

6. Italy, not Germany, invaded Ethiopia in 1935 and annexed the country in 1936. King refers to Haille Selassie I (1892–1975), the last emperor of Ethiopia, who fled to England when the Italians invaded. After the British liberated Ethiopia in 1941, Selassie reclaimed the throne. He was deposed in 1974.

7. Benito Mussolini was executed on 28 April 1945.

8. Arnold Toynbee, *A Study of History* (1934–1961).

9. King refers to Edward Gibbon's *The History of the Decline and Fall of the Roman Empire.*

This morning I want to have you think about some of the things that are just as true in history as we find the truth in the natural law. The coming of the heat with the south wind, the coming of the rain with the gathering of the clouds.[10] There are some things that are as basic and as structural in history, as in nature. If we do not know these things, we are in danger of destroying ourselves and destroying the world. If we are to discern the signs of, the times in which we live we must understand a basic truth; that evil carries the seed of its own destruction. Ultimately there is a checkpoint in the Universe, there is at the end of the road of evil a sign which says, "Dead end street. You won't get through here." If you see evil riding high, do not worry, one day it will be cut down.

Go with me back across the centuries of French history. Watch the kings as they exploit and trample over the people of France thinking only about themselves and their families and their welfare. Louis XIV, his wife, Marie Antoinette, had literally wagons of meat to feed their dogs. The begging masses of people went hungry. In a few short years that same Louis XVI and his wife were beheaded by his own people.[11]

It is the long story of history "Evil carries the seed of its own destruction.

The evil system of colonization got started in the world and the great nations of Europe moved into Asia and Africa exploiting the people economically, and dominating them politically. It came to the point that the vast majority of the people of Asia and Africa were dominated by some foreign power. Finally the people fought for an end and won. Britian had under its domination more than sixty million people in Asia and Africa but not today. Evil carries the seeds of its own destruction. There is a process in the Gods universe. God still reigns in history.

You know, we know about another evil don't we? It started in 1619 right here in this nation our foreparents were brought here to slave from the soil of Africa. For more than Two Hundred Forty years africa was raped and plundered, her native kingdoms disorganized, her people and rulers demoralized. We lived with that system right here for 244 years and then for a period it looked like we were going to get out with the signing of the Emancipation Proclamation.[12] But we were only half way out.

It looked like we were doomed to stay in slavery and segregation for ever. But evil carries the seed of its own destruction. God spoke through nine men in 1954, on May 17. They examined the legal body of segregation and pronounced it constitutionally dead and ever since then things have been changing.[13] We can go to places all over the South that we could not go last year. Why? Because evil carries the seed of its own destruction. And I am convinced that segregation is just as dead as a doornail and the only thing I am uncertain about is how costly the segregationalist will make the funeral.

---

10. Cf. Luke 12:54, 55.

11. Louis XVI was executed on 21 January 1793. Marie Antoinette suffered the same fate on 16 October 1793.

12. Abraham Lincoln issued the Emancipation Proclamation on 22 September 1862.

13. On 17 May 1954, the United States Supreme Court ruled, in the case of *Brown v. Board of Education* et al., 347 U.S. 483, that segregation in education was unconstitutional.

The old order is passing away. Evil carries the seed of its own destruction. William 28 June–
Cullen Bryant caught it and said "Truth across the earth will rise again."[14] Carlisle 3 July 1955
caught it and said, "No lie can live forever."[15] James Russell Lowell caught it and said,
"Truth forever on the scaffold, wrong forever on the throne, and yet that scaffold sways
the future, and behind the dim unknown stands God within the shadow keeping watch
above his own."[16] The Bible caught it right, "You shall reap what you sow."[17] Evil carries the seed of its own destruction and that is just as true as the rising and the setting
of the sun. If we understand the facts of nature, let us understand the facts of history.

TD. CSKC: Sermon file, folder 79, "Discerning the Signs of History."

---

14. Bryant, "The Battlefield" (1839).
15. Thomas Carlyle, *The French Revolution* (1837).
16. Lowell, "The Present Crisis" (1844).
17. Cf. Galatians 6:7 and 2 Corinthians 9:6.

"The Task of Christian Leadership Training
for Education in the Local Community"

[28 June–3 July 1955?]
[Atlantic City, N.J.?]

*King traveled to Atlantic City on 28 June to attend the National Sunday School
and Baptist Training Union Congress.[1] The subject matter of the following undated,
typed manuscript indicates that it may have served as the basis for an address at the
conference. King lays out three primary challenges facing local communities: economics, religious sectarianism, and race. He criticizes "the attempt on the part of Negroes
to build up a class system within the bounds of the Negro race." King calls for leaders
who are open-minded and intelligent to address spiritual and physical needs and to
exhibit moral authority.*

About two weeks ago, a little more than five hundred Negro young men and
women graduated from the six institutions of higher learning in my home City,
Atlanta, Georgia.[2] In that City a little more than six hundred boys and girls received
high school diplomas. I am all but sure that this same thing happened in numerous
other communities of our nation.

---

1. In a letter written 28 June 1955, King indicated he was departing for the convention (see King to
Benjamin Elijah Mays, 28 June 1955, in *Papers* 2:562–563). The National Sunday School and Baptist
Training Union Congress was a division of the National Baptist Convention.

2. King most likely refers to Atlanta University, Clark College, Morehouse College, Morris Brown College, Spelman College, and Gammon Theological Seminary, all historically black institutions in Atlanta
during the 1950s.

Does this mean anything to you as ministers, as laymen, as leaders, as potential leaders, and as followers of Christ? Does it mean something worth while and far reaching to you or does it impress you as merely another phenomenon taking place in this moving world of activity? Does it mean that you will go out with a rebellious air saying that education is harmful or does it mean that or does it mean that you will attempt to synthesize education and religion, realizing that the problems of the local community are so gigantic in extent and chaotic in detail that it will take a good dose of education mixed with a good dose of religion to solve them.

Before discussing the task of Christian leaders for education in the local community, let us define the community and set forth some of the pressing problems that are present within the local community.

By community is meant a given territory within which people live together, sharing daily [*common?*] life. They possess a common language, means of transportation, a web of custom, folklore and tradition, and a marked degree of social coherence. Now what are some of the problems that we are faced with in every community? I might say while passing that the problems of the local community are reflexions of the problem of the world community. So that each of these problems that will be discussed as characteristic of the local community are also characteristic of the world community on a larger scale.

First, we are faced with that glaring economic problim. It radiates in our communities like the rays of the beaming sun. In every community people are hungry, unemployment is rising like a tidal wave, housing conditions are embarrassingly poor, crime and juvenile delinquency are spreading like the dew drops on an early fall morning. All of these conditions result from the economic problem. Moreover, the economic problem has brought about one of the major conflicts of our time, the conflict between capital and labor. This internal war between labor and capital is a basic problem within every community.

I would not be so naive as to say, as the communist do, that if we solve the economic problem all problems will be solved. But we will have to admit with the communist that the economic problem is a major problem. Too often have we in America taken necessities from the masses to give luxeries to the classes. Have we been all together fair to the laboring man, that man who has to work sometimes until his hands are all but porched and his eyebrows all but scorched. Our failure to give the laboring man a fair break is the very reason why capitalism is her death bed in America.

There is a second problem which each community is faced with, namely, the religious problem. It expresses itself in the narrow sectarianism which is so rampant. The dissention between the denominations of the Protestant church, some two hundred fifty or more is quite appalling. Many of these various denominations stand out with an authoritative voice saying, "we are right and everybody else is wrong." Every minister is aware of the problem in the local community. This Civil War within the Protestant Faith makes the larger conflict between Catholicism and Protestantism much more extensive.

There is a third problem present within each of our communities which is so ostensible that it hardly needs explaination, namely, the race problem. It is this problem that threatens the well-being of Christianity as an influential power in world affairs. In practically every community men of color are being still being surpressed economically, politically and socially. We continue to recite our democratic creeds but fail to practice them in deeds.

This race problem has brought about another problem which is just as anti-Christian as its source, namely, the attempt on the part of Negroes to build up a class system within the bounds of the Negro race. This has lead many Negroes who have had educational and economical advantages to exploit and even discriminate the Negroes who have not had these advantages. We the oppressed, instead of profiting by the mistakes of the oppressors, have fallen victims of the philosophy of the oppressors. This practice is deep within the fiber of the local community and its advocators are increasing daily. This brings us next to the question of the task of Christian Leaders for Education in the local community. In other words, what type of leaders are needed to face these perplexing problems which are found in the local community? In the face of these problems what type of leaders are needed to put over a worthwhile educational program in the community?

First, every Christian leader has the task of being open-minded. Have not our Christian leaders too often been advocators of narrow sectarianism? Have not our educational programs in the community been to Baptist, to Methodist, to Presbyterian, and not to Christian. Has not this internal war between the diverse denomination caused a lapse in community progress. Christian leaders must come to see that problems of the local community are so intricite that it will take the united effort of all denominations to solve them. Christian leaders must come to see that God is not a denominational God, and that in the final analysis we are all in the same boat. Although we differ in minute detail, such as ritual and minor doctrine, we should be working forward to the coming of God's Kingdom in earth. This plea for ecumenical minded leaders cannot be exaggerated, for everywhere one turns he sees narrow minded leaders.

A second task facing Christian leaders is that of being intelligent. By intelligence I mean the ability to keep abreast with the problems of a changing culture. This demand for intelligence is somewhat inevitable, for how can we interpret the situation in the community without a knowledge of them. It is the job of every leader to keep up with the changing trends through intellectual discipline. I realize that there are many who would agree that the Christian leader only has the job of being sincere and pious, but sincerity and piety are not enough, as important as they are. We must remember that the same Jesus that said love the Lord thy God with all thy heart and soul also said love God with all thy mind.[3] Some of the most crucial periods in history have been those periods when we loved God with our hearts and souls and failed to love him with our minds.

The third specific task of the Christian leader is that he must deal with people as whole beings, not as fragments. He must not see individuals as "souls" divorced from the material secular bodies. He must come to see that man is a Psyco-Physical being, and that his body is as important as his soul. Somehow we must come to see that Christianity is a two way road. On the one hand, we must attempt to chang men's souls so that society will be changed. On the other hand, we must attempt to change society so that the soul will have a chance. How can we be concerned with the souls of men and not be concerned with the conditions that damn their souls.

---

3. Cf. Matthew 22:37.

How can we be concerned with men being true and honest and not concerned with the economic conditions that made them dishonest and the social conditions that make them untrue.[4] Too often do we become so absorbed in a future good "over yonder" that we forget the present evil over here.

Finally, the Christian leader must be consecrated. There is a dire need for leaders who have been touched by the hand of the Divine. Too many leaders make religion only a one day affair, something that they put on Sunday morning and hang up in the closet on Sunday night. Too many leaders have only been innoculated with a mild form of Christianity. We stand today in dire need of a moral voice able to call forth all its powers. The weakness of leaders today is that they exercise no moral authority. They are picking around the surface of our really vital problems. We need leaders today who are able to convince the secular world that we are engaged in the most dangerous, the most daring and at the same time the most necessary business on earth, that of saving men from moral bankruptcy. What we need today is more spiritual engineers to guide this train of religion. When our leaders will have reached this point we will sail safely into the harbor of God's Kingdom. This is our overwhelming responsibility and our profound challenge.

TD. CSKC: Sermon file, folder 36, "Sermon Notes."

---

4. Fosdick, *The Hope of the World*, p. 25: "I plead instead for a church that shall be a fountainhead of a better social order. Any church that pretends to care for the souls of people but is not interested in the slums that damn them, the city government that corrupts them, the economic order that cripples them, and international relations that, leading to peace or war, determine the spiritual destiny of innumerable souls—that kind of church, I think, would hear again the Master's withering words: 'Scribes and Pharisees, hypocrites!' "

"Worship,"
Sermon at Dexter Avenue Baptist Church

[*7 August 1955*]
[*Montgomery, Ala.*]

King notes in this handwritten, dated sermon that effective worship should "cause us to serve our fellow man in every day life."[1] *After pointing out the possibility of worshiping God on one's own, King highlights the value of public worship: "Here the employer and the employee, the rich and the poor, the white collar worker and the common laborer all come* [together] *in a vast unity. Here we come to see that*

---

1. King wrote "Preached at Dexter, Aug. 7 1955" on the file folder containing this sermon. He delivered a version of this sermon at Dexter on 28 April 1957 (King, The Rewards of Worship, pp. 293–302 in this volume). For another sermon on worship, see King, "Worship at Its Best," Sermon at Dexter Avenue Baptist Church, 14 December 1958, pp. 350–351 in this volume.

Dr. [*William Ernest*] Hocking of Havard Uni has said that "all life can be reduced to work and worship—what we do ourselves, and what we let the higher than ourselves do."[2] Worship is as natural to the human family as the rising of the sun is to the cosmic order. Men always have worshipped and always will worship. In some form or other, ~~it~~ worship is found everywhere, in all ages and among all peoples. Buddhism, a religion ~~without~~ theoretically without a God, would impress us as a religion that excludes worship; yet in every country where Buddhism is dominant, worship is present. Confucius urged his followers not to have much to do with the gods; yet immediately after his death his followers deified him and today millions worship him. If today one crosses the borders of Christianity into the plain of Mohammedanism he will find formal prayer five times daily. This tendency to worship is one of the elemental functions of human life.

Not only do we find worship in religious realms, but we find it in other realms of life. Even the man who theoretically denies the existence of God worships something. Werever one gives his total personality unreservingly to something elsse he worships that something, and convinces himself that that something is higher than himself. In this sense one can worship any material thing, from a diamond ring to a human demogogue.

This morning I would like to speak of worship in the Christian religion and to the Christian God, notwithstanding the fact that worship cannot be confined to the Christian religion neither to the Christian God.

First, we may ask, what is worship? I can give a partial answer to this question by saying what worship is not. Worship is not entertainment. Of course many of our churches would leave us with the impression that worship is entertainment. How often do we find ministers who are mere showmen giving the people what they want rather than what they need. How often do we find the minnister going in the pulpit depending on the volume of his voice rather that the content of his message. How often do we find our prayers uttered for the entertaiment of the listeners rather than for the sincere communication with God. How often do we select songs in our worship periods which appeal to the feet & hands rather than to the heart and mind. This tendency to reduce our worship periods to mere entertaining periods has sapped the very vitality of spiritual fervor from the root of the church. The living water of the Holy spirit fails to flow through the stream of our churchs. Of course the irony of the whole matter is that the very people who make worship an entertaining center are the people who are convinced that their actions reveal the holy spirit. They have confused overt emotionalism with the true holy spirit. This misinterpretation of the holy spirit has caused many to fail to see value of a sensible sermon. Moreover, it has caused many to loss appreciation for real music. We have

---

2. Fosdick, *Successful Christian Living,* pp. 173–174: "Professor Hocking is right in saying that all man's life can be reduced to two aspects, work and worship—what we do ourselves, and what we let the higher than ourselves do to us."

strayed away from those song that were written out of the souls of men, and jumped to those songs which are written merely for comercial purposes. At this point there is a great deal that we can learn from Catholacism. No one can doubt the fact that the Catholics have mastered the art of worship. On many occasions I have been in Catholic churches and it felt as if the very atmosphere blew the wind of the holy spirit. There was something in the very atmosphere that motivated one to worship.

Not only is worship not entertainment but it is not to be confused with service. When one worships God he is not necessarily serving God. Worship only prepares one for service. We must not think that after worship we have totally fulfilled our Christian duty. If worship does not cause us to serve our fellow man in every day life and see the worth of human personality then the whole process is as "sounding brass and a tinkling cymbal."[3]

What then is worship from a positive angle? Worship is a silent communication with God. It is the awareness of the creator on the part of the creature. This definition of worship makes it very clear that worship is not totallaly a public affair, but it may also be private. The sound of great music might cause us to worship in our bedrooms. The reading of profound and lasting literature might cause us to worship at our studies. The observation of the beauties of nature might cause us to worship it the midnight hours. Have you ever been in an airoplan that somehow seeped above the clouds? As you looked up you could see nothing but the dark deep blue of the skies and as you looked below you could see nothing but the shining silvery sheets of the clowds and somehow you cried in amazement—O God, how beautiful nature. This is worship Have you ever been out late at night when somehow you could look above the man-made lights of the city into the lofty blue with all its majestic grandeur and there you saw the stars as they appeared to shinning silver pins sticking in the magnificent blue pin cusion. Somehow you begin to ask, "do these stars shine from their cold, serene, and passionless height totally indifferent to the joys and sorrows of men? Finally you could answer, O no, for behind those swinging laterns of eternity," is a purpose that embraces all mankind. This, my friends was worship. Have you ever the singing of the birds early in the morning? They somehow filled our ears with melodious music that out-sounded the wrestling of the jostling winds. This was a woshipful experience. Whenever we are carried our of ourselves by something greater than ourselves and give ourselves to that something then we are worshipping.

Although private worship is significant and uplifting it must not be a stopping point. A worship period on the radio cannot be a subsitute for a worship period in

---

3. Cf. 1 Corinthians 13:1. In the same folder as this sermon, King filed an outline also titled "Worship" which further emphasized the point that worship is not entertainment (King, "Worship," Sermon outline, 7 August 1955). He added at this point in the outline that worship is also "not passive superficial dignity. There are many people who have caught the contagious disease of 'spectatoritis.' Such persons are only spectators or onlookers but not participants. Such persons watch the minister and choir indulge in prayer and praise. They come to see what is going on rather than to help create, give direction and enrichment to what is going on. The mood of the true worshiper is not passive, but active. He comes not just to get but to give, not to observe, but to participate; not just to see what is going on, but to contribute to what is going on. Many receive nothing from their formal devotion because they suffer from spectatoritis."

a church. Worship at its best is a social experience where people of all leavels of life come together and communicate with a common father. Here the employer and the employee, the rich and the poor, the white collar worker and the common laborer all come to-gether in a vast unity. Here we come to see that although we have different callings in life we are all the children of a common father, who is the father of both the rich and the poor. This fellowship and sense of oneness that we get in public worship cannot be surpassed.

What does worship do for us? Worship helps us to transcend the hurly-burly of everyday life and dwell in a transcendent realm. Worship is the type of escape that is both heathy and normal.

2. Through worship ones worse self comes face to face with his better self, and the better self comes face to face with something still better still. No man can be at his best unless he stands over and over again in the presence that which superior to his best[4]

{3. Howard Thurmond}[5]

AD. CSKC: Sermon file, folder 4, "Worship."

---

4. In the sermon outline, King concluded with these words: "So in a real sense worship is the highest of all activities. It must therefore be taken seriously, following a definite pattern. Worship is not only the mother of the arts, but is also an art itself."

5. King may refer to observations on worship made by Howard Thurman in a 1949 sermon titled "The Commitment": "The center of our undertaking, the heart of our commitment, summarizes itself in terms of the worship of God . . . I mean [by] the worship of God, the immediate awareness of the pushing out of the barriers of self, the moment when we flow together into one, when I am not male or female, yellow or green or black or white or brown, educated or illiterate, rich or poor, sick or well, righteous or unrighteous—but a naked human spirit that spills over into other human spirits as they spill over into me. Together, we become one under the transcending glory and power of the spirit of the living God" (Thurman, "The Commitment," *The Growing Edge,* March 1949).

"Looking Beyond Your Circumstances," Sermon at Dexter Avenue Baptist Church

[*18 September 1955*]
[*Montgomery, Ala.*]

King illuminates the challenges of African American life in this handwritten manuscript: "His birth automatically throws him into the tragic circumstances of segregation and [discrimination]."[1] *Acknowledging the temptation to turn painful situations into contempt, he writes, "The Negro who experiences bitter and*

---

1. On the file folder containing this document, King wrote "Preached at Dexter, Third Sun in Sept. 1955."

agonizing circumstances as a result of some [ungodly] white person is tempted to look upon all white persons as evil." Rather than capitulating to difficulties, King urges a strong and patient faith in God: "We as Negroes may often have our highest dreams blown away by the jostling winds of a white man's prejudice, but wait on the Lord."

I had fainted unless I had believed to see the goodness of the Lord in the land of the living—Ps. 27:13[2]

Life constantly presents each of us with circumstances which are beyond our control. <u>There is a point in every man's life beyond which the gift of choice cannot reach</u>. There is an area in which every man must bow to the surging swept of life's determinism. Even the most extreme indeterminist must admit that there are areas in which man's life is determined. Freedom is always within limits. Our freedom must operate within the framework of an already existent determinism. <u>We are continually confronted with circumstances which we did not have the freedom to choose, but which we are forced to deal</u>.

These piercing and almost always unwanted circumstances take many form. The child that is born in India has no choice as to his social status. At the moment of his birth he is automatically thrust into the circumstance of a caste system. The Negro that is born in America has no choice as to his social, political and economic status. His birth automatically throws him into the tragic circumstances of segregation and discrimanation. The persons who are forced to live with some dread disease, in most cases, did not choose such circumstances, they were thrust upon them. When we stand and see a loved one carried away by the chilly winds of death, we do not choose it, but it a circumstance that we must accept. These are but few of the myriad circumstances that life thrusts upon us. They come so often to blot out the hightening joy of life's noon, leaving us grouping in the bleak and desolate moments of life's evening.

One of the great temptations of life is to become too absorbed in one's circumstances. There are many people whose visions are turned totally inward, and they can never see beyond their particular circumstances. This always leads to tragic consequences. Whenever a man looks merely at his circumstances he ends up in despair, disillusionment and cynicism. Indeed this is one of the causes of suicide and schizophenic personalities. In the former case the individual becomes so absorbed in his tragic circumstances that he can see no way out other than getting rid of the ~~source~~ center of all circumstances, namely, life itself. In the latter case the individual becomes so absorbed in his circumstances that the personality gradually becomes thinner and thinner, ultimately spliting and disintegrating under the pressing load.

The great burden of life, then, is to master the art of looking beyond one's circumstances. Ultimately, the test of a man's life is how he responds to his circumstances.

One day the Psalmist was meditating ~~upon~~ on his circumstances. He remem-

---

2. Psalm 27:13.

bered the moments when roaring waters of trouble poured upon him in staggering torrents. He remembered days when his enemies came upon like tidal waves, leaving him sinking in the rushing waters of defeat. He had noticed on so many occasions how the wicket were elevated to the throne of prosperity, while the righteous were trodden and crushed by the iron feet of suffering. In the midst of these circumstances, the Psalmist crys out: "I had fainted, unless:* I had believed to see the goodness of the Lord in the land of the living."[3]

By fainting here the Psalmist does not mean physical collaspe; rather he means spiritual collaspe. He is saying in substance: "I would have lost my courage and spirit; I would have fallen into a state of dejection; I would have collasped spiritually; I would have fallen under the sultry sweltering heat of cynicism if I had looked only at my particular circumstances. But I gained the courage to look beyond my circumstances, and by so doing I was able to see the goodness of God winning its victory in history."

What are the specific gains in looking beyond your circumstances? First it helps one to see reality as a whole. The person who fails to look beyond his circumstances is tempted to judge the whole of reality on the basis of a partial view of reality. It leaves one vulnerable to the fallacy of generalization. The girl who has an unfortunate love affair with some ill mannered man is tempted to conclude that all men are no good, if she does not look beyond her circumstances. {The man who has a tragic disappointment is tempted to conclude that all life is meaningless.} The Negro who experiences bitter and agonizing circumstances as a results of some ongodly white person is tempted to look upon all whites persons as evil, if he fails to look beyond his circumstances. But the minute he looks beyond his circumstances and sees the whole of the situation, he discovers that ~~many~~ some of the most implacable and vehement advocates of racial equality are consecrated white persons. We must never forget that such a noble organization as the National Association for the Advancement of Colored People was organized by whites, and even to this day gains a great deal of ~~its~~ support from northern and southen white persons.[4] The most vocal and impetuous abilitionists were not negroes, but whites.[5] As a race we fail to see this if we get bogged down in the partial view of our particular circumstances. Airplane[6]

One of the most noble characters of all the Old Testament was Elijah. The tragedy of his life was that he allowed himself to become victimized with the chronic

---

3. Psalm 27:13. King wrote this quote on a separate sheet of paper and probably intended to link it to the asterisk in the document: "Behind that unless is an affirmation of cosmic significance. Behind that unless is a radiant star of hope that brings light to every cloud of despair. Behind that unless is a joyous daybreak that comes to end every ~~night~~ bewildering night."

4. In 1909 white civil rights supporters joined African Americans in founding the National Association for the Advancement of Colored People (NAACP). They included Mary White Ovington, Oswald Garrison Villiard, Henry Moscowitz, Leonora O'Reilly, and William English Walling.

5. King may refer to radical abolitionists such as William Lloyd Garrison (1805–1879) and John Brown (1800–1859).

6. In notes for another version of this sermon, King wrote: "The plane trip—No wind of [*adversity*] can stop him. No [*storm*] of failure can [*overwhelm*] him" (King, When Your A String Breaks, 1959, p. 355 in this volume).

disease of over absorbsion in his circumstances. He started out in the venture of life with courage and hope. In one majestic sweep he ascended to the hights of prophecy. But then one day he found that his circumstances had brought disappointment and difficulty. ~~The cloud of perplexity was hovering~~ All of the sunshine of joy had been obscured from his vision by the cloud of perplexity that was hovering so low. In the midst of this Elijah fainted spiritually. The lamp of hope was gradually flickering. One day while lying under a tree he said to God, "take away my life. I am disgusted. All The people have forsaken thee. They have torn down the altars. They have slain the prophets. I am now the only one left who has not turned to Baal." You remember God's response to Elijah. He asks: "What doest thou here? . . . Go to Damascus." In other word God is saying to Elijah, "What are you doing bogged down in your circumstances. No wonder you are cynical and blue. Get up and look beyond your circumstances—go to Damascus." God also reveals to Elijah that because ~~has become the victim~~ of his over absorption in his circumstances he has become the victim of an unwarented generalization; He feels that all the prophets have deserted God. But God affirms to Elijah in terms bristling with certainty that there are seven thousand prophets that have never bowed their knees to Baal.[7]

This, then, is the first advantage of looking beyond your circumstances. It enables us to see our particular experiences in the light of the totality of all experiences.

{The second gain that comes from looking beyond ones circumstances is that of seeing that your particular circumstances, however tragic, are not unique.}

The third gain that comes from looking ~~for~~ beyond one's circumstances is that of being able to see the ultimate triumph of goodness ~~a fixed~~ structure of goodness that can master every circumstance. There is something inherently unstable about our present circumstances. They cant be depended on. Even if our circumstances happen to be fortunate we cannot bet on them. We may abound in the grandeur of riches today and starve in the cluches of poverty tomorrow. We may be elevated to the throne of popularity today and dropped in the abyss of obscurity tomorrow. We may be at the pinnacle of good health this week and in a few weeks sink to the nadir of bad health. There is something tenuous, elusive, and vascilating about circumstances. So whenever we look merely at our circumstances we end up with a frustration shrouded with devastating cynicism. This is why it is necessary to look beyond our circumstances for something fixed and permanent which can master every circumstance. This was what the Psalmist did. When he looked beyond his circumstances he was able to see the permanent structure of God's goodness which could master every circumstance in this life. Herein lies our hope. This is why the simon-pure Christian can stand up in his circumstances and never be overcome by them. He has faith in a God that can master every circumstance, and he knows that God's goodness will ultimately win out over every state of evil in the universe. God is working every moment in history for the triumph of goodness. ~~Wait therefore on the Lord~~. So as the Psalmist says: "Wait on the Lord."[8]

---

7. Cf. 1 Kings 19:1–18.

8. Psalms 27:14; 37:34.

In an inscription to the Kings in a copy of Thurman's 1955 book *Deep River*, Howard Thurman writes, "The test of life is often found in the amount of pain we can absorb without spoiling [*our?*] joy."

Many will probably ask, Why do we have to wait? Why doesn't God streighten out things right now? The answer is found in the fact that God seems to work in strides. He does not do things all at once. Even the Gensis writer realized this. In his conception God could have spoken and the whole universe would have come into being all at once, but instead he chose to spread it out over six days.[9] Apparently God sees that his purpose in the universe can best be realized by working in strides. An all at once method of creation would not give man a chance to grow and develope. He would be a blind automaton. So God chooses to work in strides. This is why a theory of evolution should never freigten us. May it not be that God is working through the evolutionary process.

Wait, therefore, on the Lord. Your circumstance may ~~be~~ seem to overwelm you now, but wait on the Lord. Some disappointing experience may have you shivering in the cold winter of despair, but wait on the Lord. We as Negroes may often have our highest dreams blown away by the jostling winds of a white man's prejudice, but wait on the Lord you may now be quivering in the midst of the chilley winds of adversity, but wait on the Lord.

Isaiah waited on him, and in the dark and dreary day of the exile he could cry out: "The grass may whither, the flowers may fade away, but the word of our Lord shall stand forever."[10] Job waited on him[11]

AD. CSKC: Sermon file, folder 121, "Looking Beyond Your Circumstance."

---

9. Genesis 1.

10. Isaiah 40:8.

11. King refers to the perseverance of Job's faith in God despite overwhelming adversity.

"Pride Versus Humility:
The Parable of the Pharisee and the Publican,"
Sermon at Dexter Avenue Baptist Church

[*25 September 1955*]
[*Montgomery, Ala.*]

King draws upon George Buttrick's interpretation of Jesus' parable in this handwritten sermon. He observes that "the perpetrators of many of the greatest evils in our society worship Christ," and uses the jurors in the Emmett Till case as an example of those who "worship Christ emotionally and not morally." [1]

---

1. Buttrick, *The Parables of Jesus*, pp. 87–91. On the inside of the file folder in which he kept this sermon, King wrote "Preached at Dexter, Sept (4th Sun), 1955."

In order to understand the revolutionary teaching of this parable, it is necessary to understand the positions which the Pharisee and Publican held in the community. The Pharisee was by far one of the most respected persons in the community. He was distinguished as a pillar of the Church and as a citizen of highest character.[3] On the basis of strict adherence to the ~~Jewish~~ Mosaic law, he was certainly the "good" man of his community. The Publican, on the other hand, was looked upon as one of the disgraceful characters of the community. And yet the parable implies throughout that Jesus condemns the Pharisee—the good man—and approves the Publican—the sinner. The stand was not only unorthodox, but revolutionary. It was a staggering blow to the accepted judgments of that day. It was an appalling affront to the high-ups in the intricate ecclesiastical machinery.

Now the question is, Why did Jesus condemn the Pharisee and approve the Publican?

The first thing that caused Jesus to look askance at the Pharisee was that he confused ceremonial piety with geniune religious living. His logic seems to have been this: "I go to the synagogue regularly. I pay ten per cent of my income to the church, and I fast twice in the week; therefore I am a religious man, and I must be better than the publican, because he doesn't do any of these things." Jesus says the Pharisee is wrong because he attempted to incarcerate religion within the walls of religious observances; he made ceremonialism an end rather than a means to an end.

There are basically two sides to the religious life—the inward and the outer. The inward side of religion is the actual relationship between the I and the thou; it is the devotion of the individual to that object which concerns him ultimately. The outward side of religion is an expression of this concern through ritualistic and ceremonial means. Now the great danger confronting the religious man is that he will allow the outer side of religion to become a substitute for the inner side. There is the danger that actual contact with God will be lost beneath a maze of external formality. There is the danger that the fresh flowing stream of religion will be overwelmed by ritualistic tributaries and ceremonial eddies flowing in. There is the danger that the ceremonial demands of Sunday will become substitutes for the ethical demands of Monday.

This was one of the basic errors of the Pharisee. He thought that the fulfilling of religious ceremony was a religious end. But ceremony is a religious means; it is a junction, not a terminus. Genuine religion is more than a ceremonial act, more than a Sunday form, more than a ritualistic observance; it it an attitude to life.

Jesus condemned this over-emphasis on the ceremonial, because he knew the omminus effects would it could ~~engender~~ lead to. He saw that it could be the springboard of a religion which ~~worshipped Christ emotionally~~ substitutes emotions

---

2. Luke 18:9–14 recounts the parable of the Pharisee and the Publican in which Jesus called for sincerity and humility before God.

3. Buttrick, *The Parables of Jesus,* p. 87: "The Pharisee was a pillar of the Church, an ardent patriot, and respected in his community as a citizen of highest character."

for moral. This is what we are seeing in the world today—countless millions of people worshipping Christ emotionally but not morally. Great imperialistic powers, like Britian, France, and Holland, which have [~~trumpeled~~] trodden and crushed Africa and Asia with the "iron feet of oppression, worship Christ. The white men who lynch Negroes worship Christ. That jury in Mississippi, which a few days ago in the Emmett Till case, freed two white men from what might be considered one of the most brutal and inhuman crimes of the twentieth century, worships Christ.[4] The perpetrators of many of the greatest evils in our society worship Christ. These ~~trouble is that all~~ people, like the Pharisee, go to church regularly, ~~they~~ pay their tithes and offerings, and observe religiously the various ceremonial requirements. The trouble with these people, however, is that they worship Christ emotionally and not morally. They cast his ethical and moral insights behind the gushing smoke of emotional adoration and ceremonial piety.

To those who would follow such a religion, we can God saying through the prophets: "Get out of my face. Your incense is an abomination unto me, your feast day trouble me. When you spread forth your hands, I will hide my face. When you make your loud prayer, I will not hear. Your hand are full of blood."[5] Again he says: "Take away from me the noise of thy songs; for I will not hear the melody of thy viols. But let judgment run down as waters and righteousness as a mighty stream."[6] This is always God's respons to those who would make ceremonial piety a substitute for genuine religious living.

This is the danger of Phariseeism and the continual threat that hoovers over every religious expression.

Another thing that Jesus found wrong with the Pharisee was that he compared himself to another to that other's disparagement. The Pharisee looked at the Publican and said in substance, "I thank thee that I am not like that poor devil." The Pharisee makes the Publican "a dark foil for his gleaming whiteness."[7] But the truely religious man never does this. Instead he finds himself saying with Richard Baxter, as he watches a poor wretch go off to prison, "There but for the grace of God go I."[8] Whenever a man lives close to God he is able to see ~~in his~~ soul the slumbering giants of evil always on the verge of awaking in his soul; he discovers staggering tides of badness which are capable of rising to flood propotions. Consequently, he cannot boast like the Pharisee, and whenever he sees humanity [*strikeout illegible*] at its worse the inner voices of his soul cry out, "But for the grace of God, I to would be like that."

What the Publican needed was not condemnation, but encouragemet. We never

---

4. Till, a fourteen-year-old African American from Chicago, was lynched during the summer of 1955 in Money, Mississippi, for allegedly whistling at a white woman. On 23 September 1955, an all-white jury in Sumner, Mississippi, took just over an hour to acquit Roy Bryant and J. W. Milam of Till's murder.

5. Cf. Isaiah 1:13–16.

6. Amos 5:23–24.

7. Buttrick, *The Parables of Jesus,* p. 88: "The poor publican, standing at a distance, is thus dragged into the 'prayer' as a dark foil for the Pharisee's gleaming whiteness."

8. This quote is sometimes attributed to English clergyman Richard Baxter (1615–1691), although its source is Puritan martyr John Bradford (1510–1555). While in prison, Bradford watched criminals go to their execution and exclaimed, "But for the grace of God there goes John Bradford" (*The Writings of John Bradford* [Cambridge: University Press, 1853], p. xliii).

help others by condemning them. Mere condemnation is always wrong. The evil is to be condemned, but not the person who does it, though he may have to be restrained and punished because of the evil he does. Mere condemnation tends to set up an impassible gulf between ~~the condemned~~ us and the condemned person. As the Psychoanalyse Jung has said so well in the last chapter of his book <u>Modern Man in Search of a Soul</u>, speaking of patient who come to him concerned about their guilt feelings:

> Condemnation does not liberate, it oppresses. I am the oppressor of the person I condemn, not his friend and fellow sufferer. . . . Modern man has heard enough about guilt and sin. He is sorely beset by his own bad conscience and wants rather to learn how he is to reconcile himself with his own nature, how he is to love the enemy in his own heart and call the wolf his brother.[9]

As a minister, it falls my responsibility from time to time to talk with people concerning their problems, mistakes, and guilt feelings. I try never to embark upon such conversations with an attitude of condemnation and passing judgment; I seek not to appear before them with the holy-art-I attitude. Every councilor must to create for the patient a permissive atmosphere.[10] He must learn to ~~project~~ imagine himself in the patients situation, never condemning or being shocked, trying to understand and helping the person to make a new start. The truely religious man who tries to help others will say, in effect, "I cannot condemn you, for I have erred too many times myself, but I can tell you of Jesus who forgave me, and I can show you the upward path which I and trying to follow."

The Pharisee did not do this. He saw his brother stumble on the rugged paths of life, and rejoiced in his falling. He watched his brother being crushed by the battering-rams of his passions, and gained his ego-satisfaction there from.

{The Pharisee regarded God as a corporation in which he had [*earned?*] a considerable block of stock, so that at any moment he might be invited to become a director. His prayer told God that he was waiting for well deseved honors.

The Publican had a soul open to God, while the pharisee was locked in himself}[11]

{<u>Here</u>} Once a man has confronted God, he can never turn on one who has stumbled and fallen, and feel superior. ~~Perhaps~~ He comes to see that he might be thinking things and doing things that are just as bad. Never forget that if sin were punished by society on the basis of God's assessement of sin, we would all be in jail. How we turn up our noses at those who commit sins like stealing or drunkenness or other crimes of the criminal courts. But often we do things far worse. We may never rob a bank, but how often do we rob our fellows of their good names through mali-

---

9. C. G. Jung, *Modern Man in Search of a Soul*, pp. 234–235, 237.

10. Psychologist Carl R. Rogers stressed that effective client-centered therapy was enhanced "if the counselor creates a warm and permissive atmosphere in which the individual is free to bring out any attitudes and feelings which he may have, no matter how unconventional, absurd, or contradictory these attitudes may be" (Rogers, "Significant Aspects of Client-Centered Therapy," *American Psychologist* 1 [October 1946]: 416).

11. King wrote the main body of this document in pencil. This concluding section was written in pen.

cious gossip. We may never become drunkards, but how often have we staggered before our dearest friends intoxicated with a bad temper. We may never murder a person with some physical weapon, but how often have husbands killed the spirits of wives and wives killed the spirits of husbands with the deadening bullet of mental cruelty. On the basis of God's standard we all deserve to be punished.

All of this the Pharisee failed to see. It is no wonder that Jesus condemned his attitude.

Let us look at a third reason why Jesus condemned the attitude of the Pharisee—and I think here we find the crux of the whole story, the most important thing we are to learn. Jesus condemned the Pharisee because he was a victim of inordinate spiritual pride. From this tragic attitude stemms all of the other faults of the Pharisee. Pride, as it is used here, is not "snobbishness" or respect for achievement. Pride has a much more comprehensive meaning. It is more akin to the idea of self-sufficiency, or as Webster's dictionary puts it, "inordinate self-esteem." Spiritual pride is the worst of sins, because it imagines that sin can be conquered by the efforts of man. The Pharisee felt that he had saved himself by the doing of a few good deeds. ~~Every that~~ Everything that he says is centered in himself. His whole philosophy of life is wrapped up in the one word "I." He uses the word "God," but it is only a perfunctory prelude to a paean of self-praise. He first congratulates himself on his virtues of omission.[12] Then he informs [~~heaven~~] heaven of his virtues of commission. Herein was his mistake. His virtue was negative. His goodness was mummery.[13] His virtue was so cankered with pride that it was almost rotten.[14]

But the story takes of another Character. He stood afar off as one unworthy to be the neighbor of a righteous man.[15] He looked upon himself with agonizing shame. He was aware that the sin of his nature had ~~brought about~~ separated him, not only from himself and his neighbors, but also from God.[16] In the midst of this deep awarness and this dreadful shame he cries out to ~~God~~ heaven: "God be merciful unto me a sinner."

The minute he says this Jesus came to the terse conclusion of the matter: "I say unto you, This man went down[17]

AD. CSKC: Sermon file, folder 59, "Pride Versus Humility (Parable of Publican and Pharisee)."

---

12. Buttrick, *The Parables of Jesus,* p. 88: "He used the word 'God,' but it was only a glance in the general direction of heaven to prelude a paean of self-praise. He first congratulated himself on his virtues of omission."

13. Buttrick, *The Parables of Jesus,* p. 89: "His abstentions from wrong having been listed, the Pharisee next informed heaven of his virtues of commission. . . . His virtue was negative! His goodness was mummery!"

14. Buttrick, *The Parables of Jesus,* p. 88: "The Pharisee's virtue was so cankered by pride that it was almost rotten."

15. Buttrick, *The Parables of Jesus,* p. 89: "He 'stood afar off' as one unworthy to be the neighbor of a righteous man."

16. Buttrick, *The Parables of Jesus,* p. 89: "The Publican by his own confession was infamously separated from all others by his sin."

17. Buttrick, *The Parables of Jesus,* pp. 89–90: "Then the terse conclusion of the matter: . . . 'I say unto you, This man went down to his house justified rather than the other.'"

"The Impassable Gulf
(The Parable of Dives and Lazarus),"
Sermon at Dexter Avenue Baptist Church

2 October 1955
[*Montgomery, Ala.*]

King uses Jesus' parable to convince his listeners that the disparity between fortune and misfortune is unjust and that they should work to bridge that gap. He charges that "Dives is the white man who refuses to cross the gulf of segregation and lift his Negro brother to the position of first class citizenship, because he thinks segregation is a part of the fixed structure of the universe." In this sermon, King echoes George Buttrick's lecture on the parable.[1]

Luke 16:19–31

This dramatic parable, told in first century Palestine, has long been stenciled on the mental sheets of succeeding generations. It was this parable which served as the spark setting off the humanitarian flame in the life of Albert Schweitzer. He concluded that Africa, so long exploited and crushed by Western civilization, was a beggar lying at Europe's doorstep, so he willingly relinquished the charming melodies of Bach on the organ and the prestige that comes from an attractive professorship in one of Europe's greatest universities, to establish a hospital in Africa. This parable has that kind of power.

We must not take this story as a theology of the after life. It is not a Baedeker's guide to the next world.[2] Its symbols are symbols and not literal fact. Jesus accepted the Hereafter as a reality, but never sought to describe it.[3] There is always the danger that we will transform mythology into theology. We must remember that there is always a penumbra of mystery which hovers around every meaningful assertion about God and the after life. He who seeks to describe the furniture of heaven and the temperature of hell is taking the mystery out of religion and incarcerating it in the walls of an illogical logic.[4] Jesus had no such intentions. He was merely telling a parable to get over a basic truth about this life. He who takes this parable as a description of the history and geography of the after life "is transplanting it violently from its native soil to a barren literalism where it cannot live.

---

1. Buttrick, *The Parables of Jesus,* pp. 137–146. Someone other than King wrote "Preached at Dexter Oct. 2 1955" above the sermon's title.

2. German publisher Karl Baedeker began producing a series of travel handbooks in the mid-nineteenth century.

3. Buttrick, *The Parables of Jesus,* p. 139: "Let it be remembered that the story is a parable. Its symbols are symbols, not literal facts. Jesus took for granted a Hereafter, but did not describe it."

4. Reinhold Niebuhr, *The Nature and Destiny of Man: A Christian Interpretation* (New York: Charles Scribner's Sons, 1943), 2:294: "It is unwise for Christians to claim any knowledge of either the furniture of heaven or the temperature of hell; or to be too certain about any details of the Kingdom of God in which history is consummated."

First of all, let us get the picture vividly in our minds. There are two main characters in this drama: Dives, the Rich man and Lazarus, the beggar at his gates. Dives dresses in the finest clothes. He is richly housed in a palatial home, and richly fed with the best of foods. Then Lazarus enters in ghastly contrast. He lies outside the rich man's gate, and is not only very poor, but is very ill, covered with sores, and is so weak that he cannot even push the unclean dogs away when they come and lick his sores. His circumstances are so tragic that he counts it good fortune to be fed with crumbs from the rich man's table.[5]

The second scene of the drama is cast in the next world. Lazarus is now in Abraham's bosom, and Dives is in torment. Dives requests that Lazarus may come and ease his torment, by bringing one drop of water. But Father Abraham answers, "No, you had your good things in the earth life which Lazarus had only evil things, and now the situation is reversed. Besides all this," says Abraham, "there is now a gulf between us and you which is fixed."[6]

So we can see that is is Dives who ends up being condemned in this parable. We are naturally forced to raise the question, Why?

There is no hint that Dives was condemned because he gained his wealth by dishonest means.[7] From all indications he gained his wealth from the discipline of an industrious life. He probably had the genius for wise investment. His wealth did not come through some corrupt racket or vicious exploitation.

Moreover, Dives was not a bad man by the world's accepted standards.[8] He was probably well respected in his community. He possessed at least a modicum of humaness. He probably dispensed the customary charities. The fact that the beggar was brought to his gate daily implies that he had been fed.[9]

There is no implication in that parable that being rich was Dives' crime. We must remember that Dives in hell was talking to Abraham in heaven, and Abraham was considered the richest man of his day. Dives' riches would have hardly been more than the interest which Abraham received from his boundless extension of his wealth. So this is not a parable condemning wealth. Jesus never concems wealth per se. It is the inordinate worship of wealth that he condemns. Jesus always warned men that wealth is highly dangerous. But if the possessor of wealth does not allow it to suggest a false security and regards himself as a steward, then wealth can be a rich opportunity.[10]

---

5. Buttrick, *The Parables of Jesus*, pp. 137–138: "There are two main characters: the unnamed Rich Man and Lazarus, the beggar at his gates. We see the Rich Man richly clothed—his outer garment was dyed in the costly purple of the murex; his inner garment was woven from Egyptian flax. We see him richly housed—'gates' betokens the portico of a palatial home. We see him richly fed and living merrily. Then Lazarus enters in ghastly contrast. He is daily carried to the Rich Man's porch. His rags do not cover his ulcerated body. Unclean dogs which infest the street come to lick his sores, and he has no strength to drive them off. He counts it good fortune to be fed with scraps from the Rich Man's table."

6. Luke 16:25–26.

7. Buttrick, *The Parables of Jesus*, p. 138: "Dives was not unscrupulous; the story gives no hint that he came by his wealth dishonestly."

8. Buttrick, *The Parables of Jesus*, p. 138: "He was not cruel in the word's accepted meaning."

9. Buttrick, *The Parables of Jesus*, p. 138: "The fact that a beggar was brought there daily implies that he had been fed. . . . Dives dispensed the customary charities."

10. In a handwritten version of this sermon that King filed in the same folder, he crossed out the fol-

There is nothing inherently vicious about wealth, and there is nothing inherently vir-

tuous about poverty. If there is a hell there will be plenty poor folks in it.

What, then, were the sins that lead to Dives' damnation.

First, Dives over absorption in self prevented him from seeing others. He was victimized with the tragic disease of egocentrism. He passed Lazarus every day, but he never really <u>saw</u> him.[11] He was too much absorbed in himself to be able to see. He was a man of large affairs, and he had to think of his stacks and banks, his ouse and estate. Soon Dives was so close to himself that he couldn't see Lazarus, although the beggar was as near him as the doorstep. Dives became locked up in Dives. He became so involved in his possessions that he became over-absorbed in the possessor. Dives' crime was not his wealth but inordinate self-love.[12]

Secondly, Dives was condemned because his selfishness caused him to lose the capacity to sympathize. There is nothing more tragic than to find a person who can look at the anguishing and diplorable circumstances of fellow human beings and not be moved. Dives' wealth had made him cold and calculating; it had blotted out the warmth of compassion. Dives could look at men crushed by the battering rams of circumstance and not be moved. Dives could watch hungry fellowmen smothering in the air-tight cage of poverty and not be moved. Dives could watch his brothers being blown assunder by the chilly winds of adversity and not be moved. He saw men hungry and fed them not; he saw men sick and visited them not; he saw men naked and clothed them not. And so he was not fit for the Kingdom of God. He was only fit for a place of torment.[13]

Finally, Dives' greatest sin was that he accepted the inequalities of circumstance as being the proper conditions of life. There is a gulf that originates in the accident of circumstance. Circumstances make it possible for some people to get an education, while other people are denied the opportunity. Circumstances make some people rich, social prestige, while others are left gnawing on the crumbs of obscurity. There are certain gulfs in life which originate in the accident of circumstance. So in the parable Lazarus was poor, not because he wanted to be, but because tragic circumstances had made him so. On the other hand, Dives was rich because fortunate circumstances had made him so. There is a circumstantial gulf between Lazarus and Dives. Now Dives' sin was not that he made this gulf between him and Lazarus; this gulf had come into being through the accidents of circumstance. The sin of Dives was that he felt that the gulf which existed between him and Lazarus was a proper condition of life. Dives felt that this was the way things were to be. He took the "isness" of circumstantial accidents and transformed them

---

lowing words in this sentence: "But if the possessor of wealth does not allow it to ~~bind him to himself~~ suggest a false security . . ." (King, "The Impassable Gulf [The Parable of Dives and Lazarus]," 2 October 1955).

11. Buttrick, *The Parables of Jesus*, p. 138: "He passed Lazarus several times a day, but he never really *saw* him."

12. Buttrick, *The Parables of Jesus*, p. 138: "Being rich was not his crime; being rich, the story hints, was his opportunity. His crime was worldly self-love."

13. Cf. Matthew 25:41–46.

into the "oughtness" of a universal structure.[14] He adjusted himself to the patent inqualities of circumstance.

Dives is the white man who refuses to cross the gulf of segregation and lift his Negro brother to the position of first class citizenship, because he thinks segregation is a part of the fixed structure of the universe. Dives is the India Brahman who refuses to bridge the gulf between himself and his brother, because he feels that the gulf which is set forth by the caste system is a final principle of the universe. Dives is the American capitalist who never seeks to bridge the economic gulf between himself and the laborer, because he feels that it is the natural for some to live in inordinate luxury while others live in abject poverty.

Dives sin was not that he was cruel to Lazarus, but that he refused to bridge the gap of misfortune that existed between them. Dives sin was not his wealth; his wealth was his opportunity. His sin was his refusal to use his wealth to bridge the gulf between the extremes of superfluous, inordinate wealth and abject, deadning poverty.

So when Dives cries to Abraham to send him one drop of water at Lazarus' hands, Abraham replies: "There is a fixed gulf between you now." There was a time that Dives could have bridged the gulf. He could have used the engineering power of love to build a bridge of compassion between him and Lazarus. But he refused. Now the gulf is fixed. The gulf is now an impassable gulf. Time has run out. The tragic words, too late, must now be, marked across the history of Dives' life.

The Bible talks about another gulf. This time it is a gulf between God and man. This gulf originated in the circumstance of sin. In this situation God is the Dives; He is the rich man, rich in grace, rich in love, rich in power. Man is the Lazarus, poor in power, covered with the sores of sin, lying at the gates of God's throne, begging for the crumbs of God's grace. Man, like Lazarus, was too weak to bridge the gap. He was not totally helpless. He had enough power left to at least struggle up to the gate and desin the bread of grace. But he could not bridge the gulf; only God could do this. The beauty of the Christian gospel is that God, the divine omnipotent Dives is not like the Dives of the parable. He is always seeking to bridge the gulf. He is not so concerned with himself that He overlooks others. The Christian God is not the God of Aristotle that merely contemplates upon himself; he is not only a self-knowing God, but he is an ever loving God. He does not think that the gulf that exists between him and man is a proper condition of life. He knows that the gulf should not exist. So at the climax of the Christian gospel we find God in Christ seeking to bridge the gulf. This is the meaning of that dramatic scene that took place on Calvery. The cross is the boundless bridge of God's love connecting time and eternity, man and God.

Whenever we find God, He is seeking to bridge the gulf. Said Paul, "God was in Christ reconciling the world unto himself."[15] Said the writer of the fourth gospel, "For God so loved the world that He gave His only begotten Son . . . "[16] said John

---

14. Cf. Niebuhr, *Beyond Tragedy,* pp. 137–138.
15. 2 Corinthians 5:19.
16. John 3:16.

the Revelator, "Behold I stand at the door and knock . . . "[17] God is life's supreme Dives that seeks to bridge that gap between himself and every Lazarus.

The story doesn't end here. It ends only as it is reproduced in the life of man. "As I loved you, so love the bretheren."[18] In other words, God is saying, "As I have bridged the gulf between man and God, so bridge you the gulf between man and man. Each of us is a potential Dives, maybe not rich in material goods, but rich in education, rich in social prestige, rich in influence, rich in charm. At our gate stands some poor Lazarus who has been deprived of all of these. There is a gulf. But the gulf can be bridged by a little love and compassion. Bridge the gulf before it becomes too late. It is now passable. But it can become impassable.

THD. CSKC: Sermon file, folder 56, "The Impassable Gulf."

---

17. Revelation 3:20.
18. Cf. John 13:34.

"The One-Sided Approach
of the Good Samaritan"

[20 November 1955]
[Montgomery, Ala.]

In this handwritten sermon outline, King urges his listeners to combine compassion for victims of injustice with efforts to bring about social change.[1] He criticizes the Good Samaritan as one who "sought to [soothe] the effects of evil, without going back to uproot the causes."

I   Introduction—
   (A) Over the centuries the parable of the Good Samaritan has been cited as ~~the~~ a definition of Christian social responsibility.[2] There is probably no description of what it means to be a good neighbor more widely known
   B.   Point out the virtue of the Good Samaritan in contrast to the Levite & Priest[3]
   C   Jesus told the story for one purpose only, and we are not to take it as a total description of our social [*responsibility?*]
   D   The shortcomings of the parable in describing true neighborliness.

---

1. A 20 November 1955 program from Dexter's Sunday morning service indicates that King preached "The One-Sided Approach of the Good Samaritan."
2. Luke 10:25–37 recounts the parable.
3. Levites were assigned to assist the priests and to perform sanctuary duties in the Temple.

    E.   Although the parable says nothing concerning [*where?*] [*strikeout illegible*] The Levite and the Priest might have been going; ~~let us imagine~~ it is quite probable the Levite was on his way to Jerico to make a survey of crime in the vicinity, and perhaps the priest was en route to Jerusalem to serve on the National Committe for the Improvement of Public Highways.[4] So by a slight stretch of the imagination, or at least for argument sake, quite an excellent case can be made for the priest and Levite. Before we completely condemn the Levite and the Priest we should consider this.

II   But not only is it possible to ~~see the possible~~ elevate the roles of the Priest and Levite; it is also easy to see the shortcomings in the conduct of the Samaritan.

    (a) There is no suggestion that the Samaritan ~~organized~~ sough to investigate the lack of police protection on the Jerico Road. Nor did he appeal to any public officials to set out after the robbers and clean up the Jerico road. Here was the weakness of the good Samaritan. He was concerned [*merely?*] with temporary reliff, not with thorough reconstruction. He sought to sooth the effects of evil, without going back to uproot the causes.

III   Now, without a doubt Christian social responsibility includes the sort of thing the good Samiritan did. So we give to the United Appeals, the Red Cross, to all types of unfortunate conditions.[5] In the midst of such staggering and appalling conditions we cannot afford to "pass by on the other side."[6] Like the good Samitan we must always stand ready to decend to the depth of human need. The person who fails to look with compassion upon the thousands of individuals left wounded by life's many roadsides is not only unethical, but ungodly. Every Christian must ply the good Samaritan

IV   But there is another aspect of Christian social responsibility which is just as compelling. It seeks to tear down unjust conditions and build anew instead of patching things up. It seeks to clear the Jerico road of its robbers as well as caring for the victims of robbery.

AD. CSKC: Sermon file, folder 44, "The One-Sided Approach to the Good Samaritan."

---

4. In an incomplete draft filed in the same folder as this sermon, King wrote "Give Liston Pope's analysis" at this point in the outline (King, "The One-Sided Approach of the Good Samaritan," Sermon outline, 20 November 1955). Pope wrote that Jesus "was an emissary to all people, associating with despised groups (including Samaritans) without discrimination . . . and illustrating neighborliness with a story of a merciful act by a Samaritan" (Pope, *The Kingdom Beyond Caste* [New York: Friendship Press, 1957], p. 149). Liston Pope was a professor of social ethics at Yale University, and served as dean of its Divinity School from 1949 until 1962.

5. The United Appeal was a fund-raising campaign for local charities.

6. Cf. Luke 10:31–32.

[*4 December 1955*]
[*Montgomery, Ala.*]

Preaching to his Dexter congregation on the eve of the Montgomery bus boycott, an
event triggered by the 1 December arrest of Rosa Parks, King draws upon a 1947
sermon by Robert McCracken.[1] King seeks to elucidate "the awful silence of heaven"
in the face of evil such as "imperialistic nations trampling over other nations with
the iron feet of oppression." He used this metaphor to tremendous effect the following
evening at the first mass meeting of the Montgomery Improvement Association
(MIA).[2]

{Isaiah 45:15}[3]

I   Introduction—Long centuries ago, when proud Babylon ruled the world, the
Great Isaiah cried, "Verily thou art a God that hidest thyself, O God of Israel, the
Savior." How often through the centuries has this cry risen to human lips. of late
We ourselves have not been unfamiliar with it.[4] We have seen imperialistic
nations trampling over other nations with the iron feet of oppression. We have
seen evil in the form of calamitous wars, which left battlefields painted with
blood, filled nations with ophrans and widows, ~~and~~ stacked up national debts
higher than mountains of gold, and sent men home psychologically wrecked
and physically handicapped. And God did not intervene. The awful silence of
heaven remained unbroken. We appealed to God in desperate tones to intervene and defend his right.[5] But still evil continued to rise to astronomical proportions. Our generation feels afresh what Keats called "the giant agony of the
world"[6] Small wonder that some like H. G. Wells complained bitterly "He is an
ever-absent help in time of trouble."[7] And others cried out with the earnest
believer Carlyle: "God sits in heaven and does nothing."[8]

---

1. According to a Dexter program from 4 December 1955, King delivered a version of this sermon. King
kept a copy of McCracken's 27 April 1947 sermon "Why Does God Hide Himself?" in his homiletic file.

2. The overflow crowd reacted with thundering applause when King exclaimed, "And you know, my
friends, there comes a time when people get tired of being trampled over by the iron feet of oppression"
(King, MIA Mass Meeting at Holt Street Baptist Church, 5 December 1955, in *Papers* 3:72).

3. "Verily, thou art a God that hidest thyself, O God of Israel, the Savior."

4. McCracken, "Why Does God Hide Himself?": "How often through the centuries that cry has risen
to human lips! Of late we ourselves have not been unfamiliar with it."

5. McCracken, "Why Does God Hide Himself?": "And God did not intervene. The awful silence of
heaven remained unbroken. We pleaded with Him to manifest Himself and defend the right."

6. John Keats, "The Fall of Hyperion: A Dream" (1819).

7. McCracken, "Why Does God Hide Himself?": "What wonder that some like H. G. Wells complained
bitterly, 'He is an ever-absent help in time of trouble.' "

8. In the sermon "Having a Faith That Really Works," Harry Emerson Fosdick wrote: "In a depressed
mood Carlyle said once, 'God sits in heaven and does nothing' " (Fosdick, *What Is Vital in Religion* [New
York: Harper & Brothers, 1955], p. 12). King and Fosdick paraphrase Thomas Carlyle's *Sartor Resartus*
(1836), p. 163.

II   In a real sinse every true believer has had to accept the fact that he is worshiping a God that is partially hidden.

1. Consider how God hides himself in nature. In saying this I am not forgetting the fact that for many nature is the very handiwork of God.[9] (The Romantic poets)[10] But this is only one side of the picture. Nature is often cruel. Think of the pain and suffering inflicted upon thousands of people by some dread disease which they are not responsible for. Think of the disatrous effects of floods and tonadoes. Where is God when all of this is happening. "Verily he is a God that hideth himself."

2. Consider how God hides himself in history. Cromwell said to the man whom he appointed to tutor his son, "I would have him taught a little history."[11] We know why he said what he did. He believed that the study of history inclined one to a sane, balanced and reverent judgement But not all lessons that history teaches are lessons that inspire and quicken faith. So often When we look through the long corridors of history, what do we find?[12]—might winning out over right, Christ on a Cross and Caesar in a palace; truth on the scaffold and wrong on the throne, the just suffering while the unjust prosper.[13]

AD. CSKC: Sermon file, folder 107, Why Does God Hide Himself.

---

9. McCracken, "Why Does God Hide Himself?": "Consider how He hides Himself in nature. In saying that I do not forget that for many nature is the very handwriting of God."

10. The Romantic poets of the late eighteenth and early nineteenth centuries, such as William Wordsworth and Percy Bysshe Shelley, looked to nature for inspiration and fulfillment.

11. Oliver Cromwell (1599–1658) was a Puritan politician and military leader during the English Civil War, which led to the defeat of King Charles I. Cromwell ruled England as Lord Protector from 1653 until 1658. In 1649 Cromwell wrote to his son's mentor, Richard Mayor, "I would have him mind and understand business, read a little history, study the mathematics and cosmography" (*The Letters and Speeches of Oliver Cromwell with Elucidations by Thomas Carlyle*, vol. 1 [London: Methuen, 1904], p. 451).

12. McCracken, "Why Does God Hide Himself?": "Consider, too, how God hides Himself in history. Cromwell said to the man whom he appointed to tutor his son, 'I would have him taught a little history.' We know why he said what he did. He believed that the study of history inclined one to a sane, balanced and reverent judgment. But not all the lessons that history teaches are lessons that inspire and quicken faith. So often when we delve into the story of the past, what do we find?"

13. King underlined a paraphrase of James Russell Lowell's 1844 poem "The Present Crisis" in his copy of McCracken's "Why Does God Hide Himself?": "Might triumphing over right, the race to the swift and the battle to the strong, truth on the scaffold and wrong on the throne, Christ on a Cross and Caesar in a palace" (p. 39).

[*1 January 1956*]
[*Montgomery, Ala.*]

With the boycott approaching its second month, King draws on two sermons by
Frederick M. Meek to offer a message of hope to the people of Dexter.[1] He reveals his
own struggle in the midst of despair: "There are times that I get despondent, and
wonder if it is worth it. But then something says to me deep down within God is
able." King acknowledges that God does not offer a problem-free life, but he concludes
with words of encouragement: "If you have a proper faith in God he will give you
something within which will help you to stand up amid your problems."

"Now unto Him that is able to keep you from falling—Jude 1:24[2]

This is the beginning of a New year. It is a time when the startling Facts of yesterday and the hightening expectations of tomorrow join hands in the pressing
urgency of today. There is no better way to begin this year than with the conviction
that there is a God of Power Who is able to do exceeding abundantly thing in our
lives and in the life of the universe.[3] To believe in and to live by the fact that "God is
able" ~~gives~~ is to transform life's impending sunsets into glittering sunrises. The conviction that "Our God is able" is a conviction stressed and exulted in, over and over
again in [*both?*] the New and Old Testaments.[4] This conviction stands at the cente
of our Christian faith. Theologically, it is expressed in the doctrine of the omnipotence of God. The God that we worship is not a weak God, He is not an incompetent God and consequently he is able to beat back gigantic mountains of opposition
and to bring low prodigious hill tops of evil.[5] The ringing cry of the Christian faith
is that our God is able.

There are times when each of us is forced to question the ableness of our God.
When we notice the stark and colossal realities of evil—that something that Keats

---

1. A Dexter program for 1 January 1956 indicates that King delivered this sermon. He filed copies of
Meek's sermons in the same file folder as this document (Meek, "Our God Is Able, a sermon preached
in Old South Church in Boston," 4 January 1953; Meek, "Perhaps Your God Is Not Big Enough, a sermon preached in Old South Church in Boston," 11 October 1953). For a more developed version of this
sermon, see King, Draft of Chapter XIII, "Our God Is Able," *Strength to Love*, July 1962–March 1963, pp.
527–534 in this volume.

2. "Now unto him that is able to keep you from falling, and to present you faultless before the presence of his glory with exceeding joy." This is also the biblical text for Meek's sermon "Our God Is Able."

3. Cf. Ephesians 3:20.

4. Meek, "Our God Is Able": "Meanwhile 'Our God is able' is a conviction stressed and exulted in,
over and over and over in the New Testament."

5. Meek, "Our God Is Able": "Believe me, it is not a weak God, it is not an incompetent God with
Whom we have to deal." In his copy of Meek's sermon, King underlined this sentence and next to it
wrote the Roman numeral I.

To Dr. Martin Luther King, theological scholar, devoted minister of the Gospel, wise Christian statesman, in whose courageous faith, hope and love the light of Christ shines brightly;

in admiration, pride and affection,

L. Harold DeWolf.

May 3, 1957.

L. Harold DeWolf, King's advisor at Boston University, lauds King in this inscription written on the front cover page of his 1955 book *Trends and Frontiers of Religious Thought,* as a "theological scholar, devoted minister of the Gospel, wise Christian statesman, in whose courageous faith, hope and love the light of Christ shines brightly . . ." (3 May 1957).

called "the giant agony of the world," when we notice the long [*ruthlessness?*] of earthquakes and tonadoes, when we behold ills like insanity that fall on individuals even at birth, when we are forced to experience the grim tragedies of war and man's inhumanity to man, we find ourselves asking, why does all of this exist if God is able to prevent it.[6] This morning we are not able to go into the "whyness" of evil. Such a venture would require another sermon altogether. [*Yet?*] we can say that in spite of these glaring dimensions of evil, and the occasional doubts that come to all of us there is the perenial conviction that "our God is able."

I   Let us notice first that our God is able to sustain the vast scope of the cosmic order

(1) Living in an age when science has carved highways through the stratosphere, and almost totally annihilated distance, we are tempted to say only man is able.

(2) We think about the fact that there are jet planes which fly at a rate of 1000 to 1500 miles per hour. That's faster than the speed of sound. You can see a jet coming, but it has passed you before you ~~see~~ hear it.

(3) Many of the commercial airlines are now ordering jets. It will soon be possible to leave London at 1:00 P.M. and arrive in New York City the preceding 10:00 A.M. That's really moving. But when we look at this in terms (of) cosmic speed, this is barely moving

(4) Our earth is moving around the sun so fast that ~~if~~ the fastest jet racing it would be left behind 66 thousand miles in the first hour of the race

(5) Since I started talking to you about five minutes ago you and our earth have hurtled through space more than 5,500 miles

(6) We look out at the sun which astronomer tell us is the center of the universe. Our earth revolves around this sun once each year . . . traveling ~~at a~~ 584,000,000 miles in that year at a rate of 66,700 miles per hour or 1,600,000 miles per [*strikeout illegible*] day.

(7) This time tomorrow you will be 1,600,000 miles from where you are at this hundreth of a second.

(8) There is the sun. It often looks near. But it is 93,000,000 miles from the earth. In six month we will be on the other side of that sun, 93,000,000 miles beyond it. And in a year from now we will have swung completely around it and back to where we are now.[7]

(9) We we notice the vastness of the cosmic [*order?*] . . . we must cry out, "Our God is able."

II   Let us notice again that God is able to subdue all the powers of evil.

(1) One of the things that we [*soon?*] notice about our universe is that it presents itself in a strange dualism good and evil, right and wrong, light and darkness, happiness and pain, life and death. There is a tension or a strug-

---

6. King cites a line from John Keats, "The Fall of Hyperion: A Dream" (1819).

7. This illustration mirrors one that Meek related in "Perhaps Your God Is Not Big Enough."

gle at the core of the universe. All the great religion have discovered this conflict: Hinduism (illusion & reality); Zoroastrianism (light and darkness; Platonism (spirit and matter) traditional Judaism & Christianity (God & Satan)[8]

(2) Yet Xn insist that in the long struggle between good and evil, good ultimately emerges as the victor. Evil must ultimately give way to the powerful, insurgent forces of Good.

(3) This is ultimately the hope that keeps us going. Much of my ministy has been given to fighting against social evil. There are times that I get despondent, and wonder if it is worth it. But then something says to me deep down within God is able. you need not worry. So this morning I say to you we must continue to struggle against evil, but dont wory, God is able. Dont worry about segregation. It will die because God is againt it.

(4) Whenever God is against a thing it cannot survive. Give Victor Hugo's description of Waterloo. He asks "Was it possible that Napolean should win this battle? I answer no. Because of Wellington? No. But because of God. Waterloo is not a battle; it is a change in the front of the universe."[9] Waterloo is the symbol of the eternal doom of every Napolean

III

III God is able, finally, to give us inner resources to confront the trials and difficulties of life.

(1) This is about all that religion can garantee. I dont want to fool you this morning. I cannot say to [*you?*] that if you have faith in God, you will have no problem, or misfortune but I can say if you have a proper faith in God he will give you something within which will help you to stand up amid your problems.

(2) Qute passage "all things work together."[10]

(3) Give illustration of Seminary Professor.

AD. CSKC: Sermon file, folder 11, "Our God Is Able."

---

8. Fosdick, "How Believe in a Good God in a World Like This?" in *Living Under Tension* (New York: Harper & Brothers, 1941), p. 216: "All the great religions have so pictured life in terms of conflict. Hinduism called it a conflict between reality and illusion; Zoroastrianism a conflict between light and darkness; Platonism a conflict between spirit and matter; traditional Judaism and Christianity a conflict between God and Satan." A central element of Zoroastrianism, a religion founded in Persia as early as 1000 BCE, is the constant struggle between the evil spirit of darkness and the god of light and goodness.

9. Meek, "Perhaps Your God Is Not Big Enough": "Victor Hugo is describing the Battle of Waterloo. And Hugo concludes his description with these words: 'Was it possible that Napoleon should win this battle? I answer 'No.' Because of Wellington? 'No.' Because of Blucher? 'No.'—because of God. Waterloo is not a battle; it is a change in the front of the universe." See also Victor Hugo, *Les Misérables* (New York: A. L. Burt, 1862), pp. 337–338.

10. Romans 8:28: "And we know that all things work together for good to them that love God, to them who are the called according to his purpose."

"How Believe in a Good God in the Midst of Glaring Evil"

[*15 January 1956*]
[*Montgomery, Ala.*]

King delivered a version of this sermon to his Dexter congregation a few days after the MIA voted to boycott city buses indefinitely.[1] He draws upon a Crozer paper, "Religion's Answer to the Problem of Evil," to construct this handwritten outline.[2] King readily acknowledges the existence of evil as a force in the world and its deleterious effect on Christian faith but concludes by offering various rationales for belief in God despite the reality of evil.

I   Introduction—We come face to face this morning with an old question: How can we believe in a good God in the midst of glaring evil. Many centuries ago Job confronted this problem. In the glorious days of Greek culture Sophocles wondered how the gods could look complacently down on so much suffering and pain.[3] There is hardly a person here this morning who has not asked this question in some form. There are times when we all experience the heightening joy and soothing warmth of life's summers. At such moments we dont think about the problem of evil. But at other times we experience the bleak and desolate chill of life's winter. At such a time we are prone to cry with the earnest believer Carlyle, "God sits in his heaven and does nothing."[4]
We seek to live by the faith that our God is all-good and all-powerful. But on every hand the facts of life seem to contradict this faith.

(1) Nature is often cruel with its floods and tornadoes, with the long ruthlessness of the evolutionary process, with dread diseases like cancer and ills like insanity. As John Stuart Mill said, "Nearly all the things which men are hanged and imprisoned for doing to one another are nature's every day performances. Nature kills, burns, starves, freezes, poisons.[5]

(2) Nature is apparently non-moral. It makes no distinction between the evil

---

1. On 12 January, the MIA elected to continue the bus boycott after the city rejected their most recent proposal "to assure all passengers equal treatment" (To the Commissioners of the City of Montgomery, 9 January 1956, in *Papers* 3:97–98). Dexter's program for 15 January 1956 indicates King preached this sermon.

2. King, "Religion's Answer to the Problem of Evil," 27 April 1951, in *Papers* 1:416–433.

3. Sophocles (ca. 496–406 BCE) was one of classical Athens's three great tragic playwrights, along with Aeschylus and Euripides.

4. King cites lines from Thomas Carlyle's *Sartor Resartus* (1836), p. 163.

5. Mill, *Three Essays on Religion* (1874), pp. 28–29: "In sober truth, nearly all the things which men are hanged or imprisoned for doing to one another, are nature's every day performances . . . Nature impales men, breaks them as if on the wheel, casts them to be devoured by wild beasts, burns them to death, crushes them with stones like the first Christian martyr, starves them with hunger, freezes them with cold, poisons them by the quick or slow venom of her exhalations." King used this paraphrase of Mill's quote in a 27 April 1951 paper for Davis (see note 1 to "Religion's Answer to the Problem of Evil," in *Papers* 1:416).

and the good. It is true that it sends its rain on the just and the unjust, but the obverse is also true, it sends its floods and tonadoes on the good and the evil.[6]

(3) The world seems positvily immoral at times. The innocent suffer for the deeds of the evil

In the midst of all of this we are prone to ask where is God. How can we reconcile an all-good and all-powerful God with the glaring facts of evil. This is the question the men have struggled to answered in every generation. The answered to this problem can be broken down to about four.

(1) Dualism is perhaps the simplest answer.

(2) The second answr may be called the legalistic. It rest on the principle of retribution. The universe rest on law and evil is simply the results of wrongdoing. Judaism used this in its view that goodness brings prosperity.[7]

(3) There is the position absolute idealism in its various forms.

   (a) Looked at from the whole it is not evil.[8]

   (b) Christian science view.[9]

(4) The disciplinary view. Pain and sorror are here to develop character.[10]

Now the real question is Why do we believe in a good God in the midst of glaring evil.

(A) The first reason is because disbelief in a good God presents more problems than it solves. It is difficult to explain ~~evil~~ the presence of evil in the world of a good God, but it is more difficult to explain the presence of good in a world of no God.

   1. The [*vast?*] & orderly structure of the cosmic order.

   2. Michael Angelo

   3. Handel

   4. Plato

   5. Shakespeare

   6. A great person or a child where did it come from

   7. Going out look at the stars

(B) The second reason why we believe in a good God is that all the suffering and pain we bear come from four factors, and all four of these factor are necessary for the existence of a good world.

---

6. Cf. Matthew 5:45.

7. King, "Religion's Answer to the Problem of Evil," in *Papers* 1:418: "A second view explains physical evils as a punishment for moral evils. Such a view rests in the principle of retribution. This view goes back to the old Deuteronomic idea that prosperity follows piety and righteous."

8. King, "Religion's Answer to the Problem of Evil," in *Papers* 1:420: "There is a fourth position which explains evil as incomplete good. Absolute idealists like Hegel and his followers have been strong proponents of this view."

9. The Church of Christ, Scientist teaches that sickness, evil, and sin are all merely illusions, with no basis in reality. The Church's founder, Mary Baker Eddy (1821–1910), espoused the benefits of spiritual healing through prayer over the practices of medical science.

10. King, "Religion's Answer to the Problem of Evil," in *Papers* 1:419: "A third view explains nonmoral evils as disciplinary rather than penal. Here the purpose of evil is to reform or to test rather than to punish. . . . Character often develops out of hardship."

1. First, the freedom of will
2. Second, the evolutionary nature of the world
3. Third, the law-abidingness of the universe
4. Fourth, the intermeshed relationships of human life.

AD. CSKC: Sermon file, folder 70, "Christ the Center of our Faith" / "How to Believe in a Good God in the Midst of Glaring Evil."

"Redirecting Our Missionary Zeal"

[22 January 1956]
[Montgomery, Ala.]

In this handwritten outline King criticizes the hypocrisy of international missionary efforts in light of domestic racial injustice: "The paradox of it all is that the white man considers himself the supreme missionary. He sends [millions] of dollars to the foreign field. And in the midst of that he tramples over the Negro."

"Go ye therefore into all the world and preach the gospel . . . [1]

I   Intro—Ever since the dawn of the Christian era, Christians have considered it a serious part of their basic responsibility to carry the gospel of Jesus Christ into all the world and to every creature

II   This is one of the things that distinguishes Christianity from the other great religions of the world. Most of the other great religions have had profound admiration for their founders, but they do not consider it a seriou part of their responsibility to carry the message of their founders into all the world.— Buddism, Hinduism, Judaism, Mohammedanism

III   Christianty has never been content to wrap itself up in ~~any particular society~~ the garments of any particular society.[2]

IV   If there is any one word that characterizes our creed it is go. It started with Jesus and continued with Paul.
Go ye into all the world
I must need you through [*word illegible*]

V   Now, this demand to carry the gospel to every creature has long since been known as missionary work. From the beginning Christians have been considered missionaries

---

1. Cf. Matthew 28:19. Dexter's 22 January 1956 program indicates that King preached this sermon.
2. In a similar sermon filed in the same folder, King followed this point with a reminder: "Use the ill. of something being to good to hold. (A secret or a piece of cake being so good that it must be shared). The Gospel is good news" (King, "The Mission of the Church," 1953–1956). King also considered this illustration in "Propagandizing Christianity," Sermon at Dexter Avenue Baptist Church, 12 September 1954, pp. 184–187 in this volume.

VI Now two impressions got out about the missionary which have come down to us.
  1. The use of the phrase "into all the world" ~~go~~ has ~~to often~~ left many with the impression that missionary work is only foreign.
      a. State the untruth of this.
  2. It has often been looked upon as the occasional work of a few Christians or a particular society.
      a. State the untruth of this

VII All that I am saying leads to this—along with our work on the foreign field we must begin to do missionary work right here. Each of us must do this. And we must begin with the white man.

VIII He is pagan in his conceptions What is more pagan than . . . Milan & Bryant are church members[3]

IX The paradox of it all is that the white man considers himself the supreme missionary. He sends millios of dollars to the foreign field. And in the midst of that he tramples over the Negro
  (a) Tell story of Church in Florida.[4] They went into the temple singing
  (b) No wonder Mathma Ghandi said to someone that the greatest enemy that Christ has in India is Xn.[5]
  (c) Shakespeare's "Who steal my purse steals trash."[6]
  (D) It seems that we can hear the almighty God saying yor hands are full of blood.[7]

X Now how are we to do this
  (1) A good missionary understand the situation of those he seeks to help as goes back to the root of the problem.
  (2) Love him
  (3) Sit down and preach to him

XI Conclusion—Be maladjusted[8]

AD. CSKC: Sermon file, folder 27, "The Mission of the Church."

---

3. On 23 September 1955, J. W. Milam and Roy Bryant were found not guilty of the murder of fourteen-year-old Emmett Till.

4. King may refer to a story that a law school principal told Howard Thurman during his 1935 visit to Ceylon: "One of my students who went to your country sent me a clipping telling about a Christian church in which the regular Sunday worship was interrupted so that many could join a mob against one of your fellows. When he had been caught and done to death, they came back to resume their worship of their Christian God" (Thurman, *Jesus and the Disinherited*, pp. 14–15).

5. King may refer to a story told by E. Stanley Jones in *The Christ of the Indian Road*. When Jones asked Gandhi how Christianity could become more a part of Indian culture, Gandhi suggested that Christians "live more like Jesus Christ," that they refrain from toning down their religion, that they "put [*their*] emphasis on love," and finally, that they "study the non-Christian religions and culture more sympathetically" (Jones, *The Christ of the Indian Road*, pp. 118–120). In "The Mission of the Church" (1953–1956), King noted, "Use the exp of a chicken being clipped by his own wings."

6. Shakespeare, *Othello*, act 3, sc. 3.

7. Cf. Isaiah 1:15.

8. King would elaborate on this notion of being maladjusted to unjust laws and social conditions throughout his life; for an example, see King, The Christian Way of Life in Human Relations, Address Delivered at the General Assembly of the National Council of Churches, 4 December 1957, pp. 322–328 in this volume.

"It's Hard to Be a Christian"

[*5 February 1956*]
[*Montgomery, Ala.*]

Just a few days after his home in Montgomery was bombed, King delivered a sermon to his Dexter congregation that may have been based on this handwritten outline.[1] He refers to the story of the Good Samaritan, noting: "The question of the Samaritan was[:] What will happen to this man if I [don't] stop to help him. Ultimately the thing that determines whether a man is a Christian is how he answers this question." King concludes: "Taking up the cross is the voluntary or deliberate choice of putting ourselves without reservation at the service of Christ and his kingdom; it is putting our whole being in the struggle against evil, whatever the cost."

"If any man will come after me, let him deny himself, and take up his cross, and follow me." Mt. 16:24[2]

(1) One of the most prevalent illusions of modern life is the belief that it is easy to be a Christian. In so many quarter Christianity has been relegated to a bundle of sentimental teachings

(2) The popular preachers of our day are men like [*Norman Vincent*] Peale.

(3) So Xn ends up little more than a glorified "aspin tablet" an opiate of the people[3]

(4) We have substituted a cushion for a cross. We have substituted the soothing lemonade of escape for the bitter cup of realits. We have a high blood prussure of creeds and an anemia of deeds

(5) We are regimenting men not regenerating them. This is seen quite clearly in so many of our churches
The shouting church
The dignified chuch

(6) Theynl do it every Sunday[4]
Quote E. Stanley Jones[5]

---

1. On 30 January 1956 the MIA filed a federal suit challenging the segregation of Montgomery buses. Later that evening, while King addressed a crowd of two thousand at a mass meeting at First Baptist Church, his home was bombed. He rushed home to find his wife, Coretta, and their daughter, Yolanda, unharmed. King then urged the crowd gathered outside his home to remain nonviolent. For more on this, see Joe Azbell, "Blast Rocks Residence of Bus Boycott Leader," 31 January 1956, in *Papers* 3:114–115. Dexter's program from 2 February 1956 indicates King preached "It's Hard to Be a Christian."

2. Matthew 16:24.

3. Karl Marx, "Contribution to the Critique of Hegel's *Philosophy of Right:* Introduction" (1844).

4. King refers to a poem from Harry Emerson Fosdick's sermon "Christianity Not a Form But a Force," in *A Great Time to Be Alive*, p. 89. For this poem's text, see King, "A Religion of Doing," Sermon at Dexter Avenue Baptist Church, 4 July 1954, p. 172 in this volume.

5. King may refer to a quote by E. Stanley Jones that King also used in an earlier sermon: "We are inoculating the world with a mild form of Christianity, so that it is now practically immune against the real thing" (see note 6 to King, "A Religion of Doing," 4 July 1954, p. 172 in this volume).

Jesus never left men with such illusions. He made it crystal clear that his gospel was difficult

I   It demands that we subordinate our clamoring egos to the pressing concerns of God's Kingdom This is the meaning of self-denial. There is nothing vague and ambiguous about the word "deny". It is appallingly sharp and clear. It means what it says. It is saying "no" to

Xn is hard because it demands a dangerous and costly altruism. It demands that the "I" be immersed in the deep waters of "thou"

your "self" in order to say "yes" to God. It is subjecting the whole structure of your ego to the demands of God's ~~ego~~.

(a) Now this is not easy. This is where most of us miss the mark.

(b) Tell the story of the Good Samaritan The question of the Levite & Priest: What will happen to me if I stop to help this man. The question of the Samaritan was; What will happen to this man if I dont stop to help him. Ultimately the thing that determines whether a man is a Christian is how he answers this question.

(c) Here is a boy or girl, confronted with some undesirable habit. To often the first question that is asked is, What will happen to me, my popularity, my social acceptance is I dont do this. How many times have we degraded our characters trampled over principles because we were more concerned about our selfish desires than about the transcendent principles of God.

(D) There are many white people who are for justice and fair play, but they are afraid to speak. (Give example of preachers.)

(E) Christianity is hard because it demands a dangerous and costly altruism; It demands that the "I" be immersed in the deep waters of the "thou"

II   There is a second point in this text which well illustrates the hardness of the Christian life. It is the word "cross."

(a) Jesus is not giving some mechanical scheme to be his disciple. Nor is he giving some ritualistic form such as wearing a cross.

(b) Jesus is not speaking of burdins we are forced to bear A burden is the inevitable load which life lays on every man.

(c) Taking up the cross is the voluntary or deliberate choice of putting ourselves without reservation at the service of Christ and his kingdom; it is putting our whole being in the struggle against evil, whatever the cost.

AD. CSKC: Sermon file, folder 144, "Meaning of Civil Disobedience."

"Faith in Man"

[*26 February 1956*]
[*Montgomery, Ala.*]

*In the following two handwritten outlines, King urges his listeners to remain aware
of the evil potential of human nature while maintaining faith in the individual's
ability to rise above the limitations of heredity, environment, and injustice. In the
first outline, King cites two recent events as reasons for holding a pessimistic view
of "the nature and destiny of man": the lynching in 1955 of Emmett Till and the
recent rioting at the University of Alabama in response to the admission of the
school's first African-American student, Autherine Lucy. He argues however that,
despite human shortcomings, Jesus "saw within this sea of humanity not a dead
sea of impossibilities, but an ocean of [infinite] possibilities and potentialities."
A newspaper report of the sermon quotes King as hopefully predicting that the bus
boycott will end in a victory that will ripple out beyond Montgomery: "It will be a
victory for justice, a victory for fair play and a victory for democracy."* [1]

"Faith in Man" I

I   Intro:—

(a) One of the things that we are [~~noticing~~] witnessing in our age is a growing
pessimism concerning the nature and destiny of man. Man has lost faith in
himself. ~~There are~~ And so many would cry out with the writer who referred
to man as "a cosmic accident"[2] Other would affirm with the cynical writer
that "man is the supreme clown of creation." Still others would affirm
with Jonathan Swift than "man is the most pernicious little race of odious
vermin . . . "[3]

(b) At many points it is quite understandable why it is difficult for us to have
faith in man. Man has often made such a poor showing of himself. Within
a generation we have fought two world wars. We have seen man's tragic
inhumanity to man. We have looked to Missippii and seen supposedly
Christian and civilized men brutally mudering the precious life of a little
child[4] We have looked to Alabama and seen a ruthless mob take the pre-

---

1. The *New York Times* covered King's sermon in an article about the bus boycott and King's 21 February indictment with eighty-eight other leaders of the Montgomery movement on misdemeanor charges (Wayne Philips, "Negro Pastors Press Bus Boycott by Preaching Passive Resistance," *New York Times*, 27 February 1956; Indictment, *State of Alabama v. M. L. King, Jr., et al.*, 21 February 1956, in *Papers* 3:132–133).

2. Cf. C. S. Lewis, *Answers to Questions on Christianity* (Hayes, England: Electric & Musical Industries Fellowship, 1944), p. 10.

3. Jonathan Swift (1667–1745) was an author and Anglo-Irish satirist. King cites the words of King Brobdingnag to Gulliver in Swift's *Gulliver's Travels* (London: Hamish Hamilton, 1947), p. 140: "I cannot but conclude the bulk of your natives to be the most pernicious race of little odious vermin that nature ever suffered to crawl upon the surface of the earth."

4. King refers to the lynching of fourteen-year-old Emmett Till in Money, Mississippi.

cious law of the land and crush it blow of their tragic whims and caprises.[5] We have seen England trampling over India with the iron feet of oppression. We have seen the British and the Dutch and the Belgians and the French crushing Africa with the battering rams of exploitation.

(c) Yet, in the midst of this Christianity insist that there is hope for man. Christianity has always insisted that man's plight is never so low that it cant be better.

(D) This was certainly expressed in the life of Jesus. Throughout his ministry Jesus revealed a deep faith in the possibilities of human nature. He saw within this sea of humanity not a dead sea of impossibilities, but an ocean of infinte possibilities and potentialities.

(E) This is expressed very beautifully in a passage in the ~~fourth~~ first chaptr of John. Jesus is presented talking to Peter. Now you remember Peter was undependable, vascilating so fickle in his ever changing moods. But Jesus says to him in substance altough you are Simon now, you will be Peter. It did not look like it. And it was a long time in coming. But it did come. He was saying to Peter "actually you are like sand, but potentially you are a rock.[6]

AD. CSKC: Sermon file, folder 66, "Accepting Responsibility for Your Actions" / "Faith in Man."

"Faith in Man" II

I Introduction

(1) In our age there is a growing pessimism about the nature and destiny of man. Man is fastly losing faith in himself. Many would be in accord with the writer who spoke of man as the supreme clown of creation. (quote other poets[7]

(2) ~~There was a time when man had to much~~ Such a pessimistic attitude toward man is far out of line with the Christian religion. Christianity has always insisted that man's plight is never so low that it cant be better. We might go so far as to say that Christianity stands or falls with its power change human nature

---

5. Students rioted at the University of Alabama on 6 February to protest Lucy's court-ordered admission. The University expelled Lucy, allegedly for her protection. It later reinstated her by order of the court only to expel her again, this time for allegedly making accusations against school officials. The court that had ordered Lucy's reinstatement later upheld the University's actions. For more on Autherine Lucy, see note 2, King to Fred Drake, 7 February 1956, in *Papers* 3:128.

6. Cf. John 1:40–42 (*The Bible: An American Translation; The Old Testament*, trans. J. M. Powis Smith; *The New Testament*, trans. E. J. Goodspeed [Chicago: University of Chicago Press, 1944]). Subsequent cites of biblical verses from Goodspeed's translation of the New Testament are noted as GOODSPEED, in parentheses.

7. King quoted Psalm 8, Shakespeare's *Hamlet*, and Thomas Carlyle's *French Revolution* in an introduction to a similar sermon (see King, "What Is Man?" Sermon at Dexter Avenue Baptist Church,11 July 1954, p. 175 in this volume).

(3) Throughout his ministry Jesus revealed his deep faith in the possibilities of human nature

(4) Text[8]

Jesus knew that God had given man certain creative powers and had endowed him with with high and noble virtues; and that these virtues and powers could be made living realities in the life of man if he properly reponded to the Grace of God.

II Let us state at the outset that there is always the danger of man having to much faith in himself.

(a) Modern humanism

(b) Extreme liberal Theology

(c) Man's faith in Man must never come to the point of the deification of Man.

D. True Christian Position

(1) Man is a creature. No matter how much he advances cuturally, he is still a creature

III Faith in man consist in the following beliefs

1. A belief in the possibility of human nature being changed.

(a) Some deny the possibility of being changed after adolesence

2. A belief in man's better self being able to master his evil self

3. A belief in man's capacity to rise above his hereditary and environmental circumstances.

(A) Many men are environmentalist and hereditary determinist

(B) A roll of men who have risen above their environment.[9]

IV Conclusion: If men are willing to submit their wills to God's will and to cooperate with him in his divine purpose, we will be able to turn the world upside down, outside in, and right side up.

AD. CSKC: Sermon file, folder 66, "Accepting Responsibility for Your Actions" / "Faith in Man."

---

8. King may have used John 1:40–42 (GOODSPEED) as his text, as he did in the previous sermon outline, "Faith in Man."

9. In another sermon which King filed in the same folder as both versions of "Faith in Man," he cited Marian Anderson, Roland Hayes, Abraham Lincoln, John Bunyan, Franklin D. Roosevelt, and Helen Keller as examples of those who overcame conditions of environment and heredity to make noble contributions to society (King, "Accepting Responsibility for Your Actions," 26 July 1953, pp. 139–172 in this volume).

King, Rev. Horace W. B. Donegan, Bishop of New York *(left)*,
and the Rev. James A. Pike *(right)* chat before the "Day of
Prayer and Thanksgiving" service at the Cathedral of St. John
the Divine in New York to commemorate anniversary of the
Brown v. Board of Education decision, 17 May 1956. Courtesy
of Bettman/CORBIS.

King delivers "The Death of Evil Upon the Seashore" at the Cathedral of
St. John the Divine before 12,000 people, 17 May 1956. Photo by Frank
Mastro; courtesy of Bettman/CORBIS.

"When Peace Becomes Obnoxious"

[18 March 1956]
[Montgomery, Ala.]

King delivered this sermon from Dexter's pulpit the day before his trial for violating Alabama's anti-boycott law.[1] He begins this handwritten outline by recounting that, after Autherine Lucy's expulsion from the University of Alabama, many celebrated the relative quiet that followed days of rioting at the University. King condemns this calm as "the type of peace that stinks in the nostrils of the almighty God." He recounts a conversation with someone who suggested the bus boycott was destroying race relations and peace in the community, and responds: "Yes it is true that if the Negro [accepts] his place, accepts exploitation, and injustice, there will be peace. But it would be an obnoxious peace." Louisville Defender editor Frank L. Stanley, who was in Montgomery covering the trial, reproduced a version of this sermon outline in his newspaper on 29 March 1956.[2]

Mt. 10:34–36[3]

I   A few weeks ago, a federal judge handed down an edict which stated in substance that the university of Alabama could no longer deny admission to persons because of their race. With the handing down of this decision, a brave young lady by the name of Autherine Lucy was accepted as the first Negro student to be admitted in the history of the university of Alabama. This was a great moment and a great decision. But with the announcement of this decision, the vanguards of the old order began to emerge. The forces of evil began to congeal. As soon as Autherine Lucy walked on the campus, a group of spoiled students lead by Leonard Wilson and a vicious group of outsiders began threatning her on every hand.[4] Crosses were burned. Eggs and bricks were thrown at

---

1. Dexter's 18 March 1956 program indicates King preached this sermon. King's trial began on 19 March 1956. Judge Eugene Carter found King guilty after a four-day trial and sentenced him to either pay a $500 fine plus court costs or serve 386 days in jail. The sentence was suspended following an appeal by King's attorney (Testimony in *State of Alabama v. M. L. King, Jr.*, 22 March 1956, in *Papers* 3:183–196).

2. King, "When Peace Becomes Obnoxious," Sermon Delivered on 18 March 1956 at Dexter Avenue Baptist Church, 29 March 1956, in *Papers* 3:207–208. The published version follows the wording of this handwritten outline. In a 3 April 1956 letter, King wrote to Stanley to thank him for his "fine" coverage of the Montgomery movement and to "express my deepest appreciation for your interest in our cause and for the interest you have stimulated in Alpha men all over the country." Stanley was national president of King's fraternity, Alpha Phi Alpha, at the time of this letter.

3. Matthew 10:34–36: "Think not that I am come to send peace on earth: I came not to send peace, but a sword. For I am come to set a man at variance against his father, and the daughter against her mother, and the daughter in law against her mother in law. And a man's foes shall be they of his own household."

4. University of Alabama officials expelled Leonard Wilson in mid-March because of his "unwarranted and outrageous attacks . . . upon the integrity of the president and faculty and officers of the university" ("Segregation: That Defiant Sophomore," *Newsweek*, 26 March 1956, p. 25). Wilson was head of the Citizens Council of West Alabama and a sophomore at the University of Alabama.

her. The mob even jumped on top of the car in which she was riding. Finally the president and trustees of the university of Alabama asked Autherine to leave for her own safety and the safety of the university. The next day after Autherine was dimissed the paper came out with this headline: "Things are quiet in Tuscaloosa today. There is peace on the campus of the university of Alabama."[5] Yes things were quiet in Tuscaloosa. yes there was peace on the campus, <u>but it was peace at a great price. It was peace that had been purchased</u> at the exorbitant price of an inept trustee board succoming to the whims and carprices of a vicious mob. It was peace that had been purchased at the price of allowing mobocracy to reign supreme over democracy. It was peace that had been purchased at the price of ~~the~~ capitulating to the forces of darkness. This is the type of peace that all men of goodwill hate. It is the type of peace that is obnoxious. It is the type of peace that stinks in the nostrils of the almighty God.

II   Now let me hasten to say that this is not a concession to or a justification for physical war. I can see no moral justification for war. I believe absolutely and positively that violence is self-defeating. War is devastating. And we know now that if we continue to use these weapons of destruction, our civilization will be plunged accross the abyss of destruction.

III However, there is a type of war that every Christian is involved in. It is a spiritual war. It is a war of ideas. Every true Christian is a fighting passifist. In a very profound passage, which has been often misunderstood, Jesus utters this. He says "Think not that I am come to bring peace. I come not to bring peace, but a sword." {Mt 10:34–36} Certainly he is not saying that he comes not to bring peace in the higher sense. What he is saying is: "I come not to bring this peace of escapism, this peace that fails to confront the real issues of life, the peace that makes for stagnant complacency." Then he says, I come to bring a sword—not a physical sword. Whenever I come a conflict is precipitated between the old and the new, between justice and injustice, between the forces of light and the forces of darkness. "I come to declare war on evil. I come to declare war on injustice.

IV   This text is saying in substance Peace is not merely the absence of some negative force—war, tensions, confusion but it is the presence of some positive force—justice, goodwill, the power of the kingdom of God.

(a) I had a long talk the other day with a man about this bus situation. He discussed the peace being destroyed in the community, the destroying of good race relations. I agreed that it is more tension now. But peace is not merely to absence of this tension, but the presence of justice. And even if we didn't have this tension, we still wouldn't have positive peace. Yes it is true that if the Negro accept his place, accepts explotation, and injustice, there will be peace. But it would be an obnoxious peace. It would be a peace that boiled down to stagnant complacity, deadening passivity and

---

5. An editorial in the 7 February 1956 *Tuscaloosa News* concluded: "Yes, there's peace on the University campus this morning. But what a price has been paid for it!"

(b) If peace means this, I dont want peace:

    (1) If peace means accepting second class citizen ship I dont want it

    (2) If peace means keeping my mouth shut in the midst of injustice and evil, I dont want it

    (3) If peace means being complacently adjusted to a deadning staus quo, I dont want peace.

    (4) If peace means a willingness to be exploited economically, dominated polically, humiliated and segregated, I dont want peace.

    In a passive non-violent manner we must revolt against this peace.

    Jesus says in substance, I will not be content until justice, goodwill, brotherhood, love yes, the kingdom of God are established upon the earth. This is real peace. Peace is the presence of positive good.

V   Finally, never forget that there is an ~~The~~ inner peace that comes as a result of doing God's will.

Our Father God, who dost overarch our fleeting years with thine eternity and dost undergird our weakness with thy strength, in the midst of the pressures of another day, as we face its vast concerns.

Above all else save us from succumbing to the tragic temptation of Of becoming cynical

AD. CSKC: Sermon file, folder 111, "When Peace Becomes Obnoxious."

"Fleeing from God"

[*29 April 1956*]
[*Montgomery, Ala.*]

After Montgomery officials pledged to enforce state and city segregation laws despite a recent Supreme Court decision declaring such measures unconstitutional, the MIA unanimously voted at its 26 April meeting to continue the bus boycott.[1] *The following Sunday, in a sermon based on these two handwritten documents, King considers the story of Jonah to reflect on the human urge to flee from responsibility and from God. According to a newspaper account of the service, King prayed that God would give Montgomery's city commission the "wisdom to see the vision of goodness in the Cradle of the Confederacy."*[2]

---

1. King, Address to MIA Mass Meeting at Day Street Baptist Church, 26 April 1956, in *Papers* 3:230–232.

2. Art Carter, "Rev. King Is 'King' in Montg'ry," *Baltimore Afro-American*, 12 May 1956. The document is dated from this newspaper article.

"Fleeing from God"

Jonah 1:3 F[3]

One of the strange facts of human life is the fact that there is within every man an underlying urge to escape God. This is true not only of the rabit atheist, but also of the devout theist. We may not be aware of this in our conscious minds, but deep down within the hidden chambers of the sub-conscius there is the mad desire to flee from the presence of the Almighty God.

On the one hand, this attempt to escape God stemns from man's desire to hid his innomost nature. Every psychiatrist is familiar with the tremendous force of resistance in each personality against self-revelation. Nobody wants to be <u>known</u>, even when he knows that his health and salvation depend on it. ~~Nobody wants to be known~~ There is something within all of us that we wish to hid, something that we wish to remain private. But when we stand in the presence of the Almighty God, that which is humanly private becomes divinely public. God looks with eyes that see everything; He peers into man's ground and depth. Our entire inner life, our thoughts and desires, our feelings and imaginations, are known by God. Who does not hate a companion who is always present on every rock Who does not want to break through the prison of such a perpetual companionship.

Another reason why man seeks to escape God is because he doesn't want to follow the commands of God. God's commands are exacting, final and ultimate. Man in his finite, frail and sinful nature seeks to escape these exacting demands.

Man's perennial attempt to flee from God is pictured graphically in the book of Jonah.

a. Tell the story

AD. CSKC: Sermon file, folder 63, "Fleeing from God & When God Seems to Deceive Us."

"Fleeing from God," Sermon outline

Text Jonah 1:3 F

I   Introd—Modern man's quest to flee from God.
     Tell the story.
II   Ways modern man has sought to flee God
     1.   Running to the city of science
          a.   But this not the way (The atomic bomb)
     2.   Going to the city of pleasure
     3.   Going to the city of moral relativism

---

3. Jonah 1:3: "But Jonah rose up to flee unto Tarshish, from the presence of the Lord, and went down to Joppa; and he found a ship going to Tarshish; so he paid the fare thereof, and went down into it, to go with them unto Tarshish from the presence of the Lord." The succeeding verses tell of Jonah's flight from God's command to go to the city of Nineveh to condemn its sinfulness, and his eventual submission to this task.

King poses with mothers and babies during a baby pageant at Dexter Avenue Baptist Church in July 1956. Courtesy of Boston University.

{All of this has caused a storm. Whenever man seeks to flee from God a storm develops.}

Whenever God places responsibility upon man he cant escape it and the more he tries the more frustrated he becomes.

Quote the Psalmist, "If I assend into the heavens . . ." [4]

God's will is inflexible. Even after Johnah had gone through all of thies mishaps, God still stood before Jonah saying Go to Ninevah. [5]

AD. CSKC: Sermon file, folder 63, "Fleeing from God & When God Seems to Deceive Us."

---

4. Cf. Psalm 139:8.
5. Cf. Jonah 3:1–2.

"Living Under the Tensions of Modern Life," Sermon Delivered at Dexter Avenue Baptist Church

[September 1956]
[Montgomery, Ala.]

The emotionally and physically trying bus boycott was in its tenth month when King delivered a sermon with this title. He laments: "Oh, I know all of us sometimes worry about our particular situation. We worry about the fact that we live now amid the tension of the Southland. We worry about what will, what's going to happen in this whole struggle toward integration." He appeals to them to draw on resources of strength and hope: "How is it that we can keep walking in Montgomery? How is it that we can keep burning out our rubber? How is it that we can keep living under tension? And we can cry out to the nation, 'We can do it because we know that as we walk God walks with us.'" The following text is taken from an audio recording of the service.

[*Gap in recording*] use as the subject this morning, "Living Under the Tensions of Modern Life."[1] We use as a basis for our discussion together the twenty-eighth verse of the eleventh chapter of the gospel as recorded by St. Matthew: "Come unto me, all ye that labor and are heavy laden, and I will give you rest."

There can be no gainsaying of the fact that modern life is characterized by endless tensions. On all levels of life, men are experiencing disruption and conflict, self-destruction and meaninglessness. And if we turn our eyes around our nation, we discover that the psychopathic wards of our hospitals are filled today. Fear and anxiety have risen to the throne of modern life and very few persons escape the influence of their powerful domination. It is probably true to say that we live today in one of the most, if not the most, frustrated generations of all human history. Now what accounts for this tension, this anxiety, this confusion so characteristic of modern life? What is the causal basis for all of the tensions of our modern world? I will say that if we are to find the cause we must look for more than one cause and it's a plurality of causes that have all conjoined to make for the tensions of our generation.

First, there is a tension that comes as a results of the competitive struggle to make a living. It is true to say that our whole capitalistic economy is based on the profit motive under more or less competitive conditions. And whether we want to or not, we all find ourselves engaged in the competitive struggle to make a living. Sometimes we come to the point of feeling that life is a sort of endless struggle to pay bills and to pay taxes and to buy food to eat. We go to work to make the money to buy the food to gain the strength to go back to work, and life sometimes seems to be an

---

1. Harry Emerson Fosdick's sermon "Living Under Tension" may have inspired the title of King's sermon (Fosdick, *Living Under Tension*, pp. 1–10). King's secretary Maude Ballou made a September 1956 entry in her diary, referring to a sermon with this title: "Went to hear Martin preach yesterday. Inspiring, meaningful and timely" (Ballou, Diary, July–26 November 1956).

endless chain of monotony, an endless round of sameness. The competitive struggle to make a living makes for tensions throughout modern life, and that is why Karen Horney, the great psychologist, contends that it is this struggle to make a living in the competitive structure of our economic system that makes for the neurotic personality of our times.[2] There is some truth there, that tension grows out of the competitive struggle to make a living in this modern world.

Then again, we find that that tension grows out of the whole of modern urbanization and the industrial structure of our modern life. We live in an age in which men live in big cities and mass populations. It is a machine age in which we have vast industrial [*orders?*]. And there is a danger that men will feel in such a system that they are lost in the crowd. So men get in the big cities and feel a sense of lostness, feel that they are lost amid all of the vast numbers that they encounter every day. And then, there is a danger that men will feel that they are mere cogs in a vast industrial machine because it is an industrial world, and man so often becomes depersonalized; the machine becomes the end. This sense of not belonging, this sense of loneliness, characterizes modern life. And so many of us are lonely in a crowd because there is that basic drive that characterizes the whole of human nature: to want to belong, to have a sense of status. And there is so much in our modern world that makes us feel that we don't belong, that we are merely cogs in a vast industrial wheel that moves on.

And then, there is a tension that results from the fears accompanying a war-torn world. We find ourselves today standing amid the threat of war at every hand, and we often wonder what will happen. We feel at times that the future is uncertain, and we look out and feel that the future is shrouded with impenetrable obscurities, that we don't know how things will turn out. Every young man that grows up in this world has to face the fact that he just doesn't know how the future will turn out because there is the endless round of preparing for war. And we know today that through atomic development we have now come to the point that we tread a narrow [*word inaudible*] that skirts a blazing inferno that Dante could never dictate.[3] We know that we stand today at any moment to be plunged across the abyss of atomic destruction. And all of that causes us to fear and live in tension and agony, wondering how things will turn out. This is a part of the general fear and tension and anxiety of modern life.

Then, there is the tension that comes as a results of man's general finite situation. Man has to face the fact that he's finite, that he is inevitably limited, that he's caught up within the categories of time and space. And he faces this thing that he may not be. That's why one great school of modern philosophy, known as existentialism, cries out that the great threat of modern life is the threat of nonbeing and every man has to live under the threat of nonbeing, that he must face this fact soon or later in his life, that hovering over him is the threat of nonbeing.[4] He finds his self asking with Shakespeare, "To be or not to be, that's the question," but he faces the

---

2. Karen Horney, *The Neurotic Personality of Our Time* (New York: W. W. Norton, 1937).

3. King refers to Dante Alighieri's *Inferno* (1314), the first volume of his epic poem *Divine Comedy*.

4. King may refer to Jean-Paul Sartre's *Being and Nothingness* (New York: Philosophical Library, 1956).

fact that he may not be.[5] And he knows that there will come a moment that he will have to go into his room and pull down the shades and turn out the lights and take off his shoes and walk down to the chilly waters of death. And he confronts this *threat* of nonbeing that drives through the whole structure of modern life. And because of that he lives in tension and dismay and despair because he knows that hanging over him is the cloud of nonbeing, the threat of nothingness. He wonders, "Where does it go from here?" This is the tension of modern life, and these things account for the tension. These things all come together and leave all of us standing amid the tension of modern life.

But then in the midst of all of that, a voice rings out through all of the generations saying, "Come unto me, all ye that labor and are heavy laden, and I'll give you rest." That voice cries out to us saying, "Come unto me, all ye that are laboring every day trying to make a living. You're caught in this round of life, in this chain of life. All of those who are laboring trying to explain life, all of those who are laboring under all of the problems of life, those who are heavy laden with burdens of despair, those who are laden with fear, those who are laden with anxieties and disappointment, *come* unto me and I will give you rest." That's the voice that comes crying out to modern life, which gives us a little solace to carry us on. And if we didn't hear that voice, we couldn't make it. That voice simply says to us that the answer to the tension of modern life is to sufficiently commit ourselves to Christ and to be sure that we have a truly religious bit of life. For until a man discovers a religious attitude of life, he lives life in eternal frustration, and he finds himself crying out unconsciously with Shakespeare's Macbeth that "Life is a tale told by an idiot, full of sound and fury, signifying nothing."[6] Until he gets some *religion*, he cannot stand up amid the tensions of modern life. That is why H. G. Wells can cry out and say that a man who is not religious begins at nowhere and ends at nothing.[7] For religion is like a mighty wind that knocks down doors and breaks down walls and makes that possible, and even easy, which seems difficult and impossible. It is religion, it is a proper religious faith that is the answer to the tensions of life.

I have a statement here from a man you should know, the great psychiatrist Jung, who was greatly influenced by Sigmund Freud, but who went a little beyond Freud. But most of his life spent, had been spent counseling people who have confronted the problems of life, the agony of modern life. And this is what Jung says. He says:

> During the past thirty years, people from all the civilized countries of the earth have consulted me. I have treated many hundreds of patients, the larger number being Protestants, the smaller number Jews, and not more than five or six believing Catholics. Among all my patients, in the second half of life—that is to say over thirty-five—there has not been one whose problem in the last resort was not that of finding a religious outlook on life.[8]

---

5. Shakespeare, *Hamlet*, act 3, sc. 1.

6. Shakespeare, *Macbeth*, act 5, sc. 5.

7. Cf. Wells, *Mr. Britling Sees It Through*, p. 442.

8. C. G. Jung, *Modern Man in Search of a Soul*, p. 264. Fosdick also quoted Jung in his essay "The Principle of Self-Acceptance" (Fosdick, *On Being a Real Person*, p. 74).

That's not a preacher talking; that's a psychiatrist talking. That's a psychoanalyst talking. He's saying, in substance, that people face the frustrations and bewildering experiences in life so often because they do not have the proper religious bent on life. So the experiences of life come before them as mighty winds and knock them down because they have nothing within to face them. Facing the tensions of modern life through the proper religious faith. That's what Jesus is saying, "Come unto me. Sufficiently commit yourself to religion, and you will make it."

Now what does religion give us? What does genuine religion give us? What is it that Christ gives us to help us face the tensions of life and to stand up amid the tensions of life? What is it that he gives us to keep us going? What is it that genuine religion has to offer for us to live the difficult [*reign?*] of life? I think the first thing is that religion gives us a capacity to accept ourselves. And I think that is one of the first lessons that all of us should learn, the principle of self-acceptance.[9] This accounts for one of the big problems in modern life. So many people have been plunged across the abyss of emotional fatalism because they did not learn this simple lesson, the lesson of self-acceptance. So many of us hide this tragic gap between our desired self and our actual self. We find ourselves living life trying to be what we are not and what we can't be. So genuine religion says to us in no uncertain terms, "Accept yourself." You cannot be anybody else. You can't be me and I can't be you. And your great prayer in life should be, "Lord help me to accept my tools. However dull they are, help me to accept them. And then Lord, after I have accepted my tools, then help me to set out and do what I can do with my tools." For there is a bit of latent creativity within all of us, seeking to break forth, and that creativity is often blocked because we are trying to be somebody else, trying to be what we aren't. There is nothing more tragic than to see an individual whose ambitions outdistance his capacity. That's a tragic sight.

So that we have in life this responsibility to be sure that we are willing to face our capacities as they are and do the best we can with them, and that's all God requires. That's all that stands before you is to do it well. And when you stand before the judgment of all eternity, there is a great reward: "Well done, thy good and faithful servant. You have been good, faithful over a few things. Come up high, and I'll make you rule over many."[10] That is true for the two-talent man as well as the five-talent man, and it would have been true of the one-talent man if he had used it.[11]

We must live by this principle of self-acceptance. Oh, I know a lot of things in life that I would like to have, and I just have to face the fact that I don't have them and live by it. That means accepting everything, even your looks. I wish the Lord had made me tall, tan, and handsome, and it would have been much better for my sake. I would have enjoyed that the mirror would have been much more meaningful to me. But I can't spend all of my life worrying because the Lord didn't make me that

---

9. Fosdick discussed religion's role in promoting self-respect in "The Principle of Self-Acceptance" (Fosdick, *On Being a Real Person*, pp. 73–78).

10. Cf. Matthew 25:21, 23.

11. King refers to Jesus' parable of the talents, in which he praises those with five and two talents for using them constructively but condemns the person with one talent for burying it in the ground (Matthew 25:14–30).

way. We must come with that bit of humor to see that *we* must accept *ourselves* as we are. That becomes the first lesson of life, and genuine religion gives us that so that we rise above the *competitive* tension of life because we accept ourselves as we are, and we begin to say like Moses said in *Green Pastures*, "Lord, I ain't much but I's all I got."[12] And we live by that principle, and you live through life with a harmony that men all around you can never understand because you learned a great secret, the secret and the principle of self-acceptance.

But not only that, high religion, genuine religion, gives you the capacity to accept the realities of life, not only yourself but the external circumstances that beat up against you in life. That is one of the things that makes, also, for a lot of the problems of modern life: that so many people have not mastered this art of accepting life in a balanced perspective. We must come to see that life is a pendulum swinging between two opposites—a pendulum swinging between disappointment and fulfillment, between success and failure, between joy and sorrow. And that's life. And we never mask the life, and we think that life must be only joyous and happy and that we must live in terms of fulfillment. Disappointment is just as much a part of life as fulfillment. Failure is just as much a part of life as success, sorrow as much a part of life as joy. That is the thing that religion helps us to see. That is the greatness of Jesus. And he goes one day out, standing amid the Good Friday's light. He knows that Good Friday much as a part, is as much a part of life as Easter, and life somehow is a pendulum swinging between Good Friday and Easter, swinging between agony and triumph, swinging between darkness and light. And he who learns that has learned the lesson of life; so that he doesn't break down when he faces the other side of the pendulum. When the bitter moment of life come, he doesn't break down nor does he get overjoyous when the sweet moment of life come because he knows that this is the endless trend of life.

This is the way it moves. This is what carries life on. Why it is that way maybe we do not fully understand, but it is. Religion says, "Yes, there is a crown you wear, but before the crown you wear there is a cross you must bear." We learned that when we learned to live close to Jesus, and we go unto Christ. He gives us the rest that comes for learning, from learning this lesson, that life is a pendulum, and it can throw us around and throw us [*wild when we let it?*]. But one day we might be rich, and that doesn't bother us. One day we might be poor, and that doesn't bother us. One day we might be happy, and that doesn't particularly bother us; and one day we might be unhappy, and that doesn't particularly bother us because we know that life is going to swing right back to the other opposite.

We learned that and we learned then to live with a harmony, with an inner peace, that the world can't understand. That is why Jesus says, "My peace I leave with you, not as the world giveth."[13] The world can't understand this peace for it is an inner peace; it is a tranquil soul amid the external accidents of circumstance. Christ gives us that. If we will only come unto Him, He gives us the capacity to accept the oppo-

---

12. Cf. Marc Connelly, *The Green Pastures: A Fable* (New York: Farrar & Rinehart, 1929), p. 68. See also Fosdick, *On Being a Real Person*, p. 78: "Says Noah in the play *Green Pastures*, 'I ain' very much but I'se all I got.'"

13. John 14:27.

sites of life. Not only that. Religion at its best, and when we go unto Christ we discover this, that there is something called forgiveness for the sins we commit. That too is a great release, isn't it? That is another lesson that we must all learn if we are to live amid the tensions of modern life.

The psychologists tell us on every hand that a lot of people are frustrated and disillusioned today because they have inner guilt feelings, and these inner feelings of guilt begin to accumulate. You know enough about psychoanalysis, I'm sure, to understand what they're talking about, for when they talk about this thing they're talking about something realistic. Freud used to talk about this thing in his psychological system about [*words inaudible*] man here having an impression, and if it doesn't become an expression it becomes a repression. But all of the psychologists tell us that it's dangerous to repress our emotions, that we must always keep them on the forefront of consciousness. And we must do something else—not repress but sublimate. That's another big psychological word that we use in the modern world: sublimation. But religion gives you the art of sublimation, and so you don't repress your emotions, you substitute the positive for the negative of repression. You sublimate instead of repressing, and that is what religion gives us when we go unto Christ. There is something saying to us at all times that you can be forgiven. If you commit a sin you don't have to give your life in a long state of worrying about it because you're going to make mistakes. That's normal. It's altogether human to sin and to make mistakes and to fall short of the mark. But what religion says that when you fall short of the mark, if you will humble yourself and *bow* before the feet of Jesus and confess your sins, then he gives you a sense of forgiveness, and you can stand up with it and keep going. And you no longer get bogged down in the past, but you move on in the future. That's the way to live life.

I was talking with a young lady some few weeks ago who had made a grave mistake she felt in life, and she hated to face [*the public?*]. She hated to face anybody, and she hated to face herself. And here she was with this guilt feeling deep down within her, afraid to face herself and afraid to face life. And I said to her, "You must see something else. You made a mistake, yes, but all of us make them. Maybe ours are not seen as much as yours. Maybe yours is glaring, and it's a mistake that everybody could see, but in our private lives all of us make them just as bad." And if I say to you this morning, "Bow down before the feet of Jesus, and there is your God, of Jesus, with the grace of God expressed in his being that will forgive us and say to us, 'Rise up and go on.'" That's what Jesus said to that woman when those men stood around her to cast their stones and they wanted to [*words inaudible*]. Jesus looked at them and said, "He who is without sin cast the first stone." They began to drop their stones and run from that situation because they knew deep down within that they too were involved in the guilt of life. But then Jesus looked at that lady and said, "Go and sin no more," as if to say, "Don't get bogged down in the path and worry because you've committed adultery. Everybody has committed it, but turn around into the future and move on out, and you will become somebody because you have accepted my grace and my forgiving power."[14]

---

14. Cf. John 8:3–11.

There is a man lost in the foreign country of life, but then something comes to him and it says he came to himself. But he didn't stop there, that passage says that he got up and decided to walk up the dusty road that he had once come down. And as he started up that road, there was at the end of that road a father with an out-stretched arm saying, "Come home, and I will accept you." And he reaches back and gets the fatted calf and said, "Come on into the fold, and you can be made all over again."[15] And that is the meaning of repentance. It means a right about-face, not only feeling sorry for your sins but turning around and deciding to move on and not do it anymore. And if you make the same mistake again, you try to turn around again and go on. And that is the joy, and that is the great example that the Christian religion gives to us. Christ says, "I will forgive you seventy times seven. I'll keep on forgiving you if you will keep on repenting."[16] This saying gives you a balanced life. That's just good psychology that Jesus discovered years ago. He is saying simply what psychiatrists are saying today: keep your emotions on the forefront of conscious, and don't repress them because if you keep on doing that you will have a deep sense of guilt that will make a morbid personality and you will become a civil war fighting against yourself. "Come unto me, all ye that labor and are heavy laden with sin, and I will give you the rest of forgiveness."

And then finally, I must conclude now. There is something else that religion does. There is something else that Jesus does. It reminds us that at the center of the universe is a God who is concerned about the welfare of his children. Religion gives us that. High religion gives it in terms of a great personality. Religion at its best does not look upon God as a process, not as some impersonal force that is a mere moral order that guides the destiny of the universe. High religion looks upon God as a personality. Oh, it's not limited like our personalities. God is much higher than we are. But there is something in God that makes it so that we are made in his image. God can think; God is a self-determined being. God has a purpose. God can reason. God can love.

Aristotle used to talk about God as "Unmoved Mover," but that's not the Christian God. Aristotle's God is merely a self-knowing God, but the Christian God is an other-loving God. He reaches out with His long arm of compassion and love and embraces all of His children. It gives life a meaning and a purpose that it could never have without Him. I say that if there is not a God, there ought to be one; and since there ought to be a God, there is a God; and if man doesn't find the God of the universe, he'll make him a God. He's got to find something that he would wor-ship and give his ultimate allegiance to. And I say this morning that the Christian religion talks about a God, a personal God, who's concerned about us, who is our Father, who is our Redeemer. And this sense of religion and of this divine compan-ionship says to us, on the one hand, that we are not lost in a universe fighting for goodness and for justice and love all by ourselves. It says somehow that although we live amid the tensions of life, although we live amid injustice, no matter what we live amid, it's not going to be like that always.

---

15. King refers to the parable of the prodigal son in Luke 15:11–32.
16. Cf. Matthew 18:21–22.

There's a good dose of psychology there. And I'm glad the slaves were the greatest psychologists that America'd ever known, for they learned something that we must always learn. And they said it in their broken language, "I'm so glad that trouble don't last always."[17] They had learned something in their lives. And that's what real, determined faith in God gives you. Gives you the conviction that although trouble is rampant, that although you stand amid the forces of injustice, it will not last always because God controls the universe. And you can live without tension then. You can live under it.

Oh, I know all of us sometimes worry about our particular situation. We worry about the fact that we live now amid the tension of the Southland. We worry about what will happen, what's going to happen in this whole struggle toward integration. We hear those who will come on the television and say that the brain of the Negro is less than that of white, that it is inferior. We hear those who say that they will use any means to block the Negro from his advance. They attempt to keep the Negro segregated and exploited and keep him down under the iron yoke of oppression. And we begin to wonder, and sometimes I know we ask the question: "Why is it? Why does God leave us like this? Seventeen million of his children here in America, leaving us under these conditions, why is it?" But then there is something that comes out on the other side and says to us that it ain't gonna last always. There is that conviction that grows, "I'm so glad that segregation don't last always." And there is something that cries out to us and says that Kasper and Engelhardt and all of the other men that we hear talking—grim men that represent the death groans of a dying system—and all that they are saying are merely the last-minute breathing spots of a system that will inevitably die.[18] For justice rules this world, love and goodwill, and it will triumph. They begin to wonder over the nation, how is it that we can keep walking in Montgomery? How is it that we can keep burning out our rubber? How is it that we can keep living under tension? And we can cry out to the nation, "We can do it because we know that as we walk God walks with us." [*Congregation:*] (Yes)

We know that God is with us in all of the experiences of life. And we can walk and never get weary because we know that there is a great camp meeting in the promised land of freedom and justice.[19] Then it gives us this faith in God, gives us the assurance that in nothing we confront in life do we stand alone, for there is cosmic companionship. As we face our individual troubles, as we face our individual problems, there is a God that stands with us. And isn't that consoling that at last long we can find something permanent, for we live in life and life is so elusive. As I've said it

---

17. In the published version of King's sermon "Knock at Midnight," King attributed this quote to Howard Thurman (King, *Strength to Love*, pp. 49, 144; Thurman, *Deep River: Reflections on the Religious Insight of Certain of the Negro Spirituals* [New York: Harper & Brothers, 1955], pp. 28–29).

18. King refers to vocal segregationist John Kasper, who aggressively opposed integration in Clinton, Tennessee in the fall of 1956, and Alabama State Senator Sam Engelhardt, Jr., who was chair of the Central Alabama Citizens' Council and authored the 1956 Alabama Placement Act, designed to circumvent the implementation of *Brown v. Board of Education* (see Martin Luther King, Jr., Robert E. DuBose, H. J. Palmer, H. H. Hubbard, S. S. Seay, and Ralph Abernathy to the Montgomery County Board of Education, 28 August 1959, in *Papers* 5:272).

19. King paraphrases the spiritual "There's a Great Camp Meeting."

is this pendulum swinging between joy and sorrow, between disappointment and fulfillment, but there is something beyond all of that which is permanent. If we put our ultimate faith in that, we don't worry about anything. Oh, when we get our ultimate faith in God, everything in life can come to us, and yet we don't despair because we know that there is something permanent.

And I say to you this morning I'm not going to put my ultimate faith in these little gods that are here today and gone tomorrow. I'm not going to put my ultimate faith in a few dollars and cents and a few Cadillac cars and Buick convertibles. I'm going to put my ultimate faith in the God of the universe who is the same yesterday, today, and forever.[20] When all of these gods have passed away, He's still standing. And He is the eternal companion.

And now I can understand what the old people meant. They cried out in their poetic manner, not being able to talk about God in philosophical and theological categories. They could only talk about him in terms of their particular poetic imaginations expressed in the scripture. They could cry out throughout all the ages, "He's a rock in a weary land and a shelter in the time of storm. He is a lily of the valley and a bright and morning star." And then when they gave out they wouldn't stop there because they gave out a language and they just started crying out, "He's my everything. He's my sister and my brother; He's my mother and my father. He's all together lovely; He's fairest among ten thousand. And I'm going to worship Him forever because I believe that He can guide us throughout life."[21] Come unto me, all ye that are laborers, beat down and burdened down because of the problems of modern life. Come unto me and I will give you the rest that will carry you through the generations. I will give you a peace that the world can never understand. My peace I leave with you, not as the world giveth, but a peace that passeth all understanding.[22] God grant, if we will discover this, we will be able to live amid the tensions of modern life.

Oh God, our gracious heavenly [*recording interrupted*] Grant, oh God, that we will accept ourselves and accept the realities of life. And learn to come to thee for forgiveness so that we can wash our guilt away, then devote our whole lives to Thee. Grant, oh God, that as we do this, we will rise out of the tensions of modern life. We can live in the world, and yet above it. We can live in the tension, and yet beyond it. In the name and spirit of Jesus, we pray. Amen.

At. MLKEC: ET-32.

---

20. Cf. Hebrews 13:8.
21. King cites Charles W. Fry's hymn "The Lily of the Valley" (1881).
22. Cf. Philippians 4:7 and John 14:27.

[*October 1956?*]
[*Montgomery, Ala.?*]

During October 1956, King began a series of sermons at Dexter on the parable of the prodigal son.[1] He incorporates ideas gleaned from Buttrick and J. Wallace Hamilton in this handwritten outline.[2]

I   This is probly the most familiar of all of the parables of Jesus. George Mury has said that this parable is "the most divinely tender and the most humanly touching story ever told on earth. This is no exaggration. No story more instantly touches the nerve of actual life. It is the story of a boy who churned his life into fleshly mess and is condemned by it and is finally saved.[3]

II   Tell the story.[4] As we look at the Prodical, let us look not as spectators. The Prodical is a faithful reflection of life everywhere, in every age.

III   The one word that can describe all of this boys mistakes is the word "illusion". He was the tragic victim of a threefold illusion
What is an illusion. It is an imange in the mind's eye which has no corresponding existnce in reality.

    A.   The first illusion is his mind was that pleasure is the end of life; that the satisfaction of the senses is the end of existence. This is an old illusion

        (1) The Hedonist
        (2) Epicurus
        (3) Ecclesiates[5]
        (4) Omar Khayyam
{The moving Finger writes and Having writ, moves on

---

1. A report titled "Travels with the Pastor" in the 17 October 1956 *Dexter Echo* indicates that King delivered a series of sermons on the prodigal son. This outline may represent King's first sermon of the series.

2. Buttrick, *The Parables of Jesus*, pp. 189–194; Hamilton, *Horns and Halos in Human Nature* (Westwood, N.J.: Revell, 1954), pp. 25–34. King annotated a copy of Hamilton's book and kept it in his personal library. He also drew significantly from Hamilton in another sermon outline on this theme (Prodigal Son, Sermon outline, 1964–1968).

3. Buttrick, *The Parables of Jesus*, p. 189: " 'The most divinely tender and most humanly touching story ever told on our earth,' says George Murray. The appraisal is not extravagant. . . . No story more instantly touches the nerve of actual life. . . . The boy who has churned his life into a fleshly mess is condemned by it, and saved." For George Murray's words, see Murray, *Jesus and His Parables* (Edinburgh: T. & T. Clark, 1914), p. 163.

4. Luke 15:11–32. In Jesus's parable of the prodigal son, a son takes his share of his father's estate and squanders it on indulgent pleasures. He is still welcomed home after becoming destitute.

5. Hamilton paraphrased Ecclesiastes 2:4–11 in his analysis of the prodigal son, which King underlined in his copy of the sermon: "Away back in antiquity a man wrote it down and got it recorded in the Bible: 'I tried it,' he said. 'I made a business of happiness. I worked hard at the game, surrounded myself with all the pleasures the senses could provide, withheld not my heart from any joy. Then one day I drew a line under it, added it up, and all I got was zero, nothing. All is vanity, a striving after the wind' " (*Horns and Halos in Human Nature*, p. 31).

Neither tears nor wit can cancel out a line of it!

"A Book of verses underneath the Bough, A jug of wine, a loaf of Bread an Thou}[6]
"The saddest people in the world," wrote Winchell, "are those sitting in joints making believe they are having a good time." This Broadway street [*of fools?*][7]

  B. The second illusion was the feeling on the part of the prodical that he was independent; that he could live life happily outside his fathers house and his fathers will.

  C. He was a victim of the illusion that freedom is liscnce.

AD. MLKJP-GAMK: Vault Box 6.

---

6. King quotes from Khayyám's *Rubáiyát* 71 and 12 (pp. 50 and 31). Hamilton also cited these two verses to exemplify "the philosophy of the prodigal" (*Horns and Halos in Human Nature,* p. 29).

7. King probably refers to journalist Walter Winchell, whose syndicated gossip column "On Broadway" ran in newspapers from 1924 until 1963.

"The Fellow Who Stayed at Home"

[October 1956?]
[Montgomery, Ala.?]

King bases the following handwritten outline on J. Wallace Hamilton's sermon "That Fellow Who Stayed at Home," which deals with the prodigal son's older brother.[1] King removed this chapter from his annotated copy of Hamilton's book, Horns and Halos in Human Nature, *and kept the torn pages in the same file folder as this sermon. In the outline below, King observes that the elder brother "failed to realize that he was [committing] sins as damaging to the soul as the coarser sins of the younger brother."*

They began to be merry—that is a fitting climax.[2] The elder brother is a sudden discord, but without him the story would have been untrue to life. The year has its winter storms, the glow of day is followed by the gloom of night;

I He possessed a sort of unattractive goodness that was deeply repulsive. True he stayed at home, did the chores, kept the rules. He wasted no money nor scarred his soul with dissipation—But he was undesirable nevertheless. He did the right things but in the wrong spirit.[3]

---

1. Hamilton, *Horns and Halos in Human Nature,* pp. 163–173. The 17 October 1956 *Dexter Echo* noted that King was scheduled to preach a sermon series on the prodigal son. This sermon may represent King's second sermon in that series.

2. Cf. Luke 15:24.

3. Hamilton, *Horns and Halos in Human Nature,* p. 166: "Let us begin with the most obvious fact about him—that, for all his respectability, *he illustrates a kind of ungracious, unattractive goodness that is much too common.* True, he stayed at home, did the chores, kept the rules, performed his duty. He sowed no wild

minister had called for those who felt the need of prayer to linger after the service at the altar of the church. In the quiet, came a number, among them two men from opposite sides of the church. Without notice of each other, they knelt at the altar to pray. When, after a few moments, they arose, they looked at each other in startled recognition. When before they had faced each other one was a judge pronouncing sentence, the other a man who, in the frailties of his flesh, had run afoul of the law. Here, however, at the altar of the church, before the higher tribunal of Christ's spirit, they both stood in common need. And in the bountiful mercy of God they clasped hands in the common fraternity of the forgiven.

So we leave the great parable with the definite feeling that our Lord was talking about us. If He missed us in the first part He reached us in the second; and over it all is still the boundless love of the Father within whose house our restless souls find their true home.

① ➝the tragedy of the elder brother was that he was contaminated with the sin of pride of egotism. He did good deeds, but from bad motive. He did the right thing, but in the wrong spirit. He would have given to the united appeals, but his generosity at this point would have been merely to feed his pride.

173

② His spiritual pride had drained from him the capacity to love. He could not call his brother brother.

In the margin of James Wallace Hamilton's sermon "That Fellow Who Stayed at Home," from his 1954 book *Horns and Halos in Human Nature*, King writes, "The tragedy of the elder brother was that he was contaminated with the sin of pride of egotism. . . . His spiritual pride had drained from him the capacity to love. He could not call his brother brother" (p. 173).

a. The little girls prayer—Lord, Make all good people nice[4]

b. The solo spoiled by the accompaiment[5]

c. My former church member

D. Homes are often broken by that. "Incompatibility" is the lawyers word for the offensive nagging of people who are smugly moral and piously unbending. God save us from a stuffed-shirt morality. It is not enough to be good; to be Christian we must be good in a nice way.[6]

II He failed to realize that he was commiting sins as damaging to the soul as the coarser sins of the younger brother

There are two types of sin: sins of passions and sins of disposition or sins of the flesh and sins of the spirit. Sins of the flesh would include such things as drunkedness, adultry, stealing, gambling, profanity. Sins of spirit include sins of envy jealousy, bad temper, self-centeredness and social callousness "The publicans and the harlots go into heaven before you."[7]

{The Church has been harder on profanity than on prejudice. It has denounced drunkenness more than stinginess. It was unchristian to gamble, but not to [*own?*] slaves}[8]

III His spiritual pride drained from him the capacity to love. He could not call his [*brother brother?*][9]

5. [*page torn*]

So often people will do a good thing, and then spoil it by some ugly twist of the spirit[10] We often see this in the Church. Some people will faithfully perform some

---

oats, wasted no money nor scarred his soul with dissipation—all of which was definitely in his favor. But he was a sourpuss, none the less. Not the kind of man you would want to go fishing with, not a good example of righteousness; touchy, stingy, churlish, thoroughly wrapped up in himself, *he did the right things, all of them in a wrong spirit that repels and pushes you away.*" At the end of Hamilton's sermon "That Fellow Who Stayed at Home," King wrote the following: "1) The tragedy of the elder brother was that he was contaminated with the sin of pride of egotism. He did good deeds, but from bad motives. He did the right thing, but in the wrong spirit. He would have given to the united appeals, but his generosity at this point would have been merely to feed his pride" (Hamilton, *Horns and Halos in Human Nature,* p. 173).

4. In his 14 July 1963 sermon, The Sinner Who Stayed at Home, King mentioned a little girl's prayer: "Lord, make all the bad people good and make all the good people nice."

5. Hamilton, *Horns and Halos in Human Nature,* p. 166: "A lovely young woman stood in the circle singing a solo. Around her was the band—the drum, trombone, and cymbals. From the occasional notes he caught from the singer, he judged the girl had an exceptionally fine voice. He wanted to hear more of it, but the blare of the trumpet and the pounding of the drum smothered the solo and drowned out its beauty. So it is with the goodness of some people—they ruin the solo by the accompaniment."

6. Hamilton, *Horns and Halos in Human Nature,* p. 167: "Homes are often broken by that. 'Incompatibility' is the lawyers' word for the offensive nagging of people who are smugly moral and piously unbending. God save us from a stuffed-shirt morality! It is not enough to be good; to be Christian we must be good in a nice way." King underlined the last sentence in this passage.

7. Cf. Matthew 21:31–32.

8. Hamilton, *Horns and Halos in Human Nature,* pp. 168, 170: "The Church has attached more guilt to the sins of passion than to the subtler sins of disposition. We have been harder on profanity than on prejudice. . . . It was unchristian to gamble, but not unchristian to own slaves."

9. King wrote on the last page of his copy of Hamilton's sermon "That Fellow Who Stayed at Home": "His spiritual pride had drained from him the capacity to <u>love</u>. He could not call his brother brother" (Hamilton, *Horns and Halos in Human Nature,* p. 173).

10. Hamilton, *Horns and Halos in Human Nature,* p. 166: "They do a good thing, and then spoil it by some ugly twist of the spirit."

fine service in the Church but grumble so much about it, seek their own interest in it, or want so much public recognition for it that they destroy a beautiful act with the wrong spirit, And you have the feeling they are not doing it for the sake of Christ but for their own.

AD. CSKC: Sermon file, folder 60, "The Fellow Who Stayed at Home."

Garden of Gethsemane, Sermon Delivered at Dexter Avenue Baptist Church

[*14 April 1957*]
Montgomery, Ala.

In this Palm Sunday sermon, King declares, "You can stand up amid despair. You can stand up amid persecution. You can stand up amid disappointment. You can stand up even amid death. But you don't worry because you know God is with you. You have made the transition. You have faced life's central test."[1] *Vowing to replicate Jesus' obedience to God's will, King cries, "Wherever He leads me, I will follow. I will follow Him to the garden. I will follow Him to the cross if He wants me to go there." The following text is taken from an audio recording of the service.*

[*Choir singing*]
There is hardly anyone here this morning who has not at some time been pushed to the rugged edges of life. There have been times that all of us felt that a cloud of despair had come to blot out the joyous glitter of a distant star of hope. So often we have been left standing amid the surging murmur of life's restless sea. We have been frustrated and disillusioned, bewildered and on the brink of despair.[2] There have been times that we felt like giving up. We felt that we couldn't make it any longer. This has been an experience characterizing the lives of men and women in all generations—religious men, unbelieving men. For instance, we turn back to the pages of the Old Testament and we hear an earnest believer like Isaiah in the midst of the Babylonian exile crying, "Verily thou art a God that hidest thyself, O God of Israel."[3]

We can run the long gamut of biography and come up to modern life. And we can hear an earnest believer like Carlyle saying, "It seems that God sits in his heaven and does nothing."[4] We can turn to a noble writer and literary genius like

---

1. The following Sunday, King commented that he had preached a sermon on Jesus' experience in the garden of Gethsemane "just last week," indicating that he delivered this homily on 14 April 1957 (King, Questions That Easter Answers, 21 April 1957, p. 288 in this volume).

2. In early 1957 supporters of segregation bombed four African American churches as well as the parsonages of MIA vice president Ralph Abernathy and white minister Robert Graetz. In March 1957 the MIA put out a leaflet titled "Segregation Hasn't Been Licked" that depicted the damage (in *Papers* 4:4).

3. Cf. Isaiah 45:15.

4. King paraphrases Thomas Carlyle, *Sartor Resartus,* p. 163.

Shakespeare and hear him crying out through the lips of Macbeth that "Life is a tale told by an idiot, full of sound and fury, signifying nothing."[5] We can hear that noble Negro poet in the midst of the streak of his poetic genius, crying out about life:

> A crust of bread and a corner to sleep in.
> A minute to smile and an hour to weep in.
> A pint of joy to a peck of trouble.
> And never a laugh but the moans come double
> And that is life.[6]

We can hear a pessimistic philosopher like Schopenhauer crying out amid the despair of his life that life is "an endless pain with a painful end."[7] And the strange thing is that we all come to those moments when we feel like crying out with these believers and these disbelievers of distant days. We feel like giving up, and life is now standing on the rugged edges. And we stand on the brink of despair.

I would like to take your minds back across the centuries this morning to our Lord and Master and at least demonstrate the fact that even Jesus confronted this experience when life was pushed out to the rugged edges, when the deep cloud of despair surrounded him at every point. He had lived for about thirty-two years. And he had gone around doing good: healing the sick, feeding the poor, preaching the gospel to the captives.[8] And in the midst of all of that, he was coming to a point that men wanted to get rid of him. We can see him on that day when he was getting ready to go to Jerusalem. Jerusalem was the center of Palestine at that time; it was the center of the religious world. And now, at the culmination of his ministry, he prepares to go to Jerusalem. And we can see the crowds as they greet him. He is entering Jerusalem now, the triumphant entry. And we can hear them as they cry— cry their loud hosannas.[9]

This is Palm Sunday you see. This is the day that people praise Jesus. This is the day that people talk about the good things he's done. This is the day for loud and vociferous hosannas. But Jesus know, knew that this was just the beginning of that week. He knew that before that week was over, that he would move from the loud hosannas to the dark and deep voice of "crucify him!"[10] He knew that before that week was over that he would move from the high mountain of praise to the deep valley of condemnation. He knew that before that week was over that the glorious sunrise that had characterized his Palm Sunday would be transformed into a dark sunset that would bring in Good Friday. He knew that. So he prepared himself for it.

---

5. Shakespeare, *Macbeth*, act 5, sc. 5.

6. King recites Paul Laurence Dunbar's poem "Life" (1895).

7. King may be referring to Arthur Schopenhauer, *The World as Will and Idea*, 3:462: "In the whole of human existence suffering expresses itself clearly enough as its true destiny. Life is deeply sunk in suffering, and cannot escape from it; our entrance into it takes place amid tears, its course is at bottom always tragic, and its end still more so."

8. Cf. Luke 4:18.

9. Cf. Matthew 21:1–9. "Hosanna" is an ancient Hebrew exclamation that means "pray, save [us]!"

10. Cf. Mark 15:12–14.

And it is an interesting thing that Jesus was aware of the fact that this was ahead and he set out and he went on. He didn't stop. He knew that this would come through his Jerusalem experience but he went on. The Bible tells us that just before facing the darkest moment of his life, before facing Good Friday, he went out and decided to talk with God. And it is standing there with all of its glaring dimensions, it stands there in the form of a garden of Gethsemane.

And when he came to this point and Jesus realized that he had to face death, when he realized that there were those around who would seek to destroy him and take his life, he went to pray. He took some of his friends with him. And we can see him as he prepares to go into that garden, and he says to his friends, "Watch and wait while I pray." And he went into there, into the garden to pray and he came back first and discovered that his friends were asleep.[11] This is the mystery and the strange thing of life, that when we come to the difficult moments of life, when we come to the crisis situations of life, we always have to face it alone. One preacher preached a sermon on this very text and he called it "The Loneliness of Christ."[12] And isn't this the true picture of life? That the time that we need our friends most, that is the time that they seem so unconcerned and so apathetic. Even at our best our friends misunderstand us. And when we come to the moment that we need them most, we find them asleep. That seems to be the long commentary of life. He had to confront it alone.

Oh, it is true that in many of the experiences of life our friends help us and they give us kind and consoling words. The story comes down from the late Dr. George Truett of Texas that a big fire broke out one day in a large hotel in a southern city.[13] And in the midst of this fire, the fire engines came out from all over. It became so extensive that fire engines from other cities had to be called in. And there they stood with their nets and their ladders fighting the fire. And it came to a point that it seemed that the fire was out, and they were pulling the ladders down and they were letting the nets in and getting ready to leave. The fire was now under control and had been put out. It lasted for several hours. And now everything was clear. And it was under control. Just the time that the people were leaving, all of the persons working there prepared to leave. They were getting on the trucks, ready to drive off. And just at that moment, a little voice was heard screaming to the top of its voice. And at the moment everybody stopped, wondering where this voice was coming from. And they looked up to the top of that hotel, some fifteen or sixteen stories, and there at the top of the hotel they saw the face of a little white girl on the very top floor. And immediately the fire chief called the firemen back. And he called forth the youngest and bravest fireman and he said to him, "Go up and rescue this little girl." They placed the ladders back, the nets were waiting and the crowd came back, standing there, in all of the tension and the anxiety of the moment. The young

---

11. Cf. Matthew 26:36–45.

12. King may refer to Frederick William Robertson's (1816–1853) sermon "The Loneliness of Christ," in *Sermons Preached at Trinity Chapel, Brighton, by the late Rev. Frederick W. Robertson, M.A.* (Leipzig, Germany: Bernhard Tauchnitz, 1861), pp. 227–241.

13. King refers to an illustration in George W. Truett's sermon "What to Do with Life's Burdens" (Truett, *A Quest for Souls*, p. 22).

fireman started ascending the ladder and going up and up and up until he reached the top. And he got there and reached in the window and rescued the little girl. And he started back down the ladder.

As he descended the ladder, everything seemed all right. But then he got about middleways the ladder. At that moment the fire that they thought was out broke out again. Flames began to leap from all sides and billows of smoke began to break forth. And the young brave fireman lost his courage. He lost his strength and he began to falter there on the ladder and everybody stood there in fear, wondering what would happen. They were afraid that the fireman would fall, they were afraid that he would lose his hold and that he would fall there and kill himself and kill the little girl. The fire chief came forth at that time. He called forth all of the firemen around and he cried out in terms that rang out all over the space that they stood in: "Cheer him on!" [*recording interrupted*] and finally the cheers from the ground reached the ladder, the middle, where the young man was with the little girl. The cheers reached his ears. And when he heard the cheers from below, something happened to him. And he began to brace up, he began to regain his courage. He began to regain his faith and he regained his strength. And when he heard those cheers and they came close to him, he started once more to descend the ladder. And as a result of the cheers, as a result of the support from below, he was able to come on down the ladder and bring the little girl safely to the end.

Oh, my friends, so often in life we come to tragic experiences; the cheers and encouraging words of our friends and loved ones help us on. We are able to regain our courage and to regain our strength and to regain our power because of the cheers of friends. But we can't always depend on that. Suppose Jesus had depended on that? He would have never made it through. Did not his friend Peter deny him?[14] Did not his friend Judas betray him?[15] Did not his other friends run on back to Galilee?[16] When Jesus had to stand amid the darkness of Pilate's judgment hall, there were no cheers.[17] When Jesus had to confront the darkness of the cross, there were no cheers. When Jesus had to stand amid Golgotha's hill, there were no cheers.[18] He had to face it all alone.

And this is the tragic picture of life, that at our darkest moments our friends often go to sleep. The time that we need them most is the time that we don't find them. Oh, our friends are often with us in our days of triumph. They are always with us in our days of victory, in our days of popularity. But so often our friends leave us standing alone when we stand in the midst of defeat. So often our friends leave us standing alone when we stand amid the dark experiences of life. So Jesus confronted the long story of history, that when we come to the darkest moments of life, when we come to the crisis situations of life, we have to stand alone. For even our best friends are so often apathetic and non-concerned, unconcerned. Even our best friends leave us at the moment that we need them most.

---

14. For an example of Peter's denials of Jesus, see Matthew 26:69–75.
15. For an example of Judas' betrayal of Jesus, see Luke 22.
16. Cf. Matthew 26:56.
17. Cf. Matthew 27:2, 11–26.
18. Cf. Matthew 27:33–50.

So he faced this experience. He went there in [*recording interrupted*] "Father, if thy be willing let this cup pass from me."[19] Jesus didn't want to die. Now maybe you misinterpreted Scripture if you think Jesus wanted to die. As some fundamentalists would say Jesus came in the world [*knowing in the beginning?*], knowing that he was going to die, that he desired to die. But that's not true, according to the Scripture. It says in glaring terms that Jesus didn't want to die. [*recording interrupted*] "Father, if it is thy will, let this cup pass from me." In other words, "Father, keep me from dying. Keep this bitter experience from coming to me." And that was altogether a human experience. We have so often projected Jesus so far into the divine realm that we have forgotten about his humanity. Jesus not only experienced the glow of the divine, but also the tang of the human. And Jesus there, with his human nature, cries out, "Save me. I don't want to die. Take this cup from me."

There is nothing abnormal about that. That's altogether human. No young, normal human being wants to die. No normal human being wants to face the disappointments of life. Philosophers have told us throughout the generations that there is something of a surge and a quest for happiness and to avoid pain on the part of human nature. All of human beings have a desire to fulfill life through pleasure and happiness rather than through pain. That's the natural, normal desire.

Here is a mother whose son is getting ready to go off to war, whose son is getting ready to be taken away to the far-flung battlefields of the world. That mother has to face the thought and the possibility of her son never coming back again. And it is altogether normal and natural for that mother to pray to God to save her son. Nothing abnormal about that. It's altogether natural for that mother to pray to God, "Let this cup pass from me."

Yes, here is a person facing some incurable disease, caught up in bed for years and years and years with a disease that seems never to pass away. And it is altogether normal and natural for that person in the midst of the agony of life to cry out, "God, let this bitter cup pass from me."

Here is a young lady, who has always had the desire for life, and all of its beauty fulfilling itself in marriage, with all of the beauty that goes along with it. Here she comes to an age that it seems that that opportunity will not come. It is altogether natural and normal for that young lady to cry out to God, "Let this cup pass from me."

Here is a beautiful couple, married and always brought up with all of the longings and all of the aspirations of beautiful and noble children. It seems that because of biological difficulties, it isn't working out. It's altogether normal for that couple to cry out to God, "Let this cup pass from me! Oh, God, how much I desire children." There is nothing abnormal, there is nothing unnatural for men and women in the darkest moments of life to cry out to God, "Let this cup pass from me." That's a normal, *natural* desire.

And there we find Jesus, in the midst of his humanity, in the midst of his naturalness, crying out to God, "Let this cup pass from me. I don't want this disappointment. I don't want to die. Let it pass from me." But then it didn't stop there. There

---

19. Cf. Matthew 26:39.

was something after that. We read after that "nevertheless," "nevertheless." And after that "nevertheless" is the essence of religion. After that "nevertheless" is the ultimate test of one's devotion to God. After that "nevertheless" is the ultimate test of one's character. After that "nevertheless" is the ultimate test of one's loyalty. "Let this cup pass from me, nevertheless, not my will, but Thy will be done."

And this, you see, is the central test of an individual's life. This is the test. How one moves out from "let this cup pass from me" to "nevertheless."[20] This determines your life. This determines how you will live it. This determines how the very destiny of your life unfolds, how you are able to move from "let this cup pass from me" to "nevertheless." This is the great transition, and this is the test of an individual's life. This is the central test of life. We must learn the rigorous test of moving from "let this cup pass from me" to "nevertheless." Few people learn the lesson. And they end up in all of the misery and all of the agony and all of the frustration of life because they can't quite jump from one to the other. They live life on "let this cup pass from me." And they try to, when they see that the cup is still there, they try to get away from it through diverse methods and manners. And they end up more frustrated. They try the method of escapism. And sometimes in trying to get rid of this cup, some disappointment, some other experience, they take certain attitudes and they take certain things that they think will help them escape the experience. That is why some people become dope addicts and others become alcoholics because they do not have the power and the stamina to make the transition. And in an attempt to solve it themselves, they take something to escape. And they find themselves unable to face the responsibilities of life, and that presents a crisis. And so, in an attempt to get away from this difficult decision of facing responsibilities, they try to escape.

But the tragedy is that you can never escape. And these things only serve as temporary alleviations, not ultimate solutions to the problem. And that becomes merely a sort of passing answer to an ultimate problem. And the psychologists tell us that this is no answer, for it is a tragic answer. People who try the method of escapism when they face a bitter cup end up in psychological maladjustment. They tell us that the more and more we try to escape the difficult decisions of life, the thinner and thinner our personalities become, until ultimately they split. That's one of the reasons for schizophrenic personality. Have you seen people who have used so long methods of escape and escape and escape until their personalities have become split? It is because this is no answer.

One must learn to make the transition from "let this cup pass from me" to "nevertheless, not my will, but Thy will be done." And God grant this morning as you go out and face life with all of its decisions, as you face the bitter cup which you will inevitably face from day to day, God grant that you will learn this one thing and that is to make the transition from "this cup" to "nevertheless." This, you see, is the test of your religion. This, you see, is the thing that determines whether you go through life devoted to an eternal cause or whether you go through life depending on your own finite answers which really turn out to be no answers. This is the thing that

---

20. Fosdick, "Facing Life's Central Test," in *A Great Time to Be Alive*, p. 218: "And the central test of our lives now is whether we can take that next step—'Nevertheless.'"

determines whether you can rise out of your egocentric predicament to devotion to a higher cause. This is what Jesus was able to do and this is the lesson that he presents to us today and in all generations, the way to make the transition.

And do you know how he made it? Simply through a positive and constructive and abiding faith in God. That was the way he made the transition. He didn't depend on his friends. Your friends will deceive you a lot. You can't depend on that in all of the experiences of life. If you're going to depend on friends, the transition is difficult and almost impossible sometimes. He didn't depend on money, because he didn't have that. Money can't make this transition for you. And oh, haven't we looked through life and we see people with so many of the things that we call great? They are successful out in terms of man's standards for success and yet they can't make the transition. I read so often, here is somebody here with all of the wealth, all of the beautiful homes that one could expect, all of the money that one could think of. And yet we see them committing suicide and we wonder what happened. It is because they thought money could make the transition. Here is somebody with all of the culture, all of the academic achievements that one could ever attain. And yet we see them frustrated and disillusioned, cynical about life. It is because they thought philosophical judgments and scientific rationalizations could make the transition. But that can't do it.

Oh, my friends, this morning my answer to you is that God is the answer. Are you standing amid trials and tribulations? Well, God is the answer. Are you disappointed with something about life? God is the answer. Are you standing amid some experience that seems so dark that you will never get through? God is the answer. Young man, are you standing amid life and trying to make some great decision and it seems that the decision can't be made and you're giving your life to something low and yet you cry out for the high? Well, God is the answer. Are you looking for some way to run through the streets of life and remain calm amid war? Well, God is the answer. That is the only answer that I have for you this morning. And Jesus had the answer. He had it a long time ago. And this is the thing that carries us over. This is the thing that makes the transition.

I can look back at Job and I can see him as a young man with all of the riches of life, with a beautiful family, with all of the wealth in terms of cattle and other things that anybody could desire in life, with all of the happiness that one could think of. And then one day, all of these things left: his cattle gone, all of his wealth gone, his family gone, all of these things taken from him. And there he stands in life. There he stands before the universe stripped of everything that he had once had.[21] And I can hear him as he cries out in some form, "Let this cup pass from me." Oh, it's dark for Job now. I can hear his wife as she comes up to him and said: "Job, curse God and die. Just curse him."[22] And I can see Job in the midst of his despair, as he cries out: "Oh, that I knew where I could find him, that I might come to his dwelling. And I will set my case in order before him. Oh, I'm tired of this thing, it's dark for me. I can't face it!"[23] But then I can see Job as he turns to God, and he turns away from

21. Cf. Job 1–2.
22. Cf. Job 2:9.
23. Cf. Job 23:3–4, 16–17.

himself, and he gets away from his wife. And I can hear him cry out, "Though he slay me, yet will I trust him."[24] I can hear him crying out again, "I know that my Redeemer liveth and that he shall stand forth on the latter day of the judgment."[25] I'm talking about turning to God this morning.

I can hear Jeremiah at one time crying out, "Cursed be the day that I was born.[26] I'm tired of this thing, Lord, all of my enemies surrounding me, and it seems that I'm defeated on every hand." But I can hear that same Jeremiah crying out again, "The word of God is upon me like fire shut up in my bones. And I know, I know that somehow this God is my God. And He's going to stand with me."[27]

I can hear Habakkuk crying out on one time, "And it's mighty dark for me Lord. And I can see the wicked prospering on every hand. And it seemed that the longer we try to live good, the more we suffer. I'm tired of this, Lord! And I'm going to sit on the watchtower and just wait until you answer me."[28] But then I can hear that same Habakkuk once more crying out after he had turned to God that, "The Lord God is my strength and my refuge. He makes my feet like hind's feet and causes me to walk across high places."[29]

I can hear even Jesus himself, standing amid the agony and darkness of Good Friday, standing amid the darkness of the cross. And out of the pain and the agony and the darkness of that cross we hear him saying, "My God, my God, *why* hast Thou forsaken me?"[30] But then, in the midst of that he turns to God. And he keeps his eyes on God. He keeps his vision on God. And *out* of the midst of all of that, *that isn't the last* word that we hear from the cross. For out of the midst of the darkness and the agony of the cross, we hear something else. We hear a voice saying, "Into Thy hands I *commend* my spirit."[31] And then we can hear him saying, "Not my will, but thy will be done."

Now you got to learn that, my friends, and when you learn that you can stand up amid any condition because you know that *God* is with you no matter what happens. You can stand up amid despair. You can stand up amid persecution. You can stand up amid disappointment. You can stand up even amid death. But you don't worry because you know God is with you. You have made the transition. You have faced life's central test.

And so I'm going away this morning, I don't know about you, but I'm going away determined that wherever He leads me, I will follow.[32] I will follow Him to the garden. *I will follow* Him to the cross if He wants me to go there. I will follow Him to the dark valleys of death if He *wants* me to go there. *Not my will,* but Thy will be done. And when you can cry that, you stand up amid life with an *exuberant* joy. And you know that God walks with you. Even though you walk through the valley of the

---

24. Cf. Job 13:15.
25. Cf. Job 19:25.
26. Cf. Jeremiah 20:14.
27. Cf. Jeremiah 20:9–11.
28. Cf. Habakkuk 1:13–2:1.
29. Cf. Habakkuk 3:19.
30. Cf. Matthew 27:46.
31. Cf. Luke 23:46.
32. King refers to William A. Ogden's hymn "Where He Leads I'll Follow" (1885).

shadow of death, you know that *God* is there.[33] Even though you stand amid the [*giant?*] shadow of disappointment, you don't despair because you know God is with you. Father, let this cup pass from me. It's dark down here. Tired sometimes, disappointing experiences all around, sickness, facing the death of loved ones, facing disappointment, highest dreams often shattered, highest hopes often blasted. Let this cup pass from me, nevertheless, not my will, but Thy will be done. And somehow you've given us a way to live when we say that. We remain stable amid the storm. There is an equilibrium that comes. And while the others all around fall down in despair, and even suicide, and even death, we keep going and keep singing:

> Amazing grace! how sweet the sound
> That saves a wretch like me!
> I once was lost, but now I'm found;
> Was blind, but now I see.[34]

And we can keep singing that because we have decided to cry, "Not my will, but Thy will be done."

Let us pray. Oh, God our gracious Heavenly Father, in the glory of this Palm Sunday, help us to realize the darkness of the week ahead, with its Gethsemane, yes, with its Calvary, with its dark cross. Oh, God, help us to realize though that in the midst of this, there is a way out as we face life's central test, the test of making the transition from "Let this cup pass from me" to "nevertheless." God grant that we will discover that it can only be faced by giving our ultimate allegiance to Thee and to a religious view of life. Help us to realize that God is the answer. In the midst of all of our trials and tribulations, God is the answer. In the midst of all of our disappointments, God is the answer. Help us to live with that philosophy. And by that we will be able to live until we meet Thee in all of Thy eternities. In the name and spirit of Jesus we pray. Amen.

At. MLKEC: ET-66.

---

33. Cf. Psalm 23:4.
34. King quotes John Newton's hymn "Amazing Grace" (1779).

Questions That Easter Answers, Sermon
Delivered at Dexter Avenue Baptist Church

[*21 April 1957*]
Montgomery, Ala.

Building upon his Palm Sunday message Garden of Gethsemane, King contemplates the resurrection of Jesus in this Easter sermon. He mourns the unremitting savagery and hate in Montgomery and throughout the South: "<u>Why</u> is it, God? <u>Why</u> is it simply because some of your children ask to be treated as first-class human beings they are <u>trampled</u> over, their homes are bombed, their <u>children</u> are pushed from their *classrooms, and sometimes little children are thrown in the deep waters of Mississippi?" King admonishes his congregation to believe that, despite the crucifixion, Jesus' resurrection signals the inexorable triumph of good over evil, including the evil of segregation: "As I look over the world, as I look at America, I can see Easter coming in race relations. I can see it coming on every hand. I see it coming in Montgomery." The following text is taken from an audio recording of the service.*

[*Choir singing*]

We come once more to Easter Day. And one begins to wonder what this day means. For some, Easter is little more than a fashion show. [*Congregation:*] (*Amen*) For others, Easter is little more than a national holiday with no semblance of a religious holy day. We look upon Easter in diverse ways. And as I look over this congregation this morning and see the beautiful hats and the beautiful dresses and all of the things that go to commercialize Easter, I wonder if we really know the real meaning of it. But in the midst of all of that I imagine that most of you assembled here this morning for something deeper and something more meaningful than outer show. Easter is a day above all days. It surpasses the mystery and marvel of Christmas with all of the glory of the incarnation. It asserts that man's extremity is God's opportunity. It affirms that what stops us does not stop God and that miracle is as much a part of the end as of the beginning. Above all, Easter provides answers to the deepest queries of the human spirit. Easter symbolizes an event that provides answers to questions that have puzzled the probing minds of philosophers and theologians over the generations. You raise basic questions about the universe and about life and about all of the mysteries attached to it. And the Christian faith comes back confirming in words that echo across the generations that Easter has the answer. And I want to deal with some of these questions this morning, some of the questions that Easter answers, questions that we raise sometimes consciously and sometimes unconsciously.

One of the first questions that we find ourselves raising, Is the life of man immortal? Oh, from time to time we try to get by this question. You see this is, at bottom, the question, If a man dies, shall he live again?[1] This question is as old as the primitive gropings of ancient man and as modern as a morning's newspaper. "If a man dies, shall he live again?" It is a question of immortality. We try sometimes to be nonchalant about it. Or we might even agree with H. G. Wells that it is an irrelevant question, it is the height of [*egotism?*] to talk about immortality of the soul.[2] Oh, we try to be agnostic about it sometimes and say we just don't know; it isn't important anyway. But then one day, death invades our home and snatches away from us a loving, devoted friend. One day we come to the moment that we see our devoted loved one fade away. As Carlyle said concerning his mother, "Like the last pale circle of the moon fading in the deep seas."[3]

---

1. Cf. Job 14:14.

2. For the full text of Wells's thoughts, see *First and Last Things: A Confession of Faith and a Rule of Life* (New York: G. P. Putnam's Sons, 1908), p. 110.

3. In Carlyle's translation of Goethe's *Sorrows of Werther*, a passage reads: "Then, contemplating the

And in that moment, we can't be nonchalant. In that moment, we are not exactly agnostic. In that moment, we unconsciously cry out for the meaning of this thing. And there is something deep down within our souls that revolts against saying good-bye forever. We begin to ask, Is the ultimate destiny of man a rendezvous with the dust? Is the spirit of man extinguished at death like a candle guttered by a passing wind? We begin to wonder if death is a state of nothingness that leads us finally to a meaningless existence with no reality.

Then comes Easter to answer the question. Easter comes out ringing in terms that we all hear if we seek to hear it, that the soul of man is immortal. Through the resurrection of Jesus Christ we have fit testimony that this earthly life is not the end, that death is just something of a turn in the road, that life moves down a continual moving river, and that death is just a little turn in the river, that this earthly life is merely an embryonic prelude to a new awakening, that death is not a period which ends this great sentence of life but a comma that punctuates it to more loftier significance. That is what it says. That is the meaning of Easter. That is the question that Easter answers—that death is not the end. (*Amen*)

And as we think this morning, as we think in the mornings to come, about the immortality of the soul, here is the answer. For we have the testimony of reason on our side. Rationality tells us somehow that God would not make a universe and bring man across the centuries unfolding through the evolutionary process from a watery existence to the marvelous height of personality. And something tells us that God wouldn't cut it off now that he has planted within our lives an infinite responsibility and we need infinite time to fulfill it. (*Yeah*) Easter rings out and says to us with all of the rationality that can be mustered up that man lives on, that death is not the end, and somehow those who have left us along the way of life, those who have gone on into the distant eternities are not gone forever. We will see them again. And that is the marvelous and beautiful meaning of this faith. That is the first question that Easter answers—that life is immortal, that death is not the end.

We begin to wonder also about the reality of the invisible. And one of the big questions of life is whether the material is ultimately real or the spiritual is ultimately real. This has been the great question of philosophy through the generations, and philosophers have usually split up at this point. Some have been materialist, and some have been idealist. The materialist insisting that matter is the ultimate reality—those things which you see and touch and feel, those things which you can apply your five senses to. The idealist, on the other hand, insisted that mind is the ultimate reality, that spirit, that intangible forces are ultimately real. Then Easter comes unto us and says we take sides with the idealist, that these earthly, mundane, material things will pass away, that as you look at them they look like something permanent but they are just here for a season and then they go on, but there are these invisible, these intangible things that stand forever.

Oh, as we look at them, as we look at the visible things, we tend to think that this is all. As Professor Sorokin of Harvard says, we live in a sort of sensate civilization

pale moon, as she sinks beneath the waves of the rolling sea, the memory of bygone days strikes the mind of the hero" (*The Works of J. W. von Goethe*, ed. Nathan Dole, trans. Thomas Carlyle and R. D. Boylan [Boston: Wyman-Fogg, 1901], p. 87).

and we tend to think that just the things that we see, just the things that we touch, just the things that we can apply our five senses to, have existence.[4] But Easter comes and says that isn't true. You walk out at night, and you look up at the beautiful stars as they bedeck the heavens like swinging lanterns of eternity, and somehow you think you see all. But oh no, you can never see the law of gravitation that holds them there. You look at this building, and you look at its beautiful architecture, and you think you see all. You look out and you walk out this morning, and you look over at the beautiful capitol building and all of the surrounding buildings, and you think you see all. The materialist would say that's about all. But oh no, you don't see all. You can never see the mind of the architect who drew the blueprint. You can never see the faith and the hope and the love of the individuals who made this church possible. You can see the external bricks; you can see the building, but you cannot see the internal forces that brought it into being.

You look up here this morning and hear somebody talking and you cry out, "Yes, I see you, M. L. King." But I'm here to tell you this morning that you don't see me. (*No*) You look here, and you see my body. You see my external being. You see something that's merely a manifestation of something else. But the real me, you can never see. (*Amen*) You can never see that something that the psychologists call my personality. (*Yeah*) You can never see my mind. You can never see my ideas. You can only see my body, and my body can't think. My body can't reason. My body only moves at the dictates of my mind. And so this morning, Easter tells us that everything that we see is a shadow cast by that which we do not see. The invisible is a shadow cast by the invisible. Easter cries out to us that the idealists are right, that it is ultimately mind, personality, *spiritual* forces that are eternal and not merely these material things that we look about and see. For, one day, the gigantic mountains will pass away. One day, even the stars that bedeck the heavens will move out of their course. One day, the beautiful building of Dexter will not stand here. But there is something that will stand. There is faith, there is love, there is hope, there is something beyond the external that will stand through the ages.[5] The Christian faith says this is the testimony of Easter—that Christ on the day that he walked with a group of men on the Emmaus road was a little more real than he was the day before, the days before that, that he walked with them in the flesh, for there is something now that takes him into the spiritual realm.[6] And he's more real now than he was before. So Easter comes and says to us that the invisible forces are the forces that are ultimately real and the visible forces are merely shadows cast by the invisible.

There is another question that we like to raise; it is the question of whether life is doomed to futility and frustration. We wonder whether life has meaning or whether it is doomed to final frustration and futility, and some people have con-

---

4. Pitirim Alexandrovitch Sorokin (1889–1968) was a Russian-born sociologist who characterized twentieth-century Western industrial society as "sensate," possessing a reality that is perceived largely through the senses.

5. Cf. 1 Corinthians 13:13 (MOFFATT, RSV).

6. Luke 24. On the day of the Resurrection, two disciples met the risen Jesus on the Emmaus road. When they broke bread with him, Jesus vanished. They then returned to Jerusalem and told of their encounter, saying, "The Lord is risen indeed."

cluded that it is doomed to final frustration and futility. Some people feel that life is nothing more than a pendulum swinging between frustration and futility, and ultimately, it has no meaning. It's just a pendulum swinging. You've read of the pessimistic philosopher Schopenhauer, and he builds a whole philosophy on that in his book *The World as a Will and an Idea.* He builds a whole philosophical system on this fact, that life is nothing but a pendulum swinging between boredom and futility.[7] It is nothing but a boring, disillusioning, bewildering statement. But then Easter comes to us and tells us that that isn't true. And one can discover meaning in this life through the resurrection of Jesus Christ and that all of the disappointments of life can be transformed into meaningful experiences.

Oh, this morning are you disappointed by something? Are you disappointed about some experience that you've had in life? Well, don't give up in despair. You're just in Good Friday now, but Easter is coming. Are you disappointed about some great ideal that you had and you felt that you would have achieved by now, but you have not achieved it? You have somehow been caught in the moment. You have somehow been caught at a point at which it seems that you can't get out. Well, don't give up in despair. If you will just wait, Easter will come. This morning, have you had some high and noble ideals? Have you had some high and noble hopes, and it seems that they have been blasted by the years? Well, don't give up. Don't despair, because Easter is coming. And this is the thing that men through the generations have learned when they live close to Jesus Christ, that Easter can emerge, and that all of the darkness of Good Friday can pass away.

There are some people who find themselves in the experiences of Good Friday. And Good Friday is something of an inevitable transition of life. But if you look at life in all of its reality, you see it at one moment swinging back toward the beautiful days of Palm Sunday. There you hear the loud hosannas; there you stand in your state of happiness and joy and fulfillment in everything. But then you discover that life again swings over to Good Friday. This is a part of life. That is the dark part, that is the disappointment, that is the delusion, the disillusioning side of life. And some people swinging over from Palm Sunday to Good Friday give up in despair. They run to the rivers and cry out, "I can't take it." And sometimes they even jump in because Good Friday's on them, and they have lived so long in the midst of Palm Sunday.

But if you live close to Jesus Christ, there is something that cries out to you, "If you can just stand up with the Good Friday, there is another day that emerges." There is an Easter that comes out. And there is an Easter that comes and blocks out all of the darkness of Good Friday. (*Yeah*) There is an Easter that comes on the scene and blocks out all of the crucifixion that establishes itself on Good Friday. If you can just hold on, the pendulum swings back and forth, but it has a fulfillment. We find ourselves in the thesis of Palm Sunday, and then we move over into the antithesis of Good Friday. But Jesus Christ, with all of his beauty and all of his eloquence, rings out across the centuries and says, "There is a synthesis in Easter." And this means

---

7. King refers to Schopenhauer, *The World as Will and Idea* (London: Routledge & Kegan Paul, 1883), 1:402: "Life swings like a pendulum backwards and forwards between pain and ennui."

that life is meaningful, that life is not doomed to frustration and futility but life can end up in fulfillment in the life and the resurrection of our Lord and Savior Jesus Christ.

There is another question that men like to ask: Is the universe on the side of the forces of justice and goodness? Sometimes it looks dark and sometimes people come to feel that the universe is on the other side, that the universe seems to say "Amen" to the forces of injustice, and that the voices of the universe seem to cry out "Hallelujah" to the forces of godlessness. And oh, it looked dark for men centuries ago, looked like everything that they had stood for had gone.

Just last week, we thought about the darkness and the agony and the disappointment that Jesus suffered.[8] We can see him as he goes into the garden to pray, as he cries out, "Oh God, Father, let this cup pass from me."[9] That was a dark moment. And the interesting thing about it and the thing that we can never forget is that that cup didn't pass. It reminds us that everything we pray for will not come. It reminds us that sometimes we can ask for our highest hopes to be fulfilled and God doesn't always fulfill them. The cup didn't pass. And it looked mighty dark, didn't it?

But on the next morning, the next afternoon, after standing in Pilate's judgment hall, he had to go out and face the darkness of the cross.[10] Huge symbols accompanied the event. The Bible paints it in vivid terms: it looked like the whole universe got dark.[11] The disciples themselves were disappointed, and they decided to run on back to Galilee. This Savior, this leader, this teacher that had lived with them so many years, they felt was now defeated. And the universe to them, at that time, seemed to have no meaning. The universe was now justifying injustice. The universe was now on the side of godlessness. The universe was on the side of the forces of evil now. We can see Jesus there dying on the cross amid two thieves.[12] (*Yeah*) The most righteous man that ever entered human history (*Yeah*) dying a most ignominious death. We look at him there and all that goes with goodness, all that goes with nobility, all that goes with that which is sublime, seems to be crushed now. And that was a dark moment. (*Yeah*) But thank God the crucifixion was not the last act in that great and powerful drama. There is another act. And it is something that we sing out and cried and ring out about today. Thank God a third day came.[13] (*Yeah*) Thank God a day came when Good Friday had to pass. (*All right*)

And that's what our religion says to us—that Good Friday may occupy the throne for a day, but ultimately it must give way to the triumphant beat of the drums of Easter. (*Yeah*) It says to us that somehow nagging tares may come in to stand in the way of stately wheat but one day the tares must pass away and the wheat will grow on.[14] (*Yeah*) It says to us sometimes a vicious mob may take possession and crucify

---

8. King refers to his Palm Sunday sermon Garden of Gethsemane, 14 April 1957, pp. 275–283 in this volume.

9. Cf. Matthew 26:39.

10. Matthew 27:2, 11–26.

11. Matthew 27:45.

12. Matthew 27:38.

13. According to Christian tradition, Jesus rose from the dead on the third day after his crucifixion.

14. Cf. Matthew 13:24–30. King refers to the parable of the wheat and tares in which a farmer's

the most meaningful and sublime and noble character of human history. It says to us that one day that same Jesus will rise up and split history into A.D. and B.C. (*Yeah*) so that history takes on a new meaning. That's what Easter says to us (*Yeah*), that the forces of darkness, the forces of evil, the forces of *justice must finally* come to the light and must finally come to the forefront. And the forces of darkness and evil must finally pass away. (*Yeah*) Thank God that truth crushed to earth (*Yeah*) will rise again.[15] (*Yeah*)

You know every now and then, my friends, I doubt. Every now and then I get disturbed myself. Every now and then I become bewildered about this thing. I begin to despair every now and then. And wonder why it is that the forces of evil seem to reign supreme and the forces of goodness seem to be trampled over. Every now and then I feel like asking God, Why is it that over so many centuries the forces of injustice have *triumphed* over the Negro and he has been forced to live under oppression and *slavery* and exploitation? *Why* is it, God? *Why* is it simply because some of your children ask to be treated as first-class human beings they are *trampled* over, their homes are bombed, their *children* are pushed from their classrooms, and sometimes little children are thrown in the deep waters of Mississippi?[16] Why is it, oh God, that that has to happen? I begin to despair sometimes, it seems that Good Friday has the throne. It seems that the forces of injustice reign supreme. But then in the midst of that something else comes to me.

And I can hear something saying, "King, you are stopping at Good Friday, but don't you know that Easter is coming? (*Yeah*) *Don't worry* about this thing! You are just in the midst of the transition now. You are just in the midst of Good Friday now. But I want you to know, King, that *Easter* is coming! One day truth will rise up and reign supreme! (*Yeah*) One day *justice* will rise up. One day all of the children of God will be able to stand up on the *third* day and then cry, 'Hallelujah, Hallelujah' (*Yeah*) because it's the Resurrection day." (*That's the truth*)

And when I hear that I don't despair. I can cry out and sing with new meaning. This is the meaning of Easter; it answers the profound question that we confront in Montgomery. And if we can just stand with it, if we can just live with Good Friday, things will be all right. For I know that Easter is coming and I can see it coming now. As I look over the world, as I look at America, I can see Easter coming in race relations. I can see it coming on every hand. I see it coming in Montgomery. I see it coming in Alabama. I see it coming in Mississippi. Sometimes it looks like it's coming slow, but it's still coming. (*Yeah*) And when it comes, it will be a great day, for all of the children of God will be able to stand up and cry, "This is God's day. All hail the power of Jesus's name."[17] This is the meaning of it.

---

enemy sowed noxious weeds in his wheat field. The farmer instructed his servants to wait until harvest time to separate the tares from the wheat and to burn it.

15. Cf. William Cullen Bryant, "The Battlefield" (1839).

16. King refers to the January 1957 bombing of the homes of bus boycott leaders and ministers Robert Graetz and Ralph Abernathy and of several black churches. Unexploded dynamite was also discovered on King's porch during the period after the bus boycott. He also alludes to the violence that accompanied school desegregation efforts and the 1955 lynching of Emmett Till, whose brutalized body was found in Mississippi's Tallahatchie River.

17. King cites Edward Perronet's hymn "All Hail the Power of Jesus' Name" (1779).

And I want to tell you one more thing, and then I'm concluding. People are always asking, "What is the most durable power in the universe? And the fact is that Easter answers that question too. You wonder about it. What is it that is the heartbeat of the moral cosmos? What is it? Philosophers have tried to grapple with it over the years, and they moved back, and maybe Heraclitus comes out and says that it's pleasure.[18] Maybe somebody else comes out and points out to certain moral established principles. But I tell you I want to reach out and get one morally established principle for you, and said that that is the basic and underlying principle of the universe, that is the most durable power in the world. And do you know what that is? It's the power of love. Easter tells us that. Sometimes it looks like the other powers are much more durable. Then we come to see that isn't true. But the most durable, lasting power in this world is the power to love.[19] And my friends, it seems to me that history tells us that. History's a running commentary of it. We have seen the forces of military power hold the throne for a while, haven't we? And it looked like this was the most durable power in the world. It seemed that might made right. It seemed that somehow the more guns and the more ammunition you could get, the greater the power was, the greater the durability of it. Then at every point in history, we have been able to see that this kind of power passes away.

Just the other day, I stood over the tomb of Napoleon in Paris, one of the most beautiful sights in the world.[20] The greatest tomb erected to a man anywhere in the world. It can only be matched or outmatched by the Taj Mahal in India, but that's to a woman. And here that statue, that great tomb stands to a great hero, to a great warrior, to a great military genius. And as I looked there I could not only think of its beauty. But my mind for the moment went back across the centuries. I thought about Alexander the Great with all of his military power; then I said, "He came to his end." I went on back even more and started thinking of the great warrior, Asia's Genghis Khan.[21] I said that all of his power came to an end. Went back to the Caesars and thought about the great power of the Roman Empire. Then I said, "Even it came to its end by the sword, for he who lives by the sword, will die by the sword."[22] And all of the glory of Rome had to fall one day, and I could see the hordes of Visigoths marching through Rome in 510 A.D. Rome fell.[23] My mind went on back to Charlemagne, said, "He's gone."[24]

Then I started thinking of Napoleon himself. My mind ran across his life. I could see him, at the age of nineteen, walking across the banks of the Seine River con-

---

18. King mistakenly cites Heraclitus rather than Epicurus, whose philosophy is identified with the pursuit of pleasure.

19. King expanded on this theme in a sermon, from which *Christian Century* published an excerpt (King, "The Most Durable Power," Sermon at Dexter Avenue Baptist Church on 6 November 1956, 5 June 1957, pp. 302–303 in this volume).

20. King visited Paris on 18–21 March 1957 following a trip to celebrate Ghana's independence.

21. Genghis Khan (1162–1227) was a political leader and conqueror who united the Mongol tribes and created an empire that stretched from the Caspian Sea to the Sea of Japan.

22. Cf. Matthew 26:52.

23. The Visigoths sacked Rome in 410 CE. The last Roman emperor, Romulus, died in 476 CE.

24. Charlemagne unified Western Europe in the late years of the eighth century and was crowned the first Holy Roman Emperor by Pope Leo III in 800 CE. His sons divided his empire after his death in 814 CE.

templating suicide. I could see him later as he stood there around France in 1795, just at a youthful age as he came into the situation to quiet a mob. I could see him again in 1796 as he took over the army and led them to Italy, and with a group of inexperienced, ill-fed, ill-paid men, he was able to win the victory. I could see him again in 1798 when he marched into Egypt and Syria, how in the midst of that battle he was able to conquer these nations with ease. I could see him again in 1799, and he became dictator with the title of First Consul. I could see him again in 1800 as he marched into Austria, and there at the battle of Marengo, brought into being one of the greatest victories of his career. I could see him again in 1804, and he became the emperor. I could see him again in 1812, standing with all of his power. Then I saw him a year later move over into the battle of Leipzig. And I could see that same Napoleon going down, that Napoleon that had conquered more nations than *any warrior* that had ever lived. And I watched him as he marched to Waterloo. I could see Napoleon, with *all* of his military power, *dying* and *faltering* with his army at Waterloo. I said to myself, "This is the doom of every Napoleon. This is the doom of every man and every nation that feels that victory can ultimately come through force."

In the midst of that, as Coretta and I walked away from that building, I decided that my mind had to go back a little beyond that. It went back about twenty centuries. And I could see a little boy being born. I could see him at the age of thirty years old going out on his Galilean mission. He didn't have any armies with him. (*That's right*) He didn't have many followers with him. (*Come on*) He didn't even have a hundred percent cooperation from them, for one of them betrayed him and another went around and condemned, denied it, denied that he knew him.[25] And all of them deserted him at the end. But I thought about it. And I watched him as he walked around the hills of Galilee just doing good, just preaching the gospel to the brokenhearted, healing the sick and raising the dead. And I just watched him. I looked at him, and I said, "Now, he doesn't have a band [*following him?*]. He has no great army! He has no great military power." Then I can see him go with another kind of army. I can hear him as he says somehow to himself, "I'm just going to put on the breastplate of righteousness. And I'm going take the ammunition of love and the whole armor of God, and I'm just gonna march."[26] And my friends, he started marching. And after he marched a little while, he came to his Waterloo. Good Friday came, and there he was on the cross. That was his Waterloo. But the difference is that Napoleon's Waterloo ended with Waterloo. (*Amen*) Jesus's Waterloo ended transforming Waterloo. (*Amen*) And *there* came that third day. And this was the [*time?*] that he was able to reign supreme. His Waterloo couldn't stop him. He stopped Waterloo. And this became the *beginning* of his influence. This became the most powerful moment of his life. (*Yeah*)

[*As?*] I walked away from that building, I could hear choirs singing everywhere. On this side, it seemed that I could hear somebody saying:

---

25. For an example of Judas' betrayal of Jesus, see Luke 22. For an example of Peter's denials of Jesus, see Matthew 26:69–75.

26. Cf. Ephesians 6:11–17.

All hail the power of Jesus's name!
Let angels prostrate fall; (*That's the truth*)
Bring forth the royal diadem,
And crown him Lord of all.[27] (*Yeah*)

Then I could hear another choir on the other side, singing:

Jesus shall reign *where'er* the sun
Does his successive journeys run; (*Yes he will*)
His kingdom spread from *shore* to shore
Till moons shall wane and wax no more.[28] (*Amen*)

And then I could hear another choir over here singing:

In Christ there is no east or west,
In *Him* no north or south,
But one great brotherhood of love
Throughout the whole wide world.[29]

And then off from the distance, I could hear something else singing, "Hallelujah, hallelujah! He's King of Kings and Lord of Lords, hallelujah, hallelujah!" (*Yeah*) And then I could hear the echo singing, "He shall reign forever and ever (*Yes Lord*), hallelujah, hallelujah!"[30] (*Yeah*)

This is the Easter message; this is the question that it answers. It says to us that love is the most durable power in the world (*Yeah*) than all of the military giants, all of the nations that [*base?*] their way on military power. I wish this morning that you would go tell Russia, go tell America, go tell the nations of the world that atomic bombs cannot solve the problems of the universe. Go back and tell them that hydrogen bombs cannot solve the problems of the world, but it is only through love and devotion to the justice of the universe that we can solve these problems. And then we can go away saying in terms that cry out across the generations that "God reigns, he reigns supreme, the Lord God omnipotent reigneth."[31] He reigns because he established his universe on moral principles. And through the love that he revealed through Jesus Christ, things move on. These are the questions that Easter answers. God grant that as you seek to answer them you will catch the spirit of Jesus in Easter and live life with an exuberant joy.

Oh God, our gracious Heavenly Father, we come on this Easter morning, thanking Thee for revealing to us the ultimate meaning and the ultimate rationality of the universe. We thank you, this morning, for your Son, Jesus, who came by to let us know that love is the most durable power in the world, who came by to let us know that death can't defeat us, to take the sting out of the grave and death and make it

---

27. King quotes the hymn "All Hail the Power of Jesus' Name" (1779).
28. King quotes Isaac Watts's hymn "Jesus Shall Reign Where'er the Sun" (1719).
29. King quotes John Oxenham's hymn "In Christ There Is No East or West" (1908).
30. King quotes excerpts from the "Hallelujah Chorus" of George Frideric Handel's 1741 oratorio *Messiah;* see also Revelation 19:16, 11:15.
31. Cf. Revelation 19:6.

possible for all of us to have eternal life. We thank you, oh God. And God grant that we will be grateful recipients of thy eternal blessings. In the name and spirit of Jesus, we pray. Amen.

At. MLKEC: ET-20.

The Rewards of Worship, Sermon Delivered at Dexter Avenue Baptist Church

[28 April 1957]
[Montgomery, Ala.]

King encourages his congregation to appreciate participation in communal worship. He highlights several rewards of worship: it elevates participants beyond the dull monotony of life; it satisfies the human need for companionship; and it provides the resources to face life's difficulties. "I'm so glad whenever Sunday morning comes about, and I can hear something within saying, 'Let us go into the house of the Lord,' because sometimes I get a little arrogant out in the world," King proclaims. "But when I get up enough nerve to come to the house of God, it cries out in my soul and my conscience begins to ring out. And something says to me that 'You're made for the everlasting, born for the stars, created for eternity.'" The following text was taken from an audio recording of the service.[1]

"I was glad when they said unto me, Let us go into the house of the Lord."[2] Dr. [*William Ernest*] Hocking, a former professor of philosophy at Harvard University, has said somewhere that all life is divided into work and worship, what we do ourselves and what we let the higher-than-ourselves do.[3] Worship is as much a part of the human organism as the rising of the sun is to the cosmic order. Men always have worshiped, and men always will worship. This has been true in every nation; it has been true in every age; it has been true in every culture. Men find themselves unconsciously worshiping God. Buddhism, a religion theoretically without a god, would give one the impression that it is devoid of worship, but if you go into any land today where Buddhism is present, you will find worship also present. You will remember centuries ago that Confucius urged his followers not to worship and not to be concerned about the gods. But as soon as Confucius died, his followers deified him, and today hundreds and thousands of people worship Confucius.

If you will wander across the borders of Christianity into the plains of Mohammed-

---

1. This recording was dated according to an audio inventory of the Martin Luther King, Jr., Library and Archive at the King Center in Atlanta, Georgia.

2. Psalm 122:1.

3. Fosdick, *Successful Christian Living*, pp. 173–174: "Professor Hocking is right in saying that all man's life can be reduced to two aspects, work and worship—what we do ourselves, and what we let the higher than ourselves do to us."

anism, you will discover there men and women praying five times a day. Just the other day, Mrs. King and I were in Kano, Nigeria, which is a Muslim town, and we spent a day and a night there and went around that town.[4] And it was an interesting thing to notice the people as they ran back and forth to the temple. They call it the mosque. And we were out sightseeing one day, and the young man who was driving for us disappeared, and we asked the guide what happened to him. And he said, "He's gone over to pray. And this is our custom—that five times a day we go to the mosque to pray."

This seems to be the elemental function, or rather the elemental longing, of human nature. This quest and this desire to somehow be attached to something beyond self. And this isn't only true of the so-called religious man. Every man worships. It isn't only true of the man who is a devotee to Christianity or Mohammedanism or Sikhism or Hinduism or Jainism or Buddhism or any of the great religions of the world. It is true even of the so-called irreligious man. Voltaire was right, that if a man can't find God, he'll make him a god.[5] And somehow, no man can be satisfied with the sheer longing and worship of self. There must be something beyond self because there is this inner drive and this inner urge for some power outside. Men may be atheists philosophically, but they can never be psychologically. And even if a man disbelieves in God in the top of his mind, he inevitably believes in God in the bottom of his heart because there is something within the very psychological makeup of human nature that demands a god. And if man can't find the legitimate God of the ages, he makes him one. It might be some abstract something out here that he calls humanity. It might be something that he calls communism. But pretty soon he gets his relics and his saints, and he bows down before [*Joseph*] Stalin and Lenin [*Vladimir Ilyich Ulyanow*] and [*Karl*] Marx and somebody else because there is that basic drive and that basic urge that cries out for the eternal and something beyond self. Man is innately religious; man worships unconsciously.

But the important thing is to be sure that the worship drive is directed into the proper channel. That is the thing that we must always be concerned about—that our worship drive is directed into the proper channel so that we must be sure that we worship nothing short of the eternal God of the universe. And so many men have found themselves directing their worship instincts into improper, illegitimate channels. And they have ended up frustrated and disillusioned because their god wasn't big enough. Their god was a little too small.

And so this morning, I'm thinking in terms of a worship that is directed into the proper channel and the type of worship that does something to the soul. I'm thinking of the type of worship that is directed towards the eternal God whose purpose changes not. And it is this type of worship that is very rewarding. It is this type of worship that the Psalmist was talking about, I'm sure, when he said, "I was glad when they said unto me, 'Let us go into the house of the Lord,'" for the kind of worship that I'm talking about is a rewarding worship and he was glad to get to it. It has all

---

4. Following his trip to Ghana, King visited Nigeria 12–14 March 1957.
5. Voltaire, *Épîtres à l'auteur du livre des "Trois Imposteurs"* (1877): "If God did not exist, it would be necessary to invent him."

of the rewards that come to the point of making life meaningful. It lifts us above something to something higher.[6]

And I want you to think with me on the rewards of worship when it is directed into the proper channel. What does it do? So many of us worship God in diverse ways, ways that really have no basic meaning. And we get nothing out of it, and we begin to wonder why. It is because we aren't worshiping properly. You see, worship is not entertainment, for instance, and so often we have made worship merely a sort of passing state of entertainment. Oh, I go into so many places. How easy do we face the temptation of making worship merely a state of entertainment? How many preachers of the gospel go into the pulpit more concerned about the volume of their voices and how they can twist their moan to the point of entertaining the people? How much of our music has been relegated to a sort of gospel bebop where men do not get the real quality of religion but they are thrown out to a sort of secular, meaningless, jazzy type of thing that throws God out on the periphery of life? That isn't real music. That isn't real religion. That isn't real worship. It's merely entertainment.

Oh, we are not supposed to enjoy church. We are supposed to appreciate it. We enjoy entertainment; we enjoy a show. And I realize that so often our worship services degenerate into a sort of show, a sort of ecclesiastical circus where men merely show themselves off with their secular methods that have no meaning. That isn't worship. Men wonder why they don't get anything out of it. It is because it is a merely an arena of entertainment. Also, worship is not a state of cold, abstract dignity where men come to reveal what they do not know, thinking that they know. It is not a place where we come to show ourselves but we come to unfold ourselves to the Almighty God and to the ever-flowing power of His grace. And so many of us have made religion and the church little more than a sort of secular social club with a thin veneer of religiosity. And it becomes a sort of cold religion, devoid of all of the fire and power and passion and fervor that goes with real worship. So worship is neither entertainment nor is it cold, abstract, meaningless dignity. Worship is the everlasting, eternal cry for the eternal and almighty God. Worship is something of man's quest for the eternal and his communion with the Almighty. And only then is it meaningful. It has its rewards when it comes to that point.

Now, what are some of the these rewards of worship that I'm trying to think about this morning? I think the first reward of worship is that it lifts one above the dull monotony of life. That is what worship does at its best. It is one of the best forms of escape. We are always trying to find ways to escape the monotony of life. We're always trying to run from the dullness and the dull problem of sameness, and we use so many methods to do this. Some people run out into a mad world of pleasure. Some people get themselves involved and involved in the round and round of existence, trying to get away from it. But religion comes out and says that worship is the best channel. It is the best means of escape from the dull monotony of life, and every man needs this, every woman needs this. Oh, so often life is a sort of round of

---

6. King also preached on the merits of "true" worship in "Worship at Its Best," Sermon at Dexter Avenue Baptist Church, 14 December 1958, pp. 350–351 in this volume.

going to work to make the money, to buy the bread, to gain the strength to go back to work. And oh, how tiring that can be, just going around in a circle, working, making money, going back to work, making more money. And life becomes somewhat monotonous. It becomes a dull round of sameness. And there is something tired, there is something tiring and dull about it. There is something monotonous, and it can even become frustrating.

And oh, I'm so glad when Sunday comes around. And I'm so glad when it is said to me, "Let us go into the house of the Lord." For this is the moment that this dull round can be broken and I can forget about making a living and all of the problems that surround life and come into the house of God and gain a little bread, a little spiritual bread that is much more powerful than that physical or material bread that we work so hard to gain. You see, after all, the acquisitive desires of human nature are insatiable. And the more you get, the more you want. And life loses its full meaning because we get out in here trying to satisfy our desires and then we satisfy our desires and then more desires crop up. We get a thousand dollars, and we want five thousand. We get five thousand, and we want ten thousand. And then we get a million, and we want two million. And we get two million, and we want five million. And there is that round of life. These acquisitive desires of human nature finding themselves insatiable. And all of this becomes dull and monotonous.

There needs to be something to bring us to a balance, and that is what worship does. Worship lifts us above the round, the dull round, if you please, of existence and places us in tune with the infinite. And it is a beautiful break. Haven't you seen people in life work all the time? All the time. And they get so busy that nothing counts but their work. They work all the time and all the time, and they kill their health. They kill their everything. They kill their internal being. And they never find time to break off from the chain of work and come into the house of God, not realizing that by coming into house of God every Sunday it gives them a little more power to do the work a little better. But they get so involved in the chain of existence and making a living and producing a record and producing this within the working routine, that life loses something. And oh, those persons walk the streets of life with a dull meaningless existence, and they begin to wonder why. It is because they only fulfill one side of the great polar, the great pendulum of life which swings between work and worship. They begin to worship, and their worship becomes their work. It is not this legitimate work which moves over from the worship, but work itself becomes worship. But worship at its best breaks us aloose from that, and it gives us a power to go back once more and pick up the work and keep going. It lifts us above the dull round of monotonous sameness, and it gives us something that makes us one with the infinite. And gives us renewed power and strength to carry on. That is one of the great rewards of worship.

Not only that, worship provides the most thorough channel of fellowship that we can ever find. There is always the desire in human life for fellowship, and worship provides that in a way that we find it nowhere else. It provides the most thorough avenue of fellowship that we can find anywhere. [*Motorcycle is heard in background*] Don't worry about the motorcycle, we're having worship in here. We're trying to worship now. You see, that's what I'm talking about. The motorcycles have taken us away from worship. Worship somehow provides for us the channels of fellowship that we can find nowhere else, and this is something that life needs so much. We go all of the week, and we're involved in our work; we are involved in all of these things of life that we must do to make our living. And somehow we need to break away from that and forget about all of that and come to a point where we become united with God. And that's what worship does, you see. It provides fellowship to the highest degree.

Now somebody says to me, "I'm sure that that is true and we don't have to go to church to worship. We can worship at home. We can turn on the radio. They have sermons on the radio on Sunday. And there are many experiences that we can have at home and out in the regulars, the avenues of life that will provide as much worship as we can get at church." Well, I agree that it's true we can worship at home in some form; we can worship outside in some form. No one can look at the beauties of nature and fail to worship, if that person has any type of sensitive capacity for the divine. And one looks at the beauty of the sunset. And one notices the beautiful stars as they bedeck the heavens. And one notices the clouds and the skies with all of their radiant beauty. And one listens to a Wagnerian opera or a Beethoven symphony.[7] One has to worship if one has any sense of the urgency of the divine. I grant you that.

But my friends, these, none of these can be substitutes for going into the house of God and worshiping God there. Why? Because worship at its best is a social experience where men come together in a deep sense of fellowship and where they forget themselves, where they forget their offices, where they forget their life's work and come here and meet the divine, and this is the beauty of worship. And at its best, men come and realize that they are the children of a common father. This is the one place where we come and forget our degrees. And we come and forget our, the fact that we are Professor This or Dr. That or Attorney This or Mr. This. This is the one place where we come before God and forget our stations in life. It provides the best channel of fellowship, where men of all levels of life come together in a sense of unity and oneness. And they come to see that they are not doctors here. They come to see that they are not lawyers here. They come to see that they are not Ph.D.'s here, but they are all children of a common father. And worship brings us together where we somehow forget our external attachments. And I'm so glad when Sunday comes. Don't have to worry about titles. Don't have to worry about all of these things that we have in the external world that makes for our positions and our prestige and our this-and-that. This is where we come and bow before the Almighty God and forget these things because before God they aren't important anyway.

The important thing is that we are united and one with Him. And as one great Lord said as he wandered into the Church of England and the ushers moved along and tried to make the way clear and find a special seat, and he looked over to the usher and said, "No, don't do this, for there are no lords here." And that is what the house of God means, that there is no special person there, but that all men come before the throne of God and realize something that makes them one. And this is the rewarding aspect of it. We are not rich here. We are not poor here. We are not educated here. We are not uneducated here. We are not young here. We are not old

---

7. King refers to nineteenth-century German composers Richard Wagner and Ludwig van Beethoven.

here. But we are all one in Christ Jesus. And worship gives us that leveling reality that makes our lives united with our brothers because our lives are united with God. It provides that for us. [*recording interrupted*] It brings us into relationship with that which is better than the best that we have in ourselves, and thereby, it provides us with a spiritual humility that we need to live life at its best.

You see, when we are moving around in everyday life, we have nothing to compare ourselves to but our brothers and sisters round about us. And in so many instances, we are a little better than they are. Sometimes our morals are better; sometime our characters are better. And that gives us a sense of arrogance sometimes, a sense of spiritual pride. And we look over here and say, "I'm so glad that I'm not like other men. I thank God that I'm not like these people."[8] That's what happens when we just live from Monday to Saturday because we see so many people that we are a little better. We are not drunkards. We do not indulge in the things that our society considers bad. And so we are better than they are on the basis of societal norms. But then we come to the church of God on Sunday. And the norm of comparison is no longer our brother beside us, but the norm of comparison becomes the life and the teachings and the principles of Jesus Christ. And we discover there that there is something wrong in our souls. There is something that causes us to cry out when we walk into the church. [*recording interrupted*] "God of love, be merciful unto me a sinner."[9] Out in life you cried, "Thank God that I'm not like other men," but when you come in here you discover that you're a sinner because your norm of comparison is different. Out in the world, you compare yourselves with the mundane agencies, with your brothers and sisters round about you. But when you come in here, you discover that there is a tragic gap between the "oughtness" and the "isness."[10] You discover that there is a tragic gap between what you actually are and what you know that you ought to be. You discover when you come in here that your best self is separated from that other self, that worse self. And you see there something of a civil war within dividing you up, making you schizophrenic, making you split up against yourself.[11] That's what happens when you come here. And no man is ever at his best until he stands over and over again in the face of his better best, that which is better than his best. And that is what happens when you come here.

The house of God provides you with a norm of comparison which *far* outdistances that norm which you discover in everyday life. You begin to sit down before the Almighty and discover what you're made for. We forget out in life, don't we? We move around every day, and it's so easy for us to forget. We forget what we are made for because our lives are so bent on the earthy, so bent on those things which pass by in everyday life, and we so easily forget. Then when somebody cries out to us, "Let us go into the house of the Lord," there is something there that reminds. Every now and then, we discover. Every now and then, we hear something calling us to the hills. Every now and then, something cries out in our souls for the peaks.

---

8. Cf. Luke 18:11.
9. Cf. Luke 18:13.
10. Cf. Reinhold Niebuhr, *Beyond Tragedy*, pp. 137–138.
11. Fosdick, *On Being a Real Person*, p. 52.

Every now and then, we begin to breathe the stars. Every now and then, we discover that we are made for eternity. And this is what the church does for us. This is what the house of God does. It reminds us that we are not made for the valleys and the plains, but we are made for the hills and the mountains and the peaks. And when we go into the house of God that truth comes ringing out to us with new meaning. It comes over and over again.

And so I'm so glad whenever Sunday morning comes about, and I can hear something within saying, "Let us go into the house of the Lord," because sometimes I get a little arrogant out in the world. I think I'm a pretty good fellow. And I move around the streets of life and see so many things that I don't do and I'm proud about it, but then I come into the house of God and discover that I'm not so good after all. And that there are so many areas that I could improve in. And something cries out saying, "King, you are not made for the plains, but you are made for the mountains. You are not made for the far country, but you're made for your Father's house." And so long as I stay out in the world, I miss that. But when I get up enough nerve to come to the house of God, it *cries* out in my soul and my conscience begins to ring out. And something says to me that "You're made for the everlasting, born for the stars, created for eternity." That is what worship does. It throws you in relationship to the best that reality offers, and your norm of comparison becomes greater than all of the things that you can find in everyday life.

There is a final thing. And it is a great thing. Worship provides us with the strength and the power to face the most difficult situations of life. It gives us hope amid despair. It gives us something to keep us going and it gives us something to cause us to smile while other men all around are falling down in despair. Worship gives us that. And that's one of the great things about it. And we need this more than anything else.

Sometimes, my friends, you feel like this—that you don't need God. Life is beautiful. It's something like the launching of a ship. That ship stands there getting ready to pull out. And you notice the bands, the cheering and enthusiastic crowds. And they stand there with all of the beauty, the flags very high. This is the beginning, and everything is beautiful. But before that ship reaches its last harbor, it will be faced with long, drawn-out storms, howling and jostling winds, and tempestuous seas that make the heart stand still. And I say to you, life is like that. And before you reach the last harbor of life, you will be forced to stand amid the surging moment of life's restless sea. The chilly winds of adversity will blow all around you. The jostling winds of despair will be in the midst of you. And if you don't have a little something on the inside, you won't be able to make it. Religion gives you something on the inside to stand up.

And I think that's what it means at bottom. Religion never has guaranteed, it doesn't promise you that you aren't going to have any trouble in life, any trials and tribulations. You have a misconception of religion.[12] That's a sort of escape religion. That's the sort of religion that becomes what the Marxists would call the opiate of

---

12. Meek, "Strength in Adversity, A sermon preached in the Old South Church in Boston," 19 April 1953: "It is a misunderstanding and a misinterpretation of Christianity to imagine that Christianity's promise is that it will free us from life's crises." King filed a copy of Meek's homily in his sermon file.

the people.[13] That's the sort of religion that moves away from the realities of life, but religion at its best has never said that. Oh, there are some preachers who write their books on a guide to confident living. And they produce their "How" cards. And they tell you just the formula to follow and everything will work out all right. And they will talk about the power of positive thinking.[14] And religion becomes a sort of shadowy sort of thing; it becomes a thing that escapes the realities of life. It's a sort of "How," and so the Gospel is a sort of "Go ye into all of the world, and keep your blood pressure down, and I will teach you how to relax."[15] That's all the Gospel is for these people, but that isn't the Gospel. That isn't religion. Religion has a cross in it, and it says that before you can get to Easter you must go by way of Good Friday. That's religion at its best. It has *never* guaranteed that you wouldn't have the cross. Yes, there is a crown you wear, but before that there is a cross you bear. Religion says that at its best, but it says also that if you are sufficiently committed to God and His way you gain the power and the strength to stand up amid any condition that comes. And men through the ages have been able to prove that. And no matter how great the problems were, if they had faith in God, they were able to stand up.

And I know some of you this morning looking at me, some of you have experienced that. I know there have been moments that you went into life and stood before the universe thinking that you couldn't make it. Some great problem came before you, some disappointing experience, something that took away from you the best that you wanted, and you just felt that you couldn't make it. You didn't know how you were going to make it. Somehow you got enough strength and enough courage to get up on Sunday morning and run by the church of God. You got there, and you heard the sweet music of eternity. You heard a word from the scripture. You heard something from the lips of the Almighty God, and that gave you new strength and new power to carry on. "I was glad when they said unto me, 'Let us go into the house of God,'" because there is something in the house of God that gives us power and strength to stand up amid all of the tragic and difficult experiences of life.

Oh, you know the story of William Cowper, the great hymn writer, the story of how he wrote that great hymn, "God Moves in a Mysterious Way." It's said that one day he got tired, decided that he wanted to give up. Life had lost something of its meaning to him, and he had had a disappointing experience, and he didn't want to face life any longer. And in the midst of this, his emotions ran wild, and he decided to commit suicide. It's said that he walked down the banks of the Seine River in Paris, and there he stood with one foot on the bank and one foot across, getting ready to jump in the river. As he stood there, he could hear within a voice saying, "Don't jump. Don't jump." And so he decided, "Well, I'll do it another way." And he decided to go over and get a cup and drink some poison, and this would be the thing that would destroy his life in a little or no time. And he got the cup, and he

13. Karl Marx, "Contribution to the Critique of Hegel's *Philosophy of Right:* Introduction" (1844).

14. King refers to Norman Vincent Peale's book *The Power of Positive Thinking* (New York: Prentice-Hall, 1952).

15. King parodies Matthew 28:19–20: "Go ye therefore, and teach all nations, baptizing them in the name of the Father, and of the Son, and of the Holy Ghost: Teaching them to observe all things whatsoever I have commanded you: and, lo, I am with you always, even unto the end of the world. Amen."

decided to drink the poison, but as he put the cup to his lips there was something saying, "Don't drink. Don't drink."

And though he was about to give up in all types of despair and do everything, he said, "What can I do now?" And he ran on home and he said, "I know what I can do. I can end it very quickly. I'll get a pistol, and I'll shoot a bullet through my skull, and that will end it very quickly." And he went home, and he got his pistol. And he put it there and he started to shoot, but there was something in, within saying, "Don't shoot. Don't shoot." And here he stood, *wanting* to die, *wanting* to take his life, and yet there is something saying, "Don't do it!" His conscience is beating him; something is gripping him. Wanting to die, yet he can't die.

And he decided to just walk the streets. It is said that as he walked the street in the solemn quietness of the night he walked by one of the great cathedrals of Paris. And just out of curiosity he decided to go in, and he heard some singing in there. And then after getting in there for a few moments, he saw a man mount the throne, and he started talking about the man who could make a way out of no way. He heard him talking about the man of Galilee who could transform darkness into light. He heard him talking about one who was the light amid all of the dark moments of life. He heard him talking about one who was the way, the truth, and the life.[16]

And it is said that Cowper at that moment gained a new courage; he gained new strength. And he walked out on the outside of that great cathedral and took a seat on the steps. And there under the glaring light of the night he scratched across the pages of history some great words, as if to say, I know why I couldn't drink that poison. I know why I couldn't jump in that river. I know why I couldn't shoot that gun. It is because:

> God moves in a mysterious way,
> His wonders to perform;
> He plants His footsteps in the sea
> And rides above the storm.
>
> Judge not the Lord in feeble sense
> But judge Him by His grace,
> Behind the crowning providence
> He hides a smiling face.[17]

That's what worship does. It helps us to adjust to the most difficult experiences of life. And so let us go out this morning, glad that men said to us, glad that somebody said to us this morning, "Let us go into the house of the Lord. I was glad when they said unto me, Let us go into the house of the Lord."

Oh God, our gracious Heavenly Father, we thank Thee for the privilege above all privileges, and that is the privilege to worship Thee. Grant that we will never misuse worship, that we will direct it in the proper channel and receive all of the great

---

16. Cf. John 14:6.

17. Cowper wrote the hymn "God Moves in a Mysterious Way" in 1774 and composed the anti-slavery poem "The Negro's Complaint" (1788), which King often quoted.

rewards that come as a result of our kneeling before Thee in humble submission and worshiping Thee throughout the whole wide world. In the name and spirit of Jesus, we pray. Amen.

At. MLKEC: ET-62.

"The Most Durable Power,"
Excerpt from Sermon at Dexter Avenue Baptist
Church on 6 November 1956

5 June 1957
Chicago, Ill.

This excerpt was published in the 5 June 1957 Christian Century.[1]

Always be sure that you struggle with Christian methods and Christian weapons. Never succumb to the temptation of becoming bitter. As you press on for justice, be sure to move with dignity and discipline, using only the weapon of love. Let no man pull you so low as to hate him. Always avoid violence. If you succumb to the temptation of using violence in your struggle, unborn generations will be the recipients of a long and desolate night of bitterness, and your chief legacy to the future will be an endless reign of meaningless chaos.

In your struggle for justice, let your oppressor know that you are not attempting to defeat or humiliate him, or even to pay him back for injustices that he has heaped upon you. Let him know that you are merely seeking justice for him as well as yourself. Let him know that the festering sore of segregation debilitates the white man as well as the Negro. With this attitude you will be able to keep your struggle on high Christian standards.

Many persons will realize the urgency of seeking to eradicate the evil of segregation. There will be many Negroes who will devote their lives to the cause of freedom. There will be many white persons of good will and strong moral sensitivity who will dare to take a stand for justice. Honesty impels me to admit that such a stand will require willingness to suffer and sacrifice. So don't despair if you are condemned and persecuted for righteousness' sake. Whenever you take a stand for truth and justice, you are liable to scorn. Often you will be called an impractical idealist or a dangerous radical. Sometimes it might mean going to jail. If such is the case you must honorably grace the jail with your presence. It might even mean physical death. But if physical death is the price that some must pay to free their

---

1. King derived the title of this sermon from Harry Emerson Fosdick's "The Most Durable Power in the World" (*Successful Christian Living,* pp. 86–96). King annotated a copy of Fosdick's book and kept it in his personal library. A few months earlier King had published an article entitled "Nonviolence and Racial Justice" in the February 1957 *Christian Century* (in *Papers* 4:118–122).

children from a permanent life of psychological death, then nothing could be more Christian.

I still believe that standing up for the truth of God is the greatest thing in the world. This is the end of life. The end of life is not to be happy. The end of life is not to achieve pleasure and avoid pain. The end of life is to do the will of God, come what may.

I still believe that love is the most durable power in the world. Over the centuries men have sought to discover the highest good. This has been the chief quest of ethical philosophy. This was one of the big questions of Greek philosophy. The Epicureans and the Stoics sought to answer it; Plato and Aristotle sought to answer it. What is the *summum bonum* of life?[2] I think I have discovered the highest good. It is love. This principle stands at the center of the cosmos. As John says, "God is love."[3] He who loves is a participant in the being of God. He who hates does not know God.

From a sermon preached in Montgomery, Alabama, November 6, 1956.

PD. *Christian Century* 74 (5 June 1957): 708–709.

---

2. *Summum bonum* is Latin for "highest good."
3. 1 John 4:8, 16.

"Overcoming an Inferiority Complex," Sermon Delivered at Dexter Avenue Baptist Church

[*14 July 1957*]
[*Montgomery, Ala.*]

This sermon was the first of a series concerning "Problems of Personality Integration" that King preached during the summer of 1957.[1] He uses the story of Jesus's inter-action with Zacchaeus, a diminutive tax-collector, as a means of encouraging his listeners to accept themselves, to devote their lives to a greater purpose, and to develop an abiding faith. "It's so easy for us to feel that we don't count, that we are not sig-nificant, that we are less than," King tells the congregation. "We stand every day before a system which says that to us. But I say to you this morning, you should go out with the assurance that you belong and that you count and that you are some-body because God loves you." In developing the sermon, King incorporates ideas found in Harry Emerson Fosdick's essay "The Principle of Self-Acceptance."[2] This transcription is taken from an audio recording of the service.

---

1. "Members Enjoying Sermon Series," *Dexter Echo*, 7 August 1957.
2. Fosdick, *On Being a Real Person*, pp. 52–78. King annotated his copy of this book and kept it in his personal library. Benjamin Mays also dealt with this theme of African American inferiority in a similar way ("Inferiority Among Negroes," *Pittsburgh Courier*, 10 May 1947).

This morning I want to discuss with you a very practical problem, and I want to try to deal with it in a practical manner. We're using as the subject "Overcoming an Inferiority Complex." "Overcoming an Inferiority Complex." There is hardly anyone here this morning who has not at some time experienced a deep feeling of inadequacy. How many of us have been almost overwhelmed by an appalling sense of inferiority? This is one of those experiences that seems to run the whole gamut of human life. Some years ago a survey was taken, a psychological survey on the hundreds of college students, and it was revealed that more than ninety percent of those students suffered from a nagging, frustrated feeling of inferiority.[3]

Certainly many of the great men of history have been dogged with this feeling of inadequacy. Take, for example, Sir Walter Scott. Many of us feel that his *Ivanhoe* is one of the greatest tales ever told.[4] But there were times in the early life of Sir Walter Scott that he was discouraged because he wanted to be a poet. And he used to look and read the works of Lord Byron, and he would become envious and felt greatly inadequate because he couldn't do what Byron was doing.[5] And in the early years of his life, Sir Walter Scott was so overwhelmed with a sense of inadequacy that he was ashamed of his first writings and had most of them published anonymously.

It is probably true that the inferiority complex is one of the most stagnating and strangulating and crushing conditions of the human personality. It distorts the personality and plunges it into the abyss of inner conflicts. And so one of the first things that individuals must do to integrate themselves and to be sure that their personalities are integrated is to seek to overcome a feeling of inferiority. This is one of the first and basic conditions of life.

Now there are several ways that we do this, and one of the most beautiful examples in all scripture of an individual who was plagued with a sense of inferiority and who later overcame that sense of inferiority because of his devotion and allegiance to Jesus Christ is found in the passage that I read this morning for our scripture lesson. You will remember that Zacchaeus was a man who felt a deep sense of inferiority because of his size. He was small; he was a very little man. And because of this he felt inferior. He felt that he did not belong. He felt that he was not accepted. And so he decided to get back at society, to pay society back by turning to some method of gaining attention, and this was to become a tax collector. He turned to Roman culture and became a tax collector. And after becoming a tax collector he made big money, and he tried to live a life foreign to his actual nature. You will remember also that in the midst of this condition he had an experience with Jesus.[6] But he tried to get away from his sense of inferiority by paying society back and being something that he wasn't.

---

3. Fosdick, *On Being a Real Person*, p. 61: "One study of 275 college men and women revealed that over 90% of them suffered from gnawing, frustrated feelings of deficiency." In his copy of Fosdick's book, King bracketed this section and wrote "imp" in the margin. This study was cited in psychologist Gordon Allport's book *Personality: A Psychological Interpretation* (New York: Henry Holt, 1945), p. 174. Allport's book was included on George W. Davis's bibliography for his course Religious Development of Personality (Davis, "Selected bibliography, Religious Development of Personality," 12 September–22 November 1950).

4. Sir Walter Scott, Scottish novelist and poet, published *Ivanhoe* in 1791.

5. George Gordon, Lord Byron, was a nineteenth-century English Romantic poet.

6. Cf. Luke 19:1–10.

Now throughout life we see these conditions quite similar to that of Zacchaeus. Many people express it in different forms, and this sense of inferiority is caused by many different things. Some people feel a sense of inferiority because they are physically handicapped. And some people feel a sense of inferiority because of ill health. Other people feel a sense of inferiority because they lack social charm. Others feel a sense of inferiority because they are not attractive externally. And others feel a sense of inferiority because of love failures and because of moral failures.[7] There are many things and manifold reasons why individuals fall down under the load of an inferiority complex. And one of the great challenges of life is to properly overcome a sense of inferiority.

Now people try many methods to overcome inferiority; like Zacchaeus they try different things which are not constructive. For instance, some people try to overcome their inferiority complex by turning to or fleeing to a world of fantasy and daydreaming and the world of illusion. And you will find a lot of people doing that. They attempt to get away from the realities of life by daydreaming or by turning to a world of illusion. And so the things that they cannot do in actual life they believe that they are doing it anyway through daydreaming. And so they find themselves the victims of endless and meaningless and crippling daydreams.[8] That is one of the reasons that many people become drunkards. They start out trying to get away from an inferiority complex, and that's the way they try to drowned it out. And so in the midst of their inferiority complex, they turn to drunkardness, and they become what they are not when they are sober. They get drunk in order to escape the feeling of limitation, the feeling of handicap. And this is a way, a method, they feel, of getting away from the conditions of actual life.

Now we all know the dangers of this method of overcoming inferiority complex. It is dangerous in the sense that it leads to divisions within one's personality. Psychologists tell us that the more individuals attempt to escape the realities of life through daydreaming and drunkardness the thinner and thinner their personalities become until ultimately they split. And they have a big word; they call it the schizophrenic personality. This is the split personality. Individuals become so accustomed and absorbed in running away from the conditions of life, in trying to escape their actual selves, that their personalities actually become so thin that they split and the real self recedes into the background.

I remember very vividly, when I was in school in Boston, one of my very dear friends had a nervous breakdown. And he had to be taken away to a mental institution, and I visited him on several [*occasions?*] [*recording interrupted*] overcome an inferiority complex by using the method of the fox in *Aesop's Fables*. That is by calling all grapes sour that they can't reach.[9] You find a lot of people who live life by

---

7. Fosdick, *On Being a Real Person*, p. 61: "The areas of their conscious inferiority were manifold— physical incompetence, ill health, unpleasant appearance, lack of social charm, failure in love, low-grade intellectual ability, moral failure, and guilt."

8. Fosdick, *On Being a Real Person*, p. 63: "Others deal with this tension between the actual and the desired self by fantasy. Unable in the real world to secure their longed-for eminence, they retreat into the world of daydream."

9. Fosdick, *On Being a Real Person*, p. 62: "Others, like the fox in Aesop's fable, handle the problem of bitterly felt inferiority by calling sour all grapes they cannot reach."

belittling other people. They get a sort of inner satisfaction and a sense of superiority by pulling everybody else down. That is how they live; that is how they overcome their sense of inferiority. They belittle everybody else, and their lives are based on a negative. They live a life of criticism and a life of negativism. They find something wrong with everybody else who lives in the universe. Now, when you see people like that, these are persons victimized with an inferiority complex, and they are trying to overcome that inferiority complex in the wrong way.

And so often you will find a young fellow who is weak and frail condemning all athletics. And so often you will find the individual who has no self-control calling everybody who has self-control a prude or something like that. And so often you will find a person who could not finish school or who did not have opportunity to get an education calling everybody with education a person who's trying to be a big shot or a person who's stuck up. So often you will find an unattractive young lady calling every beautiful young lady supercilious and selfish and stuck up. So often people find within other people belittling elements because they are trying to justify their sense of inadequacy and their inferior feelings.[10] This is one of the ways that people use to overcome an inferiority complex. That, too, is a destructive way.

There's another way—I call this the "smoke-screen" method. People try to overcome a sense of inferiority by giving the impression that they are superior. And you see people, you think they have a superiority complex. It isn't that. They have basically an inferiority complex, and they try to give the world the impression that they are really superior, so they boast all the time. They talk about how much they have. They talk about how much money they have, how much education they have, how much they can do. They brag and boast, and they are cocky all of the time.[11] Occasionally you will find a husband in the home who is dictatorial, and he has to convince his wife all the time that he's the boss, and he's going to run things and he knows more than she knows. Now he isn't superior; he's really inferior, and he is trying to overcome his inferiority through the impression that he is superior. These are the methods that people so often use in an attempt to overcome an inferiority complex. But as I said, these are the unhealthy methods.

Now let us turn for the few moments left to what I would call the healthy ways of overcoming a sense of inferiority, using as our basis the situation of Zacchaeus as he confronted Jesus. That passage says that Jesus went home with Zacchaeus, and I can imagine that Jesus said several things to him. As I know Jesus, I can about think of the things that he said to Zacchaeus. Zacchaeus, in his feeling of littleness, in his physi-

---

10. Fosdick, *On Being a Real Person*, pp. 62–63: "The frail youth discounts athletics; the debauchee, really suffering from a sense of guilt, scoffs at the self-controlled as prudes; the failure at school or college, deeply humiliated, scorns intellectuals as 'high-brows'; the girl without charm exaggerates her liability, dresses crudely, adopts rough manners, deliberately looks her worst, professing lofty disdain of charm as triviality. A major amount of cynicism springs from this source. Watch what people are cynical about, and one can often discover what they lack, and subconsciously, beneath their touchy condescension, deeply wish they had."

11. Fosdick, *On Being a Real Person*, p. 62: "Some deal with it by the smoke-screen method. Feeling miserably inferior, and not wanting others to know it, the shy become aggressive, the embarrassed effusive, and the timid bluster and brag. The boastful, cocky, pushing man may seem afflicted with an exaggerated sense of his superiority, whereas in fact he is covering under a masquerade of aggressiveness a wretched feeling of inadequacy."

cal littleness, in his lack of physical stature, developed this deep sense of inferiority. And Jesus went home with him that day, and I can imagine the first thing Jesus said to Zacchaeus: " Zacchaeus, come down from that tree, and accept yourself as you actually are. Don't try to be anybody else except yourself. And if you will do that, Zacchaeus, you will be able to face every condition of life with a healthy attitude."

Now it seems to me that that is the first way to overcome an inferiority complex—the principle of self-acceptance. That's a prayer that every individual should pray: "Lord, help me to accept myself." Every man should somehow say, "I, John Doe, accept myself with all of my inherited abilities and handicaps. I accept those conditions within my environment which cannot be altered or which I cannot control. And after accepting these I go back to myself and see what I can do with myself." And this is a healthy attitude of life. So many people are busy trying to be somebody else, and that is what accounts for their frustration. There is within every man a bit of latent creativity seeking to break forth, and it is often blocked because we are busy trying to be somebody else. So this is the first way to overcome an inferiority complex: accept yourself. That means accept your looks. It means accept your limitations in every area. It means what it says: "Accept your actual self." And where the conflict really comes is that individuals find a sort of impassable gulf between their actual selves and their desired selves. And that is when an inferiority complex breaks out in morbid proportions—when individuals come to see that there is such a tremendous gap between their actual selves and their desired selves. And the thing that every individual should pray to the Almighty God for is to give them that sense of acceptance of the actual self with all limitations and with all of the endowments that come as the results of our being born in this world.

We should ask God to help us to accept ourselves and to use our tools no matter how dull they are. I've used this example quite often. I remember when I was in college; I was taking a very difficult course, that many of you have taken I'm sure, called statistics, and I've never been a great mathematician.[12] And we had the job, you know, of finding the mead, mode, and medium, and standard deviation. And I remember that I had a classmate who is now the bursar, I mean the registrar, of Morehouse College, and he had a tremendous faculty for taking up things in the mathematical realm and doing them in just a few minutes. And I thought that I was to do it just like he did it. He could do it in just a few minutes. And I was going to do this thing like Leif Cain. I was gonna do this thing just like he did it. I knew I had the capacity of Leif Cain, and he would turn it out. And I discovered that I would try to do it in the same length of time, and I didn't get it. And I finally had to accept the fact, and it was kind of difficult at first, but I had to come to see that Leif Cain had a better mind than I had. He had a better capacity for grasping this particular thing. And so while he could do it in one hour, I had to spend three hours in doing it.[13] I had to just come down to the point of accepting myself and my dull tools and doing it the best that I could, and this is the thing that every individual must do.

We must come to see that we can accept ourselves and live life in a healthy manner.

---

12. King received an incomplete in Statistics at Morehouse in the fall of 1947 and earned a C in Principles and Methods of Statistics in the spring of 1948.

13. Leif Cain graduated in 1948 from Morehouse College, where he later served as bursar and assistant treasurer.

A Ford trying to be a Cadillac is absurd. But if a Ford accepts itself, it can be just as durable as a Cadillac, and it can turn many curves that a Cadillac can't even make, and park in many places that a Cadillac could never get in and can take off with a speed that a Cadillac can never take off with. And in life some people are Cadillacs, and other people are Fords. And when the Ford learns to accept itself as a Ford, it can do things that the Cadillac could never do. This is the thing that Jesus told Zacchaeus: "Zacchaeus, accept yourself and you will be able to overcome any sense of inferiority."

Now along with that point, I'm sure Jesus added this: "That you must remember, Zacchaeus, that anything that you do for the upbuilding of humanity is significant no matter how small you think it is. Don't consider your work insignificant. Consider it of cosmic significance." All of the people of the world cannot do the so-called big things. Some of us will have to be content to do the so-called little things, but we must do the little things in a big way. We must do the ordinary things in an extraordinary manner. And we overcome our sense of inferiority by doing just this—by somehow accepting what we have to do and doing that thing well. No matter how small you consider it, you can dignify anything. I have a friend around on Hall Street, Urelee Gordon who shines shoes occasionally.[14] And I just love to go there to get a shoeshine. He can do more with just shining shoes than most people can do with their Ph.D.'s. He can get more music out of a rag shining shoes than Louis Armstrong can get out of a trumpet. And I just love to see him shine shoes. He has dignified shoeshining. And that is what men and women must come to see—that anything can be dignified if the way that you do it and the enthusiasm that you put in it. As I like to say, if it falls your lot to be a street sweeper in life, sweep streets like Raphael painted pictures.[15] Sweep streets like Michelangelo carved marble. Sweep streets like Beethoven composed music. Sweep streets like Shakespeare wrote poetry. Sweep streets so well that all the hosts of heaven and earth will have to pause and say, "Here lived a great street sweeper who swept his job well."[16] And then you come to see the meaning of Douglas Malloch's words:

> If you can't be a pine on the top of the hill
> Be a shrub in the valley—but be
> The best shrub on the side of the rill,
> Be a bush if you can't be a tree.
>
> If you can't be a highway, just be a trail,
> If you can't be the sun be a star,
> It isn't by size that you win or you fail—
> Be the best of whatever you are![17]

And when you do that you overcome this sense of inferiority. You become like the squirrel who stood before the mountain one day. He looked up and noticed its gigantic peaks and its curvaceous slopes. He stood back and said, "Talents differ; all

---

14. Urelee Gordon was the proprietor of the Gordon Shoe Shine Parlor in Montgomery.
15. Raphaello Sanzio (1483–1520) was a prominent Italian Renaissance painter.
16. At an Atlanta NAACP rally on 1 January 1957, King attributed this illustration to Benjamin Mays (King, "Facing the Challenge of a New Age," in *Papers* 4:79).
17. King paraphrases Douglas Malloch's poem "Be the Best of Whatever You Are" (1926).

is well and wisely put. If I cannot take a forest on my back neither can you crack a nut."[18] When you see that, the squirrel gives us a philosophy to live by, that all of us can do something that somebody else can't do. You take that and do it well. And when you do that all of the eternity strikes silent, and the angels shout for joy, saying that this is an individual who has discovered the way to live life.

I imagine Jesus said another thing to Nicodemus, I mean, to Zacchaeus. He probably said, " Zacchaeus, you must master, to put it in our modern psychological terms, substitutionary compensation. You must learn that even though you are inadequate at certain points, you can take those inadequate points and transform them into something adequate. You can compensate, to use another modern psychological phrase, you can sublimate and take these inadequacies and somehow transform them into something meaningful and something constructive." So the young lady who is unattractive, who is homely, can develop a charm and an inner beauty and a personality that all of the world will have to respect.[19] And haven't you seen individuals who are not blessed with the beauty of human nature, who are not blessed with external beauty, but they developed a sort of soul beauty? And when you looked at them, you did not look at their external countenance, but you looked within, and you saw there a beauty that even the person with external beauty could never comprehend. This is the thing that is so significant and so vital: substitutionary compensation. Here is a young man who's shy and who's all but diffident. Because of that maybe he feels that he has no place in life. He can't get over his shyness. But maybe he can take that shyness and direct it into the channel of great scientific research and great artistic development and leave a lasting contribution to humanity that all men must be proud of. There are ways that even individuals with inadequacies can transform them into amazingly adequate points. And I'm sure Zacchaeus heard these words from the Master: "Zacchaeus you may be short, you may be little, your stature may be unequal to that of other men, but you have within you the possibilities of an equality that the world can always respect. You can substitute. You can compensate."

There is another vital thing which I am sure Jesus said to Zacchaeus. He probably said to him, "Zacchaeus, come down out of the tree, and give yourself to some ideal and some purpose greater than yourself. And by absorbing yourself in some cause, in some principle, in some ideal greater than yourself, you overcome your sense of inferiority."[20] So many people feel inferior because they have their egos on their hands.[21] The ego stands out as a sore thumb, oversensitive and easily hurt. The thing that individuals must do somehow is push the ego in the background by becoming absorbed in great causes and in great ideals and in great principles. I

---

18. Fosdick, *Meaning of Prayer* (New York: Association Press, 1949), p. 80: "As in Emerson's parable of the mountain and the squirrel, he can be undismayed by the special excellence of another, and can say as the squirrel did to the mountain, 'If I cannot carry forests on my back, Neither can you crack a nut.'" Fosdick referred to Ralph Waldo Emerson's poem "Fable" (1847).

19. Fosdick, *On Being a Real Person*, pp. 65–66: "Even so, however, a substitutionary compensation is almost always possible. The homely girl may develop the more wit and charm because she is homely."

20. Reinhold Niebuhr, *Moral Man and Immoral Society* (New York: Charles Scribner's Sons, 1932), p. 257: "The individual must strive to realise his life by losing and finding himself in something greater than himself."

21. Fosdick wrote an essay titled "Getting Oneself Off One's Hands" (*On Being a Real Person*, pp. 79–107).

Overcoming an Inferiority Complex

There is hardly a person here this morning who has not at times experienced a deep feeling of inadequacy. How many of us have been almost overwhelmed with an appalling sense of inferiority. One study of 275 college students revealed that more than 90% of them suffered from gnawing frustrated feelings of inadequacy. The feeling of inferiority has dogged the steps of many a great man. Take the example of Sir Walter Scott. Many consider his Ivanhoe one of the best tales ever written, yet what a discouraged young man Sir Walter Scott was, for he wanted to be a poet. He was so overwhelmed with the feeling of inferiority that

Handwritten sermon outline King may have used to preach "Overcoming an Inferiority Complex" at Dexter (14 July 1957).

he was ashamed of his first writings and published some of them anonymously.

The inferiority complex is one of the most stagnating and strangulating psycological conditions. It distorts the personality, and plunges one into the abyss of inner conflict. In a real sense ones personality integration is determined by the way he handles his sense of inadequacy.

The situations that give rise to the sense of inferiority are manifold indeed — physical hadicaps, ill health, unpleasant appearance, lack of social charm, failure in love, lack of high intellectual ability.

We turn to the New Testament for the best example of a man who first mishandled his sense of inferiority and then successfully overcome it when he fell one day under the influence of Christ. Zacchaeus' ~~comp~~ felt a sense of inferiority because of his size; he was an extremely little ~~man~~.

1. Other People go further than Zacchaeus; they turn ~~to~~ many unhealthy ~~ways~~ to handle the problem of inferiority.

2. Some of the ways persons handle the problem

A. ~~Some~~ deal with it by fleeing into a world of fantasy and illusion. ~~They~~ become in a daydreaming world what they cannot be in actual life.

(1) Daydreaming — ~~Can~~ be a useful faculty; it can furnish harmless escape from loneliness and struggle; but when it becomes an escape from the realities of life it is harmful.

(2) Drinking — the reason why many people become habitual drunkards is to overcome their feeling of inferiority. Through drink they become what they cannot be when sober. By drink a man seeks to lift himself from his actual limitations into the comforting illusion of greatness and grandeur.

(3) The danger of these methods is that they cloxing temporary glory without peace. It leads to split personalities

B. Others, like the Fox in Aesop's fable, handle the problem by calling sour all grapes they cannot reach. They belittle everything that seems to be beyond their reach, that is superior to the

think that is what Jesus meant when he said, "He who seeks to find his life shall lose it, and he who loses his life for my sake shall find it."[22] In other words, he who seeks to find his ego will lose his ego, but he who loses his ego in some great cause greater than his ego shall find his ego. This is the thing that challenges us.

We look back across the years, and we see a great man like Abraham Lincoln. We see the great contribution that he made to humanity and to history. You must never forget that up until he was forty-five years old Abraham Lincoln was one of the most discouraged men that ever lived. He felt a sense of insignificance. He ran for the state legislature and was defeated there. He went into business and failed there and spent seventeen years of his life paying off the debt of a worthless partner. He met the girl that he so passionately loved and wanted to marry, and she died. In 1846 he ran for Congress and was elected, and two years later he was defeated. He ran for the United States Senate, was defeated there. In 1856 he ran for the vice presidency of the United States and was defeated there. And two years later Douglas defeated him again. Lincoln was about to feel that he was insignificant, that he did not count, that he did not belong. Then Lincoln, one day, became interested in the slavery issue, and he gave his life to this cause. He became embedded in this cause. And because of his being embedded in this cause, in giving himself to this cause and losing himself into this cause, he became a great man. He was finally elected the president of the United States, and today all history adores him as one of its most noble citizens. There stands a monument to him in Washington no one can hardly enter without shedding tears.[23]

When H. G. Wells was called upon to list the seven great men of history, he'd look back and picked Jesus of Nazareth.[24] He'd look back to Greece and pick Socrates. He had looked over to India and picked Mahatma Gandhi, but he said, "Before I stop, I must turn my eyes to America and pick Abraham Lincoln." This man became great because he absorbed himself in a cause greater than himself. And so many people have a sense of inferiority today because they aren't doing anything. They aren't doing anything but going to work and coming home and sitting down thinking of themselves, and their life is lived in a mirror room where everywhere they look they see themselves. And so they live a life of inferiority which leads to morbid and tragic ends. This is so important. This is so vital, to lose yourself in a cause greater than yourself and give yourself to it.

---

22. Cf. Matthew 10:39, 16:25.

23. Fosdick, "A Man Is What He Proves to Be in an Emergency," in *On Being Fit to Live With*, pp. 155–156: "Once there was a man in Springfield, Illinois, who ran for the legislature and was defeated. Then he entered business, and failed, and spent seventeen years paying the debts of a worthless partner. He fell passionately in love with the girl of his choice who loved him in return, and then she died. He was elected to Congress in 1846 and served one term but was defeated when he ran for re-election. Next, he tried to get an appointment to the United States Land Office and failed. Then, becoming a candidate for the United States Senate, he was defeated. In 1856 as a candidate for the vice presidency he was beaten, and two years later Douglas defeated him again. And when at last he became President, the first thing that happened was a great war that he would have given his life to prevent. What a lifetime of testing! But in Washington there is a Memorial to him that some of us can hardly enter without tears."

24. Benjamin Mays, "Non-Violence," *Pittsburgh Courier*, 28 February 1948: "Some years ago, H. G. Wells named six great men of history. They were: Buddha, Asoka, Aristotle, Jesus, Roger Bacon and Abraham Lincoln"; see also Bruce Barton, "H. G. Wells on the Six Greatest Men in History," *Strand Magazine* (September 1922): 214.

There is a final point. I'm sure Jesus said to Zacchaeus, "If you really want to overcome this sense of inferiority, develop an abiding religious faith." Because there is something about religion that gives you a sense of belonging. I'm sure you've read of the great psychoanalyst Carl Jung. Jung said some years ago, "Of all of the hundreds and thousands of patients that have come to me for treatment and counsel over the past few years, I think I can truly say that all of them past the middle of life had conditions which could be cured by the proper religious faith."[25] That isn't a preacher talking. That's a psychoanalyst talking. Irreligion somehow leaves us standing in a blind universe. It says to us somehow that human life is nothing but a cosmic accident on a minor planet, a sort of haphazard by-product of blind forces.[26] Says to us somehow that man is nothing but a tiny vagary of whirling electrons, a wisp of smoke from a limitless smoldering. But then religion comes over and says, "Oh no," that this universe has meaning and that every individual in this universe counts and every individual in this universe has significance because there is a God who guides the destiny of life. There is a God who stands at the center of the universe, and he who discovers this principle begins to live.

And I would say to you this morning that you have an opportunity to feel that you're somebody if you develop early the proper religious faith. In our society, in which it's so easy for us to feel that we don't count, in which it's so easy to feel that we are sort of depersonalized cogs in a vast industrial machine, this has vital significance. And this has a lot of significance for the race problem and for every Negro who stands in America. It's so easy for us to feel inferior because we have lived so long amid the tragic midnight of injustice and oppression. This is one thing that the great social psychologists have been saying across the past few years—that segregation generates a feeling of inferiority, that it gives the individuals under the system an inferiority complex. We can hear it ringing from Dr. Gordon Allport of Harvard and Dr. Gardner Murphy of Columbia, from Dr. Kenneth Clark of New York University, that these inferior feelings develop because of the system of segregation.[27] And it's so easy for us to feel that we don't count, that we are not significant, that we are less than. We stand every day before a system which says that to us. But I say to you this morning, you should go out with the assurance that you belong and that you count and that you are somebody because God loves you. And that becomes a hope. That is the vital point. When men can see the true meaning of the great religion of the ages, they can find a new sense of dignity and a new sense of belonging. And they can walk through life with a self-respect, with a sense of dignity that nothing can take from them.

---

25. King paraphrases C. G. Jung, *Modern Man in Search of a Soul*, p. 264; see also Fosdick, *On Being a Real Person*, p. 74.

26. C. S. Lewis, *Answers to Questions on Christianity*, p. 10.

27. Harvard professor Gordon Willard Allport wrote *The Nature of Prejudice* (Cambridge: Addison-Wesley Publishing, 1954). Columbia University psychology professor Edgar Gardner Murphy wrote *Problems of the Present South*, which considered the emotional, intellectual, and social barriers that keep African Americans and whites from seeing themselves and each other as they are (New York: Macmillan, 1904). Kenneth Bancroft Clark was a social psychologist who taught at the City College of New York and whose 1950 study on the effects of racial segregation on children was used by the Legal Defense Fund of the National Association for the Advancement of Colored People (NAACP) in its case, *Brown vs. Board of Education* (1954). In an 1989 oral history, Clark reminisced about his "wonderful debates" with King on the

That was what happened around slavery. People lived amid the dark days of slavery. So many things stood there to discourage them, but the old preacher would come up with his broken language. He would look out to them and said, "Friends, you ain't no nigger. You ain't no slave, but you God's chillun."[28] And that gave them something to make another week. They knew in many instances that they had to go out into the field and work all day from camp to camp. They knew that they would be beaten and trampled over and kicked about. Sometimes the women knew that they had to give up their bodies to satisfy the biological urges of the old, mean, white boss. They knew that as soon as their children were born they would be snatched from their hands like a hungry dog snatches a bone from a human hand. They lived amid the darkness and the anger and the anguish of slavery, and sometimes I'm sure they felt like giving up. Then they got something within their soul; their religion began to ring out to them. They did not know anything about the lasting traditions of intellectual systems. They had probably never heard of Plato or Aristotle. They could have never understood Einstein's theory of relativity. They knew nothing about a compound or complex sentence. They didn't know the difference between "you does" and "you don't," but they knew God. They knew that the God that they had heard about in the New Testament was not a God that would subject some of his children and exalt the others. And so although they knew that some days they had to go out into the field in their bare feet, that didn't stop them. And they could sing in their broken language:

> I got shoes, you got shoes,
> All of God's chillun got shoes.
> When I get to heaven gonna put on my shoes
> And just walk all over God's heaven.
>
> I got a robe, you got a robe,
> All of God's chillun got a robe.
> When I get to heaven gonna put on my robe
> And just gonna shout all over God's heaven.[29]

They had something that kept them going. And I say to you this morning go out of this church with a new faith in yourself, with a new self-confidence, with a new sense of dignity, knowing that there is a God in this universe who loves all of his children. And although [*recording interrupted*]

At. MLKEC: ET-62.

---

philosophy of nonviolence and "about telling the masses of blacks that they should 'love the oppressor.'" He reflected further, saying, "No matter how you define it, no matter how many of the Greek words you use to differentiate the various kinds of love, let's face the fact that oppressed human beings do not react to oppression by philosophy" (Clark, "Reminiscences of Kenneth Bancroft Clark," interview by Ed Edwin, Oral History Research Office, Columbia University, New York, 1989, pp. 282–283).

28. Thurman, *Jesus and the Disinherited,* p. 50: "When I was a youngster, this was drilled into me by my grandmother. The idea was given to her by a certain slave minister who, on occasion, held secret religious meetings with his fellow slaves. How everything in me quivered with the pulsing tremor of raw energy when, in her recital, she would come to the triumphant climax of the minister: 'You—you are not niggers. You—you are not slaves. You are God's children.'"

29. King quotes the spiritual "All God's Chillun Got Wings."

The Mastery of Fear

King delivered "The Mastery of Fear" as the second in his series on "Problems of Personality Integration."[1] He kept the following three handwritten documents in the same file folder. In each, King urges his listeners to openly confront their fears. He incorporates quotations found in Harry Emerson Fosdick's sermon "The Conquest of Fear," Fosdick's essay "Dealing with Fear and Anxiety," a newspaper column by Benjamin Mays, and Robert McCracken's sermon "What to Do with Our Fears?"[2]

The Mastery of Fear, Sermon notes

[21 July 1957]
[Montgomery, Ala.]

They are part of the fee we pay for [*citizen?*]

1. Of primary importance in dealing with fear is making a practice of looking fairly and squarly at the object of our dread.[3] Emerson "He has not learded the lesson of life who does not eveyday surmount a fear."[4]

One of the chief services of ministers and psychiatrists is to be listening-posts, where crammed bosoms, long burdendd with surreptitious fears, can unload themselves.[5]

Fear of dark, of water, of closed places, of high place, of cats, of Friday, of walking undr a ladder, fear of resposinblity; of old age and death[6]

Get them in open and sometimes laugh at them. Dr Sadler said "Ridicule is the master cure of fear and axiety."

2. There is an area of fear which mist be mastered with goodwill and love.

3. It is overcome by possessing adequate interior Resources

The cure of fear is Faith[7]

AD. CSKC: Sermon file, folder 45, "Mastering Our Fears."

---

1. "Members Enjoying Sermon Series," *Dexter Echo*, 7 August 1957.

2. Fosdick, *The Hope of the World*, pp. 59–68; Fosdick, *On Being a Real Person*, pp. 108–132; Mays, "Two Fears," *Pittsburgh Courier*, 20 July 1946; McCracken, *Questions People Ask*, pp. 122–129.

3. McCracken, *Questions People Ask*, p. 125: "The first is that we make a practice of looking fairly and squarely at our fears." Fosdick, *On Being a Real Person*, p. 112: "Of primary importance in dealing with fear is the need of getting out into the open the object of our dread and frankly facing it."

4. Ralph Waldo Emerson, "Courage," in *Society and Solitude* (1870). Fosdick also used this quote in *On Being a Real Person*, p. 115.

5. Fosdick, *On Being a Real Person*, p. 113: "One of the chief services of ministers and psychiatrists is to be listening-posts, where crammed bosoms, long burdened with surreptitious fears, can unload themselves."

6. Fosdick, *The Hope of the World*, p. 63: "Fear of the dark, fear of water, fear of closed places, fear of open places, fear of altitude, fear of death, fear of hell, fear of cats, fear of Friday the thirteenth, fear of walking under a ladder—anybody who knows that hinterland and slum district of the mind knows how tragic it is."

7. Fosdick, *On Being a Real Person*, p. 132: "It was a psychiatrist, Dr. Sadler, who, having said in one place, 'Ridicule is the master cure for fear and anxiety,' struck a deeper note when he said in another, 'The only known cure for fear is *faith*.'" For the source of this quote, see William S. Sadler, *The Mind at Mischief* (New York: Funk & Wagnalls, 1929), p. 43.

[21 July 1957]
[Montgomery, Ala.]

I   Int. There is probably no emotion that plagues and crumbles the human personality more than that of fear. Every where we turn we ~~meet~~ see that monster fear; every road we travel we meet that monster fear. Fear expresses itself is such diverse forms—fear of others, fear of oneself, fear of growing old, fear of death, fear of change, fear of disease and poverty; Russia fears America and America fears Russia, the young lady fears that she will not be married, the ~~impure~~ wrongdoer fears that he will get caught.[8] Every where we turn we see that monster fear; every road we travel we meet that monster fear. Fear begins to accumulate to the point that at last many face what psychiatrists call phobophobia, the fear of fear, being afraid of being afraid.[9] Fear of death. The terrifying spectacle of atomic warfare has put Hamelet's words "To be or not to be" on millions of trembling lips.[10] Fear has risen to such extensiv propotions in ~~the~~ contemporary ~~world~~ life that one of the leading psychiatrists of the world has said: "If fear were abolished from modern life, the work of the psychotherapist would be nearly gone."[11]

II   Text: It seems that Jesus had an amazing insight into the tragic and ominous effects that can flow forth from fear. He was continually saying to his followers "fear not" "Be not afraid" Be not anxious"

III   Now we must make it clear that the admonition Be not afraid does not mean get rid of all fear. Without fear the human race could have never survived Fear is the elemental alarm system of the human organism which make it sensitive to the first sign of danger. Fear of darkness, fear of pain, fear of ignorance, fear of war.[12]

IV   Fear is a powerfully creative force. The fear of ignorance leads to education etc . . . Every saving invention and every intellectual advance has behind it as a part of its motivation the desire to avoid or escape some dreaded thing. And so Angelo Patri is right in saying, "Education consist in being afraid at the right time."[13] So if by "a fearless man" we mean one who is not afraid of anything, we

---

8. Fosdick, *The Hope of the World*, pp. 60–61: "Everywhere, all the time, men and women face fear— fear of others, fear of themselves, fear of change, fear of growing old, fear of disease and poverty . . ."

9. Fosdick, *The Hope of the World*, p. 61: " . . . and at last many face what the psychiatrists call phobophobia, the fear of fear, being afraid of being afraid."

10. Shakespeare, *Hamlet*, act 3, sc. 1. King wrote this sentence in a second pen.

11. Fosdick, *On Being a Real Person*, p. 111: "When it becomes terror, hysteria, phobia, obsessive anxiety, it tears personality to pieces. Dr. J. A. Hadfield says: 'If fear were abolished from modern life, the work of the psychotherapist would be nearly gone.' " For a similar quote, see Fosdick, *The Hope of the World*, p. 65. For Hadfield's words, see J. A. Hadfield, *The Psychology of Power* (New York: Macmillan, 1924), p. 36.

12. Fosdick, *The Hope of the World*, p. 59: "Fear is the elemental alarm system of the human organism, one of our primary and indispensable instincts."

13. Fosdick, *On Being a Real Person*, p. 110: "Angelo Patri is right in saying, 'Education consists in being afraid at the right time.' " Fosdick may have gotten this quote from William H. Burnham's book *The Nor-*

are picturing, not a wise man, but a defective mind. There are normal and abnormal fears

V   So the difficulty of our problem is that we are not to get rid of fear altogether, but we must harness it and master it.[14] Like fire it is a useful and necessary servant, but a runious master. It is fear when it becomes terror, panic and chronic anxiety that we must seek to eliminate

VI How do we master fear

    A. Of basic importance in mastering fear is the need of getting out in the open the object of our fear and frankly facing it. Human life is full of secret fears.

    B. A further step in mastering fear is to remember that it always involves the misuse of the imagination

AD. CSKC: Sermon file, folder 45, "Mastering Our Fears."

"Mastering Our Fears"

[*21 July 1957?*]
[*Montgomery, Ala.?*]

I   Introduction

    a. The universality and oldness of fear

    b. The prevelance of fear everywhere

        (1) Russia fears America and America Russia

        (2) Mangement fears labor and labor [*management?*]

        (3) The Negro fears the White man and the White man the [*Negro?*][15] Everywhere we turn we ~~meet~~ see that monster fear; every road we travel we meet that moster fear—fear of others, fear of the future, fear of change, fear of old age, fear of disease—and at last many come to that chronic state of what the psychiatrists call phobophobia, the fear of fear, being afraid of being afraid.[16] And so our homes, institutions, prisons, churches are filled with people who are hounded by day and harrowed by night because of some fear that lurks ready to spring into action as soon as one is alone, or as soon as the lights go out

    C. Jesus realized both the gravity and the disastrous effects of fear in human life. He said again and again "Be not afraid," "Be not anxious." All of this shows his clairvoyance into many a broken and hopeless life.[17]

---

mal Mind (New York: D. Appleton, 1924), p. 417. Patri, an educator and expert on child psychology, disavowed any use of fear in child-rearing (*Child Training* [New York: D. Appleton, 1922], pp. 19, 250).

    14. Fosdick, *The Hope of the World*, p. 60: "Indeed, this is the difficulty of our problem, that our business is not to get rid of fear but to harness it, curb it, master it."

    15. Morehouse president Benjamin Mays devoted his 20 July 1946 newspaper column to the issue of fear: "Thousands of Negroes live in physical fear of what the white man might do to them. . . . The fear on the part of many white people is equally disturbing and must be overcome" ("Two Fears," *Pittsburgh Courier*).

    16. Cf. Fosdick, *The Hope of the World*, pp. 60–61.

    17. Fosdick, *The Hope of the World*, p. 59: "Jesus, however, while he did say, 'Go, and sin no more,' said

So that one of the great questions of life is how to harness fear.

H

II Let me say first that ~~fear in itself is not an~~ we should not seek to eliminate fear altogethr. We could not survive without some fear. There is a constructive use of fear.

  (a) Fear is the elemental alarm system of the human organism[18]

  (b) In modern life fear helps us through.

  Although there is some fear that is necessay, there is some fear that is ruinous and destructive.

Our problem is not to get rid of fear altogether, but to harness it master it.[19] How do we harness fear.

III For one thing, a great deal of fear can be overcome by living a clean and upright moral life.[20]

  (1) [*strikeout illegible*] Many of the fears of the modern world can be traced back to moral wrongdoing.

  (2) The garden of Eden[21]

  (3) There seems to be a moral imperative or moral consciousness in every man. Whenever he lives out of harmony with this moral imperative guilt feelings begin to emerge. Then fear arrives.

    (a) the fear of the white man

IV Again, we can overcome fear through goodwill and love. So the New Testament says: "Perfect love casteth out fear.[22]

  (a) Now you are asking what relation does love have to fear. Let us look at ourselves. ~~The~~ There are within all of us tides of evil which [*can?*] rise to flood proportions and the slumberig giant . .

  Someone is asking what relation does love have to fear. Let us look at our selves. There are within tides of

  But did you ever stop to realize that this envy and jealousy grow out of fear. We are not jealous of people and then fea them, but we fear them first and then become jealous and envious—We are afraid of the superiority of others, afraid that

  (b) How true this is in international relations.

    (1) The basic cause of war is fear. Of course there are other causes—economic, political, racial,—but they all spring from and are shot through with fear.[23]

---

again and again, 'Fear not,' 'Be not afraid,' 'Be not anxious,' which shows his clairvoyance into many a broken and hopeless life."

  18. Cf. Fosdick, *The Hope of the World*, p. 59.

  19. Cf. Fosdick, *The Hope of the World*, p. 60.

  20. Fosdick, *The Hope of the World*, p. 61: "One primary condition is a clean and upright life, for if we could be rid of the fears that follow moral wrongdoing we should be a long way out of our problem."

  21. Fosdick gave an account of the story of the Garden of Eden in "The Conquest of Fear" (*The Hope of the World*, p. 61).

  22. Cf. 1 John 4:18.

  23. In his 20 July 1946 *Pittsburgh Courier* column "Two Fears," Mays asserted, "Fear is the greatest enemy of mankind. It is the foundation of many wars."

(2) We are accostomed to hearing that hate cause war. But the sequence of events is generally quite otherwise—first fear, then war, then hate. Fear of another nation attack, fear of another nations economic supremacy, fear of lost markets.

(3) The old remedy for fear was great armaments. But how futile. Instead of being a remedy great armament has become a cause for fear. It is only love that will solve the problem.

{I of basic importance in mastering fear is making a practice of looking fairly and squarly at the object of our fear.[24] "Ridicule is the master cure of fear"[25]

II A great deal of fear can be overcome by living a clar and upright moral life[26]

III Fear is mastered through love. A common cause of fear is the awareness of inadequate [*resources?*]

IV Fear is mastered through faith.}

V Finally, fear is overcome by the possesion of adequate interior resources. So many people are attempting to face the strain and tensions of life with~~out~~ inadequate interior resources.

(1) Now it is true that many fears which people possess they are not responsible for. There fears got an ~~early~~ long start in them from early childhood from unfortunate accident and unwise parents. The are only two fears which a baby is born with—fear of falling and fear of loud noises. Every other fear is accumulated—name the fears.[27] Every parent is responsible

(2.) But beneath all of this is the fact that most people do not have the proper spiritual equipment to face the tensions of life.

3. This is what religion gives a man. It gives him internal resources to face the problems of life.

It gives him the awaness the he is a child of God. He knows that he is

ADf. CSKC: Sermon file, folder 45, "Mastering Our Fears."

---

24. Cf. McCracken, *Questions People Ask*, p. 125; cf. Fosdick, *On Being a Real Person*, p. 112.

25. Cf. Fosdick, *On Being a Real Person*, p. 132.

26. Cf. Fosdick, *The Hope of the World*, p. 61.

27. Fosdick, *The Hope of the World*, p. 63: "A normal baby's fear instinct has only two expressions, the dread of falling and the dread of a loud noise. That is all. Every other fear we possess we have accumulated since . . . We parents have few duties more sacred than to see to it that our children do not catch from us unnecessary and abnormal fears."

The Christian Way of Life in Human Relations, Address Delivered at the General Assembly of the National Council of Churches

[*4 December 1957*]
[*St. Louis, Mo.*]

In his second of two addresses during the annual meeting of the National Council of the Churches of Christ in the U.S.A., King charges that "all too many ministers are still silent while evil rages."[1] *He calls on church leaders to be "maladjusted" to social injustice and asserts that "the aftermath of nonviolence is the creation of the beloved community, while the aftermath of violence is tragic bitterness." The following text is taken from an audio recording of the event at St. Louis's Kiel Auditorium.*[2]

It is impossible to look out into the wide arena of American life without noticing a real crisis in race relations. This crisis has been precipitated, on the one hand, by the determined resistance of reactionary elements in the South to the Supreme Court's momentous decision outlawing segregation in the public schools. This resistance has often risen to ominous proportions. The legislative halls of the South ring loud with such words as "interposition" and "nullification."[3] In many states, the Ku Klux Klan is on the march again, and also there are the White Citizens Councils.[4] Each of these organizations is determined to preserve segregation at any cost and, thereby, defy the desegregation rulings of the Supreme Court. All of these forces have conjoined to make for massive resistance.

The crisis has been precipitated, on the other hand, by the radical change in the Negro's evaluation of himself. It is probably true to say that there would be no crisis in race relations if the Negro continued to think of himself in inferior terms and

---

1. In a 16 April 1957 letter, J. Quinter Miller, an assistant general secretary of the National Council of Churches, invited King to speak at its General Assembly on 4 December 1957, and at the Council's public session of the Division of Christian Life and Work the preceding evening (King, The Oneness of Man in American Intergroup Relations, Address delivered at the National Council of Churches Division of Christian Life and Work visitors program, 3 December 1957). King accepted Miller's invitation on 1 May 1957. As part of a session on "Oneness in Christ Across the Races," King delivered this 4 December 1957 address to the General Assembly after a speech by Yale Divinity School dean Liston Pope, then participated in a panel discussion (National Council of the Churches of Christ, Program, Public Meeting of the General Assembly, 4 December 1957). King's address was covered in a front-page article in the conference newspaper ("'Silent Good' People Called to Repent with 'Noisy Bad' People," *The Assemblyan: Official Newspaper of the General Assembly of the National Council of Churches,* 5 December 1957). He was also scheduled to speak at Washington University's Graham Memorial Chapel on the morning of this address ("Martin Luther King to Speak Tomorrow," *Student Life: Washington University in St. Louis,* 3 December 1957).

2. A transcription of this speech was later published in *Presbyterian Life* 11 (8 February 1958): 11–13.

3. King highlights legal strategies advocated by southern political leaders to thwart enforcement of federal laws and the Supreme Court's *Brown v. Board of Education* decisions of 1954 and 1955.

4. Citizens Councils were anti–civil rights groups; the first Council was formed in Indianola, Mississippi, in July 1954 in response to the *Brown v. Board of Education* decision.

patiently accepted injustice and exploitation. But it is at this very point that the change has come.

For many years, the Negro tacitly accepted segregation. The system of slavery and segregation caused many Negroes to feel that perhaps they were inferior. Indeed this is the ultimate tragedy of segregation. It not only harms one physically, but it injures one spiritually. It scars the soul and distorts the personality. It inflicts the segregator with a false sense of superiority, while inflicting the segregated with a false sense of inferiority.[5]

But through the forces of history, something happened to the Negro. He came to feel that he was somebody. He came to believe and to know that the important thing about a man is not his specificity but his fundamentum, not the color of his skin or the texture of his hair, but the texture and quality of his soul. And so there has been a revolutionary change in the Negro's evaluation of his nature and destiny and a concomitant determination to achieve freedom and human dignity, whatever the cost may be.

This determination of Negro Americans to win freedom from all forms of oppression springs from the same deep longing for freedom that motivates oppressed peoples all over the world. The rhythmic beat of the deep rumbling of discontent from Asia and Africa is at bottom a quest for freedom and human dignity on the part of people who have long been the victims of colonialism and imperialism.

The struggle for freedom on the part of oppressed people in general, and the American Negro in particular, is not suddenly going to disappear. It is sociologically true that privileged classes rarely ever give up their privileges without strong resistance. It is also sociologically true that once oppressed people rise up against their oppression, there is no stopping point short of full freedom. And so realism impels us to admit that the struggle will continue until freedom is a reality for all of the oppressed peoples of the world. Since the struggle will continue, the basic question which confronts the oppressed peoples of the world is this: How will the struggle against the forces of injustice be waged?

Now there are two possible answers to this question. One is to resort to the all too prevalent method of physical violence and corroding hatred. Violence appears to have become the inseparable twin of Western materialism. It has even become the hallmark of its grandeur. Violence nevertheless solves no social problems; it merely creates new and more complicated ones. Occasionally violence brings temporary victory but never permanent peace. There is still a voice crying through the vista of time saying to every potential Peter, "Put up your sword."[6] History is replete with the bleached bones of nations and communities that failed to follow this command. If

---

5. King's discussion of the effects of segregation is similar to Benjamin Mays's observation in a 1955 speech, "The Moral Aspects of Segregation": "The chief sin of segregation is the distortion of human personality. It damages the soul of both the segregator and the segregated. It gives the segregated a feeling of inherent inferiority which is not based on facts, and it gives the segregator a feeling of superiority which is not based on facts" (William Faulkner, Benjamin E. Mays, and Cecil Sims, *Three Views of the Segregation Decisions* [Atlanta: Southern Regional Council, 1956], p. 15). King kept a copy of this book in his personal library.

6. Cf. John 18:11.

the American Negro and other victims of oppression succumb to the temptation of using violence in the struggle for freedom, unborn generations will be the recipients of a long and desolate night of bitterness, and their chief legacy to the future will be an endless reign of meaningless chaos.

The alternative to violence is a method of nonviolent resistance. This method is nothing more and nothing less than Christianity in action. It seems to me to be the Christian way of life in solving problems of human relations. You will well remember that this method was made famous in our generation by Mohandas K. Gandhi, who used it to free his country from the political domination and economic exploitation inflicted upon it by the British Empire. This method has also been used in Montgomery, Alabama, under the leadership of ministers of several denominations, to free 50,000 Negroes from the long night of bus segregation.

Several basic things can be said about nonviolence as a method of bringing about better racial conditions. First, this is not a method of cowardice or stagnant passivity. It does resist. It is true that this method is passive, or non-aggressive, in the sense that the nonviolent resister is not aggressive physically toward his opponent. But his mind and emotions are always active, constantly seeking to persuade the opponent that he is mistaken. This method is passive physically, but it is strongly active spiritually.

The second basic fact about this method is that it does not seek to defeat or humiliate the opponent, but to win his friendship and understanding. The nonviolent resister must often voice his protest through non-cooperation or boycotts, but he realizes that non-cooperation and boycotts are not ends within themselves; they are merely means to awaken the sense of moral shame within the opponent. But the end is redemption. The end is reconciliation. The aftermath of nonviolence is the creation of the beloved community, while the aftermath of violence is tragic bitterness.

A third fact that characterizes the method of nonviolence is that the attack is directed at forces of evil rather than persons caught in the forces. It is evil that we are seeking to defeat, not the persons victimized with evil. Those of us who struggle against racial injustice must come to see that the basic tension is not between races. As I like to say to the people in Montgomery, Alabama, "The tension in this city is not between white people and Negro people. The tension is at bottom between justice and injustice, between the forces of light and the forces of darkness. And if there is a victory it will be a victory not merely for 50,000 Negroes, but a victory for justice, a victory for freedom, a victory for the forces of light. We are out to defeat injustice and not white persons who may happen to be unjust."

A fourth point that must be brought out concerning the method of nonviolence is that this method not only avoids external physical violence, but also internal violence of spirit. At the center of nonviolence stands the principle of love. In struggling for human dignity, the oppressed people of the world must not become bitter or indulge in hate campaigns. To retaliate with hate and bitterness would do nothing but intensify the existence of hate in the universe. Along the way of life, someone must have sense enough and morality enough to cut off the chain of hate. This can only be done by projecting the ethic of love to the center of our lives.

In speaking of love at this point, we are not referring to some sentimental or affectionate emotion. It would be nonsense to urge men to love their oppressors in an affectionate sense. Love in this connection means understanding goodwill. The

Greek language comes to our aid in dealing with this problem. There are three words in the Greek New Testament for love. And first, there is *eros*. In platonic philosophy *eros* meant the yearning of the soul for the realm of the gods. It has come now to mean a sort of aesthetic or romantic love. Second, there is *philia*. It meant intimate affection between personal friends. *Philia* denotes a sort of reciprocal love. The person loves because he is loved.

When we speak of loving those who would oppose us, we refer neither to *eros* nor *philia*. We speak of a love which is expressed in the Greek word *agape*. *Agape* means nothing sentimental or basically affectionate. It means understanding, creative, redeeming goodwill for all men.[7] It is an overflowing love which seeks nothing in return. It is not set in motion by any quality or function of its object. It is purely spontaneous, unmotivated, groundless, and creative. It is the love of God operating in the human heart. When we rise to love on the *agape* level, we love men not because we like them, not because their attitudes and ways appeal to us, but we love them because God loves them. Here we rise to the position of loving the person who does the evil deed while hating the deed that the person does.

A fifth basic fact about the method of nonviolent resistance is that it is based on the conviction that the universe is on the side of justice. It is this deep faith in the future that causes a nonviolent resister to accept suffering without retaliation. He knows that in his struggle for justice he has cosmic companionship.

Now I am aware of the fact that there are devout believers in nonviolence who find it difficult to believe in a personal God. But even these persons believe in the existence of some creative force that works for togetherness, whether we call it a principle of concretion as in Whitehead; a process of integration as Henry Nelson Wieman; Being Itself as Paul Tillich; an impersonal Brahma as Hinduism; or a personal being of boundless power and infinite love.[8] We must believe that there is a creative force in this universe that works to bring the disconnected aspects of reality into a harmonious whole. There is a creative power that works to bring low gigantic mountains of evil and pull down prodigious hilltops of injustice. This is the faith that keeps the nonviolent resister going through all of the tension and suffering that he must inevitably confront.

And those of us who call the name of Jesus Christ find something at the center of our faith which forever reminds us that God is on the side of truth and justice. Yes, there is an event which reminds us that Good Friday may occupy the throne for a day, but ultimately it must give way to the triumphant beat of the drums of Easter. Evil may so shape events that Caesar will occupy the palace and Christ a cross, but

---

7. Harry Emerson Fosdick, "On Being Fit to Live With," in *On Being Fit to Live With,* pp. 6–7: "Love in the New Testament is not a sentimental and affectionate emotion as we so commonly interpret it. There are three words in Greek for love, three words that we have to translate by our one word, love. *Eros*— 'erotic' comes from it—that is one. . . . *Philia*—that is another Greek word. It meant intimate personal affectionateness and friendship. . . . But the great Christian word for love is something else: *agape*. . . . *agape* means nothing sentimental or primarily emotional at all; it means understanding, redeeming, creative good will." King cited Paul Tillich's 1951 work *Systematic Theology* in his dissertation as another source of this concept (note 201 to King, "A Comparison of the Conceptions of God in the Thinking of Paul Tillich and Henry Nelson Wieman," in *Papers* 2:441).

8. King refers to theologians Alfred North Whitehead (1861–1947), Henry Nelson Wieman (1884–1975), and Paul Johannes Tillich (1886–1965).

one day that same Christ will rise up and split history into A.D. and B.C., so that even the life of Caesar must be dated by His name. There is something in this universe which justifies Carlyle in saying, "No lie can live forever."[9] There is something in this universe which justifies William Cullen Bryant in saying, "Truth, crushed to earth, will rise again."[10] There is something in this universe that justifies James Russell Lowell in saying:

> Truth forever on the scaffold,
> Wrong forever on the throne.
> Yet that scaffold sways the future,
> And behind the dim unknown
> Stands God, within the shadows,
> Keeping watch above His own.[11]

And so in Montgomery, Alabama, we can walk and never get weary because we know that there will be a great camp meeting in the promised land of freedom and justice.[12]

I cannot close this message without saying to you that the problem of race is indeed America's greatest moral dilemma. The churches are called upon to recognize the urgent necessity of taking a forthright stand on this crucial issue. If we are to remain true to the gospel of Jesus Christ, we cannot rest until segregation and discrimination are banished from every area of American life. I am aware of the fact that many churches have already taken a stand. This great body, the National Council of Churches, has condemned segregation over and over again and has requested its constituent denominations to do likewise. I am not unmindful of the fact that many individual ministers, even in the South, have stood up with dauntless courage. And in passing I would like to express my personal appreciation to the ninety ministers of Atlanta, Georgia, who so courageously signed the noble statement calling for compliance with the law and an opening of the channels of communication between the races.[13]

All of these things are marvelous and deserve our highest praise. But we must admit that these courageous stands from the churches are still far too few. The sublime statements of the major denominations on the question of human relations move all too slowly to the local churches and actual practice. All too many ministers are still silent while evil rages. It may well be that the greatest tragedy of this period of social transition is not the glaring noisiness of the bad people, but the appalling silence of the good people. It may be that our generation will have to repent not only for the diabolical actions and vitriolic words of the children of darkness, but

---

9. Carlyle, *The French Revolution* (1837).

10. Bryant, "The Battlefield" (1839).

11. Lowell, "The Present Crisis" (1844).

12. King refers to the spiritual "There's a Great Camp Meeting."

13. Eighty Atlanta ministers signed a six-point public statement on race relations in the wake of resistance to school desegregation in Little Rock, Arkansas. The declaration called for the preservation of free speech and public school systems, obedience to the law, an end to race hatred, the maintenance of communication between races, and the use of prayer to resolve the difficulties ("Ministers List 6 Principles for Race Peace," *Atlanta Daily World,* 3 November 1957).

also for the crippling fears and tragic apathy of the children of light. It is one of the tragedies of history that the children of darkness are often wiser in their generation, more zealous, conscientious and determined, than the children of light.[14] And so I would like to call upon each of you to go away from this meeting with a restless determination to make the ideal of brotherhood a reality in this nation and all over the world.

There are certain technical words in the vocabulary of every academic discipline which tend to become cliches and stereotypes. Psychologists have a word which is probably used more frequently than any other word in modern psychology. It is the word "maladjusted." This word is the ringing cry out of the new child psychology—"maladjusted." Now in a sense all of us must live the well-adjusted life in order to avoid neurotic and schizophrenic personalities. But there are some things in our social system to which I'm proud to be maladjusted and to which I call upon you to be maladjusted. I never intend to adjust myself to the viciousness of mob rule. I never intend to adjust myself to the evils of segregation or the crippling effects of discrimination. I never intend to adjust myself to an economic system that will take necessities from the masses to give luxuries to the classes. I never intend to adjust myself to the madness of militarism and the self-defeating effects of physical violence. And my friends, I call upon you to be maladjusted to all of these things, for you see, it may be that the salvation of the world lies in the hands of the maladjusted. The challenge of this hour is to be maladjusted. Yes, as maladjusted as the prophet Amos, who in the midst of the tragic injustices of his day, could cry out in words that echo across the generations: "Let judgement run down like waters and righteousness like a mighty stream."[15] As maladjusted as Lincoln, who had the vision to see that this nation could not exist half slave and half free.[16] As maladjusted as [*Thomas*] Jefferson, who in the midst of an age amazingly adjusted to slavery, could cry out in terms lifted to cosmic proportions: "All men are created equal and are endowed by their creator with certain unalienable rights, and among these are life, liberty and the pursuit of happiness." Yes, as maladjusted as Jesus of Nazareth, who looked at the men of his generation and said: "Love your enemies. Bless them that curse you, pray for them that despitefully use you."[17] Who could stand up amid the intricate and fascinating military machinery of the Roman Empire, and say, "He who lives by the sword will perish by the sword."[18]

The world is in desperate need of such maladjustment. And through such courageous maladjustment, we will be able to emerge from the bleak and desolate mid-

---

14. Cf. Luke 16:8.

15. Amos 5:24.

16. Abraham Lincoln, "'A House Divided Against Itself Cannot Stand,' Speech in acceptance of nomination as United States Senator, made at the close of the Republican State Convention, Springfield, Ill., 16 June 1858," in *Life and Works of Abraham Lincoln*, ed. Marion Mills Miller (New York: Current Literature Publishing, 1907), 3:35–46.

17. Cf. Matthew 5:44.

18. Cf. Matthew 26:52. King's discussion of "maladjustment" reflects the influence of Fosdick, who wrote of a prisoner of conscience who refused to be "well-adjusted to a state of society that denied such elemental rights as religious liberty" (*On Being a Real Person*, p. 205); Fosdick, *The Hope of the World*, p. 112: "The deepest obligation of a Christian, I should suppose, is to be maladjusted to the status quo."

night of man's inhumanity to man into the bright and glittering daybreak of freedom and justice. And this will be the day when we will be able to sing by the grace of God, the kingdom of this world has become the kingdom of our Lord and His Christ, and He shall reign for ever and ever. Hallelujah, Hallelujah.[19] [*sustained applause*]

At. RRL-ViRUT.

---

19. King quotes excerpts from the "Hallelujah Chorus" of Handel's oratorio *Messiah* (1741); see also Revelation 11:15.

"The Christian Doctrine of Man," Sermon Delivered at the Detroit Council of Churches' Noon Lenten Services

[*12 March 1958*]
Detroit, Mich.

On 1 March 1957 Detroit Council of Churches executive director G. Merrill Lenox invited King to preach during the Council's 1958 Noon Lenten series.[1] This was the third sermon that King delivered during that series.[2] He encourages the congregation to adopt a "realistic" view of humanity, by recognizing that man is "a biological being, injected with spirit, made in the image of God." However, he charges that "man has misused his freedom" and laments, "We deal with problems today just as people dealt with them two thousand years ago. We go to the battlefield to solve our problems. The only difference is that we are progressively evil. People two thousand years ago used to kill you with bow and arrows; we do it now with atomic bombs." The following text is taken from an audio recording of the service.

I would like to take just a moment to say what a great spiritual experience this has been for me. And I want to express my personal appreciation to each of you for your kind expressions and for your cooperative spirits. I will remember these three days for many, many years to come. Now, I am also grateful to Doctor Lenox and the

---

1. King agreed to the offer in a 24 April 1957 letter; this was his first appearance. The Noon Lenten series, initiated in 1920, featured nationally renowned ministers and broadcast their sermons on Detroit radio station WWJ. The 1957 series included preachers such as Morehouse College president Benjamin Mays, James Albert Pike of St. John the Divine Cathedral, and radio minister Ralph Sockman. King would also preach during the 1961 Noon Lenten Services (see King, The Man Who Was a Fool, 6 March 1961 and Loving Your Enemies, 7 March 1961, pp. 411–419 and 421–429 in this volume, respectively).

2. King preached at three noon services between 10 and 12 of March 1958 (see Detroit Council of Churches, Announcement, "Noon Lenten Services," 19 February–3 April 1958).

Detroit Council of Churches for extending the invitation. I have been deeply impressed with the Council here and the great work that is being done by Dr. Lenox and his staff. I am familiar with most of the church councils across the country, and I can say that the Detroit Council is the most active Council of Churches that I know about in anywhere in this country. And this is due to the great work, the unselfish labor, of Dr. Lenox and his staff, and I want to express my appreciation to them for this great and noble work. And I hope you will continue to cooperate with the Council here in the great work for the kingdom of God. I cannot close these introductory remarks without saying that it gives me a great deal of humility to stand in the spot, the pulpit, occupied from Sunday to Sunday by Dr. Henry Hitt Crane.[3] By all standards of measurement, Dr. Crane is one of the great preachers of our age, and if there is any man anywhere in this world who is a Christian, it's Henry Hitt Crane. So it is a great honor to stand in this spot today and all of the three days.[4]

This afternoon I would like to talk about "The Christian Doctrine of Man."[5] I guess you wonder why one would be talking about man during the Lenten season, but it is important for us to know who we are—to know what Jesus thought about man. The cross reveals two basic things it seems to me. On the one hand, it is a revelation of the amazing heights to which man can ascend by the grace of God. On the other hand, it is an expression of the tragic and demonic depths to which man can sink. The question, What is man? is one of the most important questions confronting any generation. The whole political, social, and economic structure of a society is largely determined by its answer to this pressing question. Indeed, the conflict which we witness in the world today between totalitarianism and democracy is at bottom a conflict over the question, What is man?[6]

In our generation the asking of this question has risen to heightening proportions. But although there is widespread agreement in asking the question, there is fantastic disagreement in answering it. For instance there are those who think of man as a pretty low creature. For them he's little more than a misguided animal. We

---

3. Henry Hitt Crane (1902–1977) served as pastor of Detroit's Central Methodist Church from 1938 to 1958.

4. King had filled Central Methodist's pulpit the previous year during the church's summer preaching series and would be a regular participant in the summer series in the coming years (Program, Sunday services, 18 August 1957; Central Methodist Church, Announcement, "Summer preaching program," 6 July–7 September 1958; King, Loving Your Enemies, Sermon delivered at Central Methodist Church, 23 August 1959; Central Methodist Church, Announcement, "Summer preaching program," 26 June–4 September 1960). Like the Noon Lenten series, Central Methodist's summer series featured prominent ministers and spokespersons, such as George Buttrick and Norman Thomas.

5. King developed antecedents for this sermon, alternatively titled "What Is Man?" while a student at Crozer (Sermon Introductions, 30 November 1948–16 February 1949, pp. 83–84 in this volume and "What Is Man," Sermon notes I and II, 1948–1954). He delivered versions of it while an associate pastor at Ebenezer and early in his ministry at Dexter ("Radio Sermons," 26 July–6 September 1953, and "What Is Man," 11 July 1954, pp. 136 and 174–179 in this volume, respectively).

6. In the published version of this sermon, King elaborated that "the conflict we witness between totalitarianism and democracy is fundamentally centered on this: Is man a person or a pawn? Is he a cog in the wheel of the state or a free, creative being capable of accepting responsibility?" (*Strength to Love*, p. 87).

may refer to these persons as the pessimistic naturalists.[7] Some of them would cry out that man is the supreme clown of creation. Another would say that man is a cosmic accident—a disease on this planet not soon to be cured.[8] Another would say that man is the most pernicious little race of ominous vermin that nature ever suffered to walk across the face of the earth.[9] These people don't see very much in him. And when I'm speaking of man at this point I must make it clear that I'm not talking about the male sex; this is generic in its setting including men and women.

There are those on the other hand who would lift man to almost idealistic proportions and almost to the level of a god.[10] And so they would cry out with Shakespeare's Hamlet, "What a piece of work is man, how noble in faculty, how infinite in reason, in form and moving how express and admirable. In apprehension how like a god; in action how like an angel. The beauty of the world; the paragon of animals."[11]

There are others who seek to be realistic in the doctrine of man. They see something of a strange dualism, a dichotomy, a split-up in man, a mixture.[12] And so they would cry out with Carlyle that there are depths in man which go down to the lowest hell and heights which reach the highest heaven. For are not both heaven and hell made out of Him, everlasting miracle and mystery that He is.[13] One day the Psalmist looked out; he noticed the vastness of the cosmic order. He noticed the stars as they bedeck the heavens like swinging lanterns of eternity. He noticed the moon as it stood in all of its scintillating beauty, and he says, "Now in the midst of all of this, what is man?" He has an answer. He comes out and says, "Thou hast made him a little lower than the angels and crowned him with glory and honor."[14] The more modern translations—the Moffatt, the Goodspeed, and the Revised Standard Version—which say, "Thou hast made him a little less than God; Thou hast made him a little less than divine."[15] This is the realistic approach. And I think it was this realistic

---

7. In the published version of this sermon, King expanded on this point: "Those who think of man purely in materialistic terms argue that man is simply an animal, a tiny object in the vast, ever-changing organism called nature, which is wholly unconscious and impersonal. His whole life may be explained in terms of matter in motion. Such a system of thought affirms that the conduct of man is physically determined and that the mind is merely an effect of the brain" (*Strength to Love,* p. 87).

8. C. S. Lewis, *Answers to Questions on Christianity,* p. 10.

9. Jonathan Swift, *Gulliver's Travels* (1726).

10. At this point in the published version, King wrote: "Humanism is another answer frequently given to the question, 'What is man?' Believing neither in God nor in the existence of any supernatural power, the humanist affirms that man is the highest form of being which has evolved in the natural universe" (*Strength to Love,* pp. 87–88).

11. Shakespeare, *Hamlet,* act 2, sc. 2.

12. In the published version, King wrote: "There are those who, seeking to be a little more realistic about man, wish to reconcile the truths of these opposites, while avoiding the extremes of both. They contend that the truth about man is found neither in the thesis of pessimistic materialism nor the antithesis of optimistic humanism, but in a higher synthesis. Man is neither villain nor hero; he is rather both villain and hero" (*Strength to Love,* p. 88).

13. Thomas Carlyle, *The French Revolution* (1837).

14. Cf. Psalm 8:4–5; Psalm 8:5 in *The New Testament of Our Lord and Savior Jesus Christ: Revised Standard Version* (New York: Thomas Nelson & Sons, 1946); cites of biblical verses from this translation are noted as RSV, in parentheses.

15. Cf. Psalm 8:5 (GOODSPEED) and Psalm 8:6 (MOFFATT).

King at the pulpit of Holt Street Baptist Church in Montgomery, 1958. Photo by Charles Moore; courtesy of Black Star.

course that Jesus followed in his thinking about man. For he saw man in his whole being as that being with great possibilities for goodness and also possibilities for evil.

Now let us take this realistic approach and try to work out the Christian doctrine of man. Let us begin by stating something that is very obvious, and that is, man is a biological being with a physical body. I guess this is why the Psalmist can say, "Thou hast made him a little less than God, a little less than divine." You see when we think of God, we don't think of a being with a body; we don't think of a being with a nervous system in any biological sense. We don't think of a being with hands in any physical sense. We think of God as a being of pure spirit. But man, that being a little less than God, has a body; he's in nature. And he can never totally disown his kinship from animated nature. The facts in favor of the theory of evolution are so conclusive that to deny them would mean standing in the face of the most obvious evidence. Man is a biological being with a material body. Now the Bible said God made him that way, and since God made him that way it must be good because when we turn over in the book of Genesis we read everything that God makes is good, so there is nothing wrong with having a body—nothing wrong with it.

And this is one of the things that distinguishes the Christian doctrine of man from the Greek doctrine. The Greeks under the impetus of Plato felt that the body was something inherently depraved, inherently evil, and that somehow the soul could not reach its full maturity until it had broken aloose from the prison of the body. But this was never the Christian doctrine. The Christian doctrine did not consider the body as the principle of evil; Christianity says the will is the principle of evil. And so in Christianity the body is sacred. The body is significant. This means that in any Christian doctrine of man we must forever be concerned about man's physical well-being. Jesus was concerned about that. He realized that men had to have certain physical necessities. One day he said, "Man cannot live by bread alone."[16] [*Congregation:*] (*Yeah*) But the mere fact that the "alone" was added means that Jesus realized that man could not live without bread. (*Yes*) So as a minister of the gospel, I must not only preach to men and women to be good, but I must be concerned about the social conditions that often make them bad. (*Yeah*) It's not enough for me to tell men to be honest, but I must be concerned about the economic conditions that make them dishonest. (*Amen*) I must be concerned about the poverty in the world. I must be concerned about the ignorance in the world. I must be concerned about the slums in the world. (*Amen*) It's all right to talk about the new Jerusalem, but I must be concerned about the new Detroit, the new New York, the new Atlanta. (*Amen, Tell it*) It's all right to think of a city and the street flowing with milk and honey, but religion must be concerned about those streets in this world where individuals go to bed hungry at night. (*Right, Amen*) And any religion that professes to be concerned about the souls of men and fails to be concerned about the economic conditions that corrupt them, the social conditions that damn them, the city governments that cripple them, is a dry, dead, do-nothing religion in need of new blood.[17] And it justly deserves the criticism of the Marxists as nothing

---

16. Cf. Matthew 4:4.
17. Cf. Fosdick, *The Hope of the World*, p. 25.

but an opiate of the people.[18] Because it fails to see one basic fact—that man is a biological being with a physical body.

But we can't stop here in the doctrine of man. Some people stop right here. Marxism would stop right here. Communism would stop right here and say that man is made merely for collective profit, so to speak. The whole economic interpretation of history is the way it looks at it.[19] There are those who would stop right here—the naturalistic and materialistic thinkers. Man is little more than an animal for these thinkers. Some years ago a group of chemists who had a flair for statistics decided to work out in terms of the market values of that particular day the worth of man—the worth of his bodily makeup. And after they had worked several days and several weeks, they came out with this conclusion: that the average man has enough fat in him to make about seven bars of soap, enough iron to make a medium-size nail, enough lime to whitewash a chicken coop, enough sugar to fill a shaker, enough phosphorous to make about twenty-two hundred match tips, and enough magnesia for a dose of magnesium, and a little sulphur. And when all of this was added up in the market values of that day it came to ninety-eight cents.[20] [*laughter*] That's all you could get out of man's bodily stuff, his bodily makeup. Now, the standards of living are higher now, and I guess maybe you could get a dollar ninety-eight cents for the average man. But think of this: man's bodily makeup being worth only ninety-eight cents, that's it. But can you explain the literary genius of Shakespeare in terms of ninety-eight cents? Can you explain the artistic genius of Michelangelo in terms of ninety-eight cents? Can you explain the musical genius of Beethoven in terms of ninety-eight cents? Can you explain the spiritual genius of Jesus of Nazareth in terms of ninety-eight cents? Can you explain the mystery of the human soul and the magic of the human heart in terms of ninety-eight cents? (*Oh, no*) Oh, no. There is something within man that cannot be calculated in terms of dollars and cents. (*Amen, Yeah, Amen*) There is something within man that cannot be reduced to biological terms. Man is more than a tiny vagary of whirling electrons or a wisp of smoke from a limitless smoldering. Man is a child of God. (*Amen, Amen*)

And therefore we must bring into a Christian doctrine of man this second point: man is a being of spirit. He has a mind, he has rational capacity, he can think.[21] And this is what distinguishes man from his animal ancestry. This is his uniqueness. As you look out through nature it seems that mind and matter run on two parallel lines, but when it comes to man, they intersect. And this is man's uniqueness. He's in nature and yet above nature. He's in time and yet above time. And this is what makes him different. This is what the Psalmist means when he says, "Thou hast, hath crowned him with glory and honor." This is what Jesus sees within man when he talks about

---

18. King cites Karl Marx, "Contribution to the Critique of Hegel's *Philosophy of Right:* Introduction" (1844).

19. In the published version, King expanded on this idea: "The Marxists, for instance, following a theory of dialectical materialism, contend that man is merely a producing animal who supplies his own needs and whose life is determined largely by economic forces" (*Strength to Love*, p. 89).

20. Cf. Fosdick, *Successful Christian Living*, pp. 265–266.

21. Regarding man's rational capacity, King added in the published version: "He moves up 'the stairs of his concepts' into a wonder world of thought. Conscience speaks to him, and he is reminded of things divine" (*Strength to Love*, p. 90).

the great heights to which man can ascend. Man is a being of spirit. He can think a poem and write it; he can think a symphony and compose it; he can think up a great civilization and go out and create it. This is man. He's God's marvelous creation. And because he has rational capacity you can't quite hem him in. He has a mind, and he can't be limited by his body. You can take his body if you please and put it in Bedford's prison, but pretty soon his mind will break out through the bars (*Amen*) and come back and scratch across the pages of history *A Pilgrim's Progress*.[22] (*Amen, Yeah*) You can bring him down in his wretched old age, and his body's all but worn out, vision all but gone, but in the midst of that, in the person of a [*George Frideric*] Handel, he can look up and imagine that he hears the angels singing and come back and scratch across the pages of history a "Hallelujah Chorus." (*Amen, Yeah*) You just can't hold him down. (*Yeah*) Man is God's marvelous creation. (*Amen, Yeah*) Somehow he can leap oceans, break through walls, transcend the categories of time and space.[23] The stars may be marvelous, but not as marvelous as the mind of man that comprehended them. Man is made to have dominion over the things of the world. There's another thing that comes under this point, and that is man is made in the image of God.[24] (*Amen, Amen*) This is what the biblical writers mean. They mean that somehow man has a capacity—the unique capacity—to have fellowship with God. He has rational capacity, and therefore there is something within man that is god-like—he can have communion with Him. (*Amen*)

I must rush on to bring about another basic point that must stand out in any Christian doctrine of man. He is a biological being, injected with spirit, made in the image of God, but some of that image is gone. Man is free and I don't have time to go into that. We just accept that as a presupposition that man can choose between alternatives. He isn't guided by instinct as the lower animals merely. But he's free: he can choose between the high and the low, the good and the evil. But man has misused his freedom.[25] And so there is that other point that must stand out in any Christian doctrine of man. And that is, man is a sinner in need of God's grace. (*Yes, Amen*) We don't like to hear this. We hate to recognize the fact that we are sinners. But what does this Lenten season reveal to us other than the fact that we are sinners in need of God's grace—in need of repentance. Oh, we try to get by it, and we try to call it different names, and we bring into being the new psychology; and we try to use that to get by this term "sin." We say it's inner conflicts; we say it's phobias. And

---

22. King refers to John Bunyan.

23. In the published version, King wrote: "By his ability to reason, his power of memory, and his gift of imagination, man transcends time and space" (*Strength to Love*, p. 90).

24. Genesis 1:26–27.

25. In the published version, King elaborated: "This is what the Bible means when it affirms that man is made in the image of God. The *imago dei* has been interpreted by different thinkers in terms of fellowship, responsiveness, reason, and conscience. An abiding expression of man's higher spiritual nature is his freedom. Man is man because he is free to operate within the framework of his destiny. He is free to deliberate, to make decisions, and to choose between alternatives. He is distinguished from animals by his freedom to do evil or to do good and to walk the high road of beauty or tread the low road of ugly degeneracy." He continued: "To avoid being victimized by an illusion born of superficiality, it should be said that we err when we assume that because man is made in the image of God, man is basically good. Through his all too prevalent inclination for evil, man has terribly scarred God's image" (*Strength to Love*, p. 90).

we say the conflict is between what the psychologist [*Sigmund*] Freud would call the id and the superego. But when we look at ourselves hard enough, we come to see that the conflict is between God and man.[26] (*Amen, Yes, Amen*) There is something within all of us that causes us to cry out with Ovid the Latin poet, "I see and approve the better things of life, but the evil things I do."[27] There is something within all of us that causes us to cry out with Plato that "the personality is like a charioteer with two headstrong horses each wanting to go in different directions."[28] There is something in all of us that causes us to cry out with Saint Augustine, "Lord make me pure, but not yet."[29] There is something within all of us that causes us to agree with the apostle Paul, "The good that I would I do not, the evil that I would not that I do."[30] (*Yeah, Amen*)

This is man's plight. Somehow the "isness" of our present natures is out of harmony with the eternal "oughtness" that forever confronts us.[31] So we are sinners. It isn't because we don't know. We know truth, and yet we lie. (*Right on*) We know how to be honest and yet we are dishonest. (*Yeah, Amen*) We know how to be just and yet we are unjust. We are unfaithful to those that we should be faithful to; we are disloyal to those that we should be loyal to. (*Amen*) All we like sheep have gone astray.[32] (*Amen, Yeah*) When I look at myself hard enough, I don't feel like crying out, "Lord I thank thee that I'm not like other men," but I find myself crying out, "God be merciful unto me a sinner."[33] (*Amen, Yeah*) And we see this sinfulness of man bounding through the universe. Because of our sinfulness we have come to the point, producing an age of guided missiles and misguided men. We have allowed our civilization to outdistance our culture. The means by which we live outdistance the ends for which we live. And when it comes to our collective life, our sinfulness is even greater. As individuals we are sinful but when we interact in society, it becomes even greater. One theologian looking at this problem could write a book, *Moral Man and Immoral Society*.[34] Oh, when society becomes a reality before us we see sin in all of its glaring dimensions. People tend to think sometimes that we are evolving to a better height, or we are getting better inevitably, but I don't know about that. We deal with problems today just as people dealt with them two thousand years ago. We go to the battlefield to solve our problems. The only difference is that we are progressively evil. People two thousand years ago used to kill you with bow and arrows; we do it now with atomic bombs. (*Yeah, Amen*) And somehow we find ourselves in this state of sinfulness. One racial group tramples over another racial group with the iron feet of oppression. (*Yeah*) One nation tramples over another nation with injustice and

---

26. In the published version, King added this sentence: "These concepts only serve to remind us that engulfing human nature is a tragic, threefold estrangement by which man is separated from himself, his neighbors, and his God. There is a corruption in man's will" (*Strength to Love*, p. 91).

27. Ovid *Metamorphoses* 7.20.

28. Plato *Phaedrus* 246a–247c.

29. Cf. Augustine *Confessions* 8.7.

30. Romans 7:19.

31. Cf. Reinhold Niebuhr, *Beyond Tragedy*, pp. 137–138.

32. Isaiah 53:6.

33. Cf. Luke 18:9–14.

34. King refers to Reinhold Niebuhr and his 1932 publication.

evil and all that we can think of. We leave the battlefields of the world painted with blood, stack up national debts higher than mountains of gold, send men home psychologically deranged and physically handicapped, and fill our nations with orphans and widows. (*Yeah, Amen*) When we look at our collective life, we must cry out, "We are sinners. (*Yeah, Amen, Sinners*) We need to repent."[35] (*Amen, Yes*)

This afternoon as I come to my conclusion, there is still a voice crying out, "Repent. The kingdom of God is at hand."[36] (*Yeah, Amen*) And as we stand in this season of the year, this is the hour that we should repent. Let us come to see that man isn't made for the low places. Man is made for the stars, created for the everlasting, born for eternity. Jesus revealed to us that we are made for that which is high, noble, and good.[37] (*Amen*) And we must go out and seek it at every moment. There is a boy, who goes up to his father and says, "Father, give me my goods." And we see that boy walking down the road, going to a far country. After being there a while—wasting his substance, wasting his life, wasting all—a famine breaks out. And he ends up in a hog's pen. That parable tells us something.[38] It says to us that man is not made for the far country of evil, and as long as he finds himself going there he will end up frustrated, bewildered, and disillusioned.[39] Every time man goes to the far country of evil, a famine breaks out.[40] (*Amen, Yeah, Amen*) And what is the neu-, what can we consider the neurotic tendencies of our times—the frustration, the fears, and the suspicions—but expressions of the famine that has broken out in our world because we have separated ourselves from God? (*Yeah, Amen*)

But that parable doesn't end there. It said one day that boy came to himself. And when he came to himself he decided to rise up. And somehow we can see him as he

---

35. In a version of this sermon, which he submitted for publication in *Strength to Love*, King further lamented the evil tendencies of collective humanity: "Man collectivized in the group, the tribe, the race, and the nation often sinks to levels of barbarity unthinkable even among lower animals. We see the tragic expression of Immoral Society in the unspeakable savagery of Hitler's Germany, in nations trampling over other nations with the iron feet of oppression, in a doctrine of white supremacy which plunges millions of black men into the abyss of exploitations, and in the horrors of two world wars which have left battlefields drenched with blood, national debts higher than mountains of gold, men psychologically deranged and physically handicapped, and nations filled with widows and orphans. Man is a sinner in need of God's forgiving grace. This is not deadening pessimism; it is Christian realism" (Draft of Chapter XI, "What Is Man?" *Strength to Love*, July 1962–March 1963).

36. Matthew 4:17.

37. In the published version of this sermon, King wrote: "Despite man's tendency to live on low and degrading planes, something reminds him that he is not made for that. As he trails in the dust, something reminds him that he is made for the stars. As he makes folly his bedfellow, a nagging inner voice tells him that he is born for eternity. God's unbroken hold on us is something that will never permit us to feel right when we do wrong or to feel natural when we do the unnatural" (*Strength to Love*, p. 91).

38. King refers to the parable of the prodigal son (Luke 15:11–32).

39. In the published version, King wrote: "The farther he moved from his father's house, the closer he came to the house of despair. The more he did what he liked, the less he liked what he did" (*Strength to Love*, p. 91).

40. In the draft of this sermon that King submitted for publication, he continued: "Modern man has strayed to numerous far countries—secularism, materialism, and sexuality, only to mention a few. Racial injustice is one of the far countries to which man has [*journeyed*] with almost unrelenting passion over the last few centuries. His journey has brought a moral and spiritual famine in Western civilization. But it is not too late to return home" (Draft of Chapter XI, "What Is Man?" July 1962–March 1963).

says to himself, "I have a father back home. I have a father back home with food and other things to spare. I'm not made for this. I'm not made to dwell here. I will rise up and go back to my father." We can see him walking up the dusty road that he had once come down. Had a little speech and he had practiced this speech and he had planned to make it. But you know the beautiful thing is that he never did get a chance to make that speech. (*Amen*) Before he could get home, there was a father there waiting with outstretched arms (*Amen, Yeah*), saying, "Come home and I will accept you." And he runs down the road to meet him.

This is what happens any time that man decides to rise up. This is what happens any time a nation or an individual decides to rise up. The God of the universe stands there in all of His love and forgiving power saying, "Come home. (*Yeah, Amen, Amen*) Western civilization, you have strayed away into the far country of colonialism and imperialism. You have taken one billion six hundred million of your brothers in Asia and Africa, dominated them politically, exploited them economically, segregated and humiliated them. You have trampled over them. But western civilization, if you will rise up now and come out of this far country of imperialism and colonialism and come on back to your true home, which is freedom and justice, I'll take you in. (*Yeah, Oh amen*) America, I had great intentions for you. I had planned for you to be this great nation where all men would live together as brothers—a nation of religious freedom, a nation of racial freedom. And America, you wrote it in your Declaration of Independence. You meant well, for you cried out, 'All men are created equal and endowed by their creator with certain unalienable rights. (*Yeah*) Among these are life, liberty, and the pursuit of happiness.' (*Preach*) But in the midst of your creed, America, you've strayed away to the far country of segregation and discrimination. (*Say it, Amen*) You've taken sixteen million of your brothers, trampled over them, mistreated them, inflicted them with tragic injustices and indignities.[41] But America, I'm not going to give you up. If you will rise up out of the far country of segregation and discrimination (*Amen*), I will take you in, America. (*Amen, Amen*) And I will bring you back to your true home." (*Amen*)

And when a nation decides to do that, when an individual decides to do that, somehow the morning stars will sing together (*Amen, Yeah*), and the sons of God will shout for joy. (*Yeah, Amen*)

> To every man there openeth a way and ways and a way.
> The high soul climbs the high way. And the low soul gropes the low.
> And in between on the misty flats, the rest drift to and fro.
> But to every man there openeth a high and a low way.
> Every man decideth which way his soul shall go.[42]

God grant that under the spirit of Jesus the Christ you will choose a high way. (*Amen, Lord*) Eternal God our Father, we thank Thee for the inspiration of Jesus.

---

41. King used different language in the published version of this sermon: "In the far country of segregation and discrimination, you have oppressed nineteen million of your Negro brothers, binding them economically and driving them into the ghetto, and you have stripped them of their self-respect and self-dignity, making them feel that they are nobodies" (*Strength to Love*, p. 92).

42. King quotes John Oxenham's poem "The Ways" (1916).

(*Amen*) Grant that we will follow His way and recognize that we are made for the high places. (*Amen*) And grant that we will rise up out of the low, far countries of evil and return to the father's house. And now unto Him who is able to keep us from falling and to present us faultless before our father's throne, to Him be power and authority, majesty and dominion, now, henceforth, and forevermore. Amen.

At. MDCC-MiDW-AL.

Paul's Letter to American Christians, Sermon Delivered to the Commission on Ecumenical Missions and Relations, United Presbyterian Church, U.S.A.

[3 June 1958]
[Pittsburgh, Pa.]

King began to deliver versions of this sermon, written as early as 1956, as national speaking opportunities increased.[1] He uses the form of a New Testament Pauline epistle to challenge the American church, as Frederick Meek had done previously in his "A Letter to Christians."[2] King preached the following version at the inaugural convention of the newly established United Presbyterian Church, U.S.A. He assumes Paul's voice and questions whether Americans' "spiritual progress has been commensurate with your scientific progress." King warns the gathered Presbyterian leaders against racial segregation within their church as well as the schisms and "narrow sectarianism" within Protestantism that threatens to destroy "the unity of the body of Christ." He concludes by urging those involved in the struggle for justice, white as well as black, to remain nonviolent and to grow in their capacity for love, even for the oppressor. The following text is taken from an audio recording of the address.

Mr. Chairman, distinguished platform associates, ladies and gentlemen, I need not pause to say how very delighted I am to be here this morning and to be a part of this very rich fellowship. I want to express my personal appreciation to the Board of Missions for extending this invitation and making it possible for me to share in this

---

1. Charles W. Kelly, pastor emeritus of Tuskegee's Greenwood Missionary Baptist Church, extolled King's 7 September 1956 delivery of this sermon at the seventy-sixth annual meeting of the National Baptist Convention in Denver, writing: "You spoke as a prophet and seer which you are—The imaginative 'Letter from St. Paul' to American Xns was as vivid and real as any of the Pauline Epistles" (Kelly to King, 8 September 1956, in *Papers* 3:366). King preached a nearly identical version of this sermon at Dexter the following November (King, "Paul's Letter to American Christians," Sermon Delivered at Dexter Avenue Baptist Church, 4 November 1956, in *Papers* 3:414–420). Between 1956 and 1962, he delivered this sermon at least fifteen times.

2. King annotated a copy of Meek's homily "A Letter to Christians" and kept it in his sermon file ("A Letter to Christians, A sermon preached in Old South Church in Boston," 21 February 1954).

great meeting. I must apologize for being late this morning but I am sure you will forgive me when you realize that I didn't get in town until about six o'clock this morning
after riding all night on trains and planes with a minimum of sleep. I can assure you
if I had been in town earlier I would have been here on time this morning. But certainly it is a real pleasure and privilege to greet you this morning and to be here.

Now, since this is an overseas breakfast, naturally we are concerned about world
issues—issues confronting the Christian church, issues facing our whole missionary
enterprise. But I'd like to discuss with you this morning some of the problems confronting our nation. And before you accuse me of being provincial here, let me say to
you that our nation is a part of the world, and before the problems of the world are
solved, we must solve the problems of our nation, for we are caught in an inescapable
network of mutuality. Whatever affects one directly, it affects all indirectly. Missionaries
tell us every day that the missionary undertaking is made more difficult in so many
instances because of the gap in our national life between practice and profession. And
so I want to discuss some of the problems that we confront in our nation and problems that must be solved if our missionary efforts are to be meaningful.

What I have to say this morning will be in the form of a letter. I would like to
share with you an imaginary letter which comes from the pen of the Apostle Paul,
and the postmark reveals that it comes from the island of Crete.[3] After opening the
letter, I discovered that it was written in ill-formed, sprawling Greek.[4] At the top of
the letter was this inscription: "Please read when the people assemble themselves
together and pass on to the other churches."[5] For many weeks now I have been
laboring with the translation. At times it has been difficult, but now I believe I have
deciphered its true meaning. And if in presenting the letter the contents sound
strangely Kingian instead of Paulinian, attribute it to my lack of complete objectivity rather than Paul's lack of clarity.

It is miraculous indeed that the Apostle Paul should be writing a letter to you
and to me nearly nineteen hundred years after his last letter appeared in the New
Testament.[6] How this is possible is something of an enigma wrapped in mystery. The
important thing, however, is that I can imagine the Apostle Paul writing a letter to
American Christians in 1958 A.D. And here is the letter as it stands before me:

I, an apostle of Jesus Christ, by the will of God, to you who are in America, grace
and peace be unto you through our Lord and Savior, Jesus Christ.[7]

For many years I have longed to be able to come to see you. I have heard so much

---

3. Meek also said that his letter from Paul was "postmarked on the island of Crete," although Paul did
not write any of his epistles from there (Meek, "A Letter to Christians"). The Book of Titus, however, was
written by Paul to his disciple who was serving a young church on Crete. In his 4 November 1956 version
of this sermon, King preached that Paul wrote the letter in the Greek city of Ephesus (*Papers* 3:415).

4. The Pauline epistles were written in Koine Greek.

5. Meek, "A Letter to Christians": "Please read on the day when the people assemble themselves
together, and then pass on to the other churches."

6. Meek, "A Letter to Christians": "But by what strange miracle he should be writing to you and me
nearly 1900 years after the date of his last letter in the New Testament, I cannot imagine—and I do not
really care."

7. Paul began many of his letters, including Ephesians and Colossians, with this type of salutation.

of you and of what you are doing. I have heard of the fascinating and astounding advances that you have made in the scientific realm. I have heard of your dashing subways and flashing aeroplanes. Through your scientific genius you have been able to dwarf distance and place time in chains. Yes, you have been able to carve highways through the stratosphere, and so that in your world it is possible to eat breakfast in New York City and supper in Paris, France. I have also heard of your skyscraping buildings with their prodigious towers steeping heavenward. I have heard of your great medical advances which have resulted in the curing of many dread plagues and diseases and, thereby, prolonging your lives and making for greater security and physical well-being. All of that is marvelous. You can do so many things in your day that I could not do in the Greco-Roman world of my day. In your age you can travel distances in one day that it took me three months to travel. That is wonderful. You have made tremendous strides in the area of scientific and technological development.

But America, as I look at you from afar, I wonder whether your moral and spiritual progress has been commensurate with your scientific progress. Your poet Thoreau used to talk about improved means to an unimproved end.[8] How often this is true. You have allowed the material means by which you live to outdistance the spiritual ends for which you live. You have allowed your mentality to outrun your morality. You have allowed your civilization to outdistance your culture, and through your scientific genius you have made of the world a neighborhood. But through your moral and spiritual genius, you have failed to make of it a brotherhood. And so, America, I would urge you to bring your moral advances in line with your scientific advances.

I am impelled to write you concerning the responsibilities laid upon you to live as Christians in the midst of an unchristian world. This is what I had to do. This is what every Christian has to do.[9] But I understand that there are many Christians in America who give their ultimate allegiance to man-made systems and customs. They are afraid to be different. Their great concern is to be accepted socially. They live by some such principle as this: "Everybody is doing it, so it must be all right." Morality is merely group consensus. In your modern sociological lingo, the mores are accepted as the right ways. You have unconsciously come to believe that right is discovered by taking a sort of Gallup Poll of the majority opinion, and how many are giving their ultimate allegiance to this way.[10]

But American Christians, I must say to you, as I said to the Roman Christians years ago, "Be not conformed to this world, but be ye transformed by the renewing of your mind."[11] Or as I said to the Philippian Christians, "Ye are a colony of heaven."[12] This means that although you live in the colony of time your ultimate

---

8. Henry David Thoreau, *Walden; or Life in the Woods* (1854), p. 57.

9. Meek, "A Letter to Christians": "I am impelled to write to you about the demands that are laid upon you to live as Christians in the midst of the sub-Christian world of your day. That is what I had to do—live in an unChristian world. That is what we all have to do."

10. King wrote at the end of his copy of "A Letter to Christians": "They tell me that there are some among you particularly one by the name of McCarthy, who has caused Christian to be afraid to speak out against social evils. They tell me that even some of the preachers have lost the prophetic note."

11. Cf. Romans 12:2.

12. Cf. Philippians 3:20 (MOFFATT).

allegiance is to the empire of eternity. You have a dual citizenry. You live both in time and eternity, both in heaven and earth.[13] Therefore, your ultimate allegiance is not to the government, not to the state, not to the nation, not to any man-made institution. The Christian owes his ultimate allegiance to God, and if any earthly institution conflicts with God's will, it is your Christian duty to take a stand against it. You must never allow the transitory, evanescent demands of man-made institutions to take precedence over the eternal demands of the Almighty God.

I understand that you have an economic system in America known as capitalism, and through this economic system you have been able to do wonders. You have become the richest nation in the world, and you have built up the greatest system of production that history has ever known. All of this is marvelous. But Americans, there is the danger that you will misuse your capitalism. I still contend that money can be the root of all evil.[14] It can cause one to live a life of gross materialism, and I'm afraid that many among you are more concerned about making a living than making a life.[15] You are prone to judge the success of your professions by the index of your salary and the size of the wheel base on your automobile rather than the quality of your service to humanity.

The misuse of capitalism can also lead to tragic exploitation. This has so often happened in your nation. They tell me that one-tenth of one percent of the population controls more than forty percent of the wealth. Oh, America, how often have you taken necessities from the masses to give luxuries to the classes? If you are to be truly a Christian nation, you must solve this problem. Now, you cannot solve the problem by turning to communism, for communism is based on an ethical relativism and a metaphysical materialism that no Christian can accept. But you can work within the framework of democracy to bring about a better distribution of wealth. You can use your powerful economic resources to wipe poverty from the face of the earth. God never intended for a group of people to live in superfluous, inordinate wealth while others live in abject, deadening poverty. God intends for all of His children to have the basic necessities of life, and He has left in this universe enough and to spare for that purpose. So I call upon you to bridge the gulf between abject poverty and superfluous wealth.

I would that I could be with you in person so that I could say to you face to face what I am forced to say to you in writing. Oh, how I long to share your fellowship.[16]

Let me rush on to say something about the church. America, I must remind you,

---

13. Meek, "A Letter to Christians": "Your citizenship is two-fold—on earth and in heaven, in time and in eternity, of the kingdoms of men and of the kingdom of God." On that page of his copy of Meek's sermon, King wrote, "Remember that your citizenship is twofold—It is true that you live in the colony of time. But you must get your orders from the empire of eternity."

14. Cf. 1 Timothy 6:10.

15. On the last two pages of his copy of "A Letter to Christians," King noted, "I understand that you have a economic system called capitalism and it has wrought many good fruits, such as giving you the greatest production system in the world. It has also bought many evils. Since I am not an economist I cannot criticism it from an economic point of view but only from an economic one (1) exploitation (2) a gross materialism."

16. Meek, "A Letter to Christians": "I would to God that I could be with you in person, so that I could say to your face—and more too—what I am writing."

as I have said to so many others, that the church is the body of Christ, and so when the church is true to its nature, it knows neither division nor disunity. But I am disturbed about what you are doing to the body of Christ. They tell me that in America you have within Protestantism more than 256 denominations. The tragedy is not so much that you have such a multiplicity of denominations but that most of them are warring against each other with a claim to absolute truth.[17] I am not calling for uniformity, America; I am calling for unity. This narrow sectarianism is destroying the unity of the body of Christ. You must come to see that God is not a Baptist, God is not a Methodist, God is not a Presbyterian, God is not an Episcopalian. God is bigger than all of our denominations. You must come to see that, America.

But I must not stop with a criticism of Protestantism. I am disturbed about Roman Catholicism. This church stands before the world with its pomp and power, insisting that it possesses the only truth. It incorporates an arrogance that becomes a dangerous spiritual arrogance. It stands with its noble pope who somehow rises to the miraculous heights of infallibility when he speaks *ex cathedra*.[18] But I am disturbed about a person or an institution that claims infallibility in this world. I am disturbed about any church that refuses to cooperate with other churches under the pretense that it is the only true church. I must emphasize the fact that God is not a Roman Catholic and that the boundless sweep of his revelation cannot be limit to the Vatican. Roman Catholicism must do a great deal to mend its ways.[19] I understand that you have in your nation what is known as the National Council of Churches. And all over the world now there is a World Council of Churches, and I would urge you to continue to cooperate with all of these bodies. More than anything else, they continually remind us that we are all one in Christ Jesus. And that at bottom, although we differ in certain credal systems and certain doctrinal forms, there is a unity that makes us all one.

There is another thing that disturbs me to no end about the American church—you have a white church, and you have a Negro church.[20] You have allowed segregation to creep into the doors of the church. How can such a division exist in the true body of Christ? You must face the tragic fact that when you stand at eleven o'clock on Sunday morning to sing "In Christ There Is No East or West," you stand in the most segregated hour of Christian America.[21] They tell me that there is more integration in the entertaining world, in sports arenas, in other secular agencies,

---

17. A *Chicago Daily Tribune* article reported that King praised the creation of the United Presbyterian Church, U.S.A. "as a move away from the 'multiplicity of denominations' within American Protestantism. The tragedy of having so many of them, he said, is that 'most of them are warring against each other with a claim to absolute truth'" ("Presbyterian White Groups O.K. Negroes," 4 June 1958).

18. *Ex cathedra*, or "from the chair," signifies the pronouncement of church doctrine, particularly that coming from the pope of the Roman Catholic Church.

19. King mitigated his harsh criticism of divisive sectarianism, particularly of Catholicism, in the published version of this sermon (King, *Strength to Love*, pp. 129–130).

20. On the last page of his copy of Meek's sermon, King wrote, "The division in the churches appalls me (i.e. Negro and White)."

21. King refers to John Oxenham's hymn "In Christ There Is No East Or West" (1908). In the November 1956 version of this sermon at Dexter, King cited the hymns "All Hail the Power of Jesus Name" and "Dear Lord and Father of All Mankind" (*Papers* 3:417).

than there is in the Christian church. How appalling that is. I understand that there are Christians among you who try to justify segregation on the basis of the Bible. They argue that the Negro is inferior by nature because of Noah's curse upon the children of Ham.[22] Oh, my friends, this is blaspheming. This is against everything that the Christian religion stands for. I must say to you, as I have said to so many Christians before, that in Christ there is neither Jew nor Gentile, bond nor free, male nor female, for we are all one in Christ Jesus.[23] Moreover, I must reiterate the words that I uttered on Mars' Hill: "God that made the world and all things therein hath made of one blood all nations of men for to dwell on all the face of the earth."[24]

And so Americans, I am impelled to urge you to get rid of every aspect of segregation. The broad universalism standing at the center of the gospel makes both the theory and practice of segregation morally unjustifiable. Segregation is a blatant denial of the unity which we all have in Christ. It substitutes an I-It relationship. [*recording interrupted*] relationship.[25] The segregator relegates the segregated to the status of a thing rather than elevate him to the status of a person. The underlying philosophy of Christianity is diametrically opposed to the underlying philosophy of segregation, and all the dialectics of the logicians cannot make them lie down together. I praise your Supreme Court for rendering a great decision just a few years ago.[26] And I am happy to know that so many persons of goodwill have accepted the decision as a great moral victory. And I understand that there are some brothers among you who have risen up in open defiance. And I hear that their legislative halls ring loud with such words as "nullification" and "interposition." They have lost the true meaning of democracy and Christianity. So I would urge each of you to plead patiently with your brothers and tell them that this isn't the way. With understanding goodwill, you are obligated to seek to change their attitudes. Let them know that in standing against integration they are not only standing against the noble precepts of your democracy but also against the eternal edicts of God Himself. Yes America, there is still the need for an Amos to cry out to the nation, "Let judgment roll down as waters, and righteousness as a mighty stream."[27]

Now, I know there are those among you who are talking about gradualism and moderation. They are saying to you that you must slow up in the move for freedom and justice. I would say to you, America, if moderation means moving on towards the goal of justice and freedom, with wise restraint and calm reasonableness, then moderation is a great virtue that all men of goodwill must seek to achieve in this tense period of transition. But if moderation means slowing up in the move for justice and capitulating to the whims and caprices of the guardians of a deadening status quo, then moderation is a tragic vice which all men of goodwill must condemn.

---

22. Genesis 9:24–25.

23. Galatians 3:28.

24. Acts 17:24, 26.

25. In his 4 November 1956 version of this sermon at Dexter, King said at this point in the sermon, "It substitutes an 'I-it' relationship for the 'I-thou' relationship" (*Papers* 3:418).

26. King probably refers to *Brown v. Board of Education* (1954).

27. Amos 5:24.

You must say to your brothers all over America that you have a moral obligation to press on, and because of your love for America and your love for democracy, you must press on. You must realize that out of the two billion five hundred million people in this world, about one billion six hundred million of them are colored, living on two continents, mainly Asia and Africa—six hundred million in China, four hundred million in India and Pakistan, two hundred million in Africa, a hundred million in Indonesia, more than eighty-six million in Japan. For years, these people have been the victims of colonialism and imperialism, and now they are breaking aloose. They are breaking loose from all of this, and they are saying in no uncertain terms that racism and colonialism must go. So if your nation is to be a first-class nation, she can no longer have second-class citizens.

May I say just a word to those of you who are struggling against this evil in America. Always be sure that you struggle with Christian methods and Christian weapons. Never succumb to the temptation of becoming bitter. As you press on for justice, be sure to move with dignity and discipline, using only the weapon of love. Let no man pull you so low as to make you hate him. Always avoid using violence in your struggle, for if you succumb to the temptation of using violence unborn generations will be the recipients of a long and desolate night of bitterness and your chief legacy to the future will be an endless reign of meaningless chaos. Remember, America, that there is still a voice crying out through the vista of time, saying to every potential Peter, "Put up your sword."[28] And history is replete with the bleached bones of nations. History is cluttered with the wreckage of communities that fail to follow this command. And so violence is not the way.

In your struggle for justice [*recording interrupted*] or even to pay him back for injustice that he has heaped upon you.[29] Let him know that you are merely seeking justice for him as well as yourself. Let him know that the festering sore of segregation debilitates a white man as well as a Negro. With this attitude, you will be able to keep your struggle on high Christian standards.

Many persons will recognize the urgency of seeking to eradicate the evil of segregation. There will be many Negroes who will devote their lives to the cause of freedom. There will be many white persons of goodwill and strong moral sensitivity who will dare to take a stand for justice. Honesty impels me to admit that such a stand requires willingness to suffer and sacrifice, so don't despair if you are condemned and persecuted for righteousness' sake.[30] Whenever you take a stand for truth and justice, you are liable to scorn. Often you will be called an impractical idealist or a dangerous radical. Sometimes it might mean going to jail. If such is the case, you must honorably grace the jail with your presence. It might even mean physical death for some. But if physical death is the price that some must pay to free their children from a permanent life of psychological death, then nothing could be more Christian.

---

28. John 18:11.

29. In his 4 November 1956 version of this sermon at Dexter, King elaborated, "In your struggle for justice, let your oppressor know that you are not attempting to defeat or humiliate him, or even pay him back for injustices that he has heaped upon you" (*Papers* 3:418).

30. Cf. Matthew 5:10.

Don't worry about persecution, America. You are going to have that if you stand up for a great principle. I can say this with some authority because my life was a continual round of persecutions. After my conversion, I was rejected by the disciples at Jerusalem. Later, I was tried for heresy at Jerusalem. I was jailed at Philippi, beaten at Thessalonica, mobbed at Ephesus, and depressed at Athens.[31] But yet I am still going. I came away from each of these experiences more persuaded than ever before that neither life nor death, angels nor principalities, things present nor things to come shall be able to separate us from the love of God, which is in Christ Jesus our Lord.[32] I still believe that standing up for the truth of God is the greatest thing in the world. This is the end of life, America. The end of life is not to be happy. The end of life is not to achieve pleasure and to avoid pain. The end of life is to do the will of God, come what may.

I must bring my writing to a close, now. Timothy is awaiting me to deliver this letter, and I must take leave for another church.[33] But just before leaving, I must say to you, as I said to the church at Corinth, that I still believe that love is the most durable power in all the world.[34] Over the centuries men have sought to discover the highest good. This has been the chief quest of ethical philosophy. This was one of the big questions of Greek philosophy. The Epicureans and the Stoics sought to answer it. Plato and Aristotle sought to answer it. What is the *summum bonum* of life?[35] I think I have an answer, America. I think I have discovered the highest good. It is love. This principle stands at the center of the cosmos. As John says, "God is love."[36] And so he who loves is a participant in the being of God. He who hates does not know God.[37]

So American Christians, you may master the intricacies of the English language. You may possess all of the eloquence of articulate speech. But even if you speak with the tongues of men and angels and have not love, you are become as sounding brass or a tinkling cymbal.

You may have the gift of prophecy and understand all mysteries.[38] You may be able to break into the storehouse of nature and bring out many insights that men never dreamed were there. You may ascend to the heights of academic achievement so that you will have all knowledge. You may boast of your great institutions of learning and the boundless extent of your degrees. But all of this amounts to absolutely nothing devoid of love.

Yes, America, you may give your goods to feed the poor. You may give great gifts

---

31. Cf. 2 Corinthians 11:22–30. In his copy of Meek's sermon, King wrote on the last page, "Those of you who are living the Christian life may sometimes be persecuted, but don't worry, for God will give you power to withstand it. I myself have had a deal of trouble living the life for Christ. I was tried for heresy at Jerusalem, etc."

32. Cf. Romans 8:39.

33. Meek, "A Letter to Christians": "(Timothy tells me that I must finish my writing because the winged machine that is to carry this letter to you will be here shortly.)"

34. Cf. 1 Corinthians 13:13 (MOFFATT, RSV).

35. *Summum bonum* is Latin for "the greatest good."

36. 1 John 4:8, 16.

37. Cf. 1 John 4:7–8.

38. Cf. 1 Corinthians 13:1–2.

to charity. You may tower high in philanthropy, but if you have not love, it means nothing. You may even give your body to be burned and die the death of a martyr. And your spilled blood may be a symbol of honor for generations yet unborn, and thousands may praise you as history's supreme hero. But even so if you have not love, your blood was spilled in vain. You must come to see that it is possible for a man to be self-centered in his self-denial and self-righteous in his self-sacrifice. He may be generous in order to feed his ego and pious in order to feed his pride. Man has a tragic capacity to relegate a heightening virtue to a tragic vice. Without love, benevolence becomes egotism and martyrdom becomes spiritual pride.

So the greatest of all virtues is love.[39] This is the thing that kept the early church moving. This is the thing that kept us moving amid the days of persecution around the Greco-Roman world. Men and women would look at us and cry out, "What is it that makes you so happy? Is it in your ecclesiastical machinery?" And we could answer, "No." "Is it in your dogmas? Is it in your creeds?" And we could answer, "No." "What is it then?" We could cry out, "We are happy because we have passed from death unto life." "Why?" "Because we love; that is it." This is the thing that must keep the church moving, and America, let me say to you that this is the meaning of the cross. That event on Calvary is more than a meaningless drama that took place on the stage of history. It is a telescope through which we look out into the long vista of eternity and see the love of God breaking forth into time. It is an eternal reminder to a power-drunk generation that love is a most durable power in the world and that is, at bottom, the heartbeat of the moral cosmos. Only through achieving this love can you expect to matriculate into the university of eternal life.

I must say good-bye now. I hope this letter will find you strong in the faith.[40] It may be that I will not get to see you in America, but I will meet you in God's eternity.

And now unto Him who is able to keep us from falling.[41] And now unto Him who is able to lift us from the fatigue of despair to the buoyancy of hope. And now unto Him who is able to solve the race problem if we will cooperate with Him. And now unto Him who is able to transform this cosmic energy into constructive force. Now unto Him who is able to transform this midnight of injustice into a glowing daybreak of freedom and justice. To Him be power and authority, majesty and dominion, now, henceforth, and forever more.[42]

This is the letter, and now comes the living of it.[43] [*sustained applause*]

At. PCUSAP-PPPrHi.

---

39. Cf. 1 Corinthians 13:13 (MOFFATT, RSV).

40. Meek, "A Letter to Christians": "I trust that the letter finds you well and strong in the faith. I must take my leave now, and in God's eternity we shall all meet." At the bottom of this page of his copy of Meek's sermon, King wrote, "Love is still the principle thing You may have towering skyscrapers, ~~and~~ but without love it is nothing. You may have all knowledge, all philosophical profundity, but without love."

41. Jude 1:24.

42. Cf. Jude 1:25.

43. Meek, "A Letter to Christians": "Now comes the living of it."

[14 September 1958]
[Chicago, Ill.]

King penned this sermon outline for the Youth Sunday Services of the Woman's Convention Auxiliary, National Baptist Convention. A report of the proceedings described King as "the Mahatma Gandhi—in the present day American race crisis."[1] Written on stationery of the Woman's Auxiliary, it is based on Jesus' illustration of a neighbor's response to a persistent friend seeking bread at midnight. Drawing on D. T. Niles's homily "Evangelism," King notes that while many look to the church during their time of need, "hundreds & [thousands] of men and women in quest for the bread of social justice" leave disappointed.[2] King later prepared a full version of this sermon for publication in Strength to Love.[3]

Luke 11:6 [4]

Int. It is midnight in the parable; ~~and~~ it is also midnight in our world today. Man is exper today a darkness so deep that he can hardly see which way to turn.[5] The best minds of our day, the most prophetic voices, are saying that today ~~we stand~~ our civilization stands at the midnight of its revolving cycle. It is a dark age and a dark world in which we live

I.

1. It is midnight in the social order. Within a generation we have fought two world wars, and there is always hovering over us the treat of another war. The deep rumblings of discontent from around our globe are obvious signs of the social diruption of our age.

    As we look out on the international horizon we see the nations of the world engaged in a collosal and bitter contest for supremacy, which might easily result in the annihilation of the whole human race. We look out and see that atomic warfare has just begun and bacteriological warfare yet unused. These ~~instruments~~ weapons are so powerful that a city like Chicago can be wiped off the globe in a matter of seconds. It seems that all of these

---

1. National Baptist Convention of the United States of America, *The Record of the Seventy-eighth Annual Session of the National Baptist Convention U.S.A. Incorporated and the Woman's Auxiliary* (1958), p. 357.

2. King wrote "A Knock at midnight" on the copy of Niles's homily that he kept in his sermon file (D. T. Niles, "Evangelism," Address at the second assembly of the World Council of Churches, 16 August 1954). Niles later published this sermon as "Summons at Midnight" (Niles, *Christian Century* [5 October 1954]: 1037–1039).

3. King, Draft of Chapter VI, "A Knock at Midnight," July 1962–March 1963, pp. 494–504 in this volume.

4. Luke 11:5–6: "And he said unto them, Which of you shall have a friend, and shall go unto him at midnight, and say unto him, Friend, lend me three loaves; For a friend of mine in his journey is come to me, and I have nothing to set before him?"

5. Niles, "Evangelism": "It is midnight in the parable. It is also midnight in the world today. The night is so deep that everything has become just an object to be avoided, and obstacle in the dark against which men must take care not to bump."

> . . . Through such souls alone
> God stooping shows sufficient of his light
> For us i' the dark to rise by. And I rise.

That is the essence of the gospel. We say it about Christ:

> God stooping shows sufficient of his light
> For us i' the dark to rise by.

Close by showing that religion does not clear up all the answers. At the heart of of our religion is the deepest mystery of all, the cross, where love was nailed to a tree by hate

At the end of Fosdick's sermon called "The Mystery of Life," from his 1958 book *Riverside Sermons,* King writes, "Close by showing that religion does not clear up all the answers. At the heart of our religion is the deepest mystery of all, the cross, where love was nailed to a tree by hate" (p. 27).

things may conspire to bring an untimely death to the human family on this globe.

2. It is also midnight in the psychological order. People are more worried and frustrated than [~~every~~?] ever before. The psychopathic wards of our hospital are full. Minister and psychiatrist are busy

a. Notice the best sellers In psychology: <u>Man Against Himself</u>; <u>The</u> [*Neurotic?*] <u>Personality of time</u>; <u>Modern Man in Search of a Soul</u>[6]

It is [*Sigmund*] Freud who is the popular phychologist.

b. In Religion

<u>Peace of Soul</u>, <u>Peace of Mind</u>, <u>A Guide to Confident Living</u>[7]

The popular preachers today are those who can preach great sermons on "How to relax" etc. "How to keep your

All of this is a fit testamony to the fact that it is midnight in the inner lives of men and women.

3. It is midnight in the moral order. Midnight is a time when all colors loss their distinctiveness and become merely a dirty ~~shade of grade~~ gray.[8] All moral principles have lost their distinctions Nothing is right or wrong absolutely for modern man. It is just a matter of what the majority of the people are doing. Everybody is doing it so it must be alright. So we have developed a generation of moral cowards Midnight is a time when everything is relative Midnight also causes us to feel that nothing is really right but to get by. And nothing really wrong but to get caught

II But as in the parable so in our world today, the deep darkness of the midnight is interupted by the sound of a knock. And in our day it is the knock of the world on the door of the church.[9] And more than anybody else in the church the minister is aware of the knock. quite strange isnt it that man at midnight will be knocking on the door of the church

There are more people members of the church today than ever before. 97,000,000. Compare that with the fact that in 1929 there were only 50,000,000. That is an increase of more than 90% and the population in that time has increased only 31%.

And you remember the parable said that the man wanted three loaves of bread. And stragly enough modern man is in quest for three loaves. It is spritual bread

a bread of faith—Modern man is so often a faithless being

b bread of hope—Modern man has lost hope in the future and in his destiny

c. bread of love—

6. Karl A. Menninger, *Man Against Himself* (New York: Harcourt, Brace, 1938); Karen Horney, *The Neurotic Personality of Our Time;* C. G. Jung, *Modern Man in Search of a Soul.*

7. Fulton J. Sheen, *Peace of Soul;* Joshua Loth Liebman, *Peace of Mind;* Norman Vincent Peale, *A Guide to Confident Living* (New York: Prentice-Hall, 1948).

8. Niles, "Evangelism": "Besides, at midnight every colour loses its distinctiveness and becomes merely a dirty shade of grey." Above this sentence, King wrote "discuss moral relativism" on his copy of Niles's sermon.

9. Niles, "Evangelism": "But, as in the parable, so in our day, the tense silence of the midnight is disturbed by the sound of a knock. It is the door of the Church on which somebody is knocking."

Isnt it strange that in the midnight hous of his life when he has stood in the darkness of our generation, in the darknes of our age. [*He?*] groups through the streets of life and runs to the church of God to find a little bread.

III When he first knocked he was left disappointed
   Hundreds & thousand of men and women in quest for the bread of social justice going ~~into~~ to the church only to be disappointed.
   (a) Look at South Africa—Lead on by a Dutch Reform Protestant Preacher.[10]
   (b) Look at the British Empire and her exploitation of India—The Church of England sanctioned it.
   (c) The white man in America—11 Oclock is the segregated hour in Christian America[11]

AD. CSKC: Sermon file, folder 8, "A Knock at Midnight."

---

10. Daniel François Malan, a clergyman in the Dutch Reformed Church and prime minister of South Africa from 1948 until 1954, instituted his nation's policy of apartheid.

11. National Council of Churches official Helen Kenyon labeled eleven o'clock on Sunday morning as "the most segregated time" in the United States ("Worship Hour Found Time of Segregation," *New York Times*, 4 November 1952; see also Robert J. McCracken, "Discrimination—The Shame of Sunday Morning," p. 4).

"Worship at Its Best,"
Sermon at Dexter Avenue Baptist Church

[14 December 1958]
[Montgomery, Ala.]

Recognizing that worship is an elemental component of all religions, King delineates its three fundamental aspects.

Int: There is hardly any drive in human nature more elemental than the practice of worship. Everywhere man appears [*to be?*] as a worshipping creature. Whether he is a Buddhist praying in his temple, a Confucianist bowing in his shrine, a Moslem knealing in his mosques, a Jew worshiping in his synagogue, or a Christian prasing God in his Cathedral, man is a worshiping creature.[1]

---

1. Fosdick, *Successful Christian Living*, p. 165: "Man everywhere appears as a worshiping creature. Some of us have prayed with Buddhists in their temples, bowed with Confucianists in their shrines, knelt with Moslems in their mosques, worshiped many a time in synagogues, and with all sorts of Christians have shared devotion." King wrote "Preached at Dexter, Dec. 14, 1958" on the folder containing this outline and Fosdick's sermon, which King had torn out of *Successful Christian Living*.

Since worship is such a basic part of the human response, we may well ask, What 14 Dec 1958 is distinguishs true from false worship? What is worship at its best?

Worship at its best consist of a threefold look

I   The upward look—seeing God high and lifted up. In our day it means going to Church and partaking of the sacramnts.

II   The inward look—"I am a man of unclean lips."[2] It brings us in contact with the highest and least in reality. We begin to say as Iago said abot Cassio;

> He hath a daily beauty in his life
>
> that makes me ugly[3]

Worship makes us aware of life's undying dream. (See Miller, The Great Realities, p 24, 32)[4]

III The outward look—"Here am I O lord send me"[5] If worship does not lead to service it is meaningless.

"Why call ye me Lord Lord and do not the things I command.[6]

> Quote the prophets
>
> Amos
>
> Miches
>
> Jermiah about subtituting worship for service.

'What doth the Lord requre of thee but to do justly, love mercy."[7]

Be not deceived, God is not mocked by empty hymn anthem, and prayer.[8] God cannot be placated by pious observances.[9]

AD. CSKC: Sermon file, folder 62, Worship at Its Best.

---

2. Cf. Isaiah 6:5.

3. William Shakespeare, *Othello*, act 5, sc. 1.

4. King cites two references made to persistent dreams by Samuel Miller in *The Great Realities* (New York: Harper & Brothers, 1955). Miller writes: "Under it all there is a dream, perhaps a bit hard to remember, but a dream that will not die completely, however much it is neglected or compromised," and further states, "This lasting dream which tortures and torments us with its undying hopes, ill treated and neglected as it is, stands embedded in the reality of our human state" (Miller, *The Great Realities*, pp. 24, 32). Samuel Howard Miller was minister of the Old Cambridge Baptist Church from 1935 until 1959, when he became dean of Harvard Divinity School.

5. Cf. Isaiah 6:8.

6. Cf. Luke 6:46.

7. Cf. Micah 6:8. In King's notes on this verse, he wrote: "Here again we find one of the high water marks of the O.T. The divine demand upon men is expressed in terms of elemental simplicity—justice and kindness between man and man, and a humble walk with God. This was religion as Micah saw it. [¶] Jehovah's good will is served not by a careful observance of the ritual, or by the bringing of sacrifices, whatever may be their intrinsic value, but by a life in accord with the principles of righteousness, by the diligent practice of kindness and brotherliness, and by a living fellowship with God in the spirit of humility. Few notions so sublime have been conceived in the whole history of religion" (King, Notecards on topics from Micah, 22 September 1952–28 January 1953).

8. Fosdick, *Successful Christian Living*, p. 172: "'Be not deceived; God is not mocked' by empty hymns, anthems, and prayers." Cf. Galatians 6:7.

9. Micah 6:8. King underlined Fosdick's use of this phrase in his annotated copy of *Successful Christian Living*, p. 172.

King greets parishioners, 1958. Photo by Flip Schulke; courtesy of Black Star.

"Christ Our Starting Point,"
Sermon at Dexter Avenue Baptist Church

[21 December 1958]
[Montgomery, Ala.]

In this handwritten outline for a sermon he delivered at Dexter Avenue Baptist Church, King emphasizes the importance of beginning life with Christ: "When you start with Christ you go the second mile; you give a cup of cold water; you stop on the [Jericho] road and help your brother; and you even love your enemies."[1]

Rev. 1:2 [2]

I   Intro:
    (A) The necessity of the right starting point in life. The starting point determnis the ending point.
    (b) Our starting point should be an absolute. We must not begin with relativism.
II   Christianity has always insisted that Christ is the proper starting point. Some

---

1. The 21 December 1958 Dexter program indicates King preached "Christ, Our Starting Point." He also wrote "Preached at Dexter Dec. 21, 1958" on the file folder containing this sermon.
2. "Who bare record of the word of God, and of the testimony of Jesus Christ, and of all things that he saw." King wrote this biblical citation in a second pen.

would argue with this by saying God is the starting point. But if we start with God we start with our ideas about him.

    A.   But Christ telles us what God is like. God is Christlike.[3]

    B.   Christ is the moral and spiritual ultimate

III When we start with Christ several things happen

    A.   We place a new value on ourselves and our possibilities. We are never hopeless about our plight. Christ reminds us that we can be better than we are. We place new value on the dignity ad worth[4]

    B   When you start with Christ you go the second mile; you give a cup of cold water; you stop on the Jerico road and help your brother; and you even love your enemies . . . "[5]

    C.   We come to see that there is a reliable dependable God in the universe whose purpose changeth not.[6]

        (1) We are not thrown out as ophrans on the planet. We are not alone in our struggle. We can depend on him.

        (2) So we can live without fear. If we are always worring about death, or the future, or what will happen [*tomorrow?*] we have the wong starting point.

    D.   Conclusion: So we have a hope. Old secourities may fall, but we have a hope. Fried may desert us, but we have a hope. Even western civilization may crumble and decay, but we have a hope

        I can hear you asking now what is it. Is it your econic security, no

My hope is built on nothing less Than Jesus' blood and righteousness; I dare not trust the sweetest frame, But wholly lean on Jesus' name.

When darkness seems to hide his face I rest on his unchanging grace; In every high and stormy gale, My anchor holds with-in the veil.—On Christ[7]

AD. CSKC: Sermon file, folder 94, "Christ, Our Starting Point."

---

3. King may be referring to John 10:36–38: "Say ye of him, whom the Father hath sanctified, and sent into the world, Thou blasphemest; because I said, I am the Son of God? If I do not the works of my Father, believe me not. But if I do, though ye believe not me, believe the works: that ye may know, and believe, that the Father is in me, and I in him."

4. King wrote this sentence in a second pen.

5. Cf. Matthew 5:41, 10:42; Luke 10:25–37; and Matthew 5:44.

6. Cf. Malachi 3:6.

7. King quotes Edward Mote's hymn "My Hope Is Built" (1834). He added this entire reference to the hymn in a second pen.

When Your A String Breaks

King asserts that God's grace enables one to turn liabilities into opportunities.[1]
Noting that "we as a people have the handicap of oppression and injustice,"
King draws inspiration from the resilience of slaves, whose "bottomless [vitality]
transformed the fatigue of despair into the buoyancy of hope."

II Cor 12:9 And he said unto me, My grace is sufficient for thee: for my strength is made perfect in weakness[2]

I   I would like to start my sermon this morning by referring to a violin—that gently beautiful instrument that pours forth cosmically melodious music.

II   This is life—to have your A string snap and finish on three strings.[3]

III   The A string may break in sone childhood exp.

     a   Some parents do not understand the critical importance of the emotial experiences of childhood, and the child grows up with supicion, distrust, fear anxiety and vinditveness. <u>His spiritual problem will be to deal with this</u>.

     b.   Or here is a man who in youth had all the natural ambitions of young manhood for success but who now reconizes that he will not arive at the desired goal Again and again he has steped on the gas, but the sped is not in him. Nature did not equip him with eight cylinders or with six—only four, and those none to good.

     B.   The A string may break in some physical hadicap blind, cripple for life

     C.   The A string may break in being inflicted with the lonliness of standing up in a great cause

     D.   The A string may break as a result of personal relations—Here is a life that wanted love and missed it. Here is a young couple that wanted a beatiful marriage. Here is a family where a child was greeted as a blessing, but became an inward agony. epilepsy—eye trouble.

II   Paul experiece. "My grace is sufficient."

V.   How do we deal with this. Where is the grace that is sufficient to us

     A.   We must honestly confront the experience of having our A string [*snap?*]. Dont run from it. Place your handicap ~~daringly~~ at the forfront of your mind and stare daringly stare at it. "How may I transform this liability into an asset."

     B.   Another important way to deal with the problem is to develop the capacity

---

1. King wrote the first page of this outline on the verso of a 3 November 1959 letter ripped in half. Although missing the sender's name, the text indicates the author was Thomas H. Randall. King wrote the last two pages of the sermon on a sheet of Southern Christian Leadership Conference (SCLC) stationery that was torn in half.

2. Cf. 2 Corinthians 12:9.

3. King's sermon file contained his handwritten note about the violinist Ole Bull, who continued to play when his A string broke (King, When Your A String Breaks, Sermon notes, 1959).

to make our limitations our opportunities. We must take our handicaps and use them as the raw material out of which we mold and create something meaningful Transform the dungeon of handicap into a haven of creativity

    (1) The boy in Jamacai

    (2) Roosevelt[4]

    (3) Lincoln[5]

    (4) Beetovan, Milton, Handle[6]

C. However sevely our handicaps we can always make a spiritual contribution to the world. We as a people have the handicap of oppression and injustice.

    1. Call the rol of Negrors[7]

    2. Slavery—they survived.

    3. Their bottomless vitaliy tranformed the fatigue of despair into the buoyancy of hope

D. The plane trip—No wind of advesity can stop him. No stom of failure can overwelm him

E. Lagston Hughes[8]

F. The meaning of grace

AD. CSKC: Sermon file, folder 82, "Making It in on Broken Pieces."

---

4. King may refer to President Franklin Delano Roosevelt's ability to pursue a successful political career despite his paralysis.

5. In his sermon "Overcoming an Inferiority Complex," King observed that a young Abraham Lincoln had been "one of the most discouraged men that ever lived" until he gave his life to the cause of anti-slavery (King, "Overcoming an Inferiority Complex," 14 July 1957, p. 314 in this volume).

6. King may refer to Ludwig van Beethoven's deafness and the blindness of John Milton and George Frideric Handel. King also referred to Milton's blindness in Unfulfilled Hopes, Sermon Delivered at Dexter Avenue Baptist Church, 5 April 1959, p. 363 in this volume.

7. In a sermon filed in the same folder as this document, King listed Booker T. Washington, Roland Hayes, and Mary McLeod Bethune as African Americans who "demonstrate to us that we can make it in on broken pieces" (King, "Making It in on Broken Pieces," 4 August 1963).

8. King may be referring to Langston Hughes's 1922 poem "Mother to Son," as he does in the prepared text of the 1957 speech, "The Montgomery Story" (King, "The Montgomery Story," Address at 47th Annual NAACP convention, 27 June 1956, in *Papers* 3:310). He preceded the poem with the comment, "We must continue to move on in the face of every obstacle."

I'm Going To: Procrastination

[*1959*]

In this handwritten sermon outline, King advises against waiting to do the
right thing.[1]

Ananius the High Priest
Tertullus[2]

1. This text reveals the tragic gulf between knowlege of what is right and the doing of what is right.[3]
   a) Quote Socrates[4]
2. Felix failed to see the power and decisiveness of habit
3. Another point that we must see here is indecision is at bottom decision. We cannot remain undecided. Felix forget the most pertinacious facts in life, that while a man may hold his opinions in suspense he cannot hold his living in suspense. We may not succeed in making up our minds, but we cant help making up our lives. Life cannot be reduced to a pure science. Pure science does well in keeping itself tentative, openminded uncommitted
   (1) define decision
   (2) Life does hold up (Smoking, Wheat
4. Felix failed to see that there is such a thing as a lost opportunity
   (1) Time runs out
   (2) The fact of Death—Kings die
       a.   Civilizations—[*Arnold*] Toynbee
              Americas danger—Triplet (racism, nationalism militarism)
       B.   The Bible tells the story
              a   The Lost Sheep[5]
              b.   The man who was a fool[6]
              c.   Dives[7]

---

1. King penned this outline on the verso of deacon Thomas H. Randall's August 1959 report on his rounds as Dexter's church visitor (Randall to King, August 1959). On the folder containing this document, King wrote "I'm Going to Procrastination," and, on the top of the document, King wrote, "I Going To."

2. According to Acts 24:1–8, the Jewish high priest Ananias and the orator Tertullus brought charges of sedition against Paul before Felix, the Roman procurator who oversaw the region of Judah.

3. Cf. Acts 24:24–27.

4. King may be citing a paraphrase of a speech by Socrates found in Plato's *Apology* 38a: "The unexamined life is not worth living" (Plato, *Apology*, trans. B. Jowett, in *Plato* [New York: Walter J. Black, 1942], p. 56).

5. Luke 15:3–7.

6. Luke 12:16–21. King developed a sermon with this title (King, The Man Who Was a Fool, 6 March 1961, pp. 411–419 in this volume; King, *Strength to Love*, pp. 51–57).

7. King refers to the parable of Dives and Lazarus found in Luke 16:19–31. He had developed a sermon on this topic (see King, "The Impassable Gulf [The Parable of Dives and Lazarus]," Sermon at Dexter Avenue Baptist Church, 2 October 1955, pp. 235–239 in this volume).

C. Personal experience
 1. Russel Roberts[8]
 2. Lillian Smith[9]

AD. CSKC: Sermon file, folder 83, "I'm Going To Procrastination."

---

8. Russell A. Roberts served as pastor of Shiloh Baptist Church in Atlantic City, N.J. and conducted a public fast in support of the Montgomery bus boycott ("Fasting and Praying," *Pittsburgh Courier*, 24 March 1956).

9. Lillian Smith was a Southern white writer whose controversial 1944 novel *Strange Fruit* featured an interracial relationship. For more on King's personal relationship with Smith, see Smith to King, 10 March 1956, in *Papers* 3:168, and note 1, Dexter Avenue Baptist Church to King, 24 October 1960, in *Papers* 5:528.

Unfulfilled Hopes

[*5 April 1959*]
[*Montgomery, Ala.*]

King draws on themes from Frederick Meek's homily "Strength in Adversity."[1] In an audio recording of the sermon, King expounds on these ideas using the story of the Apostle Paul's "blasted hopes and shattered dreams."[2] He reflects on attending Little Rock Central High School's 1958 commencement exercises and describes the "creative" and "dynamic will" of African Americans who have overcome the challenges of slavery and racism. "Out of these black men and these black women came something that keeps the generations going," King remarks. "If they had turned to the first method of bitterness, it wouldn't have come. If they had withdrawn and turned to silent hate, it wouldn't have come."

Unfulfilled Hopes, Sermon outline

I   Our sermon today brings us face to face with one of the most persistent realities in human experience. Very few people are priveledged to live life with all of their dreams realized and all of their hopes fulfilled. Who has not had to face the agony of blasted hopes and shattered dreams

II We may turn back to the life of the Apostle Paul and find a very potent exam-

---

1. King wrote "Unfulfilled Hopes" on the file folder containing this outline and also wrote this title on his personal copy of Meek's sermon (Meek, "Strength in Adversity, A sermon preached in the Old South Church in Boston," 19 April 1953). The 5 April 1959 Dexter program indicates that King preached the sermon "Unfulfilled Hopes."

2. King would later title this sermon "Shattered Dreams" (King, Draft of Chapter X, "Shattered Dreams," *Strength to Love*, July 1962–March 1963, pp. 514–527 in this volume).

ple of this problem of unfullfilled hopes In the Fifteenth Chapter of his letter to the Christians at Rome, Paul writes this: "When I take my journey into Spain, I will come unto you"[3] It was one of Paul's greatest hopes to go to Spain, the edge of the then known world, [*strikeout illegible*] where he could further spread the Christian gospel. And on his way to Spain, he planned to visit ~~Rome~~ that vallient group of Christians in ~~the city of~~ Rome, the capital city of the world. He looked forward to the day that he would have personal fellowship with those people whom he greeted in his letter as "Christians in the household of Caesar."[4] The more he thought about it, the more his heart exuded with joy. All of his attention now would be turned toward the preparation of ~~going to~~ carrying the gospel to the city of Rome with its many gods, and to Spain, the end of the then known world.[5]

But notice what happened to this [*glowing?*] dream and this promising hope which gripped Pauls life. Paul ~~never got to Spain did get to Rome~~ never got to Rome in the sense that he had hoped. He ~~got~~ went there only as a prisoner and not as a free man. He spent his days in that ancient city in a little prison cell, held captive because of his daring faith in Jesus Christ.[6] And Paul ~~never saw~~ was never able to walk the dusty roads of Spain, or to see its curvasious slopes, or watch its busy coast life, because he died a mytres death in Rome before his hope could be fulfilled.[7] The story of Pauls life was the tragic story of blasted hopes and unfillfilled dreams.

This is the persistent story of life. There is hardly anyone here this morning who has not set out for some distant Spain, some momentous goal, some glorious realization, only to find that he had to settle for far less. We were never able to walk as free men through the streets of our Rome. Instead we were [*forced?*] to to live our lives in a little confining cell which circumstance had built around us.[8]

III   What does one do under such circumstances

3. Romans 15:24.

4. Cf. Philippians 4:22.

5. Meek, "Strength in Adversity": "Paul had high hopes of going to Spain, the edge of the then known world, that he might take there his word about the Christian Gospel. And on the way he planned to visit the Christian folk in Rome, the capital city of the world. Paul wanted to see that little valiant group of Christians, folk whom he saluted in his letter as 'Christians in the household of Caesar.' The more he thought about his planned journey, the more his heart was warmed by it. Imagine, Rome with its many gods and with its great power, subject to the Christian Gospel."

6. Cf. Acts 28:16–17.

7. Meek, "Strength in Adversity": "Paul *did get* to Rome, but he went as a prisoner and not as a free man. Paul lived in Rome at the expense of the Roman government in a prison cell, held captive because of his faith. And Paul never saw the mountains and the plains and the coast life of Spain, because he died a martyr's death before the hope of his mission could ever be fulfilled." Someone other than King wrote the word "martyr's" next to the misspelled word "mytres."

8. Meek, "Strength in Adversity": "How many of us in one way or another have dreamed our dreams of going to Spain, of fulfilling some far reaching hope, of doing valiantly for a great cause. But we never reached the Spain of our dreams. We had to settle for a far shorter journey. We were never able to wander freely about the streets of our Rome. Instead, we looked out through the little windows of some confining cell which the circumstances of life had built around us."

a. It is quite possible for one to seek to solve this problem by making everything and everybody atone for one's predicament. All of their frustration are distilled into a core of bitternes that expressess itsefe in hardness of attitude and a total mercilessnes. They take out their disappointment on someone else. You have seen people like that
   (1) cruel to their mate
   (2) inhuman to children
   In short they are mean.
      (a) they are bitter
      (b) They are cynical
      (c) they are loveless
      (D) They find fault in everything and everybody. They always complain. They have a demonical grudge against life.[9]

b. Some people try to deal with the problem by withdrawing completely into themselves.

c. The final alternative is creative. It involves the exercise of a great and creative will.[10]

AD. CSKC: Sermon file, folder 12, "Unfulfilled Hopes."

Unfulfilled Hopes,
Sermon Delivered at Dexter Avenue Baptist Church

Our sermon today brings us face to face with one of the most persistent realities in human experience. Very few people are privileged to live life with all of their dreams realized and all of their hopes fulfilled. Who here this morning has not had to face the agony of blasted hopes and shattered dreams?

One of the best examples of this problem is found in the life of the Apostle Paul. In the fifteenth chapter of the Book of Romans, which we read in the scripture lesson for the morning, we find Paul writing these words to the Roman Christians: "Whenever I go into Spain, I will come unto you." In other words, "Whenever I go to Spain, I will stop by to see you." This was one of the high hopes of Paul's life, the desire to go to Spain, the edge of the then known world, and carry the gospel of Jesus Christ to that distant land. And on his way to Spain he would stop by to see the Christians in Rome, the capital city of the world. He looked forward to the day that he would have personal fellowship with that little group of people that he referred to in the greetings of his letter as "Christians in the household of Caesar." This was his great hope. This was his great dream. And all of his life now would be turned

---

9. Thurman, *Deep River,* p. 37: "It is quite possible to become obsessed with the idea of making everything and everybody atone for one's predicament. All one's frustrations may be distilled into a core of bitterness and disillusionment that expresses itself in a hardness of attitude and a total mercilessness—in short, one may become mean. You have seen people like that. They seem to have a demoniacal grudge against life." King paraphrased this text on the verso of a 12 October 1960 letter from Coretta Scott King to Velma Hall.

10. King added this final section (beginning with Roman numeral III) in a second pen.

toward the preparation of going to Spain and carrying the gospel there and of going to Rome, the capital of the world. This was his dream. This was his hope.

But let us notice what happened to this hope that gripped the life of Paul, to this dream that saturated his being. We will read the scripture carefully and delve into the history of Paul's life. We discover that Paul never got to Rome in the sense that he desired. He only got to Rome as a prisoner and not as a free man. He had to spend his days in Rome in a little cell because of his daring faith in the gospel of Jesus Christ. Not only that, Paul never got to travel the dusty roads of Spain, to notice its curvaceous slopes and the busyness of its coast life, because he died a martyr's death in Rome. The story of Paul's life is the story, the tragic story, of unfulfilled hopes and shattered dreams.

But in a real sense, my friends, this is the persistent story of life. Almost everybody here this morning has started out on some distant trip to reach some distant Spain, to achieve some distant goal, to realize some distant dream, only to discover that life stopped far short of that. We never got an opportunity to walk as free men in the Romes of our lives. We ended up so often confined in a little cell that had been built up around us by the forces of circumstance.[11] This is the story of life.

This reveals to us that there is a tragic element in life. We must never overlook it. If the early Christian church didn't overlook it, we must not overlook it. The early Christians, they were bringing together the books of the Bible, did not leave out of the gospel the event that took place on Calvary Hill. That was a tragic event. It was a dark moment in history. And the universe crucified its most noble character. We must never forget that that stands at the center of the Christian gospel which reveals to us that there is an element of tragedy in life, there is a cross at the center of it. That as we face life and all of its problems, we see this element as tragic. Life is not a great symphony with all of the instruments playing harmoniously together. We will look at it long enough, we will discover that there is a jangling discord in life that has somehow thrown the symphony out of whack. The nagging, prehensile tentacles of evil are always present, taking some of the meaning out of life.

Many people have often looked at this, and they've gotten frustrated about it, and they've wondered if life had any justice in it. Long years ago the philosopher Schopenhauer looked at it. He said that life is nothing but a tragic comedy played over and over again with slight changes in costume and scenery.[12] Long time ago Shakespeare's Macbeth looked at it. He said that life has no meaning in the final analysis. Why? Because life turns out to be sound and furied in so many instances.[13] A good while ago, even in our own nation, Paul Laurence Dunbar looked at it. And all that he could come out with was saying:

> A crust of bread and a corner to sleep in,
> A minute to smile and an hour to weep in,
> A pint of joy to a peck of trouble,

---

11. Cf. Meek, "Strength in Adversity."

12. King paraphrases segments of Arthur Schopenhauer's chapter "On History" in *The World as Will and Idea*, 3:224–227.

13. Shakespeare, *Macbeth*, act 5, sc. 5: "Life's . . . a tale / Told by an idiot, full of sound and fury, / Signifying nothing."

And never a laugh that the moans come double;
And that is life![14]

We've looked at this so often, and we've become frustrated, wondering if life has any justice. We look out at the stars; we find ourselves saying that these stars shine from their cold and serene and passionless height, totally indifferent to the joys and sorrows of men. We begin to ask, Is man a plaything of a callous nature, sometimes friendly and sometimes inimical? Is man thrown out as a sort of orphan in the terrifying immensities of space, with nobody to guide him on and nobody concerned about him? These are the questions we ask, and we ask them because there is an element of tragedy in life.

We come back to that point of our text and of our prophet. We come to the point of seeing in life that there are unfulfilled hopes. There are moments when our dreams are not realized. And so we discover in our lives, soon or later, that all pain is never relieved. We discover, soon or later, that all hopes are never realized. We come to the point of seeing that no matter how long we pray for them sometimes, and no matter how long we cry out for a solution to our problems, no matter how much we desire it, we don't get the answer. The only answer that we get is a fading echo of our desperate cry, of our lonely cry. So we find Jesus in the Garden of Gethsemane praying that the cup would be removed from him.[15] But he has to drink it with all of its bitterness and all of its pain. We find Paul praying that the thorn would be removed from his flesh, but it is never removed, and he is forced to go all the way to the grave with it.[16] And so in this text, we find Paul wanting to go to Spain with a, for a noble purpose, to carry the gospel of Jesus Christ to Spain. Paul never gets to Spain. He ends up in Rome, not as a free man but as a man in prison. This is the story of life. In so many instances, it becomes the arena of unrealized dreams and unfulfilled hopes, frustration with no immediate solution in the environment.

Now, the question that I want to try to grapple with you this, with this morning is this: what do you do when you find your dreams unrealized, your hopes unfulfilled, and you see no basic solution in your environment to the problem that you are facing? How do you deal with it?

Now, some people deal with this problem, as you well know, by getting caught up in the response of bitterness. They feel that the best way, they end up dealing with their frustration by taking out their anger with the universe, their anger with life, on other people and other things. In short, they become mean.

Have you ever seen mean people? Now, sometimes you take a good psychological analysis of that person. You look back, and you discover that that person had a distant Spain in mind that he wanted to go to, and he had a great hope and a great desire and because of the forces of circumstance something happened and he never got to that Spain. And he ended up confined in a little cell of life that had been brought up and built up around him by the very forces of circumstance. And

---

14. King quotes from Dunbar's poem "Life" (1895).
15. Matthew 26:39.
16. 2 Corinthians 12:7–10.

now he lives in his cell, bitter and angry with life, and he has a sort of demonical grudge against life. This is his response. And he seeks to solve his frustration by taking all of this out on other people. And so maybe sometimes he's mean to his children, or he's mean to his wife, or she's mean to her husband, or mean to people round and about because he can't find life itself. Life is intangible in a sense; it's invisible. We, we, we don't see life; we see the manifestations of life. And you can never take life and hit life and beat up on life. And so he discovers that he can't get life itself to beat on and pay back for what the universe has done to him, so he finds people that are tangible, and he finds things that are tangible, and he takes this bitterness and this hate out on these things. And this is the solution to his problem, he thinks. The bitterness within, and the anger, he becomes angry with the universe. And he fights the universe through people and things. This is one way that people deal with this problem of unfulfilled hopes. They react with bitterness and mercilessness and meanness.

Well, there is another way that people often follow. They may withdraw completely into themselves. This is often a way that people use. They withdraw completely within themselves, and very happily they build the walls around themselves, and they don't allow anybody to penetrate. And they develop detachment into a neat and fine art. And so they look out into the world through eyes that have burned out. They end up with a cold and dead stare. They solve their problem, they feel, through the silence of hate. They are neither happy nor unhappy. They are just indifferent.[17] You've seen people like this, broken down by the storms of life, beat down by the weight of circumstance. And they are not fighting it with bitterness on the one hand, but they are fighting it with a silent hate. They withdraw from people, and they withdraw from the world. They withdraw from everything and turn totally within. This, they feel, is a solution to the problem. But that isn't it.

There is another way, which I think is a more creative way. And that is, it involves the exercise of a great and dynamic will.[18] This is the individual who stands up in his circumstances and stands up amid the problem, faces the fact that his hopes are unfulfilled. And then he says, "I have one thing left. Life has beaten it down; it has broken away from me many things, sometime my physical body. But at least it has left me with a will, and I will assert *this,* and I *refuse* to be stopped. Even if Rome and Spain are blocked off of my itinerary, I refuse to be stopped."[19] And this is the man who stands up in the greatness of life. He discovers the power and the creativity of the human will, and he faces any circumstance with the power and the force of his will. And he has a sort of *dogged* determination. This is what Paul Tillich, the great philosopher and theologian of our age, means when he writes a book entitled *The*

---

17. Thurman, *Deep River,* p. 38: "Or such persons may withdraw completely into themselves. Very carefully they build a wall around themselves and let no one penetrate it. They carry the technique of detachment to a highly developed art. Such people are not happy, nor are they unhappy, but are completely indifferent. They look out on life through eyes that have burned out, and nothing is left but a dead, cold stare."

18. Thurman, *Deep River,* pp. 38–39: "The final alternative is creative—thought of in terms of a second wind. It involves the exercise of a great and dynamic will."

19. Meek, "Strength in Adversity": "We cannot, we must not, stop even though Spain and Rome are crossed off our itinerary."

Courage to Be.[20] He says in that book that all around man is the threat of nonbeing. The man who has adjusted to modern life, the man who lives with creativity in the modern world, is the individual who stands amid the thrust of nonbeing and has the courage to be, in spite of all. And this is the way that Paul faced his problem. This is the way that any great Christian faces his problem. The hopes are not fulfilled, and the dreams are not realized. He says that I have one thing left and that is the power of the will. And I refuse to be stopped. I'll stand up amid life and the circumstances of life. Every now and then it will beat me, push me to this side and to that side, but I will stand up to it. I will not be stopped.

The other day we were flying to London.[21] I remember the pilot said to us that the flight coming back from London would be four hours longer than the flight going over to London. You know, these jet planes can go from New York to London in five hours and a half, but it takes them about nine hours to get back from London to New York. He said, now, the reason it is like this is that going over to London, you, you, you have a tailwind and it helps you to get in there fast. But coming back from London to New York you have strong headwinds, and that slows you up; it makes it kind of difficult to get in. You can't go in with the same speed, to go from London to New York. But I started thinking about the fact that if, even if that plane is four hours late, it battles through that wind somehow, and it gets to New York. That's the important thing. It gets off at London earlier, and it gets to New York later, but it does get to New York because it gets in itself the power to endure and go through the wind, even when they are pushing against them.

And this, I think, we find in this a parallel to life: that often we have strong tailwinds, and we move through life with ease, and things work in our favor, and everything is bright, and everything is happy. The sunshine of life is glowing radiantly in our eyes. These are bright and marvelous and happy days. But there will come moments when life will present headwinds before you. It seems that as you move something is blocking you. Circumstance after circumstance, disaster after disaster, stand in your path and beat up against you. And who is the man of creativity? He is the man who is *determined* to move on in spite of the headwinds. And who says somehow, "I might get in late, but I'm gonna get in because I have a *strong* and determined will in spite of the winds of circumstance that blow against me." Now, this is what Paul did in his own life. And this is what we have to do. We must get within ourselves, cultivate within ourselves, the power of a dynamic will and have the determination to move on amid every circumstance.

When we study history, when we read biography, we find it is a running commentary on this. We appreciate John Milton. We read *Paradise Lost* and *Paradise Regained* with great joy and great appreciation, but we appreciate it even more when we discover that he wrote it when he was blind.[22] We read Longfellow as he translates Dante [*Alighieri*]. We think of the greatness, this poet translating the works of another great poet. Then, we appreciate Longfellow even more when even we dis-

---

20. Paul Tillich, *The Courage to Be* (New Haven: Yale University Press, 1952).

21. On 3 February 1959, the Kings and SCLC historian Lawrence D. Reddick flew from New York City to London as they began a six-week trip to India and the Middle East.

22. John Milton lost his sight in 1651.

cover that a few days before he started translating Dante, the dress of his wife accidentally caught fire. And he tried desperately to put the fire out, but he couldn't put it out. It injured her to the point that she died a few days later. Here, we see that wifeless, motherless man sitting in his lonely room, turning to the translation of Dante in order to bring meaning in life.[23] And he did it well. We see Helen Keller, and we appreciate her. We appreciate her even more when we discover that here is a person been thrown into a little cell of blindness and deafness, can't see, can't hear, but yet in spite of that she wouldn't be stopped. She was determined to be in the midst of nonbeing. She was determined to assert her will in the midst of tragic circumstances. And even though she didn't achieve the Spain of sight to see the beauties of nature, she achieved an inner sight, which all of the men and women of this world appreciate. We will but look and see these individuals. We will see them with a beauty and a power.

I remember just last year I was out to Little Rock, Arkansas, at the time of the commencement exercise at Central High School, and I had the privilege of going in that evening.[24] I think they had only about eight or ten Negroes who were able to get in because they had to have invitations; and Ernest Green, who was the only Negro graduate, extended an invitation, and I went into that commencement. There were many things there that I remember, but one of the things that I remember more than anything else is that, as they were going across the platform getting their diploma, I remember very vividly a student going up on the arms of two other students. He had been taken out of a little chair going up, and I heard noises and shouts and cheers all over the grandstand. I am sure that for no athlete that had ever played out there in that field, in that stadium, I am sure that they had never gotten cheers like this boy got. And I watched him as he went up. And here was a boy who, I understand, started out in school, and he did an excellent job, was one of the star students of his class. One day when he was in class at Central High, and he was there, and the teacher didn't know him. The teacher said, "Stand up." And he said, "I'm sorry, I haven't stood up since I was four years old." But that boy had something else: the power of a creative will. His body was broken. The forces of circumstance had inflicted pain upon him. The forces of circumstance had taken something away from him that he desperately longed for, I'm sure. Some Spain that would given him, would have given him a certain physical integration that he wanted, I'm sure. Yet, he didn't have it. But he had one thing left. And that was the power of a dynamic will. This is what can take you through.

I look back over the dark days of slavery. Let nobody fool you about it. We can romanticize all we want to about the beauty of slavery. There are those who would

---

23. Henry Wadsworth Longfellow published his 1867 translation of Dante's *Divine Comedy* after his wife Fanny Appleton burned to death in a household accident in 1861.

24. Little Rock's Central High School was the center of a national controversy in September 1957 when Governor Orval Faubus deployed the Arkansas national guard to prevent the enrollment of nine black students. President Eisenhower eventually commanded the national guardsmen to uphold the *Brown* decision and desegregate the high school. The "Little Rock Nine" successfully entered Central High on 25 September. For King's response to the use of military troops in Little Rock, see King to Dwight D. Eisenhower, 25 September 1957, in *Papers* 4:278.

still try to romanticize about the beauty of slavery, and they, they have their minds back to those good old days. Slavery was a tragic thing. All that the Negro had to look forward to was rows of cotton, sizzling sun, the whip of the boss, and the barking of bloodhounds. This is what he faced. It is tragic to be cut off from some things, but there is nothing more tragic than to be cut off from your language, cut off from your family, cut off from your roots.[25] This is what the Negro faced—going over in ships out of Africa, huddled up in ships, not able even to talk to each other, thrown up and brought over to distant countries to work, nothing in their past to hold on to. Yet, they are thrown here, all of the Spains of their lives pulled out, caught up in a Rome of prisonous slavery. And this is where they had to live. That's enough to beat anybody down, keep them from ever becoming anything, hold them back, and keep them from ever giving to history any contribution. That's enough, isn't it?

They had something left. The little preacher who didn't know his English grammar, who had never heard of Plato or Aristotle, who could never understand Einstein's theory of relativity, he'd look at them and say to them, "Now, you ain't no nigger. You ain't no slave but you God's children."[26] They went out, they left feeling that they were God's children, that they had a will to carry them on even amid the darkness of slavery. And sometime they would begin to walk around the field, and they knew that it was dark in their lives. They knew that they had to walk there so often in bare feet, but they pictured the day when they would lay down their burdens and they could sing, "I'm so glad that troubles don't last always."[27] And then you could hear an echo saying, "And I know my robe going to fit me well because I tried it on at the gates of hell. By and by, by and by, I'm gonna lay down my heavy load."[28] These people, because of their creative, dynamic will, gave to this world something to keep it going, and they have given to this world contributions that the world will always have to be proud of. What gave to America the spiritual, which is the only original and creative music in this nation, gave to this world generations of young men and young women who've made marvelous contributions. For out of the black men and women of these dark days came a Marian Anderson, a Roland Hayes, and a Paul Robeson, to sing until the very fiber of men's souls is shaken. Out of these men and women came a Ralph Bunche to stand as one of the great diplomats of the world.[29] Out of these men came a Booker T. Washington and a W. E. B.

25. Thurman, *Deep River*, p. 35: "For the slave, freedom was not on the horizon; there stretched ahead the long road down which there marched in interminable lines only the rows of cotton, the sizzling heat, the riding overseer with his rawhide whip, the auction block where families were torn asunder, the barking of the bloodhounds—all this, but not freedom. Human slavery has been greatly romanticized by the illusion of distance, the mint julep, the long Southern twilight, and the lazy sweetness of blooming magnolias. But it must be intimately remembered that slavery was a dirty, sordid, inhuman business. . . . There is no more hapless victim than one who is cut off from family, from language, from one's roots."

26. King may have drawn this anecdote from Thurman's *Jesus and the Disinherited*, p. 50.

27. King refers to the spiritual "I'm So Glad Trouble Don't Last Always."

28. King refers to the spiritual "Bye and Bye."

29. In 1950 Ralph J. Bunche received the Nobel Peace Prize for his diplomatic efforts on behalf of the United Nations during the 1948–1949 Arab-Israeli War. He corresponded with King during the Montgomery bus boycott (Bunche to King, 22 February 1956, and 21 November 1956, in *Papers* 3:134, 436, respectively).

Du Bois as great educators.[30] *Out* of these black men and black women came Charles Drew to *save* us with blood plasma all over this world.[31] Out of these black men and out of these black women came an E. Franklin Frazier to interpret sociologically the trends of our age.[32] *Out* of these black men and these black women came a Paul Laurence Dunbar, a Countee Cullen, and a Langston Hughes to write poetry so that we can identify ourselves with reality through poetry.[33] Out of these black men and these black women *came* something that keeps the generations going. If they had turned to the first method of bitterness, it wouldn't have come. If they had withdrawn and turned to silent hate, it wouldn't have come. But it came because of the creativity of the will and the dynamic quality of it, and the determination to stand up, amid all of those forces, amid all of the darkness of human circumstance.

And whenever a man comes to this point, he brings reality into the very center of his existence, and he brings new meaning and delight in the universe. And you know, strangely enough when you come to this point, you don't worry about suffering. You don't die because you don't get to Spain. You come to see that suffering might make you stronger and bring you closer to the Almighty God.

> The tree that never had to fight,
> For sun and sky and air and light,
> That stood out in the open plain
> And always got its share of rain,
> Never became a forest king,
> But lived and died a scrubby thing.
>
> The man who never had to toil
> By mind or hand in life's turmoil,
> But always won his share
> Of sky and sun and light and air,
> Never became a manly man,
> But lived and died as he began.

And never forget,

> Good timber does not grow in ease.
> The stronger the wind, the tougher the tree.
> The farther sky, the greater length.
> The rougher the storm, the greater strength.

---

30. Educator Booker T. Washington (1856–1915) founded Tuskegee Institute in 1881 and was a major spokesperson for African Americans at the turn of the twentieth century. Scholar and activist W. E. B. Du Bois (1868–1963) authored the groundbreaking book on African American life, *Souls of Black Folk* (1903). He was a founder of the National Association for the Advancement of Colored People (NAACP) and edited the organization's journal *Crisis* until 1934. During the bus boycott he sent a poem to King (Du Bois to King, March 1956; see also King to Du Bois, 19 March 1956, in *Papers* 3:180).

31. Charles Drew (1904–1950) was a surgeon who is recognized for his work with blood plasma and blood banks.

32. Sociologist E. Franklin Frazier (1894–1962) authored *The Negro Family in the United States* (1939). In a 28 November 1960 letter, Frazier solicited information from King on "the work which your church is doing concerning marriage and family relations."

33. King refers to poets Dunbar, Cullen (1903–1946), and Hughes (1902–1967).

By sun and wind, by rain and snows,
In tree and men, good timber grows.

Where thickest stand the forest grows
We find the patriarchs of both
And they hold converse with the stars,
Whose broken branches show the scars
Of many winds and much of strife.
This is the common law of life.[34]

Discover this. Go out anew into the experiences of life. I assure you that you will meet your Spain, in the sense that you will never get there. You might get to your Rome as a prisoner, not as a free man. But if you have the power and the dynamics of a human will, nothing in all this world can stop you. Why? Because you refuse to be stopped. You have the dogged determination to exist and the courage to be. Let us pray.

Oh God, our gracious, heavenly Father, we thank Thee for the creative insights in the universe. We thank Thee for the lives of great saints and prophets in the past, who have revealed to us that we can stand up amid the problems and difficulties and trials of life and not give in. We thank Thee for our foreparents, who've given us something in the midst of the darkness of exploitation and oppression to keep going. And grant that we will go on with the proper faith and the proper determination of will, so that we will be able to make a creative contribution to this world and in our lives. In the name and spirit of Jesus we pray. Amen. [*Invitation omitted*][35]

At. MLKEC: ET-61.

---

34. Cf. Douglas Malloch, "Good Timber" in *Be the Best of Whatever You Are* (Chicago: Scott Dowd, 1926), p. 31.

35. For an example of King's invitation to baptism, see final paragraph of "Man's Sin and God's Grace (1954–1960?), p. 391 in this volume.

My Call to the Ministry

7 August 1959
[*Montgomery, Ala.*]

Joan Thatcher, publicity director of the American Baptist Convention, asked King to compose this statement. In her request, Thatcher noted, "Apparently many of our young people still feel that unless they see a burning bush or a blinding light on the road to Damascus, they haven't been called."[1]

---

1. Thatcher to King, 30 July 1959. Maude Ballou enclosed this statement in a 7 August 1959 reply to Thatcher. Thatcher's letter indicated that King's message was to be included in a leaflet for the January 1960 observance of Life Service Sunday.

My call to the ministry was neither dramatic nor spectacular. It came neither by some miraculous vision nor by some blinding light experience on the road of life. Moreover, it did not come as a sudden realization. Rather, it was a response to an inner urge that gradually came upon me. This urge expressed itself in a desire to serve God and humanity, and the feeling that my talent and my commitment could best be expressed through the ministry. At first I planned to be a physician; then I turned my attention in the direction of law. But as I passed through the preparation stages of these two professions, I still felt within that undying urge to serve God and humanity through the ministry. During my senior year in college I finally decided to accept the challenge to enter the ministry. I came to see that God had placed a responsibility upon my shoulders and the more I tried to escape it the more frustrated I would become. A few months after preaching my first sermon I entered theological seminary.[2] This, in brief, is an account of my call and pilgrimage to the ministry.

Martin Luther King, Jr.

THD. MLKP-MBU: Box 21.

---

2. King preached his trial sermon at Ebenezer in the fall of 1947 and was ordained in February 1948. He graduated from Morehouse College in May of that year and entered Crozer Theological Seminary the following September.

"Divine and Human Mutuality"
"Man's Helplessness Without God"

[*9 August 1959*]
[*Montgomery, Ala.*]

King offers two possible titles for this handwritten sermon outline. He criticizes those who rely too much on their own power, as well as those who "wait on God to do every-thing" and believe they "don't need to do anything about the race problem."[1]

I   Introduction—One of the things that has characterized human life through the centuries has been man persistnt attempt to remove evil from the face of the earth. Very seldom has man, collectively or individually, thoroughly adjusted himself to evil. In spite of all of his rationalizations, compromises, and alibis, man knows that the "is" is not the ought and the actual is not the possible. Though he often treasure in his heart the evils of sensuality, selfishness and cruelty, something within him reminds him that they are intruders. Even and again man in his deepest attachment to evil is reminded of a higher destiny and

---

1. A 9 August 1959 Dexter program indicates that King preached the sermon "Man's Helplessness Without God."

a more nobl alleigence. Man's attachment to hankering after the demonic is always disturbed by his longing for the divine. As he seeks to adjust to the demands of time, he knows that eternity is ultimate habitat, and even while dwelling in the lowest valley something reminds him that he is made for the highest star. When man comes to himself he sees evil as a foreign invader that must be driven from the native soils of his life before he can achieve moral and spiritual dignity.

But the problem that has always confronted man is his inability to conquer evil by his own power. He is constantly asking is pathetic amazingment, "Why can I not cast it out?"[2] Why can I not remove this evil from my life?"

These question are reminescent of an event that took place during the life of Christ. The event took place immediately after Christ's transfirguration Give the details of the story[3]

Jesus ends up telling the disciples that the reason of their failure is they they have been trying to do by themselves what they can only do when he is behind them, when their nature are so open that His strength can freely flow through them. This is the meaning of faith.

II   This bring us again to the question, how can evil be cast out? There are two ideas that men have usually held about the way evil is to be eliminated and the world saved.

   A.   One idea is that man must do it by his own power.
       (1) What man can do through education and legislation
       (2) ~~The beginning of~~ This philosophy had its beginning with the Renaissance. Then came the Age of Reason. The earth would be changed by reason not religion. They envisioned the whole world being cleansed of crime, poverty and slavery and war by reason alone.[4]
       (3) Modern Humanism—The cult of modern science
       (4) The words of Invictus[5]
       (5) The most aggressive avocate of this doctrine is Marxism
       (6) Yet in the midst of all of this optimism and humanism, the evils have persistnled. And today this people are crying in utter bewilderment, "Why could not we cast it out." "Since 1914 on tragic event has followed another . . . "[6]

2. Cf. Matthew 17:18–19.

3. Cf. Matthew 17:14–21.

4. Hamilton, *Horns and Halos*, pp. 62–63: "The Renaissance, on the other hand, went too far in excessive optimism. . . . Perhaps the most optimistic book ever written was published on the eve of the French Revolution by a French humanist Condorcet. . . . He thought the whole earth would speedily be changed, not by religion but by reason. It was to be 'the age of reason.' . . . He visioned the whole world cleansed of crime and poverty and slavery and war by reason and reason alone."

5. King most likely refers to William Ernest Henley's poem "Invictus" (1875), which concludes: "It matters not how strait the gate, / How charged with punishments the scroll, / I am the master of my fate: / I am the captain of my soul."

6. In the published version of the sermon "The Three Dimensions of a Complete Life," King wrote, "Reinhold Niebuhr has said: 'Since 1914 one tragic event has followed another as if history were designed to refute the vain delusions of modern man' " (*Strength to Love*, p. 74; see also Niebuhr, *Faith and History* [New York: Charles Scribner's Sons, 1949], pp. 6–7).

B. The other idea says that man must wait on God to do everything.

(1) Let men lie still, purely submissive and God in his good time will bring salvation.

(2) The one sided emphasis of the Reformation
Man, they said, is so depraved that he can do nothing, but wait on God.

(3) This emphasis has lead to a purely other wordly religion (Religion does deal with man ultimate concern, but also his preliminary) It has ~~postptoned~~ postponed redemption to beyond the skys. By emphasizing man's heplesness and stresing the need for concentrating his efforts on getting his soul prepared for the world to come it has paralyzed social reform, and divorced religion from life. No wonder the Marxist call religion an opiate

(4) The idea in everyday life of wait on the Lord
(3) you dont need a doctor
(2) you dont need to do anything about race problem.

(5) This idea ends up a failure. Waiting on the Lord still leves evil present. This view two is a lack of faith.

C. Then in the failure of these two ideas came another which is distinctly different from either.

AD. CSKC: Sermon file, folder 9, "Divine and Human Mutuality."

"The Conflict in Human Nature," Sermon at Dexter Avenue Baptist Church

[16 August 1959]
[Montgomery, Ala.]

King draws on J. Wallace Hamilton's sermon "Horns and Halos in Human Nature" to develop this handwritten introduction.[1]

"The good that I would, I do not . . . "[2]

Introduction: These words from the pen of the apostle Paul tell us a great deal about the nature of human nature. Paul, through the undisputed authority of experience, had learned something basic about man. The theology of Paul is not a systematic formulation that he quietly worked out through persistnt contmplation. Rather, it is a system that grows out of his experience. Paul had tried desprately to live up to the demands of the law. And yet in the midst of all of his attempts, he failed. The good that he wanted to do, he couldn't do, and the evil he didn't want to do, he found himself doing. This was his tragic and helpless plight.

---

1. King wrote "Preach at Dexter August 16, 1959" on the folder containing this sermon.
2. Cf. Romans 7:19.

now. "Father, forgive them, for they know not what they do. They are ignorant. They are not themselves."

So, when I get the blues about human nature and when I am tempted to lose faith in people or in the future, I turn to Christ. He keeps me believing in common people. He keeps me believing in the future. More than that, he keeps me believing in myself.

Sermon

I *[illegible]* an expression of *[illegible]* the tension
  a. Philosophical expression
  b. Psychological expression
  c. Biblical expression of the *[illegible]*

II The text which reveals the tension clearly

III Examples of this tension in practical everyday life.

IV The persistent tendency to overlook this duality — either we overstress the evil or we overstress the good.
  1. Reformation — overstress the evil.
  2 Renaissance. " " " good.

V Christianity calls for realism at this point. By realistically recognizing our plight we can rise up to an sen

King outlines the sermon "The Conflict in Human Nature" in his copy of Hamilton's 1954 book *Horns and Halos in Human Nature,* concluding "Christianity calls for realism at this point. By realistically recognizing our plight we can rise up to our [*selves?*]" (p. 67).

This experience in the life of Paul is a persistnt experience in the life of all. There is a basic conflict in human nature. ~~Me~~ Man is not all good, and not all bad—a mixture and a conflict. Whenever man seeks the high there is the drundry of the low. Whenever he seeks to [*strikeout illegible*] commune with the stars, he feels the blinding gust of dust blocking his vision. Mans quest for the divine is interupted by the nagging movements of the demonic. From Adam on, the story of man is one of magnificent devotion and shameful degregation.[3]

The pages of literature, both acient and modern, abound with illustration of this conflict.[4]

Man is false of spirit, bloody of hand, a wolf in greediness, a lion in prey[5]

AD. CSKC: Sermon file, folder 84, "The Conflict in Human Nature."

---

3. Hamilton, *Horns and Halos,* p. 59: "From Adam on, it is the story of magnificent devotion and shameful degradation."

4. Hamilton, *Horns and Halos,* p. 60: "You see it in literature," referring to "that everlasting warfare in man between the halos and the horns."

5. Hamilton, *Horns and Halos,* p. 60: " 'Man is false of spirit, bloody of hand; a fox in stealth, a wolf in greediness, a lion in prey.' " Cf. Shakespeare, *King Lear,* act 3, sc. 4.

"A Tough Mind and a Tender Heart"

[*30 August 1959*]
[*Montgomery, Ala.*]

King elaborates on a dichotomy found in Gerald Hamilton Kennedy's sermon "The Mind and the Heart" to explore the need for tough-minded and tender-hearted Christians.[1] *Citing inaccurate media portrayals of prime ministers Kwame Nkrumah of Ghana and Jawaharlal Nehru of India, King regrets that most individuals do not look beyond the "subjective appraisals of the newspaper headlines to the actual truth of the situation." He warns, "The shape of the world today does not permit us the luxury of* [soft mindedness]. *A nation of soft minded men is purchasing its own spiritual death through an* [installment] *plan." King also targets "those hard hearted* [individuals] *among us who feel that the only way to deal with oppression is to rise up against the opponent with physical violence and corroding hatred." He directs his listeners to "another way which* [combines tough mindedness] *with tender heartedness. It is tough minded enough to resist evil. It is tender hearted to*

---

1. Kennedy, *The Lion and the Lamb: Paradoxes of the Christian Faith* (New York: Abingdon-Cokesbury Press, 1950), pp. 161–171. In his copy of Kennedy's book, King wrote "The tough mind & the tender Heart" above the title of the sermon, "The Mind and the Heart." While King uses Kennedy's categories of "soft mind," "tough mind," "hard heart," and "tender heart," the body of King's sermon is different than Kennedy's. On the folder containing this sermon, King wrote "Preached at Dexter, August 30, 1959."

resist it with love. It [avoids] the complacency and the donothingism of the soft minded and the violence and bitterness of the hard hearted." King submitted a more complete version of this handwritten sermon outline for publication in Strength to Love.[2]

Text: "Behold I send you forth as sheep in the midst of wolves; be ye therefore wise as serpents and harmless as doves."[3]

I. Introduction: open with quote from French philosopher.[4] Show how the demands of the good life require toughness of mind and tenderness of heart.

II Let us consider first the need for a tough mind.

A. Definition of tough mind—(use <u>Religion in Changing world</u>)[5] No one can doubt that this is a great need

B. Very few people achieve this toughness of mind. But All to many are content with the soft mind. It is a rarity to find ~~anyone~~ one willing to engage in hard, serious thinking. There is an almost universal quest for easy answer, and half baked solutions. Nothing pains some people more than the idea of having to think

C. Man's soft mindedness is expressed in his unbelievable gullibility. The soft minded person believes anything. Take an attitude toward advertizements. We ~~may seldom pause to~~ can be so easily lead to buy a product [*words illegible*] because a television and radio advertizement pronounces it better than any other. Advetizers have long since learnd that most people are soft minded, so they have developed special skill to create phrases and slogans that will penetrate the thin ~~layer~~ mind of the average reader or listener.

This undue guillibility is also seen in the tendency of many to accept the printed word of the press as final truth. They fail to see that even facts can be slanted and truth can be distorted. So President Nkru of Ghana is considered a ruthless dictator by many because the American press has carefully disseminated this idea.[6] Prime Nehru is consider a a non committed

---

2. See King, Draft of Chapter I, "A Tough Mind and a Tender Heart," July 1962–March 1963, pp. 459–466 in this volume.

3. Matthew 10:16.

4. King most likely refers to the quote he used to introduce the version of this sermon he submitted for publication: "A French philosopher once said that 'No man is strong unless he bears within his character antitheses strongly marked'" (King, "A Tough Mind and a Tender Heart," July 1962–March 1963, p. 459 in this volume). The quote mirrors lines from an E. Stanley Jones book that King annotated and kept in his personal library (Jones, *Mahatma Gandhi: An Interpretation* [New York: Abingdon-Cokesbury Press, 1948], p. 17).

5. In his book *Religion in a Changing World*, Abba Hillel Silver said, "Our lives need much more than a precise, eager and powerful intellect. They need not only knowledge which is power, but wisdom which is control. They need not only truth which is light, but goodness which is warmth" (Silver, *Religion in a Changing World* [New York: Richard R. Smith, 1930], p. 172).

6. During the summer of 1959, articles ran in the *New York Times* characterizing Nkrumah's government as "moving in great strides toward authoritarian rule" (see Henry Tanner, "Ghana Is Divided on Type of Rule," 4 July 1959). Kwame Nkrumah, prime minister (1957–1960) and president (1960–1966) of Ghana, was overthrown in a military coup in 1966. King met Nkrumah during his March 1957

ingrate because the press has given the impression that his [*strikeout illegible*] policy of non ~~of positive neutralism~~ alignment is is at bottom a negative commitment to nothing.[7] Many social revolution in the world growing out of the legitimate aspiration of man for political independence, economic security and human dignity are all too often believed to be communist inspired because a large segment of the press reports it as such.

Very few peopl have the toughness of mind that drives them to look beyond the inevitable biases and ~~prejudices~~ subjective appraisals of the newspaper headlines to the actual truth of the situation

The soft minded are susceptible to belief in all kinds of superstitions. Almost any irrational fear can invade the soft mind without any sign of resistance—fear of Friday the thirthenth, fear of a black cat crossing one's path, A few month ago I noticed for the first time that the hotel in which I have stayed on several occasions did not have a thirteenth floor. On inquiring from the elevation driver the reason for this omission he said, "most large hotels follow this practice because of the fear of that so many people have in staying on the 13 floor. Actually the 14th floor is the 13th but we could never state it, because no one would stay there.

D. The soft minded always fears change. The most pain of all pain for them is the pain of a new idea. They get a security in the status-quo. Give example of white man

E. Soft mindedness has often invaded the ranks of religion. This is why religion has been all to slow in accepting new truth.

(1) Galileo's experience[8]

(2) The theory evolution was considered blasphemous, and there are still those religionist who, in spite of the most definitive evidence, reject this theory with religious passion

(3) Higher Criticism of the Bible[9]

(4) Reason in Religion

(5) All of this has lead to the [*widespread?*] belief that there is a conflict between science and religion. This isn't true. There may be a conflict between soft minded religionist and tough minded scientist, but not science and religion.

---

visit to Ghana to celebrate the nation's independence. He reflected on this experience in his sermon "The Birth of a New Nation," Sermon at Dexter Avenue Baptist Church, 7 April 1957, in *Papers* 4:155–167.

7. Jawaharlal Nehru, the first prime minister of independent India (1947–1964), developed a foreign policy during the Cold War that included nonalignment with both the United States and the Soviet Union. On 10 February 1959, during a trip to India, King dined with Nehru (see King, "Notes for Conversation between King and Nehru," in *Papers* 5:130).

8. The Inquisition sentenced mathematician and astronomer Galileo Galilei (1564–1642) to life imprisonment, served under house arrest, for affirming heliocentric theories found heretical by the Catholic Church.

9. In the draft of this sermon submitted for publication in *Strength to Love,* King elaborated on higher criticism (King, "A Tough Mind and a Tender Heart," July 1962–March 1963, p. 462 in this volume).

F. We have all seen the ominous consequecs of this type of soft mindedness in the modern world
   (1) Dictator after Dictor has capitalized on it, and as a result lead human-ity more than once to blistering fires of barbarism. It came to its most tragic expression in Hitler. (Quote from <u>Mein Kamph</u>)[10]
   (2) ~~The cancer of Race prejudice is also produced~~ [*strikeout illegible*] Soft mindedness is also one of the basic causes for race prejudice. They always pre-judge a race of people. {Life was an eternal mirror in which he saw only himself; and not a window through which he saw other selves.}
       (a) Racial [*prejudice?*] grows out of fears. which are grounless
       (b) Quote Abraham Curse and the soft mind believe[11]
       (c) The Negro is [*criminal?*]. He doesn't stop to see that these condi-tions are environmental.
       (D) intermarriage
       (e) ~~Ruth Re~~ Superiority of the white in spite of Ruth Benedict and M. Mead.[12]
       (f) Show how politician capitalize on this[13]
G. There is little hope for us in our personal or collective lives until we become tough minded enought to rise about the shackles of half-truth and legends. The shape of the world today does not permit us the luxury of soft minded. A nation of soft minded men is purchasing its own spiritual death through an instalment plan.

II But we must not stop with the cultivation of a tough mind. The gospel also demands a tender heart. Tough mindedness without tender heartedness is cold, and and detached. It leaves one life hardened by like a pepetual without the warmth of spring and the gentle heat of summer. There is nothing more tragic than to see a person who has risen to the displined heights of tough minded and has sunk to the passionless depths of hard heartedness.
A. The ~~harted~~ hard hearted person ~~experiences~~ truly loves. He only engages in a crude utilitarian love, which is not love at all. (Define Uti love)[14] He only loves himself. He has never experienced the beaty of friendship

---

10. In the published version of "A Tough Mind and a Tender Heart," King wrote: "Adolf Hitler real-ized that softmindedness was so prevalent among his followers that he said, 'I use emotion for the many and reserve reason for the few.' In *Mein Kampf* he asserted: 'By means of shrewd lies, unremittingly repeated, it is possible to make people believe that heaven is hell—and hell, heaven. . . . The greater the lie, the more readily will it be believed'" (*Strength to Love*, pp. 3–4).

11. In the draft, King discusses Noah's curse upon the children of Ham (King, "A Tough Mind and a Tender Heart," July 1962–March 1963, p. 462 in this volume).

12. Ruth Fulton Benedict (1887–1948) and Margaret Mead (1901–1978) were anthropologists whose studies of non-Western societies rejected the notion of cultural superiority.

13. In the draft, King identified politicians who relied on the soft-mindedness of their constituency, such as Arkansas governor Orval Faubus (King, "A Tough Mind and a Tender Heart," July 1962–March 1963, p. 463 in this volume).

14. King defined utilitarian love as "love at the lowest level" in which "one loves another for his use-fullness to him." He labeled this type of love as "crude [*selfishness*]" (King, "Levels of Love," 14 August 1960).

B. The hard hearted person has no genuine compassion. He is unconcerned about the pains and misfortunes of his brothers. He passes by un-
fortnate men every day, but he never realy sees them. He sees men hungry and feeds them not; he sees men nacked and [*clothes?*] them not; he
sees men sick and visits them not.[15] He becomes cold, self-centered and
heartless. If he decides to gives to a worth charity, he gives his dollar and
not his spirit.

C. The hard hearted h individual never see people as people. They become
objects and inpersonal cogs in some ever turning wheel. If he is a hard
headed business man people become mere producers of dollar. They are
digits, numbers etc (see Butrick.[16]

D. Jesus told many parables to illustrate the characteric of the hard hearted.
The good Samaritan was good because he was tough minded enough to
gain economic security and tender hearted enough to have compassion
for wounded brother on life's highway.[17] The rich fool was foolish not
because he wasn't tough minded but because he wasn't tender hearted.[18]
Life was an eternal mirror in which he saw only himself, and not a window through which he saw other selves. Dives went to hell not because he
was wealthy but because he was not tender hearted enough to see
Lazarus. He went to hell because he was so hard hearted that he guarded
compassion and made no move to bridge the gulf between himself and
his brother.[19]

E So Jesus reminds in a striking way that the good life demand combinding
the toughness of th serpent with the tenderness of the dove. To have
sepernt like qualities devoid of dove-like qualities is to be passionless, mean
and selfish. To have dove like qualities without serpent like qualities is to be
sentimental, aimless, and empty. We must combind in our characters
antithesis strongly marked.

F. This text has a great deal of bearing on our struggle for racial justice. We as
Negroes must combind tough mindeness and tender heartedness if we
are to attain the goal of freedom and equality. There are those soft minded
individuals among us who feel that the only way to deal with oppression
is to adjust it. They acquise to the fate of segregation. They have been
oppressed so long that they have become conditioned to oppression. Like
Shakepeare' Hamlet . . .[20] But this isn't thy way. It is only for soft minded
cowards. its

---

15. Cf. Matthew 25:41–46.

16. King may refer to George Buttrick's analysis of Jesus's parable of the rich man and the beggar
(Buttrick, *Parables of Jesus*, pp. 137–146).

17. Cf. Luke 10:25–37.

18. Cf. Luke 12:16–21.

19. Cf. Luke 16:19–31.

20. Cf. *Hamlet*, act 3, sc. 1. King referred to this quote in the version of this sermon he submitted for
publication, "A Tough Mind and a Tender Heart," July 1962–March 1963, p. 464 in this volume).

There are ~~still other~~ those hard hearted ind. among us who feel that the only way to deal with oppression is to rise up against the opponent with physical violence and corroding hatred. They have allowed themselves to become bitter. But this is not the way. It creates many more social problems than it solves

There is another way which cobinds tough mindnes with tender heartedness. It is tough minded enough to resist evil. It is tendered hearted to resist it with love. It avoid the complacency and the donothingism of the soft minded and the violence and bitterness of the hard hearted.[21]

III Conclusion I cannot close without close without applying to meaning of our text to the nature of God. The greatness of our God lies in the fact that he is both tough minded and tender hearted. This tough mindednes of God is expressed in an austere masculinity. The tender heartedness of God is expressed in a gentel feminty. He possesses the firmness of a father and the softness of a mother. The Bible stresses both the tough midedness of God—his justice and Wrath—and the tender mindedness of God—his love and grace. God has two strong arms—one that is strong enough to surround us with justice and one that is gentle enough to surround us with grace. On the one hand the Bible pictures God as a stern Judge who punishes Israel for he wayward deeds On the other hand he is a loving father who gladly forgives a Prodigal Son and gives his only begotten son to redeem man.[22] I am so thankful this [*morning?*] that we worship a God who is both TM and TH. If God were only TM he would be a cold and passionless despot, who sits in so far off heaven "contemplating all"— as Tennyson has it in his <u>Palace of Art</u>.[23] He would be an Aristul [*Aristotelian?*] unmoved mover or an Hegelian impersonal absolute who was merely self-knowing, but not other loving. If God were only TH he soft and sentimental unable to function when things go wrong and incapable of controling what he has made. He would be like H. G. Wells' God in <u>God the Invisible King</u> who is a lovable Being who with unrelenting passion desire to make a good world, but finds himself helpless before the surging powers of evil.[24] No, God is neither hard hearted nor soft minded. He is tough minded enough to transcend the world. He is tender hearted enough to be immanent in it—He leves us not alone in our agonies and struggles. He seek us in dark places and suffers with us and for us in our tragic prodigality

There are times when we need to know that God is a God of justice. When evil forces rise to the throne and slumbring [*giants?*] of injustice rise up in the earth, we need to know that there is a God of Justice who can cut them down like a green hay there and leave them withering like the grass.[25] But there are

---

21. In the draft of this sermon submitted for publication in *Strength to Love,* King identified this "third way" as "non-violent resistance."

22. Cf. Luke 15:11–32 and John 3:16.

23. Alfred Lord Tennyson, "The Palace of Art" (1832).

24. H. G. Wells, *God The Invisible King* (New York: Macmillan, 1917).

25. Cf. Psalm 37:2.

times when as need to know that God is a God of love and mercy When we are staggered by th chill winds of andversity and th battering storms disappointment; When through our folly and sin we stray into some destructive far country and are frustrated because of a strange [*homesickness?*], we need to know that there is Someone who loves us, who understands, and who who can will give us another chance. When days grow dark and nights grow dreary we can be thankful that our God is not a one- sided incomplete God, but he combinds in his nature a creative synthesis of love and justice which can lead us through life's dark valley to sun lit pathways of hope and fulfillment.

AD. CSKC: Sermon file, folder 17, "A Tough Mind and a Tender Heart."

To William E. Newgent

20 October 1959
[*Montgomery, Ala.*]

In a 12 October letter, a member of the Fellowship of Reconciliation (FOR) asked King for biblical citations used by segregationists "to back up their stand."[1] King directs him to two passages, cautioning that their use is "a glaring misrepresentation of what the Scripture teaches."[2]

Mr. William E. Newgent
17- 67th Avenue, S.E.
Washington 27, D.C.

Dear Mr. Newgent:

This is just a note to acknowledge your letter making inquiry of the passages of scripture that the segregationists use in an attempt to justify their position. One argument that they used is that the Negro is inferior by nature because of Noah's curse upon the children of Ham.[3] As you well know, this is a misinterpretation of an incident that is recorded in the Book of Genesis. The 17th Chapter and 26th Verse

---

1. William Edgar Newgent (1914–2001) had previously written King a 20 April 1956 letter during the Montgomery bus boycott because he was concerned by reports that King had been asked to resign his Dexter pastorship. In his reply to Newgent, King responded that his congregation backed him "one-hundred per cent" (King to Newgent, 26 April 1956, in *Papers* 3:229).

2. In an undated handwritten outline King maintained that Christian ministers must "speak out on the segregation issue" because some individuals "attempt to justify segregation on the basis of the Bible" (King, "Why the Christian Must Oppose Segregation," 1954–1964).

3. King refers to Genesis 9:24–25: "And Noah awoke from his wine, and knew what his younger son had done unto him. And he said, Cursed be Canaan; a servant of servants shall he be unto his brethren."

4. "And hath made of one blood all nations of men for to dwell on all the face of the earth, and hath determined the times before appointed, and the bounds of their habitation."

of the Book of Acts is used also.[4] It is the last part of this verse that is used which states "and hath determined the times before appointed, and the bounds of their habitation." You may read this whole passage and see it is a glaring misrepresentation of what the Scripture teaches. These are but two of the many arguments that are used.

Yours very truly,

Martin L. King, Jr.

TLc. MLKP-MBU: Box 32.

To Samuel McCrea Cavert

27 November 1959
[*Montgomery, Ala.*]

Responding to a request by Pulpit Digest *for a sermon on race relations, King declines, explaining that he had not had an opportunity to write out a complete sermon on this topic for several years.*[1]

Dr. Samuel McCrea Cavert
PULPIT DIGEST
159 Northern Boulevard
Great Neck, New York

Dear Dr. Cavert:

Thank you for your very kind letter of November 18, requesting me to submit a sermon that would be appropriate for either Race Relations Sunday or Brotherhood Sunday to appear in the columns of PULPIT DIGEST.[2]

First, let me say how deeply grateful I am to you for inviting me to submit a sermon to such a significant publication. Unfortunately, however, I do confront some problems concerning the possibility of submitting the type of sermon you request.

---

1. Cavert to King, 18 November 1959. Samuel McCrea Cavert (1888–1976) received a B.A. from Union College (1910) and an M.A. in philosophy from Columbia University (1914). In 1915, he obtained a B.D. from Union Theological Seminary. That same year, he was ordained as a Presbyterian minister. He served as general secretary of the Federal Council of Churches from 1921 until his retirement in 1954, when it was known as the National Council of Churches. In 1959, King accepted Cavert's invitation to join the Advisory Board of the journal's Religious Book Club (King to Cavert, 28 January 1959). *Pulpit Digest* contains sermons and articles to assist ministers in sermon preparation.

2. Race Relations or Brotherhood religious services focus on raising public awareness on race and other social issues. The National Council of Churches began sponsoring an annual Race Relations Sunday in 1922 to acknowledge the importance of interracial relations. King prepared a 10 February 1957 Race Relations Sunday message for distribution by the Council titled "For All . . . A Non-Segregated Society" (in *Papers* 4:123–125).

In this first page of his handwritten draft of "Why the Christian Must Oppose Segregation," King writes, "Since this issue of segregation is of such vast significance, I feel it my duty, as a Christian minister, to discuss it with you" (1954–1964).

Due to an extremely crowded and strenuous schedule for the last two or three years, I have not had an opportunity to write most of the sermons that I preach. In most cases I have had to content myself with a rather detailed outline. This happens to be the case with all of the sermons that I have preached on the general theme of brotherhood and race relations. I have several such sermons pretty well outlined, but I do not have a single one in a final written form. If I had time I would be more than happy to write one of these sermons in full, but several pressing responsibilities make that impossible at this time. But for these difficulties I would be more than happy to comply with your request. Please know that I regret this very deeply. I might mention that I have the complete manuscript for several of my other sermons. If you are ever desirous of having one I will be glad to submit it.

Very sincerely yours,

Martin L. King, Jr.

MLK:mlb

TLc. MLKP-MBU: Box 33A.

Man's Sin and God's Grace

[*1954–1960?*]
[*Montgomery, Ala.?*]

King describes human sin as "the tragedy of collective and social life" that requires God's grace. This sermon was probably inspired by Gerald Hamilton Kennedy's homily "Sin and Grace."[1] Invoking the story of the prodigal son, King challenges America: "You've trampled over sixty million of your precious citizens. You have called them 'dogs,' and you have called them 'niggers.' You have pushed them aside and kicked them around and pushed them in an inferior economic and political position. And now you have made them almost depersonalized and inhuman. And there you are in that far country of oppression, trampling over your children. But western civilization, America, you can come home and if you will come home, I will take you in." The following text is taken from an audio recording of the service.[2]

There is something wrong with human nature, something basically and fundamentally wrong. A recognition of this fact stands as one of the basic assumptions of our Christian faith. The picture of this glaring reality of the gone-wrongness of

---

1. King kept an annotated copy of Kennedy's *The Lion and the Lamb: Paradoxes of the Christian Faith* in his personal library and wrote "Man's Sin and God's Grace." on the top margin of page 41 of Kennedy's book. At the top of a typed draft of this sermon, King wrote, "See Kennedy's Book" (King, "Man's Sin and God's Grace," 1954–1960).

2. The dating of this recording is based on King's recollection of his seminary years and of an encounter in Atlanta, suggesting that he delivered this sermon during his tenure at Dexter.

human nature is set forth on almost every page of the Bible. The Bible pictures it in the pride and disobedience of Adam and Eve, which ends up injecting a discord in the beautiful symphony of life in a garden.[3] It pictures it in a ruthless and merciless pharaoh, caught in the clutches of a hardened heart.[4] It pictures it in the jealousy of a Saul, who ends up hating David with a bitter and dangerous hate.[5] It pictures it in the glorious career of a David, who constantly spoils that career with [*recording interrupted*] and making sex the be all and end all of life.[6] It pictures it in a Judas, who was willing to succumb to the temptation of selling his lord for a few pieces of silver.[7] It pictures it in Pilate, who sacrifices truth on the altar of his self-interest and who falls victim to the whims and caprices of a group of people who are crying out, "Crucify him."[8] Yes, it pictures it in a vicious but sincere mob hanging the world's most precious character on a cross between two thieves.[9] The Bible is clear in setting forth the tragic dimensions of the gone-wrongness of human nature.

Wherever we discover life, somehow we discover this gone-wrongness. Wherever there is a struggle for goodness, we discover, on the other hand, a powerful antagonism, something demonic, something that seems to bring our loveliest qualities to evil and our greatest endeavors to failure. Theologians have referred to this over the years as "sin." That is something that stands at the core of life, this element of sin. And whenever we think about man we must think of this tragic fact—that man is a sinner. Sin is this revolt against God; sin is at bottom separation. It is alienation. It is a creature trying to project himself to the status of the creator. It is the creature's failure to accept his limitations and, thereby, reach out for something higher to integrate his life, and it ends up in tragic separation.

Man is a sinner before the Almighty God. That is one of the basic facts of the universe and one of the basic facts of life. Now, we've tried to get away from this in the modern world; we hate to hear this word "sin." We try to run from it, and we try to talk about it in other terms. This is one of the weaknesses of religious liberalism, that in throwing out certain traditional concepts, which it should have thrown out—traditional concepts like the damnation of infants and a hell with a fiery furnace—it was good that liberal Christianity threw that out. I have no objection to that, for I find it very difficult and almost impossible to believe in a hell of a fiery furnace and all of that. But in throwing out these old traditional conceptions, liberalism fell victim to the danger that forever confronts any new view, and that is that it became sentimental and soft, feeling that man was evolving from a lower state to a higher state and eventually he would move on up the evolutionary ladder and throw off all of the evils and sin of his nature. Then, we came back to see that even after all of that man is still a sinner.

---

3. Genesis 3.

4. In Exodus 7–14, Pharaoh's callousness prevents him from releasing the Hebrew people.

5. 1 Samuel 18:5–11.

6. 2 Samuel 11:1–21. In a handwritten outline of this sermon, King wrote that David's career was "spoiled by tragic lust" (King, "Man's Sin and God's Grace," Sermon outline, 1954–1960).

7. Cf. Matthew 26:14–15.

8. Luke 23:20–21.

9. Matthew 27:38.

We face the new psychology, and it furnished us with a lot of words and a lot of phrases to explain certain weaknesses of human nature, and so we very easily dismiss the word "sin." And we start talking about phobias and inhibitions, and we reached over to Freudian psychology and said that it's a conflict between the id and the superego. But when man got through talking in terms of all of his bombastic psychological phrases, he discovered that, at bottom, he was still a sinner before the Almighty God and that, at bottom, the conflict is not between the id and the superego but the conflict is between God and man. And the universe stands with that glaring picture of the reality of life—that man is a sinner; man is a sinner in need of God's redemptive power. We can never escape this fact.

We just need to look around a little, that's all, and we discover it everywhere. Notice this element of the gone-wrongness of human nature in our own personal lives. I don't mean for you to look out here at somebody else this morning; just look at yourself long enough, and you will discover this dimension, this tragic dimension of sin. All men, great minds, philosophers, and literary geniuses throughout the ages have pointed out, and we find ourselves having to agree with them, that there is something wrong in human nature. There is something in all of us that makes us more than one self. We are all two selves, and if you look at yourself hard enough you will discover that other self. We find ourselves split up against ourselves. We have something of what the psychologists or the psychiatrists would refer to as the schizophrenic personality. We are split personalities. There is something high in us and there is something low in us.

Plato talked about it in one of his dialogues, and he pictured the human personality as a charioteer with two headstrong horses, each wanting to go in different direction.[10] Reason was the driver, and spirit and appetite were the two horses. And here is spirit with its good desires on this side, and here is appetite with its evil dimensions over here. And each of them wanting to go in different directions. There is something true in Plato's analysis of the human situation.

There is something in all of us which causes us to cry out with Ovid, the Latin poet, "I see and approve the better things of life, but the evil things I do."[11] One day Goethe looked at himself, and he said, "It's strange that I'm one self but yet in all of this bundle of me there's enough stuff to make both a gentleman and a rogue."[12] That seems to be the characteristic of life. There is within all men this bundle of stuff that keeps us in a dichotomy, a dualism, so that we have enough in us to be both good and evil. There is enough in us to make both a gentleman and a rogue.

This is a dimension of life. H. G. Wells said one day, "I'm not so much of a human being as a civil war, and every man confronts this civil war within himself."[13] There is the complying North of his soul always in conflict with the recalcitrant South. And there is that continual battle, that civil war, the South of the soul breaking out against the North of the soul. This is man's plight. Man discovers that he has

---

10. King refers to Plato's *Phaedrus* 246a–247c.

11. Ovid *Metamorphoses* 7.20.

12. Cf. Sheen, *Peace of Soul*, p. 36.

13. Fosdick, *On Being a Real Person*, p. 52: "A modern novelist describing one of his characters says, 'He was not so much a human being as a civil war.'"

this division, this very tension at the center of his nature. Just look hard enough, and you'll discover that something. That's why Paul could say, "The good that I would I do not, and the evil that I would not, that I do."[14] And then man discovers it, and he goes out and tries to resolve the tension, and he finds himself something like Dr. Jekyll and Mr. Hyde.[15] Oh, in the day he's this respectable person; he's good and decent, a servant of humanity, but then at night he goes and puts on that other self. And there is that Mr. Hyde, that indecent self, that degrading self, that self that sinks to animalism. And there is something in all of us, although we read it in literature, that comes to the center of our lives, and we find that we are Dr. Jekyll and Mr. Hyde.

We discover that there is a private aspect of our lives forever in conflict with the personal aspects of our lives. We all have a private self that we don't want the public self to discover. There is a privacy about all of us that we are ashamed of, that we forever seek to hide, and that we would never want to become public. This is the sin of man. There is a Mr. Hyde in all of us that seeks at the night of life to go into being while pushing aside the day of life that is Dr. Jekyll, and then, the next morning it tries to become Dr. Jekyll again. Then, that night it becomes Mr. Hyde again. There is this conflict between the is-ness of our present natures and the eternal ought-ness that forever confronts us. That comes in all lives.

And so it boils down that we are sinners in need of God's redemptive power. We know truth, and yet we lie. We know how to be just, and yet we are unjust. We know how to live our lives on the plane of love, and yet we hate, or we are unfaithful to those we should be faithful to. We stand amid the high road, and yet we deliberately choose the low road. We know the ways of peace, and yet we go to war. We have resources for great economic systems where there could be equitable distributions of wealth, and yet we monopolize and take it all for ourselves and forget about our brothers. And when we come to see ourselves, we discover that all of us are sinners. "All we like sheep have gone astray."[16]

There's no point in pushing it out here, saying, "Well, I don't fit into that category," for sin takes so many areas. It not only, you see, we often see these things that are so glaring and we think they are the only sins—you know, getting drunk, or indulging in tragic lust, or going downtown robbing a bank and stealing a lot of money. That's not the only sin. I've seen people who would never rob a bank, but how many people have they robbed of their good names? I've seen people who were so good that they would never do anything in terms of stealing from their neighbors of material goods, but they'll get on the telephone and gossip about them and spread evil rumors about them. All of that's sin. I've seen people who would say they, "I don't do anything. I don't drink. I don't do this. I don't do that," and then they end up their lives bogged down in a negative because the Christian ethic is never a bundle of do-nots but it's a bushel of dos. Whenever I hear people talking about what they don't do, I wonder what do they do. It's always an

---

14. Romans 7:19.

15. Robert Louis Stevenson, *Dr. Jekyll and Mr. Hyde* (1886).

16. Isaiah 53:6. In his copy of *The Lion and the Lamb*, King underlined Kennedy's use of this biblical text and wrote underneath, "The Universality of Sin" (p. 37).

Darkness cannot drive out darkness; only light can do that. More ignorance cannot drive out ignorance; only knowledge can do that. More evil cannot drive out evil; only goodness can do that. Better start with this somewhere tomorrow: "Father, forgive us ours . . . as we forgive theirs."

"I Have Sinned"

Introduction — Modern man's attempt to get away from the fact of sin through doctrine of automatic progress and inherent goodness of man. But finally we must come back to the fact that man is a sinner.

What is sin. Sin is separation

1. Separation from self

2. Separation from others

3 Separation from God

103

At the end of the chapter "Forgive Us Our Trespasses" in his copy of Hamilton's 1954 book *Horns and Halos in Human Nature,* King writes a brief outline titled "I Have Sinned." He notes, "Modern man's attempt to get away from the fact of sin through doctrines of automatic progress and inherent goodness of man. But finally we must come back to the fact that man is a sinner" (p. 103).

affirmative. And *there is never* a time when the individual, even in his moment of highest ethical achievement, doesn't experience this disintegration, this tragic alienation from God. Every man experiences it. And that is why the saint always recognizes that he's a sinner, and the worst sinner in the world is the man who feels that he isn't a sinner. That is the point at which he's the greatest sinner. So that in our own personal lives, as we look at ourselves, as we look at the personal dimensions of our everyday living, we discover this dimension of sin. And there is something about it that causes us to know that as we look down into the deepest resources of our souls that we are in eternal revolt against God.

I don't know about you, but when I look at myself hard enough and deep enough and go on back from my public self to my private self, I don't feel like crying out with the Pharisee, "I thank Thee, God, that I'm not like other men." But I find myself saying, "Lord, be merciful unto me a sinner."[17] There is that dimension which runs the gamut of human life so that man in his personal experiences discovers this tragic dimension and this awful tendency of sin.

But you know this thing of sin grows even worse when we go out to the social dimensions of it, when we pass from the personal to the social. And that is when sin really becomes tragic. When man comes together collected in society, when persons come together and come into, bring into being this big something called society, then sin rises to even more ominous proportions. You know, individuals devoid of society are much more moral, much more rational, much more good than society itself. But it's because man is caught in society that he becomes even a greater sinner. It's very seldom that a man by himself will lynch anybody, but a mob will lynch somebody. Individual men won't do the things that a nation will do. So that when we get caught up in societal living, when we get caught up in social life, sin even grows greater.

That is why one theologian can write a book entitled *Moral Man and Immoral Society*.[18] He discovers that man as an individual is pretty good; he's not totally immoral. But when man begins to interact in society, he gets caught up in all of the evils of society. And so that is why people caught in society will do things that they probably never would do as an individual. They want to be approved socially. They get courage to do things that they could never do by themselves. The crowd is doing it, and so in order to be in social line with the crowd they do it. And so man rises to the tragic level of social sin. And then the real tragedy of man's social and collective existence is the fact that sin is almost inescapable in this level. Because you are involved in society and you are necessarily a part of the sins of society, you can't quite break off.

I was talking with a man the other night who was saying to me that he refused to pay income taxes because the nation uses such taxes for war, and I was sympathetic with his view. But I said to him, "You haven't solved the problem because by refusing to pay income tax because the nation spends its money for the evils of war you are just putting greater tax burdens on your brother. And somehow you cannot

---

17. Luke 18:9–14.
18. King refers to Reinhold Niebuhr's 1932 book.

refuse to pay taxes because you drove your car down here from Ohio, and you had to buy gas, and every time you bought gas you were paying some taxes on that gas, and you were helping to support war even while you bought gas." Man can never escape evil in his life. He is a part of the structure of society and so he must be a part of all the greed of society; he's a part of all the wars of society; and even if he's a pacifist, he's still contributing to the very thing that he's revolting against. This is the tragedy of collective and social life—that man *never* gets out of sin because he's caught up in society, and he can't get out of society because if he got out of that he wouldn't be man.

Social psychologists tell us that the thing that makes an individual a person is that he interacts with other persons, and man never becomes man until he interacts. That baby comes into being, but that baby comes to be a personality as it interacts with others around it. And so man can never get away from man and society. And yet as he stands in society, he's caught up in all of the evils of society, all of the sins of society. This is the tragedy of man's predicament—that even on every level of his movement he's caught in sin and he supports evil. And I can never be what I ought to be until you are what you ought to be, and you can never be what you ought to be until I am what I ought to be. That is the interaction, the togetherness of humanity and that makes the level of social sin even more tragic.

Now, that looks kind of bad, and I'm about to conclude now. I know you say, "Now you stand there on a somber note. You've said to us that we are sinners; we are caught in the clutches of sin in our personal lives and in our social lives." And yes, if we stop there, I assure you that we would be in a pretty tragic predicament, that man's life would be a life of nothingness, a life of endless pessimism. So that we can't stop there. And that's something of the beauty of the Christian faith, that it says that in the midst of man's tragic predicament, in the midst of his awful inclination towards sin, God has come into the picture and has done something about it. That's the beauty of our faith. It says that standing over against the tragic dimensions of man's sin is the glorious dimensions of God's grace. Where sin abounded, grace abounded even more exceedingly.[19] That's the Christian faith. On the one hand it is the most pessimistic religion in the world, for it recognizes the tragic and awful dimensions of man's sin. But on the other hand it is the most optimistic religion in the world, for it recognizes the heightening dimensions of God's grace and how God's grace can come in and pick up. So that over against man's sin stands God's grace. Christianity, therefore, becomes the greatest pessimistic optimistic religion in the world. It's a combination of a pessimistic optimism; it sees over against man's sinfulness, man's tragic state, the graciousness of God's mercy, and His love and His forgiving power.

God's grace stands over man's sin. Now, the grace of God is not just some passing phrase, not just some old concept that we should be ashamed to use now. It's not just some mechanical concept that has no deep meaning. Grace has a very vital place in any life. It has a very vital place in understanding the whole predicament

---

19. Cf. Romans 5:20. Kennedy used this biblical citation as the basis for his sermon "Sin and Grace" (*The Lion and the Lamb,* p. 35).

of man and the whole predicament of the universe, for you can never understand life until you understand the meaning of the grace of God. The whole of life hinges on the ever flowing power and ever flowing stream of God's grace. Grace is just that something that God gives us. It's a gift that we don't merit, that we don't deserve, but which we so desperately need. That's grace, and none of us could live without it.

To give a practical example of grace, I remember when I was in theological seminary. We were having final exam in a course in philosophical theology, which turned out to be a very difficult course. It turned out that after the exam was over, we, everybody in the class—I think about twenty-five or thirty-five students were in the class—and all of us flunked the exam; all of us did a very poor job. You see, in graduate school, when you make a C you flunk. So all of us made under eighty, everybody, so we had all flunked the course. But then I never will forget Dr. Davis came back to that class.[20] He told us about it, and there we were sitting there, sorrowful, feeling that we were going to have to take philosophical theology over again. And he said, "Well, you've been a loyal class, and I think, at bottom, maybe I should do something about this. And you will notice on your books that I have added ten points; to every examination I've added ten points." I got my little blue book and I noticed up there at the top, "75." Then under there I noticed the word "grace" and then it had "10" under there, right across from "grace." And then there was a line there, and it said "85" under there. And that happened for every examination, there was this additional ten points, so that all of us were able to get by and pass the examination and get through the course. That was grace.

Now, he didn't have to do that. We didn't deserve it; we didn't merit that. But we so desperately needed it to pass that course and to finish that seminary. And this was the grace that carried us through. This is the meaning of God's grace. As we stand amid the great examination of life, confronting *all* of the experiences of life, we stand writing our answers to all of the issues of life, but in *all* of our very being we flunk the exam; we make mistakes; we are not prepared. Our ingenuity is too weak; we are too finite to pass it. And yet God reaches out and looks at us in our tragic state and says to us, "If you will have faith in me, if you will be loyal enough to come to class, I will *add* a little to your examination so that you can pass and stand up amid life with all of the beauty and all of the glory of life, and you can get through." And that's the thing that brings us through life. That's something that we don't merit, that's something that we don't deserve, but that's something that we so desperately need in order to survive and pass the ultimate examination of life, which lifts us from the seminary of life to the broad university of experience and eternal life. This is what God gives us, and it only comes through His grace, His free gift.

Have you ever done anything, and you felt that you had become a shame to yourself? You feel a sense of shame before your family and before society, and you felt that your integrity never would come back? That your life now was an endless process of meaninglessness and that everything that turned against you, and as you

---

20. During King's final year at Crozer Theological Seminary, he took two courses in philosophical theology with George W. Davis: Philosophy of Religion and Advanced Philosophy of Religion. King received an A in both courses.

walked the streets you were ashamed to look at anybody, and you felt that everybody was looking at you with scorn? And you went to bed at night, and you tried to pray that you wouldn't think about it or you wouldn't dream about it, but even in the midnight hours you would wake up and discover that it was still plaguing you? And then, at that moment, you decided to try another method; you decided to turn this thing over to God and lay yourself bare before the Almighty God, and something happened to you, and you could walk out before life and before your family and before yourself and your friends with new meaning. Looked like the life had taken on something new, and you wondered what happened. That was the grace of God. Something that you didn't deserve, something that you didn't merit, but something that you so desperately needed in order to live through the experiences of life.

I talked with a young lady some two or three years ago who had had a tragic, or made a tragic mistake in life, she felt, and she felt that her life was now bare and meaningless. Life had no meaning; her family was disappointed with her; friends were disappointed, and relatives were disappointed; everybody was disappointed. And she was ashamed to face life, ashamed to stand up before anybody because of this great mistake. Then I looked at her, having known her for a number of years, and I said to her first, "Here's one thing you've got to do—you've got to forget about this mistake that you made back here. Don't get bogged down in the past. You've got to look forward to the future now. You've got to outlive it. And let this sense of guilt you have serve as only an impetus for you to keep going and outlive and renew your experiences." And then I said to her, "Try this. I know it sounds kind of vague and old-timey for a young person to say this to another young person, but you know, one day just try this, just, just get off to yourself, and close all of the doors, and get off in some privacy, and just sit there, meditate on this thing, and, and then decide to lay your life bare before the Almighty God. Just decide to turn it over to Him, and decide that you have come to the limit, that you can't solve this thing, and just leave it to God."

I saw that young lady two days ago in Atlanta. I was talking to her about this very same thing, and here was a new person, young lady now, who lives all of the glory of life, very happy, a very happy family relationship, having forgotten about this experience. And she said, "Somehow it just passed away. And I don't even think about it too much now. It doesn't cross my mind hardly." Oh, I could look at her and say to myself that was the grace of God. That's what the grace of God does. It gives us that something that we so desperately need to live this difficult and this often trying experience of human life.

And there is another thing about it. There's a boy who leaves home and runs off to a far country, and he throws away everything that he has. He wastes everything that he has—all of his virtue, all of his time, all of his money, and everything else. And there he is in a hog's pen, getting ready to eat of the food that the hogs eat. But then something comes to him, he comes to himself and says, "I'm no hog. I'm the son of a father back home." And he decides to run back home and go back to his father. But you know the beauty of that thing is, that parable talks about a father standing back home and almost looking out, seeing that boy as he trudges back up the dusty road that he had once gone down. When that boy gets home, the father looks about and says, "Servants, go ahead and bring the fatted calf, for my son is back home and we are going to celebrate tonight." He didn't deserve that. That father had every right in the world to look at that son and say, "I'm through with it, through with you. You deceived me; you disappointed me; you did everything against my will." But instead of doing that the father said, "Come back home. Come in and be elevated into this home, for you are my son and I still love you." And that's what Jesus is saying; that's what the Gospel is saying; that's the meaning of grace—that no matter how low we sink, no matter how far we go, God still stands there saying, "If you come back home, I'll take you in."[21]

Western civilization, you've gone into the far country of imperialism and colonialism. You have trampled over more than one billion six hundred million of the people of the world. You have exploited them economically; you have dominated them politically, trampled over them, humiliated them, and segregated them. And there you are in this far country of exploitation. But oh, western civilization, if you will rise up now and come home, I'll take you in. And I will make of you a great civilization so that you can inject new meaning into the veins of this world and of this civilization.

America, you've done that. You've trampled over sixty million of your precious citizens. You have called them "dogs," and you have called them "niggers." You have, you have pushed them aside and kicked them around and pushed them in an inferior economic and political position. And now you have made them almost depersonalized and inhuman. And there you are in that far country of oppression, trampling over your children. But western civilization, America, you can come home and if you will come home, I will take you in. And I will bring the fatted calf and I will cry out to all of the eternities, "Hallelujah," for my nation has come home.

Drunkard man, you've gone to the far country of drunkenness; you've gone to the far country of gambling; you've gone to the far country of everything that is low and evil and degrading your own personal life. But if you will rise up and come home, I'll take you in. You don't deserve it; you don't merit it, but you so desperately need it in order to live. And so when we do that, and we discover the meaning of this thing, this powerful grace that comes to offset this tragic sin, we can cry out with John Newton:

> Amazing grace! how sweet the sound
> That saves a wretch like me.
> I once was lost but now I'm found;
> Was blind but now I see.
>
> 'Twas grace that taught my heart to fear,
> but not only that, 'twas grace my fears relieved.

Isn't that the beauty of it? It teaches us how to fear, and yet, it relieves those very same fears. And then we can talk about:

> Through many dangers, toils, and snares,
> I have already come;
> 'Twas grace that brought me safe thus far,
> And it is grace that will lead me home.[22]

---

21. Cf. Luke 15:11–32.

22. King quotes stanzas of John Newton's 1779 hymn "Amazing Grace."

Where sin abounded, grace abounded even more exceedingly.

Oh God, our gracious heavenly Father, help us to see the meaning of this grace, and help us to realize that in our sinful lives there is some hope, there is a way out through Thy powerful and ever flowing grace. In the name and spirit of Jesus we pray. Amen.

We open the doors of the church now. Probably there is someone here this morning who feels the need of this grace, feels the need of this Christ, who forever gives this grace. Who this morning will accept it? He might be leading you this morning. Will you be able to say, "Where He leads me, I will follow. Wherever He leads me, I will follow."[23] As we sing this beautiful hymn, hymn number 164, I want somebody to make a decision this morning. I look over this congregation, and I see those who need to make the decision. Where He leads me, I will follow. Who will make that decision? Come in and accept the Christ as your personal savior. For all of His powerful grace, let us stand.

At. MLKEC: ET-31.

---

23. King refers to Ernest W. Blandy's 1890 hymn "Where He Leads Me."

IV: EBENEZER BAPTIST CHURCH

"The Three Dimensions of a Complete Life," Sermon Delivered at Friendship Baptist Church

[*28 February 1960*]
Pasadena, Calif.

Shortly after leaving Dexter to join his father as co-pastor of Ebenezer Baptist Church in Atlanta, King delivered the following sermon at Marvin T. Robinson's Friendship Baptist Church as part of a Southern Christian Leadership Conference (SCLC) fund-raising trip to southern California.[1] While introducing King, Robinson lauded him for "making a signal contribution to our American way of life, the equality of man, and the dignity of the individual," and assured King, "We rejoice when you rejoice, and when you are in trouble we are also in trouble."[2]

Expanding on a version of this sermon that he delivered in 1954 as a candidate for Dexter's pastorate, King reflects on many of his experiences, including the successful bus boycott and his 1959 journey to the Holy Land and India.[3] He also lambasts white racism: "Many of our white brothers are concerned only about the length of life, their preferred economic positions, their political power, their so-called way of life. If they would ever rise up and add breadth to length, the other-regarding dimension to the self-regarding dimension, we would be able to solve all of the problems in our nation today." The following text is taken from an audio recording of the service.

[*Choir singing*]

My good friend Reverend Robinson, distinguished guests, members and friends of the Friendship Baptist Church of Pasadena, I am certainly delighted to have the privilege and pleasure of being with you today and of being a part of this worship experience. As your pastor said, I have been invited to Friendship on a number of occasions, and each time some previous long-standing commitment stood in the

---

1. Robinson (1914–2001) was the pastor of Friendship Baptist Church from 1954 until 1971. In a 6 February 1960 letter to Los Angeles Baptist Ministers Conference president P. J. Ellis, King accepted an invitation to speak at an afternoon rally and benefit for the Southern Christian Leadership Conference (SCLC) on 28 February at Timothy M. Chambers's Zion Hill Baptist Church in Los Angeles. He also indicated that he would fill the pulpit at Friendship Baptist Church that morning. Later that day King preached "Going Forward by Going Backward" at G. H. B. Charles's Mt. Sinai Baptist Church ("Huge Crowds Attend M. L. King Rallies," *Los Angeles Sentinel*, 3 March 1960).

2. King's five-day speaking tour was arranged by Maurice Dawkins, chair of the California Ministers Christian Leadership Conference on Civil Rights, and also included stops in Bakersfield and San Diego (Dawkins to King, 17 February 1960; Murlene Whitley to King, 9 March 1960; Wayne A. Neal to King, 1 March 1960). On 27 February King attended a dinner organized by Morehouse alumni. He reportedly discussed the need for nonviolence in order to win white support. He explained that "violence for independence is all right" but "non-violence is much more practical in trying to obtain integration" (Brad Pye, Jr., "Martin Luther King Hits L.A.'s Geranium Leaders," *Los Angeles Sentinel*, 3 March 1960; "Morehouse Alumni Host M. L. King," *Los Angeles Sentinel*, 3 March 1960). Friendship Baptist contributed $1,000 to SCLC. King's densely scheduled West Coast visit, which attracted overflow crowds at every stop, raised over $5,000 for the organization.

3. King, "The Dimensions of a Complete Life," Sermon at Dexter Avenue Baptist Church, 24 January 1954, pp. 150–156 in this volume.

way. But I am very happy that at long last I found it possible to come to this community and to the church of my good friend Marvin Robinson and my friends of Pasadena. (*Nice, Amen*)

I bring you greetings this morning from the Southern Christian Leadership Conference, an organization constituting leaders from all across the Southland [*Congregation:*] (*Oh yes*), leaders who are working in a determined, courageous yet Christian manner (*Praise the Lord*) to achieve full equality for the Negro people of the South. (*Praise the Lord*) Naturally, in seeking to do this, we face tremendous odds and tremendous difficulties, but we go on with the faith that what we are doing is right not only for the Negro people of the nation but for the soul of America. (*Praise the Lord, Amen*) For I am convinced that our struggle is not the struggle merely for the freedom of seventeen or eighteen million black men and black women, but it is a struggle to save the soul of the United States. (*Praise the Lord, Amen*) Therefore, what we are doing, it seems to me, is something that the government of this nation should welcome (*Amen, Amen*) because America cannot remain a first-class nation so long as she has second-class citizens. (*Amen, Amen*) I solicit your support for our work in the South, your moral support and your financial support. One of the things that we are trying to do through our Conference, along with other things, is to increase the number of Negro registered voters in the South, feeling that if this is done many of our problems can be solved on the local level. There are potentially five million Negro voters in the South, and out of that number there are only one million three hundred thousand. And so as you can see we have a long, long way to go. (*Amen*) But we're going to keep working with grim and bold determination until our people and your brothers and sisters have the ballot. (*Amen*)

Now, naturally, it takes a lot of time and energy and money to do this because it means getting people into the various communities and into the various counties to conduct voting clinics and block campaigns in order to do the job. And therefore, we are expanding our staff in order to do this, and I solicit your cooperation and your continued support and your prayers. For in a real sense the Negro cannot be free in Pasadena or Los Angeles until the Negro is free in Jackson, Mississippi and Montgomery, Alabama. (*Amen, Amen*) We are all involved in a single struggle. (*Yes, Yes*)

I would also like to bring greetings to you from a little city that you may have heard of along the way of life. It's called Montgomery, Alabama. (*Amen*) Although I'm not living in Montgomery now I am still intimately involved in the struggle there and in the affairs of the city, still associated with the Montgomery Improvement Association, and so I would like to bring greetings and special greetings from the fifty thousand Negro citizens of Montgomery who, just a few years ago, came to see that it is ultimately more honorable to walk in dignity than ride in humiliation.[4] (*Amen*) A people who decided to substitute tired feet for tired souls (*Amen*) and walk the streets of Montgomery until the sagging walls of bus segregation were finally crushed. (*Amen, Amen, Amen*) And I'm happy to report this morning that the buses of Montgomery, Alabama are thoroughly integrated. And after three hundred and eighty-one days of suffering and sacrifice, Negro passengers can sit any-

---

4. King continued to serve on the MIA's executive board after his departure from Montgomery.

where on the buses that they want to. (*Amen, Amen*) We were able to achieve this significant victory not only because of our sacrifices but because millions of people of good will all over this nation and all over the world were willing to walk with us (*Yes*), and above all God walked with us. (*That's it, Amen, Oh Lord*) Therefore, a new day is developing in Alabama and all over our nation.

I would like to have you think with me for the moments left from the subject "The Three Dimensions of a Complete Life." From time to time, we hear that in order for certain things to be complete they must be three-dimensional. I think you occasionally hear this from Hollywood—that in order for the movie or the picture to be complete today it needs to be three-dimensional. And I would like to attempt to set forth the thesis this morning that if life is to be complete it too must be three-dimensional.

Many, many centuries ago a man by the name of John was in prison out on a lonely, obscure island called Patmos, and in such a setting he was deprived of every freedom but the freedom to think. And so out there in that dark and desolate situation he had a rendezvous with eternity (*Yes, Oh yes*), and he looked up and imagined that he saw something. (*Oh, Praise the Lord*) He wrote about it over in the Book of Revelation. He said, "I saw a new heaven and a new earth (*That's it, That's it, Oh yes*) descending out of heaven from God (*Praise the Lord*); I saw the new Jerusalem."[5] (*Yes*) One of the greatest glories of this new city of God that John saw was its completeness. (*Oh yes, Yes*) It was not partial and one-sided (*All right, Amen*), but it was complete in all three of its dimensions. (*All right, Yes*) And so in describing the city over in the twenty-first chapter of Revelation in the sixteenth verse, John says this: "The length and the breadth and the height of it are equal." (*Amen, Praise the Lord, Come on*) In other words, this new city of God, this city of ideal humanity is not an unbalanced entity (*Well*), but it is complete on all sides. (*Praise the Lord, praise the Lord*) Now, John is saying something here quite significant. For many of us the Book of Revelation is a difficult book, puzzling to decode, and we tend to think of it as something of a great enigma wrapped in mystery, and I guess if you look at the Book of Revelation as a record of actual historical occurrences it is a difficult book shrouded with impenetrable mysteries. (*Oh yes*) But if you will look beneath the peculiar jargon of vocabulary of the author and the prevailing symbolism, you will see in the Book of Revelation many eternal truths which forever challenge us. (*Amen, Amen, Well*) And one such truth is the truth of this text, for what John is really saying is this: that life as it should be and life at its best is a life that is complete on all sides. (*Amen, Amen, Come on*) And so there are three dimensions of any complete life to which we can fitly give the words of our text: length, breadth, and height. (*Right*) Now, the length of life, as we shall use it here, is not its duration, not how long it lasts, not how long you live, but it is the push of a life forward to achieve its inner powers and ambitions. It is the, it is the inward concern for one's own welfare. (*Oh yes*) The breadth of life is the outreach, the outward concern for the welfare of others; and the height of life is the upward reach for God. (*Amen, Amen*) If life is to be complete, these three must be together; in other words, life at its best is

---

5. Cf. Revelation 21:2.

something of a triangle. At one angle stands the individual person; at the other angle stands other persons; and at the tip top stands the supreme infinite person— God. (*Yes, Amen*) If your life is to be complete, all three must work harmoniously together and be properly cultivated (*Praise the Lord, Yes*), for the complete life is the three-dimensional life. (*Well*)

Now, let us look for the moment at the length of life. I have said that this is a dimension of life in which the individual is concerned with developing his inner powers. In a sense, this is the selfish dimension of life, and there is such a thing as rational and moral self-interest. If you aren't concerned about yourself, you aren't really going to be concerned about other selves. (*Oh yes, That's right*) Some years ago, a brilliant Jewish rabbi, Joshua Liebman, wrote a book entitled *Peace of Mind*, and he has a chapter in that book entitled "Love Thyself Properly."[6] (*All right*) And what he says in substance in that chapter is that before you can love other people adequately you got to love your own self properly. (*Amen*) Many people have been plunged into the abyss of emotional fatalism because they didn't love themselves properly. (*Praise the Lord, All right*) And, therefore, we have a legitimate right to be concerned about ourselves, and we must be so concerned about ourselves that we set out early in life to discover what we are made for (*Amen, All right*), for God has called up all of us to do something. He has given all of us certain abilities, and we must use them; after we discover them, we must use them well. (*Praise the Lord, All right*) Some maybe have five talents, some two, some one, but the important thing is that you do the best with whatever you have. (*That's it, Amen, Oh yes*) And there is always a "well done" waiting (*Well*), well done by good and faithful servants, when the job is done.[7] So we must set out to discover (*Yes*) what we are called to do and what we are made for, and then after we discover it, we should set out to do it with all of the strength and all of the power that we have in our system. (*Well, Oh help him*) When you discover your life's worth (*All right*), set out to do it so well that the living, the dead, or the unborn (*Oh Lord*) couldn't do it better. (*Praise the Lord, Yes, Amen*) And no matter what it is, never consider it insignificant because if it is for the upbuilding of humanity (*Yes*) it has cosmic significance. (*Amen, Yes*) And so if it falls your lot to be a street sweeper (*That's it, Well*), sweep streets like Rafael painted pictures. Sweep streets like Michelangelo carved marble. (*Amen, Well*) Sweep streets like Beethoven composed music. (*Oh yeah, Have mercy*) Sweep streets (*Amen*) like Shakespeare wrote poetry. (*Amen*) Sweep streets so well that all the hosts of heaven and earth will have to pause and say, "Here lived a great street sweeper (*That's it, Amen*) who swept his job well."[8] (*Praise the Lord, Amen*) Douglas Malloch put it in a beautiful little poem:

> If you can't be a pine on the top of the hill, be a shrub in the valley
> But be the best little shrub (*That's right*) on the side of the rill.
> Be a bush if you can't be a tree. (*Yes*)
> If you can't be a highway, just be a trail.

---

6. Liebman, *Peace of Mind*, pp. 38–58.
7. Cf. Matthew 25:14–30.
8. King once attributed this illustration to Benjamin Mays (King, "Facing the Challenge of a New Age," 1 January 1957, in *Papers* 4:79).

If you can't be the sun, be a *star.* (*Amen*)
For it isn't by size that you win or you fail,
Be the best of whatever you are.[9] (*Yes, Amen, All right*)

And when you do this you've mastered the length of life. (*Oh yes, Well*) This onward push to the end of realizing your inner capacity (*All right*) is a length of a man's life. But don't stop here. (*Praise the Lord, All right*) It's dangerous to stop with the length of life. (*Praise the Lord*) And some people never get beyond this first dimension; they live life as if nobody else lived in the world but themselves. (*Yes, All right, Praise the Lord, Well*) And other people become mere steps by which they climb to their personal ends and ambitions. And if they manage to get around to loving, it becomes a utilitarian love; they love only those people that they can use. (*Yes, That's right, that's right*) My friends, I say to you this morning that there is nothing more tragic than to see an individual bogged down in the length of life (*That's it, That's it*), devoid of the breadth. And so we must add breadth to length.

Now, the breadth of life is that dimension in which we are concerned about others. As I've said, it is the outward concern for the welfare of others. (*Oh yes*) And I submit to you this morning that an individual hasn't begun to live until he can rise above the narrow confines of his individualistic concerns to the broader concerns of all humanity. (*Oh yes*) One day a man went running up to Jesus, and he wanted to raise some significant questions. (*Praise the Lord, Well*) He got around finally to the question: "Who is my neighbor?" (*Well*) Now, that could have very easily led to a philosophical debate. It could have very easily ended up in the abstract. That question could have been left out somewhere in midair (*Well, All right*), but Jesus immediately pulled that question out of midair and placed it on a dangerous curb between Jerusalem and Jericho.[10] (*Oh yes*) And he talked about a certain man (*Praise the Lord*), a certain man that fell among thieves. (*Sure enough, sure enough*) He went on to say that three men passed by. (*Sure enough, sure enough, Well*) One was a priest; one was a Levite. (*Well*) And they passed by on the other side; they didn't stop to help him. And finally another man came (*Well*), a man of another race (*Yes, All right*), and he stopped and helped the man there on the ground, and history had said that he was a good man.[11] Now, he was good because he had the capacity to project the "I" into the "thou." He was good because he could rise above the length of life and incorporate the breadth. (*Praise the Lord, Yes*) Now, we have a lot of theories about why these other two men passed by on the other side. Sometimes we say that they were probably busy going to some church meeting and they just didn't have time (*Yes, Well*); that's a possibility. And then it's possible that they could have been going down to Jerusalem, to Jericho, to establish a Jericho road improvement association. I don't know; that's a possibility. [*laughter*]

But the fact is that they passed by on the other side. And I have another theory when I use my imagination about this thing. You know it's possible that they passed on by because they were afraid. (*Amen, Well*) You see, the Jericho road is a danger-

---

9. King recites lines from Douglas Malloch's poem, "Be the Best of Whatever You Are" (1926).
10. Cf. Buttrick, *The Parables of Jesus,* p. 150.
11. Luke 10:25–37.

ous road. A few months ago, about eight months ago, Mrs. King and I were in Jerusalem, and we rented a car and drove down from Jerusalem to Jericho.[12] (*Yeah*) Now, you know that Jerusalem is way above sea level, some twenty-six hundred feet above sea level, and Jericho is a thousand feet below sea level. (*That's right*) And I said to my wife as we were driving around this Jericho road that this is the, it's easy to understand why Jesus used it as a setting for his parable. This is a meandering, curvy, dangerous road, and it's very conducive for robbery and that type of thing. (*Well, All right*) And I could easily see then why Jesus used it as the occasion, and something said to me then that it's possible that those brothers that passed by on the other side were really afraid because it is dangerous on the Jericho road. And first, they could have thought that if they stopped and helped the man the robbers were still around, and they might have come out there, robbed them, and beat them, and left them there. (*Well*) Or they could have thought that the man on the ground was a faker and that he really was there in order to get them over there, and something would happen to them. (*Well, All right*) So that the first question that the Levite raised, the first question that the priest raised was "If I stop to help this man, what will happen to me?" (*Well, All right*) The good Samaritan by the very nature of his concern reversed the question: "If I do not stop to help this man, what will happen to him?" Therefore, he was a great man because he had the mental equipment for a dangerous altruism. He was a great man because he could rise above (*Yes*) his self-concern (*Well*) to the broader concern of his brother. (*Oh yes*) He was a great man because he saw the power of the breadth of life (*Yes*), not only the length of life. (*That's it*)

And my friends, I am convinced that this is the basis of our problem in the area of race relations today. This is our problem in the South, and this is our problem over the United States. Many of our white brothers are concerned only about the length of life, their preferred economic positions, their political power, their so-called way of life. If they would ever rise up and add breadth to length, the other-regarding dimension to the self-regarding dimension, we would be able to solve all of the problems (*Amen*) in our nation today. And I say this morning that the United States of America may go out in the world and produce all that she can possibly bear, possibly produce in guided missiles. She may astound the world with her great production system. She may fascinate men all over the world with her great resources or wealth, but if men and women of this nation (*All right*) [*will?*] [*gap in tape*] all of God's children are significant. (*Amen*) The United States of America will be relegated to a second-rate power in this world (*Amen*), and all of her words will be as sounding brass and a tinkling cymbal, and all of her achievements will be null and void. (*Yes*) And when the history books are written in the future years, historians will have to say, "America *died* because too many of her people were concerned about the *length* of life (*Well*) and not concerned about the *breadth* of life." (*Amen, Praise the Lord*) This is the challenge facing our nation today. (*Well, Oh yes*)

And is it only necessary within a nation; it's necessary on the international hori-

---

12. For a further description of this trip, see King, A Walk Through the Holy Land, Easter Sunday Sermon Delivered at Dexter Avenue Baptist Church, 29 March 1959, in *Papers* 5:164–175.

zon (*Well, All right*), for the breadth of life simply means that every individual and every nation realize that nobody can live alone in this world. (*Yes*) We are all made to live together. (*Well, Oh yes, All right*) It was my good fortune to journey over to that great country in the Far East known as India a few months ago, and it was the most rewarding experience to move around that great nation and meet the great leaders of that country, from Prime Minister Nehru on down to the village councilmen (*Well*), and then to talk with the ordinary people of that country in the villages around.[13] (*All right*) It was a most rewarding experience. But as I stood there in that great country (*Yes*), I say to you this morning that there were those depressing moments, for how can one avoid being depressed (*All right*) when he sees with his own eyes millions of people going to bed hungry at night? How can one avoid being depressed when he sees with his own eyes millions of people sleeping on the sidewalks at night? Had no beds to sleep in, no houses to sleep in. In Calcutta alone, more than a million people sleep on the sidewalk every night. In Bombay, more than six hundred thousand people sleep on the sidewalks at night. How can one avoid being depressed when he discovers that out of India's population about four hundred million people, more than three hundred million make a annual income of less than sixty dollars a year? And most of these people have never seen a doctor or a dentist.

And as I stood there and noticed these conditions, something within me cried out (*Lord*), "Can we in America stand idly by and not be concerned about these conditions?" And some answer came out saying, "Oh no" (*All right*), because the destiny of the United States is tied up with the destiny of India. (*Oh yeah, Well*) And, therefore, we should use our vast resources of wealth to aid these undeveloped countries that are undeveloped because the people have been dominated politically (*Well*), exploited economically, segregated, and humiliated across the centuries by foreign powers. (*Well*) And I found myself saying maybe we in the United States have spent far too much money in establishing military bases around the world rather than establishing bases of genuine concern and understanding. (*That's right, Yes*) And all I'm saying this morning is that all life is interrelated. (*Well*) We are caught in an inescapable network of mutuality; whatever affects one individual directly, it affects all indirectly. (*Yes, Well, Oh yeah, All right*) Therefore [*recording interrupted*] life. (*Oh yes*)

But don't stop here either. (*Well, That's it*) Some people never get beyond the first two dimensions of life. (*Praise the Lord, Well*) They develop their inner power brilliantly. They have a concern for humanity in many instances. Sometimes they love humanity so much that they conclude that humanity is God. These are the people who find themselves seeking to live life without a sky. (*Oh yes, All right*) But I say to you this morning that if life is to be complete, the individual must reach up beyond his self-interest, the individual must reach up beyond humanity (*All right*) and reach up high enough to discover God. (*Praise the Lord, Amen*) Now, I know some of you are asking now, "Reverend, why would you mention this dimension?

---

13. While visiting India during February 1959, King dined with India's prime minister Jawaharlal Nehru (King, "Notes for Conversation between King and Nehru," in *Papers* 5:130).

Why do you bring this up? You're in church, and we're in church, and the fact that we're here in such large numbers, and the fact that we're in church means that we believe in God, and why would you mention this?" (*Well*) Well, there is some truth in that. The fact that you are here means, I guess, that at least you agree that there is a God. But you know there is a distinction between intellectual assent and real belief. (*Amen, Yes, Amen*) Intellectual assent is merely agreeing that something is true; belief is acting like it is true. (*That's right, All right*) And so often we find people who agree that there is a God, and they pay lip service to God, but they live as if there is no God in the universe. (*Oh yes, Amen, Lord have mercy*) These are the people who have a high blood pressure of creeds and an anemia of deeds. [*laughter*] And so the atheism that pervades our society today is not theoretical atheism so much but practical atheism—living as if there is no God.

And how often do we find ourselves paying lip service to God but not life service? (*That's right*) We just become involved in other things. We become so involved in getting our big cars and our big bank accounts and our beautiful homes that we unconsciously forget about this third dimension. (*That's it, That's right*) We become so involved in looking at the man-made lights of the city that we unconsciously forget to look up and think about that great cosmic light. (*Well*) It gets up early in the morning in the eastern horizon and paints its technicolor across the blue, a light that man could never make. (*That's it, that's it*) We become so involved in looking at our skyscraping buildings, and we unconsciously forget to think about the gigantic mountains (*That's it*) kissing the sky (*That's it*), something that man could never make. (*Oh yes*) We become so involved and fascinated (*Well*) about our radar and our televisions (*Well*) that we unconsciously forget to think about the beautiful stars that bedeck the heavens, like swinging lanterns of eternity (*Oh yeah, That's it*), something that man could never make. (*Well, Amen*) We become so involved and fascinated by man's progress in the scientific realm (*Well, Yes sir*), we unconsciously find ourselves believing that man can usher in a new world unaided by any divine power. (*Well, Oh yes*) And so when we turn around and come to ourselves we discover that we've gone a whole day's journey not knowing that God isn't with us. (*Well, That's it, Oh yes, Yes, Oh yes*) But I submit to you (*Well*) that if life is to be complete (*That's it*) we must discover God. (*That's it, Oh yes*)

And don't worry about our new scientific developments. We must continue to break out and break into the storehouse of nature and bring out many precious insights (*Well, That's right*), but never believe that because of our new developments in the scientific realm God's being is diminished. (*Well, All right*) But I tell you today God is still around. (*That's it, Oh yes*) Even if we can't see Him, He's still here. (*Praise the Lord, praise the Lord*) The great things in this universe you can never see. Go out and look at the stars at night, and you think you see all. Oh no! You can never see the law of gravitation that holds them there. (*That's it, that's it*) Run out into your city; look at the beautiful buildings, if you will, and all of the beautiful architecture. Look at this church, if you will, with its beautiful architecture, and maybe you think you see all. Oh no! (*Well, All right*) You can never see the mind of the architect who drew the blueprint. (*That's right*) You can never see the faith and the hope and the love of the individual who made it so. (*Well, That's it*)

This morning I see you (*That's it*) saying to yourselves, "We see Martin Luther King." And I hate to disappoint you. You don't see Martin Luther King (*All right*); you see my body. (*Talk, talk, Come on, come on*) You can never see my mind; you can

King, King Sr. *(center)*, and Fred Shuttlesworth *(right)* at Ebenezer
Baptist Church, 1960. Courtesy of Donald Uhrbrock/Timepix.

never see my personality (*That's it, that's it*); you can never see the me which makes
me me. (*Oh yes, Come on*) So in the final analysis, everything that you see in this universe is a shadow cast by that which you do not see. (*Yes, Sure enough*) Visible is a
shadow cast by the invisible. (*Yes*) So this morning I can cry out to you that even
though we can't see God He's *still* around! (*Yes*) God is still here. (*All right, All right*)
And so if we are to live a complete life, let us discover Him. And if you will discover
this God (*Praise the Lord*), things will change in life. (*Oh yes, Oh yes*) People all
around you will wonder how you are able to make it amid the dark and desolate
moments. (*Oh yes, All right*) In the midst of the difficulties (*Yes*), you will be able to
stand up with an inner calmness. (*Well, Oh yes*)

403

A reporter asked me some days ago (*What*), "Dr. King, aren't you afraid living in the tension of the South and the daily threats that you and your family get (*Well*) and all of the harassment that you have to constantly go through? How is it that you keep going?" (*Well, Yes, All right*) And I said to him, "I have but one answer. (*Praise the Lord, That's it*) First, I think that this cause is right. (*Well, All right*) And since it is right I believe that God is with it because God is on the side of right. (*Amen, Amen, Yes*) And therefore, I can go on with a faith (*Well, Praise the Lord*) that because God is with the struggle for the good life (*Well, Oh yes*), victory is inevitable." (*Sure enough*) No matter what comes (*All right*), no matter how difficult the moments may be (*Well, Praise the Lord, Oh yes*), if you gain this feeling that God is with you (*Well, Yes*), all of the powers in hell below (*That's it, That's it, Amen, Oh yes*) and all of the evils and the principalities of evil can't destroy you because you have a faith. (*That's right*)

And, therefore, I leave you by saying, "I have a faith." (*That's right, Oh yes, Oh yes*) Somebody is crying out, "Where is that faith? Is it in good health?" No. (*Praise the Lord, Well, All right*) For I have lived just a few years but I've come to see that you can't depend on good health. (*That's all right, Sure enough*) You may be in good health today and plunged to the nadir of bad health tomorrow. (*Sure enough, Oh yes*) You may be elevated to the heights of physical security today (*Sure enough, Yes*) and tomorrow inflicted with some incurable disease (*Yes*) that will be with you the remainder of your days. (*Yes, Sure enough*) So my faith is not in good health (*Sure enough*), but I have a faith. (*Talk to me, Yes*) "Is it in a long life?" No. (*Well, Praise the Lord, Yes*) But I have come to see now that I'm involved in a dangerous struggle for my people (*Sure enough, sure enough, Yes*), and I don't know what the future holds in that sense. (*All right*) Maybe I will not get to see my three score years and ten. (*Sure enough, Come on*) So now I've come to the conclusion that I can't put my ultimate faith in a long life, but I have a faith. (*Sure enough, All right, Oh yeah*) "Is your faith in economic security?" No. (*Sure enough, Well*) For dollars are here today and gone tomorrow. (*Sure enough, sure enough, Oh yes, Yes Lord*) My faith is not in the dollar, but I have a faith. (*Talk, Yes*) "Is it in the United States of America?" No. (*Sure enough, sure enough, Well*) For every now and then I think about America and I get worried about it. (*Sure enough, sure enough, Oh yeah, That's it*) So my ultimate faith is not in America (*Sure enough, sure enough*), but I have a faith. (*Oh yes*) "Is your ultimate faith in Western civilization?" No. (*Well, Lord help him*) But I look at Western civilization, and I wonder sometimes if Western civilization will be able to survive. (*Oh yes, Sure enough, sure enough*) When I go back and read Gibbon's *Decline and Fall of the Roman Empire*, I find that the parallels between Western civilization and the Roman empire are frightening.[14] (*Sure enough, sure enough*) And I'm not so sure now whether Western civilization will be able to survive, but I have a faith. (*Sure enough, Yes, Sure enough, sure enough*)

"Is your faith in organized religion?" Not totally. (*Catch your breath*) Yes, my faith is in the church, within the church, that spiritual (*Yes*) church (*Oh yes*), but sometimes I get worried about our particular churches. We are busy warring among ourselves (*Oh yes, Sure enough*), caught up in narrow sectarianism, giving out sanction to the status quo. (*Yes*) Slavery couldn't have survived in America if the church hadn't

---

14. Edward Gibbon, *The History of the Decline and Fall of the Roman Empire* (1776–1788).

sanctioned it. (*That's it, that's it*) Segregation would be dead as a doornail in the South today if the Southern white church took a stand against it. (*Sure enough, sure enough*) So today I say to you that my ultimate faith is not in organized religion, but I have a faith. (*Yes*) "What is that faith?" (*Sure enough*) I say to you this morning that my faith is in the eternal *God* (*All right*), whose purpose changes not. (*Sure enough, sure enough*) So I can cry out:

> Oh God, our help in ages past (*Talk, Yes*),
> our hope for years to come (*Sure enough, Sure enough*),
> our shelter in the time of storm,
> and *our* eternal home: (*Sure enough, sure enough*)

> Before the hills in order stood,
> or earth received her frame,
> from everlasting Thou art God,
> to endless years the same.[15]

This is my faith. And I choose to go on through my days with this faith. I tell you if you catch it, you will be able to rise from the fatigue of despair to the buoyancy of hope. (*Yes*) Love yourself; you are commanded to do that. (*Well*) That is the length of life. (*Well*) Love your neighbor as you love yourself (*Oh yeah*); you are commanded to do that. That's the breadth of life. (*Well, Oh yes*) But never forget that there is a first and even greater commandment: Love the Lord thy God with all thy *heart* (*Oh yes*), with all thy *soul* (*Yes*), and with all thy *mind*. (*Yes*) *That* is the height of life. And when you do this, you'll live the complete life. Thank God for John who, centuries ago, out on a lonely obscure island, caught vision of the new Jerusalem. And God grant to those of us who are left to live life, who have kept the vision (*Oh yes*) and decide to move toward that city of complete life in which the length, and the breadth (*Oh yes*), and the height are equal. (*Oh yes, Yes, Amen, My Lord*)

At. JBC.

---

15. Isaac Watts, "O God Our Help in Ages Past" (1719).

"Love in Action" I

[*3 April 1960*]
[*Atlanta, Ga.*]

Throughout his pastoral career, King developed several sermons on love, including this handwritten outline exploring forgiveness and living in accordance with God's teaching.[1]

---

1. King later developed this sermon further and included it in a thematic series (King, "Levels of Love," Sermon Delivered at Ebenezer Baptist Church, 16 September 1962, pp. 437–445 in this volume).

"Then said Jesus, Father, forgive them, for they know not what they do."[2]

Introduction: Notice closely the word with which our text opens: "Then." The verse which immediately precedes it reads thus, "And when they were come to the place, which is called Clavery, there they crucified Him; and the malefactors, one on the right hand and the other on the left."[3] Then, said Jesus, Father, forgive them. "Then"—when he was ~~the victim of man's most~~ dying ~~ign A~~ most ignominous death. "Then"—when he was being plunged into the abyss of nagging agony. "Then—when man had stooped to his worst. "Then"—when the wicket hands of the creature had dared to crucify the only begotten son of the creator. "Then"—when the vileness of the human heart was displayed in climactic devilry. Then, said Jesus, Father Forgive them Behind that then could have been another reaction. Then he could have said, "Father, get even with them. Then he could have said, "Father let loose the mighty thunderbolts of righteous wrath and slay them. Then he could have said, "Father open the flood gates of justice, and let the staggering avalance of retribution pour upon them." But this is not his response. Though subjected to unspeakable shame, though suffering excruciating pain, though despised, rejected, hated, nevertheless, He cries, "Father, forgive them."

Let us notice two basic lessons from this text

I   It is an expression of Jesus' ability ~~to~~ to live in the closest detail the sublime philosophy which his lip had proclaimed Match his sublime teachings with matchless living.[4]

    (a) One of the tragedies of life is that very few men match their profession with practice[5]

    (b.) He had spoken about love (Love your enemies) and forginess.[6]

    (c) Then comes the moment of testing. Will he reveal the love and forgiveness that he has talked about. He responds by proving that his deeds are equal to his words.[7]

He would also submit a version of this sermon for publication (King, Draft of Chapter IV, *Strength to Love,* "Love in Action," July 1962–March 1963, pp. 486–494 in this volume). According to a 3 April 1960 program from Ebenezer, King preached the sermon "Love in Action."

2. Luke 23:34.

3. Luke 23:33.

4. In a later version of this sermon that King kept in his sermon file, he continued: "This was Jesus finest hour, this was his heavenly response to his earthly rendezvous with destiny We sense the greatness of this prayer by contrast. Nature does not forgive. It is caught in the finality of its impersonal structure. In spite of the agonizing pleas of men trapped in the path of an onrushing hurricane or the anguishing cry of a builder falling from the scaffold, nature expresses only a cold, serene and passionless indifference" (King, Love and Forgiveness, Sermon notes, 20 May 1964).

5. In another outline of this sermon, King wrote, "How often are our lives characterized by a high blood pressure of Creeds and an anemia of deeds" (King, Love in Action II, 3 April 1960).

6. Matthew 5:44.

7. In the other outline, King continued, "Jesus affirmed a higher law from the cross. He knew that an eye for an eye would leave everybody blind. He did not seek to overcome evil with evil. He overcame evil with good. What a magnificent lesson. Generations will rise and fall. Men will continue to worship the god of revenge and bow before the altar of retaliation; but ever and again this noble lesson of Calvery will be a nagging reminder that only goodness can drive out evil" (King, Love in Action II, 3 April 1960).

It is an expression of Jesus awareness of man's stupidity. They know not what
they do.

(a) over some of the most shameful tragedies of history [*hang?*] these words.[8]

(b) Individually, I feel like saying Father be merciful to me a fool[9]

AD. CSKC: Sermon file, folder 120, "Love in Action" / "Father Forgive."

---

8. Fosdick, "Crucified by Stupidity," in *The Hope of the World*, p. 223: "over the most shameful tragedies of history, as over the cross of Christ, the judgment stands: 'They know not what they do.'"

9. Cf. Luke 18:13. In his sermon notes, King concluded at this point, "A second lesson comes to us from Jesus prayer on the cross. It is an expression of man's intellectual and spiritual blindness. 'They know..' Blindness was their trouble; enlightenment was their need. Jesus was naild to the cross not simply by badness but also by blindness. The men who [*cried*] 'crucify him' were not bad men but rather blind men. This tragic blindness expresses itself in many ominous ways in our own day. I. Some men feel that war is the answer to the problems of the world. Sincerity & conscientiousness in themselves are not enough. Nothing in all the world is more dangerous than sincere ignorance and conscientious stupidity. The church must urge men to be kindhearted & sincere" (King, Love and Forgiveness, 20 May 1964).

"The Seeking God"

[*2 October 1960*]
[*Atlanta, Ga.*]

Referring to Jesus' parable of the lost sheep, King declares God's active concern and love for every individual: "Every man from a [bass*] black to a treble white is significant on God's keyboard."*[1]

Based on the parable of the Lost Sheep
Luke 15:1–7

Introduction—There is a desperate question on the lips of every individual. It is a poinant insistent question. In no life can the question be finally dismissed. The question is simply this—What is God like? "The Power that rolls the planets on their course and draws the line of death across our human days—Who is He?" "Our dearest faith, our ghastliest doubt"—What is he like.[2] The majestic Power that is the heartbeat of the cosmos—Who is he. This is the desperate, stinging, poignant question flowing from the lips of every man

---

1. This sermon was King's announced topic for this date (Ebenezer Baptist Church, Press release, "'The Seeking God' King Jr.'s Topic at Ebenezer," 1 October 1960).

2. Buttrick, *The Parables of Jesus*, p. 179: "'What is God like?' . . . the Power Who rolls the planets on their course and draws the line of death across our human days—Who is He? 'Our dearest faith, our ghastliest doubt'—what is He like?"

The Seeking God
Based on the parable of the Lost Sheep
Luke 15:1-7

Another
introduction
can be "where
is God." As
Carlyle said
"God sits in
Heaven and
does nothing

Introduction — There is a desperate question on the lips of every individual. It is a poignant insistent question. In our life can the question be finally dismissed. The question is simply this — What is God like? "The Power that rolls the planets on their course and draws the line of death across our human days — Who is He?" "Our dearest faith, our ghastliest doubt" — What is he like. The majestic Power that is the heartbeat of the cosmos — Who is he. This is the desperate, stinging, poignant question flowing from the lips of every man.

Jesus answered the question. He answered it in terms that every man of this generation could understand. "God," he says, "is like a Good Shepherd." Indeed lead us into this pasture of mortal life. He knows that folly by which we wander. He seeks us through pain and peril. And finally

he is the
cosmic Shepherd that

On this first page of a handwritten draft for the sermon "The Seeking God," based on the parable of the lost sheep, King writes, "What is God like? . . . This is the desperate, stinging, poignant question flowing from the lips of every man." Jesus, King says, answers that God "is like a Good Shepherd."

Jesus answered the question. He [*answered?*] it in terms that every man of his generation could understand. "God," he says, "is like a Good Shepherd."[3] Indeed he is the Cosmic Shepard that lead us into this pasture of mortal life. He knows that folly by which we wander. He seeks us through pain and peril. And finally he leads us through the Valley of the Shadow, His lifted rod our guide.[4] This aspect of God's nature is set forth so beautifully in the parable of the lost Sheep.

{Another introduction can be "where is God." as Carlyle said "God sits in Heaven and does nothing}[5]

The basic message of this parable is set forth in three points.[6]

I It emphasizes ~~mans tragic tendency to become lost~~ the tragedy of being lost. There is nothing more tragic than to see a person who has wandered so far from the fold of his destiny that he ~~ends up in the maze of present circumstances~~ ends up with a complete loss of a sense of direction.

    (a) Now notice that this sheep was not lost by deliberate choice.[7] There is nothing in the parable to indicate that the sheep consciously strayed away from the fold. He was probably just nibbling sweet grass. Like the sheep, men follow the lure of the moment—this transitory thrill of pleasure, that passing enrichment—until at last they reach the deep darkness of a lost night.[8]

    {As a counselor of people I have come to see that most personal problem do not grow out of a deliberate choice

        (1) The alcoholic starts as a social drinker—Yale Report.[9]

        (2) Dope addiction starts in the quest for a new experience

        (3) Marriage infidelity starts in the enjoyment of being flattered}[10]

    b. Now what does being lost really mean. It means [*strikeout illegible*] being on the wrong road.

II The second basic point brought out in this parable is that God is unwearily persistent in seeking the lost. Indeed this is the crux of the parable. It only deals with the lostness of man in order to reveal the amazing propotions of God's seeking love.

---

    3. Cf. John 10:11, 14.

    4. Cf. Psalm 23:4; Buttrick, *The Parables of Jesus*, p. 179: "He is like a shepherd! He led us into this pasture of mortal life. He knows the folly by which we wander, drawn by this pleasant tuft and that lush watercourse, until the night is on us and the mountains rise like walls of rock. He seeks us through pain and peril. He will lead us at the last through the Valley of the Shadow, His lifted rod our guide!"

    5. Carlyle, *Sartor Resartus*, p. 163; King inserted this reference to Thomas Carlyle in a second pen.

    6. Buttrick, *The Parables of Jesus*, p. 180: "The message of the story—this avowal of God's love—is concentrated in three of its words." Buttrick explored the significance of the following words: "lost," "seeking," and "until" (*The Parables of Jesus*, pp. 180–181).

    7. Buttrick, *The Parables of Jesus*, p. 180: "Sometimes they are lost like sheep, not from viciousness or deliberate choice but from weak will and heedlessness."

    8. Buttrick, *The Parables of Jesus*, p. 180: "Like sheep, men follow the zest of the moment—this transitory thrill of pleasure, that passing enrichment—until they reach darkness and the brink of the precipice!"

    9. King may be referring to information from a 1959 Yale University conference on alcoholism (Program, "Ministers' conference on the problems of alcohol," 18 October–20 October 1959).

    10. King added these bracketed lines in a second pen.

    (a) We tend to think that the seach is on man's part, but it is the other way around. Prayer, for instance, is really man response to God.

    (b) Aristotle's God[11]

    (c) God is not an absentees God. He is not the God that sits in his heaven and does nothing. Throughout the Bible, from the beginning of the O.T. to the end of the New, we find God trudging [*thru?*] the hedges and highways of history seeking to find to lost[12]

IV Finally, this parable teaches the endless preciousness of the individual to God. "There is joy in heaven over <u>one</u> sinner[13]

    (a) There is so much in our moden life to refute this principle

        (1) men and women [*hovered?*] up in big cities & big industrial areas

        (2) Communism as a threat to individualism

        (3) Out of this emphasis of the worth of the ind grew democracy

    (b) The Christian gospel is committed, once and for all, to the worth of the individual. By his cross, Christ has bound all men into an inextricably bond of brotherhood, and stamped on all men the indelible imprint of preciousness.

    (c) All men are significant. The one lost is as significant as the ninety and nine. Every man from a base black to a treble white is significant on God's keyboard.[14] The important thing about a man is not his specificity, but his fundamentum.

In the final analysis this parable tells us that there is somebody in the universe who cares. This is what the hymn writer meant when he said; Jesus cares[15]

AD. CSKC: Sermon file, folder 51, "The Seeking God (Parable of Lost Sheep)."

---

11. King's subject index file contained a notecard in which he cited "Knudson, DOG, 298" below the title "Aristotle's God" (King, Notecards on Aristotle, U.S. policy on Asia, Atheism, and Augustine, 1951–1955). Albert C. Knudson argued that Aristotle's God was not a personal god: "He is a shining ideal which attracts the world, and in this sense the world loves him, but he does not love the world. He stands aloof from it. There is no reciprocal intercourse between him and men" (Knudson, *The Doctrine of God* [New York: Abingdon Press, 1930], pp. 281, 298).

12. Cf. Luke 14:23.

13. Luke 15:7; King added this sentence in a second pen.

14. In a 1955 published sermon Robert J. McCracken remarked, "Aggrey, that great Negro Christian, said: 'You can play some sort of tune on the white keys of a piano; you can play some sort of tune on the black keys of a piano; but to produce real harmony you must play both the black and white keys'" (McCracken, "Discrimination—The Shame of Sunday Morning," *The Pulpit* [February 1955]: 6). James E. Kwegyir Aggrey, born in Gold Coast, became an AME Zion Church minister and theologian after migrating to the United States in 1898.

15. King added the last two sentences in a second pen. He may be referring to Frank E. Graeff's 1901 hymn "Does Jesus Care?": "Oh yes, He cares, I know He cares, / His heart is touched with my grief; / When the days are weary, the long nights dreary, / I know my Saviour cares."

January 1961
Chicago, Ill.

On 20 November 1960, Ebony *managing editor Era Bell Thompson conducted a*
telephone interview with King on "current opinions regarding hell" and published his
response in an article in the magazine's January 1961 issue.[1]

Rev. Martin Luther King Jr., Baptist, Atlanta. Says the man who has had his share of
hell on earth: "I do not believe in hell as a place of a literal burning fire. Hell, to me,
is a condition of being out of fellowship with God. It is man's refusal to accept the
Grace of God. It is the state in which the individual continues to experience the
frustrations, contradictions and agonies of earthly life. Hell is as real as absolute
loneliness and isolation."[2]

PD. *Ebony* (January 1961): 52.

---

1. Thompson to King, 21 November 1960. The *Ebony* article included responses by other notable
ministers such as Adam Clayton Powell, Gardner C. Taylor, Howard Thurman, Benjamin Mays, and J. H.
Jackson.

2. Thompson's letter contained a longer version of King's reply that included his observation on the
nature of heaven: "On the other hand, heaven is the state in which man finds himself in eternal ~~fri~~ fellowship with God. It is a release from the trials and tribulations of life. . . . Heaven is as real as friendship
or an idea" (King, Draft, What Happened to Hell? 21 November 1960).

The Man Who Was a Fool,
Sermon Delivered at the Detroit Council
of Churches' Noon Lenten Services

[*6 March 1961*]
Detroit, Mich.

At the invitation of G. Merrill Lenox, director of the Detroit Council of Churches,
King preached this sermon at the city's Central Methodist Church as part of the
Council's 1961 Noon Lenten series.[1] *Drawing on George Buttrick's explication of*
Jesus' parable of the rich fool, he warns against the pursuit of material possessions:
"There is always the danger that we will judge the success of our professions by the size
of the wheel base on our automobiles and the index of our salaries rather than the
quality of our service to humanity." In contrast to this preoccupation with individual

---

1. Lenox to King, 14 April 1959. King accepted in a 30 April 1959 letter.   411

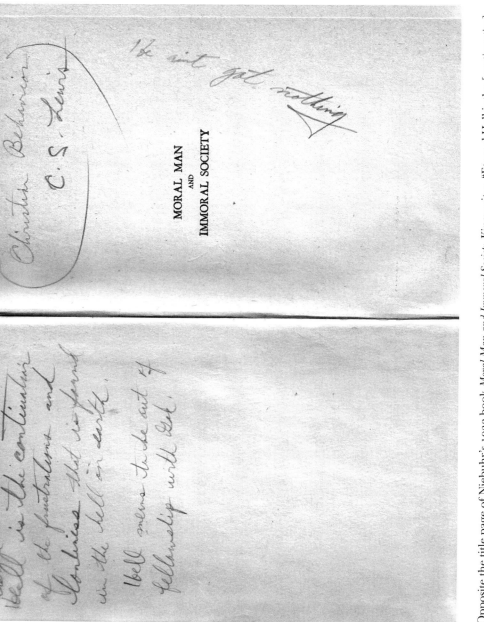

Opposite the title page of Niebuhr's 1932 book *Moral Man and Immoral Society*, King writes, "Eternal Hell is the [*continuation*] of the frustrations and [*loneliness*] that is found in the hell on earth. Hell means to be out of fellowship with God."

accumulation, he notes the importance of human interdependence, urging the United States to place its excess grain "in the wrinkled stomachs of the hundreds and millions of people who go to bed hungry at night. And we can store it there free of charge." King challenges white racism but also adds, "Black supremacy is based on a great deal of foolishness. It is the foolish notion that the black man has made all of the contributions of civilization and that he will one day rule the world." He attributes the rich fool's spiritual death to his failure "to realize his dependence on God" and concludes, "We must all learn to live together as brothers, or we will all perish together as fools." The following text is taken from an audio recording of the service.[2]

I need not pause to say how very delighted I am to be here today and to be a part of this Lenten series. At one time I felt that I wouldn't get here today because about this time yesterday morning I could hardly talk. I came down over the weekend with a very bad cold and a hoarseness that I have never known before. So I will have to ask you to indulge me with a rather hoarse voice. But it is always a great privilege and pleasure to be in Detroit and to be a part of the Lenten program. I remember the wonderful and rich experience which came to me just two years ago when I was a part of the Lenten series.[3]

Now, as we think of our Christian commitment, as we think of deepening our Christian commitment, I would like to share with you a dramatic little story, packed with spiritual significance. It is a story of a man who dreamed a dream that could never come true. It is a story of a man who, on the basis of all standards of modernity, would have been considered an eminently successful man. And yet Jesus called him a fool. This familiar story is preserved for us in the gospel as recorded by Saint Luke. The main character in the drama is a certain rich man. His grounds had brought forth plentifully. He didn't know where to store his goods. And like a bolt out of the blue, it occurred to him that he could tear down his old barns and build new and larger ones. And then he would say to his soul, "Thou hast much goods laid up for many years. Take thine ease. Eat, drink, and be merry." And then the story goes on to tell us that at the very heyday of his prosperity this man died. And God says, "Thou fool, this night, thy soul is required of thee."[4]

This is the story. This story is so terribly relevant in its implications and so profoundly meaningful in its conclusions. Think of it. If this man lived in Detroit today, he would be a big shot. [*Congregation:*] (*Yes*) He would be a key figure. (*Yes*) And yet a Galilean peasant had the audacity to call him a fool. Now, there was nothing here to tell us that he was called a fool because he came about his wealth, or rather that

---

2. The audio tape begins with a voice announcing the sermon's date. King had also given this sermon at Chicago's Sunday Evening Club on 29 January 1961, and the preaching journal *The Pulpit* published this version in its June 1961 issue (pp. 4–6). King later included a version of this sermon in *Strength to Love* (pp. 51–57).

3. King preached during the 1958 series (King, "The Christian Doctrine of Man," Sermon Delivered at Detroit Council of Churches' Noon Lenten Services, 12 March 1958, pp. 328–338 in this volume). He participated in the 1959 summer preaching series at Central Methodist Church.

4. Luke 12:16–21.

he gained his wealth through dishonest means. From all indications, this man was a hard worker. He was very industrious; he had probably invested wisely. It doesn't seem that he trampled over other men with iron feet of oppression. There is nothing in the parable which tells us that this man was a fool because he had money and because he was wealthy, for Jesus never makes a sweeping indictment against wealth.[5] It is always the misuse of wealth that Jesus condemns (*That's right*), for wealth is amoral like any other force, such as the force of electricity. It can be used for good or evil.

Now it is true that one day a man came to Jesus wanting to raise certain questions about eternal life, and Jesus said to that man, "Sell all."[6] But at that point he was prescribing individual surgery and not setting forth a universal diagnosis.[7] There is never a sweeping indictment against all wealth in the New Testament. As I said, it is the misuse of wealth that Jesus constantly condemns. And so there is nothing inherently vicious about wealth, and there is nothing inherently virtuous about poverty. I am sure that if there is a hell there will be plenty poor folk in it. [*laughter*] (*That's right*) Why then did Jesus call this man a fool? Where do we find the basic reasons for this?

It seems to me that the first reason that Jesus called this man a fool was because he allowed the "within" of his life to be absorbed within the "without" of his life. Each of us lives on two levels, so to speak, and we operate within two realms—the "within" and the "without." The "within" of life is what we use. It deals with the techniques and devices, instrumentalities and mechanisms, by means of which we live—in short, the material stuff that is necessary for our existence. This is the "without" of life—the car we drive, the house we live in, the clothes we wear, and all of those material objects that are necessary for our earthly survival. Then there is a "within" of life. And this is that realm of spiritual ends, which expresses itself in art, literature, morality and religion, for which, at best, we live.

Now, the foolishness of this man consisted in the fact that he allowed the "within" of his life to become absorbed in the "without." In other words, he allowed the means by which he lived to become, to absorb the ends for which he lived. He allowed his civilization to outdistance his culture. And so he was a victim of that something that Thoreau referred to when he said, "Improved means to an unimproved end."[8] He failed to keep a line of distinction between "him" and "his." He failed to keep a line of demarcation between his life and his livelihood.[9] And there is always the danger that we will find ourselves caught up in this foolishness. We must always be careful in America because we live in a capitalistic economy, which stresses the profit motive and free enterprise. And there is always the danger that we

---

5. Buttrick, *The Parables of Jesus*, p. 128: "Certain it is that Jesus made no sweeping indictment of material wealth."

6. Luke 18:18–22.

7. Buttrick, *The Parables of Jesus*, p. 128: "It is true that He bade the rich young ruler 'sell all' and follow; but He was then prescribing an individual surgery, not a universal rule."

8. Thoreau, *Walden; or, Life in the Woods*, p. 57.

9. Buttrick, *The Parables of Jesus*, p. 130: "But the Rich Man thought so persistently and with such concentration about his 'goods' that the necessary line of distinction between *him* and *his* was erased. His life was lost in his livelihood."

will be more concerned about making a living than making a life. There is always the danger that we will judge the success of our professions by the size of the wheel base on our automobiles and the index of our salaries rather than the quality of our service to humanity. There must always be a line of distinction between the "within" and the "without" of life.[10]

You see this man was foolish because the richer he became materially, the poorer he became spiritually and intellectually. He may have been married, but he didn't really love his wife. He may have given her all of the material necessities of life, but he deprived her of that something which she needed more than anything else, namely love and affection. He may have had children, but he didn't really appreciate them. It's possible that he had many volumes of books stored around his mansion, but he never read them. He may have had access to great music, but he never listened to it. And so his eyes were closed to the majestic grandeur of the stars. And somehow his ears were closed to the melodious sweetness of great music. His mind was closed to the insights of the poets and prophets and philosophers. And therefore his title was justly merited. He was a fool because he failed to keep a line of distinction between the "within" and the "without" of life.

But not only that. This man was a fool because he failed to realize his dependence on others. If you will read that soliloquy in the Book of Luke, you will notice that there are about sixty words used. And as you read the monologue, you will discover that this man uses "I" and "my" more than thirteen times.[11] He had said "I" and "my" so much that he had lost the capacity to say "we" and "our," and so he was inflicted with the cancerous disease of egotism. He was a fool because he failed to realize that wealth is always a result of the commonwealth.[12] He talked as if he could plow the fields alone. He talked as if he could build the barns alone. He failed to realize the interdependent structure of reality.

And so often we fail to see this. Something should remind us before we can finish eating breakfast in the morning we are dependent on more than half of the world. We get up in the morning and go to the bathroom and reach over for a sponge, and that's handed to us by a Pacific Islander. Then we reach over for a bar of soap, and that's given to us at the hands of a Frenchman. And then we reach up for our towel, and that's given to us by a Turk. And then we go to the kitchen for breakfast, getting ready to go to work. Maybe this morning we want to follow the good old American tradition, and we drink coffee. That's poured in our cups by a South American. Or maybe we are desirous of having tea. Then we discover that that's poured in our cup by a Chinese. Or maybe we want cocoa this morning, and then we discover that that's poured in our cup by a West African. Then we reach over for a piece of toast, only to discover that that's given to us at the hands of an English-speaking farmer, not to mention the baker. And so before we finish eating breakfast in the morning,

10. Buttrick, *The Parables of Jesus,* p. 133: "So Jesus ended the story in a terse sentence which once more sharply drew the line between the 'within' and 'without' of our lives."

11. Buttrick, *The Parables of Jesus,* p. 130: "His soliloquy as translated in our version occupies sixty-one words. 'I' occurs six times in that brief monologue, and 'my' or 'thine' (addressed to himself) six times."

12. Buttrick, *The Parables of Jesus,* p. 131: "The rich man reached affluence mainly by reason of the *commonwealth.*"

we are dependent on more than half of the world.[13] (*That's right*) But this man didn't realize that. (*Right on*) And any man who fails to see the interdependent structure of reality is really a fool. (*Yes, Amen, Tell it*)

Now, this text has a great deal of bearing on our struggle in race relations in our nation, indeed all over the world. (*Amen*) For what is white supremacy but the foolish notion that God made a mistake and stamped an eternal stigma of inferiority on a certain race of people? What is white supremacy but the foolishness of believing that one race is good enough to dominate another race? (*Tell it, Yeah*) What is white supremacy but the foolish notion (*Oh yeah*) of believing that certain people are to be relegated to the status of things rather than being elevated to the status of persons? (*Hallelujah, Amen*) There is no greater foolishness than the foolishness that accompanies our inhumanity to man. And the converse is also true. Black supremacy is based on a great deal of foolishness. (*Amen, Tell it*) It is the foolish notion that the black man has made all of the contributions of civilization and that he will one day rule the world. I am convinced, as I have said so often, that as Negroes we must work passionately and unrelentingly for first-class citizenship, but we must never use second-class methods to gain it. (*Amen*) We must not seek to rise from a position of disadvantage to one of advantage, thus subverting justice. Not substituting one tyranny for another, but we must seek to achieve democracy for everybody. (*Yes*) God is not interested merely in the freedom of black men and brown men and yellow men; God is interested in the freedom of the whole human race (*Yeah, Amen*) and the creation of a society where all men will live together as brothers and every man (*Oh yeah*) will respect the dignity and the worth of human personality. (*Yeah*) Whenever we fail to believe this, we indulge in a tragic foolishness. (*Yes*)

Now in our international life this text has a great deal of bearing. It means so much to us in America, at least it should. For all here in America, we have goods stored up. And so often our grounds bring forth plentifully. (*Yes*) And constantly we find ourselves asking, "Where can we store these surplus goods?" (*Yeah*) At times we find ourselves pulling down our old barns, building new and larger ones. At other times we find ourselves spending more than a million dollars a day to store surplus food and find ourselves asking, "Where, or What can we do with all of these goods?" There is an answer. (*Yes*) I saw the answer when I traveled in Africa.[14] I saw the answer when I traveled in India a few months ago and saw millions of people sleeping on the sidewalks at night.[15] I saw the answer when I traveled in South America

---

13. Leslie Weatherhead, *Why Do Men Suffer?* (New York: Abingdon-Cokesbury, 1936), pp. 69–70: "When I rise and go to my bath, a cake of soap is handed me by a Frenchman, a sponge is handed me by a Pacific Islander, a towel by a Turk, my underclothes by one American or an Englishman, my outer garments by another. I come down to breakfast. My tea is poured out by an Indian or a Chinese. My porridge is served by a Scottish farmer. My toast I accept at the hands of an English speaking farmer, not to mention the baker. My marmalade is passed to me by a Spaniard, my banana by a West Indian. I am indebted to half the world before I have finished breakfast." King paraphrased Weatherhead in a school paper, and wrote this quote and the attribution to Weatherhead on a notecard titled "Brotherhood" (King, Six Talks Based on *Beliefs that Matter* by William Adams Brown, 15 February 1950 in *Papers* 1:282, and Personal notecards on "B" topics, 1948–1954).

14. King visited Liberia, Ghana, and Nigeria in March 1957.

15. King visited India in the spring of 1959.

this past summer.[16] Where can we store these surplus goods? In the wrinkled stomachs of the hundreds and millions of people who go to bed hungry at night. And we can store it there free of charge. (*Yeah, Yes sir*)

And I am convinced that maybe in America we've used too much of our wealth to establish military bases around the world rather than establishing bases of genuine concern and understanding. (*Yes*) All I am saying is simply this: that all life is interrelated. We are tied in a single garment of destiny, caught in an inescapable network of mutuality. And whatever affects one directly, affects all indirectly. As long as there is poverty in the world, no man can be totally rich, even if he has a billion dollars. (*Yeah*) As long as diseases are rampant and millions of people cannot expect to live more than twenty-eight years, no man can be totally healthy, even if he just got a clean bill of health from Mayo Clinic.[17] Strangely enough (*Yeah*), I can never be what I ought to be until you are what you ought to be, and you can never be what you ought to be until I am what I ought to be. (*Yeah*) This is the way the world is made. I didn't make it that way. You didn't make it that way. We all found it that way. (*Yes, yes*) John Donne caught this years ago and placed it in graphic terms: "No man is an island entire of itself. Every man is a piece of the continent, a part of the main." And then he goes on toward the end to say, "Any man's death diminishes me, because I am involved in mankind. And therefore never send to know for whom the bell tolls. It tolls for thee."[18]

And there was a final reason why this man was foolish. He failed to realize his dependence on God. Go back again and read his words. He talked as if he regulated the seasons. He talked as if he produced the rain. He talked as if he controlled the setting and the rising of the sun. This man was a fool because he felt that he was the creator instead of a creature. And so he sought to live life without a sky. He sought to live life merely on the horizontal plane, devoid of the vertical. Now there is nothing new about this foolishness. It is still alive today. We find it in a collective sense at times when whole nations rise up and say that God is an irrelevant item on the agenda of life. This is something of what communism says; it talks about its dialectical materialism, and thinks of the whole of reality being pulled on by certain economic, materialistic forces. And so God is eliminated from the whole program of life. But not only do we find theoretical denials; at times we find another type of atheism, which is even worse. It is a practical atheism, living as if there is no God. (*Amen*) A part of the secularism and the materialism of modern life is found in this practical atheism, not where the individual denies the existence of God with his lips, not where the individual goes through the intellectual process of arguing this question of the reality of God, where the individual affirms the reality of God with his lips and denies His existence with his life. This is an even greater type of atheism and a more dangerous type.

In spite of our theoretical denials, in spite of our inordinate worship of things, we continue to have those spiritual experiences which cannot be explained in materi-

---

16. King visited Brazil, Argentina, and Venezuela between 29 June and 6 July 1960.

17. The Mayo Clinic in Rochester, Minnesota, has a Nobel Prize-winning medical staff.

18. King recites a section from John Donne's "Meditation XVII," *Devotions Upon Emergent Occasions* (1624).

alistic terms. In spite of our denial of the existence of the unseen, in spite of our living in what Professor Sorokin of Harvard called the "sensate civilization," ever now and again something comes to remind us that the unseen is the real. And so we go out in life and look about. Maybe at night we look up at the beautiful stars as they bedeck the heavens like swinging lanterns of eternity, and we conclude that we see all. But then something comes to remind us that we don't see all, for we can never see the law of gravitation that holds them there. (*Yeah*) We look at this beautiful church and its beautiful architectural designs, and for a moment we think we see all. Oh no, we can never see the mind of the architect who drew the blueprint. We can never see the hope and the love and the faith of the individuals who made it so. You look up this morning, and I can hear you saying, "I see Martin Luther King." I hate to disappoint you. You see my body. (*Amen, Right on, Yeah*) You see the external manifestations of my personality, but you can never see my mind. You can never see my personality; you can never see the me that makes me me. Everything that we see is a shadow cast by that which we do not see. (*Yeah*) And so maybe Plato was right; the visible is a shadow cast by the invisible.[19] (*Right on*)

Therefore, all of our new knowledge, as important as it is, cannot decrease God's being. All of our new knowledge can banish God neither from the microcosmic [*compass?*] of the atom nor from the vast, unfathomable ranges of interstellar space. Living in a universe in which we are forced to measure stellar distance in light years (*Right*) and confronted with the illimitable expanse of the solar system in which stars are five hundred million million miles from the earth, in which heavenly bodies travel at incredible speed, and in which the ages of planets are reckoned in terms of billions of years, modern man is forced to cry out with the Psalmist of old: "When I behold the heavens, the work of thy hands, the moon and the stars and all that thou hast created, what is man that thou art mindful of him? (*Yeah*) And the son of man that thou rememfereth him?"[20] God is still around. (*Yes, He is*) And all of our new knowledge cannot decrease His being one iota. And when we discover Him, and when we allow Him to be the central force in our lives, we begin to live with new meaning (*Amen*), for there is something about this faith in God that lifts us from the fatigue of despair to the buoyancy of hope (*Yeah*), that can transform dark and desolate valleys into sunlit paths of joy. Then we come to know that as we struggle for the good life, we do not struggle alone but that we have cosmic companionship. (*Yes*) When we believe in God sure enough, we know that there is a power in this universe working at every moment to bring low gigantic mountains of injustice and to pull down prodigious hilltops of evil. There is something in this universe (*Oh yeah*) which justifies Carlyle in saying, "No lie can live forever."[21] There is something in this universe which justifies James Russell Lowell in saying:

> Truth forever on the scaffold,
> Wrong forever on the throne (*Yes*),
> Yet that scaffold sways the future,

---

19. Plato *Republic* 515c.
20. Psalm 8:3–4.
21. Thomas Carlyle, *The French Revolution* (1837).

And behind the dim unknown,
Standeth God within the shadow,
Keeping watch above His own.[22] (*Oh yes*)

There is something in this universe which justifies William Cullen Bryant in saying, "Truth crushed to earth will rise again."[23] And when we discover this (*Yes*), we live life with new meaning.

This man was a fool because he didn't realize this. And then the story comes to a dramatic end. It says that when this man had come to the heyday of his prosperity and his stock had accrued the greatest amount of interest, and somehow his Cadillac car was shining with all of its radiance, and when his palatial home stood out in all of its impressive proportions, it tells us that he died. And maybe that added drama to it, the fact that he came to physical death at this moment, but even if he hadn't died at this moment, he was already dead. (*Yeah*) And the cessation of breathing in his life was but the belated announcement of an earlier death of the spirit. He died when he failed to keep a line of distinction between the "within" and the "without" of life. (*Amen*) He died when he failed to realize his dependence on others. He died when he failed to realize his dependence on God.

And whenever we do that, whenever an individual does that, he, too, is engaged in a tragic foolishness. And it may well be that Jesus was talking about our acquisitive generation. Yes, we have the privilege of having things and many things. Through our scientific genius, we have been able to dwarf distance and place time in chains. Yes, we've been able to carve highways through the stratosphere. There is the danger now that we will forget something even more important, for in spite of all of our material and technological advances we have not learned the simple lesson of living together as brothers. The alternative to understanding goodwill, to a world of brotherhood, to world government, to disarmament, may well be a civilization plunged into the abyss of annihilation. We must all learn to live together as brothers, or we will all perish together as fools. (*That's right*) There is still a voice crying through the vista of time saying, "What shall it profit a man, what shall it profit a nation, to gain the whole world of means, color televisions, electric lights, automobiles, and subways, and lose the end, the soul."[24] This is the message. And if we as a nation will but discover this, if we as individuals will but turn away from this foolishness, the morning stars will sing together (*Amen*) and the sons of God will shout for joy. (*Amen*)

May we pray? The Lord bless thee and keep thee. The Lord make His face to shine upon thee and be gracious unto thee. (*Oh yes*) The Lord lift up the light of His countenance unto thee and be with thee forever and ever more.[25] Amen.

At. MAWC.

---

22. Lowell, *The Present Crisis* (1844).
23. Bryant, "The Battlefield" (1839).
24. Cf. Mark 8:36.
25. Numbers 6:24–26.

King sits in his study, 1960. Photo by Henri Cartier-Bresson;
courtesy of Magnum Photos, Inc.

King and Dora McDonald in his study, 1960. Photo by Henri Cartier-Bresson; courtesy of Magnum Photos, Inc.

Loving Your Enemies,
Sermon Delivered at the Detroit Council of Churches' Noon Lenten Services

[*7 March 1961*]
Detroit, Mich.

King delivered this oft-given sermon at Central Methodist Church as his second message of the week for the Noon Lenten Services.[1] He argues that Jesus' command to love one's enemies was not "the pious injunction of a utopian dreamer" but the words of a "practical realist." Noting that love is a display of strength, King asserts: "Put us in jail, and we will go in with humble smiles on our faces, still loving you. Bomb our homes and threaten our children, and we will still love you. . . . But be assured that we will wear you down by our capacity to suffer." The following text is taken from an audio recording of the service.[2]

---

1. King's schedule for his Detroit visit included Noon Lenten sermons on 6 and 7 March (Lenox to King, 15 February 1961). Detroit's radio station WWJ broadcast abridged versions of both sermons King preached during the Lenten series (Detroit Council of Churches, Announcement, "Noon Lenten services," 15 February–30 March 1961).

2. King later published a version of this sermon (King, *Strength to Love*, pp. 34–41).

Again let me say how happy I am to be here and to be a part of this Lenten program once more. And I want to express my personal appreciation to my good friend Dr. [*G. Merrill*] Lenox for extending the invitation. I would also like to express my personal appreciation to him for the great work that he is doing through the Detroit Council of Churches.

I travel over the country a great deal speaking for various Councils of Churches, and certainly all of them are doing good jobs, and I don't want to minimize any. But I think I can say without fear of successful contribution, contradiction, that I don't know any council that is doing a better job and that has a more dynamic program than the Detroit Council of Churches. And I'm sure that that is due a great deal to the dynamic leadership of Dr. Lenox.

I regret so much that I cannot be with you tomorrow, but as has already been explained, I will have to go back, and I've had to change my schedule somewhat because of the heavy demands and because of the many responsibilities in the South.[3] But I'm sure that you will want to come back tomorrow to hear my good friend, Dr. Banks, who is certainly one of the distinguished and outstanding preachers of our nation.[4] And it is good for Detroit to have a man of his caliber in this community, and I'm sure that you will want to hear him tomorrow.

Now this afternoon I would like to have you think with me on a passage of scripture that has been a great influence in my life and a passage that I have sought to bring to bear on the whole struggle for racial justice, which is taking place in our nation. The words are found in the fifth chapter of the gospel as recorded by Saint Matthew. And these words flow from the lips of our Lord and Master: "Ye have heard it said of old that thou shall love thy neighbor and hate thine enemy. But I say unto you, love your enemies. Bless them that curse you. Do good to them that hate you, and pray for them that despitefully use you, that ye may be the children of your Father which is in heaven."[5]

These are great words, words lifted to cosmic proportions. And over the centuries men have argued that the actual practice of this command just isn't possible. Years ago the philosopher Nietzsche contended that this command illustrates that the Christian ethic is for weak men, not for strong men, and certainly not for the superman.[6] And he went on to argue that it was just additional proof that Jesus was an impractical idealist who never quite came down to earth.

But we have come to see today that, far from being the practical, the impractical idealist, Jesus is the practical realist, and the words of this text stand before us with new urgency. And far from being the pious injunction of a utopian dreamer, this command is an absolute necessity for the survival of our civilization. Yes, love is the

---

3. Originally scheduled to be in Detroit for three days, King cited health concerns and the growing demands of the civil rights movement in shortening the stay to two days, 6–7 March (King to Lenox, 15 February 1961).

4. King refers to Allen A. Banks, pastor of Second Baptist Church.

5. Matthew 5:43–45.

6. King may refer to Friedrich Nietzsche, *The Antichrist,* trans. H. L. Mencken (New York: Knopf, 1918), p. 43: "The weak and the botched shall perish: first principle of *our* charity. And one should help them to it. What is more harmful than any vice?—Practical sympathy for botched and the weak—Christianity. . . ."

key to the solution of the problems of our world, love even for enemies. Since this is a basic Christian command and a basic Christian responsibility, it is both fitting and proper that we stop from time to time to analyze the meaning of these arresting words. And so we may well begin by raising the practical "how"—How do we go about loving our enemies?

There are many things that we must do in order to love our enemies, but I would like to suggest just three. Seems to me that the first thing that the individual must do in order to love his enemy is to develop the capacity to forgive with a naturalness and ease. If one does not have the capacity to forgive, he doesn't have the capacity to love.

Now it is assumed that the individual or the group who is our enemy has done something to hurt us. That individual has mistreated us or has mistreated our group, so to speak, and this creates a conflict situation. Now, the only way to grapple with this conflict situation is that the mistreated person, the hurt person, the injured person, must develop the capacity to forgive, for it is only the individual who is injured or who is hurt that can forgive. The person who hurts must repent, but the person who is hurt is the one that must forgive. And it is through this method that we are able to restore the moral balance of society or individual relationships, for in the final analysis, forgiveness means a willingness to go any length to restore a broken relationship.

Now you'll hear people saying from time to time, "I will forgive you, but I won't forget." [*Congregation:*] [*laughter*] Well if you won't forget, you haven't forgiven because forgiveness means forgetting. Now it doesn't mean forgetting in the sense that you completely erase the misdeed out of your mind. This may be impossible. But it means that you erase it from your mind in the sense that it no longer serves as a determining factor in the future relationship, so that one can only forgive when he forgets.

Again we hear people saying, "I will forgive you but I won't have anything to do with you." There again, one hasn't forgiven if he will not have anything to do with the person or the group that he is supposedly forgiving because forgiveness means reconciliation. Forgiveness means the development of a new relationship. And I submit to you that the first way that one can go about loving his enemy neighbor is to develop the capacity to forgive.

The second thing is this. In order to love the enemy neighbor we must recognize that the negative deed of the enemy does not represent all that the individual is. His evil deed does not represent his whole being. If we look at ourselves hard enough, and if we look at all men hard enough, we see a strange dichotomy, a disturbing schizophrenia. We are divided against ourselves, split up so to speak. There is something within all of us which causes us to cry out with Ovid the Latin poet, "I see and approve the better things of life, but the evil things I do."[7] There is something within all of us that causes us to agree with Plato that "the human personality is like a charioteer with two headstrong horses each wanting to go in different directions."[8] There is something within all of us that causes us to cry out with St.

---

7. Ovid *Metamorphoses* 7.20.
8. Plato *Phaedrus* 246a–247c.

Augustine in his *Confessions* from time to time, "Lord, make me pure, but not yet."[9] [*laughter*] Or we find ourselves crying out with the Apostle Paul, "The good that I would I do not, and the evil that I would not that I do."[10] Or we cry out with Carlyle that "there are depths in man which go down to the lowest hell and heights which reach the highest heaven, for are not both heaven and hell made out of Him, everlasting miracle and mystery that He is."[11]

And there is within all of us something of this division. And psychologists have tried to analyze it. Sigmund Freud calls it a conflict between the id and the superego. Theologians call it a conflict between God and man. But whatever we call it, we realize soon or later that the "isness" of our present natures is out of harmony with the eternal "oughtness" that forever confronts us.[12] And this means that there is some good in the worst of us [*Congregation:*] (*Amen*) and some evil in the best of us. (*Amen*) And when we come to see this we begin to love all men. And we see an element of good even in the person who is seeking to defeat us and even in the person of the group that hates us most.

And finally we come to see that there is within every man the image of God, and no matter how much it is scarred, it is still there.[13] And so when we come to recognize that the evil act of our enemy neighbor is not the whole being of our enemy neighbor, we develop the capacity to love him in spite of his evil deed.

The other thing that we must do in order to love the enemy neighbor is this: we must seek at all times to win his friendship and understanding rather than to defeat him or humiliate him. There may come a time when it will be possible for you to humiliate your worst enemy or even to defeat him, but in order to love the enemy you must not do it. For in the final analysis, love means understanding goodwill for all men and a refusal to defeat any individual. And so somehow love makes it possible for you to place your vision and to center your activity on the evil system and not the individual enemy who may be caught up in that system. And so you set out to defeat segregation and not the segregationist. You set out to defeat the evil system of communism and not the communist. And there is a great deal of difference there. And there must be an active love for the individuals who may be caught up in an evil unjust system while we continue to work passionately and unrelentingly to do away with the system itself.

The Greek language comes to our aid when we seek to analyze the meaning of love with special reference to our enemies. There are three words in the Greek language for love. There is the word *eros,* for instance. And the word *eros* refers to a sort of aesthetic love. Plato uses it a great deal in his dialogues—a yearning of the soul for the realm of the divine. And it has come to us to mean a sort of romantic love,

---

9. Augustine *Confessions* 8.7.

10. Romans 7:19.

11. Thomas Carlyle, *The French Revolution* (1800).

12. Cf. Reinhold Niebuhr, *Beyond Tragedy,* pp. 137–138: "The problem of maturity is not only to achieve unity amidst complexity of impulses but to overcome the particular conflict between the IS and the OUGHT of life, between the ideal possibilities to which freedom encourages man and the drive of egoism, which reason sharpens rather than assuages."

13. Genesis 1:27.

and so in that sense we all know about *eros*. We've experienced it, and we've read about it in all of the beauties of literature. In a sense Edgar Allan Poe was talking about *eros* when he talked about his beautiful Annabel Lee with a love surrounded by the halo of eternity.[14] In a sense, Shakespeare was talking about *eros* when he said, "Love is not love which alters when its alteration finds, or bends with the remover to remove. It is an ever-fix'ed mark that looks on tempest and is never shaken. It is a star to every wandering bark."[15] This is beautiful. This is *eros*, a vital type of love.

Then the Greek language talks about *philio*, which is another level of love that is a sort of intimate affection between personal friends. It is friendship. And so on this level you love because you are loved. It's a reciprocal love. You love the people that you like.

Then the Greek language has another word. It calls it *agape*. *Agape* is more than romantic love. *Agape* is more than friendship. *Agape* is understanding, redemptive goodwill for all men. *Agape* is an overflowing love, a spontaneous love, which seeks nothing in return. And theologians would say that it is the love of God operating in the human heart. When you rise to love on this level you love all men, not because you like them, not because their ways appeal to you, not because they are worthful to you, but you love all men because God loves them. And you rise to the noble heights of loving the person who does the evil deed while hating the deed that the person does.[16]

And I think this is what Jesus means when he says, "Love your enemies." And I'm so happy he didn't say, "Like your enemies," because it's kind of difficult to like some people. [*laughter*] Like is sentimental; like is an affectionate sort of thing. And you can't like anybody who's bombing your home and threatening your children. It's hard to like a senator who's spending all of his time in Washington standing against all of the legislation that will make for better relationships and that will make for brotherhood.[17] It's difficult to like them. But Jesus says, "Love them," and love is greater than like. Love is understanding, redemptive, creative goodwill for all men. And so Jesus was expressing something very creative when he said, "Love your enemies. Bless them that curse you. Pray for them that despitefully use you."

Now for the moments left, let us turn from the practical "how" to the theoretical "why," and ask the valid, the vital and valid question, Why should we love our enemies? Because this is an important question.

I would say the first reason, and I'm sure Jesus had this in mind, we should love our enemies is this: to return evil for evil only intensifies the existence of hate and evil in the universe. And somewhere along the way of life, somebody must have

---

14. Edgar Allan Poe, "Annabel Lee" (1849).

15. Shakespeare, "Sonnet 116" (1609).

16. Harry Emerson Fosdick, *On Being Fit to Live With*, pp. 6–7: "Love in the New Testament is not a sentimental and affectionate emotion as we so commonly interpret it. There are three words in Greek for love, three words that we have to translate by our one word, love. *Eros*—'erotic' comes from it—that is one. . . . *Philia*—that is another Greek word. It meant intimate personal affectionateness and friendship. . . . But the great Christian word for love is something else: *agape*. . . . *agape* means nothing sentimental or primarily emotional at all; it means understanding, redeeming, creative good will."

17. King probably refers to Senator James O. Eastland (D-Miss) as he does in "Levels of Love," 16 September 1962, p. 441 in this volume.

sense enough, somebody must have morality enough, somebody must have religion enough, to cut off the chain of hate and evil. And this can only be done by meeting hate with love. For you see in a real sense, if we return hate for hate, violence for violence, and all of that, it just ends up destroying everybody. And nobody wins in the long run. And it is the strong man who stands up in the midst of violence and refuses to return it. It is the strong man, not the weak man, who stands up in the midst of hate and returns love.

Some time ago, my brother and I were driving from Atlanta, Georgia, to Chattanooga, Tennessee. He was driving the car, and it was late at night, and for some reason most of the drivers were discourteous that night. They just didn't dim their lights as they approached our car. Everybody was forgetting to dim lights that night. And my brother got angry, and he said, "I know what I'm going to do. The next car that comes along this highway and fails to dim its lights, I'm going to refuse to dim mine, and I'm going to keep these lights on in all of their glaring outpour." And I looked up and I said, "Wait a minute. Don't you do that. For if you refuse to dim your lights, there will be a little too much light on this highway [*laughter*], and may end up in destruction for all of us. Somebody will have to have sense enough on this highway to dim their lights." [*laughter*] And maybe here we find an analogy to the whole struggle of life. Somebody must have sense enough to dim their lights. (*Right*) Hate begets hate. Force begets force. Violence begets violence. Toughness begets toughness. And it is all a descending spiral ending in destruction for everybody.

And so Jesus is right. (*Yes*) Love is the answer. The other point is this: that we should love our enemies because hate damages the personality and injures the soul. So often we talk about what hate does to the hated person or to the hated group, and we think of the damages that we find in the hate process as it moves toward the object of hate. So when we look in our nation and we look in the South in particular, we began to talk about how much it damages the Negro for the white man to hate him, and what this hate on the part of the white group is doing to destroy the Negro, and what it is doing to destroy the physical comfort, and the individual's freedom, and the collective freedom of the Negro. And that is true, it does destroy this. But so often we overlook the fact that hate is as damaging to the subject of hate as it is to the object of hate. Hate damages a white man, in many instances, more than it damages the Negro, for it does something to the personality; it does something to the soul. And this is why I say that our struggle in the United States today is not merely a struggle to free the Negro, but it is a struggle to free our white brothers from their fears, from their prejudices, from their hate, and all of those attitudes that destroy and damage the soul.

Some time ago, I was reading a book, or rather an essay by Dr. E. Franklin Frazier, the outstanding sociologist of Howard University, and it's called "The Pathology of Racial Prejudice." And he has a very interesting illustration in there. He shows that you find many persons who are filled with hate very normal in many of their relationships. But when they become, when they come to the point of interacting with Negroes, they interact in a very pathological manner. And he gave the illustration of a very aristocratic, wealthy white woman in Virginia who had this beautiful, palatial home, and a Negro went by one day to see her, to talk with her on some matters. And she happened to have been a mulatta, very fair, and the white lady didn't know that she was a Negro. She invited her in and had her to sit on this beautiful, expensive sofa. And they were seated in the living room and they talked and talked and had a genuine fellowship. And then the Negro woman left. A few days later, the white woman discovered that this was a Negro woman that had been in her house, that she had maybe an ounce of Negro blood, and that made her Negro. So she discovered this and after she discovered that she had entertained a Negro on that fine sofa, she went and burned it up. Now this is what hate will do. It leads to pathological ends.[18]

All the psychologists have been telling us this, haven't they? They tell us today that we must love or perish. And they tell us that there is something about hate that disrupts the personality, that makes for inner conflicts and guilt feelings and, thereby, develops neurotic personalities. But long ago Jesus realized this. Jesus realized that hate does something to the personality of the hater, and so the individual who hates can't see right. The individual who hates can't walk right. The individual who hates loses his sense of objectivity and his sense of values. And so for the individual who hates, the beautiful becomes ugly, and the ugly becomes beautiful. The true becomes false, and the false becomes true. The evil becomes good, and the good becomes evil. The person who hates loses the power of rationality and objectivity. And so again Jesus was right—love your enemies. (*Yeah*) Bless them that curse you. Pray for them that despitefully use you because hate can destroy the personality.

And finally, we must love our enemies because hate, or rather because love has within its very power transforming qualities. And we notice hate and think about it. Hate serves to destroy. Love serves to build up. Hate seeks destructive ends. Love seeks constructive ends. Hate seeks to annihilate. Love seeks to convert. Hate seeks to live in monologue. Love seeks to live in dialogue. And it is only through love that we are able to redeem and transform the enemy neighbor.

And so when Jesus says, "love the enemy," he's saying love the enemy because there is something about love that can transform, that can change, that can arouse the conscience of the enemy. And only by doing this are you able to transform the jangling discords of society into a beautiful symphony of brotherhood and understanding. We've seen examples of this—many cases in history and in biography. We look back at our own history, and we think of Abraham Lincoln, the great president of the United States, one of the great men of history. When H. G. Wells stopped one day to discover the six great men of history, after he had looked around the world, he had to choose Abraham Lincoln as one of the six great men of history.[19]

Abraham Lincoln was a great man. You remember when he was running for president of the United States, there was a man who hated Lincoln. He went around the country saying very nasty and evil things about Lincoln. And sometimes he got very low in his words; he would go so far as to say, "You don't want this tall, lanky, ignorant man as your president." Abraham Lincoln was aware of all of this. He was aware of all of the words that were being uttered by this man. The man's name was [*Edwin M.*] Stanton. Finally, Abraham Lincoln was elected president of the United

---

18. E. Franklin Frazier, "The Pathology of Race Prejudice," *Forum* 77 (1927): 856–862.

19. Mays, "Non-Violence," *Pittsburgh Courier*, 28 February 1948.

States. And then came that day when he had to select his cabinet. And do you know what Abraham Lincoln did when he started selecting his cabinet? He looked around the country and decided to choose a man by the name of Stanton as his secretary of war. Abraham Lincoln's advisors looked over to him and said, "Are you crazy? Are you foolish? Do you know what this man has been saying about you?" Abraham Lincoln said, "Yes, I've read his words, and I've heard about them. But after looking over the country, I find that he's the best man for the job." Few months later, Abraham Lincoln was assassinated. Many great words were uttered concerning Abraham Lincoln, but one of the finest tributes ever paid Abraham Lincoln, some of the greatest words ever uttered concerning the life of Abraham Lincoln, were uttered by this man by the name of Stanton. And he scratched across the pages of history that "now belongs to the ages." Suppose Abraham Lincoln had hated Stanton, suppose he had returned evil for evil [*recording interrupted*][20]

[*Recording resumes*] must learn to say to all those reactionaries who have brought, blocked the road to progress: We will match your capacity to inflict suffering by our capacity to endure suffering. We will meet your physical force with soul force. Do to us what you will, and we will still love you. We cannot in all good conscience obey your unjust laws because non-cooperation with evil is as much a moral obligation as is cooperation with good. And so put us in jail, and we will go in with humble smiles on our faces, still loving you. Bomb our homes and threaten our children, and we will still love you. Send your propaganda agents around the country and make it appear that we are not fit morally, culturally, and otherwise for integration. And we will still love you. Send your hooded perpetrators of violence into our communities at the midnight hours, and drag us out on some wayside road and beat us and leave us half dead, and we will still love you. (*That's right*) But be assured that we will wear you down (*Yes indeed*) by our capacity to suffer. (*Yes*) And one day we will win our freedom, but not only will we win freedom for ourselves, we will so appeal to your heart and conscience that we will win you in the process. (*Yes, Lord*) And our victory will be a double victory. This seems to me the only answer and the only way to make our nation a new nation and our world a new world. Love is the absolute power.

Years ago, Napoleon said something like this: "Alexander, Caesar, Charlemagne, and I have built great empires. But upon what did they depend? They depended upon force. But years ago Jesus built an empire that depended upon love. And even to this day, millions will die for him."[21] And that is the meaning of love. As we watch Jesus the Christ and see him as he starts out standing amid the intricate and fascinating military machinery of the Roman Empire, it seems that we can hear him say-

---

20. In his 17 November 1957 version of this sermon, King continued: "Abraham Lincoln would have not transformed and redeemed Stanton. Stanton would have gone to his grave hating Lincoln, and Lincoln would have gone to his grave hating Stanton. But through the power of love, Abraham Lincoln was able to redeem Stanton. [¶] That's it. There is a power in love that our world has not discovered yet. Jesus discovered it centuries ago. Mahatma Gandhi of India discovered it a few years ago, but most men and most women never discover it. For they believe in hitting for hitting; they believe in an eye for an eye, and a tooth for a tooth; they believe in hating for hating. But Jesus comes to us and says, 'This isn't the way'" ("Loving Your Enemies," Sermon Delivered at Dexter Avenue Baptist Church, in *Papers*: 4:322).

21. King kept a handwritten version of this illustration, drawn from Henry H. Halley, in his sermon file (King, "Conclusion," 1948–1954; Halley, *Pocket Bible Handbook* [Chicago: H. H. Halley, 1941], p. 321).

ing, "I will not use these methods. I will just take the ammunition of love and put on the breastplate of righteousness and the whole armor of God. And just start marching."[22] And this was what he did. And through this approach he was able to shake the hinges from the gates of the Roman Empire. And through his life, he was able to transform history and split history into A.D. and B.C. so that today we can hear the glad echo of heaven sing:

> Jesus shall reign where'er sun
> Does its successive journeys run;
> His Kingdom spread from shore to shore,
> Till moon shall wane and wax no more.[23]

And this is the meaning of the cross as we move toward Easter. It is not just a meaningless drama taking place on the stage of history, but it is a telescope through which we look out into the long vista of eternity and see the love of God breaking forth into time. It is an eternal reminder to a power-drunk generation, a generation growing in nuclear and atomic weapons, saying love is the only way. (*Yeah*) Love is the only answer. And so this morning, as I look into your eyes, as I lift my eyes beyond you and look into the eyes of the peoples of the world, I love you. I would rather die than hate you. (*Amen*) And I believe that my spirit can meet your spirit, and your spirit, through this process, will meet my spirit; and through this collision of spirits, the kingdom of God will finally emerge. (*Amen*) There is still a voice crying even this day, saying, "Love your enemies. (*Yes*) Bless them that curse you. (*Yes*) Do good to them that hate you. Pray for them that despitefully use you." (*Yes*) And only through this method can you matriculate into the university of eternal life.

Oh God, our gracious heavenly Father, we thank Thee for the inspiration of Jesus the Christ. And grant that we will love Thee with all of our hearts, souls, and minds, and love our neighbors as we love ourselves, even our enemy neighbors.[24] And we ask Thee, Oh God, in these days of emotional tension, when the problems of the world are gigantic in extent and chaotic in detail, to be with us in our going out and our coming in, in our rising up and in our lying down, in our moments of joy and in our moments of sorrow, until the day when there shall be no sunset and no dawning.[25] Amen.

At. MAWC.

---

22. Cf. Ephesians 6:11–17.
23. King quotes Isaac Watts's hymn "Jesus Shall Reign" (1719).
24. Cf. Mark 12:30–31.
25. Cf. Psalm 121:8 and Psalm 139:2–3.

King greets parishioner Carolyn Hunt at Riverside Church in New York, 14 August 1961.
Photo by Jim Mooney; courtesy of the *New York Daily News*.

Sermons on Secrets

King delivered a sermon series on secrets at Ebenezer in the winter of 1961 that may have included the following three handwritten documents.[1] The first two outlines may have formed the basis for a sermon on married happiness. Here, King bemoans the fact that "marriage has lost something of its spiritual creative meaning, and in many cases has become little more than a monotonous endurance contest between two people." In the third manuscript, King calls for contentment in the midst of life's tensions by pointing to the example of the apostle Paul who "[learned] to live from within instead of from without" and trusted in God to provide a "[changeless] structure of goodness in the universe, which transcends every circumstance."

---

1. Ebenezer Baptist Church, Press release, "'The Secret of Adjustment,' King Jr's Topic at Ebenezer," 1 December 1961.

[*19 November 1961*]
[*Atlanta, Ga.*]

Every well-thinking American is deeply concerned about the decadent state into which the American family is falling.[2] For ~~so many peo~~ some time now both religious and secular thinkers have sought to find the cause and cure of this disintegration that is gradually mortifying the American family.

Marriage has lost something of its spiritual creative meaning, and in many cases has become little more than a monotonous endurance contest between two people. So many marriages have set out for the city of utopia, only to end up in the city of Reno.[3] So many young people have entered marriage with great hopes and challenging dreams, only to find their hopes blasted and [*their?*] dreams shattered.

We do not have to look far to see the tragic consequences of this breakdown in the modern family. It means that hundred and thousands of young people are forced to be brought up in broken homes. The possible psychological difficulties arising from such broken homes are almost inculculable.

This breakdown in the modern family also means the possible loss of our national security. Family life is still the basic unit ~~of~~ in the life of the nation, and on healthy family life depends the moral and spiritual life of the nation.

1. Happy marriage requires that both husbad and wife shall have some real understanding of the nature of marriage.
    a. Many young people go into marriage expecting too much
    b. Happy marriage is not something that you find
    c. Marriage is a state of adjustment
2. Married happiness requires that husband and wife shall have some understanding of the nature of man and the natue of a woman.

AD. CSKC: Sermon file, folder 76, "The Crisis in the Modern Family."

---

1. Ebenezer Baptist Church, Press release, "'The Secret of Adjustment,' King Jr's Topic at Ebenezer," 1 December 1961.

2. King's announced Sunday morning sermon topic was "Secrets of Married Happiness," which was "to carry a special message to all people seeking a closer family circle and Christian fellowship with our fellowmen" (Ebenezer Baptist Church, Press release, "Martin Luther King Jr at Ebenezer Sunday," 18 November 1961).

3. From the 1920s through the 1950s, spouses seeking to end their marriages flocked to Reno, Nevada, due to the state's liberal divorce statutes.

"What Then Are Some of the Secrets of Happy Marriage"

[19 November 1961?]
[Atlanta, Ga.?]

I   A happy marriage requires that a husband and wife shall have some understanding of the nature of man and the nature of a woman.[4] Many a young couple after marriage find themselves completely at a loss to understand each other. They conclude that they have made a mistake. The real truth is that they have never learnd that a man and a woman differ decidedly in taste, opinion and temperament.

A man's wold is largely one of action. He is never happy unless he can measure his success or failure in terms of conquest in the exterior world. On the other hand, despite all her success in the exterior word, a woman is never happy outside an emotional world. She is most at home in the world of love and maternity.

Woman is subjective, realistic, concrete

Man is objective abstract and general

Every woman has her world of love, devotion and sympathy, and wise is the man who understands and appreciates it. Man has his world of action and creativity and wise is the wife who understands it. Instead of feeling jealous of it and the time it takes from her, she encourages her husband to achieve success in the exterior world.

II   Married happiness require that both husband and wife shall have some [*understanding?*] of the real nature of marriage itself. Often people go into marriage expecting to much and end up disappointed

    1.   People who say they never had a conflict

Dean Sperry of Harvard said once that he would "be prepared to reduce by fifty percent the divorces in the modern world if he could have young couples entering marriage know in advance that "differences were bound to spring up and that they are a sign of love's health rather than its mortal ill."[5]

III   Successful [*marriages?*] must be built on mutual compromise.

    1.   You can always have your way

    2.   Man must no longer consider himself [*boss?*]

    3.   There must be patience and forgiveness

No marriage can be succesful unless in it are two people who love each other even after they have forfeited any natural right to be loved; who forgive each other's obvious sins, awkwardness, and foolishness, who in spite of all which is hidden to other people see somethig worth while in each other and help to bring it out through mutual patience, kindness and understandig.

IV   Each individual must instill within himslf a new awarness of the sacredness.

Marriage fo so many has been relegated to a state of sexual experiment when people live together until the facination has worn off. Hollywod has

---

4. King wrote this outline on the verso of a 1961 letter and a 1961 conference schedule.

  5. William L. Sperry was dean of Harvard Divinity School from 1922 until 1953.

become the Holy City for many American, and thousands have bowed before its shrine, feeling that the more divorces the receive, the more they would receive the grace of [*glamour?*]. Love has been eliminated as a necessity for marriage, and in its place has appeard such thing as economic security, status and physical attraction. All of these thing have lead to a [*disregard?*] for the sacredness of [*marriage?*] Marriage is holy ground. It sanctifies the privilege of sharing in creative life. Through its portals men and women enter the realm of their immortality. Marriage is not an arrangement of convenience, to be entered into at will and dissolved at whim. It is a holy covenant between two souls pledged to revere one another, to face life's [*tasks?*] together, to face life's sorrow and struggle together, to build a [*home?*] and to shield, and love the offspring of their union.[6]

AD. CSKC: Sermon file, folder 76, "The Crisis in the Modern Family."

"The Secret of Adjustment"

[*2 December 1961*]
[*Atlanta, Ga.*]

"I have learned in whatever state I am to be content." Philippians 4:11.

I   Introduction: One may well characterize life as a pendulum swinging between opposites. joy and sorrow, hope and despair, poverty and wealth, sickness and health success and failure, popularity and obscurity.

   a. One moment we are in joy, and in a flash we experience sorrow.
      One day we are wealthy, and then we are poor.
      One day we are popular, another day we are hardly known

   b. This is the structure of life. Life is something of the strife of opposites Nobody ever absolutely escapes this [*tension?*]

   c. Every individual is in a constant struggle seeking to deal constructively with this tension. Ultimately an ind. is judged by the way he handles this tension. The adjustment of the individual depends on his ability to handle this tension

   D. Methods used to deal with the tension

      (1) Most people attmpt to deal with the tension by attempting to freeze one side of the opposite The gear themselves for living with one side of the opposite.

         (a) So there are persons who are geared only to live ~~under categories~~ by those opposites that fall under the category of fulfillment.

---

6. Abba Hillel Silver, *Religion in a Changing World*, pp. 162–163: "Marriage, it maintains, is holy ground. . . . It sanctifies the privilege of sharing in creative life. Through its portals men and women enter the realm of their immortality. . . . Marriage is not an arrangement of convenience, physical or financial, to be entered into at will and dissolved at whim. . . . It is a holy covenant between two souls pledged to revere one another, to face life's tasks together, sorrow, struggle and disillusionment, to be each others complement, to build a home and to shield and love the offspring of their union."

The Secret Of Adjustment

"I have learned in whatever state I am to be content." Philippians 4:11.

I Introduction: One may well characterize life as a pendulum swinging between opposites. joy and sorrow, hope and despair, poverty and wealth, sickness and health success and failure, popularity and obscurity.

a. One moment we are in joy, and in a flash we experience sorrow.

One day we are wealthy, and then we are poor.

One day we are popular, another day we are hardly known

b. This is the structure of life. Life is something of the strife of opposites Nobody ever absolutely escapes this tension

c. Every individual is in a constant struggle

Consequently when the darker moments of life come, they are knocked off of balance.

 (b) There are other persons who are geared only to live by those opposites that fall under the category of darkness. Consequently, when the sunshine of life comes they aren't prepared for it.

 (c) Neither of [*these methods?*] brings proper [*adjustment?*]

II The Apostle Paul confronted this problem Certainly no man has confronted the omnipresence of life's opposites any more than Paul. Probably he confronted the opposites of disappointment much more than the opposites of fulfillment. Yet in his own life he discovered the secret which every man must discover if he is to live the adjusted life. In Phillipians 4:11 he rings out with words which ~~sound over~~ echo across the generations: "I have learned in whatsoever state I am, therewith to be content." This is the secret of adjustment

III What did Paul mean by this? What had he learned.

 A. First, Paul did not mean that he had learned to become complacent There is nothing in the life of Paul which could characterize him as a complacent man. Gibbon in his "Decline and Fall of the Roman Empire" say, Paul has done more to promote the idea of freedom and liberty than any man who set foot on western soil."[7] This does not sound like a complacent man. So Paul is not telling us that the way to become adjusted to the opposites of life is through stagnant complacency. If complacency were considered a sign of adjustment, I would advocate maladjustment as the ideal and supreme virtue of life, leaving adjustment as a deadning and tragic vice.

 b. Secondly, in declaring that he had learned to be content, Paul did not mean that he had merely become resigned to his fate. There are those who look upon man as the plaything of a callous nature sometimes friendly and sometimes inimical. They feel that the only way to solve the prolems of life is to give up in the struggle and become resigned to [*strikeout illegible*] fate. Such persons give up in the struggle of life.

 c. What then, I repeat, had Paul learned? He meant that he had leaned to stand up amid the opposites of life and not despair. He had had every sort of experience. He had ranged from the lowest valleys to the highest mountaintop. But he declares: "These circumstances have not controlled me; I have learned to control them." Paul had discovered the distinction between a tranquil soul and the outward accidents of circumstance. He had leaned to live from within instead of from without.

IV How did Paul learn to be contented.

 a. Paul found contentment because he believed that over against ~~the changing structure~~ changeableness of circumstances, There is a ~~perma~~ changless structure of goodness in the universe, which transcends every circumstance.

AD. CSKC: Sermon file, folder 115, "The Secret of Adjustment & The Meaning of Easter."

---

7. Edward Gibbon, *The History of the Decline and Fall of the Roman Empire* (1776–1788).

435

King preaches in front of the Ebenezer Baptist Church choir, 1960. Courtesy of Donald Uhrbrock/Timepix.

"Without a Preacher"

[*1962*]

King penned this outline, which explores the importance of a preacher's spiritual guidance, on the verso of a form for a 19 February 1962 speaking engagement.[1]

Introduction: Definition of Preacher and Preaching. See Keighton's [*book?*][2]

I Without a preacher we would be tempted to be satified with our evil ways.[3] But the preacher reminds us that in our individual and collective lives that where we are is never where we ought to be. Without a preacher we would be satified with the vally, but he reminds us that we are made for the stars

---

1. Shirley Bird to Charlotte Sander, 19 February 1962.

2. King may refer to Keighton's definition of preaching in his book *The Man Who Would Preach* ([New York: Abingdon Press, 1956], pp. 19–20). In his copy of the book, which he kept in his personal library, King underlined several passages including: "The sermon is what takes place in the lives of our hearers, and preaching is influencing human lives."

3. Cf. Romans 10:14.

II   Without a Preacher we would conclude that we could lift ourselves by our own botstraps.

III   Without a preachr we would conclude that man is the center of the universe. So many things have happened recently to give us the impression that man can do anything. (Give examples)

AD. CSKC.

"Levels of Love,"
Sermon Delivered at Ebenezer Baptist Church

16 September 1962
Atlanta, Ga.

In this sermon, prepared as part of a series on love, King urges his congregation to move beyond varieties of love that involve self-interest, such as romantic love and friendship. He cites a recent conversation with a white man in Albany who claimed the tension of the civil rights movement had caused him to not "love Negroes like I used to." King's unspoken retort is, "You never did love Negroes because your love was a conditional love. It was conditioned upon the Negro staying in his place, and the minute he stood up as a man and as somebody you didn't love him anymore." Instead he recommends a higher kind of love that extends even to segregationists and recommends that his congregation "rise to agape . . . an all-inclusive love. It is the love of God operating in the human heart." The following text is taken from an audio recording of the service.[1]

I hope that at this moment you will not utter a word unless that word is uttered to God. For the moment you will rise above the miasma and the hurly-burly of everyday life and center your vision on those eternal verities, those eternal values that should shape our destiny. Life is difficult. It is the road we travel, but in traveling this road we encounter rough places. At points it's a meandering road; it has its numerous curves; it has its hilly places; and we struggle to get over the hills. Sometimes it's painful; sometimes it's trying. But [*somehow?*] we have a faith, and we have a belief that even though the road of life is meandering and curvy and rough and difficult, we can make it if God guides us and leads us. We go on with that faith, and we can keep on keeping on. We can smile when others all around us are giving up in despair. Lead me. Guide me. Be with me as I journey the road of life.

May we open our hearts and spirits now as we listen to the words from the choir. [*choir sings*]

This morning I would like to continue the series of sermons that I'm preaching

---

1. A voice at the beginning of the tape states the day and date, gives King's name, and identifies the sermon as "Levels of Love." This was King's announced sermon topic for 16 September 1962 ("Martin Luther King, Jr., at Ebenezer Sunday," *Atlanta Daily World*, 15 September 1962).

on love. I'll preach a sermon this morning that I preached in this pulpit some two years ago, but one that I've had a chance to give some more thought to.[2] And one that I hope will clear up some of the things that we have been discussing in the two previous sermons. You remember we started the series preaching from the subject "Loving Your Enemies." The second sermon in the series was "Love in Action," based on the prayer of Jesus Christ on the cross: "Father, forgive them for they know not what they do."[3]

And I'd like to use as the subject this morning "Levels of Love," trying to bring out the meaning of the various types of love. Certainly, there is no word in the English language more familiar than the word "love." And yet in spite of our familiarity with the word, it is one of the most misunderstood words. In a sense it is an ambiguous term. And we often confuse when we begin to grapple with the meaning of love and when we attempt to define it. And I think a great deal of the confusion results from the fact that many people feel that love can be defined in one category, in one pattern, in one type. But in order to understand love and its meaning and its many sides, its qualities, we must understand that there are levels of love. And this is what I would like to set forth this morning as my thesis and try to give these various levels of love.

First, there is what I would refer to as utilitarian love. This is love at the lowest level. Here one loves another for his usefulness to him. The individual loves that person that he can use. A great deal of friendship is based on this, and this why it is meaningless pseudo-friendship, because it is based on this idea of using the object of love. [*Congregation:*] (*That's right*) There are some people who never get beyond the level of utilitarian love. They see other people as mere steps by which they can climb to their personal ends and ambitions, and the minute they discover that they can't use those persons they disassociate themselves, they lose (*All right*) this affection that they once had for them. (*That's right*)

Now we can easily see what is wrong with this love. Number one—it is based on true selfishness, for in reality the person who engages in utilitarian love is merely loving himself (*That's right*) through somebody else. The second thing wrong with it is that it ends up depersonalizing persons. The great philosopher Immanuel Kant said, in what he called his categorical imperative, that "every man should so live that he treats every other man as an end and never as a means."[4] Kant had something there because the minute you use a person as a means you depersonalize that person, and that person becomes merely an object. This is what we do for things. We use things, and whenever you use somebody you, in your own mind, thingify that person. A great Jewish philosopher by the name of Martin Buber wrote a book entitled *I and Thou,* and he says in that book that life at its best is always on the level of

---

2. This was also King's announced sermon topic for 14 August 1960 ("'Levels of Love' to Be Subject at Ebenezer," *Atlanta Daily World*, 13 August 1960).

3. "Dr. King Jr. to Preach on 'Love Your Enemies' at Ebenezer Sunday," *Atlanta Daily World*, 18 August 1962; "'Love in Action,' King Jr.'s Topic at Ebenezer Sunday," *Atlanta Daily World*, 1 September 1962; Luke 23:34.

4. "Accordingly the practical imperative will be as follows: So act as to treat humanity, whether in thine own person or in that of any other, in every case as an end withal, never as a means only" (Kant, *Fundamental Principles of the Metaphysic of Morals,* trans. Thomas K. Abbott [Indianapolis: Bobbs-Merrill, 1949], p. 46).

"I and Thou," and whenever it degenerates to the level of "I and It," it becomes dangerous and terrible.[5] Whenever we treat people not as thous, whenever we treat a man not as a him, a woman not as a her but as an it, we make them a thing, and this is the tragedy of this level of love. This is the tragedy of racial segregation. In the final analysis, segregation is wrong not merely because it makes for physical inconveniences, not merely because it leaves the individuals who are segregated with inferior facilities, but segregation is wrong, in the final analysis, because it substitutes an I-It relationship for the I-Thou relationship and relegates persons to the status of things. This is utilitarian love. And the other thing wrong with it is that it is always a conditional love, and love at its best is always unconditional.

I talked with a white man in Albany, Georgia, the other day, and when we got down in the conversation he said, "The thing that worries me so much about this movement here is that it's creating so much tension, and we'd had such peaceful and harmonious race relations." And then he went on to say, "I used to love the Negro, but I don't have the kind of love for them that I used to have. You know, I used to give money to Negro churches. And even the man who worked for me, I would give him something every year extra; I'd give him a suit. But I just don't feel that way now. I don't love Negroes like I used to." And I said to myself, "You never did love Negroes (*That's right*) because your love was a conditional love. It was conditioned upon the Negro staying in his place, and the minute he stood up as a man and as somebody, you didn't love him anymore because your love was a utilitarian love that grew up from the dark days of slavery and then almost a hundred years of segregation." This is what the system has done, you see. (*Yes*) It makes for the crudest level of love. Utilitarian love is the lowest level of love.

Now there is another type of love which is real love, and we're moving on up now into genuine, meaningful, profound love. It is explained through the Greek word *eros*. Plato used to use that word a great deal in his dialogues as a sort of yearning of the soul for the realm of the divine. But now we see it as romantic love, and there is something beautiful about romantic love. When it reaches its height there is nothing more beautiful in all the world. A romantic love rises above utilitarian love in the sense that it does have a degree of altruism, for a person who really loves with romantic love will die for the object of his love. A person who is really engaged in true romantic love will do anything to satisfy the object of that love, the great love. We've read it about in all of the beauties of literature, whether in ancient or medieval days. We could read about it in a Romeo and Juliet, Anthony and Cleopatra, Tristan and Isolde, beauty of romantic love. Edgar Allan Poe talks about it in his beautiful "Annabel Lee" with the love surrounded by the halo of eternity.[6] I've quoted for you before those great words of Shakespeare which explain the beauty of romantic love:

> Love is not love which alters when it alteration finds,
> Or bends with the remover to remove:
> It is an ever-fix'ed mark

---

5. Buber, *I and Thou* (1937).
6. Poe, "Annabel Lee" (1849).

That looks on tempests and is never shaken;
It is the star to every wandering bark.[7]

Oh, it's a beautiful love. There is something about romantic love that lifts it above the crude level of utilitarian love.

But I must warn you that romantic love is not the highest love. And we must never forget this. With all of its beauty this can't be the highest form of love because it is basically selfish. This is often difficult to think about, but it is true. You love your lover because there is something about that person that attracts you. If you are a man, it may be the way she looks. It may be the way she talks. It may be her glowing femininity. It may be her intellectual qualities. It may be other physical qualities— something about her that attracts you. If you are a woman it may be something about that man that attracts you, and even if you can't put it in words you end up saying, "I don't quite know what it is, but I just know that he moves me." [*laughter*] This is the, this is romantic love. It's a selfish love. And so with all of its beauty it can never be considered the highest quality of love.

Well, there is another type of love, certainly on the same level of romantic love, and that is mother's love. (*That's right*) Oh, when life presents it in its beauty, it gives us something that we never forget, for there is nothing more beautiful than the loving care, the tender concern, and the patience (*That's right*) of a real mother. (*That's right*) This is a great love, and life would be ugly without it. Mother's love brings sunshine into dark places. (*Yes*) And there is something about it that never quite gives up. (*Amen, That's right*) The child may wander to some strange and dark far country, but there's always that mother who's there waiting (*Yes Lord*) and even her mind journeys to the far country. (*Yes Lord*) No matter what the mistake is, no matter how low the child sinks, if it's a real mother, she still loves him. (*Praise Him, Lord*) How beautiful it is. (*Oh yes*) It has been written about, too, in beautiful glowing language. We've read about it. We've seen it in beautiful stories. It is a great love.

There is another level of love that I would like to mention this morning. But before mentioning that let me say that even mother's love can't be the highest. (*That's right*) We hate to hear that, I guess, but you see, a mother loves her child because it is her child. (*That's right*) And if she isn't careful, she can't quite love that other person's child like she loves her child. (*That's right*) Even mother's love has a degree of selfishness in it. (*Yes*)

Well, we move on up to another level of love that is explained in another Greek word, the word *philio,* which is the sort of intimate affection between personal friends. This is friendship. In a sense it moves a little higher, not because the love itself is deeper, not because the person who is participating in the love is any more genuine of concern, but because its scope is broader, because it is more inclusive. You see, romantic love, at its best, is always between two individuals of opposite sex, but when we rise to friendship a man can love a man, a woman can love a woman. Friendship becomes one of the most beautiful things in all the world. One can have five friends, ten friends, twenty friends, and jealousy does not creep in as the hori-

---

7. Shakespeare, "Sonnet 116" (1609).

zon broadens and as the group enlarges. (*That's right*) In romantic love, always, jealousy emerges when the one individual moves towards a love act with another individual and rightly so. Then in friendship, which is not based on sex, which is not based on physical attraction, one has risen to another level of love where they stand side by side and become united because of a common interest in something beyond themselves. In romantic love, the individuals in love sit face to face absorbed in each other. In friendship the individuals sit side by side absorbed in some great concern and some great cause and some great issue beyond themselves, something they like to do together. It may be hunting. It may be going and swimming together. It may be discussing great ideas together. It may be in a great movement of freedom together. Friendship is beautiful. (*Yes Lord*) There is a beauty about it that will always stand. There is nothing more beautiful in all the world than to see real friendship, and there isn't much of it either. (*That's right*) You labor a long time to find a real genuine friend (*Yes Lord, Preach it*), somebody who's so close to you that they know your heartbeat. I must hasten to say that as we discuss these levels of love we must remember that one can be involved in several levels simultaneously. A young lady who loves her husband is engaged in romantic love, but at the same time she will have some children later—she engages in mother's love, and if she's really a wonderful person she's a good friend of her husband. So that one can engage in romantic love and mother's love and friendship simultaneously. This is a beautiful level.

But even friendship can't be the highest level of love because there is something about friendship that is selfish. You love people that you like. And it's hard to be friendly with Mr. [*James O.*] Eastland.[8] It's hard to be friendly with Mr. Marvin Griffin if you believe in democracy.[9] Friendship is always based on an affection for somebody that you like, and it's difficult to like Mr. Griffin. It's difficult to like Mr. Eastland because we don't like what they are doing. But this would be a terrible world if God hadn't provided us with something where we could love Mr. Griffin even though it's impossible for us to really like him. And friendship limits the circle even though it enlarges the circle over romantic and mother's love. It limits it because it says that the friend is the person who has mutual concerns and the person that you like to be with, that you like to talk with (*That's right*), that you like to deal with.

Well, there is a love that goes a little higher than that. We refer to that as humanitarian love. It gets a little higher because it gets a little broad and more inclusive. The individual rises to the point that he loves humanity. And he rises to the point of saying that within in every man there is a divine spark. He rises to the point of saying that within every man there is something sacred and so all humanity must be loved. And so when one rises to love at this point he does get a little higher because he is seriously attempting to love everybody. But it still can't be the highest point because it has a danger point. It is impersonal; it says I love this abstract something called humanity, which is never quite concretized in an individual. Dostoyevsky, the great Russian novelist, said once in one of his novels, "I love humanity in general so

8. Eastland served in Congress from Mississippi in 1941 and from 1943 until 1978, using his power as chair of the Senate Judiciary Committee to block civil rights legislation.

9. Griffin served as governor of Georgia from 1955 to 1959.

much that I don't love anybody in particular."[10] [*laughter*] So many people get to this point. It's so easy to love an abstraction called humanity and not love individual human beings. And how many people have been caught in that. (*That's right*) Think of the millions of dollars raised by many of the white churches in the South and all over America sent to Africa for the missionary effort because of a humanitarian love. And yet if the Africans who got that money came into their churches to worship on Sunday morning they would kick them out. (*Yes they would*) They love humanity in general, but they don't love Africans in particular. [*laughter*] (*That's right*) There is always this danger in humanitarian love—that it will not quite get there. The greatness of God's love is that His love is big enough to love everybody and is small enough to love even me. (*That's right*) And so humanitarian love can't be the highest.

Let me rush on to that point which is explained by the Greek word *agape. Agape* is higher than all of the things I have talked about. Why is it higher? Because it is unmotivated; it is spontaneous; it is overflowing; it seeks nothing in return. It is not motivated by some quality in the object. Utilitarian love is motivated by a quality in the object, namely the object's usefulness to him. Romantic love is motivated by some quality in the object, maybe the beauty of the object or the quality that moves the individual. A mother's love is motivated by the fact that this is her child, something in the object before her. Move on up to friendship, it is motivated by that quality of friendliness and that quality of concern that is mutual. Go on up to humanity, humanitarian love, it is motivated by something within the object, namely a divine spark, namely something sacred about human personality. But when we rise to *agape,* to Christian love, it is higher than *all* of this. It becomes the love of God operating in the human heart. (*Amen, Yes Lord*) The greatness of it is that you love every man, not for your sake but for his sake. And you love every man because God loves him. (*Amen, That's right*) And so it becomes all inclusive. The person may be ugly, or the person may be beautiful. The person may be tall, or the person may be short. The person may be light, or the person may be dark. The person may be rich, or the person may be poor. The person may be up and in; the person may be down and out. The person may be white; the person may be black. The person may be Jew; the person may be Gentile. The person may be Catholic; the person may be Protestant. In other words, you come to the point of loving *every* man and becomes an all-inclusive love. It is the love of God operating in the human heart. And it comes to the point that you even love the enemy.[11] (*Amen*) Christian love does something that no other love can do. It says that you love every man. You hate the deed that he does if he's your enemy and he's evil, but you love the person who does the evil deed.

And so this is the distinction that I want you to see this morning. And on all other levels we have a need love, but when we come to *agape* we have a gift love. And so it is the love that includes everybody. And the only testing point for you to know whether you have real genuine love is that you love your enemy (*Yeah*), for if you fail

---

10. Cf. Fyodor Dostoyevsky, *The Brothers Karamazov* (New York: Modern Library, 1937), p. 56: "But it has always happened that the more I detest men individually the more ardent becomes my love for humanity."

11. Cf. Matthew 5:44.

King preaches at Ebenezer Baptist Church, 1960. Courtesy of
Donald Uhrbrock/Timepix.

to love your enemy there is no way for you to fit into the category of Christian love. You test it by your ability to love your enemy.[12]

And so this is what we have before us as Christians. This is what God has left for us. He's left us a love. As He loved us, so let us love the brother. And therefore, I'm convinced this morning that love is the greatest power in all the world. Over the centuries men have asked about the highest good; they've wanted to know. All of the great philosophers have raised the question, "What is the *summum bonum* of life? What is the highest good?" Epicureans and the Stoics sought to answer it. Plato and Aristotle sought to answer it. What is that good that is productive and that produces every other good? And I am convinced this morning that it is love. God is light. God is love. And he who hates does not know God. But he who loves, at that moment, rises to a knowledge of God.[13]

And so you may be able to speak well, you may rise to the eloquence of articulate speech, but if you have not love you are become as sounding brass or the tinkling cymbal. (*Yes Lord*) You may have the gift of prophecy so that you can understand all mysteries. You may break into the storehouse of nature and bring out many insights that men never knew were there. You may have all knowledge so that you build great universities. You may have endless degrees. But if you have not love it means nothing. Yes, you may give your gifts and your goods to feed the poor. You may rise high in philanthropy, but if you have not love, your gifts have been given in vain. Yes, you may give your body to be burned (*All right*), and you may die the death of a martyr. You may have your blood spilt, and it will become a symbol of honor for generations yet unborn. But if you have not love, you're blood was spilt in vain.[14] (*All right*) We must come to see that it is possible to be self-centered in our self-sacrifice and self-righteous in our self-denial. We may be generous in order to feed our ego. We may be pious in order to feed our pride. And so without love, spiritual pride becomes a reality in our life, and even martyrdom becomes egotism.

Love is the greatest force in all the world. And this is why Jesus was great. He realized it in his life, and he took this force and split history into A.D. and B.C. so that all history has to sing about him and talk about him because he made love the center of his life. And what does the cross mean? It means that God's love shines before us through that cross in all of its dimensions. And so "when I survey the wondrous cross on which the Prince of Glory died, I count my richest gains but loss and pour contempt on all my pride. Were the whole realm of nature mine that were a present far too small. Love so amazing, so divine, demands my life, my all, and my all."[15] This is our legacy. This is what we have. And may we go on with a love in our hearts that will change us and change the lives of those who surround us. And we will make this old world a new world. And God's kingdom will be a reality.

We open the doors of the church now. Someone here this morning needs to accept the Christ. Someone needs to make a decision for Him. If you have the faith, He has the power. Who this morning will come? Just as you are, will you come? Just

---

12. King draws upon Harry Emerson Fosdick's discussion of *agape* in *On Being Fit to Live With* (pp. 6–7).
13. Cf. 1 John 4:7–8.
14. Cf. 1 Corinthians 13:1–3.
15. King cites Isaac Watts's 1707 hymn "When I Survey the Wondrous Cross."

as you are, will you come? And make this church not only a place to come as a regular attending person but a spiritual home. Who this morning will make that decision as we sing this great hymn, "Just As I Am?"[16] Wherever you are, will you accept Christ? By Christian experience baptism [*words inaudible*]. Wherever you are, you come this morning. God's love stands before us. God's love is always ready. He's calling you now. Make the church the center of your life, for here, we come to the mercy seat. Here, you learn the great realities of life. [*Congregation sings*]

Now let us stand for the next stanza, and if you are there we still bid you come wherever you are. Who will come this morning? Just as I am, wherever you are, will you come? Is there one who will accept Christ this morning?

Now let us sing that last stanza, and as we prepare to sing, I make this last plea. There is someone here this morning without a church home. There is someone here this morning standing between two opinions. There is someone here this morning who lives in Atlanta, who was a Christian back home, but who is not united with a church in this city. We give you this opportunity, in the name of Christ, to come as we sing this last stanza. This is the hour for you to decide. [*Congregation sings*]

God bless you [*recording interrupted*]

At. MLKEC: ET-72.

---

16. King refers to Charlotte Elliot's hymn "Just As I Am" (1836).

"Can a Christian Be a Communist?"
Sermon Delivered at Ebenezer Baptist Church

30 September 1962
Atlanta, Ga.

While insisting that "no Christian can be a communist," King calls on his congregation to consider communism "a necessary corrective for a Christianity that has been all too passive and a democracy that has been all too inert." Frustrated by the church's unwillingness to take a stand against racial discrimination, he complains, "This morning if we stand at eleven o'clock to sing 'In Christ There Is No East or West,' we stand in the most segregated hour of America." King also admonishes individuals unwilling to commit to social justice: "If you haven't discovered something that you will die for, you aren't fit to live." The following text is taken from an audio recording of the service.[1]

---

1. A voice at the beginning of the tape states that the recording's date is 30 September 1962. See also "'Can a Christian Be a Communist?' King's Topic at Ebenezer Sunday," *Atlanta Daily World*, 29 September 1962. King included a version of this sermon titled "How Should a Christian View Communism?" in *Strength to Love* (pp. 93–100).

[*Gap in tape*] elicit your undivided attention as I attempt to discuss with you one of the vital issues of our day. It is a rather controversial subject, and yet I think it is the responsibility of the preacher to keep his congregation informed on the major issues of the day, to bring the kind of tenets of our gospel to bear on these various issues. Now, this will not be the traditional sermon with a text, and you may feel when it's over that it's more of an academic lecture than a moving sermon. But I think it is important for me to discuss the question of communism with you, and so I am using as a subject from which to preach, "Can a Christian Be a Communist?"

Now, there are at least three reasons why I feel obligated as a Christian minister to talk to you about communism. The first reason grows out of the fact that communism is having widespread influence in the contemporary world. Like a mighty tidal wave, it has moved through China, Russia, eastern Europe, and now has rolled within ninety miles of the borders of our nation.[2] More than a billion of the peoples of the world believe in communism. And many of these people have accepted it as a new religion, and they are willing to surrender their total being to this system. A force so potent cannot be ignored.

A second reason that I feel compelled to talk about communism this morning is that it is the only serious rival of Christianity.[3] The other historic and great religions of the world such as Judaism, Mohammedanism, Buddhism, and Hinduism may stand as alternatives to Christianity. But for the most formidable competitor that Christianity faces in the world today, we must look to communism. No one conversant with the hard facts of modern life can deny the truth that communism is Christianity's most serious rival.

The third reason that I feel compelled to talk about communism this morning is that it is unfair and certainly unscientific to condemn a system of thought without knowing what that system of thought says and without knowing why it is wrong and why it is evil. So, for these reasons, I choose to talk about this troubling issue.

Now, let us begin by answering the question which our sermon topic raises: Can a Christian be a communist? I answer that question with an emphatic "no." These two philosophies are diametrically opposed. The basic philosophy of Christianity is unalterably opposed to the basic philosophy of communism, and all of the dialectics of the logician cannot make them lie down together. They are contrary philosophies.

How, then, is communism irreconcilable with Christianity? In the first place, it leaves out God and Jesus Christ. Communism is avowedly secularistic and materialist.[4] The great philosopher of communism, Karl Marx, based his total philosophy on what he called dialectical materialism. There was a philosopher by the name of [*Georg Wilhelm Friedrich*] Hegel who had used what he called the dialectical system to analyze

---

2. King refers to the 1959 Cuban revolution and Cuban president Fidel Castro's embrace of communism. In October 1962 President Kennedy set up a military blockade to compel the Soviet Union to remove its ballistic missiles from Cuba.

3. Robert J. McCracken, *Questions People Ask*, p. 164: "No one in touch with the realities of the contemporary situation will deny that in the crisis confronting civilization Christianity's most formidable competitor and only serious rival is Communism."

4. McCracken, *Questions People Ask*, p. 168: "Because it is avowedly secularistic and materialistic."

concepts, and Karl Marx was willing to take Hegel's dialectic. And then he studied another man by the name of Feuerbach, a German philosopher.[5] This man was a materialist. And so he took the materialism of this man and added it to the dialectic that he got from Hegel, and this is why his system is called dialectical materialism.

Now, what is materialism? It says in substance that the whole of reality can be explained in terms of matter in motion. In other words, it says that the basic stuff of reality is the material stuff. Materialism says, in substance, that idealism is wrong when it talks about the ultimate reality of mind and spirit and all of that. Karl Marx was a materialist, and he believed that the whole of human history moved on, driven by economic forces. This was his idea. There was no place in that system for God, and so from that moment on, communism became an atheistic system. And to this very day it is atheistic. It denies the existence of God. And if one goes to Russia, even today, he will find many of the churches full on Sunday morning, but we know that in spite of that, the Russian government has had a campaign against religion, and against God and belief in God, ever since the revolution in 1917.

So that no Christian can be a communist because communism leaves out God. It regards religion psychologically as wishful thinking, regards religion intellectually as the product of fear and ignorance. And it regards religion historically as an instrument serving the ends of exploiters. This is what communism teaches about religion. And so, in a real sense, we disagree with this because we believe that history is moved not by economic forces but by spiritual forces. [*Congregation:*] (*Amen, Yeah*) We believe that there is a God (*Pray on*) in this universe (*Yes sir, Yes*), a God who loves his children, and a God who works through history for the salvation of man. (*Pray on*) Consequently, we can't accept communism at that point.

A second reason that we can't accept communism is that its methods are opposed to Christianity. (*Pray on*) Since for the communist there is no divine government or no absolute moral order, there are no fixed, immutable principles. So force, violence, murder, and lying are all justifiable means to bring about the millennial end. Lenin, the man who was something of the technician of communism, putting the philosophy of Karl Marx into practical action, said on one occasion, "We must be ready to employ trickery, deceit, and lawbreaking, withholding and concealing truth."[6] That the followers of Lenin have been willing to act upon these instructions is a matter of history. For communism the end justifies the means.

There again we can't go along with this. We believe that there are certain moral principles in this universe that are eternal and absolute. We believe that there are some things right and there are some things wrong. It's wrong to lie. It always has been wrong, and it always will be wrong. It's wrong to hate. (*Yes sir*) It always has been wrong, and it always will be wrong. It's wrong to throw away the precious lives that God has given us in riotous living. It was wrong in 1800 B.C., and it's wrong in 1962 A.D. It's wrong in Russia. It's wrong in China. It's wrong in India. It's wrong in New York. It's wrong in Atlanta. (*Yeah*) We believe that there are some things right, eternally and absolutely so, and there are some things wrong. Then we don't believe

---

5. Ludwig Feuerbach (1804–1872) was a critic of Hegel's idealism.

6. McCracken, *Questions People Ask,* pp. 168–169: "'We must be ready,' wrote Lenin, 'to employ trickery, deceit, lawbreaking, withholding and concealing truth.'"

that the end justifies the means if those means happen to be bad. For we know that the end represents the means in process and the ideal in the making. The end is preexistent in the means. And so destructive means cannot bring about constructive ends. Immoral methods cannot achieve moral goals. And so we disagree with the ethical relativism of communism.

In the third place, we have to disagree with communism because the end of communism is the state. I should qualify this by saying that the state in communist theory is a temporary reality, an interim reality, which is to be eliminated when the classless society emerges. (*Yeah, yeah*) Karl Marx talks of that day when there will be a classless society. The ruling class, or rather the workers, what he called the proletariat, will through the revolution take power from the ruling class, which were the producers or the capitalists. And finally they will come to power, and through their power, they will establish a classless society. He says that while you are on the way to this classless society the state is the end. Man becomes only a means to that end. And if any man's so-called rights or liberties stand in the way of that end, they are simply swept aside. And so in the communistic system, you do not have freedom of the press. You do not have freedom of speech. You do not have freedom of assembly. All of these things are under the scrutiny of the state, which is manipulated through the party. And whatever the Party says, that must be done. All of the freedoms that are dear to us are denied. Man has to be a servant, a dutiful and submissive servant of the state. The state is omnipotent and supreme, and so if one lived in Russia today, he couldn't just get up and make a speech against the Communist Party. (*Right*) If one lived in Russia today, he could not write a book saying certain things without the condemnation of the Party; he may be searched and even killed. (*Yeah*) You remember the great book that Pasternak wrote, and you remember the problems that he faced because there were within that book some things that they didn't like in Russia.[7] It had some criticisms of the system.

We know that the most creative moments in history are those moments when individuals are left free to think. The thing that makes man man is his freedom. This is why I could never agree with communism as a philosophical system because it deprives man of freedom. And if a man is not free, he is not fully man. If a man does not have the capacity to deliberate, to decide, and to respond, as Paul Tillich would say, he is not a man, for a man is man because he is free. And, therefore, communism is on the wrong road because it denies freedom.

And so for these three reasons, I am convinced that no Christian can be a communist. These two systems are opposed to each other. These two systems are contradictory. We must try to understand communism. We must love communists. But never can we accept communism and be true Christians.

Yet, we must realize that there is something in communism which challenges us all. It was the late Archbishop of Canterbury, William Temple, that referred to communism as a Christian heresy. I want you to follow me as I go through this other aspect of the message. By this he meant that communism had laid hold on certain truths which are essential parts of the Christian view of things but that it had bound

---

7. King refers to Boris Pasternak's novel *Dr. Zhivago* (New York: Pantheon, 1958).

up with them concepts and practices which no Christian can ever accept or profess.[8] In other words, although communism can never be accepted by a Christian, it emphasizes many essential truths that must forever challenge us as Christians. Indeed, it may be that communism is a necessary corrective for a Christianity that has been all too passive and a democracy that has been all too inert.

Communism should challenge us to be more concerned about social justice. However much is wrong with communism, we must admit that it arose as a protest against the hardships of the underprivileged. *The Communist Manifesto,* which was published in 1847 by Marx and Engels, emphasizes throughout how the middle class has exploited the lower class. Communism in society is a classless society. Along with this goes a strong attempt to eliminate racial prejudice. Communism seeks to transcend the superficialities of race and color (*Yeah*), and you are able to join the Communist Party whatever the color of your skin or the quality of your blood, the quality of blood in your veins. (*Yeah, Right on*)

No one can deny that we need to be concerned about social justice. (*Yeah*) Karl Marx arouses our conscience at this point. Karl Marx was born a Jew in a rabbinic family. Somewhere along the way as a child, he must have heard his parents reading the words of Amos: "Let justice roll down like waters and righteousness like a mighty stream."[9] Then, when he was six years old, his parents became Christians, and somewhere along the way he must have heard them reading over the New Testament: "Ye do it unto the least of these, ye do it unto me."[10] So with this passionate concern for social justice, Christians are bound to be in accord. Such concern is implicit in the Christian doctrine of the Fatherhood of God and the brotherhood of man.[11] Christians are always to begin with a bias in favor of a movement which protests against unfair treatment of the poor, but surely Christianity itself is such a protest. *The Communist Manifesto* might express a concern for the poor and the oppressed, but it expresses no greater concern than the manifesto of Jesus, which opens with the words, "The spirit of the Lord is upon me, because He hath anointed me to preach the gospel to the poor; He has sent me to heal the brokenhearted, to preach deliverance to the captive, recovering the sight of the blind; to set at liberty them that are bruised, to proclaim the acceptable year of the Lord."[12] And so a passionate concern for social justice must be a concern of the Christian religion.

---

8. Cf. McCracken, *Questions People Ask,* pp. 165–166: "William Temple, the late Archbishop of Canterbury, was a distinguished philosopher and a man of affairs. He was a great Christian as well as a great churchman. From all over Christendom men looked to him for light and leading. He once described Communism as a 'Christian heresy.' What did he mean by that? He meant that Communism had laid hold on certain truths which are an essential part of the Christian scheme of things and which every Christian should acknowledge and profess, but that it had bound up with them concepts and practices which no Christian can ever acknowledge or profess."

9. Amos 5:24.

10. Cf. Matthew 25:40.

11. McCracken, *Questions People Ask,* p. 166: "With a passionate concern for social justice Christians are bound to be in the completest accord. It is implicit in the Christian doctrines of the Fatherhood of God, the Brotherhood of man, the infinite worth of the human soul and explicit in passage after passage of the Bible."

12. Luke 4:18–19.

We must admit that we, as Christians, have often lagged behind at this point. Slavery could not have existed in the United States for almost 250 years if the church had really taken a stand against it. Segregation could not exist today in the United States if the church took a stand against it. (*Well*) Mr. Meredith would be in the University of Mississippi right now (*Say it*) if the church of Mississippi had taken a stand against segregation.[13] (*Preach brother*) The tragic fact is that, in spite of Mr. Barnett's defiance of the Supreme Court of the land and the moral law of the universe, we haven't heard a single word from the churches of Mississippi.[14] (*All right*) This morning if we stand at eleven o'clock to sing "In Christ There Is No East or West" (*Yeah*), we stand in the most segregated hour of America.[15] (*Yes it does*)

Oh, we have a high blood pressure of creeds and an anemia of deeds, and this is the tragedy facing us today. We must admit that the church has often lagged behind, that the church has too often been an institution serving to crystallize the patterns of the status quo. Oh, we've identified the name of Christ with so many evil things. I heard Mr. Barnett saying the other day that he had to do what he was doing because of the righteousness that had been handed down from God through Jesus Christ. I said to myself, "Isn't it tragic that we will take the name of Christ, identify it with so many evils of history. Oh, how we've lost Christ." You remember the words of Shakespeare's *Othello*. As he stood there before the villain Iago, cried out, "Who steals my purse steals trash; 'tis something, nothing; 'twas mine, 'tis his, has been the slave of thousands. But he who filches from me my good name robs me of that which might enrich him but makes me poor indeed."[16] (*Yes*) This is what we've done to Christ. (*Yes*) We robbed him of his good name. (*Yeah*) And we've identified that name with segregation. We've identified that name with exploitation and with oppression and with so many of the evils of history.

This is why Karl Marx one day looked out, and this is why others following him have looked out and decided to say, "Religion is the opiate of the people."[17] It has too often been the opiate of the people. Too often the churches talk about a future good over yonder and not concerned about the present evil over here. Oh, I tell you this morning, and I believe in immortality. (*Yes sir*) I believe in it firmly and absolutely. But I'm tired of people telling me about the hereafter and they don't tell me about the here. (*Yeah*) You can't say hereafter (*Yeah*) without saying here. It's all right to talk about silver slippers in a symbolic sense over in heaven, but give me some shoes to wear down here. (*Preach it brother*) It's all right to talk about long white robes over yonder, but give me some clothes to wear down here. It's all right to talk

---

13. Riots broke out at the University of Mississippi on 30 September 1962, the evening before James Meredith enrolled as its first black student.

14. King refers to Mississippi governor Ross Barnett's staunch opposition to Meredith's admission to the university.

15. King refers to John Oxenham's hymn "In Christ There Is No East or West" (1908). National Council of Churches official Helen Kenyon labeled eleven o'clock on Sunday morning as "the most segregated time" in the United States ("Worship Hour Found Time of Segregation," *New York Times*, 4 November 1952; see also Robert J. McCracken, "Discrimination—The Shame of Sunday Morning," p. 4).

16. Cf. Shakespeare, *Othello*, act 3, sc. 3.

17. Karl Marx, "Contribution to the Critique of Hegel's *Philosophy of Right*: Introduction" (1844).

about streets flowing with milk and honey over yonder, but I want to see men living in decent homes right here in this world. (*Amen*) It's all right to talk about all of these things in terms of a new Jerusalem, but I want to see a new Atlanta, a new New York, a new America, and a new world right here. (*Amen*)

This is what we've got to see—that the church has a social gospel that it must be true to. We must certainly work with individuals and seek to change the soul; that's very important. But we've got to deal with these social conditions that corrupt the soul, and any religion that professes to be concerned about the souls of men and not concerned about the city government that damns the soul (*Yeah*), the economic conditions that corrupt the soul, the slum conditions, the social evils that cripple the soul, is a dry, dead, do-nothing religion (*Amen*) in need of new blood. It is already spiritually dead, and the only thing I'm certain about it is the day that it will be dead.[18] (*All right*) We've got to see that we are challenged to have a greater social consciousness in this church. We must be concerned about the gulf between superfluous wealth and abject, deadening poverty. One does not have to be a communist to be concerned about this. I would say to you this morning that one-tenth of one percent of the population of this nation controls almost fifty percent of the wealth, and I don't mind saying that there's something wrong with that.

I don't mind saying this morning that too often in capitalism we've taken necessities from the many to give luxuries to the few. *I* will never be content, I will never rest until all of God's children can have the basic necessities of life. (*Amen, amen, amen*) Oh, they tell me, and I think it's true, that Atlanta has the finest homes for Negroes of any city in the United States. (*Yeah*) That's true. Never forget that all these fine homes you see represent less than five percent of the Negro population of Atlanta. I'm not concerned about five percent of the Negroes living all right. (*Well*) I want to see *all* of God's children (*Yeah*) with a decent home and three square meals a day and *able* to educate their children. (*Amen*) God wants this for everybody. (*Yes Jesus*) And I will never be content as long as somebody over here can make five hundred thousand dollars a year, and I've met black men and women down in Mississippi who make less than five hundred dollars a year. (*Amen, Brother, keep it going*) Something wrong with that. (*Yes Jesus*) And I see hungry boys and girls in this nation and other nations and think about the fact that we spend more than a million dollars a day storing surplus food. (*Yes*) And I say to myself, "I know where we can store that food free of charge—in the wrinkled stomachs of the millions of people in our nation and in this world who go to bed hungry at night." (*Hungry at night*) And God has left enough and to spare in this world for all of his children to have the basic necessities of life. (*Yes*)

There is another thing. Marx reveals the danger of the profit motive as the sole basis for an economic system. We must heed this challenge. I'm afraid that there are too many people in America concerned about making a living rather than making

---

18. Harry Emerson Fosdick, *The Hope of the World,* p. 25: "Any church that pretends to care for the souls of people but is not interested in the slums that damn them, the city government that corrupts them, the economic order that cripples them, and international relations that, leading to peace or war, determine the spiritual destiny of innumerable souls—that kind of church, I think, would hear again the Master's withering words: 'Scribes and Pharisees, hypocrites!'"

a life. (*Yes, Yes*) I'm afraid this morning there are too many medical doctors concerned about making a big salary and getting a big home and a fine car than there are about healing the sick bodies of men. (*Yes*) I'm afraid that there are too many school teachers in America more concerned about the check that comes at the first of the month than introducing their students to the great, inexhaustible treasuries of knowledge and loving them and watching them grow. I'm afraid that there are too many preachers in the pulpit (*Yes*) more concerned (*Yes*) about their anniversaries (*Yes*) than they are about saving the souls of man. (*Yeah*) I'm afraid, my friends (*Yes, Go on*), that we are prone to judge the success of our profession by the size of the wheel base (*Yes*) of our automobiles (*That's right*) rather than the size of our service to humanity. (*All right*) Something is telling us today (*That's true*) that there is something more than making a lot of money. (*Yeah*) We must make money to live, but we must always remember that money is just an ingredient in the objective which we seek in life. (*Yes*) And if we don't see that, we'll make money-making an end rather than a means. (*Amen*) Jesus said, "I know you need it. I know you need money. I know you have need of clothes. I know you need a car to ride in. I know you need a home to live in and to sleep in. I know that you have need of all these things. (*Yeah*) But seek ye first the kingdom of God. (*Yes*) Seek ye first righteousness (*Righteousness*), and *all* of these (*Yes*) things will be added unto you."[19] (*Add them Lord*) And this is what we must do. (*Yes*)

Let me rush on now toward my conclusion and say this. We are challenged to dedicate and devote our lives to the cause of Christ as the communists do to communism. We cannot accept their creed, but we must admire their dream (*Yeah*) and their readiness to sacrifice themselves to the very utmost and even to lay down their lives for a cause that they believe in, a cause that they believe is going to make the world a better place. One watches that zeal, and one has to say, "Why is it that Christians don't have this zeal? (*Amen*) Why is it that we don't have this zeal for Christ? Why is that we don't have this sense of purpose, this sense of dedication for his kingdom?" Oh, these problems that we face in America and the world wouldn't be here today if we were as dedicated to Christianity as we ought to be. And it may well be that communism is in this world today because Christians haven't been Christian enough and democracies haven't been democratic enough. (*Well*) It may well be that the success of communism is due to the failure of Christians to live up to the basic principles of Christianity. (*Yeah*) [*Words inaudible*] communists will take their system, and they will go out, and they will dedicate themselves to the path of winning others to communism. (*Well, Well*) They will go out in cell groups and work day and night trying to convert somebody to communism. We'll go day in and day out, year in and year out and never speak to anybody about Jesus Christ. (*Well*) We've got to bring some lost boy or girl, some lost man or woman, into the church and into the kingdom.

If I would ask each of you here this morning to raise your hand if you've spoken to somebody about Christ, and about the church, and about the kingdom, and tried to bring them in (*Yeah*), I would be ashamed to see (*Yeah*) the small number of

19. Cf. Matthew 6:32–33.

hands that would go up if you were really being true. Then they get together, communists, and study Marx and Lenin and Stalin and all of the thinkers of communism. They study at night and in the day. They know their creed. (*Yeah*) And yet we can't get Christians to read the Bible. (*Well, Yeah*) They won't come to Sunday School. (*Yeah*) They won't come to Baptist Training Union. (*Amen*) And *I* submit to you that every person sitting in church this morning is biblically and is religiously illiterate. (*Yeah*) If I'd ask somebody here this morning, where is the Book of Exodus? you'd say it's in the New Testament. If I'd ask you, where the Book of Revelation? you may say it's the first book in the Bible, in the Old Testament. Our children come up religiously illiterate. (*Yeah*) Adults go through life religiously and biblically illiterate. We don't study about it. We don't have this zeal. We don't have this concern. Oh, there is a voice saying to us this morning (*Yes it is, Yes it is*), "You shall be my witnesses." (*Yes*) That means that if we are to be witnesses for Christ we've got to talk about it. (*Yeah*) We've got to be willing to convert others. (*Yes it is*)

The word "witness" in the New Testament has three meanings. You start out in the Gospels, the Book of Acts. The word "witness" means just verbal affirmation, talking about the life and the death and the resurrection of Jesus Christ. We've got to talk about this [*gospel?*]. (*Yes, we do*) You know talking can help sometimes; don't let anybody fool you. Hitler used to say that even if you tell a lie, tell a big one, and if you tell it long and loud enough, you'll convince everybody that it is true, even yourself. And he took that method and convinced the German people that the Jews were the cause of all of their misfortunes (*Well*) and led that great nation with all of its great minds to the killing of six million Jews. (*Well*) Now, if a man could tell a *lie* and turn a nation upside-down toward an evil end, it seems that we could tell the truth about Jesus Christ and turn this world right side-up. (*Yeah*) Let's talk about it some.

Then, the word "witness" goes on, and it says that not only that, when you get to the Pauline epistles, it means living a triumphant life. It's not enough to talk about it; you've got to live about it. (*Yeah*) Too many people have religion on Sunday, but it doesn't apply to Monday. If they'll do it every Sunday, they'll be all right on Monday, just a little song they've acquired.[20] But if one is to be a witness for Jesus Christ, he must live this thing. (*Yes Lord*) He must not only preach a sermon (*Well*) with words, but he must preach it with his life (*Amen*) so that his very walking down the street is the embodiment of the principles of Jesus Christ. (*Yeah*)

And then finally open the Book of Revelation. The word "witness" means being willing to die for the cause of Jesus Christ. (*Yes Lord*) This morning, my friends, we must believe that there is something so dear, something so precious, something so eternal, that we'll die for it. (*That's right*) And if you haven't discovered something that you will die for, you aren't fit to live. (*That's right*) You may be thirty, as I've said so often, at that moment some great principle stands before you, some great truth, some great decision, and you fail to take a stand because you are afraid that (*Well,*

---

20. Fosdick, *A Great Time to Be Alive,* p. 89: "Gratefully appreciating the genuine faith and character in our churches, yet when one surveys the scene as a whole, one understands the lines of a modern poet about our worshiping congregations: 'They do it every Sunday, / They'll be all right on Monday; / It's just a little habit they've acquired.'"

Well) something will happen to you or that you will be killed and you want to live a few more years. (*Yeah*) Well, you might go on and live until eighty, but I submit to you that you were just as dead at thirty as you are at eighty and the cessation of breathing in your life is merely the belated announcement of an earlier death of the spirit. (*Yeah*)

You died when you failed to stand up for something. (*Yes sir*) You died when you failed to give yourself to some great principle. (*Yes, yes*) You *died* when you refused to stand up against segregation. (*Tell it preacher*) You died (*Preach*) when you refused to stand up against some great evil of society. (*Evil*) Somebody's calling us this morning (*Yes*), saying "Go preach my gospel. (*Yes*) You shall be witnesses unto me in Samaria (*Yes*), Judea, and unto every part of the earth, carry this gospel (*Pray on*) into the villages, to the hedges and the highways (*Yes*), and tell men about Jesus."[21]

And if we will do this, we will make this old world a new world. (*New world, Yes*) We won't have to worry (*Right on*) about communism. (*Nope*) We won't have to be stocking up on nuclear weapons, for that can't defeat communism. (*Yes*) It can never be defeated with ammunition. It can never be defeated with missiles. (*Amen*) The only way that we can defeat communism is to get a better idea, and we have it in our democracy. (*Yeah*) We have it in our Christianity. And if we will live by it (*Yeah*), we won't have to worry about communism. And men the world over will join hands as brothers, and they will walk this earth knowing that we are all God's children. (*Yeah*) Once again, we will be able to sing, not only in Ebenezer on Sunday morning. (*Well*) We will hear the very angels in heaven stop silent and the eternity stand still. (*Yes, Yes*) And we will hear Peter cry out (*Yes*), "The kingdom of this world has become the kingdom of our Lord and Christ. And He shall reign forever and ever. Hallelujah (*Yeah*), hallelujah!" (*Oh, Yes*)[22]

This is our faith, and this is our hope. We open the doors of the church now. Someone here this morning needs Christ. Someone here needs to follow Him. Who this morning will accept Him? We have a challenge; we have a faith. We don't need communism. We have it within our religion and within our faith, if we would only live it, if we would only be true to Jesus Christ. This is it. Who this morning will accept Him, as we come to the invitational hymn, hymn number 229, "Jesus Is Calling."[23] You here this morning, wherever you are, Jesus is calling. [*Music*] Are you here this morning? We bid you come. Who this morning will come make a decision to Christ? Come and unite with this church. Who will this morning? [*words inaudible*] [*Congregation sings*]

At. MLKEC: S-10.

---

21. Cf. Luke 14:23.

22. King quotes excerpts from the "Hallelujah Chorus" from Handel's oratorio *Messiah;* see also Revelation 11:15.

23. King refers to Fanny Crosby's hymn "Jesus Is Tenderly Calling You Home" (1883).

V: STRENGTH TO LOVE, DRAFTS

Editorial Note

King submitted the following ten documents as part of the seventeen chapters included in his book of collected sermons, *Strength to Love*.[1] He originally discussed producing this book with Harper Brothers publishing house in 1957 but, due to his commitments to the Montgomery Improvement Association, Southern Christian Leadership Conference, and to his pastoral responsibilities, was unable to complete work on the sermon drafts until early in 1963. King's sermon file and the collection of his papers at Boston University's Howard Gottlieb Archival Research Center contain numerous drafts of each sermon he prepared for submission to the press. King first wrote out each sermon in longhand and his secretary, Dora McDonald, typed these drafts, which King amended by hand and then sent to Melvin Arnold, his editor at Harper. Those drafts were returned with comments; King further amended the edited drafts and resubmitted his revised versions for the book. The documents reproduced here represent the first typed draft that King sent his publisher and hence demonstrate close to the original language found in these sermons.

Arnold and Charles Wallis, another Harper's editor, made substantial changes to these drafts in the course of editing the manuscript. Most of their revisions were at the level of copyediting. However, these editors also modified King's words out of a concern that his prose was too hard-hitting or, in some cases, politically too radical. Arnold expressed similar worries about King's reputation when he edited *Stride Toward Freedom*, King's 1958 memoir of the Montgomery bus boycott. "I learned what the enemies of freedom and liberalism can do. Therefore, I made—and am now making—every attempt to see that not even a single sentence can be lifted out of context and quoted against the book and the author."[2] In particular, Arnold and Wallis muted King's criticisms of colonialism and capitalism, and his statements opposing war and the arms race.[3] Their treatment of King's sermons significantly altered the tone and, in some cases, the intent. The editors' major textual deletions have been restored in the ten documents presented here and are printed in a different font. Other significant editorial changes appear in document footnotes.[4]

King ultimately agreed to these changes. He strove to have his spiritual message accessible to a wider audience, one that was already familiar with his political oratory, and to reinforce his identity as a religious figure as well as a social activist.

---

1. We are publishing the first typed draft versions of ten of the seventeen chapters that appeared in the first edition of *Strength to Love*. Six of the remaining homilies are represented in this volume by transcriptions of audio-recorded sermons that King delivered as a mature preacher. "My Pilgrimage to Nonviolence," the final sermon published in the book, appears in earlier volumes (*Papers* 4:473–481, and 5:419–425). For the published versions of all seventeen sermons, see King, *Strength to Love* (New York: Harper & Row, 1963).

2. Arnold to King, 5 May 1958, in *Papers* 4:404.

3. For examples of these statements, see King, Draft of Chapter VIII, "Death of Evil Upon the Seashore," and Draft of Chapter IV, "Love in Action," July 1962–March 1963, pp. 508–509 and 490–491 in this volume, respectively.

4. See p. 468 for a sample of the copyediting alterations made in the first typed draft manuscript. Text enclosed in square brackets represents deleted or rewritten material. Insertions and other text changes are penciled in above and below the typed text line.

Table of Contents for *Strength to Love*

---

5. The asterisk indicates that the first typed draft of the chapter is not included in this section.

King, Christine King Farris *(left)*, and Alberta Williams King *(right)* at a book signing for
Strength to Love, June 1963. Courtesy of Clayborne Carson collection.

Draft of Chapter I,
"A Tough Mind and a Tender Heart"

[*July 1962–March 1963*]
[*Atlanta, Ga.*]

*King urges his readers to balance reason and compassion in this sermon, a version of
which he delivered on 30 August 1959.*[1] *Elaborating on a biblical text and concepts
used by Gerald Hamilton Kennedy, King characterizes soft-mindedness or gullibility
as "one of the basic causes of race prejudice" and calls for nonviolent resistance as a
means of "opposing the unjust system while loving the perpetrators of the system."*[2] *He
concludes by rejoicing that "we worship a God who is both tough minded and tender
hearted" in that "he combines in his nature a creative synthesis of love and justice which
can lead us through life's dark valleys into sun-lit pathways of hope and fulfillment."*

---

1. "A Tough Mind and a Tender Heart," pp. 372–378 in this volume.
2. Kennedy, *The Lion and the Lamb*, pp. 161–171.

Text: Matthew 10:16[3]

A French philosopher once said that "No man is so strong unless he bears within his character antitheses strongly marked."[4] The strong man is the man who can hold in a {living blend} strongly marked opposites. Very seldom do men achieve this blance of ~~opposition~~ opposites. The idealists are not usually realistic, and the realists are not usually idealistic. The militant are not usually passive, and the passive are not usually militant. The humble are very seldom self-assertive and the self-assertive are rarely humble. But life at its best is a creative synthesis. It is the bringing together of opposites into fruitful harmony. As the philosopher [*Georg Wilhelm Friedrich*] Hegel said, "truth is found neither in the thesis nor the antithesis, but in an emergent synthesis which reconciles the two."[5]

Jesus recognized the need for this blending of opposites. He knew that his disciples were going out to take his message into a difficult and hostile world. He realized that they would confront the recalcitrance of political officials, and the intransigence of the protectors of the old order. He knew that they would confront cold and arrogant men whose hearts had been hardened by the long winter of traditionalism. So He said to them: "Behold, I send you forth as sheep in the midst of wolves." Then he goes on to give them a formula for action: "be ye therefore wise as serpents, and harmless as doves." It is pretty difficult to imagine a single person having the characteristics of the serpent and the dove simultaneously; but this is what Jesus expects.[6] We must combine the toughness of the serpent with the softness of the dove. In other words, Jesus is saying that individual life at its best requires the possession of a tough mind and a tender heart.

Let us consider first the need for a tough mind. This is that quality of life characterized by incisive thinking, realistic appraisal, and decisive judgment. The tough mind is sharp and penetrating. It breaks through the crust of legends and myths, and sifts the true from the false. The tough minded individual is astute and discerning. He has about him a strong, austere quality that makes for firmness of purpose and solidness of commitment.[7]

No one can doubt that this toughness of mind is one of man's greatest needs. **So few people ever achieve it. All too many are content with the soft mind.** It is a rarity indeed to find men willing to engage in hard, solid thinking. There is an almost universal quest for easy answers, and half-baked solutions. Nothing pains some people more than the idea of having to think.

This prevalent tendency to lean toward soft mindedness is found in man's unbe-

---

3. "Be ye therefore wise as serpents, and harmless as doves."

4. E. Stanley Jones, *Mahatma Gandhi: An Interpretation*, p. 17: "A French philosopher once said that 'no man is strong unless he bears within his character antitheses strongly marked.'" King annotated a copy of Jones's book and kept it in his personal library.

5. King refers to Hegel's system of dialectical logic.

6. Kennedy, *The Lion and the Lamb*, p. 169: "It may be a little difficult to imagine the serpent and the dove as characteristic of the same person, but this is what Jesus expects of us."

7. Kennedy, *The Lion and the Lamb*, p. 162: "Realistic thinking always has a bleak, austere quality about it."

lievable gullibility. Take our attitude toward advertisements. We can be so easily lead to purchase a product because a television or radio advertisement pronounces it better than any other. Advertisers have long since learned that most people are soft minded, and they capitalize on this susceptibility with skillful and effective slogans.

This undue gullibility is also seen in the tendency of all too many readers to accept the printed word of the press as final truth. Very few people realize that even our authentic channels of information, the press, the platform and the pulpit, in many instances, do not give us objective and unbiased truth. **So President [*Kwame*] NKrumah of Ghana is considered a ruthless dictator because the American press has carefully dissimulated this idea. The great statesman and scholar, Prime Minister [*Jawaharlal*] Nehru of India, is ofren considered a non-committed ingrate because some segments of the American press have given the impression that his policy of non-alignment is at bottom a {vascilating} commitment to nothing. Many social revolutions in the world growing out of the legitimate aspirations of oppressed people for political independence, economic security and human dignity are considered Communist inspired because conservative element of the American press report them as such.** Very few people have the toughness of mind to judge critically, to discern the true from the false, the fact from the fiction. Our minds are constantly being invaded by legions of half-truths, prejudices, and false facts. One of the great needs of mankind is to be lifted above the morass of false propaganda.

The soft minded individuals are prone to be susceptible to all kinds of superstitutions. Their minds are constantly invaded by irrational fears. These phobias range from fear of Friday the thirteenth to fear of a black cat crossing one's path. A few months ago I was stopping in one of the large hotels of New York City. As the elevator made its upward climb the lighted sign within designated the number of each floor. I noticed for the first time that there was no thirteenth floor; the sign revealed that floor fourteen followed floor twelve. On ~~inquiry~~ {inquiring} from the elevator driver the reason for this omission he said: "This practice is followed by most large hotels because of the fear of numerous people to stay on a thirteenth floor." And then he went on to say, "the foolishness of the fear is the fact that the fourteenth floor is actually the thirteenth, and yet we could never designate it so, because no one would stay there." These are just some of the fears that leave the soft mind haggard by day and haunted by night.

The soft minded always fears change. They get a security in the status quo. They have an almost morbid fear of the new. For them, the most pain of all pain is the pain of a new idea. An elderly segregationist in the south was reported to have said a few days ago: "I have come to see now that desegregation is inevitable. But I pray God that it will not take place until I die." He feared living with the change. The soft minded person always wants to freeze the moment, and hold life in the gripping yoke of sameness.

Soft mindedness has often invaded the ranks of religion. This is why religion has all too often closed its eyes to new discoveries of truth. Through edicts and ~~bills~~ {bulls}, inquisitions and excommunications, the church has attempted to {prorogue} truth and place an impenetrable stone wall in the path of the truth-seeker. **So, many new truths, from the findings of Capernicus and Galileo [*Galilei*] to the Darwinian theory of evolution, have been rejected by the church with dogmatic**

passion.[8] The historical ~~philosophical~~ {philological} criticism of the Bible is looked upon by the soft minded as a blasphemous act, and reason is often looked upon as the exercise of a corrupt faculty which has no place in religion. The soft minds have re-written the Beatitudes to read: "Blessed are the pure in ignorance for they shall see God."[9]

All of this has lead to the widespread belief that there is a conflict between science and religion. But this isn't true. There may be a conflict between soft minded religionists and tough minded scientists, but not between science and religion. Their respective worlds are different and their methods are dissimilar. Science investigates. Religion interprets. Science gives man knowledge which is power. Religion gives man wisdom which is control. Science deals mainly with facts. Religion deals mainly with values. The two are not rivals. They are each other's complement. Science keeps religion from sinking into the mores of crippling {irrationalism} and paralyzing obscurantism. Religion prevents science from falling into the marsh of obsolete materialism and moral nihilism.

We do not have to look very far to see the dangers of soft mindedness. We have seen its ominous consequences in the modern world. Dictator after dictator has capitalized on soft mindedness, and lead men to acts of barbarity and terror that are unthinkable as existing {realities} in civilized society. It came to its most tragic expression in Adolph Hitler. He realized that soft mindedness was so prevelant among his followers that he said on one occasion: "I use emotion for the man and reserve reason for the few." In <u>Mein Kamph</u>, he asserted:[10]

Soft mindedness is also one of the basic causes of race prejudice. The tough minded always examines the facts before they reach conclusions; in short they post-judge. The tender minded will reach a conclusion before they have examined the first fact; in short they pre-judge, hence they are prejudiced. All race prejudice is based on fears, suspicions, and misunderstandings that are usually groundless. **So there are those who are soft minded enough to believe that the Negro is inferior by nature because of Noah's curse upon the children of Ham.**[11] There are those who are soft minded enough to believe in the superiority of the white race and the inferiority of the Negro race in spite of the tough minded research of anthropologists like Margaret ~~Mild~~ {Mead} and Ruth Benedict revealing the falsity of such a notion. There are those who are soft minded enough to argue that racial segregation should be maintained because Negroes lag behind in academic, health and moral standards. They are not tough minded enough to see that if there are lagging standards in the Negro they are themselves the result of segregation and discrimination. They are not discerning enough to see that it is both rationally unsound and socio-

---

8. The Polish astronomer Nicolas Copernicus (1473–1543) disputed the theory of a geocentric universe.

9. King parodies Matthew 5:8: "Blessed are the pure in heart: for they shall see God."

10. A summary of a section from *Mein Kampf* was added in the published version: "By means of shrewd lies, unremittingly repeated, it is possible to make people believe that heaven is hell—and hell, heaven. . . . The greater the lie, the more readily will it be believed" (King, *Strength to Love*, p. 4); cf. Adolf Hitler, *Mein Kampf* (Boston: Houghton Mifflin, 1943), pp. 176–186.

11. Genesis 9:24–25.

logically ~~untelable~~ {untenable} to use the tragic effects of segregation as an argument for its continuation. All too many politicians in the south recognize this disease of soft mindedness which engulfs their constituency, and with insidious zeal they make inflammatory statements and disseminate distortions and half-truths which result in arousing abnormal fears and morbid antipathies within the minds of uneducated and underprivileged whites, leaving them in such a state of confusion that they are led to acts of meanness and violence. that no normal person would commit. **Little Rock, Arkansas will always remain as a shameful reminder to the American people that this nation can sink to deep dungeons of moral degeneracy when an irresponsible, power-thirsty head of a state appeals to a constituency that is not tough minded enough to see through his malevolent designs.**[12]

There is little hope for us in our personal and collective lives until we become tough minded enough to break loose from the shackles of prejudice, half-truths, and downright ignorance. The ~~hope~~ {shape} of the world today does not permit us the luxury of soft mindedness. A nation or a civilization that continues to produce soft minded men is using an installment plan to purchase its own spiritual death.

But we must not stop with the cultivation of a tough mind. The gospel also demands a tender heart. Tough mindedness without tender heartedness is cold and detached. It leaves one's life like a perpetual winter devoid of the ~~warmt~~ warmth of spring and the gentle heat of summer. There is nothing more tragic than to see a person who has risen to the disciplined heights of tough mindedness and has at the same time sunk to the passionless depths of hard heartedness.

The hard hearted person never truly loves.[13] He only engages in a ~~cross~~ {crass} utilitarian love which sees other people mainly in relationship to ~~other~~ their usefulness to him. He never experiences the beauty of friendship because he is too cold to have affection for another and too self-centered to have joy in another's joy and sorrow in another's sorrow.[14] So he ends up as an isolated island with no outpouring of love to link him with the mainland of humanity.

The hard hearted person has not the capacity for genuine compassion. He is unconcerned about the pains and sufferings of his brothers. He passes by unfortunate men every day, but he never really sees them. **He confronts men hungry and feeds them not; he passes men naked and clothes them not; he finds men sick and visits them not.**[15] If he decides to give to a wothwhile charity, he gives his dollars and not his spirit. **He becomes cold, self-centered and heartless.**

The hard hearted individual never sees people as people. He sees them only as objects and impersonal cogs in some every turning wheel. If it is the vast wheel of industry, he sees men as hands rather than persons. If it is the massive wheel of big

---

12. King refers to the resistance by city and state officials to desegregating the schools in Little Rock, Arkansas.

13. In King's personal copy of *The Lion and the Lamb*, he underlined the phrase "For when the heart becomes hard, we are shut off from love . . . " He also wrote in the margin next to these words, "It shuts us off from love" (Kennedy, *The Lion and the Lamb*, p. 168).

14. In his copy of Kennedy's book, King wrote, "It shuts us off from true friends" next to a paragraph on hardheartedness (*The Lion and the Lamb*, p. 168).

15. Cf. Matthew 25:35–36.

city life, he sees men as digits in a multitude. If it is the deadly turning wheel of army life, he sees men as numbers in a regiment. He ends up depersonalizing individual life, and seeing men as little more than useful things.[16]

Jesus told many parables to illustrate the characteristics of the hard hearted. The rich fool was condemned not because he wasn't tough minded but because he wasn't tender hearted.[17] For him, life became an eternal mirror in which he saw only himself, and not a window through which he saw other selves. Dives went to hell not because he was wealthy, but because he was not tender hearted enough to see Lazarus. He went to hell because he quenched compassion and made no attempt to bridge the gulf between himself and his brother.[18]

So Jesus reminds us in a striking way that the good life demands combining the toughness of the serpent with the tenderness of the dove. To have serpent-like qualities {devoid} of dove-like qualities is to be passionless, mean and selfish. To have dove-like qualities without serpent-like qualities is to be sentimental, anemic and aimless. We must combine in our characters antithesis strongly marked.

This text has a great deal of bearing on our struggle for racial justice. We as Negroes must combine tough mindedness and tender heartedness if we are to move creatively toward the goal of freedom and justice. There are those soft minded individuals among us who feel that the only way to deal with oppression is to adjust to it. They follow the way of acquiescence and resign themselves to the fate of segregation. In almost every pilgrimage up freedom's road some of the oppressed prefer to remain oppressed.[19] Almost 2800 years ago Moses set out to lead the children of Israel from the slavery of Egypt to the freedom of the Promised Land. He soon discovered that slaves do not always welcome their deliverers. They would rather bear those ills they have, as Shakespeare pointed out, than flee to others that they know not of.[20] They prefer the "fleshpots of Egypt" to the ordeals of emancipation.[21] But this is not the way out. This soft minded acquiescence is the way of the coward. My friends, we cannot win the respect of the white people of the South or the peoples of the world if we are willing to sell the future of our children for our personal and immediate safety and comfort. Moreover, we must learn that the passive acceptance of an unjust system is to cooperate with that system, and thereby become a participant in its evil. **Noncooperation with evil is as much a moral obligation as is cooperation with good.**

There are those hard hearted individuals among us who feel that our only way out is to rise up against the opponent with physical violence and corroding hatred. They have allowed themselves to become bitter. But this also is not the way out. Violence often brings about momentary results. Nations have frequently won their independence in battle. But as I have said to you so many times before, in spite of temporary victories, violence never brings permanent peace. It creates many more

---

16. In the published version: "He depersonalizes life" (p. 5).
17. Luke 12:16–21.
18. Luke 16:19–31.
19. In the published version: "They prefer to remain oppressed" (p. 5).
20. Shakespeare, *Hamlet,* act 3, sc. 1.
21. Cf. Exodus 16:3.

social problems than it solves.[22] So I am convinced that if we succumb to the temptation of using violence in our struggle for freedom, unborn generations will be the recipients of a long and desolate night of bitterness, and our chief legacy to them will be an endless reign of meaningless chaos. There is still a voice echoing through the vista of time saying to every potential Peter, "Put up your sword."[23] History is cluttered with the wreckage of nations that failed to follow this command.

There is a third way open to us in our quest for freedom, namely, non-violent resistance. It is a way that combinds tough mindedness and tender heartedness. It aaoids the complacency and donothingness of the soft minded and the violence and bitterness of the hard hearted. **It is tough minded enough to resist evil. It is tender hearted enough to resist it with love and nonviolence.** It seems to me that this is the method that must guide our action in the present crisis in race relations. Through nonviolent resistance we will be able to rise to the noble heights of opposing the unjust system while loving the pertetrators of the system. We must work passionately and unrelentingly for full stature as citizens, but may it never be said, my friends, that we used inferior methods to gain it. We must never come to terms with falsehood, malice, hate or violence.

I cannot close this morining without applying the meaning of the text to the nature of God. The greatness of our God lies in the fact that he is both tough minded and tender hearted. He has qualities of austerity and qualities of gentleness. The Bible is always clear in stressing both attributes of God. It expresses his tough mindedness in his justice and wrath. It expresses his tender heartedness in his love and grace. So God has two outstretched arms—one that is trong enough to surround us with justice and one that is gentle enough to surround us with grace. On the one hand God is a God of justice who punishes Israel for her wayward deeds. On the other hand he is a forgiving father whose heart is filled with unutterable joy when a prodical son returns home.

I am thankful this morning that we worship a God who is both tough minded and tender hearted. If God were only tough minded he would be a cold passionless despot who sits in some far off heaven—"contemplating all"—as Tennyson puts ~~in~~ {it} in Palace of Art.[24] He would be like Aristotle's "unmoved mover" who was merely self knowing, but not ~~ever~~ {other} loving. If God were only tender hearted he would be so soft and sentimental that he would be unable to function when things go wrong and incapable of controlling what he has made. He would be like H. G. Wells' God in God The Invisible King who is a lovable Being strongly desirous of making a good world, but finds himself helpless before the surging powers of evil. No, God is neither hard hearted or soft minded. He is tough minded enough to transcend the world. He is tender hearted enough to be in it. He leaves us not alone in our agonies and struggles. He seeks us in dark places and suffers with us and for us in our tragic prodigality.

---

22. The preceding seven sentences were condensed in the published version: "And there are hardhearted and bitter individuals among us who would combat the opponent with physical violence and corroding hatred. Violence brings only temporary victories; violence, by creating many more social problems than it solves, never brings permanent peace" (p. 6).

23. Cf. John 18:11.

24. Alfred Lord Tennyson, "The Palace of Art" (1832).

There are times when we need to know that God is a God of justice. When **evil forces rise to the throne and** slumbering giants of injustice emerge in the earth, we need to know that there is a God of power who can cut them down like the grass, and leave them ~~withing~~ witherine like the green herb.[25] When our most tireless efforts fail to stop the surging sweep of **some monster of** oppression, we need to know that there is a God in this universe whose matchless strength is a fit contrast to the sordid weakness of man. But there are times when we need to know that God is a God of love and mercy. When we are staggered by the chilly winds of adversity and battered by the raging storms of disappointment; when through our folly and sin we stray into some destructive far country and are frustrated because of a strange feeling of home-sickness, we need to know that there is Someone who loves us, who really cares, who understands, and who will give us another chance. When day grows dark and nights grow dreary we can be thankful that our God **is not a one-sided, incomplete God, but he** combines in his nature a creative {synthesis} of love and justice which can lead us through life's dark valleys into sun-lit pathways of hope and fulfillment.

TADd. MLKP-MBU: Box 120.

---

25. Cf. Psalm 37:2.

Draft of Chapter II,
"Transformed Nonconformist"

[*July 1962–March 1963*]
[*Atlanta, Ga.*]

Originally titled "Mental and Spiritual Slavery," this sermon was composed during King's early years assisting his father at Ebenezer.[1] He later revised the sermon and gave it this title.[2] King maintains that the church's sanction of social evils such as race discrimination and economic exploitation demonstrates that it has "more often conformed to the authority of the world than to the authority of God." He chastises the church's tendency to retreat "behind the isolated security of stained glass windows" and rebukes ministers who have "joined the enticing cult of conformity." In contrast, King praises "the early Christians" as "nonconformists in the truest sense" but warns that "nonconformity is always costly" and "may mean losing a job. It may mean having to answer to your six-year old daughter when she asks, 'Daddy, why do you have to go to jail so much.'"

---

1. King's announced sermon topic at Ebenezer on 7 September 1952 was "Mental and Spiritual Slavery" ("Rev. King, Jr. Will Deliver Last Summer Sermon Sun.," *Atlanta Daily World*, 6 September 1952). He also delivered "Mental and Spiritual Slavery" at Dexter in May 1954 (pp. 167–170 in this volume).

2. "Transformed Nonconformist," November 1954, pp. 195–198 in this volume.

"And be not conformed to this world: but be ye transformed by the renewing of your mind." Romans 12:2.

"Do not conform" is adifficult advice for anyone living in the modern world. The pressure of the crowd is constantly pouring upon us with torrential force. Our minds and feet are unconsciously conditioned to move by the rhythmic beat of the drums of the <u>status-quo</u>. So many forces in our world are saying if you want to live a respectable life, just conform! Don't take a stand for unpopular causes; and don't allow the glaring search light of public opinion to catch you standing in an isolated minority of two or three. Choose the line of least resistance. Conform![3] Even some of our intellectual disciplines are attempting to convince us of the necessity of conforming. Some philosophical sociologists have gone so far as to tell us that morality is merely group consensus, and that the folkways are the right ways. Certain psychologists would go so far as to say that the best way maladjusted people can solve their problem is to learn to conform to this world. If they will only think and act like other people, they will achieve mental and emotional adjustment.[4] So success, recognition, conformity are the bywords of the modern world. Everybody seems to be seeking the anesthetizing security of being identified with the majority.

But in spite of this prevailing tendency to conform, we as Christians have a mandate to be nonconformists. The Apostle Paul, a man who knew the reality of the Christian faith, counseled us, "Be not conformed to this world, but be ye transformed by the renewing of your mind." We as Christians are commanded to live differently. We are called to be people of conviction and not conformity; people of moral nobility and not social respectability. We are called to a higher loyalty, to a more excellent way.

Indeed, every true Christian is a citizen of two worlds: the world of time and the world of eternity. We find outselves in the paradoxical situation of having to be in the world and yet not of the world. As Paul said in another letter: "We are a colony of heaven."[5] The Christians to whom Paul was writing understood that figure, for their city of Phillippi was a Roman colony. Whenever Rome wanted to Romanize a province, it took a small colony of people and planted them there to spread Roman law, Roman culture, and Roman customs. These people stood as a powerful, creative minority spreading the gospel of Roman culture.[6] Even though they lived in

---

3. The preceding four sentences were condensed in the published version: "Many voices and forces urge us to choose the path of least resistance, and bid us never to fight for an unpopular cause and never to be found in a pathetic minority of two or three" (King, *Strength to Love*, p. 8).

4. The preceding two sentences were altered in the published version: "Some psychologists say that mental and emotional adjustment is the reward of thinking and acting like other people" (p. 8). Will, "Men Who Live Differently," p. 5: "Some of our philosophical sociologists have gone even further and have told us that morality is only group consensus. In sociological lingo, this means that there is little difference between folkways and morals. In plain language, it means that you tell the difference between right and wrong by a sort of Gallop poll method of finding what the majority thinks. The answer of certain psychologists to all maladjusted people is, similarly, to learn to conform to this world. If we only will dress and act and think like other people, then we shall be happy and mentally healthy."

5. Cf. Philippians 3:20 (MOFFATT).

6. Fosdick, *The Hope of the World*, pp. 5–6: "Do you remember what Paul called them in his letter to the Philippians? 'We are a colony of heaven,' he said. The Philippean Christians would understand that

"TRANSFORMED NONCONFORMIST"

["And] be not conformed to this world: but be ye transformed by the renewing of your mind." Romans 12:2.

in a generation when crowd pressures have

"Do not conform" is [a]difficult advice [for anyone living in
the modern world. The pressure of the crowd is constantly pouring upon us with torrential force. Our minds and feet are] unconsciously conditioned to move [by] the rhythmic [beat of the drums]
our minds and feet *to* *drumbeat*
of the status-quo. [So] many forces [in our world are saying if you
voices and urge us to choose the path of least resistance, and bid us never to
want to live a respectable life, just conform! Don't take a stand
fight for an unpopular cause and never to be found in a pathetic
for unpopular causes; and don't allow the glaring search light of public
opinion to catch you standing in an isolated] minority of two or three.
[Choose the line of least resistance. Conform!]¶ Even [some] of our
certain
intellectual disciplines [are attempting to convince us of the [necessity
persuade *need to conform.*
of conforming.] Some philosophical sociologists [have gone so far as
to tell us] that morality is merely group consensus[,] and that the folk-
suggest
ways are the right ways. [Certain] psychologists [would go so far as to
Some *say that*
say that the best way maladjusted people can solve their problem is
to learn to conform to this world. If they will only think and act like
other people, they will achieve] mental and emotional adjustment. [So]
is the reward of thinking and acting like other people.
¶ success, recognition, [and] conformity are the bywords of the modern world[.] [where
Everybody seems to [be seeking] the anesthetizing security of being
one *crave*
identified with the majority.

[But] in spite of this prevailing tendency to conform, we as

another country their ultimate allegiance was to Rome. While this analogy has its weaknesses—if for no other reason than that it is placed in the framework of a system that has become a symbol of injustice and exploitation, viz., colonialism—it does point out the responsibility of the Christian in an unchristian world. We are sent out as pioneers to imbue an unchristian world with the ideals and way of living of a higher order and a more noble realm.[7] Even though we live in the colony of time we are ultimately responsible to the empire of eternity. In other words, as Christians we must never give our ultimate loyalty to any time-bound custom or idea of earth. There is a higher reality at the heart of our universe to which we must be conformed—God and his kingdom of love.

This command not to conform comes not merely from Paul, but also from our Lord and Master Jesus Christ. He was the world's most dedicated nonconformist. **It was nonconformity that led him to Pilate's judgment hall. It was nonconformity that caused him to be nailed on a cross between two thieves.** His ethical nonconformity still stands before the conscience of mankind as a nagging reminder of a higher order and a ~~more ennobling~~ {nobler} destiny.[8] When an affluent society would drive us to believe that happiness consisteth in the size of our automobiles, the impressiveness of our houses, and the expensiveness of our clothes, Jesus reminds us that "a man's life consisteth not in the abundance of the things which he possesseth."[9] When we would yield to the temptation of a world rife with sexual promiscurity and gone wild with a philosophy of self-expression, Jesus tells us that adultery is sinful and that "whosoever looketh on a woman to lust after her hath committed adultery in his heart."[10] When we refuse to suffer for righteousness, and choose to follow the path of comfort rather than conviction, we hear Jesus saying "Blessed are they which are persecuted for righteousness' sake: for their's is the kingdom of heaven."[11] When we in our moments of spiritual pride feel that we have reached the peak of moral excellence, Jesus says to us, "The tax collectors and the harlots go into the kingdom of God before you."[12] When we, through compassionless detachment and arrogant individualism fail to be concerned about the needs of the ~~masses~~ underprivileged, we hear the Master saying, "if ye do it unto the least of these, ye do it unto me."[13] When we allow the spark of revenge in our souls to rise to flame proportions and live our lives with a burning hatred for our enemies, Jesus says to us:

---

figure, for their city of Philippi was a Roman colony. When Rome wanted to Romanize a new province, it took Roman people and planted them as a colony in the midst of it. There, as a powerful minority, they stood for Roman law, Roman justice, Roman faith, and Roman custom, leaven in the lump of the province, until the whole province was leavened."

7. Fosdick, *The Hope of the World*, p. 6: "They were a minority thrown out, as pioneers, in the midst of an unchristian world to represent the ideals, faiths, and way of living of a nobler realm until the earth should be the Lord's and the fulness thereof."

8. The preceding five sentences were condensed in the published version: "This command not to conform comes, not only from Paul, but also from our Lord and Master, Jesus Christ, the world's most dedicated nonconformist, whose ethical nonconformity still challenges the conscience of mankind" (p. 9).

9. Cf. Luke 12:15.

10. Cf. Matthew 5:28.

11. Cf. Matthew 5:10.

12. Cf. Matthew 21:31.

13. Cf. Matthew 25:40.

"Love your enemies, bless them that curse you, and pray for them that persecute you."[14] **When we would seek to build our nations on military power and put our abiding trust in a policy of massive retaliation, Jesus reminds us that "he who lives by the sword will perish by the sword."[15]** Everywhere, and at all times, the love ethic of Jesus will stand as a radiant light to show up the ugliness of our stall conformity.

In spite of this imperitive demand to live differently, we are producing a generation of the mass mind. We have moved from the extreme of rugged individualism to the even greater extreme of rugged collectivism. Instead of making history we are made by history. The philosopher Nietzsche once said that every man is a hammer or an anvil.[16] That is to say every man either molds society or is molded by society. Who can doubt that most men today are anvils continually being molded by the patterns of the majority. **One great preacher has used the difference between the thermometer and the thermostat to point up the problem. The thermometer merely records the temperature. If it is seventy or eighty degrees, it registers that and that is all. On the other hand the thermostat transforms the temperature. If it is too cool in the house you simply push the thermostat up a little and it makes it warmer. In other words, the thermometer is an indicator simply registering what is; the termostat is a regulator which transforms the is into what ought to be.[17]** It is tragic, indeed, that most people, Christians in particular, are merely thermometers indicating and registering the temperature of the majority opinion, rather than thermostats serving to transform and regulate the temperature of society.

Millions of people fear nothing more terribly than to take a position which stands out sharply and clearly from the prevailing opinion. The great ambition of the average person is to take a position that is so ambiguous that it will include everything and so popular that it will include everybody.[18] Along with this has grown an inordinate worship of bigness. We live in an age of "jumboism" where men find security in that which is large and extensive—big cities, big buildings, big corporations.[19] This worship of size has caused many to fear being identified with a minority idea. There are those who have high and noble ideals, but they never reveal them for fear of being different from the majority. There are many sincere white people in the South who privately oppose segregation and discrimination, but they never take a public stand against it for fear of standing alone. There are millions of peo-

---

14. Cf. Matthew 5:44.

15. Cf. Matthew 26:52.

16. Frederick Nietzsche, *Thus Spake Zarathustra*, p. 123: "Ye know only the sparks of the spirit: but ye do not see the anvil which it is, and the cruelty of its hammer!" In the published version, King quotes Henry Wadsworth Longfellow, *Hyperion* (1892): "In this world a man must either be anvil or hammer" (King, *Strength to Love*, p. 10).

17. For this illustration, see Henry Hitt Crane, *These Prophetic Voices*, pp. 26–40.

18. Eugene Austin, "The Peril of Conformity," *The Pulpit* (October 1952), p. 13: "Millions of Americans fear nothing more terrible than to be identified with a position that standouts out, sharp and clear, as different, setting them apart from other men. . . . Increasingly the typical ambition of the 'middle-brow' is to belong to something that is big enough to swallow up individual differences, ambiguous enough to include anything, and popular enough so that everybody will want to belong."

19. Fosdick, *The Hope of the World*, p. 4: "Again, this truth of Jesus is deflected from many modern minds because of our worship of bigness. One of my friends calls it 'Jumboism.'"

ple in our country who are tired of the arms race and deeply disturbed by the fact that the "military industrial complex" often shapes the policy of our nation, but they will never take a public stand against it for fear of being in am minority stance.[20] There are countless millions of loyal Americans who honestly feel that "Red China" should be a member of the United Nations, but they dare not say it for fear of being called a Communist sympathizer. There are thousands, yea millions of people in this country who, in spite of believing in capitalism, have come to see that it must undergo a deep seated change and that there must be a better distribution of wealth, but they would never take a stand for this position for fear of being called a bad name.[21] In the realm of personal morals, there are numerous young people who have developed undesirable habits, not because they wanted to, not even because they enjoyed them, but because they were ashamed to say "no" when the rest of the group was saying "yes." Everywhere we turn we find only a dearth of people who have the audacity to express their convictions publicly. Most people allow themselves to be "astronomically intimidated."

We can see the disastrous possibilities of this blind conformity that has engulfed our nation. It leads to a suspiciousness of any individual who still insists on ~~talking~~ taking a stand for what he believes. Indeed, this is exactly what has happened. So great is our suspicion of these people that we wrecklessly curb their civil liberties. If a man believes vigorously in peace and is foolish enough to say it and carry a picket sign in its behalf, he is liable to be called before the Senate Committee on Internal Security.[22] If a southern white person sincerely believes in the American dream of the dignity and worth of human personality, and is daring enough to invite a Negro to his home and joins the Negro as an ally in his struggle for freedom, he is in danger of being called before the House Un-American Activities Committee.[23] He most certainly must be a Communist if he believes in brotherhood.[24]

---

20. In the published version: "Millions of citizens are deeply disturbed that the military-industrial complex too often shapes national policy, but they do not want to be considered unpatriotic" (p. 10). In his farewell presidential address on 17 January 1961, President Dwight D. Eisenhower trumpeted the importance of a perpetual state of war-readiness and of maintaining a vast "military-industrial complex" (Eisenhower, "Farewell Radio and Television Address to the American People," 17 January 1961, in *The Public Papers of the Presidents of the United States: Dwight D. Eisenhower, 1960–1961* [Washington, D.C.: U.S. Government Printing Office, 1961], p. 1038).

21. In the published version: "A legion of thoughtful persons recognizes that traditional capitalism must continually undergo change if our great national wealth is to be more equitably distributed, but they are afraid their criticisms will make them seem un-American" (pp. 10–11).

22. The Senate Committee on Internal Security was created by the McCarran Act of 1950, passed over a veto by President Harry Truman, and required communist organizations to register with the Attorney General. The committee targeted civil rights and anti-war groups among others that they labeled communist-front organizations.

23. Established in 1938, the House UnAmerican Activities Committee became a standing Congressional committee in 1946 and became known for its investigations into communist activity in the late 1940s and 1950s, particularly in the film industry and in labor unions.

24. The preceding paragraph was altered in the published version: "Blind conformity makes us so suspicious of an individual who insists on saying what he really believes that we recklessly threaten his civil liberties. If a man, who believes vigorously in peace, is foolish enough to carry a sign in a public demonstration, or if a Southern white person, believing in the American dream of the dignity and worth of human personality, dares to invite a Negro into his home and join with him in his struggle for freedom,

That great American, Thomas Jefferson, said on one occasion: "I have sworn upon the altar of God eternal hostility against every form of tyranny over the mind of man."[25] In these days of McCarthyism, John Birch Societies and White Citizens' Councils, these are rather dangerous words, and if Jefferson were alive today and lived these words out in real life situations, he would be investigated by numerous congressional committees.[26] We have allowed the light of independent thinking to grow dim, and the lamp of individualism to burn slowly out.[27] If we continue to go down this dangerous path of thought-control, business-control, and freedom-control, we will land inevitably in a dark abyss of facism.

Nowhere is the tragic tendency to conform more evident than in the church. The church has often been an institution serving to crystalize and conserve the patterns of the majority opinion. **We find it all too often blessing a status quo that needs to be blasted and reassuring a social order that needs to be reformed.** The mere fact that slavery, racial segregation, war and economic exploitation have been sanctioned by the church is fit testimony to the fact that the church has more often conformed to the authority of the world than to the authority of God. The church is called to be the moral guardian of the community, yet it is so often the preserver of that which is immoral and unethical. The church is called to take a stand against social evils, but it so often remains silent behind the isolated security of stained glass windows. The church is called to lead men to the highway of brotherhood and summon them to rise above the narrow confines of race and class, but it is so often found comforting men in their prejudices and giving their theories of racial exclusiveness biblical and religious sanction.[28]

Even we preachers have often joined the enticing cult of conformity. We, too, have often yielded to the success symbols of the world, feeling that the size of our ministry must be measured by the size of our automobiles.[29] So often we turn into showmen, **distorting the real meaning of the gospel,** in an attempt to appeal to the whims and caprices of the crowd. We preach soothing sermons that bypass the weightier matters of Christianity. We dare not say anything in our sermons that will question the respectable views of the comfortable numembers of our congregations. **If you want to get ahead in the ministry, conform! Stay within the secure walls**

---

he is liable to be summoned before some legislative investigation body. He most certainly is a Communist if he espouses the cause of human brotherhood!" (p. 11).

25. Jefferson to Doctor Rush, 23 September 1800, in *Memoir, Correspondence, and Miscellanies, From the Papers of Thomas Jefferson,* vol. 3, ed. Thomas Jefferson Randolph (Charlottesville, Va.: F. Carr, 1829), p. 56.

26. The John Birch Society is an ultraconservative organization founded in 1958 to fight the perceived threat of communism in the United States. Among its activities during the 1960s was the distribution of literature attacking proposed civil rights legislation.

27. The preceding two sentences were altered in the published version: "To the conformist and the shapers of the conformist mentality, this must surely sound like a most dangerous and radical doctrine. Have we permitted the lamp of independent thought and individualism to become so dim that were Jefferson to write and live by these words today we would find cause to harass and investigate him?" (p. 11).

28. In the published version: "Called to lead men on the highway of brotherhood and to summon them to rise above the narrow confines of race and class, it has enunciated and practiced racial exclusiveness" (p. 11).

29. In the published version "parsonage" replaced the word "automobiles" (p. 12).

of the Sanctuary. Play it safe. How many ministers of Jesus Christ have sacrificed truth on the altar of their self-interest, and, like Pilate, yielded their convictions to the demands of the crowd.[30]

We need to recapture something that the early Christians had. They went out aglow with a radical gospel. They were nonconformists in the truest sense of the word. They never allowed their actions to be shaped by the mundane patterns of this world. They were willing to sacrifice fame or fortune or life itself for a cause they knew was right. They were quantitatively small but qualitatively big. In those days Christianity was powerful. It stopped barbaric evils like infanticide and brought an end to the bloody gladiatorial shows. **Its views on war were clearly known because of the refusal of every Christian to take up arms.** At that time the church was still a numerical minority. But then it began to grow in numbers until it finally captured the Roman Empire. Gradually it became so entrenched in wealth and worldly prestige that it began to dilute the strong demands of the gospel and to conform to the status quo of the world. Ever since that time the church has been like a weak and ineffectual trumpet making uncertain sounds, rather than a strong trumpet sounding a clarion call for truth and righteousness. If the church of Jesus Christ is to regain its power, and its message its authentic ring, it must go out with a new determination not to conform to this world.

The hope of a secure and livable world lies in the disciplined and dedicated nonconformists, set not on the preservation of any status quo, but set on building, with God's help, an order of justice peace and brotherhood. **The world has always moved forward on the feet of its nonconformists. It was the nonconformists who stood forthrightly against slavery. It was a nonconformist like Socrates who, having drank the hemlock paved the way for academic freedom.[31] It was the nonconformists who fought for popular education and the freedom of scientific research. It was the nonconformists that fought for religious liberty.** In any cause that concerns the progress of mankind put your faith in the nonconformist.

In his essay on "Self Reliance," Emerson says that a man is not a man unless he can be a nonconformist.[32] The Apostle Paul reminds us that a Christian cannot be truly Christian unless he is a nonconformist. The Christians who blindly accept the opinions of the majority and who out of fear and timidity follow a path of expediency and social approval are really mental and spiritual slaves. In the words of James Russell Lowell:

> They are slaves who fear to speak, for
> the fallen and the weak;
> They are slaves who will not choose,
> hatred, scoffing, and abuse,
> Rather than in silence shrink,
> From the truth they needs must think;

---

30. Cf. Mark 15:15.

31. Socrates (469–399 BCE) was sentenced by an Athenian court to carry out his own execution by drinking hemlock.

32. Ralph Waldo Emerson, *Self Reliance* (1841): "Whoso would be a man must be a nonconformist."

They are slaves who dare not be,
In the right with two or three.[33]

Now let us make it clear that non-conformity in itself may not be good. There is a type of bad nonconformity which has neither transforming nor redemptive power. There is no saving value in being a non-conformist for its own sake. Often being a nonconformist represents just a form of exhibitionism by people who could not get attention in any other way. So Paul gives us the formular for constructive nonconformity in the second half of the text. "Be ye transformed by the renewing of your mind." In other words nonconformity can only be creative ~~when~~ when it is controlled and directed by a transformed life. In order to be a constructive nonconformist we must accept a new mental outlook. We must so open our lives to God in Christ that he makes us new creatures. Jesus' phrase for this experience was the new birth. So only when we have been born again can we be true nonconformists.[34] We are called upon not merely to be nonconformist, but to be transformed nonconformists.

If we go out merely to be nonconformists we are in danger of becoming cold, hardhearted, and self-righteous.[35] XSomeone has said "I love reforms but hate reformers." So often reformers are nonconformists who have not been transformed. Their revolt against the evils of society often causes them to become annoyingly rigid and unreasonably impatient. **They talk about unselfish righteousness in the most self-righteous way. They talk about God's love in the most hateful way.** It is only through an inner spiritual transformation that we find the strength to revolt vigorously against the evils of the world and yet remain humble and loving. The transformed nonconformists will never fall into the sort of patience which ~~will nev~~ is an excuse for doing nothing about social evils and individual sin. On the other hand his very transformation saves him from the irresponsible words which estrange without reconciling and the hasty judgment which is blind to the necessity of social process. The transformed nonconformist will recognize that social change cannot come overnight, but he will work as if it is a possibility the next morning.

The most pressing need of this hour is a dedicated circle of transformed nonconformists. Today our planet teeters on the brink of atomic annihilation. Dangerous passions of pride, hatred, and selfishness still sit contentedly on the throne of our lives, and wounded truth and love are still lying prostrate on the rugged hills of nameless ~~colonies~~ calvaries. Men are still genuflecting before the false gods of nationalism and materialism. If our world is to be saved from its pending doom it will come not through the complacent adjustment of the conforming majority but through the creative maladjustment of a nonconforming minority. **If the world is to be lifted from the morass of confusion and chaos it will be done by**

---

33. Lowell, "Stanzas on Freedom" (1892).

34. Cf. John 3:3–7.

35. The preceding four sentences were condensed in the published version: "This experience, which Jesus spoke of as the new birth, is essential if we are to be transformed nonconformists and freed from the cold hardheartedness and self-righteousness so often characteristic of nonconformity" (p. 13).

men who have succeeded in standing above the world so that God can lift it through them.

Professor [*Julius Seelye*] Bixler reminded us some years ago of the danger of overstressing the well-adjusted life.[36] Everybody is passionately seeking to be well adjusted; nobody wants to be maladjusted. There is probably no word in modern psychology that is used more than the word maladjusted. It is the word most frequently on the lips of the child psychologist. In a sense we must all seek to live the well adjusted life in order to avoid neurotic and schiozophrenic personalities. But there are some things in our world to which all men of good will must be maladjusted until the good society is realized.[37] **As for me I must confess that there are some things to which I'm proud to be maladjusted.** I never intend to become adjusted to the evils of segregation and the crippling effects of discrimination. I never intend to become adjusted to the moral degeneracy of religious bigotry and the corroding effects of narrow sectarianism. I never intend to adjust myself to economic conditions that **will take necessities from the many a to give luxuries to the few.**[38] I never intend to become adjusted to the insanities of militarism and the self-defeating effects of physical violence.

The world is in dire need of a society of the creative maladjusted. It may well be that the salvation of our world lies in the hands of such a creative minority. We need men today **as maladjusted as the prophet Amos, who in the midst of the injustices of his day could cry out in words that echo across the centuries: "Let justice roll down like waters and righteousness like a mighty stream;"** as maladjusted Shadrach, Meshach, and Abednego who, in the midst of an order from King Nebuchadnezzar to bow down and worship the golden image, said in unequivocal terms: "If it be so, our God whom we serve is able to deliver us, but if not we will not bow;" as maladjusted as Abraham Lincoln who had the vision to see that this nation could not survive half slave and half free; as maladjusted as Thomas Jefferson, who in the midst of an age amazingly adjusted to slavery could scratch across the pages of history these profound and eloquent words: "We hold these truths to be self-evident that all men are created equal; that they are endowed by their Creator with certain unalienable rights; that among these are life, liberty and the pursuit of happiness;" as maladjusted even as our Lord who, in the midst of the intricate and fascinating military machinery of the Roman Empire, **emerged from a wilderness temptation to establish a political kingdom by [*strikeout illegible*] firmly saying: "Get thee behind me Satan," and** reminded his followers that "he who lives by the sword shall perish by the sword."[39] Through such maladjustment we may be able to call an already decadent generation back to those things which make for peace.

---

36. Fosdick, *The Hope of the World,* p. 112: "Professor Seelye Bixler, of Harvard University, has lately made some shrewd comments on our new psychological talk about the well-adjusted life."

37. The preceding five sentences were condensed in the published version: "Everybody passionately seeks to be well-adjusted. We must, of course, be well-adjusted if we are to avoid neurotic and schizophrenic personalities, but there are some things in our world to which men of goodwill must be maladjusted" (p. 14).

38. The published version refers to "economic condition that deprive men of work and food" (p. 14).

39. Cf. Amos 5:24, Daniel 3:17–18, Luke 4:1–13, and Matthew 26:52.

Now there is a warning signal. Honesty impels me to admit that transformed nonconformity is always costly, and it is never altogether comfortable. It may mean walking through the valley of the shadow of suffering. It may mean losing a job. It may mean having to answer your six-year old daughter when she asks, "Daddy, why do you have to go to jail so much," Well, this is it! But after all this is what we as Christians are pledged to do. We are gravely mistaken if we feel that Christianity is a religion to protect us from the pain and agony of mortal existence. Christianity has always insisted that **there is a Good Friday before every Easter, and that** the cross we bear always precedes the crown we wear. It has said in unmistakable terms that to be a Christian one must take up his cross, with all of its difficulties, all of its agonizing and tragedy-packed content, and carry it until that very cross leaves its marks upon us and redeems us to that more excellent way which can be opened up only by suffering.

In these days of world-wide confusion, **when the forces of evil have risen to gigantic and ominous proportions,** there is a dire need for men and women who will gird their courage and do battle with all their hearts, souls and minds. We need Christians who will say as John Bunyan said to his jailor when, after he had spent twelve years in jail, he was promised freedom if he would agree to quit preaching: "I am determined, Almighty God being my help and shield, yet to suffer, if frail life shall continue so long, even till the moss grow over my eyebrows, rather than to violate my faith and make a continual butchery of my conscience."[40]

We must make a choice. Will we continue to march by the beat of the drums of conformity and respectibility, or will be listen to the beat of another drum in the distance and with a heroic daring of the w soul set our feet to move by its echoing sounds? Will we **be so bent on worldly success and social acceptqbility that we will** march only by the music of time, or will we risk criticism, abuse and being out of step with the majority in order to march by the soul-saving music of eternity? The challenge faces us today more than ever before: "Be not conformed to this world but be transformed by the renewing of your minds."

TADd. MLKP-MBU: Box 120.

---

40. William Hamilton Nelson, *Tinker and Thinker: John Bunyan 1628–1688* (New York: Willett, Clark & Colby, 1928), p. 169: "I wish that instead of trying to side-step and live softly we would say as he said when they offered him liberty at the price of his convictions: 'But if nothing will do, unless I make of my conscience a continual butchery and slaughter-shop, unless, putting out my own eyes, I commit me to the blind to lead me, as I doubt is desired by some, I have determined, the Almighty God being my help and shield, yet to suffer, if frail life might continue so long, even till the moss shall grow on mine eyebrows, rather than thus to violate my faith and principles.'"

The story begins in a theological controversy and ends in a description of first aid at a roadside. It arises in a question of eternal life and works out to a payment for room and board at a hotel.

The Goodness of the Good Samaritan

I. Introduction — One day a certain lawyer came to Jesus and said, "What shall I do to inherit eternal life."

(a) He is asking about a quality of this life.

(b) How does one attain this life

(c) Jesus replies; "you are a lawyer, you ought to know. What is written in the law"

D He thinks a moment, and then cries out; "Thou shalt love the Lord Thy God . . . ,

(E) And Jesus looks up and says; "Thou chast answered right. This do and thou shalt live.

(F) But the lawyer still wasn't content. He had to prove to the people that he wasn't to be minimized. And so he asks; "Who is my neighbor."

(G) Jesus immediately lifted this question out of midair and placed it on

In the top margin of this page of his outline for "The Goodness of the Good Samaritan," King notes, "The story begins in a theological controversy and ends in a description of first aid at a roadside. It arises in a question of eternal life and works out to a payment for room and board at a hotel" (28 November 1960).

Draft of Chapter III,
"On Being a Good Neighbor"

[*July 1962–March 1963*]
[*Atlanta, Ga.*]

Expanding on a 28 November 1960 outline titled "The Goodness of the Good Samaritan," this sermon draft hews closely to George Buttrick's themes in his lecture on the Good Samaritan.[1] King lauds the Samaritan's altruism, which enabled him to look beyond "accidents of race, religion and nationality" and applies the parable's message to race relations, acknowledging that laws "may not change the heart, but they can restrain the heartless." To effect true change, King submits, "Something must happen so to touch the hearts and souls of men that they will come together because it is natural and right." Finally, in a passage deleted from the published version, he commends his readers to "go out with the conviction that all men are brothers, tied in a single garment of destiny."

Luke 10:25–37

This morning I would like to talk with you about a good man. He is a man whose ~~exp~~ exemplary life will always stand ~~as the conscience of mankind~~ as a flashing light to plague the dozing conscience of mankind. His goodness was not found in his passive commitment to a particular creed, but in his active participation in a life saving deed. His goodness was not found in the fact that his moral pilgrimage had reached its destination point, but in the fact that he made the love ethic a reality as he joureyed life's highway. He was good because he was a good neighbor.

The ethical concern of this man is expressed in a magnificent little story. It is a story which begins with a theological discussion on the meaning of eternal life and ends with a concrete expression of compassion on a dangerous road. Jesus was asked the question by a man who had been trained in the details of Jewish law: "Teacher, what shall I do to inherit eternal life." The retort is ~~promp~~ prompt. "What is written in the law? How readest thou?" The scribe thinks a moment and then recites articulately: "Thou shalt love the Lord thy God with all thy heart, and with all thy soul, and with all thy strength, and with all thy mind; and thy neighbor as thy self." Then came the decisive word from Jesus: "you have answered right; this do, and thou shalt live."

The scribe was left standing before Jesus and the people in a state of chagrin. "Why, the people could ask, "would an expert in law raise a question that even the ~~nov~~ novice ~~could~~ could answer." So, in order to prove that he was not to be minimized, the scribe sought to show Jesus that his reply was far from conclusive. "Desiring to justify himself," he said, "And who is my neighbor?"[2] It was obvious that

---

1. Buttrick, *The Parables of Jesus,* pp. 148–156.

2. Buttrick, *The Parables of Jesus,* p. 150: "Jesus' reply, as he would demonstrate, was far from conclusive. So, 'desiring to justify himself,' he said, 'And who is my neighbor?' "

the scribe was now taking up the cudgels of debate.[3] It would have been so easy for the ~~question~~ inquiry to ~~look to an~~ end up in an abstract theological discussion. But Jesus immediately pulled the question out of mid-air and placed it on a dangerous curve between Jerusalem and Jerico.[4]

He told the story of "a certain man" who went down from Jerusalem to Jerico. As he made his journey he fell among robbers [*who?*] stripped him and beat him, and departed, leaving him half dead. By chance a certain Priest appeared, but he left the wounded man to his fate by passing by on the other side. A few minutes later a Levite approach the scene, and like the Priest he passed by on the other side. Finally, a certain Samaritan appeared—a half-breed, a man of another race, a man with whom the Jews had no dealings. But when he saw the wounded man he was moved with compassion.[5] He went to the man and administered first aid. He placed him on his beast, "and brought him to an inn, and took care of him."

"Who is my neighbor?" "I do not know his name," says Jesus. "He is anyone to whom you prove to be neighborly. He is anyone lying in need on life's roadside. He is neither a Jew nor a Gentile; he is neither a Russian nor an American; he is neither Negro nor white. He is 'a certain man'—any man lying needy on one of the numerous Jerico roads of life." So Jesus ends up defining a neighbor not in a theological definition but in a life situation.[6]

We may well ask what constituted the goodness of the good Samaritan. Why will he always stand as an inspiring paragon of neighborly virtue? It seems to me that this man's goodness can be described in one word—<u>altruism</u>. The good Samaritan was altruistic to the core. The dictionary defines altruism as "regard for, and devotion to, the interest of others." Indeed, the Samaritan was great because he made the first law of his life not self preservation, but other preservation.[7]

Let us notice first that the Samaritan had the capacity for a <u>universal altruism</u>. He ~~looked beyond the accidents of~~ had the piercing insight to see beyond the [*eternal?*] accidents of race, religion and nationality. **He saw a fellow human being in need.** ~~He saw first a human being who became a Jew by accident.~~ One of the great tragedies of man's long trek up the highway of history ~~is~~ has been his ~~ever-present~~ all to prevelant tendency to limit his neighborly concern to the race, the tribe, the class ~~and~~ or the nation. Not only was the god of early Old Testament days a tribal god, but the ethic was a tribal ethic. Thou shall not kill meant thou shall not kill a fellow Israelite, but for God-sake kill a Philistine. Greek democracy only applied to ~~the~~ a certain aristocracy, and not to the horde of Greek slaves ~~by~~ whose labors built

---

3. Buttrick, *The Parables of Jesus,* p. 149: "Perhaps in self-confidence he was taking up the cudgels of debate."

4. Buttrick, *The Parables of Jesus,* p. 150: "He lifted the question out of the atmosphere of controversy, since in that atmosphere real questions can never be settled, and set it down—where? He set it down on a dangerous road in Palestine!"

5. Buttrick, *The Parables of Jesus,* p. 151: "'But a certain Samaritan . . .' He was a half-breed, of a race which the Jews counted religiously in disrepute and with which they had 'no dealings.' But 'when he saw him, he was moved with compassion.'"

6. Luke 10:25–37.

7. In the published version: "The Samaritan was good because he made concern for others the first law of his life" (King, *Strength to Love,* p. 17).

the City States.[8] [*strikeout illegible*] The universalism standing at the center of the Declaration of Independence has been shamefully negated by America's appalling tendency to substitute some for all. **The ugly practices of our nation reveal that** numerous people north and south still believe that the affirmation "All men are created equal" means all white men are created equal. Our unswerving devotion to monopoly capitalism makes us concerned about the economic ~~tribal god, but the ethic was a tribal ethic~~ security of the captains of industry, and not the laboring men whose sweat and skills keep the wheels of industry rolling.

We can immediately see the devastating consequeces of this narrow, group centered concern. It means that one ~~doesn't~~ not mind what happens to the people outside his group. If an American is concerned only about his nation, he will not be concerned about what happens to the peoples of Asia, Africa or South America. Isn't this why nations can engage in the madness of war without the slightest sense of penitence? Isn't this why it is a national crime to murder a citizen of your own nation, but an act of heroic virtue to murder the citizens of another nation in war? If members of the American Medical Association and the National Manufacturers Associations are concerned only with their interests, they will not be concerned about what happens to the working man. They will pass by on the other side while thousands of people are stripped of their jobs and left displaced on some Jerico road as a result of the faces of automation. They will see every move for a better distribution of wealth and a better life for the working man as an act of creeping socialism.[9] If a white man is concerned only about his race, he will not be interested in what happens to the Negro. He will notice the Negro being robbed of his personhood, stripped of his sense of dignity, beaten by hooded perpetrator of violence and left dying on some wayside road, and yet he will pass by on the other side.[10] Some time ago an autobile carrying several members of a Negro college basketball team had an accident on a southern highway. Three of the fellows were severely injured. An ambulance was immediately called. On arriving at the scene of the accident the driver of the abulance, who happened to have been white, noticed that the injured boys were Negroes. He quickly said in unconcerned terms that it was not his policy to service Negroes and off he went. ~~When a~~ The driver of a passing automobile was gracious enought to take the boys to the nearest hospital. When the attending physician noticed that his incoming dying patients were Negroes he told the driver in rather belligerant terms, "we dont take niggers in this hospital." When the boys finally arrived at a "colored" hospital in a town about fifty miles away one was

---

8. Buttrick, *The Parables of Jesus,* p. 150: "The Greeks held the 'barbarian' in similar contempt; they denied the title 'neighbor' even to the horde of Greek slaves (human goods and chattels) on which the City States were built."

9. The preceding three sentences were altered in the published version: "If manufacturers are concerned only in their personal interests, they will pass by on the other side while thousands of working people are stripped of their jobs and left displaced on some Jericho road as a result of automation, and they will judge every move toward a better distribution of wealth and a better life for the working man to be socialistic" (p. 18).

10. The preceding two sentences were altered in the published version: "If a white man is concerned only about his race, he will casually pass by the Negro who has been robbed of his personhood, stripped of his sense of dignity, and left dying on some wayside road" (p. 18).

dead upon arrival and the other two died thirty and fifty minutes later respectively. The lives of all three could have probably been saved if they had been treated immediately. This is just one of the thousands of inhuman incidents that are the every day occurences of the south. It is an unbelievable expressions of the [*strikeout illegible*] barbaric consequences of any tribal-centered, national-centered or racial-centered ~~view~~ ethic.

The ultimate tragedy of this narrow provincialism is that it causes one to see people as entities, in short as things. So seldom do we see people in their true <u>human-ness</u>. ~~Our vision is so often limited to the external~~ We suffer from a sort of spiritual myopia which so often limits our vision to external accidents. We see men as Jews or Gentiles, Catholics or Protestants, Chinense or American, Negroes or whites. We fail to see them as fellow human beings made out of the same basic stuff as we are, molded by the same divine image. The Priest and the Levite saw only a bleeding body, not a human being made in their own likeness.[11] But the good Samaritan will always stand before us as a nagging reminder that we must remove the cateracks of provincialism from our spiritual eyes and see men as men. If the Samaritan had seen the wounded man as a Jew first he would not have stopped. The Jews and the Samaritan had no dealings. He saw a human being first who became a Jew by accident. The good neighbor will look beyond the external accidents long enough to see those inner qualies that make all men human, and therefore brothers.

Let us notice second that the good Samaritan possessed the capacity for a <u>dangerous altruism</u>. He risked his life to save a brother When we use our imagination concerning the reason why the Priest and the Levite ~~didn't~~ did not stop to help the wounded man, numerous things come to mind. Perhaps they were ~~too busy with~~ [*strikeout illegible*] in a hurry to get to an important ecclesiastical [*strikeout illegible*] meeting ~~and~~ for which they could not afford to be late. [*strikeout illegible*] Perhaps their temple regulations demanded ~~they~~ that they touch no human body ~~so many~~ for several hours before their temple function began. Or, they could have been on their way to a meeting to organize a Jerico Road Improvement Association. Certainly this was a real need. It is not enough to aid the wounded man on the Jerico Road. It is also necessary to work to change the conditions of the ~~Jerico~~ Road which made robbery possible. Philanthropy is marvelous, but it must not cause the philanthropist to overlook the need for working to remove many conditions of economic injustice which make philanthropy necessary. So maybe the Priest and the Levite felt that it was better to cure injustice from the causal source than to get bogged down with one individual effect. All these are probable reasons for their failure to stop. But there is another possibility which is often overlooked. It is possible that they were afraid. The Jerico Road ~~is~~ was a ~~deg~~ dangerous road. Some month ago Mrs. King and I were in Jerusalem. We rented a car and drove down from Jerusalem to Jerico. As we traveled ~~that~~ slowly down that meandering [*mountainous?*] road I said to my wife, "I can very easily see why Jesus used this road as the setting for his parable." Jerusalem was some two thousand feet ~~miles~~ above sea level

---

11. The phrase "made in their own likeness" was altered in the published version to "like themselves" (p. 19).

and Jerico was some one thousand feet below it. This upward or downward climb was made in a distance of less than twenty miles. Its many sudden curves made the road condusive for ambushing and exposed the traveler to unforseen attack. The road came to be known as the Bloody Pass.[12] So it is possible that the Priest and the Levite were afraid that if they stopped they too would ~~haveha~~ be ~~en~~beatten; for couldn't the robbers still be around? Or maybe the man on the ground was just a faker, using a pretended wounded condition to draw passing travlers to his side for quick and easy ~~seizure~~ seizure. So I can imagine that the first question which the Priest and the Levite asked was: "If I stop to help this man, what will happen to me?" Then the good Samaritan came by, and by the very nature ~~of the very nature~~ of his concern reversed the question: "If I do not stop to help this man, what will happen to him?" The good Samaritan was willing to engage in a dangerous altruism. In his very life he raised the question that always emerges from the good man. We so often ask, "what will happen to my job, my pretige or my status if I take a stand on this issue? If I take a stand for justice and truth, will my home be bombed, will my life be threatened or will I be jailed? What will happen to me?" The good man always reverses the question. Albert Switzer [*Schweitzer*] did not ask "what will happen to my pretige and security as a university Professor and my status as a Back Organist if I go to work with the people of Africa, but what will happen to these millions of people who have been wounded by the forces of injustice if I do not go to them?"[13] Abraham Lincoln did not ask, "what will happen to me if I issue the emancipation Proclamation and bring an end to chattle slavery, but what will happen to the union and millions of Negro people if I fail to do it?" The Negro professional does not ask, "what will happen to my secure position, my middle class status or my personal safty if I participate in the movement to end the system of segregation, but what will happen to the cause of justice and the masses of Negro people ~~who will never see the light of dignity or~~ who have never experienced the warmth of economic security ~~until the~~ if I do not participate actively and courageously in the movement?

The ultimate measure of a man is not where he stands in moments of confort and moment of convinience, but where he stands in moments of challenge and moment of controversy. The true neighbor is the man who will risk his position, his prestige and even his life for the welfare of others. His altruism ~~is~~ will not be limited to safty places, but it will move through dangerous valleys and hazzardous pathways to lift some bruised and beaten brother to a higher and more noble life.

Let us look at the neighborly Samaritan once more. He was good because he possessed the ability to engage in <u>excessive altruism</u>. He got down ~~from his beast~~ on the ground, bound up the wounds of the man with his own hands, and set him on his

---

12. For King's account of his drive on the Jericho Road, see A Walk Through the Holy Land, 29 March 1959, in *Papers* 5:166. Buttrick, *The Parables of Jesus*, p. 150: "Jerusalem was some two thousand feet above sea level and Jericho over one thousand feet below it. The twenty miles between the cities wound through mountainous country, whose limestone caves offered ambush for brigand bands, and whose sudden turns exposed the traveler to unforeseen attack. The road became known as the 'Bloody Pass.'"

13. In 1913, Schweitzer established a hospital in Lambaréné, French Equatorial Africa and remained there for much of his life. In 1952, he was awarded the Nobel Peace Prize for his work. Schweitzer was also an organist who specialized in the works of composer J. S. Bach.

own beast. It would have been much easier for him to ~~have~~ pay an ambulance to take the unfortunate man to the hospital, rather than risk having his neatly trimmed suit stained with blood.[14]

True altruism is more than the capacity to pity one in need; it is the capacity to sympathize. Pity may be little more than an impersonal concern which prompts the sending of a material check. But true sympathy is personal concern which demands the giving of ones soul. Pity may arise out of a concern for a big abstraction called humanity. Sympathy grows out of a concern for "a certain man," a particular human being lying needy at life's roadside. Sympathy is feeling with the person in need— his pain, his agony, his burdens. Our missionary efforts have often failed because they were based on pity, rather than true compassion. Instead of seeking to do something with the African and Asian peoples, we have to often sought to do something for them. This expression of pity devoid of genuine sympathy leads to a new form of paternalism which no self repecting person can accept. ~~Millions of dollars~~

Dollars may ~~be wonderful, but unless they~~ have the potential for helping some wounded child of God on life's Jerico Road, but unless those dollars are distributed by compassionate fingers they will enrich neither the giver nor the receiver. Millions of [*missionary?*] dollars have gone to Africa from the hands of Church people who would die a million deaths before they would [*strikeout illegible*] allow an African the priviledge of worshipping in their congregations. Million of Peace Corp dollars are going to Africa as a result of the votes of some men who would fight unrelentingly to prevent African Ambassadors from holding membership in their diplomatic club or establish residency in their particular neighborhood. The Peace Corp will fail if it seeks to do something for the undeveloped peoples of the world; it will succeed if it seek creatively to do something ~~creative~~ with them.[15] It will fail if it is a negative gesture to defeat communism; it will succeed if it is a positive thrust to wipe povrty, ignorance and disease from the face of the earth. Soon we will come to see that money devoid of love is like salt devoid of savor; it is good for nothing but to be trodden under the foot of men. **It may buy material bread, but the bread that it buys will soon decay.** True neighborliness requires [*strikeout illegible*] personal concern. The Samaritan not only ~~eased the hurt of the~~ used his physical hands to bind up the wounds of the robbed man's body, ~~with his physical hands,~~ but he released an overflowing love to bind up the wounds of his broken spirit. ~~by his comforting love~~.

Another expression of the excessiveness of the Samaritan's altruism was his willingness to go far beyond the call of duty. Not only did he bind up the man's wounds, but he put him on his beast and carried him to an inn. On leaving the [*strikeout illegible*] inn he left some money and made it clear that if any other financial needs arose he would gladly meet them. "Whatsoever thou spendest more, I, when I come back,

---

14. Buttrick, *The Parables of Jesus*, p. 153: "It would have been easier to be compassionate by proxy— to have phoned the hospital and despatched an ambulance. But *he* bound up the wounds with his own hands. *He* himself poured in oil and wine. *He* placed the unfortunate on *his own* beast."

15. In this sentence the word "undeveloped" was replaced with "underprivileged" in the published version (p. 21). With Executive Order 10924, President John F. Kennedy established the Peace Corps in 1961 "to help foreign countries meet their urgent needs for skilled manpower," maintaining that decent living standards are "the foundation of freedom and a condition of peace."

will repay thee." His love was complete. He could have stopped so much sooner than this and more than fulfilled any possible rule about one's duty to a wounded stranger. He went not only the second, but the third mile.

Dr. Harry Emerson Fosdick has made a most impressive distinction between enforceble and unenforceable obligations.[16] The former are obligation which can be regulated by the codes of society and the vigorous implementation of law enforment agencies. These are the obligations which are ~~spead out over spelled out on~~ spelled out on thousands of law book pages, ~~and if they are the broken~~ breakage of which has filled numerous prisons. But then are those unenforceable obligations which the laws of society cant reach. They deal with inner attitudes, genuine person-to person relations, and expressions of compassion which ~~laws~~ law books cannot regulate and jails cannot rectify. They are obligations which can be ~~dalt~~ dealt with only by ones commitment to an inner law, a commandment written on the heart. Man made laws are needed to assure justice, but a higher law ~~must~~ is needed to produce love. No code of conduct ever written by man can make a father love his children and a husband have affection for his wife. The law court may compell him to provide physical bread for the family, but it cannot make him provide the bread of love. A good father must be obedient to the unenforceable. The good Samaritan will always remain the conscience of mankind because he was obedient to that which could not be enforced. No law in the world could have made him do what he did. No ~~made~~ man made code could have produced such unallayed compassion, such efflorescent love, such thorough altruism. ~~The ultimate test of~~ The ultimate test of a man's goodness is whether he is obedient to the unenforceable.[17]

In our nation today a mighty struggle is taking place. It is a struggle to conquer the reign of a evil monster called segregation and its inseparable twin called discrimination—a monster that has wandered through this land for well-nigh one hundred years, stripping millions of Negro people of their sense of dignity and robbing them of their birthright of freedom. **A great deal of our so called race problem will be solved in the realm of enforceable obligations.** Let us never succumb to the temptation of believing that legislation and judicial decrees can play no major roll in bringing about desegregation. It may be true that morality cannot be legislated, but behavior can be regulated. Judicial decrees may not change the heart, but they can restrain the heartless. The law cannot make an employer love me, but it [*strike-out illegible*] can keep him from refusing to hire me because of the color of my skin. The habits if not the hearts of people have been and are being altered everyday by legislative acts, judicial [*decisions?*] and executive orders from the President.[18] So let

---

16. In Fosdick's sermon "The Cross and the Ordinary Man," he considered "enforceable and unenforceable obligations," referring to a speech by Lord Moulton from July 1924 in which Moulton espoused the importance of being "obedient to the unenforceable" (Fosdick, *Successful Christian Living*, pp. 210–219; see also Lord John Fletcher Moulton, "Laws and Manners," *Atlantic Monthly* [July–December 1924]:1).

17. The preceding three sentences were condensed in the published version: "No law in the world could have produced such unalloyed compassion, such genuine love, such thorough altruism" (p. 22).

18. President Kennedy signed Executive Order 11063 on 20 November 1962, which called for equal opportunity in housing. King wrote that "the housing order is a good-faith step in the right direction"

us not be misled by those who argue that segregation cannot be ended by the force of law. **It is already being ended by legislative and executive acts ~~already~~ presently in effect.**

But acknowledging this we must go on to admit that the ultimate solution to the race problem lies in the ability of men to be obedient to the unenforceable. Court orders and federal enforcement ~~agencies~~ agencies will be of inestimable value in achieving desegregation. But desegregation is only a partial, though necessary, step toward the ultimate goal which we seek to realize. Desegregation will break down the legal barriers, and bring men together physically. But something must happen so to touch the hearts and souls of men that they will come together because it is natural and right. In other words, our ultimate goal is integration which is genuine intergroup and interpersonal living. Only by producing a nation committed to the inner law of love can this goal be attained. A vigorous enforcement of civil rights laws can bring an end to segregated public facilities which stand as barriers to a truly desegregated society, but it cannot bring an end to the blindness, fear, prejudice, pride and irrationality which stand as barriers to a truely integrated society. These dark and demonic responses of the spirit can only be removed when men will ~~listen to decency~~ become possessed ~~if~~ by that invisible, inner law which ~~says~~ will etch in their ~~spirits~~ hearts the conviction that all men are brother and that love is mankind's most potent weapon for personal and social transformation. True integration will come only when men are true neighbors, willing to be obedient to unenforceable obligations.

Today more than ever before men of all races and men of all nations are challenged to be neighborly. The call for a good neighbor policy on the part of the nations of the world is more than an ephemeral shibboleth, it is the call to a way of life which will transform our almost cosmic elegy into creative fulfillment.[19] No longer can we engage in the luxury of passing by on the other side. Such folly was once moral failure; today it can ~~lead~~ only lead to universal suicide. **The alternative to a world of brotherhood to match [*strikeout illegible*] its geographical neighborhod may well be a civilization plunged into an inferno more devastating than anything Dante could ever envision.**[20] We cannot long survive living spiritually apart in a world that is geographically one. **As you leave this place of worship my friends go out with the conviction that all men are brothers, tied in a single garment of destiny.** In the final analysis I must not ignore the wounded man on life's Jerico Road because he is ~~appart~~ a part of me and I am ~~apart~~ a part of him. His agony diminishes me and his salvation enlarges me.

In our quest to make neighborly love a reality in our lives we have not only the inspiring example of the good Samaritan, but we have the magnanimous life of our Christ to guide us. ~~His death on the Cross of Calvary was a single event expressing a threefold altruism. He died for all men, which made his death a uni-~~

---

toward "the fulfillment of a campaign pledge made by the then-Senator Kennedy," but he lamented that "the order does not go far enough" (see King, "JFK's Executive Order," *New York Amsterdam News,* 22 December 1962).

19. Cf. Judges 12:5–6.

20. King refers to Dante Alighieri and the first volume of his epic poem *Divine Comedy, Inferno* (1314).

~~versal altruism. He died in excruciating pain which was an expression of his will-~~
~~ingness to engage in the most dangerous altruism. Mankind had been robbed~~
[*strikeout illegible*] ~~of his virtue by demonic forces, and left inflicted with deaden-~~
~~ing wounds of sin~~. He lived his days in a persistent concern for the welfare of others. His altruism was universal in that he saw all men as brothers. He was a neighbor to the publicans and the sinners. **When he addressed God in the Lord's Prayer
he ~~says~~ said "Our Father" which ~~lifts~~ immediately lifted God above the category of
a tribal deity concerned only about one race of people.** His altruism was willing to
travel dangerous roads in that he was willing to ~~risk~~ [*strikeout illegible*] ~~popularity~~
relinquish fame fortune and even life itself for a cause he knew was right. His
altruism was excessive in that he didn't have to die on a cross. His death on
Calvery will always stand as history's ~~f~~ most magnificent expression of obedience
to the unenfoceable.[21]

> When I survey the wondrous Cross
> Were the whole Realm of nature mine.[22]

ADd. MLKJP-GAMK: Vault box 3.

---

21. The preceding three sentences were altered in the published version: "His altruism was dangerous, for he willingly traveled hazardous roads in a cause he knew was right. His altruism was excessive, for
he chose to die on Calvary, history's most magnificent expression of obedience to the unenforceable"
(p. 24).
22. King quotes Isaac Watts's hymn "When I Survey the Wondrous Cross" (1707).

Draft of Chapter IV, "Love in Action"

[July 1962–March 1963]
[Atlanta, Ga.]

*King uses Jesus' words from the cross to preach forgiveness in the face of humanity's
ignorance, citing war, slavery, and segregation as manifestations of a "tragic
blindness." In particular, he decries those who "go on blindly believing in the eternal
validity of an evil called segregation and the timeless truth of a myth called white
supremacy. What a tragedy! Millions of Negroes have been crucified by conscientious
blindness." King developed this sermon from an outline from which he preached in the
spring of 1960.[1]*

Father, forgive them; for they know not what they do.
Luke 23:34.

---

1. King, "Love in Action" I, 3 April 1960, pp. 405–407 in this volume.

There are probably no words in all the New Testament that express more clearly and solemnly the magnanimity of Jesus' spirit than that sublime utterance from the cross—"Father forgive them, for they know not what they do." Here we see love at its best.

It is impossible to understand the great meaning of Jesus' prayer without noticing the word with which the text opens. It is the word "then." The verse which immediately precedes it reads thus: "And when they were come to the place, which is called Calvery, there they crucified Him, and the malefactors, one on the right hand and the other on the left."[2] Then, said Jesus, Father, forgive them. "Then"—when he was dying, a most ignomious death. "Then"—when he was being plunged into the abyss of nagging agony. "Then" when man had stopped to his worst. "Then"—when the wicked hands of the creature had dared to crucify the only begotten son of the creator. Then, said ~~Jesu~~ Jesus, Father forgive them. Behind that "then" could have been another reaction. Then he could have said, "Father, get even with them." Then he could have said, "Father let loose the mighty thunderbolts of righteous wrath and destroy them in their tracks." Then he could have said, "Father open the flood gates of justice and let the staggering avalanche of retribution pour upon them them.[3] But this was not his response. Though subjected to inexpressible agony, though suffering excruciating pain, though despised and rejected, nevertheless, He cries, "Father forgive them."

Let us notice two basic lessons from this text.

First, it is a marvelous expression of Jesus' ability to match words with actions. One of the great tragedies of life is that men seldom bridge the gulf between practice and profession, between doing and saying. There is that persistent schizophrenia which leaves so many of us tragically divided against ourselves. On the one hand we proudly profess certain sublime and noble principles, but on the other hand, we sadly practice the very antithesis of those principles. How often are our lives characterized by a high blood pressure of creeds and an anemia of deeds? We talk eloquently about our commitment to the principles of Christianity and yet we live our lives saturated with the practices of paganism. We proudly profess our devotion to democracy, and yet we sadly practice the very opposite of the democratic creed. We talk passionately about peace, and yet at the same time we assiduously prepare for war. We make our fervent pleas for the high road of justice, and yet we tread unflinchingly the low road of injustice. This strange dicotomy, this agonizing gulf between the ought and the is, stands out as the long and tragic story of mah's earthly pilgrimage.

But when we turn to the life of Jesus we find the gulf bridged. Never in all history have we found a more sublime example of the consistency of word and deed. During his ministry around the sunny villages of Galilee, Jesus had talked passion-

---

2. Cf. Luke 23:33.

3. The preceding four sentences were altered in the published version: "That 'then' might well have been otherwise. He could have said, 'Father, get even with them,' or 'Father, let loose the mighty thunderbolts of righteous wrath and destroy them,' or 'Father, open the flood gates of justice and permit the staggering avalanche of retribution to pour upon them'" (*Strength to Love*, p. 25).

ately about forgiveness. This strange doctrine awakened the questioning mind of Peter. "How oft," he asked, "shall my brother sin against me, and I forgive him? Seven times." Peter wanted to keep it legal and statistical. But Jesus responded by affirming that there is no limit to forgiveness. "I say not unto thee until seven times: but until seventy times seven."[4] In other words, forgiveness is not a matter of quantity, but a matter of quality. One cannot forgive four hundred and ninety times without it becoming a part of the habit structure of one's being. Forgiveness is not an occasional act; it is a permanent attitude. **This was what Jesus taught his disciples.**

Jesus had also admonished his followers to love their enemies and pray for them that despitefully used them.[5] This doctrine had fallen upon the ears of many of his hearers like strange music from a foreign land. Their ears were not attuned to the tonal qualitites of such amazing love. They had been taught to love their friends and hate their enemies. Their lives had been conditioning to seek redress in the time-honored technique of retaliation. And Yet Jesus continued to teach them that only through a creative love for their enemies could they be children of their father in Heaven.

So Jesus consistently taught his disciples that love and forgiveness were absolute necessities for spiritual maturity. Now the moment of testing emerges. Christ, the innocent Son of God, lies in painful agony on ~~a~~ {an} uplifted Cross. What place is there for love and forgiveness now? How will Jesus act? What will he say? The answer to these questions burst forth in majestic splendor. Jesus lifts his head up amid the wreath of thorns that encircles his brow and cries out in words lifted to cosmic proportions: "Father, forgive them; for they know not what they do." Indeed, this was Jesus finest hour; this was his heavenly response to his earthly rendezvous with destiny.

One can only see the greatness of this prayer by contrast. Nature does not forgive. It is caught in the finality of its own impersonal structure. In spite of the agonizing plea of the men trapped in the path of the rushing hurricane or the anguishing cry of the builder falling from the scaffold, nature must stand with a cold, serene, andpassionless indifference. She must do everlasting honor to her fixed, immutable laws. When these laws are violated, she has no alternative but to follow inexorably her path of unifornity. Nature does not and cannot forgive.

Man is slow to forgive.[6] We live by the philosophy that life is a matter of getting even and saving face. We genuflect before the altar of revenge. Samson, eyeless at ~~Goya~~ {Gaza}, prays fervently for his enemies, but only for their utter destruction.[7] The potential beauty of human life is constantly made ugly by man's ever recurring tendency to sing the song of retaliation.

Society is even less prone to forgive.[8] It has to have its standards, norms and mores. It has to have its legal checks and judicial restraints. Those who fall below the

---

4. Cf. Matthew 18:21–22.
5. Matthew 5:44.
6. In the published version: "Or contrast Jesus' prayer with the slowness of man to forgive" (p. 27).
7. Cf. Judges 16:28.
8. In the published version: "Or contrast the prayer with a society that is even less prone to forgive" (p. 27).

standards and those who disobey the laws are often left in a dark abyss of condemnation with no hope for another chance. Ask the innocent young lady, who, as a result of a moment of overriding passion, becomes the mother of an illegitimate child, and she will tell you that society is slow to forgive. Ask the public figure, who through a moment's carelessness betrays the public trust, and he will tell you that society is slow to forgive. Go to any prison and ask its numerous inhabitants, who, through small misdemeanors and large felonies have written shameful ~~lives~~ {lines} across the pages of their lives, and they will cry from behind the bars that society is slow to forgive. Go to that same prison and make your way to death row and ask those tragic victims of criminality as they prepare to make their pathetic walk to the electric chair, and they will cry from a dark and hopeless cell that society does not forgive. What is capital punishment but ~~societys's~~ society's final assertion that it is determined not to forgive.

This is the persistent story of life. Look down through the centuries and see how the oceans of history are made turbulent by the ever-rising tides of revenge. "Life for life, eye for eye, tooth for tooth, hand for hand, foot for foot." Man has never risen above this idea of the <u>lex talionis</u>.[9] In spite of the fact that the law of revenge solves no social problems, men continue to go its disastrous way. History is cluttered with the wreckage of nations and individuals that followed this self-defeating path.

Jesus eloquently affirmed from the cross a higher law. He knew that the old eye for an eye philosophy would end up leaving everybody blind.[10] He did not seek to overcome evil with evil. He overcame evil with good. Although crucified by hate, he responded with a radical love.[11]

What a magnificent lesson! Generations will continue to rise and fall; men will continue to worship the god of revenge and bow before the alter of retaliation; but ever and again this noble lesson from Calvary will come as a nagging reminder that only goodness can drive out evil, and only love can conquer hate.

There is a second lesson that comes to us from Jesus' prayer on the Cross. It is an expression of Jesus' awareness of man's intellectual and spiritual blindness. "They know not what they do," said Jesus. Blindness was their trouble. Enlightenment was their need. We must recognize that Jesus was nailed to the cross not simply by sin but by blindness. The man who cried "crucify him" were not bad men but blind men.[12] The ~~piercing~~ {jeering} mob that lined the roadside which led to the cross was not composed of evil people but blind people. They knew not what they did. What a tragedy![13]

History abounds with illustrations of this shameful tragedy. Centuries ago a sage

---

9. *Lex talionis* is Latin for "law as retaliation." This principle that criminals should receive precisely the injuries they inflict upon their victims was most famously established in the legal code of Hammurabi, the sixth king of Babylon (1792–1750 BCE).

10. Matthew 5:38.

11. The word "radical" was replaced by "aggressive" in the published version (p. 28).

12. Cf. Mark 15:12–14.

13. Fosdick, *The Hope of the World,* p. 222: "Jesus was put to death not simply by sin but by stupidity. . . . Those angry men before Pilate, crying 'Crucify him!' did not know what they did. What a tragedy! Those people by the roadside jeering at the staggering figure under his heavy cross did not know what they did."

named Socrates was forced to drink the hemlock. The men who called for his death were not bad men with demonic blood running through their veins. On the contrary, they were sincere and [*respectable?*] citizens of Greece. They sincerely thought Socrates an atheist because his idea of God had a philosophical depth that went beyond tratitional concepts.[14] It was not badness but blindness that killed Socrates. The Apostle Paul was not a bad man when he was ~~presenting~~ persecuting Christians.[15] He was a sincere conscientious devotee of Israel's faith. He thought he was right. He persecuted Cheistians not because he was devoid of sincerity but because he was devoid of enlightenment. The Christians who engaged in infamous persecutions and shameful Inquisitions were not evil men but misguided men.[16] The churchmen who felt that they had an edict from God to stand in the way of scientific progress, whether in the form of a Copernican revolution or a ~~Davinis~~ Darwinian theory of evolution, were not mischeivous men, but misinformed men.[17] And so Christ's words from the Cross may be written in sharply etched terms across some of the most inexpressible tragedies of history: "They know not what they do."

This tragic blindness expresses itself in so many ominous ways in the modern world. There are those who still feel that war is the answer to the problems of the world. They are not evil people. On the contrary, they are good respectable citizens whose ideas are dressed in the garments of patriotism. They talk in terms of brinkmanship and a balance of terror. They sincerely feel that a continuation of the arms race will do more good than harm.[18] So they passionately call for bigger ~~boms~~ {bombs}, larger nuclear stockpiles, and faster ballistic missiles.

Wisdom should tell them that war is obsolete. There may have been a time that war could serve as a negative good in the sense of preventing the spread and growth of an evil force. But the present destructive power of modern weapons of warfare eliminates the possibility of war serving even as a negative good. If we assume that life is worth living and that man has a right to survive, then we must find an alternative to war. In a day when Sputniks are dashing through outer space and guided ballistic missiles are carving highways of death through the stratosphere, no nation can win a war.[19] A so-called limited war can leave nothing but a calamitous legacy of human suffering, political turmoil, and spiritual disillusionment. A world war (God forbid) will leave nothing but the smouldering ashes of a human race whose folly

---

14. Fosdick, *The Hope of the World*, p. 223: "The Athenians who made Socrates drink the hemlock, far from being bad, were among the most earnest, conscientious, religious people of their day. But they stupidly thought Socrates an atheist because his idea of God was so much greater than the popular opinion."

15. Acts 9:1–28.

16. The Catholic Church began forcibly suppressing heresy throughout Europe in the thirteenth century, and the Inquisition continued for hundreds of years. Most notably in Spain under the rule of King Ferdinand V and Queen Isabella I, judges of the Inquisitions interrogated Catholic heretics, Jews, and Muslims and forced them to convert often under threat of torture, exile, and execution.

17. In the published version the phrase "natural selection" replaced "evolution" (p. 29).

18. The phrase "do more good than harm" was replaced by "be conducive to more beneficent than maleficent consequences" (p. 29).

19. Sputniks were a series of unmanned satellites initially launched by the Soviet Union in the late 1950s. The word "sputniks" was replaced by "vehicles" in the published version (p. 29).

led inexorably to an untimely death. **So the alternative to disarmament and the suspension of nuclear tests may well be a civilization plunged into the abyss of ~~civilization~~ annihilation.** And yet there are those who sincerely feel that disarmament is an evil and international negotiation is an abominable waste of time. Today our world is threatened with the grim prospect of atomic annihilation because ~~those~~ there are still too many men who know not what they do.

Notice how the truth of this text is revealed in race relations. Slavery was perpetuated in America not merely by human badness but also by human blindness. True, the causal basis for the system of slavery must be traced back, to a large extent, to the economic factor. But men soon convinced themselves that a system which was so economically profitable must have been morally justifiable. They began to formulate elaborate theories of racial superiority. Their rationalizations were contrived to clothe obvious wrongs in the beautiful garments of righteousness. It was this tragic attempt to give moral sanction to an economically profitable system that gave birth to the doctrine of white supremacy. Religion and the Bible were used as instruments to crystalize the status quo. Science was used as a tool to prove the biological inferiority of the Negro. Even philosophical logic was used to give intellectual credence to the system of slavery. Someone who had read the logic of the philosopher Aristotle place ~~this~~ {the} argument of the inferiority of the Negro in the framework of an Aristotelian syllagism. The argument went thusly: All men are made in the image of God; God, as everybody knows, is not a Negro; Therefore, the Negro is not a man. So men took the insights of religion, science, and philosophy and conveniently twisted them to give sanction to the doctrine of white supremacy. This idea was soon imbedded in every etextbook and preached in practically every pulpit. It became a structured part of the culture. Soon men embraced this philosophy not as the rationalization of a lie but as the expression of a final truth. They sincerely came to believe that the Negro was inferior by nature and that slavery was ordained by God. In 1857 the system of slavery was given its greatest legal boost when the Supreme Court of the United States rendered the Dred Scott decision. The Court affirmed that the Negro had no rights that the white man was bound to respect. The Judges that rendered this decision were not wicked men. On the contrary, they were decent and dedicated men. But they were victims of spiritual and intellectual blindness. They knew an not what they did. The whole system of slavery was largely perpetuated by sincere ignorance.[20]

This tragic blindness is found in racial segregation—the not too distant cousin of slavery. Some of the most vigorous defenders of segregation are sincere in their beliefs and earnest in their motives. It is true that some men are segregationist merely for reasons of of political expediency and economic gain. But all of the resistance to integration is not the rear guard action of professional bigots. There are some who sincerely feel that what they do in attempting to preserve segregation is best for themselves, their children, and their nation. In most instances they are good church people, anchored in the religious faith of their mothers and fathers.

---

20. The word "ignorance" was replaced with "though spiritually ignorant persons" in the published version (p. 30).

Pressed for a religious indication for their conviction, they will argue that God was the first segregationist. "Red birds and blue birds don't fly together," they contend. They sincerely feel that their views about segregation can be rationally explained and morally justified. Pressed for a justification for their belief in the inferiority of the Negro, they will turn to some pseudo work of science and sincerely argue that the Negroes' brain is smaller than the white man's brain. They do not know, for they refuse to know, that the idea of an inferior or superior race has been refuted by the best evidence of the science of anthropology. Great anthropoligists like Ruth Benedict, Margaret Mead and Melvin Herskonicts have all agreed that there ~~are no inferior or superior races, but inferior and superior individuals in all races.~~ [21]{while there may be inferior and superior individuals in all races, there is no superior or inferior race.} Again, the segregationists refuse to know that science has revealed that there are four types of blood and that these four types are found within every racial group. They go on blindly believing in the eternal validity of an evil called segregation and the timeless truth of a myth called white supremacy. What a tragedy! Millions of Negroes have been crucified by conscientious blindness. Like Jesus on the Cross, we must look lovingly at our oppressors and say: "Father forgive them, for they know not what they do."

From all that I have attempted to say it should be clear now that sincerity and conscientiousness are not enough. History has proven that these noble virtues can be relegated to tragic vices. There is nothing more dangerous in all the world than sincere ignorance and conscientious stupidy. As Shakespeare said:

"For sweetest things turn sourest by their deeds;
Lilies that fester smell far worse than weeds."[22]

As the chief moral guardian of the community, the church must implore men to be good and well-intentioned. It must extoll the virtues of kind-heartedness and conscientiousness. But somewhere along the way it must remind men that goodness and conscientiousness without intelligence may be the brutal forces that will lead to shameful crucificions. The church must never tire of reminding men that they have a moral responsibility to be intelligent.

We must admit that the Church has often overlooked this moral demand for enlightenment. At times it has talked as if ignorance is a virtue and intelligence a crime. Through its obscurantism, closed mindedness, and obstinacy to new truth, the church has often unconsciously encouraged its worshippers to look askance upon intelligence.

But if we are to call ourselves Christians, we had better avoid intellectual and moral blindness. Throughout the New Testament we are reminded of the need for enlightenment. We are commanded to love God not only with our hearts and souls, but also with our minds.[23] **Jesus bids his disciples not only to be as harmless as**

---

21. Melville J. Herskovits (1895–1963) was an American anthropologist who studied African and African American culture. His book *The Myth of the Negro Past* explored racial myths of the time (New York: Harper & Brothers, 1941).

22. Shakespeare, "Sonnet 94" (1609).

23. Cf. Matthew 22:37.

doves but also as wise as serpents.[24] When the Apostle Paul ~~noticed~~ {notices} the blindness of many of his opponents, he says: "I ~~beat~~ {bear} them witness that they have a zeal for God, but not according to knowledge."[25] Over and over again the Bible reminds us of the danger of zeal without knowledge and sincerity without intelligence.

So we see that we have a mandate not only to conquor sin but to conquer ignorance. Modern man is presently having a rendezvous with chaos not merely because of human badness but also because of human stupidity. If Western civilization continues to degenerate until it, like twenty four of its ~~prede~~ predecessors, falls hopelessly into the bottomless void of liquidation, it will be due not only to its undeniable sinfulness, but also to its appalling blindness.[26] If American democracy should gradually disentegrate, it would be due as much to a lack of insight as to a lack of commitment to right. If modern man continues to flirt unhesitatingly with war and eventually transforms his earthly habitat into an inferno that even Dante ~~can~~ could not imagine, it will result not only from downright badness, but also from downright stupidity.[27]

"They know not what they do," said Jesus. Blindness was their besetting trouble. And the crux of the matter lies here: we do need to be blind. Unlike physical blindness that is usually inflicted upon individuals as a result of natural forces outside their control, intellectual and moral blindness is an ill which man inflicts upon himself. by his tragic misuse of freedom and his failure to use his mind to its fullest capacity.[28] **There is plenty information available if we consider it as serious a moral obligation to be intelligent as to be sincere.** One day we will learn that the heart can never be totally right if the head is totally wrong. **This is not to say that the head can be right if the heart is wrong.** Only through the bringing together of head and heart—intelligence and goodness—can man rise to a filfillment of his true essence. Neither is this to say that one must be a philosopher or a posseor of extensive academic training before he can achieve the good life. I know many people of limited formal training who have amazing intelligence and foresight. The call for intelligence is a call for open-mindness, sound judgment, and love for truth. It is a call for men to rise above the stagnation of close-mindness and the paralysis of gullibility. No one need be a profound scholar to be open-minded. No one need be a keen academician to engage in an addiduous search for truth.

Light has come into the world. There is a voice crying through the vista of time calling men to walk in the light. Man's earthly life will be reduced to a tragic cosmic elegy if he fails to heed this call. "This is the condemnation," says John, "that light is come into the world, and men loved darkness rather than light."[29]

---

24. Cf. Matthew 10:16. Fosdick, *The Hope of the World*, p. 227: "If we are to call ourselves Christians, we had better not be stupid. Who was it said that his disciples were to be as wise as serpents and as harmless as doves? Jesus."

25. Cf. Romans 10:2.

26. King may be elaborating on an idea expressed by Arnold Toynbee in a twelve-volume work of comparative analysis on world civilizations throughout history, *A Study of History* (1934–1961), as he did in his sermon "First Things First" (2 August 1953, p. 145 in this volume).

27. King refers to Dante Alighieri and the first volume of his epic poem *Divine Comedy, Inferno* (1314).

28. In the published version, the word "ill" was replaced by "dilemma" (p. 32).

29. John 3:19.

So Jesus was right about those men who crucified him. They knew not what they did. They were inflicted with a terrible blindness.

Let us leave with a true picture of the Cross. Many quiet afternoons I have walked into this Sanctuary and looked meditatively at the illumined Cross above the altar. Every time I look at that Cross I am reminded of the greatness of God and the redemptive power of Jesus Christ. I am reminded of the beauty of sacrificial love and the majesty of ~~unsnerving~~ unswerving devotion to truth. It causes me to cry out with John Browning:[30]

> "In the Cross of Christ I glory, Towering o'er
> the wrecks of time; all the light of sacred
> story Gathers round its head sublime."[31]

It would be wonderful if I could look at the Cross and emerge with only this sublime reaction. But somehow I can never turn my eyes from that Cross without realizing that it symbolizes a strange mixture of greatness and smallness, of good and evil. As I behold that uplifted Cross I am not only reminded of the unlimited power of God, but also of the sordid weakness of man. I not only think of the glory of the divine, but of the tang of the human. I am reminded not only of Christ at his best, but also of man at his worst.

We must continue to see the Cross as a magnificant symbol of love conquering hate, and light overcoming darkness. But in the midst of this glowing affirmation, let us never forget that our Lord and Master was nailed to that Cross because of human blindness. Those who crucified him knew not what they did.

TADd. MLKP-MBU: Box 120.

---

30. In the published version, the phrase "cry out" was replaced with "say" (p. 33).
31. King cites John Bowring's hymn "In the Cross of Christ I Glory" (1825).

Draft of Chapter VI, "A Knock at Midnight"

[July 1962–March 1963]
[Atlanta, Ga.]

In this sermon, delivered as early as 1958, King speaks candidly about the church's inability to meet the challenges of modern life and the needs of those seeking religious solace.[1] He charges, "How often has the church left men disappointed at midnight, while it slept quietly in a chamber of pious irrelevancy." In particular, King criticizes the black church for being either one that "reduces worship to entertainment" or that offers "a loaf of stale bread that has been

---

1. King, "A Knock at Midnight," 14 September 1958, pp. 348–350 in this volume.

hardened by the winter of morbid class consciousness." King, nonetheless, remains hopeful about the church's potential to serve the needy, saying, "We must provide them with the fresh bread of hope, and imbue them with the conviction that God is still working with this old sinful world, and he has the power to [wring] the good out of the evil."

"Which of you who has a friend will go to him at midnight and say to him, Friend, lend me three loaves; for a friend of mine has arrived on a journey, and I have nothing to set before him."
(Luke 11: 5, 6)

Although this is a parable dealing with the power of persistent prayer, there is much in it that can serve as a basis for analyzing many of the problems of the modern world and the role of the church in grappling with them. The first thing we notice in the parable is that it is midnight. It is also midnight in the world today. The darkness is so deep that we hardly see which way to turn.[2]

It is midnight in the social order. As we look out on the international horizon we see the nations of the world engaged in a colossal and bitter contest for supremacy. Within a generation two world wars have been fought, and the clouds of another war are constantly hovering dangerously low. Man now has within his possession atomic and nuclear weapons that can completely destroy any of the major cities of the world in a matter of seconds. In spite of this, the arms race continues at breakneck speed. Nuclear tests continue to explode in the atmosphere with the grim prospect that the very air we breathe will be poisoned by radioactive fallout. Bigger and faster missiles continue to carve highways of death through the stratosphere. There is the ever present danger that all of these conditions and weapons will yet conspire to bring about the total annihilation of the human race.

In the past when we have confronted midnight in the social order we have turned to science for help. And little wonder! Science has saved us on so many occasions. When we were in the midnight of physical limitations and material inconvenience it was science that lifted us to the bright morning of physical and material comfort. When we were in the midnight of crippling ignorance and superstition, it was science that brought us to the daybreak of objective appraisal and creative analysis.[3] When we were caught in the midnight of dread plagues and diseases, it was science, through surgery, sanitation and the wonder drugs, that lifted us to the bright day of physical health, thereby prolonging our lives and making for greater security and physical well being. So it is quite easy to understand why men turn to science when the problems of the world are so ghastly in detail and ominous in extent.[4]

---

2. D. T. Niles, "Evangelism," 16 August 1954: "It is midnight in the parable. It is also midnight in the world today. The night is so deep that everything has become just an object to be avoided, and obstacle in the dark against which men must take care not to bump."

3. The phrase "objective appraisal and creative analysis" was replaced by "the free and open mind" in the published version of this sermon (King, *Strength to Love*, p. 43).

4. In the published version: "How naturally we turn to science in a day when the problems of the world are so ghastly and ominous" (p. 43).

But alas! Science cannot rescue us this time, because the scientist themselves are caught in the terrible midnight of our age. Indeed it was science that gave us the very instruments that can lead today to universal suicide. So modern man continues to face a dreary and frightening midnight in the social order.

This midnight in man's external collective life has brought about midnight in his internal individual life. It is midnight in the psychological order. Everywhere there are people who are harrowed by day and haunted by night with paralyzing fears. Deep clouds of anxiety and depression are floating in so many of our mental skies. Indeed people are more emotionally disturbed today than at any other period of human history. The psycopathic wards of our hospitals are more crowded than ever before. The most popular psychologists today are the psychoanalysts. The best sellers in psychology are books like <u>Man Against Himself, The Neurotic Personality of Our Times</u>, and <u>Modern Man in Search of a Soul</u>. The best sellers in religion are such books as <u>Peace of Mind</u> and <u>Peace of Soul</u>.[5] The most popular preachers are those who can preach soothing sermons on "How To Be Happy" and "How To Relax." Some have been tempted to re-translate Jesus' command to read "Go ye into all the world and keep your blood pressure down and lo I will make you a well-adjusted personality."[6] All of this is indicative of the fact that it is midnight in the inner lives of men and women.

It is also midnight in the moral order. Midnight is a time when all colors lose their distinctiveness and become merely a dirty shade of gray.[7] In so many instances moral principles have lost their distinctiveness. Nothing is absolutely right or absolutely wrong for modern man; it is just a matter of what the majority of people are doing. For most people right and wrong are merely relative to their likes and dislikes and the customs of their particular community. We have unconsciously taken Einstein's theory of relativity, which properly described the physical universe, and applied it to the moral and ethical realm.

Midnight is a time when everybody is desperately seeking to avoid getting caught. It is the hour when hardly anybody is concerned about obeying the ten commandments; everybody is passionately seeking to obey the eleventh commandment— "thou shall not get caught." According to the ethic of midnight the only sin is to get caught and the only virtue is to get by. It's all right to lie, but do it with real finesse; it's all right to steal, but be a dignified stealer, so that if you are caught it becomes embezzelement rather than robbery; it's all right even to hate, but dress your hate up in the garments of love and make it appear that you are loving when you are

---

5. King cites Karl A. Menninger, *Man Against Himself;* Karen Horney, *The Neurotic Personality of Our Time;* C. G. Jung, *Modern Man In Search of a Soul;* Joshua Loth Liebman, *Peace of Mind;* and Fulton J. Sheen, *Peace of Soul.*

6. King parodies Mark 16:15–16: "And he said unto them, Go ye into all the world, and preach the gospel to every creature. He that believeth and is baptized shall be saved; but he that believeth not shall be damned." Halford Luccock, "Life's Saving Tension," in *Marching Off the Map* (New York: Harper & Brothers, 1952), p. 75: "They are almost on the verge of rewriting the Scriptures to read, 'If any man will come after me, let him relax,' or 'Go into all the world and keep down your blood pressure.'"

7. Niles, "Evangelism": "Besides, at midnight, every colour loses its distinctiveness and becomes merely a dirty shade of grey."

actually hating.[8] So in place of the Darwinian survival of the fittest, many have sub-stituted a philosophy of the survival of the slickest. This has led to a tragic break-down of moral standards. And so the midnight of moral degeration grows deeper and deeper.

But, as in the parable, so in our world today, the deep darkness of the midnight is interrupted by the sound of a knock. It is the door of the Church on which mil-lions of people are knocking.[9] In this country church rolls are larger than ever before. More than 100,000,000 people are at least paper members of some church or Synagogue. Compare this with the fact that in 1929 there were only 50,000,000 church members. This represents an increase of 100 percent, while the population only increased 31 percent during the same period. Recent visitors to Soviet Russia, a country whose official policy is atheistic, have reported that the churches of that nation are not only bulging over with people Sunday after Sunday, but that they are growing every day. Harrison Salisbury, in a recent article in the New York Times on religious life in Russia, stated that the officials of the Communist party are becom-ing disturbed over the fact that so many young people are expressing a growing interest in the church and religion.[10] After forty years of the most vigorous efforts to suppress religion, the hierarchy of the Communist party is now faced with the inescapable fact that millions of people are knocking on the door of the church.

Now this numerical growth of the Church is not to be over-emphasized. We must not succumb to the temptation of confusing spiritual power with big numbers. Jumboism, as someone has called it, is an utterly fallacious standard in measuring positive power.[11] An increase in quantity does not necessarily represent an increase in quality. A bigger membership does not necessarily represent a bigger commit-ment to Christ. It has almost always been the creative, dedicated minority that has made the world better. But in spite of the fact that the numerical growth of the church does not necessarily represent a concommitant growth in ethical commit-ment, it does mean that millions of people feel that the Church can provide an answer to the deep confusion that has encompassed their lives. It is still the one familiar landmark to which the weary traveller by midnight comes. It is the one house which stands where it has always stood, the house to which the man travelling at midnight either comes or refuses to come. Some decide not to come.[12] But the many who come and knock are desperately seeking a little bread to tide them over.

Like the man in the parable, they are asking for three loaves of bread. They want

---

8. In the published version: "It is all right to steal, if one is so dignified that, if caught, the charge becomes embezzlement, not robbery. It is permissible even to hate, if one so dresses his hating in the gar-ments of love that hating appears to be loving" (p. 44).

9. Niles, "Evangelism": "But, as in the parable, so in our day, the tense silence of the midnight is dis-turbed by the sound of a knock. It is the door of the Church on which somebody is knocking."

10. King may refer to the fifth in a series of articles by Salisbury: "Khrushchev's Russia—5: Anti-Semitism and Religious Upsurge Are Said to Baffle the Soviet Regime," New York Times, 12 September 1959.

11. Fosdick, The Hope of the World, p. 4: "Again, this truth of Jesus is deflected from many modern minds because of our worship of bigness. One of my friends calls it 'Jumboism.'"

12. Niles, "Evangelism": "That is still the one familiar landmark to which the traveller by midnight comes. . . . It is the one house which stands where it has always stood, the house to which the man trav-elling at midnight either comes or refuses to come. Many decide not to come."

the bread of faith. Living through a generation of so many colossal disappointments, **with one towering frustration piled on another,** so many men have lost faith in God, faith in man, and faith in the future. Many feel somewhat like Wilberforce felt in 1801 when he said: "I dare not marry—the future is so unsettled;" or as William Pitt felt in 1806 when he said: "There is scarcely anything round us but ruin and despair."[13] In the midst of this staggering disillusionment, many are crying out for the bread of faith.

There is also a deep longing for the bread of hope. Many who lived in the early days of this century did not feel the need of seeking this bread. Living in the days of the first telephones, the first automobiles, and the first airplanes caused them to grow up with a radiant optimism. They worshiped at the shrine of **Herbert Spencer's doctrine of** inevitable progress.[14] They believed that every new scientific achievement was lifting man to higher levels of perfection. But then came a series of tragic developments which revealed the selfishness and corruption of man, and pointed out with frightening clarity the truth of Lord Acton's dictum: "Power tends to corrupt. Absolute power corrupts absolutely."[15] This awful discovery led to one of the most colossal breakdowns of optimism in history. For so many people, young and old, the light of hope has gone out, and they roam wearily in the dark chambers of pessimism. Many have concluded that life has no meaning. There are those who would agree with the philosopher [*Arthur*] Schopenhauer in saying: "Life is an endless pain with a painful end;" or as he said on another occasion: "Life is a tragic-comedy played over and over again with only slight changes in costume and scenery."[16] Others would cry out with Shakespeare's Macbeth:

> Life is a tale told by an idiot, full of sound
> and fury, signifying nothing.[17]

But in spite of the inevitable moments when all seems hopeless, men know that without some sense of hope they are really dead while they live. So in agonizing desperation they are crying for the bread of hope.

Then there is the deep longing for the bread of love. Everybody wants to love and be loved. He who feels that he isn't loved feels that he is nobody, that he doesn't count. So much has happened in the modern world to make men feel that they don't belong. **Caught in the chains of injustice and the mannacles of discrimination,**

---

13. William Wilberforce (1759–1833) was a British politician who worked for the abolition of slavery. William Pitt, the Younger (1759–1806), British prime minister from 1783 to 1801 and again from 1804 to 1806, opposed the slave trade.

14. Herbert Spencer (1820–1903) was an English philosopher who advocated the application of progressive evolutionary theory to all branches of knowledge.

15. John E. E. Dalberg-Acton, "Acton-Creighton Correspondence," in *Essays on Freedom and Power* (Boston: The Beacon Press, 1948), p. 364.

16. King refers to Schopenhauer, *The World as Will and Idea*, vol. 3, p. 462: "In the whole of human existence suffering expresses itself clearly enough as its true destiny. Life is deeply sunk in suffering, and cannot escape from it; our entrance into it takes place amid tears, its course is at bottom always tragic, and its end still more so." King also paraphrases segments of Schopenhauer's chapter "On History" in *The World as Will and Idea*, vol. 3, pp. 224–227.

17. Shakespeare, *Macbeth*, act 5, sc. 5.

many of us are left feeling that we are things rather than persons. Living in big cities, and mass populations, many of us are driven to believe that we are merely depersonalized cogs in a vast industrial wheel. Living in a world which has become so oppressively impersonal, many of us have come to feel that we are little more than a number. Ralph Borsodi has given an arresting picture of a world where numbers have replaced persons. He writes that today the modern mother is often merely maternity case No. 8434, and her child, after being fingerprinted and footprinted, becomes No. 8003. At the other end of life a modern funeral in a large city becomes an event in Parlor B on a certain day, with Preacher No. 14, singer No. 87, rendering music. No. 174, flowers and decorations Class B. Frustrated because of this growing tendency to reduce man to a card in a vast index, modern man is in a desperate search for the bread of love.

When the man in the parable knocked on the door of his friend and asked for the three loaves of bread, he received the impatient retort: "Don't bother me! The door is fastened, and my children and I have gone to bed; I cannot get up and give you any." **In other words, this man was left disappointed at midnight.** How often have men experienced a similar disappointment when they knocked on the door of the Church at midnight. How often has the church left men disappointed at midnight, while it slept quietly in a chamber of pious irrelevancy. Millions of Africans have patiently knocked on the door of the Christian church seeking the bread of social justice. In almost every instance they have either been ignored altogether, or told to wait later—later almost always meaning never. In America millions of Negroes starving for the want of the bread of freedom have knocked over and over again on the door of the so-called white churches. They have usually confronted a cold indifference and a blatant hypocrisy. Even the white religious leaders who have a heartfelt desire to open the door and provide the bread are often more cautious than courageous and more prone to follow the expedient path than the ethical path. It is one of the shameful tragedies of history that the institution which should be removing man from the midnight of racial segregation is itself a participant in creating and perpetuating the midnight.

Men caught in the terrible midnight of war have often knocked on the door of the Church to find the bread of peace. In almost every instance the church has left them disappointed. Hardly anything has revealed the pathetic irrelevancy of the church in present-day world affairs as its stand on war. In the midst of a world gone mad with arms buildups, {chauvinistic} passions, and imperialistic exploitation, the church has stood by, either endorsing these activities or remaining appallingly silent. During the last two world wars the national churches often functioned as the ready lackeys of the state. They sprinkled holy water upon the battleships and joined the mighty armies in singing "praise the Lord and pass the ammunition."[18] A weary world pleading desperately for peace has often found the church giving moral sanction to war.

Then there are those who have gone to the church for the bread of economic justice. How often has the church left men standing in the frustrating midnight of

---

18. King refers to Frank Loesser's 1943 song "Praise the Lord and Pass the Ammunition."

economic deprivation. In so many instances it has so aligned itself with the privileged classes and defended the <u>status quo</u> that it found it impossible to answer the knock at midnight. We must never forget the lesson of the Greek Church in Russia. This church allied itself with the <u>status quo</u> and became so inextricably bound with the despotic czarist regime, that it was impossible to get rid of the corrupt political and social system without getting rid of the church. This is the fate of every ecclesiastical organization that allies itself with the <u>status-quo</u>.[19]

The church must be reminded once again that {it} is not to be the master or the servant of the state, but the conscience of the state. It must be the guide and the critic of the state,—never its tool. **As long as the church is a tool of the state it will be unable to provide even a modicum of bread for men at midnight.** If the church does not recapture its prophetic zeal and cease to be an echo of the <u>status-quo</u> it will be relegated to an irrelevant social club with no moral or spiritual authority. If the church does not participate actively in the struggle for peace, economic and racial justice, it will forfeit the loyalty of millions and cause men everywhere to know that it is an institution whose will is atrophied. But if the church will free itself from the the shackles of a deadening status-quo, and, recovering its great historic mission, will proceed to speak and act fearlessly and insistently on the questions of justice and peace, it will enkindle the imagination of mankind. It will fire the souls of men and imbue them with a glowing and ardent love for truth, justice and peace. Men far and near will then see the church as that great fellowship of love which provides light and bread for lonely travellers at midnight.

In speaking of the laxity of the church, I must not overlook the fact that the so-called Negro church has often left men disappointed at midnight. I say so-called Negro church, because ideally, there can be no Negro or white church. It is to the everlasting shame of the American church that white Christians developed a system of racial segregation within the church, and inflicted so many indignities upon its Negro worshippers that they had to go out and organize their own churches. There are two types of Negro churches that have failed to provide bread at midnight. One is a church that burns up with emotionalism and the other is a church that freezes up with classism. The former is a church that reduces worship to entertainment, and places more emphasis on volume than on content. It confuses spirituality with muscleality. The danger of this church is that its members will end up with more religion in their hands and feet than in their hearts and souls. So many people have gone by this type of church at midnight, and it had neither the vitality nor the relevant gospel to feed their hungry souls. The other type of Negro church that leaves men unfed at midnight is a church that develops a class system within. It boasts of the fact that it is a dignified church, and most of its members are professional people. It takes pride in its exclusiveness. In this church the worship service is cold and meaningless. The music is dull and uninspiring. The sermon is little more than a

---

19. Peter the Great (1682–1725) partially incorporated the Russian Orthodox Church into the government's administrative structure by replacing the independent Patriarchate of Moscow, the body of church fathers, with the Holy Synod, a collective body subordinate to the tsar. The Church remained a functionary of the tsar until the Bolshevik Revolution (1917) when the new Soviet state abolished the state religion and suppressed religious education.

nice little essay on current events. If the pastor says too much about Jesus Christ the members begin to feel that he is taking the dignity out of the pulpit. If the choir sings a Negro spiritual, the members bow their head in shame feeling that this is an affront to their class status.[20] The tragedy of this type of church is that it fails to see that worship at its best is a social experience with people of all levels of life coming together to realize their oneness and unity under God. **This church ends up losing the spiritual force of the "whosoever will let him come" doctrine, and is little more than a social club with a thin veneer of religiosity.**[21] When men have gone by this church at midnight they have either been ignored altogether because of their limited education or they have been given a loaf of stale bread that has been hardened by the winter of morbid class consciousness.

As we turn to the parable again we notice that in spite of the man's initial disappointment he continued to knock on the door of his Friend. **This is so true of men's experience with the church. How bitterly men and women speak about their disappointment with the church. But in spite of being left disappointed, many continue to knock. In the parable the man continued to knock so patiently and diligently that the man within finally opened the door and gave him bread.** Because of his importunity—his persistence, his urgent plea—he was able to persuade his Friend to open the door. **It is very doubtful that the man in need of bread would have continued to knock on the friend's door if he had had the slightest notion that there was no bread in his house. He would have left immediately after the Friend impatiently told him to leave. But even though he was at first disappointed he continued to knock because he knew that some bread was in that house.** Many men continue to knock on the door of the church at midnight, even though the church has so bitterly disappointed them, because they know deep down within that the bread of life is there.

The greatest challenge facing the church today is to keep the bread fresh and remain a Friend to men at midnight. The church must proclaim God's son as the hope of the world. Jesus Christ is the hope of men in all of their complex personal and social problems.[22] Many will continue to come by the church in quest for an answer to life's problems. Many young people will knock on the door who are perplexed by the uncertainties of life, confused by the disappointments of life and disillusioned by the ambiguities of history. Some will come who were torn from their schools and careers during the war and thrown into dirty, filthy trenches. Some will come who have been crippled, gassed, or blinded in the dark horrors of war. They will wander here in the midnight of gloom and hopelessness. We must provide them with the fresh bread of hope, and imbue them with the conviction that God **is still working with this old sinful world, and he** has the power to ring the good out of the evil. Some will come tortured with a nagging sense of guilt as a result of their

---

20. In the published version the phrase "bow their head in shame feeling that this is" was replaced with the word "claim" (p. 48).

21. Cf. Mark 8:34.

22. The preceding three sentences were condensed in the published version: "The church today is challenged to proclaim God's Son, Jesus Christ, to be the hope of men in all of their complex personal and social problems" (p. 48).

wandering in the midnight of ethical relativism and commitment to the doctrine of self-expression. We must lead them to Christ where they can find the fresh bread of forgiveness. Some will knock who are moving toward the evening of life and are tormented with the fear of death. We must provide them with the bread of faith in immortality, so that they will realize that this earthly life is merely an embryonic prelude to a new awakening **and that death is not a period which ends this great sentence of life, but a comma that punctuates it to more loftier significance.**

Midnight is a confusing hour, and one in which it is difficult to be faithful; **but the relevancy and power of the church will be measured by its capacity to meet the needs of those who come at midnight.** The most inspiring word that the church can say to men at midnight is that no midnight is here to stay. The weary traveller by midnight who is asking for bread is really asking for the dawn.[23] Our eternal message of hope is that dawn will come. **Midnight is only a temporary development in the cycle of life's day.** Our slave foreparents realized this. They were never unmindful of the fact of midnight, for there was always the rawhide whip of the overseer and the auction block where families were torn asunder to remind them of its reality. So when they thought of midnight with all of its agonizing darkness they sang:

> Oh, Nobody knows de trouble I've seen;
> Sometimes I'm up, sometimes I'm down
> Oh, yes, Lord,
> Sometimes, I'm almost to de groun',
> Oh, yes, Lord.
> Oh, nobody knows de trouble I've seen,
> Glory Hallelujah.[24]

But even though emcompassed by a staggering midnight, they had faith to believe that morning would come. When thinking of this they would sing:

> I'm so glad trouble don't last alway.
> O my Lord, Oh my Lord, what shall I do?[25]

Here we see a positive belief in the dawn which uses the midnight of life as the raw material out of which it creates its own strength. This was the growing edge of hope that kept the slaves going amid the most barren and tragic circumstances.[26]

In the final analysis, faith in the dawn grows out of faith in God. It grows out of the conviction that God is good and God is just. When one believes this he knows that the contradictions of life are neither final nor ultimate. Therefore, he can walk through the dark night with a sense of being safe and being secure. He lives with the

---

23. Niles, "Evangelism": "Midnight is a difficult hour in which to be faithful or successful: but we shall find grace as we seek to minister to the real need of him who comes to us in the midnight. For the traveller by midnight who is asking for bread is really asking for the dawn."

24. King quotes a verse from the spiritual "Nobody Knows the Trouble I've Had."

25. King refers to the spiritual "I'm So Glad Trouble Don't Last Always."

26. The preceding two sentences were condensed in the published version: "Their positive belief in the dawn was the growing edge of hope that kept the slaves faithful amid the most barren and tragic circumstances" (p. 49).

radiant conviction that all things work together for good for those that love God. He knows that even the most starless midnight may be the darkest moment just before the dawn of some great fulfillment.

I recall a very meaningful experience during the bus boycott in Montgomery, Alabama. At the beginning of the boycott we were able to set up a voluntary carpool to assist in getting the people to and from their jobs. After we had struggled for eleven long months and our carpool had worked extraordinarily well, Mayor [*William*] Gayle introduced a resolution instructing the city's legal department to "file such proceedings as it may deem proper to stop the operation of car pool or transportation system growing out of the bus boycott." The hearing was set for Tuesday, November 13.

Our regular weekly mass meeting was scheduled the night before the hearing. I had the responsibility of going before the mass meeting to warn the people that the car pool would probably be enjoined. I knew that they had willingly suffered for nearly twelve months, but how could they function at all with the car pool destroyed? Could we ask them to walk back and forth every day to their jobs? And if not, would we then be forced to admit that the protest had failed in the end? For the first time I almost shrank from appearing before them.

The evening came, and I mustered up enough courage to tell them the truth. I tried, however, to end on a note of hope. "We have moved all of these months," I said, "with the daring faith that God was with us in our struggle. The many experiences of days gone by have vindicated that faith in a marvelous way. We must go out with the same faith tonight. We must believe that a way will be made out of no way." But in spite of these words, I could feel the cold breeze of pessimism passing through the audience. It was a dark night—darker than a thousand midnights. It was a night in which the light of hope was about to fade away and the lamp of faith about to flicker.

Tuesday morning found us in court before Judge [*Eugene*] Carter. The city argued that we were operating a "private enterprise" without a franchise. Our lawyers argued brilliantly that the carpool was a voluntary "share-a-ride" plan provided as a service by Negro churches without a profit. As the hearing proceeded it was obvious that Judge Carter was going to rule in favor of the city.

As chief defendant I sat at the front table with the lawyers. Around twelve o'clock—during a brief recess—I noticed unusual commotion in the courtroom. Mayor Gayle was called to the back room. Several reporters moved excitedly in and out of the room.

Instantly a reporter came up to me with a paper in his hand.

"Here is the decision that you have been waiting for, read this release."

Quickly, with a mixture of anxiety and hope, I read these words: "The United State Supreme Court today unanimously ruled bus segregation unconstitutional in Montgomery, Alabama."[27] At this moment my heart began to throb with an inexpressible joy. The darkest hour of our struggle had indeed proved to be the first

---

27. On 13 November 1956, the United States Supreme Court ruled, in the case of *Gayle et al., Members of the Board of Commissioners of Montgomery, Ala., et al. v. Browder, et al.* 352 U.S. 203; 77 (1956) that the segregation of Montgomery buses was unconstitutional.

hour of victory. Someone shouted from the back of the courtroom: "God Almighty has spoken from Washington."[28]

The night before we were in a confusing midnight, but now daybreak had come.

Yes, the dawn will come. Disappointment, sorrow and despair are all born in midnight, but we may be consoled by the fact that morning will come. "Weeping may tarry for a night," says the Psalmist, "but joy cometh in the morning."[29] This is the faith that will adjourn the assemblies of hopelessness, and bring new light into the dark chambers of pessimism.

TADd. MLKP-MBU: Box 119A.

---

28. King recounts this story in his book *Stride Toward Freedom*, pp. 158–160.
29. Cf. Psalm 30:5.

Draft of Chapter VIII,
"The Death of Evil Upon the Seashore"

[*July 1962–March 1963*]
[*Atlanta, Ga.*]

King finds inspiration in ideas presented in Phillips Brooks's "The Egyptians Dead Upon the Seashore" for this sermon, a version of which he delivered at Dexter in 1955.[1] In a sentence deleted from the published version, King announces his faith in a just universe: "A mythical Satan, through the work of a conniving serpent, may gain the allegiance of man for a period, but ultimately he must give way to the magnetic redemptive power of a humble servant on an uplifted cross." Retelling the tale of the Jewish exodus from Egypt and the death of the Egyptian army that symbolized "the death of inhuman oppression and unjust exploitation," he draws a parallel with the U.S. Supreme Court's 1954 Brown v. Board of Education decision, affirming that "the Red Sea was opened and the forces of justice marched through to the other side." King concludes, "There is a Red Sea in history that ultimately comes to carry the forces of goodness to victory, and that same Red Sea closes in to bring doom and destruction to the forces of evil."

Text: "And Israel saw the Egyptians dead upon the seashore.
Exodus 14:30.

---

1. King, "Death of Evil Upon the Seashore," Sermon at Dexter Avenue Baptist Church, 24 July 1955; Brooks, *Selected Sermons*, pp. 105–115. King also preached a version of this sermon on 17 May 1956 in New York City ("The Death of Evil Upon the Seashore," Sermon Delivered at the Service of Prayer and Thanksgiving, Cathedral of St. John the Divine, in *Papers* 3:256–262).

There is hardly anything more obvious than the fact that evil is present in the universe. It projects its nagging, prehensile tentacles into every level of human existence. We may debate over the origin of evil, but only the person victimized with a superficial optimism will debate over its reality. Evil is with us as a stark, grim, and colossal reality.

The Bible affirms the reality of evil in unmistakable terms. Symbolically, it pictures it in the conniving work of a serpent which comes to inject a discord into the harmonious symphony of life in a garden.[2] Through the warnings of the prophets, it sees evil in callous injustices and ugly hypocrisy. At the center of the New Testament, it sees it in a misguided mob hanging the world's most precious character on a cross between two thieves.[3] The Bible is crystal clear in its perception of evil.[4]

Jesus was not unmindful of the reality of evil. While he never sought to give a theological explanation for the origin of evil, he never explained it away. In the parable of the tares Jesus made it clear that the tares were tares.[5] They were not illusions or errors of the mortal mind. They were real weeds disrupting the orderly growth of stately wheat. Whether sown by Satan or by man's misuse of his own freedom, the tares were poisonous and deadly evil. Jesus said in substance concerning the choking weeds: "I do not attempt to explain their orgin, but they are the work of an enemy."[6] Jesus realized that the force of evil was as real as the force of good.

But we need not stop with the Bible's glaring examples to establish the reality of evil. We need only look out into the wide arena of everyday life. We have seen evil in tragic lust and inordinate selfishness.[7] We have seen it in high places where men are willing to sacrifice truth on the altars of their self-interest. We have seen it in imperialistic nations trampling over other nations with the iron feet of oppression.[8] We have seen it clothed in the garments of calamitous wars which left battlefields

---

2. Cf. Genesis 3.

3. Cf. Matthew 27:35–38.

4. This paragraph was condensed in the published version: "Affirming the reality of evil in unmistakable terms, the Bible symbolically pictures the conniving work of a serpent which injects discord into the harmonious symphony of life in a garden, prophetically denounces callous injustice and ugly hypocrisy, and dramatically portrays a misguided mob hanging the world's most precious Person on a cross between two thieves. Crystal clear is the biblical perception of evil" (King, *Strength to Love*, p. 58).

5. Cf. Matthew 13:24–30.

6. Buttrick, *The Parables of Jesus*, pp. 65–66: "But if evil is not explained, it is not explained away. The tares are tares. They are not immature grain. They are not imaginary. They are weeds and poisonous. They positively war against a good harvest. Whether we call the power that sows them 'devil' or the wrong choice of human freewill, that power is the foe of our souls: 'An *enemy* hath done this.' Tares have entered the field—whether sown by Satan or by our perversion of a God-given liberty; and life will be clarified if we fixedly regard them as a hostile growth, and resolve to be rid of them. To regard evil as illusory solves no problems. . . . Jesus says of the choking weeds of life: 'I do not account for them, but they are the work of an 'enemy.'"

7. The preceding three sentences were condensed in the published version: "Within the wide arena of everyday life we see evil in all of its ugly dimensions. We see it expressed in tragic lust and inordinate selfishness" (p. 59). In the 1955 version of the sermon, King added, "We have seen it walk the streets of Montgomery" (King, "Death of Evil Upon the Seashore," 24 July 1955).

8. This sentence was altered in the published version: "We see it in imperialistic nations crushing other people with the battering rams of social injustice" (p. 59).

drenched with blood, filled nations with widows and orphans, and sent men home physically handicapped and psychologically wrecked. We have seen evil in all of its tragic dimensions.[9]

So in a sense, the whole of life is the history of a struggle between good and evil. There seems to be a tension at the very core of the universe. All the great religions have recognized this tension. Hinduism called it a conflict between illusion and reality; Zoroastrianism looked upon it as a conflict between the god of light and the god of darkness; **Platonism called it a conflict between spirit and matter;** traditional Judaism and Christianity called it a conflict between God and Satan.[10] Each of these religions realized that in the midst of the upward thrust of goodness there is the downward pull of evil.

Christianity is clear, however, in affirming that in the long struggle between good and evil, good eventually emerges as the victor. Evil is ultimately doomed by the powerful, inexorable forces of good. Good Friday may occupy the throne for a day, but eventually it must give way to the triumphant music of the trumpets of Easter.[11] **A mythical Satan, through the work of a conniving serpent, may gain the allegiance of man for a period, but ultimately he must give way to the magnetic redemptive power of a humble servant on an uplifted cross.** Degrading tares may choke the sprouting necks of growing wheat for a season, but eventually the harvest will come and separate the evil tares from the good wheat. Evil may so shape events that Ceasar will occupy a palace and Christ a cross, but one day that same Christ will rise up and split history into A.D. and B.C., so that even the life of Caesar must be dated by his name. Biblical religion recognized long ago what William Cullen Bryant came to see: "Truth crushed to earth will rise again;" and what [*Thomas*] Carlyle came to see: "No lie can live forever."[12]

A graphic example of this truth is found in an incident in the early history of the Hebrew people. You will remember that at a very early stage in her history the children of Israel were thrown into the bondage of physical slavery under the gripping yoke of Egyptian rule. Egypt was the symbol of evil in the form of humiliating oppression, ungodly exploitation and crushing domination. The Israelites symbolized goodness in the form of devotion and dedication to the God of Abraham, Isaac and Jacob. These two forces were in a continual struggle against each other—Egypt struggling to maintain her oppressive yoke and Israel struggling to gain freedom

---

9. The preceding two sentences were altered in the published version: "We see it clothed in the garments of calamitous wars which leave men and nations morally and physically bankrupt" (p. 59).

10. Fosdick, *Living Under Tension,* p. 216: "All the great religions have so pictured life in terms of conflict. Hinduism called it a conflict between reality and illusion; Zoroastrianism a conflict between light and darkness; Platonism a conflict between spirit and matter; traditional Judaism and Christianity a conflict between God and Satan." A central element of Zoroastrianism, a religion founded in Persia as early as 600 BCE, is the constant struggle between the evil spirit of darkness and the god of light and goodness.

11. This sentence was altered in the published version: "Good Friday must give way to the triumphant music of Easter" (p. 59).

12. Bryant, "The Battlefield" (1839); Carlyle, *The French Revolution* (1837). This quote from Carlyle, which King used regularly, was corrected in the published version: " 'No lie you can speak or act but it will come, after longer or shorter circulation, like a bill drawn on Nature's Reality, and be presented there for payment—with the answer, No effects' " (p. 59).

from the chains of slavery. For years the struggle continued. The Pharoahs stubbornly refused to respond to the cry of Moses. Plague after plague swept through the Pharoah's domain, and yet they insisted on following their recalcitrant path. This tells us something about evil that we must never forget. It never voluntarily relinquishes its throne. Evil is stubborn, hard and determined. It never gives up without a bitter struggle and without the most persistent and almost fanatical resistance.[13] But there is a checkpoint in the universe. Evil cannot permanently organize itself. So after a long and trying struggle the Israelites, through the providence of God, were able to cross the Red Sea, and thereby get out of the hands of Egyptian rule. But like the old guard that never surrenders, the Egyptians, in a desperate attempt to prevent the Israelites from escaping, had their armies to go in the Red Sea behind them. As soon as the Egyptians got into the dried up Sea the parted waters swept back upon them, and the turbulence and momentum of the tidal waves soon drowned all of them. As the Israelites looked back all they could see was here and there a poor drowned body beaten upon the seashore.[14] For the Israelites, this was a great moment. It was the end of a frightful period in their history.[15] It was a joyous daybreak that had come to end the long night of their captivity.

This story symbolizes something basic about the universe. Its meaning is not found in the drowning of a few men, for no one should rejoice at the death or defeat of a human being. This story, at bottom, symbolizes the death of evil. It was the death of inhuman oppression and unjust exploitation.

The death of the Egyptians upon the seashore is a glaring symbol of the ultimate doom of evil in its struggle with good. There is something in the very nature of the universe which is on the side of Israel in its struggle with every Egypt. There is something in the very nature of the universe which ultimately comes to the aid of goodness in its perennial struggle with evil.[16] The New Testament is right when it affirms: "No chastening for the present seemeth to be joyous, but grievous: nevertheless, afterward it yieldeth the peaceable fruit of righteousness."[17] Pharaoh exploits the children of Israel until they are relegated to the status of things rather than persons—nevertheless afterward! Pilate yields to the crowd and crucifies Christ on a cross between two thieves—nevertheless afterward.[18] The early Chris-

---

13. The preceding eight sentences were condensed in the published version: "Egypt struggled to maintain her oppressive yoke, and Israel struggled to gain freedom. Pharaoh stubbornly refused to respond to the cry of Moses, even when plague after plague threatened his domain. This tells us something about evil that we must never forget, namely that evil is recalcitrant and determined, and never voluntarily relinquishes its hold short of a persistent, almost fanatical resistance" (pp. 59–60).

14. Exodus 14:21–30.

15. Brooks, *Selected Sermons*, p. 105: "The parted waves had swept back upon the host of the pursuers. The tumult and terror, which had rent the air, had sunk into silence, and all that the escaped people saw was here and there a poor drowned body beaten up upon the bank, where they stood with the great flood between them and the land of their long captivity and oppression. It meant everything to the Israelites. . . . It was the end of a frightful period in their history."

16. The preceding three sentences were condensed in the published version: "The death of the Egyptians upon the seashore is a vivid reminder that something in the very nature of the universe assists goodness in its perennial struggle with evil" (p. 60).

17. Cf. Hebrews 12:11.

18. Cf. Matthew 27:35–38.

tians are thrown to the lions and carried to the chopping blocks until man's inhumanity to man becomes barbaric and unbelievable—nevertheless afterward.[19]

There is something in this universe which justifies Shakespeare in saying:

> "There's a divinity that shapes our ends,
> Routh-hew them how we will."[20]

and [*James Russell*] Lowell in saying,

> "Though the cause of Evil prosper, yet
> t'is truth alone is strong;"[21]

and [*Alfred*] Tennyson in saying,

> "Good shall fall at last—far off—at last, to
> all, And every winter change to spring."[22]

Notice how we have seen the truth of this text revealed in the contemporary struggle between good, in the form of freedom and justice, and evil, in the form of oppression and colonialism. There are approximately 2,800,000,000 people in the world today. The vast majority of these people are found in Asia and Africa. More than 1,800,000,000 of the peoples of the world are found on these two continents. Just fifteen years ago most of the Asian and African peoples were colonial subjects. They were dominated politically, exploited economically, segregated and humiliated by some foreign power. For years they protested against these grave injustices. Almost every territory in Asia and Africa had some courageous Moses who pleaded with undying passion for the freedom of his people. For some twenty years Mahatma Gandhi, **the Saint of India,** pleaded unrelentingly with the Viceroys, and Governors General, the Prime Ministers and the Kings of England to let his people go. Like the Pharaohs of old, the leaders in power turned deaf ears on these agonizing pleas. Even so great a statesman as Winston Churchill responded to Gandhi's cry for independence by saying: "I did not become his Majesty's First Minister to preside over the liquidation of the British Empire."[23] So for years the struggle continued between two determined forces—the colonial powers struggling to maintain political and economic domination and the Asian and African peoples struggling to gain freedom and independence. In a real sense this has been one of the most momentous and critical struggles of the twentieth century.[24]

---

19. The preceding three sentences were altered in the published version: "Pharaoh exploits the children of Israel—*nevertheless afterward!* Pilate yields to the crowd which crucifies Christ—*nevertheless afterward!* The early Christians are thrown to the lions and carried to the chopping blocks—*nevertheless afterward!*" (p. 60).

20. Shakespeare, *Hamlet,* act 5, sc. 2.

21. James Russell Lowell, "The Present Crisis" (1844).

22. Alfred Lord Tennyson, *In Memoriam A. H. H.* (1850).

23. For a news report and transcript of this speech, see "Prime Minister Churchill's Speech," *New York Times,* 11 November 1942.

24. The preceding two sentences were altered in the published version: "The conflict between two

But in spite of the resistance and recalcitrance of the colonial powers, we have seen the gradual victory of the forces of justice and human dignity. Twenty five years ago there were only three independent countries in the whole continent of Africa. Today there are thirty two countries in Africa that have risen to the status of independence. Just fifteen years ago the British Empire had under its political domination more than 650,000,000 people in Asia and Africa. But today that number has been reduced to less than 60,000,000. Yes, the Red Sea has opened, and the vast majority of the oppressed masses from Asia and Africa have won their independence from the Egypt of colonialism, and are now free to move toward the promised land of economic and cultural stability. As they look back they clearly see the evils of colonialism and imperialism dead upon the seashore.

In our own struggle for freedom and justice in this country we have gradually seen the death of evil. In 1619 the Negro was brought to American as a slave. He was brought here from the soils of Africa.[25] For more than two hundred years Africa was raped and plundered, her native kingdoms disorganized and her people and rulers demoralized. Throughout slavery the Negro was treated in a very inhuman fashion. He was a thing to be used not a person to be respected. He was merely a depersonalized cog in a vast plantation machine.[26] **The famous Dred Scott decision of 1857 well illustrated the status of the Negro during slavery.[27] In this edict the Supreme Court of the nation said that the Negro was not a citizen of the United States, but that he was property subject to the dictates of his owner. It stated farther that the Negro had no rights that the white man was bound to respect.**

But in spite of the Dred Scott decision from so powerful a body as the United States Supreme Court, there were those who had a nagging conscience about slavery. They knew that such an unjust system was a strange paradox in a nation founded on the principle that all men are created equal. In 1820, six years before his death, Thomas Jefferson wrote these melancholy words:

> "But the momentous question (slavery), like a fire bell in the night awakened and filled me with terror. I considered it at once as the knell of the Union. I regret that I am now to die in the belief that the useless sacrifice of themselves by the generation of 1776 to acquire self-government and happiness to their country is to be thrown away, and my only consolation is to be that I live not to weep over it."[28]

---

determined forces, the colonial powers and the Asian and African peoples, has been one of the most momentous and critical struggles of the twentieth century" (p. 61).

25. The preceding two sentences were condensed in the published version: "In 1619, the Negro was brought to America from the soils of Africa" (p. 61).

26. The preceding three sentences were condensed in the published version: "In America, the Negro slave was merely a depersonalized cog in a vast plantation machine" (p. 61).

27. *Scott v. Sandford* (1857).

28. Jefferson to John Holmes Monticello, 22 April 1820, in *Memoir, Correspondence, and Miscellanies, From the Papers of Thomas Jefferson*, vol. 4, ed. Thomas Jefferson Randolph (Charlottesville, Va.: F. Carr, 1829), pp. 323–324.

There were numerous abolishionists who, like Jefferson, were tortured in their hearts by the question of slavery. With keen perception they saw that the immorality of slavery degraded the white master as well as the Negro.

Then came the day when Abraham Lincoln had to face this matter of slavery squarely. His torments are well known, his vacillations were facts. Yet he searched his way to the conclusions embodied in these words, "in giving freedom to the slave we assure freedom to the free, honorable alike in what we give and what we preserve."[29] On this moral foundation Lincoln personally prepared the first draft of the Emancipation Proclamation. This powerful executive order brought an end to chattel slavery. The world significance of the Emancipation Proclamation was colorfully described by that great American, Frederick Douglas, in these words,

> "It recognizes and declares the real nature of the contest and places the North on the side of justice and civilization. . . . Unquestionably the first of January, 1863 is to be the most memorable day in American annals. The Fourth of July was great, but the First of January, when we consider it in all its relations and bearings, is incomparably greater. The one had respect to the mere political birth of a nation; the last concerns the national life and character and is to determine whether that life and character shall be radiantly glorious with all high and noble virtues, or infamously blackened forevermore."[30]

But in spite of the far reaching consequences of the Emancipation Proclamation, it did not bring full freedom to the Negro. While he enjoyed certain political and social opportunities during the days of reconstruction, the Negro soon discovered that these were short lived, and that the Pharaohs of the south were still determined to keep him in slavery. Certainly the Emancipation Proclamation brought him nearer the Red Sea for his passage out of Egypt, but it did not carry him across it. The system of racial segregation came into being backed up by a decision from the United States Supreme Court in 1896.[31] Segregation turned out to be a new form of slavery covered up with certain niceties of complexity. The great struggle of the last half century has been between the forces of justice trying to end the evil system of segregation and the forces of injustice trying to maintain it. ThePharoahs have used legal maneuvors, economic reprisals and even physical violence to hold the Negro in the Egypt of segregation. Despite the patient cry of many a Moses, they refused to let the Negro people go.

But now we are seeing a massive change. A few years ago, through a world shaking decree by the nine justices of the United States Supreme Court, the Red Sea was opened and the forces of justice marched through to the other side.[32] In this deci-

---

29. U.S. Congress, *Message of the President of the United States to the Two Houses of Congress*, 37th Congress, 3d sess., House Document 1 (Washington, D.C., 1862). The endnote in *Strength to Love* mistakenly identifies this speech as "Annual message to Congress 1 December 1820" (p. 144).

30. Douglass, *Douglass' Monthly* (1 January 1863): 1.

31. King refers to *Plessy v. Ferguson* 163 U.S. 537; 16 S. Ct. 1138; 41 L. Ed. 256 (1896).

32. King refers to *Brown v. Board of Education* (1954). The phrase "the forces of justice marched through to the other side" was altered in the published version: "the forces of justice are moving to the other side" (p. 63).

sion the Court affirmed that the old Plessy decision of 1896 must go; that separate facilities are inherently unequal; and that to segregate a child on the basis of race is to deny the child equal protection of the law. This decision came as a great beacon light of hope to millions of disinherited people. As we look back we see the forces of segregation gradually dying on the seashore. The problem is far from solved. There are still gigantic mountains of opposition ahead. But at least we have left Egypt, and with patient yet firm determination we can reach the promise land. Evil in the form of injustice and exploitation cannot survive forever. There is a Red Sea in history that ultimately comes to carry the forces of goodness to victory, and that same Red Sea closes in to bring doom and destruction to the forces of evil.[33]

All of this tells us something basic about life and history. It reminds us that evil carries the seed of its own destruction. In the long run right defeated is stronger than evil triumphant. The great historian, Charles A. Beard, was once asked to give the major lessons that he had learned from history. He answered by saying that he had learned four. Here they are: "First, whom the gods would destroy they must first make mad with power. Second, the mills of God grind slowly, yet they grind exceeding small. Third, the bee fertilizes the flower it robs. Fourth, when it is dark enough you can see the stars."[34] This is not a preacher talking, but a hard-headed historian. His long and painstaking study of history revealed to him that evil has a self-defeating quality. It can go a long way, but then it reaches its limit. There is something in this universe that Greek mythology referred to as the goddess of Nemesis.[35]

We must be careful not to engage in a superficial optimism at this point. We must not conclude that the death of a particular evil means that there will be a moment in history when all evil will lie dead upon the seashore. We must remember that all progress is precarious, and the solution of one problem leaves us standing face to face with another problem. The kingdom of God as a universal reality remains "not yet." Sin exists on every level of man's existence. Because of this, the death of one tyranny presents the threat of the emergence of another tyranny.

But just as we must avoid a superficial optimism, we must also avoid a crippling pessimism. Even though all progress is precarious, there can be real social progress within limits. Even though man's moral pilgrimage may never reach a destination point on earth, his never ceasing strivings can bring him closer and closer to the city

---

33. In the sermon's 1955 version, King accounted for the tenacity of discrimination and segregation, saying: "I can imagine that those Egyptians struggled hard to survive in the Red Sea. They probably saw a ~~long~~ {log} here and even a straw there, and I can imagine them reaching desperately for something as light as a straw trying to survive. This is what is happening to segregation today. It is caught in the midst of a mighty Read Sea, and its advocators are reaching out for every little straw in an attempt to survive. This accounts for the passing of so many absurd laws by our southern legislators. We need not worry, however, for the passing of such laws is indicative of the fact that the advocators of segregation have their backs against the wall. Segregation is drowning today in the rushing waters of historical necessity."

34. Fosdick, "What Keeps Religion Going?" in *Riverside Sermons* (New York: Harper & Brothers, 1958), p. 156: "Professor Charles A. Beard, one of the leading historians of our time, was asked sometime since what major lessons he had learned from history, and he answered that he had learned four. Here they are: 'First, whom the gods would destroy they first make mad with power. Second, the mills of God grind slowly, yet they grind exceedingly small. Third, the bee fertilizes the flower it robs. Fourth, when it is dark enough you can see the stars.'"

35. Nemesis is the ancient Greek goddess of retribution or just punishment.

of righteousness. Even though the kingdom of God may remain "not yet" as a universal reality in history, it may exist in the present in isolated forms, such as in judgment, in personal devotion, and in some group life. "The Kingdom of God," says the New Testament, "is in the midst of you."[36]

Above all, we must be reminded anew that God is at work in his universe. He is not outside the world looking on with a sort of cold indifference. He is here on all the roads of life striving in our striving. Like an ever loving Father, he is working through history for the salvation of his children. So as we struggle to defeat the forces of evil, we do not struggle alone; we have cosmic companionship. The God of the universe struggles with us.[37] In the final analysis evil dies on the seashore not merely because of man's endless struggle against it, but because of God's power to defeat it.

Someone may ask, this morning, why is God so slow in conquering the forces of evil? Why did God allow Hitler to kill six million Jews? Why did God allow slavery to last in America two hundred and forty-four years? Why does God allow blood thirsty mobs to lynch Negro men and women at will, and drown Negro boys and girls at whim? Why doesn't God break in and smash the evil schemes of wicked men?

I do not pretend to understand all of the ways of God and his particular timetable in grappling with evil. Perhaps if he dealt with evil in the overbearing way that we wish he would, God would be defeating his ultimate purpose. He would be making us blind automatoms rather than responsible human beings. God has made us persons and not puppets. In doing this, he had to relinquish a bit of his sovereignty and impose certain limitations upon Himself. If his children were to be free, they would have to make the doing of his will a voluntary choice. Therefore, God cannot impose his will upon his children and maintain his purpose for man. If what God did through sheer omnipotence defeated his purpose, it would be an expression of weakness rather than power. Indeed, power is the ability to fulfill purpose. Action which defeats purpose is weakness.

But whatever the reason for God's unwillingness to deal with evil with an oberbearing immediacy, it does not mean that he is doing nothing. We weak and finite human beings are not alone in our quest for the triumph of righteousness. There is, as Matthew Arnold said, a "power, not ourselves, which makes for righteousness."[38]

We must also remember that as God works to defeat the forces of evil, he does not forget his children who are the victims of these evil forces. He gives us the interior resources to bear the burdens and tribulations of life. When we are in the darkness of some oppressive Egypt, God is a light unto our path. He imbues us with the strength to endure the ordeals of Egypt and he gives us the courage and power to make the journey ahead. When the lamp of hope begins to flicker and the candle of faith begins to run low, he restoreth our souls and gives us renewed vigor to carry

---

36. Luke 17:21 (RSV).

37. The preceding two sentences were condensed in the published version: "As we struggle to defeat the forces of evil, the God of the universe struggles with us" (p. 64).

38. Matthew Arnold, *Literature and Dogma* (New York: Macmillan, 1914), p. 27: "At the time they produced those documents which give to the Old Testament its power and its true character, the *not ourselves* which weighed upon the mind of Israel, and engaged its awe, was the *not ourselves* by which we get the sense for *righteousness,* and whence we find the help to *do right.*"

on. He is with us not only in the noon time of fulfillment, but also in the midnight of despair.

When Mrs. King and I were in India some months ago, we spent a lovely weekend in the State of Karala, the southernmost point of that vast country.[39] While there we went to the beautiful beach of Cape Comorin. In India this beach on the Cape is called "lands end," because this is actually where the land of India comes to an end. There is nothing before you but the broad expanse of the rolling waters. It is one of the most beautiful spots in all the world. It is a point at which three great bodies of water met—the Indian Ocean, the Arabian Sea and the Bay of Bengal. Mrs. King and I took a seat on a huge rock that was slightly protruded into the ocean. We sat there enthralled by the vastness of the ocean and its terrifying immensities. We noticed the waves as they unfolded in almost rhythmic succession. As the rolling waters would smash against the bottom of the rock on which we were seated, they had a sort of oceanic music that brought sweetness to the ear. In this beautiful setting we turned our eyes to the west and saw the magnificent sun standing like a great cosmic ball of fire. It was gradually going down and down. Since we could see nothing before us but water, it appeared that the sun would sink into the very ocean itself.[40] Just as it was almost out of sight, Mrs. King touched me and said, "look Martin, isn't it beautiful!" I looked around and there I saw another ball standing in all of its scintilating beauty. It was the moon. As the sun appeared to be sinking into the ocean, the moon appeared to be rising out of the ocean. I looked back to the west and watched the sun as it finally passed completely out of sight, and noticed how darkness gradually engulfed the earth. At this point I looked again to the east and the moon was still rising, and its radiant light was shining supreme.

I said to my wife, "this is a real analogy of what often happens in life." We all have experiences when the light of day goes out and we are left standing in some dark and desolate midnight—moments when our noblest dreams are shattered and our highest hopes are blasted; moments when we are the victims of some tragic injustice and some terrible exploitation.[41] During these moments our spirits are almost eaten away by gloom and despair; we feel that there is no light anywhere. But ever and again, when these moments come, we find ourselves taking the eastward look, only to discover that there is another light which shines even in the darkness. Something happens to transform "the spear of frustration into a shaft of light."[42]

This would be a miserable, terrible and unbearable world if God had only one light. But we can be consoled by the fact that God has two lights—a light to guide us in the brightness of the day when hopes are fulfilled and circumstances are favorable and a light to guide us in the darkness of the midnight when frustrations are

---

39. For more on the Kings' journey to India, see Introduction, in *Papers* 5:4–12.

40. The preceding three sentences were altered and condensed in the published version: "To the west we saw the magnificent sun, a great cosmic ball of fire, appear to sink into the very ocean itself" (p. 65).

41. In the published version: "We have experiences when the light of day vanishes, leaving us in some dark and desolate midnight—moments when our highest hopes are turned into shambles of despair or when we are the victims of some tragic injustice and some terrible exploitation" (p. 65).

42. Cf. Thurman, *Deep River,* p. 39. The preceding two sentences were condensed in the published version: "But ever and again, we look toward the east and discover that there is another light which shines even in the darkness, and 'the spear of frustration' is transformed 'into a shaft of light' " (p. 66).

real and the slumbering giants of gloom and hopelessness are on the verge of rising up in our souls. Therefore we never need walk in darkness. This was what the Psalmist meant when he said:

> "Whither shall I go from thy spirit? Or whither shall I flee from thy presence? If I ascend up into heaven, thou art there: If I make my bed in hell, behold, thou art there. If I take the wings of the morning, and dwell in the uttermost part of the sea; even there shall thy hand lead me, and thy right hand shall hold me. If I say, surely the darkness shall cover me; even the night shall be light about me. Yea, the darkness hideth not from thee; but the night shineth as the day: the darkness and the light are both alike to thee."[43]

This is the faith that will keep us going in our struggle to escape the bondage of every evil Egypt. This is the faith that will be a lamp unto our weary feet and a light unto our meandering path.[44] If such a faith ever leaves the spirit of man, he will stand in immediate candidacy for nonbeing, and his highest dreams will go silently to the dust.[45]

TDd. MLKP-MBU: Box 119A.

---

43. Psalm 139:7–12.

44. Cf. Psalm 119:105.

45. This sentence was altered in the published version: "Without such faith, man's highest dreams will pass silently to the dust" (p. 66). In the 1955 version, King concluded the sermon by turning from his analysis of segregation to one of "our own personal lives. There is not only an Egypt out in the world, but there are Egyptians in our souls. What is your Egyptian? Is it some corroding passion? Years, years ago you became its captive. Perhaps you cannot at all remember when. Perhaps . . . you were born into its captivity." King then reflected on the moment when "the conviction broke out within you like burning fire that this Egyptian could be conquered; that it could pass out of existence, finally dying upon the seashore." He ended the sermon with the observation: "Isn't this the peculiar insistence of the christian religion? It is our conviction that if an individual sufficiently commits himself to Christ he can conquer any Egyptian that might well up in his soul. Christ is histories eternal Red Sea who, on the one hand, stands as Savior and Redeemer aiding the forces of good to escape some evil Egypt, and on the other hand, as judge condemning the forces of evil to ultimate doom. . . . My friends, get out of Egypt! Get something done! Realize that your life is not made to be dominated by evil Egyptians Go out and leave your Egyptian dead. Your ultimate destiny is the promised land."

Draft of Chapter X, "Shattered Dreams"

[July 1962–March 1963]
[Atlanta, Ga.]

King blends thoughts on unmet expectations from preachers Frederick Meek, Leslie Weatherhead, Howard Thurman, and J. Wallace Hamilton in this sermon. He writes that African Americans have "long dreamed of freedom," and asserts, "Moreover, through our suffering in this oppressive prison and our non-violent struggle to get out of it, we may give the kind of spiritual dynamic to western civilization that it so desperately needs to survive." As in the version of this sermon

he preached at Dexter in 1959, King elaborates on the apostle Paul's unfulfilled   July 1962–
desire to travel to Spain.[1] *He asks the congregation to learn from Paul's "unwanted*   March 1963
and unfortunate circumstance . . . in developing the capacity to accept the finite
disappointment and yet cling to the infinite hope."

"When I take my journey into Spain, I will come unto you." Romans 15:24.

Our sermon today brings us face to face with one of the most agonizing problems of human experience. Very few, if any, of us are able to see all of our hopes fulfilled. So many of the hopes and promises of our mortal days are unrealized. **Each of us, like Shubert, begins composing a symphony that is never finished.**[2] There is much truth in George Frederick Watts' imaginative portrayal of Hope in his picture entitled Hope. He depicts Hope as seated atop our planet, but her head is sadly bowed and her fingers are plucking one unbroken harp string.[3] Who has not had to face the agony of blasted hopes and shattered dreams?

If we turn back to the life of the Apostle Paul, we find a very potent example of this problem of disappointed hopes.[4] In his letter to the Christians at Rome Paul wrote: "When I take my journey into Spain, I will come unto you." It was one of Paul's greatest hopes to go to Spain, the edge of the then known world, where he could further spread the Christian gospel. And on his way to Spain, he planned to visit that valiant group of Christians in Rome, the capital city of the world. He looked forward to the day that he would have personal fellowship with those people whom he greeted in his letter as "Christians in the household of Caesar."[5] The more he thought about it the more his heart exuded with joy. All of his attention now would be turned toward the preparation of carrying the gospel to the city of Rome with its many gods, and to Spain, the end of the then known world.[6]

But notice what happened to this noble dream and this glowing hope that

---

1. King, Unfulfilled Hopes, Sermon Delivered at Dexter Avenue Baptist Church, 5 April 1959, pp. 359–367 in this volume. King annotated the chapter titled "Shattered Dreams" in his personal copy of J. Wallace Hamilton's *Horns and Halos in Human Nature* (pp. 25–34).

2. Franz Schubert (1797–1828), an Austrian composer, completed only two movements of his eighth symphony.

3. British sculptor and painter George Frederick Watts produced "Hope" in 1886; George A. Buttrick, *Sermons Preached in a University Church* (New York: Abingdon Press, 1959), p. 110: "Thus George Frederick Watts depicts Hope herself as seated atop our planet indeed, but with head forlornly bowed and her fingers plucking one unbroken harp string."

4. The phrase "If we turn back to the life of the Apostle Paul" was replaced by "In Paul's letter to the Roman Christians" in the published version (King, *Strength to Love*, p. 78).

5. The preceding two sentences were altered in the published version: "On his return he wished to have personal fellowship with that valiant group of Roman Christians" (p. 78).

6. In the published version: "His preparations now centered in carrying the gospel to the capital city of Rome and to Spain at the distant fringe of the empire" (p. 78). Meek, "Strength in Adversity": "Paul had high hopes of going to Spain, the edge of the then known world, that he might take there his word about the Christian Gospel. And on the way he planned to visit the Christian folk in Rome, the capital city of the world. Paul wanted to see that little valiant group of Christians, folk whom he saluted in his letter as 'Christians in the household of Caesar.' The more he thought about his planned journey, the more his heart was warmed by it. Imagine, Rome with its many gods and with its great power, subject to the Christian Gospel."

joy. [All of his attention now would be turned toward the preparation
His preparations now centered in
of] carrying the gospel to the *capital* city of Rome [with its many gods] and to
Spain, *at the distant fringe of the empire.* the end of the then known world.]

[But notice what happened to this noble dream and this *what a* glowing
hope *stirred within* [that gripped] Paul's [life]. *heart! But* *according to the pattern of his hopes* He never got to Rome [in the sense that
Because of his daring faith in Jesus Christ, he was indeed taken there but
he had hoped. He went there only *as* a prisoner and [not as a free man.]
was held captive
He spent his days in that ancient city in a little prison cell[G] [held captive

because of his daring faith in Jesus Christ. Neither was Paul able to]
Nor did he ever *look upon*
walk the dusty roads of Spain, nor [see] its curvacious slopes, nor watch
He was put to death, we presume, as *for Christ*
its busy coast life[B] [because he died] a martyr['s death] in Rome. [The story
is a
of] Paul's life [was the] tragic story of a shattered dream [and a blasted hope.]
mirrors many similar
Life [is full of this] experience. [There is hardly anyone here

this morning who has not set out for some distant Spain, some momentous
cap
goal, *or* some glorious realization, only to [find that we had to] settle for
learn at last that he must
much less? We [were] never [able to] walk as free men through the streets
circumstances decree that we live within
of our Rome[.] Instead [we were forced to live our lives in a] little con-
Written across our lives is
fining cell [which circumstance had built around us. / Life seems to have] a
within *runs* *vein.*
fatal flaw[B] and history [seems to have] an irrational and unpredictable
Like Abraham, we too sojourn in the land of promise, but so often we do not become "heirs with him of the same promise." Always
[streak. Ultimately we all die not having received what was promised. *our reach exceeds our grasp.*

Our dreams are constantly tossed and blown by staggering winds of

disappointment.]
struggling for *to achieve* *Mahatma Gandhi*
[Mahatma Gandhi,] after [long] years [of struggle for] independence, *witnessed*
cap
[dreamed of a united India, only to see that dream trampled over by a]
and the subsequent
bloody religious war between the Hindus and the Moslems [which led to

Edited typescript of second page of the sermon "Shattered Dreams" (Chapter X, *Strength to Love*).

gripped Paul's life. He never got to Rome in the sense that he had hoped. He went there only as a prisoner and not as a free man. He spent his days in that ancient city in a little prison cell, held captive because of his daring faith in Jesus Christ. Neither was Paul able to walk the dusty roads of Spain, nor see its curvacious slopes, nor watch its busy coast life, because he died a martyr's death in Rome.[7] The story of Paul's life was the tragic story of a shattered dream **and a blasted hope.**

Life is full of this experience. There is hardly anyone here this morning who has not set out for some distant Spain, some momentous goal, some glorious realization, only to find that we had to settle for much less. We were never able to walk as free men through the streets of our Rome. Instead we were forced to live our lives in a little confining cell which circumstance had built around us.[8] Life seems to have a fatal flaw, and history seems to have an irrational and unpredictable streak. Ultimately we all die not having received what was promised. Our dreams are constantly tossed and blown by staggering winds of disappointment.[9]

Mahatma Gandhi, after long years of struggle for independence, dreamed of a united India, only to see that dream trampled over by a bloody religious war between the Hindus and the Moslems which led to the division of India and Pakistan.[10] Woodrow Wilson dreamed of a league of nations, but he died with the dream shattered. The Negro slaves of America longed for freedom with all their passionate endeavors, but many died without receiving it. Jesus, prayed in the garden of Gethsemane that the cup might pass, but he had to drink it to the last bitter dregs.[11] The Apostle Paul prayed fervently for the "thorn" to be removed from his flesh, but he went to his grave with this desire unfulfilled.[12] **Shattered dreams! Blasted hopes! This is life.**

---

7. Meek, "Strength in Adversity": "Paul *did* get to Rome, but he went as a prisoner and not as a free man. Paul lived in Rome at the expense of the Roman government in a prison cell, held captive because of his faith. And Paul never saw the mountains and the plains and the coast life of Spain, because he died a martyr's death before the hope of his mission could ever be fulfilled."

8. Meek, "Strength in Adversity": "How many of us in one way or another have dreamed our dreams of going to Spain, of fulfilling some far reaching hope, of doing valiantly for a great cause. But we never reached the Spain of our dreams. We had to settle for a far shorter journey. We were never able to wander freely about the streets of our Rome. Instead, we looked out through the little windows of some confining cell which the circumstances of life had built around us."

9. The preceding two sentences were replaced in the published version: "Like Abraham, we too sojourn in the land of promise, but so often we do not become 'heirs with him of the same promise.' Always our reach exceeds our grasp" (p. 79).

10. The Muslim state of Pakistan was founded as a provision of the Indian Independence Act of 1947. Immediately following independence, border disputes and religious conflicts erupted between India and Pakistan, killing hundreds of thousands and displacing millions. The preceding sentence was altered in the published version: "After struggling for years to achieve independence, Mahatma Gandhi witnessed a bloody religious war between the Hindus and the Moslems, and the subsequent division of India and Pakistan shattered his heart's desire for a united nation" (p. 79).

11. Cf. Matthew 26:39.

12. Cf. 2 Corinthians 12:7–10; Howard Thurman, *Deep River,* pp. 34–35: "Jesus, in the garden of Gethsemane, prayed that the cup might pass, but he had to drink it to the last bitter dregs. The Apostle Paul prayed for the 'thorn' to be taken from his flesh, but he had to carry the thorn to his grave." In the published version the phrase "he went to his grave with this desire unfulfilled" was replaced with "the pain and annoyance continued to the end of his days" (p. 79).

What does one do under such circumstances? This is a central question, for we must determine how to live in a world where our highest hopes are not fulfilled.

It is quite possible for one to seek to deal with this problem by distilling all his frustrations into a core of bitterness and resentment of spirit. The persons who follow this path develop a hardness of attitude and a coldness of heart. They develop a bitter hatred for life itself. In fact, hate becomes the dominant force in their lives. They hate God, they hate the people around them, and they hate themselves. Since they can't corner God or life, they take out their vengeance on other people. If they are married they are extremely cruel to their mate. If they have children, they treat them in the most inhuman manner. When they are not beating them, they are screaming at them; and when they are not screaming at them, they are cursing them. In short, they are mean.[13] They love nobody and they demand no love. They trust no one and do not expect anyone to trust them. They find fault in everything and everybody. They always complain. You have seen people like this. They are cruel, vindictive and merciless.[14]

The terrible thing about this approach is that it poisons the soul and scars the personality. It does more harm to the person who harbours it than to anyone else. Many physical ailments are touched off by bitter resentment. Medical science has revealed that many cases of arthritis, gastric ulcer and asthma are caused by the long continuance of emotional poison in the mind. They are often psychosomatic, that is to say, they show in the body, but they are caused in the mind. There can be no doubt that resentment is a harmful reaction to disappointment and capable of setting up actual physical illness.[15]

Another possible reaction to the experience of blasted hopes is for the individu-

---

13. Thurman, *Deep River*, p. 37: "It is quite possible to become obsessed with the idea of making everything and everybody atone for one's predicament. All one's frustrations may be distilled into a core of bitterness and disillusionment that expresses itself in a hardness of attitude and a total mercilessness—in short, one may become mean. You have seen people like that. They seem to have a demoniacal grudge against life." King also paraphrased this passage in a handwritten note for a sermon; see King, Notes on *Deep River* by Howard Thurman, October 1960.

14. The preceding twelve sentences were altered in the published version: "Because he cannot corner God or life, he releases his pent-up vindictiveness in hostility toward other people. He may be extremely cruel to his mate and inhuman to his children. In short, meanness becomes his dominating characteristic. He loves no one and requires love from no one. He trusts no one and does not expect others to trust him. He finds fault in everything and everybody, and he continually complains" (p. 79). King's notes on *Deep River* also included these words: "They trust no one and have no interest in doing so. . . . For them life is essentially evil, and they are essentially vengeful. . . . They have nothing to lose because they have lost everything" (King, Notes on *Deep River*, October 1960).

15. The preceding four sentences were altered in the published version: "Medical science reveals that such physical ailments as arthritis, gastric ulcer, and asthma have on occasion been encouraged by bitter resentments. Psychosomatic medicine, dealing with bodily sicknesses which come from mental illnesses, shows how deep resentment may result in physical deterioration" (p. 80). Leslie Weatherhead, "The Nature of Christ's Temptations," in *The Key Next Door* (New York: Abingdon Press, 1960), pp. 50–51: "I must speak very carefully here, but it is known that arthritis is sometimes touched off by resentment. . . . it would be foolish to overlook the fact that some illnesses are what we now delight to call psychosomatic. That is to say, they show in the body, but they are caused or touched off in the mind, and arthritis is one of them. Asthma is another; the gastric ulcer is another. . . . There can be no doubt that resentment, long harbored in the mind, is a faulty reaction to grief and capable of setting up actual physical illness."

als to withdraw completely into themselves. They become absolute introverts. They allow no one to come into their lives and they refuse to go out to others. Such persons give up in the struggle of life. They lose the zest for living. They attempt to escape the disappointments of life by lifting their minds to a transcendent realm of cold indifference. Detachment is the word that may describe them. They are too unconcerned to love and they are too passionless to hate. They are too detached to be selfish and too lifeless to be unselfish. They are too indifferent to experience moments of joy and they are too cold to experience moments of sorrow.[16] In short, such people are neither dead nor alive; they merely exist. Their eyes behold the beauties of nature, and yet they do not see them. Their ears are subjected to the majestic sounds of great music, and yet they do not hear it. Their hands gently touch a charming little baby, and yet they do not feel him. There is nothing of the aliveness of life left in them; there is only the dull motion of bare existence. Their disappointed hope leads them to a crippling cynicism. With Omar Khayyam they would affirm:

> "The Worldly Hope men set their
> Hearts upon turns to ashes—or it
> prospers; and anon,
> Like Snow upon the Desert's dusty Face
> Lighting a little Hour or two—is gone."[17]

One can very easily see the danger of this reaction. It is, at bottom, based on an attempt to escape life. Psychiatrists tell us the more individuals attempt to engage in these escapes from reality the thinner and thinner their personalities become until ultimately they split. This is one of the causal sources of the schiophrenic personality.

Another way that people respond to life's disappointments is to adopt a philosophy of fatalism. This is the idea that whatever happens must happen, and that all events are determined by necessity. Fatalism implies something foreordained and inescapable. The people who subscribe to ~~The~~ this philosophy follow a course of absolute resignation. They resign themselves to what they consider their fate. They see themselves as little more than helpless orphans thrown out in the terrifying immensities of space. Since they believe that man has no freedom, they seek neither to deliberate nor to make decisions. They wait passively for external forces to deliberate and decide for them. They never actively seek to change their circumstances, since they believe that all circumstances, like the Greek tragedies, are controlled by irresistible and foreordained forces. Often the fatalists are very religious people who see God as the determiner and controller of destiny. **Everything, they feel, is God's will, however evil it happens to be.** This view is expressed in the verse of one of our Christian hymns:

> "Though dark my path and sad my lot,
> Let me be still and murmur not,

---

16. The repetition of the phrase "they are" in the preceding three sentences was omitted in the published version (p. 80).

17. Khayyám, *Rubáiyát*, XVI.

But breathe the prayer divinely taught,
Thy will be done."[18]

So the fatalists go through life with the conviction that freedom is a myth. They end up with a paralyzing determinism, saying that we are

"But helpless Pieces of the Game He plays
Upon this chequer-board of Night and Days,

and that we need not trouble our minds about the future—**"Who knows?" Nor about the past, for**

"The Moving Finger writes, and having writ
moves on. . . . Neither tears not wit can
cancel out a line of it."[19]

For one to sink in the quicksands of this type of fatalism is both intellectually and psychologically stiffling. Since freedom is a part of the essence of man, the fatalist, in his denial of freedom, becomes a puppet and not a person. He is right in his conviction that there is no absolute freedom, and that freedom always operates within the framework of predestined structure. Thus a man is free to go north from Atlanta to Washington or South from Atlanta to Miami. But he is not free to go north to Miami or South to Washington. Freedom is always within destiny. But there is freedom. We are both free and destined. Freedom is the act of deliberating, deciding and responding within our destined nature. Even if destiny prevents our going to some attractive Spain, there still remains in us the capacity to take this disappointment, to {answer} it, to make our individual response to it, to stand up to it and do something with it. Fatalism doesn't see this. It leaves the individual stymied and helplessly inadequate for life.

But even more, fatalism is based on a terrible conception of God. It sees everything that happens, evil and good alike, as the will of God. Any healthy religion will rise above the idea that God wills evil. It is true that God has to permit evil in order to preserve the freedom of man. But this does not mean that he causes it. That which is willed is intended, and the idea that God intends for a child to be born blind, or that God gives cancer to this person and inflicts insanity upon another is rank heresy. Such a false idea makes God into a devil rather than a loving Father. So fatalism is a tragic and dangerous way to deal with the problem of unfulfilled dreams.[20]

What, then, is the answer? We must accept our unwanted and unfortunate circumstance and yet cling to a radiant hope. The answer lies in developing the capacity to accept the finite disappointment and yet cling to the infinite hope. In speak-

---

18. King quotes Charlotte Elliott's hymn, "My God and Father! While I Stray" (1834).

19. King quotes from Khayyám, *Rubáiyát,* LXIX and LXXI. The final line in the published version of this sermon read: "nor all your Piety nor Wit / Shall lure it back to cancel half a Line, / Nor all your Tears wash out a Word of it" (p. 81).

20. The phrase "as are bitterness and withdrawal" was inserted at the end of this sentence in the published version (p. 82).

ing of acceptance, I do not mean the grim, bitter acceptance of those who are fatalistic. I mean the kind of acceptance that Jeremiah achieved as expressed in the words, "this is my grief and I must bear it."[21]

This means sitting down and honestly confronting your shattered dream. Don't follow the escapist method of trying "to put it out of your mind." This will lead to repression which is always psychologically injurious. Place it at the forefront of your mind and stare daringly at it. Then ask yourself, "how can I transform this liability into an asset?" "How can I, confined in some narrow Roman cell, unable to reach life's ~~Rome~~ {Spain}, transform this cell from a dungeon of shame to a haven of redemptive suffering." Almost anything that happens to us can be woven into the purposes of God. It may lengthen our cords of sympathy. It may break our self-centered pride. Even the cross, which was willed by wicked men, was woven by God into the redemption of the world.

Many of the world's most influential characters have transformed their thorns into a crown. Charles Darwin was almost always physically ill. Robert Louis Stevenson was inflicted with tuberculosis. Helen Keller was blind and deaf.[22] But they did not respond to these conditions with bitter resentment and grim fatalism. Rather they stood up to life, and, through the exercise of a dynamic will, transformed a negative into a positive.[23] [*George Frideric*] Handel confronted the most difficult and trying circumstances in his life. Says his biographer: "His health and his fortunes had reached the lowest ebb. His right side had become paralyzed, and his money was all gone. His creditors seized him and threatened him with imprisonment. For a brief time he was tempted to give up the fight—but then he rebounded again to compose the greatest of his inspirations, the epic "Messiah." So, the "Hallelujah Chorus" was born, not in a desired Spain, but in a narrow cel of undesirable circumstances.

Wanting Spain and getting a narrow cell in a Roman prison, how familiar an experience that is! But to take the Roman prison, the broken, the left-over of a disappointed expectation, and make of it an opportunity to serve God's purpose, how much less familiar that is![24] Yet, powerful living has always involved such a victory over one's own soul and one's situation.

We as a people have long dreamed of freedom, but we are still confined to an oppressive prison of segregation and discrimination.[25] Must we respond to this disappointed hope with bitterness and cynicism? Certainly not, for this will only distort and

---

21. Cf. Jeremiah 10:19.

22. Fosdick, *On Being a Real Person*, p. 6: "Charles Darwin, as he himself said, 'almost continually unwell'; Robert Louis Stevenson, with his tuberculosis; Helen Keller, blind and deaf."

23. The preceding six sentences were condensed in the published version: "Many of the world's most influential personalities have exchanged their thorns for crowns. Charles Darwin, suffering from a recurrent physical illness; Robert Louis Stevenson, plagued with tuberculosis; and Helen Keller, inflicted with blindness and deafness, responded not with bitterness or fatalism, but rather by the exercise of a dynamic will transformed negative circumstances into positive assets" (p. 82).

24. The preceding two sentences were condensed in the published version: "How familiar is the experience of longing for Spain and settling for a Roman prison, and how less familiar the transforming of the broken remains of a disappointed expectation into opportunities to serve God's purpose!" (p. 83).

25. The word "Negroes" replaced "as a people" in the published version (p. 83).

poison our personality. Must we conclude that the existence of segregation is a part of the will of God, and thereby resign ourselves to the fate of oppression. Of course not, for such a course would be blasphemy, because it attributes to God something that should be attributed to the devil. Moreover, to accept passively an unjust system is to cooperate with that system; thereby the oppressed become as evil as the oppressor. Our most fruitful course of action will be to stand up with a courageous determination, moving on non-violently amid obstacles and setbacks, facing disappointments and yet clinging to the hope. It will be this determination and final refusal to be stopped that will eventually open the door of fulfillment. While still in the prison of segregation we must ask, "How can I turn this liability into an asset?" It is possible that, recognizing the necessity of suffering, we can make of it a virtue. To suffer in a righteous cause is to grow to our humanity's full stature.[26] If only to save ourselves from bitterness, we need the vision to see the ordeals of this generation as the opportunity to transfigure ourselves and American society. Moreover, through our suffering **in this oppressive prison** and our non-violent struggle to get out of it, we may give the kind of spiritual dynamic to western civilization that it so desperately needs to survive.

Of course some of us will die having not received the promise of freedom. But we must continue to move on. On the one hand we must accept the finite disappointment, but in spite of this we must maintain the infinite hope. This is the only way that we will be able to live without the fatigue of bitterness and the drain of resentment.

This was the secret of the survival of our slave foreparents. Slavery was a low, dirty, inhuman business. When the slaves were taken from Africa, they were cut off from their family ties, and chained to ships like beasts. There is nothing more tragic than to cut a person off from his family, his language, and his roots.[27] In many instances, during the days of slavery, husbands were cut off from wives and children were separated from parents. The women were often forced to satisfy the biological urges of the master himself, and the slave husband was powerless to intervene.[28] Yet, in spite of these inexpressible cruelties, our foreparents continued to live and develop. Even though they could expect nothing the next morning but the long rows of cotton, the sweltering heat and the rawhide whip of the overseer, they continued to dream of a better day.[29] They accepted the fact of slavery and yet clung to the hope of freedom. Their hope continued even amid a seemingly hopeless situation. They

---

26. The preceding two sentences were condensed in the published version: "By recognizing the necessity of suffering in a righteous cause, we may possibly achieve our humanity's full stature" (p. 83).

27. Thurman, *Deep River*, p. 35: "But it must be intimately remembered that slavery was a dirty, sordid, inhuman business. When the slaves were taken from their homeland, the primary social unit was destroyed, and all immediate tribal and family ties were ruthlessly broken . . . There is no more hapless victim than one who is cut off from family, from language, from one's roots."

28. Thurman, *Deep River*, p. 36: "In instance after instance, husbands were sold from wives, children were separated from parents; a complete and withering attack was made on the sanctity of the home and the family. Added to all this, the slave women were constantly at the mercy of the lust and rapacity of the master himself, while the slave husband or father was powerless to intervene."

29. Thurman, *Deep River*, p. 35: "For the slave, freedom was not on the horizon; there stretched ahead the long road down which there marched in interminable lines only the rows of cotton, the sizzling heat, the riding overseer with his rawhide whip, the auction block where families were torn asunder, the barking of the bloodhounds."

took the pessimism of life and filtered it in their own souls and fashioned it into a creative optimism that gave them strength to carry on. With their bottomless vitality they continually transformed the darkness of frustration into the light of hope. They had the "courage to be."[30]

When I first flew from New York to London, it was in the days of the propellor type aircraft. The flight over took 9½ hours. (The jets can make the flight in six hours.) On returning to the States from London I discovered that the flying time would be twelve hours and a half. This confused me for the moment. I knew that the distance returning to New York was the same as the distance from New York to London. Why this difference of three hours, I asked myself. Soon the pilot walked through the plane to greet the passengers. As soon as he got to me I raised the question of the difference in flight time. His answer was simple and to the point. "You must understand something about the winds," he said. "When we leave New York," he continued, "the winds are in our favor; we have a strong tail wind. When we return to New York from London, the winds are against us; we have a strong head wind." And then he said, "don't worry though, these four engines are fully capable of battling the winds, and even though it takes three hours longer we will get to New York." Well, life is like this. There are times when the winds are in our favor— moments of joy, moments of great triumph, moments of fulfillment. But there are times when the winds are against us, times when strong head winds of disappointment and sorrow beat unrelentingly upon our lives.[31] We must decide whether we will allow the winds to overwhelm us or whether we will journey across life's mighty Atlantic with our inner spiritual engines equipped to go in spite of the winds. This refusal to be stopped, this "courage to be," this determination to go on living "in spite of," is the God in man. He who has made this discovery knows that no burden can overwhelm him and no wind of adversity can blow his hope away. He can stand anything that can happen to him.

Certainly the Apostle Paul had this type {of} "courage to be." His life was a continual round of disappointments. He started out for Spain and ended up in a Roman prison. He wanted to go to Bithynia but ended up in Troas.[32] Everywhere he turned he faced broken plans. He was jailed, mobbed beaten and shipwrecked in his gallant program of ~~preaching~~ spreading the gospel of Christ. But he did not allow these conditions to overwhelm him.[33] "I have learned," he said, "in whatsoever state I am, therewith to be content."[34] Paul did not mean that he had learned to be

---

30. King invokes the title to Paul Tillich's book *The Courage to Be.*

31. The preceding three sentences were altered in the published version: "At times in our lives the tail winds of joy, triumph, and fulfillment favor us, and at times the head winds of disappointment, sorrow, and tragedy beat unrelentingly against us" (p. 84).

32. Cf. Acts 16:7–9.

33. In the published version, the preceding five sentences were altered: "On every side were broken plans and shattered dreams. Planning to visit Spain, he was consigned to a Roman prison. Hoping to go to Bithynia, he was sidetracked to Troas. His gallant mission for Christ was measured 'in journeyings often, in perils of waters, in perils of robbers, in perils by mine own countrymen, in perils by the heathen, in perils in the city, in perils in the wilderness, in perils in the sea, in perils among false brethren.' Did he permit these conditions to master him?" (pp. 84–85).

34. Philippians 4:11.

which to close, he said, "We're leaving now for France, the trenches, and maybe to die." He didn't mean to say that. Looking around embarrassedly, he said, "Can anybody tell us how to die?" There was an awkward pause as though he had said the wrong thing, and a period of strange silence in which nobody said anything. Then someone walked quietly to the piano and began to sing the aria from "Elijah"—"O Rest in the Lord." In the quiet that followed, as deep called unto deep, every man's soul was making its way back to some half-remembered thing to which he always had belonged.

This is it. This is the Life. "Thou hast made us for Thyself, O God, and restless are our souls until they rest in Thee...."

SHATTERED DREAMS

Not many days after the younger son gathered all together, and took his journey ...   LUKE 15:13.

"NOT MANY DAYS after..." What was he doing in those few days while he was getting ready to be off? He was dreaming, dreaming a strange, wild dream. He was thinking of that far country and what it held for him. His imagination had gone prodigal before he did. In his dreams he had pictured the far land before he arrived there.

A wonderful, wonderful mystery are dreams, the life that goes on in the mind, the picture-making power of imagination. Everyone carries around in him his own private movie theater. If you could open the skull of a person and watch the flow of thought for any given half hour, day or night, the images, the ideas, the little pictures flashing on and off the screen of consciousness, you would see a stranger and more entertaining sight than you will ever see in any movie theater.

Dreams are the stuff of which life is made. All great things are born there—art, music, books, buildings. "All that we glory in," said Edwin Markham, "was once a dream"—a little picture in the mind. Garibaldi's mother named him, in his

King writes an outline about dreams that do not come true next to a chapter titled "Shattered Dreams" in his copy of Hamilton's 1954 book *Horns and Halos in Human Nature* (pp. 24–25).

complacent. There is nothing in the life of Paul which could characterize him as a complacent man. [*Edward*] Gibbon in his <u>Decline and Fall of the Roman Empire</u> says, "Paul has done more to promote the idea of freedom and liberty than any man who set foot on western soil." This does not sound like a complacent man. So Paul is not saying that he had learned to dwell in a valley of stagnant complacency. Neither is he saying that he had learned to resign himself to some tragic fate. Paul meant that he had learned to stand up amid the disappointment of life without despairing. He had discovered the distinction between a tranquil soul and the outward accidents of circumstance. He had learned to live from within instead of from without.[35]

The person who makes this magnificent discovery will, like Paul, be the recipient of true peace. Indeed, he will possess that peace which passeth all understanding.[36] The peace which the world understands is that which comes with the removal of the burden or the pain. It is a peace which only comes on beautiful summer days, when the skies are clear and the sun shines in all of its scintilating beauty. It is a peace that comes when the pocketbook is filled and the body has no aches or pains. It is a peace that can only come by reaching the Spain of one's hope and staying out of the filthy jail. But this is not true peace. Real peace is something inward, a tranquility of soul amid terrors of trouble. It is inner calm amid the howl and rage of outer storm. True peace is like a hurricane. Around its circomference rages howling and jostling winds of destruction, while at its center all is serenely quiet. This is why true peace passeth all understanding. It is easy to understand how one can have peace when everything is going right, and one is "up and in." But it is difficult to understand how one can have unruffled tranquility when he is "down and out," when the burden still lies heavy upon one's shoulders, when the pain still throbs annoyingly in one's body, when the prison cell still surrounds one with unbearable agony, and when the disappointment is inescapably real. True peace is peace amid story, tranquility amid disaster. It is a calm that exceeds all description and all explanation.[37]

Peace was Jesus' chief legacy. He said, "peace I leave with you, my peace I give

---

35. The previous six sentences were altered in the published version: "Does this sound like complacency? Nor did he learn resignation to inscrutable fate. By discovering the distinction between spiritual tranquillity and the outward accidents of circumstance, Paul learned to stand tall and without despairing amid the disappointments of life" (p. 85).

36. Cf. Philippians 4:7.

37. The preceding paragraph was altered in the published version: "Each of us who makes this magnificent discovery will, like Paul, be a recipient of that true peace 'which passeth all understanding.' Peace as the world commonly understands it comes when the summer sky is clear and the sun shines in scintillating beauty, when the pocketbook is full, when the mind and body are free of ache and pain, and when the shores of Spain have been reached. But this is not true peace. The peace of which Paul spoke is a calmness of soul amid terrors of trouble, inner tranquillity amid the howl and rage of outer storm, the serene quiet at the center of a hurricane amid the howling and jostling winds. We readily understand the meaning of peace when everything is going right and when one is 'up and in,' but we are baffled when Paul speaks of that true peace which comes when a man is 'down and out,' when burdens lie heavy upon his shoulders, when pain throbs annoyingly in his body, when he is confined by the stone walls of a prison cell, and when disappointment is inescapably real. True peace, a calm that exceeds all description and all explanation, is peace amid storm and tranquillity amid disaster" (p. 85).

unto you."[38] **This peace is there for us to ~~iner~~ inherit if we will only accept it through faith.** Paul at Philippi, body beaten and bloody, incarcerated in a dark and desolate dungeon, feet chained and spirit tired, could joyously sing the songs of Zion at midnight.[39] The early Christians, with the fierce faces of hungry lions standing before them and the excruciating pain of the chopping block only a step away, could face these pending disasters rejoicing that they had been ~~dem~~ deemed worthy to suffer disgrace for the sake of Christ. The Negro slaves, standing tiredly in the sizzling heat with the whip lashes freshly etched on their backs could sing triumphantly, "By and by I'm gwin to lay down this heavy load."[40] This was peace amid storm.[41]

In the final analysis our ability to deal creatively with shattered dreams and blasted hopes will be determined by the extent of our faith in God. A genuine faith will imbue us with the conviction that there is a God beyond time and a Life beyond Life. Thus we know that we are not alone in any circumstance, however dismal and catastrophic it may be. God dwells with us in life's confining and oppressive cells. And even if we die there having not received the earthly promise, he will walk with us down that mysterious road called death, and lead us at last to that indescribable city that he has prepared for us. Let us never feel that God's creative power is exhausted by this earthly life, and his majestic love is locked within the limited walls of time and space. This would be a strongly irrational universe if God did not bring about an ultimate wedding of virtue and fulfillment. This would be an ~~absurdly~~ absurdly meaningless universe if death turned out to a blind alley leading the human race into a state of nothingness. God, through Christ has taken the sting from death, and it no longer has dominion over us.[42] This earthly life is merely an embryonic prelude to a new awakening, and death is an open door that leads us into life eternal.

With this faith we can accept nobly what cannot be changed, and face disappointments and sorrow with an inner poise. We will have the power to absorb the most excruciating pain without losing our sense of hope. We will then know that in life and death, God will take care of us.[43]

> "Be not dismayed, what-ere betide,
> God will take care of you.
> Beneath his wings of live abide,
> God will take care of you."
>
> "Thro' days of toil when heart doth fail,
> God will take care of you.
> When dangers fierce your path assail,
> God will take care of you."

---

38. John 14:27.

39. Cf. Acts 16:22–25.

40. King quotes from the spiritual "Bye and Bye."

41. In the published version: "These are living examples of peace that passeth all understanding" (p. 85).

42. Cf. 1 Corinthians 15:55–57.

43. This sentence was omitted and the previous sentence continued "for we know, as Paul testified, in life or in death, in Spain or Rome, 'that all things work together for good to them that love God, to them who are the called according to his purpose'" (p. 86).

"God will take care of you, through every day,
"O're all the way.
He will take care of you,
God will take care of you."[44]

{But helpless pieces of the game he plays upon this chequer Board of Nights and days.}[45]

TAHDd. MLKP-MBU: Box 119A.

---

44. King quotes Civilla D. Martin's hymn "God Will Take Care of You" (1904).
45. Khayyám, *Rubáiyát*, LXIX.

Draft of Chapter XIII, "Our God Is Able"

[*July 1962–March 1963*]
[*Atlanta, Ga.*]

King reminds his readers that "God is able to subdue all the powers of evil" and that "evil does not have the final word." As examples of this, King discusses the disintegration of colonialism in Africa and Asia and the slow but sure decline of legal segregation in this country, noting that they "represent the passing of a system that was born in injustice, nurtured in inequality and raised in exploitation." He recounts a transformative experience from the bus boycott during a night when, he admits, "I was ready to give up." As King prayed for guidance, he heard "the quiet assurance of an inner voice saying: 'Stand up for righteousness, stand up for truth; and God will be at your side forever.'" King preached a version of this sermon during the early days of the Montgomery bus boycott.[1]

"Now unto Him that is able to keep you from falling . . ." Jude 1:24

At the center of the Christian faith is the conviction that there is a God of Power in the universe who is able to do exceedingly abundant things in nature and history. This conviction is stressed over and over again in the Old and New testaments.[2] Theologically, it is expressed in the doctrine of the omnipotence of God. The God that we worship is not a weak and incompetent God.[3] He is able to beat back gigan-

---

1. King, "Our God Is Able," 1 January 1956, pp. 243–246 in this volume.
2. Meek, "Our God Is Able, A sermon preached in the Old South Church in Boston," 4 January 1953: "Meanwhile 'Our God is able' is a conviction stressed and exulted in, over and over and over in the New Testament."
3. Meek, "Our God Is Able": "Believe me, it is not a weak God, it is not an incompetent God with Whom we have to deal."

tic waves of opposition and bring low prodigious mountains of evil. The ringing cry of the Christian faith is that God is able.

There are those who would seek to convince us that only man is able. This desperate attempt to substitute a man-centered universe for a God-centered universe is not exactly new.[4] It had its beginning in the sixteenth century with the coming of the Renaissance and the so-called Age of Reason. Gradually man came to feel that God was an unnecessary item on the agenda of life.[5] Then came the Industrial Revolution in England. This revolution brought certain gadgets and contrivances into being which further convinced man that God was irrelevant.[6] And so the laboratory began to replace the church, and the scientist became a substitute for the prophet. The whole chorus of modernity joined, with Swinburne, in the singing of a new song: "Glory to man in the highest! for man is the master of things."[7]

The devotees of the new man-centered religion pointed to the spectacular advances of modern science as justification for their faith. Through science and technology man has assiduously enlarged his body. Through the telescope and television he has enlarged his eyes. Through the telephone, radio, and microphone he has strengthened his voice and ears. Through the automobile and airoplane he has lengthened his legs. Through the wonder drugs he has prolonged his life. Pointing to these amazing achievements, numerous people contended that only man was able.

But alas! Something has happened to shake the faith of those who made the laboratory "the new cathedral of men's hopes." The instruments that they yesterday worshiped as gods today contain cosmic death, and there is the danger that all of us will be plunged into the abyss of annihilation. No, man is not able to save himself or the world, and unless he is guided by God's spirit his new-found scientific power will be transformed into a devastating Frankenstein that will bring his earthly life to ashes.

There are other forces that at a times cause all of us to question the ableness of God. When we notice the stark and colossal reality of evil in the world—that something that Keats calls "the giant agony of the world;"—when we notice the long ruthlessness of ~~flanks~~ {floods} and tornadoes wiping away people as if they were weeds in an open field; when we behold ills like insanity falling on some individuals at birth leaving them living their days in a tragic cycles of meaninglessness; when we experience the madness of war and the barbarity of man's inhumanity to man; we find ourselves asking why do all of these things occur if God is able to prevent

---

4. In the published version of this sermon the phrase "this desperate" was replaced by the word "their" (King, *Strength to Love,* p. 101).

5. The preceding two sentences were altered in the published version: "It had its modern beginnings in the Renaissance and subsequently in the Age of Reason, when some men gradually came to feel that God was an unnecessary item on the agenda of life" (p. 101).

6. The preceding two sentences were combined and the phrase "This revolution brought certain gadgets and contrivances into being which further convinced man that" was replaced by "others questioned whether" in the published version (p. 101).

7. King quotes the final line of Algernon Charles Swinburne's poem "Hymn of Man" (1871). In the published version the phrase "the whole chorus of modernity" was replaced by "not a few" (p. 101).

them.[8] **Can a God who is both all-powerful and all-loving allow such glaring evils to exist? To answer this question would require another sermon altogether.** It would mean a lengthy discussion on that problem that has plagued the mind of man since the days of ancient philosophy, namely the problem of evil. So this morning I can only say in passing that much of the evil which we experience in the world is due to man's folly and ignorance, the misuse of his freedom.[9] Beyond this, I can only assert that there is and always will be a penumbra of mystery surrounding God, and what appears evil for the moment may have a purpose that our finite minds are incapable of comprehending. So in spite of the pressure of evil and the occasional doubts that lurk in our minds we are constantly driven back to the conviction that our God is able.[10]

Let us notice first that God is able to sustain the vast scope of the physical universe. Here again, we are tempted to feel that man is the true master of the physical universe. When we notice man-made jet planes compressing into minutes distances that once took days and man-made space ships carrying cosmonauts through outer space at a speed of 18,000 miles per hour, we begin to wonder if God is not being replaced in his mastery of the cosmic order.

But before we go too far in our man-centered arrogance, let us take a broad look at the universe.[11] We will soon discover that our man made instruments are barely moving in comparison to the movement of the God created solar system. Think about the fact, for instance, that the earth is moving around the sun so fast that the fastest jet racing it would be left behind sixty-six thousand miles in the first hour of the race. Since I started preaching this sermon, about seven minutes ago, our earth and you have hurtled through space more than eight thousand miles.[12] ~~Nature~~ {Notice} the sun which scientists tell us is the center of the solar system. Our earth revolves around this cosmic ball of fire once each year, traveling 584,000,000 miles in that year at the rate of 66,700 miles per hour or 1,600,000 miles per day. This means that this time tomorrow we will be 1,600,000 miles from where we are at this hundredth of a second. Look at that sun again. It may look rather near. But it is

8. King cites a line from John Keats, "The Fall of Hyperion: A Dream" (1819). This sentence was altered in the published version: "The stark and colossal reality of evil in the world—what Keats calls 'the giant agony of the world'; ruthless floods and tornadoes that wipe away people as though they were weeds in an open field; ills like insanity plaguing some individuals from birth and reducing their days to tragic cycles of meaninglessness; the madness of war and the barbarity of man's inhumanity to man—why, we ask, do these things occur if God is able to prevent them?" (p. 102).

9. The preceding two sentences were altered in the published version: "This problem, namely, the problem of evil, has always plagued the mind of man. I would limit my response to an assertion that much of the evil which we experience is caused by man's folly and ignorance and also by the misuse of his freedom" (p. 102).

10. In the published version the phrase "are constantly driven back to" was replaced by "shall wish not to surrender" (p. 102).

11. The phrase "go too far in" was replaced by "are consumed too greatly by" in the published version (p. 102).

12. This sentence was altered in the published version: "In the past seven minutes we have been hurtled more than eight thousand miles through space" (p. 103). This illustration mirrored one that Meek related in "Perhaps Your God Is Not Big Enough, A sermon preached in the Old South Church in Boston," 11 October 1953.

888888888888

8888888888888888

93,000,000 miles from the earth. In six months from now we will be on the other side of the sum,—93,000,000 miles beyond it—and in a year from now we will have swung completely around it and back to where we are right now. So when we behold the illimitable expanse of the solar {system} in which we are compelled to measure stellar distance in light years, and in which heavenly bodies travel at incredible speed, we are forced to look beyond man and affirm anew that God is able.

Let us notice again that God is able to subdue all the powers of evil. In affirming that God is able to conquer evil we are admitting its reality. Christianity has never dismissed evil as illusory or an error of the mortal mind. It sees it as a force that has objective reality. But it contends that evil does not have the final word. It carries the seed of its own destruction.[13] There is a checkpoint in the universe. Evil cannot permanently organize itself. History is the long and tragic story of evil forces rising high only to be crushed by the battling rams of the forces of justice.[14] There is a law in the moral world,—a silent, invisible imperative—akin to the laws in the physical world, which reminds us that life will only work a certain way. The Hitlers and the Mussolinis may have their day, and for a period they may wield great power, spreading themselves like a green bay tree, but soon they are cut down like the grass and wither as the green herb.[15]

Go back to another century. Victor Hugo is describing the Battle of Waterloo in <u>Les Miserables</u>. He concludes his graphic account with these pointed words: "Was it possible that Napoleon should win this battle?[16] I answer 'No.' Because of Wellington? 'No.' Because of Bluchen? 'No.'—because of God. Waterloo is not a battle; it is a change in the front of the universe."[17] In a real sense, Waterloo is a symbol of the doom of every Napoleon. It is an eternal reminder to a generation drunk with military power that in the long run of history might does not make right and the power of the sword cannot conquer the power of the spirit.

Let us look at our own day. We saw an evil system known as colonialism soar high. Like a plague, it swept across Africa and Asia, bringing more than 1,600,000 people under its gripping yoke.[18] **Like any system of oppression, colonialism is evil because it is based on a contempt for life. It stripped millions of people of their self-respect, robbed them of their sense of dignity, and treated them as if they were**

---

13. Meek, "Our God Is Able": "The very evil that threatens our destruction carries within it the seeds of its own doom."

14. The preceding six sentences were condensed in the published version: "It reckons with evil as a force that has objective reality. But Christianity contends that evil contains the seed of its own destruction. History is the story of evil forces that advance with seemingly irresistible power only to be crushed by the battling rams of the forces of justice" (p. 103).

15. Cf. Psalm 37:2.

16. In the published version, this quotation was introduced with the phrase "in his graphic account of the Battle of Waterloo in *Les Misérables,* Victor Hugo wrote" (p. 103).

17. Victor Hugo, *Les Misérables,* pp. 337–338; see also Meek, "Perhaps Your God Is Not Big Enough": "Victor Hugo is describing the Battle of Waterloo. And Hugo concludes his description with these words: 'Was it possible that Napoleon should win this battle? I answer "No." Because of Wellington? "No." Because of Blucher? "No."—because of God. Waterloo is not a battle; it is a change in the front of the universe.'"

18. In the published version, these three sentences were replaced with: "An evil system, known as colonialism, swept across Africa and Asia" (p. 104).

things rather than persons. But then the quiet invisible law began to operate. As Prime Minister MacMillan said, "the wind of change began to blow."[19] The powerful colonial empires began to disintegrate like stacks of cards, and new, independent nations began to emerge like refreshing oases in deserts sweltering with the heat of injustice. In less than fifteen years independence has swept through Asia and Africa like an irresistible tidal wave, releasing more than 1,500,000 people from the crippling manacles of colonialism.

In our own nation we have seen an evil system known as segregation rise to the throne. For almost one hundred years this unjust system has inflicted the Negro with a sense of inferiority, robbed him of his personhood, and denied him life, liberty and the pursuit of happiness.

For all of these years segregation has been the Negroes' burden and America's shame. But as on the world scale, so in our nation, the wind of change began to blow. **Since May 17, 1954, when the Supreme Court rendered its historic decision,** one event has followed another to bring a gradual end to the system of segregation. So that today we can all but say with certainty that segregation is dead and the only question left now is how costly the south will make the funeral.

These great changes taking place in the world today are not just political and sociological shifts. They represent the passing of a system that was born in injustice, nurtured in inequality and raised in exploitation. They represent the inevitable decay of any system based on principles out of harmony with the moral laws of the universe. When in future generations men look back upon these turbulent, tension-packed days through which we are passing, they will see God working through history for the salvation of man; **they will see the gradual fulfillment of Isaiah's prophecy: "Every valley shall be exhaulted and every mountain shall be made law; the rough places shall be made plain, and the crooked places straight; and the glory of the Lord whall be revealed;"** they will see that God was working through some men who had the vision to see that no nation could survive half slave and half free.[20]

Yes, God is able to conquer the evils of history. His control is never usurped. **His ways may seem slow, but his mills are grinding exceedingly fine.**[21] If at times we begin to despair because of the relatively slow progress being made in ending racial discrimination, **and become disappointed because of the silence of people whose support is so urgently needed,** and because of the undue cautiousness of the federal government, let us gain consolation from the fact that God is able, and in our sometimes difficult and lonesome walk up freedom's road, we do not walk alone, but God walks with us. He has placed in the very structure of this universe certain absolute moral laws. No matter how much we try, we cannot defy or break them; if

---

19. King refers to a controversial speech British prime minister Harold Macmillan delivered to the South African Parliament on 3 February 1960 in which he frankly criticized the system of apartheid. Macmillan said of the growing national consciousness in African nations that a "wind of change is blowing through the continent" and that South Africa must "come to terms with it" (Leonard Ingalls, "Macmillan, in South Africa, Censures Apartheid Policy," *New York Times*, 4 February 1960).

20. Cf. Isaiah 40:4–5.

21. Euripides *Bacchae* 882–887.

we disobey them, they end up breaking us. The force of evil may temporarily conquer truth, but truth has a way of ultimately conquering its conqueror. Our God is able. James Russell Lowell was right:

> Truth forever on the scaffold
> Wrong forever on the throne
> Yet that scaffold sways the future,
> And behind the dim unknown,
> Stands God within the shadow
> Keeping watch above His own.[22]

Let us notice finally that God is able to give us interior resources to confront the trials and difficulties of life. Each of us confronts circumstances in life which compel us to carry heavy burdens of sorrow, moments when jostling winds of adversity come with hurricane force and glowing sunrises are transformed into darkest nights. There are moments when our highest hopes are blasted and our noblest dreams are shattered.

Christianity has never overlooked these experiences of disappointment. They will inevitably come. Like the rythmic alternation in the natural order, life has ~~its glittering daybreaks and its desolate midnight;~~ {the glittering sunlight of its summers and the piercing chill of its winters,} its moment of unutterable joy and its moments of overwhelming sorrow. Like the everflowing waters of the river, life has its moments of flood and its moments of drought. When these dark moments of life emerge, many find themselves crying out with Paul Lawrence Dunbar:[23]

> A crust of bread and a corner to sleep in;
> A minute to smile and an hour to weep in;
> A pint of joy to a peck of trouble
> And never a laugh that the[24]
> and that is Life.[25]

Admitting that moments will inevitably come when the weight of problems and staggering disappointments will invade ~~your~~ {our} lives, Christianity goes on to affirm that God is able to give us the power to meet them. He is able to give us the inner equilibrium to stand up amid the trials and burdens of life. He is able to provide inner peace amid outer storms. This inner stability of the man of faith was Christ's chief legacy to his disciples. He left them with neither material resources nor a magical formula that would exempt them from suffering and persecution. But he left them an imperishable gift: "My peace I leave with thee."[26] This is that peace which passeth all understanding.

---

22. Lowell, "The Present Crisis" (1844).

23. The preceding two sentences were altered in the published version: "Life brings periods of flooding and periods of drought. When these dark hours emerge, many cry out with Paul Laurence Dunbar" (p. 105).

24. In the published version: "And never a laugh but the moans come double" (p. 105).

25. Dunbar, "Life" (1895).

26. Cf. John 14:27.

We may feel at times that we don't need God, but then one day the storms of disappointment will begin to rage, the winds of disaster will begin to blow, and the tidal waves of grief will beat up against our lives, and if we don't have a deep and patient faith our emotional lives will be ripped to shreds. Now, this is why there is so much frustration in the world. We are relying on gods rather than God. For years we have genuflected before the god of science, only to find that it has given us the atomic bomb, producing fears and anxieties that science can never mitigate. We have worshipped the god of pleasure only to find that thrills play out and sensations are short-lived. We have bowed before the god of money only to find that there are things that money can't buy—love and friendship—and that in a world of possible depressions, stock market crashes, and bad business investments, money is a rather uncertain deity. No, these transitory gods are not able to save us or bring happiness to the human heart. Only God is able. It is faith in Him that we must re-discover in this modern world. With this faith we can transform bleak and desolate valleys into sun-lit paths of joy, and bring new light into the dark chambers of pessimism. Is someone here this morning moving toward the evening of life and afraid of that something called death? Why? God is able. Is someone here this morning all but on the brink of despair because of some grave disappointment?—the death of a loved one, the breaking of a marriage, the waywardness of a child. Why? God is able to give you the power to endure that which cannot be changed. Is someone here afraid of a bad health? Why? If it comes, God is able.[27]

As I come to the conclusion of my message I would like for you to indulge me as I mention a personal experience.[28] The first twenty-four years of my life were years packed with fulfillment. I had no basic problems or burdens. Because of concerned and loving parents who provided for my every need, I sailed through high school, college, theological school and graduate school without a single interruption. It was not until I came to this community and became a part of the leadership of the bus protest that I really confronted the trials of life. Almost immediately after the protest started we began to receive threatening telephone calls and letters in our home. Sporadic in the beginning, they increased as time went on. When these incidents started, I took them in stride, feeling that they were the work of a few hotheads who would soon be discouraged when they discovered that we would not fight back. But as the weeks passed, I began to see that many of the threats were in earnest. Soon I felt myself faltering and growing in fear.

One night toward the end of January I settled into bed late, after a strenuous day.[29] My wife had already fallen asleep and just as I was about to doze off the telephone rang. An angry voice said, "Listen, nigger, we've taken all we want from you;

---

27. The preceding three sentences were altered in the published version: "Is someone here anxious because of bad health? Why be anxious? Come what may, God is able" (p. 106). Meek, "Our God Is Able": "'Am I afraid of death? Why? "Our God is able."' 'Am I afraid of ill health? Why? Suppose it comes. "Our God is able" as others have proven.' 'Have I been hurt, defeated, battered by life? Yes. But, "Our God is able."'"

28. The phrase "like for you to indulge me as I mention" was replaced by "wish you to permit" in the published version (p. 106).

29. In the published version: "After a particularly strenuous day, I settled in bed at a late hour" (p. 107).

before next week you'll be sorry you ever came to Montgomery." I hung up, but I couldn't sleep. It seemed that all of my fears had come down on me at once. I had reached the saturation point.

I got out of bed and began to walk the floor. Finally I went to the kitchen and heated a put of coffee. I was ready to give up. **With my cup of coffee sitting untouched before me** I tried to think of a way to move out of the picture without appearing a coward. In this state of exhaustion, when my courage had all but gone, I decided to take my problem to God. With my head in my hands, I bowed over the kitchen table and prayed aloud. The words I spoke to God that midnight are still vivid in my memory. "I am here taking a stand for what I believe is right. But now I am afraid. The people are looking to me for leadership, and if I stand before them without strength and courage, they too will falter. I am at the end of my powers. I have nothing left. I've come to the point where I can't face it alone."

At that moment I experienced the presence of the Divine as I had never experienced Him before. It seemed as though I could hear the quiet assurance of an inner voice saying: "Stand up for righteousness, stand up for truth; and God will be at your side forever." Almost at once my fears began to go. My uncertainty disappeared. I was ready to face anything.[30] The outer situation remained the same, but God had given me the inner calm to face it.

Three nights later, on January 30, as you know, our home was bombed. Strangely enough, I accepted the work of the bombing calmly. My experience with God a few nights before had given me the strength to face it.[31]

Yes, God is able to give us the interior resources to face the storms and problems of life. Go out this morning and let this affirmation be our ringing cry. It will give us courage to face the uncertainties of the future. It will give our tired feet new strength as we continue our forward stride toward the city of freedom. When our days become dreary with low hovering clouds and our nights become darker than a thousand midnights, let us remember that there is a great benign Power in the universe whose name is God, and He is able to make a way out of no way, and transform dark yesterdays into bright tomorrows. This is our hope for becoming better men. This is our mandate for seeking to make a better world.

TADd. MLKP-MBU: Box 119A.

---

30. King recounts this story of his vision in *Stride Toward Freedom,* pp. 134–135; see also "King Says Vision Told Him to Lead Integration Forces," 28 January 1957, in *Papers* 4:114–115.

31. This sentence was altered in the published version: "My experience with God had given me a new strength and trust" (p. 107).

Draft of Chapter XIV,
"The Mastery of Fear or Antidotes for Fear"

[July 1962–March 1963]
[Atlanta, Ga.]

King first developed a sermon on the subject of fear during the early years that King assisted his father at Ebenezer.[1] In this sermon, developed from one that he preached at Dexter in 1957, he draws on the work of Riverside Church ministers Harry Emerson Fosdick and Robert McCracken, and theologians Paul Tillich and Joshua Liebman, to offer ways to conquer modern fears.[2] King identifies fear as a major cause of war and prescribes love as its remedy: "Only love, understanding and organized goodwill can cast out fear. Or to put it another way, not [armament] but disarmament will cast out fear, and disarmament will never become a reality until enough goodwill and good faith are released to make mutual trust a reality."

"There is no fear in love, but perfect love casts out fear. For fear has to do with punishment, and he who fears is not perfected in love." I John 4:18

"For God hath not given us the spirit of fear; but of power, and of love, and of a sound mind." II Timotny 1:7

Today it has become almost a truism to call our time an "age of fear." In these days of terrifying change, bitter international tension and chaotic social disruption, who has not experienced the paralysis of crippling fear? Everywhere there are people depressed and bewildered, irritable and nervous all because of the monster of fear. Like a nagging hound of hell, fear follows our every footstep, leaving us tormented by day and tortured by night.

Our fears assume many different disguises and dress themselves in strangely different robes. There are those superstitious fears that range from the fear of walking under a ladder to a fear of Friday the thirteenth. There are those fears that fall under the category of "personal anxiety." Everywhere we find men and women facing these fears. They fear bad health; so they begin to find evidence of disease in every meaningless symptom. They fear growing old; so they dose themselves with a succession of drugs advertised to keep them young. When they are not worried about their physical health, they are worried about their personalities. They fear others and they fear themselves; so thay are driven through life with a sense of insecurity, a lack of self-confidence, and a nagging feeling of failure. They end up with what the psychologists call an inferiority complex. Strangely enough there are those who fear success; so they wander aimlessly down

---

1. King's announced sermon topic for 20 August 1950 was "Conquest of Fear" ("Rev. M. L. King, Jr. At Ebenezer Sunday," *Atlanta Daily World*, 19 August 1950).

2. King, "The Mastery of Fear," 21 July 1957, pp. 317–321 in this volume. King may have gotten the original title for this sermon from Fosdick (see Fosdick, "The Conquest of Fear," in *Hope of the World*, pp. 59–68).

the frittering road of excessive drink and sexual promiscuity. How many people have allowed endless fears to transform the sunrise of love and peace into a sunset of inner depression!

Sometimes our fears are dressed in the garments of mental phobias. These nagging phobias take many forms—fear of water, fear of high places, fear of closed rooms, fear of darkness and fear of being alone. These phobias continue to accumulate until at last many face what the psychiatrists call phobiaphobia—the fear of fear, being afraid of being afraid.

Then there are those economic fears which are especially real in this highly competitive society. Karen Horney has set forth the thesis that most of the psychological problems of our age grow out of this gnawing economic fear.[3] Many men are tormented by the possible or actual failure of their businesses. Others are tortured by the uncertainty of the stock market. Numerous people are plagued with the fear of unemployment and the collapse of their careers because of a force called automation. **One of the tragic things about unemployment is that it crushes a man's sense of pride, drowns his spirit, and leaves him standing before his wife and children as a disastrous failure. How real and frustrating are our economic fears!**

There are, above all, the religious and ontological fears. They are at [*strikeout illegible*] bottom the fear of death and nonbeing.[4] The atomic bomb and nuclear weapons have lifted the fear of death to morbid proportions. More than anything else, the haunting spectacle of possible nuclear annihilation has saturated our day with "the spirit of fear." Hamlet's soliloquy, "to be or not to be," is the desperate question falling from many trembling lips.[5] Indicative of the intensity of this contemporary fear of death is the mad quest to build fallout shelters; but the fear increases even more when sober assessment reminds us that a shelter would be of little use against a sizeable H-bomb. In agonizing desperation we petition our governments to increase the nuclear stockpile; but we soon discover that this fanatical quest to maintain "a balance of terror" increases rather than diminishes fear, for it leaves all nations frightfully at tip-toe stance not quite knowing which diplomatic faux pas will result in the pushing of the fatal bottom. **The fear of death leaves so many people wandering through a bleak dungeon with no hope for reaching an exit sign.**

So the problem of fear is one of the most serious problems of modern life. It leaves so many people psychologically wrecked and spiritually dejected. It drains one's energy and depletes one's resources. This is why Emerson said, "He has not learned the lesson of life who does not every day surmount a fear."[6]

Now this does not mean that we should seek to eliminate fear altogether from human life. Such an undertaking would not only be humanly impossible but practically undesirable. Fear is the elemental alarm system of the human organism

---

3. King probably refers to Horney's book *The Neurotic Personality of Our Time.*

4. In the published version, the word "nonbeing" was replaced by "racial annihilation" (King, *Strength to Love,* p. 109).

5. Shakespeare, *Hamlet,* act 3, sc. 1.

6. Ralph Waldo Emerson, *Society and Solitude* (1870); see also Fosdick, *On Being a Real Person,* p. 115.

which warns us of approaching dangers.[7] Without it man could not have survived in the primitive world, nor could he survive in the modern world.

Fear is a powerfully creative force. Every great invention and every intellectual advance has behind it as a part of its motivation the xdesire to escape some dreaded thing. The fear of darkness caused man to discover the secret of electricity. The fear of pain led to the marvelous discoveries of medical science. The fear of ignorance was one reason that man built great institutions of learning.[8] The fear of war was one of the forces behind the birth of the United Nations. Angelo Patri was right in saying, "Education consist in being afraid at the right time."[9] If we were to take away man's capacity to fear, we would take away his capacity to grow, invent and create. Some fear is normal, necessary, and creative.

But it must be borne in mind that there are abnormal fears which are emotionally ruinous and psychologically destructive. The best illustration of the difference between normal and abnormal fear was given by Sigmund Freud himself. A person tramping through the heart of an African jungle, he said, should quite properly be afraid of snakes. That is normal and self-protective. But if a person suddenly begins to fear that snakes are under the carpet of his city apartment, then his fear is abnormal, neurotic.[10] Are not most of our fears so based? Psychologists tell us that a normal child is born with only two fears—the fear of falling and the fear of loud noises—and all others are environmentally acquired. Most of these acquired fears turn out to be snakes under the carpet.[11]

When we speak of getting rid of fear we are referring to this chronic abnormal, neurotic fear. Normal fear protects us; abnormal fear paralyzes us. Normal fear is a friend that motivates us to improve our individual and collective welfare; abnormal fear is an enemy that constantly poisons and distorts our inner lives. So our problem is not to get rid of fear but to harness and master it.

How, then, is it to be mastered?

---

7. Fosdick, *On Being a Real Person*, p. 110: "Fear is every animal's elemental alarm-system, so sensitively keyed that at the first sign of danger the organism snaps into readiness for flight or fight."

8. Fosdick, *On Being a Real Person*, pp. 110–111: "Indeed, fear can be a powerfully creative motive. In a profound sense schools spring from fear of ignorance, industry from fear of penury, medical science from fear of disease. Every saving invention, from a lighthouse to sulfanilamide, and every intellectual advance, whether in engineering or economic theory, has behind it as part of its motivation the desire to avoid or escape some dreaded thing."

9. Fosdick, *On Being a Real Person*, p. 110: "Angelo Patri is right in saying, 'Education consists in being afraid at the right time'"; see also note 13 to King, The Mastery of Fear, 21 July 1957, pp. 318–319 in this volume.

10. Liebman, *Peace of Mind*, pp. 84–85: "The best illustration of the difference between normal and neurotic fear was given by Sigmund Freud himself. A person in an African jungle, he said, may quite properly be afraid of snakes. That is normal and self-protective. But if a friend of ours suddenly begins to fear that snakes are under the carpet of his city apartment, then we know that his fear is neurotic. . . . Are not most of our fears so based? Suppose we scrutinize that large body of fears coming under the heading of 'personal anxiety.' Oftener than not, they turn out to be snakes under the carpet"; McCracken, *Questions People Ask*, p. 124: "If I were tramping through the heart of an African jungle I should very naturally and properly be afraid of snakes. If in my Riverside Drive apartment I were living in terror of snakes under the carpet I would be at the mercy of a fear that is neurotic."

11. Fosdick, *On Being a Real Person*, p. 114: "As infants we started with fear of two things only—falling and a loud noise, and all other fears have been accumulated since."

First we must face our fears without flinching. We must honestly ask ourselves why we are afraid. The confrontation will, to some measure, grant us power. We can never cure fear by the method of escapism. Nor can it be cured by repression. The more we attempt to ignore and repress our fears, the more we multiply our inner conflicts **and cause the mind to deteriorate into a slum district.**

Psychiatrists tell us that by looking squarely and honestly at our fears we discover that many of them are the residues of some childhood need or apprehension. Here is a person, for instance, haunted by a fear of death or the thought of punishment in the after life. By honestly facing this fear the person soon discovers that it is a projection of an early childhood experience of being punished by parents, locked in a room, seemingly deserted. As an adult he unconsciously projected this childhood experience of aloneness and punishment into the whole of reality. Or take the example of the man plagued with the fear of inferiority and social rejection. By looking squarely at this fear he soon discovers that it is rooted in a childhood experience of parental rejection. He was the son of a self-centered mother and a busy, preoccupied father. The mother felt that his coming interfered with her endless social functions. Quietly, and quite unconsciously, he was rejected. In his rejection he felt an enormous bitterness toward life. **In an attempt to express this resentment he engaged in excessive temper tantrums and was severely punished. He found that he could get no attention unless he concealed his bitterness. Conceal it he did. He gained a degree of approval by transforming himself into a dependent, subservient creature who always concealed his true feelings. So he came into maturity with a terrible sense of inadequacy. He had ability of his own, but he was afraid to express it because all of his childhood attempts at self-assertion had brought punishment and rejection. And so by looking at his fears in the light he discovered that they were rooted in unexpressed resentment which, since his childhood, he had repressed.**

So let us take our fears one by one and look at them fairly and squarely. By bringing them to the forefront of consciousness, we may find them to be more imaginary than real. Some of them will turn out to be snakes under the carpet. Let us remember that more often than not, fear involves the misuse of the imagination. By getting our fears in the open we may end up laughing at some of them, and this is good. As one psychiatrist has said: "Ridicule is the master cure for fear and anxiety."[12]

We can master fear not only by facing it and understanding it; we can master it through courage. Courage has always been considered a supreme virtue. Plato considered it that element of the soul which bridges the cleavage between reason and desire. Aristotle considered it the affirmation of one's essential nature. Thomas Aquinas considered it the strength of mind capable of conquering whatever threatens the attainment of the highest good. **The stoics considered it the affiamation of one's essential being in spite of desires and anxieties.**

So courage is the power of the mind to overcome fear. Fear, unlike anxiety, has a

---

12. Fosdick, *On Being a Real Person*, p. 132: "It was a psychiatrist, Dr. Sadler, who, having said in one place, 'Ridicule is the master cure for fear and anxiety,' struck a deeper note when he said in another, 'The only known cure for fear is *faith*'"; see also Sadler, *The Mind at Mischief*, p. 43.

definite object which can be faced, analyzed, attacked and endured.[13] So often the object of our fear is fear itself. "Nothing," says Seneca, "is terrible in things except fear itself."[14] And Epictetus says, "for it is not death or hardship that is a fearful thing, but the fear of death and hardship."[15] Courage can take the fear produced by a definite object into itself and thereby conquer the fear involved. "Courage," says Paul Tillich, "is self-affirmation 'in spite of' . . . that which tends to hinder the self from affirming itself."[16] It is self-affirmation in spite of death and non-being. He who acts courageously takes the fear of death into his self affirmation and acts upon it. This courageous self affirmation which is a sure remedy for fear is not to be confused with "selfishness." Self-affirmation includes the right self-love and the right love of others. Erich Fromm has pointed out in convincing terms that the right self-love and the right love of others are interdependent, and that selfishness and the abuse of others are equally interdependent.[17]

Courage is that quality which enables us to stand up to any fear. It is the final determination not to be stopped or overwhelmed by any object, however frightful it may be. Many of our fears are very real, and not mere snakes under the carpet. Trouble is a reality in this strange medley of life and dangers lurk beneath our every move. Accidents do occur and bad health stands as an ever threatening possibility. Death is a stark, grim and inevitable reality. We do ourselves and our neighbors a great disservice when we try to prove that there is nothing in this world to be frightened at. In this conundrum of life evil and pain are inescapable realities. The things that make for fear are close to all of us. These forces that threaten to negate life must be met and challenged by a daring "courage to be." Courage is the power of life to affirm itself in spite of its ambiguities. It involves the exercise of a great and creative will. It is a bottomless resourcefulness that ultimately enables a man to hew out of the mountain of despair a stone of hope. Courage is the inner determination to go on in spite of obstacles and frightening situations; cowardice is the submissive surrender to the forces of circumstance. The man of courage never loses the zest for living even though his life situation is zestless; the cowardly man, overwhelmed by the uncertainties of life, loses the will to live. Courage breeds creative self-affirmation; cowardice breeds destructive self-abnegation. Courage faces fear and

---

13. Tillich, *The Courage to Be*, p. 36: "Fear, as opposed to anxiety has a definite object . . . which can be faced, analyzed, attacked and endured."

14. This quote from Seneca was replaced in the published version with a Henry David Thoreau quote: "Nothing is so much to be feared as fear" (King, *Strength to Love*, p. 111); see also *The Writings of Henry David Thoreau, 1850–September, 1951*, ed. Bradford Torrey (Boston: Houghton Mifflin, 1906), p. 468.

15. Epictetus, *Discourses and Enchiridion*, trans. Thomas Wentworth Higginson (New York: Walter J. Black, 1944), p. 86: "For it is not death or pain that is to be dreaded, but the fear of pain or death." Paul Tillich quoted both Seneca and Epictetus (*The Courage to Be*, p. 13).

16. Tillich, *The Courage to Be*, p. 3: "The courage to be is the ethical act in which man affirms his own being in spite of those elements of his existence which conflict with his essential self-affirmation."

17. Erich Fromm makes this argument in the section about "Self-Love" in the second chapter of his book *The Art of Loving* ([New York: Harper & Brothers, 1956], pp. 57–63); Tillich, *The Courage to Be*, p. 22: "Erich Fromm has fully expressed the idea that the right self-love and the right love of others are interdependent, and that selfishness and the abuse of others are equally interdependent."

thereby masters it; cowardice represses fear and is thereby mastered by it. So we must constantly build dykes of courage to ward off the flood of fear.

Fear is also mastered through love. The New Testament is right in saying, "there is no fear in love, but perfect love cast out fear." Now the word "love" in the New Testament is not something soft, anemic and sentimental. It is a very strong love that could carry Christ to a cross and send Paul sailing unembittered through the angry seas of persecution. It is love facing evil with an infinite capacity to take it without flinching, to overcome the world by the cross.

Now what does all of this have to do with the fears so prevalent in the modern world such as the fear of war, the fear of economic displacement, the fears accompanying racial injustice, and the fears associated with personal anxiety?[18] It has so much to do with them that we can find an illustration at almost any point. Hate is rooted in fear and the only cure for fear-hate is love. Take our deteriorating international situation. It is shot through with the poison darts of fear—Russia fears America and America fears Russia; China fears India and India fears China; the Arabs fear the Israelis and the Israelis fear the Arabs. The fears are numerous and varied—fear of another nation's attack, fear of another nation's scientific and technological supremacy, fear of another nation's economic power, fear of lost status and power. Fear is one of the major causes of war. We usually think that war comes from hate, but a close scrutiny of responses will reveal a different sequence of events—first fear, then hate, then war, then deeper hatred. If a nightmarish nuclear war engulfs our world—God forbid—it will not be because Russia and America first hated each other, but because they first feared each other.

Our method for dealing with this fear has been to arm ourselves to the <u>n</u>th degree. So the two contending camps of the world are engaged in a fever-packed arms race. Expenditures for defense continue to rise to mountain proportions.[19] **Nuclear tests continue to ~~curve~~ carve vertical highways of death through the atmosphere, and atomic submarines continue to cut horizontal pathways of destruction through the rolling seas.** Greater arms will cast out fear, the nations seem to say. But alas! Large armaments have not cast out fear. They have only produced greater fear. So we are called back in these turbulent, panic-stricken days to that wise affirmation of the New Testament: "Perfect love casts out fear." Greater armaments are not the remedy for fear; only love, understanding and organized goodwill can cast out fear. Or to put it another way, not armanent but disarmament will cast out fear, and disarmament will never become a reality until enough goodwill and good faith are released to make mutual trust a reality.

Our own problem of racial injustice must be solved by this same formula. The whole system of racial segregation is buttressed by a series of irrational fears—fear

---

18. This sentence was altered in the published version: "But does love have a relationship to our modern fear of war, economic displacement, and racial injustice?" (p. 112).

19. The preceding three sentences were altered in the published version: "What method has the sophisticated ingenuity of modern man employed to deal with the fear of war? We have armed ourselves to the nth degree. The West and the East have engaged in a fever-pitched arms race. Expenditures for defense have risen to mountainous proportions, and weapons of destruction have been assigned priority over all other human endeavors" (p. 112).

of losing a preferred economic position, fear of losing social status, fear of intermarriage, fear of adjusting to a new situation. Numerous white people spend sleepless nights and haggard days attempting to fight these corroding fears. They seek to cast out the fear by diverse methods. Some follow the path of escape. They seek to ignore the question of race relations altogether. They close their minds on this issue and allow nothing to go in or out. Others seek to deal with fear by placing faith in such legal maneuvers as interposition and nullification. They fanatically go down the slippery road of massive resistance. Still others seek to drown the fear by engaging in acts of violence and meanness toward Negroes. **These barbaric acts arose their sense of guilt, and they end up trying to drown the guilt feeling by engaging even more in the guilt evoking act.** But how futile are all of these remedies! Instead of reducing fear, they bring deeper and more pathological fears, fears that leave the victims inflicted with strange psychoses and peculiar cases of paranoia. Neither repression nor massive resistance nor aggressive violence will cast out the fear of integration; only love and goodwill can do that.

If our white brothers are to master fear they must depend not only on their commitment to the way of love but also on the love the Negro generates toward them. Only through our adherence to love and nonviolence can the fear of the white community be mitigated. A guilt-ridden white minority lives in fear that if the Negro should ever attain power, he would act without restraint or pity to revenge the injustices and brutality of the years. It is something like a parent who continually mistreats a son. One day that parent raises his hand to strike the son, only to discover that the son is now as tall as he is. The parent is suddenly afraid—fearful that the son will use his new physical power to repay his parent for all the blows of the past.

The Negro, once a helpless child, has now grown up politically, culturally, and economically. Many white men fear retaliation. The job of the Negro is to show them that they have nothing to fear, that the Negro understands and forgives and is ready to forget the past. He must convince the white man that he seeks justice, <u>for both himself and the white man</u>. A mass movement exercising love and nonviolence is an object lesson in power under discipline, a demonstration, to the white community that if such a movement attained a degree of strength, it would use its power creatively and not vengefully.

What is the cure, then, of this morbid fear of integration? We know the cure— God help us to achieve it! Love casts out fear.

This truth has a great deal of bearing on our personal anxieties. What are some of us afraid of? We are afraid of the superiority of other people, afraid of failure, afraid that we will be the objects of scorn or disapproval on the part of those whose opinions we value most. Envy, jealousy, a lack of self-confidence, a feeling of insecurity, and a haunting sense of inferiority are all rooted in fear. We are not jealous of people and then fear them; we first fear them and then we become jealous of them. What is the cure for these annoying fears that poison our personal lives? Again it is a deep and abiding commitment to the way of love. "Perfect love casts out fear."

Hatred and bitterness can never cure the disease of fear; only love can do that. Hatred paralyzes life; love releases it. Hatred confuses life; love harmonizes it. Hatred darkens life; love lights it. **Hatred has ~~cronic~~ chronic eye trouble — it cannot see very far; love has sound eyes — it can see beneath the surface and beyond the outer masks.**

A final way to master fear is through faith. One of the commonest sources of fear is the consciousness of deficient resources and of consequent inadequqcy for life. All too many people are attempting to face the tension of life with inadequate inner resources. While on a recent vacation in Mexico, Mrs. King and I rented a boat and went deep sea fishing. Having limited money to spend we rented a rather cheap boat that was old and ill-equipped. At first we gave this no thought. But after getting about ten miles from shore the clouds began to hover low and the howling winds began to blow in fierce fury. Immediately we were afraid because we knew that we had an inadequate boat that was not able to stand strong amid a storm. As we made our way back to the shore we were inflicted every minute with a paralyzing fear. Multitudes of people are in such a situation. Heavy winds, weak boats—they are afraid.

Many of our fears, particularly the abnormal ones, can be dealt with by the skills of psychiatry. This relatively new discipline pioneered by Sigmund Freud is a vital means of investigating the sub-conscious drive of men, and of discovering how and why these fundamental energies are diverted into neurotic channels. It can help us to look unflinchingly at our inner selves, and with searching fingers to probe out the causes of our failures and fears. Much of our fearful living, however, moves in a realm where the service of psychiatry is ineffectual unless the psychiatrist is a man of religious faith. For the trouble with us is simply that we are attempting to face fear without faith; we are attempting to sail through the stormy seas of life without strong spiritual boats. This is why one of the leading physicians and psychiatrists of America said: "The only known cure for fear is faith."[20] The abnormal fears and phobias that express themselves in <u>neurotic anxiety</u> can be cured by psychiatry, but the fear of death, nonbeing and nothingness which expresses itself in <u>existential anxiety</u> can only be cured by a positive religious faith. Such a faith imbues us with a sense of the trustworthiness of the universe, and a feeling of relatedness to God. A positive religious faith does not leave us with the illusion that we will be exempted from pain and suffering, nor does it imbue us with the idea that life is a drama of unalloyed comfort and untroubled ease; rather it instills us with the inner equilibrium to face the strains, burdens and fears that will inevitably come.

Irreligion tells us that we are alone in this strange conumdrum of life, orphans thrown out amid the terrifying immensities of space. It leaves us with the idea that the universe is without purpose or intelligence, **a blind mechanism moved by blind forces, that man is the plaything of a callous nature, the accidental product of a fortuitous interplay of atoms and electrons, that history is the tragic arena of never ceasing conflict and the endless cycle of monotonous meaninglessness.** Such a view of life and history drains courage and exhausts the energies of men. **It causes a man to live through the dark night of the soul where the shadows of inner depression are luridly etched in his aimless paths.** He feels something of the aloneness and emptiness that Tolstoi felt before his conversion. In his <u>Confession</u>, he writes:

---

20. Cf. Sadler, *The Mind at Mischief*, p. 43; see also Fosdick, *On Being a Real Person*, p. 132.

> There was a period in my life when everything seemed to be crumbling, the very foundations of my convictions were beginning to give way, and I felt myself going to pieces. There was no sustaining influence in my life and there was no God there, and so every night before I went to sleep, I made sure that there was no rope in my room lest I be tempted during the night to hang myself from the rafters of my room; and I stopped from going out shooting lest I be tempted to put a quick end to my life and to my misery.[21]

At this stage of his life Tolstoi, like so many people, lacked the sustaining influence which comes from the conviction that this universe is guided by a benign intelligence whose infinite love embraces all mankind.

Religion endows us with the conviction that we are not alone in this vast, uncertain universe. Beneath and above the shifting sands of time, the uncertainties that darken our days, and the vicissitudes that cloud our nights is a wise and loving God. This universe is not a tragic expression of meaningless chaos but a marvelous display of orderly cosmos—"The Lord hath in wisdom founded the earth, He hath established the heaven in understanding."[22] Man is not a wisp of smoke from a limitless smoldering, but a child of God created "a little lower than the angels."[23] Above the manyness of time stands the one eternal God, with wisdom to guide us, strength to protect us and love to keep us. His boundless love supports and contains us as {the} a mighty ocean contains and supports the tiny drops of every wave. With a surging fullness he is forever moving toward us, seeking to fill the little creeks and bays of our lives with unlimited resources. This is religion's everylasting diapason, its eternal answer to the enigma of existence. Any man who finds this cosmic sustenance can walk the highways of life without the fatigue of pessimism and the weight of morbid fears.

Herein lies the answer to the neurotic fear of death that plagues so many of our lives. Let us face the fear that the atomic bomb has aroused with the faith that we can never travel beyond the arms of the Divine. Death is inevitable. It is a democracy for all of the people not an aristocracy for some of the people—kings die and beggars die; young men die and old men die; learned men die and ignorant men die. We need not fear it. The God who brought our whirling planet from primal vapor and has led the human pilgrimage for low these many centuries can most assuredly lead us through death's dark night into the bright daybreak of ~~eternity~~ eternal life. His will is too perfect and his purposes are too extensive to be contained in the limited receptacle of time and the narrow walls of earth. Death is not the ultimate evil; the ultimate evil is to be outside God's love. We need not join the mad rush to purchase an earthly fallout shelter. God is our eternal fallout shelter.

Jesus always stressed the trustworthiness and love of God when he dealt with the problem of fear. He knew that nothing could separate man from God's love. In the tenth chapter of Matthew we read his majestic words:

---

21. King paraphrases part of the fourth chapter of Tolstoy's book *My Confession and The Spirit of Christ's Teaching* (1887).

22. Cf. Proverbs 3:19.

23. Cf. Psalm 8:5 and Hebrews 2:7.

Fear them not therefore: for there is nothing covered, that shall not be revealed; and hid, that shall not be known. . . . And fear not them which kill the body; but are not able to kill the soul; but rather fear him which is able to destroy both soul and body in hell. Are not two sparrows sold for a farthing? And one of them shall not fall on the ground without your Father. But the very hairs of your head are all numbered. Fear ye not therefore, ye are of more value than many sparrows.[24]

Man, for Jesus, is not mere flotsam and jetsam in the river of life. He is a child of God, and it is unreasonable to assume that God whose creative activity is expressed even in such details as the hairs of a man's head, would exclude from his concern the life of man himself.[25] The idea that God is mindful of the individual is of tremendous value in dealing with the poisonous disease of fear. It gives one a sense of worth, belonging and at-homeness in the universe.

During the bus protest in Montgomery, Alabama, one of the most dedicated participants was an elderly Negro woman that we affectionately called Mother Pollard. Although poverty-stricken and uneducated, she was amazingly intelligent and possessed a deep understanding of the meaning of the movement. Once she was asked several weeks of walking whether she was tired. "My feets is tired," she answered, "but my soul is rested." This was just one example of her ungrammatical profondity. One Monday evening, after having gone through a tension-packed week which included being arrested and receiving numerous threatening calls, I went to the mass meeting depressed and fear-stricken. In my address I tried desperately to give an overt impression of strength and courage, **but deep down within the soil of my inner life was the nagging serpent of fear which left me poisoned with the fangs of depression.** At the end of the meeting, Mother Pollard came to the front of the church and said, "Come here son." I immediately walked over and gave her a big hug. Then she said "something is wrong with you. You didn't talk strong tonight." Seeking to keep my fears to myself I retorted, "Oh, no, Mother Pollard, nothing is wrong. I am feeling as fine as ever." "Now you can't fool me," she said; "I knows something is wrong. Is it that we ain't doing things to please you? or is it that the white folks is bothering you?" Before I could answer she looked directly into my eyes and said, "I don told you we is with you all the way." And then with a countenance beaming with quiet certainty she concluded, "but even if we aint with you, God's gonna take care of you." Everything in me quivered with the pulsing tremor of raw energy when she uttered these consoling words.

Mother Pollard has now passed on to glory. Since that dreary night in 1956 I have known very few quiet days. I have been tortured without and tormented within by the raging fires of tribulation. Day in and day out I have been forced to stand up amid howling winds of pain and jostling storms of adversity. **Times without number I have learned that life has not only sun-lit moments of joy but also fog-packed moments of sorrow;** but as the years have unfolded the majestic words of Mother Pollard have come back again and again to give light and peace to **the hinterlands of** my troubled soul. "God's gonna take care of you." This is the faith that can trans-

---

24. Cf. Matthew 10:26–31.
25. Luke 12:7.

form the whirlwind of despair into the soothing breeze of hope. There is an old familiar motto which says: "Fear knocked at the door. Faith answered. There was no one there."[26]

July 1962– March 1963

TADd. MLKP-MBU: Box 120A.

---

26. George A. Buttrick, "Anxiety and Faith," in *Sermons Preached in a University Church* (New York: Abingdon Press, 1959), p. 43: "Fear knocked at the door. Faith answered. There was no one there."

Draft of Chapter XV,
"The Answer to a Perplexing Question"

[July 1962–March 1963]
[Atlanta, Ga.]

King preached a version of this sermon in 1959.[1] Rejecting claims that human action alone can purge the world of evil, he denies that "God in his good time will redeem the world." He maintains that this belief, which focuses on salvation in the afterlife, "has [led] to a dangerously irrelevant church" that "is little more than a country club where people assemble to hear and speak pious platitudes." Rather, King asserts, "The unit of power for moral victory is God filling man and man opening his life by faith to God, as the gulf opens itself to the overflowing waters of the river. Racial justice is a real possibility in this nation and in the world." Several passages of this sermon reflect the thoughts of J. Wallace Hamilton and Phillips Brooks.

"Why Could Not We Cast Him Out?" Mt. 17:19

One of the things that has characterized human life through the centuries has been man's persistent attempt to remove evil from the face of the earth. Very seldom has he thoroughly adjusted himself to evil. In spite of all of his rationalizations, compromises and alibis, man knows that the "is" is not the ought and the actual is not the possible. Though he often allows the evils of sensuality, selfishness and cruelty to rise up aggressively in his soul, something within reminds him that they are intruders. Ever and again man in his deepest attachment to evil is reminded of a higher destiny and a more noble allegiance. Man's hankering after the demonic is always disturbed by his longing for the divine. As he seeks to adjust to the demands of time, he knows that eternity is his ultimate habitat. When man comes to himself

---

1. King preached this sermon under a different title (King, "Divine and Human Mutuality" / "Man's Helplessness Without God," 9 August 1959, pp. 368–370 in this volume).

545

he knows that evil is a foreign invader that must be driven from the native soils of his soul before he can achieve moral and spiritual dignity.

But the problem that has always frustrated man has been his inability to conquer evil by his own power. He is constantly asking in pathetic amazement, "Why can I not cast it out?" "Why can I not remove this evil from my life?"

This agonizing, perplexing question is reminiscent of an event that took place during the life of Jesus Christ. The event occured immediately after Christ's transfiguration.[2] Jesus comes down from the mountain and finds a little boy in wild convulsions. His disciples were desperately trying to cure the unhappy child. The more they tried to heal him the more they discovered their own inadequacies, and the pathetic limitations of their power. At the point at which they are about to give up in despair, their Lord appears on the scene. The father of the child turns to him in utter desperation; he tells him of the failure of the disciples.[3] And then Jesus "rebuked the devil; and he departed out of him: and the child was cured from that very hour." At this point "the disciples came to Jesus apart, and said, why could not we cast him out." They wanted an explanation for their obvious limitations. Jesus tells them that the reason of their failure is their unbelief.[4] He says: "If you have faith as a grain of mustard seed, ye shall say unto this mountain, "Remove hence to yonder place; and it shall remove; and nothing shall be impossible unto you."[5] In other words, Jesus was saying to his disciples that the reason for their failure was that they were trying to do by themselves what they could only do when they so surrendered their natures to God that his strength could freely flow through them. **This is what Jesus means by faith.**

This brings us again to the question, how can evil be cast out? There are two ideas that men have usually held about the way evil is to be eliminated and the world saved.

One idea is that man must remove evil with his own power. It is the strange conviction that if man goes on thinking, inventing and governing he will be able to conquer by his own strength and ingenuity the nagging forces of evil. Just give people a fair chance, and a decent education, and they will save themselves. This idea has swept across the modern world like a plague ushering God out and escorting man

---

2. Cf. Matthew 17:1–20.

3. The words "turns to him in utter desperation; he tells him" were replaced by "told Jesus" in the published version (King, *Strength to Love*, p. 119).

4. Phillips Brooks, "Why Could Not We Cast Him Out?" in *Sermons Preached in English Churches* (New York: E. P. Dutton, 1903), pp. 181–182: "The words belong, as you remember, to the story of what immediately followed Christ's transfiguration. The Lord comes down from the mountain on which he has been glorified and finds a poor lunatic boy in convulsions at the mountain's foot. His disciples are trying to cure the unhappy child. How we can see their helplessness! Their association with Jesus had taught them to believe that such affliction could be cured, but when they tried they could not do it. Still the poor boy raved on. At last, when they are ready to give up in despair, their Master comes in sight. The father of the child turns eagerly to Him; he tells Him how the disciples had failed; and then Jesus 'rebuked the devil; and he departed out of him: and the child was cured that very hour.' Then it was that 'the disciples came to Jesus apart, and said, Why could we not cast him out?' They could not accept their own failure. They must have an explanation for their weakness. And Jesus tells them that the reason for their failure is their unbelief."

5. Matthew 17:20.

in, substituting human ingenuity for inner guidance.[6] Where it had its beginning is not clearly known. It is always difficult to get back to the one causal root of an idea in history. Some say it had its beginning with the Renaissance, when the age of reason was substituted for the age of religion. Others contend that it got under way with Darwin's <u>Origin of Species</u>, which substituted the idea of evolution for the idea of creation.[7] Still others think it started with the industrial revolution, which substituted material comfort for physical inconvenience.[8] But wherever it got started, the idea of the adequacy of man to solve the evils of history captured the minds of millions of people. Out of it came the easy optimism of the 19th century and the idea of inevitable progress. Out of it came Rousseau's doctrine of "the original goodness of human nature."[9] Out of it came the conviction of the French humanist, Condorcet, that the whole world would soon be cleansed of crime, poverty and war by reason alone.[10]

With this glowing faith in the power of reason and science, modern man went out to change the world. Instead of thinking about God and the human soul, he turned his attention to the outer world and its possibilities. Through test tubes, microscopes and telescopes, he observed it, analyzed it, and explored it. Soon the laboratory became his sanctuary and the individual scientists his priests and prophets. In the words of a modern humanist, many confidently affirmed: "The future is not with the churches but laboratories, not with prophets but with scientists, not with piety but with efficiency. Man is at last becoming aware that he alone is responsible for the realization of the world of his dreams, that he has within himself the power for its achievement." **Like a mighty Judge** modern man has subpoenaed nature to appear before the judgment seat of scientific investigation. There can be no gainsaying of the fact that his work in the scientific laboratories has paid off with unbelievable advances in power and comfort. It has produced machines

---

6. In the published version, the word "inner" was replaced by "divine" (p. 119).

7. Charles Darwin, *On the origin of species by means of natural selection, or, The preservation of favoured races in the struggle for life* (1859).

8. The preceding five sentences were condensed in the published version: "Some people suggest that this concept was introduced during the Renaissance when reason dethroned religion, or later when Darwin's *Origin of Species* replaced belief in creation by the theory of evolution, or when the industrial revolution turned the hearts of men to material comforts and physical conveniences" (p. 119).

9. The philosopher Jean-Jacques Rousseau argued in "Discourse on the Origin of Inequality" that compassion is the universal source for innate human goodness (Rousseau, *The Social Contract and Discourses* [1762]).

10. The French philosopher and political scientist Condorcet maintained that human progress based on science and reason would proceed indefinitely (Condorcet, *Sketch for a Historical Picture of the Progress of the Human Mind* [1795]). The preceding four sentences were condensed in the published version: "At any rate, the idea of the adequacy of man to solve the evils of history captured the minds of people, giving rise to the easy optimism of the nineteenth century, the doctrine of inevitable progress, Rousseau's maxim of 'the original goodness of human nature,' and Condorcet's conviction that by reason alone the whole world would soon be cleansed of crime, poverty, and war" (p. 119). Hamilton, *Horns and Halos*, pp. 62–63: "The Renaissance went too far in excessive optimism. . . . Out of that came the easy optimism of the 19th century and the idea of automatic progress—Spencer's philosophy, Rousseau's 'rights of man,' and 'the original goodness of human nature.' Perhaps the most optimistic book ever written was published on the eve of the French Revolution by a French humanist Condorcet. . . . He visioned the whole world cleansed of crime and poverty and slavery and war by reason and reason alone."

that think and gadgets that contain immeasurable power. Its matchless achievements are seen soaring majestically through the skies, standing impressively on the land, and moving stately on the seas.

But in spite of these astounding new scientific developments, the old evils continue to exist. Modern man has had to witness his age of reason being transformed into an age of terror. The old evils of selfishness and hatred have not been removed by an enlargement of ~~an~~ {our} educational system and an extension of our legislative policies. **The threat of atomic and nuclear warfare is more frighteningly real today than ever before.** And so a once optimistic generation now stands asking in utter bewilderment: "Why could not we cast it out?"

The answer to this question is rather simple. Man by his own power can never cast evil out of the world. The humanist's hope is an illusion. It is based on too great an optimism concerning the inherent goodness of human nature. There are thousands of sincere and dedicated people outside the churches working unselfishly through various humanitarian movements to cure the world of its social evils. I would be the last to condemn these people because they have not yet found their way to God, for I would rather that a man be a committed humanist than an uncommitted Christian. But so many of these dedicated people, having no one but themselves to save, {themselves} end up disillusioned and pessimistic. They are disillusioned because they started out with a great illusion. For them there is no sinner or no sin. Human nature is essentially good, and the only evil is found in systems and institutions; just enlighten people and free them from the crippling yoke of poverty, and they will save themselves. All of this sounds wonderful and soothingly pleasant. But it is an illusion wrapped in superficiality. It is a kind of self-delusion which causes the individual to ignore a basic fact about human nature.[11]

None of this is to minimize the importance of science and the great contribution of the Renaissance. We needed them to lift us from the stagnating valleys of superstitions and half-truths to the sun-lit mountains of creative analysis and objective appraisal. The unquestioned authority of the church in scientific matters needed to be challenged. Too often had it engaged in a paralyzing obscurantism. Through shameful inquisitions the church sought to circumscribe truth and place unsurmountable obstacles in the path of the truth-seeker. This had to be rectified. Without the Renaissance and the Age of Reason we would still be wandering in a confusing wilderness of antiquated, scientific notions. Nevertheless they went to far in optimism. In its earnest attempt to free the mind of man, the Renaissance forgot about man's capacity for sin.[12]

The other idea concerning the way evil is to be removed from the world says that man must wait on God to do everything. Man must lie still, purely submissive,

---

11. The preceding seven sentences were altered in the published version: "But so many of these dedicated persons, seeking salvation within the human context, have become understandably pessimistic and disillusioned, because their efforts are based on a kind of self-delusion which ignores fundamental facts about our mortal nature" (p. 120).

12. The preceding five sentences were altered in the published version: "But the exalted Renaissance optimism, while attempting to free the mind of man, forgot about man's capacity for sin" (p. 121).

and God in his good time will redeem the world.[13] This idea is rooted in a pessimistic doctrine of human nature. It has cropped up many times in the history of Christianity. It was prominent in the Reformation. This great spiritual movement which led to the birth and development of Protestantism was concerned about moral and spiritual freedom. It served as a necessary corrective for a medieval church that had become all too corrupt and stagnant.[14] Its doctrines of justification by faith and the priesthood of all believers are towering principles which we as Protestants must forever affirm. But in its doctrine of human nature the Reformation overstressed the corruption of man. While the Renaissance went to far in optimism, the Reformation went too far in pessimism.[15] The renaissance so concentrated on the goodness of man that it overlooked his capacity for evil. The Reformation so concentrated on the wickedness of man that it overlooked his capacity for goodness. While it was right in affirming the sinfulness of human nature and man's incapacity to save himself, the Reformation wrongly went to the extreme of believing that the image of God had been completely erased from man.

This led to the Calvinistic doctrine of the total depravity of man.[16] It led to a resurrection of the terrible idea of infant damnation. So depraved was human nature, said the Calvinist, that every baby born in the world was a candidate for damnation; and if he died in infancy without baptism he would burn in hell forever.[17] Certainly this was carrying the idea of man's sinfulness too far.

This lopsided Reformation theology has often led to a purely other-worldly religion. **It has caused many churches to ignore the "here" and emphasize only the "yonder."** By stressing the utter hopelessness of this world and emphasizing the need for the individual to concentrate his efforts on getting his soul prepared for the world to come, it has ignored the need for social reform, and divorced religion from life.[18] **It sees the Christian gospel as only concerned with the individual soul.** Recently a church was seeking a new minister and the pulpit committee listed several qualifications that he should possess. The first qualification was: "He must be able to preach the true gospel and not talk about social issues." This emphasis has lead to a dangerously irrelevant church. It is lit-

---

13. The preceding two sentences were altered in the published version: "The second idea for removing evil from the world stipulates that if man waits submissively upon the Lord, in his own good time God alone will redeem the world" (p. 121).

14. The preceding five sentences were altered in the published version: "Rooted in a pessimistic doctrine of human nature, this idea which eliminates completely the capability of sinful man to do anything, was prominent in the Reformation, that great spiritual movement which gave birth to the Protestant concern for moral and spiritual freedom and served as a necessary corrective for a corrupt and stagnant medieval church" (p. 121).

15. Hamilton, *Horns and Halos,* p. 62: "The Reformation went too far in pessimism."

16. The word "doctrine" was replaced by "concept" in the published version (p. 121). Hamilton, *Horns and Halos,* p. 62: "The result was an extreme Calvinism, the teaching of the total depravity of human nature."

17. This sentence was altered in the published version: "So depraved is human nature, said the doctrinaire Calvinist, that if a baby dies without baptism he will burn forever in hell" (p. 121).

18. This sentence was altered in the published version: "By ignoring the need for social reform, religion is divorced from the mainstream of human life" (p. 121).

tle more than a country club where people assemble to hear and speak pious platitudes.[19]

This one-sided emphasis of the Reformation overlooks the fact that the gospel deals with the whole man—his body as well as his soul. It is in danger of setting up a tragic dichotomy between the sacred and the secular, the god of religion and the god of life.[20] If the church is to be worthy of its name it must become the fountain-head of a better social order. It must seek to transform not only individual lives, but also the social situation. It must be concerned not only about individual sin but also about social situations that bring to many people anguish of spirit and cruel bondage.[21]

The idea that man must wait on God to do everything has lead to a tragic misuse of prayer. He who feels that God must do everything will end up asking him for anything. Some people see God as little more than "a cosmic bellhop" that they will call on for every trivial need. Others see God as so omnipotent and man as so powerless that they end up making prayer a substitute for work and intelligence. A man said to me the other day: "I believe in integration, but I know it will not come until God gets ready for it to come. You Negroes should stop protesting and start praying." Well I'm sure we all need to pray for God's help and guidance in this integration struggle. But we will be gravely misled if we think it will come by prayer alone. **God will never allow prayer to become a substitute for work and intelligence.** God gave us minds to think and breath and body to work, and he would be defeating his own purpose if he allowed us to obtain through prayer what can come through work and intelligence. No, it is not either prayer or human effort; it is both prayer and human effort. Prayer is a marvelous and necessary supplement of our feeble efforts but it is a dangerous and callous substitute. Moses discovered this as he struggled to lead the Israelites to the Promised Land. God made it clear that he would not do for them what they could do for themselves. In the Book of Exodus we read: "And the Lord said unto Moses, Wherefore criest thou unto me? Speak unto the children of Israel, that they go forward."[22]

We must pray earnestly for peace. But along with our prayers we must work vigorously for disarmanent and suspension of nuclear tests.[23] We must use our minds as rigorously to work out a plan for peace as we have used them to work out a plan for war. We must pray with unceasing passion for the emergence of racial justice. But along with this we must use our minds to develop a program and organize ourselves into mass non-violent action and use every resource of our bodies and souls to end **the long night of** racial injustice. We must pray unrelentingly for economic

---

19. The preceding two sentences were altered in the published version: "This is a blueprint for a dangerously irrelevant church where people assemble to hear only pious platitudes" (p. 121).

20. The preceding two sentences were altered in the published version: "By disregarding the fact that the gospel deals with man's body as well as with his soul, such a one-sided emphasis creates a tragic dichotomy between the sacred and the secular" (pp. 121–122).

21. The preceding three sentences were altered in the published version: "To be worthy of its New Testament origin, the church must seek to transform both individual lives and the social situation that brings to many people anguish of spirit and cruel bondage" (p. 122).

22. Cf. Exodus 14:15.

23. The term "nuclear tests" was replaced by "weapon testing" in the published version (p. 122).

justice. But along with our prayers we must work diligently to bring into being those social changes that will make for a better distribution of wealth. We must use our minds to develop a sort of massive Marshall Plan that will aid the undeveloped countries of the world to emerge from the long and bitter winter of poverty to the warm spring of economic stability.[24]

All of this reveals the fallacy of the idea that God alone will rid the earth of evil. Man, sitting complacently by the wayside, and expecting to see God cast evil out of the world, will see no such thing. No prodigious thunderbolt will come dashing out of the sky to blast evil away. No mighty army of angels will decend from heaven and force men to do what their wills have led them not to do. Throughout the Bible God is pictured not as an Omnipotent Czar who makes all of the decisions for his subjects nor as a cosmic tyrant who uses gestapo-like methods to invade the inner lives of men; he is rather pictured as a loving Father who stands ever ready to give exceedingly abundant things to his children if they will freely accept.[25] It is always clear that man must do something. "Stand up on your feet," says God to Ezekiel, "and I will speak to you."[26] Man is not a helpless invalid who is left in a valley of total depravity until God pulls him out; he is rather an upstanding human being whose vision has been impaired by the cataracts of sin and whose soul has been weakened by the virus of pride. But there is enough vision left for man to lift his eyes unto the hills, and there is enough of God's image left for man to turn his weak and sin-battered life toward the Great Physician, the curer of the disease of sin.

So we can see the real weakness of the idea that God will do everything. It is based on a false conception of God and a false conception of man. It makes God so absolutely sovereign that man is absolutely helpless. It makes man so absolutely depraved that he can do nothing but wait on God. It sees the world as so contaminated with sin that God totally transcends it and only touches it here and there through a mighty invasion. This view ends up with a God who is a despot, ~~a dictator and not a Father.~~ {and not a Father.} It ends up with such a pessimism concerning human nature that it leaves man little more than a helpless worm crawling through the morass of an evil world. ~~But neither God nor man is like this.~~ {But} Man is ~~not~~ {neither} totally depraved, ~~and~~ {nor is} God ~~is not~~ an almighty dictator. We must ~~continue to~~ {surely} affirm the majesty and sovereignty of God, ~~We must continue to declare with unmistakable clarity that God is all-powerful and all-knowing. But~~ {but} this should not lead us to believe that God is an Almighty Monarch who will impose his will upon us. ~~He has made us persons with freedom, free to choose the good and therefore free to choose what is not good.~~ {and deprive us of the freedom to choose what is good or what is not good.} He will not thrust himself upon us. ~~Like the~~

---

24. The Marshall Plan (1947), named after secretary of state George C. Marshall, was an economic program intended to aid in Europe's reconstruction after World War II. The preceding three sentences were altered in the published version: "We must pray unrelentingly for economic justice, but we must also work diligently to bring into being those social changes that make for a better distribution of wealth within our nation and in the undeveloped countries of the world" (p. 122).

25. The phrase "stands ever ready to give exceedingly abundant things to his children if they will freely accept" was replaced by "gives to his children such abundant blessings as they may be willing to receive" in the published version (p. 123).

26. Cf. Ezekiel 2:1.

~~Father in the parable of the prodical son, God will not~~ {nor} force us to stay home when our minds are bent on journeying to some degrading far country. But he follows us in ~~our shabby defilement~~ {love}, and ~~if and~~ when we come to ourselves and turn our tired feet back to the Father's house, he stands waiting with outstretched arms of forgiveness.[27]

Therefore we must never feel that God will, through some breathtaking miracle or a wave of the hand, cast evil out of the world. As long as we believe this we will pray unanswerable prayers and ask God to do things that he will never do. The belief that God will do everything for man is as untenable as the belief that man can do everything for himself. It, too, is based on a lack of faith. We must learn that to trust God with the expectation that he will do everything while we do nothing is not faith, but superstition.

What, then, is the answer to life's perplexing question? How can evil be cast out of our individual and collective lives? If the world is not to be purified by God alone or by man alone, who, then, will do it?

The answer to this question is found in an idea which is distinctly different from the two we have been discussing. It is not either God or man that will bring about the world's salvation. It is both man and God, made one by a marvelous unity of purpose, by an overflowing love and the free gift of himself on the part of God, by perfect obedience and receptivity on the part of man—these two together can transform the old into the new, and drive out the deadly cancer of sin.

The principle which opens the door for God to work through man is faith. This is what the disciples lacked as they stood at the foot of the mountain desperately trying to remove the nagging evil from the body of the sick child. Jesus reminded them that they failed because they had been trying to do for themselves what they could only do when he was behind them, when their very lives were open receptables, as it were, into which God's strength could be freely poured.

In the Scripture two types of faith in God are clearly set forth. One may be referred to as the mind's faith in God; the individual intellect ~~asserts~~ {assents} to the belief that God exists. The other may be referred to as the heart's faith in God; the whole man is here involved in a trusting act of self-surrender to God. It is this latter type of faith that man must have in order to know God. The mind's faith in God is directed toward a theory. The heart's faith in God is centered in a person. **In a real sense faith is total surrender to God.** Gabriel Marcel has said that faith is really <u>believing in</u> rather than <u>believing that</u>. It is "opening a credit; which puts me at the disposal of the one in whom I believe." If I believe, he says, "I rally to; with that sort of interior gathering of oneself which the act of rallying implies."[28] Faith is the act of opening one's life to God. It is openess on all sides and at every level to the Divine inflow.

This is what the Apostle was getting at in his doctrine of salvation by faith. For him, faith is man's capacity to accept God's offer through Christ to rescue us from the bondage of sin. God, in his magnanimous love, offers to do for us what we can't

---

27. Luke 15:11–32.

28. King refers to the thoughts of the French existentialist Gabriel Marcel on spiritual faith (Marcel, *Creative Fidelity*, trans. Robert Rosthal [New York: Farrar, Straus, 1964], p. 134).

do for ourselves. The humble and willing acceptance of this offer is faith. **Indeed, faith is the willing acceptance of a free gift. It is accepting our acceptance. It is reaching out to take in. It is man's whole nature wide open to God.**

So it is by faith that we are saved. Man filled with God and God operating through man will bring unbelievable changes in our individual and social lives. As we look out into our world we see that social evils have risen to ominous proportions. They have left millions of men wandering through a dark and murky corridor with no sight of an exit sign. Others have come dangerously close to being plunged {into} a dark abyss of psychological fatalism. If these deadly, paralyzing evils are to be removed from the world it will be done neither by God alone or man alone; it will be done at last by a humanity perfectly united with God through obedience. The unit of power for moral victory is God filling man and man opening his life by faith to God, as the gulf opens itself to the overflowing waters of the river.[29] Racial justice is a real possibility in this nation and in the world. But it will not come by our frail and often misguided efforts alone; neither will it come by a mighty act of God in which he imposes his will on wayward men. It will come when enough people will open their lives to God, and allow him to pour his triumphant Divine energy into their souls. Our long and noble dream of a world of peace may yet become a reality. But it will come neither by man working alone or God breaking in to crash the wicked schemes of men. Peace will come when men so open their lives to God that he will fill them with love, mutual respect, and understanding goodwill. Yes, ~~even~~ social salvation can only come through faith—man's willing acceptance of God's mighty gift.

Let me turn for a moment to an application of all that I have been saying to our individual lives. Many of you here know something of what it is to struggle with sin. Year by year you became aware of a terrible sin that was taking possession of your life. It may have been slavery to drink, untruthfulness, impurity or selfishness. As the years unfolded the vice grew bolder and bolder.[30] You know {knew} all along that it was an unnatural intruder. And you said to yourself "one day I am going to rise up and drive this evil out. I know it is wrong. It is destroying my character and embarrassing my family." At last the day came. You made a New Year's resolution that you would get rid of the whole base thing. And then the next New Year came around and you were doing the old evil. Can you remember the surprise and disappointment that gripped you when you discovered that after all of your sincere efforts the old habit was still there.[31] In utter amazement you found yourself asking, "why could not I cast it out?"

---

29. The preceding five sentences were altered in the published version: "Social evils have trapped multitudes of men in a dark and murky corridor where there is no exit sign and plunged others into a dark abyss of psychological fatalism. These deadly, paralyzing evils can be removed by a humanity perfectly united through obedience with God. Moral victory will come as God fills man and man opens his life by faith to God, even as the gulf opens to the overflowing waters of the river" (pp. 124–125).

30. The phrase "grew bolder and bolder" was replaced by "widened its landmarks on your soul" in the published version (p. 125).

31. The preceding four sentences were altered in the published version: "At last you determined to purge yourself of the evil by making a New Year's resolution. Do you remember your surprise and disappointment when you discovered, three hundred and sixty-five days later, that your most sincere efforts had not banished the old habit from your life?" (p. 125)

In this moment of despair you decided to take your problem to God. Instead of asking him to work through you, you said: "God you must solve this problem for me. I can't do anything about it." As the days and months unfold{ed} you discover{ed} that the evil is {was} still with you. God would not cast it out, for he never takes away sin without the cordial co-working of sinful men. No, the problem could not be solved by your standing idly by waiting on Lod {God} to do all of the work.

What, then, is the way out? Not by our own efforts, and not by a purely external help from God. One cannot remove an evil habit by mere resolution; nor can it be [*strikeout illegible*] done by simply calling on God to do the job. It can be done only when a man lifts himself up until he can put his will into the hands of God's will as an instrument. This is the only way to be delivered from the accumulated weight of evil. It can only be done when we allow the energy of God to be let loose in our souls.

May we go out today big in faith, strong in our determination to be new creatures. God has made his free offer through Jesus Christ.[32] "If any one is in Christ," says Paul, "he is a new creation; the old has passed away, behold, the new has come."[33] In other words, if any man is in Christ he is a new person. His old self has gone. He becomes a divinely transformed son of God.

One of the great glories of the Gospel is that Christ has transformed so many men, and made sons of nameless prodigals. He transformed a Simon of Sand into a Peter of Rock.[34] He changed a persecuting Saul into an Apostle Paul.[35] He changed a lust-fested Augustine into a Saint Augustine. Tolstoi's beautiful confession in "My Religion" is the experience of men in every nation and every tribe: "Five years ago I came to believe in Christ's teaching, and my life suddenly became changed: I ceased desiring what I had wished before, and began to desire what I had not wished before. What formerly had seemed good to me appeared bad, and what had seemed bad appeared good. . . . The direction of my life, my desires became different: what was good and bad changed places."[36]

Herein we find the answer to a perplexing question. Evil can be cast out. But it will not be removed by man alone nor by a Dictatorial God who invades our lives. It will be removed when we will open the door and allow God through Christ to enter. "Behold I stand at the door and knock," sayeth the Lord, "if any man will open the {door} I will come in to him and sup with him and he with me."[37] God is too cour-

---

32. The previous two sentences were replaced in the published version: "God has promised to co-operate with us when we seek to cast evil from our lives and become true children of his divine will" (pp. 125–126).

33. 2 Corinthians 5:17 (RSV).

34. John 1:42.

35. Acts 9:1–28.

36. King cites the opening paragraph of the introduction to Tolstoy's book *My Religion* (trans. Huntington Smith [London, Walter Scott, 1900], p. 1). This discussion of Tolstoy was altered in the published version: "The measured words of Leo Tolstoi's confession in *My Religion* reflect an experience many have shared: 'Five years ago faith came to me; I believed in the doctrine of Jesus, and my whole life underwent a sudden transformation. What I had once wished for I wished for no longer, and I began to desire what I had never desired before. What had once appeared to me right now became wrong, and the wrong of the past I beheld as right . . . My life and my desires were completely changed; good and evil interchanged meanings'" (p. 126).

37. Revelation 3:20.

teous to break the door down. But if we will open it there will be a divine and human confrontation that will transform dark yesterday into bright tomorrows, and turn the ruin of sin into glorious victory.[38]

TADd. CSKC: Sermon file, folder 96, Dr. King's Letters.

---

38. The preceding two sentences were altered in the published version: "God is too courteous to break open the door but when we open it in faith believing, a divine and human confrontation will transform our sin-ruined lives into radiant personalities" (p. 126).

VI: UNDATED HOMILETIC MATERIAL

Note on Dating

The sermons published in this section are a sampling of homiletic documents from King's sermon file that may represent some of his early efforts at sermon preparation. Mainly handwritten sermon outlines and notes on general theological themes, these documents contain few internal or external references by which to date them definitively. While many are written on lined, loose-leaf paper of the type King commonly used during his school years at Crozer Theological Seminary (1948–1951) and Boston University (1951–1954), the documents cannot be linked to a specific class or professor and so are assigned a range date of 1948–1954: between the time he was ordained in February 1948 and when he delivered his January 1954 trial sermon at Dexter Avenue Baptist Church in Montgomery. A few documents do contain references to authors and books that appear on syllabi for courses King took at Crozer and Boston, and so their range date is adjusted accordingly. King filed almost half of these outlines and notes in a folder titled "Sermons Not Preached."

Sermon outlines were a primary mode of King's sermon preparation and presentation through much of his life. In a letter to *Pulpit Digest* editor Samuel M. Cavert, King remarked, "Due to an extremely crowded and strenuous schedule for the last two or three years, I have not had an opportunity to write most of the sermons that I preach. In most cases I have had to content myself with a rather detailed outline."[1] While many of the outlines published here may not have become part of King's sermon repertoire, their content is evident in other sermons that he composed. King readily drew on early sermon material for phrases, concepts, and general inspiration, especially after the Montgomery bus boycott put him in great demand as a preacher and civil rights advocate. Coretta Scott King remembered that "in his later years he almost always preached from an outline."[2] While working from outlines was an issue of expediency for King, it may also have been a stylistic choice. Without a prepared text, King could draw freely on the biblical texts, hymns, illustrations, anecdotes, and set pieces that he had honed over the years, as well as add references to recent events and current cultural topics to keep his sermons fresh.

---

1. King to Cavert, 27 November 1959, pp. 379–381 in this volume.
2. Coretta Scott King, *My Life with Martin Luther King, Jr.*, p. 115.

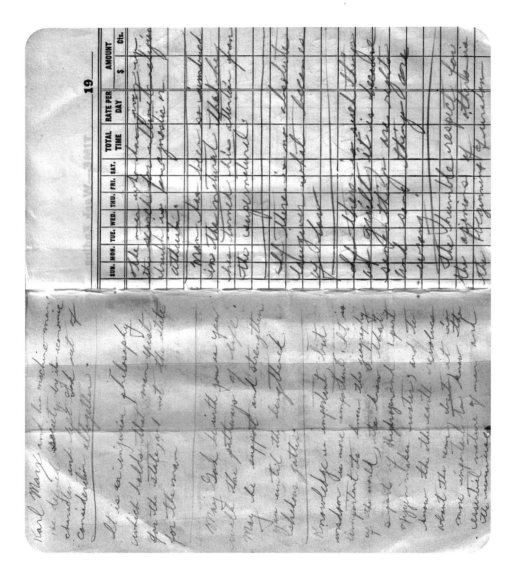

King used a weekly time book to record his thoughts on a variety of topics (1948–1954).

In these handwritten notes, King mentions several sources for sermon ideas including the course textbook Christian Beginnings *by Morton Scott Enslin, his Crozer professor, and course notes from George W. Davis's* Christian Theology for Today.[1] *King wrote these miscellaneous thoughts on several different types of paper and kept them in a folder titled "Sermon Notes."*

Facing Catastrophe with Faith and courage
(text—Therefore will not we fear, though the earth is removed, and though the mountain be carried <u>away</u> into the midst of the sea . . . the Lord of hosts is with us; the God of Jacob is our refuge."[2]

A Man Is What He Proves To be in A Crisis. (Ghandi: He taked of non voilence and forgiveness all of his life. But the real quality of his life came in the great crisis when he could forgive a man who had assisinated him.)[3]

God's Search For Man
1 Kings 18:27[4]
    What is God doing during the long ages in which men are seeking him? Does He leave man to do all the seeking? That would be like the scene on Mount Carmel when the Priest of Baal could not get an answer from their God and Elijah kept baiting them with Satirical suggestions, telling them to call a little louder, because their God might be absent minded or even asleep. The point of such excellent satire was that the living and true God is not like that. (Use to Poem, the Hond of Heaven[5]
                        Death couldn't hold him
Easter Sermon Acts 2:24 Moffett[6]

---

1. Enslin assigned his book *Christian Beginnings* (New York: Harper & Brothers, 1938) for his class The Gospels, which King took in the spring of 1949. King completed Davis's course Christian Theology for Today on 15 February 1950.

2. Cf. Psalm 46:2, 7. King drew a line below this entry, separating it from the following one. He placed several other lines between entries in this document, which are indicated in the transcription by an extra line of space.

3. Indian independence leader Mohandas K. Gandhi was killed by Nathuram Godse on 30 January 1948. On notecards he titled "Religion and Peace of Soul," King also referred to "Gandhi's dying prayer for his murderer" (King, 1948–1954). In his 28 February 1948 column, Benjamin Mays wrote of Gandhi, "He died practicing what he preached. The press stated that when falling, he gave a sign which meant 'forgive'" ("Non-Violence," *Pittsburgh Courier*).

4. "And it came to pass at noon, that Elijah mocked them, and said, Cry aloud; for he is a god: either he is talking, or he is pursuing, or he is in a journey, or peradventure he sleepeth, and must be awaked."

5. Francis Thompson, "The Hound of Heaven" (1893): "'Ah, fondest, blindest, weakest, / I am He Whom thou seekest! / Thou dravest love from thee, who dravest Me.'"

6. Acts 2:24 (MOFFATT): "but God raised him by checking the pangs of death. Death could not hold him."

Why death could not hold him

1. His mind was to great for the grave

2. His love was to great for the grave

3. His character was to great for the grave.
> Jesus was more powerful on the day of pentacost six weeks after his death than he was in Jerusalem on Palm Sunday

The Life of Jesus is like a drama—see Enslin pp 374–375[7]

3. Two Challenging questions/can he be found in research {this sumer)}
> Can God Be known
> What think ye of Christ

These are two questions which we all face as ministers

We can know about God, but we can never know God.

The power of the Infinite in the finite
> (The Hand of God)

* The Jungles Of Life

Jeremiah 12:5.[8] See Prostant Pulpit.[9]

What is Authority in Christianity?
> It is Christ within you, which is love. Not the Bible, not the pope in Rome, but love

> If I would go to Gemany and speak in English no matter how loud and how long I talk the people would not understand me. But if I struck four chords of music everyone of the could could understand the emotion which I am attempting to convey. As we set out in life we must strick the chord of God's eternal sound which is love and it will be understood by all people.

Sermon

1. Why does History Move?

Int.   Why cant we freeze history.
> 1. Hegel—Absolute working toward Divine consciousness[10]
> 2. [*Karl*] Marx—Internal contradiction of matter.
> 3. Christianity—God moves History

We always move round the One, but we do not always fix our gaze upon It. We

---

7. Enslin, *Christian Beginnings*, pp. 374–375: "As the narrative proceeds, the tone of excitement heightens, until in the last pages—the dreadful days in Jerusalem—there is no let down or breathing space till the very end, the death. His enemies are victorious; his body is put in a rock-cut tomb. The curtain falls with the audience speechless. Then after a quick moment the curtain rises again for an instant."

8. "If thou hast run with the footmen, and they have wearied thee, then how canst thou contend with horses? and if in the land of peace, wherein thou trustedst, they wearied thee, then how wilt thou do in the swelling of Jordan?"

9. King may refer to Arthur John Gossip's sermon based on Jeremiah 12:5 titled "But When Life Tumbles In, What Then?" in *The Protestant Pulpit: An Anthology of Master Sermons from the Reformation to Our Own Day*, ed. Andrew Watterson Blackwood (New York: Abingdon Press, 1947), pp. 198–204.

10. Georg Friedrich Wilhelm Hegel (1770–1831) was a German philosopher who argued that history reveals a dialectical nature, that of two contrasting ideas combining into a synthesis through time and ultimately culminating in the discovery of God, the Absolute Spirit.

are like a choir of singers standing round the conductor, who do not always sing in tune, because their attention is diverted to some external object. When they look at the conductor, they sing well and are really with him. So we always move round the One. If we did not, we should dissolve and cease to be. But we do not always look toward the One. When we do, we attain the end of our existence and our rest; and we no longer sing out of tune, but form in truth a divine choir about the One: Plotinus[11]

Kinds Of Christian

1. Institutional Christians (solitary)

2. Intellectual Christians (and seekers of after religion

3. There are experiential
4. There are inheritance Christian.
Going Forward by Going Back—The paradox.
       Luke 2:45[12]

"John is Arisen, even the John I Beheaded" Mark 6:16.[13]
Good text on conscience.
Series Of Sermons on Sin—See Theology II (notes[14]

Nathan's parable.—II Samuel 11 and 12. The story of Davids adultery is not written so much to show Davids wicket, but to show the moral courage of Nathan. Nathan had the moral courage to stand out against the evil of King in the court. The story is Nathan centered rather than David centered

How To Find God.
(1) God is manifest in the world and its creatures. This is natural theology
(2) God is found in the stream of History. He is found in Christ and the Prophets. This is dogmatic theology.
(3) He is found in Soul secret and direct experience of God. This is mystical theology. For a well rounded religious life we should have a part of all of these. Not all of one.
Sub—Invinsibles For Cataclysmic Times
II Kings 18:20[15] A cleansing element.

---

11. Plotinus (204?–270 CE) was a Roman philosopher who developed the concepts of neoplatonism.
12. "And when they found him not, they turned back again to Jerusalem, seeking him." King developed this into a complete sermon (see King, "Going Forward by Going Backward," Sermon at Dexter Avenue Baptist Church, 4 April 1954, pp. 159–163 in this volume). In his personal copy of *The New Testament of Our Lord and Savior Jesus Christ: Revised Standard Version*, King wrote the words "Going Forward by Going Backward" next to Luke 2:41–47.
13. "But when Herod heard thereof, he said, It is John, whom I beheaded: he is risen from the dead."
14. King's notes from Davis's course include the following topic headings: "Sin and its Relation to Man," "The Nature of Sin," "The Christian Consciousness of Sin," "The Result of Sin," "Sin in Relation to God," and "The Process of Forgiving Sin" (Class notes, Christian Theology for Today, 29 November 1949–15 February 1950).
15. "Thou sayest (but they are but vain words), I have counsel and strength for the war. Now, on whom dost thou trust, that thou rebellest against me?"

the thing that we choose now might be the very thing that will piece you in later life

{Preach this summer} Trying God in A moment Of Crisis

(Lord let the cup pass from me)[16]

Here Jesus will was in conflict with God's will[17]

I am convinced that for men who love the risks of faith and the divine adventure, who can live hard and like it, the ministry presents the noblest and most rewarding of careers. The task is especially difficult in these days, and it is a good thing for the ministry and for the Christian Church that the task is so challenging, and that it taxes every power of manhood. Nothing is to be gained by making the entrance into the ministry easy

Remember the strange question that Jesus put to the paralytic. The afficted men had begged Jesus to heal him. But, instead of complying at once, the Master asks a question: "Wilt thou be made whole?"[18] What a question to ask a cripple! Might not Jesus have known, even without the man's spoken plea, that he sincerely desired to be made strong? But no, no necessarily so; for there are som advantages in being a cripple. A cripple is not expected to work. He need carry no responsibility. He does not have to stand up to the pressure and demands of life, like the well man. His frinds are very tender; they wait on him, eagerly fulfilling his every wish. Hence it happens occasionally that sick peopl unconsciously fall in love with being sick. They feel, subconsciously of course, that the advantages of being sick are more to be desired than the disadvantages of being healthy. Psychology has demonstrated again and again that some people do not get well because deep down in their sub-conscious selves they do not want to! Do you really want the health which will mean work and responsibility Are you prepared to accept the consequences of being a well man.

{~~Every~~ all the universe is in some way the expression of the life of God.}

The universe is indeed a unity—a oneness [*will?*] many. Of course, for conven-ience study we divide this universe into chemistry and physics, biology and botany, and the other sciences. It must be remembered however, that when we study one of these sciences we are getting only a partial view of the whole. It is like living in a large house when, desiring to see the surrounding world outside, we go first to one window and then to another But we are looking at the same world

{There is no loss of energy or matter says science. There is no death. What we call death always turns out to be a change of form, or a different expression of life.} Two gases unite to form what we call water. At a given temperature it becomes solid. Again it become a liquid, and with its change of rising temperature, disappears in a

---

16. Cf. Matthew 26:39. King would use this passage as the basis for other sermons ("A Way Out," 22 May 1949, and Garden of Gethsemane, Sermon Delivered at Dexter Avenue Baptist Church, 14 April 1957, pp. 90–94 and 275–283, in this volume, respectively).

17. After this entry, another person expanded the outline with references to materialism, wealth, pleasure, luck, astrology, and idleness.

18. Cf. John 5:6.

vapor, uniting with other elements for other forms. But in all the series of changes,
not a particle of matter, nor a throb of energy has been destroyed

I would rather fail in a movement that will ultimately succeed than to succeed in a movement that will ultimately fail
{Subject Insatiable Hopes}
Luke 24:13–31[19]

How

What was it that Christ did to give the follower a ray of hope even though their desires had not been satisfied

What does Jesus ofer to man to man him optimistic when all of the desires of his life seem to be optimistic
1. Belief in the whole Christ
2. Belief in history.
3. Fellowship

~~Johna~~ Jonah
I Intro
II When man revolt against the will of God disaster is inevitable
1. What is the will of God
1. Judaism's approach
2. Approach of chatholic church
3. Christ's approach—Law of Love
III You are inevitably your brothers Keeper[20]

We need a spare tire so if anything happens we may use it.
Luke:22:42[21]

Theme—What resources can we have in a moment of crisis that will keep us stable

Here Jesus' will is out of harmony with God's will. What did he do to make his will coincide with God's

In a moment of crisis what spiritual resources do we have.
I Some try evasion
1. Feet—disciples
2. drinking—
3. suicide
4. Friends—your best friend might be your worse enemy

---

19. Luke 24:13–31 recorded Jesus's encounter, after His resurrection, with two disciples on the road to Emmaus. King used this story in the sermon Questions That Easter Answers, 21 April 1957, pp. 283–293 in this volume.

20. Genesis 4:9.

21. "Saying, Father, if thou be willing, remove this cup from me: nevertheless not my will, but thine, be done." King developed this passage and theme into a full sermon (King, Garden of Gethsemane, 4 April 1957, pp. 275–283 in this volume.

1950–1954 Jesus Conquers Time

We ar victims of time.

Jesus identified himself with something that transcended time.

"On Facing the Challenge of a difficult situation"

    See Fosdicks', "Making the Best Out of a Bad Mess" in <u>Hope of the World</u>[22]

    Sub—Pride of Achievement

The record of King Uzziah illustrates it. Listen: His name spread far abroad; for he was marvelously helped, till he was strong. But when he was strong, his heart was lifted up to his own destruction."[23]

    Success breeds a sense of self-sufficiency Men no longer feel need of God. Then they fall.

    see Sockman "The Higher Happiness p. 30, 31.[24]

    Sub.—The Omnipotence of God

    Text "He telleth the number of the stars . . . He healeth the broken in heart."[25]

    God is powerful in the physical and the Spiritual realms.

    See Chp 2 in Weatherhead's—<u>Why Do Men Suffer</u>[26]

    Sub.—The Lord God Omnipotent Reigneth

    Text Rev 19.6[27]

See Prostant pulpit p. 238[28] {* preach to preachers}

AHD. CSKC: Sermon file, folder 49, "Sermon Notes."

---

22. On an attached notecard, King wrote this reference to a sermon in Harry Emerson Fosdick, *Hope of the World*, pp. 117–125. He also delivered the sermon "Making the Best of a Bad Mess" at Ebenezer on 24 April 1966.

23. Cf. 2 Chronicles 26:15–16.

24. Ralph W. Sockman, *The Higher Happiness* (New York: Abingdon-Cokesbury Press, 1944), p. 31: "Success breeds a sense of self-sufficiency. Men no longer feel the need of God. Then they fall." Sockman also considered racial prejudice: "Or think how the pride of race poisons human relationships. When a person has nothing else of which to be proud, he can always fall back on his race, provided, of course that he is white and Aryan. And how much of our race prejudice is fomented by people who have little else but race to distinguish them!"

25. Psalm 147:3–4.

26. Weatherhead, *Why Do Men Suffer?* pp. 26–46. Weatherhead titled his second chapter "Is God Omnipotent?"

27. "And I heard as it were the voice of a great multitude, and as the voice of many waters, and as the voice of mighty thunderings, saying, Alleluia; for the Lord God omnipotent reigneth."

28. King refers to the first page of Joseph Fort Newton's sermon "Reconciliation" in *The Protestant Pulpit*, p. 238.

"The Relevance of the Holy Spirit"
A very good sermon esp for preachers
For central points see DeWolf TLC, 272 F.[1]

"The Meaning of Salvatin"
Salvation implies three things

(1) It brings about a new relationship with ourselves

(2) It brings about a new relationship with God.

(3) It brings about a new relationsship with other persons
See DeWolf, TLC, 287 F[2]

"The Mission of the Church"[3]
See DeWolf, TLC, 322F[4]

"The Kingdom as Present and yet to Come"
Use a double text: "The Kingdom of God is within you"[5]
the kingdom will come in the future
I   Definition of the Kingdon
II   The Kingdom As Present
III The Kingdom not yet
See DeWolf TLC, 299F[6]

God Is A Spirit
Text: "God is a spirit . . ."[7]
The assertion has three meaning

---

1. King refers to a subsection of chapter 32 in L. Harold DeWolf's book *A Theology of the Living Church* titled "Significance of Belief in the Holy Spirit." DeWolf wrote: "The doctrine of the Holy Spirit is a guarantee within the ancient Christian tradition itself of every man's right and obligation to look beyond tradition. For there is always 'new truth yet to break forth,' not only through new study of the Bible, but also through other channels, from the God in whom is all truth and who speaks anew in every age" (*A Theology of the Living Church*, p. 273). This document is dated based on the publication date of DeWolf's 1953 book. He was King's dissertation advisor at Boston University.

2. King refers to chapter 34, titled "The New Birth" (DeWolf, *A Theology of the Living Church*, pp. 287–296). DeWolf examined the importance of being "born anew" from psychological, ethical, and theological perspectives. Each of these, he argued, revealed that salvation "involves change within the individual, change in his relation to God and change in his relation to other persons" (pp. 287–288).

3. King developed a full sermon with this title (see King, "The Mission of the Church," 1953–1956).

4. King refers to a section of chapter 37 titled "Purpose of the Organized Church." DeWolf critiqued false conceptions of the church's purpose, bemoaning those who equate it with "the whole kingdom of God," while noting the church exists to nurture and express Christian love (DeWolf, *A Theology of the Living Church*, pp. 322–326).

5. Cf. Luke 17:21.

6. King refers to chapter 35, titled "The Kingdom as Present and Growing." DeWolf discussed a "Definition of the Kingdom," "The Kingdom Present," and "The Kingdom Not Yet." He defined the Kingdom as the "reign of God" in which the "supreme uniting principle is love." "The kingdom is, in some respects and in some human experience, already present" for God is present and active even now. He cautioned, however, that the continued presence of sin is "grim evidence that the kingdom has not come" (DeWolf, *A Theology of the Living Church*, pp. 299–305).

7. Cf. John 4:24.

"The Relevance of the Holy Spirit"
A very good sermon esp. for preachers

For central points see De Wolf
TLC, 272 F.

"The Meaning of Salvation"

Salvation implies three things
(1) It brings about a new relationship with ourselves
(2) It brings about a new relationship with God,
(3) It brings about a new relationship with other persons

See De Wolf, TLC, 287F

"The Mission of the Church"
    See De Wolf, TLC, 322F

"The Kingdom as Present and yet to Come"

Use a double text: "The Kingdom of God is within you"
the kingdom will come in the future

I Definition of the Kingdom

II The Kingdom As Present

III The Kingdom not yet

See DeWolf T L C, 299F

God Is A Spirit

Text: "God is a spirit . . ."

The assertion has three meaning

1. God is above that which is material and Physical

2. God is not impeded by the wolddness of flesh.

3. There is an ethical and rational side
to his nature.

See Knudson, R T O T, Ch II

1. God is above that which is material and Physical

2. God is not impeded by the weakness of flesh.

3. There is an ethical and rational side to his nature.
   See Knudson, RTOT, Ch IV[8]

AD. CSKC: Sermon file, folder 50, Sermons Not Preached.

---

8. In Albert Knudson's book *The Religious Teaching of the Old Testament*, chapter 4 is titled "The Spirituality of God." He wrote: "The word 'spirituality' as applied to God has at least three distinct meanings. It means that God is a spirit distinguished from material or physical existence. It means that he is free from the weakness of flesh, and is a supramundane power, superior to the forces of nature. It means also that there is an inner side to his personality, a rational and ethical side, and that it is here that his essential nature is to be found" (Knudson, *The Religious Teaching of the Old Testament*, p. 93).

Wedding Prayer and Marriage Ceremony

[1948–1954]

King may have prepared the following two documents early in his career to use as a standard prayer and ceremonial text for weddings throughout his ministry. He may have used them to officiate in one of his first marriage ceremonies, the 22 August 1948 wedding of Samuel P. Long and Ruth Bussey at Thankful Baptist Church in Decatur, Georgia.[1]

"Wedding Prayer"

O God our gracious heavenly father, who art the originator of all life; whose presence brings happiness to every condition; whose favor sweetens every relation. We beseech thy blessings upon these thy servants as they embark upon the great sea of matrimony. Grant that the ship of their marriage will be well anchored and guided by the proper compass, so that ~~when the tidal wave of a new experince emerges and the jostling winds of adjustmnt~~ they will be able to emerge successfully into the great habor of peace, happiness and oneness. Give them a deep awareness of the sacredness of this venture. In an age when so many men and women would make marriage a mere perfectory act with no divine and sacred value, when myriad hollywood would arise to make of marriage a mere seasonable plaything which must occur at least four or five times in a life time, in such an age help then to realize that marriage is man's greatest perogative, for it is in and through it that thou hast given man the priveledge to aid thee in thy creative activity. Help them to see the primacy of love in this venture. Grant that they will realize that without it a marrige can be dropped into the abyss of

---

1. "Bussey-Long Wedding of Wide Interest in Atlanta, Decatur," *Atlanta Daily World*, 4 September 1948.

meaninglessness where each peson will experience the bleekness of nagging despair, but with it the marrige can be lifted to ~~heavenly paradise where exhuberant joy will reign without ceasing~~ the radiant level of life's most exciting venture.

AD. CSKC: Sermon file, folder 97.

Marriage Ceremony

Today you embark upon the sacred seas of matrimony. Marrige is not a physical arrangement to be entered at will and dissolved at whim; it is holy ground that must be entered reverently. Through its portals men and women enter the realm of their immortality. Indeed, marriage is man's greatest perogative, for it is in and through it that God has allowed us to aid him in his creative activity.

Today you become the hiers of a legacy of togetherness. Together you will dream dreams. Together you will make plans. Together you will face moments of unutterable joy. Together you will face moments of inespressible sorror. Dispair not when the inevitable moments of personality adjustment arise, for they may be the stepping stones to a higher levels of self completion. Be not dismayed when the booyancy of fulfillment is transformed into the fatigue of disappointment, for this is a part of the changing scenery of life. Like the ever flowing water of the river, life has its moments of drought and its moments of flood. Like the ever changing cycle of the seasons life has the piercing chill of its winters and the soothing ~~warth~~ warmth of its ~~winters~~ summers.

If you feel that the fountain of love is running dry in your marriage, seek desperately to fill it anew; for without love marriage is like a parched and dryed up dessert without the refreshing oasis of happiness If you are tempted to stumble from the mountain of love, seek passionately to reach the high places again; for without truth marrige is like a ship without a compass.

Love, trust, loyalty and mutual respect are the pillars upon which the temple of marriage must be built. If these elements are there the storms may come and the winds may blow, but they will not upset the temple of your marrige, for it is founded upon a solid rock.

AHD. MLKJP-GAMK: Box 123.

"God's Relation to the World"

[*1948–1954*]

Text Neh. 9:6 "Thou, even thou art Lord alone; thou hast made heaven . . . the earth, and things that are therein . . . and thou preservest them all."[1]

Rom 11:36 "For of him, and through him, and to him, are all things."

---

1. Cf. Nehemiah 9:6. On a notecard, King elaborated: "Here Nehemiah affirm emphatically that God

Int. These passages reveal that the Bible represents God's relation to the world under three aspects: creation, conservation and transformation We may treat these three sucessively

I God created the World. Without him it would not have come into being

1. The world is not a reality that came into being through the accidental interplay of atoms and electrons

   The world is not an eternal reality which always has been and always will be.

2. Rather the world came into being by an act of God. God decided to create the world

3. He created <u>ex nihilo</u>[2] (Compare to what man creates which is alway out of something else)

4. Although God created the world he isn't dependent on it. God is a being who depends on nothing, but upon whom everything else is dependent.[3] As the late Archbishop of Canterbury, Dr. William Templ used to say "God minus the world equals God; the world minus God equals nothing."[4] (At this point use the illustration of the Lord's statement to Moses "I am")[5]

   Prior to the appearance of self conscious beings on this earth, God was. Prior to all organic life, God was. Long before the hills in order stood or earth received her frame, God was. Before the appearance of the sun, the moon the planets and the stars, God was.[6]

II God conserves the world. Syn. (Maintain sustain, uphold, defend, protect)

God is not like an architect who lays the foundation of his world and then leaves He is not like a clockmaker that mechanically wound this clock of the world and left it to tick on its own accord: God is not like a ~~far~~ spectator that sits in some far off cosmic grandstand frequently looking in on the game of human life. Rather God is an active part of the game itself sustaing and protecting it, and without God's continual sustaing power this game of life could not be played. In God "we live and move and have our being."[7] Without God the whole cosmos would crumble to nothingness. Without God our human efforts

---

is a creator. He created all the heavens, the earth, and the seas. This emphasis on God's creative power runs throughout the Old Testament. Whenever men look upon God as creator of all the universe they have risen to the level of monotheism whether they realize it or not. Nehemiah showed many nationalistic biases on the one hand, but with this theory of God as creator of the universe, he was recognizing a universal God" (King, Notecards on topics from Ezra and Nehemiah, 22 September 1952–28 January 1953).

2. *Ex nihilo* is Latin for "out of nothing."

3. In notes on this topic, King continued, "First, God created the physical world; without Him it would not have come into being, but He is in no way dependent on it (forcibly expressed in Jeremiah's comparison of the potter and the clay [*Jeremiah*] 18:6)" (King, "God's Relation to the World," Sermon notes, 1948–1954; cf. Jeremiah 18:6).

4. William Temple, *Nature, Man and God* (London: Macmillan, 1934), p. 435: "The World – God = 0; God – the World = God."

5. Exodus 3:14.

6. King invokes Isaac Watts's hymn "Our God, Our Help in Ages Past" (1719).

7. Acts 17:28.

would turn to ashes and our sunrises into darkest night. Without God the whole drama of human life would be a meaningless myth.[8] God is forever on the scene sustaining and protecting us.

III God will transform the world to its ideal state, in fullfilment of his ultimate purpose.

    1. God created the world with the hope that man would live in rightness and in accord with his will. ~~However he did not force rightness on man; rather he gave him free will~~ But in order to make him true man rather than an automaton he gave him free will; i.e. the possibility to choose. The tragedy came when man misused his freedom. Since that time the whole of human history has been a persistent struggle between two diametrically opposed forces; good and evil.

AD. CSKC: Sermon file, folder 28, "God's Relation to the World."

---

8. In notes for this sermon, King wrote that God's "conserving power is expressed in Job thus: 'If he were to withdraw His spirit to Himself, and to gather His breath to Himself, all flesh would expire at once, and man would return to the dust' (Job 34:14, 15)" (King, "God's Relation to the World," 1948–1954).

"All That We Are, We Owe"

[1948–1954]

I.   Introduction

One of the most potent facts of human life is the fact that man ~~amid all his independency~~ is basically a dependent being. This fact is reveald from the earliest days of infancy to the declining days of old age. No man ever makes it by himself. In fact it is this vey element of dependency that makes man man. for no individual becomes a personality until it interacts with other personalities. In our fickle moments we may feel that we are what we are by our own achievments, but in our sober moments we know deep down in our selves that we did not make ~~it alone~~ ourselves. This is another way of saying: "All that We are, We owe."[1]

Certainly this is not in accord with much of our contemporary thinking. Many modern thinkers would state our theme in the direct opposite: "All that we are, we have achieved." There is a school of modern philosophy called existentialism which starts out with the premise that man creates himself. Says it most outstanding exponent: "It is a doctrine according to which existence preceded, and eternally creates, the essence. Man first exists, and in choosing himself he creates himself: in acting

---

1. King may have drawn this phrase from Horatius Bonar's hymn "All That I Was, My Sin, My Guilt" (1845). The first stanza reads: "All that I was, my sin, my guilt, / My death, was all my own; / All that I am I owe to Thee, / My gracious God, alone."

he makes himself."[2] Stated in more concrete terms this theory merely says that man is the measure of all things; man, rather than God, creates himself; and that whatever man is he himself achieved. But no Christian can believe this. From the deeps of our moral consciousness springs the conviction that what we are, we owe.

AD. CSKC: Sermon file, folder 118, "Sermon Material."

---

2. King refers to the French philosopher Jean-Paul Sartre: "What is meant here by saying that existence precedes essence? It means that, first of all, man exists, turns up, appears on the scene, and, only afterwards, defines himself" (Jean-Paul Sartre, *Existentialism*, trans. Bernard Frechtman [New York: Philosophical Library, 1947], p. 18). King encountered existentialism in Christian Theology for Today, a class at Crozer, and recorded a paraphrase of this Sartre quote on notecards written during his years at Boston University (King, Class notes, Christian Theology for Today, 13 September–23 November 1949, and Personal notecards on "E" topics, 1948–1954).

"God the Inescapable"

[1948–1954]

Text: 139th Psalm

Introd—The quest of Modern man to escape God.

How do men attempt to escape God? The Psmst gives the ways men attempt to escape in his assertions of how man cant escape God

I   If I ascnt to the heavens. Many many attempt to [*ascend to?*] to a heaven of perfection, of absolute justice in which <u>God</u> is not wanted. The heaven of utopia.

II   If I make Sheol my bed, thou art there.[1] Sheol, the habitation of the dead, is where man often runs to escape God. There are those who long for death in order to escape the divine command. But death is no escape

III Go to the ends of the sea. This is the way in which our technical civilization tries to liberate itself from God. Going ahead and ahead conquering more space, always active, always planning. But God hands have fallen upon us, it has fallen heavil and destructively on our fleeting civilization

IV   If I say darkness shall covr me, night shall hide me all around, yet darkness is not darness to thee, the night is as bright as the day. Fleeing into darkness or forgetting God is no escape from him. Even if you deny him he gives you the truth to make the denial.

~~Conc. That's~~ Conclusion: There is no escape from God by forgetting him. "Where could I go from thy Spirit, where could I flee from thy face." Let your minds like maddening water run back to the sea of divinity. Just as we cant be lawless without law we cant be Godless without God.

AD. CSKC: Sermon file, folder 63, "Fleeing from God & When God Seems to Deceive Us."

---

1. *Sheol* is the Hebrew word for "afterlife."

Success and Failure

Brethren, I count not myself to have
apprehended. — Philippians 3:13

Here is a frank confession of failure

Yet this confession of failure produces
no depression on the man who makes it.

What is the explination of this
contradiction?
The answer is found in the next verse

Phi 3: 8 (that I may) — 10. Here was
a confession of failure which could be
made without humility but with pride

For — and here is what the passage says —
The only way to produce real joy and
permenent satisfaction is to fail in
reaching something that is is beyond us
rather than to succeed in doing something
that is beyond us that lies within our
reach. What we succeed in doing
does not cause us to rejoice.
God cares more for our high failures
than for our easy successes

King concludes a brief outline for "Success and Failure" by proclaiming, "God cares more for our high failures than for our easy successes."

"Getting Caught in the Negative"
"The Peril of Emphasizing a Negative"
"Accentuating the Positive"

[1948–1954]

Text: Act 15:1 Except ye be circumcised after the manner of Moses, ye cannot be saved."

This was the position taken by Jewish Christians when Gentiles began coming into the Church. The placed their whole emphasis on a negative. Jews and Gentiles alike believed in the gospel but while the Gentiles dispensed with the Law the Jews did not, and they staked everything on the mere denial of a position held by others. Nothing can ever come out of bare negation, and there is always the danger that it may take the place of what you positively believe

(1) The are sects today that are quite outmolded for any intelligent person, and yet this same sect can produce some of the finest types of Christin character. The reason is that with all their narrowness they hold fast to some positive truths; but too often they are not content with that and take to denouncing all views that differ from their own. In course of time this mere antagonism becomes their religion, and then they merely cumber the ground.

(2) The principle holds good in the case of other sects which pride themselves on their liberalism. They have broken away from an outworn mode of thought, and this is well; but in their emancipation they contrast themselves with those who are not so favoured. They cease to have much interest in what they do believe, and are satisfied with not believing what other people do.

Conclusion: The real argument against most forms of scepticism is not that they are false, but that they are empty. It can matter little to anybody what you do not believe. The question always arises when you have condemned the errors of other men, what truth can you put in their place Jesus could say "ye have hard it said of old . . . but I say."[1] He didn't stop with a mere criticism of the past, but he went on with a positive affirmation.

Dont get bogged down in the negative. Christianity must forever offer to the world a dynamic positive.

It is interesting to note that these Jewish Christians spend all their time opposing Paul.[2] Their Christianity was wholly negative, with the result that it ceased to count, and the movement went forward without it. It had given the new religion to the world, and seemed destined to mould and direct it, but it fell by the wayside. It is a tragedy which has many parallels in history, and religious history generally. Movements which began gloriously and brought liberty and new life have died as mere obstructions, not because they had outlived their usefulness but because they allowed themselves to drift into mere negation. The thing they stood for was forgot-

---

1. Jesus repeated this phrase several times in Matthew 5.

2. Cf. Acts 14:19–15:6.

The Foolishness of Preaching

1 Cor 1:21

I. Preaching gives [illegible] insecure people (young and old) a new bent on life.

II. Preaching stirs within men a desire to change the social situation.

III. Preaching continually reminds men of the unconditioned ground of their being.

It is through the Foolishness of preaching that many have found a new way of life which bring joy and peace.

On the front and back of a notecard titled "The Foolishness of Preaching," King writes, "Preaching stirs within men a desire to change the social situation" and that "It is through the Foolishness of preaching that many have found a new way of life which [*brings*] joy and peace" (1948–1954).

ten in the effort to hinder some other movement which was working for the same object in a different way. What the world demands is always the positive thing, however it may be presented, and those who do nothing to advance it are ruthlessly pushed aside.

AD. CSKC: Sermon file, folder 50, Sermons Not Preached.

[*1948–1954*]

Text "For whomsoever hath, to him shall be given; and whomsoever hath not, from him shall be taken even that whinch he seems to have.[1]

Introduction— ~~Show how this applies in the practical realm~~. This came immediately after the parable of the talents.[2] Jesus was anouncing a law of accumulation. It was a sort of "survival of the fittest" law. He saw it as a law covering the whole of life. This is a fertile universe

    Show how this truth is revealed in the practical realm. The rich get richer; the poor poorer; The more knowledge a man has the more the sources of learning open to him on all sides. The man who is being praised get more praise. The man who has many friends has many running to him. To him who has friends friends are given.

I   The realm issue of our text appears, however, in its application to the moral life or the spiritual life. Goodness and badness have the same law of accumulation.

    1.   The more a man gives himself to goodnss the more other avenues of goodness open to him.

        a.   The more honest one is the more easier it is to be honest

        b.   The more true etc . . .

        c.   The more just etc . . .

        Show how the law of habit applies here

    2.   The a man gives himself to evil, the more avenues of evil open to him.

        a.   The more he lies the easier it is to lie

        b.   The more he hate the easier it is to hate.

My friend there is a law of accumulation by which sin and goodness increase each after its own kind. There is something that makes the good grow better and the evil worse.

II   Since this is a law of life, what can we say is the value of this ~~principle~~ fundamental truth.

    Its value lies in the fact that in whatever direction a man choses to develope his life he has the aid of the universe. If a man chooses to be bad the universe multiplies his badness. On the other hand if a man reconigzes his badness and tries to be good, he finds all the world declaring a disposition towards him, helping him on in the way which he has chosen.

      Go out and undertake some duty

      Go out and give yourself to some great ideal

      ~~God~~ out and find you lost soul

      Go out and serve humanity

      Go out and be good

And in the grasping of any of these you will gain aid from the univese itself, which continually gives to him that has.

---

1. Cf. Matthew 25:29.

   2. Matthew 25:14–30.

And then you will grow and accumulate until you [*strikeout illegible*] accumulate
that chrished gift of standing before the throne of God.

AD. CSKC: Sermon file, folder 50, Sermons Not Preached.

"The Distinctions in God's Creation"

[*1948–1954*]

God said: Let there be light . . . And he divided the light from the darkness[1]

{See Introduction to Thomas Aquinas, p. 259F[2]}

I   Here it is made clear that the multitudes of things in the universe stem from God. God created many things

(1) Views that distinction does not come from God.

If God makes these distinction they must be good, for God did not create evil.

II   Why there is distinction: Because God brought things into being in order that his goodness might be represented by his creatures. And because his goodness could not be represented by one creature alone, He produced many and diverse creatures.[3]

1.   The various mountains

2.   Oceans

3.   Solar system. (Some are warning about the result if ther is life on Mars. But I dont. It just give additional proof . . .)

4.   Flowers

5.   Humains Beings Black, red, yellow, white

III   These distinction were not made to be in conflict. They were made to exist together. "God says after his creation "and it was good." meaning all of it is good. (The view of Ralph Lintons.)[4] (It is a shame that we cant appreciate the richness of God)

There can be unity without uniformity

Black and white can live together. Our biological differences are but varing expressions of the richness and complexity of the divine nature.

AD. CSKC: Sermon file, folder 50, Sermons Not Preached.

---

1. Cf. Genesis 1:3–4.

2. Anton C. Pegis, ed., *Introduction to Saint Thomas Aquinas* (New York: Modern Library, 1948). The section on Aquinas's work *Summa Theologica* includes a chapter entitled "On The Distinction of Things in General" (pp. 259–266).

3. Pegis, *Introduction to Saint Thomas Aquinas,* p. 261: "And because His goodness could not be adequately represented by one creature alone, He produced many and diverse creatures, so that what was wanting to one in the representation of the divine goodness might be supplied by another."

4. Anthropologist Ralph Linton wrote that "most anthropologists agree there will be no Negro problem in another two hundred years; by then there will not be enough recognizable Negroes left in this country to constitute a problem" (Linton, "The Vanishing American Negro," *American Mercury* 64 [February 1947]: 133–139).

[*1948–1954*]

". . . His father saw him, and had compassion, and ran, and fell on his neck, and kissed him." [1]

I   Int. This mornig I want to talk to you about the meaning of sin. This sermon is only addressed to those persons who are conscious of moral wrongdoing. If you have no uneasy stirrings of conscience about your attitude toward anything or your relationship ~~toward~~ with anybody, then this sermon does not apply to you.

But before you conclude that this sermon does not apply to you, you had better be certain what we mean by "sin". Usually when we think of sin we think of [*a list?*] of gross iniquities—murder, robbery, adultry, drunkenness. But we must add to this category at least three other categories

(1) There are sins of temperament—vindictiveness, stubborness, jealously, bad temper, malacious gossip. How much more prevalent they are; how much more harm they do.

(2) There are sins of social attitude

(3) There are the sins of neglect. It is not alone the things that we do, but the things we have left undone that haunt us—the letters we did not write, the words we did not speak, the opportunity we did not take. How often Jesus stressed this sin. What was wrong with that one talent man who buried his talent. What did he do? That was the trouble—he did nothing; he missed his chance.[2]

So here they are—sins of passion, sins of temperment, sins of social attitude, sins of neglect. I suspect that every one here fits into one of these categories: So stay with us; you too need forgiveness

II   The need for forgiven. No man's sin is ever done with until it has come through this process of forgiveness

(1) Aeschylus' Orestes[3]

(2) The Scarlet—Arthur Dimmesdale[4]

(3) Psychiatry—Most of the cases of metal derangement of a functional type are due to a sense of guilt.

III   What, then, is forgiveness

(A.) First of all it is a pardon. It is a fresh start, another chance, a new beginning.

(B.) Second, forgiveness is a process of life <u>and</u> the Christian weapon of social

---

1. Cf. Luke 15:20.

2. Cf. Matthew 25:14–30.

3. Aeschylus (525–456 BCE) was an Athenian dramatist whose works included the trilogy *Oresteia*. The protagonist, Orestes, murdered his mother and her lover, but was eventually forgiven by the Areopagus thanks to the intervention of Athena, the goddess of wisdom.

4. At the end of Nathaniel Hawthorne's *Scarlet Letter* (1850), Reverend Arthur Dimmesdale revealed that he was the father of Hester Prynne's illegitimate child and asked God to forgive them both.

redemption. Forgiveness is alway spoken of for others. Give Peter's attempt to put it in legal and statistical terms.[5]

Here then is the Christian weapon against social evil. We are to go out with the spirt of forgiveness, heal the hurts, right the wrongs and change society with forgiveness. Of course we dont think this is practical.

This is the solution of the race problem.

(C)

ADf. CSKC: Sermon file, folder 16, "Meaning of Forgiveness" / "Questions Easter Answers"

---

5. King may refer to Matthew 18:21–22: "Then came Peter to him, and said, Lord, how oft shall my brother sin against me, and I forgive him? till seven times? Jesus saith unto him, I say not unto thee, Until seven times; but, Until seventy times seven."

"I Sat Where They Sat"

[1948–1954]

Ez 3:15[1]

Introd—Ezekial as a prophet of the exile. He had the priveledge of sitting where those of the exile sat.

I   Consider the fact that unless you sit where others sit you really can inspire them.

(a) Give the example of the numerous problems of people. Unless you can put yourself in the place of that person you can really help them. You are not to be then with the "holier than thou atitude"
{Use this as second point}

(b) Give the example of modern counciling methods. The councilor must create a "permissive atmosphere"[2]

II   Consider again that unless you sit where others sit you cannot really ~~under~~ know them or understand them.

(a) Race relations. If the white man was closer to the Negro he would know more about the Negro and understand him better.

(b) Intercultural relations. The missionary movement would be better off if missionay sat where the natives sat.

AD. CSKC: Sermon file, folder 50, Sermons Not Preached.

---

1. Ezekiel 3:15: "Then I came to them of the captivity at Tel-abib, that dwelt by the river of Chebar, and I sat where they sat, and remained there astonished among them seven days."
2. Rogers, "Significant Aspects of Client-Centered Therapy," p. 416.

Moral Absolutism

To begin with Scripture lays down at its beginning the categories of good and evil: "God saw everything which he had made, and behold it was very good" (Gen 1:31); "It is not good that the man should be alone" (Gen. II:18) There is good and there is not good.

So radical is the distinction, that the prophet Isaiah denounces as sunk to the last stage of perversity those who in his eye confounded the two: "Woe unto them that call evil good, and good evil; that put darkness for light, and light for darkness..." Right is right and wrong is wrong and never the twain shall meet. All the dialectics of the logician cannot make them lie down together. I there is an eternal difference between good and evil.

II Ways modern man perverts this truth

   1. Psychologically justifying the righteousness of the wrong

   2. Ethical relativism.

   3. Says one "Whatever satisfies me; and whatever I can do and continue to live with myself is right for me."

III God's judgment is forever before us in the sense that he has set an absolute moral law in our midst.

Judgment is ultimately the sentence that a man passes upon himself for refusing to recognize this eternal law. Judgment is not some far off day in the future; but it is forever present. When I refuse to love or to be just I am passing judgment upon myself.

See Brightman's Moral Laws for a list of these eternal moral laws.

[margin: At least this is what the writer of the Fourth Gospel meant]

In a sermon outline titled "Moral Absolutism," King writes, "[*Judgment*] is ultimately the sentence that a man passes upon himself for refusing to recognize this eternal law" and in the margin next to this point he clarifies, "At least this is what the writer of the Fourth Gospel meant" (1948–1954).

[*1948–1954*]

Text Luke 22:24F He that is greatest among you, let him be as the younger; and he that is chief as he that doth serve." [1]

Introduction—Many would affirm that men reach their highest leval of productivity under competitive conditions.

(1) Show how the principle applies in practical affairs (in school seeking a grade)

(2) Show how our whole economic structure is built up it.

Now Jesus himself saw the power that competition held over men. He did not ignore it. Yet he does something with the conception of competition that hadn't been done before. He takes the conception which has been used for lower purposes and recues it from many of its dangers, by suggesting a higher method of its use. This is how he applied the term to his disciples. He saw them in danger of using it for low purposes. They wanted to compete for reputation and position—"which of them should be accounted greatest?" Jesus say No. If you must use the power of competition; If you must compete with one another; make it as noble as you can by using it on noble things. Use it for a fine unselfish thing. "He that is greatest among you shall serve." Use it for human good. Who shall be the most useful. Compete with one another in humility. See which can be the truest sevant." It seems that Christ says "Use it, but use it for higher and holier purposes. Use it not to surpass one another in esteem, but use it to increase the amount of usefulness and brothr-help.

I Such conceptions of competition lead to the surprinsig and enobling position that there can be competition without hate and jealously. Behold! you can struggle to beat and yet rejource to be beaten. What is abolished is not competition, but the object of competition is altered.

(A) Suppose this teaching of Jesus should be accepted by all of this great world of competing men. Here are these rival hearts all eager to outstrip each other. But now the object is different. Not now who shall be ~~right~~ richest, or who shall have the bigest car, or who shall be the most powerful or learned—but who shall be most absolutely devoted to the good of fellow-men.

(B) Imagige the chage that would come about if the Churches applied this truth. Now we are bogged not in competitive denominationalism which is destroying the warm blood of the Protestant Church. "Which of them shall be accounted greatest." Let the churches stop trying to outstrip each other in the number of their adherents, the size of its sanctuary, the abundance of wealth. If we must compete let us compete to see which can move toward

---

1. Cf. Luke 22:24–26: "And there was also a strife among them, which of them should be accounted the greatest. And he said unto them, The kings of the Gentiles exercise lordship over them; and they that exercise authority upon them are called benefactors. But ye shall not be so: but he that is greatest among you, let him be as the younger; and he that is chief, as he that doth serve." King wrote and then struck out the word "Lifting" next to the title "Noble Competition."

the greatest attaiment of truth, the greatest service of the poor, and the greatest salvation of the soul and bodies of men.

    If the Church entered this kind of competition we can imagine what a better world this would be.

(C) Suppose the teaching of Jesus should be accepted by the competing nations of the world, particularly Russia and Amica. They would no longer compete to see which could make the bigger Atom bombs, or which could best perpetuate its imperialism, but which could best serve humanity. This would be a better world.

AD. CSKC: Sermon file, folder 50, Sermons Not Preached.

"The Danger of Mis Guided Goodness"

[*1948–1954*]

I   Int.

    A. One of the basic functions of the Christian Church is to keep alive a certain degree of moral sensitivity. See the Church must of necessity urge men to be good, to be sincere, to be conscientious. There are basic moral principles. But they are not enough. To say of a man that he is conscientious and means well, important though that is, does not cover the ground. Not only must we be good, but we must be intelligent.[1] Every man has a moral obligation to be intelligent. Quote Socrates[2] One of the most dangerous forces in the world is misguided goodness

    B. Some of the most shameful tragedies of human history have been commtted, not by bad, people, but by good consciencious people who didn't know what they did

       (1) those who made Scrates drink the hemlock

       (2) The crusades[3]

       (3) the people that threatned Galilio [*Galileo Galilei*]

       (4) The trial of Joan of arc[4]

       (4)

---

1. Harry Emerson Fosdick, *The Hope of the World*, p. 223: "To say of a man there that he is conscientious and means well, important though that is, does not cover the ground. He must not be stupid."

2. King may be citing a paraphrase of a speech by Socrates found in Plato's *Apology* 38a: "The unexamined life is not worth living."

3. The Crusades were military campaigns carried out by European Christians intermittently between 1096 and the late thirteenth century to conquer and convert non-Christians and recapture Jerusalem and the Holy Land.

4. Jeanne d'Arc (1412–1431) led French troops during the Hundred Years' War but was later tried and burned at the stake for heresy and witchcraft. Fosdick, *The Hope of the World*, p. 223: "The Athenians who made Socrates drink the hemlock, far from being bad, were among the most earnest, conscientious, religious people of their day. . . . So, in intention, the crusades were not so much wicked as stupid; the people who threatened Galileo with torture were not wicked but stupid; the judges at the trial of Joan of Arc were not bad but senseless, and over the most shameful tragedies of history, as over the cross of Christ, the judgment stands: 'They know not what they do.'"

C. The text.[5] A profound passage comes out of one of Paul's ~~experience~~   1948–1954
Epistle to give something of a scriptural sanction to our theme.

AD. CSKC: Sermon file, folder 87, Why the Christian Must Oppose Segregation.

---

5. King may refer to Romans 10:2 as he does in the sermon Sincerity Is Not Enough, 3 June 1951, pp. 119–120 in this volume.

"The Unknown Great"

[*1948–1954*]

I   Introduction

     A   In every epoch of human history and in every civilization there are certain names that stand out and that are not forgotten.
         1.   Hebrew culture—Moses and Abraham
              Prophets—[*Isaiah?*] Jeremiah, Ezekiel
         2.   Early Christian—Paul Peter
         3.   Greek culture—Socrates, Plato and Aristotle
              Lit. Aeschylus, Euripedes, Aristophanes[1]
         4.   Roman civilizaton—Ceasars Lucresius, Augustine[2]
         5.   Middle Ages—
     B.   The contributions of these individuals have been great and lasting and history would be at a lost without them. But in every age there have been a group of men and women whose contributions have been equally significant, but whose names have passed into the dim unknown. They have gone down in history forgotten and unknown. They have faded into the dark halls of oblivion.

        A clear example of this is found in our text for the morning.
     C.   Text—Ecclesiastes 9:14–16[3]

II   Let us notice first that the course of history is not changed by the creative work of a single individual but by the cooperative endeavor of a group of individual
         1.   The minor prophets prepared the way for the greater prophets[4]

---

1. Aeschylus (525–456 BCE), Euripides (ca. 484–406 BCE), and Aristophanes (ca. 450–ca. 388 BCE) were renowned Athenian playwrights.

2. Lucretius (ca. 96–ca. 55 BCE) was an influential Roman poet.

3. "There was a little city, and few men within it; and there came a great king against it, and besieged it, and built great bulwarks against it: Now there was found in it a poor wise man, and he by his wisdom delivered the city; yet no man remembered that same poor man. Then said I, Wisdom is better than strength: nevertheless the poor man's wisdom is despised, and his words are not heard."

4. King refers to the minor prophets whose lives were documented in the twelve shorter books of prophecy in the Old Testament: Hosea, Joel, Amos, Obadiah, Jonah, Micah, Nahum, Habakkuk, Zephaniah, Haggai, Zechariah, and Malachi. By greater prophets, he refers to Isaiah, Jeremiah, and Ezekiel.

2. Paul was not the only missionary
3. Reformation was not started by Martin Luther
4. The abolition of slavery had been advocated long before Lincoln.
5.

III Let us notice again that ~~behind~~ the work of the individuals whose greatness remains known is ~~the~~ so often made possible by the work of [*strikeout illegible*] individuals whose names are not remembemed and not know

1. Doing a little in a big way
2. Marion Anderson[5]
3. The Captain of the ship—We could not survive without someone doing the dirty work.

AD. CSKC: Sermon file, folder 118, "Sermon Material."

---

5. In his sermon "Conquering Self-Centeredness" King discussed Marian Anderson's acknowledgment of her mother's sacrifice: "Let us never forget that Marian Anderson, that great contralto, is there today because somebody in the background helped her to get there. Because there was that mother who was willing to work days and nights until her eyebrows were all but parched and her hands all but scorched in order that her daughter could get her training and an education" (King, Sermon Delivered at Dexter Avenue Baptist Church, 11 August 1957, in *Papers* 4:255).

"Human Freedom & Divine Grace"

[*1948–1954*]

Text: Son of man stand upon your feet and I will speak to you. Ez[1]

Int. This text stress the point that the redemptive process is one of coopertion between man and God.[2] Human freedom and divine grace are not opposing entities, but they interpenetrate. God is saying to Ezekial in substance, "you are free and so use your freedom to help yourself and after you reached the limits of your freedom by doing all that yo can I will step in and help you." Here we avoid both the extremes of humanisn and determism.

I The Meaning of Freedom: It is presupposed in the ethical life. ~~It means that you have the possibility of contrary choices.~~

---

1. Cf. Ezekiel 2:1: "And he said unto me, stand upon thy feet that I might speak with thee." In King's dissertation while discussing Tillich's notion of human freedom, he draws on the words from a dissertation by Jack Boozer ("The Place of Reason in Paul Tillich's Conception of God" [Ph.D. dissertation, 1952], pp. 62–63): "Man has in a sense left the divine ground to 'stand upon' his own feet" (King, "A Comparison of the Conceptions of God in the Thinking of Paul Tillich and Henry Nelson Wieman," in *Papers* 2:532–533).

2. The theme of this sermon aligns closely with one of the major issues King discussed in his dissertation regarding Paul Tillich. In addition, some of the phrases used in this sermon come directly from notes taken for DeWolf's History of Christian Doctrine course taken during the 1952–1953 school year. This correlation indicates a sermon date between 1952 and 1953.

(1) illustrate from concrete experience. You can love or hate
(2)
(1) Show what freedom does not mean
 (a) it does mean that character and enviroment and hereditary have no influence on a persons conduct.
 (b) it does not mean that the will is causelesss.
(2) Freedom means the possibility of contrary choics
 (1) you may love or hate
 (2) you may be

However Freedom is not absolute. The human will is weak and vacillatory. And this limitation carries with it the need of divine grace to complete the salvation process[3]

II The Meaning of Divine Grace: Man experiences a gap between his ideals and his actions. He cannot in his own strength bridge the gulf that separates the ideal and the real, and so he seeks divine aid. The limitations of his own power drives him to God.[4]

Divine grace thus supplements human freedom and the two co-operate in man's redemption.[5]

see Knudson, DOR, 158–168.[6]

AD. CSKC: Sermon file, folder 50, Sermons Not Preached.

---

3. Albert C. Knudson, *The Doctrine of Redemption* (New York: Abingdon-Cokesbury Press, 1933), p. 165: "The exercise of freedom is not absolute. The human will is weak and vacillating. It is limited in numerous ways, and this limitation carries with it a need of redemptive grace quite as real as would the complete absence of the power of self-determination." King was assigned this book for George W. Davis's class at Crozer on the history of Christian thought (Davis, "Bibliography and assignments in History of Christian Thought," 29 November 1949–15 February 1950).

4. Knudson, *The Doctrine of Redemption*, p. 166: "He cannot in his own strength bridge the gulf that separates the ideal from the real; and so he seeks the divine aid. The limitation of his own power drives him to God."

5. Knudson, *The Doctrine of Redemption*, p.167: "Divine grace thus supplements human freedom and the two co-operate in man's redemption." King included this quote from a chapter titled "Freedom" in Knudson's book in his notes for L. Harold DeWolf's Boston University class History of Christian Doctrine (see King, Notes on the free will controversy and other topics, 4 February–22 May 1953).

6. King's cites a subsection titled "Metaphysical Freedom" from the chapter "Freedom" (Knudson, *The Doctrine of Redemption*, pp. 158–168).

"The Human Tension"

Text: "The good that I would I do not and the evil . . . "[1]

Introduction—Our thinking goes back to Paul this morning.
 (1) Show Paul struggle with himself in attempting to fulfill the law
 (2) Show how out of this experience grew the text.

Show how Paul's experience is a continual experience in the life of all.
 1. Quote Ovid[2]
 2. Quote Goethe[3]
 3 Quote Augustine[4]
 4. Quote Plato[5]
 5.

There is, therefore, the perennial tension between what we ought to be and what we actually are.

We are forever aware that the "isness" of our being is far from the "oughtness" of our highest ideals. The "isness" of our present nature is out of propotion to the eternal "oughtness" forever confronting us.[6]

I. How is this tension removed
 1. Accept the fact that you are in need and that you do have an evil element in your nature. Dont try to rationalize and make it right.
 2. Without alibi and pretense lay your life before God.
 3. God will give you his grace. You will have power that you didn't know that you had. This is what Paul did and the result after Demascus was amazing. Conversion for didn't just begin on Demascus; he had been troubled about it long before.[7]

The God of the universe forevr stands before us knocking. Who will open the door. He is there to help you. He doesn't just stand at the door, but he knocks. If you open the door he will come in an help you release the tension.[8]

AD. CSKC: Sermon file, folder 67, The Human Tension.

---

1. Cf. Romans 7:19.

2. King probably refers to Ovid *Metamorphoses* 7.20, as he does in Man's Sin and God's Grace, 1954–1960, p. 383 in this volume.

3. King probably refers to a quote by Goethe as used in Sheen's book *Peace of Soul*, p. 36: "Goethe regretted that God had made only one man of him when there was enough material in him for both a rogue and a gentleman." He also made this reference in the sermon "Mastering Our Evil Selves" / "Mastering Ourselves," 5 June 1949, p. 95 in this volume.

4. King probably refers to Augustine *Confessions* 8.7, as he does in "Creating the Abundant Life," 26 September 1954, p. 190 in this volume.

5. King probably refers to Plato's analysis of the conflicted personality from *Phaedrus* 246a–247c, as he does in Man's Sin and God's Grace, 1954–1960, p. 383 in this volume.

6. Cf. Niebuhr, *Beyond Tragedy*, pp. 137–138.

7. Paul's conversion experience as recorded in Acts 9:1–22 occurred on the road to Damascus.

8. Cf. Revelation 3:20.

Be ye Perfect

"Be ye perfect even as your father in heaven is perfect."

I. The word perfect here is to be defined by the context. ~~Jesus has been speaking of love~~ Jesus is not demanding rational perfection or even moral perfection in the sense that God is morally perfect. Jesus has been speaking of love for enemies as well as friends, and also points out that God is good not only to the just but also to the unjust. The conclusion is that to be a true son of the heavenly father one must be thoroughgoing in the exercise of love, as God is, without reservation or discrimination. He must not, like the scribe of Luke 10:29 try to justify himself by saying, "yes, but who is my neighbor?" What Jesus demanded was impartial love like God's for all men

II. Expound on the meaning of Christian love.

In sermon notes titled "Be Ye Perfect," King considers Jesus' command from Matthew 5:48 and concludes, "to be a true son of the heavenly father one must be thoroughgoing in the exercise of love, as God is, without reservation or discrimination" (1948–1954).

[*1948–1954*]

There can be no gainsaying of the fact that prayer is as natural to the human organism as the rising of the sun is to the cosmic order. Samuel Johnson was once asked what the strongest argument for prayer was, and he replied, "Sir, there is no argument for prayer."[1] Now Johnson did not mean by this that prayer is irrational, far from it; he meant, rather, to stress the fact the prayer is first of all a native tendency. Prayer is indigenous to the human spirit. It represents a throbbing desire of the human heart. As [*Thomas*] Carlyle stated in a letter to a friend: "Prayer is and remains the native and deepest impulse of the soul of man."[2] We often try to call prayer "absurd and presumptuous."[3] But a yearning so agelong and deep-rooted cannot be slain by a couple of adjectives. Men have often tried to dismiss it by affirming that pressing rigidity of natural law makes it impossible. But such a declaration is unconvincing; for there is something deep down within us that makes us know that God works in a paradox of unpredictable newness and trustworthy faithfulness. And so even the most devout atheist will at times cry out for the God that his theory denies. Men always have prayed and men always will pray.

Although prayer is native to man, there is the danger that he will misuse it. Although it is a natural outpouring of his spirit, there is the danger that he will use it in an unnatural way.

I.   Never make prayer a substitute for work and intelligence.

    (1) (a) There are three way to cooperate with God prayer must be a suppliment and not a substitute

          (b) The would be musician

          (C) The Farmer

          (D) Passing an exam

          (E) Calling a doctor when sick

          (F) Prayer for civil rights

    (2) Prayer is no substitute for intelligence

          (a) knowledge of classics of culture didn't come through prayer

          (b) creative insights of medical science didn' come through prayer

          (c) knowledge of astronomy

    (3) We make God a cosmic bell hop a universal errand boy.

          In that dramatic scene when the Israelites are confronted with the Red Sea in front and the Egyptian armies behind, Moses goes away to pray. God says, "Go Forward."[4]

---

1. Fosdick, *The Meaning of Prayer,* p. 1: "Samuel Johnson once was asked what the strongest argument for prayer was, and he replied, 'Sir, there is no argument for prayer.'" Samuel Johnson (1709–1784) was a British poet, critic, and essayist.

2. Fosdick, *The Meaning of Prayer,* p. 1: "As Carlyle stated it in a letter to a friend: 'Prayer is and remains the native and deepest impulse of the soul of man.'"

3. Immanuel Kant's reflection on the act of prayer contained these words ("Prayer," in *Lectures On Ethics,* Louis Infield, trans. [New York and London: Century, 1930], pp. 98–103).

4. Cf. Exodus 14:10–15.

II Never ~~make~~ pray for anything which if done would injure somebody else.
    (1) Dont pray for God to help you get even with your enemy.
    (2) The white man often prays to God to help him oppress the Negro.
    (3) Dont pray that your country will win the war.
III Never pray for God to change the fixed laws of the universe

AD. CSKC: Sermon file, folder 166, "The Misuse of Prayer."

"What Shall We Do to Be Saved?"

[*1948–1954*]

Intro: I would like to set forth the thesis this evenig that the question "What Shall we do to be saved?" is but a collectivized extension of the question What shall I do to be saved.[1] The pocess of social salvation is the same as the process of individual salvation

I   The first thing necessary for ind. salvation is an honest recognition of one's estranged and sinful condition. One can never be saved until he recognizes the fact that he needs to be saved. Christian theology has always insisted that man is a sinner, that there is something wrong with human nature. The whole doctrine of original sin came into being to explain this gonewronness in human nature.
    a.   No one can ever get well until he recognizes that he is sick.
    b.   ~~The story of the~~ This same thing is true in the [*social situation?*]

ADf. CSKC: Sermon file, folder 102.

---

1. Cf. Acts 16:30.

"O That I Knew Where I Might Find Him!"

[*1951–1954*]

King argues in this handwritten sermon that seeking God is difficult due to the "cruelties of nature," the "ambiguities of history," and the prevalence of modern scientific achievement. Despite these challenges to knowing God, King maintains, "In Jesus we have the clearest picture of what God is like." Referring to his "recent Seminary days," he reminisces, "Everyday I would sit [on] the edge of the campus by the side of the river and watch the beauties of nature. My friends in this experience I saw God."

The Necessity of the New Birth

1. Nic. was a big shot. Big shots need to be born again.

2. Jesus realized that all men needed to be born again. In some sense all men are sinners. Whether it is due to original sin I don't know, but the fact remains that man is a sinner.

3. How can a man be changed when he is old. i.e. old in his habits. Habits are easy to start, but difficult to stop.

4. In order to be changed one must first admit that he has an ailment, and that he needs to be changed.

5. Then he must proceed to help himself. But here he realized that he can't do it alone.

6. So he must turn to God, and God will aid you. God says to every man if you really want to be true I'll help you to be true. If you etc.

Here is the true meaning of Grace.
If we really want to improve God injects within us the power to do it.

Quote amazing Grace

On notecards titled "The Necessity of the New Birth," King discusses religious rebirth. He concludes, "Here is the true meaning of Grace. If we really want to improve[,] God injects within us the power to do it" (1948–1954).

These words flow from the lips of that noble character of the Old testamen— Job.[1] They are words expressing a longing that has been apart of man's nature ever since ~~the dawn of recorded history~~ man has been man The search for God has been man's perennial search. Indeed the search has often been a difficult and devious one, yet amid all of its difficulties many have continued to search for that unfailing source of eternal value.[2] ~~In this great religious odyssey many have fallen out on the way, some disillusioned and some content~~.

We do not have to look far to see why this search is a difficult one. On every hand it seems that God hides himself. As the Great Isaiah cried long age, "Verily thou art a God that hidest thyself, the Savior."[3] Notice how it seems that God hides himself in nature. Nature is often cruel. "Nearly all the things which men are hanged or imprisoned for doing to one another," says John Stuart Mill, "are nature's every day performances. Nature kills, burns, starves, freezes, poisons." (1)[4] Not only nature, but it seems that God hides himself in history. If we look through the corridors of history what do we find? Jesus on a cross and Caesar in a palace; truth on the scaffold and wrong on the throne; the just suffering while the ~~evil~~ unjust prosper.[5] Indeed, it was essentially these conditions which caused Job to seek the whereabouts of God. The whole book of Job may be said to be an attempt to answer the question, Why do the righteous suffer?[6]

Not only is our search for God made difficult by the cruelties of nature—and the ambiguities of history, but also by the very nature of modern scientific society. In our scietific age we have become so conditioned to material things, those things which we can see, feel, and touch, that we unconsciously find it difficult to believe that anything non-material can have objective existence. It is easy to believe that the sun is shinning because we can see that, but it is hard to believe that there is a purposive being behind that sun because we cant see it. And so our doubts begin to multiply.

So we must admit that the search for God is not an ~~difficult~~ easy one: It requies illumined visions, broad understanding, and penetrating eyes. It requires power of endurance, lasting patience, and purity of heart. [*strikeout illegible*] The man who has not found God is the man who has not looked far and long enough; he is the man who has looked in the wrong place. Be ye well assured that God is not found in a

---

1. Job 23:3: "Oh that I knew where I might find him! that I might come even to his seat!"

2. While at Crozer, King wrote a paper titled "The Place of Reason and Experience in Finding God" for George W. Davis's course Christian Theology for Today (13 September–23 November 1949 in *Papers* 1:230–236). In his opening paragraph, King wrote, "Man is a metaphysical animal ever longing for answers to the last questions. This in some way accounts for mans continual search for the object of religious faith known as God. The search has often been a difficult and devious one, yet amid all of its difficulties many have continued to search for the unfailing source of eternal value."

3. Cf. Isaiah 45:15.

4. King inserted a footnote at the bottom of the page: "1. Three Essays On Religion, p. 28"; see Mill, *Three Essays on Religion*, pp. 28–29.

5. King cites lines from James Russell Lowell's "The Present Crisis" (1844).

6. In a final exam, King asks, " Why do the righteous suffer? In other words, how can a good God allow so much evil to exist in the world? Are not the goodness of good and the existence of evil incompatible ideas? These are questions which baffle the writer of Job. The existence of evil calls his faith into question" (King, Final examination answers, Religious Teachings of the Old Testament, 22 September–28 January 1953, in *Papers* 2:168).

microscope; he is not found in a ~~the~~ [*strikeout illegible*] telescope; he is not found in an argument. Where then must one turn to find God?

First let us consider God's presence in nature. Surely there is something in the unruffled calm of nature which reveals the almighty God. This fact has been recognized by religionists of all ages. Some have gone so far as to identify God with nature, arguing that God is nature and nothing more. Certainly we must avoid any such heresy, for this (Reconcile the cruelties of nature with God revealing himself in it) Christian religion its at ~~its~~ best insists that God is more than nature and that he cannot be limited to the transitoriness of time and space. Yet although God is beyond nature he is also immanent in it. Long centuries age the great Psalmist exclaimed, "The heavens declare the glory of God; and the firmament sheweth his handywork."[7] ~~Here, surely is the place to start looking for God.~~ And so the true seeker who has gone through the necessary preparation cannot open his eyes without seeing God. Probably many of us who have been so urbanized and modenized need at times to get back to the simple rural life and commune with nature. In such a setting the finding of God will not be difficult. We fail to find God because we are too conditioned to seeing man made skyscrapers, electric lights, aeroplanes, and subways. We need sometimes to get away from the man-made lights of the city and place our eyes on that eternal light which man can never invent. We need sometimes to ~~close our ears to~~ get away from the noisy tunes of the man-made street cars and subways and open our ears to the malodious vioices of the birds and the wistling [*strikeout illegible*] sounds of the jostling wind.

I can remember very vividly how, in my recent Seminary days, I was able to strengthen my spiritual life through communing with nature. The seminary campus is a beautiful sight, ~~and~~ peticularly so in the spring. And it was at this time of the year that I made it a practice to go out to the edge of the campus ~~at least~~ every afternoon for at least an hour to ~~and~~ commune with nature. On the side of the campus ran a little tributary from the Deleware river. Everyday I would sit ~~by~~ [*on?*] the edge of the campus by the side of the river and watch the beauties of nature. My friends in this experience I saw God. I saw him in birds of the air, the leaves of the tree, the movement of the rippling waves. I can certainly now declare with Carlyle, "Nature is the time vesture of God that reveals him to the wise and hides him from the foolish."[8]

Sometimes go out at night and look up at the stars as they bedeck the heavens like shinning silver pins sticking in a magnificant blue pin cusion. There is God. Sometimes watch the sun as it gets up in the morning and paints its technicolor across the eastern horizen. There is God. Sometimes watch the moon as it walks across the sky as a queen walks across her masterly ~~mantion~~ mansion. There is God. Henry Ward Beecher was right:

> Nature is God's tongue. He speaks by summer and by winter. He can manifest himself by the wind, by the storm, by the calm. Whatever is sublime and potent, whatever is sweet and gentle, whatever is fear-inspiring, whatever is soothing,

---

7. Psalm 19:1.
8. Carlyle, *Sartor Resartus,* p. 265.

whatever is beautiful to the eye or repugnant to the taste, God may employ. The heavens above, and the procession of the seasons as they month by month walk among the stars, are various manifestations of God.[9]

Come further, now, and consider ~~how~~ that God is found in history. As stated above it is not at all easy to believe that God is present in history. Considering the anomalies of history one might logically ask, Is history rational? Is there any purpose in history? Long ago Marcus Aurelius finding no progress whatsoever in history, wrote, "Everything now is just as it was in the time of those whom we have buried." (Meditations, IX, 14)[10] He finds the present pageant of history to be exactly the same as its past drama. All that differs is the actors.

But such a passimistic view of history is certainly to narrow for the man who looks at the whole. From the pessimism of Marcus Aurelius we turn to the realism of the poet Tennyson and cry with him: "thro' the ages one increasing purpose runs." (Locksley Hall, line 137).[11] If our visions are broad enough we are able to see that the light of God shines through history as the blossom shines through the bud. At times the light might seem dim, yet it shines. "The mills of the gods grind slowly but exceedingly fine."[12] There is in this universe something of what the ancient Greeks called Nemesis—the doom the falls inevitably upon arrogance and pride.[13] Throughout history we have seen the Nemesis at work. In recent times we saw it pull Hitler's Nazidom down from its high horses to a place of shame and ~~pity~~ ruin. As Theodor Mommsen, the historian, wrote: History has a Nemesis for every sin."[14]

What more is the Nemesis than the workings of God. It is God working for the ultimate triumph of the kingdom of righteousness. We human beings are not alone the originators and backers of goodness in this world. There is, as Matthew Arnold said, a "power, not ourselves, which makes for righteousness."[15]

The key to history is lost when we separate God from the stream of events. And this, for the simple reason that, while history shows man in action, it also discloses to open mind and sensitive heart the unwearied action of the living God, yet toiling to establish his kingdom over all the earth The man who fails to see God in history is the man who is spiritually blind.

Finally we may find God in Jesus Christ. Fron the earliest days of the Christian era

---

9. Henry Ward Beecher (1813–1887), was a nineteenth century preacher and abolitionist. His 1869 sermon "The Hidden Christ" evoked this connection between God and nature (*The Original Plymouth Pulpit,* ed. T. J. Ellenwood [New York: Fords, Howard, & Hulbert, 1893], pp. 275–288).

10. Marcus Aurelius (121–180 CE) was the Roman emperor from 161 to 180 CE. He wrote *The Meditations* in 167 CE.

11. Alfred Lord Tennyson, *Locksley Hall* (1872): "Yet I doubt not thro' the ages one increasing purpose runs, / And the thoughts of men are widen'd with the process of the suns." Tennyson (1809–1892) was appointed poet laureate of England in 1850.

12. Euripides *Bacchae* 882–887.

13. In Greek mythology Nemesis, the goddess of retribution, handed down the divine justice of the gods, which was often visited upon the proud.

14. Theodor Mommsen (1817–1903), a German historian best known for his multi-volume *History of Rome* (1887), was awarded the 1902 Nobel Prize in literature.

15. Matthew Arnold, *God and the Bible* (London: Smith, Elder, 1891), p. xxvii: "Our God is the Eternal not ourselves that makes for righteousness."

1 Our live are filled these hectic days with small trivialities and large catastrophes

2. Ever and again we have experiences by which existence is validated. Such are mountain heights and oceanic depths are the stuff out of which life is made.

3. Today we are surrounded by the fear of bombs more awful then the hell of Dante.

4. The Eternal command of God comes like spring across our winter-hardened lives.

5 For so many people, as T.S. Eliot has pointed out, the only way to have fellowship with one another is at the cocktail party, when the threshold of consciousness is lowered to a point or T....

In two pages of sermon notes, King considers some of the "small trivialities and large catastrophes" of modern life (1948–1954).

6. In these days of emotional faustration we often feel that we are helpless puppets pulled by the the strings of a very twitchy, thiweldered world

7. Today men so often have anemic opinions, rather then full bodied convictions

until now men have affirmed that God was supremely reveald in Christ. The divinity of Christ has been ~~the~~ one of the chief connerstones of the Christian tradition. It has been insisted that with the coming of Jesus a bit of eternity came into time [*strikeout illegible*] in order that time might become eternal. In other word, we are only saying that God is Christlike. This, my friends, is the ultimate meaning of the doctrine of the Trinity. It affirms that in some mysterious way God and Christ are one in substanse. And so to experience one is to experience the other. To know Christ is to know God.

Those who are serious about finding God this morning I bid you turn to Christ. In him you will find the personification of all that is high noble and God, and consequently you will find God. In Jesus we have the clearest picture of what God is like.

Strangely enough, Christian have insisted that this presence of God in Christ is culminated in the crucifixion and resurrection. [*strikeout illegible*] The most astounding fact about Christ's crucifixion is that it has been for Christians the supreme revelation of God's love—"God commendeth his own love toward us, in that, while we were yet sinners, Christ died for us."[16] It is quite difficult to see the love of God in such a shameful tragedy, isn't it? Certainly it requires penetrating eyes to see God in such a setting. Yet Christians throughout the ages have found him there. They have seen in the cross a ~~God who~~ revelation of a God who takes the initiative, a God who is always before hand with men, seeking them before they seek him. Jesus presents to us a "seeking" God whose very nature it is to go the whole waey into the wilderness in quest of man.

This morning I challenge you to seek God with open hearts and open minds and I assure you that he will be found. We do not have to look far to fim him, for he is near by

"Speak to him, thou, for he hears, and Spirit with spirit can meet—
Closer is he than breathing, and nearer than hands and feet.[17]

The Cross is at one and the same time the depth of human sin and the hight of divine love.

AD. CSKC: Sermon file, folder 6, "Finding God."

---

16. Romans 5:8.
17. Alfred Lord Tennyson, "The Higher Pantheism" (1869).

"The Peril of the Sword"

[*1955–1960?*]

King explores ideas about nonviolence that he developed more fully in speeches and sermons delivered after the start of Montgomery bus boycott.[1] In this handwritten outline, King advocates nonviolence and says of confronting an oppressor, "The true aim should be to convert him, to change his understanding and his sense of values."

I   Introduction—the existence of evil in the universe
     Because of this evil disputes and conflicts arise between individuals. The ques-
     tion which every individual and every nation confronts soon or later is, how will
     I deal with this evil force.

II   Now one method is the method of violence. The sword method This is the pop-
     ular method. To this method Jesus said, "He who lives by the sword shall perish
     by the sword."[2] History is replete with the bleached bones of natios. So this
     method carries the seed of its own destruction. It is perilous Over against this
     stands the method of non-violence. It resist just as strongly as the violent method.

III (a) The method of violence assumes that evil can overcome evil. It confront a
          negative with a negative. Retailatory violence does nothing but multiplies
          the existence of Man and his deeds are two distinct things.
     1.   The use of the sword presuppese that evil can overcome evil.
          The doer of the deed must always be respectd.
     2.   The aim of the sword is to defeat injure and humiliate an oppressor. But
          the true aim should be to convert him, to change his understanding and
          his sense of values.

AD. CSKC: Sermon file, folder 5, "Man's Sin and God's Grace" / "The Peril of the Sword."

---

1. For example, see King, "When Peace Becomes Obnoxious," 18 March 1956, pp. 257–259 in this
volume. In an October 1960 letter which King wrote while in the Georgia State prison in Reidsville, he
requested that Coretta King bring him this and seventeen other "sermons from my file" (see King to
Coretta Scott King, 26 October 1960, *Papers* 5:531–532).
   2. Cf. Matthew 26:52.

God in History: Four Proverbs

[*1959–1968*]

*King mentions his September 1958 stabbing as he reflects on lessons that can be
learned from life and history.*[1]

Ps. 37:1–3[2]

I   The first truth which the centuries have to tell us is summed up in the ~~pro~~ old
     Greek proverb: "Whom the gods destroy, they first make <u>mad</u>."[3] The Bible says

---

1. King wrote the sermon title on the folder containing this handwritten outline. After his stabbing,
he did not return to active preaching until late 1958.
   2. Psalm 37:1–3: "Fret not thyself because of evildoers, neither be thou envious against the workers
of iniquity. For they shall soon be cut down like the grass, and wither as the green herb. Trust in the Lord,
and do good; so shalt thou dwell in the land, and verily thou shalt be fed."
   3. King most likely drew the main points of this homily from a sermon by Harry Emerson Fosdick,

the same thing in two familiar passages: "<u>Pride</u> goeth before destruction" "Whosover <u>exhalts</u> himself shall be <u>abased</u>."[4]

This is saying in substance, when a man <u>loses his head over his</u> own importance, he has taken the first step on the road to his own self destruction

The process is easy to describe. A man does good work for a period, he is praised for it, he receives awards, he becomes popular. But then he becomes drunk with power inflated with vanity, and wrecks himself.

    A.   [*Benito*] Mussolini

    B.   Napoleon [*Bonaparte*]

II   The mills of God grind slowly, but they grind exceedingly small."[5] Evil and injustice may seem strong for a time but they do not endure. Right is right and wrong is wrong; it is never [*right?*] to do wrong and wrong always brings its own punishment.

    A.   [*Adolf*] Hitler

    B.   Colonialism

    C.   Slavery

III There is another truth that history has to teach us: "The bee alway fertilizes the flower which it robs."

    A.   Negroes like R. Hayes & M. <u>Anderson</u>[6]

    B.   Poverty

    C.   The bee of war <u>robed</u> the flower of civilization of <u>those who have in there faces the</u> ~~flow~~ <u>blossom of youth</u>.

IV There is a final truth which Dr. Beard tells us history has to teach.[7] "When it gets dark enough you can see the stars. Sunlight always hides the depths of the heavens; you cannot see the Milky Way in daytime, but the darkness of the night unveils the North Star by which we chart our course.

    A.   Buyan, Milton, Beetoven, Handel[8]

    B.   Personal sins & errors

    C.   Personal tragedies/my stabbing[9]

    D.   What is the darkest [*century?*] on record

AD. CSKC: Sermon file, folder 77, "God In History (Four Proverbs)."

"What Keeps Religion Going?" Fosdick wrote: "Professor Charles A. Beard, one of the leading historians of our time, was asked sometime since what major lessons he had learned from history, and he answered that he had learned four. Here they are: 'First, whom the gods would destroy they first make mad with power. Second, the mills of God grind slowly, yet they grind exceedingly small. Third, the bee fertilizes the flower it robs. Fourth, when it is dark enough you can see the stars'" (Fosdick, *Riverside Sermons*, p. 156). King annotated his copy of Fosdick's book, which he kept in his personal library.

    4. This phrase is found in both the Old and New Testaments; for example, see Proverbs 16:18 and Matthew 23:12.

    5. Cf. Euripides *Bacchae* 882–887.

    6. King refers to singers Roland Hayes and Marian Anderson.

    7. Historian Charles Austin Beard (1874–1948) was noted for emphasizing a relationship between politics and economics in historical analysis.

    8. In other sermons, King refers to those individuals' ability to triumph over adversity. For an example of this, see King, Unfulfilled Hopes, 5 April 1959, p. 363 in this volume.

    9. Izola Ware Curry stabbed King during a book-signing in New York City on 20 September 1958.

ADDENDUM

Messages Following the Stabbing

On 20 September 1958 Izola Curry, a mentally disturbed black woman, stabbed King with a letter opener as he signed copies of Stride Toward Freedom, *at a Harlem department store.[1] Following the assault, he received a deluge of mail and telegrams, including this correspondence recently acquired by the King Papers Project from United Nations under-secretary general Ralph J. Bunche and civil rights advocate Ruth H. Bunche, vice president Richard M. Nixon, author John Steinbeck, and entertainer Harry Belafonte.[2] Steinbeck states, "You are very valuable to our whole perplexed and anxious species. Get well quickly. We need you, for you too are an accident—one of those fortunate accidents that have permitted us to survive our stupidities and our blundering."*

From Ruth H. and Ralph J. Bunche

20 September 1958
Kew Gardens, N.Y.

DR MARTIN LUTHER KING = HARLEM HOSPITAL PATIENT =

WE ARE CONFIDENT THAT YOUR GREAT SPIRITUAL AS WELL AS PHYSICAL STRENGTH, AND YOUR COURAGE, WILL LEAD YOU TO A SPEEDY RECOVERY STOP PLEASE ACCEPT OUR DEEP SYMPATHY AND WARMEST GOOD WISHES STOP =

RUTH AND RALPH BUNCHE[3]

PWSr. CSKC.

---

1. For more on King's stabbing and recovery, see Introduction, in *Papers* 4:34–35.

2. Upon his 24 October return to Montgomery, King acknowledged "the vast outpouring of sympathy and affection that came to me literally from everywhere—from Negro and white, from Catholic, Protestant and Jew, from the simple, the uneducated, the [*celebrities*] and the great" (King, Statement Upon Return to Montgomery, 24 October 1958, in *Papers* 4:513–514).

3. Ralph J. Bunche, the first African American Nobel Peace Prize winner, and his wife, Ruth, had been King's supporters since the Montgomery bus boycott. Ralph Bunche contributed to a fund used to defray King's expenses following his stabbing (see note 1, King to A. Philip Randolph, 8 November 1958, in *Papers* 4:527). Ruth Bunche served as a co-chair for the Youth March for Integrated Schools on 25 October 1958, held during King's convalescence (see note 1 to King, Address at Youth March for Integrated Schools in Washington, D.C., Delivered by Coretta Scott King, in *Papers* 4:514).

JOHN STEINBECK · 206 East Seventy-second Street, New York 21, N. Y.

September 23, 1958

My dear Reverend King:

The knowledge that you are flooded with messages does not decrease my wish to add a few drops to the torrent.

When the news came of your accident, and it was an accident, as you were the first to point out, I found myself bewildered and angry. Your service to negros is obvious, but I and many others know your importance to white people. Having erred in ethics and morals as well as in judgment, we react as my little boys sometimes do when they are being "bad." After a mistake they act their crimes and search for another to justify the first. You have showed the good, but more important, the practical way — in fact the only possible way.

After my first confused anger, I knew as you must have known from the first, that history sometimes uses strange instruments, in this case a sad and troubled woman. But who could have foreseen that the savagery of the cross as a deterrent to civil unrest would become the symbol of love and a flag of truce in a world of hatred.

Your accident provides a climate for evaluation and re-evaluation. I am sorry for your pain but very sure that you accept it as a part of the pattern without which no human step toward dignity and understanding is ever taken.

you are very valuable to our whole perplexed and
anxious species. Get well quickly. We need you, for
you too are an accident, one of those fortunate
accidents that have permitted us to survive our stupidities
and our blundering.

          yours gratefully
            John Steinbeck

From Richard M. Nixon

22 September 1958
Washington, D.C.

Dr. Martin Luther King, Jr.
Harlem Hospital
Lenox Avenue and 136th Street
New York, New York

Dear Dr. King:

I was terribly distressed to learn of the attack that was made on you in New York Saturday. To have this incident added to all of the unfortunate indignities which have been heaped upon you, is indeed difficult to understand.

I can only say that the Christian spirit of tolerance which you invariably display in the face of your opponents and detractors will in the end contribute immeasurably in winning the support of the great majority of Americans for the cause of equality and human dignity to which we are dedicated.[4]

Mrs. [*Pat*] Nixon joins me in sending our best wishes to you and Mrs. King.

Sincerely,

[*signed*] Richard Nixon
Richard Nixon

TLS. CSKC.

From John Steinbeck

23 September 1958
New York, N.Y.

My dear Reverend King:

The knowledge that you are flooded with messages does not decrease my wish to add a few drops to the torrent.

When the news came of your accident, and it was an accident, as you were the first to point out, I found myself bewildered and angry. Your service to negros is obvious, but I and many others know your importance to white people. Having

---

4. King first met Nixon on 5 March 1957 in Accra, Ghana, during that nation's independence ceremonies. Later that spring, the two men met in Washington, D.C., to discuss the pending Civil Rights Act of 1957. There, King demanded that Nixon deliver a speech in the South endorsing African American voting rights (Statement on Meeting with Richard M. Nixon, 13 June 1957, in *Papers* 4:222–223). King sent Nixon an inscribed copy of *Stride Toward Freedom*, writing, "Through our conversation and correspondence, I know of your interest in the Civil Rights problem facing our nation. I sincerely hope this contribution to the discussion may, in some measure, help the many sincere people seeking a just and democratic solution" (King, Inscriptions on complimentary copies of *Stride Toward Freedom*, November 1958).

erred in ethics and morals as well as in judgement, we react as my little boys sometimes do when they are being "bad" After a mistake they set their chins and search
for another to justify the first. You have showed the good, but more important, the
practical way—in fact the only possible way.

After my first confused anger, I knew as you must have known from the first, that
history sometimes uses strange instruments, in this case a sad and troubled woman.
But who could have for seen that the savagery of the Cross as a deterrent to civil
unrest would become the symbol of love and a flag of truce in a world of hatred.

Your accident provides a climate for evaluation and reevaluation I am sorry for
your pain but very sure that you accept it as a part of the pattern without which no
human step toward dignity and understanding is ever taken.

You are very valuable to our whole perplexed and anxious species. Get well
quickly. We need you, for you too are an accident—one of those fortunate accidents
that have permitted us to survive our stupidities and our blundering.

Yours gratefully,

[*signed*] John Steinbeck[5]

ALS. CSKC.

From Harry Belafonte

29 September 1958
Rome, Italy

= REV MARTIN LUTHER KING
HARLEM HOSPITAL NYK

WE WERE SHOCKED WHEN WE HEARD OF THE INCIDENT IN NEW YORK HAVE TRIED
TO CALL YOU BUT BEEN UNABLE TO REACH YOU WE ARE DEEPLY THANKFUL THAT
YOU HAVE BEEN SPARED PLAN TO RETURN FIRST WEEK OF OCTOBER WILL SEE YOU
WUB003 INTL 2/58 = THEN IF THERE IS ANYTHING MY WIFE OR I CAN POSSIBLY DO
PLEASE DO NOT HESITATE TO CALL UPON US THE MEMBERS OF MY TRAVELING MUSI-

---

5. In his 21 October 1958 reply to Steinbeck, King acknowledged that Steinbeck's "genuine concern
and moral support come as a great lift to me and are of inestimable value in giving me the strength and
courage to face the ordeal of this trying period." John Steinbeck (1902–1968) was born in Salinas, California and attended Stanford University from 1919 until 1925. Steinbeck was awarded the 1940 Pulitzer
Prize for his novel *Grapes of Wrath* (1939), and was honored with the Nobel Prize in Literature in 1962
for his body of work, which included *Of Mice and Men* (1937), *Their Blood Is Strong* (1938), and *East of Eden*
(1952).

CAL SAFARI SEND THEIR BEST WISHES AND HOPES FOR A SPEEDY RECOVERY[6] MY WIFE
[*JULIE*] AND I JOIN THEM AND THE GREATER MAJORITY OF THE WORLD IN THE SAME[7]
WISHES AND HOPES

HARRY BELAFONTE

PWSr. CSKC.

---

6. Belafonte was making his first European concert tour with a traveling troupe at the time (Howard Taubman, "Belafonte Sings at Brussels Fair," *New York Times*, 6 September 1958). On the day that he sent this wire, Belafonte publicly condemned Arkansas governor Orval Faubus's strident resistance to school desegregation in Little Rock, saying, "America will survive Faubus in the same way as Europe survived Hitler" ("Belafonte, in Rome, Denounces Faubus," *New York Times,* 30 September 1958).

7. A supporter of King's since the Montgomery bus boycott, Harry Belafonte participated in the 25 October Youth March for School Integration during King's recovery (King, Address at Youth March for Integrated Schools, in *Papers* 4:514).

The following list represents the sermon file folders in the order that they were first encountered. Quote marks for a folder's title indicate King's handwritten titling. Contents of each folder are listed by author, title, King Papers Project identification number, and number of pages (complete bibliographic information is contained in the Calendar of Documents). The order of the documents within each folder represents that originally found. Boldface type indicates inclusion in this volume. All sermon file documents were acquired in June 2006 by Morehouse College in Atlanta, Georgia.

Folder 1: "Loving Your Enemies"
    King, Martin Luther, Jr. "Love Your Enemies." 571110-004. 15 pp.
    King. "Loving Your Enemies." 520831-000. 4 pp.
    King. "Conclusion." 540000-103. 3 pp.
    Ferris, Theodore P. "The Doctrine of Original Goodness." 620527-000. 6 pp.
    Thurman, Howard. "We Believe." 591211-002. 2 pp.
    Thurman, Howard. "We Believe." 591218-002. 2 pp.
Folder 2: Death of Evil
    King. "The Death of Evil Upon the Seashore." 560517-001. 5 pp.
    King. "The Death of Evil Upon the Seashore." 560517-017. 7 pp.
    King. "The Death of Evil Upon the Seashore." 560517-022. 4 pp.
Folder 3: "Illustrations and Meditations"
    King. "Religion and Peace of Soul." 540000-088. 4 pp.
Folder 4: "Worship"
    King. "Worship." 550807-000. 11 pp.
    Fosdick, Harry Emerson. *Successful Christian Living: Sermons on Christianity Today* (pp.7–8). 370000-011. 2 pp.
    King. "Worship," Sermon outline. 550807-001. 2 pp.
Folder 5: "Man's Sin and God's Grace" / "The Peril of the Sword"
    King. "The Peril of the Sword." 600000-003. 2 pp.
Folder 6: "Finding God"
    King. "O That I Knew Where I Might Find Him!" 540000-070. 7 pp.
Folder 7: Shattered Dreams
    King. Draft of chapter X, "Shattered Dreams," *Strength to Love*. 630300-045. 12 pp.
Folder 8: "A Knock at Midnight"
    Niles, D. T. "Evangelism." 540816-000. 7 pp.
    King. "A Knock At Midnight." 590729-008. 2 pp.
    King. "A Knock at Midnight." 580914-003. 7 pp.
Folder 9: "Divine and Human Mutuality"
    King. "Divine and Human Mutuality" / "Man's Helplessness Without God." 590809-002. 7 pp.
Folder 10: "Communism's Challenge to Christianity"
    King. "Communism's Challenge to Christianity." 530809-001. 4 pp.
    King. "Communism's Challenge to Christianity," Sermon outline. 530809-002. 5 pp.
Folder 11: "Our God Is Able"

King. Draft of chapter XIII, "Our God Is Able," *Strength to Love*. 630300-054. 26 pp.

King. "Our God Is Able," Sermon outline. 610400-013. 3 pp.

King. "Our God Is Able." 560101-002. 9 pp.

King. "The Eternal Significance of Christ." 540000-106. 2 pp.

King. "Radio Sermons." 530906-004. 2 pp.

Meek, Frederick M. "Our God Is Able, A sermon preached in Old South Church in Boston." 530104-000. 8 pp.

Meek, Frederick M. "Perhaps Your God is Not Big Enough, A sermon preached in the Old South Church in Boston." 531011-000. 8 pp.

Folder 12: "Unfullfilled Hopes"

King. Unfulfilled Hopes, Sermon outline. 590405-003. 6 pp.

Folder 13: "A Way Out"

King. "A Way Out." 490522-001. 12 pp.

King. Notes on *Deep River* by Howard Thurman. 601000-029. 1 p.

King, Coretta Scott. Letter to Velma B. Hall. 601012-006. 1 p.

Folder 14: "Transformed Non-Conformist"

King. "Transformed Nonconformist." 541100-004. 5 pp.

King. "Transformed Nonconformist," Sermon outline. 541100-003. 3 pp.

Will, James E. "Men Who Live Differently." 510700-003. 3 pp.

Smith, A. Milton. "A Militant Christianity." 590000-149. 1 p.

"The Tempest." 510400-000. 2 pp.

Folder 15: Untitled

Morningside Baptist Church. "1962 Budget." 620000-018. 2 pp.

Folder 16: "The Meaning of Forgiveness" / "Questions Easter Answers"

King. "The Meaning of Forgiveness." 540000-128. 3 pp.

Folder 17: "A Tough Mind and A Tender Heart"

King. "A Tough Mind and a Tender Heart," Sermon outline. 590830-003. 6 pp.

King. Draft of chapter I, "A Tough Mind and a Tender Heart," *Strength to Love*. 630300-071. 26 pp.

King. "A Tough Mind and a Tender Heart." 590830-002. 10 pp.

Folder 18: "False Gods We Worship"

King. On Worshiping False Gods. 550100-003. 5 pp.

King. "The False God of Nationalism." 530712-001. 2 pp.

King. "The False God of Science." 530705-000. 2 pp.

King. The False God of Pleasure. 550100-005. 2 pp.

King. "The False God of Money." 530719-000. 4 pp.

Folder 19: Book Inscription

Davis, George W. *Existentialism and Theology* (Inscription by Davis). 570000-067

Folder 20: Justice Without Violence

King. "Justice Without Violence." 570403-021. 10 pp.

Folder 21: "The Three Dimensions of a Complete Life"

King. "The Three Dimensions of a Complete Life." 540124-003. 8 pp.

King. "The Dimensions of a Complete Life." 540124-002. 8 pp.

King. "The Dimensions of a Complete Life." 590531-002. 12 pp.

King. Notes on "Meditation XVII," *Devotions Upon Emergent Occasions by John Donne*. 540000-151. 1 p.

Folder 22: "What Is Man?"

King. "What Is Man?" 540711-000. 11 pp.

King. What Is Man? Sermon notes. 540711-001. 2 pp.

King. Prayer. 600000-204. 1 p.

King. "Remember Who You Are!!" 561206-015. 12 pp.

King. "What Is Man?" Address at the Chicago Sunday Evening Club. 580112-001. 3 pp.

King. Remember Who You Are, Sermon notes. 561206-016. 1 p.

Denver Area Council of Churches. Program, "Holy week service." 620418-000. 4 pp.

King. Draft, "What Is Man?" 590000-042. 16 pp.

Folder 23: Negro and the American Dream

King. The Negro and the American Dream, Excerpts of address at the annual Freedom Mass Meeting of the North Carolina State Conference of branches of the NAACP. 600925-000. 5 pp.

Folder 24: Bible 252

Kelsey, George D. Study questions, Bible. 470500-002. 6 pp.

King. Class notes, Bible. 470500-003. 35 pp.

King. Examination answers, Bible. 470500-004. 9 pp.

King. Examination answers, Bible. 470523-000. 6 pp.

King. Examination answers, Bible. 461203-000. 6 pp.

King, Christine. "Religion: The Characters of Samuel, Saul, David, and Solomon." 480500-000. 3 pp.

Folder 25: Untitled

King. Notes on Foreword by H. H. McConnell to *How to Make an Evangelistic Call.* 470000-013. 1 p.

Hiltner, Seward. *How to Make an Evangelistic Call.* 470000-026. 24 pp.

Folder 26: Christian Century June 22, 1960

Stein, Edward V. "Persons in a Depersonalized Age." 600622-004. 4 pp.

Folder 27: "The Mission of the Church"

Dexter Avenue Baptist Church. Program, Sunday services. 560122-000. 4 pp.

King. "Redirecting Our Missionary Zeal." 560122-002. 4 pp.

King. "The Mission of the Church." 560000-081. 3 pp.

Folder 28: "God's Relation to the World"

King. "God's Relation to the World," Sermon outline. 540000-110. 4 pp.

King. "God's Relation to the World," Sermon notes. 540000-109. 2 pp.

Folder 29: Untitled

SCLC. "' . . . I have decided to start with myself,' Tenth anniversary convention banquet." 670814-001. 5 pp.

Folder 30: Untitled

SCLC. *Newsletter* 1, no. 7. 620900-003. 4 pp.

SCLC. *Newsletter* 1, no. 10. 630700-003. 8 pp.

SCLC. *Newsletter* 1, no. 11. 630800-004. 8 pp.

SCLC. *Newsletter* 1, no. 12. 630900-004. 12 pp.

King. "Epitaph and Challenge." 631200-000. 1 p.

SCLC. *Newsletter* 2, no. 4. 640100-003. 12 pp.

Folder 31: Untitled

[*SCLC*]. Draft, *Newsletter.* 620900-017. 4 pp.

King, and William G. Anderson. Statement on violence in Albany, Ga. and declaration of Day of Penance. 620725-001. 1 p.

Folder 32: Untitled

SCLC. Press release, "Martin Luther King, Jr., and other southern leaders set to speak at series of New York protest meetings." 610602-008. 4 pp.

Folder 33: Untitled

King. Press release, Statement calling for executive order declaring segregation illegal. 610605-001. 2 pp.

Folder 34: Untitled

King. Give Us the Ballot. 570517-000. 5 pp.

Folder 35: Untitled

University of Bridgeport. Citations for recipients read on the occasion of the conferral of the honorary degree of Doctor of Laws. 610604-006. 4 pp.

Folder 36: "Sermon Notes"

Kelsey, George D. "The Present Crisis in Negro Ministerial Education." 480119-000. 4 pp.

King. Sermon Conclusions. 490216-023. 4 pp.

King. Sermon Sketches III. 490216-025. 2 pp.

King. "Karl Barth." 500215-036. 3 pp.

King. "The Task of Christian Leadership Training for Education in the Local Community." 550703-000. 5 pp.

King. Sermon Sketches I. 490216-018. 4 pp.

King. Sermon Introductions. 490216-022. 4 pp.

King. "Will Capitalism Survive?" 500215-035. 3 pp.

King. "The Limitation of Experience." 500215-018. 3 pp.

King. "Science Surpasses the Social Order." 510504-041. 2 pp.

King. "Is the Church the Hope of the World?" 500215-034. 4 pp.

King. Sermon Sketches II. 490216-021. 3 pp.

King. "The Purpose of Religion." 510500-049. 3 pp.

King. "An order for the baptism of adults." 500215-038. 4 pp.

King. "Preaching Ministry." 481124-006. 6 pp.

Sockman, Ralph W. "What the World Wants Most, a radio address." 480411-000. 5 pp.

Sockman, Ralph W. "Lest We Forget, a radio address." 480530-000. 5 pp.

Bonnell, John Sutherland. "The Source of Inner Strength, a radio address." 480314-000. 5 pp.

Bonnell, John Sutherland. "Prayer—A Cosmic Power, a radio address." 480307-000. 5 pp.

Sockman, Ralph W. "Prepared for the Best, a radio address." 480118-000. 6 pp.

Bonnell, John Sutherland. "Faith that Moves Mountains, a radio address." 480215-000. 5 pp.

Religious Book Club. *Bulletin.* 490900-004. 5 pp.

Folder 37: "Desegregation and the Future"

King. "Desegregation and the Future." 561215-005. 8 pp.

Folder 38: "Addresses by Others"

Jackson, J. H. "Address at the eightieth annual session of the National Baptist Convention, U.S.A., Inc." 600908-002. 35 pp.

Jackson, J. H. "Address at the seventy-ninth annual session of the National Baptist Convention, U.S.A., Inc." 590910-004. 26 pp.

Kelsey, George D. "The Lord of Life." 600629-004. 5 pp.

Smith, Lillian. "Are We Still Buying a New World with Old Confederate Bills?" 601016-002. 8 pp.

Jackson, J. H. "Annual address at the seventy-sixth annual session of the National Baptist Convention, U.S.A., Inc." 560906-003. 33 pp.

Folder 39: Untitled

King. The Negro and the American Dream. 600925-000. 5 pp.

Graham, Frank Porter. "Students 'Standing Up' for the American Dream." 600800-003. 1 p.

Jones, Lewis W. "Problems in the Segregated South." 601015-001. 14 pp.

Jones, Lewis W. Letter to Martin Luther King, Jr. 601101-013. 2 pp.

Folder 40: "Lecture on Philosophy of Nonviolence"

Yungblut, John. Letter to Martin Luther King, Jr. 610116-006. 3 pp.

"Nonviolence and the will of God, a church school elective course for four Sundays." 600000-088. 11 pp.

Folder 41: The Man Who Was A Fool

King. "The Man Who Was a Fool." 610600-000. 3 pp.

Folder 42: "Old Testament"

King. Class notes, Introduction to the Old Testament. 481124-005. 60 pp.

Folder 43: "Beyond Condemnation"

King. "Beyond Condemnation." 541100-007. 7 pp.

Folder 44: "The One-Sided Approach to the Good Samaritan"

King. "The One-Sided Approach of the Good Samaritan," Sermon outline. 551120-002. 2 pp.

King. "The One-Sided Approach of the Good Samaritan." 551120-003. 3 pp.

Folder 45: "Mastering Our Fears"

King. "The Mastery of Fear," Sermon outline. 570721-003. 4 pp.

King. The Mastery of Fear, Sermon notes. 570721-004. 2 pp.

King. "Mastering Our Fears." 570721-005. 5 pp.

Folder 46: "The Good Samaritan"

King. "The Goodness of the Good Samaritan." 601128-018. 4 pp.

Folder 47: Mis Sermons

Demere, Charles. "Partnership with God." 630519-000. 4 pp.

Folder 48: The Prodigal Son

King. Prodigal Son, Sermon outline. 680000-086. 1 p.

Folder 49: "Sermon Notes"

King. "The Philosophy of Life Undergirding Christianity and the Christian Ministry." 510500-047. 3 pp.

King. Sermon Notes and Outlines I. 540000-142. 14 pp.

Bosley, Harold A. "We Believe in the Church." 490700-001. 2 pp.

Folder 50: Sermons Not Preached

King. "Human Freedom and Divine Grace." 540000-115. 2 pp.

King. "Getting Caught in the Negative" / "The Peril of Emphasizing a Negative" / "Accentuating the Positive." 540000-102. 2 pp.

King. "Unity." 540000-127. 4 pp.

King. "Cooperative Competition" / "Noble Competition." 540000-130. 2 pp.

King. "What is Salvation?" 540000-187. 2 pp.

King. "Men's Day Sermon." 490303-000. 2 pp.

King. Sermon Notes and Outlines II. 540000-095. 3 pp.

King. "Moral Absolutism." 540000-118. 1 p.

King. "Be Ye Perfect." 540000-123. 1 p.

King. "The Call of Christ" / "Follow Me." 540000-114. 1 p.

King. "I Sat Where They Sat." 540000-129. 1 p.

King. "The Eternality of God Versus the Temporality of Man." 540000-108. 1 p.

King. Man's Highest Value. 540000-112. 1 p.

King. "Science and Religion." 510500-077. 2 pp.

King. "The Law of Spiritual Accumulation." 540000-119. 2 pp.

King. "Salvation Through Despair" / "Life's Fulfillment through Despair." 540000-113. 1 p.

King. "The Distinctions in God's Creation." 540000-126. 1 p.

King. A Man to Fill the Gap. 540000-117. 1 p.

Folder 51: "The Seeking God (Parable of Lost Sheep)"

King. "The Seeking God." 601002-001. 5 pp.

Folder 52: Father Forgive Them

King. Love and Forgiveness, Sermon notes. 640520-002. 4 pp.

Folder 53: "Man's Sin and God's Grace"

King. "Man's Sin and God's Grace." 600000-215. 14 pp.

King. "Man's Sin and God's Grace," Sermon outline. 600000-214. 2 pp.

Folder 54: The Drum Major Instinct

King. "The Drum-Major Instinct," Sermon outline. 680204-001. 3 pp.

If I Can Help Somebody. 680000-087. 1 p.

"One Solitary Life." 680000-088. 1 p.

Folder 55: "Propagandizing Christianity"

King. "Propagandizing Christianity." 540912-001. 6 pp.

King. Sincerity Is Not Enough. 510603-002. 2 pp.

King. "Propagandizing Religion." 540000-134. 2 pp.

Folder 56: "The Impassable Gulf"

King. "The Impassable Gulf (The Parable of Dives and Lazarus)." 551002-003. 7 pp.

King. "The Impassable Gulf (The Parable of Dives and Lazarus)." 551002-004. 14 pp.

King. Notes on Dives. 551002-006. 1 p.

Folder 57: Luke 2:28

King. After Christmas, What? 521228-000. 2 pp.

Folder 58: Sermon: Paul's Letter to American Christians

King. "Paul's Letter to American Christians." 561104-000. 7 pp.

Folder 59: "Pride versus Humility (Parable of Publican and Pharisee)"

King. "Pride Versus Humility: The Parable of the Pharisee and the Publican." 550925-001. 13 pp.

King. "Pride Versus Humility: Parable of the Pharisee and the Publican," Sermon outline. 550925-002. 2 pp.

Folder 60: "The Fellow Who Stayed at Home"

Hamilton, J. Wallace. "That Fellow Who Stayed at Home." 540000-023. 4 pp.

King. "The Fellow Who Stayed at Home." 561000-016. 2 pp.

Folder 61: We Would See Jesus
King. "We Would See Jesus," Sermon notes. 670507-002. 1 p.
Folder 62: Worship at Its Best
King. "Worship at Its Best." 581214-002. 3 pp.
Fosdick, Harry Emerson. "Why Worship?" in *Successful Christian Living* (pp. 165–175). 370000-003. 11 pp.
Folder 63: "Fleeing from God & When God Seems to Deceive Us"
King. Notecard on Philip Sidney. 540000-186. 1 p.
King. "The Necessity of the New Birth." 540000-098. 3 pp.
King. "God the Inescapable." 540000-131. 4 pp.
King. "Eternal Life." 540000-107. 2 pp.
King. "Fleeing From God." 560429-008. 2 pp.
King. "Fleeing from God," Sermon outline. 560429-009. 1 p.
Folder 64: Sermon Material
King. Notes, "Man Incurably Religious" by John White Chadwick. 680000-084. 1 p.
Folder 65: Untitled
King. "On Being Unashamed of the Gospel," Sermon outline. 641004-001. 4 pp.
Program, "Community mass meeting." 640722-003. 1 p.
King. Fruitful Tension. 600000-169. 1 p.
King. "If." 600000-199. 1 p.
King. A Knock at Midnight, Sermon outline. 640800-011. 6 pp.
King. The Mixture in Human Nature. 540000-180. 1 p.
King. Notes, Address at community mass meeting at the Masonic Temple. 640722-000. 1 p.
Folder 66: "Accepting Responsibility for Your Actions" / "Faith in Man"
King. "Accepting Responsibility for Your Actions." 530726-002. 5 pp.
King. "Faith in Man" I. 560226-007. 3 pp.
King. "Faith in Man" II. 560226-008. 3 pp.
Folder 67: The Human Tension
King. "The Human Tension." 540000-120. 2 pp.
Folder 68: "Opportunity, Fidelity, and Reward"
King. "Opportunity, Fidelity, and Reward." 550100-006. 4 pp.
King. Opportunity, Fidelity, and Reward, Sermon outline. 550100-007. 1 p.
Folder 69: "God's Love"
King. "God's Love." 540905-003. 3 pp.
Folder 70: "Christ the Center of Our Faith" / "How Believe in a Good God in the Midst of Glaring Evil"
King. "Christ, The Center of Our Faith." 550000-000. 3 pp.
King. "How Believe in a Good God in the Midst of Glaring Evil." 560115-003. 5 pp.
Folder 71: "Creating the Abundant Life" / "A Moment of Difficult Decision"
King. "Creating the Abundant Life." 540926-001. 9 pp.
King. "A Moment of Difficult Decision." 540000-048. 1 p.
King. Creating the Abundant Life, Sermon outline. 540000-138. 2 pp.
King. Notes, "Be the Best of Whatever You Are" by Douglass Malloch. 540000-139. 1 p.
King. Notes on Clarence Darrow. 540000-140. 1 p.
King. The Sea of Life. 540000-178. 1 p.

Folder 72: "Who is Truly Great"
Folder empty
Folder 73: "New Wine in New Bottles"
King. "New Wine in New Bottles." 541017-006. 4 pp.
Marshall, Peter. "Let's Keep Christmas." 540000-043. 2 pp.
Folder 74: "The Future of Integration"
Atkins, C. B. Letter to Martin Luther King, Jr. 620612-000. 4 pp.
King. "The Road to Freedom." 610000-026. 2 pp.
King. "The Future of Integration." 601211-005. 12 pp.
Folder 75: "Facing Life's Inescapables"
King. "Facing Life's Inescapables." 490303-001. 6 pp.
Folder 76: "The Crisis in the Modern Family"
King. "The Crisis in the Modern Family." 550508-000. 8 pp.
King. "Secrets of Married Happiness." 611119-000. 3 pp.
**King. "What Then Are Some of the Secrets of Happy Marriage." 611119-001.
5 pp.**
Folder 77: "God in History (Four Proverbs)"
King. God in History: Four Proverbs. 680000-094. 2 pp.
Folder 78: "Keep Moving From This Mountain"
King. "Other Mountains." 550515-001. 1 p.
King. "Founders Day Address, Keep Moving From This Mountain." 600410-001.
13 pp.
King. Outline, Founders Day address, Keep Moving From This Mountain.
600410-002. 3 pp.
Folder 79: "Discerning the Signs of History"
King. "Discerning the Signs of History," Sermon notes. 550626-002. 2 pp.
King. "Discerning the Signs of History," Sermon outline. 550626-003. 5 pp.
King. "Discerning the Signs of History." 550626-004. 3 pp.
Folder 80: "God's Judgment on Western Civilization" / "The Vision of a World
Made New"
King. "God's Judgment on Western Civilization," Sermon notes II. 570300-024.
1 p.
King. "The Vision of a World Made New." 540909-002. 6 pp.
King. God's Judgment on Western Civilization. 570300-017. 4 pp.
King. God's Judgment on Western Civilization, Sermon notes I. 570300-019.
6 pp.
Folder 81: How to Deal with Disappointment
King. "How to Deal With Grief and Disappointment," Sermon outline.
650523-002. 3 pp.
Folder 82: "Making It In on Broken Pieces"
King. "Making It in on Broken Pieces." 630804-001. 4 pp.
King. "When Your A String Breaks." 590000-046. 3 pp.
[*Randall, Thomas H.*]. Letter to Martin Luther King, Jr. 591103-010. 1 p.
Folder 83: "I'm Going To Procrastination"
Randall, Thomas H. Letter to Martin Luther King, Jr. 590800-007. 1 p.
King. I'm Going To: Procrastination. 590000-048. 2 pp.
Folder 84: "The Conflict in Human Nature"
King. "The Conflict in Human Nature." 590816-001. 3 pp.

Folder 85: Antidotes for Fear
  King. Draft of chapter XIV, "Antidotes for Fear," *Strength to Love.* 630300-061.
    13 pp.
Folder 86: "A Look to the Future"
  [*Rustin, Bayard*]. "The Nature of the Present Crisis." 570000-060. 3 pp.
  [*Levison, Stanley D.*]. "A Wind is Rising." 570400-012. 3 pp.
  [*Rustin, Bayard*]. "Notes on Nonviolence." 570000-061. 5 pp.
  King. "For All . . . A Non-Segregated Society, A message for Race Relations Sun-
    day." 570210-001. 4 pp.
Folder 87: Why the Christian Must Oppose Segregation
  King. "Why the Christian Must Oppose Segregation." 640000-145. 2 pp.
  King. "The Danger of Mis Guided Goodness." 540000-133. 1 p.
Folder 88: Untitled
  King. Draft of chapter XI, "What Is Man?" *Strength to Love.* 630300-048. 8 pp.
  King. Draft, Annual report, Dexter Avenue Baptist Church. 581130-003. 21 pp.
Folder 89: Untitled
  King. Draft, Invocation at funeral of John Wesley Dobbs. 610902-001. 6 pp.
Folder 90: Untitled
  King. Draft of chapter I, "A Tough Mind and a Tender Heart," *Strength to Love.*
    630300-012. 10 pp.
  King. Draft, What Is Man? 590000-074. 2 pp.
  Advertisement, "A business primer for Negroes." 480000-043. 8 pp.
Folder 91: "Religion of Doing"
  [*Hughes, Hugh Price*]. "The City of Everywhere." 540704-001. 2 pp.
  King. "A Religion of Doing." 540704-000. 6 pp.
Folder 92: From Coretta Scott King to Miss Jackson
  Folder empty
Folder 93: "Paul's Letter to American Christians"
  King. "Paul's Letter to American Christians." 560000-183. 11 pp.
Folder 94: "Christ, Our Starting Point"
  King. "Christ Our Starting Point." 581221-002. 3 pp.
Folder 95: "Carbon Copies of Final Draft" / Howard University Rankin Memorial
Chapel, Wash, D.C., November 9, 1958
  King. Draft of chapter IV, "Love in Action," *Strength to Love.* 630300-024. 14 pp.
  King. Draft of chapter XVII, "Pilgrimage to Nonviolence," *Strength to Love.*
    630300-068. 10 pp.
  King. Draft of chapter V, "Loving Your Enemies," *Strength to Love.* 630300-027.
    13 pp.
  King. Draft of chapter XVI, "Paul's Letter to American Christians," *Strength to
    Love.* 630300-067. 10 pp.
  King. Draft of chapter XII, "How Should A Christian View Communism?"
    Strength to Love. 630300-052. 11 pp.
  King. Draft of chapter IX, "Three Dimensions of a Complete Life," *Strength to
    Love.* 630300-044. 14 pp.
  King. Draft of chapter VI, "A Knock At Midnight," *Strength to Love.* 630300-033.
    16 pp.
  King. Draft of chapter XV, "The Answer to a Perplexing Question," *Strength to
    Love.* 630300-065. 14 pp.

King. Draft of chapter III, "On Being a Good Neighbor," *Strength to Love.* 630300-020. 11 pp.

King. Draft of chapter XIII, "Our God Is Able," *Strength to Love.* 630300-057. 11 pp.

King. Draft of chapter VIII, "The Death of Evil Upon the Seashore," *Strength to Love.* 630300-040. 12 pp.

Folder 96: Dr. King's Letters

[*Wallis, Charles L.*]. Editorial notes on *Strength to Love.* 621003-007. 6 pp.

Arnold, Melvin. Letter to Martin Luther King, Jr. 621005-004. 1 p.

King. Draft of chapter XV, "The Answer to a Perplexing Question," *Strength to Love.* 630300-063. 17 pp.

Folder 97: Untitled

Meek, Frederick M. "The Protestant Witness, A sermon preached in the Old South Church in Boston." 521026-000. 8 pp.

King. "Going Forward By Going Backward." 540404-001. 5 pp.

King. "Wedding Prayer." 540000-197. 2 pp.

King. "The Death of Evil Upon the Seashore." 560517-017. 7 pp.

King. "Prayers." 530906-003. 12 pp.

King. Draft, *Strength to Love.* 630300-010. 30 pp.

Meek, Frederick M. "A Letter to Christians, A sermon preached in the Old South Church in Boston." 540221-001. 8 pp.

Rust, Henry. "God's Order—Man's Disorder." 610528-001. 4 pp.

Folder 98: "Some Things that We Must Do"

King. "Some Things We Can Do." 571205-006. 6 pp.

Folder 99: The Death of Evil Upon the Seashore

King. "The Death of Evil Upon the Seashore." 560517-001. 5 pp.

Folder 100: "Sermons by Other Ministers"

The Pulpit 22. 511000-001. 32 pp.

Meek, Frederick M. "How Are We to Live in Days Like These? Fulfill the Disciplines of the Faith, A sermon preached in the Old South Church in Boston." 520330-000. 7 pp.

Meek, Frederick M. "On Loan to God, A sermon preached in the Old South Church in Boston." 530405-000. 7 pp.

Meek, Frederick M. "Evading Responsibility, A sermon preached in the Old South Church in Boston." 530329-000. 8 pp.

Meek, Frederick M. "The Christian and His Occupation, A sermon preached in the Old South Church in Boston." 521130-001. 11 pp.

Meek, Frederick M. "The Hindrances to the Christian Life, A sermon preached in the Old South Church in Boston." 521019-000. 7 pp.

Sockman, Ralph W. "Taking Our Chances, a radio address." 490522-000. 5 pp.

Bonnell, John Sutherland. "Courage to Face Life, a radio address." 470302-000. 5 pp.

Malik, Charles. "Asia and Africa Ask Searching Questions." 540818-000. 8 pp.

Meek, Frederick M. "Institutions and Men, A sermon preached in Old South Baptist Church in Boston." 530308-000. 8 pp.

Meek, Frederick M. "Going Back to the Place of Vision, A sermon preached in the Old South Church in Boston." 531004-000. 6 pp.

Elderveld, Peter. "Peace Amid War, a radio message." 520928-000. 12 pp.

Meek, Frederick M. "The Lord Hath Need of Him, A sermon preached in the Sermon File Old South Church in Boston." 530315-000. 8 pp.

The Philosophy of Life Undergirding Christianity and the Christian Ministry. 510500-057. 1 p.

King. "The ministry as it looks to me." 510500-038. 1 p.

King. "Success and Failure." 540000-121. 1 p.

King. Sermon titles II. 540000-183. 1 p.

King. Three Levels of Fellowship. 500528-000. 1 p.

King. "Three Stages of Life." 510500-043. 1 p.

King. Sermon titles I. 540000-182. 2 pp.

King. Four Sorts of Men. 540000-124. 2 pp.

King. "The Philosophy of Life Undergirding Christianity and the Christian Ministry," Outline. 510500-039. 1 p.

Folder 101: The Death of Evil Upon the Seashore

King. "The Death of Evil Upon the Seashore." 560517-001. 5 pp.

King. "The Death of Evil Upon the Seashore." 550724-002. 8 pp.

King. "Paul's Letter to American Christians." 561104-000. 7 pp.

Folder 102: Untitled

King. "What Shall We Do to Be Saved?" 540000-179. 1 p.

King. "Paul's Letter to American Christians." 561104-004. 10 pp.

Folder 103: "The Tension between Life's Palm Sunday and Life's Good Friday"

King. Garden of Gethsemane, Sermon notes. 570414-005. 5 pp.

King. The Tension Between Life's Palm Sunday and Life's Good Friday. 600410-005. 3 pp.

Folder 104: Organizations—Let.

King. Address at the Peace Parade and Rally. 670325-001. 15 pp.

Luna, Benjamin Laureano. "La Doctrina de America." 670325-005. 2 pp.

Folder 105: "Making the Best of a Bad Mess"

King. "Making the Best of a Bad Mess." 660424-005. 3 pp.

King. When Your A String Breaks, Sermon notes. 590000-094. 1 p.

Morse, Wayne. Interview by Bill Plymat on Vietnam. 670000-087.

Folder 106: "Sermons"

King. An Unforeseen Event. 600000-179. 2 pp.

King. Statement on arrest of ministers. 581027-012. 1 p.

King. "What Should Be Our Attitude Toward Mystery." 680000-083. 2 pp.

King. "The Foolishness of Preaching." 540000-104. 2 pp.

King. Tribute to supporter. 590000-058. 2 pp.

King. "Not Many Days After . . . " 680000-085. 4 pp.

SCLC. Layout, "The Crusader." 590100-008. 3 pp.

King. Love, the Only Force. 540000-189. 1 p.

Michigan Christian Advocate. "Truth Never Dies." 540000-099. 1 p.

King. "God Is Light." 540000-149. 1 p.

King. "The God that Jesus Revealed." 540000-190. 2 pp.

Folder 107: Why Does God Hide Himself

King. "Why Does God Hide Himself." 551204-001. 3 pp.

Folder 108: Unrealized Sufficiencies

"Unrealized Sufficiencies." 510500-079. 7 pp.

Folder 109: "Levels of Love"

619

King. "The Meaning of Easter," Sermon outline. 620422-002. 2 pp.

King. "Levels of Love." 600814-001. 4 pp.

King. "Levels of Love," Sermon notes. 540000-077. 1 p.

Folder 110: "Mastering Our Evil Selves"

King. "Is It Unchristian to Judge Others?" Sermon outline. 660700-003. 2 pp.

King. "Mastering Our Evil Selves" / "Mastering Ourselves." 490605-001. 16 pp.

King. Small Trivialities and Large Catastrophes. 680000-095. 2 pp.

King. Is It Unchristian to Judge Others? Sermon notes. 660700-004. 2 pp.

King. Notes, Eulogy for C. R. Lyons. 670000-066. 1 p.

Folder 111: "When Peace Becomes Obnoxious"

King. "When Peace Becomes Obnoxious." 560318-008. 8 pp.

Folder 112: "First Things First"

King. "First Things First." 530802-001. 2 pp.

King. "God's Kingdom First." 530802-002. 3 pp.

Folder 113: "Mental Slavery"

King. "Mental and Spiritual Slavery" I. 540500-007. 2 pp.

Folder 114: "Splinters and Planks"

King. "Splinters and Planks." 490724-000. 9 pp.

Folder 115: "The Secret of Adjustment / The Meaning of Easter"

King. "The Secret of Adjustment." 611202-001. 6 pp.

Folder 116: Conditions for Entering the Kingdom

King. "Conditions for Entering the Kingdom." 540000-111. 2 pp.

Folder 117: Jan. 16, 1966

King. Transformed Nonconformist. 660116-002. 15 pp.

Folder 118: "Sermon Material"

King. "When God Seems to Deceive Us." 540000-100. 1 p.

King. "All That We Are, We Owe." 540000-116. 2 pp.

King. "The Unity of Mankind." 540000-184. 2 pp.

King. "The Weaknesses of Liberal Theology" I. 480000-031. 3 pp.

King. Notes on *Christianity and Our World* by John C. Bennett. 520516-018. 1 p.

Crozer Theological Seminary. "Student chapel order of service." 500127-000. 2 pp.

King. Sincerity Is Not Enough, Sermon outline. 510603-003. 1 p.

King. Index of Sermon Topics. 510504-043. 6 pp.

Quotes for sermons. 540000-191. 1 p.

King. "The Unknown Great." 540000-143. 2 pp.

King. Acceptance Address at Dexter Avenue Baptist Church. 540502-001. 2 pp.

King. "Beyond Condemnation," Sermon notes. 541100-008. 1 p.

King. What Is Man?, Sermon notes I. 540000-181. 1 p.

Folder 119: "Civilization's Greatest Need" / "Faith in Man"

King. "Civilization's Great Need." 490000-039. 3 pp.

King. "Civilization's Great Need." 490000-031. 2 pp.

Folder 120: "Love in Action" / "Father Forgive Them"

King. "Love in Action" I. 600403-003. 4 pp.

Folder 121: "Looking Beyond Your Circumstance"

King. "Looking Beyond Your Circumstances." 550918-001. 13 pp.

Folder 122: MLK Speech 3/31/68

King. "Remaining Awake Through a Great Revolution." 680331-002. 11 pp.
Folder 123: Untitled
"Integrationist Dr. King Praises Priests' Bus Ride." 611000-002. 1 p.
Progressive National Baptist Convention, Inc. Program, "Second annual session."
    630908-001. 4 pp.
King. "Advance excerpts." 630630-000. 3 pp.
"King Pickets Scripto Plant Thirty Minutes." 641220-000. 1 p.
"Scripto, Union to Hold Meeting on December 21." 641216-000. 2 pp.
"Dexter Avenue has Meeting." 551102-004. 1 p.
"King: Boycott All Mississippi Goods." 641211-004. 1 p.
"Strikers Meet At Ebenezer." 641203-001. 1 p.
Black, Charles A. "Scripto Strikers Here Call For World-Wide Boycott of Scripto."
    641212-002. 1 p.
"Scripto, Union Meeting Today." 641203-000. 1 p.
"Scripto Boycott Backed By SCLC." 641222-002. 1 p.
Greene, Tom. "Labor Council Backs Strike At Scripto." 641211-003. 1 p.
Folder 124: Untitled
"Martin Luther King Column" V. 600218-017. 3 pp.
[*King*]. The Social Organization of Nonviolence. 591000-015. 5 pp.
King. Mental and Spiritual Slavery II. 540500-006. 4 pp.
King. Draft, Introduction, *Why We Can't Wait.* 640500-028. 4 pp.
American Negro culture. 540000-087. 6 pp.
Folder 125: Article—Martin L. King
King. "The Burning Truth in the South." 600500-000. 3 pp.
King. "Fumbling on the New Frontier." 620303-000. 4 pp.
Folder 126: Speeches by Dr. King, Montgomery, 1956
King. "The Montgomery Story." 560627-009. 13 pp.
Folder 127: Speeches—MLK
King. "Justice Without Violence." 570403-021. 10 pp.
King. "Nonviolent Procedures to Inter-Racial Harmony." 561016-003. 8 pp.
Folder 128: Speech 1/17/59 Mt. Tabo AME Z Church
Women's Missionary Society of the Mt. Tabo AME Zion Church. Program,
    "Women sharing in Kingdom Building." 600117-003. 4 pp.
Folder 129: The Pulpit—1961 (June) Article by Dr. King
The Pulpit: A Journal of Contemporary Preaching 32. 610600-017. 28 pp.
Folder 130: "Acceptance Speech of Spingarn Metal"
King. "Remarks in acceptance of the forty-second Spingarn Medal at the forty-
    eighth annual convention of the NAACP." 570628-001. 14 pp.
Folder 131: Speeches—MLK, Jr. Atlanta Summit Conference Dec. 15, 1963
King. "A Challenge to the Churches and Synagogues." 630117-006. 17 pp.
King. Address at the Pilgrimage for Democracy. 631215-000. 8 pp.
Draft, Program, Pilgrimage for Democracy. 631215-007. 1 p.
Folder 132: "Nonviolent Bus Integration / First Address made to SCLC by MLK, Jr."
King. Draft, Letter to Grover C. Hall. 570111-034. 2 pp.
Southern Leaders Conference. "A Statement to the South and Nation."
    570111-008. 8 pp.
Folder 133: Articles by MLK Jr.
King. "The President Has the Power: Equality Now." 610204-000. 4 pp.

Folder 134: Speech—Hungry Club 12/15/65

> King. "A Great Challenge Derived from a Serious Dilemma." 651215-000. 14 pp.

Folder 135: "Facing the Challenge of a New Age"

> King. "Facing the Challenge of a New Age." 561203-000. 20 pp.

Folder 136: Speech—Spingarn Medal M.L.K.

> Emrich, Richard S. M. "Remarks on presentation of the forty-second Spingarn Medal to Rev. Dr. Martin Luther King, Jr. at the NAACP forty-eighth annual convention." 570628-006. 4 pp.

> King. "Remarks in acceptance of the forty-second Spingarn Medal at the forty-eighth annual convention of the NAACP." 570628-001. 14 pp.

> NAACP. "Fortieth Spingarn Medal Awarded to Dr. Carl Murphy." 550624-002. 43 pp.

Folder 137: "The Christian Way of Life in Human Relations" / "Nonviolence and Racial Justice"

> King. Draft, "The Christian Way of Life in Human Relations." 571204-012. 7 pp.

> King. "Nonviolent Procedures to Inter-Racial Harmony." 561016-003. 8 pp.

> Bowles, Chester. Letter to Martin Luther King, Jr. 571231-002. 2 pp.

Folder 138: Untitled

> King. Pilgrimage to Nonviolence. 600413-014. 10 pp.

> Hill, Daniel G. Letter to Martin Luther King, Jr. 570221-008. 1 p.

> Muste, A. J. Letter to Martin Luther King, Jr. 580923-004. 1 p.

> Crozer Theological Seminary. *Bulletin 51: The Voice Issue.* 591000-014. 16 pp.

> Fey, Harold Edward. Letter to Martin Luther King, Jr. 591231-000. 1 p.

Folder 139: "Articles on 'Sit-ins' and Civil Rights Debate"

> National Council of the Protestant Episcopal Church. "Background paper on the student 'sit-in' protest movement in the light of the church's authoritative statements." 600401-008. 15 pp.

> Congress of Racial Equality. "The meaning of the sit-ins." 600801-007. 6 pp.

> United Presbyterian Church. "Dynamic for Teaching." 600000-075. 4 pp.

> Southern Regional Council. *New South* 15. 600300-008. 16 pp.

> "Let Us Kneel-in Together!" 600824-006. 2 pp.

> Baker, Ella J. Letter to Student leader. 600408-011. 1 p.

> Westfeldt, Wallace. "Settling a Sit-in." 600700-014. 12 pp.

> Fleischman, Harry. "Summary of CCD mass media committee meeting." 600323-007. 3 pp.

> "The Terrible Meek." 600406-015. 2 pp.

> Posey, Barbara Ann. "Why I Sit In." 600900-004. 4 pp.

> Jewish Labor Committee. "A Tribute to the Organized Labor Movement." 600326-003. 6 pp.

> King. Notes on sit-ins, the presidential election, and Harry S. Truman. 600400-017. 13 pp.

> Southern Regional Council. "The Student Protest Movement, Winter 1960." 600225-006. 20 pp.

> *The Progressive* 24. 600400-016. 50 pp.

> Lewis, Anthony. "Human Background of the Civil Rights Issue." 600214-004. 4 pp.

Folder 140: Integrated Bus Suggestions

> King and William J. Powell. "Integrated bus suggestions." 561219-001. 1 p.

Folder 141: "The Negro's Reevaluation of His Nature & Destiny & The Declaration of Independence and the Negro"

King. Draft, Our Struggle. 560400-022. 10 pp.

Folder 142: "Articles: The Negro's New Economic Life, Hughes The Negro Voter, White"

White, Theodore Harold. "The Negro Voter: Can He Elect a President?" 560817-001. 6 pp.

Folder 143: Untitled

Inter-Civic Council. "ICC diary, part V." 560822-007. 2 pp.

Koch, Melvin. Letter to Martin Luther King, Jr. 560820-005. 2 pp.

Nolde, O. Frederick. "That All May Be One, A message for Race Relations Sunday." 530208-000. 4 pp.

Helton, R. L. Letter to Martin Luther King, Jr. 560800-012. 4 pp.

Payne, Ethel L. "King Raps Jim Crow Dixie Rule." 560422-004. 1 p.

King. Draft, For All—A Non-Segregated Society. 560904-009. 7 pp.

Gallagher, Buell G. "For . . . Healing of the Nations, A message for Race Relations Sunday." 540214-001. 4 pp.

National Council of the Churches of Christ in the United States of America. "Brethren—Dwell Together In Unity, A message for Race Relations Sunday." 550213-000. 4 pp.

King. For All—A Non-Segregated Society, Sermon outline. 560904-010. 2 pp.

Folder 144: "Meaning of Civil Disobedience"

King. "It's Hard to Be a Christian." 560205-003. 6 pp.

Dunbar, Leslie W. "Civil Disobedience." 610207-004. 12 pp.

Dewees, Gisela H. Letter to Billy Graham. 601129-005. 1 p.

Herriford, John H. Letter to Martin Luther King, Jr. 601111-001. 2 pp.

[*King*]. Draft, Letter to Daisy Bates. 580900-010. 1 p.

Wofford, Harris. "The Law and Civil Disobedience." 591120-008. 4 pp.

King. Draft, Letter to Gordon M. Tiffany. 580900-009. 1 p.

SCLC. "Possible conference schedule." 581002-011. 1 p.

Folder 145: December 20, 1958

King. Draft, Address at the Religious Leaders Conference. 590511-012. 5 pp.

King. Letter to W. Averell Harriman. 581100-014. 1 p.

King. "An appeal to Negro and white men of goodwill." 580900-015. 2 pp.

Religious Leaders Workshop. "Workshop leader's guide." 590511-011. 3 pp.

King. Draft, Letter to twelve southern governors. 581200-009. 3 pp.

King. Letter to A. J. Muste, Norman Thomas, A. Philip Randolph, and James L. Hicks. 581200-008. 1 p.

Memo regarding Jimmy Wilson. 580904-019. 3 pp.

Killens, John Oliver. Letter to Martin Luther King, Jr. 580914-002. 1 p.

Folder 146: Dr. Martin Luther King—Columns

"Martin Luther King Column" I. 600217-014. 3 pp.

"Martin Luther King Column" II. 600217-015. 3 pp.

"Martin Luther King Column" III. 600217-016. 3 pp.

"Martin Luther King Column" IV. 600217-017. 3 pp.

Duckett, Alfred. Letter to Martin Luther King, Jr. 600218-013. 2 pp.

Folder 147: January 21, 1960

"Martin Luther King Column," I. 600217-014. 3 pp.

"Martin Luther King Column," IV. 600217-017. 3 pp.

"Martin Luther King Column," II. 600217-015. 3 pp.

Folder 148: "Speech on Voting"

[*King*]. Draft, "Introductory remarks to both parties." 600707-006. 2 pp.

[*King*]. Draft, "Proposals to both parties." 600707-005. 2 pp.

Wood, James R. Press release, "Dr. King addresses mass meeting." 600820-001. 1 p.

King. Outline, Address at Jefferson County Armory. 600823-006. 1 p.

Rustin, Bayard. Letter to Martin Luther King, Jr. 600707-009. 1 p.

Rustin, Bayard. Letter to Martin Luther King, Jr. 600707-010. 1 p.

[*SCLC*]. "Challenge to new age, importance of voting." 600700-006. 2 pp.

King. Address at NAACP Mass Rally for Civil Rights. 600710-001. 2 pp.

Folder 149: "Speeches"

Johnson, Charles S. "A Southern Negro's View of the South." 560923-001. 4 pp.

King. "The Peril of Superficial Optimism in the Area of Race Relations." 550619-002. 1 p.

Gelb, Phillip. "The Most Significant Story—Montgomery, Ala." 560227-016. 8 pp.

King. Statement on the end of the Montgomery Bus Boycott. 561220-000. 1 p.

Lautier, Louis. "Baptists." 570910-006. 2 pp.

Lindsay, James B. Letter to Martin Luther King, Jr. 561010-018. 1 p.

Fellowship of Reconciliation. *Fellowship* 22. 561100-009. 35 pp.

Huberman, Leo, and Paul M. Sweezy. "On Segregation: The Crisis in Race Relations, Two Nations—White and Black." 560600-022. 23 pp.

Southern Regional Council. "Next Steps in the South: Answers to Current Questions." 560000-192. 20 pp.

Fitz-Gibbon, Bernice. "Tips for Would-Be Women Bosses." 560923-002. 1 p. (fragment).

Fellowship of Reconciliation. "Freedom, the South, and Nonviolence." 560410-010. 6 pp.

Prattis, Percival Leroy. "Horizon: Family Income." 561013-000. 1 p.

Boddie, J. Timothy. "Cleric tells why disorder swept Baptist convention." 570910-007. 1 p.

Folder 150: "Speeches"

King. "The Negro Past and Its Challenges for the Future." 540000-092. 10 pp.

Negro ministers of Montgomery and their congregations. Letter to the Montgomery public. 551225-001. 4 pp.

Montgomery Improvement Association. "The Montgomery bus protest." 560000-103. 1 p.

Folder 151: How My Mind Has Changed

King. Draft, "How My Mind Has Changed in the Last Decade." 600413-024. 28 pp.

King. Notes, "How My Mind Has Changed" series. 600413-025. 8 pp.

King. Draft, "How My Mind Has Changed in the Last Decade." 600413-023. 18 pp.

King. "How My Theology Has Changed." 600413-021. 2 pp.

Folder 152: "Church Notes"

King. Annual report, Dexter Avenue Baptist Church. 551031-000. 28 pp.

Dexter Avenue Baptist Church. "Financial statement for October through
March." 550408-000. 11 pp.
Folder 153: Summaries of Speakers #4 #5 #6
Thomas, Norman. "Civil Liberty: A Look Back and Ahead." 541128-000. 3 pp.
Schuyler, George Samuel. "Views—Reviews." 540000-029. 1 p.
Folder 154: Untitled
Starr, Edward C. "The pastor and his reference library." 510415-000. 3 pp.
"Bibliography—Christian Theology." 540000-192. 52 pp.
Folder 155: "Bank Statements"
First National Bank of Montgomery. Statement of account for Martin Luther
King, Jr. 541213-000. 49 pp.
Folder 156: Untitled
King. Examination answers, Bible. 460326-000. 8 pp.
Folder 157: "Aesthetics"
King. Notes, "Problems of esthetics." 510203-005. 15 pp.
King. Notes, "The Relation between esthetics and science." 510203-006. 12 pp.
Folder 158: "Theological Integration"
King. Notes on ethics. 510504-038. 4 pp.
King. Notes, "Theological presuppositions of Christian social philosophy."
510504-039. 2 pp.
King. "Theological integration." 510504-040. 10 pp.
Folder 159: Speeches—Reprints in Various Magazines, M. L. King
King. Draft, Statement to the Democratic National Convention committee on
platform and resolutions. 560811-001. 2 pp.
Pond, Chomingwen. Letter to Martin Luther King, Jr. 590124-001. 5 pp.
King. "Out of the Night of Segregation." 580200-017. 4 pp.
King. "Out of the Long Night of Segregation." 580200-016. 2 pp.
King. "A View of the Dawn." 570500-002. 4 pp.
King. "Facing the Challenge of a New Age." 570200-009. 9 pp.
King. "Nonviolence and Racial Justice." 580726-001. 3 pp.
King. "The Montgomery Story." 561000-015. 4 pp.
King. The Power of Nonviolence. 580500-003. 2 pp.
Merriam, Eve. "An Evening to Remember." 571200-021. 1 p.
Simon, Paul. "Montgomery Looks Forward." 580122-014. 2 pp.
Program, "National conference on Christian education." 580822-010. 6 pp.
United Christian Movement, Inc. Program, "United Christian conference on
registration and voting." 580814-006. 18 pp.
King. "The Great Debate: Is Violence Necessary to Combat Injustice?"
600100-000. 1 p.
Fair Share Organization. Program, "Dr. Martin Luther King, Jr. in a bon voyage
to Europe." 590129-006. 26 pp.
King. The Birth of a New Age. 560000-136. 6 pp.
The National Eagle 9. 590200-017. 13 pp.
Morehouse College Bulletin 25. 571100-017. 16 pp.
Folder 160: MLK Proposed Article (Al Duckett)
King. "My Dream: Peace-God's Business and Man's." 651127-006. 4 pp.
King. "My Dream: The North: Myth of the Promised Land, Part Two, Phila-
delphia—Story of a Will and a Wall." 651127-005. 3 pp.

King. "My Dream: Great Expectations." 651127-003. 3 pp.

King. "My Dream: The North: Myth of the Promised Land." 651127-004. 4 pp.

Kittell, Donald. Letter to Martin Luther King, Jr. 651127-002. 4 pp.

Folder 161: Worship

King. Notes, "Worship." 491123-010. 11 pp.

Buffington, Willie L. "Worship: A selected bibliography." 410500-000. 15 pp.

World Council of Churches. "Proceedings, First assembly of the World Council of Churches." 480904-001. 58 pp.

"Marriage record." 540000-148. 1 p.

Folder 162: Minister's Use of Radio

[*Keighton, Robert E.*]. Examination, "Minister's Use of the Radio." 501120-000. 1 p.

Schmitz, Charles H. "Hints on Religious Music For Radio." 480000-023. 24 pp.

King. Class notes, "Minister's Use of the Radio." 501122-012. 4 pp.

Bloomquist, Earl W. "Religious broadcasts." 501122-013. 7 pp.

Folder 163: Untitled

[*King.*] "The Dialectical Character of Niebuhr's Thought and His Attitude Toward Current Social System." 540000-152. 2 pp.

King. "Jacques Maritain." 510504-028. 2 pp.

Leo XIII, Pope. *Immortale Dei: The Christian Constitution of States.* 410000-010. 33 pp.

King. Notes, Definitions of French terms. 470500-007. 1 p.

Religious Book Club. *Bulletin* 24. 510600-006. 9 pp.

The Billy Graham Evangelistic Team. "Revival in our time." 520113-000. 8 pp.

State Council for a Pennsylvania FEPC. "It's Your Law, too: Fair Employment Practices Commission." 480000-042. 6 pp.

Religious Book Club. *Bulletin* 23. 500500-003. 6 pp.

"Orders for Bently and Simon pulpit robes." 510500-078. 1 p.

Folder 164: Untitled

Kells, Robert H. Cross reference index for Sermon classification. 490000-017. 12 pp.

Folder 165: Untitled

Sheen, Fulton J. "The Theology of Conversion." 480321-002. 8 pp.

Sockman, Ralph W. "Hunger that Means Happiness, a radio address." 480307-001. 5 pp.

Bonnell, John Sutherland. "Palm Branches and a Cross, a radio address." 480321-000. 5 pp.

Sheen, Fulton J. "Repression and Self-Expression." 480229-000. 8 pp.

Sheen, Fulton J. "The Psychology of Conversion." 480307-003. 8 pp.

McCracken, Robert J. "Why Does God Hide Himself?" 470427-000. 10 pp.

McCracken, Robert J. "On Beginning from Within." 460113-000. 10 pp.

Muste, A. J. "What the Bible Teaches About Freedom: A message to the Negro Churches." 430000-017. 14 pp.

Cohn, David L. "Marrying Is Not Marriage." 471100-000. 3 pp.

Putnam, Nina Wilcox. "Divorce Is No Solution." 480800-001. 3 pp.

Morrison, A. Cressy. "Seven Reasons Why a Scientist Believes in God." 461200-000. 4 pp.

Whitman, Howard. "Let's Help Them Marry Young." 471000-001. 3 pp.

King. Letter to the editor. 561000-014. 1 p.
King. "Should F.E.P.C. become a federal law." 540000-185. 6 pp.
King. "The Weaknesses of Liberal Theology" II. 480000-032. 3 pp.
Sheen, Fulton J. "The Effects of Conversion." 480314-001. 8 pp.
Sockman, Ralph W. "The Lord of All Being, a radio address." 480321-001. 5 pp.
Heimsath. Examination questions, American Literature. 470500-005. 1 p.
Nix, William M. Form letter to Seniors. 480304-000. 4 pp.
King. "Nonviolence and Racial Justice." 580726-001. 3 pp.
Folder 166: "The Misuse of Prayer"
King. "The Misuse of Prayer." 540000-141. 4 pp.

The editors have selected those books relevant to the preparation of King's sermons and found in his home library at the time of the house's sale in the 1990s. Books published after King's death are omitted as are those books unrelated to homiletics such as school textbooks. Items containing inscriptions or King's handwritten comments are noted.

Abbey, Merrill R. *Preaching to the Contemporary Mind*. New York: Abingdon, 1963.

Abbott, Lyman. *What Christianity Means to Me: A Spiritual Autobiography*. New York: Macmillan, 1924.

Abdu'l-Baha. *Foundations of World Unity*. Wilmette, Ill.: Baha'i Publishing Trust, 1955. (Inscription by Ludmila Van Sombeck, 7/9/1962.)

Ahmad, Mirza Mubarak. *Islam in Africa*. Rabwah, Pakistan: Ahmadiyya Muslim Foreign Missions Office, 1962.

Ahmann, Mathew H., ed. *The New Negro*. Notre Dame, Ind.: Fides, 1961.

——. *Race: Challenge to Religion*. Chicago: Henry Regnery, 1963.

Albaugh, Ralph Mattern. *Thesis Writing: A Guide to Scholarly Style*. Ames, Iowa: Littlefield, Adams, 1951.

American Assembly. *The Congress and America's Future*. Englewood Cliffs, N.J.: Prentice-Hall, 1965.

The American Peoples Encyclopedia. Chicago: Spencer, 1960.

Anderson, B. M. *Social Value: A Study in Economic Theory Critical and Constructive*. New York: Houghton Mifflin, 1911.

——. *The Value of Money*. New York: Macmillan, 1917.

Anderson, Marian. *My Lord, What a Morning: An Autobiography*. New York: Viking, 1956.

Andrae, Tor. *Mohammed: The Man and His Faith*. Translated by Theophil Menzel. New York: Harper & Brothers, 1960.

Aptheker, Herbert. *And Why Not Every Man?* Berlin: Seven Seas Books, 1961.

Arbuthnot, May Hill. *Children and Books*. Chicago: Scott Foresman, 1947.

Aubrey, Edwin Ewart. *Living the Christian Faith*. New York: Macmillan, 1939. (Marginal comments by King.)

Azad, Abulkalam. *India Wins Freedom: An Autobiographical Narrative*. Bombay: Orient Longmans, 1959.

Badham, Leslie. *Love Speaks from the Cross: Thoughts on the Seven Words*. New York: Abingdon, 1955.

Bailey, Kenneth Kyle. *Southern White Protestantism in the Twentieth Century*. New York: Harper & Row, 1964.

Ballard, Austin. *Springs of the Waters: A Story of Love that Transcends All Human Barriers*. New York: Greenwich Book, 1958. (Inscription by Ballard, 1/1959.)

Balzac, Honoré de. *Old Goriot*. New York: Walter J. Black, 1945.

The Baptist Hymnal: For Use in the Church and the Home. Philadelphia: American Baptist Publication Society, 1883.

Barnette, Henlee H. *Introducing Christian Ethics*. Nashville: Broadman, 1961. (Inscription by Barnette.)

Barr, Stringfellow. *The Pilgrimage of Western Man*. New York: Harcourt, Brace, 1949. (Marginal comments by King.)

———. *The Will of Zeus: A History of Greece from the Origins of Hellenic Culture to the Death of Alexander*. Philadelphia: J. B. Lippincott, 1961. (Inscription by Harris Wofford, 10/16/1961.)

Bartlett, George Arthur. *Men, Women and Conflict: An Intimate Study of Love, Marriage, and Divorce*. New York: G. P. Putnam's Sons, 1931.

Bartlett, John. *Bartlett's Familiar Quotations*. Little, Brown, 1955. (Inscription.)

Bartlett, Robert Merrill. *They Stand Invincible: Men Who Are Reshaping Our World*. New York: Thomas Y. Crowell, 1959.

Baty, Eben Neal. *Citizen Abroad: An American Finds Out About His Country's Decade of Decline While Going Around the World by Freighter and Car*. New York: Viking, 1962. (Inscription by Baty, 7/14/1962.)

Bawany, Ebrahim Ahmed, ed. *Islam—Our Choice*. Karachi, Pakistan: Begum Aisha Bawany Wakf, 1961.

Bays, Alice Anderson. *Worship Services for Youth*. New York: Abingdon-Cokesbury, 1946.

Bell, William Kenan. *Fifteen Million Negroes and Fifteen Billion Dollars*. New York: William K. Bell, 1956. (Inscription by Bell.)

Bellamy, Edward. *Looking Backward 2000–1887*. New York: Modern Library, 1951. (Inscription by Coretta Scott, 4/7/1952; marginal comments by King.)

Benson, Mary. *South Africa: The Struggle for a Birthright*. Baltimore: Penguin Books, 1966.

Bergman, Lee. *None So Blind*. New York: Thomas Y. Crowell, 1957.

Berman, Mory. *Autumn Leaves: A Collection of Essays*. New York: Exposition, 1961. (Inscription by Berman, 6/1965.)

Berrigan, Philip. *No More Strangers*. New York: Macmillan, 1965.

Bertelsen, Aage. *October '43*. Translated by Milly Linholm and Willy Agtby. New York: G. P. Putnam's Sons, 1954. (Inscription by Bertelsen.)

Berton, Pierre. *The Comfortable Pew: A Critical Look at Christianity and the Religious Establishment in the New Age*. Toronto: McClelland & Steward, 1965.

Bhave, Vinoba A. *Talks on the Gita*. Kashi, India: Akhil Bharat Sarva Seva Sangh Prakashan, [1959].

Bibby, Cyril. *Race, Prejudice and Education*. London: William Heinemann, 1959.

Bittle, William E., and Gilbert Geiss. *The Longest Way Home: Chief Alfred C. Sam's Back-to-Africa Movement*. Detroit: Wayne State University Press, 1964.

Blackburn, Joyce. *Martha Berry: Little Woman with a Big Dream*. Philadelphia: J. B. Lippincott, 1968. (Inscription by Blackburn.)

Blaikie, W. Garden. *The Personal Life of David Livingstone*. New York: Fleming H. Revell, 1880.

Blake, William. *Songs of Innocence and Experience*. Mount Vernon, N.Y.: Peter Pauper, 1945.

Blaustien, Albert P., and Clarence Clyde Ferguson. *Desegregation and the Law: The Meaning and Effect of the School Segregation Cases*. New Brunswick, N.J.: Rutgers University Press, 1957. (Inscription by Ferguson.)

Blossom, Virgil T. *It Has Happened Here*. New York: Harper & Brothers, 1959.

Boak, A. E. R., Albert Hyma, and Preston Slosson. *The Growth of Western Civilization.*
New York: Appleton-Century-Crofts, 1951. (Marginal comments by King.)

Bocaccio, Giovanni. *Tales from The Decameron.* Translated by Richard Addington. New York: Garden City, 1930.

Bonhoeffer, Dietrich. *Letters and Papers from Prison.* Edited by Eberhard Bethge, translated by Reginald H. Fuller. New York: Macmillan, 1962.

Bontemps, Arna. *Black Thunder.* Berlin: Seven Seas, 1964.

The Book of Mormon. Translated by Joseph Smith. Monogahela, Pa.: Church of Jesus Christ of Latter-Day Saints, 1954. (Inscription by Timothy Dom Bucci, 11/8/1965.)

———. Translated by Joseph Smith. Salt Lake City, Utah: Church of Jesus Christ of Latter-Day Saints, 1950.

Booth, Charles Octavius. *Plain Theology for Plain People.* Philadelphia: American Baptist Publication Society, 1890.

Booth, L. Venchael, ed. *Who's Who in Baptist America: In the National Sunday School and Baptist Training Union Congress.* Cincinnati: Western, 1960. (Inscription by Booth, 6/21/1960.)

Bose, Nirmal Kumar. *Studies in Gandhism.* Calcutta: Indian Associated Publishers, 1947. (Inscription, 2/17/1959.)

Bosley, Harold Augustus. *He Spoke to Them in Parables.* New York: Harper & Row, 1963. (Marginal comments by King.)

The Boston University Philosophical Club. *Philosophical Forum: An Annual.* Vol. 1. Edited by Sheldon C. Ackley. Boston: The Boston University Philosophical Club, 1943.

Bowen, Catherine Drinker. *John Adams and the American Revolution.* Boston: Little, Brown, 1950.

Boyle, Sarah Patton. *The Desegregated Heart: A Virginian's Stand in Time of Transition.* New York: William Morrow, 1962.

———. *For Human Beings Only: A Primer of Human Understanding.* New York: Seabury, 1964.

Braden, Anne. *The Wall Between.* New York: Monthly Review, 1958. (Inscription to Coretta Scott King by Braden, 4/1960.)

Bradford, Roark. *Ol' Man Adam an His Chillun; Being the Tales They Tell about the Time When the Lord Walked the Earth Like a Natural Man.* New York: Grosset & Dunlap, 1928.

Branscomb, B. Harvie. *The Gospel of Mark.* New York: Harper & Brothers, 1937.

Brightman, Edgar Sheffield. *An Introduction to Philosophy.* Rev. ed. New York: Henry Holt, 1925. (Marginal comments by King.)

Brooke, Edward William. *The Challenge of Change: Crisis in Our Two-Party System.* New York: Little, Brown, 1966. (Inscription by Brooke.)

Brooks, Phillips. *New Starts in Life, and Other Sermons.* New York: E. P. Dutton, 1896. (Marginal comments by King.)

———. *Sermons Preached in English Churches.* New York: E. P. Dutton, 1893. (Marginal comments by King.)

Brown, Jacob Tileston. *Theological Kernels: A Question-Book of Bible Doctrines and Baptist Church Polity with Scripture Reference.* Nashville: National Baptist Publishing Board, 1903. (Inscription by J. H. Lowe.)

Brown, Roscoe C. *Little Charlie Browne: The Genesis, Arts, and Revelations of Charles*

F. M. Browne. Washington, D.C.: Roscoe C. Brown, 1957. (Inscription by Brown, 11/6/1957.)

Bryant, Alice Franklin. *Religion for the Hardheaded*. New York: Dodd, Mead, 1953. (Inscription by Bryant, 11/10/1957.)

Bucci, Timothy Dom. *Apostasy and Restoration*. Monongahela, Pa.: The Church of Jesus Christ of Latter-Day Saints, 1962. (Inscription by Bucci.)

Buchman, Frank Nathan Daniel. *Remaking the World: The Speeches of Frank N. D. Buchman*. London: Blandford, 1953.

Buckingham, Walter S. *Automation: Its Impact on Business and People*. New York: Harper & Brothers, 1961. (Inscription by Buckingham, 5/2/1961.)

Buckmaster, Henrietta. *Freedom Bound*. New York: Macmillan, 1965.

Buddhadatta, A. P., ed. *Dhammapadam: An Anthology of Sayings of the Buddha*. Colombo, Ceylon: Colombo Apothecaries, [1950]. (Inscription, 12/23/1964.)

Bunche, Ralph J. *The World Significance of the Carver Story*. Indianola, Iowa: Simpson College, 1956.

Bunker, R. F. *Seven Canvases*. New York: Vantage, 1963. (Inscription by Bunker, 12/1964.)

Bunzel, John H., ed. *Issues of American Public Policy*. Englewood Cliffs, N.J.: Prentice Hall, 1964.

Burns, W. Haywood. *The Voices of Negro Protest in America*. New York: Oxford University Press, 1963. (Inscription by Alfred Duckett, 9/1963.)

Bury, J. B. *A History of Greece to the Death of Alexander the Great*. New York: Modern Library, 1961.

Buskes, Johannes Jacobus. *Martin Luther King*. Den Haag, Netherlands: Bruseman, 1965.

Buttrick, George Arthur. *Sermons Preached in a University Church*. New York: Abingdon, 1959. (Marginal comments by King.)

Buttrick, George Arthur, ed. *The Interpreter's Bible*. Vols. 1–4, 6, 10. New York: Abingdon, 1952–56.

———. *The Interpreter's Dictionary of the Bible*. New York: Abingdon, 1962.

Bynner, Witter. *The Way of Life According to Laotzu: An American Version*. New York: John Day, 1944.

Cabot, Richard C., and Russell L. Dicks. *The Art of Ministering to the Sick*. New York: Macmillan, 1950.

Cahn, Edmond Nathaniel. *The Predicament of Democratic Man*. New York: Macmillan, 1961.

Cain, Alfred E., ed. *Negro Heritage Reader for Young People*. New York: Educational Heritage, 1964.

———. *The Winding Road to Freedom: A Documentary Survey of Negro Experiences in America*. New York: Educational Heritage, 1964.

Calverton, V. F., ed. *The Making of Society: An Outline of Sociology*. New York: Modern Library, 1937.

Campbell, Marie Sears. *Inspirational Guidance*. N.p.: Published by author, 1964. (Inscription by Campbell, 1/25/1965.)

Canzoneri, Robert. *"I Do So Politely": A Voice from the South*. Boston: Houghton Mifflin, 1965.

Carnegie, Amos Hubert. *Faith Moves Mountains: An Autobiography*. Washington, D.C.: Published by author, 1950.

Carr, Robert K. *Federal Protection of Civil Rights: Quest for a Sword*. Ithaca, N.Y.: Cornell University Press, 1947. (Inscription by Carr.)

Carter, Charlotte, and Herbert Dyson Carter. *Future of Freedom*. Gravenhurst, Ontario: Northern Book House, 1963.

Carter, Mark. *"Okay America."* Los Angeles: Delmar, 1963. (Inscription, 1964.)

Case, Shirley Jackson. *The Evolution of Early Christianity: A Genetic Study of First-Century Christianity in Relation to Its Religious Environment*. Chicago: University of Chicago Press, 1927.

Cattermole, R., and H. Stebbing, eds. *The Sacred Classics*. Vol. 19. Piccadilly, England: John Hatchard & Son, 1835.

Christian Science Hymnal with Seven Hymns Written by the Reverend Mary Baker Eddy. Boston: Christian Science Publishing Society, 1932. (Inscription by Hillabee Hardin.)

Christly Mental Doctrine. *The Truth in a Book*. Mexico City: Christly Mental Doctrine, 1961.

Christmas, Walter, ed. *Negroes in Public Affairs and Government*. New York: Educational Heritage, 1965.

Clark, Kenneth B. *Prejudice and Your Child*. Boston: Beacon, 1963.

Clark, Thomas Curtis, ed. *Today Is Mine: A Manual of Devotion*. New York: Harper & Brothers, 1950. (Inscription to Mr. & Mrs. Martin Luther King, Sr. by Nannie H. Burroughs, 11/22/1951.)

Clark, Thomas D., and Albert D. Kirwan. *The South Since Appomattox: A Century of Regional Change*. New York: Oxford University Press, 1967.

Clarke, Arthur C. *Childhood's End*. New York: Ballantine Books, 1953.

Clayton, Edward T. *The Negro Politician: His Success and Failure*. Chicago: Johnson, 1964. (Inscription by Clayton.)

Cleaver, Eldridge. *Soul On Ice*. New York: Dell, 1968.

Cleland, James T. *Wherefore Art Thou Come? Meditations on the Lord's Supper*. New York: Abingdon, 1961.

Close, Upton. *Behind the Face of Japan*. New York: D. Appleton-Century, 1942.

Cokes, George Louis. *The Eagle and the Cross: The Racial Problem in Perspective*. New York: Exposition, 1965. (Inscription by Cokes, 2/9/1966.)

Collins, LeRoy. *The South and the Nation*. Atlanta: Southern Regional Council, 1960.

Committee of First Amendment Defendants. *Behind the Bars for the First Amendment*. New York: Committee of First Amendment Defendants, 1960.

The Constitution of the United States, with the Amendments; also, The Declaration of Independence. New York: International, 1942.

Conwell, Russell H. *Acres of Diamonds*. Philadelphia: Temple University Press, 1959. (Inscription by Millard E. Gladfelter.)

Coon, Carleton Stevens, and Edward E. Hunt. *The Living Races of Man*. New York: Alfred A. Knopf, 1965.

Copeland, Lewis. *Everyday Reference Library: An Encyclopedia of Useful Information*. Chicago: J. G. Ferguson, [1957].

Cousins, Norman, Robert McAfee Brown, Hermann J. Muller, Everett E. Gendler, and Thomas Merton. . . . *Therefore Choose Life*. Santa Barbara, Calif.: Center for the Study of Democratic Institutions, 1965. (Inscription by Gendler.)

Cowles, Gardner. *The Crucial Problem of Communications.* Indianola, Iowa: Simpson College, 1955.

Craig, Clarence Tucker. *The Beginning of Christianity.* New York: Abingdon-Cokesbury, 1943.

Craig, Robert Morris. *The Natural Order for Human Existence.* Kansas City, Mo.: Brown-White-Lowell, 1956. (Inscription by Craig, 2/21/1957.)

Craven, Thomas. *Famous Artists and Their Models.* New York: Pocket Books, 1949.

Cuban, Larry. *The Negro in America.* Chicago: Scott, Foresman, 1964.

Cudjoe, S. D. *Aids to African Autonomy: A Review of Education and Politics in the Gold Coast.* London: College Press, 1950. (Inscription.)

Cunliffe, John W., James Francis Pyre, and Karl Young, eds. *Century Readings in English Literature.* New York: Century, 1929.

Cunningham, Eugenia Isabella. *Make Bright the Memories.* As Told to Sara Sprott Morrow. Nashville: Southern Publishing Association, 1954.

Dabbs, James McBride. *The Southern Heritage.* New York: Alfred A. Knopf, 1958. (Marginal comments by King.)

————. *Who Speaks For The South?* New York: Funk & Wagnalls, 1964.

Dannett, Sylvia G. L. *Profiles of Negro Womanhood.* Vol. 1, *1619–1900.* New York: American Book–Stratford, 1964.

Davies, Alfred T., ed. *The Pulpit Speaks on Race.* New York: Abingdon, 1965. (Inscription by Davies, 5/26/1965.)

Davies, A. Powell. *The Meaning of the Dead Sea Scrolls.* New York: New American Library, 1956.

Davis, George W. *Existentialism and Theology: An Investigation of the Contribution of Rudolf Bultmann to Theological Thought.* New York: Philosophical Library, 1957. (Inscription by Davis, 12/22/1958; marginal comments by King.)

Davis, Jerome. *Religion in Action.* New York: Philosophical Library, 1956. (Inscription by Davis.)

Davis, Jerome, ed. *Peace or World War III.* New York: Greenwich Book, 1968. (Inscription by Davis.)

Davis, John P., ed. *The American Negro Reference Book.* 2 vols. New York: Educational Heritage, 1966.

Dawn Bible Students Association. *Behold Your King: A Herald of Christ's Presence.* East Rutherford, N.J.: Dawn Bible Students Association Press, 1948.

————. *Studies in the Scriptures.* Series 1, *The Plan of the Ages.* East Rutherford, N.J.: Dawn Bible Students Association Press, 1955.

————. *Why God Permits Evil.* East Rutherford, N.J.: Dawn Bible Students Association Press, n.d.

Day, Albert Edward. *An Autobiography of Prayer.* New York: Harper & Brothers, 1952.

de Hartog, Jan. *The Hospital.* New York: Atheneum, 1964.

Dei-Anang, Michael. *Africa Speaks: A Collection of Original Verse with an Introduction on Poetry in Africa.* Accra: Guinea, 1959.

Deissmann, D. Adolf. *Paulus: Eine Kultur- und religionsgeschichtliche Skizze.* Tübingen, Germany: J. C. B. Mohr, 1925. (Marginal comments by King.)

Deming, Barbara. *Prison Notes.* New York: Grossman, 1966.

Desai, Neera. *Women in Modern India.* Bombay: Vora, 1957.

Desai, Ram, ed. *Christianity in Africa as Seen by Africans.* Denver: Alan Swallow, 1962.

Desmond, James. *Nelson Rockefeller: A Political Biography.* New York: Macmillan, 1964.
(Inscription by Nelson Rockefeller.)

DeWaters, Lilian. *The Atomic Age.* Stamford, Conn.: Published by author, 1945.

———. *Gems.* Stamford, Conn.: Hycliff, 1937. (Inscription by DeWaters, 1963.)

———. *Light: Companion Volume to "God is All."* Stamford, Conn.: Published by author, 1950.

———. *The Narrow Way.* Stamford, Conn.: Published by author, 1945.

———. *Our Sufficient Guide: A Study of the Bible.* Stamford, Conn.: Published by author, 1924.

DeWolf, L. Harold. *The Enduring Message of the Bible.* New York: Harper & Brothers, 1960. (Inscription by DeWolf, 4/13/1960.)

———. *Trends and Frontiers of Religious Thought.* Nashville: National Methodist Student Movement, 1955. (Inscription by DeWolf, 5/3/1957; marginal comments by King.)

Dexter, Harriet Harmon. *What's Right with Race Relations.* New York: Harper & Brothers, 1958.

Dhawan, Gopinath. *The Political Philosophy of Mahatma Gandhi.* Ahmedabad, India: Navajivan, 1951. (Marginal comments by King.)

Dickens, Charles. *Christmas Stories.* Cleveland: World Syndicate, [1939]. (Inscription to Christine King from Alberta Williams King.)

Diwakar, Ranganath Ramachandra. *Satyagraha: Its Technique and History.* Bombay: Hind Kitabs, 1946. (Inscription by Ralph O. Blackwood.)

Dodge, Ralph E. *The Unpopular Missionary.* Westwood, N.J.: Fleming H. Revell, 1960.

Dostoyevsky, Fyodor. *The Brothers Karamazov.* Translated by Constance Garnett. New York: Modern Library, [1929].

———. *Crime and Punishment.* New York: Signet Books, 1949.

Douglas, William O. *America Challenged.* New York: Avon, 1960. (Inscription by Ingeborg Teek-Frank, 4/12/1964.)

Douglass, Frederick. *My Bondage and My Freedom.* New York: Miller, Orton & Mulligan, 1855.

Dumond, Dwight Lowell. *A Bibliography of Antislavery in America.* Ann Arbor, Mich.: University of Michigan Press, [1961].

Dunbar, Paul Laurence. *The Complete Poems of Paul Laurence Dunbar.* New York: Dodd, Mead, 1934.

Duncan, Patrick. *South Africa's Rule of Violence.* London: Methuen, 1964. (Inscription by Duncan.)

Durant, Will. *The Story of Philosophy: The Lives and Opinions of the Greater Philosophers.* New York: Simon & Schuster, 1933. (Marginal comments by King.)

Dushaw, Amos I. *When Mr. Thompson Got to Heaven.* Brooklyn, N.Y.: Tolerance, 1954. (Inscription by Dushaw, 12/17/1956.)

Eaton, Allen Hendershott. *Immigrant Gifts to American Life: Some Experiments in Appreciation of the Contributions of Our Foreign-Born Citizens to American Culture.* New York: Russell Sage Foundation, 1932.

Eaton, Ralph M., ed. *Descartes Selections.* New York: Charles Scribner's Sons, 1955. (Marginal comments by King.)

Eckenrode, H. J., and Bryan Conrad. *James Longstreet: Lee's War Horse.* Chapel Hill, N.C.: University of North Carolina Press, 1936.

Edel, Abraham. *The Theory and Practice of Philosophy*. New York: Harcourt, Brace, 1946. (Marginal comments by King.)

Ehle, John. *The Free Men*. New York: Harper & Row, 1965.

Eisenman, Abram. *Why I Should Be President*. Savannah, Ga.: Savannah Sun, 1963. (Inscription by Eisenman, 12/16/1963.)

El Sermón del Cristo. N.p., n.d. (Inscription by Maria A. de Fajardo.)

Elder, John. *Prophets, Idols and Diggers: Scientific Proof of Bible History*. Indianapolis, Ind.: Bobbs-Merrill, 1960.

Ellison, Ralph. *Invisible Man*. New York: New American Library, 1964.

Embree, Edwin R. *American Negroes: A Handbook*. New York: John Day, 1942.

Emerson, Ralph Waldo. *A Modern Anthology*. Edited by Alfred Kazin and Daniel Aaron. New York: Dell, 1958.

————. *Essays and Addresses*. Edited by Benjamin A. Heydrick. Chicago: Scott, Foresman, 1919. (Marginal comments by King.)

Enslin, Morton Scott. *Christian Beginnings*. New York: Harper & Brothers, 1938.

Essien-Udom, Essien Udosen. *Black Nationalism: A Search for an American Identity*. Chicago: University of Chicago Press, 1962.

Evans, Lancelot, ed. *Emerging African Nations and Their Leaders*. Vol. 1, *Burundi to Liberia*. New York: Educational Heritage, 1964.

Exman, Eugene. *The Brothers Harper: A Unique Publishing Partnership and Its Impact upon the Cultural Life of America from 1817 to 1853*. New York: Harper & Row, 1965. (Inscription by Exman, 5/6/1965.)

Fair, Ronald L. *Many Thousand Gone: An American Fable*. New York: Harcourt, Brace & World, 1965.

Fairchild, Fred Rogers, Norman Sydney Buck, and Edgar Stevenson Furniss. *Elementary Economics*. Vol. 1. New York: Macmillan, 1937.

Farmer, James. *Freedom—When?* New York: Random House, 1965. (Inscription by Farmer, 1/27/1966.)

Faulkner, William. *The Sound and the Fury*. New York: New American Library, 1959.

Faulkner, William, Benjamin Elijah Mays, and Cecil Sims. *Three Views of the Segregation Decisions*. Atlanta: Southern Regional Council, 1956. (Marginal comments by King.)

Fayette County Project Volunteers. *Step By Step: Evolution and Operation of the Cornell Students' Civil-Rights Project in Tennessee, Summer, 1964*. New York: W. W. Norton, 1965.

Ferm, Vergilius, ed. *An Encyclopedia of Religion*. New York: Philosophical Library, 1945.

Ferraby, John. *All Things Made New: A Comprehensive Outline of the Baha'i Faith*. Wilmette, Ill.: Baha'i Publishing Trust, 1960.

Fosdick, Harry Emerson. *A Great Time to Be Alive: Sermons on Christianity in Wartime*. New York: Harper & Brothers, 1944. (Marginal comments by King.)

————. *The Hope of the World: Sermons on Christianity Today*. New York: Harper, 1933. (Marginal comments by King.)

————. *On Being A Real Person*. New York: Harper & Brothers, 1943. (Marginal comments by King.)

————. *On Being Fit to Live With: Sermons on Post-War Christianity*. New York: Harper & Brothers, 1946. (Marginal comments by King.)

————. *Riverside Sermons*. New York: Harper & Brothers, 1958. (Marginal comments by King.)

———. *Successful Christian Living.* New York: Harper & Brothers, 1937. (Marginal comments by King.)

Frank, Waldo. *The Rediscovery of Man: A Memoir and a Methodology of Modern Life.* New York: George Braziller, 1958.

Franklin, James Henry. *The Never Failing Light.* New York: Missionary Education Movement of the United States & Canada, 1933.

Fredericksen, Dick. *Democracy, Revolution and Civil Disobedience,* 1955.

Freedman, David Noel, and G. Ernest Wright, eds. *The Biblical Archaeologist Reader.* Garden City, N.Y.: Doubleday, 1961.

Freedom House Public Affairs Committee. *A Survey of the Progress of Freedom in 1967.* New York: Freedom House, 1967.

Friedenberg, Edgar Z. *Coming of Age in America: Growth and Acquiescence.* New York: Random House, 1965.

Friedlander, M., ed. *The Illustrated Jerusalem Bible.* Jerusalem: Jerusalem Bible, 1958. (Inscription by Edward Bassings, 7/20/1966.)

Friedrich, Walter. *Leben und Wirken.* Berlin: Friedensrat der Deutschen Demokratischen Republik, 1963.

Fuller, Carlos Greenleaf. *Be Not Afraid.* Central Square, N.Y.: Published by author, 1958.

Fuller, David Otis. *Spurgeon's Illustrative Anecdotes.* Grand Rapids, Mich.: Zondervan, 1945.

Fund for Adult Education. *Education for Public Responsibility.* White Plains, N.Y.: Fund for Adult Education, [1959].

Gaines, Gartrell J. *Where Do We Stand?: The Negro in the South Today.* New York: Vantage, 1957. (Inscription by Gaines.)

Galbraith, John Kenneth. *The New Industrial State.* Boston: Houghton Mifflin, 1967.

Gandhi, Mahatma. *The Collected Works of Mahatma Gandhi.* Edited by Jairamdas Doulatram. 2 vols. New Delhi: Ministry of Information and Broadcasting, 1958. (Inscription by Doulatram, Vol. 1, 2/11/1959.)

———. *The Collected Works of Mahatma Gandhi.* Vol. 2. New Delhi: Ministry of Information and Broadcasting,1959.

———. *Conquest of Self.* Bombay: Thacker, 1946. (Inscription by Kaka Kalelkar, 2/12/1959.)

———. *The Mind of Mahatma Gandhi.* Compiled by R. K. Prabhu and U. R. Rao. London: Oxford University Press, [1946]. (Inscription, 2/10/1959.)

———. *Non-Violence in Peace and War.* Vol. 1. Ahmedabad, India: Navajivan, [1948].

———. *Satyagraha in South Africa.* Ahmedabad, India: Navajivan, 1950. (Inscription by Lawrence Dunbar Reddick.)

———. *Selected Letters.* Translated by Valji Govindji Desai. Ahmedabad, India: Navajivan, 1949. (Inscription by Ingeborg Teek- Frank, 11/2/1960.)

Gandhi, Mahatmaand Pyarelal. *The Epic Fast.* Ahmedabad, India: Mohanlal Maganlal Bhatt, 1932. (Inscription by Pyarelal, 3/6/1959.)

Gandhi Smarak Nidhi. *Gandhi Smarak Nidhi: Its Work and Plans.* New Delhi, July 1960.

Gandhiji and Mani Bhavan, 1917–1934. Bombay: Mani Bhavan Gandhi Sangrahalaya, 1960.

Gardner, John William. *Self-Renewal: The Individual and the Innovative Society*. New York: Harper & Row, 1963.

Garrett, Constance. *Growth in Prayer*. New York: Macmillan, 1950.

Garrison, Winfred Ernest. *A Protestant Manifesto*. New York: Abingdon-Cokesbury, 1952.

Garry, Ralph, F. B. Rainsberry, and Charles Winick, eds. *For The Young Viewer: Television Programming for Children . . . At the Local Level*. New York: McGraw-Hill, 1962.

George, Henry. *Progress and Poverty*. New York: Robert Schalkenbach Foundation, 1962.

Georgia Conference on Educational Opportunities. *Georgia's Divided Education*. Atlanta: Georgia Conference on Educational Opportunities, 1960.

Gibran, Kahlil. *Tears and Laughter*. Edited by Martin L. Wolf. Translated by Anthony Rizcallah Ferris. New York: Philosophical Library, 1949.

Gift, Maye Harvey, and Alice Simmons Cox, eds. *Race and Man: A Compilation*. Wilmette, Ill.: Baha'i Publishing Committee, 1943.

Gih, Andrew. *Twice Born—and Then?: The Autobiography and Messages of Rev. Andrew Gih*. Edited by Ruth J. Corbin. London: Marshall, Morgan & Scott, 1954.

Gillispie, Charles Coulston. *Genesis and Geology: A Study in the Relations of Scientific Thought, Natural Theology, and Social Opinion in Great Britain, 1790–1850*. New York: Harper & Brothers, 1959.

Ginzberg, Eli, ed. *The Nation's Children 3: Problems and Prospects*. New York: Columbia University Press, 1960.

Gist, Noel Pitts, and L. A. Halbert. *Urban Society*. New York: Thomas Y. Crowell, 1946. (Marginal comments by King.)

Gittelsohn, Roland Bertram. *Consecrated Unto Me: A Jewish View of Love and Marriage*. New York: Union of American Hebrew Congregations, 1965. (Inscription by Gittelsohn and Emily and Kivie Kaplan, 12/5/1965.)

———. *A Jewish View of God*. Washington, D.C.: B'nai B'rith Youth Organization, 1965.

Goguel, Maurice. *Jesus and the Origins of Christianity*. Vol. 1, *Prolegomena to the Life of Jesus*. Translated by Olive Wyon. New York: Harper & Brothers, 1960.

Golden, Harry. *You're Entitle'*. New York: World, 1962. (Inscription by Golden, 7/16/1962.)

Goldfarb, Samuel J. *How From a Monkey I Became a Man*. Sarasota, Fla.: Good Neighbor, 1964. (Inscription by Goldfarb, 8/15/1964.)

Goodspeed, Edgar J. *The Apocrypha: An American Translation*. Chicago: University of Chicago Press, 1938.

Goold, F. E. *You Will Come Back: A Conversation about Reincarnation and Karma*. Ontario, Canada: F. E. Goold, 1958.

Gopani, Amritlal Savchand, trans. *Ujjwala-Wani: Religious Sermons Delivered by Bala Brahmacharini Pravarttini Mahasatiji Ujjvalakumvarji at Seth Meghji Thobhan Jain Dharmasthanak, Kandavadi, Bombay in 1948 AD During Her Four Months' Stay in the Monsoon*. Bombay: Girdharlal Damodar Daftary Ravichand Sukhlal Shah Ramaniklal Kasturchand Kothari, n.d.

Gordon, Ernest. *Through the Valley of the Kwai*. New York: Harper & Brothers, 1962. (Inscription by Gordon.)

Goudge, Elizabeth, ed. *A Book of Comfort: An Anthology*. New York: Coward-McCann, 1964.

Gould, Samuel B. *Knowledge Is Not Enough*. Yellow Springs, Ohio: Antioch Press,
1959. (Inscription.)

Graham, Billy. *The Seven Deadly Sins*. Grand Rapids, Mich.: Zondervan, 1955.

Greenough, Ruth Hornblower. *The Bible for My Grandchildren*. Vol. 2. N.p.: privately printed, 1955. (Inscription by National Bible Guild, Inc., 3/1956.)

Gregg, Richard Bartlett. *A Discipline for Nonviolence*. Ahmedabad, India: Navajivan, 1954.

———. *A Philosophy of Indian Economic Development*. Ahmedabad, India: Navajivan, 1958.

———. *The Power of Non-violence*. Ahmedabad, India: Navajivan, 1949.

———. *The Self Beyond Yourself*. New York: J. B. Lippincott, 1956.

———. *Which Way Lies Hope?: An Examination of Capitalism, Communism, Socialism and Gandhiji's Programme*. Ahmedabad, India: Navajivan, [1957].

Griffith, Helen. *Dauntless in Mississippi: The Life of Sarah A. Dickey*. North Hampton, Mass.: Metcalf, 1966.

Griffith, Leonard. *The Eternal Legacy: From An Upper Room*. New York: Harper & Row, 1963.

Group for the Advancement of Psychiatry. *Psychiatric Aspects of School Desegregation*. New York: Group for the Advancement of Psychiatry, May 1957. (Inscription.)

Grund, Francis J. *Aristocracy in America: From the Sketch-book of a German Nobleman*. New York: Harper Torchbooks, 1959.

Gunther, John. *Inside Europe Today*. New York: Harper & Brothers, 1961.

———. *Inside Russia Today*. New York: Harper & Brothers, 1958.

———. *Inside U.S.A*. New York: Harper & Brothers, 1947.

Haile, Pennington. *The Eagle and the Bear: The Philosophic Roots of Democracy and Communism*. New York: David McKay, 1965. (Inscription by Haile, 1/1965.)

Hall, Fred S., ed. *Social Work Year Book 1935*. New York: Russell Sage Foundation, 1935.

Hall, Fred S., and Mabel B. Ellis, eds. *Social Work Year Book 1929*. New York: Russell Sage Foundation, 1930.

Hallowell, John H. *Main Currents in Modern Political Thought*. New York: Henry Holt, [1950].

Hamilton, Edith. *Witness to the Truth: Christ and His Interpreters*. New York: W. W. Norton, 1957.

Hamilton, James Wallace. *Horns and Halos in Human Nature*. Westwood, N.J.: Fleming H. Revell, 1954. (Inscription by Hamilton; marginal comments by King.)

Hanna, Hilton E., and Joseph Belsky. *The 'Pat' Gorman Story . . . Picket and the Pen*. New York: American Institute of Social Science, 1960. (Inscription by Hanna, 2/26/1961.)

Hannau, Hans W. *Jamaica*. Munich: Wilhelm Andermann Verlag, 1962.

Hansberry, Lorraine. *The Sign in Sidney Brustein's Window*. New York: Random House, [1965]. (Inscription by Robert Nemiroff, 6/2/1965.)

Hansen, Harry, ed. *The World Almanac and Book of Facts*. New York: New York World-Telegram, 1959.

Hapgood, Hutchins. *The Spirit of the Ghetto: Studies of the Jewish Quarter of New York*. New York: Funk & Wagnalls, 1965.

Hargis, Billy James. *Communist America: Must It Be?* Tulsa, Okla.: Christian Crusade, 1960.

Harris, Mark. *Trumpet To The World.* New York: Reynal & Hitchcock, 1946.

Harris, Marvin. *Portugal's African "Wards": A First-hand Report on Labor and Education in Mozambique.* New York: American Committee on Africa, 1960.

Harvard University Graduate School of Education, Center for Field Studies. *Schools for Hartford.* Cambridge, Mass.: Harvard University Press, [1965].

Hastings, James, and John A. Selbie, eds. *A Dictionary of the Bible: Dealing with its Language, Literature and Contents, Including the Biblical Theology.* Vol. 4. New York: Charles Scribner's Sons, 1903.

Hausmann, Marzelius. *Under the Red Star.* Berne, Ind.: Published by author, 1958. (Inscription by Isobel Houseman, 1966.)

Hazelton, Roger. *New Accents in Contemporary Theology.* New York: Harper & Brothers, 1960.

Heick, O. W., and J. L. Neve. *History of Protestant Theology.* Vol. 2 of *A History of Christian Thought,* edited by J. L. Neve. Philadelphia: Muhlenberg, 1946.

Henderson, Algo D., and Dorothy Hall. *Antioch College: Its Design for Liberal Education.* New York: Harper & Brothers, 1946.

Hendrick, George. "Dr. King's Pilgrimage to Nonviolence." *Gandhi Marg* 3 (January 1959): 63–65.

Here's How by Who's Who. Cleveland: Bonne Bell, 1965.

Hersey, John. *Here to Stay.* New York: Bantam Books, 1964.

Heussenstamm, Karl. *Creative Spirit.* New York: Philosophical Library, 1961. (Inscription by Heussenstamm, 6/14/1962.)

Higginson, Thomas Wentworth. *Army Life in a Black Regiment.* With a new introduction by Howard N. Meyer. New York: Collier, 1962. (Inscription by Meyer.)

Hirsch, Richard G. *There Shall Be No Poor. . . .* New York: Commission on Social Action of Reform Judaism, 1965.

Hobbes, Thomas. *The Metaphysical System of Hobbes in Twelve Chapters from "Elements of Philosophy Concerning Body" Together with Briefer Extracts from "Human Nature" and "Leviathan."* Edited by Mary Whiton Calkins. Chicago: Open Court, 1910.

Hochhuth, Rolf. *The Deputy.* Translated by Richard and Clara Winston. New York: Grove, 1964.

Hodges, David Julian. *The P Formation.* N.p.: Published by author, 1956. (Inscription by Hodges, 9/1961.)

Hoffer, Eric. *The True Believer: Thoughts on the Nature of Mass Movements.* New York: Harper & Brothers, 1951.

Holdridge, Herbert C. *How to Gain Freedom From Economic Slavery.* Sherman Oaks, Calif.: Holdridge Foundation, 1961.

The Holy Bible, Authorized King James Version. Philadelphia: National Bible, 1945. (Inscription by Katherine King, 6/10/1947; marginal comments by King.)

Hooper, Van B., ed. *Words Eternal.* Milwaukee, Wis.: Ideals, 1962.

Hopkins, Charles Howard. *The Rise of the Social Gospel in American Protestantism, 1865–1915.* New Haven, Conn.: Yale University Press, 1940.

Horace, Lillian B. *Sun-Crowned: A Biography of Doctor Lacey Kirk Williams.* N.p.: L. Venchael Booth, 1964. (Inscription by L. Venchael Booth.)

Horsch, John, ed. *Symposium on War.* Scottdale, Pa.: Mennonite Publishing House, 1927.

Horton, Walter Marshall. *Christian Theology: An Ecumenical Approach.* New York:
Harper & Brothers, [1955]. (Marginal comments by King.)

Howard, Peter. *Frank Buchman's Secret.* Garden City, N. Y.: Doubleday, 1961.

Hoyle, Fred. *The Nature of the Universe.* New York: New American Library, 1963.

Huddleston, Trevor. *Naught for Your Comfort.* New York: Macmillan, 1963.

Huie, William Bradford. *Three Lives for Mississippi.* New York: Whitney Communications Corporation Books, 1965.

Hunter, Allan A. *Courage in Both Hands.* New York: Fellowship of Reconciliation, [1951].

————. *White Corpuscles in Europe.* Chicago: Willett, Clark, 1939.

Hunter, Edward. *The Black Book on Red China.* New York: Bookmailer, 1958.

Huntley, Thomas Elliott. *When People Behave Like Sputniks, As I Saw Them.* New York: Vantage, 1960. (Inscription by Huntley, 1/16/1961.)

Hutchins, Robert Maynard, ed. Great Books of the Western World. Vol. 23, *"The Prince" by Nicolo Machiavelli: "Leviathan; or, Matter, Form, and Power of a Commonwealth Ecclesiastical and Civil" by Thomas Hobbes.* Chicago: William Benton, 1952.

Hutchinson, Paul, and Winfred E. Garrison. *20 Centuries of Christianity: A Concise History.* New York: Harcourt, Brace, 1959.

Hutchison, John Alexander. *The Two Cities: A Study of God and Human Politics.* Garden City, N.Y.: Doubleday, 1957.

Information Please Almanac 1957. New York: Macmillan, 1956.

Integrating the Urban School. New York: Teacher's College, Columbia University, 1963.

International Ladies' Garment Workers' Union. *Equal Opportunity Union Made.* New York: International Ladies' Garment Workers' Union, [1962].

Irwin, Inez Haynes. *Up Hill with Banners Flying.* Penobscot, Me.: Traversity, 1964.

Jabhat al-Tahrir al-Qami. *Algeria: Questions and Answers.* New York: Algerian Office, June 1960.

Jackson, James E. *The View from Here.* New York: Publishers New Press, 1963.

Jacobsen, Gertrude Ann, and Miriam H. Lipman. *An Outline of Political Science.* College Outline Series. New York: Barnes & Noble, 1949.

James, Clifford L. *An Outline of the Principles of Economics.* 5th ed. College Outline Series. New York: Barnes & Noble, 1940.

————. *New Outline of the Principles of Economics.* College Outline Series. New York: Barnes & Noble, 1949.

Jefferson, Thomas. *The Life and Morals of Jesus of Nazareth.* New York: Wilfred Funk, 1944.

Jews and the Jewish People: Collected Materials from the Soviet Press. London: Contemporary Jewish Library, 1965.

Johns, Joseph P. *Kosciuszko: A Biographical Study with a Historical Background of the Times.* Detroit: Endurance, 1965.

Johns, R. Elizabeth. *Refinement by Fire: The Story of a Project that May Change the Face of the Nation.* N.p.: Council for Christian Social Action, [1965].

Johnson, Lyndon B. *My Hope for America.* New York: Random House, 1964. (Inscription by Johnson, 12/18/1964.)

Johnson, Paul Emanuel. *Psychology of Religion.* New York: Abingdon, 1959.

Jones, E. Stanley. *The Christ of the American Road.* New York: Abingdon-Cokesbury, [1944]. (Marginal comments by King.)

———. *Mahatma Gandhi: An Interpretation.* New York: Abingdon-Cokesbury, 1948. (Marginal comments by King.)

Jones, Rufus Matthew. *Rufus Jones Speaks to Our Time: An Anthology.* Edited by Harry Emerson Fosdick. New York: Macmillan, 1951.

———. *Spirit in Man.* Berkeley, Calif.: Peacock, 1963.

Jordan, Lewis Garnett. *The Baptist Standard Church Directory and Busy Pastor's Guide.* Nashville: Sunday School Publishing Board, 1929.

Jowett, J. H. *Thirsting for the Springs: Twenty-Six Weeknight Meditations.* New York: Hodder & Stoughton, 1903.

Jung, C. G. *Psychologie und Erziehung: Analytische Psychologie und Erziehung Konflikte der kindlichen Seele Der Begabte.* Zurich: Rascher, 1950. (Marginal comments by King.)

The Junior Instructor: A Treasure House of Adventure for Boys and Girls. Lake Bluff, Ill.: United Educators, 1962.

Kalb, Barry. "'Rankin Brigade' Ponders Results of March." *Evening Star* (Washington, D.C.), 16 January 1968.

Karlikow, Abraham S. *Jews in Arab Countries.* New York: American Jewish Committee, 1968.

Karon, Bertram P. *The Negro Personality: A Rigorous Investigation of the Effects of Culture.* New York: Springer, 1964.

Keating, Edward M. *The Scandal of Silence.* New York: Random House, 1965.

Kegley, Charles W., and Robert W. Bretall, eds. *The Library of Living Theology.* Vol. 1, *The Theology of Paul Tillich.* New York: Macmillan, 1952. (Marginal comments by King.)

Keighton, Robert E. *The Man Who Would Preach.* New York: Abingdon, 1956. (Marginal comments by King.)

Kelso, Louis O., and Patricia Hetter. *Two-Factor Theory: The Economics of Reality.* New York: Vintage Books, 1968.

Kendrick, Mari [Gardener, George K.]. *Operation Hair Tonic.* New York: Pageant, 1957. (Inscription by Mari Kendrick.)

Kennedy, Gerald. *The Lion and the Lamb: Paradoxes of the Christian Faith.* New York: Abingdon-Cokesbury, 1950. (Marginal comments by King.)

Kennedy, John F. *Profiles in Courage.* New York: Pocket Books, 1957.

Kennedy, Robert F. *The Enemy Within.* New York: Popular Library, 1960.

Kepler, Thomas Samuel. *The Meaning and Mystery of the Resurrection.* New York: Association Press, 1963.

Key, V. O., Jr. *Southern Politics in State and Nation.* New York: Alfred A. Knopf, 1949.

Keyes, Kenneth S. *How to Develop Your Thinking Ability.* New York: McGraw-Hill Book, 1950.

Khan, Muhammad Zafrulla. *Islam: Its Meaning for Modern Man.* New York: Harper & Row, 1962.

Killens, John O. *Youngblood.* New York: Dial, 1954. (Inscription by Killens, 6/6/1956.)

———. *Youngblood.* New York: Pocket Books, 1955. (Inscription by Killens, 9/12/1957.)

King, Donald Barnett, and Charles W. Quick, eds. *Legal Aspects of the Civil Rights Movement.* Detroit: Wayne State University Press, 1965.

King, Henry Churchill. *Letters on the Greatness and Simplicity of the Christian Faith.* Boston: Pilgrim, 1906. (Inscription.)

The Kingdom, the Power, and the Glory: Services of Praise and Prayer for Occasional Use in Churches. New York: Oxford University Press, 1933. (Inscription by Margaret and Eliot Porter, 1/15/1961.)

Kirkland, Edward C. *A History of American Economic Life,* rev. ed. New York: F. S. Crofts, 1946.

Klein, Roger H., ed. *Young Americans Abroad.* New York: Harper & Row, 1963.

Knox, Raymond Collyer. *Knowing The Bible.* New York: Macmillan, 1929.

Knox, Vicesimus. *Christian Philosophy; or, An Attempt to Display, by Internal Testimony, the Evidence and Excellence of Revealed Religion.* London: John Hatchard, 1835.

Koestler, Arthur. *Darkness at Noon.* Translated by Daphne Hardy. New York: New American Library, 1948.

Korngold, Ralph. *Citizen Toussaint.* New York: Hill & Wang, 1965. (Inscription by Piri Korngold, 8/1965.)

Kripalani, J. B. *Class Struggle.* Wardha, India: Akhil Bharak Sarva Seva Sangh Prakashan, 1958.

———. *The Gandhian Way.* 3rd rev. ed. Bombay: Vora, 1945. (Inscription by Kripalani, 2/11/1959.)

———. *The Indian National Congress.* Bombay: Vora, 1946.

———. *Planning and Sarvodaya.* Rajghat, India: Sarva Seva Sangh Publication, [1957]. (Inscription by Kripalani, 2/11/1959.)

Kunstler, William Moses. *. . . And Justice For All.* Dobbs Ferry, N.Y.: Oceana, 1963. (Inscription by Kunstler, 3/31/1963.)

———. *Deep in My Heart.* Forewords by James Foreman and Martin Luther King, Jr. New York: William Morrow, 1966.

L'Hommedieu, Howard W. *One-Sentence Economics and World Leprosy: The Untaught Science.* Arlington Heights, Ill.: Public Press, 1963. (Inscription by L'Hommedieu, 7/21/1964.)

Lang, Serge. *The Scheer Campaign.* New York: W. A. Benjamin, 1967.

Lanther, H. C. *The Fifth Horseman.* Vol. 1, *The Road to Sodoma.* New York: Carlton, 1961. (Inscription by Lanther.)

Laubach, Frank C. *How to Teach One and Win One for Christ: Christ's Plan for Winning the World; Each One Teach and Win One.* Grand Rapids, Mich.: Zondervan, 1964.

Lecomte du Noüy, Pierre. *Human Destiny.* New York: Longmans, Green, 1947.

Le Ghait, Edouard. *No Carte Blanche to Capricorn: The Folly of Nuclear War Strategy.* New York: Bookfield House, 1960.

Lee, Gloria. *The Going and the Glory.* Auckland: Heralds of the New Age, [1966].

Libby, Violet Kelway. *Henry Dunant: Prophet of Peace.* New York: Pageant, 1964. (Inscription by Libby, 11/25/1964.)

Lichtenberger, Arthur. *The Day Is At Hand.* New York: Seabury, 1964.

Lifton, Robert Jay. *Death in Life: Survivors of Hiroshima.* New York: Random House, 1967.

Linscott, Robert N., ed. *The Best American Humorous Short Stories.* New York: Random House, 1945.

Lipman, Eugene J., and Albert Vorspan, eds. *A Tale of Ten Cities: The Triple Ghetto in American Religious Life.* New York: Union of American Hebrew Congregations, 1962. (Inscription by Lipman and Vorspan, 7/16/1962.)

Liska, Rudolph. *Unity with Creative Living Dramatics.* Chicago: Liska, 1958. (Inscription by Liska.)

Littlechild, Mary J. *"Creation" and "Reason and Re-A-Son."* Kingston, Canada: Maxwell Printers & Lithographers, 1964.

Lohaus, Adam. *Survival and Caesar at the Grassroots: Our Sociological Rat Race.* New York: Carlton, 1964. (Inscription by Lohaus, 2/1965.)

Lord, Walter. *The Past That Would Not Die.* New York: Harper & Row, 1965.

Lowenstein, Allard K. *Brutal Mandate: A Journey to South West Africa.* New York: Macmillan, 1962.

Lowry, Charles Wesley. *To Pray Or Not to Pray! A Handbook for Study of Recent Supreme Court Decisions and American Church-State Doctrine.* Washington, D.C.: University Press of Washington, D.C., 1963. (Inscription by Tom Sander.)

Luccock, Halford Edward. *In the Minister's Workshop.* New York: Abingdon-Cokesbury, 1944. (Marginal comments by King.)

———. *Preaching Values in the Epistles of Paul.* Vol. 1, *Romans and First Corinthians.* New York: Harper & Brothers, 1959. (Marginal comments by King.)

Lynn, Kenneth S., ed. *The Professions in America.* Boston: Houghton Mifflin, 1965.

Lyttle, Bradford. *National Defense Thru Nonviolent Resistance.* Chicago: Steib, 1958.

Macgregor, George Hogarth Carnaby. *The New Testament Basis of Pacifism.* New York: Fellowship of Reconciliation, 1954.

MacLennan, David Alexander. *Resources for Sermon Preparation.* Philadelphia: Westminster, 1957.

Maddux, Rachel. *Abel's Daughter.* New York: Harper & Brothers, 1960.

Magruder, Frank Abbott. *American Government: A Textbook on the Problems of Democracy.* Boston: Allyn & Bacon, 1950.

Maguire, John David. "Broken Fellowship and the Godly Fact." Reprint from *Foundations* 5 (April 1962). (Inscription by Maguire.)

Man One Family: Excerpts from "Race and Man." Wilmette, Ill.: Baha'i Publishing Committee, 1943.

Manshardt, Clifford, ed. *The First Decade, August 15, 1947–August 15, 1957: A Symposium Commemorating the Tenth Anniversary of Indian Independence.* New Delhi: United States Information Service, 1957. (Inscription by Swami Vishwananda, 3/10/1959.)

Maritain, Jacques. *Von Bergson Zu Thomas Von Aquin: Acht Abhandlungen über Metaphysik und Moral.* Cambridge, Mass.: Schoenhof Verlag, 1945.

Markowitz, Sidney L. *What You Should Know About Jewish Religion, History, Ethics, and Culture.* New York: Citadel, 1955.

Martin, Bernard. *The Healing Ministry in the Church.* Richmond, Va.: John Knox, 1960.

Martin, Rose Hinton. *Endearing Endeavors.* New York: Pageant, 1960. (Inscription by Martin.)

Marty, Martin E. *The New Shape of American Religion.* New York: Harper & Brothers, 1959.

Marty, Martin E., and Dean G. Peerman, eds. *New Theology No. 1.* New York: Macmillan, 1964.

Mason, Alpheus Thomas. *Free Government in the Making: Readings in American Political Thought.* New York: Oxford University Press, 1965.

Mathews, Isaac George. *The Religious Pilgrimage of Israel.* New York: Harper & Brothers, 1947.

Mays, Benjamin Elijah. *A Brief Summary of Fifteen Years at Morehouse.* Atlanta: More-house College, 1955.

———. *Seeking to Be Christian in Race Relations.* New York: Friendship, 1957. (Inscription by Mays, 2/12/1957.)

Mazar, Benjamin. *The World of the Bible.* Philadelphia: Educational Heritage, 1964.

Mazo, Earl. *Richard Nixon: A Political and Personal Portrait.* New York: Harper & Brothers, 1959.

Mboya, Tom. *The Kenya Question: An African Answer.* London: Fabian Colonial Bureau, 1956. (Inscription by Mboya.)

McCallum, James Dow, ed. *The Revised College Omnibus.* New York: Harcourt, Brace, 1939. (Marginal comments by King.)

McCollum, Lee Charles. *History and Rhymes of the Lost Battalion.* New York: Bucklee, 1939.

McGill, Ralph. *The South and the Southerner.* Boston: Little, Brown, 1963. (Inscription by J. C. Herrin; marginal comments by King.)

McGinnis, Frederick A. *The Education of Negroes in Ohio.* Wilberforce, Ohio: 1962. (Inscription by McGinnis, 2/26/1965.)

McGovern, Ann. *Runaway Slave: The Story of Harriet Tubman.* New York: Four Winds, 1965.

McKeon, Richard, ed. *Introduction to Aristotle.* New York: Modern Library, 1947. (Marginal comments by King.)

McKinney, Richard I. *Religion in Higher Education Among Negroes.* New Haven, Conn.: Yale University Press, 1945.

McNeil, Jesse Jai. *As Thy Days So Thy Strength.* Grand Rapids, Mich.: William B. Eerdmans, 1961.

McNeill, Marion Lucius. *Drink Deep of Life.* New York: Vantage, 1958. (Inscription by Randolph McNeill.)

Meir, Golda. "Israel and the Arab Challenge." *New York Herald Tribune,* 17 February 1958.

Melanchthon, Philip. *The Loci Communes of Philip Melanchthon.* Translated by Charles Leander Hill. Boston: Meador, 1944.

Meland, Bernard Eugene. *Seeds of Redemption.* New York: Macmillan, 1947.

Merchant, Francis. *The Transformation of Society.* Boston: Bruce Humphries, 1960.

Meredith, Ronald R. *Hurryin' Big For Little Reasons.* New York: Abingdon, 1964. (Inscription by Meredith.)

Merriam, Eve. *Montgomery, Alabama, Money, Mississippi and Other Places.* New York: Cameron Associates, 1956. (Inscription by Merriam, 5/25/1956.)

Merton, Thomas. *The Black Revolution.* Atlanta: Southern Christian Leadership Conference, 1963.

Mill, John Stuart. *Principles of Political Economy.* Edited by J. Laurence Laughlin. New York: D. Appleton, 1886.

Millea, Thomas V. *Ghetto Fever.* Milwaukee, Wis.: Bruce, 1968.

Miller, Carl Wallace. *A Scientist's Approach to Religion.* New York: Macmillan, 1947. (Marginal comments by King.)

Miller, Clifford L. *Wings Over Dark Waters.* New York: Great Concord, 1954. (Inscription by Miller.)

Miller, J. R. *Bethlehem to Olivet: The Life of Jesus Christ Illustrated by Modern Painters.* Edited by W. Shaw Sparrow. New York: Hodder & Stoughton, 1908.

Miller, Randolph Crump. *Christian Nurture and the Church.* New York: Charles Scribner's Sons, 1961.

Milton, John. *Paradise Lost.* Garden City, N.Y.: Doubleday, 1960.

Mochalski, Herbert. *Der Mann in der Brandung: Ein Bildbuch um Martin Niemöller.* Frankfurt: Stimme-Verlag, 1962. (Inscription by student group, 8/10/1964.)

Moltmann, Jürgen. *Theology of Hope.* New York: Harper & Row, 1967. (Inscription by Moltmann.)

Montagu, Ashley. *On Being Human.* New York: Henry Schuman, 1951. (Marginal comments by King.)

Morison, Samuel Eliot. *The Oxford History of the American People.* New York: Oxford University Press, 1965.

Morrison, A. Cressy. *Man Does Not Stand Alone.* Rev. ed. New York: Fleming H. Revell, 1947. (Marginal comments by King.)

Morrison, Charles Clayton. *Can Protestantism Win America?* New York: Harper & Brothers, 1948.

Moskin, J. Robert. *Morality in America.* New York: Random House, 1966.

Muelder, Walter George. *Foundations of the Responsible Society.* New York: Abingdon, 1959.

Mumford, Lewis, Tom Stoner, Norman Cousins, et al. *Breakthrough to Peace.* Introduction by Thomas Merton. Norfolk, Conn.: J. Laughlin, 1962.

Muzumdar, Haridas Thakordas. *Mahatma Gandhi: Peaceful Revolutionary.* New York: Charles Scribner's Sons, 1952. (Inscription by M. Rama Lal, 3/29/1956.)

Narayan, Jayaprakash. *From Socialism to Sarvodaya.* Rajghat, India: Akhil Bharat Sarva Seva Sangh Prakashan, 1958.

Narayan, Shriman. *One Week with Vinoba.* New Delhi: Indian National Congress, 1956. (Inscription by Narayan, 3/8/1959.)

———. *The Two Worlds.* Bombay: Hind Kitabs, 1950. (Inscription by Narayan, 3/8/1959.)

Nason, Elias. *The Life and Times of Charles Sumner: His Boyhood, Education, and Public Career.* Boston: B. B. Russell, 1874.

National Advisory Committee on Farm Labor. *Poverty on the Land in a Land of Plenty.* New York: National Advisory Committee on Farm Labor, 1965.

Neil, William. *Harper's Bible Commentary.* New York: Harper & Row, [1962].

The New Covenant: Commonly Called the New Testament of Our Lord and Savior Jesus Christ; Revised Standard Version. New York: Thomas Nelson & Sons, 1946. (Marginal comments by King.)

New York Herald Tribune. *Israel After 10 Years.* New York: New York Herald Tribune, [1958].

Nicoll, W. Robertson, ed. *The Expositor's Greek Testament.* Vols. 3–5. Grand Rapids, Mich.: William B. Eerdmans, 1952.

Niebuhr, H. Richard. *The Kingdom of God in America.* New York: Harper & Brothers, 1959.

Niebuhr, Reinhold. *Moral Man and Immoral Society.* New York: Charles Scribner's Sons, 1947. (Marginal comments by King.)

Nielsen, Waldemar A. *African Battleline: American Policy Choices in Southern Africa.* New York: Harper & Row, 1965.

Niles, D. T. *Upon the Earth: The Mission of God and the Missionary Enterprise of the Churches.* New York: McGraw-Hill, 1962.

Nininger, Ruth. *Growing a Musical Church.* Nashville: Broadman, 1947.

Oates, Whitney Jennings, and Charles Theophilus Murphy. *Greek Literature in Translation.* New York: Longmans, Green, 1946.

O'Connor, Elizabeth. *Journey Inward, Journey Outward.* New York: Harper & Row, 1968. (Inscription by O'Connor.)

Ohrn, Arnold T., ed. *Tenth Baptist World Congress, Rio de Janeiro, Brazil, June 26–July 3, 1960: Official Report.* Nashville: Broadman, 1961.

Oldroyd, Osborn H., ed. *Words of Lincoln.* Washington, D.C.: Published by author, 1895.

Olsen, Otto H. *Carpetbagger's Crusade: The Life of Albion Winegar Tourgee.* Baltimore: John Hopkins, 1965.

One Nation Indivisible: A Television Report on the Racial Crisis. New York: Westinghouse Broadcasting, [1968].

Padmore, George. *Pan-Africanism or Communism?: The Coming Struggle for Africa.* London: D. Dobson, 1956. (Inscriptions by Padmore, C. L. R. James, and David Pitt.)

Palmer, Vernon U. *The New Grand Army.* New York: Vantage, 1965. (Inscription by Palmer, 12/24/1965.)

Papini, Giovanni. *The Devil.* Translated by Adrienne Foulke. New York: E. P. Dutton, 1954. (Inscription.)

Pappenheim, Fritz. *The Alienation of Modern Man: An Interpretation Based on Marx and Tönnies.* New York: Monthly Review, 1959. (Inscription by Pappenheim, 2/1963.)

Parkhill, Forbes. *Mister Barney Ford: A Portrait in Bistre.* Denver: Sage Books, 1963. (Inscription by Parkhill, 1/6/1964.)

Parks, Willis B. *The Possibilities of the Negro in Symposium.* Atlanta: Franklin, 1904.

Paterson, John. *The Praises of Israel: Studies Literary and Religious in the Psalms.* New York: Charles Scribner's Sons, 1950.

Patterson, Haywood, and Earl Conrad. *Scottsboro Boy.* Garden City, N.Y.: Doubleday, 1950.

Patterson, Lindsay, ed. *The Negro in Music and Art.* New York: Publishers Co. [1967].

Patterson, William L., ed. *We Charge Genocide: The Historic Petition to the United Nations For Relief from a Crime of The United States Government against the Negro People.* New York: Civil Rights Congress, 1952. (Inscription by Patterson, 3/25/1956.)

Paul, William. *Analysis and Critical Interpretation of the Hebrew Text of the Book of Genesis: Preceeded by a Hebrew Grammar, and Dissertations. . . .* Edinburgh: William Blackwood & Sons, 1852.

Paulding, James E. *Sometime Tomorrow.* New York: Carlton, 1965. (Inscription by Paulding.)

Pearl, Jack. *Stockade.* New York: Trident, 1965. (Inscription by Pearl.)

Pearson, Robert E. *No Share of Glory.* Pacific Palisades, Calif.: Challenge, 1964.

Penn, I. Garland, and J. W. E. Bowen. *The United Negro: His Problems and His Progress; Containing the Addresses and Proceedings the Negro Young People's Christian and Educational Congress, Held August 6–11, 1902.* Atlanta: D. E. Luther, 1902.

Peto, Frank D. *The Cosmic Way.* Houston: F. Hajos, 1959. (Inscription by Peto.)

Pettigrew, Thomas H., Jr. *The Kunu-ri (Kumori) Incident.* New York: Vantage, 1963. (Inscription by Pettigrew, 7/28/1963.)

Philippou, A. J., ed. *The Orthodox Ethos: Essays in Honour of the Centenary of the Greek Orthodox Archdiocese of North and South America.* Oxford, England: Holywell, 1964.

Phillips, J. B. *Plain Christianity and Other Broadcast Talks.* New York: Macmillan, 1954.

Pine, L. G., ed. *The Author's and Writer's Who's Who.* London: Burke's Peerage, [1960].

Pire, Dominique-Georges. *Building Peace.* London: Transworld, 1967.

Plimpton, Ruth T. *Operation Crossroads Africa.* New York: Viking, 1962.

Poling, Daniel A. *A Preacher Looks at War.* New York: Macmillan, 1943.

Porter, Katherine Anne. *Ship of Fools.* Boston: Little, Brown, 1945.

Powell, Adam Clayton, Sr. *Riots and Ruins.* New York: Richard R. Smith, 1945. (Inscription by Powell.)

President's Committee on Equal Employment Opportunity. *Report to the President.* Washington, D.C.: U.S. Government Printing Office, 1963.

Price, Margaret. *The Negro Voter in the South.* Atlanta: Southern Regional Council, 1957.

Pyarelal. *A Nation Builder at Work.* Ahmedabad, India: Navajivan, 1952.

———. *A Pilgrimage for Peace: Gandhi and Frontier Gandhi among N.W.F. Pathans.* Ahmedabad, India: Navajivan, 1950.

———. *Mahatma Gandhi: The Last Phase.* Ahmedabad, India: Navajivan, 1958. (Inscription by Richard Bartlett Gregg, 12/2/1958.)

———. *Thoreau, Tolstoy, and Gandhiji.* Calcutta: A. K. Banerji, 1958.

Pye, Ernest. *The Biography of a Mind: Bosworth of Oberlin.* New York: Bosworth Memorial Committee of the Board of Sponsors, 1948. (Inscription to Vernon Johns by Pye, 5/16/1949.)

Quimby, Chester Warren. *The Great Redemption: A Living Commentary on Paul's Epistle to the Romans.* New York: Macmillan, 1950. (Marginal comments by King.)

Raines, Robert Arnold, ed. *Creative Brooding.* New York: Macmillan, 1966.

Rall, Harris Franklin. *According to Paul.* New York: Charles Scribner's Sons, 1945. (Marginal comments by King.)

Ralph, John Robertson. *The Happy Bondage.* New York: Vantage, 1956.

Ramachandran, G. *A Sheaf of Gandhi Anecdotes.* Bombay: Hind Kitabs, 1945.

Ramsey, Paul. *Christian Ethics and the Sit-In.* New York: Association Press, 1961.

Randall, John H. Jr., and Justus Buchler. *Philosophy: An Introduction.* College Outline Series. New York: Barnes & Noble, 1948.

Ransome, William Lee. *An Old Story for this New Day and Other Sermons and Addresses.* Richmond, Va.: Central, 1954. (Inscription by Ransome; marginal comments by King.)

Ray, Benoy Gopal. *Gandhian Ethics.* Ahmedabad, India: Navajivan, 1950.

Read, David Haxton Carswell. *Sons of Anak: The Gospel and the Modern Giants.* New York: Charles Scribner's Sons, 1964.

Read, Florence Matilda. *The Story of Spelman College.* Atlanta, 1961. (Inscription by Landonia Gettell, 10/20/1963.)

Reaves, Laurie. *Lo! The Poor Innocents.* New York: Carlton, 1963.

Redding, J. Saunders. *No Day of Triumph.* New York: Harper & Brothers, 1942.

Render Unto Caesar: A Collection of Sermon Classics on All Phases of Religion in Wartime. New York: Lewis Publishing, 1943.

Reyburn, Hugh Adam. *The Ethical Theory of Hegel: A Study of the Philosophy of Right.* Oxford: Clarendon, 1921. (Marginal comments by King.)

Reznikoff, Charles. *Testimony: The United States, 1885–1890*. New York: New Directions, 1965.

Ricardo, David. *The Principles of Political Economy and Taxation*. Edited by Ernest Rhys. New York: Everyman's Library, 1933.

Riedel, Otto. *Gewissensnot; Roman*. Berlin: Evangelische Verlagsanstalt, 1964.

Robert, Henry M. *Robert's Rules of Order*. Chicago: Scott, Foresman, 1951.

Roberts, Oral. *This Is Your Abundant Life in Jesus Christ: Bible Studies in Abundant Life*. Tulsa, Okla.: Abundant Life, 1961.

Robinson, James Harvey. *An Introduction to the History of Western Europe*. Vol. 2, *The Emergence of Existing Conditions and Ways of Thinking*. Boston: Ginn, 1934.

Robinson, James Harvey, and Charles A. Beard. *History of Europe, Our Own Times: The Eighteenth and Nineteenth Centuries, the Opening of the Twentieth Century, the World War, and Recent Events*. Rev. ed. Boston: Ginn, 1927.

Robinson, James Herman. *Tomorrow Is Today*. Philadelphia: Christian Education, 1954.

Robinson, John A. T. *In the End God*. London: Fontana Books, 1968.

Rogers, Edward. *Living Standards: A Christian Looks at the World's Poverty*. London: SCM Press, 1964.

———. *Poverty on a Small Planet: A Christian Looks at Living Standards*. New York: Macmillan, [1965].

Rollins, Wayne G. *The Gospels: Portraits of Christ*. Philadelphia: Westminster, 1963.

Rosenthal, A. M. *Thirty-eight Witnesses*. New York: McGraw-Hill, 1964.

Roumain, Jacques. *Masters of the Dew*. Translated by Langston Hughes and Mercer Cook. New York: Reynal & Hitchcock, 1947. (Inscription, 4/27/1957.)

Rovner, Maurice B., J. Alexis Fenton, and Louis Kalvin. *Vitalized American History*. New York: College Entrance Book, 1949.

Rowlingson, Donald T. *Jesus the Religious Ultimate*. New York: Macmillan, 1961.

Rudwick, Elliott M. *Race Riot at East St. Louis, July 2, 1917*. Carbondale, Ill.: Southern Illinois University Press, 1964.

Runes, Dagobert D., ed. *The Dictionary of Philosophy*. New York: Philosophical Library, [1942].

Sandburg, Carl. *Abraham Lincoln: The Prairie Years and the War Years in Three Volumes*. Vol. 1: *The Prairie Years*. New York: Dell, 1960.

Saruya, Kaname. *Amerika no Kokujin: Sono Kunan No Rekishi*. Tokyo: Kobundo, [1964]. (Inscription.)

Sayers, Dorothy L. *Creed or Chaos?* New York: Harcourt, Brace, 1949.

School of Visual Arts. *Children at Play*. New York: School of Visual Arts, 1964.

Schwarcz, Ernest. *Paths to Freedom Through Nonviolence: A Study of East-West Conflict and the Methods of Nonviolent Resistance*. Vienna: Sensen-Verlag, 1959.

Schweitzer, Albert. *Out of My Life and Thought: An Autobiography*. Translated by C. T. Compton. New York: New American Library, 1961.

Scott, Michael. *A Time To Speak*. Garden City, N.Y.: Doubleday, 1958. (Inscription by Scott, 10/24/1958.)

Scott, Robert, and Williams Curtis Stiles. *Cyclopedia of Illustrations for Public Speakers: Containing Facts, Incidents, Stories, Experiences, Anecdotes, Selections, etc. for Illustrative Purposes, with Cross-references*. New York: Funk & Wagnalls, 1911.

Seiss, Joseph Augustus. *The Apocalypse: A Series of Special Lectures on the Revelation of Jesus Christ, with Revised Text.* Vol. 2. 9th ed. New York: Charles C. Cook, 1906.

Seljouk, M. A. *Corpses.* London: Gerald Duckworth, 1966.

Sen, Priyaranjan. *Gandhism.* Calcutta: A. Mukherjee, 1957. (Inscription by Sen, 2/15/1959; marginal comments by King.)

Seuell, Malchus M. *The Black Christ, and Verse.* Downey, Calif.: Elena Quinn, 1957. (Inscription by Seuell, 11/1957.)

Seventeen Magazine. *The Seventeen Book of Prayer.* New York: Macmillan, 1965.

Shahani, Ranjee Gurdarsing. *Mr. Gandhi.* New York: Macmillan, 1961.

Sharma, Jagdish Saran. *Mahatma Gandhi: A Descriptive Bibliography.* Delhi: S. Chand, 1955. (Inscription by R. R. Diwakar, 3/8/1959.)

Sharpe, Dores Robinson. *Call to Christian Action.* New York: Harper & Brothers, 1949. (Inscription by Sharpe.)

Shaw, Alexander Preston. *Christianizing Race Relations: As a Negro Sees It.* Los Angeles: Wetzel Publishing, 1928.

Shaw, S. B. *Children's Edition of Touching Incidents and Remarkable Answers to Prayer.* Guthrie, Okla.: Faith, 1895.

Shipler, Guy Emery, ed. *Sermons of Goodwill: The Churchman's First Series on Brotherhood and Goodwill.* New York: Association Press, 1948. (Inscription to Stanley D. Levison by Shipler, 5/1955.)

Shridharani, Krishnalal. *War Without Violence: A Study of Gandhi's Method and Its Accomplishments.* New York: Harcourt, Brace, 1939.

Shub, David. *Lenin: A Biography.* Edited by Donald Porter Geddes. New York: New American Library, 1950.

Silberman, Charles E. *Crisis in Black and White.* New York: Random House, 1964. (Marginal comments by King.)

Silver, Abba Hillel. *Religion in a Changing World.* New York: Richard R. Smith, 1931. (Marginal comments by King.)

Silver, Minnesota. *Rhymes of a Rambler.* Edited by John J. Kohn. New York: John J. Kohn, 1964. (Inscription by Kohn, 2/2/1965.)

Silverman, Morris, ed. *Passover Haggadah: With Explanatory Notes and Original Readings.* Hartford, Conn.: Prayer Book, 1959. (Inscription by Silverman.)

Silverman, William B. *The Still Small Voice Today: Jewish Ethical Living.* Book 2. New York: Behrman House, 1957. (Inscription by Silverman.)

Simon, Charlie May. *A Seed Shall Serve: The Story of Toyohiko Kagawa, Spiritual Leader of Modern Japan.* New York: E. P. Dutton, 1958.

Simon, Paul. *Lovejoy: Martyr to Freedom.* St. Louis, Mo.: Concordia, 1964. (Inscription by Simon 8/28/1964.)

Simons, Menno. *The Cross of Christ.* Scottdale, Pa.: Mennonite Publishing House, 1946.

Sin-Pfaeltzer, Marianne, and Max Kruse. *Fred und Peter: Eine Geschichte aus unseren Tagen.* Bern: Verlag Hallwag, 1966. (Inscription by Sin-Pfaeltzer, 12/1966.)

Sinclair, Upton. *The Cup of Fury.* Great Neck, N.Y.: Channel, 1960. (Inscription, 10/21/1960.)

Sindler, Allan P., ed. *Change in the Contemporary South.* Durham, N.C.: Duke University Press, 1963.

Singh, Ranbir. *Glimpses of the Divine Masters.* New Delhi: International Traders Organization, 1965. (Inscription by A. S. Bhatia.)

Singleton, George A. *The Autobiography of George A. Singleton*. Boston: Forum, 1964.

Smith, Adam. *An Inquiry Into the Nature and Causes of the Wealth of Nations*. Edited by Ernest Rhys. 2 vols. Everyman's Library. New York: E. P. Dutton, 1931.

Smith, David Eugene. *Number Stories of Long Ago*. London: Ginn, 1957.

Smith, Donald Hugh. "Martin Luther King, Jr.: Rhetorician of Revolt." Ph.D. diss., University of Wisconsin, 1964. (Inscription by Smith.)

Smith, Ed. *Where To, Black Man? An American Negro's African Diary*. Chicago: Quadrangle Books, 1967.

Smith, Ivory Harvey, and Isabelle Tolbert Smith. *Life Lines: A Collection of Inspiring Poetry and Prose*. Charlotte, N.C.: Observer Printing House, 1952. (Inscription by Ivory Harvey and Isabelle T. Smith.)

Smith, J. M. Powis. *William R. Harper's Introductory Hebrew Method and Manual*. Rev. ed. New York: Charles Scribner's Sons, 1922.

Smith, Joseph R. *Sin Corner and Joe Smith: A Story of Vice and Corruption in Chicago*. New York: Exposition, 1963. (Inscription by Smith, 2/24/1966.)

Smith, Lillian Eugenia. *Our Faces, Our Words*. New York: W. W. Norton, 1964. (Inscription by Smith, 11/12/1964.)

Smith, Thomas I. *A Soldier's Theology*. Philadelphia: Dorrance, 1943.

Snowden, James H. *Snowden's Sunday School Lessons*. New York: Macmillan, 1924.

Sobel, Lester A., ed. *Civil Rights: 1960–63: The Negro Campaign to Win Equal Rights and Opportunities in the United States*. New York: Facts on File, 1964.

Soman, R. J. *Peaceful Industrial Relations, Their Science and Technique*. Ahmedabad, India: Navajivan, 1957.

Soule, George. *The Shape of Tomorrow*. New York: New American Library, 1958.

Southern Regional Council. *Race and Law Enforcement: A Guide to Modern Police Practices*. Atlanta: Southern Regional Council, 1952.

Spalding, Samuel Charles. *I've Had Me a Time! with Autobiographical Sketch, Selected Poems, and Sermons*. Great Barrington, Mass.: Friends of Gould Farm, 1961. (Inscription by Spalding.)

Spike, Robert W. *The Freedom Revolution and the Churches*. New York: Association Press, 1965.

Spock, Benjamin. *Baby and Child Care*. New York: Pocket Books, 1963.

Spring, Howard. *Hard Facts*. New York: Viking, 1944.

Stats, Jeanette. *The Extension of Legal Services to the Poor: Conference Proceedings*. Washington, D.C.: U.S. Government Printing Office, 1964.

Steele, John Dorman. *A Brief History of the United States for Schools*. New York: A. S. Barnes, 1875.

Steiner, Stan. *The New Indians*. New York: Harper & Row, 1968.

Stewart, John T. *The Deacon Wore Spats: Profiles from America's Changing Religious Scene*. New York: Holt, Rinehart & Winston, 1965.

Stidger, William L. *Planning Your Preaching*. New York: Harper & Brothers, 1932.

Stone, Chuck. *Tell It Like It Is*. New York: Trident, 1967.

Stone, Irving. *Lust for Life: The Novel of Vincent van Gogh*. New York: Pocket Books, [1946].

Stormer, John A. *None Dare Call It Treason*. Florissant, Mo.: Liberty Bell, 1964.

Strauss, Lewis L. *Men and Decisions*. New York: Popular Library, 1963.

Strickler, G. B. *Sermons*. New York: Fleming H. Revell, 1910.

Stringfellow, William. *A Private and Public Faith*. Grand Rapids, Mich.: William B. Eerdmans, 1962. (Inscription by Stringfellow, 6/24/1963.)

———. *My People Is the Enemy: An Autobiographical Polemic*. New York: Holt, Rinehart & Winston, 1964. (Inscription by Stringfellow.)

Studensky, Paul. *Teachers' Pension Systems in the United States: A Critical and Descriptive Study*. The Institute for Government Research: Studies in Administration. New York: D. Appleton, 1920.

Student Nonviolent Coordinating Committee. *A Chronology of Violence and Intimidation in Mississippi Since 1961*. Atlanta: Student Nonviolent Coordinating Committee, [1964].

Swing, Raymond. *In the Name of Sanity*. 3rd ed. New York: Harper & Brothers, 1946.

Tagore, Rabindranath. *Visva-Bharati and Its Institutions*. Santiniketan, India: Publinbihari Sen, 1956. (Inscription, 2/15/1959.)

Tan, Yun-shan. *Twenty Years of the Visva-Bharati Cheena-Bhavana, 1937–1957*. Santiniketan, India: Sino-Indian Cultural Society of India, 1957.

Taylor, Charles L. *Let the Psalms Speak*. Greenwich, Conn.: Seabury, 1961.

Texas Standing Committee on Youth Participation, Governor's Committee for the White House Conference on Children and Youth. *Texas Youth Participation*. Houston: Governor's Office, 1959.

Theobald, Robert. *Free Men and Free Markets*. New York: Clarkson N. Potter, 1963.

Thomad, G. W. C. *The Circle and the Cross*. New York: Abingdon, 1964.

Thomallo, Clifford F. *Strangers In My House*. New York: Pageant, 1959. (Inscription by Thomallo, 9/20/1959.)

Thompson, Daniel C. "The Formation of Social Attitudes." Reprint from *American Journal of Orthopsychiatry* 32 (January 1962).

Thompson, Richard. *Race and Sport*. London: Oxford University Press, 1964.

Thurman, Howard. *Deep River: Reflections on the Religious Insight of Certain of the Negro Spirituals*. Rev. ed. New York: Harper & Brothers, 1955. (Inscription by Thurman; marginal comments by King.)

———. *Footprints of a Dream: The Story of the Church for the Fellowship of All Peoples*. New York: Harper & Brothers, 1959. (Inscription by Kivie Kaplan, 10/27/1960.)

———. *The Growing Edge*. New York: Harper & Brothers, 1956. (Inscription by Thurman.)

Tillich, Paul. *The Protestant Era*. Translated by James Luther Adams. Chicago: University of Chicago Press, 1948. (Marginal comments by King.)

———. *The Shaking of the Foundations*. New York: Charles Scribner's Sons, 1948. (Marginal comments by King.)

———. *Systemic Theology*. Vol. 2, *Existence and the Christ*. Chicago: University of Chicago Press, 1957. (Marginal comments by King.)

Tittle, Ernest Fremont. *Christians in an Unchristian Society*. New York: Association Press, 1940.

Titus, Harold Hopper, and Morris T. Keeton. *The Range of Ethics: Introductory Readings*. New York: American Book, 1966.

Tolstoy, Leo. *What Men Live By, and Where Love Is, There God Is Also*. Westwood, N.J.: Fleming H. Revell, 1959.

Tumin, Melvin A. *Desegregation: Resistance and Readiness*. Princeton, N.J.: Princeton University Press, 1958. (Inscription by Tumin.)

Turnbull, Andrew. *Thomas Wolfe*. New York: Charles Scribner's Sons, 1967.

Turner, John Roscoe. *Introduction to Economics*. New York: Charles Scribner's Sons, 1919.

Twain, Mark. *The Adventures of Tom Sawyer*. New York: New American Library, 1876.

Under the Banner of Leninism: A Symposium. Prague: Peace and Socialism, 1961.

The Union Prayerbook for Jewish Worship. Part 1. Rev. ed. Cincinnati: Central Conference of American Rabbis, 1942.

U.S. Commission on Civil Rights. *Administration of Justice*. Vol. 2. Washington, D.C.: U.S. Government Printing Office, 1965.

———. *Education*. Washington, D.C.: U.S. Government Printing Office, 1961.

———. *Housing*. Washington, D.C.: U.S. Government Printing Office, 1961.

———. *The New Orleans School Crisis*. Washington, D.C.: U.S. Government Printing Office, [1961].

———. *Report on Maryland: Employment*. Washington, D.C.: United State Commission on Civil Rights, 1964.

———. *Reports on Apprenticeship*. Washington, D.C.: United States Commission on Civil Rights, 1964.

U.S. Congress. House. *Brief of Contestants Urging the Vacating of the Contested Seats and the Holding of New Elections*. New York: Hecla, 1965.

U.S. Congress. House. Committee on Education and Labor. *Impact of Automation on Employment: Hearings Before the Subcommittee on Unemployment and the Impact of Automation*. 87th Cong., 1st sess. Washington, D.C.: U.S. Government Printing Office, 1961.

U.S. President's Committee on Civil Rights. *To Secure These Rights: The Report of the President's Committee on Civil Rights*. Washington, D.C.: U.S. Government Printing Office, 1947. (Inscription by Robert K. Carr.)

Unnithan, T. K.K.N. *Gandhi and Free India: A Socio-Economic Study*. Groningen, Netherlands: J. B. Wolters, 1956. (Inscription, 5/17/1958.)

Van Bracht, Thieleman. *The True and the False Church: As Outlined in the Bloody Theatre, or Martyrs Mirror*. 2nd ed. Compiled by Menno Sauder. Elmira, Canada: Menno Sauder, 1944.

Van Dusen, Henry P. *World Christianity: Yesterday, Today, Tomorrow*. New York: Friendship, 1947.

Van Dyke, Henry. *The Story of the Other Wise Man*. Westwood, N.J.: Fleming H. Revell, 1966.

Van Vechten, Carl. *Nigger Heaven*. New York: Alfred A. Knopf, 1926.

Vaughan, Curtis M. *Faubus' Folly: The Story of Segregation*. New York: Vantage, 1959. (Inscription by Vaughan.)

Vining, Elizabeth Gray. *Friend of Life: The Biography of Rufus M. Jones*. Berkeley, Calif.: Peacock, 1958.

Violi, Unicio Jack. *Greek and Roman Classics*. New York: Monarch, [1965]. (Marginal comments by King.)

Voltaire. *Candide or Optimism*. Translated by John Butt. Baltimore: Penguin Books, 1952.

Vorspan, Albert. *Giants of Justice*. New York: Union of American Hebrew Congregations, 1960. (Inscription by Vorspan, 10/27/1960.)

Voss, Carl Hermann. *Rabbi and Minister: The Friendship of Stephen S. Wise and John Haynes Holmes*. New York: World, 1964. (Inscription by Voss, 9/7/1964.)

Wadiyar, Jaya Chamarajendra. *Dattatreya: The Way and the Goal.* London: George Allen & Unwin, [1957]. (Inscription by Wadiyar.)

Walker, David. *David Walker's Appeal, in Four Articles; Together With a Preamble, to the Coloured Citizens of the World, But in Particular, and Very Expressly, to Those of the United States of America.* Edited by Charles M. Wiltse. New York: Hill & Wang, 1965.

Walker, Kath. *We Are Going: Poems.* Brisbane: Jacaranda, 1964. (Inscription by Walker, 5/1964.)

Walker, Rollin H. *The Modern Message of the Psalms.* New York: Abingdon, 1938.

Walker, Stanley. *Dewey: An American of This Century.* New York: McGraw-Hill, 1944.

Walker, Thomas Calhoun. *The Honey-Pod Tree: The Life Story of Thomas Calhoun Walker.* New York: John Day, 1958.

Walker, Williston. *A History of the Christian Church.* Student's ed. New York: Charles Scribner's Sons, 1954. (Marginal comments by King.)

Ward, Baldwin H., ed. *Year: 1964 Encyclopedia News Annual; Events of the Year 1963.* New York: Year, 1964.

Ward, Barbara. *The Rich Nations and the Poor Nations.* New York: W. W. Norton, 1962.

Washington, Vivian E. *Mount Ascutney.* New York: Comet, 1958. (Inscription by Washington, 10/1/1958.)

Weatherhead, Leslie Dixon. *When the Lamp Flickers.* New York: Abingdon-Cokesbury, 1948. (Marginal comments by King.)

Webb, W. L., ed. *The Bedside "Guardian" 16: A Selection from "The Guardian" 1966–67.* London: Collins, 1966. (Inscription by W. J. Weatherby.)

Wedel, Theodore O. *The Christianity of Main Street.* New York: Macmillan, 1950.

Wentzel, Fred D. *Epistle to White Christians.* Philadelphia: Christian Education, 1948. (Inscription by Wentzel.)

Wesley, Charles H. *The History of Alpha Phi Alpha: A Development in Negro College Life.* Washington, D.C.: Foundation Publishers, 1950.

———. *History of Alpha Phi Alpha: A Development in College Life.* 8th ed. Washington, D.C.: Foundation Publishers, 1957. (Inscription by Wesley, 8/12/1957.)

———. *The History of Sigma Pi Phi: First of the Negro-American Greek-letter Fraternities.* Washington, D.C.: Association for the Study of Negro Life & History, 1954.

West, Don. *The Road Is Rocky.* New York: New Christian Books, [1951].

Whale, J. S. *Victor and Victim: The Christian Doctrine of Redemption.* New York: Cambridge University Press, 1960. (Marginal comments by King.)

Wheatley, Melvin E. *Going His Way.* Westwood, N.J.: Fleming H. Revell, 1957. (Inscription by Wheatley.)

White House Conference on Children and Youth. "Conference Proceedings." Golden Anniversary White House Conference on Children and Youth, March 27–April 2, 1960. Washington, D.C., 1960.

———. "Focus on Children and Youth." Golden Anniversary White House Conference on Children and Youth, March 27–April 2, 1960. Washington, D.C., 1960.

———. "Reference Papers on Children and Youth." Golden Anniversary White House Conference on Children and Youth, March 27–April 2, 1960. Washington, D.C., 1960.

———. "Recommendations: Composite Report of Forum Findings, Golden Anniversary White House Conference on Children and Youth," March 27–April 2, 1960. Washington, D.C., 1960.

———. "The States Report on Children and Youth." Golden Anniversary White

House Conference on Children and Youth, March 27–April 2, 1960. Washington, D.C., 1960.

Whittemore, Reed. *Ways of Misunderstanding Poetry.* Washington, D.C.: Library of Congress, 1965. (Inscription by Joseph and Lillian Jenkins, 1965.)

Wilcox, Mary. *Iowa the Tall.* Mason City, Iowa: Collison Agency, 1963. (Inscription by Jim Collison.)

Williams, Chancellor. *Have You Been to the River?* New York: Exposition, 1952. (Inscription by Williams, 9/30/1958.)

———. *The Raven.* Philadelphia: Dorrance, 1943. (Inscription by Williams, 8/14/1958.)

Williams, Robert F. *Negroes with Guns.* Edited by Marc Scheifer. New York: Marzani & Munsell, 1962.

Williams, Tennessee. *Suddenly Last Summer.* New York: New American Library, 1960.

Wilson, Grove. *Great Men of Science: Their Lives and Discoveries.* New York: New Home Library, 1944.

Wilson, Minter Lowther. *Heart Throbs from the Bench.* Boston: Christopher, 1950. (Inscription by Wilson.)

Wines, Emma M., and Marjory W. Card. *"Come to Order!" Essentials of Parliamentary Practice and Group Discussion.* New York: Odyssey, 1941.

Wofford, Harris. "Nonviolence and the Law." *Gandhi Marg* 3 (January 1959): 27–35.

Wolf, William J. *The Almost Chosen People: A Study of the Religion of Abraham Lincoln.* Garden City, N.Y.: Doubleday, 1959.

Wolpert, Stanley. *Nine Hours to Rama.* New York: Bantam Books, 1963.

Woodburne, Angus Stewart. *The Theory of Knowledge from Locke to Kant.* London: Oxford University Press, 1930. (Marginal comments by King.)

Wright, George Ernest, and Floyd Vivian Filson, eds. *The Westminster Historical Atlas to the Bible.* Philadelphia: Westminster, 1945. (Marginal comments by King.)

Wright, Harry K. *Civil Rights U.S.A.: Public Schools, Southern States, 1963, Texas.* Staff report submitted to the United States Commission on Civil Rights. Washington, D.C.: The Commission, [1964].

Wright, James Frederick Church. *The Louise Lucas Story: This Time Tomorrow.* Montreal: Harvest House, 1965. (Inscription by Wright, 2/21/1966.)

Wright, Nathan. *The Song of Mary.* Boston: Bruce Humphries, 1958. (Inscription by Wright.)

Wright, William Kelley. *A History of Modern Philosophy.* New York: Macmillan, [1947]. (Marginal comments by King.)

Wynne-Tyson, Esmé. *The Philosophy of Compassion: The Return of the Goddess.* London: Vincent Stuart, 1962.

Yates, Elizabeth. *Howard Thurman: Portrait of a Practical Dreamer.* New York: John Day, 1964. (Inscription by Howard Thurman.)

Year's Pictorial History of the American Negro. New York: Year, 1965.

Young, Whitney M. *To Be Equal.* New York: McGraw-Hill Book, 1964.

Yourcenar, Marguerite. *Fleuve profond, sombre rivière: Les "Negro Spirituals" comentaires et traductions.* Paris: Gallimard, 1964.

Each volume of *The Papers of Martin Luther King, Jr.* includes a Calendar of Documents that provides an extensive list of significant King-related material for the period. The calendar includes research material relevant to the study of King's life and work that was not selected for publication in the volume. Because the content of King's sermon file is historically significant, the calendar for this volume includes all documents found in this file, except those published in the volume, as well as other documents related to King's sermon preparation and delivery. It is generated from an online database maintained at the King Project's office.

Owing to space constraints, full bibliographic citations are not provided in editorial annotations: instead, complete references for individual documents mentioned in headnotes, footnotes, and the Introduction are found only in the calendar. The majority of the calendar is composed of significant King-authored homiletic material such as speeches, sermons and sermon outlines, and articles. It also contains selected correspondence, school papers, and other ephemera regarding King's ministry. This calendar contains over four dozen undated sermon outlines that have been assigned range dates corresponding to the years of King's graduate education (1948–1954). The calendar also includes citations to documents that became available after the publication of previous volumes of *The Papers of Martin Luther King, Jr.* covering that time period. Only those photographs or illustrations that appear in the volume are listed in the calendar. They are indicated by boldface type.

Each calendar entry provides essential bibliographic information about the document. Italics and brackets indicate information determined by the editors based on evidence contained in the document; when the evidence is not conclusive question marks are used as well. Each entry adheres to the following format:

Date	Author (Affiliation). Document Title. Date. Place of origin. (Physical description codes) Number of pages. (Notes.) Archival location. King Papers Project identification number.
8/2/1953	King, Martin Luther, Jr. "God's Kingdom First." [*8/2/1953*]. [*Atlanta, Ga.*](TD) 3 pp. CSKC: Sermon file, folder 112, "First Things First." 530802-002.

DATE. The date in the left margin is intended to aid the reader in looking up specific documents. Complete date information is provided in the entry. In those cases where the original bears no date the editors have assigned one and enclosed it in brackets. Those documents bearing range dates are arranged after precisely dated documents, unless logic dictates another order. The date of photographs is presented without brackets if the donor provided a date. The date of published or printed papers is the date of publication or public release rather than the date of composition.

AUTHOR. A standardized form of an individual's name (based on *Anglo-American Cataloging Rules*, 2d ed.) is provided in both the author and title fields. Forms of address are omitted unless necessary for identification, such as a woman who used only her husband's name. For photographs, the photographer is considered the author. Since King's script is distinctive, his unsigned handwritten documents are identified as of certain authorship. Institutional authorship is provided when appropriate.

AFFILIATION. Affiliation information is provided if the author wrote in his or her capacity as an official of an organization. No brackets or italics have been used in the affiliation field (except for periodical titles).

TITLE. Titles enclosed in quotation marks have been drawn directly from the document with minor emendations of punctuation, capitalization, and spelling for clarity. Phrases such as "Letter to," "Photo of," are used to create titles for otherwise untitled documents; in such titles, sentence style capitalization is used and names are standardized. The use of the word "delivered" in the titles of speeches and sermons connotes an audio version. Published versions of earlier speeches contain the date of delivery in the title.

PLACE OF ORIGIN. This field identifies where the document was completed or, in the case of a published document, the place of publication. If the document does not contain the place of origin and the information can be obtained, it is provided in brackets; such information is offered only for documents written by King or those written on his behalf.

PHYSICAL DESCRIPTION. This field describes the format of presentation, type of document, version of document, and character of the signature (see List of Abbreviations, pp. 61–63). Documents that consist of several formats are listed with the predominant one first.

LENGTH. The number of pages or the duration of a recording is indicated.

NOTES. In this optional field, miscellaneous information pertaining to the document is provided. This information includes enclosures to a letter, routing information, (e.g., "Copy to King"), and remarks concerning the legibility of the document or King's or his professors' authorship of marginalia. For tapes, information about the media used is also indicated in this field.

ARCHIVAL LOCATION. The location of the original document is identified using standard abbreviations based on the Library of Congress's codes for libraries and archives (see List of Abbreviations, pp. 61–63). When available, box numbers or other archival location identification are provided. Titles of file folders in the sermon file are enclosed in quotation marks if written by King. Many of the documents published and referred to in this volume, including all sermon file documents, with the archival codes CSKC, CSKCH, and MLKJP-GAMK: Vault are part of a large collection of King material acquired in June 2006 by Morehouse College in Atlanta, Georgia.

IDENTIFICATION NUMBER. The nine-digit identification number, based on the date, uniquely identifies the document.

1937	Fosdick, Harry Emerson. "Why Worship?" From: *Successful Christian Living: Sermons on Christianity Today*. New York: Harper & Brothers, 1937, pp. 165–175. (PHD) 11 pp. CSKC: Sermon file, folder 62, Worship at Its Best. 370000-003.	Calendar

1937 · Fosdick, Harry Emerson. "Why Worship?" From: *Successful Christian Living: Sermons on Christianity Today*. New York: Harper & Brothers, 1937, pp. 165–175. (PHD) 11 pp. CSKC: Sermon file, folder 62, Worship at Its Best. 370000-003.

1937 · Fosdick, Harry Emerson. *Successful Christian Living: Sermons on Christianity Today.* New York: Harper & Brothers, 1937, pp. 7–8. (PHD) 2 pp. CSKC: Sermon file, folder 4, "Worship." 370000-011.

1937 · **Fosdick, Harry Emerson. *Successful Christian Living: Sermons on Christianity Today.* New York: Harper & Brothers, 1937, pp. 80–81. (PHD) (Marginal comments by King.) CSKCH. 370000-011.**

10/17/1940 · King, Martin Luther (Atlanta Missionary Baptist Association, Inc.). Moderator's Annual Address. 10/17/1940. From: *Minutes of the 36th Annual Session of the Atlanta Missionary Baptist Association, 10/15/1940–10/17/1940.* Cartersville, Ga. (PD) 3 pp. CKFC. 401017-000.

1941 · Leo XIII, Pope. *Immortale Dei: The Christian Constitution of States.* 1941. New York: Paulist Press, 1941. (PD) 33 pp. CSKC: Sermon file, folder 163. 410000-010.

5/1941 · Buffington, Willie L. (Crozer Theological Seminary). "Worship: A selected bibliography." 5/1941. Chester, Pa. (TD) 15 pp. CSKC: Sermon file, folder 161, Worship. 410500-000.

1943 · Muste, A. J. (Abraham Johannes). *What the Bible Teaches About Freedom: A Message to the Negro Churches.* New York: Fellowship of Reconciliation, [*1943*]. (PHD) 14 pp. CSKC: Sermon file, folder 165. 430000-017.

1944 · **Luccock, Halford Edward. *In the Minister's Workshop.* New York: Abingdon-Cokesbury Press, 1944, pp. 38–39. (PHD) (Marginal comments by King.) CSKCH. 440000-006.**

1/13/1946 · McCracken, Robert J. (Robert James). (Riverside Church). "On Beginning from Within." 1/13/1946. New York, N.Y. (PD) 10 pp. CSKC: Sermon file, folder 165. 460113-000.

3/26/1946 · King, Martin Luther, Jr. (Morehouse College). Examination answers, Bible. 3/26/1946. [*Atlanta, Ga.*] (AHDS) 8 pp. (Marginal comments by George D. Kelsey.) CSKC: Sermon file, folder 156. 460326-000.

12/1946 · Morrison, A. Cressy. "Seven Reasons Why a Scientist Believes in God." 12/1946. New York, N.Y. From: *Reader's Digest*, December 1946, pp. 11–14. (PD) 4 pp. CSKC: Sermon file, folder 165. 461200-000.

12/3/1946 · King, Martin Luther, Jr. (Morehouse College). Examination answers, Bible. 12/3/1946. [*Atlanta, Ga.*] (AHDS) 6 pp. (Marginal comments by George D. Kelsey.) CSKC: Sermon file, folder 24, Bible 252. 461203-000.

1947 · Hiltner, Seward. *How to Make an Evangelistic Call.* New York: Federal Council of the Churches of Christ in America, 1947. (PD) 24 pp. CSKC: Sermon file, folder 25. 470000-026.

1947 · King, Martin Luther, Jr. Notes on Foreword by H. H. McConnell to *How to Make an Evangelistic Call.* [*1947*]. (AD) 1 p. CSKC: Sermon file, folder 25. 470000-013.

1947 · **Niebuhr, Reinhold. *Moral Man and Immoral Society: A Study in Ethics and Politics.* New York: Charles Scribner's Sons, 1947. (PHD) (Marginal comments by King.) CSKCH. 470000-025.**

3/2/1947 · Bonnell, John Sutherland. "Courage to Face Life, a radio address." 3/2/1947. Copy in: *National Vespers*, 1946–1947. New York, N.Y. (TTa) 5 pp. CSKC: Sermon file, folder 100, "Sermons by Other Ministers." 470302-000.

4/27/1947 · McCracken, Robert J. (Robert James). (Riverside Church). "Why Does God Hide Himself?" 4/27/1947. New York, N.Y. (PHD) 10 pp. CSKC: Sermon file, folder 165. 470427-000.

5/1947 · Heimsath (Morehouse College). Examination questions, American Literature. 5/1947. (TD) 1 p. CSKC: Sermon file, folder 165. 470500-005.

5/23/1947 · King, Martin Luther, Jr. (Morehouse College). Examination answers, Bible. 5/23/1947. [*Atlanta, Ga.*] (AHD) 6 pp. (Marginal comments by George D. Kelsey.) CSKC: Sermon file, folder 24, Bible 252. 470523-000.

9/1946–5/1947 · [*Kelsey, George D.*] (Morehouse College). Study questions, Bible. [*9/1946–5/1947*]. (THD) 6 pp. (Marginal comments by King.) CSKC: Sermon file, folder 24, Bible 252. 470500-002.

9/1946–5/1947 · King, Martin Luther, Jr. (Morehouse College). Class notes, Bible. [*9/1946–5/1947*]. [*Atlanta, Ga.*] (AD) 35 pp. CSKC: Sermon file, folder 24, Bible 252. 470500-003.

9/1946–5/1947 · King, Martin Luther, Jr. (Morehouse College). Examination answers, Bible.

[*9/1946–5/1947*]. [*Atlanta, Ga.*] (AHD) 9 pp. (Marginal comments by George D. Kelsey.) CSKC: Sermon file, folder 24, Bible 252. 470500-004.

9/1945–5/1947   King, Martin Luther, Jr. (Morehouse College). Notes, Definitions of French terms. [*9/1945–5/1947*]. [*Atlanta, Ga.*] (AD) 1 p. CSKC: Sermon file, folder 163. 470500-007.

10/1947   Whitman, Howard. "Let's Help Them Marry Young." 10/1947. New York, N.Y. From: *Reader's Digest*, October 1947, pp. 2–4. (PD) 3 pp. CSKC: Sermon file, folder 165. 471000-001.

11/1947   Cohn, David L. "Marrying Is Not Marriage." 11/1947. New York, N.Y. From: *Reader's Digest*, November 1947, pp. 71–73. (PD) 3 pp. CSKC: Sermon file, folder 165. 471100-000.

1948   **Photo of Martin Luther King, Jr. and Martin Luther King. [*1948*]. [*Atlanta, Ga.*] (Ph) 1 p. CKFC. 480000-014.**

1948   Schmitz, Charles H. *Hints on Religious Music for Radio*. New York: Northern Baptist Convention, 1948. (PD) 24 pp. CSKC: Sermon file, folder 162, Minister's Use of Radio. 480000-023.

1948   State Council for a Pennsylvania FEPC. "It's Your Law, too: Fair Employment Practices Commission." [*1948*]. Philadelphia, Pa. (PD) 6 pp. CSKC: Sermon file, folder 163. 480000-042.

1948   Advertisement, "A Business Primer for Negroes." [*1948*]. New York, N.Y. (PHD) 8 pp. CSKC: Sermon file, folder 90. 480000-043.

1/18/1948   Sockman, Ralph W. "Prepared for the Best, a radio address." 1/18/1948. New York, N.Y. Copy in: *National Radio Pulpit*, 1947–1948. (TTa) 6 pp. CSKC: Sermon file, folder 36, "Sermon Notes." 480118-000.

1/19/1948   Kelsey, George D. "The Present Crisis in Negro Ministerial Education." 1/19/1948. Atlanta, Ga. (TD) 4 pp. CSKC: Sermon file, folder 36, "Sermon Notes." 480119-000.

2/15/1948   Bonnell, John Sutherland. "Faith that Moves Mountains, a radio address." 2/15/1948. New York, N.Y. Copy in: *National Vespers*, 1948. (TTa) 5 pp. CSKC: Sermon file, folder 36, "Sermon Notes." 480215-000.

2/29/1948   Sheen, Fulton J. (Catholic University of America). "Repression and Self-Expression." 2/29/1948. Washington, D.C. From: *The Catholic Hour*, 29 February 1948. (PHD) 8 pp. (Marginal comments by King.) CSKC: Sermon file, folder 165. 480229-000.

3/4/1948   Nix, William M. (Morehouse College). Form letter to Seniors. 3/4/1948. Atlanta, Ga. (TLS) 4 pp. (Includes enclosures.) CSKC: Sermon file, folder 165. 480304-000.

3/7/1948   Bonnell, John Sutherland. "Prayer—A Cosmic Power, a radio address." 3/7/1948. New York, N.Y. Copy in: *National Vespers*, 1947–1948. (THTa) 5 pp. CSKC: Sermon file, folder 36, "Sermon Notes." 480307-000.

3/7/1948   Sockman, Ralph W. "Hunger that Means Happiness, a radio address." 3/7/1948. New York, N.Y. Copy in: *National Radio Pulpit*, 1947–1948. (TTa) 5 pp. CSKC: Sermon file, folder 165. 480307-001.

3/7/1948   Sheen, Fulton J. (Catholic University of America). "The Psychology of Conversion." 3/7/1948. Washington, D.C. From: *The Catholic Hour*, 7 March 1948. (PD) 8 pp. CSKC: Sermon file, folder 165. 480307-003.

3/14/1948   Bonnell, John Sutherland. "The Source of Inner Strength, a radio address." 3/14/1948. New York, N.Y. Copy in: *National Vespers*, 1948. (TTa) 5 pp. CSKC: Sermon file, folder 36, "Sermon Notes." 480314-000.

3/14/1948   Sheen, Fulton J. (Catholic University of America). "The Effects of Conversion." 3/14/1948. Washington, D.C. From: *The Catholic Hour*, 14 March 1948. (PD) 8 pp. CSKC: Sermon file, folder 165. 480314-001.

3/21/1948   Bonnell, John Sutherland. "Palm Branches and a Cross, a radio address." 3/21/1948. New York, N.Y. Copy in: *National Vespers*, 1948. (TTa) 5 pp. CSKC: Sermon file, folder 165. 480321-000.

3/21/1948   Sockman, Ralph W. "The Lord of All Being, a radio address." 3/21/1948. New York, N.Y. Copy in: *National Radio Pulpit*, 1947–1948. (TTa) 5 pp. CSKC: Sermon file, folder 165. 480321-001.

3/21/1948   Sheen, Fulton J. (Catholic University of America). "The Theology of Conversion." 3/21/1948. Washington, D.C. From: *The Catholic Hour*, 21 March 1948. (PHD) 8 pp. (Marginal comments by King.) CSKC: Sermon file, folder 165. 480321-002.

4/11/1948   Sockman, Ralph W. "What the World Wants Most, a radio address." 4/11/1948.

New York, N.Y. Copy in: *National Radio Pulpit*, 1947–1948. (TTa) 5 pp. CSKC: Sermon file, folder 36, "Sermon Notes." 480411-000.

5/30/1948   Sockman, Ralph W. "Lest We Forget, a radio address." 5/30/1948. New York, N.Y. Copy in: *National Radio Pulpit*, 1947–1948. (TTa) 5 pp. CSKC: Sermon file, folder 36, "Sermon Notes." 480530-000.

9/1944–5/1948   King, Christine. "Religion: The Characters of Samuel, Saul, David, and Solomon." [*9/1944–5/1948*]. (THD) 3 pp. CSKC: Sermon file, folder 24, Bible 252. 480500-000.

8/1948   Putnam, Nina Wilcox. "Divorce Is No Solution." [*8/1948*]. New York, N.Y. From: *Reader's Digest*, August 1948, pp. 60–62. (PD) 3 pp. CSKC: Sermon file, folder 165. 480800-001.

8/22/1948   De Kalb Co. (Ga.) Marriage certificate for Samuel Preston Long, Jr., and Ruth Argenis Bussey. 8/22/1948. De Kalb County, Ga. (TFmS) 1 p. (Filed 11/6/1949.) SLP. 480822-000.

8/23/1948–
9/4/1948   World Council of Churches. Proceedings, "First assembly of the World Council of Churches." 8/23/1948-9/4/1948. New York, N.Y. (THD) 58 pp. (Marginal comments by King.) CSKC: Sermon file, folder 161, Worship. 480904-001.

9/14/1948–
11/24/1948   King, Martin Luther, Jr. (Crozer Theological Seminary). Class notes, Orientation for juniors. [*9/14/1948–11/24/1948*]. [*Chester, Pa.*] (AD) 20 pp. MLKP-MBU: Box 115. 481124-003.

**9/14/1948–
11/24/1948**   **King, Martin Luther, Jr. (Crozer Theological Seminary). Class notes, Introduction to the Old Testament, including Palestine map. [*9/14/1948–11/24/1948*]. [*Chester, Pa.*] (AD) 60 pp. CSKC: Sermon file, folder 42, "Old Testament." 481124-005.**

**9/14/1948–
11/24/1948**   **King, Martin Luther, Jr. (Crozer Theological Seminary). "Preaching Ministry." [*9/14/1948–11/24/1948*]. [*Chester, Pa.*] (AHDS) 6 pp. (Marginal comments by Robert E. Keighton.) CSKC: Sermon file, folder 36, "Sermon Notes." 481124-006.**

1949   Kells, Robert H. Cross Reference Index for Sermon classification index. 1949. Mt. Rainier, Md. (PD) 12 pp. CSKC: Sermon file, folder 164. 490000-017.

1949   **King, Martin Luther, Jr. "Civilization's Great Need." [*1949*]. (TD) 2 pp. CSKC: Sermon file, folder 119, "Civilization's Greatest Need" / "Faith in Man." 490000-031.**

11/30/1948–
2/16/1949   King, Martin Luther, Jr. (Crozer Theological Seminary). Class notes, Preparation of the Sermon. [*11/30/1948–2/16/1949*]. [*Chester, Pa.*] (AD) 11 pp. MLKP-MBU: Box 113. 490216-000.

11/30/1948–
2/16/1949   King, Martin Luther, Jr. (Crozer Theological Seminary). "The Danger in Worshipping Jesus," Sermon introduction I. [*11/30/1948–2/16/1949*]. [*Chester, Pa.*] (AD) 2 pp. MLKP-MBU: Box 113. 490216-001.

11/30/1948–
2/16/1949   King, Martin Luther, Jr. (Crozer Theological Seminary). "The Danger in Worshipping Jesus," Sermon introduction II. [*11/30/1948–2/16/1949*]. [*Chester, Pa.*] (AD) 1 p. MLKP-MBU: Box 113. 490216-024.

11/30/1948–
2/16/1949   King, Martin Luther, Jr. (Crozer Theological Seminary). Class notes I, Great Theologians. [*11/30/1948–2/16/1949*]. [*Chester, Pa.*] (AD) 21 pp. MLKP-MBU: Box 115. 490216-011.

11/30/1948–
2/16/1949   King, Martin Luther, Jr. (Crozer Theological Seminary). Class notes II, Great Theologians. [*11/30/1948–2/16/1949*]. [*Chester, Pa.*] (AD) 7 pp. MLKP-MBU: Box 115. 490216-014.

11/30/1948–
2/16/1949   King, Martin Luther, Jr. (Crozer Theological Seminary?). Sermon Sketches III. [*11/30/1948–2/16/1949?*]. [*Chester, Pa.?*] (AHD) 2 pp. (Marginal comments by Robert E. Keighton.) CSKC: Sermon file, folder 36, "Sermon Notes." 490216-025.

3/1949   Thurman, Howard. "The Commitment." 3/1949. San Francisco, Calif. From: *The Growing Edge*, March 1949. (PD) 3 pp. ABPC. 490300-001.

3/3/1949   King, Martin Luther, Jr. "Men's Day Sermon." [*3/3/1949*]. (AD) 2 pp. CSKC: Sermon file, folder 50, Sermons Not Preached. 490303-000.

5/22/1949   Sockman, Ralph W. "Taking Our Chances, a radio address." 5/22/1949. New York, N.Y. Copy in: *National Radio Pulpit*, 1948–1949. (THTa) 5 pp. CSKC: Sermon file, folder 100, "Sermons by Other Ministers." 490522-000.

7/1949   Bosley, Harold A. "We Believe in the Church." 7/1949. Chicago, Ill. From: *The Pulpit* (July 1949): 159–160. (PD) 2 pp. CSKC: Sermon file, folder 49, "Sermon Notes." 490700-001.

9/1949   Religious Book Club. *Bulletin* 22. 9/1949. New York, N.Y. (PHDf) 5 pp. CSKC: Sermon file, folder 36, "Sermon Notes." 490900-004.

9/13/1949– 11/23/1949   King, Martin Luther, Jr. (Crozer Theological Seminary). "The Place of Reason and Experience in Finding God." [*9/13/1949–11/23/1949*]. [*Chester, Pa.*] (THD) 8 pp. (Marginal comments by George W. Davis.) MLKP-MBU: Box 112. 491123-003.

9/13/1949– 11/23/1949   King, Martin Luther, Jr. (Crozer Theological Seminary). Class notes, Christian Theology for Today. [*9/13/1949–11/23/1949*]. [*Chester, Pa.*] (AD) 80 pp. MLKP-MBU: Box 113. 491123-006.

9/13/1949– 11/23/1949   King, Martin Luther, Jr. (Crozer Theological Seminary). Notes, "Worship." [*9/13/1949–11/23/1949*]. [*Chester, Pa.*] (AD) 11 pp. CSKC: Sermon file, folder 161, Worship. 491123-010.

1/27/1950   Crozer Theological Seminary. "Student chapel order of service." 1/27/1950. (THD) 2 pp. CSKC: Sermon file, folder 118, "Sermon Material." 500127-000.

11/29/1949– 2/15/1950   [*Davis, George W. (Washington)*] (Crozer Theological Seminary). "Bibliography and assignments in History of Christian Thought." [*11/29/1949–2/15/1950*]. (THD) 8 pp. (Marginal comments by King.) MLKP-MBU: Box 115. 500215-024.

11/29/1949– 2/15/1950   King, Martin Luther, Jr. (Crozer Theological Seminary). Notes, Development of Christian ideas. [*11/29/1949–2/15/1950*]. [*Chester, Pa.*] (TAHD) 46 pp. JOG. 500215-027.

11/29/1949– 2/15/1950   King, Martin Luther, Jr. (Crozer Theological Seminary). Class notes, Christian Theology for Today. [*11/29/1949–2/15/1950*]. [*Chester, Pa.*] (TAD) 28 pp. MLKP-MBU: Box 106. 500215-030.

11/29/1949– 2/15/1950   King, Martin Luther, Jr. (Crozer Theological Seminary). "An order for the baptism of adults." [*11/29/1949–2/15/1950*]. [*Chester, Pa.*] (AHDS) 4 pp. (Marginal comments by Robert E. Keighton.) CSKC: Sermon file, folder 36, "Sermon Notes." 500215-038.

5/1950   Religious Book Club. *Bulletin* 23. 5/1950. New York, N.Y. (PD) 6 pp. CSKC: Sermon file, folder 163. 500500-003.

9/1950   [*Crozer Theological Seminary*]. "Syllabus in Christian education." [*9/1950*]. (TD) 1 p. (Enclosed in 500908-000.) CSKC. 500900-003.

9/1950   [*Crozer Theological Seminary*]. "Syllabus in applied Christianity." [*9/1950*]. (TD) 2 pp. (Enclosed in 500908-000.) CSKC. 500900-005.

9/1950   [*Crozer Theological Seminary*]. "Syllabus for the history of Christianity." [*9/1950*]. (THD) 3 pp. (Enclosed in 500908-000.) CSKC. 500900-006.

9/1950   [*Crozer Theological Seminary*]. "Syllabus in Christian theology." [*9/1950*]. (TD) 2 pp. (Enclosed in 500908-000.) CSKC. 500900-007.

9/1950   [*Crozer Theological Seminary*]. "Syllabus in New Testament." [*9/1950*]. (TD) 1 p. (Enclosed in 500908-000.) CSKC. 500900-008.

9/1950   [*Crozer Theological Seminary*]. "Syllabus in Old Testament." [*9/1950*]. (TD) 1 p. (Enclosed in 500908-000.) CSKC. 500900-009.

9/1950   [*Crozer Theological Seminary*]. "Syllabus in preaching and worship." [*9/1950*]. (TD) 1 p. (Enclosed in 500908-000.) CSKC. 500900-013.

9/7/1950– 9/8/1950   Crozer Theological Seminary. "Comprehensive examinations." [*9/7/1950– 9/8/1950*]. Chester, Pa. (TD) 2 pp. (Contains enclosures 500900-003, -005, -006, -007, -008, -009, -013.) CSKC. 500908-000.

11/20/1950   [*Keighton, Robert E. (Robert Elwood)*] (Crozer Theological Seminary). Examination, "Minister's Use of the Radio." 11/20/1950. (TD) 1 p. CSKC: Sermon file, folder 162, Minister's Use of Radio. 501120-000.

9/12/1950– 11/22/1950   King, Martin Luther, Jr. (Crozer Theological Seminary). Class notes, Religious Development of Personality. [*9/12/1950–11/22/1950*]. [*Chester, Pa.*] (AD) 22 pp. MLKP-MBU: Box 106. 501122-003.

9/12/1950– 11/22/1950   [*Davis, George W. (Washington)*] (Crozer Theological Seminary). "Selected bibliography, Religious Development of Personality." [*9/12/1950–11/22/1950*]. (THD) 2 pp. (Marginal comments by King.) MLKP-MBU: Box 106. 501122-008.

9/12/1950– 11/22/1950   King, Martin Luther, Jr. (Crozer Theological Seminary). Class notes, Minister's Use of the Radio. [*9/12/1950–11/22/1950*]. [*Chester, Pa.*] (AD) 4 pp. CSKC: Sermon file, folder 162, Minister's Use of Radio. 501122-012.

9/12/1950– 11/22/1950   Bloomquist, Earl W. "Religious broadcasts." [*9/12/1950–11/22/1950*]. (TD) 7 pp. CSKC: Sermon file, folder 162, Minister's Use of Radio. 501122-013.

9/25/1950– 2/3/1951   King, Martin Luther, Jr. (University of Pennsylvania). Notes, "Problems of esthetics." [*9/25/1950–2/3/1951*]. [*Philadelphia, Pa.*] (AHD) 15 pp. CSKC: Sermon file, folder 157, "Aesthetics." 510203-005.

9/25/1950–
2/3/1951

King, Martin Luther, Jr. (University of Pennsylvania). Notes, "The Relation between esthetics and science." [*9/25/1950–2/3/1951*]. [*Philadelphia, Pa.*] (AD) 12 pp. CSKC: Sermon file, folder 157, "Aesthetics." 510203-006.

11/28/1950–
2/15/1951

King, Martin Luther, Jr. (Crozer Theological Seminary). Class notes, Philosophy of Religion. [*11/28/1950–2/15/1951*]. [*Chester, Pa.*] (AD) 75 pp. MLKP-MBU: Box 113. 510215-001.

4/1951

"The Tempest." 4/1951. From: *Spelman Messenger*, April 1951, pp. 19–20. (PD) 2 pp. CSKC: Sermon file, folder 14, "Transformed Non-Conformist." 510400-000.

4/15/1951

Starr, Edward C. (Crozer Theological Seminary). "The Pastor and His Reference Library." 4/15/1951. (TD) 3 pp. CSKC: Sermon file, folder 154. 510415-000.

9/1948–5/1951

King, Martin Luther, Jr. (Crozer Theological Seminary). "The Ministry As It Looks to Me." [*9/1948–5/1951*]. [*Chester, Pa.*] (AD) 1 p. CSKC: Sermon file, folder 100, "Sermons by Other Ministers." 510500-038.

9/1948–5/1951

King, Martin Luther, Jr. (Crozer Theological Seminary?). "The Philosophy of Life Undergirding Christianity and the Christian Ministry," Outline. [*9/1948–5/1951?*]. [*Chester, Pa.?*] (AD) 1 p. CSKC: Sermon file, folder 100, "Sermons by Other Ministers." 510500-039.

9/1948–5/1951

The Philosophy of Life Undergirding Christianity and the Christian Ministry. [*9/1948–5/1951?*]. (AD) 1 p. CSKC: Sermon file, folder 100, "Sermons by Other Ministers." 510500-057.

9/1948–5/1951

King, Martin Luther, Jr. [*Crozer Theological Seminary?*]. "Three Stages of Life." [*9/1948–5/1951?*]. [*Chester, Pa.?*] (AD) 1 p. CSKC: Sermon file, folder 100, "Sermons by Other Ministers." 510500-043.

9/1948–5/1951

"Orders for Bently & Simon pulpit robes." [*9/1948–5/1951*]. Chester, Pa. (PTD) 1 p. CSKC: Sermon file, folder 163. 510500-078.

9/1948–5/1951

"Unrealized Sufficiencies." [*9/1948–5/1951*]. (THD) 7 pp. CSKC: Sermon file, folder 108, Unrealized Sufficiencies. 510500-079.

11/28/1950–
5/4/1951

[*Davis, George W. (Washington)*] (Crozer Theological Seminary). Bibliography and term assignments, Philosophy of Religion and Advanced Philosophy of Religion. [*11/28/1950–5/4/1951*]. (THD) 4 pp. (Marginal comments by King.) MLKP-MBU: Box 113. 510504-000.

2/20/1951–
5/4/1951

Smith, Kenneth L. (Crozer Theological Seminary). Syllabus, Christianity and Society. [*2/20/1951–5/4/1951*]. (THD) 4 pp. (Marginal comments by King.) MLKP-MBU: Box 112. 510504-005.

2/20/1951–
5/4/1951

"The ethical implications of the atomic bomb," Paper for Christianity and Society. [*2/20/1951–5/4/1951*]. (THD) 2 pp. MLKP-MBU: Box 112. 510504-015.

2/20/1951–
5/4/1951

King, Martin Luther, Jr. (Crozer Theological Seminary). Class notes, Christian Social Philosophy II. [*2/20/1951–5/4/1951*]. [*Chester, Pa.*] (AD) 53 pp. CSKC. 510504-024.

2/20/1951–
5/4/1951

King, Martin Luther, Jr. (Crozer Theological Seminary). "Jacques Maritain." [*2/20/1951–5/4/1951*]. [*Chester, Pa.*] (TD) 2 pp. CSKC: Sermon file, folder 163. 510504-028.

2/20/1951–
5/4/1951

King, Martin Luther, Jr. (Crozer Theological Seminary?). Notes on ethics. [*2/20/1951–5/4/1951?*]. [*Chester, Pa.?*] (AD) 4 pp. CSKC: Sermon file, folder 158, "Theological Integration." 510504-038.

2/20/1951–
5/4/1951

King, Martin Luther, Jr. (Crozer Theological Seminary). Notes, "Theological presuppositions of Christian social philosophy." [*2/20/1951–5/4/1951*]. [*Chester, Pa.*] (AD) 2 pp. CSKC: Sermon file, folder 158, "Theological Integration." 510504-039.

2/20/1951–
5/4/1951

King, Martin Luther, Jr. (Crozer Theological Seminary). "Theological integration." [*2/20/1951–5/4/1951*]. [*Chester, Pa.*] (AD) 10 pp. CSKC: Sermon file, folder 158, "Theological Integration." 510504-040.

**2/20/1951–
5/4/1951**

King, Martin Luther, Jr. (Crozer Theological Seminary?). Index of Sermon Topics. [*2/20/1951–5/4/1951?*]. [*Chester, Pa.?*] (AFm) 6 pp. CSKC: Sermon file, folder 118, "Sermon Material." 510504-043.

6/1951

Religious Book Club. *Bulletin* 24. 6/1951. New York, N.Y. (PD) 9 pp. CSKC: Sermon file, folder 163. 510600-006.

7/1951

Will, James E. "Men Who Live Differently." 7/1951. From: *The Pulpit* 22 (July 1951): 5–7. (PD) 3 pp. CSKC: Sermon file, folder 14: "Transformed Non-Conformist." 510700-003.

10/1951

The Pulpit 22. 10/1951. Chicago, Ill. (PD) 32 pp. CSKC: Sermon file, folder 100, "Sermons by Other Ministers." 511000-001.

1/13/1952   The Billy Graham Evangelistic Team. "Revival in our time." 1/13/1952. Washington, D.C. (PHD) 8 pp. CSKC: Sermon file, folder 163. 520113-000.

3/11/1952   [*DeWolf, L. Harold (Lotan Harold)*] (Boston University). Examination questions, Religious Teaching of the New Testament. 3/11/1952. (TD) 1 p. CSKCH. 520311-000.

3/30/1952   Meek, Frederick M. "How Are We to Live in Days Like These? Fulfill the Disciplines of the Faith, A sermon preached in the Old South Church in Boston." 3/30/1952. (PD) 7 pp. CSKC: Sermon file, folder 100, "Sermons by Other Ministers." 520330-000.

4/4/1952   [*DeWolf, L. Harold (Lotan Harold)*] (Boston University). Examination questions, Religious Teaching of the New Testament. 4/4/1952. (THD) 1 p. (Marginal comments by King.) CSKCH. 520404-001.

4/7/1952   **Scott, Coretta. Inscription to Martin Luther King, Jr. 4/7/1952. (ALS) 1 p. CSKCH. 520407-000.**

5/13/1952   [*DeWolf, L. Harold (Lotan Harold)*] (Boston University). Examination questions, Religious Teaching of the New Testament. 5/13/1952. (THD) 1 p. (Marginal comments by King.) CSKCH. 520513-000.

1/23/1952–   King, Martin Luther, Jr. (Boston University). Notes on *Christianity and Our World* by
5/16/1952   John C. Bennett. [*1/23/1952–5/16/1952*]. [*Boston, Mass.*] (AD) 1 p. CSKC: Sermon file, folder 118, "Sermon Material." 520516-018.

6/11/1952   National Council of the Churches of Christ in the United States of America. "The Churches and Segregation: An Official Statement and Resolution Adopted by the General Board." 6/11/1952. New York, N.Y. (PD) 4 pp. CSKCH. 520611-000.

7/14/1952   King, Martin Luther, Jr. Letter to Coretta Scott. [*7/14/1952*]. Atlanta, Ga. (ALS) 2 pp. CSKC. 520714-000.

9/28/1952   Elderveld, Peter. "Peace Amid War, a radio message." [*9/28/1952*]. From: *Back to the God Hour*, 28 September 1952. Chicago, Ill. (PD) 12 pp. CSKC: Sermon file, folder 100, "Sermons by Other Ministers." 520928-000.

10/19/1952   Meek, Frederick M. "The Hindrances to the Christian Life, A sermon preached in the Old South Church in Boston." 10/19/1952. (PD) 7 pp. CSKC: Sermon file, folder 100, "Sermons by Other Ministers." 521019-000.

10/26/1952   Meek, Frederick M. "The Protestant Witness, A sermon preached in the Old South Church in Boston." 10/26/1952. (PD) 8 pp. CSKC: Sermon file, folder 97. 521026-000.

10/26/1952   People's Baptist Church. Program, "Fifty-ninth anniversary." 10/26/1952. Portsmouth, N.H. (PD) 4 pp. PBC-NhPoAA. 521026-001.

11/30/1952   Meek, Frederick M. "The Christian and His Occupation, A sermon preached in the Old South Church in Boston." 11/30/1952. (PD) 11 pp. CSKC: Sermon file, folder 100, "Sermons by Other Ministers." 521130-001.

1/4/1953   Meek, Frederick M. "Our God Is Able, A sermon preached in the Old South Church in Boston." 1/4/1953. (PHD) 8 pp. (Marginal comments by King.) CSKC: Sermon file, folder 11, "Our God Is Able." 530104-000.

1/25/1953   Meek, Frederick M. "What Is Our Mission? A sermon preached in the Old South Church in Boston." 1/25/1953. (PHD) 8 pp. (Marginal comments by King.) CSKC. 530125-000.

9/22/1952–   King, Martin Luther, Jr. (Boston University?). Notecards on topics from Ezra and
1/28/1953   Nehemiah. [*9/22/1952–1/28/1953?*]. [*Boston, Mass.?*] (AD) 18 pp. CSKC. 530128-033.

9/22/1952–   King, Martin Luther, Jr. (Boston University?). Notecards on topics from Micah.
1/28/1953   [*9/22/1952–1/28/1953?*]. [*Boston, Mass.?*] (AD) 18 pp. CSKC. 530128-042.

9/22/1952–   King, Martin Luther, Jr. (Boston University?). Notecards on topics from I Samuel.
1/28/1953   [*9/22/1952–1/28/1953?*]. [*Boston, Mass.?*] (AD) 10 pp. CSKC. 530128-051.

2/8/1953   National Council of Churches in Christ in the United States of America. "That All May Be One, A message for Race Relations Sunday." 2/8/1953. New York: National Council of Churches in Christ in the United States of America (PD) 4 pp. CSKC: Sermon file, folder 143. 530208-000.

3/8/1953   Meek, Frederick M. "Institutions and Men, A sermon preached in the Old South Church in Boston." 3/8/1953. (PD) 8 pp. CSKC: Sermon file, folder 100, "Sermons by Other Ministers." 530308-000.

3/15/1953   Meek, Frederick M. "The Lord Hath Need of Him, A sermon preached in the Old South Church in Boston." 3/15/1953. (PD) 8 pp. CSKC: Sermon file, folder 100, "Sermons by Other Ministers." 530315-000.

3/29/1953   Meek, Frederick M. "Evading Responsibility, A sermon preached in the Old South

Church in Boston." 3/29/1953. (PD) 8 pp. CSKC: Sermon file, folder 100, "Sermons by Other Ministers." 530329-000.

4/5/1953   Meek, Frederick M. "On Loan to God, A sermon preached in the Old South Church in Boston." 4/5/1953. (PD) 7 pp. CSKC: Sermon file, folder 100, "Sermons by Other Ministers." 530405-000.

4/19/1953   Meek, Frederick M. "Strength in Adversity, A sermon preached in the Old South Church in Boston." 4/19/1953. (PHD) 8 pp. (Marginal comments by King.) CSKC. 530419-000.

2/4/1953–
5/22/1953   King, Martin Luther, Jr. (Boston University?). Notes on the free will controversy and other topics. [2/4/1953–5/22/1953?]. [*Boston, Mass.?*] (AD) 4 pp. MLKP-MBU: Box 114. 530522-023.

8/2/1953   King, Martin Luther, Jr. "God's Kingdom First." [*8/2/1953*]. [*Atlanta, Ga.*] (TD) 3 pp. CSKC: Sermon file, folder 112, "First Things First." 530802-002.

8/9/1953   King, Martin Luther, Jr. "Communism's Challenge to Christianity," Sermon outline. [*8/9/1953*]. [*Atlanta, Ga.*] (AD) 5 pp. CSKC: Sermon file, folder 10, "Communism's Challenge to Christianity." 530809-002.

10/4/1953   Meek, Frederick M. "Going Back to the Place of Vision, A sermon preached in the Old South Church in Boston." 10/4/1953. (PD) 6 pp. CSKC: Sermon file, folder 100, "Sermons by Other Ministers." 531004-000.

10/11/1953   Meek, Frederick M. "Perhaps Your God is Not Big Enough, A sermon preached in the Old South Church in Boston." 10/11/1953. (PHD) 8 pp. (Marginal comments by King.) CSKC: Sermon file, folder 11, "Our God Is Able." 531011-000.

1954   **Hamilton, James Wallace. *Horns and Halos in Human Nature.* Westwood, N.J.: Fleming H. Revell Co., 1954, p. 173. (PAHDS) (Inscription by Hamilton. Marginal comments by King.) CSKCH. 540000-031.**

1954   Hamilton, James Wallace. "That Fellow Who Stayed at Home." From: *Horns and Halos in Human Nature.* Westwood, N.J.: Fleming H. Revell, 1954, pp. 163-168. (PHDf) 4 pp. (Marginal comments by King.) CSKC: Sermon file, folder 60, "The Fellow Who Stayed at Home." 540000-023.

1954   Schuyler, George Samuel. "Views—Reviews." [*1954?*]. Pittsburgh, Pa. From: *Pittsburgh Courier.* (PD) 1 p. CSKC: Sermon file, folder 153, Speakers. 540000-029.

1953–1954   **King, Martin Luther, Jr. Sermon Notes and Outlines II. [*1953–1954*]. (AD) 3 pp. CSKC: Sermon file, folder 50, Sermons Not Preached. 540000-095.**

1/24/1954   **King, Martin Luther, Jr. "The Dimensions of a Complete Life," Sermon at Dexter Avenue Baptist Church. [*1/24/1954*]. [*Montgomery, Ala.*] (AD) 8 pp. CSKC: Sermon file, folder 21, "The Three Dimensions of a Complete Life." 540124-002.**

1/24/1954   King, Martin Luther, Jr. "The Three Dimensions of a Complete Life." [*1/24/1954*]. [*Montgomery, Ala.*] (AD) 8 pp. CSKC: Sermon file, folder 21, "The Three Dimensions of a Complete Life." 540124-003.

2/14/1954   National Council of Churches in Christ in the United States of America. "For . . . Healing of the Nations, A message for Race Relations Sunday." 2/14/1954. New York: National Council of Churches in Christ in the United States of America (PD) 4 pp. CSKC: Sermon file, folder 143. 540214-001.

2/21/1954   Meek, Frederick M. "A Letter to Christians, A sermon preached in the Old South Church in Boston." 2/21/1954. (PHD) 8 pp. (Marginal comments by King.) CSKC: Sermon file, folder 97. 540221-001.

5/2/1954   **King, Martin Luther, Jr. Acceptance Address at Dexter Avenue Baptist Church. [*5/2/1954*]. Montgomery, Ala. (AD) 2 pp. CSKC: Sermon file, folder 118, "Sermon Material." 540502-001.**

5/21/1954   Robinson, Jo Ann Gibson (Women's Political Council). Letter to W. (William) A. Gayle. 5/21/1954. Montgomery, Ala. (TLcS) 1 p. MCDA-AMC. 540521-000.

7/4/1954   [*Hughes, Hugh Price*]. "The City of Everywhere." [*7/4/1954*]. (TD) 2 pp. CSKC: Sermon file, folder 91, "Religion of Doing." 540704-001.

7/11/1954   King, Martin Luther, Jr. What Is Man? Sermon notes. [*7/11/1954*]. [*Montgomery, Ala.*] (AD) 2 pp. CSKC: Sermon file, folder 22, "What is Man?" 540711-001.

8/16/1954   Niles, D. T. "Evangelism," Address at the second assembly of the World Council of Churches." 8/16/1954. (THD) 7 pp. (Marginal comments by King.) CSKC: Sermon file, folder 8, "A Knock at Midnight." 540816-000.

8/18/1954   Malik, Charles. "Asia and Africa Ask Searching Questions," Address at the second assembly of the World Council of Churches. 8/18/1954. (TD) 8 pp. CSKC: Sermon file, folder 100, "Sermons by Other Ministers." 540818-000.

10/31/1954   Dexter Avenue Baptist Church. Program, "The installation of Rev. Martin L. King, Jr. as pastor of Dexter Avenue Baptist Church." 10/31/1954. Montgomery, Ala. (PHD) 11 pp. CKFC. 541031-000.

11/1954   King, Martin Luther, Jr. "Transformed Nonconformist," Sermon outline. [*11/1954*]. [*Montgomery, Ala.*] (AD) 3 pp. CSKC: Sermon file, folder 14, "Transformed Non-Conformist." 541100-003.

11/1954   King, Martin Luther, Jr. "Beyond Condemnation," Sermon notes. [*11/1954*]. [*Montgomery, Ala.*] (AD) 1 p. CSKC: Sermon file, folder 118, "Sermon Material." 541100-008.

11/28/1954   Thomas, Norman. "Civil Liberty: A Look Back and Ahead." 11/28/1954. New York, N.Y. From: *New York Times Magazine*, 28 November 1954. (PDf) 3 pp. CSKC: Sermon file, folder 153, Speakers. 541128-000.

10/13/1954–   First National Bank of Montgomery. Statement of account for Martin Luther King,
12/13/1954   Jr. 10/13/1954–12/13/1954. Montgomery, Ala. (PHFm) 49 pp. CSKC: Sermon file, folder 155, "Bank Statements." 541213-000.

1948–1954   Marshall, Peter. "Let's Keep Christmas." [*1948–1954*]. (TD) 2 pp. CSKC: Sermon file, folder 73, "New Wine in New Bottles." 540000-043.

1948–1954   King, Martin Luther, Jr. "A Moment of Difficult Decision." [*1948–1954*]. (AD) 1 p. CSKC: Sermon file, folder 71, "Creating the Abundant Life" / "A Moment of Difficult Decision." 540000-048.

1948–1954   King, Martin Luther, Jr. "Levels of Love," Sermon notes. [1948–1954]. (AD) 1 p. CSKC: Sermon file, folder 109, "Levels of Love." 540000-077.

1948–1954   American Negro culture. [*1948–1954*]. (TDf) 6 pp. CSKC: Sermon file, folder 124. 540000-087.

1948–1954   King, Martin Luther, Jr. "Religion and Peace of Soul." [*1948–1954*]. (AD) 4 pp. CSKC: Sermon file, folder 3, "Illustrations and Meditations." 540000-088.

1948–1954   Michigan Christian Advocate. "Truth Never Dies." [*1948–1954*]. (PD) 1 p. CSKC: Sermon file, folder 106, "Sermons." 540000-099.

1948–1954   King, Martin Luther, Jr. "When God Seems to Deceive Us." [*1948–1954*]. (AD) 1 p. CSKC: Sermon file, folder 118, "Sermon Material." 540000-100.

1948–1954   King, Martin Luther, Jr. "Conclusion." [*1948–1954*]. (AD) 3 pp. CSKC: Sermon file, folder 1, "Loving Your Enemies." 540000-103.

1948–1954   King, Martin Luther, Jr. "The Foolishness of Preaching." [*1948–1954*]. (AD) 2 pp. CSKC: Sermon file, folder 106, "Sermons." 540000-104.

1948–1954   King, Martin Luther, Jr. Notes on Philosophy and Religion. [*1948–1954*]. (AD) 12 pp. CSKC. 540000-105.

1948–1954   King, Martin Luther, Jr. "The Eternal Significance of Christ." [*1948–1954*]. (AD) 2 pp. CSKC: Sermon file, folder 11, "Our God Is Able." 540000-106.

1948–1954   King, Martin Luther, Jr. "Eternal Life." [*1948–1954*]. (AD) 2 pp. CSKC: Sermon file, folder 63, "Fleeing from God & When God Seems to Deceive Us." 540000-107.

1948–1954   King, Martin Luther, Jr. "The Eternality of God Versus the Temporality of Man." [*1948–1954*]. (AD) 1 p. CSKC: Sermon file, folder 50, Sermons Not Preached. 540000-108.

1948–1954   King, Martin Luther, Jr. "God's Relation to the World," Sermon notes. [*1948–1954*]. (AD) 2 pp. CSKC: Sermon file, folder 28, "God's Relation to the World." 540000-109.

1948–1954   King, Martin Luther, Jr. "Conditions for Entering the Kingdom." [*1948–1954*]. (ADf) 2 pp. CSKC: Sermon file, folder 116, Conditions for Entering the Kingdom. 540000-111.

1948–1954   King, Martin Luther, Jr. Man's Highest Value. [*1948–1954*]. (AD) 1 p. CSKC: Sermon file, folder 50, Sermons Not Preached. 540000-112.

1948–1954   King, Martin Luther, Jr. "Salvation through Despair" / "Life's Fulfillment through Despair." [*1948–1954*]. (AD) 1 p. CSKC: Sermon file, folder 50, Sermons Not Preached. 540000-113.

1948–1954   King, Martin Luther, Jr. "The Call of Christ" / "Follow Me." [*1948–1954*]. (AD) 1 p. CSKC: Sermon file, folder 50, Sermons Not Preached. 540000-114.

1948–1954   King, Martin Luther, Jr. A Man to Fill the Gap. [*1948–1954*]. (AD) 1 p. CSKC: Sermon file, folder 50, Sermons Not Preached. 540000-117.

1948–1954   King, Martin Luther, Jr. "Moral Absolutism." [*1948–1954*]. (AD) 1 p. CSKC: Sermon file, folder 50, Sermons Not Preached. 540000-118.

1948–1954   King, Martin Luther, Jr. "Success and Failure." [*1948–1954*]. (AD) 1 p. CSKC: Sermon file, folder 100, "Sermons by Other Ministers." 540000-121.

1948–1954   King, Martin Luther, Jr. "Be Ye Perfect." [*1948–1954*]. (AD) 1 p. CSKC: Sermon file, folder 50, Sermons Not Preached. 540000-123.

1948–1954   King, Martin Luther, Jr. Four Sorts of Men. [*1948–1954*]. (AD) 2 pp. CSKC: Sermon file, folder 100, "Sermons by Other Ministers." 540000-124.

1948–1954	King, Martin Luther, Jr. Sermon notes on Zacchaeus. [*1948–1954*]. (AD) 2 pp. CSKC. 540000-125.	Calendar
1948–1954	King, Martin Luther, Jr. "Unity." [*1948–1954*]. (AD) 4 pp. CSKC: Sermon file, folder 50, Sermons Not Preached. 540000-127.	
1948–1954	King, Martin Luther, Jr. "Propagandizing Religion." [*1948–1954*]. (AD) 2 pp. CSKC: Sermon file, folder 55, "Propagandizing Christianity." 540000-134.	
1948–1954	King, Martin Luther, Jr. Creating the Abundant Life, Sermon outline. [*1948–1954*]. (AD) 2 pp. CSKC: Sermon file, folder 71, "Creating the Abundant Life" / "A Moment of Difficult Decision." 540000-138.	
1948–1954	King, Martin Luther, Jr. Notes on "Be the Best of Whatever You Are" by Douglas Malloch. [*1948–1954*]. (AD) 1 p. CSKC: Sermon file, folder 71, "Creating the Abundant Life" / "A Moment of Difficult Decision." 540000-139.	
1948–1954	King, Martin Luther, Jr. Notes on Clarence Darrow. [*1948–1954*]. (AD) 1 p. CSKC: Sermon file, folder 71, "Creating the Abundant Life" / "A Moment of Difficult Decision." 540000-140.	
1948–1954	King, Martin Luther, Jr. "Is There a God." [*1948–1954*]. (AD) 2 pp. MLKP-MBU: Box 118. 540000-144.	
1948–1954	King, Martin Luther, Jr. "Developing a Life-Purpose," Sermon outline. [*1948–1954*]. (AD) 2 pp. MLKP-MBU: Box 118. 540000-145.	
1948–1954	King, Martin Luther, Jr. Developing a Life-Purpose, Sermon notes. [*1948–1954*]. (AD) 2 pp. MLKP-MBU: Box 118. 540000-150.	
1948–1954	King, Martin Luther, Jr. "Life's Blueprint." [*1948–1954*]. (AD) 1 p. MLKP-MBU: Box 118. 540000-146.	
1948–1954	King, Martin Luther, Jr. "Divine Nostalgia." [*1948–1954*]. (AD) 1 p. MLKP-MBU: Box 118. 540000-147.	
1948–1954	"Marriage record." [*1948–1954*]. (TFm) 1 p. CSKC: Sermon file, folder 161, Worship. 540000-148.	
1948–1954	King, Martin Luther, Jr. "God Is Light." [*1948–1954*]. (AD) 1 p. CSKC: Sermon file, folder 106, "Sermons." 540000-149.	
1948–1954	King, Martin Luther, Jr. Notes on "Meditation XVII," *Devotions Upon Emergent Occasions* by John Donne. [*1948–1954*]. (AD) 1 p. CSKC: Sermon file, folder 21, "The Three Dimensions of a Complete Life." 540000-151.	
1951–1954	[*King, Martin Luther, Jr.*] (Boston University). "The Dialectical Character of Niebuhr's Thought and His Attitude Toward Current Social System." [*1951–1954*]. [*Boston, Mass.*] (TD) 2 pp. CSKC: Sermon file, folder 163. 540000-152.	
1948–1954	King, Martin Luther, Jr. Personal notecards on "B" topics. [*1948–1954*]. (AD) 39 pp. CSKC. 540000-154.	
1948–1954	King, Martin Luther, Jr. Personal notecards on "E" topics. [*1948–1954*]. (AD) 48 pp. CSKC. 540000-157.	
1948–1954	King, Martin Luther, Jr. Personal notecards on "M" topics. [*1948–1954*]. (AD) 102 pp. CSKC. 540000-165.	
1948–1954	King, Martin Luther, Jr. The Sea of Life. [*1948–1954*]. (AD) 1 p. CSKC: Sermon file, folder 71, "Creating the Abundant Life" / "A Moment of Difficult Decision." 540000-178.	
1948–1954	King, Martin Luther, Jr. The Mixture in Human Nature. [*1948–1954*]. (AD) 1 p. CSKC: Sermon file, folder 65. 540000-180.	
1948–1954	King, Martin Luther, Jr. What Is Man? Sermon notes I. [*1948–1954*]. (ADf) 1 p. CSKC: Sermon file, folder 118, "Sermon Material." 540000-181.	
1948–1954	King, Martin Luther, Jr. "What Is Man," Sermon notes II. [*1948–1954*]. (AD) 1 p. MLKP-MBU: Box 115. 540000-193.	
1948–1954	King, Martin Luther, Jr. Sermon titles I. [*1948–1954*]. (AD) 2 pp. CSKC: Sermon file, folder 100, "Sermons by Other Ministers." 540000-182.	
1948–1954	King, Martin Luther, Jr. Sermon titles II. [*1948–1954*]. (AD) 1 p. CSKC: Sermon file, folder 100, "Sermons by Other Ministers." 540000-183.	
1948–1954	King, Martin Luther, Jr. "The Unity of Mankind." [*1948–1954*]. (AD) 2 pp. CSKC: Sermon file, folder 118, "Sermon Material." 540000-184.	
1948–1954	King, Martin Luther, Jr. "Should F.E.P.C. Become a Federal Law." [*1948–1954*]. (TAHDS) 6 pp. CSKC: Sermon file, folder 165. 540000-185.	
1948–1954	King, Martin Luther, Jr. Notecard on Philip Sidney. [*1948–1954*]. (AD) 1 p. CSKC: Sermon file, folder 63, "Fleeing from God & When God Seems to Deceive Us." 540000-186.	
1948–1954	King, Martin Luther, Jr. "What is Salvation?" [*1948–1954*]. (AD) 2 pp. CSKC: Sermon file, folder 50, Sermons Not Preached. 540000-187.	

10/2/1955   King, Martin Luther, Jr. (Dexter Ave. Baptist Church). "The Impassable Gulf (The
             Parable of Dives and Lazarus)." [*10/2/1955*]. Montgomery, Ala. (AD) 14 pp.
             CSKC: Sermon file, folder 56, "The Impassable Gulf." 551002-004.

10/2/1955   King, Martin Luther, Jr. Notes on Dives. [*10/2/1955*]. [*Montgomery, Ala.*] (AD) 1 p.
             CSKC: Sermon file, folder 56, "The Impassable Gulf." 551002-006.

10/30/1955   Dexter Avenue Baptist Church. Program, Sunday services. 10/30/1955. Mont-
             gomery, Ala. (TD) 4 pp. MLKP-MBU: Box 76. 551030-000.

10/1/1954–   King, Martin Luther, Jr. "Annual report, Dexter Avenue Baptist Church."
10/31/1955   10/1/1954–10/31/1955. Montgomery, Ala. (TAHD) 28 pp. CSKC: Sermon
             file, folder 152, "Church Notes." 551031-000.

10/27/1955– "Dexter Avenue has Meeting." [*10/27/1955–11/2/1955?*]. Montgomery, Ala.
11/2/1955   From: *Montgomery Advertiser.* (PD) 1 p. CSKC: Sermon file, folder 123. 551102-
             004.

11/17/1955   King, Martin Luther, Jr. Telegram to Coretta Scott King. [*11/17/1955*]. Mont-
             gomery, Ala. (PWSr) 1 p. CSKC. 551117-000.

11/17/1955   Abernathy, Ralph, and Juanita Abernathy. Telegram to Coretta Scott King.
             [*11/17/1955*]. Montgomery, Ala. (PWSr) 1 p. CSKC. 551117-001.

11/20/1955   Dexter Avenue Baptist Church. Program, Sunday services. 11/20/1955. Mont-
             gomery, Ala. (THD) 4 pp. (Marginal comments by King.) MLKP-MBU: Box 76.
             551120-000.

11/20/1955   King, Martin Luther, Jr. "The One-Sided Approach of the Good Samaritan," Ser-
             mon outline. [*11/20/1955*]. [*Montgomery, Ala.*] (AD) 2 pp. CSKC: Sermon file,
             folder 44, "The One-Sided Approach to the Good Samaritan." 551120-002.

11/20/1955   Dexter Avenue Baptist Church. Program, Installation services. 11/20/1955. Mont-
             gomery, Ala. (TD) 3 pp. MLKJP-GAMK: Box 76. 551120-004.

12/4/1955   Dexter Avenue Baptist Church. Program, Sunday services. 12/4/1955. Mont-
             gomery, Ala. (TD) 4 pp. DABCC. 551204-000.

12/25/1955   Negro ministers of Montgomery and their congregations. Letter to the Mont-
             gomery public. [*12/25/1955*]. Montgomery, Ala. (THD) 4 pp. CSKC: Sermon
             file, folder 150, "Speeches." 551225-001.

12/25/1955   Dexter Avenue Baptist Church. Program, Sunday services. 12/25/1955. Mont-
             gomery, Ala. (TD) 4 pp. DABCC. 551225-003.

1951–1955   King, Martin Luther, Jr. (Boston University). Notecards on Aristotle, U.S. policy on
             Asia, Atheism, and Augustine. [*1951–1955*]. [*Boston, Mass.*] (AD) 8 pp. CSKC.
             550000-040.

1956   MIA. "The Montgomery bus protest." [*1956*]. Montgomery, Ala. (TD) 1 p. CSKC:
             Sermon file, folder 150, "Speeches." 560000-103.

1956   King, Martin Luther, Jr. "Paul's Letter to American Christians." 1956. [*Montgomery,
             Ala.*] (TAHD) 11 pp. CSKC: Sermon file, folder 93, "Paul's Letter to American
             Christians." 560000-183.

1956   Southern Regional Council. "Next Steps in the South: Answers to Current Ques-
             tions." 1956. Atlanta, Ga. (PHD) 20 pp. CSKC: Sermon file, folder 149,
             "Speeches." 560000-192.

1956   King, Martin Luther, Jr. Paul's Letter to American Christians, Sermon outline.
             [*1956*]. [*Montgomery, Ala.*] (ADf) 2 pp. CSKC. 560000-193.

1/1/1956   Dexter Avenue Baptist Church. Program, Sunday services. [*1/1/1956*]. Mont-
             gomery, Ala. (TD) 4 pp. DABCC. 560101-001.

1/15/1956   Dexter Avenue Baptist Church. Program, Sunday services. 1/15/1956. Mont-
             gomery, Ala. (TD) 4 pp. MLKP-MBU: Box 76. 560115-000.

1/22/1956   Dexter Avenue Baptist Church. Program, Sunday services. 1/22/1956. Mont-
             gomery, Ala. (TD) 4 pp. CSKC: Sermon file, folder 27, "The Mission of the
             Church." 560122-000.

2/5/1956   Dexter Avenue Baptist Church. Program, Sunday services. [*2/5/1956*]. Mont-
             gomery, Ala. (TD) 4 pp. DABCC. 560205-002.

2/26/1956   Dexter Avenue Baptist Church. Program, Sunday services. 2/26/1956. Mont-
             gomery, Ala. (TDf) 1 p. DABCC. 560226-006.

2/27/1956   Gelb, Phillip. "The Most Significant Story—Montgomery, Ala." 2/27/1956. (TTa)
             8 pp. CSKC: Sermon file, folder 149, "Speeches." 560227-016.

3/1956   Barbour, J. Pius (*National Baptist Voice*). "Meditations on Rev. M.L. King, Jr., of Mont-
             gomery Ala." 3/1956. Chester, Pa. From: *National Baptist Voice*, March 1956, p. 4-
             5. (PD) 2 pp. MLKP-MBU: Box 80. 560300-002.

3/1956   [*Du Bois, W. E. B. (William Edward Burghardt)*]. Letter to Martin Luther King, Jr.
             [*3/1956?*]. (TLc) 1 p. WEBD-MU. 560300-021.

3/11/1956	Dexter Avenue Baptist Church. Program, Sunday services. 3/11/1956. Montgomery, Ala. (TDf) 2 pp. DABCC. 560311-004.	
3/18/1956	Dexter Avenue Baptist Church. Program, Sunday services. 3/18/1956. Montgomery, Ala. (TD) 4 pp. DABCC. 560318-007.	
4/1956	King, Martin Luther, Jr. Draft, Our Struggle. [4/1956]. [Montgomery, Ala.] (TADd) 10 pp. (Draft of 4/1956 *Liberation*.) CSKC: Sermon file, folder 141, "The Negro's Reevaluation of His Nature & Destiny & The Declaration of Independence and the Negro." 560400-022.	
4/3/1956	King, Martin Luther, Jr. Letter to Frank L. Stanley. 4/3/1956. [Montgomery, Ala.] (TLc) 1 p. DABCC. 560403-001.	
4/10/1956	Fellowship of Reconciliation. "Freedom, the South, and Nonviolence." [4/10/1956]. New York, N.Y. (PD) 6 pp. CSKC: Sermon file, folder 149, "Speeches." 560410-010.	
4/20/1956	Newgent, William E. Letter to Martin Luther King, Jr. 4/20/1956. Washington, D.C. (TLS) 1 p. MLKP-MBU: Box 63. 560420-009.	
4/13/1956– 4/22/1956	Payne, Ethel L. (Afro American Youth International Rotary Club, Inc.). "King Raps Jim Crow Dixie Rule." [4/13/1956–4/22/1956]. New York, N.Y. (TD) 1 p. CSKC: Sermon file, folder 143. 560422-004.	
3/1956–4/1956	**Weiner, Dan. Photo of Martin Luther King, Jr. in front of Dexter Avenue Baptist Church. [3/1956–4/1956]. Montgomery, Ala. (Ph) 1 p. NNCIP. 560400-004.**	
3/1956–4/1956	**Weiner, Dan. Photo of Martin Luther King, Jr. and a Dexter Avenue Baptist Church parishioner. [3/1956–4/1956]. Montgomery, Ala. (Ph) 1 p. NNCIP. 560400-025.**	
5/17/1956	The Cathedral Church of St. John the Divine. Program, "A Service of Prayer and Thanksgiving." 5/17/1956. New York. (PHD) 4 pp. MLKP-MBU: Box 80. 560517-011.	
5/17/1956	King, Martin Luther, Jr. "The Death of Evil Upon the Seashore," Sermon at the Cathedral of St. John the Divine. 5/17/1956. New York, N.Y. (PD) 5 pp. CSKC: Sermon file, folder 2, Death of Evil. 560517-001.	
5/17/1956	King, Martin Luther, Jr. "The Death of Evil Upon the Seashore," Sermon at the Cathedral of St. John the Divine. 5/17/1956. New York, N.Y. (TAD) 7 pp. CSKC: Sermon file, folder 97. 560517-017.	
5/17/1956	King, Martin Luther, Jr. "The Death of Evil Upon the Seashore," Sermon at the Cathedral of St. John the Divine. 5/17/1956. New York, N.Y. (TAD) 4 pp. (Draft of 6/1956 *National Baptist Voice*.) CSKC: Sermon file, folder 2, Death of Evil. 560517-022.	
5/17/1956	**Mastro, Frank (International News Photo). Photo of Martin Luther King, Jr. at Cathedral of St. John the Divine. 5/17/1956. New York, N.Y. (Ph) 1 p. UPIR-NNBETT. 560517-019.**	
5/17/1956	**International News Press. Photo of Martin Luther King, Jr., Horace W. B. Donegan, and James A. (James Albert) Pike at the Cathedral of St. John the Divine. 5/17/1956. New York, N.Y. From: *Birmingham World*, 1 June 1956. (Ph) 1 p. UPIR-NNBETT. 560517-014.**	
6/1956	King, Martin Luther, Jr. "The Death of Evil Upon the Seashore," Sermon at the Cathedral of St. John the Divine on 5/17/1956. 6/1956. Nashville, Tenn. From: *National Baptist Voice*, June 1956, pp. 10, 14. (PD) 2 pp. MLKJP-GAMK. 560600-023.	
6/1956	Huberman, Leo, and Paul M. Sweezy. "On Segregation: The Crisis in Race Relations, Two Nations—White and Black." 6/1956. New York, N.Y. (PHD) 23 pp. (Marginal comments by King.) CSKC: Sermon file, folder 149, "Speeches." 560600-022.	
6/27/1956	King, Martin Luther, Jr. (MIA). "The Montgomery Story," Address at the Forty-seventh NAACP Annual Convention. 6/27/1956. San Francisco, Calif. (TD) 13 pp. CSKC: Sermon file, folder 126, Speeches by Dr. King, Montgomery, 1956. 560627-009.	
7/1956	**Photo of Martin Luther King, Jr., judging prettiest baby contest. [7/1956]. Montgomery, Ala. (Ph) 1 p. MLKP-MBU: Box 43. 560700-007.**	
8/1956	Peters, William. "Our Weapon Is Love." 8/1956. New York, N.Y. From: *Redbook*, August 1956, pp. 42–43, 71–73. (PD) 5 pp. 560800-006.	
8/1956	**Photo of Martin Luther King, Jr. 8/1956. From: *Redbook*, August 1956, p. 41. (PPh) 1 p. 560800-009.**	
8/1956	Helton, R. L. Letter to Martin Luther King, Jr. [8/1956]. Burbank, Calif. (ALS) 4 pp. CSKC: Sermon file, folder 143. 560800-012.	

8/11/1956   King, Martin Luther, Jr. (MIA). Draft, Statement to the Democratic National Convention committee on platform and resolutions. 8/11/1956. [*Chicago, Ill.*] (TDd) 2 pp. CSKC: Sermon file, folder 159, Speeches—Reprints in Various Magazines, M. L. King. 560811-001.

1956   King, Martin Luther, Jr. The Birth of a New Age, Address at the fiftieth anniversary of Alpha Phi Alpha Fraternity, Inc. in Buffalo, N.Y. on 8/11/1956. 1956. Chicago, Ill. From: Wesley, Charles H., *Golden Anniversary Story of Alpha Phi Alpha Fraternity, Inc.* Chicago: Alpha Phi Alpha, 1956, pp. 85–90. (PD) 6 pp. CSKC: Sermon file, folder 159, Speeches—Reprints in Various Magazines, M. L. King. 560000-136.

8/17/1956   White, Theodore Harold. "The Negro Voter: Can He Elect a President?" 8/17/1956. From: *Collier's*, 17 August 1956. (PDf) 6 pp. CSKC: Sermon file, folder 142, "Articles: The Negro's New Economic Life, Hughes The Negro Voter, White." 560817-001.

8/20/1956   Koch, Melvin (Young Men's Christian Association (YMCA)). Letter to Martin Luther King, Jr. 8/20/1956. Berkeley, Calif. (TALS) 2 pp. CSKC: Sermon file, folder 143. 560820-005.

8/22/1956   Inter-Civic Council. "ICC diary, part V." 8/22/1956. Tallahassee, Fla. (THD) 2 pp. (Marginal comments by King. 560904-009 on verso.) CSKC: Sermon file, folder 143. 560822-007.

9/4/1956   King, Martin Luther, Jr. "For All—A Non-Segregated Society." [*9/4/1956*]. [*Montgomery, Ala.*] (AD) 9 pp. MLKP-MBU: Box 119A. 560904-008.

9/4/1956   King, Martin Luther, Jr. Draft, For All—A Non-Segregated Society. [*9/4/1956*]. [*Montgomery, Ala.*] (ADd) 7 pp. (Verso of 560822-007.) CSKC: Sermon file, folder 143. 560904-009.

9/4/1956   King, Martin Luther, Jr. For All—A Non-Segregated Society, Sermon outline. [*9/4/1956*]. [*Montgomery, Ala.*] (AD) 2 pp. CSKC: Sermon file, folder 143. 560904-010.

9/6/1956   Jackson, J. H. (Joseph Harrison) (National Baptist Convention of the United States of America). "Annual address at the seventy-sixth annual session of the National Baptist Convention, U.S.A., Inc." 9/6/1956. Denver, Colo. (PHD) 33 pp. CSKC: Sermon file, folder 38, "Addresses By Others." 560906-003.

9/23/1956   Johnson, Charles S. "A Southern Negro's View of the South." 9/23/1956. New York, N.Y. From: *New York Times Magazine*, 23 September 1956. (PD) 4 pp. CSKC: Sermon file, folder 149, "Speeches." 560923-001.

9/23/1956   Fitz-Gibbon, Bernice. "Tips for Would-Be Women Bosses." 9/23/1956. New York, N.Y. From: *New York Times Magazine*, 23 September 1956. (PDf) 1 p. CSKC: Sermon file, folder 149, "Speeches." 560923-002.

10/1956   King, Martin Luther, Jr. Letter to the editor. 10/1956. Montgomery, Ala. From: *Fisk News*, October 1956. (PL) 1 p. CSKC: Sermon file, folder 165. 561000-014.

10/1956   King, Martin Luther, Jr. "The Montgomery Story," Address at the thirteenth annual Institute on Race Relations at Fisk University on 7/12/1956. 10/1956. Nashville, Tenn. From: *Fisk News*, October 1956, pp. 5-8. (PD) 4 pp. CSKC: Sermon file, folder 159, Speech—Reprints in Various Magazines, M. L. King. 561000-015.

10/10/1956   Lindsay, James B. Letter to Martin Luther King, Jr. 10/10/1956. Cortland, N.Y. (ALS) 1 p. CSKC: Sermon file, folder 149, "Speeches." 561010-018.

10/13/1956   Prattis, Percival Leroy. "Horizon: Family Income." 10/13/1956. Pittsburgh, Pa. From: *Pittsburgh Courier*, 13 October 1956. (PD) 1 p. CSKC: Sermon file, folder 149, "Speeches." 561013-000.

10/16/1956   King, Martin Luther, Jr. "Nonviolent Procedures to Inter-Racial Harmony." [*10/16/1956*]. [*Cortland, N.Y.*] (TD) 8 pp. CSKC: Sermon file, folder 127, Speeches—MLK, and folder 137, "The Christian Way of Life in Human Relations" / "Nonviolence and Racial Justice." 561016-003.

10/17/1956   Dexter Avenue Baptist Church. *Dexter Echo* 1, no. 8. 10/17/1956. (THD) 4 pp. LDRP-NN-Sc: Box 2. 561017-008.

11/1956   Fellowship of Reconciliation. *Fellowship* 22. 11/1956. New York, N.Y. (PD) 35 pp. CSKC: Sermon file, folder 149, "Speeches." 561100-009.

11/4/1956   King, Martin Luther, Jr. "Paul's Letter to American Christians, A Sermon Preached in the Dexter Avenue Baptist Church." 11/4/1956. Montgomery, Ala. (PD) 7 pp. CSKC: Sermon file, folder 58, Sermon: Paul's Letter to American Christians. 561104-000.

11/4/1956   King, Martin Luther, Jr. "Paul's Letter to American Christians, Sermon Preached in the Dexter Avenue Baptist Church." 11/4/1956. Montgomery, Ala. (TAD) 10 pp. CSKC: Sermon file, folder 102. 561104-004.

7/1956– 11/26/1956
Ballou, Maude L. Diary. 7/1956–11/26/1956. (AD) 48 pp. LDRP-NN-Sc: Box 11. 561126-017.

12/3/1956
King, Martin Luther, Jr. (MIA). "Facing the Challenge of a New Age," Address at the first annual Institute on Nonviolence and Social Change. 12/3/1956. Montgomery, Ala. (THD) 20 pp. CSKC: Sermon file, folder 135, "Facing the Challenge of a New Age." 561203-000.

12/6/1956
King, Martin Luther, Jr. (Dexter Avenue Baptist Church). "Remember Who You Are!!" Sermon at Howard University. 12/6/1956. Washington, D.C. (TAD) 12 pp. CSKC: Sermon file, folder 22, "What Is Man?" 561206-015.

12/6/1956
King, Martin Luther, Jr. Remember Who You Are, Sermon notes. [12/6/1956]. (AD) 1 p. CSKC: Sermon file, folder 22, "What Is Man?" 561206-016.

12/2/1956– 12/9/1956
Howard University. Program, "Religious emphasis week." 12/2/1956–12/9/1956. Washington, D.C. (PHD) 4 pp. MLKP-MBU: Box 80. 561209-001.

12/10/1956
Hill, Daniel G. (Howard University). Letter to Martin Luther King, Jr. 12/10/1956. Washington, D.C. (TLS) 1 p. MLKP-MBU: Box 82. 561210-016.

12/15/1956
King, Martin Luther, Jr. "Desegregation and the Future." [12/15/1956]. [New York, N.Y.] (TADf) 8 pp. CSKC: Sermon file, folder 37, "Desegregation and the Future." 561215-005.

12/19/1956
King, Martin Luther, Jr., and William J. Powell. (MIA). "Integrated bus suggestions." 12/19/1956. Montgomery, Ala. (TD) 1 p. CSKC: Sermon file, folder 140, Integrated Bus Suggestions. 561219-001.

12/20/1956
King, Martin Luther, Jr. (MIA). Statement on Ending the Montgomery Bus Boycott. 12/20/1956. [Montgomery, Ala.] (TD) 1 p. CSKC: Sermon file, folder 149, "Speeches." 561220-000.

1953–1956
King, Martin Luther, Jr. "The Mission of the Church." [1953–1956]. (AD) 3 pp. CSKC: Sermon file, folder 27, "The Mission of the Church." 560000-081.

1957
[Rustin, Bayard]. "The Nature of the Present Crisis." [1957]. (THD) 3 pp. (Marginal comments by King.) CSKC: Sermon file, folder 86, "A Look to the Future." 570000-060.

1957
[Rustin, Bayard]. "Notes on Nonviolence." [1957]. (TAD) 5 pp. CSKC: Sermon file, folder 86, "A Look to the Future." 570000-061.

1957
Davis, George W. (Washington). *Existentialism and Theology: An Investigation of the Contribution of Rudolf Bultmann to Theological Thought.* New York: Philosophical Library, 1957. (PAHDS) (Inscription by Davis, 12/22/1958. Marginal comments by King.) CSKC: Sermon file, folder 19, Book Inscription. 570000-067.

1/6/1957
Dexter Avenue Baptist Church. Program, Sunday services. 1/6/1957. Montgomery, Ala. (THD) 4 pp. BRP-DLC. 570106-000.

1/10/1957– 1/11/1957
Southern Leaders Conference. "A Statement to the South and Nation." 1/10/1957–1/11/1957. Atlanta, Ga. (THD) 8 pp. (Marginal comments by King. 570111–034 on verso.) CSKC: Sermon file, folder 132, "Nonviolent Bus Integration" / First Address to SCLC by MLK, Jr. 570111-008.

1/11/1957
King, Martin Luther, Jr. Letter to Grover C. Hall. [1/11/1957]. [Atlanta, Ga.] (ALd) 2 pp. (Verso of 570111-008.) CSKC: Sermon file, folder 132, "Nonviolent Bus Integration." / First Address Made to SCLC by MLK, Jr. 570111-034.

1/13/1957
King, Martin Luther, Jr. The Ways of God in the Midst of Glaring Evil, Sermon delivered at Dexter Avenue Baptist Church. [1/13/1957]. Montgomery, Ala. (F) 10 min. (1 videocassette.) CBSNA-NNCBS. 570113-007.

1/20/1957
King, Martin Luther, Jr. "Paul's Letter to American Christians," Sermon delivered at Ebenezer Baptist Church. [1/20/1957]. [Atlanta, Ga.] (At) 29 min. (1 sound cassette: analog.) MLKEC: ET-31. 570120-003.

2/1957
King, Martin Luther, Jr. Paul's Letter to American Christians, Sermon at Ebenezer Baptist Church on 1/20/1957. 2/1957. Atlanta, Ga. From: *Ebenezer Messenger,* February 1957. (TD) 2 pp. EBCR. 570200-002.

2/1957
King, Martin Luther, Jr. "Facing the Challenge of a New Age," Address on 12/3/1956. 2/1957. New York, N.Y. From: *Fellowship* 23 (February 1957): 3–11. (PD) 9 pp. CSKC: Sermon file, folder 159, Speeches—Reprints in Various Magazines, M. L. King. 570200-009.

2/5/1957
Arnold, Melvin (Harper & Brothers). Letter to Martin Luther King, Jr. 2/5/1957. New York, N.Y. (TLS) 1 p. MLKP-MBU: Box 2. 570205-000.

2/10/1957
King, Martin Luther, Jr. (Dexter Avenue Baptist Church). "For All . . . A Non-Segre-

gated Society, A message for Race Relations Sunday." 2/10/1957. New York, N.Y.
(PD) 4 pp. CSKC: Sermon file, folder 86, "A Look to the Future." 570210-001.

2/21/1957   Hill, Daniel G. (Howard University). Letter to Martin Luther King, Jr. 2/21/1957. Washington, D.C. (THLS) 1 p. (Marginal comments by King. 600413-014 on verso.) CSKC: Sermon file, folder 138. 570221-008.

2/28/1957   King, Martin Luther, Jr. (Dexter Avenue Baptist Church). Letter to Melvin Arnold. 2/28/1957. [*Montgomery, Ala.*] (THLc) 1 p. MLKP-MBU: Box 2. 570228-000.

3/1957   King, Martin Luther, Jr. God's Judgment on Western Civilization. [*3/1957*]. Gold Coast (AD) 4 pp. CSKC: Sermon file, folder 80, "God's Judgment on Western Civilization" / "The Vision of a World Made New." 570300-017.

3/1957   King, Martin Luther, Jr. God's Judgment on Western Civilization, Sermon notes I. [*3/1957*]. (AD) 6 pp. CSKC: Sermon file, folder 80, "God's Judgment on Western Civilization" / "The Vision of a World Made New." 570300-019.

3/1957   King, Martin Luther, Jr. "God's Judgment on Western Civilization," Sermon notes II. [*3/1957*]. (AD) 1 p. CSKC: Sermon file, folder 80, "God's Judgment on Western Civilization" / "The Vision of a World Made New." 570300-024.

3/1/1957   Lenox, G. Merrill (Detroit Council of Churches). Letter to Martin Luther King, Jr. 3/1/1957. Detroit, Mich. (TLS) 4 pp. (Includes enclosure.) MLKP-MBU: Box 38A. 570301-015.

4/1957   [*Levison, Stanley D.*]. "A Wind is Rising." [*4/1957*]. (TD) 3 pp. CSKC: Sermon file, folder 86, "A Look to the Future." 570400-012.

4/3/1957   King, Martin Luther, Jr. "Justice Without Violence," Helmsley Lecture I at Institute for Adult Education, Brandeis University. 4/3/1957. [*Waltham, Mass.*] (TD) 10 pp. CSKC: Sermon file, folder 20, Justice Without Violence and Sermon file, folder 127, Speeches—MLK. 570403-021.

4/7/1957   King, Martin Luther, Jr. (Dexter Avenue Baptist Church). "The Birth of a New Nation." [*4/7/1957*]. Montgomery, Ala. (THTa) 22 pp. MLKJP-GAMK: Box 107. 570407-002.

4/14/1957   King, Martin Luther, Jr. Garden of Gethsemane, Sermon notes. [*4/14/1957*]. [*Montgomery, Ala.*] (AD) 5 pp. CSKC: Sermon file, folder 103, "The Tension between Life's Palm Sunday and Life's Good Friday." 570414-005.

4/16/1957   Miller, J. Quinter (National Council of the Churches of Christ in the United States of America). Letter to Martin Luther King, Jr. 4/16/1957. New York, N.Y. (TLS) 2 pp. MLKP-MBU: Box 66. 570416-007.

4/24/1957   King, Martin Luther, Jr. (MIA). Letter to G. Merrill Lenox. 4/24/1957. [*Montgomery, Ala.*] (TLc) 1 p. MLKP-MBU: Box 38A. 570424-015.

5/1957   King, Martin Luther, Jr. "A View of the Dawn," Address on 4/24/1957. 5/1957. New York, N.Y. From: *Interracial Review* 30 (May 1957): 82–85. (PD) 4 pp. CSKC: Sermon file, folder 159, Speeches—Reprints in Various Magazines, M. L. King. 570500-002.

5/1/1957   King, Martin Luther, Jr. (MIA). Letter to J. Quinter Miller. 5/1/1957. [*Montgomery, Ala.*] (TLc) 1 p. MLKP-MBU: Box 66. 570501-008.

5/17/1957   King, Martin Luther, Jr. Give Us the Ballot, Address at the Prayer Pilgrimage for Freedom. 5/17/1957. Washington, D.C. (TD) 5 pp. CSKC: Sermon file, folder 34. 570517-000.

6/3/1957   Ballou, Maude L. Letter to Russell Roberts. 6/3/1957. [*Montgomery, Ala.*] (TLc) 1 p. MLKP-MBU: Box 64. 570603-022.

6/5/1957   King, Martin Luther, Jr. "The Most Durable Power, Sermon at Dexter Avenue Baptist Church on 11/6/1956." 6/5/1957. Montgomery, Ala. (THD) 2 pp. (Draft of *Christian Century*, 6/5/1957). MLKJP-GAMK: Box 107. 570605-001.

6/9/1957   King, Martin Luther, Jr. "The Quest for Freedom." [*6/9/1957*]. [*Montgomery, Ala.*] (THD) 7 pp. LDRP-NN-Sc: Box 2. 570609-001.

6/28/1957   King, Martin Luther, Jr. "Remarks in acceptance of the forty-second Spingarn Medal at the Forty-eighth annual convention of the NAACP." 6/28/1957. Detroit, Mich. (TD) 14 pp. CSKC: Sermon file, folder 130, "Acceptance Speech of Spingarn Metal," and folder 136, Speech—Springarn Medal M.L.K. 570628-001.

6/28/1957   Emrich, Richard S. M. (Richard Stanley Merrill) (Diocese of Michigan). "Remarks on presentation of the Forty-second Spingarn Medal to Rev. Dr. Martin Luther King, Jr. at the NAACP Forty-eighth annual convention." 6/28/1957. Detroit, Mich. (TD) 4 pp. CSKC: Sermon file, folder 130, "Acceptance Speech of Spingarn Metal" and folder 136, Speech—Springarn Metal M.L.K. 570628-006.

7/14/1957   **King, Martin Luther, Jr. (Dexter Avenue Baptist Church). "Overcoming an Inferiority Complex," Sermon notes. [7/14/1957]. [*Montgomery, Ala.*] (AD) 4 pp. CSKC. 570714-002.**

8/7/1957   Dexter Avenue Baptist Church. *Dexter Echo* 2, no. 4. 8/7/1957. Montgomery, Ala. (TD) 4 pp. DABCC. 570807-000.

8/11/1957   King, Martin Luther, Jr. "Conquering Self-Centeredness," Sermon delivered at Dexter Avenue Baptist Church. [8/11/1957]. Montgomery, Ala. (At) 37.9 min. (2 sound cassettes: analog.) MLKEC: ET-58. 570811-000.

8/18/1957   Central Methodist Church. Program, Sunday services. 8/18/1957. Detroit, Mich. (PHD) 2 pp. CSKC. 570818-000.

9/10/1957   Lautier, Louis. "Baptists." 9/10/1957. Baltimore, Md. From: *Baltimore Afro-American*, 10 September 1957. (PD) 2 pp. CSKC: Sermon file, folder 149, "Speeches." 570910-006.

9/10/1957   Boddie, J. Timothy (Shiloh Baptist Church). "Cleric tells why disorder swept Baptist convention." 9/10/1957. Baltimore, Md. From: *Baltimore Afro-American*, 10 September 1957. (PD) 1 p. CSKC: Sermon file, folder 149, "Speeches." 570910-007.

11/1957   *Morehouse College Bulletin* 25. 11/1957. Atlanta, Ga. (PD) 16 pp. CSKC: Sermon file, folder 159, Speeches—Reprints in Various Magazines, M. L. King. 571100-017.

11/6/1957   King, Martin Luther, Jr. (Dexter Avenue Baptist Church). "Things that are God's," Sermon at Dexter Avenue Baptist Church on 10/27/1957. 11/6/1957. Montgomery, Ala. From: *Dexter Echo* 2, 6 November 1957. (TD) 2 pp. CKFC. 571106-000.

11/6/1957   Dexter Avenue Baptist Church. *Dexter Echo* 2, no. 8. 11/6/1957. Montgomery, Ala. (TD) 4 pp. CKFC. 571106-004.

11/10/1957   King, Martin Luther, Jr. "Love Your Enemies," Sermon at forty-first annual convocation of the school of religion at Howard University. 11/10/1957. Washington, D.C. (TATa) 15 pp. (Enclosed in 571228-000.) CSKC: Sermon file, folder 1, "Loving Your Enemies." 571110-004.

11/17/1957   Dexter Avenue Baptist Church. Program, Sunday services. 11/17/1957. Montgomery, Ala. (TD) 6 pp. DABCC. 571117-000.

11/17/1957   King, Martin Luther, Jr. "Loving Your Enemies," Sermon delivered at Dexter Avenue Baptist Church. [11/17/1957]. [*Montgomery, Ala.*] (At) 41.7 min. (1 sound cassette: analog.) MLKEC: ET-1. 571117-002.

11/17/1957   King, Martin Luther, Jr. Loving Your Enemies, Sermon at Dexter Avenue Baptist Church. [11/17/1957]. Montgomery, Ala. (THTa) 14 pp. MLKJP-GAMK. 571117-006.

12/1957   Merriam, Eve. "An Evening to Remember." 12/1957. From: *American Judaism* (December 1957): 18. (PD) 1 p. CSKC: Sermon file, folder 159, Speeches—Reprints in Various Magazines, M. L. King. 571200-021.

12/1/1957   Dexter Avenue Baptist Church. Program, Sunday services. 12/1/1957. Montgomery, Ala. (TD) 4 pp. DABCC. 571201-000.

12/3/1957   King, Martin Luther, Jr. The Oneness of Man in American Intergroup Relations, Address delivered at the National Council of Churches Division of Christian Life and Work Visitors Program. [12/3/1957]. [*St. Louis, Mo.*] (At) 34 min. (1 sound cassette: analog.) MLKJP-GAMK:T-10. 571203-001.

12/3/1957   King, Martin Luther, Jr. "The Oneness of Man in American Intergroup Relations," Address at the National Council of Churches Division of Christian Life and Work Visitors Program. [12/3/1957]. [*St. Louis, Mo.*] (AD) 15 pp. MLKP-MBU: Box 120A. 571203-002.

12/4/1957   National Council of the Churches of Christ in the United States of America. Program, "Public Meeting of the General Assembly." 12/4/1957. St. Louis, Mo. (PD) 3 pp. NCCP-PPPrHi: Box 2. 571204-008.

12/4/1957   King, Martin Luther, Jr. Draft, "The Christian Way of Life in Human Relations." [12/4/1957]. [*St. Louis, Mo.*] (TADf) 7 pp. CSKC: Sermon file, folder 137, "The Christian Way of Life in Human Relations" / "Nonviolence and Racial Justice." 571204-012.

12/5/1957   King, Martin Luther, Jr. "Some Things We Can Do." [12/5/1957]. [*Montgomery, Ala.*] (AD) 6 pp. CSKC: Sermon file, folder 98, "Some Things That We Must Do." 571205-006.

12/1/1957–12/6/1957   National Council of the Churches of Christ in the United States of America. "General assembly program outline." [12/1/1957–12/6/1957]. (PHDf) 5 pp. NCCP-PPPrHi: Box 2. 571206-005.

| 12/8/1957 | Dexter Avenue Baptist Church. Program, Sunday services. 12/8/1957. Montgomery, Ala. (TD) 4 pp. DABCC. 571208-000. | Calendar |

12/8/1957 — Dexter Avenue Baptist Church. Program, Sunday services. 12/8/1957. Montgomery, Ala. (TD) 4 pp. DABCC. 571208-000.

12/22/1957 — Dexter Avenue Baptist Church. Program, Sunday services. 12/22/1957. Montgomery, Ala. (TD) 4 pp. DABCC. 571222-000.

12/28/1957 — Giltner, John H. (*Journal of Religious Thought*). Letter to Martin Luther King, Jr. 12/28/1957. Washington, D.C. (TLS) 1 p. (Contains enclosure 571110-004.) MLKP-MBU: Box 64A. 571228-000.

12/31/1957 — Bowles, Chester. Letter to Martin Luther King, Jr. 12/31/1957. Essex, Conn. (TLS) 2 pp. (Contains enclosure 571231-006.) CSKC: Sermon file, folder 137, "The Christian Way of Life in Human Relations" / "Nonviolence and Racial Justice." 571231-002.

12/31/1957 — Bowles, Chester. "Article for *Saturday Evening Post*." 12/31/1957. (TD) 20 pp. (Enclosed in 571231-002.) MLKP-MBU: Box 43. 571231-006.

1/12/1958 — King, Martin Luther, Jr. (Dexter Avenue Baptist Church). "What Is Man?" Address at the Chicago Sunday Evening Club. 1/12/1958. Chicago, Ill. (TTa) 3 pp. CSKC: Sermon file, folder 22, "What Is Man?" 580112-001.

1958 — **Schulke, Flip. Photo of Martin Luther King, Jr. greeting parishioners. [*1958*]. (Ph) 1 p. BStPC. 580000-056.**

1958 — **Moore, Charles (Black Star). Photo of Martin Luther King, Jr. at the pulpit of Holt Street Baptist Church. [*1958*]. Montgomery, Ala. (Ph) BStPC. 580000-057.**

1958 — **Fosdick, Harry Emerson. *Riverside Sermons*. New York: Harper & Brothers, 1958, p. 27. (PHD) (Marginal comments by King.) CSKCH. 580000-080.**

1/13/1958 — King, Martin Luther, Jr. (Dexter Avenue Baptist Church). A Great Time to Be Alive, Address delivered at Beth Emet the Free Synagogue. [*1/13/1958*]. Evanston, Ill. (At) 44.3 min. (1 sound cassette: analog.) MLKEC: ET-16. 580113-005.

1/13/1958 — King, Martin Luther, Jr. A Great Time to Be Alive. [*1/13/1958*]. (TDf) 4 pp. MLKP-MBU: Box 119. 580113-006.

1/19/1958 — Dexter Avenue Baptist Church. Program, Sunday services. 1/19/1958. Montgomery, Ala. (TD) 4 pp. CKFC. 580119-000.

1/22/1958 — Simon, Paul. "Montgomery Looks Forward." 1/22/1958. Chicago, Ill. From: *Christian Century* 75 (22 January 1958): 104–105. (PD) 2 pp. CSKC: Sermon file, folder 159, Speeches—Reprints in Various Magazines, M. L. King. 580122-014.

2/1958 — King, Martin Luther, Jr. "Out of the Long Night of Segregation." 2/1958. New York, N.Y. From: *Missions* 156 (February 1958): 22–23. (PD) 2 pp. CSKC: Sermon file, folder 159, Speeches—Reprints in Various Magazines, M. L. King. 580200-016.

2/1958 — King, Martin Luther, Jr. "Out of the Night of Segregation." 2/1958. Philadelphia, Pa. From: *Lutheran Woman's Work* 51 (February 1958): 9–11, 30. (PD) 4 pp. CSKC: Sermon file, folder 159, Speeches—Reprints in Various Magazines, M. L. King. 580200-017.

2/16/1958 — Dexter Avenue Baptist Church. Program, Sunday services. 2/16/1958. Montgomery, Ala. (TD) 4 pp. DABCC. 580216-000.

3/2/1958 — Dexter Avenue Baptist Church. Program, Sunday services. 3/2/1958. Montgomery, Ala. (TD) 4 pp. DABCC. 580302-000.

3/3/1958 — Lenox, G. Merrill (Detroit Council of Churches). Letter to Martin Luther King, Jr. 3/3/1958. Detroit, Mich. (TLS) 1 p. (Contains enclosure 580403-004.) MLKP-MBU: Box 38A. 580303-007.

3/16/1958 — Dexter Avenue Baptist Church. Program, Sunday services. 3/16/1958. Montgomery, Ala. (TD) 4 pp. DABCC. 580316-000.

3/17/1958 — Lenox, G. Merrill (Detroit Council of Churches). Letter to Martin Luther King, Jr. 3/17/1958. Detroit, Mich. (TAHLS) 2 pp. MLKP-MBU: Box 38A. 580317-004.

3/18/1958 — Giltner, John H. (Howard University). Letter to Martin Luther King, Jr. 3/18/1958. Washington, D.C. (THLS) 1 p. (Contains enclosure 580318-003.) MLKP-MBU: Box 28. 580318-002.

3/18/1958 — King, Martin Luther, Jr. "Love Your Enemies," Sermon at Howard University on 11/10/1957. [*3/18/1958*]. [*Washington, D.C.*] (PAD) 5 pp. (Enclosed in 580318-002. Marginal comments by King.) MLKP-MBU: Box 28. 580318-003.

3/23/1958 — Dexter Avenue Baptist Church. Program, Sunday services. 3/23/1958. Montgomery, Ala. (TD) 4 pp. DABCC. 580323-000.

2/19/1958–4/3/1958 — Detroit Council of Churches. Announcement, "Noon Lenten services." 2/19/1958–4/3/1958. Detroit, Mich. (PD) 1 p. (Enclosed in 580303-007.) MLKP-MBU: Box 38A. 580403-004.

4/6/1958   Dexter Avenue Baptist Church. Program, Sunday services. 4/6/1958. Montgomery, Ala. (TD) 4 pp. DABCC. 580406-000.

4/13/1958   Dexter Avenue Baptist Church. Program, Sunday services. 4/13/1958. Montgomery, Ala. (TD) 4 pp. DABCC. 580413-000.

4/29/1958   Hill, Daniel G. (Howard University). Letter to Martin Luther King, Jr. 4/29/1958. Washington, D.C. (TLS) 1 p. MLKP-MBU: Box 28. 580429-006.

5/1958   King, Martin Luther, Jr. The Power of Nonviolence, Address on 6/24/1957. 5/1958. New York, N.Y. From: *Intercollegian* 75 (May 1958): 8–9. (PD) 2 pp. CSKC: Sermon file, folder 159, Speeches—Reprints in Various Magazines, M. L. King. 580500-003.

5/4/1958   Dexter Avenue Baptist Church. Program, Sunday services. 5/4/1958. Montgomery, Ala. (TD) 4 pp. DABCC. 580504-000.

5/11/1958   Dexter Avenue Baptist Church. Program, Sunday services. 5/11/1958. Montgomery, Ala. (TD) 4 pp. DABCC. 580511-000.

5/25/1958   Dexter Avenue Baptist Church. Program, Sunday services. 5/25/1958. Montgomery, Ala. (TD) 4 pp. DABCC. 580525-001.

6/1/1958   Dexter Avenue Baptist Church. Program, Sunday services. 6/1/1958. Montgomery, Ala. (TD) 4 pp. DABCC. 580601-000.

6/15/1958   Dexter Avenue Baptist Church. Program, Sunday services. 6/15/1958. Montgomery, Ala. (TD) 3 pp. DABCC. 580615-000.

6/22/1958   Dexter Avenue Baptist Church. Program, Sunday services. 6/22/1958. Montgomery, Ala. (TD) 4 pp. DABCC. 580622-000.

6/29/1958   Dexter Avenue Baptist Church. Program, Sunday services. 6/29/1958. Montgomery, Ala. (TD) 4 pp. DABCC. 580629-000.

7/6/1958   Dexter Avenue Baptist Church. Program, Sunday services. 7/6/1958. Montgomery, Ala. (TD) 4 pp. DABCC. 580706-000.

7/26/1958   King, Martin Luther, Jr. (MIA). "Nonviolence and Racial Justice." 7/26/1958. Philadelphia, Pa. From: *Friends Journal* 4 (26 July 1958): 442–444. (PD) 3 pp. CSKC: Sermon file, folder 159, Speeches—Reprints in Various Magazines, M. L. King, and folder 165. 580726-001.

8/3/1958   Dexter Avenue Baptist Church. Program, Sunday services. 8/3/1958. Montgomery, Ala. (TD) 4 pp. DABCC. 580803-001.

8/10/1958   Dexter Avenue Baptist Church. Program, Sunday services. 8/10/1958. Montgomery, Ala. (TD) 4 pp. DABCC. 580810-000.

8/14/1958   United Christian Movement, Inc. Program, "United Christian conference on registration and voting." 8/14/1958. Shreveport, La. (PD) 18 pp. CSKC: Sermon file, folder 159, Speeches—Reprints in Various Magazines, M. L. King. 580814-006.

8/17/1958   Dexter Avenue Baptist Church. Program, Sunday services. 8/17/1958. Montgomery, Ala. (TD) 4 pp. DABCC. 580817-000.

8/19/1958–
8/22/1958   Program, "National conference on Christian education." 8/19/1958–8/22/1958. Lafayette, Ind. (PD) 6 pp. CSKC: Sermon file, folder 159, Speeches—Reprints in Various Magazines, M. L. King. 580822-010.

9/1958   King, Martin Luther, Jr. (SCLC). Draft, Letter to Gordon M. Tiffany. [*9/1958*]. (TLd) 1 p. CSKC: Sermon file, folder 144, "Meaning of Civil Disobedience." 580900-009.

9/1958   [*King, Martin Luther, Jr.*]. Draft, Letter to Daisy Bates. [*9/1958*]. (TLd) 1 p. CSKC: Sermon file, folder 144, "Meaning of Civil Disobedience." 580900-010.

9/1958   King, Martin Luther, Jr. "An Appeal to Negro and White Men of Goodwill." [*9/1958*]. [*Montgomery, Ala.*] (TD) 1 p. CSKC: Sermon file, folder 145, December 20, 1958. 580900-015.

8/26/1958–
9/4/1958   Memo regarding Jimmy Wilson. [*8/26/1958–9/4/1958*]. (TL) 3 pp. CSKC: Sermon file, folder 145, December 20, 1958. 580904-019.

9/7/1958   Dexter Avenue Baptist Church. Program, Sunday services. 9/7/1958. Montgomery, Ala. (TD) 4 pp. DABCC. 580907-000.

7/6/1958–
9/7/1958   Central Methodist Church. Announcement, "Summer preaching program." 7/6/1958–9/7/1958. Detroit, Mich. (PD) 5 pp. MDCC-MiDW-AL: Box 8. 580907-003.

9/11/1958   Sheeder, Franklin I. (Franklin Irvin) (United Church of Christ). Letter to Martin Luther King, Jr. 9/11/1958. Philadelphia, Pa. (TLS) 1 p. MLKP-MBU: Box 69. 580911-006.

9/14/1958   Killens, John Oliver. Letter to Martin Luther King, Jr. 9/14/1958. Brooklyn, N.Y. (TAHLS) 1 p. CSKC: Sermon file, folder 145, December 20, 1958. 580914-002.

9/19/1958	King, Martin Luther, Jr. Letter to Franklin I. (Franklin Irvin) Sheeder. 9/19/1958. [*Montgomery, Ala.*] (TLc) 1 p. MLKP-MBU: Box 69. 580919-006.	Calendar

9/19/1958   King, Martin Luther, Jr. Letter to Franklin I. (Franklin Irvin) Sheeder. 9/19/1958. [*Montgomery, Ala.*] (TLc) 1 p. MLKP-MBU: Box 69. 580919-006.   Calendar

9/20/1958   Kelsey, George D. (Drew University). Letter to Martin Luther King, Jr. 9/20/1958. Madison, N.J. (ALS) 1 p. CSKC. 580920-009.

9/20/1958   Jackson, Mahalia. Telegram to Martin Luther King, Jr. [*9/20/1958*]. Chicago, Ill. (PWSr) 1 p. CSKC. 580920-011.

9/21/1958   Scott, Fannie E. Telegram to Martin Luther King, Jr. [*9/21/1958*]. New York, N.Y. (PWSr) 1 p. CSKC. 580921-006.

9/21/1958   Johnson, Mordecai W. (Mordecai Wyatt). Telegram to Martin Luther King, Jr. [*9/21/1958*]. Washington, D.C. (PHWSr) 1 p. CSKC. 580921-010.

9/22/1958   Siciliano, Rocco C. (United States. White House). Letter to Martin Luther King, Jr. 9/22/1958. Washington, D.C. (TLS) 1 p. CSKC. 580922-011.

9/22/1958   Peale, Norman Vincent (Marble Collegiate Church). Letter to Martin Luther King, Jr. 9/22/1958. New York, N.Y. (THLS) 1 p. CSKC. 580922-013.

9/23/1958   Muste, A. J. (Abraham Johannes) (Fellowship of Reconciliation). Letter to Martin Luther King, Jr. 9/23/1958. New York, N.Y. (TALS) 1 p. CSKC: Sermon file, folder 138. 580923-004.

9/23/1958   Steinbeck, John. Letter to Martin Luther King, Jr. 9/23/1958. New York, N.Y. (ALS) 2 pp. CSKC. 580923-006.

9/23/1958   Goldstein, Israel (Congregation B'nai Jeshurun). Letter to Martin Luther King, Jr. 9/23/1958. New York, N.Y. (TLS) 1 p. CSKC. 580923-008.

9/24/1958   Shuttlesworth, Fred L. Telegram to Martin Luther King, Jr. [*9/24/1958*]. Gary, Ind. (PHWSr) 1 p. CSKC. 580924-012.

9/25/1958   Reeves, Ambrose. Letter to Martin Luther King, Jr. 9/25/1958. Johannesburg, South Africa (THL) 1 p. CSKC. 580925-004.

9/25/1958   Burroughs, Nannie Helen. Telegram to Martin Luther King, Jr. 9/25/1958. Washington, D.C. (PHWSr) 1 p. CSKC. 580925-005.

10/1/1958–   [*SCLC*]. "Possible conference schedule." [*10/1/1958–10/2/1958*]. (TDf) 1 p.
10/2/1958   CSKC: Sermon file, folder 144, "Meaning of Civil Disobedience." 581002-011.

10/3/1958   Dahlberg, Edwin T. (Edwin Theodore) (National Council of the Churches of Christ in the United States of America). Letter to Martin Luther King, Jr. 10/3/1958. St. Louis, Mo. (TLS) 1 p. CSKC. 581003-008.

10/15/1958   King, Martin Luther, Jr. Letter to James R. Robinson. 10/15/1958. [*Brooklyn, N.Y.*] (TLc) 1 p. CSKC. 581015-007.

10/17/1958   King, Martin Luther, Jr. Letter to Norman Vincent Peale. 10/17/1958. [*Brooklyn, N.Y.*] (TLc) 1 p. CSKC. 581017-022.

10/17/1958   King, Martin Luther, Jr. Letter to Lena Horne. 10/17/1958. [*Brooklyn, N.Y.*] (TLc) 1 p. CSKC. 581017-023.

10/17/1958   King, Martin Luther, Jr. Letter to Jo Ann Gibson Robinson. 10/17/1958. [*Brooklyn, N.Y.*] (TLc) 1 p. CSKC. 581017-024.

10/17/1958   King, Martin Luther, Jr. Letter to Rumsey M. McGregor. 10/17/1958. [*Brooklyn, N.Y.*] (TLc) 1 p. CSKC. 581017-029.

10/20/1958   King, Martin Luther, Jr. Letter to W. Averell (William Averell) Harriman. 10/20/1958. [*Brooklyn, N.Y.*] (TLc) 1 p. CSKC. 581020-008.

10/21/1958   King, Martin Luther, Jr. Letter to John Steinbeck. 10/21/1958. [*Brooklyn, N.Y.*] (TLc) 1 p. CSKC. 581021-004.

10/23/1958   King, Martin Luther, Jr. Letter to George D. Kelsey. 10/23/1958. [*Brooklyn, N.Y.*] (TLc) 1 p. CSKC. 581023-012.

10/23/1958   King, Martin Luther, Jr. Letter to Robert S. Graetz and Jeanie Graetz. 10/23/1958. [*Brooklyn, N.Y.*] (TLc) 1 p. CSKC. 581023-014.

10/24/1958   Wentzel, Fred D. (Christian Education Press). Letter to Martin Luther King, Jr. 10/24/1958. Philadelphia, Pa. (TLS) 1 p. MLKP-MBU. 581024-007.

10/27/1958   King, Martin Luther, Jr. Statement on arrest of ministers. [*10/27/1958*]. [*Montgomery, Ala.*] (AD) 1 p. CSKC: Sermon file, folder 106, "Sermons." 581027-012.

10/29/1958   King, Martin Luther, Jr. Letter to Edwin T. (Edwin Theodore) Dahlberg. 10/29/1958. [*Montgomery, Ala.*] (TLc) 1 p. CSKC. 581029-013.

10/30/1958   Laird, James H. (Central Methodist Church). Letter to Martin Luther King, Jr. 10/30/1958. Detroit, Mich. (THLS) 1 p. MLKP-MBU: Box 37A. 581030-011.

11/1958   King, Martin Luther, Jr. Inscriptions on complimentary copies of *Stride Toward Freedom*. [*11/1958*]. Montgomery, Ala. (THD) 2 pp. MLKP-MBU: Box 118. 581100-013.

11/1958   King, Martin Luther, Jr. Letter to W. Averell (William Averell) Harriman. [*11/1958*]. [*Montgomery, Ala.*] (TLc) 1 p. CSKC: Sermon file, folder 145, December 20, 1958. 581100-014.

677

11/1958		King, Martin Luther, Jr. Inscription to Harry Emerson Fosdick. [*11/1958*]. [*Montgomery, Ala.*] (ALS) 1 p. PrRE. 581100-021.
11/1958		King, Martin Luther, Jr. "What Negroes Can Learn from History." [*11/1958*]. [*Montgomery, Ala.*] (AD) 2 pp. MLKP-MBU: Box 119. 581100-023.
11/1/1957– 11/30/1958		King, Martin Luther, Jr. Draft, Annual report, Dexter Avenue Baptist Church. [*11/1/1957–11/30/1958*]. [*Montgomery, Ala.*] (TAHDd) 21 pp. CSKC: Sermon file, folder 88. 581130-003.
12/1958		King, Martin Luther, Jr. Letter to A. J. (Abraham Johannes) Muste, Norman Thomas, A. Philip (Asa Philip) Randolph, and James L. Hicks. [*12/1958*]. [*Montgomery, Ala.*] (THLd) 1 p. CSKC: Sermon file, folder 145, December 20, 1958. 581200-008.
12/9/1958		King, Martin Luther, Jr. Letter to Fred D. Wentzel. 12/9/1958. [*Montgomery, Ala.*] (TLc) 1 p. MLKP-MBU: Box 52. 581209-007.
12/14/1958		Dexter Avenue Baptist Church. Program, Sunday services. 12/14/1958. Montgomery, Ala. (TD) 4 pp. DABCC. 581214-000.
12/21/1958		Dexter Avenue Baptist Church. Program, Sunday services. 12/21/1958. Montgomery, Ala. (THD) 4 pp. DABCC. 581221-000.
12/28/1958		Dexter Avenue Baptist Church. Program, Sunday services. 12/28/1958. Montgomery, Ala. (TD) 4 pp. DABCC. 581228-000.
10/1958– 12/1958		King, Martin Luther, Jr. Draft, Letter to twelve southern governors. [*10/1958–12/1958*]. (TLd) 3 pp. CSKC: Sermon file, folder 145, December 20, 1958. 581200-009.
1959		King, Martin Luther, Jr. "Hopeful Signs on the Human Relations Horizon." [*1959*]. [*Montgomery, Ala.*] (AD) 5 pp. MLKJP-GAMK: Box 108. 590000-000.
1959		King, Martin Luther, Jr. Draft, "What Is Man?" [*1959*]. [*Montgomery, Ala.*] (TADd) 16 pp. CSKC: Sermon file, folder 22, "What Is Man?" 590000-042.
1959		King, Martin Luther, Jr. Draft, What Is Man? [*1959*]. [*Montgomery, Ala.*] (TDf) 2 pp. CSKC: Sermon file, folder 90. 590000-074.
1959		King, Martin Luther, Jr. When Your A String Breaks, Sermon notes. [*1959*]. [*Montgomery, Ala.*] (AD) 1 p. CSKC: Sermon file, folder 105, "Making the Best of a Bad Mess." 590000-094.
1/1959		SCLC. Layout, "The Crusader." [*1/1959*]. (AD) 3 pp. CSKC: Sermon file, folder 106, "Sermons." 590100-008.
1/4/1959		Dexter Avenue Baptist Church. Program, Sunday services. 1/4/1959. Montgomery, Ala. (TD) 4 pp. DABCC. 590104-000.
1/11/1959		Dexter Avenue Baptist Church. Program, Sunday services. 1/11/1959. Montgomery, Ala. (TD) 4 pp. DABCC. 590111-000.
1/18/1959		Dexter Avenue Baptist Church. Program, Sunday services. 1/18/1959. Montgomery, Ala. (TD) 4 pp. DABCC. 590118-000.
1/24/1959		Pond, Chomingwen (Garrett Biblical Institution). Letter to Martin Luther King, Jr. 1/24/1959. Evanston, Ill. (APLS) 5 pp. CSKC: Sermon file, folder 159, Speeches—Reprints in Various Magazines, M. L. King. 590124-001.
1/28/1959		King, Martin Luther, Jr. Letter to Samuel McCrea Cavert. 1/28/1959. [*Montgomery, Ala.*] (TLc) 1 p. MLKP-MBU: Box 68. 590128-024.
1/29/1959		Fair Share Organization. Program, "Dr. Martin Luther King, Jr. in a bon voyage to Europe." 1/29/1959. Gary, Ind. (PD) 26 pp. CSKC: Sermon file, folder 159, Speeches—Reprints in Various Magazines, M. L. King. 590129-006.
2/1959		*The National Eagle* 9. 2/1959. Hartford, Mich. (PHD) 13 pp. CSKC: Sermon file, folder 159, Speeches—Reprints in Various magazines, M. L. King. 590200-017.
2/8/1959		Dexter Avenue Baptist Church. Program, Sunday services. 2/8/1959. Montgomery, Ala. (TD) 4 pp. DABCC. 590208-000.
2/25/1959		Bristol, James E. Letter to Dorothy Bristol. 2/25/1959. Bangalore, India (TAHLc) 2 pp. AFSCR-PPAFS. 590225-001.
3/22/1959		Dexter Avenue Baptist Church. Program, Sunday services. 3/22/1959. Montgomery, Ala. (TD) 4 pp. DABCC. 590322-000.
3/22/1959		King, Martin Luther, Jr. Palm Sunday Sermon on Mohandas K. Gandhi. 3/22/1959. [*Montgomery, Ala.*] (THTa) 11 pp. MLKJP-GAMK. 590322-001.
3/29/1959		Dexter Avenue Baptist Church. Program, Sunday services. 3/29/1959. Montgomery, Ala. (THD) 4 pp. DABCC. 590329-000.
3/29/1959		King, Martin Luther, Jr. A Walk Through the Holy Land, Easter Sunday Sermon delivered at Dexter Avenue Baptist Church. [*3/29/1959*]. [*Montgomery, Ala.*] (At) 47.3 min. (1 sound cassette: analog.) MLKJP-GAMK: T-17. 590329-001.

4/5/1959	Dexter Avenue Baptist Church. Program, Sunday services. 4/5/1959. Montgomery, Ala. (TD) 4 pp. DABCC. 590405-000.	Calendar

4/12/1959   Dexter Avenue Baptist Church. Program, Sunday services. 4/12/1959. Montgomery, Ala. (TD) 4 pp. DABCC. 590412-001.

4/12/1959   Mount Vernon First Baptist Church. Program, Installation of Alfred Daniel King. 4/12/1959. Newnan, Ga. (PHD) 4 pp. (Marginal comments by King.) MLKP-MBU: Box 82. 590412-004.

4/14/1959   Lenox, G. Merrill (Detroit Council of Churches). Letter to Martin Luther King, Jr. 4/14/1959. Detroit, Mich. (THLS) 1 p. MLKP-MBU: Box 38A. 590414-001.

4/19/1959   King, Martin Luther, Jr. "The Dimensions of a Complete Life," Address at the Chicago Sunday Evening Club. 4/19/1959. Chicago, Ill. (TD) 5 pp. SCLCR-GAMK: Box 27. 590419-001.

4/26/1959   Dexter Avenue Baptist Church. Program, Sunday services. 4/26/1959. Montgomery, Ala. (TD) 3 pp. DABCC. 590426-000.

4/30/1959   King, Martin Luther, Jr. Letter to G. Merrill Lenox. 4/30/1959. [*Montgomery, Ala.*] (TLc) 1 p. MLKP-MBU: Box 38A. 590430-006.

5/1959   King, Martin Luther, Jr. "Sermons for Future Weeks." [*5/1959*]. [*Montgomery, Ala.*] (AD) 1 p. MLKP-MBU: Box 116. 590500-000.

5/3/1959   Dexter Avenue Baptist Church. Program, Sunday services. 5/3/1959. Montgomery, Ala. (TD) 4 pp. DABCC. 590503-000.

5/10/1959   Dexter Avenue Baptist Church. Program, Sunday services. 5/10/1959. Montgomery, Ala. (TD) 4 pp. DABCC. 590510-000.

5/11/1959   Religious Leaders Conference. "Workshop leader's guide." [*5/11/1959*]. (TD) 3 pp. CSKC: Sermon file, folder 145, December 20, 1958. 590511-011.

5/11/1959   King, Martin Luther, Jr. Draft, Address at the Religious Leaders Conference. [*5/11/1959*]. [*Montgomery, Ala.*] (THADfd) 5 pp. CSKC: Sermon file, folder 145, December 20, 1958. 590511-012.

5/17/1959   Dexter Avenue Baptist Church. Program, Sunday services. 5/17/1959. Montgomery, Ala. (TD) 3 pp. DABCC. 590517-000.

5/18/1959   King, Martin Luther, Jr. Letter to D. Elton Trueblood. 5/18/1959. [*Montgomery, Ala.*] (TLc) 1 p. MLKP-MBU: Box 38A. 590518-002.

5/29/1959   Ballou, Maude L. Letter to Victor G. Backus. 5/29/1959. [*Montgomery, Ala.*] (TLc) 1 p. (Contains enclosure 590531-002.) MLKP-MBU: Box 38A. 590529-005.

5/31/1959   Dexter Avenue Baptist Church. Program, Sunday services. 5/31/1959. Montgomery, Ala. (TD) 3 pp. DABCC. 590531-000.

5/31/1959   King, Martin Luther, Jr. "The Dimensions of a Complete Life," Sermon at Dillard University. [*5/31/1959*]. [*New Orleans, La.*] (TD) 12 pp. (Enclosed in 590529-005.) CSKC: Sermon file, folder 21, "The Three Dimensions of a Complete Life." 590531-002.

6/1/1959   Trueblood, D. Elton (Earlham College). Letter to Martin Luther King, Jr. 6/1/1959. Richmond, Ind. (TLS) 1 p. MLKP–MBU: Box 38A. 590601-005.

6/1/1959   King, Martin Luther, Jr. Letter to Ben L. Rose. 6/1/1959. [*Montgomery, Ala.*] (TLc) 1 p. MLKP-MBU: Box 68. 590601-013.

6/14/1959   Dexter Avenue Baptist Church. Program, Sunday services. 6/14/1959. Montgomery, Ala. (THD) 4 pp. DABCC. 590614-000.

6/14/1959   Dexter Avenue Baptist Church June Club. "Church covenant." 6/14/1959. (TD) 2 pp. MLKJP-GAMK: Vault Box 8. 590614-002.

6/21/1959   Dexter Avenue Baptist Church. Program, Sunday services. 6/21/1959. Montgomery, Ala. (TD) 4 pp. DABCC. 590621-000.

6/28/1959   Dexter Avenue Baptist Church. Program, Sunday services. 6/28/1959. Montgomery, Ala. (TD) 4 pp. DABCC. 590628-000.

7/19/1959   Dexter Avenue Baptist Church. Program, Sunday services. 7/19/1959. Montgomery, Ala. (TD) 3 pp. DABCC. 590719-000.

7/26/1959   Dexter Avenue Baptist Church. Program, Sunday services. 7/26/1959. Montgomery, Ala. (TD) 4 pp. DABCC. 590726-000.

7/26/1959   King, Martin Luther (Ebenezer Baptist Church). Religious indecision. [*7/26/1959*]. (THD) 4 pp. MLKP-MBU: Box 113. 590726-001.

7/27/1959   Arnold, Melvin (Harper & Brothers). Letter to Martin Luther King, Jr. 7/27/1959. New York, N.Y. (TL) 1 p. MLKP-MBU: Box 2. 590727-002.

7/29/1959   King, Martin Luther, Jr. "A Knock at Midnight." [*7/29/1959*]. [*Montgomery, Ala.*] (AD) 2 pp. CSKC: Sermon file, folder 8, "A Knock at Midnight." 590729-008.

7/30/1959   Thatcher, Joan (American Baptist Convention). Letter to Martin Luther King, Jr. 7/30/1959. New York, N.Y. (TLS) 1 p. MLKP-MBU: Box 21. 590730-000.

8/1959	Randall, T. H. (Thomas Hamilton) (Dexter Avenue Baptist Church). Letter to Martin Luther King, Jr. [*8/1959*]. (TLfS) 1 p. (590000-048 on verso, pp. 356–357 in this volume.) CSKC: Sermon file, folder 83, "I'm Going To Procrastination." 590800-007.
8/2/1959	Dexter Avenue Baptist Church. Program, Sunday services. 8/2/1959. Montgomery, Ala. (TD) 4 pp. DABCC. 590802-000.
8/7/1959	Ballou, Maude L. Letter to Joan Thatcher. 8/7/1959. [*Montgomery, Ala.*] (TLc) 1 p. (Contains enclosure 590807-005.) MLKP-MBU: Box 21. 590807-000.
8/9/1959	Dexter Avenue Baptist Church. Program, Sunday services. 8/9/1959. Montgomery, Ala. (TD) 4 pp. DABCC. 590809-000.
8/14/1959	Dabbs, James McBride (Southern Regional Council). Letter to Martin Luther King, Jr. 8/14/1959. Mayesville, S.C. (TLS) 1 p. SCLCR-GAMK: Box 3. 590814-003.
8/16/1959	Dexter Avenue Baptist Church. Program, Sunday services. 8/16/1959. Montgomery, Ala. (TD) 4 pp. DABCC. 590816-000.
8/23/1959	King, Martin Luther, Jr. Loving Your Enemies, Sermon delivered at Central Methodist Church. [*8/23/1959*]. Detroit, Mich. (At) 21.5 min. (1 sound cassette: analog.) MiDCUMA. 590823-002.
8/27/1959	King, Martin Luther, Jr. Letter to Edward C. Stone. 8/27/1959. [*Montgomery, Ala.*] (TLc) 1 p. MLKP-MBU: Box 70. 590827-007.
8/30/1959	Dexter Avenue Baptist Church. Program, Sunday services. 8/30/1959. Montgomery, Ala. (TD) 3 pp. DABCC. 590830-000.
8/30/1959	King, Martin Luther, Jr. "A Tough Mind and a Tender Heart," Sermon outline. [*8/30/1959*]. [*Montgomery, Ala.*] (ADf) 6 pp. CSKC: Sermon file, folder 17, "A Tough Mind and a Tender Heart." 590830-003.
9/2/1959	Arnold, Melvin (Harper & Brothers). Letter to Martin Luther King, Jr. 9/2/1959. New York, N.Y. (TLS) 1 p. MLKP-MBU. 590902-000.
9/6/1959	Dexter Avenue Baptist Church. Program, Sunday services. 9/6/1959. Montgomery, Ala. (THD) 5 pp. DABCC. 590906-000.
9/10/1959	Jackson, J. H. (Joseph Harrison) (National Baptist Convention of the United States of America). "Address at the seventy-ninth annual session of the National Baptist Convention, U.S.A., Inc." 9/10/1959. San Francisco, Calif. (PHD) 26 pp. (Marginal comments by King.) CSKC: Sermon file, folder 38, "Addresses by Others." 590910-004.
9/27/1959	Dexter Avenue Baptist Church. Program, Sunday services. 9/27/1959. Montgomery, Ala. (TD) 4 pp. DABCC. 590927-001.
9/29/1959	King, Martin Luther, Jr. Letter to Melvin Arnold. 9/29/1959. [*Montgomery, Ala.*] (TLc) 1 p. MLKP-MBU: Box 2. 590929-000.
10/1959	Crozer Theological Seminary. *Bulletin 51: The Voice Issue.* 10/1959. Chester, Pa. (PHD) 16 pp. CSKC: Sermon file, folder 138. 591000-014.
10/1959	[*King, Martin Luther, Jr.*]. The Social Organization of Nonviolence. [*10/1959*]. [*Montgomery, Ala.*] (THD) 5 pp. (Draft of 10/1959 *Liberation.*) CSKC: Sermon file, folder 124. 591000-015.
10/5/1959	Arnold, Melvin (Harper & Brothers). Letter to Martin Luther King, Jr. 10/5/1959. New York, N.Y. (TLS) 1 p. MLKP-MBU. 591005-000.
10/12/1959	Newgent, William E. Letter to Martin Luther King, Jr. 10/12/1959. Washington, D.C. (TLS) 1 p. MLKP-MBU: Box 32A. 591012-012.
10/18/1959	Dexter Avenue Baptist Church. Program, Sunday services. 10/18/1959. Montgomery, Ala. (TD) 3 pp. DABCC. 591018-000.
10/18/1959–10/20/1959	Program, "Ministers' conference on the problems of alcohol." 10/18/1959–10/20/1959. (TD) 50 pp. CtY-D: Group 73. 591020-000.
11/1/1959	Dexter Avenue Baptist Church. Program, Sunday services. 11/1/1959. Montgomery, Ala. (TD) 4 pp. DABCC. 591101-000.
11/3/1959	[*Randall, T. H. (Thomas Hamilton)*] (Dexter Avenue Baptist Church). Letter to Martin Luther King, Jr. 11/3/1959. Montgomery, Ala. (TALf) 1 p. (590000-046 on verso, pp. 354–358 in this volume.) CSKC: Sermon file, folder 82, "Making It in on Broken Pieces." 591103-010.
11/15/1959	Dexter Avenue Baptist Church. Program, Sunday services. 11/15/1959. Montgomery, Ala. (TD) 4 pp. DABCC. 591115-000.
11/18/1959	Cavert, Samuel McCrea (*Pulpit Digest*). Letter to Martin Luther King, Jr. 11/18/1959. Great Neck, N.Y. (TLSr) 1 p. MLKP-MBU: Box 33A. 591118-000.
11/20/1959	Wofford, Harris. "The Law and Civil Disobedience." 11/20/1959. (THD) 4 pp.

(Marginal comments by King.) CSKC: Sermon file, folder 144, "Meaning of Civil Disobedience." 591120-008.

11/29/1959   Dexter Avenue Baptist Church. Program, Sunday services. 11/29/1959. Montgomery, Ala. (TD) 3 pp. DABCC. 591129-000.

12/2/1959   Arnold, Melvin (Harper & Brothers). Letter to Martin Luther King, Jr. 12/2/1959. New York, N.Y. (TLS) 1 p. MLKP-MBU. 591202-005.

12/11/1959   Thurman, Howard (Boston University). "We Believe." 12/11/1959. Boston, Mass. (THD) 2 pp. (Marginal comments by King.) CSKC: Sermon file, folder 1, "Loving Your Enemies." 591211-002.

12/18/1959   Thurman, Howard (Boston University). "We Believe." 12/18/1959. Boston, Mass. (TD) 2 pp. CSKC: Sermon file, folder 1, "Loving Your Enemies." 591218-002.

12/20/1959   Dexter Avenue Baptist Church. Program, Sunday services. 12/20/1959. Montgomery, Ala. (TD) 4 pp. CKFC. 591220-000.

12/27/1959   Dexter Avenue Baptist Church. Program, Sunday services. 12/27/1959. Montgomery, Ala. (TD) 3 pp. CKFC. 591227-000.

12/31/1959   Fey, Harold Edward (*Christian Century*). Letter to Martin Luther King, Jr. 12/31/1959. Chicago, Ill. (TLS) 1 p. CSKC: Sermon file, folder 138. 591231-000.

1946–1959   Smith, A. Milton (First Church of the Nazarene). "A Militant Christianity." [*1946–1959*]. (PDf) 1 p. CSKC: Sermon file, folder 14, "Transformed Non-Conformist." 590000-149.

1956–1959   King, Martin Luther, Jr. Tribute to supporter. [*1956–1959?*]. [*Montgomery, Ala.*] (AD) 2 pp. CSKC: Sermon file, folder 106, "Sermons." 590000-058.

1960   United Presbyterian Church. "Dynamic for Teaching." [*1960*]. New York, N.Y. (PD) 4 pp. CSKC: Sermon file, folder 139, "Articles on 'Sit-ins' and Civil Rights Debate." 600000-075.

1960   **Cartier-Bresson, Henri (Magnum Photos). Photo of Martin Luther King, Jr. [*1960*]. Atlanta, Ga. (PPh) 1 p. NNMAGPC. 600000-155.**

1960   **Cartier-Bresson, Henri (Magnum Photos). Photo of Martin Luther King, Jr. and Dora E. McDonald in his study at Ebenezer. [*1960*]. Atlanta, Ga. (Ph) 1 p. NNMAGPC. 600000-165.**

1960   **Diehl, William. Photo of Martin Luther King, Jr., Coretta Scott King, Yolanda Denise King, and Martin Luther King, III. 1960. Atlanta, Ga. (Ph) 1 p. RUSIA-DNA. 600000-216.**

1960   King, Martin Luther, Jr. "If." [*1960*]. [*Atlanta, Ga.*] (AD) 1 p. (verso of 600300-016) CSKC: Sermon file, folder 65. 600000-199.

1/1960   King, Martin Luther, Jr. "The Great Debate: Is Violence Necessary to Combat Injustice?" 1/1960. Louisville, Ky. From: *Southern Patriot,* January 1960, p. 3. (PD) 1 p. CSKC: Sermon file, folder 159, Speeches—Reprints in Various Magazines, M. L. King. 600100-000.

1/1960   Hughes, Langston. "Prayer for the Mantle-piece." 1/1960. (TDS) 1 p. (Enclosed in 600118-001.) MLKP-MBU: Box 30A. 600100-002.

1/1960   Hughes, Langston. "Merry-go-Round." [*1/1960*]. (TDS) 1 p. (Enclosed in 600118-001.) MLKP-MBU: Box 30A. 600100-003.

1/3/1960   Dexter Avenue Baptist Church. Program, Sunday services. 1/3/1960. Montgomery, Ala. (TD) 4 pp. CKFC. 600103-000.

1/17/1960   Dexter Avenue Baptist Church. Program, Sunday services. 1/17/1960. Montgomery, Ala. (THD) 4 pp. (Marginal comments by King.) MLKP-MBU: Box 82. 600117-000.

1/17/1960   Women's Missionary Society of the Mt. Tabo AME Zion Church. Program, "Women Sharing in Kingdom Building." 1/17/1960. Marion, Ala. (TD) 4 pp. CSKC: Sermon file, folder 128, Speech 1/17/59 Mt. Tabo A.M.E. Z. Church. 600117-003.

1/18/1960   Hughes, Langston. Letter to Martin Luther King, Jr. 1/18/1960. (TLS) 1 p. (Contains enclosures 600100-002 and 600100-003.) MLKP-MBU: Box 30A. 600118-001.

1/28/1960   Exman, Eugene (Harper & Brothers). Letter to Martin Luther King, Jr. 1/28/1960. New York, N.Y. (TLS) 1 p. MLKP-MBU: Box 2. 600128-000.

1/31/1960   Dexter Avenue Baptist Church. Program, Sunday services. 1/31/1960. Montgomery, Ala. (TD) 4 pp. MLKP-MBU: Box 24. 600131-000.

1/31/1960   Dexter Avenue Baptist Church. A Salute to Dr. and Mrs. Martin Luther King, Jr. 1/31/1960. Montgomery, Ala. (At) 180 min. (3 sound cassettes: analog.) MLKEC: ET-55 & ET-56. 600131-005.

2/1/1960   MIA. Program, "A Testimonial of Love and Loyalty." 2/1/1960. Montgomery, Ala. (PHD) 4 pp. LDRP-NN-Sc: Box 3. 600201-000.

2/6/1960   King, Martin Luther, Jr. Letter to P. J. Ellis. 2/6/1960. [*Atlanta, Ga.*] (TLc) 2 pp. MLKP-MBU: Box 47A. 600206-001.

2/14/1960   Lewis, Anthony. "Human Background of the Civil Rights Issue." 2/14/1960. New York, N.Y. (PD) 4 pp. (Reprint of 2/14/1960 *New York Times Magazine*.) CSKC: Sermon file, folder 139, "Articles on 'Sit-ins' and Civil Rights Debate." 600214-004.

2/17/1960   Dawkins, Maurice A. (California Ministers Christian Leadership Conference on Civil Rights). Letter to Martin Luther King, Jr. 2/17/1960. Los Angeles, Calif. (THLS) 2 pp. MLKP-MBU: Box 23A. 600217-003.

2/17/1960   "Martin Luther King Column" I. [*2/17/1960*]. (TDd) 3 pp. CSKC: Sermon file, folder 146, Dr. Martin Luther King—Columns, and folder 147, January 21, 1960. 600217-014.

2/17/1960   "Martin Luther King Column" II. [*2/17/1960*]. (THDd) 3 pp. CSKC: Sermon file, folder 146, Dr. Martin Luther King—Columns, and folder 147, January 21, 1960. 600217-015.

2/17/1960   "Martin Luther King Column" III. [*2/17/1960*]. (THDd) 3 pp. CSKC: Sermon file, folder 146, Dr. Martin Luther King—Columns, and folder 147, January 21, 1960. 600217-016.

2/17/1960   "Martin Luther King Column" IV. [*2/17/1960*]. (THDd) 3 pp. CSKC: Sermon file, folder 146, Dr. Martin Luther King—Columns, and folder 147, January 21, 1960. 600217-017.

2/18/1960   Duckett, Alfred (Alfred Duckett Associates). Letter to Martin Luther King, Jr. 2/18/1960. New York, N.Y. (TLS) 2 pp. (Contains enclosure 600218-017.) CSKC: Sermon file, folder 146, Dr. Martin Luther King—Columns. 600218-013.

2/18/1960   "Martin Luther King Column" V. [*2/18/1960*]. (TDd) 3 pp. (Enclosed in 600218-013.) CSKC: Sermon file, folder 124. 600218-017.

2/21/1960   Chicago Sunday Evening Club. Program, "Order of service." 2/21/1960. Chicago, Ill. (PD) 4 pp. MLKJP-GAMK: Box 123A. 600221-004.

2/21/1960   Quinn Chapel, The Original Forty Club, and Alpha Phi Alpha Fraternity, Inc. Announcement, "A special service of worship in observance of Brotherhood Week." 2/21/1960. Chicago, Ill. (THDc) 1 p. (Contains enclosure 600221-006.) AJC-ICHi: Box 40. 600221-005.

2/21/1960   Quinn Chapel. "Archibald J. Carey, Jr. Award." 2/21/1960. (TDc) 1 p. (Enclosed in 600221-005.) AJC-ICHi: Box 40. 600221-006.

2/25/1960   Southern Regional Council. "The Student Protest Movement, Winter 1960." 2/25/1960. (TD) 20 pp. CSKC: Sermon file, folder 139, "Articles on 'Sit-ins' and Civil Rights Debate." 600225-006.

3/1960   *New South* 15. 3/1960. Atlanta, Ga. (PD) 16 pp. CSKC: Sermon file, folder 139, "Articles on 'Sit-ins' and Civil Rights Debate." 600300-008.

3/1/1960   Neal, Wayne A. (San Diego County Council of Churches). Letter to Martin Luther King, Jr. 3/1/1960. San Diego, Calif. (THLS) 1 p. (Marginal comments by King.) MLKP-MBU: Box 32. 600301-000.

3/9/1960   Whitley, Murlene. Letter to Martin Luther King, Jr. 3/9/1960. Bakersfield, Calif. (TLc) 1 p. MLKP-MBU: Box 73A. 600309-012.

3/15/1960   King, Martin Luther, Jr. Letter to Archibald J. (Archibald James) Carey. 3/15/1960. [*Atlanta, Ga.*] (TLc) 1 p. MLKP-MBU: Box 22. 600315-016.

3/15/1960   Conger, Richard Stockton. Letter to Martin Luther King, Jr. 3/15/1960. Princeton, N.J. (THLS) 1 p. MLKJP-GAMK: Box 22. 600315-019.

3/20/1960   Tabernacle Baptist Church. Program, Sunday services. 3/20/1960. Detroit, Mich. (PTD) 6 pp. CSKC. 600320-002.

3/23/1960   Fleischman, Harry. "Summary of CCD mass media committee meeting." New York, N.Y. 3/23/1960. (TDS) 3 pp. CSKC: Sermon file, folder 139, "Articles on 'Sit-ins' and Civil Rights Debate." 600323-007.

3/25/1960   King, Martin Luther, Jr. Letter to Marvin Robinson. 3/25/1960. [*Atlanta, Ga.*] (TLc) 1 p. MLKP-MBU: Box 68. 600325-004.

3/26/1960   Jewish Labor Committee. "A Tribute to the Organized Labor Movement." 3/26/1960. New York, N.Y. (PD) 6 pp. CSKC: Sermon file, folder 139, "Articles on 'Sit-ins' and Civil Rights Debate." 600326-003.

4/1960   *The Progressive* 24. 4/1960. Madison, Wis. (PD) 50 pp. CSKC: Sermon file, folder 139, "Articles on 'Sit-ins' and Civil Rights Debate." 600400-016.

4/1960   King, Martin Luther, Jr. Notes on sit-ins, the presidential election, and Harry S. Truman. [*4/1960*]. [*Atlanta, Ga.*] (AD) 13 pp. CSKC: Sermon file, folder 139, "Articles on 'Sit-ins' and Civil Rights Debate." 600400-017.

4/1/1960	National Council of the Protestant Episcopal Church. "Background paper on the student 'sit-in' protest movement in the light of the church's authoritative statements." 4/1/1960. New York, N.Y. (TD) 15 pp. CSKC: Sermon file, folder 139, "Articles on 'Sit-ins' and Civil Rights Debate." 600401-008.
4/3/1960	Ebenezer Baptist Church. Program, Sunday services. 4/3/1960. Atlanta, Ga. (TD) 4 pp. MLKJP-GAMK: Vault Box 9. 600403-000.
4/3/1960	King, Martin Luther, Jr. Love in Action II. [4/3/1960]. [Atlanta, Ga.] (AD) 2 pp. MLKJP-GAMK: Box 123. 600403-001.
4/6/1960	"The Terrible Meek." [4/6/1960]. (TD) 2 pp. (Reprint of 4/6/1960 Christian Century.) CSKC: Sermon file, folder 139, "Articles on 'Sit-ins' and Civil Rights Debate." 600406-015.
4/8/1960	Baker, Ella (SCLC). Letter to Student leaders. 4/8/1960. Atlanta, Ga. (TLc) 1 p. CSKC: Sermon file, folder 139, "Articles on 'Sit-ins' and Civil Rights Debate." 600408-011.
4/10/1960	King, Martin Luther, Jr. "Founders Day Address," Keep Moving from This Mountain. [4/10/1960]. Atlanta, Ga. (TD) 13 pp. CSKC: Sermon file, folder 78, "Keep Moving From This Mountain." 600410-001.
4/10/1960	King, Martin Luther, Jr. Outline, Founders Day Address, Keep Moving from this Mountain. [4/10/1960]. [Atlanta, Ga.] (AD) 3 pp. CSKC: Sermon file, folder 78, "Keep Moving From This Mountain." 600410-002.
4/10/1960	King, Martin Luther, Jr. The Tension Between Life's Palm Sunday and Life's Good Friday. [4/10/1960]. [Atlanta, Ga.] (AD) 3 pp. CSKC: Sermon file, folder 103, "The Tension between Life's Palm Sunday and Life's Good Friday." 600410-005.
4/13/1960	King, Martin Luther, Jr. Pilgrimage to Nonviolence. [4/13/1960]. (TADd) 10 pp. [Atlanta, Ga.] (Verso of 570221-008.) CSKC: Sermon file, folder 138. 600413-014.
4/13/1960	King, Martin Luther, Jr. "How My Theology Has Changed." [4/13/1960]. [Atlanta, Ga.] (AD) 2 pp. CSKC: Sermon file, folder 151, How My Mind Has Changed. 600413-021.
4/13/1960	King, Martin Luther, Jr. Draft, "How My Mind Has Changed in the Last Decade." [4/13/1960]. [Atlanta, Ga.] (ADfd) 18 pp. (Draft of 4/13/1960 Christian Century.) CSKC: Sermon file, folder 151, How My Mind Has Changed. 600413-023.
4/13/1960	King, Martin Luther, Jr. Draft, "How My Mind Has Changed in the Last Decade." [4/13/1960]. [Atlanta, Ga.] (ADd) 28 pp. (Draft of 4/13/1960 Christian Century.) CSKC: Sermon file, folder 151, How My Mind Has Changed. 600413-024.
4/13/1960	King, Martin Luther, Jr. Notes, "How My Mind Has Changed" series. [4/13/1960]. [Atlanta, Ga.] (AD) 8 pp. CSKC: Sermon file, folder 151, How My Mind Has Changed. 600413-025.
4/20/1960	Ballou, Maude L. Letter to Daniel G. Hill. 4/20/1960. [Atlanta, Ga.] (TLc) 1 p. MLKP-MBU: Box 40. 600420-004.
4/21/1960	King, Martin Luther, Jr. Letter to David S. Evans. 4/21/1960. [Atlanta, Ga.] (TLc) 1 p. MLKP-MBU: Box 24. 600421-000.
5/1960	King, Martin Luther, Jr. "The Burning Truth in the South." 5/1960. Madison, Wis. From: The Progressive 24 (May 1960): 8–10. (PD) 3 pp. CSKC: Sermon file, folder 125, Article—Martin L. King. 600500-000.
5/1/1960	**Uhrbrock, Donald (Time Inc.). Photo of Martin Luther King, Jr., Fred L. Shuttlesworth, and Martin Luther King, Sr. [5/1/1960]. Atlanta, Ga. (Ph) 1 p. NNTI. 600501-001.**
6/2/1960	Arnold, Melvin (Harper & Brothers). Letter to Martin Luther King, Jr. 6/2/1960. New York. N.Y. (TLS) 1 p. MLKP-MBU: Box 2. 600602-000.
6/22/1960	Stein, Edward V. "Persons in a Depersonalized Age." 6/22/1960. Chicago, Ill. From: Christian Century (22 June 1960): 744–746. (PHD) 4 pp. CSKC: Sermon file, folder 26, Christian Century June 22, 1960. 600622-004.
6/29/1960	Kelsey, George D. "The Lord of Life." [6/29/1960]. Rio de Janeiro, Brazil (THD) 5 pp. CSKC: Sermon file, folder 38, "Addresses by Others." 600629-004.
4/1960–6/1960	King, Martin Luther, Jr. (Ebenezer Baptist Church). "Going Forward By Going Backward," Address at the Chicago Sunday Evening Club on 2/21/1960. 4/1960–6/1960. Nashville, Tenn. From: A.M.E. Church Review 77 (April 1960–June 1960): 62-67. (PD) 6 pp. 600600-018.
7/1960	[SCLC]. "Challenge to new age, importance of voting." [7/1960]. (TD) 2 pp. CSKC: Sermon file, folder 148, "Speech on Voting." 600700-006.
7/1960	Westfeldt, Wallace. "Settling a Sit-in." [7/1960]. Nashville, Tenn. (PD) 12 pp. CSKC: Sermon file, folder 139, "Articles on 'Sit-ins' and Civil Rights Debate." 600700-014.

7/1/1960–
7/7/1960
    [*King, Martin Luther, Jr.*]. Draft, "Proposals to both parties." [*7/1/1960–7/7/1960*]. (TAHDd) 2 pp. (Enclosed in 600707-010.) CSKC: Sermon file, folder 148, "Speech on Voting." 600707-005.

7/1/1960–
7/7/1960
    [*King, Martin Luther, Jr.*]. Draft, "Introductory remarks to both parties." [*7/1/1960–7/7/1960*]. (TAHDd) 2 pp. (Enclosed in 600707-010.) CSKC: Sermon file, folder 148, "Speech on Voting." 600707-006.

7/1/1960–
7/7/1960
    Rustin, Bayard. Letter to Martin Luther King, Jr. [*7/1/1960–7/7/1960*]. (TADdI) 1 p. (Enclosed in 600707-010.) CSKC: Sermon file, folder 148, "Speech on Voting." 600707-009.

7/1/1960–
7/7/1960
    Rustin, Bayard. Letter to Martin Luther King, Jr. [*7/1/1960–7/7/1960*]. (TADdS) 1 p. (Contains enclosures 600707-005, 600707-006, & 600707-009.) CSKC: Sermon file, folder 148, "Speech on Voting." 600707-010.

7/10/1960
    King, Martin Luther, Jr. (SCLC). Address at NAACP Mass Rally for Civil Rights. 7/10/1960. Los Angeles, Calif. (TD) 2 pp. CSKC: Sermon file, folder 148, "Speech on Voting." 600710-001.

7/24/1960
    Ebenezer Baptist Church. Program, Sunday services. 7/24/1960. Atlanta, Ga. (TD) 4 pp. MLKP-MBU: Box 24. 600724-000.

7/1960–8/1960
    Graham, Frank Porter (United Nations). "Students 'Standing Up' for the American Dream." 7/1960–8/1960. Atlanta, Ga. From: *New South*, July–August 1960. (PDf) 1 p. CSKC: Sermon file, folder 39. 600800-003.

8/1/1960
    Congress of Racial Equality. "The meaning of the sit-ins." 8/1/1960. (THD) 6 pp. CSKC: Sermon file, folder 139, "Articles on 'Sit-ins' and Civil Rights Debate." 600801-007.

8/14/1960
    King, Martin Luther, Jr. "Levels of Love." [*8/14/1960*]. [*Atlanta, Ga.*] (AD) 4 pp. CSKC: Sermon file, folder 109, "Levels of Love." 600814-001.

8/20/1960
    Wood, James R. (SCLC). Press release, "Dr. King addresses mass meeting." 8/20/1960. Louisville, Ky. (TD) 1 p. CSKC: Sermon file, folder 148, "Speech on Voting." 600820-001.

8/23/1960
    King, Martin Luther, Jr. Outline, Address at Jefferson County Armory. 8/23/1960. Louisville, Ky. (TD) 1 p. CSKC: Sermon file, folder 148, "Speech on Voting." 600823-006.

8/24/1960
    "Let Us Kneel-in Together!" 8/24/1960. Atlanta, Ga. (PD) 2 pp. (Reprint of 8/24/1960 *Christian Century*.) CSKC: Sermon file, folder 139, "Articles on 'Sit-ins' and Civil Rights Debate." 600824-006.

9/1960
    Posey, Barbara Ann. "Why I Sit In." 9/1960. New York, N.Y. (Reprint of 9/1960 *Datebook*.) (PD) 4 pp. CSKC: Sermon file, folder 139, "Articles on 'Sit-ins' and Civil Rights Debate." 600900-004.

9/1/1960
    Uhrbrock, Donald (Time Inc.). Photo of Martin Luther King, Jr. and Ebenezer Baptist Church choir. [*9/1/1960*]. Atlanta, Ga. (Ph) 1 p. NNTI. 600901-007.

9/1/1960
    Uhrbrock, Donald (Time Inc.). Photo of Martin Luther King, Jr. [*9/1/1960*] Atlanta, Ga. (Ph) 1 p. NNTI. 600901-008.

6/26/1960–
9/4/1960
    Central Methodist Church. Announcement, "Summer preaching program." 6/26/1960–9/4/1960. Detroit, Mich. (PD) 4 pp. MLKP-MBU: Box 37A. 600904-001.

9/5/1960
    King, Martin Luther, Jr. Paul's Letter to American Christians, Sermon delivered at DePauw University School of the Prophets. 9/5/1960. [*Greencastle, Ind.*] (At) 35.9 min. (1 sound cassette: analog.) InGrD. 600905-000.

9/8/1960
    Jackson, J. H. (Joseph Harrison) (National Baptist Convention of the United States of America). "Address at the eightieth annual session of the National Baptist Convention, U.S.A., Inc." 9/8/1960. Philadelphia, Pa. (PHD) 35 pp. CSKC: Sermon file, folder 38, "Addresses by Others." 600908-002.

9/25/1960
    King, Martin Luther, Jr. The Negro and the American Dream, Excerpts of address at the annual Freedom Mass Meeting of the North Carolina State Conference of branches of the NAACP. 9/25/1960. Charlotte, N.C. (TAD) 5 pp. CSKC: Sermon file, folder 23. 600925-000.

10/1960
    King, Martin Luther, Jr. Notes on *Deep River* by Howard Thurman. [*10/1960*]. [*Atlanta, Ga.*] (AD) 1 p. (On verso of 601012-006.) CSKC: Sermon file, folder 13, "A Way Out." 601000-029.

10/1/1960
    Ebenezer Baptist Church. Press release, "'The Seeking God' King Jr.'s topic at Ebenezer." [*10/1/1960*]. (TD) 1 p. EBCR. 601001-003.

10/2/1960
    King, Martin Luther, Jr. (Ebenezer Baptist Church). "The Seeking God." [*10/2/1960*]. [*Atlanta, Ga.*] (AD) 5 pp. CSKC: Sermon file, folder 51, "The Seeking God (Parable of Lost Sheep)." 601002-001.

1/15/1961	King, Martin Luther, Jr. "Three Dimensions of a Complete Life," Sermon at Woodland Hills Community Church. [*1/15/1961*]. [*Woodland Hills, Calif.*] (TTa) 8 pp. FODC. 610115-002.
1/16/1961	Yungblut, John (Religious Society of Friends). Letter to Martin Luther King, Jr. 1/16/1961. Atlanta, Ga. (THLS) 3 pp. CSKC: Sermon file, folder 40, "Lecture on Philosophy of Nonviolence." 610116-006.
2/4/1961	King, Martin Luther, Jr. "The President Has the Power: Equality Now." 2/4/1961. New York, N.Y. (PD) 4 pp. (Reprint of 2/4/1961 *The Nation*.) CSKC: Sermon file, folder 133, Articles by MLK Jr. 610204-000.
2/7/1961	Dunbar, Leslie W. (Southern Regional Council). "Civil Disobedience." 2/7/1961. Richmond, Ind. (TD) 12 pp. CSKC: Sermon file, folder 144, "Meaning of Civil Disobedience." 610207-004.
2/15/1961	Lenox, G. Merrill (Detroit Council of Churches). Letter to Martin Luther King, Jr. 2/15/1961. Detroit, Mich. (THLS) 2 pp. (Includes enclosure.) MLKP-MBU: Box 38A. 610215-008.
2/15/1961	King, Martin Luther, Jr. Letter to G. Merrill Lenox. 2/15/1961. [*Atlanta, Ga.*] (TLc) 1 p. MLKP-MBU: Box 38A. 610215-009.
2/24/1961	Lenox, G. Merrill (Detroit Council of Churches). Letter to Martin Luther King, Jr. 2/24/1961. Detroit, Mich. (AHLS) 1 p. (Marginal comments by King.) MLKP-MBU: Box 38A. 610224-005.
3/1961	King, Martin Luther, Jr. (Ebenezer Baptist Church). Questions that Easter answers. [*3/1961*]. [*Atlanta, Ga.*] (ADd) 3 pp. CSKC. 610300-002.
3/8/1961	King, Martin Luther, Jr. Letter to G. Merrill Lenox. 3/8/1961. [*Atlanta, Ga.*] (TLc) 2 pp. (Includes enclosure.) MLKP-MBU: Box 38A. 610308-011.
3/15/1961	Lenox, G. Merrill (Detroit Council of Churches). Letter to Martin Luther King, Jr. 3/15/1961. Detroit, Mich. (TLS) 1 p. MLKP-MBU: Box 38A. 610315-003.
3/23/1961	King, Martin Luther, Jr. Letter to Lillian Miles. 3/23/1961. [*Atlanta, Ga.*] (THLc) 1 p. MLKP-MBU: Box 55. 610323-006.
2/15/1961– 3/30/1961	Detroit Council of Churches. Announcement, "Noon Lenten services." 2/15/1961–3/30/1961. Detroit, Mich. (PD) 1 p. MDCC-MiDW-AL: Box 8. 610330-008.
4/1961	King, Martin Luther, Jr. "Our God Is Able," Sermon outline. [*4/1961?*]. [*Atlanta, Ga.?*] (AD) 3 pp. CSKC: Sermon file, folder 11, "Our God Is Able." 610400-013.
4/1/1961	Ebenezer Baptist Church. Press release, Theme for Easter Sunday services. 4/1/1961. Atlanta, Ga. (THD) 1 p. EBCR. 610401-000.
4/8/1961	Ebenezer Baptist Church. Press release, "'The Meaning of Freedom,' Dr. King Jr.'s subject Sunday at Ebenezer." 4/8/1961. Atlanta, Ga. (TD) 1 p. EBCR. 610408-001.
4/19/1961	King, Martin Luther, Jr. Address delivered to Christian Ethics class at Southern Baptist Theological Seminary. [*4/19/1961*]. [*Louisville, Ky.*] (At) 42 min. (1 sound cassette: analog.) KyLoS. 610419-014.
4/19/1961	King, Martin Luther, Jr. "The Church on the Frontier of Racial Tension," Gay Lecture delivered at Southern Baptist Theological Seminary. 4/19/1961. Louisville, Ky. (At) 47.2 min. (1 sound cassette: analog.) KyLoS. 610419-015.
5/5/1961	Exman, Eugene (Harper & Brothers). Letter to Martin Luther King, Jr. 5/5/1961. New York, N.Y. (TLS) 1 p. MLKP-MBU: Box 56A. 610505-002.
5/6/1961	Ebenezer Baptist Church. Press release, "'The Other Prodigal Son,' Dr. King Jr.'s topic Sunday." 5/6/1961. Atlanta, Ga. (TD) 1 p. EBCR. 610506-001.
5/13/1961	Ebenezer Baptist Church. Press release, "'Crisis in the Modern Family,' Dr. King Jr's topic at Ebenezer." 5/13/1961. Atlanta, Ga. (TD) 1 p. EBCR. 610513-002.
5/28/1961	Rust, Henry. "God's Order—Man's Disorder." 5/28/1961. Whittier, Calif. (THDf) 4 pp. CSKC: Sermon file, folder 97. 610528-001.
6/1961	King, Martin Luther, Jr. (Ebenezer Baptist Church). "The Man Who Was a Fool," Sermon at the Chicago Sunday Evening Club on 1/29/1961. 6/1961. Chicago, Ill. From: *The Pulpit* 32 (June 1961): 4-6. (PD) 3 pp. CSKC: Sermon file, folder 41, The Man Who Was a Fool. 610600-000.
6/1961	*The Pulpit*, 32. 6/1961. Chicago, Ill. (PD) 28 pp. CSKC: Sermon file, folder 129, The Pulpit—1961 (June) Article by Dr. King. 610600-017.
6/2/1961	SCLC. Press release, "Martin Luther King, Jr., other southern leaders set to speak at series of New York protest meetings." 6/2/1961. Brooklyn, N.Y. (THD) 4 pp. CSKC: Sermon file, folder 32. 610602-008.
6/4/1961	University of Bridgeport. Citations for recipients read on the occasion of the conferral of the honorary degree of Doctor of Laws. 6/4/1961. Bridgeport, Conn. (TD) 4 pp. CSKC: Sermon file, folder 35. 610604-006.

6/5/1961	King, Martin Luther, Jr. (SCLC). Press release, Statement calling for executive order declaring segregation illegal. 6/5/1961. New York, N.Y. (THD) 2 pp. CSKC: Sermon file, folder 33. 610605-001.	Calendar
6/10/1961	Ebenezer Baptist Church. Press release, " 'Mastering Our Fears,' Dr. King Jr.'s topic at Ebenezer Sunday." 6/10/1961. Atlanta, Ga. (THD) 1 p. EBCR. 610610-001.	
8/5/1961	Ebenezer Baptist Church. Press release, "Dr. Martin Luther King, Jr. at Ebenezer Sunday." 8/5/1961. Atlanta, Ga. (TD) 1 p. EBCR. 610805-003.	
8/6/1961	King, Martin Luther, Jr. (Ebenezer Baptist Church). "Paul's Letter to American Christians." [8/6/1961]. [Atlanta, Ga.] (TD) 10 pp. MLKP-MBU. 610806-000.	
8/8/1961	McDonald, Dora E. Letter to Shirley Bird. 8/8/1961. [Atlanta, Ga.] (TLc) 1 p. MLKP-MBU: Box 46. 610808-007.	
8/14/1961	**Mooney, Jim (*New York Daily News*). Photo of Martin Luther King, Jr. greeting Riverside Church congregation. [*8/14/1961*]. New York, N.Y. (PPh) 1 p. CHAC. 610814-003.**	
7/1961–9/1961	King, Martin Luther, Jr. (Ebenezer Baptist Church). "The Man Who Was a Fool," Sermon at the Chicago Sunday Evening Club on 1/29/1961. 7/1961–9/1961. Nashville, Tenn. From: *A.M.E. Church Review* 78 (July–September 1961): 82-86. (PD) 5 pp. (Reprint of 6/1961 *The Pulpit*.) 610900-005.	
9/2/1961	King, Martin Luther, Jr. Invocation delivered at funeral of John Wesley Dobbs at Big Bethel AME Church. [9/2/1961]. Atlanta, Ga. (At) 6.7 min. (1 sound cassette: analog.) JWD-ARC-LNT. 610902-000.	
9/2/1961	King, Martin Luther, Jr. Draft, Invocation at funeral of John Wesley Dobbs. [9/2/1961]. [Atlanta, Ga.] (ADd) 6 pp. CSKC: Sermon file, folder 89. 610902-001.	
9/2/1961	Ebenezer Baptist Church. Press release, "Dr. King, Jr. at Ebenezer Sunday." 9/2/1961. Atlanta, Ga. (TD) 1 p. EBCR. 610902-006.	
9/9/1961	Ebenezer Baptist Church. Press release, "Martin Luther King, Jr. at Ebenezer Sunday." 9/9/1961. Atlanta, Ga. (THD) 1 p. EBCR. 610909-000.	
9/16/1961	Ebenezer Baptist Church. Press release, " 'Where Is God Found,' King Jr., at Ebenezer Sunday." [9/16/1961]. Atlanta, Ga. (TD) 1 p. EBCR. 610916-002.	
9/30/1961	Ebenezer Baptist Church. Press release, " 'Making Life Worth Living,' Martin Luther King's topic at Ebenezer Sunday." [9/30/1961]. Atlanta, Ga. (TD) 1 p. EBCR. 610930-000.	
10/1961	"Integrationist Dr. King Praises Priests' Bus Ride." [10/1961]. [Detroit, Mich.] (PD) 1 p. CSKC: Sermon file, folder 123. 611000-002.	
10/14/1961	Ebenezer Baptist Church. Press release, "Martin Luther King, Jr. at Ebenezer Sunday." 10/14/1961. Atlanta, Ga. (TD) 1 p. EBCR. 611014-000.	
10/22/1961	King, Martin Luther, Jr. Paul's Letter to American Christians, Sermon delivered at White Rock Baptist Church. [10/22/1961]. Philadelphia, Pa. (At) 41.9 min. (1 sound cassette: analog.) WRBC. 611022-002.	
11/13/1961	McDonald, Dora E. Letter to H. Claude Shostal. 11/13/1961. [Atlanta, Ga.] (TLc) 1 p. MLKP-MBU: Box 57. 611113-005.	
11/13/1961	Arnold, Melvin (Harper & Brothers). Letter to Martin Luther King, Jr. 11/13/1961. New York, N.Y. (TLS) 1 p. MLKP-MBU: Box 53A. 611113-008.	
11/18/1961	Ebenezer Baptist Church. Press release, "Martin Luther King, Jr. at Ebenezer Sunday." 11/18/1961. Atlanta, Ga. (TD) 1 p. EBCR. 611118-001.	
12/1/1961	Ebenezer Baptist Church. Press release, " 'The Secret of Adjustment,' King Jr.'s topic at Ebenezer." 12/1/1961. Atlanta, Ga.(TD) 1 p. EBCR. 611201-005.	
12/2/1961	**King, Martin Luther, Jr. (Ebenezer Baptist Church). "The Secret of Adjustment." [*12/2/1961*]. [*Atlanta, Ga.*] (AD) 6 pp. CSKC: Sermon file, folder 115, "The Secret of Adjustment & The Meaning of Easter." 611202-001.**	
12/17/1961	Ebenezer Baptist Church. Press release, " 'God's Love,' Dr. King Jr. at Ebenezer." 12/17/1961. Atlanta, Ga. (THD) 1 p. EBCR. 611217-004.	
12/23/1961	Ebenezer Baptist Church. Press release, "Martin Luther King, Jr. will fill pulpit at Ebenezer Sunday." 12/23/1961. Atlanta, Ga. (TD) 1 p. MLKP-MBU: Box 47. 611223-000.	
12/27/1961	McDonald, Dora E. Letter to John Hicks. 12/27/1961. [Atlanta, Ga.] (TLc) 1 p. MLKJP-GAMK: Box 15. 611227-003.	
1962	Morningside Baptist Church. "1962 Budget." 1962. (PD) 2 pp. CSKC: Sermon file, folder 15. 620000-018.	
1/6/1962	Ebenezer Baptist Church. Press release, " 'The Ultimate Triumph of Goodness,' Martin Luther King's topic at Ebenezer." 1/6/1962. Atlanta, Ga. (TD) 1 p. EBCR. 620106-001.	

2/3/1962   Ebenezer Baptist Church. Press release, "'The Worth of Man,' King, Jr.'s topic at Ebenezer Sunday." 2/3/1962. Atlanta, Ga. (TD) 1 p. EBCR. 620203-003.

2/19/1962   Bird, Shirley (University of Texas). Letter to Charlotte Sander. 2/19/1962. Austin, Texas (TL) 2 pp. (Includes enclosure. 620000-039 on verso, p. 436 in this volume.) CSKC. 620219-001.

2/20/1962   [*McDonald, Dora E.*] Letter to Martin Luther King, Jr. [*2/20/1962*]. [*Atlanta, Ga.*] (TLc) 2 pp. MLKJP-GAMK: Box 15. 620220-002.

3/3/1962   King, Martin Luther, Jr. "Fumbling on the New Frontier." 3/3/1962. New York, N.Y. From: *The Nation* 194 (3 March 1962): 190–193. (PD) 4 pp. CSKC: Sermon file, folder 125, Article—Martin L. King. 620303-000.

3/9/1962   King, Martin Luther, Jr. Letter to Eugene Exman. 3/9/1962. [*Atlanta, Ga.*] (TLc) 1 p. CSKC. 620309-011.

4/15/1962   King, Martin Luther, Jr. Palm Sunday Prayer delivered at Ebenezer Baptist Church. 4/15/1962. Atlanta, Ga. (At) 6.5 min. (1 sound cassette: analog.) MLKEC. 620415-001.

4/18/1962   Denver Area Council of Churches. Program, "Holy week service." 4/18/1962. Denver, Colo. (TD) 4 pp. CSKC: Sermon file, folder 22, "What Is Man?" 620418-000.

4/22/1962   King, Martin Luther, Jr. "The Meaning of Easter," Sermon delivered at Ebenezer Baptist Church. [*4/22/1962*]. [*Atlanta, Ga.*] (At) 32 min. (1 sound cassette: analog.) MLKEC: S-1. 620422-001.

4/22/1962   King, Martin Luther, Jr. "The Meaning of Easter," Sermon outline. [*4/22/1962*]. [*Atlanta, Ga.*] (AD) 2 pp. CSKC: Sermon file, folder 109, "Levels of Love." 620422-002.

4/29/1962   **Associated Press. Photo of Martin Luther King, Jr., Karl Barth, and James I. McCord. 4/29/1962. Princeton, N.J. (Ph) 1 p. NNAPWW. 620429-001.**

4/26/1962–   Princeton University. Program, "Biennial religious conference, Integration:
4/29/1962   conscience in crisis." [*4/26/1962–4/29/1962*]. Princeton, N.J. (PD) 4 pp. CSKCH. 620429-002.

5/4/1962   McDonald, Dora E. Letter to Frank Madison Reid. 5/4/1962. [*Atlanta, Ga.*] (TLc) 1 p. (Contains enclosure 620504-011.) MLKJP-GAMK: Box 64. 620504-010.

5/4/1962   King, Martin Luther, Jr. "A Prayer." 5/4/1962. [*Atlanta, Ga.*] (TD) 1 p. (Enclosed in 620504-010.) MLKJP-GAMK: Box 64. 620504-011.

5/27/1962   Ferris, Theodore P. (Trinity Church). "The Doctrine of Original Goodness." 5/27/1962. Boston, Mass. (PHD) 6 pp. CSKC: Sermon file, folder 1, "Loving Your Enemies." 620527-000.

6/12/1962   Atkins, C. B. (Progressive Talent, Inc.). Letter to Martin Luther King, Jr. 6/12/1962. New York, N.Y. (TLS) 4 pp. (Includes enclosure.) CSKC: Sermon file, folder 74, "The Future of Integration." 620612-000.

6/17/1962   King, Martin Luther, Jr. "The Dilemma and the Challenge Facing the Negro Today," Address delivered at Zion Hill Church. [*6/17/1962*]. Los Angeles, Calif. (At) 43.7 min. (1 sound cassette: analog.) MLKEC: S-11. 620617-001.

7/25/1962   King, Martin Luther, Jr., and William G. Anderson. Statement on violence in Albany, Ga. and declaration of Day of Penance. 7/25/1962. [*Albany, Ga.*] (TAD) 1 p. CSKC: Sermon file, folder 31. 620725-001.

9/1962   SCLC. *Newsletter* 1, no. 7. 9/1962. Atlanta, Ga. (PD) 4 pp. CSKC: Sermon file, folder 30. 620900-003.

9/1962   [*SCLC*]. Draft, *Newsletter*. [*9/1962*]. (THDd) 4 pp. CSKC: Sermon file, folder 31. 620900-017.

10/3/1962   [*Wallis, Charles L.*]. Editorial notes on *Strength to Love*. 10/3/1962. (THD) 6 pp. (Enclosed in 621005-004.) CSKC: Sermon file, folder 96, Dr. King's Letters. 621003-007.

10/5/1962   Arnold, Melvin (Harper & Row). Letter to Martin Luther King, Jr. 10/5/1962. New York, N.Y. (TALS) 1 p. (Contains enclosure 621003-007.) CSKC: Sermon file, folder 96, Dr. King's Letters. 621005-004.

10/7/1962   King, Martin Luther, Jr. "The Perfect Faith," Sermon delivered at Ebenezer Baptist Church. [*10/7/1962*]. [*Atlanta, Ga.*] (At) 32.1 min. (1 sound cassette: analog.) MLKEC: S-10. 621007-000.

10/7/1962   King, Martin Luther, Jr. The Perfect Faith, Sermon notes. [*10/7/1962*]. [*Atlanta, Ga.*] (AD) 1 p. CSKC. 621007-002.

10/15/1962   McDonald, Dora E. Letter to Melvin Arnold. 10/15/1962. [*Atlanta, Ga.*] (TLc) 1 p. CSKC. 621015-005.

10/23/1962   [*McDonald, Dora E.*]. Letter to Melvin Arnold. 10/23/1962. [*Atlanta, Ga.*] (TLc) 1 p. CSKC. 621023-007.

| 11/15/1962 | Wallis, Charles L. (Keuka College). Letter to Martin Luther King, Jr. 11/15/1962. Keuka Park, N.Y. (THLS) 1 p. CSKC. 621115-004. | Calendar |

11/15/1962 [*McDonald, Dora E.*]. Letter to Melvin Arnold. 11/15/1962. [*Atlanta, Ga.*] (TLc) 1 p. CSKC. 621115-005.

11/18/1962 King, Martin Luther, Jr. "The Dimensions of a Complete Life," Sermon at Riverside Church. 11/18/1962. New York, N.Y. (PTa) 18 pp. NNRC. 621118-000.

11/26/1962 Arnold, Melvin. Telegram to Martin Luther King, Jr. 11/26/1962. New York, N.Y. (PWSr) 1 p. CSKC. 621126-010.

11/26/1962 Withers, Lucille (Harper & Row). Letter to Dora E. McDonald. 11/26/1962. New York, N.Y. (TLS) 1 p. CSKC. 621126-011.

11/29/1962 Arnold, Melvin (Harper & Row). Letter to Martin Luther King, Jr. 11/29/1962. New York, N.Y. (THLS) 1 p. CSKC. 621129-000.

12/2/1962 King, Martin Luther, Jr. The Religion of the Dawn, Sermon delivered at Ebenezer Baptist Church. [*12/2/1962*]. [*Atlanta, Ga.*] (At) 40.5 min. (1 sound cassette: analog.) MLKEC: ET-67. 621202-000.

12/3/1962 [*McDonald, Dora E.*]. Letter to Lucille Withers. 12/3/1962. [*Atlanta, Ga.*] (TLc) 1 p. CSKC. 621203-004.

12/4/1962 [*McDonald, Dora E.*]. Letter to Melvin Arnold. 12/4/1962. [*Atlanta, Ga.*] (TLc) 1 p. CSKC. 621204-002.

12/9/1962 King, Martin Luther, Jr. "A Knock at Midnight," Sermon delivered at Sixth Avenue Baptist Church. 12/9/1962. Birmingham, Ala. (At) 67.7 min (1 sound cassette: analog.) JTPP. 621209-003.

12/23/1962 King, Martin Luther, Jr. "God's Love," Sermon delivered at Ebenezer Baptist Church. [*12/23/1962*]. [*Atlanta, Ga.*] (At) 38.8 min. (1 sound cassette: analog.) MLKEC: ET-40. 621223-000.

12/26/1962 King, Martin Luther, Jr. Letter to Melvin Arnold. 12/26/1962. [*Atlanta, Ga.*] (TLc) 1 p. 64VF-CtW. 621226-002.

1/5/1963 Ebenezer Baptist Church. Press release, "Dr. King Jr. at Ebenezer, 'The Tragedy of Almost,' morning topic." 1/5/1963. Atlanta, Ga. (TD) 1 p. EBCR. 630105-001.

1/14/1963 Wallis, Charles L. (Keuka College). Letter to Martin Luther King, Jr. 1/14/1963. Keuka Park, N.Y. (TAHLS) 2 pp. (Includes enclosure. Marginal comments by King.) MLKJP-GAMK: Box 19. 630114-006.

1/17/1963 King, Martin Luther, Jr. "A Challenge to the Churches and Synagogues," Address at the National Conference on Religion and Race. 1/17/1963. Chicago, Ill. (TD) 17 pp. CSKC: Sermon file, folder 131, Speeches—MLK, Jr. Atlanta Summit Conference Dec. 15, 1963. 630117-006.

1/19/1963 Ebenezer Baptist Church. Press release, "Dr. King Jr. to fill pulpit at Ebenezer Sunday." 1/19/1963. Atlanta, Ga. (TD) 1 p. EBCR. 630119-001.

1/25/1963 Ebenezer Baptist Church. Press release, "'God's Own Love,' Dr. King's morning topic at Ebenezer." 1/25/1963. Atlanta, Ga. (TD) 1 p. EBCR. 630125-000.

2/12/1963 Photo of Martin Luther King, Jr. preaching at Ebenezer Baptist Church. [*2/12/1963*]. Atlanta, Ga. From: *Look*, 12 February 1963, p. 96. (PPh) 1 p. LMC-DLC. 630212-003.

3/1/1963 Elliott, Frank (Harper & Brothers). Letter to Martin Luther King, Jr. 3/1/1963. New York, N.Y. (TLS) 2 pp. CSKC. 630301-003.

3/10/1963 King, Martin Luther, Jr. "The Parable of Dives and Lazarus," Sermon delivered at Ebenezer Baptist Church. [*3/10/1963*]. Atlanta, Ga. (At) 27 min. (1 sound cassette: analog.) MLKJP-GAMK: T-6. 630310-000.

3/10/1963 King, Martin Luther, Jr. "The Parable of Dives and Lazarus," Sermon at Ebenezer Baptist Church. [*3/10/1963*]. [*Atlanta, Ga.*] (TTa) 25 pp. MLKJP-GAMK. 630310-001.

3/26/1963 Arnold, Melvin. Letter to Kyle Haselden. 3/26/1963. (TLS) 1 p. (Copy to King.) CSKC. 630326-000.

3/1963 King, Martin Luther, Jr. Draft, *Strength to Love*. [*3/1963*]. [*Atlanta, Ga.*] (THDd) 207 pp. MLKJP-GAMK: Vault box 8. 630300-078.

7/1962–3/1963 King, Martin Luther, Jr. Draft, *Strength to Love*. [*7/1962–3/1963*]. [*Atlanta, Ga.*] (THDf) 30 pp. CSKC: Sermon file, folder 97. 630300-010.

7/1962–3/1963 King, Martin Luther, Jr. Draft, Dedication and preface, *Strength to Love*. [*7/1962–3/1963*]. [*Atlanta, Ga.*] (ADd) 3 pp. CSKC. 630300-080.

7/1962–3/1963 King, Martin Luther, Jr. Draft, Dedication and preface, *Strength to Love*. [*7/1962–3/1963*]. [*Atlanta, Ga.*] (THDd) 2 pp. CSKC. 630300-077.

7/1962–3/1963 King, Martin Luther, Jr. Draft, Dedication and preface, *Strength to Love*. [*7/1962–3/1963*]. [*Atlanta, Ga.*] (TDc) 3 pp. MLKP-MBU: Box 120. 630300-079.

7/1962–3/1963   King, Martin Luther, Jr. Draft of chapter I, "A Tough Mind and a Tender Heart," *Strength to Love.* [*7/1962–3/1963*]. [*Atlanta, Ga.*] (ADd) 26 pp. CSKC: Sermon file, folder 17, "A Tough Mind and a Tender Heart." 630300-071.

7/1962–3/1963   King, Martin Luther, Jr. Draft of chapter I, "A Tough Mind and a Tender Heart," *Strength to Love.* [*7/1962–3/1963*]. [*Atlanta, Ga.*] (TADd) 17 pp. MLKP-MBU: Box 119A. 630300-008.

7/1962–3/1963   King, Martin Luther, Jr. Draft of chapter I, "A Tough Mind and a Tender Heart," *Strength to Love.* [*7/1962–3/1963*]. [*Atlanta, Ga.*] (THADd) 10 pp. MLKP-MBU: Box 121. 630300-011.

7/1962–3/1963   King, Martin Luther, Jr. Draft of chapter I, "A Tough Mind and a Tender Heart," *Strength to Love.* [*7/1962–3/1963*]. [*Atlanta, Ga.*] (THDd) 10 pp. CSKC: Sermon file, folder 90. 630300-012.

7/1962–3/1963   King, Martin Luther, Jr. Draft of chapter II, "Transformed Nonconformist," *Strength to Love.* [*7/1962–3/1963*]. [*Atlanta, Ga.*] (ADd) 22 pp. MLKP-MBU: Box 121. 630300-013.

7/1962–3/1963   **King, Martin Luther, Jr. Draft of chapter II, "Transformed Nonconformist," *Strength to Love.* [*7/1962–3/1963*]. [*Atlanta, Ga.*] (TADd) 15 pp. MLKP-MBU: Box 120. 630300-014.**

7/1962–3/1963   King, Martin Luther, Jr. Draft of chapter II, "Transformed Nonconformist," *Strength to Love.* [*7/1962–3/1963*]. [*Atlanta, Ga.*] (TAHDd) 10 pp. MLKP-MBU: Box 120. 630300-015.

7/1962–3/1963   King, Martin Luther, Jr. Draft of chapter II, "Transformed Nonconformist," *Strength to Love.* [*7/1962–3/1963*]. [*Atlanta, Ga.*] (TDd) 10 pp. MLKP-MBU: Box 120A. 630300-016.

7/1962–3/1963   King, Martin Luther, Jr. Draft of chapter III, On Being a Good Neighbor, *Strength to Love.* [*7/1962–3/1963*]. [*Atlanta, Ga.*] (TAHDd) 9 pp. MLKP-MBU: Box 120. 630300-018.

7/1962–3/1963   King, Martin Luther, Jr. Draft of chapter III, "On Being a Good Neighbor," *Strength to Love.* [*7/1962–3/1963*]. [*Atlanta, Ga.*] (TAHDd) 12 pp. MLKP-MBU: Box 120A. 630300-019.

7/1962–3/1963   King, Martin Luther, Jr. Draft of chapter III, "On Being a Good Neighbor," *Strength to Love.* [*7/1962–3/1963*]. [*Atlanta, Ga.*] (TDd) 11 pp. CSKC: Sermon file, folder 95, "Carbon Copies of Final Draft" / Howard University, Rankin Memorial Chapel, Wash, D.C. November 9, 1958. 630300-020.

7/1962–3/1963   King, Martin Luther, Jr. Draft of chapter IV, Love in Action, *Strength to Love.* [*7/1962–3/1963*]. [*Atlanta, Ga.*] (ADfd) 17 pp. MLKP-MBU: Box 120. 630300-021.

7/1962–3/1963   King, Martin Luther, Jr. Draft of chapter IV, "Love in Action," *Strength to Love.* [*7/1962–3/1963*]. [*Atlanta, Ga.*] (TAHDd) 13 pp. MLKP-MBU: Box 120A. 630300-023.

7/1962–3/1963   King, Martin Luther, Jr. Draft of chapter IV, "Love in Action," *Strength to Love.* [*7/1962–3/1963*]. [*Atlanta, Ga.*] (THDd) 14 pp. CSKC: Sermon file, folder 95, "Carbon Copies of Final Draft" / Howard University Rankin Memorial Chapel, Wash, D.C. November 9, 1958. 630300-024.

7/1962–3/1963   King, Martin Luther, Jr. Draft of chapter V, "Loving Your Enemies," *Strength to Love.* [*7/1962–3/1963*]. [*Atlanta, Ga.*] (ADd) 20 pp. MLKJP-GAMK: Vault box 3. 630300-025.

7/1962–3/1963   King, Martin Luther, Jr. Draft of chapter V, "Loving Your Enemies," *Strength to Love.* [*7/1962–3/1963*]. [*Atlanta, Ga.*] (TAHDd) 13 pp. MLKP-MBU: Box 120. 630300-026.

7/1962–3/1963   King, Martin Luther, Jr. Draft of chapter V, "Loving Your Enemies," *Strength to Love.* [*7/1962–3/1963*]. [*Atlanta, Ga.*] (TADd) 13 pp. CSKC: Sermon file, folder 95, "Carbon Copies of Final Draft" / Howard University Rankin Memorial Chapel, Wash, D.C. November 9, 1958. 630300-027.

7/1962–3/1963   King, Martin Luther, Jr. Draft of chapter V, "Loving Your Enemies," *Strength to Love.* [*7/1962–3/1963*]. [*Atlanta, Ga.*] (TAHDd) 10 pp. MLKP-MBU: Box 120A. 630300-028.

7/1962–3/1963   King, Martin Luther, Jr. Draft of chapter VI, "A Knock at Midnight," *Strength to Love.* [*7/1962–3/1963*]. [*Atlanta, Ga.*] (ADd) 25 pp. MLKP-MBU: Box 119A. 630300-030.

7/1962–3/1963   King, Martin Luther, Jr. Draft of chapter VI, "A Knock at Midnight," *Strength to Love.* [*7/1962–3/1963*]. [*Atlanta, Ga.*] (TAHDd) 12 pp. MLKP-MBU: Box 120A. 630300-032.

7/1962–3/1963   King, Martin Luther, Jr. Draft of chapter VI, "A Knock at Midnight," *Strength to Love.* [*7/1962–3/1963*]. [*Atlanta, Ga.*] (TADd) 16 pp. CSKC: Sermon file, folder 95, "Carbon Copies of Final Draft" / Howard University Rankin Memorial Chapel, Wash, D.C. November 9, 1955. 630300-033.

7/1962–3/1963   King, Martin Luther, Jr. Draft of chapter VII, "The Man Who Was a Fool," *Strength to Love.* [*7/1962–3/1963*]. [*Atlanta, Ga.*] (ADd) 19 pp. MLKP-MBU: Box 119A. 630300-034.

7/1962–3/1963   King, Martin Luther, Jr. Draft of chapter VII, "The Man Who Was a Fool," *Strength to Love.* [*7/1962–3/1963*]. [*Atlanta, Ga.*] (THDd) 12 pp. MLKP-MBU: Box 120. 630300-035.

7/1962–3/1963   King, Martin Luther, Jr. Draft of chapter VII, "The Man Who Was a Fool," *Strength to Love.* [*7/1962–3/1963*]. [*Atlanta, Ga.*] (TDd) 2 pp. MLKP-MBU: Box 120A. 630300-036.

7/1962–3/1963   King, Martin Luther, Jr. Draft of chapter VII, "The Man Who Was a Fool," *Strength to Love.* [*7/1962–3/1963*]. [*Atlanta, Ga.*] (TAHDd) 10 pp. MLKP-MBU: Box 119A. 630300-037.

7/1962–3/1963   King, Martin Luther, Jr. Draft of chapter VII, "The Man Who Was a Fool," *Strength to Love.* [*7/1962–3/1963*]. [*Atlanta, Ga.*] (TADd) 9 pp. MLKP-MBU: Box 120A. 630300-038.

7/1962–3/1963   King, Martin Luther, Jr. Draft of chapter VIII, "The Death of Evil Upon the Seashore," *Strength to Love.* [*7/1962–3/1963*]. [*Atlanta, Ga.*] (ADd) 23 pp. MLKP-MBU: Box 119A. 630300-074.

7/1962–3/1963   King, Martin Luther, Jr. Draft of chapter VIII, "The Death of Evil Upon the Seashore," *Strength to Love.* [*7/1962–3/1963*]. [*Atlanta, Ga.*] (TADd) 12 pp. MLKP-MBU: Box 119A. 630300-039.

7/1962–3/1963   King, Martin Luther, Jr. Draft of chapter VIII, "The Death of Evil Upon the Seashore," *Strength to Love.* [*7/1962–3/1963*]. [*Atlanta, Ga.*] (TADd) 12 pp. CSKC: Sermon file, folder 95, "Carbon Copies of Final Draft" / Howard University Rankin Memorial Chapel, Wash, D.C. November 9, 1958. 630300-040.

7/1962–3/1963   King, Martin Luther, Jr. Draft of chapter IX, "The Three Dimensions of a Complete Life," *Strength to Love.* [*7/1962–3/1963*]. [*Atlanta, Ga.*] (ADd) 25 pp. MLKP-MBU: Box 119A. 630300-041.

7/1962–3/1963   King, Martin Luther, Jr. Draft of chapter IX, The Three Dimensions of Complete Life, *Strength to Love.* [*7/1962–3/1963*]. [*Atlanta, Ga.*] (TAHDd) 16 pp. MLKP-MBU: Box 120A. 630300-042.

7/1962–3/1963   King, Martin Luther, Jr. Draft of chapter IX, "Three Dimensions of a Complete Life," *Strength to Love.* [*7/1962–3/1963*]. [*Atlanta, Ga.*] (TADd) 15 pp. MLKP-MBU: Box 120. 630300-043.

7/1962–3/1963   King, Martin Luther, Jr. Draft of chapter IX, "Three Dimensions of a Complete Life," *Strength to Love.* [*7/1962–3/1963*]. [*Atlanta, Ga.*] (TAHDd) 14 pp. CSKC: Sermon file, folder 95, "Carbon Copies of Final Draft" / Howard University Rankin Memorial Chapel, Wash, D.C. November 9, 1958. 630300-044.

7/1962–3/1963   King, Martin Luther, Jr. Draft of chapter X , "Shattered Dreams," *Strength to Love.* [*7/1962–3/1963*]. [*Atlanta, Ga.*] (ADd) 23 pp. MLKP-MBU: Box 119A. 630300-072.

7/1962–3/1963   **King, Martin Luther, Jr. Draft of chapter X, "Shattered Dreams," *Strength to Love.* [*7/1962–3/1963*]. [*Atlanta, Ga.*] (TAHDd) 16 pp. MLKP–MBU: Box 119A. 630300-073.**

7/1962–3/1963   King, Martin Luther, Jr. Draft of chapter X, "Shattered Dreams," *Strength to Love.* [*7/1962–3/1963*]. [*Atlanta, Ga.*] (TADd) 12 pp. CSKC: Sermon file, folder 7, Shattered Dreams. 630300-045.

7/1962–3/1963   King, Martin Luther, Jr. Draft of chapter X, "Shattered Dreams," *Strength to Love.* [*7/1962–3/1963*]. [*Atlanta, Ga.*] (TAHDd) 12 pp. MLKP-MBU: Box 121. 630300-046.

7/1962–3/1963   King, Martin Luther, Jr. Draft of chapter XI, "What Is Man?" *Strength to Love.* [*7/1962–3/1963*]. [*Atlanta, Ga.*] (TAHDd) 12 pp. MLKP-MBU: Box 120A. 630300-047.

7/1962–3/1963   King, Martin Luther, Jr. Draft of chapter XI, "What Is Man?" *Strength to Love.* [*7/1962–3/1963*]. [*Atlanta, Ga.*] (TDd) 8 pp. CSKC: Sermon file, folder 88. 630300-048.

7/1962–3/1963   King, Martin Luther, Jr. Draft of chapter XII, "How Should a Christian View Communism?" *Strength to Love.* [*7/1962–3/1963*]. [*Atlanta, Ga.*] (ADd) 22 pp. MLKP-MBU: Box 119A. 630300-049.

Calendar	7/1962–3/1963	King, Martin Luther, Jr. Draft of chapter XII, How Should a Christian View Communism? *Strength to Love.* [*7/1962–3/1963*]. [*Atlanta, Ga.*] (TADd) 14 pp. MLKP-MBU: Box 119A. 630300-050.
	7/1962–3/1963	King, Martin Luther, Jr. Draft of chapter XII, "How Should a Christian View Communism?" *Strength to Love.* [*7/1962–3/1963*]. [*Atlanta, Ga.*] (TAHDd) 12 pp. MLKP-MBU: Box 120A. 630300-051.
	7/1962–3/1963	King, Martin Luther, Jr. Draft of chapter XII, "How Should a Christian View Communism?" *Strength to Love.* [*7/1962–3/1963*]. [*Atlanta, Ga.*] (TADd) 11 pp. CSKC: Sermon file, folder 95, "Carbon Copies of Final Draft" / Howard University Rankin Memorial Chapel, Wash, D.C. November 9, 1958. 630300-052.
	7/1962–3/1963	King, Martin Luther, Jr. Draft of chapter XIII, "Our God Is Able," *Strength to Love.* [*7/1962–3/1963*]. [*Atlanta, Ga.*] (AHDd) 26 pp. CSKC: Sermon file, folder 11, "Our God Is Able." 630300-054.
	7/1962–3/1963	King, Martin Luther, Jr. Draft of chapter XIII, "Our God Is Able," *Strength to Love.* [*7/1962–3/1963*]. [*Atlanta, Ga.*] (TAHDd) 19 pp. MLKP-MBU: Box 120. 630300-053.
	7/1962–3/1963	King, Martin Luther, Jr. Draft of chapter XIII, "Our God Is Able," *Strength to Love.* [*7/1962–3/1963*]. [*Atlanta, Ga.*] (TAHDd) 10 pp. MLKP-MBU: Box 121. 630300-056.
	7/1962–3/1963	King, Martin Luther, Jr. Draft of chapter XIII, "Our God Is Able," *Strength to Love.* [*7/1962–3/1963*]. [*Atlanta, Ga.*] (TADd) 11 pp. CSKC: Sermon file, folder 95, "Carbon Copies of Final Draft" / Howard University Rankin Memorial Chapel, Wash, D.C. November 9, 1958. 630300-057.
	7/1962–3/1963	King, Martin Luther, Jr. Draft of chapter XIV, Antidotes for Fear, *Strength to Love.* [*7/1962–3/1963*]. [*Atlanta, Ga.*] (ADfd) 11 pp. MLKP-MBU: Box 121. 630300-058.
	7/1962–3/1963	King, Martin Luther, Jr. Draft of chapter XIV, "Antidotes for Fear," *Strength to Love.* [*7/1962–3/1963*]. [*Atlanta, Ga.*] (TAHDd) 11 pp. MLKP-MBU: Box 121. 630300-060.
	7/1962–3/1963	King, Martin Luther, Jr. Draft of chapter XIV, "Antidotes for Fear," *Strength to Love.* [*7/1962–3/1963*]. [*Atlanta, Ga.*] (TDd) 13 pp. CSKC: Sermon file, folder 85, Antidotes for Fear. 630300-061.
	7/1962–3/1963	King, Martin Luther, Jr. Draft of chapter XV, "The Answer to a Perplexing Question," *Strength to Love.* [*7/1962–3/1963*]. [*Atlanta, Ga.*] (ADd) 25 pp. MLKP-MBU: Box 121. 630300-062.
	7/1962–3/1963	King, Martin Luther, Jr. Draft of chapter XV, "The Answer to a Perplexing Question," *Strength to Love.* [*7/1962–3/1963*]. [*Atlanta, Ga.*] (TADd) 11 pp. MLKP-MBU: Box 120. 630300-064.
	7/1962–3/1963	King, Martin Luther, Jr. Draft of chapter XV, "The Answer to a Perplexing Question," *Strength to Love.* [*7/1962–3/1963*]. [*Atlanta, Ga.*] (TADd) 14 pp. CSKC: Sermon file, folder 95, "Carbon Copies of Final Draft" / Howard University Rankin Memorial Chapel, Wash, D.C. November 9, 1958. 630300-065.
	7/1962–3/1963	King, Martin Luther, Jr. Draft of chapter XVI, "Paul's Letter to American Christians," *Strength to Love.* [*7/1962–3/1963*]. [*Atlanta, Ga.*] (TADd) 17 pp. MLKP-MBU: Box 119A. 630300-066.
	7/1962–3/1963	King, Martin Luther, Jr. Draft of chapter XVI, "Paul's Letter to American Christians," *Strength to Love.* [*7/1962–3/1963*]. [*Atlanta, Ga.*] (TADd) 10 pp. CSKC: Sermon file, folder 95, "Carbon Copies of Final Draft" / Howard University Rankin Memorial Chapel, Wash, D.C. November 9, 1958. 630300-067.
	7/1962–3/1963	King, Martin Luther, Jr. Draft of chapter XVII, "Pilgrimage to Nonviolence," *Strength to Love.* [*7/1962–3/1963*]. [*Atlanta, Ga.*] (TADd) 10 pp. CSKC: Sermon file, folder 95, "Carbon Copies of Final Draft" / Howard University Rankin Memorial Chapel, Wash, D.C. November 9, 1958. 630300-068.
	7/1962–3/1963	King, Martin Luther, Jr. Draft of chapter XVII, "Pilgrimage to Nonviolence," *Strength to Love.* [*7/1962–3/1963*]. [*Atlanta, Ga.*] (TAHDd) 9 pp. MLKP-MBU: Box 121. 630300-069.
	5/19/1963	Demere, Charles (St. Bede's Episcopal Church). "Partnership with God." 5/19/1963. (TD) 4 pp. CSKC: Sermon file, folder 47, Mis Sermons. 630519-000.
	5/28/1963	Exman, Eugene (Harper & Row). Letter to Martin Luther King, Jr. 5/28/1963. New York, N.Y. (TLS) 1 p. CSKC. 630528-009.
	6/1963	**Photo of Martin Luther King, Jr., Alberta Williams King, and Christine King Farris at a *Strength to Love* book signing at Ebenezer Baptist Church. [*6/1963*]. [*Atlanta, Ga.*] (Ph) 1 p. CCCSU. 630600-000.**

6/30/1963	King, Martin Luther, Jr. "Advance excerpts," Sermon at Antioch Baptist Church. 6/30/1963. Brooklyn, N.Y. (THDc) 3 pp. CSKC: Sermon file, folder 123. 630630-000.	Calendar

6/30/1963 — King, Martin Luther, Jr. "Advance excerpts," Sermon at Antioch Baptist Church. 6/30/1963. Brooklyn, N.Y. (THDc) 3 pp. CSKC: Sermon file, folder 123. 630630-000.

7/1963 — SCLC. *Newsletter* 1, no. 10. 7/1963. Atlanta, Ga. (PD) 8 pp. CSKC: Sermon file, folder 30. 630700-003.

7/14/1963 — King, Martin Luther, Jr. The Sinner Who Stayed at Home, Sermon delivered at Ebenezer Baptist Church. [*7/14/1963*]. [*Atlanta, Ga.*] (At) 42 min. (2 sound cassettes: analog.) MLKEC: ET-2. 630714-000.

7/1/1962–7/28/1963 — King, Martin Luther, Jr. Preaching schedule. 7/1/1962–7/28/1963. [*Atlanta, Ga.*] (AD) 1 p. MLKP-MBU: Box 12. 630728-000.

8/1963 — SCLC. *Newsletter* 1, no. 11. 8/1963. Atlanta, Ga. (PD) 8 pp. CSKC: Sermon file, folder 30. 630800-004.

8/4/1963 — King, Martin Luther, Jr. "Making It in on Broken Pieces." 8/4/1963. [*Atlanta, Ga.*] (TD) 4 pp. CSKC: Sermon file, folder 82, "Making It in on Broken Pieces." 630804-001.

7/1/1962–8/25/1963 — King, Martin Luther, Jr. Preaching schedule for Ebenezer Baptist Church. [*Atlanta, Ga.*] (AD) 7/1/1962–8/25/1963. 1 p. MLKJP-GAMK: Box 12. 630825-005

9/1963 — SCLC. *Newsletter* 1, no. 12. 9/1963. Atlanta, Ga. (PD) 12 pp. CSKC: Sermon file, folder 30. 630900-004.

9/3/1963–9/8/1963 — Progressive National Baptist Convention. Program, "Second annual session." 9/3/1963–9/8/1963. Detroit, Mich. (PHD) 4 pp. CSKC: Sermon file, folder 123. 630908-001.

9/17/1963 — Arnold, Melvin (Harper & Row). Letter to Joan Daves. 9/17/1963. New York, N.Y. (TLc) 1 p. CSKC. 630917-005.

10/10/1963 — Smith, Charles R. (Mrs.) (Hoist-Master). Letter to Martin Luther King, Jr. 10/10/1963. Cassopolis, Mich. (THLS) 1 p. MLKJP-GAMK: Box 47. 631010-012.

11/1963–12/1963 — King, Martin Luther, Jr. "Epitaph and Challenge." 11/1963–12/1963. Atlanta, Ga. From: SCLC, *Newsletter* 2, November–December 1963, p. 1. (PD) 1 p. CSKC: Sermon file, folder 30. 631200-000.

12/15/1963 — King, Martin Luther, Jr. (SCLC). Address at the Pilgrimage for Democracy. 12/15/1963. Atlanta, Ga. (TD) 8 pp. CSKC: Sermon file, folder 131, Speeches—MLK, Jr. Atlanta Summit Conference Dec. 15, 1963. 631215-000.

12/15/1963 — Draft, Program, Pilgrimage for Democracy. [*12/15/1963*]. (TDd) 1 p. CSKC: Sermon file, folder 131, Speeches—MLK, Jr. Atlanta Summit Conference Dec. 15, 1963. 631215-007.

1954–1964 — King, Martin Luther, Jr. "Why the Christian Must Oppose Segregation." [*1954–1964?*]. (AD) 2 pp. CSKC: Sermon file, folder 87, Why the Christian Must Oppose Segregation. 640000-145.

1/1964 — SCLC. *Newsletter* 2, no. 4. 1/1964. Atlanta, Ga. (PD) 12 pp. CSKC: Sermon file, folder 30. 640100-003.

1/1964 — King, Martin Luther, Jr. "The Ultimate Doom of Evil," Sermon outline. [*1/1964*]. [*Atlanta, Ga.*] (AD) 3 pp. CSKC. 640100-014.

5/20/1964 — King, Martin Luther, Jr. "Love and Forgiveness," Sermon delivered to the American Baptist Convention. [*5/20/1964*]. [*Atlantic City, N.J.*] (At) 29 min. (1 sound cassette: analog.) MLKJP-GAMK: T-8. 640520-000.

5/20/1964 — King, Martin Luther, Jr. Love and Forgiveness, Sermon notes. [*5/20/1964*]. (AD) 4 pp. CSKC: Sermon file, folder 52, Father Forgive Them. 640520-002.

1/1964–5/1964 — King, Martin Luther, Jr. Draft, Introduction, *Why We Can't Wait.* [*1/1964–5/1964*]. Atlanta, Ga. (TADd) 4 pp. CSKC: Sermon file, folder 124. 640500-028.

7/22/1964 — King, Martin Luther, Jr. Notes, Address at community mass meeting at the Masonic Temple. [*7/22/1964*]. [*Jackson, Miss.*] (AD) 1 p. (Verso of 640722-003.) CSKC: Sermon file, folder 65. 640722-000.

7/22/1964 — Program, "Community mass meeting." 7/22/1964. (TD) 1 p. (640722-000 on verso.) CSKC: Sermon file, folder 65. 640722-003.

8/1964 — King, Martin Luther, Jr. A Knock at Midnight, Sermon outline. [*8/1964*]. [*Atlanta, Ga.*] (AD) 6 pp. CSKC: Sermon file, folder 65. 640800-011.

10/4/1964 — King, Martin Luther, Jr. "On Being Unashamed of the Gospel," Sermon delivered at Ebenezer Baptist Church. [*10/4/1964*]. Atlanta, Ga. (At) 31 min. (1 sound cassette: analog.) MLKEC: ET-30. 641004-000.

10/4/1964 — King, Martin Luther, Jr. "On Being Unashamed of the Gospel," Sermon outline. [*10/4/1964*]. [*Atlanta, Ga.*] (AHD) 4 pp. CSKC: Sermon file, folder 65. 641004-001.

12/3/1964   "Scripto, Union Meeting Today." [*12/3/1964*]. Atlanta, Ga. From: *Atlanta Daily World*, 3 December 1964. (PD) 1 p. CSKC: Sermon file, folder 123. 641203-000.

12/3/1964   "Strikers Meet at Ebenezer." [*12/3/1964*]. Atlanta, Ga. From: *Atlanta Daily World*, 3 December 1964. (PD) 1 p. CSKC: Sermon file, folder 123. 641203-001.

12/11/1964   Greene, Tom. "Labor Council Backs Strike At Scripto." [*12/11/1964*]. Atlanta, Ga. From: *Atlanta Journal*, 11 December 1964. (PD) 1 p. CSKC: Sermon file, folder 123. 641211-003.

12/11/1964   "King: Boycott All Mississippi Goods." [*12/11/1964*]. Atlanta, Ga. From: *Atlanta Journal*, 11 December 1964. (PD) 1 p. CSKC: Sermon file, folder 123. 641211-004.

12/12/1964   Black, Charles A. "Scripto Strikers Here Call for World-Wide Boycott of Scripto." [*12/12/1964*]. Atlanta, Ga. From: *Atlanta Inquirer*, 12 December 1964. (PD) 1 p. CSKC: Sermon file, folder 123. 641212-002.

12/16/1964   "Scripto, Union to Hold Meeting on December 21." [*12/16/1964*]. Atlanta, Ga. From: *Atlanta Daily World*, 16 December 1964. (PD) 2 pp. CSKC: Sermon file, folder 123. 641216-000.

12/20/1964   "King Pickets Scripto Plant Thirty Minutes." [*12/20/1964*]. Atlanta, Ga. From: *Atlanta Journal*, 20 December 1964. (PD) 1 p. CSKC: Sermon file, folder 123. 641220-000.

12/22/1964   "Scripto Boycott Backed by SCLC." [*12/22/1964*]. Atlanta, Ga. From: *Atlanta Journal*, 22 December 1964. (PD) 1 p. CSKC: Sermon file, folder 123. 641222-002.

5/23/1965   King, Martin Luther, Jr. "How to Deal with Grief and Disappointment," Sermon outline. [*5/23/1965*]. [*Atlanta, Ga.*] (AD) 3 pp. CSKC: Sermon file, folder 81, How to Deal with Disappointment. 650523-002.

11/27/1965   Kittell, Donald (Associated Negro Press). Letter to Martin Luther King, Jr. 11/27/1965. New York, N.Y. (TLS) 4 pp. (Includes enclosure. Contains enclosures 651127-003, 004, 005, 006.) CSKC: Sermon file, folder 160, MLK Proposed Article (Al Duckett). 651127-002.

11/27/1965   King, Martin Luther, Jr. "My Dream: Great Expectations." [*11/27/1965*]. New York, N.Y. (TD) 3 pp. (Enclosed in 651127-002.) CSKC: Sermon file, folder 160, MLK Proposed Article (Al Duckett). 651127-003.

11/27/1965   King, Martin Luther, Jr. "My Dream: The North: Myth of the Promised Land." [*11/27/1965*]. New York, N.Y. (TD) 4 pp. (Enclosed in 651127-002.) CSKC: Sermon file, folder 160, MLK Proposed Article (Al Duckett). 651127-004.

11/27/1965   King, Martin Luther, Jr. "My Dream: The North: Myth of the Promised Land, Part Two, Philadelphia—Story of a Will and a Wall." [*11/27/1965*]. New York, N.Y. (TD) 3 pp. (Enclosed in 651127-002.) CSKC: Sermon file, folder 160, MLK Proposed Article (Al Duckett). 651127-005.

11/27/1965   King, Martin Luther, Jr. "My Dream: Peace—God's Business and Man's." [*11/27/1965*]. New York, N.Y. (TD) 4 pp. (Enclosed in 651127-002.) CSKC: Sermon file, folder 160, MLK Proposed Article (Al Duckett). 651127-006.

12/12/1965   King, Martin Luther, Jr. "Is the Universe Friendly?" Sermon delivered at Ebenezer Baptist Church. [*12/12/1965*]. [*Atlanta, Ga.*] (At) 30.7 min. (1 sound cassette: analog.) MLKEC: NYC-15. 651212-004.

12/15/1965   King, Martin Luther, Jr. "A Great Challenge Derived from a Serious Dilemma," Address at the Hungry Club. 12/15/1965. Atlanta, Ga. (TD) 14 pp. CSKC: Sermon file, folder 134, Speech—Hungry Club 12/15/65. 651215-000.

1/16/1966   King, Martin Luther, Jr. Transformed Nonconformist, Sermon at Ebenezer Baptist Church. 1/16/1966. Atlanta, Ga. (TD) 15 pp. CSKC: Sermon file, folder 117, Jan. 16, 1966. 660116-002.

4/24/1966   King, Martin Luther, Jr. "Making the Best of a Bad Mess." [*4/24/1966*]. [*Atlanta, Ga.*] (AD) 3 pp. CSKC: Sermon file, folder 105, "Making the Best of a Bad Mess." 660424-005.

7/1966   King, Martin Luther, Jr. "Is It Unchristian to Judge Others?" Sermon outline. [*7/1966*]. [*Atlanta, Ga.*] (ADf) 2 pp. CSKC: Sermon file, folder 110, "Mastering Our Evil Selves." 660700-003.

7/1966   King, Martin Luther, Jr. Is It Unchristian to Judge Others? Sermon notes. [*7/1966*]. [*Atlanta, Ga.*] (AD) 2 pp. CSKC: Sermon file, folder 110, "Mastering Our Evil Selves." 660700-004.

1967   King, Martin Luther, Jr. Notes, Eulogy for C. R. Lyons. [*1967*]. [*Atlanta, Ga.*] (AD) 1 p. CSKC: Sermon file, folder 110, "Mastering Our Evil Selves." 670000-066.

1967   Morse, Wayne. Interview by Bill Plymat on Vietnam. West Des Moines, Iowa: World Peace Broadcasting Foundation, [*1967*]. (LP) CSKC: Sermon file, folder 105: "Making the Best of a Bad Mess." 670000-087.

3/25/1967	King, Martin Luther, Jr. Address at the Peace Parade and Rally. [*3/25/1967*]. Chicago, Ill. (TAD) 15 pp. CSKC: Sermon file, folder 104, Organizations—Let. 670325-001.	Calendar

3/25/1967   Luna, Benjamin Laureano. "La Doctrina de America." 3/25/1967. Chicago, Ill. From: *Tribuna de America,* 25 March 1967, pp. 4–5. (PD) 2 pp. CSKC: Sermon file, folder 104, Organizations—Let. 670325-005.

5/7/1967   King, Martin Luther, Jr. "We Would See Jesus," Sermon notes. [*5/7/1967*]. [*Atlanta, Ga.*] (AD) 1 p. CSKC: Sermon file, folder 61, We Would See Jesus. 670507-002.

8/14/1967   SCLC. "'. . . I have decided to start with myself,' Tenth anniversary convention banquet." 8/14/1967. Atlanta, Ga. (TD) 5 pp. CSKC: Sermon file, folder 29. 670814-001.

1968   If I Can Help Somebody. [*1968*]. (AD) 1 p. CSKC: Sermon file, folder 54, The Drum Major Instinct. 680000-087.

1947–1968   **King, Martin Luther, Jr. "What Is Man," Sermon outline. [*1947–1968*]. (AD) 2 pp. CSKCH. 680000-099.**

1948–1968   King, Martin Luther, Jr. Notes, "Man Incurably Religious" by John White Chadwick. [*1948–1968*]. (AD) 1 p. CSKC: Sermon file, folder 64, Sermon Material. 680000-084.

1948–1968   "One Solitary Life." [*1948–1968*]. (TDc) 1 p. CSKC: Sermon file, folder 54, The Drum Major Instinct. 680000-088.

1954–1968   **King, Martin Luther, Jr. "A Dream That Did Not Come True." [*1954–1968*]. (AD) 2 pp. CSKCH. 680000-081.**

1954–1968   **King, Martin Luther, Jr. "I Have Sinned." [*1954–1968*]. (AD) 1 p. CSKCH. 680000-082.**

1954–1968   King, Martin Luther, Jr. "What Should Be Our Attitude Toward Mystery." [*1954–1968*]. (ATD) 2 pp. CSKC: Sermon file, folder 106, "Sermons." 680000-083.

1954–1968   King, Martin Luther, Jr. "Not Many Days After . . ." [*1954–1968*]. (AD) 4 pp. CSKC: Sermon file, folder 106, "Sermons." 680000-085.

1954–1968   **King, Martin Luther, Jr. The Conflict in Human Nature, Sermon outline. [*1954–1968*]. (AD) 1 p. CSKCH. 680000-096.**

1955–1968   **King, Martin Luther, Jr. Small Trivialities and Large Catastrophes. [*1955–1968*]. (AD) 2 pp. CSKC: Sermon file, folder 110, "Mastering Our Evil Selves." 680000-095.**

1959–1968   King, Martin Luther, Jr. God in History: Four Proverbs. [*1959–1968*]. (AD) 2 pp. CSKC: Sermon file, folder 77, "God in History (Four Proverbs)." 680000-094.

1964–1968   King, Martin Luther, Jr. Prodigal Son, Sermon outline. [*1964–1968*]. [*Atlanta, Ga.*] (AD) 1 p. CSKC: Sermon file, folder 48, The Prodigal Son. 680000-086.

1966–1968   King, Martin Luther, Jr. Paul's Galatians: You Were Called to Freedom, Brethren. [*1966–1968*]. [*Atlanta, Ga.*] (TD) 4 pp. MLKJP-GAMK: Box 123. 680000-026.

2/4/1968   King, Martin Luther, Jr. "The Drum-Major Instinct," Sermon outline. [*2/4/1968*]. [*Atlanta, Ga.*] (AD) 3 pp. CSKC: Sermon file, folder 54, The Drum Major Instinct. 680204-001.

3/31/1968   King, Martin Luther, Jr. "Remaining Awake Through a Great Revolution," Sermon at the National Cathedral. 3/31/1968. Washington, D.C. (TD) 11 pp. CSKC: Sermon file, folder 122, MLK Speech 3/31/68. 680331-002.

1973   King, Martin Luther. *A Black Rebel: The Autobiography of M. L. King, Sr. As Told to Edward A. Jones.* [*1973*] (THD) 341 pp. MLKJP-GAMK. 730000-010.

INDEX

Boldfaced page numbers in entries indicate that the material can be found in documents authored by Martin Luther King, Jr. Italicized page numbers in entries indicate the location of the main biographical entry for an individual, beginning with the volume number if other than the present volume.

714

Compositor:	BookMatters, Berkeley, CA
Indexer:	Marcia Carlson Indexing Services
Text:	10/12 Baskerville
Display:	Baskerville
Printer and binder:	Edwards Brothers